# Japanese Financial Instruments and Exchange Act

## Hiroyuki Kansaku

Yoko Manzawa

Naohiko Matsuo

Sadakazu Osaki

Masakazu Shirai

Masao Yanaga

**Program
on Global Securities Market Law
at the University of Tokyo**

ZAIKEISHOHOSHA

Japanese Financial Instruments and Exchange Act

## ZAIKEISHOHOSHA,Inc
Since Nov 5, 1955

1-7-10, Ningyo-cho, Nihonbashi,
Chuo-Ku, Tokyo 103-0013, Japan

+81-3-3661-5266
zaik@oak.ocn.ne.jp
https://zaik.jp/

Copyright © 2018 Hiroyuki Kansaku, Yoko Manzawa, Naohiko Matsuo,
Sadakazu Osaki, Masakazu Shirai, Masao Yanaga

All rights reserved. No part of this publication may be reproduced,
stored in a retrieval system, or transmitted, in any form or by any means,
electronic, mechanical, photocopying, recording or otherwise,
without the prior permission in writing of ZAIKEISHOHOSHA, Inc.

First published March 2018
Printed in Japan
Typeset, printing, and binding by SO-EI PB PRINTING CO.,LTD

ISBN 978-4-88177-768-8

# Preface

This book provides a systematic introduction, in English, to the Financial Instruments and Exchange Act, which is the core of Japan's legal system for securities markets. Japan's Securities and Exchange Act was enacted in 1948 and based on securities acts in the United States, as part of its occupation policies. The Act for Partial Revision of the Securities and Exchange Act was enacted during the 164th ordinary session of the National Diet on June 7, 2006, during which the Securities and Exchange Act was significantly revised and its name was changed to the Financial Instruments and Exchange Act. By the 2006 revisions, four acts, including the Act on Regulation of Mortgage Securities Business and the Financial Futures Trading Act, were abolished and integrated into the Financial Instruments and Exchange Act. Moreover, business conduct regulations in the Act on Investment Trusts and Investment Corporations and regulations on the solicitation of investments in the Act on Regulation of Investment Advisory Business Pertaining to Securities and the Act on Regulation of Commodity Investment were absorbed into the Financial Instruments and Exchange Act. The 2006 revised act was initially applicable to securities and derivatives transactions; however, the concept of "securities" was expanded by introducing the comprehensive definition of a collective investment scheme. The concept of derivatives transactions was also expanded by including in their definition interest rate and currency swap transactions and weather derivatives. Moreover, the application scope of the Financial Instruments and Exchange Act included a wide range of operators concerning the solicitation and sale of securities and derivatives transactions and operators concerning investment services, such as asset management, investment advice, and the custody of customers' assets. Finally, the 2006 revised act strengthened disclosure systems and regulations on unfair trading, in order to secure market functions, and introduced an internal control reporting system, so as to cope with the globalization of the financial and capital markets.

Thus, the Financial Instruments and Exchange Act, after its revision in 2006, brought in both comprehensive and cross-sectional regulations of

*i*

investment services and filled gaps between regulations, both of which had been serious problems before the revision. The 2006 revised act classified investment services into type I financial instruments businesses and type II financial instruments businesses, investment management businesses, and so on and provided stepwise differences in regulations of systems for business operators to enter the financial and capital markets. As a result, the regulations adopted a flexible structure. The Financial Services and Markets Act 2000, in the United Kingdom, and the European Union's Markets in Financial Instruments Directive, in 2004, affected this regulatory framework. As a result of the 2006 revisions, the Financial Instruments and Exchange Act consolidated its social standing as the legal foundation for Japan's capital markets and investment services. Since the revisions in 2006, the Financial Instruments and Exchange Act has been revised almost every year, and the application scope of the act has been expanded further, rendering its legal system more complicated than ever before. The Financial Instruments and Exchange Act has developed as a capital market act peculiar to Japan, including regulations on takeover bids, based on the related acts in the United States, while also being affected by the related acts in the United Kingdom and the European Union.

This book is an outcome from the "Program on Global Securities Market Law (BNP Paribas)", which was established in the Faculty of Law at the University of Tokyo in October 2010 and completed in March 2016. Under the terms of the program, the theory and practice of the Financial Instruments and Exchange Act were studied comprehensively from different angles, including a comparative law approach. One of the purposes of the program was to introduce Japan's legal system for capital markets to other countries. To this end, the accomplishments of the program were summarized and translated into English.

Finally, we greatly appreciate Takeya Yoshinaga, of Zaikei Shohosha, for his devoted and sophisticated editing work, which enabled us to publish this challenging book and offer a systematic explanation of the Financial Instruments and Exchange Act in English.

Hiroyuki Kansaku
Tokyo, March 2018

# Acknowledgements

The editor and authors would like to acknowledge and thank BNP Paribas Securities (Japan) Limited and its Chairman and Representative Director, Philippe Avril, who initiated the project in 2010 to support the creation and development of an English program of Japanese Financial Instruments and Exchange Act at a Japanese university. We highly appreciate the Program Committee formed by BNP Paribas as an autonomous organization which selected the University of Tokyo for the endowment to implement the "Program on Global Securities Market Law (BNP Paribas)".

We were inspired and supported throughout the preparation of this book by the advice and encouragement of each individual member of the Program Committee; Takafumi Sato, Toru Ishiguro, Hideki Kanda, Noboru Nakagawa, Chikara Kawakita, Philippe Avril and Toru Yosano. In particular, Hideki Kanda, Professor Emeritus at the University of Tokyo and Professor at the Gakushuin University Law School, offered us invaluable suggestions and observations on substantial matters as an integral member of the Program.

We were privileged to clarify our contents on numerous points through many constructive and harmonizing comments from Nobuko Matsumoto, Professor at Gakushuin University. We are also grateful to Nishimura & Asahi partners Kazuhiro Takei and Taeko Morita, as well as to Richard Beal and Benjamin Miller from the same firm, who provided English proofreading. Finally, we would like to thank Tomoko Nunoi and Hitoshi Matsuzaki of BNP Paribas and Fumiko Inoue of the University of Tokyo, for their practical and continuous support for the publication of this book.

Hiroyuki Kansaku
Tokyo, March 2018

# Biographies

**Hiroyuki Kansaku** is a Professor of law at the University of Tokyo (2004-). He was a Professor of law at Gakushuin University (1998-2004). His principal areas of interest are corporate law, commercial law, securities and banking regulation. His recent publications include "Lectures on Financial Law (Kinyu-ho kogi), Second Edition" (Iwanami Press, 2017, co-author), "Haftung der Unternehmensleitung in Japan" in: Unternehmen im globalen Umfeld (Carl Heymanns Verlag, 2017), "Financial Law (Kinyu-ho Gaisetsu)" (Yuhi-kaku Press, 2016), "The Role of Shareholders in Public Companies, in "German and Asian Perspectives on Company Law" (Mohr Siebeck, 2016), "Alternde Gesellschaften im Recht" (Mohr Siebeck, 2015, co-editor), and "Commentary on the Financial Instruments and Exchange Act (Kinyushohintorihiki-ho Konmentar)", Vol. 4 (Shoji-homu Press, 2011, co-author). He is a member of the "Working Group on Disclosure System" and "Study Group on Financial Systems" at the Financial Services Agency and a member of the "Corporate Law Reform Section in the Legislative Council" at the Ministry of Justice.

**Yoko Manzawa** is an associate Professor at the Senshu University Faculty of Law where she teaches corporate law, corporate governance and securities regulation. She received an L.L.D. (Doctor of Laws) from the University of Tokyo. Her main research interest lies in comparative study of securities regulation between Japan, the United States, and the United Kingdom. Recent publications include "Stewardship Code and Trusteeship — Comparative study between the United States and the United Kingdom —" Shoji Homu No. 2070 (2015), pp. 23-33, "The Law of Insider Trading (Articles 166, 167, etc. of the Financial Instruments and Exchange Act)" in the Etsuro Kuromuma and Yo Ota (ed.), Ronten Taikei Kinyu Shohin Torihiki Ho [Financial Instruments and Exchange Act Commentary] 2 (Daiich Hoki, 2014) pp. 412-488, pp. 586-601; The Law of Insider Trading in the United States (Kobundo, 2011).

*v*

**Naohiko Matsuo** is an Attorney-at-law admitted in Japan & New York, Nishimura & Asahi and Visiting Professor of Law, Graduate School of Law, University of Tokyo. He was former Director and General Counsel, Financial Services Agency, Japanese Government. He is an Attorney-at-law of Nishimura & Asahi, the largest Japanese law firm, and teaches the Financial Instruments and Exchange Act (the "FIEA") as Visiting Professor of Law at the Graduate School of Law of the University of Tokyo. He entered the Japanese Ministry of Finance in 1986, and worked for the Japanese Financial Services Agency ("FSA") as Director for International Financial Markets from 2002 to 2005 and Director for the FIEA and General Counsel from 2005 to 2007. As Director for the FIEA, he was in charge of the comprehensive amendment of the former Securities and Exchange Act to the FIEA. He left the Japanese Government and joined Nishimura & Asahi in 2009. He graduated from the Faculty of Law of the University of Tokyo (LL.B.) in 1986, and the U.S. Harvard Law School (LL.M.) in 1989. He published many books and articles, in particular on the FIEA. His latest Japanese books include "Q&A on the American Financial Reform Act — All about the Dodd-Frank Act" in 2010 and "Financial Instruments and Exchange Act (Fifth Edition)" in 2018.

**Sadakazu Osaki** is Head of Research, Center for Strategic Management and Innovation, Nomura Research Institute, Ltd. and Visiting Professor of the University of Tokyo. He specializes in the regulation of capital markets. He has published several books and articles on Japanese regulation and its reforms mainly in Japanese. In addition to his job in Nomura and in the University of Tokyo, he was a member of the Financial System Council at the Financial Services Agency from 2011 to 2017. His English publication includes "Enterprise Law" (Edward Elgar, 2014, co-author), "Insider Trading: Global Developments and Analysis" (CRC Press, 2009, co-author), and "Selected Legal Issues of E-Commerce" (Kluwer Law International, 2002, co-author). He received an LL.M. from the University of London and the University of Edinburgh (with Distinction), and an LL.B. from the University of Tokyo.

**Masakazu Shirai** is a Professor of law at Doshisha University, where he

*vi*

currently teaches corporate law, securities law, and insurance law. He completed a Ph. D. in law at the University of Tokyo and an LL.M. at the University of California, Berkeley, School of Law. He also received the Shoji-home Kenkyukai Award (2012), Osumi-Kenichiro Award (2014) and M&A Forum Award (twice in 2013 & 2016). Recent publications include Nihon No Kokai Kaitsuke [Takeover Bids in Japan] (Yuhikaku, 2016, co-author), Corporate Law (Yuhikaku, 2015, co-author), M&A Ni Okeru Daisansha Iinkai No Riron To Jitsumu [Theory and Practice of Independent Committees in M&A Transactions] (Shoji-homu, 2015, co-author), Numerical Analysis of Corporate Law (Yuhikaku, 2013, co-author), Yukoteki Baishu No Bamen Niokeru Torishimariyaku Nitaisuru Kiritsu [Controlling Target Directors in Friendly Mergers and Acquisitions] (Shoji-homu, 2013).

**Masao Yanaga** is a Professor of law and accounting, University of Tsukuba. He not only passed the bar exam but is also qualified to practice as a CPA. He is the author of more than three hundred academic articles, as well as more than five hundred articles for students and practitioners. He is the author, co-author or contributor to more than 100 books, including scholarly books such as the Legal Aspects of Fair Value Accounting; Auditor Independence in appearance; and Accounting Standards and Law as well as textbooks and commentaries, e. g., Company Law; Law on Notes and Cheques; General Part of the Commercial Code and Law on Commercial Transactions; Commentary on the Company Accounting Regulation and the Implementing Regulation for the Commercial Code; Commentary on the Implementing Regulation for the Companies Act and the Electronic Public Announcement Regulation (in Japanese); and Cyber Law in Japan (3rd ed., Kluwer, 2017) (in English).

*vii*

# Contents

## Chapter 1   Introduction to the Japanese Financial Instruments and Exchange Act
### *Hiroyuki Kansaku*

A . Purposes and structure of the Japanese Financial Instruments and Exchange Act (FIEA) ·················································································2

  1 . Purposes of the FIEA ················································································2
  2 . Structure of the FIEA ···············································································5
  3 . Scope of the FIEA ·················································································10
  4 . Legal characteristics of the FIEA ·····························································14

B . Sources of the FIEA ··················································································16

  1 . The FIEA as a capital market regulation·····················································16
  2 . Other sources of capital market regulation ·················································17

C . Capital markets ························································································20

  1 . Functions of capital markets·····································································20
  2 . Primary and secondary markets································································21
  3 . Exchange markets and over-the-counter markets ·········································22
  4 . Efficiency of capital markets····································································22
  5 . Definition of capital markets and venues ···················································25
  6 . Regulatory framework of financial instruments exchange and venues ··· 31

D . Fundamental regulatory approach of the FIEA ································42

  1 . Mandatory information disclosure system – economic model under the FIEA ·····························································································42
  2 . Legal model under the FIEA – autonomy principle and self-responsibility ····································································································44
  3 . Mandatory information disclosure system ···················································45
  4 . Prohibition of market abuse····································································52
  5 . Regulation of financial instruments businesses·············································57

*ix*

E. The FIEA within the regulatory framework for financial institutions ................................................................................ 67

  1. Regulatory framework for financial institutions ........................ 67
  2. Scope of financial instruments businesses ............................ 69
  3. Separation of the financial instruments business and banking ............ 70
  4. Financial conglomerates .......................................... 72

F. Collective investment schemes .......................................... 74

  1. Meaning of collective investment schemes (CISs) .................... 74
  2. Strictly-regulated CISs .......................................... 75
  3. Investment trusts and investment corporations .................... 76
  4. CIS for asset-backed securitization ................................ 78

G. History of securities regulation in Japan ............................ 80

  1. Before World War II .............................................. 80
  2. The former Securities and Exchange Act .......................... 82
  3. The Financial Instruments and Exchange Act ...................... 91

H. Securities regulation and corporate governance ...................... 104

  1. Overview ...................................................... 104
  2. Background .................................................... 107
  3. Disclosure on corporate governance .............................. 110
  4. Internal control reports ........................................ 112
  5. Takeover bid regulation ........................................ 113
  6. Large-volume shareholdings reporting system .................... 116
  7. Proxy solicitation rule .......................................... 117

# Chapter 2  Scope of application and financial administration
*Hiroyuki Kansaku* (Part A) and *Naohiko Matsuo* (Parts B & C)

  A. Definition of "securities" and "derivatives transactions" under the FIEA ............................................................ 120

    1. Definition of "securities" ........................................ 120
    2. Definition of "derivatives transactions" .......................... 137

  B. Financial administration bodies and procedures .................... 159

1. Locus of authority for financial administration ·······························*159*

2. The Financial Services Agency (FSA) ·······························*161*

3. The Securities and Exchange Surveillance Commission (SESC)·········*164*

4. Implementation of financial administration ·······························*168*

C. International scope of application of the FIEA ·······························*180*

1. International scope of application of Japanese law ·······················*180*

2. International scope of application of the FIEA and related
regulations·······························································*182*

3. International enforcement of the FIEA and related regulations··········*187*

# Chapter 3 Disclosure requirements —— Disclosure of corporate affairs and other related matters
## *Masao Yanaga*

A. Disclosure on primary markets — notification for public offerings,
secondary distributions, specified procedures related to securities
issuance for reorganization, and specified procedures relating to
securities delivery for reorganization ·······························*192*

1. Exempted securities ·······························································*196*

2. Exemption from obligation to notify ·······························*199*

3. Notifications·······························································*210*

4. Shelf-registration system·······························································*308*

B. Regulation of transactions on primary market and provision of
information to investors ·······························································*325*

1. Regulation before notification·······························································*325*

2. Regulation after notification and provision of information to
investors ·······························································*327*

3. Specified financial instruments exchange markets and obligation to
provide and disclose specified information on securities ·······················*345*

4. Transaction regulation in secondary distributions of foreign
securities·······························································*350*

C. Written notices of securities and written notices of shelf registration
·······························································*353*

1. Obligation for submission of written notice of securities ·················· *353*
2. Submission of written notice of securities ······························· *355*
3. Written notice of changes··············································· *358*
4. Written notice of shelf registration ······································ *358*

D. Disclosure on secondary markets································· *360*

1. Persons obliged to submit annual securities reports······················ *360*
2. Extinguishment and exemption of continuous disclosure obligation ······ *363*
3. Annual securities reports················································ *369*
4. Quarterly securities reports ············································· *381*
5. Semiannual securities reports ··········································· *388*
6. Extraordinary reports ·················································· *392*
7. Internal control reports ················································ *397*
8. Confirmation letters···················································· *406*
9. Parent company's status report ········································· *408*
10. Documents substituting part of annual securities report for specified securities ······························································· *412*
11. Amendment reports, etc. ··············································· *414*
12. Foreign company reports, foreign person reports, etc.···················· *416*
13. Share buyback reports ················································· *429*
14. Disclosure of distribution in markets for professional investors ··········· *433*
15. Fair disclosure rules ··················································· *438*

E. Civil liability ······························································ *442*

1. Civil liability in offering disclosure······································· *442*
2. Civil liability in continuous disclosure····································· *459*
3. Civil liability for information provision on markets for professional investors ······························································· *467*
4. Civil liability pertaining to the provision of information in secondary distributions of foreign securities ······································· *470*

F. Administrative measures, etc. ·············································· *472*

1. Offering disclosures ···················································· *472*
2. Continuous disclosure ················································· *478*
3. Appeals against administrative dispositions ······························ *481*

*xii*

4．Urgent provisional suspension court orders and cease-and-desist orders
............................................................................................*481*

G．Criminal penalties and administrative fines ·······························*482*

　1．Submission of securities registration statements, etc. with false statements ································································································*482*
　2．Public offerings, secondary distributions, etc. without notification ········*485*
　3．Non-submission of annual securities reports, etc. ·····························*487*
　4．Submission of false copies of securities registration statements, etc. ·····*491*
　5．Non-delivery of prospectuses ··················································*492*
　6．Others ································································································*495*

H．Administrative monetary penalties ·············································*498*

　1．False statements, etc. in offering disclosures ·································*498*
　2．False statements, etc. in continuous disclosure·······························*500*
　3．Non-delivery of prospectuses in solicitation before notification, transactions before notification comes into effect, and secondary distribution of previously-disclosed securities ··················································*502*
　4．Non-submission of continuous disclosure documents ·····················*504*
　5．Administrative monetary penalties payment orders concerning markets for professionals ································································································*506*
　6．Acts of assistance in submission of false disclosure documents, etc. ·······*508*

# Chapter 4　The takeover bid system and the system of disclosure of the status of large-volume holdings
## *Masakazu Shirai*

A．The takeover bid system ···························································*512*

　1．Overview of the takeover bid system ·········································*512*
　2．Scope of application of takeover bid regulations ·····························*519*
　3．Regulations governing takeover bids ···········································*532*
　4．Ensuring effective implementation of takeover bid regulations ···········*554*
　5．Takeover bids by issuers ·····························································*558*

B．The system of disclosure of the status of large-volume holdings ····*562*

*xiii*

1. Overview of the system of disclosure of the status of large-volume holdings ··················································································562

2. The ordinary reporting system ·······················································565

3. The special reporting system·······························································580

4. Regulatory powers, administrative monetary penalties, and criminal penalties··············································································································587

# Chapter 5 Business regulations on financial instruments business operators, etc.
## *Naohiko Matsuo*

A. The concept of "financial instruments business"······························592

1. "Financial instruments business" and "financial instruments business operators"·················································································································592

2. "Registered financial institutions"················································593

3. "Financial instruments business operators, etc."···························594

4. "Financial instruments intermediary service" and "financial instruments intermediary service provider"··············································································595

5. Requirements for classification as a "business" (*gyo*) ················597

6. Acts constituting "financial instruments business"························599

7. Acts excluded from "financial instruments business"····················628

8. Categories of financial instruments business ·····························634

B. Start-up regulations for financial instruments businesses·············639

1. The registration system ······························································639

2. Comprehensiveness of start-up regulations ·································643

3. Structurally flexible start-up regulations·····································645

4. Special provisions on start-up regulations ·································646

5. Registration of financial instruments business ·····························661

6. Start-up-related regulations on financial instruments business operators, etc.·····································································································670

7. Membership in financial instruments and exchange system organizations (market infrastructure organizations) ··············································672

C. Regulations on scope of business of financial instruments business operators, etc. ·····································································································674

*xiv*

1. Regulations on scope of business of financial instruments business operators engaged in type I financial instruments business or investment management business ·······674

2. Regulations on scope of business of financial instruments business operators engaged only in type II financial instruments business or investment advisory and agency business·······676

3. Scope of business of registered financial institutions ·······677

4. Notification of concurrent holding of positions by officers and employees ·······685

5. Consolidated regulatory oversight ·······688

6. The sales representative system ·······692

# Chapter 6 Conduct regulations on financial instruments business operators, etc.
## Naohiko Matsuo

1. Structure of conduct regulations on financial instruments business operators, etc.·······700

2. Fiduciary duty and its core elements ·······711

3. Obligation to establish a conflict-of-interest management system ·······718

4. Structure of regulations on sale and solicitation·······721

5. Meaning of the term "solicitation" ·······740

6. Principle of suitability and accountability·······744

7. The Act on Sales, etc. of Financial Instruments·······749

8. Prohibition of compensation for loss, etc. ·······755

9. Regulations to prevent insider trading ·······764

10. Preventive measures against adverse effects (firewall regulations) ·····770

# Chapter 7 Regulation of exchanges and clearing and settlement organizations
## Sadakazu Osaki

A. Financial instruments exchanges ·······786

1. Role of financial instruments exchanges ·······786

2. Trading on financial instruments exchange markets ·······790

*xv*

3. Listing on the exchange markets ·················································· *793*
4. Organization of financial instruments exchanges ··························· *797*
5. Self-regulation of financial instruments exchanges ······················· *801*
6. Foreign financial instruments exchanges ···································· *807*

B. Proprietary trading systems (PTS) ············································ *808*

1. Role of proprietary trading systems (PTS) ······························· *808*
2. Removal of the ban on PTSs ·················································· *808*
3. Legislation of best execution obligation ·································· *810*

C. Financial instruments firms associations ···································· *812*

1. Importance of self-regulation in securities markets ···················· *812*
2. Authorized associations and recognized associations ··················· *813*
3. Certified investor protection organizations ···························· *816*

D. Clearing and settlement organizations ········································ *817*

1. Financial instruments clearing organizations ···························· *817*

E. Institutions for book-entry transfer of securities ························· *822*

1. From paper-based trading to book-entry system ························· *822*
2. Development of the transfer system in Japan ··························· *823*
3. Regulations concerning institutions for book-entry transfer ············ *824*

# Chapter 8　Market abuse regulation
## *Sadakazu Osaki* (Part A) and *Yoko Manzawa* (Parts B, C & D)

A. Regulation of insider trading ·················································· *828*

1. Historical background of the regulations ································· *828*
2. Contents of insider trading regulations ·································· *829*
3. Regulations aimed at preventing insider trading ························· *844*
4. Regulations for the prevention of acts of market manipulation ············ *847*

B. Market manipulation (Article 159) ············································ *851*

1. Background and purpose of enactment of Article 159 of the FIEA ······· *851*
2. Interpretation of Article 159 of the FIEA ······························· *851*
3. Liability for violation of Article 159 of the FIEA ······················· *867*

C. Prohibition on the spreading of rumors, and use of fraudulent means (Article 158 of the FIEA) ··············································································869

1. Background and purpose of enactment of Article 158 of the FIEA ·······869
2. Interpretation of Article 158 of the FIEA ·············································870
3. Legal Liability of violation of Article 158 of the FIEA ·······················882

D. General provision prohibiting "wrongful acts" (Article 157 of the FIEA) ··········································································································884

1. Background and purpose of enactment of Article 157 of the FIEA ·······884
2. Interpretation of Article 157 of the FIEA ·············································885
3. Legal liability for violation of Article 157 of the FIEA ·······················893

# Chapter 9   Enforcement under the FIEA
*Yoko Manzawa*

A. Legal basis of enforcement ·····································································896

1. Overview ······························································································896
2. Enforcement agencies ············································································898
3. Criminal penalty ···················································································904
4. Administrative disposition ·····································································907
5. Administrative monetary penalty system·················································909
6. Prohibition orders and orders for suspension issued by courts ············916
7. Civil liability ························································································918

B. Enforcement through self-regulation ······················································918

1. Japan Securities Dealers Association ······················································919
2. Financial instruments exchanges·····························································919

# Chapter 10   Proxy solicitation
*Masao Yanaga*

A. The role of proxy solicitation regulation·················································922

B. Meaning of solicitation ·········································································923

C. Exemption ··························································································924

*xvii*

D. Regulation of proxy solicitation and foreign companies ·················925

E. Details of proxy solicitation regulations ································926

  1. Delivery of proxy cards and reference documents ··················926

  2. Approval or disapproval columns in proxy cards··················928

  3. Submission of copies to the Commissioner of the Financial Services Agency ································································930

F. Other issues regarding solicitation for exercise of voting rights by proxy ····························································931

G. Items that should be stated in reference documents··················933

  1. Proxy Solicitation Cabinet Office Ordinance and material facts necessary to avoid misunderstanding ································································933

  2. General matters to be stated································································934

  3. Individual items to be stated concerning proposals submitted by the company — when solicitation is conducted by or for the issuing company 934

  4. Individual items to be stated regarding proposals submitted by companies — excluding the case where solicitation is conducted by or for the issuing company ································································945

  5. Individual items to be stated regarding proposals submitted by shareholders — when solicitation is conducted by or for the issuing company ································································948

  6. Individual items to be stated regarding proposals submitted by shareholders — excluding solicitation conducted by or for the issuing company ································································949

H. Effect of violating proxy solicitation regulations ··················950

Index ································································953

# Japanese Financial Instruments and Exchange Act

# Chapter 1

## Introduction to the Japanese Financial Instruments and Exchange Act

*Hiroyuki Kansaku*

# A. Purposes and structure of the Japanese Financial Instruments and Exchange Act (FIEA)

## 1. Purposes of the FIEA

The regulation of capital markets and financial derivatives markets in Japan has numerous sources[1] and a complicated systematic structure. The Japanese Financial Instruments and Exchange Act of 2006 (the "FIEA"), formerly the Securities and Exchange Act of 1948,[2] is at the heart of the regulatory framework for capital markets and financial derivatives markets.

Article 1 of the FIEA states its purpose, namely, *"The purpose of this Act is, among others, by developing systems for disclosure of corporate affairs and other related matters, providing for necessary matters relating to persons who engage in the financial instruments business and ensuring the appropriate operation of financial instruments exchanges, to ensure fairness in, among others, the issuance of securities and transactions of financial instruments, etc. and to facilitate the smooth distribution of securities, as well as to seek fair price formation for financial instruments, etc., through the full utilization of the functions of the capital market, thereby contributing to the sound development of the national economy and the protection of investors."*
Article 1 sets out three tiers of purposes, namely ultimate and abstract purposes, concrete purposes, and the objectives of the regulation in order to implement the first two purposes.[3]
The FIEA ultimately aims for the sound development of the national economy and protection of investors (Article 1 of the FIEA). Although

---

1   See infra B.
2   The former Securities and Exchange Act was influenced and inspired by the securities regulation in the United States, such as the Securities Act of 1933 and the Securities Exchange Act of 1934, and was largely based on them. See infra G. 2.
3   Soichiro Kojima, Keisuke Matsumoto, Kentaro Nakanishi & Atsushi Sakai, *Kinyû Shohin Torihiki Ho no Mokuteki∕ Teigi Kitei* ⟨Purposes and Definitions in the FIEA⟩; in, Naohiko Matsuo (ed.), *Kinyû Shohin Torihiki Ho · Naikaku Furei no Kaisetsu* ⟨Explanation of the FIEA and the Related Cabinet Office Ordinances⟩, pp. 16–17 (Shoji Homu, 2008).

Chapter 1　Introduction to the Japanese Financial Instruments and Exchange Act

Article 1 on its face provides for two purposes of the FIEA, its ultimate purpose is traditionally understood as to protect investors.[4] It is necessary for the protection of investors to ensure the development and maintenance of fair and efficient capital markets. Protection of investors and ensuring the proper functioning of securities and financial derivatives markets are substantially two sides of the same coin, because investors can only be protected insofar as accurate and appropriate information is offered in order for them to make reasonable investment decisions and for the markets to function well.[5] For example, theoretically, no investor can beat the markets using publicly available information to identify undervalued and overvalued stocks in securities markets if a capital market has semi-strong efficiency (defined below in C. 4), because securities prices already reflect all of the publicly-available information.[6] Investors can therefore rely on the market prices as fair prices.

The investors who seek to be protected by the FIEA are investors and prospective investors who purchase and sell securities and other financial instruments. The markets, where securities are issued and financial instruments are transacted, are subject to the regulation under the FIEA. Accurate and timely information regarding securities,[7] such as shares and corporate bonds, has to be offered to investors in order for them to make independent and rational investment decisions. On the other hand, market abuses[8] such as insider trading and market manipulation should be

---

4　Takeo Suzuki and Ichiro Kawamoto, *Shoken Torihiki Ho*, 2d. ed., ⟨Securities and Exchange Act⟩, p. 42 (Yûhikaku, 1984). On the other hand, Prof. Uemura insists that the ultimate purpose of the FIEA is to achieve efficient capital markets via fair pricing in order to fairly distribute capital and resources (Tatsuo Uemura, *Kinyû shohin torihiki ho — Mokuteki kitei no igi wo chûshin ni* [The Financial Instruments and Exchange Act — Meaning of Article 1 Prescribing the Purpose of the Act], *Horitsu no Hiroba*, Vol. 59, No. 11, p. 52 (2006)).

5　Etsuro Kuronuma, *Shoken Sijo no Kino to Fukousei Torihiki no Kisei* [The Functions of Capital Markets and the Regulation on Unfair Trading], pp. 9-13 (Yûhi-kaku, 2002). Tomonobu Yamashita/ Hideki Kanda (ed.), *Kinyû Shohin Torihiki Ho Gaisetsu* ⟨Outline of the FIEA⟩, 2d. ed., pp. 8-9 (Yûhi-kaku, 2017).

6　See infra C. 4. (b).

7　See infra Chapter 2 A. 1.

8　See infra Chapter 8.

*3*

prohibited and regulated. Regulation of disclosure and restriction of market abuses not only contributes to protecting investors, it also increases the efficiency of the markets.

The interests, rights and risks that securities, such as shares and corporate bonds, create or represent cannot be understood without information about the structure of the securities and various corporate affairs that could influence the value of the securities. Such information, which the FIEA and other rules and regulations require as necessary or appropriate in the public interest and for the protection of investors, is subject to mandatory disclosure.

Furthermore, accurate and timely information must be continuously disclosed concerning corporate affairs and securities that are listed and traded on an exchange, in order for security holders to rationally exercise their rights related to the securities, trade the securities or make other investment decisions. Efficient and fair capital markets lead to the sound development of the national economy through efficient allocation of capital and resources and by reducing transaction costs. Thus, the ultimate aims of the FIEA, namely the sound development of the national economy and protection of investors, can be simultaneously achieved.

In order to achieve these ultimate purposes, Article 1 of the FIEA also sets out three concrete purposes in the second tier. The first is to ensure fairness in, among others, the issuance of securities and the trading of financial instruments. Ensuring fairness is important for enhancing investor confidence in market integrity. The second concrete purpose is to facilitate the smooth distribution of securities. Smooth distribution is a basic requirement for liquid and efficient markets. The third concrete purpose is to obtain fair prices for financial instruments through the utilization of the functions of capital markets. The third concrete purpose was added pursuant to 2006 amendments to the FIEA. These amendments show that the FIEA focuses more and more on ensuring the proper functioning of securities and financial derivatives markets.

Article 1 of the FIEA further clarifies the regulatory objectives to achieve

*4*

Chapter 1   Introduction to the Japanese Financial Instruments and Exchange Act

the purposes of this Act. The first one is to develop systems for disclosure in terms of corporate financial affairs and other related matters. The second is to regulate and supervise persons and firms who are engaged in the financial instruments business (*kinyûshohin torihiki gyo*). The third is to ensure appropriate operation of financial instruments exchanges (*kinyûshohin torihiki jo*), on which securities, financial instruments and financial derivatives are issued and traded. The organization of the markets and the participants and intermediaries, such as financial instruments business operators and financial instruments exchanges, are regarded as the elementary regulatory objects of the FIEA in consideration of its functions.

Generally, provisions of a given act that state its purposes have little importance to the interpretation of the rest of the act.[9] Nevertheless, eventually, Article 1 of the FIEA regarding its purposes may come to affect the concrete interpretation of this Act.

Since 2006, the FIEA has regulated not only financial derivatives transactions derived from the price or worth of securities but also those derived from financial indicators or indexes, such as interest rates or foreign currencies.[10] This regulatory approach aims to distinguish between the regulation of securities and securities-related derivatives transactions, on the one hand, and that of non-securities-related financial derivatives, on the other hand. While this section mainly covers the regulatory approach to securities transactions, the background and regulatory framework and concept concerning financial derivatives is also outlined below, Chapter 2. A. 2. of this volume.

## 2. Structure of the FIEA

The FIEA consists of the following 26 chapters.

---

**9**   Makoto Saito, *Koho-teki kanten kara mita ginko kantoku hosei* [Banking regulation from the public law viewpoint], *Kinyû ho kenkyû*, No. 20, p. 64 (2004). Regarding the meaning of purpose clauses of state law, see Hiroshi Shiono, *Seitei ho ni okeru mokuteki kitei ni kansuru ichi kosatsu* [Regarding purpose clauses in state law], *Hochi Shugi no Shoso* [Various Aspects of Rule of Law], p. 44 (Yuhi-kaku, 2001).

**10**   See infra A. 3. c. and Chapter 2 A. 2.

Chapter I General Provisions
Chapter II Disclosure of Corporate Affairs and Other Related Matters
Chapter II-2 Disclosure Required for Takeover Bid
Chapter II-3 Disclosure of the Status of Large-Volume Holdings in Shares
　　　　　Etc.
Chapter II-4 Special Provisions for Procedures by Use of Electronic Data
　　　　　Processing System for Disclosure
Chapter II-5 Provision or Publication of Information on Specified Securities
Chapter II-6 Disclosure of Material Information
Chapter III Financial Instruments Business Operators, Etc.
Chapter III-2 Financial Instruments Intermediary Service Providers
Chapter III-3 Credit Rating Agencies
Chapter III-4 High Frequency Traders
Chapter IV Financial Instruments Firms Association
Chapter IV-2 Investor Protection Fund
Chapter V Financial Instruments Exchange
Chapter V-2 Foreign Financial Instruments Exchange
Chapter V-3 Financial Instruments Clearing Organization, Etc.
Chapter V-4 Securities Finance Company
Chapter V-5 Designated Dispute Resolution Organization
Chapter V-6 Trade Repository, Etc.
Chapter V-7 Specified Financial Indicator Calculation Agents
Chapter VI Regulations on Transactions of Securities
Chapter VI-2 Administrative Monetary Penalties
Chapter VII Miscellaneous Provisions
Chapter VIII Penal Provisions
Chapter VIII-2 Special Provisions for Procedures Regarding Confiscation
Chapter IX Investigation into a Criminal Case

The regulatory objectives of the FIEA are mainly classified into five categories.

The first category is the mandatory disclosure regulation. The principal means by which the FIEA regulates the issuance and transaction of securities is a mandatory disclosure system. Investors require correct and

Chapter 1   Introduction to the Japanese Financial Instruments and Exchange Act

timely information regarding securities, such as shares and corporate bonds, to make rational investment decisions. It is important in order to facilitate rational decisions to disclose information concerning securities and the issuers of those securities. Correct and timely information is part of the foundation of investor confidence and market integrity, which ensures the proper functioning of securities markets. In efficient capital markets, fair prices can be determined and capital and resources are efficiently allocated. This category covers Chapter II, II-2, II-3, II-4, II-5, and II-6. Chapter II of the FIEA creates a duty to submit a securities registration statement and securities report; specifies the information to be disclosed and form and timing of disclosure; and provides civil liability for misrepresentation or failure to disclose. An issuer of securities is not allowed to make a public offering of the securities until a securities registration statement (*yûkashoken todokedesho*) has been submitted. In Chapter II-4, there are special provisions that set out procedures for use of an electronic data processing system for disclosure according to the FIEA. Beginning in January 2003, the Financial Services Agency of Japan has operated the Electronic Disclosure for Investors' NETwork ("EDINET"). Chapter II-5 requires the provision or publication of information related to specified securities, such as asset-backed securities within the framework of structured finance. Under the amendments to the FIEA of 2017, a fair disclosure rule was introduced (Chapter II-6). Takeover bid regulation (Chapter II-2) and large-volume shareholdings reporting system (Chaper II-3) is not only related to disclosure but also to corporate control and corporate governance (H. 5. and 6.).

The second category of regulation is the supervisory regulation of the organizations and participants in securities markets and financial derivatives markets. The provision of Chapters III, III-2, III-3, III-4 (pursuant to 2017 amendments), IV, IV-2, V, V-2, V-3, V-4, V-5, V-6, and V-7 belong to this category. The FIEA regulates various organizations related to the capital markets that provide the infrastructure for capital markets, such as financial instruments exchanges (*kinyû shohin torihiki jo*; Chapter V), foreign financial instruments exchanges (*gaikoku kinyû shohin torihiki jo;* Chapter V-2), financial instruments clearing organizations (*kinyû shohin torihiki*

7

*seisan kikan*; Chapter V-3),[11] and trade repositories (*torihiki joho chikuseki kikan*; Chapter V-6). The FIEA also regulates financial intermediaries, such as financial instruments business operators (*kinyû shohin torihiki gyosha*; Chapter III), financial instruments intermediary service providers (*kinyû shohin chûkai gyosha*; Chapter III-2), credit rating agencies (*shinyo kakuzuke gyosha*; Chapter III-3), securities finance companies (*shoken kinyû kaisha*; Chapter V-4) and specified financial indicator calculation agents (*tokutei kinyû sihyo sanshutsu-sha*; Chapter V-7). The FIEA regulates the entry of these participants, as well as systems for their supervision, the scope of the participants' business and their business codes of conduct. Furthermore, self-regulatory organizations (SROs) are also regulated under the FIEA. Namely, financial instruments firms associations (*kinyû shohin torihiki gyo kyokai;* Chapter IV), financial instruments exchanges (*kinyû shohin torihiki jo*; Chapter V), and self-regulatory corporation (*jishu kisei hojin*; Chapter V) [12] are regulated as SROs. Investor protection organizations, such as investor protection funds (*toshisha hogo kikin*; Chapter IV-2) and designated dispute resolution organizations (*sitei funso kaiketsu kikan*; Chapter V-5) are also regulated under the FIEA. Under the amendments to the FIEA of 2017, regulation on high frequency traders was introduced (Chapter III-4).

The third category of regulation is the prohibition of market abuse such as insider trading or market manipulation, in order to ensure market integrity and investor confidence. Under Chapter VI, market manipulation, insider

---

11   The JSCC (Japan Securities Clearing Organization), which is a subsidiary of the Japan Exchange Group, is licensed as a financial instruments clearing organization under the FIEA. The JSCC conducts cross-market clearing operations for cash product trades executed in all stock exchange markets across Japan. In addition to trading on exchange markets, the JSCC began to offer clearing services for certain types of OTC derivatives transactions in July 2011 for credit default swaps (CDS), and expanded its services to include interest rate swaps in October 2012.

12   The Japan Exchange Regulation (JPX-R) is a subsidiary of the Japan Exchange Group (JPX), a self-regulatory corporation entrusted by the Tokyo Stock Exchange to create various self-regulations and operate to maintain and ensure the soundness and fairness of the securities market. Tokyo Stock Exchange, Inc. Rules. ⟨http://www.jpx.co.jp/english/rules-participants/rules/regulations/index.html⟩

Chapter 1   Introduction to the Japanese Financial Instruments and Exchange Act

trading, discretionary-account trading and exaggerated promotional campaigns etc. are banned. Furthermore, the FIEA generally prohibits the use of wrongful means, schemes or techniques with regard to the unfair sale, purchase, etc. of transactions of securities.

The fourth category of regulation is related to the enforcement of the FIEA. Regulation of the FIEA is enforced occasionally by administrative supervisory powers, criminal penalties or administrative monetary penalties and civil penalties. Administrative monetary penalties (*kachokin*; Chapter VI-2), penal provisions (*bassoku*; Chapter VIII), special provisions for procedures regarding confiscation (*bosshū*; Chapter VIII-2) and investigation into a criminal case (*hansoku jiken no chosa*; Chapter IX) belong to this category.

The fifth category of regulation is related to corporate control and corporate governance. Takeover bid (*kokai kaitsuke*) regulation (Chapter II-2) and large-volume shareholdings reporting systems (Chapter II-3) belong to this category. Furthermore, proxy solicitation rules, internal control reporting systems and the duty to disclose on corporate governance in securities reports are closely related to corporate control and corporate governance. A takeover bid is a means of purchasing a substantial portion of the outstanding shares of a listed company outside a stock exchange by making an offer to purchase all shares up to a specified number, offered to shareholders within a specified period at a fixed price, normally at a premium on the market price. The primary purpose of the takeover bid regulation is to secure transparency and fairness in securities transactions that are conducted outside a stock exchange and would affect corporate control. Furthermore, takeover bid regulation aims to protect the market for corporate control and to protect investors from the market viewpoint. The FIEA requires an offeror to submit a takeover bid statement (*kokai kaitsuke todokede-sho*), to issue a public notice of commencement of a takeover bid (*kokai kaitsuke kaishi kokoku*) and to provide shareholders tendering their shares with a takeover bid explanation (*kokai kaitsuke setsumei-sho*) in which the purpose and the terms and conditions of the takeover bid are specified. The target company then has to submit a report on its opinion of

*9*

the takeover bid (*iken hyomei hokoku-sho*). The takeover bid regulation aims to give shareholders an equal opportunity to sell their stock, usually at a premium on the market price.

The large-volume shareholdings reporting system is designed for the disclosure of information when a large-volume shareholding in a listed company is acquired or disposed of to reach or exceed the threshold of 5%. When the percentage of such shareholdings increases or decreases by 1% or more, such person must file a revised large-volume shareholding report indicating the change that occurred in the percentage of such holdings. This regulation aims to enhance market transparency, because changes in large-volume shareholdings would have significant effects on stock prices in the market. Furthermore, information regarding large-volume shareholdings would clarify control structure and its transformation of listed companies. Knowing the identity of major shareholders provides investors with important information, for example, with regard to imminent takeovers.

## 3. Scope of the FIEA

### a. Overview

The scope of the FIEA is mainly defined by the concepts "securities" (*yûkashoken*) and "derivatives transactions" (*derivative torihiki*).

First, public offering or secondary distribution of "securities" is subject to mandatory disclosure regulation under the FIEA. The issuer of "securities" shall submit a securities registration statement (*yûkashoken todokede-sho*) (Article 5(1) of the FIEA). Mandatory disclosure regulation varies between type I securities, which are defined as "paragraph 1 securities" and type II securities, which are defined as "paragraph 2 securities" and called deemed securities.[13] Namely, mandatory disclosure regulation was made flexible according to the class of a security depending on its liquidity.[14] Furthermore, a prospectus (*mokuromi-sho*) shall be delivered to an investor in advance of, or at the same time as, having the securities acquired or selling the securities (Article 15(2) of the FIEA). On the other hand, derivatives transactions are

---

**13**  See infra 3. b.

**14**  Hideki Kanda, *Kinyû shohin torihiki ho no kozo* [Structure of the Financial Instruments and Exchange Act], *Shoji Homu*, No. 1799, pp. 45–46 (2007).

Chapter 1  Introduction to the Japanese Financial Instruments and Exchange Act

not subject to a mandatory disclosure rule, except for covered warrant (Article 2(2) (xix) of the FIEA).[15]

Second, financial instruments business operators, who were registered by the Prime Minister according to Article 29 of the FIEA, are subject to business conduct regulation and supervisory regulation. Financial instruments business is defined by the concepts of "securities" and "derivatives transactions." For example, the following conduct or transactions are financial instruments business: (1) the sale and purchase of securities, market transactions of derivatives or foreign market transactions of derivatives, (2) intermediary, brokerage or agency service for the sale and purchase of securities, market transactions of derivatives or foreign market transactions of derivatives, (3) intermediary, brokerage or agency service for entrustment of the sale and purchase of securities or market transactions of derivatives or foreign market transactions of derivatives conducted in a financial instruments exchange market (Article 2(8) of the FIEA).

Third, market abuse regulation applies to conduct or transactions in terms of securities and derivatives transactions (Chapter VI of the FIEA).

b. Definition of "securities"[16]

As mentioned above, "securities" under the FIEA are divided into two groups depending on their liquidity, namely type I securities and type II securities. While the type I securities are characteristic of higher liquidity in the securities market, type II securities are less liquidity. Fundamentally, they conform to different type of rules with respect to disclosure requirements and financial instruments business regulations, with many exceptions. For example, type II securities are in principle not subject to mandatory disclosure regulation, except with regard to such securities whose issuer conducts investment management business that invests mainly in other securities. The "securities" are a key concept, which define the scope of the various rules and regulations under the FIEA.

Type I securities consist of securities under Article 2, paragraph 1 and some

---

**15**  Covered warrants are subject to mandatory disclosure rules as "securities".
**16**  See infra Chapter 2 A. 1.

*11*

rights or interests that are listed in Article 2, paragraph 2 as type I securities. Examples of type I securities under Article 2, paragraph 1 are as follows: Japanese government bonds (JGB), municipal bonds, specified corporate bonds prescribed in the Act on the Securitization of Assets, corporate bond certificates, share certificates and share option certificates, preferred equity investment certificates prescribed in the Act on Preferred Equity Investment by Cooperative Structured Financial Institutions, beneficiary certificates of investment trusts or foreign investment trusts prescribed in the Investment Trust and Investment Corporation Act, and beneficiary certificates in loan trusts, beneficiary certificates of beneficiary certificate-issuing trusts prescribed in the Trust Act, etc. Furthermore, type I securities also include (i) securities or certificates that have been issued by a foreign state or foreign person and are of the same nature as the above securities, (ii) securities or certificates issued by a foreign person, and representing a beneficial interest in a trust in which loan claims held by persons engaging in banking business, or persons otherwise making money loans on a regular basis are entrusted, or bearing any other similar rights, and are specified by cabinet office ordinance, (iii) option certificates pertaining to transactions which are conducted in a foreign financial instruments market, and (iv) securities or certificates that have been issued by a person with whom the above-mentioned securities or certificates are deposited and in a state other than the state in which the deposited securities or certificates were issued and which represent the rights pertaining to the deposited securities or certificates (Article 2(1) (i) to (xxi) of the FIEA). The type I securities include also some rights or interests that are listed in Article 2, paragraph 1, even where no physical certificates are issued. For example, rights or interests represented by bonds or stocks held under a book-entry transfer system are deemed equivalent to those securities listed in Article 2, paragraph 1 (Article 2 (2) of the FIEA). Furthermore, electronically recorded monetary claims and other rights designated by cabinet order as those for which it is found, when taking into consideration the liquidity thereof and other factors, equivalent to those securities listed in Article 2, paragraph 1 are included in type I securities (Article 2(2) of the FIEA).

On the other hand, type II securities namely deemed securities include (i)

Chapter 1   Introduction to the Japanese Financial Instruments and Exchange Act

beneficial interest of a trust (Article 2(2)(i) of the FIEA), (ii) rights that are claimable against a foreign person and which have the nature of the rights of beneficial interest of a trust (ibid., Article 2 (2) (ii)), (iii) membership rights of a general partnership company (*gomei kaisha*) or limited partnership company (*goshi kaisha*) or a limited liability company (*godo kaisha*) (ibid., Article 2(2)(iii)), (iv) membership rights of a foreign juridical person that have the nature of rights of a general partnership company (ibid., Article 2 (2) (iv)), (v) rights in non-strictly regulated collective investment scheme[17] based on a partnership contract,[18] an anonymous partnership agreement,[19] an investment limited partnership agreement[20] or a limited liability partnership agreement, etc. (ibid., Article 2 (2)(v) & (vi))[21]. Deemed securities (v) above cover the rights or interests in a non-strictly regulated collective investment scheme as type II securities, regardless of their legal nature or legal structure.[22] Other rights designated by cabinet order as those for which it is found, when taking into consideration the economic nature and other factors, necessary to secure the public interest or protection of investors are included in type II securities (Article 2(2)(vii) of the FIEA).

c. Definition of "derivatives transactions"[23]

The FIEA classifies financial derivatives transactions into three categories, according to the place of the transaction: market derivatives transactions, foreign market derivatives transactions; and over-the-counter (OTC) derivatives transactions (Article 2 (20) of the FIEA). Derivatives transactions are not subject to the mandatory disclosure regulation under the FIEA, unlike type I securities.

---

**17**  In a collective investment scheme, a holder of the rights can receive dividend of profits arising from the business conducted by using money invested or contributed by the investors or distribution of the assets of the invested business.

**18**  See Article 667, paragraph 1 of the Civil Code.

**19**  See Article 535 of the Commercial Code.

**20**  See Article 3, paragraph 1 of the Investment Limited Partnership Act.

**21**  See Article 3, paragraph 1 of the Limited Liability Partnership Act.

**22**  Naohiko Matsuo, *Kinyû Shohin Torihiki Ho* [Financial Instruments and Exchange Act], 5th ed., pp. 65-71 (Shojihomu, 2018).

**23**  See Chapter 2 A. 2.

*13*

"Market derivatives transactions" are futures of financial instruments or financial indexes capable of being settled by paying or receiving the difference, options to sell or purchase financial instruments, market derivatives transactions in other markets or financial index futures, etc., interest rate, currency or goods swaps and credit derivatives contracts (Article 2(21) (i) to (v) of the FIEA). These transactions are conducted on a financial instruments market in accordance with the requirements of and using the methods prescribed by the operator of the financial instruments market. Therefore, market derivatives transactions are standardized.

"Foreign market derivatives transactions" means transactions that are conducted on a foreign financial instruments market and are similar to market derivatives transactions (Article 2(23) of the FIEA).

"OTC derivatives transactions" are forwards of financial instruments or financial indicators capable of being settled by paying or receiving the difference, options to sell or purchase financial instruments, other OTC derivatives transactions, etc., interest rate or currency swaps, and credit derivatives contracts, in each case conducted neither in a financial instruments market nor a foreign financial instruments market (Article 2 (22) of the FIEA). These transactions are not conducted in a financial instruments market but face-to-face, which makes tailor-made derivatives transactions possible.[24]

## 4. Legal characteristics of the FIEA

The FIEA has various legal characteristics. The rules and regulations of the FIEA can be broken down into four categories according to the legal nature of regulation, namely, capital market regulation, supervisory regulation, criminal law and civil law.

Capital market regulation is the most characteristic of the FIEA as capital markets law, which aims to ensure the efficiency and integrity of capital markets. Mandatory disclosure regulation and market abuse regulation (e.g., prohibition of insider trading and market manipulation, etc.) are typical

---

24　See Chapter 2 A. 2. Hiroyuki Kansaku, Recent Development in the Regulation of Financial Derivatives in Japan, University of Tokyo Journal of Law and Politics, Volume 2, pp. 8-29 (Winter 2014).

Chapter 1 Introduction to the Japanese Financial Instruments and Exchange Act

capital market regulation.[25] Takeover bid regulation and large-volume shareholdings reporting system is related to capital market regulation as mandatory disclosure regulation. Furthermore, they are also related to capital market regulation in a broad sense, because they are concerned with the market for corporate control and corporate governance. Capital market regulation often accompanies supervisory enforcement and criminal sanctions and occasionally has civil law effects relating to claims for damages.

The Financial Services Agency of Japan (the "FSA") has the power not only to order various administrative dispositions but also to impose "administrative monetary penalties (*kachokin*)" in relation to breaches of the mandatory disclosure regulation or market abuse, etc.[26] Furthermore, the FIEA deals with issues related to various legal aspects of enforcement. For example, concerning the mandatory disclosure regulation, the FIEA provides for a special rule for damages due to torts in the case of failure to disclose or fraudulent disclosure of securities reports, etc., in order to lighten the burden of proof regarding negligence, damages or the causal relationship between the non-disclosure or fraudulent disclosure and damages (Articles 18, 19, 20, 21, 21-2, 21-3, 22, and 24-4 of the FIEA). The FIEA further includes many other criminal sanctions relating to securities transactions including market abuse, such as insider trading and market manipulation.

Thus, the FIEA has complex legal characteristics. The FIEA is a mixture of capital market law, supervisory regulation, criminal law, and civil law. Criminal, administrative, and eventually civil law sanctions are necessary to enforce the provisions of the FIEA and to deter parties from violation. The reason the FIEA includes a special rule for damages caused by non-disclosure or fraudulent disclosure in terms of mandatory disclosure documents is to enhance enforcement by private persons and to discourage non-disclosure and fraudulent disclosure. Enforcement by private persons is in some cases a more effective means of enforcing the FIEA than a system relying mainly on criminal sanctions and/or administrative dispositions. Nevertheless, in Japan unlike in United States, there is little effective

---

**25** Matsuo, supra note 22, p. 9.
**26** See Chapter 9.

*15*

procedural mechanism in this area dealing with the rational apathy problem, such as a class actions mechanism.[27]

# B. Sources of the FIEA

## 1. The FIEA as a capital market regulation

The Japanese Financial Instruments and Exchange Act (the "FIEA") is at the heart of the regulatory framework for capital markets and financial derivatives markets. The FIEA delegates authority for many matters to be addressed by cabinet order or cabinet office ordinance. There is one cabinet order, "Financial Instruments and Exchange Act Implementing Order", and many cabinet office ordinances, including the "Cabinet Office Ordinance on Definitions under Article 2 of the Financial Instruments and Exchange Act", "Cabinet Office Ordinance on Disclosure of Corporate Affairs, etc.", "Cabinet Office Ordinance on Disclosure on Specific Securities", "Cabinet Office Ordinance on Disclosure of Information, etc. on Issuers of Foreign Government Bonds, etc.", "Cabinet Office Ordinance on Disclosure Required for Takeover Bids for Share, etc. by Person Other than Issuer", "Cabinet Office Ordinance on Disclosure Required for Takeover Bids for Listed Share, etc. by Issuer," "Cabinet Office Ordinance on Disclosure of the Status of Large-Volume Holding in Shares, etc.", "Cabinet Office Ordinance on

---

27　Japan introduced a class action system under the Act on Special Measures Concerning Civil Court Proceedings for the Collective Redress for Property Damage Incurred by Consumers of 2013. Nevertheless, according to the lawmaker's opinion, damages in securities transactions caused by false disclosure or non-disclosure cannot be claimed using the collective redress measure, because it is not a monetary payment obligation borne by a business operator (*jigyo-sha*) against a consumer concerning a consumer contract that pertains to a claim for performance of a contractual obligation, a claim pertaining to unjust enrichment, a claim for damages based on nonperformance of a contractual obligation, a claim for damages based on a warranty against defects or a claim for damages based on a tort (limited to claims based on the provisions of the Civil Code) (Article 3(1)). Masashi Kubota, *Shûdan teki shohisha higai no kaifuku seido no sosetsu* [Establishment of Collective Redress System for Property Damage Incurred by Consumers], *Rippo to Chosa* [Legislation and Investigation], No. 336, p. 8 (2013).

Chapter 1    Introduction to the Japanese Financial Instruments and Exchange Act

Financial Instruments Business, etc.", "Cabinet Office Ordinance on Financial Instruments Exchanges, etc.", "Cabinet Office Ordinance on Financial Instruments Firms Associations, etc.", "Cabinet Office Ordinance on Financial Instruments Clearing Organizations, etc.", "Cabinet Office Ordinance on Designated Dispute Resolution Organizations under the Provisions of Chapter V-5 of the Financial Instruments and Exchange Act", "Cabinet Office Ordinance on Transactions Prescribed in Article 161-2 of the Financial Instruments and Exchange Act and Security Deposits for Said Transactions", "Cabinet Office Ordinance on Proxy Solicitation of Listed Companies' Shares" and "Cabinet Office Ordinance on Administrative Monetary Penalties under the Provisions of Chapter VI-2 of the Financial Instruments and Exchange Act", etc.

## 2. Other sources of capital markets regulation

### a. Regulation of strictly regulated collective investment schemes

The collective investment scheme (CIS) plays an important role in capital markets, because fund raising can be enhanced through securities issued by a CIS, which can intermediate and combine fundraisers and investors. Furthermore, CISs offer great business for industry and investment opportunities for investors. On the one hand, securities issued by CISs are treated as securities under the FIEA. On the other hand, the structure and distribution of the powers of CISs is partly regulated by special laws. CISs are classified into two categories based on the purposes and functions of each scheme. One category is asset management CISs, such as investment trusts, in which a special purpose vehicle (SPV) collects money and invests it in financial instruments. The other is asset-backed securitization CISs, in which a fundraiser, namely an originator, transfers particular assets to a SPV in the scheme and the vehicle issues securities.

In Japan, there are strictly regulated CISs, which are subject to strict special laws, regulations and administrative rules. There are special acts to regulate the organization of vehicles and structures for CISs and to supervise the CISs. The Investment Trust and Investment Corporation Act regulates investment trust CISs, and the Act Concerning Assets Liquidation regulates asset-backed securities CISs. The securities issued by strictly regulated CISs according to these acts are type I securities under the FIEA.[28]

*17*

These regulations govern the arrangement of the scheme, the structure and organization of the vehicle, the manner in which related parties, etc. conduct business in accordance with their obligations.

### b. Regulation of book-entry transfer system for securities

Securities listed on stock exchanges in Japan are regulated by the Act on Book-Entry Transfer of Corporate Bonds and Shares. Listed securities are transferred in this book-entry transfer system through records kept by a book-entry transfer institution (*furikae kikan*) as central securities depository and account management institutions (*koza kanri kikan*) like securities companies and banks, etc. Pursuant to the Act, shares and bonds, etc. were all dematerialized in Japan, enhancing the efficiency of trading listed securities. Under the book-entry system, a transfer of the securities is valid, only if the book-entry transfer application results in an increase in the number of securities listed in the holding column of the account of the recipient of the book-entry transfer receiver equal to the number of shares involved in the transfer. On the other hand, the participant whose recorded number of shares in its account is to be reduced as a result of the book-entry transfer shall apply to its account management institution for the book-entry transfer of the shares.

### c. Self-regulations of SROs

The role of self-regulation in exchange and capital and financial derivatives markets is increasingly important.[29] Financial instruments firms associations and financial instruments exchanges are self-regulatory organizations under the FIEA that promulgate a lot of self-regulations.

The advantages of such self-regulation by self-regulatory organizations (SROs) include: (1) The quality of rules being high and content of the rules is appropriate, because the rules are established by experts engaged in

---

**28**　Concerning type I securities, see supra A. 3. b. and infra Chapter 2 A. 1. d.

**29**　Katsuro Kanzaki, *Shoken torihiki no jishu-kisei* [Self-regulation on Securities Transactions], *Horiguchi Wataru Sensei Taikan Kinen, Gendai Kaisha Ho · Shoken Torihiki Ho no Tenkai* [Essays in Honor of Retirement for Prof. Wataru Horiguchi, Recent Development of Corporate Law and Securities Regulations], pp. 513- (Keizai Horei Kenkyû-kai, 1993).

Chapter 1　Introduction to the Japanese Financial Instruments and Exchange Act

capital markets and securities transactions and have enough information. (2) Self-regulations are promptly and timely established, reformed and lifted. (3) More effective and efficient enforcement can be realized than through enforcement by law. On the other hand, there are disadvantages to self-regulation by SROs: (1) SROs present conflicts of interest between the interests of the self-regulatory organization and the financial instruments business interests groups that are part of it, because self-regulations are established, reformed, interpreted and applied by the regulated parties themselves, such as investment firms. Self-regulations can be partial and unfair. (2) The legitimacy, consistency, and transparency of self-regulation do not compare favorably with those of laws and rules established by the nation. (3) Self-regulation by authorized SROs can be interfered with or biased by the nation,[30] blurring the respective roles and functions of hard law and soft law. (4) Self-regulation can restrict competition between members of SROs.[31]

The self-regulatory organizations under the FIEA are subject to supervision by the authorities. Therefore, SROs established under the FIEA are required by the nation to establish, interpret and enforce self-regulations and are subject to supervision by the nation (Articles 67-8, 78(2), 79-2, 84, and 87 of the FIEA).[32] The abovementioned disadvantages are mitigated by the authorization and supervision by the nation.

The Japan Securities Dealers Association, an authorized financial instruments firms association under the FIEA, promulgates self-regulations relating to customer management and internal management by association members, employees and sales representatives (*gaimu-in*) of association members, advertising, personal information protection, stocks, bonds, securitized products and other products and code of ethics.[33] The

---

30　Katsuro Kanzaki, Masashi Shitani & Yasuhiro Kawaguchi, *Kinyū Shohin Torihiki Ho* [Financial Instruments and Exchange Act], p. 29 (Seirin Shoin, 2012).

31　Kanzaki, Shitani & Kawaguchi, supra note 30, p. 29.

32　Hiroyuki Kansaku, *Global na Shihon Sijo ni okeru Soft Law to Nihon-ho heno Eikyo* [Soft Law in the Global Capital Market and its Impact on Japanese Law] in: Hiroto Dogauchi (ed.), *Gendai Ho no Dotai* [Dynamics of Contemporary Law], Vol. 4, *Kokusai shakai no hendo to ho* [Changes to International Society and Law] pp. 71-73, (Iwanami Shoten, 2015).

33　JSDA, Rules. 〈http://www.jsda.or.jp/en/rules/index.html〉

*19*

Investment Trusts Association, Japan, [34] the Financial Futures Association of Japan, [35] the Japan Investment Advisers Association, [36] and the Type II Financial Instruments Firms Association [37] each promulgate self-regulation as authorized financial instruments firms associations.

The Tokyo Stock Exchange is an authorized financial instruments exchange under the FIEA and promulgates self-regulations and related rules concerning business, trading participants, clearing and settlement, margin and loan trading, securities listings and brokerage agreement standards, etc. [38]

# C. Capital markets

## 1. Functions of capital markets

The FIEA is at the heart of the regulatory framework for capital markets and financial derivatives markets. A market is a system in which supply and demand meet. Markets allow the liquidity of securities and financial derivatives and formation of fair prices that reflect supply and demand. Securities markets generally mean the facilities through which securities are issued and traded. Companies can raise capital by issuing securities such as shares or corporate bonds in a primary market. Investors can purchase and resell their securities to invest or liquidate in a secondary market. Efficient securities markets can help to raise capital while reducing transaction costs on the one hand, and allocate capital and resources efficiently on the other hand. Among other things, it is attractive for start-up and venture capital companies to have more opportunities to raise money by convincing the

---

34 The Investment Trusts Association, Rules. ⟨http://www.toushin.or.jp/profile/article/⟩

35 The Financial Futures Association of Japan, Regulations for FX Transactions. ⟨http://www.ffaj.or.jp/en/regulation/⟩

36 ⟨http://www.jiaa.or.jp/profile/kisoku.html⟩

37 Type II Financial Instruments Firms Association, Rules. ⟨http://www.t2fifa.or.jp/teikan/index.html⟩

38 See supra note 12.

Chapter 1    Introduction to the Japanese Financial Instruments and Exchange Act

capital market of its worth. Thus, efficient markets would allocate the most financial capital to investment with the highest returns. Efficient securities markets contribute to the sound development of the national economy, which, as discussed, is the ultimate purpose of the FIEA (Article 1 of the FIEA).[39]

## 2. Primary and secondary markets

Securities markets are classified into two categories: primary markets and secondary markets. Issuers of securities can raise capital for their business by issuing their securities in a primary market. Primary market transactions are sales by a corporate issuer to investors mostly underwriters, which are called offerings of securities. Raising capital through an offering for the first time is called an initial public offering (IPO). The primary market allocates capital directly, which means it plays the central role in capital markets. There is an asymmetry of information between an issuer and investors to be corrected. Furthermore, it is usually necessary to make an effort to sell securities in the case of an IPO in a primary market in order to raise capital as planned. By contrast, there is normally less asymmetry of information in the secondary market, where already-issued securities are traded between investors. Nevertheless, there is no sharp line between public offering and secondary distribution in practice, because public offerings are generally accompanied by secondary distributions requiring sales efforts.[40]

Generally speaking, there is usually pressure to issue new securities (through a public offering) or to sell issued securities (secondary distribution) in a primary market through solicitation.[41] Issuers of securities that are publicly offered or secondarily distributed are subject to mandatory

---

**39**  See supra A. 1.

**40**  The situations deemed secondary distribution of securities by the FIEA share the element of asymmetry of information between a distributor and investors to be corrected (Article 2 (4) of the FIEA). Nagashima/ Ohno/ Tsunematsu Horitsu Jimu-sho, *Advance Kinyū Shohin Torihiki Ho* [Advanced Financial Instruments and Exchange Act], 2nd ed., pp. 115-116 (Shojihomu, 2014).

**41**  The FIEA distinguishes a "public offering" and a "secondary distribution," based on whether securities were already issued at the time of solicitation of investors. Matsuo, supra note 22, p. 120. Nevertheless, functionally, public offerings and secondary distributions are related to the primary market.

*21*

disclosure regulation called "offering disclosure (*hakko kaiji*) rules." [42]

Already issued securities can be traded in a secondary market. Secondary market transactions are sales between investors. Most of securities transactions occur in secondary markets. While issuers do not raise capital through transactions in a secondary market, investors can liquidate their investments through sales of their securities. Issuers of securities that are listed on an exchange, etc., are subject to "continuous disclosure (*keizoku kaiji*) rules." [43]

Nevertheless, conditions in secondary markets may in turn affect the primary market. Thus, primary markets are functionally connected with secondary markets.

## 3. Exchange markets and over-the-counter markets

Capital and financial markets are further divided into exchange markets and over-the-counter (OTC) markets. Securities and financial derivatives transactions take place on an exchange or directly between two investors over-the-counter (i.e., outside of the exchange or off-exchange). Securities listed on an exchange have to meet listing requirements to be listed. On the other hand, securities or financial derivatives that are not eligible for exchange trading are traded between investment firms or between customers and investment firms over-the-counter on a negotiated basis.

In practice, the boundary between exchange markets and OTC markets is becoming blurred, as recently, both securities transactions on stock exchanges and transactions on OTC markets are increasingly conducted via automated electronic trading systems.

## 4. Efficiency of capital markets

In an efficient capital market, prices fully and promptly reflect all available information at any time. This process occurs as a result of the collective investment decisions of all market participants. Therefore, all investors can

---

[42]　See infra D. 3. b. (i) and Chapter 3 A.

[43]　See infra D. 3. b. (ii) and Chapter 3 D.

Chapter 1　Introduction to the Japanese Financial Instruments and Exchange Act

theoretically use substantially the same information at the same time in an efficient capital market, if investors make rational investment decisions based on market prices. This mechanism can partly solve the problem of asymmetry of information between investors and can achieve equal opportunity for investors to buy and sell securities. This is the reason why an efficient market may be one of the best possible measures to enhance investor protection and to develop a sound national economy, both of which are ultimate purposes of the FIEA.[44]

The mandatory disclosure system under the FIEA can minimize information acquisition costs and facilitate rational investment decision-making by investors.[45] This process can lead to market efficiency.[46] The FIEA ensures that correct information is disclosed promptly and that investors can obtain that information easily.[47]

Nevertheless, the advantages of market efficiency depend on to what extent a market is efficient. The extent of capital market efficiency is measured in degrees. There are three general forms of market efficiency.

（a）　Weak-form efficiency

A capital market has weak-form efficiency when prices reflect all historical information, including historic trading patterns. The next move in the prices of securities is according to the random walk. No investor can forecast a security's future price movement from a series of past prices, because charting techniques and other approaches cannot be used to earn abnormal returns, which are defined as returns that exceed the returns earned by

---

**44** See supra A. 1.

**45** Kanzaki, Shitani & Kawaguchi, supra note 30, pp. 193-194.

**46** There is a discussion in the United States about whether a mandatory disclosure system is necessary, because issuers would voluntarily disclose and announce information without a disclosure obligation, in order to prevent suspicions among investors that unfavorable information concerning the issuer and its securities may be hidden. In Japan, the necessity of mandatory disclosure is widely accepted both in theory and in practice. Mitsuo Kondo, Kazushi Yoshihara & Etsuro Kuronuma, *Kinyū Torihiki Ho Nyūmon* [Introduction to the Financial Instruments and Exchange Act], 4th. ed. pp. 105-106, 261-262 (Shoji-homu, 2015).

**47** Kanzaki, Shitani & Kawaguchi, supra note 30, pp. 196-200.

*23*

investments with similar risks.

( b ) Semi-strong efficiency

A capital market has semi-strong efficiency when prices promptly reflect all publicly available information that could affect prices. Semi-strong efficiency is achieved through investment decisions mainly by professional investors. As a result of their investment decisions based on collection, processing and analysis of all publicly available information, prices in a semi-strong efficient market move from an uninformed to an informed level. Even professional traders cannot theoretically beat the markets by examining publicly available information for the purpose of identifying undervalued and overvalued stocks there, since all the publicly available information is reflected in the prices of securities. Nevertheless, there is room for gains through the use of insider information in a semi-strong efficient market.

( c ) Strong-form efficiency

A capital market has strong-form efficiency if prices fully reflect all information that could affect prices, even if the information is not publicly available. The fact that insider gains sometimes generate huge benefits due to insider trading suggests that capital markets in the real world do not exhibit strong-form efficiency.

Whether Japanese securities markets exhibit semi-strong efficiency or weak efficiency is disputed. While the capital markets in the US exhibit at least semi-strong efficiency according to most research,[48] there is yet little evidence that the securities markets in Japan are semi-strong form. At the least, the degree of efficiency of Japanese securities markets is generally understood to be much weaker than that in the US.[49] This could indicate that investors in Japanese securities markets may not be as protected as

---

[48] James D. Cox, Robert W. Hillman and Donald C. Langevoort, Securities Regulation, Wolters Kluwer Law & Business, 2013, pp. 93-94; On the contrary, it is disputable that trading prices reflect accurate estimates of a security's intrinsic value (*Id.*).

[49] Kenjiro Egashira, *Kigyô naiyô no Keizoku Kaiji* ⟨Continuous Mandatory Disclosure System⟩, in Shôtorihiki hô no kihon mondai ⟨Fundamental Issues on Commercial Law⟩, Yûhikaku, 2011, p 354.

Chapter 1   Introduction to the Japanese Financial Instruments and Exchange Act

investors in the US.

## 5. Definition of capital markets and venues

### a. Fundamental concept of capital markets and venues

Since the former Japanese Securities and Exchange Act was amended and the name of the Act was changed to the Financial Instruments and Exchange Act (FIEA) of 2006, the FIEA has covered securities markets and other financial derivatives markets, not only pertaining to securities but also to interest rates, currency and financial indicators, etc.

The exchange market is organized and operated by financial instruments exchanges under the FIEA. The FIEA defines the legal form of a "financial instruments exchange (*kinyû shohin torihiki jo*)" as a financial instruments membership corporation (*kinyû shohin kaiin-sei hojin)* or a stock company that has opened and operates a financial instruments market under a license granted by the Prime Minister pursuant to Article 80, paragraph 1 (Article 2 (16) of the FIEA). The financial instruments exchange operates a "financial instruments market (*kinyû shohin sijo)*," in which the sale and purchase of securities or market derivatives transactions[50] are conducted (Article 2(14) of the FIEA).

The FIEA defines "financial instruments" as follows (Article 2(24) of the FIEA); (i) securities,[51] (ii) claims based on a deposit contract or other rights, or securities or certificates indicating these claims or rights that are specified by cabinet order,[52] (iii) currencies, (iv) commodities specified by cabinet order,[53] (v) assets of which there are many of the same kind with substantial price volatility, and which are specified by cabinet order as those for which it is found necessary to secure the protection of investors with

---

**50**   See supra C. 3.

**51**   See infra Chapter 2. A. 1.

**52**   The means of payment prescribed in Article 6, paragraph 1, item 7 of the Foreign Exchange and Foreign Trade Act (*gaikoku kawase oyobi gaikoku boeki ho)*, the securities prescribed in Article 6, paragraph 1, item 11 of that Act, and the claims prescribed in item 13 of that paragraph are specified by Article 1-17 of the Financial Instruments and Exchange Act Implementing Order.

**53**   Article 1-17-2 of the Financial Instruments and Exchange Act Implementing Order.

*25*

regard to derivatives transactions pertaining thereto;[54] and (vi) standardized instruments which are created by financial instruments exchanges for the purpose of facilitating "market derivatives transactions" through standardizing interest rates, the maturity period and/or other conditions of financial instruments in (i) and (ii) above. Thus, under the FIEA, financial instruments exchanges in Japan include not only stock exchanges but also financial derivatives exchanges.

Furthermore, pursuant to the amendments to the FIEA of 2012, a financial instruments exchange is permitted to become a "comprehensive exchange (*sogo torihiki jo*)," on which both financial instruments and commodity-related derivatives can be listed and traded.[55]

b. Securities markets and venues in the FIEA

In terms of securities transactions, there are three types of securities market or venue in which securities transactions are conducted: a "financial instruments exchange market (*torihikijo kinyû shohin sijo*)"; an "over-the-counter securities market (*tento baibai yûkashoken sijo*)"; and a "proprietary trading system (PTS)." Listed securities and registered securities are traded on a financial instruments exchange market and an OTC securities market, while unlisted or unregistered securities are traded between investment firms, or between customers and investment firms in a negotiated manner.

The first type, a "financial instruments exchange market (*torihikijo kinyû shohin sijo*)" is defined by the FIEA as a financial instruments market established by a financial instruments exchange (Article 2(17) of the FIEA). A financial instruments exchange market is established and operated by a "financial instruments exchange," which is either a financial instruments membership corporation or a stock company with license granted by the

---

54  Commodities are excluded from the definition of the assets, which are covered by Article 2, paragraph 1 of the Commodity Futures Act.

55  However, markets in which only commodity-related derivatives are transacted are excluded from the definition of "financial instruments market" (Article 2(14) of the FIEA). Such commodity derivatives markets are regulated by the Commodity Futures Act (*shohin sakimono torihiki ho*).

*26*

Chapter 1   Introduction to the Japanese Financial Instruments and Exchange Act

Prime Minister under Article 80, paragraph 1 (Article 2(16) of the FIEA). On a financial instruments exchange, listed securities or financial instruments must meet the listing requirements of the exchange and be admitted to listing by the exchange. Only members of a financial instruments exchange are permitted to trade in financial instruments exchange markets (Article 111(1) of the FIEA). Investors other than investment firms can trade listed financial instruments through members of the exchange who are brokers (*toiya*) acting in their name but on their clients' account with fiduciary duties.[56] Under the FIEA, such a broker is required to be registered as a financial instruments business operator with the Financial Services Agency (FSA) of Japan (Article 29 of the FIEA).

The second type, an "over-the-counter securities market (*tento baibai yûkashoken sijo*)" is established and operated by an authorized financial instruments firms association (Article 67(2) of the FIEA).[57] On the OTC securities market, only members of authorized financial instruments firms associations can trade on their own account, but member firms may provide intermediary, brokerage or agency services in order to facilitate distribution of securities that are not listed on a financial instruments exchange, to ensure fairness of the sale and purchase or other transaction of such securities and to contribute to the protection of investors (Article 67(2) of the FIEA).

The third type is securities transactions through an electronic data processing system that is one sort of financial instruments business (Article 2(8)(x) of the FIEA). Furthermore, a large number of persons must participate simultaneously as one party in the transaction or the transaction must be conducted between a large number of participants through a PTS (proprietary trading system). The sale and purchase of securities or intermediary, brokerage or agency services in connection therewith through such a PTS is designated as a financial instruments business. The price

---

**56**   Article 551 and Article 552(2) of the Commercial Code (*sho-ho*) and Article 644 of the Civil Code (*min-po*).

**57**   "Japan Securities Dealers Association (*nihon shoken-gyo kyokai*)" is an authorized financial instruments firms association.

*27*

formation methods through a PTS are limited to auction,[58] using the trading price of the securities in the financial instruments exchange market, using the trading price of the securities published by the authorized financial instruments firms association with which the securities are registered, using the price decided by negotiation between customers, matching customer orders or offering asked and bidding quotations excluding market making (Article 2(8)(x) of the FIEA). The regulation is based on the premise that PTS is not allowed to have a price formation function like an exchange under the FIEA.[59] Therefore, provision of such service is excluded from the scope of the PTS business that is specified by cabinet order, as it may be considered inappropriate to be conducted in markets or venues other than in either a financial instruments exchange market or OTC securities market, given the huge volume of transactions (Article 2(8)(x) of the FIEA).[60]

Under the former Securities and Exchange Act (SEA), securities firms were subject to a duty to conduct all transactions of listed securities on an exchange according to the articles of exchange. The regulation purported to enhance the function of securities markets to find fair prices due to the accumulation of transactions on the exchange. The duty to conduct all trading of listed securities on the exchange was lifted and establishment and

---

**58** Article 1-10 of the Financial Instruments and Exchange Act Implementing Order limits an auction, for which the ratio of the average amount of the total transaction volume for a single business day pertaining to the sale and purchase of listed securities made in the last six months before the last day of each month to the average amount of the total transaction volume for a single business day made in all exchanges and OTC markets in the last six months, is one percent, and the ratio of the average amount of the total transaction volume for each issue of listed securities for a single business day pertaining to the sale and purchase of listed securities made in the last six months before the last day of each month to the average amount of the total transaction volume for a single business day made in all exchanges and OTC markets in the last six months, is ten percent. This requirement purports to prevent PTSs from becoming too large and important so as to rival exchange or OTC markets, because they are less regulated. Ichiro Kawamoto & Yasunami Otake, *Kinyū shohin torihiki ho tokuhon* [Guidebook on the Financial Instruments and Exchange Act], pp. 324-325 (Yūhi-kaku, 2008).

**59** Financial Services Agency of Japan, *Shisetsu torihiki system (PTS) kaisetsu to ni kakaru sisin ni tsuite* [Concerning the Guideline to Establish PTS], October 26, 2000. 〈http://www.fsa.go.jp/news/newsj/syouken/f-20001116-1.html〉

**60** Article 1-9-3 of the Financial Instruments and Exchange Act Implementing Order.

Chapter 1  Introduction to the Japanese Financial Instruments and Exchange Act

operation of a proprietary trading system (PTS) was allowed as a financial instruments business under the amendments to the former Securities and Exchange Act of 1988. Thus, PTSs are regulated as a financial instruments business but not as a financial instruments exchange in Japan. Nevertheless, even after 1988, execution of a client order outside a stock exchange was still banned unless the client specifically requested that the transaction take place outside the exchange (Article 37 of the SEA). This ban was replaced by the duty of best execution of orders of clients under the amendments to the former Securities and Exchange Act of 2004.[61]

Financial instruments business operators are required to be authorized by the Prime Minister (Article 30(1) of the FIEA) if they are going to provide PTS services, while registration but not authorization is required to conduct other financial instruments business (Article 29 of the FIEA). Since conducting a PTS service could easily come to mimic the operation of a stock exchange, it is to be strictly supervised.[62]

Indeed, it is not easy to clearly distinguish PTS services provided by a private company from the function of stock exchanges. This causes another problem: the fragmentation of securities markets.

c. Financial derivatives market and venue

There are two types of market or venue for financial derivatives transactions, namely "market derivatives transactions" and "over-the-counter derivatives transactions"; while there are three types of market or venue for securities transactions, namely "financial instruments exchange," "OTC securities market," and through "PTS." under the FIEA.

"Market derivatives transactions (*sijo derivative torihiki*)" are designated transactions conducted in a financial instruments market in accordance with requirements and using the methods prescribed by the operator of the relevant financial instruments market (Article 2(21) of the FIEA). Market

---

61  The securities firms have also been subject to determining the policy and the method for best execution since the amendments to the former Securities and Exchange Act of 2004 (Article 43-2 of the SEA).

62  Eiji Chatani, *Kinyū system kaikaku no tameno kankei horitsu no seibi-to ni kansuru horitsu no kaisetsu* [Explanation of the Act to Coordinate Related Acts for Financial System Reform], *Shojihomu*, No. 1503, p. 23.

*29*

derivatives transactions are standardized.

"Over-the-counter derivatives transactions (*tento derivative torihiki*)" are designated transactions that are conducted neither in a financial instruments market nor in a foreign financial instruments market (Article 2(22) of the FIEA).[63] The FIEA defines a "financial instruments market (*kinyû shohin sijo*)" as a market in which the sale and purchase of securities or market trading of financial derivatives is conducted (Article 2(14) of the FIEA). Thus, the scope of the definition of OTC derivatives transactions is much broader than that of the "OTC securities market", because OTC derivatives transactions include all transactions other than those which are conducted either in a domestic or a foreign financial instruments market. On the other hand, the OTC securities market is established and operated solely by an authorized financial instruments firms association, namely the Japan Securities Dealers Association.

The 2012 amendments to the FIEA require an investment firm conducting OTC financial derivatives transactions to use electronic derivatives transactions execution facilities (EDTEF) for qualified OTC financial derivatives transactions (Article 40-7 of the FIEA). The EDTEF is intended to play an important role in enhancing the transparency and oversight of the market for these certain types of OTC financial derivatives transactions. The EDTEF should help further the statutory objective of greater transparency by serving as a conduit for information regarding trading interests in selected standardized OTC financial derivatives transactions. The administration of the EDTEF is handled not as an exchange or PTS but as a type I financial instruments business under the FIEA (Article 2(8)(iv) of the FIEA).

Therefore, markets and venues for conducting derivatives transactions other than securities-based derivatives transactions consist of only two types in Japanese capital markets regulation: market derivatives transactions (namely on-exchange traded derivatives) and OTC derivatives transactions.

---

**63**  Those derivatives transactions are excluded that are specified by cabinet order as those for which it is found not to hinder the public interest or protection of investors when taking into account its content and other related factors.

*30*

Chapter 1   Introduction to the Japanese Financial Instruments and Exchange Act

In other words, there is no category of venue through PTS in terms of derivatives transactions that corresponds to a securities market and venue in Japan, while the definition of OTC derivatives transactions is sufficiently broad to cover the venue.

# 6. Regulatory framework of financial instruments exchange and venues

### a. Regulatory framework of financial instruments exchange

The establishment of a financial instruments market requires a license from the Prime Minister (Article 80 (1) of the FIEA). The operation of an exchange is subject to the supervision of the Prime Minister (Articles 148 to 153-5 of the FIEA), in consideration of its importance in organized capital markets, both for efficient financing and distribution of resources and for investor protection.

Regarding organization of a financial instruments exchange, there are two options: a membership organization or a joint stock company. Formerly, securities exchanges had to be in the form of a membership organization as a non-profit organization consisting of securities firms. However, pursuant to the amendments to the former Securities and Exchange Act of 2000, a joint stock company-type was authorized that is as a for-profit organization.

A financial instruments exchange has two functions. One is to establish and operate a financial instruments exchange market in which the fair and smooth sale and purchase of securities and market transactions of derivatives are ensured and investors are sufficiently protected through fair prices.[64] The other is to craft, interpret, execute and change self-regulation in accordance with the FIEA,[65] in order to ensure fair sale and purchase of securities and market derivatives transactions in the financial instruments exchange market, as well as to protect investors (Article 84 (1) of the FIEA).[66]

---

**64**   Matsuo, supra note 22, p. 495.
**65**   See supra B. 2. c.
**66**   Matsuo, supra note 22, pp. 506–509.

*31*

b . Regulatory framework of OTC securities market

An authorized financial instruments firms association may establish a market where registered securities are traded, as long as member firms of the association conduct such transactions on their own account or they provide intermediary, brokerage or agency services to customers.[67] This market is defined as an over-the-counter securities market under the FIEA. An OTC securities market purports to facilitate distribution of non-listed securities, to ensure fairness of the sale and purchase or other transactions of such securities and to contribute to the protection of investors (Article 67(1) of the FIEA).

An authorized financial instruments firms association may be established only by financial instruments business operators (Article 67-2(1) of the FIEA), whose members must also be financial instruments business operators (Article 68(1) of the FIEA). An authorized financial instruments firms association is a non-profit organization, which is not permitted to seek profits (Article 67-7(1) of the FIEA).[68]

c . Self-regulation

In securities markets and venues for securities transactions by investment

---

**67** There are two types of financial instruments firms associations, namely authorized financial instruments firms associations and recognized financial instruments firms associations under the FIEA. Recognized financial instruments firms associations are general incorporated associations that have been established by financial instruments business operators and granted a license by the Prime Minister. The capacities of these two types of self-regulatory organization are different. While an authorized financial instruments firms association may establish and operate an OTC securities market and hold stocks of stock company-type financial instruments exchanges (Articles 67(2) and 103-2(1) of the FIEA), a recognized financial instruments firms association is not allowed to conduct such businesses and is not allowed to hold twenty percent or more of stocks of a stock company-type financial instruments exchange. The JSDA (Japan Securities Dealers Association) is an authorized financial instruments firms association. On the other hand, the Japan Investment Advisers Association, the Investment Trust Association, Japan and the Financial Futures Association of Japan and Type II Financial Instruments Firms Associations are recognized financial instruments firms associations.

**68** The Japanese Securities Dealers Association (JSDA) that is an authorized financial instruments firms association, formerly established and operated the JSDAQ market as an OTC securities market. See infra note 82.

Chapter 1    Introduction to the Japanese Financial Instruments and Exchange Act

firms, self-regulations and the enforcement thereof play an important role. Financial instruments exchanges and financial instruments firms associations are self-regulatory organizations under the FIEA; and, in practice, they play an important role in terms of establishing, operating, and overseeing securities markets and venues by self-regulation.

( i )    Self-regulation by a financial instruments exchange

A financial instruments exchange may establish either a self-regulatory committee (Articles 105-4 to 106-2 of the FIEA) or a self-regulatory corporation (Articles 102-2 to 102-39 of the FIEA). A self-regulatory organization may be entrusted with all or part of the responsibility for self-regulation by a financial instruments exchange (Article 85 (1) of the FIEA), mainly in order to avoid conflict-of-interest issues.[69]

For example, the Tokyo Stock Exchange adopts and applies self-regulation concerning listing and delisting requirements, securities trading, timely disclosure of material corporate matters, code of corporate conduct and corporate governance code, etc. In particular, codes of corporate conduct include important self-regulations pertaining to third-party capital allotment, prohibition of stock splits that could cause turmoil in the secondary markets, regulation of the issuance of moving striking convertible bonds (MSCB), introduction of takeover defense measures, and significant transactions with controlling shareholders, etc.[70]

Concerning listing and delisting requirements, listed companies need to adhere to listing criteria established and approved by the exchange. An exchange suspends the trading of a listed security or delists a security when listing criteria are not met. Securities transactions in securities markets are monitored in order to keep trading in line with the exchange rules and to obtain fair and proper prices. An exchange requires accurate and prompt

---

**69**  Kanzaki, Shitani & Kawaguchi, supra note 30, footnote 1, p. 1104. Especially a financial instruments exchange, which is a stock company, seeks profits as a stock company on the one hand. On the other hand, it operates a financial instruments exchange market for public interests. Conflicts of interest could occur between these occasionally regarding the self-regulatory function.

**70**  Tokyo Stock Exchange, Inc., Rules. 〈http://www.jpx.co.jp/english/rules-participants/rules/regulations/index.html〉

*33*

disclosure of corporate and security information in accordance with the FIEA and the guidelines of the exchange for timely disclosure of important corporate information resulting from business activities. For example, the Tokyo Stock Exchange (TSE) also provides the "Timely Disclosure Network" (TDnet), which makes material corporate information widely available in a swift and timely manner.[71] The TSE takes appropriate measures upon discovery of any violation of its self-regulations.

Furthermore, JPX-R[72] sets forth the principles for equity financing to be observed for encouraging and facilitating high-quality equity financing in 2014. These principles are expected to prevail among shareholders and investors as well as listed companies and market professionals including broker-dealers, lawyers, CPAs (certified public accountants) and consultants.[73] In 2015, the TSE established a new corporate governance code, which rests upon a principle-based approach with the "comply or explain" rule.[74]

(ⅱ) Self-regulation of PTS business by Japan Securities Dealers Association

The PTS (proprietary trading system) business is regulated by an SRO, called the Japan Securities Dealers Association (JSDA). The JSDA established the "Rules Concerning Sale and Purchase, Etc. of Listed Share, Etc. Conducted Outside of a Financial Instruments Exchange Market,"[75] which purports to ensure fair and smooth sale and purchase, and intermediation thereof, of listed equity products conducted outside of exchanges by the PTS and to contribute to the protection of investors. The self-regulation provides for the suspension of trading, reporting and publication of trades, especially of the prices, etc.

---

71  TDnet, Company Announcements Disclosure Service. ⟨https://www.release.tdnet. info/inbs/I_main_00.html⟩

72  See supra note 12.

73  JPX, Aiming for Better Equity Financing. ⟨http://www.jpx.co.jp/english/regulation/ ensuring/listing/equity-finance/index.html⟩

74  Japan's Corporate Governance Code. ⟨http://www.jpx.co.jp/english/equities/listing/ cg/tvdivq0000008jdy-att/20150513.pdf⟩

75  ⟨http://www.jsda.or.jp/en/rules/E36.pdf⟩

Chapter 1    Introduction to the Japanese Financial Instruments and Exchange Act

d. Facts

(ⅰ) Financial instruments exchanges

In the aftermath of Japan's financial Big Bang in 1998, the scope of the securities business was extended to OTC securities derivatives trading and the provision of services through the proprietary trading systems (PTSs).[76] The introduction of the operation of PTSs was connected with the repeal of the obligation of securities firms to trade listed securities on exchanges (concentration duty of orders on an exchange). The reform enhanced not only inter-market competition between securities firms but also between exchanges.[77] The exchanges started targeting new listings around 2000, launching markets for start-up companies and growth companies whose shares they subsequently listed on other sections. The Tokyo Stock Exchange, which introduced electronic stock trading and off-floor trading, has taken a dominant position in Japan.

As of March 31, 2017, there are six financial instruments exchanges in Japan: the Tokyo Stock Exchange (TSE);[78] the Nagoya Stock Exchange (NSE); the Fukuoka Stock Exchange (FSE); the Sapporo Stock Exchange (SSE), the Osaka Exchange; and the Tokyo Financial Exchanges. The TSE, NSE, FSE, and SSE are exchanges for securities trading. The Osaka Exchange (OE) is a securities-related derivatives exchange market. The Tokyo Financial Exchange (TFE) is an exchange for financial derivatives transactions. The TSE, NSE, OE, and TFX are joint stock company-type financial instruments exchanges, while the FSE and SSE are membership-type financial instruments exchanges.

As of January 31, 2016, the total number of listed companies on the four Japanese stock exchanges stood at 3,960, of which 3,506 were on the Tokyo

---

76  See supra C. 5. b. and infra Chapter 5 A. 6.

77  See Sadakazu Osaki, *Kabushiki Sijo-kan Kyoso* [Competition of Markets for Stocks] (Daiyamondo-sha, 2000).

78  The Japan Exchange Group (JPX) was established as a holding company in January 2013. The Tokyo Stock Exchange and the Osaka Stock Exchange combined their operations under the JPX in 2013. The Osaka Stock Exchange was renamed the Osaka Exchange in March 2014. The TSE and OE are subsidiaries of the JPX. The TSE operates the First Section, the Second Section, Mothers, JASDAQ, Tokyo Pro Market and Tokyo Pro-Bond Market.

*35*

Stock Exchange (TSE). The TSE accounts for about 80% of the nation's listed stock companies. The number of foreign companies listed on the TSE is only nine.

As of December 31, 2015, the number of shares listed on all Japanese stock exchanges together is 433.3 billion[79], with a total market capitalization of ¥850.8 trillion.[80] As of December 31, 2015, the number of shares listed on the TSE is 431.3 billion, with a total market capitalization of ¥589.7 trillion.[81]

(ⅱ) OTC securities markets

At the moment, there is no OTC securities market within the meaning of the definition in the FIEA operated by an authorized financial instruments firms association. In the past, there was an OTC securities market in Japan called the JASDAQ market.[82] Nevertheless, the JASDAQ market was transformed into a financial instruments exchange (stock exchange) in 2004.

(ⅲ) Issuing market

ⅰ) Equity products

In Japan, in practice, there are four options for raising capital in an equity financing market: public offering, third-party allotment, rights offering and

---

**79** JPX, Number of Shares Listed (All Stock Exchanges). 〈http://www.jpx.co.jp/markets/statistics-equities/monthly/nlsgeu000001ekco-att/16_allse1512.pdf〉

**80** NSE, Key Statistics for Stocks (1st, 2nd & Centrex Sections). 〈http://www.nse.or.jp/market/statistics/monthly/files/gepo_kabu_1512.pdf〉; FSE, *Gyoshu-betsu Jika Sogaku* [Total Market Capitalization by Industry Sector]. 〈https://www.fse.or.jp/files/lir_ind/201512gjika.pdf〉; SSE, *Gyoshu-betsu Jika Sogaku Hyo* [List of Total Market Capitalization by Industry Sector]. 〈http://www.sse.or.jp/statistics/pdf/brand/2015/z-1512.pdf〉

**81** JPX, Key Statistics for Domestic Stocks (Total of 1st, 2nd Sections, Mothers, TOKYO PRO Market, JASDAQ Standard & JASDAQ Growth). 〈http://www.jpx.co.jp/markets/statistics-equities/monthly/nlsgeu000001ekco-att/01_sokatu1512.pdf〉

**82** The JASDAQ was originally launched as an OTC securities market in 1983. Thereafter, the JASDAQ acquired a stock exchange license and changed its name to the JASDAQ Securities Exchange in 2004, as a capital market for growth and start-up companies. JASDAQ was acquired by the Osaka Stock Exchange in 2010 and became the new JASDAQ market due to a merger with the OSE's NEO and Nippon New Market-Hercules markets. Then, the OSE merged with the TSE. See supra note 78.

*36*

Chapter 1   Introduction to the Japanese Financial Instruments and Exchange Act

the exercise of share options.[83] The total value of equity financing in listed companies via the Japanese stock exchanges was ¥1.14 trillion in 2015.[84] In 2015, the amount raised by public offering was ¥962 billion, by third-party allotment ¥163.5 billion, by rights offering ¥56 million and by exercise of share options ¥81.5 billion.[85] The issuance of new shares by listed companies that increased paid-in capital on Japanese stock exchanges totaled 4.31 billion shares in 2012, only about one-sixth of the record high of 22.42 billion shares in 2009.[86]

    ii )   Debt products
Regarding bond issuing markets, the total value of public and corporate bonds issued in 2015 amounted to ¥200.2 trillion.[87] ¥174.5 trillion or 86% of the total value was comprised of Japanese government bonds (JGB), and ¥6. 8 trillion worth of municipal bonds was publicly offered. JGBs play the predominant position in Japanese bond markets. The total value of corporate bonds publicly offered in 2015 amounted to ¥7.06 trillion. Corporate bonds are further broken down in straight bonds (¥6.8 trillion), asset-backed corporate bonds (¥50 billion) and convertible bonds (¥160 billion). The volume of bank debentures was ¥2.5 trillion in 2015.[88]

    (iv)   Trading markets
    i )   Equity products
The trading volume of stocks on all Japanese stock exchanges amounted to

---

83   Previously, the most popular means of issuing new shares was the offering of rights to existing shareholders at par value in Japanese stock markets. Nevertheless, there was no way of offering rights at par value, because the par stock was eliminated and unified in no-par stock by the reform of the Japanese Commercial Code of 2001.

84   JSDA, Equity Financing by Companies Listed in Japan (Public Stock Offerings, etc. /Domestic). 〈http://www.jsda.or.jp/shiryo/toukei/finance/index.html〉

85   JPX, Financing by Listed Companies (Annual). 〈http://www.jpx.co.jp/markets/statistics-equities/misc/06.html〉

86   Tokyo Stock Exchange, *Shôken tôkei nenpô* 〈Annual Report of Securities Statistics〉 and *Shôken tôkei geppô* 〈Monthly Report of Securities Statistics〉.

87   JSDA, *Ko-shashai Hakko-gaku / Shokan-gaku to* [Amount of Issuance and Redemption of Public and Corporate Bonds]. 〈http://www.jsda.or.jp/shiryo/toukei/ hakkou/index.html〉

88   JSDA, supra note 87.

*37*

710.5 billion units, or ¥746.2 trillion, in 2015.[89] Stock trading in Japan is extremely concentrated on the TSE. The total value of trading on the Tokyo Stock Exchange (TSE) accounted for a little under 90% of stock trading on all Japanese securities trading markets. The annual trading volume on the First Section of the TSE in 2015 was 620.2 billion units, and trading value amounted to ¥696.5 trillion.[90] On the other hand, the annual trading volume on the Second Section of the TSE in 2015 was only 36.6 billion units and trading value amounted to ¥8.3 trillion.[91] The total annual trading volume of foreign stocks on the TSE in 2015 was 42.8 million units, and the trading value was ¥29.5 billion.[92]

The average trading volume of all listed shares on the TSE amounted to 2.9 billion stocks, and the average trading value amounted to ¥3.06 trillion per one trading day in 2015.[93]

The Japan Securities Dealers Association (JSDA) promulgated "the Regulations Concerning Over-the-Counter Securities"[94] in 2005. Under these self-regulations, there are two categories: OTC-handled securities and other OTC securities. OTC-handled securities consist of securities issued by companies that have to submit securities reports under Article 24 of the FIEA, and equity products issued by companies that publish a "corporate information memorandum (*kaisha naiyo hokoku sho*)." Other OTC securities are shares based on the equity crowdfunding scheme or shareholder community scheme. Solicitation for investment is performed only via the website and e-mail with the restrictions regarding the amount of funds raised per issue and the amount of investment per investor (2014 Amendments to the FIEA).

According to the self-regulations of the JSDA, member firms are in principle

---

89  See supra note 79.
90  JPX, Annual Trading Volume & Value. ⟨http://www.jpx.co.jp/markets/statistics-equities/misc/index.html⟩
91  JPX, supra note 90.
92  JPX, supra note 90.
93  JPX, Trading Volume & Value (Total of Domestic & Foreign Stocks). ⟨http://www.jpx.co.jp/markets/statistics-equities/monthly/nlsgeu000001ekco-att/02_baibai1512.pdf⟩
94  Trading of OTC securities does not occur in the OTC securities market but over-the-counter on a negotiated basis. ⟨http://www.jsda.or.jp/en/rules/files/33_131025.pdf⟩

Chapter 1   Introduction to the Japanese Financial Instruments and Exchange Act

banned from soliciting investors for the purchase of unlisted and unregistered equity products such as shares, share options and corporate bonds with share options.[95] The ban on solicitation of unlisted and unregistered equity products aims to protect investors from the lack of information and to ensure confidence in listed or registered equity products and transactions on exchanges and OTC securities markets.[96] There is an exception pursuant to which OTC-handled securities can be solicited by investment firms, under which the information required for rational investment decisions is disclosed in accordance with the FIEA or self-regulation.

On the other hand, investment firms are permitted to solicit qualified institutional investors for the purchase of OTC securities on the condition that they do not resell their holding to anyone other than the qualified institutional investors set out in the self-regulation.[97] The JSDA requires, as self-regulation, that an issuer of OTC-handled securities disclose specified corporate information regularly in the form of a "corporate information memorandum."

Unlisted or unregistered securities can be traded in the self-regulated OTC market called Green Sheet.[98] Phoenix, the aim of which is to provide a marketplace for delisted or deregistered companies in consideration of the necessity of maintaining liquidity and at the same time providing the chance of re-listing for such companies, was spun off from the Green Sheet system in 2008. Nevertheless, the number of registered companies on Green Sheet and Phoenix is increasingly diminishing. As of the end of January 2016, only 22 securities are handled on Green Sheet[99] and one security is handled on Phoenix.[100] This is because, for one thing, stock exchanges for start-up and

---

95  Rules Concerning Over-The-Counter Securities, § 3. ⟨http://www.jsda.or.jp/en/ rules/files/33_131025.pdf⟩
96  Kanzaki, Shitani & Kawaguchi, supra note 30, pp. 776-777.
97  It is not required in private placement of unlisted or unregistered equity products to restrict sales of solicited securities to those from the person who acquired them to any other person. See infra note 123.
98  Japan Securities Research Institute, Securities Market in Japan, 2016, pp. 202-208.
99  JSDA, The Trend in Number of Issues on Green Sheet. ⟨http://www.jsda.or. jp/shiraberu/greensheet/toukei/issue.html⟩

venture businesses, such as Mothers Market in the Tokyo Stock Exchange, have more lax listing conditions than the First and Second sections of the TSE. Further, it is because insider trading regulations and disclosure obligations of transaction prices and quotation prices have applied to Green Sheet and Phoenix.[101] Green Sheet and Phoenix are expected to be abolished in accordance with a review and reform proposal report.[102] Green Sheet was abolished on March 31, 2018. Instead of Green Sheet and the Phoenix system, the concept of a shareholder community was introduced. According to this concept, only a limited number of relevant investors are included in the group for investment: a shareholder community. Insider trading regulation does not apply to the system, and the disclosure obligation is also largely mitigated due to the amendments in 2014 (Article 67-18(iv) of the FIEA, FSA Notification No. 32 of 2015).

Thus, OTC trading for equity products pertaining to unlisted or unregistered stocks occurs as an exception between investment firms. The total amount of off-exchange stock trading amounted to 5.39 billion stocks, and the total trading volume was ¥6.08 trillion during January 2016.[103]


ii) Debt products

Regarding the trading market for bonds, an overwhelming majority of bonds are traded not on an exchange but over-the-counter (OTC). During January 2016, the value of bond trades (par value) in Japan totaled ¥8,619 trillion for OTC transactions[104] and only ¥6.2 billion for on-exchange transactions.[105] The bonds are predominantly traded over-the-counter,

---

**100** JSDA, The Trend in Number of Issues on Phoenix. ⟨http://market.jsda.or.jp/shiraberu/phoenix/toukei/toukei/issue.html⟩

**101** Articles 67-18(iv) (v) (vi), 67-19, 67-20, 157, 158, 159, 165, 166 and 167 of the FIEA.

**102** JSDA, *Kabushiki tôshi-gata crowd funding oyobi green sheet meigara seido to ni kawaru aratana hijôjô kabushiki no torihiki seido no arikata ni tsuite* [Report Regarding Crowd Funding as an Investment Scheme For Stocks and Towards the New Trading System of Non-Listed Stocks Instead of Green Sheet System] (June 17, 2014).

**103** JSDA, Off-Exchange Information Network. ⟨http://offexchange.jp/offexchange/report/findMonthReport.action⟩

**104** JSDA, Trading Volume of Over-the-Counter Bonds. ⟨http://www.jsda.or.jp/shiryo/toukei/shurui/index.html⟩

Chapter 1    Introduction to the Japanese Financial Instruments and Exchange Act

because it is difficult for parties to find a matching counterparty for a particular transaction in terms of trading volume, set of bonds and other terms. Therefore, most bond transactions are conducted by negotiating and customizing the conditions individually. In most bond transactions, investment firms and dealer banks negotiate and conclude the terms of the bond transaction that is conducted over-the-counter. Thus, OTC bond trading is conducted through a decentralized process.

The total volume of OTC trading of Japanese government bonds (JGB) amounted to ¥852.8 trillion, municipal bonds to ¥3.76 trillion, corporate bonds to ¥1.60 trillion and bank debentures to ¥0.78 trillion during January 2016.[106]

The JSDA operates the Program for Publishing Reference Prices (Yields) for OTC bond transactions, which publishes quotes for publicly-offered public and corporate bonds that meet certain criteria.[107] The JSDA restricts the price movement limits for OTC bond transactions by members, in consideration of the fair price, which is calculated based on publicly offered quotes and yields. The aim is to promote the formation of fair prices and efficient and orderly trading of bonds. Additionally, the information has become widely used for mark-to-market valuation for financial reporting and tax accounting purposes and the valuation of collateral for different types of transactions.[108] The JSDA also launched the "Report/Dissemination System for Information on Corporate Bond Transactions" which has disseminated actual contract prices for OTC corporate bond transactions since 2015.[109]

---

105 JPX, Baibai-daka/ Baibai-daikin [Trading Volume & Trading Value]. 〈http://www.jpx.co.jp/markets/statistics-equities/misc/index.html〉

106 JSDA, *Koshasai Shurui Betsu Tento Baibai-daka* [Trading Volume of OTC Trading of Public and Corporate Bonds]. 〈http://www.jsda.or.jp/shiryo/toukei/shurui/index.html〉

107 JSDA, Reference Statistical Prices [Yields] for OTC Bond Transactions /Rating Matrix. 〈http://www.jsda.or.jp/en/statistics/bond-market/prices/index.html〉

108 Japan Securities Research Institute, supra note 98, p. 103.

109 JSDA, Information of Corporate Bond Transactions. 〈http://www.jsda.or.jp/en/statistics/bond-market/bond_trade/index.html〉

*41*

ⅲ） Foreign securities

A JSDA member must handle the sale and purchase of foreign securities, settlement of trade price and safekeeping of the foreign securities, etc. which are to be conducted in accordance with customers' instructions, under the provisions of an agreement on sale of foreign securities or for the agreement on sale of foreign securities for takeover bid. An association member must, in soliciting a customer for an investment in foreign securities, take due care so that the investment may be made in a manner suitable to the goals, investment experience and financial resources, etc., of the customer.

The average trading volume of foreign stocks on the TSE amounted to 175.5 thousand stocks, an average trading value of ¥121.0 thousand per one trading day.[110]

# D. Fundamental regulatory approach of the FIEA

## 1. Mandatory information disclosure system - economic model under the FIEA

Securities are not inherently valuable in themselves, since their worth comes from the claims or rights they entitle their holder to, to certain payments and to control of the issuer, such as voting rights at shareholders' meetings. Correct and timely information is required by investors to make rational investment decisions. In efficient capital markets, fair prices can be formed and found as a result of the accumulation of rational decision-making, and efficient capital markets can facilitate efficient allocation of capital and resources through fair prices.[111] This principle is based on an economic model, which can also be combined with a legal model, namely the autonomy principle in contract law and the self-responsibility principle.

The economic model on which the regulatory framework of the FIEA

---

110 JPX, Key Statistics for Foreign Stocks. 〈http://www.jpx.co.jp/markets/statistics-equities/monthly/nlsgeu000001ekco-att/01_sokatu1512.pdf〉
111 Purposes of the FIEA, see A.1 and C.4.

*42*

Chapter 1 Introduction to the Japanese Financial Instruments and Exchange Act

depends is especially premised on the belief that investors, who possess all available relevant and correct information, are able to make rational investment decisions. Investors need to collect relevant information due to the asymmetry of information between issuers and investors, and the relevant information required is common to each investor, because investors aim to maximize their own economic benefits. Nevertheless, it is difficult for each investor to collect relevant information in order to make rational investment decisions. Although the relevant information is valued by each investor, no investor will gather it for himself due to the huge costs involved. Furthermore, there are collective-action problems for most investors concerning information collection. The mandatory disclosure regulation contributes to reducing informational asymmetry and to increasing transparency, and disclosed information underpins the confidence of investors and allows them to make informed and rational decisions.[112]

Securities information tends to be underprovided, since it has a "public goods" character. Public goods are characterized by non-excludability and non-rivalry. Plenty of free-riders would also benefit from the relevant information without sharing the cost, since information is very difficult to possess exclusively. Use of the relevant information by one investor does not reduce the availability and usefulness of the information to other investors. On the other hand, an issuer of securities has information on securities and information pertaining to the issuer, which is required by investors in order to make a rational investment decision. Furthermore, an issuer has the cheapest options regarding collection and provision of relevant information. Therefore, the issuers of securities are subject to the mandatory disclosure regulation under the FIEA, even if securities are not offered by an issuer but distributed secondarily by an investment firm.

---

112 Criticism of the mandatory disclosure model comes mainly from two points of view. One comes from the efficient market hypothesis that the mandatory disclosure rule is unnecessary and imposes the harmful burden of disclosure costs. The second comes from the behavioral economics perspective and maintains that retail investors behave sometimes with a cognitive bias and act emotionally rather than rationally. Regarding cognitive bias of retail investors, the government and self-regulatory organizations in Japan are engaged in literacy promotion and investor education. See infra note 119 and 121.

*43*

Under the mandatory information disclosure system, investors are expected to act rationally and to aim to maximize their own economic benefits. Investors are assumed to always choose the option most suited to their preferences. When an investor can obtain and analyze all relevant and necessary information that is publicly available, the capital market is expected to reflect fair and correct prices.[113] Therefore, correct and timely information is necessary not only for investors to make rational investment decisions but also for an efficient capital market to form fair and correct prices. A capital market with a mandatory disclosure system will further contribute to enhancing corporate governance through the mechanism of hostile takeover bids.[114]

Information disclosed under the mandatory disclosure regulation must be correct, comprehensive and prompt; therefore nondisclosure or fraudulent disclosure is sanctioned by law and regulation.

## 2. Legal model under the FIEA – autonomy principle and self-responsibility

The abovementioned economic model, on which the mandatory disclosure system under the FIEA is based, also relates to the legal model in civil law, in which there is the autonomy principle and the self-responsibility principle. An investor who suffers a loss from a securities transaction in the capital market has to bear the loss.

The self-responsibility principle is justified by the autonomy principle, insofar as an investor can make an independent decision based on the necessary information pertaining to the securities and issuers. The mandatory disclosure rule underpins the self-responsibility principle.[115] The autonomy principle is premised on the belief that each investor acts rationally, in principle, which contributes to the efficiency and stability of securities transactions in the capital markets. When a capital market has semi-strong form efficiency, market prices reflect all publicly available information including disclosed information by issuers.[116] An investor may

---

**113** See supra C. 4.
**114** See infra H. 5.
**115** Kawamoto & Otake, supra note 58, p. 5.

Chapter 1　Introduction to the Japanese Financial Instruments and Exchange Act

rely on the market price when making a decision. The FIEA in principle permits even high-risk securities and financial instruments to be sold to retail investors, as long as mandatory disclosure is made.[117] In other words, the concept of investor protection in the FIEA is based on the traditional autonomy principle and self-responsibility principle.

The principal means by which the FIEA regulates are the mandatory disclosure regulation (3), the bans on market abuses such as insider trading and price manipulation (4), and the business conduct regulation of participants in securities and capital markets (5).

## 3. Mandatory information disclosure system

### a. Introduction

Based on the economic and legal model above, the FIEA focuses on the regulation of mandatory disclosure of information to protect investors and to enhance fair and efficient securities markets. The function of securities markets fundamentally depends on the quality and credibility of the disclosure system. In other words, the information disclosed must be correct and comprehensive.[118]

Nevertheless, it is becoming more and more apparent that an investor does not always act rationally and often acts on biased views and assumptions. There are in fact many unsophisticated investors who need to be protected. In Japan, some empirical studies have shown that investors tend to behave overconfidently in their ability to invest even in the absence of solid information.[119] These realities could undermine the premises of the above economic and legal model, on which the FIEA depends.[120]

Another topic related to the lack of investor protection is the enhancement of financial literacy. The Financial Services Agency of Japan (FSA), self-regulatory organizations and other private institutions are endeavoring to develop measures to enhance the financial literacy of non-professional

---

**116** See supra C. 4. (b).

**117** An investment firm is subject to the conduct regulation under the FIEA such as the duty to explain and suitability rule, but it is not a priori banned from selling high risk financial instruments.

**118** Kanzaki, Shitani & Kawaguchi, supra note 30, p. 203.

*45*

investors.[121]

b. Mandatory disclosure regulation
(ⅰ) Offering disclosure

The FIEA provides for two types of mandatory disclosure: offering disclosure and continuous disclosure. Under the offering disclosure system, a company that is going to publicly offer securities is required to disclose information pertaining to the securities and the issuer.

Issuers of securities are in principle subject to duties to disclose. Nevertheless, type II securities are not in principle subject to the mandatory disclosure regulation under the FIEA (Article 3(iii) of the FIEA). A type II security is subject to disclosure regulation, insofar as it represents a right or beneficial right to assets more than half of which are invested in other securities or directly in business in invested business that is mainly conducted through investment in securities (Article 3(iii) of the FIEA).[122] When the issue amount is ¥100 million or more, and the number of investors is 50 persons or more in the case of type I securities and 500 persons or more in the case of type II securities, that are "rights in a securities investment business", the issuer is subject to offering disclosure insofar as the issue does not meet the requirements of "private placements" (Articles 2(3) and 4 of

---

**119** Koichi Takeda, Toshihiko Takemura & Takashi Kozu, *Nihon no Kojin Toshi-ka no Toshi Literacy to Ishikettei Bias* [Financial Literacy and Individual Investor Behavior: Survey Evidence in Japanese Stock Market], RISS Discussion Paper Series, No. 21 (March 2012). According to the empirical study, the higher the investors' investment literacy, the lower their overconfidence bias and their propensity to avoid risk. ⟨http://www. kansai-u. ac. jp/riss/research/publications/public_files/riss_dp/RISS_DP_No. 21.pdf⟩

**120** On the other hand, the FIEA regulates the business conduct in the process of solicitation and conclusion of contracts pertaining to financial instruments. For example, the duty to explain, suitability rule and the duty to deliver a document containing material matters concerning the contract, etc. are prescribed.

**121** The Central Council for Financial Services Information published the "Financial Literacy Map" in 2014, in which the necessary financial literacy is indicated corresponding to each investor's generation. ⟨http://www.shiruporuto.jp/teach/consumer/literacy/pdf/map.pdf⟩

**122** Articles 2-9 and 2-10 of the Financial Instruments and Exchange Act Implementing Order.

Chapter 1 Introduction to the Japanese Financial Instruments and Exchange Act

the FIEA).[123] There are three categories of private placement, namely private placement for qualified institutional investors, for professional investors, and for a small number of investors.[124] The duty to disclose applies to the issuers because, first, it is they who have the information to be included in the disclosure documents;[125] and, second, because they are the beneficiaries of the issuance, as they can achieve financing through capital markets. The disclosed information is made available through a system of electronic filing and public inspection of documents organized under the FIEA called EDINET (Chapter II-4 of the FIEA).[126] This type of disclosure

---

**123** When the proceeds from the proposed offering of primary issuance or secondary distribution of shares are less than ¥100 million, the issuer is exempted from filing a securities registration statement. When the proceeds from the proposed offering of primary issuance or secondary distribution of shares are ¥10 million or greater but less than ¥100 million, and the number of investors solicited is 50 persons or more, the issuer is required to submit a statement of securities notification (*yûkashoken tsûchi-sho*). If the issuer has made an offering of the same type of securities within the previous six months and the combined number of investors solicited is 50 persons or more, the number of investors is counted based on the total issuance amounts of the offerings. The number of solicited qualified institutional investors are excluded to which the solicitation for acquisition is made and where the solicited securities are, as specified by cabinet order, not likely to be transferred from the qualified institutional investor who acquired them to any other person other than qualified institutional investors (Article 2(3)(i) of the FIEA).

**124** Private placements are the following: (a) Solicitation for acquisition which is made only to qualified institutional investors, if the solicited securities are, as specified by cabinet order, not likely to be transferred from the person who acquired them to any other person other than qualified institutional investors. (b) Solicitation for acquisition which is made only to professional investors, if the solicitation for acquisition is made based on entrustment by customers or for the investment firm and the solicited securities are not likely to be transferred from the person who acquired them to any person other than professional investors; (c) Solicitation for acquisition, if the solicited securities are not likely to be held by a large number of persons (Article 2(3)(ii) of the FIEA). In each case, solicited securities are not allowed to be equity products, which are listed on the stock exchange or registered in the OTC securities market, and the same sort of equity products were not already publicly offered (Articles 1-4 (i), 1-5-2 (ii), 1-7-4 (i), 1-8-2 (i) and 1-8-4 (iii) of the Financial Instruments and Exchange Act Implementing Order).

**125** Securities invested in a collective investment scheme are defined as specified securities under the FIEA, and there are special regulations applicable to "issuers" who have a duty to disclose.

*47*

is called indirect disclosure.

There is a similar situation concerning the asymmetry of information between distributors and investors concerning secondary distribution of securities.[127] Therefore, the FIEA defines "secondary distribution of securities (*yûkashoken no uridashi*)" as solicitations of applications to sell or purchase already-issued securities, for which the amount accounts for ¥100 million or more, and the number of investors is 50 persons or more in the case of type I securities and 500 persons or more in the case of type II securities, that are "rights in securities investment business",[128] insofar as they do not meet the requirements of "private secondary distribution" (Articles 2(4) and 4 of the FIEA), parallel to "public offering".[129] Furthermore, offering disclosure is required in cases of specified procedures relating to securities issuance or distribution for reorganization when disclosures have not been made with regard to the securities newly issued or distributed, notwithstanding disclosures that have been made with regard to shares issued by the reorganized company (Article 4(1) (ii) of the FIEA).

A public offering, secondary distribution of securities or delivery of securities through specified procedures is not allowed to be made unless the issuer has submitted a securities registration statement to the Prime Minister (Article 4(1) of the FIEA). Under the mandatory disclosure regulation, suitable amounts of information are required to be given to investors in the form of a securities registration statement (*yûkashoken todokede-sho*). Before a securities registration statement comes into effect after the waiting period

---

126 The website of EDINET is http://disclosure.edinet-fsa.go.jp/.

127 Matsuo, supra note 22, p. 118. On the other hand, some scholars insist that pressure to distribute securities is grounds for regulation. Etsuro Kuronuma, *Disclosure ni kansuru Ichi-Kosatsu* [Concerning Information Disclosure], *Egashira Sensei Kanreki Kinen, Kigyou Ho no Riron* (*2*) [Essays in Honor of Prof. Egashira, Theory of Enterprise Law Vol. 2], p. 622 (Shojihomu, 2007).

128 See supra note 122.

129 Pursuant to the amendments to the FIEA of 2009, the phrase "on uniform terms and conditions" was deleted from the definition of "secondary distribution of securities" in order to prevent regulatory arbitrage due to changing terms and conditions of secondary distribution. Matsuo, supra note 22, p. 133.

Chapter 1　Introduction to the Japanese Financial Instruments and Exchange Act

following its submission, it is prohibited to sell or to distribute the securities that are the subject of the statement to investors (Article 15(1) of the FIEA).

Thus, in the offering disclosure system, information is disclosed through the securities registration statement. Furthermore, the FIEA requires the use of a prospectus (*mokuromi-sho*) in connection with such public offerings. A prospectus must be delivered when a sales contract pertaining to securities is concluded. This type of disclosure is called direct disclosure.

(ⅱ)　Continuous disclosure

Under the continuous disclosure system, a company whose securities are listed and traded on a financial instruments exchange is required to disclose information concerning certain items periodically. It is necessary to disclose correct and sufficient pertinent information to allow others to determine a fair and efficient market price for a security. A listed company and a company whose shares are traded on an OTC securities market must file with the Prime Minister a securities report (*yûkashoken hokoku-sho*) for each business year in principle within three months after the expiration of such business year.[130] Among companies required to submit a securities report, issuers of listed securities and issuers designated by cabinet order as being similar thereto in terms of distribution conditions must file quarterly securities reports (*shihanki hokoku-sho*). Furthermore, when any material event has occurred with respect to a company that might influence the price of its securities, that company must file an extraordinary securities report (*rinji hokoku-sho*).

---

**130** A company is also required to file a securities report when (1) it issues a security that fulfills the requirements established by cabinet order as those similar to distribution conditions as listed securities; (2) it issued shares or sold outstanding shares that required filing a registration statement of securities; (3) it issues a security with more than 1,000 owners in the case of shares or other share-related securities or more than 500 owners in the case of specified securities such as rights in securities investment business at the end of each business year within the latest five years (Article 24 (1) of the FIEA, Articles 3-6 and 4-2 of the Financial Instruments and Exchange Act Implementing Order, Article 16-3 of the Cabinet Office Ordinance on Disclosure on Corporate Information, Article 26-2 of the Cabinet Office Ordinance on Disclosure on Specific Securities).

*49*

The continuous disclosure regulation has been gradually developing since 1971 [131] and is now at the center of the information disclosure system under the FIEA.

   c . Relationship and coordination of mandatory disclosure systems under the FIEA and Companies Act

   ( i ) Offering disclosure

The Japanese Companies Act requires that the terms and contents of newly issued stocks and bonds be determined by the board of directors and disclosed to shareholders by the joint-stock company. The main purpose of this regulation under the Companies Act is to protect shareholders through disclosure of the information that will be necessary and contribute to coordinating private benefits between management and shareholders, as well as between old shareholders and new shareholders. On the other hand, the FIEA provides for the mandatory disclosure system above in order to provide information that will be necessary for investors and prospective investors to make rational investment decisions. The range of information that must be disclosed under the FIEA is much wider and more extensive than that under the Companies Act. The overlap of the regulation is resolved by the coordination provision that notice and disclosure can be omitted when a company has submitted a securities registration statement to the Prime Minister [132] or delivered a prospectus to investors. [133]

   ( ii ) Continuous disclosure

The Japanese Companies Act also requires a joint-stock company to make accounting documents and to disclose certain information such as a balance sheet and profit and loss statement. Therefore, a listed company has dual financial reporting obligations: a securities report under the FIEA and accounting documents under the Companies Act. This redundancy had burdened listed companies, since the financial reporting system was

---

[131] Amendments to the former Securities and Exchange Act of 1971, 1988 and 2006.
[132] Articles 201(5) and 240(4) of the Companies Act.
[133] Articles 203(4), 242(4), and 667(4) of the Companies Act.

Chapter 1    Introduction to the Japanese Financial Instruments and Exchange Act

introduced in Japan by the reform of the Securities and Exchange Act of 1948.

Since then, the two reporting systems under the Companies Act and capital markets regulation have been coordinated; but it is not possible to unify the reporting systems into one, because the purpose of each reporting system is different. While the reporting system under the FIEA aims to disclose accurate and pertinent information concerning the securities and the state of issuers to help investors make informed and rational investment decisions, the reporting system under the Companies Act aims not only to disclose information but also to regulate the amount that can be paid to shareholders as dividends or by purchasing treasury stocks. To calculate the distributable amount (*bunpai kano gaku*), the Japanese Companies Act regulates the accounting rules and various accounting documents (*keisan shorui*), while the standard is in principle left to accounting standards.[134] The method of disclosure and reporting under the Companies Act is limited to the preparation of accounting documents, the retention of such documents at the head office, and the publication of an annual reporting summary.

Although the purposes of the reporting and disclosure systems under the Companies Act and under the FIEA are not exactly the same, coordination between the two systems has been developing. For example, Article 440, paragraphs 1, 2, and 3 of the Companies Act of 2005 provides that the duty of a joint-stock company to disclose accounting documents shall not apply to a company, which submits a securities report under the FIEA.[135]

(iii)    Timely Disclosure Network (TDnet) of the Tokyo Stock Exchange

Since 1998, the Tokyo Stock Exchange has operated a timely disclosure network (TDnet) system for the disclosure of significant information, such as earnings information, business forecast revisions, dividend forecasts, information concerning the issuance of shares or warrants, share buybacks, etc., in a timely and efficient manner through electronic processing.[136]

---

**134** Hideki Kanda, *Kaisha ho* [Corporate Law], 20th. ed., Kobun-do, pp. 281-283 (2018).
**135** Article 440(4) of the Companies Act.
**136** http://www.jpx.co.jp/listing/disclosure/index.html

Through TDnet, the Tokyo Stock Exchange receives significant information in advance on public disclosure and discloses that information to the new media, then such information is deposited in its database for public inspection.

# 4. Prohibition of market abuse

### a. Overview

The FIEA regulates against fraud in the capital markets in order to enhance the integrity of the markets and to ensure the confidence of investors. Under the prohibition of market abuse, conduct such as insider trading (*naibusha torihiki*), market manipulation (*soba sojū*), and other fraudulent transactions is included. It is essential for investor protection and investor confidence in capital markets to avert the risk of market abuse and to ensure the quality of relevant information. It is also important to introduce an effective system of enforcement against market abuse. Market abuse can be classified into four categories: general fraud, insider trading, speculative acts, and market manipulation.

Articles 157 and 158 of the FIEA generally ban fraudulent acts. Article 157 prohibits fraudulent acts with regard to the sale or purchase of securities using fraudulent measures, schemes or techniques to acquire money or other property, using a document or other representation that contains misrepresentation of important matters or omissions of statements about important matters necessary to avoid misunderstanding, etc. (Article 157 of the FIEA).[137] Article 158 bans the spreading of rumors, using fraudulent means, or committing assault or intimidation for the purpose of carrying out a public offering, secondary distribution, sale, purchase or other transaction of securities or derivatives, as well as for the purpose of influencing market prices (Article 158 of the FIEA). To make false statements or omit to make statements concerning important matters in the sale and purchase of securities is also prohibited (Article 159(2)(iii) of the FIEA).

---

**137** The general antifraud provision of Article 157 was introduced in 1948 based on securities regulation in the United States. Nevertheless, this provision has hardly been applied in Japan in contrast to the US. Matsuo, supra note 22, p. 567.

Chapter 1   Introduction to the Japanese Financial Instruments and Exchange Act

Article 159 of the FIEA prohibits one sort of market manipulation (see b. below). Market price manipulation is the act of artificially influencing securities prices, which would otherwise be determined by genuine supply and demand based on the principles of free-market competition. Market manipulation is categorized into three groups: (1) wash tradings and prearranged transactions; (2) price manipulation and misrepresentation or omission; and (3) illegal market price stabilization transactions.

The FSA restricts overly speculative acts, such as depositing money for margin transactions (Article 161-2 of the FIEA), short-selling of securities (Article 162 (1) (i) of the FIEA) and stop orders for securities, financial index futures or market option transactions (Article 162 (1) (ii) of the FIEA).[138]

Articles 166 and 167 of the FIEA prohibit insider trading by persons associated with the companies concerned. Insider trading is the sale or purchase or other type of securities transaction by an insider, with any unpublished material facts pertaining to such securities that may significantly influence the decision-making of investors before such information is publicized (see c. below).

b. Market manipulation

Market manipulation aims to influence the present market price and could impair the functioning of markets and diminish the confidence of investors. Market manipulation occurs based on information and on transactions. Information-based market manipulation is caused by the dissemination of false or misleading information, including rumors, while transaction-based market manipulation is caused by providing false or misleading signals in terms of supply of or demand for financial instruments through actual trading.

The FIEA prohibits both types of market manipulation. Information-based manipulation using a document or other representation that contains a

---

**138** Although the restriction on stop orders is to be provided by cabinet order, there is at the moment no cabinet order on this matter.

*53*

misrepresentation of important matters or omissions of statements about important matters that are necessary to avoid misunderstanding is prohibited (Article 157 of the FIEA). Spreading rumors, using fraudulent means, or committing assault or intimidation for the purpose of carrying out a public offering, secondary distribution, sale and purchase or other transaction of securities or derivatives transactions for the purpose of influencing the market price is also prohibited (Article 158 of the FIEA). Furthermore, no person may publicly report false quotations of market prices of securities (Article 168 of the FIEA), express an opinion through media (Article 169 of the FIEA), indicate that a certain advantageous purchase will be made (Article 170 of the FIEA), or represent a fixed amount of dividends (Article 171 of the FIEA).

Acts to artificially influence securities prices are prohibited as transaction-based market manipulation. Transaction-based market manipulation is categorized into three groups: (1) wash tradings and prearranged transactions (Article 159 (1) of the FIEA); (2) act for market price fluctuation (Article 159(2) (i) & (ii) of the FIEA); and[139] (3) illegal market price stabilization transactions (Article 159(3) of the FIEA).

Market manipulation is sanctioned by criminal penalty and partly by administrative monetary penalty.

c. Insider trading

Articles 166 and 167 of the FIEA prohibit insider trading by persons associated with the companies concerned. Insider trading is the sale or purchase or other type of securities transaction by a corporate insider with any unpublished material facts pertaining thereto that may significantly influence the decision-making of investors before such information is publicized. The FIEA defines an insider as a person who has come to know material facts through the performance of his/her duties or due to his/her position in a listed company, etc.

---

[139] According to the case law, any transaction with the intention of inducing sales and purchases of securities is prohibited, while a series of sales and purchases that cause the market prices of securities to fluctuate is not illegal (Supreme Court Decision on July 20, 1994).

Chapter 1   Introduction to the Japanese Financial Instruments and Exchange Act

The ban on insider trading was introduced in Japan pursuant to the amendments to the former Securities and Exchange Act of 1988. Article 157, which bans generally fraudulent act, had never been applied to insider trading in Japan, as it was too vague. Thus, under the amendments to the SEA, insider trading was specifically and precisely prohibited.[140]

The purpose of regulating insider trading is controversial. According to lawmakers, insider trading is unfair because a corporate insider could make better trades based on the undisclosed material facts than other investors.[141] Some scholars explain the purpose of insider trading regulation from the viewpoint of ensuring capital market function through enhancing the liquidity of securities and efficiency in the trading market.[142]

A corporate insider who has learned certain material facts through their relationship with a listed company must not sell or purchase the relevant securities unless the material facts are disclosed to the public in certain ways. These provisions specifically define a corporate insider subject to the prohibition of trading and material facts.

A corporate insider is a director, officer, agent or employee of a listed company, shareholder or investor who has the right to request inspection of account books, a person who has statutory authority over the company, a person who has entered into a contract with the company, etc. (Article 166 (1) (i) to (v) of the FIEA). A person who has knowledge of an unpublished material fact while he/ she is a corporate insider will continue to be subject to the insider regulation for one year from the time he/she is no longer a corporate insider (Article 166(1) of the FIEA). Furthermore, a person who learns a material fact from a corporate insider or a former corporate insider is also subject to the prohibition on insider trading (Article 166(3) of the FIEA). More specifically, only a primary information recipient is subject to

---

**140** Katsuro Kanzaki, Regulation of Insider Trading, Capital Markets and Financial Services in Japan — Regulation and Practice, Japan Securities Research Institute, pp. 20-22 (1992).

**141** Yûsuke Yokobatake, *Chikujo Kaisetsu Insider Torihiki Kisei to Bassoku* [Commentary to Insider Trading Regulation and Penal Provisions], Shojihomu, pp. 9-10 (1989).

**142** Tatsuo Uemura, *Insider Torihiki Kisei to Kaku-kai no Hanno* [Insider Trading Regulation and Response from Various Fields], Shiho, No. 53, p. 127 (1991).

*55*

the insider trading prohibition. Secondary and subsequent recipients are not subject to the prohibition in Japan.

Material facts consist of two categories. The first is facts and information regarding the company, such as a decision made by the board of directors, a loss caused by a disaster, a change in major shareholders or information on the settlement of accounts that are significantly different from those previously announced (Article 166(2) of the FIEA). The second is facts regarding a takeover bid of the company (Article 167(2) of the FIEA).[143] The FIEA defines an insider as a person who is an officer or employee of the offeror of the takeover bid, or a person who has concluded, or is in negotiations to conclude, a contract with the offeror, or the target company, etc. (Article 167(1)(i) to (vi) of the FIEA).

Insider trading is sanctioned by criminal and administrative monetary penalties.

Furthermore, the FIEA includes regulation in order to prevent insider trading. First, an officer, a director or principal shareholder owning ten percent or more of the outstanding shares of a listed company must file a report with the Prime Minister on the purchase or sale of any share, or share option of the company within fifteen days after the end of the month in which the transaction was made (Article 163(1) of the FIEA). Second, a listed company and its shareholders acting derivatively may claim to recover profits made by its officers, directors or principal shareholders from the purchase or sale of equity securities of the issuer within a six-month period, in order to prevent the wrongful use of secret information they have obtained in the course of their duty or by virtue of their position (Article 164 (1) & (2) of the FIEA). Third, a corporate insider or related person in a takeover bid may neither transmit to another person "material facts" or "facts concerning the takeover bid" nor recommend selling or purchasing equity securities of the related listed company before these facts are

---

[143] Insider trading regulation concerning information on a takeover bid is parallel to corporate insider regulation concerning material facts pertaining to an issuer. Article 167, paragraph 1, items 1 to 6 define "related persons of a takeover bid" and Article 167, paragraph 3 defines "facts concerning a takeover bid."

Chapter 1 Introduction to the Japanese Financial Instruments and Exchange Act

published for the purpose of assisting another person in making a profit or avoiding loss (Article 167-2 of the FIEA). This ban was introduced under the amendments to the FIEA of 2013, in response to the scandal concerning a public offering in which the listed companies transmitted the facts concerning the public offering to investment firms before the facts were published, and constituting untransparent trading.[144]

# 5. Regulation of financial instruments businesses

## a. Overview

The FIEA provides for the supervisory regulation of financial instruments businesses so as to protect investors and ensure the integrity of capital markets. No person may conduct a financial instruments business unless he/she is registered with the Prime Minister (Article 29 of the FIEA).[145] Entry regulation, a regulation regarding the scope of the financial instruments business and conduct regulation are the three main parts of the supervisory regulation of the financial instruments business by the FIEA.

## b. Definition and types of "financial instruments business"

( i ) Definition of "financial instruments business"

Financial instruments businesses are defined in Article 2, paragraph 8 of the FIEA as follows:

(i) Sale and purchase, or intermediary, brokerage or agency service in connection with the sale and purchase of securities or market derivatives transactions or foreign market derivatives transactions

(ii) Intermediary, brokerage or agency services in connection with the entrustment of the sale and purchase of securities or market derivatives transactions conducted in a financial instruments exchange market or the sale and purchase of securities or foreign derivatives market transactions conducted in a foreign financial

---

144 Tomoyuki Furusawa et al., *Chikujo Kaisetsu 2013 Nen Kinyū Shohin Torihiki Ho Kaisei* [Commentary of 2013 Amendments to the Financial Instruments Exchange Act], p. 2 (Shojihomu, 2014).

145 Exceptionally, a person who will provide PTS services shall receive the registration as a type I financial instruments business firm and then be authorized for the PTS services (Article 30(1) of the FIEA). See supra C. 5. b.

*57*

instruments market

(iii) Over-the-counter derivatives transactions or intermediary, brokerage or agency service in connection therewith

(iv) Brokerage for clearing of securities, etc.

(v) Underwriting of securities

(vi) Self-offering of deemed securities[146] or beneficial interests in investment trusts according to settlor's instructions, etc.

(vii) Secondary distribution of securities or solicitation to professional investors

(viii) Handling in public offerings or secondary distributions of securities, or handling in private placement of securities or solicitation to professional investors

(ix) Provision of PTS (proprietary trading system) services

(x) Investment advice concerning the value of securities or investment decisions based on an analysis of the values of financial instruments

(xi) Discretionary investment management in securities and derivatives transactions based on analysis of the values of financial instruments

(xii) Agency or intermediary services for the conclusion of an investment advisory contract or a discretionary investment contract

(xiii) Investment management mainly in securities or rights pertaining to derivatives transactions of money or other properties invested by syndicating non-strictly regulated types of collective investment schemes,[147] etc.

(xiv) Accepting cash or securities deposits from customers for securities transactions, etc.

(xv) Transfer of corporate bonds, etc. conducted in response to the opening of an account for the transfer of bonds, etc. under the Act on Book-Entry Transfer of Corporate Bonds and Shares.[148]

Self-offering of beneficial interests in investment trusts ((vi)), self-management of money invested by syndicating non-strictly-regulated types of CIS ((xiii)), accepting cash or securities ((xiv)), and transfers of corporate

---

**146** Supra A. 3. b.

**147** Infra F. 1.

**148** Infra H. 2. a.

Chapter 1    Introduction to the Japanese Financial Instruments and Exchange Act

bonds, etc. ((xv)) were newly added as financial instruments business under the FIEA.

(ⅱ)    Types of "financial instruments business" and entry regulation

The FIEA classifies financial instruments business into four types, namely type I financial instruments business (Article 28(1) of the FIEA), type II financial instruments business (Article 28(2) of the FIEA), investment advisory and agency business (Article 28(3) of the FIEA), and investment management business (Article 28(4) of the FIEA). It is necessary to be registered with the Prime Minister as a financial instruments business operator to conduct a financial instruments business (Article 29 of the FIEA). Nevertheless, one registration is sufficient even if a firm will engage in one or more types of financial instruments business.

Type I financial instruments business includes the following: sale and purchase of, market derivatives transactions of and foreign market derivatives transactions of type I securities; handling in offering or distribution, solicitation of private placement and solicitation for distribution to professional investors of type I securities; underwriting for securities; OTC derivatives transactions; PTS services and accepting cash or securities deposits, etc. The entry regulation for type I financial instruments business is stricter, as (ⅰ) many investors would participate in them otherwise, and (ⅱ) the risk and level of expertise required is high.[149]

Type II financial instruments business is as follows: self-offering or private placement of securities; sale and purchase, handling in offering, etc., of type II securities that are less liquid than type I securities; market derivatives transactions not related to securities, etc. A type II financial instruments business is subject to less strict entry regulation than type I financial instruments business, as there is little need to protect a large number of investors.

The investment advisory and agency business consists of providing investment advice and acting as an agent or broker for the conclusion of investment advisory contracts or discretionary investment contracts. The investment advisory and agency business is subject to less strict entry regulation, similar to type II financial instruments business.

---

**149** Matsuo, supra note 22, p.349.

The investment management business includes conducting discretionary investment management in securities and derivatives transactions based on analysis of the values of financial instruments, or self-management. The entry regulation for investment management business is strict, similar to type I financial instruments business.

(ⅲ) Special provision for foreign securities firms

A "foreign securities firm (*gaikoku shoken gyosha*)" is defined as a person other than a financial instruments business operator, bank, cooperative structured financial institution, etc., which is governed by the laws and regulations of a foreign state and which engages in securities-related business (*yûkashoken kanren gyo*) in a foreign state (Article 58 of the FIEA). In principle, the FIEA requires even a foreign securities firm to be registered as a financial instruments business operator to engage in the financial instruments business (Article 29 of the FIEA). Nevertheless, a foreign securities firm is permitted to conduct securities-related business vis-à-vis a financial instruments business operator or a financial institution, to conduct securities-related business from foreign jurisdictions and without any solicitation made by the foreign firm, or to negotiate on the terms and conditions of an underwriting agreement with an issuer or holder of securities if the offering is made outside of Japan (Article 58-2 of the FIEA). Furthermore, a foreign securities firm may engage in underwriting, such as through participation in an underwriting syndicate, or in market transactions on a Japanese financial instruments exchange, with approval from the Prime Minister (Articles 59 and 60 of the FIEA).

A foreign company engaging in the investment advisory business or investment management business in a foreign jurisdiction is permitted to provide investment advisory services to Japanese financial instruments business operators or registered financial institutions conducting an investment management business without registration in Japan (Article 61 of the FIEA).

(ⅳ) Special rules for funds business for qualified institutional investors

In the case of funds involving a qualified institutional investor and a maximum of 49 general investors, registration is not required. Instead, only

Chapter 1    Introduction to the Japanese Financial Instruments and Exchange Act

notification is necessary, to commence a business regarding a self-offering of securities or investment mainly in securities of money invested by syndicating non-strictly-regulated types of collective investment schemes (self-management) (Article 63(1) & (2) of the FIEA). When fund units will be solicited and sold only to not more than 50 non-professional investors, and to more than one qualified institutional investor,[150] the supervisory regulation regarding self-offering and self-management business does not apply (*tekikaku kikan toshika-to tokurei gyomu*). This special rule was expected to allow the Financial Services Agency of Japan to collect information of non-strictly-regulated CISs, such as hedge and private equity funds, while avoiding over-regulation. Nevertheless, according to the amendments to the FIEA of 2015, the supervisory regulation of funds business for qualified institutional investors was strengthened and the requirements were made more strict, since the special rule was misused to mislead or defraud general investors.

### c. Conduct regulation
####  ( i )  Overview
A financial instruments business operator namely an investment firm is subject to the regulation of business conduct standards by the FIEA and the relevant self-regulatory organization. Unlike regulations with regard to registration, the rules and regulations for business conduct standards are, in principle, comprehensive and common to all types of financial instruments business, whether type I financial instruments business or type II financial instruments business.

Business conduct regulation of a financial instruments business operator is to protect investors and to ensure the appropriateness and soundness of the financial instruments business. The scope of the financial instruments business is defined broadly, as mentioned above (D. 5. a. and b.), and business conduct regulation is systematically structured according to the four types of financial instruments business, namely type I financial instruments business (Article 28 (1) of the FIEA), type II financial instruments business (Article 28(2) of the FIEA), investment advisory and

---

**150** See infra note 154.

agency business (Article 28(3) of the FIEA), and investment management business (Article 28(4) of the FIEA). The FIEA provides for general duties and individual rules of business conduct according to the type and nature of financial instruments business.

(ⅱ) Common business conduct regulation

As for the general duties common to all four types of financial instruments businesses, each type of financial instruments business operator is subject to the duty of good faith to customers (Article 36(1) of the FIEA), prohibition on name lending (Article 36-3 of the FIEA), advertising regulation (Article 37 of the FIEA), prohibition on compensation for loss pertaining to securities transactions or derivatives transactions (Article 39 of the FIEA) and limitation on the sale and purchase of securities for professional investors with non-professional investors (Article 40-4 of the FIEA), etc. As an organizational duty, an investment firm or a registered financial institution must establish an operational control system to ensure that its business is conducted appropriately (Article 35-3 of the FIEA).

(ⅲ) Individual business conduct regulation

ⅰ) Business conduct regulation on soliciting and concluding contracts for financial instruments transactions

In the solicitation stage, prior to the conclusion of a contract for a financial instruments transaction, an investment firm or a registered financial institution must, in advance, deliver a document containing the identity of the firm, an outline of the contract, the risk of loss regarding the contract due to fluctuations in the money rate, value of currencies, quotations in the financial instruments market, and matters concerning the contents of the relevant financial instruments business that are designated by cabinet office ordinance as important matters that may have an impact on customers' investment decisions, etc. (Article 37-3(1) of the FIEA). A contract for a financial instruments transaction means a contract that is for the purpose of conducting financial instruments business with a customer as the other party or on behalf of a customer (Article 34 of the FIEA).

No person other than an investment firm, registered financial institution or person who conducts a financial instruments business in accordance with

Chapter 1  Introduction to the Japanese Financial Instruments and Exchange Act

laws and regulations shall conduct solicitation in order to conduct financial instruments business (Article 31-3-2(2) of the FIEA).

An investment firm or a registered financial institution must give the customer clear notice of whether it will deal with the customer or will act as an intermediary, broker or agent when accepting an order from a customer for the sale or purchase of securities or OTC derivatives transactions (Article 37-2 of the FIEA).

Upon the conclusion of a contract for a financial instruments transaction, an investment firm or a registered financial institution shall further, without delay, prepare and deliver a document to the customer (Article 37-4(1) of the FIEA). The matters that should be included in the document are set out in a cabinet office ordinance and include the type of underlying financial instruments or financial indicators, the volume of the transaction, the price per unit, the types of the derivatives transactions, etc.

With regard to the solicitation of OTC financial derivatives transactions, solicitation by personal visit or telephone without invitation from the customer is prohibited. This prohibition is limited to OTC financial futures and other types of OTC derivatives transactions.[151] The introduction of this regulation shows that the suitability rule and the duty to explain do not work perfectly to protect investors.

Provision of fraudulent information, provision of conclusive evaluations on uncertain matters, etc., are also prohibited in the solicitation of the conclusion of a contract for a financial instruments transaction (Article 38(i), (ii) & (ix) of the FIEA). An investment firm or a registered financial institution is required to establish and publish a policy and method for executing orders from customers for the sale or purchase of securities and derivatives

---

**151** Article 38 (iv) of the FIEA; Article 16-4 (1) of the Financial Instruments and Exchange Act Implementing Order. Solicitation is not permitted if an investment firm does not obtain confirmation from the customer prior to solicitation regarding whether it intends to accept solicitation, or if a customer has, after being solicited, manifested the intention not to conclude the contract (Article 38(v) & (vi) of the FIEA). This prohibition is limited to financial futures and other types of OTC derivatives transactions (Article 117(1) (ix) of the Cabinet Office Ordinance on Financial Instruments Business, etc.).

*63*

transactions on the best terms and conditions (Article 40-2(1) & (2) of the FIEA).

ⅱ) Duty to explain and suitability rule

When an investment firm or a registered financial institution solicits a customer, it is prohibited from conducting business in a manner that would be found to be inappropriate in light of the customer's knowledge, experience, the status of property or the purpose of concluding the contract for trading financial instruments that results in, or is likely to result in, insufficient protection of the investors (Article 40(i) of the FIEA). This prohibition is called the suitability rule. It belongs to the supervisory regulation and does not have private law effect in and of itself. Under the suitability rule, besides the duty to deliver a prospectus, the investment firm is required to provide information concerning any financial instrument that a customer is going to buy.

However, the Japanese Supreme Court has ruled that in cases where a person in charge of a customer at an investment firm solicits transactions that deviate excessively from the suitability rule, contrary to the wishes of the customer and the circumstances, and actively solicits transactions that involve obviously excessive risk, this act should be regarded as unlawful under tort law.[152] The violation of the supervisory regulation aiming to protect the investor may lead to the liability of the investment firm to compensate for the damage that resulted from the violation.

Besides the delivery of documents before and on the conclusion of a contract for a financial instruments transaction, an investment firm or a registered financial institution must explain the outline of the contract, the risk of loss with regard to the contract due to fluctuations in the money rate, value of currency quotations on the financial instruments market and matters concerning the details of the relevant financial instruments business, which are specified by cabinet office ordinance as important matters that may have

---

[152] The Japanese Supreme Court decided that the suitability rule in the FIEA provides fundamentally for a supervisory relationship between the state and investment firms, but a customer can demand compensation in tort for a loss resulting from violations of the rule if the violation is material. Supreme Court Judgment of July 14, 2005, *Minshû*, Vol. 59, No. 6, p. 1323.

Chapter 1   Introduction to the Japanese Financial Instruments and Exchange Act

an impact on customers' investment decisions, etc., in a manner and to the extent necessary to ensure that the customer understands such matters, in light of the customer's knowledge, experience, the status of his/her assets and in light of the purpose of the conclusion of the contract for the financial instruments transaction.[153]

Furthermore, a provider of a financial instrument has a civil law duty to explain under the Japanese Civil Code (*min-po*) and the Financial Instruments Sales Act (*kinyū shohin no hanbai to ni kansuru horitsu*).

iii )   Investment advisory and agency firm

An investment advisory and agency firm is subject to the general duty of care and duty of loyalty (Article 41 of the FIEA). Business conduct regulations for investment advisory and agency firms include a concrete conflict-of-interest regulation, a duty not to give advice intending to conduct a transaction on terms and conditions that are different from ordinary terms and conditions and detrimental to the customer's interests (Article 41-2 of the FIEA) and a prohibition on receiving deposit of money or securities from a customer (Article 41-4 of the FIEA), or prohibition on loans of money or securities to a customer (Article 41-5 of the FIEA), among other things.

iv )   Investment management firm

An investment management firm has the duty of loyalty and duty of care (Article 42 of the FIEA). Business conduct regulation for investment management firms includes a concrete conflict-of-interest regulation, a duty not to manage assets on terms and conditions that are different from ordinary terms and conditions and detrimental to the customer's interests (Article 42-2 of the FIEA), a self-execution duty (Article 42-3 of the FIEA), a duty to segregate customers' assets and the manager's own assets (Article 42-4 of the FIEA), a prohibition on receiving deposits of money or securities from customers (Article 42-5 of the FIEA) and a prohibition on loans of money or securities to customers (Article 42-6 of the FIEA), among other things.

---

153 Article 38 (ix) of the FIEA; Article 117 (1) (i) of the Cabinet Office Ordinance on Financial Instruments Business, etc.

*65*

ⅴ) Securities custody business

An investment firm or a recognized financial institution must conduct its securities custody business with the care of a prudent manager for customers (Article 43 of the FIEA). There is a strict duty to segregate securities deposited by customers from the company's own assets (Articles 43-2, 43-2-2 & 43-3 of the FIEA) and a restriction on furnishing customers' securities as collateral or loaning such securities to another person without the consent of the customer (Article 43-4 of the FIEA), etc.

(ⅳ) Exception — professional investors

The FIEA introduced the concept of professional investors (*tokutei toshika*) in order to establish a flexible regulatory scheme. The performance of business conduct obligations will not, in principle, apply to a contract of a financial instruments transaction, insofar as it involves only professional investors (Article 45 of the FIEA). Professional investors are, among others, (i) qualified institutional investors (*tekikaku kikan toshika*),[154] (ii) the state, (iii) the Bank of Japan, (iv) investor protection funds, etc. (Article 2(31) of the FIEA). Non-professional investors are called "general investors". Investors are classified into four categories according to their attribution; namely, (i) professional investors who cannot choose to become general investors; (ii) professional investors who can choose to become general investors; (iii) general investors who can choose to become professional investors; and (iv) general investors who cannot become professional investors.

On the other hand, some business conduct regulations does not apply to funds involving qualified institutional investors with no more than 50 non-professional investors (Article 63(1) & (11) of the FIEA). Limited

---

154 Qualified institutional investors are defined to be persons specified by the Cabinet Office Ordinance on Definitions under Article 2 of the Financial Instruments and Exchange Act as having expert knowledge of and experience with investment in securities. According to the ordinance, among other things, type I financial instruments business operators, investment management firms, banks, insurance companies, investment corporations, foreign investment corporations, etc. are included in the list of qualified institutional investors (Article 10(1) of the Cabinet Office Ordinance on Definitions under Article 2 of the FIEA).

Chapter 1   Introduction to the Japanese Financial Instruments and Exchange Act

business conduct regulations are considered necessary to ensure the fairness of transactions by professional investors, while they would not get in the way of innovation.

# E. The FIEA within the regulatory framework for financial institutions

## 1. Regulatory framework for financial institutions

Financial instruments business operators (*kinyu-shohin torihiki gyosha*) are financial institutions in a broad sense. Financial institutions in Japan are classified broadly into private financial institutions and public financial institutions (**Figure 1-1**).[155] Private financial institutions are further classified into depository financial institutions and other financial institutions. Financial instruments business operators (investment firms), as well as insurance companies, belong to the category of financial institutions other than depository financial institutions.

The classification of Japanese financial institutions depends on the supervisory regulatory framework for financial institutions in Japan. That is, depository financial institutions are regulated by the Banking Act (*ginko ho*), the Credit Associations Act (*shinyo kumiai ho*) and other special acts. Insurance companies are regulated by the Insurance Business Act (*hoken gyo ho*), and investment firms are regulated by the Financial Instruments and Exchange Act (FIEA).

The Japanese regulatory framework for financial institutions fundamentally has an institutional regulatory approach which maintains that banking, insurance, and investment business should generally be separately instituted, managed, and supervised based on individual special supervisory acts. Nevertheless, the boundaries of the definition of financial businesses are

---

**155** The number of banks is as of October 27, 2016 (Japanese Bankers Association, Financial Institutions in Japan. ⟨https://www.zenginkyo.or.jp/en/banks/financial-institutions/⟩). The number of insurance companies and investment firms is as of June 30, 2016 (FSA, *Kinyu-cho no Ichi-nen* (Heisei 27 jimu-nendo) [FSA Annual Report for Program Year 2015], pp. 676-679, 690, and 694-696).

*67*

## Figure 1-1

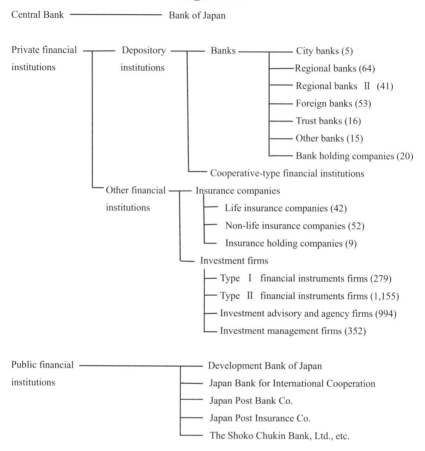

becoming more and more blurred. In particular, the regulation of the banking and securities business is becoming a mixture of an institutional regulatory approach and a functional regulatory approach due to the development of the "securitization of finance," etc. Under the functional regulatory approach, a regulator focuses on regulating a particular category of financial products or services being provided, rather than the institution providing those products or services. The FIEA is a typical example of a mixture of the institutional regulatory approach and functional regulatory approach. With the goal of establishing cross-sectional and uniform investor protection across various

Chapter 1    Introduction to the Japanese Financial Instruments and Exchange Act

financial products and services carrying considerable risk, the rule of the FIEA was extended to cover a wider range of areas, including non-strictly-regulated collective investment schemes, financial derivatives transactions, structured deposits and variable insurances, etc.

## 2. Scope of financial instruments businesses

a. Financial instruments businesses

The Financial Instruments and Exchange Act (FIEA) of 2006, a comprehensive overhaul of the former Securities and Exchange Law, defines financial instruments businesses broadly as including type I financial instruments businesses, type II financial instruments businesses, investment advisory and agency businesses, and investment management businesses (Article 28 of the FIEA). The FIEA is a mixture of the institutional regulatory approach and functional regulatory approach and covers a wide range of areas in order to provide equal and uniform investor protection across various financial products and services carrying considerable risk. Therefore, the FIEA expanded the definition of "securities" to include ownership interest in not-strictly-regulated collective investment schemes,[156] and business conduct regulation coverage is functional and cross-sectional. The FIEA has furthermore defined financial derivatives transactions broadly.[157]

Thus, the business conduct regulation of the following businesses was transferred from the former individual supervisory acts to the FIEA: the foreign securities brokers business, the financial futures business, the commodity investment business, the trust beneficial rights sales business, the investment advisory business, the business pertaining to discretionary investment contracts, the investment trust management business, the investment corporation asset management business, and the mortgage securities business.

On the other hand, to ensure a functional approach, substantially similar conduct regulation should apply to soliciting or selling deposits, insurance products or trust products, which have economically the same character as

---

**156** Supra A. 3. b. and infra Chapter 2 A. 1.
**157** Supra A. 3. c. and infra Chapter 2 A. 2.

*69*

financial instruments. The Banking Act, the Insurance Business Act and the Trust Business Act, etc. have introduced substantially the same conduct regulation regarding soliciting or selling financial products that carry considerable investment risk as under the FIEA.

b. Scope of business of investment firm: other business incidental to financial instruments business, etc.

An investment firm that conducts a type I financial instruments business or an investment management business may conduct other business incidental to such financial instruments business, such as the following: (i) the lending and borrowing of securities; (ii) money loans incidental to margin transactions; (iii) money loans secured by securities that are deposited for safekeeping by customers; (iv) agency services for customers concerning securities, etc. (*fuzui gyomu*) (Article 35(1) of the FIEA). The firm may conduct business such as (i) business pertaining to transactions on a commodity market, (ii) business pertaining to transactions conducted using fluctuations in commodity prices and other indicators, market gaps, etc., (iii) business pertaining to money lending, etc. with a notification to the Prime Minister (*todokede gyomu*) (Article 35(2) & (3) of the FIEA). The firm may furthermore engage in business for which approval has been obtained from the Prime Minister (*shonin gyomu*) (Article 35(4) & (5) of the FIEA). On the other hand, an investment firm that conducts only a type II financial instruments business or investment advisory and agent business may engage in any other business (Article 35-2(1) of the FIEA).

# 3. Separation of the financial instruments business and banking

a. Separation of the banking and securities business

The FIEA basically prohibits financial institutions such as banks or cooperative-structured financial institutions from engaging in securities-related business and the investment management business (Article 33 of the FIEA). This regulation, which is called the "separation of banking and securities business" was introduced in Japan with the enactment of the former Securities and Exchange Act of 1948. That is, Article 65 of the former Japanese Securities and Exchange Act introduced "separation of banking

Chapter 1   Introduction to the Japanese Financial Instruments and Exchange Act

and securities business" under the guidance of the General Headquarters (GHQ) of the Allied Powers in the aftermath of World War II.

The separation of banking and securities business has various rationales. First, the securities business is so risky that a bank engaged in such business is vulnerable to bankruptcy, which would harm depositors and the payment system. Therefore, banking business should be separated from securities business. Second, multiple conflicts of interest emerge when a bank engages in securities business. For example, if a bank is a creditor of an enterprise to whom it is lending, the credit risk of the enterprise would be transferred from the bank to holders of the corporate bonds that are underwritten by the bank and distributed to the public. Third, a bank may exert unfair influence over the lending enterprise and have excessive control over the industry. Fourth, banks have a competitive advantage over securities firms, because banks enjoy the protection of safety net systems such as deposit insurance and the possibility of an injection of public capital if the bank is on the brink of collapse.[158]

b. The Scope of financial instruments business conducted by banks

However, there were some exceptions to the principle of the separation of banking and securities business from the beginning, and these exceptions have been gradually expanded. For example, banks may underwrite and trade public bonds such as Japanese government bonds (JGB) on customers' accounts or on banks' accounts, though they are not allowed to engage in underwriting and trading equities and corporate bonds. The Banking Act was amended in 1981 to define the scope of financial instruments business that banks may engage in and allowed banks to engage in retail sales and the dealing of JGBs on the banking supervisory regulation side.[159]

Despite the principle of separation of banking and securities business, banks may sell and purchase securities and conduct securities-related derivatives transactions on their own trading account for the purpose of investment or a

---

[158] Hideki Kanda, Hiroyuki Kansaku & Mizuho Financial Group (ed.), *Kinyū-ho Kogi* [Lecture on Financial Law], 2nd ed., p. 259 (Iwanami-shoten, 2017).

[159] The Banking Act provides for substantially the same scope of banking business as under the FIEA. Matsuo, supra note 22, pp. 397-399.

beneficiary's account based on a trust contract, as well as on a customer's account in the case of written instructions to do so from such customer (Article 33 (1) & (2) of the FIEA). Furthermore, when banks become registered financial institutions (*toroku kinyū kikan*) with the Japanese Prime Minister, they may engage in handling intermediate sales of securities other than shares or corporate bonds, etc., derivatives transactions other than securities-related derivatives transactions, self-offerings or private placement, investment advisory and agency business and securities custodian business (Article 33-2 of the FIEA).

The FIEA regulates only the registered financial institution business and other businesses incidental thereto (e.g., Articles 44-2(2) and 52-2(1) (iii) of the FIEA). Under the FIEA the registered financial institution business includes financial instruments intermediary business (*kinyū shohin chūkai gyo*): (1) intermediary for sale and purchase of securities; (2) intermediary for entrustment of sale and purchase of securities in a financial instruments exchange market; (3) dealing in public offering or secondary distribution of securities, etc., in accordance with the firewall regulations.

Instead, the business that banks should not engage in is limited to the following businesses: (1) the sale and purchase, intermediate sale and purchase, acting as an agent in connection with, underwriting or distribution of shares, share options, corporate bonds, covered warrants, etc.; (2) handling private offerings of covered warrants related to shares; (3) conducting over-the-counter (OTC) derivatives transactions related to securities with more than 50 people; and (4) proprietary trading system (PTS) business, etc.

## 4. Financial conglomerates

The regulatory concept of the separation of banking and securities business has been modified so as to permit banking and securities business through separate legal entities within a financial conglomerate. Due to the financial systems reform of 1992, called the Japanese Big-Bang, a bank may hold a securities firm as a subsidiary and a securities firm may hold a bank as a subsidiary, which permits the construction of financial conglomerates. Financial conglomerates have numerous advantages such as economies of scale and scope and diversification of risks. They can also take advantage of

Chapter 1    Introduction to the Japanese Financial Instruments and Exchange Act

synergies to provide interrelated financial services such as deposits, loans, investment and insurance. Moreover, a conglomerate can offer customers a wide range of financial products and services called "one-stop shopping."

On the other hand, financial conglomerates have many risks. All the risks involved in transactions between member companies in a conglomerate may result in inappropriate transfers of assets, especially from banks to other group member companies which lacks liquidity, and may affect the soundness of regulated entities. Risk and reputation can easily affect other member companies as well as a conglomerate itself. From the viewpoint of customer protection, conflicts of interest and abuse of the dominant power of a conglomerate may harm customers' interests.

In response to permitting financial conglomerates,[160] the supervisory act introduced a so-called firewall regulation, such as a ban on transmission of undisclosed material information of customers across the group and on occupying dual positions as director or employee both in banks and securities firms in the same group.[161] The purposes of the firewall regulation are as follows: first, to ensure the independence and soundness of each member company in a financial conglomerate; second, to prevent and control conflicts of interest; third, to ensure fair competition between market intermediaries; and fourth, to protect investors.[162] Provisions of the firewall regulation include the arms-length transaction rule between member companies in a financial conglomerate (Articles 44-3(1)(i)(iv) and 44-3(2)(i)(iv) of the FIEA), the duty to establish a control system for conflicts of interest (Articles 44-3(1)(iii) and 44-3(2)(iii) of the FIEA) and the ban on transmission of undisclosed material information of customers across the group without the consent of the customer[163] (Article 44-3(1)(iv) of the

---

**160** The Financial Systems Reform Act of 1992 permitted a bank to hold more than half of the shares of a securities firm and a securities firm to hold more than half of the shares of the bank in a mutual fashion. Thereafter, under the amendments to the Banking Act of 1997 and the amendments to the Insurance Business Act of 1997, bank holding companies and insurance holding companies are permitted to hold more than half of the shares of a securities firm.

**161** Kanzaki, Shitani & Kawaguchi, supra note 30, pp. 950-961.

**162** See Matsuo, supra note 22, pp. 462-463.

**163** Occupying dual positions as director or employee both in a bank and a securities firm in the same group is not automatically against the ban.

*73*

FIEA, Articles 153(1)(vii) of the Cabinet Office Ordinance on Financial Instruments Business).

The firewall regulation was relaxed in 2008, because it could prevent financial conglomerates from providing various useful financial services and products to customers and from constructing the appropriate risk management and compliance system at the conglomerate-level.[164] Simultaneously, the FIEA and the Banking Act introduced the abovementioned duty of financial institutions to establish and manage a control system for conflicts of interest, which purports to prevent and correct unfair and fraudulent conduct generated by conflicts of interest.

The firewall regulation was relaxed further by the amendments to the FIEA of 2014, expanding the exemption from the regulation on the exchange of customers' information to correct overregulation.[165] The relaxation is purported to ensure the provision of various financial services at the level of the financial group for the benefit of customers.

# F. Collective investment schemes

## 1. Meaning of collective investment schemes (CISs)

The collective investment scheme (CIS) plays an important role in capital markets because fund raising can be enhanced through securities issued by a CIS, which can intermediate and combine fund raisers and investors. Furthermore, CISs offer great business for industry and investment opportunities for investors.[166] Unlike with banks and insurance companies, which are financial intermediaries in the narrow sense, a holder of securities issued by a CIS makes profit but bears risk. A CIS seems formally like a device for indirect financing, but it functions substantially as a device for

---

**164** The First Finance Division of the Financial Counsel in the Financial Services Agency, Report on Strengthening of Competition in Japanese Financial- and Capital Market ⟨*Waga kuni kinyû sihon sijo no kyosoryoku kyoka ni mukete*⟩ (18 Dec. 2007).

**165** Article 153(1) (vii) (a) and (3) (vii) & (viii) of the Cabinet Office Ordinance on Financial Instruments Business.

**166** Kanzaki, Shitani & Kawaguchi, supra note 30, pp. 976-981.

Chapter 1   Introduction to the Japanese Financial Instruments and Exchange Act

direct financing from a risk-taking perspective. Interests of CIS are treated as securities under the FIEA (Article 2 (1) (iv), (viii), (x), (xi), (xiii), (xvii), and 2 (v) of the FIEA).

The CIS is especially remarkable and expected as a tool for direct financing in Japan, where individual financial assets are mainly invested in indirect financing such as cash and deposits (52.3%) and insurance and pension reserves (29.8%), with little preference for direct financing such as shares and equities (8.6%), bonds (1.5%), investment trusts (5.0%), and others (2.9 %).[167]

CISs are classified into two categories based on the purposes and functions of the scheme. One is the CIS for asset management, such as an investment trust, in which a special purpose vehicle (SPV) collects money and invests it in financial instruments. The other is the CIS for asset-backed securitization, in which fundraiser, specially the originator, transfers a particular asset to a vehicle of the scheme and the vehicle issues securities. The distinction between a CIS for asset management and a CIS for asset-backed securitization is based on whether the investment objectives are from the outset concretely determined. Therefore, items and contents to be disclosed are different between the two types. Concerning CIS for asset management, it is difficult to disclose concrete investment objectives in advance, whereas objectives are already defined in the case of asset-backed securitization.

## 2. Strictly-regulated CISs

In Japan, there are strictly regulated CISs, which are subject to special laws, regulations and administrative rules. These regulations govern the arrangement of the scheme, the structure and organization of the vehicle, the

---

**167** The data is as of the end of September 2016. Bank of Japan, Research and Statistics Department, Flow of Funds – Overview of Japan, US, and the Euro area–, Chart 2, at 2 (December 22, 2016). In the US, cash and deposits accounts for 13.9%, insurance and pension reserves 32.1%, shares and equities 35.4%, bonds 5.1%, investment trusts 10.7 %, and others 2.8%. In the Euro area, cash and deposits accounts for 34.6%, insurance and pension reserves 34.2%, shares and equities 16.3%, bonds 3.8%, investment trusts 8.6%, and others 2.5%. ⟨http://www.boj.or.jp/en/statistics/sj/sjhiq.pdf⟩

business conduct of related parties, etc. Most important are the Investment Trust and Investment Corporation Act, the Act Concerning Assets Liquidation, and the Real Estate Syndication Act.

There are special acts to regulate the organization of vehicles and the structure of CISs and to supervise CISs. The Investment Trust and Investment Corporation Act regulates CISs for investment management, and the Act on the Securitization of Assets regulates CISs for asset-backed securitization. The ownership units of strictly regulated CISs for investment trusts and asset-backed securitization have been defined as "securities" since the amendments to the former Japanese Securities and Exchange Act of 1998. Securities are included in the definition of the type I securities under the FIEA (Article 2(1) (iv), (viii), (x), (xi), (xiii), and (xvii) of the FIEA).

## 3. Investment trusts and investment corporations[168]

CISs for asset management such as investment trusts have many advantages. First, they allow the essentially non-professional public to diversify investments in a professionally selected portfolio. Secondly, economies of scale and scope can be achieved through a collective fund. Thirdly, negotiability and transparency is ensured by regulation, which provides for the duty to issue negotiable instruments and to publish the mark-to-market net asset value of a fund on a daily basis, among other things.

Before World War II, there were similar products in the legal form of trusts, modeled after the unit trust in Great Britain. A securities firm, as settlor, transferred assets to a trust company, the trustee, in order to invest trust property in securities. Although the Trust Business Act applied to the asset management business, it could not protect investors in CISs sufficiently. For example, the Act lacks regulation regarding the duty of the settlor, who instructs the trustee on investment decisions.

After World War II, the former Securities Investment Trust Act (currently

---

**168** See in detail, Nomura Asset Management kabushiki-kaisha, *Toshi Shintaku no Homu to Jitsumu* [Legal Practice and Practice of Investment Trust], 4th. ed. (Kinyû zaisei jijo kenkyû-kai, 2008).

*76*

Chapter 1 Introduction to the Japanese Financial Instruments and Exchange Act

the Investment Trust and Investment Corporation Act; ITICA) was promulgated in 1951. Under the framework of the Act, an investment trust management company (*toshi shintaku itaku kaisha*) must be separated from a trustee, who is the custodian of the fund assets. Any investment trust that intends to invest mainly in securities is banned, unless it is based on the Act (Article 7 of the ITICA), and the investment trust property is limited to money (*kinsen shintaku*), in which settlors entrust a trustee with their money. Ultimately, the money is distributed to investors (Article 8 of the ITICA). Notwithstanding the above, the mandatory disclosure system for investment trusts was covered by the former Securities Investment Trust Act, and it is currently regulated under the Financial Instruments and Exchange Act (FIEA).

Under the amendments to the ITICA of 1967, a securities investment trust management company has been subject to the duty of loyalty and duty to disclose, even though it is not a trustee in the sense of trust law, because it is a settlor. Meanwhile, the Securities Investment Advisory Act was enacted in 1986 to regulate the business conduct of an investment advisor who makes investment decisions for investors based on an investment advisory contract or discretionary investment contract. Under the amendments to the Securities Investment Advisory Act of 1998, a registration system took the place of the licensing system in order to encourage the establishment of new funds. Distribution channels for investment trusts were expanded to financial institutions other than securities firms, such as banks and insurance companies. Outsourcing of asset management was permitted under the 1998 amendments, and investment in funds of funds was allowed in 1999. The latter amendments made it possible for investors to access the investment services of foreign asset management companies.

Meanwhile, regulations governing investment objectives were consistently weakened or lifted;[169] in particular, objectives of investment were expanded to derivatives transactions and property other than securities, such as real

---

**169** The bans on inclusion of foreign securities (1970), OTC-registered stocks (1978), forward exchange contracts (1986), derivatives with hedging purposes (1987) and derivatives with purposes other than hedging (1998) in investment trust portfolios were lifted.

*77*

estate under the 2000 amendments to the ITTCA.[170] The amendments of 2000 retitled the Investment Trust and Investment Corporation Act. Under the amendments, a corporation-type SPV was introduced as a CIS vehicle for asset management in addition to the trust-type. The introduction of corporation-type SPVs was based on the idea of enhancing competition between trusts and corporations as legal structures for CIS investment management. Furthermore, trustees are now allowed to engage in discretionary investment management of real-estate investments as well as security investment trusts. Investment trusts that are transferable on an exchange and purchase and redemptions of the creation units generally are in kind were allowed, which made possible the ETF (Exchange Traded Fund) exchangeable with gold and other products having sufficient liquidity, under the amendments to the ITTCA of 2008. Furthermore, the amendments of 2013 facilitated the merger of corporation-type SPVs by relaxing the requirements for a decision by its members. The measures of fundraising and capital strategy were enriched by lifting the ban on an investment corporation's aquisition of its own SPV units, etc.

## 4. CIS for asset-backed securitization[171]

Asset-backed securitization is a means of raising capital in exchange for cash flow in the future, which is backed by an underlying asset of an originator.[172] The underlying asset, which is difficult to transfer or liquidate, is transferred by a fundraiser, namely an originator, to a CIS. The CIS issues securities, which are normally separated into different tranches, such as preferred, mezzanine and inferior. These securities are rated by a credit

---

170 The Japan Real Estate Investment Trust (J-REIT) has been launched under these amendments since 2001 at the Tokyo Stock Exchange.

171 See in detail, Kotaro Nagasaki and Yûichiro Nukada, *Chikujo Kaisetsu Sisan Ryûdo-ka Ho* [Commentary to the Act on the Securitization of Assets], 2d. ed. (Kinyû zaisei jijo kenkyû-kai, 2008).

172 Financing similar to asset-backed finance can be realized to issue securities that are backed by a particular asset, especially a mortgage. To facilitate and to regulate issuance of such securities, the Mortgage Securities Act (*teito shoken ho*) was enacted in 1931. The Act concerning the Regulation of Business Relating to Specified Claims was enforced in 1993 and the Specified Real Estate Joint Venture Act was enacted in 1995.

Chapter 1　Introduction to the Japanese Financial Instruments and Exchange Act

rating agency, and each class has a different rating. Various credit-enhancing measures are taken to make asset-backed securities attractive, such as bank guarantees to reduce the risk involved in the cash flow generated by the underlying asset.

When the underlying asset is valuable, securities issued by the CIS, especially preferred securities can be rated higher than bonds issued by the originator. This means that the originator can raise capital in more advantageous conditions than with its own corporate bonds, whose credit rating is determined by the credit risk of the originator. Furthermore, the asset separated from the originator is easier to value than the creditworthiness of the originator itself, which leads to a reduction in the capital cost due to prompt and correct estimation of the risk.
The purposes of the transfer of the underlying asset to the CIS are as follows: first, it is to ensure bankruptcy remoteness from the originator and the holder of securities issued by the CIS; second, it is to eliminate the possibility that the underlying asset will be legally treated as collateral under the Corporate Reorganization Act, under which the rights of a secured creditor may be limited in a corporate reorganization process. As a result of this, the transfer of the asset is more likely to be legally considered not a mortgage but a "true sale."

CISs generally use corporations or trusts as vehicles for asset-backed securitization. Nevertheless, this still generates the risk of bankruptcy for the CIS. Therefore, a separate CIS is established for the sole purpose of asset-backed securitization. Furthermore, principal business is outsourced by the CIS to other companies in order to limit the risk caused by the business and to avoid its bankruptcy.

In Japan, a special act was enacted to enhance asset-backed securitization and to regulate the structure of the vehicle, the rights and duties of investors, directors and trustees, etc. In 1993, the Act Concerning the Regulation of Business Relating to Specified Claims was enacted. The Act aimed to facilitate the liquidation of lease and credit card claims by lease and finance companies and credit companies by means of asset-backed securitization,

*79*

because such companies were then restricted to raising capital by issuing corporate bonds. In 1998, the Act Concerning Liquidation of Specified Assets by Special Purpose Companies (the SPC Law) was enacted. The Act creates a juridical person solely for the purpose of asset-backed securitization called a TMK (*tokutei mokuteki kaisha*), which is not a for-profit corporation but a special juridical person (*tokushu hojin*) based on a special law. The Act was then retitled the Act Concerning Assets Liquidation and introduced TMS (*tokutei mokuteki shintaku*), which is a trust solely for the purpose of asset securitization.

# G. History of securities regulation in Japan[173]

## 1. Before World War II

Japan opened its borders after the Edo era (1603-1867) and accepted the western legal and economic system. The main purpose of westernization was to end the burden of unequal treaties imposed on Japan by western nations during the Edo era. In 1874, in the Meiji era, the Stock Trading Ordinance (*kabushiki torihiki jorei*) was enacted, modeled after the articles of the London Stock Exchange according to advice by Gustave Émile Boissonade, who is famous for being the father of the Japanese Civil Code. This was the first capital markets law in Japan. Nevertheless, the Ordinance never came into effect because the traders and other related business groups strongly objected to it.

The Stock Exchange Ordinance (*kabushiki torihiki-jo jorei*) of 1878 was promulgated instead of the Stock Trading Ordinance. The Ordinance referred back mainly to the traditional Japanese system of futures contracts for rice (*choai-mai seido*), which originated in the Edo era and had already developed.[174] The Tokyo Stock Exchange and the Osaka Stock Exchange

---

**173** Kanzaki, Shitani & Kawaguchi, supra note 30, pp. 37-106.
**174** *Dojima kome kai-jo* ⟨Dojima Futures Exchange for Rice⟩ was the first futures exchange in the world. The futures were contracts for difference; therefore, only the difference was counted after netting and settlement through a clearing house.

Chapter 1 Introduction to the Japanese Financial Instruments and Exchange Act

were established in 1878 in the legal form of joint-stock companies under the Ordinance. Also established were the Yokohama Stock Exchange in 1880, the Kobe Stock Exchange in 1882, the Kyoto Stock Exchange in 1884, and the Nagoya Stock Exchange in 1886. However, most securities trading on these exchanges were believed to be highly speculative and unsound. The stock exchanges themselves also mainly pursued profit-maximizing.[175]

The Meiji government promulgated the Exchange Ordinance (*torihiki-jo jorei*) of 1887. Notwithstanding the Ordinance's requirements that the exchanges take the legal form of membership-type organizations and the existing exchanges in the form of joint-stock companies be liquidated, the already established exchanges continued to exist. In other words, the Ordinance never became effective.

In 1893, the Exchange Act (*torihiki-jo ho*) was promulgated to supervise both stock exchanges and commodity exchanges. It regulated the organizational structure, classes and types of listed instruments and trading rules of the exchanges, etc. The Exchange Act regulated both stock exchanges and commodity exchanges. Most transactions on the exchanges were at the time still speculative because they were settled by cash settlement, not by actual delivery.


The persons subject to the Exchange Act were members of the exchange, not securities firms generally. In other words, securities firms that conducted business outside the exchange were not regulated by the Act. The Act Regarding Installment Sales Business of Securities (*Yûka-shoken kappu hanbai-gyo ho*) was promulgated in 1918 and introduced a licensing system for the business and a minimum capital requirement. Starting in 1938, business involving the brokerage and dealing of securities was regulated by the Securities Business Control Act (*Yûka-shoken gyo torisimari ho*), and the business of underwriting securities was regulated by the Securities Underwriting Business Act (*Yûka-shoken hikiuke ho*). Due to these regulations, securities firms came under supervisory control, whether they were members of an exchange or not.[176]

---

**175** Kanzaki, Shitani & Kawaguchi, supra note 30, p. 39.

*81*

In 1943, the Japan Securities and Exchange Act (*nihon torihiki jo ho*) was promulgated as one of the war-time economic policies of the government. The Stock Trading Commission (*yûka shoken torihiki iinkai*) and the Nihon Stock Exchange (*nihon shoken torihiki jo*) were established. The Japan Securities and Exchange Act regulated only the organization, trading rules and membership of stock exchanges, while the Exchange Act still regulated commodity exchanges, but its name was changed to the Commodity Exchange Act.

## 2. The former Securities and Exchange Act

### a. Enactment

After World War II, the General Headquarters (GHQ) of the Allied Powers released a memorandum regarding stock exchanges dated September 25, 1945. The resumption of business by stock exchanges, commodity exchanges and other similar facilities was banned by the memorandum, until the GHQ had concluded that a new legal framework for exchange and facilities would be established in the field of capital markets.

The former Ministry of Finance (*okura sho*) drafted the Securities and Exchange Act (*shoken torihiki ho*), which aimed to comprehensively regulate capital markets and the securities business. The bill of the Securities and Exchange Act was submitted to the Japanese Diet on condition of the approval of the GHQ. The Diet passed the bill and promulgated the Act of 1947. The Act was modeled after the Securities Act of 1933 and the Securities Exchange Act of 1934 in the United States. Nevertheless, the Act was not enacted except for Chapter 5 regarding the Securities Commission[177] because the GHQ did not ultimately approve the Act. One of the reasons the GHQ did not approve the draft was that the Act was so simple that many important matters and issues would be left to cabinet order and ordinance.

---

**176** Sales representatives of securities firms were first regulated by the Regulation on the Control of Sales Representatives of Securities (*Yûka-shoken gaimu-in torisimari kisoku*) of 1941, which introduced a registration system and a ban on unfair conduct.

**177** The Securities Commission under the Securities and Exchange Act of 1947 was not an independent commission but an advisory organization in the form of an administrative commission.

Chapter 1 Introduction to the Japanese Financial Instruments and Exchange Act

The Japanese government revised the Securities and Exchange Act of 1947 in accordance with the outline indicated by the GHQ. The Securities and Exchange Act of 1948 was totally revised to develop a modern disclosure system, including securities registration statements and prospectuses, and to introduce supervisory regulation of securities firms under a registration system, prohibition of fraudulent transactions such as market manipulation, the separation of securities business and banking, self-regulatory organizations and stock exchanges, external audit systems, etc.[178] There were 210 articles of the Act after the 1948 amendments, which was more than twice as many as in the 1947 version, which had 92 articles. The Japanese Securities Trading Commission was established as an independent commission under the Act, which administered the enforcement of the Act.

Stock exchanges were established in Tokyo, Osaka, and Nagoya in 1949. The GHQ introduced three principles on securities trading on stock exchanges in permitting the application for the establishment of stock exchanges, namely (1) all listed stocks traded by the members should be conducted on the exchange; (2) all trading on the stock exchange should be recorded via a time-ordered system; and (3) any futures trading should be prohibited. After accepting these three principles by Japanese government, the GHQ announced a policy authorizing the resumption of stock exchanges. The Securities and Exchange Act of 1948 and the three principles laid down by the GHQ provided the fundamental regulatory framework for Japanese capital markets after World War II.

b. 1952 amendments

Under the amendments to the Securities and Exchange Act of 1952, Japan's Securities Trading Commission was abolished as an independent commission and its authority was transferred to the former Ministry of Finance (*okura-sho*).

---

[178] The Act Regarding Installment Sales Business of Securities, the Securities Business Control Act and the Securities Underwriting Business Act were abolished under the revised Securities and Exchange Act in 1948.

*83*

### c. 1953 amendments

In 1953, the mandatory disclosure system for public offerings and secondary distribution of securities was simplified and relaxed, while supervisory regulation of securities firms and stock exchanges was strengthened. The ban on margin transactions was lifted.

### d. 1965 amendments

In 1965, the entry regulation for securities firms was changed from a registration system to a license system, and business conduct regulations were introduced for directors, officers, and employees of securities firms. The Minister of Finance was given authority to take measures necessary for the rectification of the violation of laws and regulations by securities firms.

### e. 1971 amendments

Under the amendments of 1971, a continuous disclosure system was developed by expanding the scope of the obligation to submit annual securities reports and introducing a semiannual and extraordinary reporting system. The scope of those persons subject to the provision regarding civil liability for falsifying securities registration statements and securities reports under the former Securities and Exchange Act was expanded to include directors or officers of the issuer and distributor of the securities, etc. The reform act of 1971 also introduced a takeover bid system[179] in Japan for the first time. A takeover bid is the act of soliciting offers for sale or other type of transfer for value of shares from many unspecified persons through public notice outside of financial instruments exchange markets (Article 27-2(6) of the current FIEA).

### f. 1981 amendments

Under the amendments of 1981, bans on securities business by banks or trust companies, etc. (financial institutions) were relaxed. Financial institutions could now conduct securities business pertaining to public bonds with authorization from the former Minister of Finance[180] and were subject to the business conduct regulation.

---

**179** See infra H. 5.

Chapter 1 Introduction to the Japanese Financial Instruments and Exchange Act

g. 1985 amendments

Under the amendments of 1985, futures pertaining to Japanese government bonds on stock exchanges were regulated, in order that securities firms or financial institutions would be able to hedge the market risk of JGBs through transactions of futures on stock exchanges. Standardized futures pertaining to JGBs were deemed to be securities according to the revised act.

h. 1988 amendments

In 1988, Japan introduced concrete and detailed insider trading regulations for the first time. Regulations regarding continuous disclosure were improved and procedures for offering disclosure were simplified. The center of the mandatory disclosure system shifted from offering disclosure to continuous disclosure. A securities registration statement and prospectus could be prepared in accordance with the "incorporation method (*kumikomi hosiki*)" or "reference method (*sansho hosiki*)," provided that the securities report was disclosed.

i. 1990 amendments

The takeover bid system was revised. The threshold for a mandatory takeover bid decreased from a 10% to a 5% shareholding following the purchase. Furthermore, a takeover bid outside the financial instruments exchange market with a change of control, namely, in principle, more than one-third of outstanding shares, became subject to the mandatory takeover bid regulation. The prior notification system was abolished, and the duration of a takeover bid was extended to enhance takeover bids. Shareholders' withdrawal rights were extended.

j. 1991 amendments

In the 1990s, the reform of the Securities and Exchange Act was accelerated, especially in accordance with global capital market regulation standards. In 1991, a disclosure system of the status of large-volume holdings in shares (the so-called 5% rule) was introduced for the first time in Japan. When the

---

**180** The authorization is not necessary when a financial institution will underwrite public bonds without any purpose for distribution.

number of shares of a listed company held by a person exceeds 5% of its outstanding shares, such large shareholder is generally required to file a large-volume shareholding report with the Minister of Finance (now the Prime Minister) within five business days from the date when such person's shareholding rate first exceeds 5%.

A rule was introduced under which a security firm must not provide property benefits to its customer in order to compensate or make up for all or part of a loss or shortfall from the relevant financial instruments transaction (*sonshitsu hoten, sonshitsu hosho*), and discretionary trading accounts were prohibited, in response to the scandal of loss compensation by securities firms only to important clients.

### k. 1992 amendments

Under the amendments of 1992, the scope of "securities" was extended to cover commercial paper (CP), beneficiary certificates of foreign loan trusts and beneficial interests in residential loan trusts, taking into account the development of the securitization of finance. Financial institutions such as banks were permitted to participate in the securities business through their subsidiaries. The legal framework for the public offering of securities was changed in order to simplify the system on the one hand and to prevent regulatory arbitrage on the other hand. Continuous disclosure was expanded to apply to unlisted or unregistered companies with more than 500 shareholders. The affairs and items to be disclosed in consolidated financial statements were expanded.

A clause providing for the general principle of fairness and honesty in the dealings with their clients and business conduct regulation, including the suitability rule, was introduced.

The Japanese Securities and Exchange Surveillance Commission (*shoken torihiki-to kanshi iinkai*) was established, and the inspection and audit system was strengthened by enhancing the functions of SROs.

### l. 1994 amendments

In 1994, a share buyback reporting system (*jiko kabuken kaitsuke jokyo hokoku sho*) and a takeover bid for shares by issuer were introduced in response to the deregulation of share buybacks in corporate law reform.

Chapter 1   Introduction to the Japanese Financial Instruments and Exchange Act

Making the determination to buy back shares was added to the list of material facts in prohibited insider dealing.

### m. 1997 amendments

In 1997, the Financial Supervisory Agency (*kinyû kantoku cho*) was established, and the authorities and functions of the supervision of financial institutions were transferred from the Ministry of Finance (*okura sho*) to the Agency. Penal provisions were strengthened in relation to violations of the duty to disclose, unfair trading, and market abuse in order to enhance the enforcement of securities and capital markets regulation. The affairs and items to be disclosed in consolidated financial statements were expanded in response to the introduction of a share option system introduced by corporate law reforms.

### n. 1998 amendments

The amendments to the former Securities and Exchange Act of 1998 were based on and part of the reform of the Japanese financial system called the " Big Bang, Japanese version." The slogan of the financial system reform was to ensure "free, fair, and global" capital markets.

The surveillance and supervisory approach shifted its emphasis from ex ante and preventative regulation to an ex-post regulation approach, according to which violations of laws and regulations would be sanctioned or rectified to ensure the financial and business soundness of securities firms.

First, entry regulations on securities firms reverted back to a registration system from a license system. OTC securities derivatives trading and PTS business was added to the list of securities businesses. The classification of PTS services as securities business was connected with the repeal of the obligation of securities firms to trade listed securities only on stock exchanges. The regulation on commissions for brokerage services was repealed, meaning the standards of commission would be determined by each securities firm in order to enhance free competition based on market principles. The restrictions on the scope of business of securities firms were relaxed so that securities firms could engage not only in the securities business and ancillary business thereto but also in qualified business and other businesses approved by supervisory authorities.

On the other hand, measures for investor protection were strengthened. The duty to segregate was introduced as part of the regulation of the business conduct of securities firms in order to protect clients' assets from misuse by officers or employees of the firms or their bankruptcy. The Investor Protection Fund (*toshika hogo kikin*) system was also launched. The scope of the definition of securities was expanded to include investment securities issued by an investment corporation that is a strictly-regulated CIS,[181] foreign investment securities, and covered warrants, etc. The ownership units of strictly-regulated CISs for investment trusts and asset-backed securitization had already been defined as "securities", and the mandatory disclosure regulation had not applied to them. Nevertheless, pursuant to the amendments of 1998, this exemption was abolished.

The disclosure system for financial reporting shifted from an individual company basis to a consolidated basis. The scope of mandatory disclosure was expanded by lowering the threshold for the duty to submit securities registration statements from 500 million yen to 100 million yen, in order to strengthen investor protection and to enhance efficiency in capital markets.

o. 2000 amendments

Under the amendments of 2000, a securities registration statement, a securities report, and other disclosure documents had to be submitted and made available for investors and prospective investors to access via the electronic disclosure system. Delivery of a prospectus could also be permitted by provision of electronic data via the Internet. A stock exchange could also take the legal form of a joint-stock company in addition to that of a membership-type organization.

p. 2003 amendments

In the 21st century, the direction of the former Securities and Exchange Act is increasingly more towards the relaxation of entry regulations and expansion of the scope of the securities business, while the business conduct regulation and prohibition of market abuse is being strengthened with

---

181 As a vehicle for strictly-regulated CISs for investment management, a company-type CIS was set up in addition to the trust-type CIS in 1998.

Chapter 1   Introduction to the Japanese Financial Instruments and Exchange Act

stricter enforcement. Since the bursting of the bubble economy in the late 1990s, the slogan "from deposit to investment" has been stressed in Japan. Under the amendments of 2003, the concept of a securities intermediary business (*shoken chûkai gyo*) was introduced to expand and diversify the distribution channels for securities. Persons or juridical persons other than financial institutions can engage in the securities intermediary business through registration with the Prime Minister.

The definition of private placement was extended as follows, in order to promote investment in venture and start-up companies. First, professional investors were excluded from the calculation of the total number of solicited investors in determining whether a given offering is a private placement to fewer than 50 persons. Second, an offering of equity securities could be the subject of a private placement for professional investors, if only purchases by professional investors are solicited and there is little possibility of the issued equity securities being transferred to investors other than professional investors. The disclosure system was strengthened for listed companies with reference to the U.S. Sarbanes-Oxley Act to increase the provision of information regarding corporate governance and risk relating to issuers.

Stock exchange holding companies could be established under these amendments in order to strengthen international competitiveness and to enhance the corporate governance of stock exchanges.

q. 2004 amendments

In 2004, the duty to seek best execution of customer orders was introduced as a business conduct standard, while an auction mechanism was permitted as one manner of determining the price in PTS. This revision purported to enhance the competition between stock exchanges and PTSs.

Furthermore, the prospectus system was improved. Rules for green sheet issuances were introduced as a special market for small and medium-sized start-up enterprises. In terms of regulation of the scope of business between banks and securities firms, restrictions on securities intermediary services by banks were lifted.

Administrative monetary penalties (*kachokin*) [182] and related trial procedures (*sinmon tetsuzuki*) were introduced in the case of false statements in issuance of disclosure documents, market price manipulation,

*89*

fraudulent securities trading and insider trading. The administrative monetary penalty system includes administrative measures to impose monetary penalties on any person, including any legal entity, who violates the abovementioned regulation, in order to achieve the administrative goal of preventing misconduct and ensuring the effectiveness of regulation. Civil liability of issuers, etc., in cases of omission or fraudulent statements in securities registration statements was strengthened by lightening the burden of proof regarding damages due to misrepresentation. The following amounts are deemed to be damage caused by a false statement: the amount calculated by deducting the average market value during the one-month after the day of announcement of the false statement from the average market value during the one-month prior to the day.

r. 2005 amendments

In 2005, a disclosure obligation on the part of the parent company of a listed company that submits no securities report was introduced. Such parent company is required to submit a document in which the identity of the company, etc., is explained (*oya kaisha-to jokyo hokoku-sho*). The scope of application of the mandatory takeover bid rule was expanded to include purchases through the ToSTNeT-1 (Tokyo Stock Exchange Trading Network) system, through which investors can execute various transactions such as block trading or basket trading for off-hour trading. The main purpose of ToSTNeT is to complement the auction market by handling orders for which smooth execution is difficult using the auction algorithms. The mandatory takeover bid rule had not applied when the one-third threshold was surpassed through ToSTNeT-1 transactions. This expansion to include ToSTNet-1 transactions occurred in the aftermath of the scandal of Livedoor vs. Nippon Broadcast Inc. Ltd.[183] In that case, Livedoor

---

**182** In program year 2015 (July 1, 2015 - June 30, 2016), the FSA ordered administrative monetary penalties in a total of 38 cases (32 cases concerning market abuses, six cases concerning false statements in securities reports, etc.). In the 2014 program year there were 48 cases; and in the 2013 program year, 48 cases. FSA, Annual Report of program year 2015 〈*Kinyu-cho no ich-nen -2016 Jimu-nendo-*〉, p. 179 (2016, November). 〈http://www.fsa.go.jp/common/paper/27/zentai/00.pdf〉

**183** Tokyo High Court Decision of 23 March, 2005, *Hanrei jiho*, No. 1889, p. 56.

Chapter 1   Introduction to the Japanese Financial Instruments and Exchange Act

purchased shares of Nippon Broadcast above the one-third threshold through ToSTNet-1 transactions, while Fuji Television offered to purchase shares of Nippon Broadcast through a takeover bid.

English-language disclosure was introduced in recognition of the globalization of securities trading and to help foreign companies to make out and submit securities reports. The scope of conduct subject to administrative monetary penalties was expanded to false statements in continuous disclosure documents.

## 3. The Financial Instruments and Exchange Act

### a. Backdrop of the FIEA

In 2006, the former Securities and Exchange Act was fundamentally revised and the title of the Act was changed to the Financial Instruments and Exchange Act (FIEA). The reform had three main purposes.[184]

The first purpose was to provide a comprehensive and cross-functional regulatory framework for the disclosure system relating to securities and supervisory regulation of financial instruments businesses, in order to cover the loopholes caused by the former approach to regulation on a sectional basis.[185]

The second purpose was to ensure the functioning of securities and financial derivatives markets to enhance the policy "from savings to investment." Under the policy of "from savings to investment," the Japanese government had already implemented policies and programs to shift to a market-based financial system with a strongly rooted securities market at its core, in which a diverse range of investors would participate.[186] According to these policies and programs, sales channels for financial instruments, including units in

---

**184**  This reform was based on the report of the first finance division of the finance council in the Financial Services Agency of Japan titled "Towards the Investment Services Act (Temporary Title)" (*Toshi service ho (kasho) ni mukete*), 22. Dec., 2005.

**185**  Hideki Kanda, *Toshi service ho toha* [What is the Investment Services Act?], Hideki Kanda, ed., *Toshi Service Ho heno Koso* [Ground Design for the Investment Services Act], pp. 2-8 (Shihon shijo kenkyû-kai, 2005).

**186**  Japan's government established "the basic policies for economic and fiscal management and reform" and "the program for structural reform of securities markets" in 2001, then "the program for promoting securities markets reform" in 2002.

*91*

investment trusts, were expanded, financial instruments and services were diversified and the fairness and transparency of the investment business were pursued. Thanks to these reforms, the allocation of household financial assets into risk-class assets, such as equities, corporate bonds and investment trusts, rose gradually.[187] On the other hand, the number and volume of complex financial instruments and transactions increased and the strengthening of investor protection rules was required. This requirement led to the enactment of the FIEA.

The third purpose was to harmonize Japanese capital market rules and regulations with global capital market standards and to enhance fair competition among investment firms.

b. Overview of the FIEA[188]

(ⅰ) Expansion of the definition of "securities" and "financial instruments businesses"

The definition of securities under the former Securities and Exchange Act was defined definitively and the definition of "securities business" was based on the concept of limited securities. The comprehensive regulatory framework would contribute to enhancing investor protection and to preventing or diminishing regulatory arbitrage.

Nevertheless, overregulation should be avoided. The FIEA introduced a non-uniform, flexible regulatory framework in consideration of the wide

---

**187** Nevertheless, the ratio of savings in the household sector is still very high in Japan. Households, including the business funds of sole proprietorships hold assets of 1,716 trillion yen, in the forms of deposits, stocks and other financial assets (Statistics Bureau, Statistical Handbook of Japan 2016, p. 48 (September 2016)). In Japan, the household sector held 54.3% of its financial assets in the form of cash and deposits, only 10.8% in stocks and other equities, 2.6% in securities other than stocks, and 28.0% in insurance technical reserves in 2010 (OECD, "Financial assets held by households", in National Accounts at a Glance 2013, OECD Publishing, Table 26-1, p. 89. ⟨http://dx. doi.org/10.1787/na_glance-2013-28-en⟩). The percentage of deposits is much higher in Japan than in other countries such as in the United States with 13.7%, Germany with 40.0% and France with 28.6%, while the percentage of stocks and other equities is much lower in Japan than in the United States with 43.4%, Germany with 18.8%, and France with 24.5% (Id., Table 26-1, p. 89).

**188** Hideki Kanda, *Kinyu-shohin torihiki ho no kozo* [The structure of the Financial Instruments and Exchange Act], *Shoji homu*, No. 1799, p. 38 (2007).

*92*

Chapter 1   Introduction to the Japanese Financial Instruments and Exchange Act

range of various sorts of securities and financial instruments business. The FIEA of 2006 introduced two types of securities, namely type I securities and type II securities.[189] The categorization is focused on the degree of negotiability and liquidity of the security. Traditional securities under the former Securities and Exchange Act (SEA), such as share certificates, corporate bonds, and share option certificates are classified as type I securities. Beneficial interests of a trust, interests or units in a collective investment scheme that is based on an anonymous partnership contract (*tokukei kumiai*) or other legal nature or structure, etc. that does not issue any certificates are comprehensively classified as type II securities. Type II securities are in principle not subject to mandatory disclosure regulation because these financial products are less liquidity.

The definition of financial instruments business is also broken down into categories in connection with the definition of securities. That is, a financial instruments business operator that deals with type I securities is classified as a type I financial instruments business operator, while a financial instruments firm that deals with type II securities is a type II financial instruments business operator.[190] The FIEA furthermore provides for supervisory regulation of investment management businesses, and investment advisory and agency businesses. The supervisory regulation under the FIEA includes entry regulation, regulation of financial conditions such as capital requirements, regulation of business conduct. Regulations are flexible and tailored to each type of financial instruments business.

( ii )   Quarterly securities reporting system

Quarterly securities reporting was introduced as a mandatory disclosure requirement and is subject to audits by certified public accountants or auditing firms. Failure to submit or submission of a false quarterly securities report is also subject to criminal or administrative monetary penalties.

---

**189** See supra A. 3. b.
**190** See supra D. 5. b.

*93*

(ⅲ) Distinction between professional investor and general investor

The definition of "professional investors (*tokutei toshika*)" was introduced (Article 2(31) of the FIEA). Professional investors are divided into qualified institutional investors, the State, the Bank of Japan and those considered professional investors, persons that meet the requirements and have filed with their investment firms based on their applications. Financial instruments business operators are exempted from certain business conduct standards obligations when a client is a professional investor. On the other hand, only professional investors may purchase in specified financial instruments markets, for example Tokyo AIM and Tokyo Pro Bond Market.[191]

(ⅳ) Takeover bid regulation

Many aspects of the takeover bid regulation were revised. The obligation of a takeover bidder to bid for all shares and to acquire all shares bids for was introduced in cases where the bidder will hold more than two-thirds of the outstanding voting shares of the target company following the purchase. The mandatory takeover bid was introduced under the amendments to the former Securities and Exchange Act of 1990 to apply to cases where an offeror will hold more than one-third of the outstanding voting shares. The scope of this mandatory takeover bid rule was also clarified and expanded, under the 2006 amendments in order to close a regulatory loophole, the amendments make clear that an offeror will hold more than one-third of the shares of the target company through a combination of transactions on financial instruments exchanges and outside the exchanges within a certain period. Furthermore, an investor has to purchase large stakes of a company through a takeover bid system if another party is already engaged in another takeover bid process targeting the company. The purpose of the acquisition, basis of the takeover bid price calculation, and special items concerning MBOs were added to the list of disclosure documents for a takeover bid. A disclosure obligation on the part of the target company was also introduced:

---

**191** See infra G. 3. c. In Japan, there are two specified financial instruments markets, namely Tokyo AIM (the former Tokyo Pro Market) and the Tokyo Pro-bond Market operated by the Tokyo Stock Exchange.

Chapter 1   Introduction to the Japanese Financial Instruments and Exchange Act

it must submit a statement of its position (*iken hyomei hokoku-sho*), in which an opinion on the takeover bid is stated. The statement may contain in addition to its opinion on the takeover bid some questions to the offeror. The takeover bidder must answer the questions in its answer (*tai shitsumon kaito hokoku-sho*). The period for the takeover bid process will now be extended where the target company so demands in the statement of its position, and the grounds for withdrawing a takeover bid were made more flexible and broader.

(ⅴ)　Disclosure of the status of large-volume shareholdings

Disclosure of the status of large-volume shareholdings has a special rule to lighten the duty on financial institutions. Namely, financial institutions could report large-volume shareholdings within 15 days for each three months when they had no intention to control the business of the issuing companies. Under the amendments of 2006, the period was shortened to within five days for each two weeks; and it was clarified that the special rule does not apply when financial institutions will make important proposals regarding the business of the issuing companies.

(ⅵ)　Internal control report and internal control audit

The internal control system was designed to ensure the effectiveness and efficiency of the enterprise's operation, the reliability of financial reporting, and compliance with applicable laws and regulations. In 2006, the FIEA introduced an internal control report and internal control audit by a certified public accountant or auditing firm for companies that are required to submit annual securities reports (Article 24-4-4(1) of the FIEA). In the internal control report, the internal system is evaluated as to whether it is in the condition necessary to ensure the appropriateness of documents in financial reports and other financial information concerning the company and the corporate group to which the company belongs.

(ⅶ)　Financial instruments exchange

A financial instruments exchange can be organized to allow the entrustment of self-regulatory operations to a "self-regulatory corporation," or the establishment of a "self-regulatory committee" to make decisions on

*95*

matters concerning self-regulatory operations for incorporated stock exchanges, in order to ensure appropriate management of self-regulatory operations by exchanges.

(viii)   Self-regulatory organization

The legal basis of various SROs, formerly contained in a number of specialized laws, was consolidated in the Financial Instruments and Exchange Act, and all SROs were vested with equivalent functions to those of the Japan Securities Dealers Association. Furthermore, a recognized investor protection association system was established, to which a certified investor protection association may apply to deal with the settlement of complaints and mediate disputes.

(ix)   Enforcement

The maximum criminal penalty was increased for violation of disclosure requirements and unfair trading in order to enhance the effectiveness of the FIEA.

c.   2008 amendments

In order to provide diverse markets in which to raise capital and to manage property, the amendments to the FIEA of 2008 introduced a specified financial instruments exchange market (*tokutei kinyû shohin torihiki-jo*), in which purchasing by non-professional investors is prohibited (Article 2(32) of the FIEA).

In view of the growth and development of the provision of financial services by financial conglomerates, the ban on interlocking directors and officers in member companies of the group, the so-called firewall regulation, was relaxed, while the duty to establish and manage a control system concerning conflicts of interest between member companies and clients was introduced. The authority to file applications for court injunctions in response to any misconduct committed by unregistered entities was granted to the Securities and Exchange Surveillance Commission.

d.   2009 amendments

In response to the financial crisis, which was triggered by the subprime

Chapter 1   Introduction to the Japanese Financial Instruments and Exchange Act

mortgage crisis in 2007 and reached its peak in the fall of 2008 with the collapse of Lehman Brothers in the United States, regulation on credit rating agencies was introduced in Japan for the first time. A voluntary registration system and business conduct, including conflict of interest, regulation was introduced.

The definition of secondary distribution (*uridashi*) of securities was revised, and its requirement of the uniform conditions was abolished, in order to prevent regulatory arbitrage resulting from small changes to the conditions. An alternative dispute resolution (ADR) system in the field of finance was established in order to resolve disputes in a short time and inexpensively outside the litigation process. The competent authority designates and supervises a dispute resolution organization, which engages in complaints processing and dispute resolution. Financial institutions must conclude contracts concerning the implementation of dispute resolution procedures with the designated dispute resolution organization.

Through the amendments, a financial instruments exchange was permitted to establish a commodities market and to hold a commodities exchange as a subsidiary company by obtaining an authorization from the Prime Minister.[192]

e. 2010 amendments

Mandatory use of central counterparties (CCPs) for clearing OTC derivatives transactions was introduced in accordance with the international discussion in the aftermath of the financial crisis, which held that the regulation of OTC derivatives transactions should be strengthened.[193] CCPs are expected to reduce counterparty risk and exposure by undertaking counter party risk and guaranteeing performance of the transactions as a central counterparty. Certain OTC derivatives such as plain vanilla interest rate swaps and iTraxx Japan CDS index transactions have to be cleared at CCP.[194] Foreign CCPs can obtain a license from the Prime Minister and

---

**192** On the contrary, a commodities exchange can establish a financial instruments market and hold a financial instruments exchange as a subsidiary company under the amendments to the Commodities Exchange Act.

**193** See the leaders statement at the G20 Pittsburg Summit. ⟨http://www.g20.utoronto. ca/summits/2009pittsburgh.html⟩

*97*

undertake financial instruments obligation assumption services. A system for data storage and reporting of trading information was also established. Investment firms and clearing organizations are required to submit trading information to the Financial Services Agency.

Significant financial conglomerates including investment firms, which hold above a one trillion Japanese yen value of total assets, were regulated and supervised.[195] First, a special financial instruments business operator must submit a notification to the Prime Minister and business reports on consolidated basis. Second, capital adequacy requirements now apply to a special financial instruments business operator on a conglomerate basis, and the power to order an investment firm to report on and inspect its subsidiaries was vested in the competent authorities.

f. 2011 amendments

In order to facilitate rights offerings, more flexible methods of delivering prospectuses in an offering of rights,[196] replacing the obligation to prepare and deliver prospectuses to all shareholders, was instituted, under which it is sufficient to submit a securities registration statement; and the fact is published in a daily newspaper. The scope of underwriting of securities was expanded to include cases in which the acquisition and exercise of unexercised share options was promised by an investment firm. Furthermore, the scope of wholesale underwriting (*moto-hikiuke*) was expanded to include a contract under which an investment firm will acquire and exercise unexercised share options. As business conduct regulation, such an underwriter must examine whether the underwriting is appropriate or not. Share option allotment without compensation has become a material fact regarding insider trading regulation.

The regulation of the investment management businesses only for professional investors was relaxed with regard to registration requirements,

---

**194** See supra note 11.

**195** See supra E 4.

**196** A rights offering is a capital increase technique where share options are allotted to all shareholders without contributions.

*98*

Chapter 1　Introduction to the Japanese Financial Instruments and Exchange Act

capital requirements, and personnel requirements. Handling of private placement of fund shares or beneficial interests in (foreign) investment trusts and (foreign) investment corporations that are type I securities, was changed so as to be treated as a type II financial instruments business instead of a type I financial instruments business, if the solicitation of offers to acquire those securities is made for professional investors and those securities are not likely to be transferred from a person who acquired them to any person other than professional investors.

g. 2012 amendments

The amendments of 2012 required financial instruments business operators to use electronic trading platforms (ETP) when entering into certain types of OTC derivatives transactions, in order to enhance market transparency. This reform has taken into account international discussions in the aftermath of the financial crisis.

Schemes employed by listed companies in making false statements have become complicated due to the assistance of external conspirators. Under the legislation prior to the revision, a person who submitted disclosure documents containing false statements was subject to criminal penalties and administrative monetary penalties, whereas a person who assisted in the submission of such documents could be charged as an accomplice of such criminal offender but was not subject to administrative monetary penalties. Under the amendments, outside collaborators should be subject to administrative monetary penalties.

Regarding insider trading regulation, the transfer of equitable interests as part of a business transfer and the delivery of treasury shares as compensation for corporate restructuring was subject to the regulation under the legislation prior to the revision. On the other hand, the succession to equitable interests as a legal effect of mergers or company split was not compared to the transferred assets. The revised act added a succession to the securities due to a merger or company split to the scope of the regulation, with the exception of where the proportion of the securities to assets for succession is not significant. On the other hand, the revised act exempted cases where treasury shares are delivered as compensation for corporate reorganizations from the regulation as with an issuance of new shares.

Through the amendments to the FIEA of 2012, the financial instruments exchange was permitted to handle commodity-related market derivatives. Type I financial instruments business operators are also permitted to intermediate any transaction on a "comprehensive exchange (*sogo torihiki-jo*),"[197] and the clearinghouse was allowed to settle and clear any transaction on the integrated exchange, regardless of the asset from which the value of the instrument was derived.

### h. 2013 amendments

The rules against the transmission of insider information and recommendation of trading of securities pertaining to the information were newly introduced for the purpose of preventing insider trading.[198] Corporate insiders with insider information ("unpublished material facts (*mikohyo jūyo jijitsu*)") must not transmit insider information or recommend trading to another person based on the information, with the intention of encouraging the person to make a profit or to avoid a loss by trading prior to publication of the information. Criminal sanctions and administrative monetary penalties are imposed on corporate insiders where trading was conducted prior to publication of the insider information. A similar regulation has been instituted concerning the prohibition of trading while possessing unpublished material facts concerning a takeover bid.

The administrative monetary penalty for violations committed by investment management firms on their client accounts was heightened in order to enhance the enforcement.

To prevent a financial crisis that may spread across financial markets, the Financial Crisis Response Council (*kinyū kiki taisaku kaigi*)[199] and an orderly

---

**197** See supra C. 5. a.

**198** The backdrop to these amendments was the scandals in which information concerning the public offering of new shares was leaked by an officer or employee of the underwriting investment firm to the financial institutions, and then the financial institutions conducted trading; however, it is unclear whether the trading was conducted knowing the unpublished material fact.

**199** This Council consists of the Prime Minister (chairman), Chief Cabinet Secretary, Minister of Finance, Minister in charge of Financial Affairs, Governor of the BOJ, and the Commissioner of the FSA.

Chapter 1   Introduction to the Japanese Financial Instruments and Exchange Act

resolution regime for financial institutions, including investment firms, based on the agreement by the G20 Summit countries were established. Liquidity is provided under the oversight of the Deposit Insurance Corporation (*yokin hoken kiko*), to ensure the performance of obligations for critical market transactions where it is considered necessary to prevent tremendous market collapse.[200] Occasionally, necessary measures for an orderly resolution[201] will be taken. In Japan, reflecting these global trends, it is necessary to establish a framework for an orderly resolution regime for financial institutions, in order to address risks that may spread across financial markets. The Prime Minister will confirm the need to implement the orderly resolution mechanism of financial institutions following the deliberations by the Financial Crisis Response Council. If losses would be incurred, the expenses shall be in principle borne ex post by the financial industry. The government may provide financial support in exceptional cases.

ⅰ. 2014 amendments

One of the major purposes of the amendments to the FIEA of 2014 was to enhance the initial public offering (IPO) of venture or start-up enterprises and to facilitate fund raising by such enterprises.

First, a regulation on crowdfunding platform operators was introduced as type Ⅰ or type Ⅱ small-amount electronic offering handling businesses (*shogaku denshi boshû toriatsukai gyosha*), according to the securities with which he/she deals. Electronic solicitation of investment in non-listed shares would be permitted only through crowdfunding for small amounts. A part of the regulation on business conduct does not apply to crowdfunding platform operators that handle only small amounts, namely less than 100 million yen, where the amount of investment per person is 500,000 yen or less and the entry regulation, including minimum capital requirement, for registration was reduced. On the other hand, crowdfunding for the purpose of investment in particular could raise concerns over harm to the interests of general investors. Therefore, platform operators are obligated to conduct due diligence on start-up enterprises and to provide information on issuers

---

**200** The measures are financial assistance and capital injection as necessary.
**201** An orderly resolution would be realized by restricting early terminations.

*101*

appropriately through the Internet for the purpose of preventing fraudulent behavior.

Second, treasury stock became exempt from the application of the regulation on the large-volume shareholdings report, since treasury stock has no voting rights and thus no influence on the issuing company in terms of control (Article 308(2) of the Companies Act).

Third, an issuing company and its officers or employees concerning fraudulent or lack of disclosure documentation in the secondary market pursuant to the FIEA was liable to investors for negligent misrepresentation, instead of strict liability. Nevertheless, the burden of proof for the negligence is imposed not on the plaintiff but on the issuing company and its officers or employees. On the other hand, liability can be pursued not only by investors who have acquired shares but also investors who have sold shares.

After a scandal concerning foreign vendors of partnership rights, regulations on a type II financial instruments business engaged in the sale of partnership rights were strengthened in order to ensure the reliability of the capital market. First, a type II financial instruments business operator was prohibited from soliciting investment in partnership rights knowing that the money invested is really used for other purposes. Second, a type II financial instruments business operator that is not a member of a self-regulatory organization (SRO) is now encouraged to join one, as they would be obligated to establish internal rules based on the relevant SRO's rules and an organizational structure for ensuring compliance with these internal rules. Third, it is required for a foreign type II financial instruments business operator to establish a business office (*eigyosho*) or office (*jimusho*) in Japan.

In the aftermath of the LIBOR manipulation scandal, the necessity of regulation on financial benchmarks has been recognized in international discussions, in order to ensure and enhance its reliability.[202] Financial benchmarks are widely used as the basis of financial transactions and have

---

**202** OICV-IOSCO, Principles for Financial Benchmarks - Final Report — (July 2013). ⟨http://www.iosco.org/library/pubdocs/pdf/IOSCOPD415.pdf⟩

Chapter 1   Introduction to the Japanese Financial Instruments and Exchange Act

great influence on the capital markets in Japan. The administrator who calculates and publicizes the specified financial indicators (*tokutei kinyū sihyo sanshutsu-sha*) must also be designated by the Prime Minister as a specified financial indicator calculation agent. The specified financial indicator calculation agent must establish operational rules, and these rules have to be authorized by the Prime Minister. The competent authority has been vested with the powers necessary to oversee the specified financial indicator calculation agent and to ensure the correctness of the specified financial indicator calculation. The TIBOR[203] (Tokyo Interbank Offered Rate) is specified as the financial indicator, and the JBA TIBOR Administration calculates and publicizes the TIBOR rate as a specified financial indicator calculation agent.[204]

j. 2015 amendments

In the case of funds involving a qualified institutional investor and a maximum of 49 non-professional investors, registration is not required; only notification is necessary, to commence a self-offering of securities business or an investment management business in securities by syndicating non-strictly-regulated types of collective investment schemes (CISs) (Article 63 of the FIEA). When fund units will be solicited and sold to not more than 50 general investors and to more than one qualified institutional investor,[205] the supervisory regulation and business conduct regulation was considerably exempted (*tekikaku kikan toshika-to tokurei gyomu*). This special rule was expected to make it easier for the Financial Services Agency to collect information on non-strictly-regulated CISs, including hedge and private equity funds, while avoiding over-regulation. Nevertheless, the special rule was misused to mislead or defraud general investors. Thus, under the

---

**203** The TIBOR consists of the "Japanese yen TIBOR" and "Euroyen TIBOR." The former reflects prevailing rates on the unsecured call market, while the latter reflects prevailing rates on the Japan offshore market. The JBA TIBOR is calculated by JBATA as a prevailing market rate based on quotes for 6 different maturities (1 week, 1 month, 2 months, 3 months, 6 months, 12 months) provided by reference banks as of 11:00 a.m. each business day. ⟨http://www.jbatibor.or.jp/english/⟩

**204** Foreign specified financial indicator calculation agents are exempted from Japanese regulation if they are adequately supervised by home-country regulators.

**205** See supra note 154.

*103*

amendments to the FIEA of 2015, the supervisory regulation of funds business for qualified institutional investors was drastically strengthened and the requirements were made stricter.[206]

k. 2017 amendments

Under the amendments to the FIEA of 2017, the fair disclosure rule was introduced for the first time in Japan. If a listed company or its officer, agent, employee, or other worker provides to the officers, etc. of an investment firm or a registered financial institution unpublished material information regarding management, business or assets of the company, which will influence the investment decision of investors significantly, the company must publicize the information concurrently. The scope of the unpublished material information is broader than that of "material facts" under the insider trading regulation. The information can be publicized via the Internet.

The revised Act has introduced a registration system for high frequency traders of listed shares. High frequency trading is defined as the sale and purchase of securities or market derivatives transactions of which an electronic data processing system makes investment decisions automatically and transmits the order thereof by using information technology in order to shorten the transmission time. A high frequency trader is subject to business conduct regulation such as the duty to establish internal control system to conduct its business appropriately. An investment firm or registered financial institution must not be entrusted with orders by non-registered high frequency traders.

# H. Securities regulation and corporate governance

## 1. Overview

Corporate governance is the system by which companies are directed and controlled. Corporate governance has two aspects: ensuring efficient and

---

**206** See supra D. 5. (b) (iv).

Chapter 1   Introduction to the Japanese Financial Instruments and Exchange Act

successful management of issuing companies and ensuring sound management in accordance with rules and regulations. The Japanese Companies Act of 2005 provides for the establishment and governance structure of a joint-stock company, the rights of shareholders, duties and liabilities of directors and officers, financial reporting, and fundamental changes such as alterations to articles of corporation, mergers, company splits, share exchanges, etc.

On the other hand, the FIEA relates also to both of the aims of corporate governance, especially from the viewpoint of disclosure, since ensuring the transparency of corporate affairs is critical for corporate governance.
The FIEA requires disclosure on corporate governance directly. The Cabinet Office Ordinance on Disclosure of Corporate Information provides for the duty to disclose information concerning corporate governance, such as the fundamental principles of the corporate governance policy, internal control systems, outside directors (*shagai torisimari-yaku*) and audit & supervisory board member (*kansa-yaku*),[207] executive compensation and share holdings, etc. in annual securities reports.[208]
The functions of an internal control system play an important role in ensuring a correct and faithful disclosure system. The internal control reporting system was introduced under the amendments to the FIEA of 2006, namely the so-called SOX Act (Japanese version), which was passed after the model of the Sarbanes-Oxley Act in the United States in response to the Enron scandal. An internal control report requires an audit certification by a certified public accountant or auditing firm. Furthermore, the representative director and CFO must submit a letter certifying that the statements contained in the annual securities report are appropriate (*kakunin-sho*).

---

**207** An audit & supervisory board (*kansa-yaku-kai*) is strictly separated from the management board. The fundamental functions of an audit & supervisory board are checking and monitoring management activities, including abuse of power by management, and reporting to a meeting of shareholders. Most of the companies listed on the Tokyo Stock Exchange are companies with an audit & supervisory board.
**208** The Cabinet Office Ordinance on Disclosure of Corporate Information, Precautions for Recording, No. 57.

Furthermore, the Tokyo Stock Exchange (TSE) has introduced a corporate governance reporting requirement. The TSE requires every listed company to submit a corporate governance report in a standard form under listing regulations, which are soft law.

Fairly-established stock prices of listed companies would put pressure on the companies for better corporate governance, typically by threat of hostile takeover. A capital market itself is affected by the degree of quality of corporate governance, since it will become more attractive for both investors and fundraisers than other markets if the listed companies on the exchange perform better and have more long-term success. It is not clear that good corporate governance would necessarily lead to long-term success, but it could increase investor confidence and thereby reduce the cost of capital. In recent years, many securities markets are interested in the enhancement of the quality of corporate governance of their listed companies, partly because of fierce competition of capital markets in the global economy. Disclosure on corporate governance could address the agency problems between management of listed companies and investors. Thus, mandatory or self-regulatory disclosure could enhance the quality of corporate governance and reduce investors' monitoring cost.

In terms of corporate control, takeover bid (*kokai kaitsuke*) regulation (Chapter II-2 of the FIEA), large-volume shareholdings report (*kabushiki tairyo hoyu hokoku*) systems (Chapter II-3 of the FIEA) and proxy solicitation regulation are closely related to corporate governance. These regulations are a key mechanism for the corporate control market, which affects corporate governance from outside a company. Generally speaking, the shareholding structure of a company affects the governance of the company. In a large publicly-held corporation, especially with dispersed ownership, individual shareholders tend to go along with management or to have rational apathy, because the cost of being involved in corporate governance normally exceeds the gains, and free-ride problems occur. However, recently, activist shareholders, such as hedge funds and private equity funds, engage and occasionally compete with management through various measures, such as dialogue with management, exercise of

Chapter 1   Introduction to the Japanese Financial Instruments and Exchange Act

shareholder's rights including voting rights or proposal rights, and takeover bids, etc.

## 2. Background

### a. Form of shareholding in Japanese listed companies

Under the Act on Book-Entry Transfer of Corporate Bonds and Shares, negotiable instruments in Japan are electronically deposited and totally dematerialized.[209] In this book-entry transfer system, investors have no opportunity to have a share certificate and opt-out of the dematerialized system.

Book-entry systems consist of a central depository institution (*furikae kikan*) and account management institutions (*koza kanri kikan*). An account management institution is able to open accounts not only in a central depository institution but also in another account management institution. Investment firms or financial institutions open a master account in an account management institution, which opens a master account for clients (*kokyaku koza*) in a central depository institution. An investor opens an account in an account management institution.

In the case of shares of publicly listed companies, the shareholder ownership rights are dematerialized and deposited in the Japan Securities Depository Center, Inc. (JASDEC) and transferred by record in JASDEC books.

The shareholder ownership rights are evidenced and transferred only by a crediting to the transferee's account. The transfer of shares is valid only if the book-entry transfer application results in an increase in the number of shares listed in the holding column of the account of the recipient of the book-entry transfer equal to the number of shares involved in the transfer. The participant whose recorded number of shares in his/her account is to be reduced as a result of the book-entry transfer shall apply to its account management institution for the book-entry transfer of the shares (**Figure**

---

**209** Hideki Kanda, Intermediated Holding of Investment Securities in Japan, in Grundmann, Merkt & Haar (eds.), Festschrift für Klaus J. Hopt zum 70. Geburtstag am 24. August 2010, Unternehmen, Markt und Verantwortung, De Gruyter, p. 3110 (2010); Changmin Chun, Cross-Border Transactions of Intermediated Securities Ch. 6. The Intermediated System in Japan, p. 285, Springer (2012).

*107*

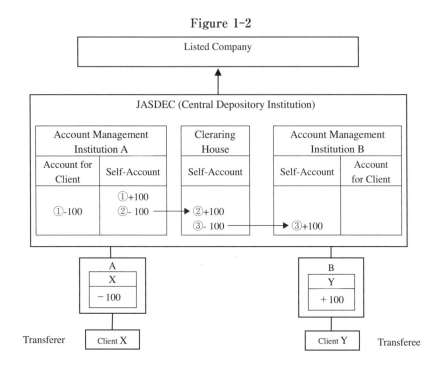

1-2).

The Japanese Companies Act provides that a shareholder must register his/her name, address, and share ownership data in a shareholders list in order to prove that he/she is entitled to his/her ownership rights in the company. JASDEC reports periodically or at the request of an issuing company the identities of investors based on reporting from low-level account management institutions to an issuing company (a general shareholder notification: *so kabunushi tsûchi*). Thus, the notified shareholders can exercise shareholder's rights such as voting rights and dividends, insofar as the issuing company records their names in the shareholders list according to the general shareholder notification. In order to exercise other rights such as filing a derivative suit or appraisal rights, a shareholder asks his/her account management institutions to convey his/her identity by having JASDEC verify their shareholding, duration of ownership and other information to the issuing company (an individual shareholder notification:

*kobetsu kabunushi tsûchi*). This means that unlike the "street-name" in other countries' intermediated securities systems, the ultimate shareholders have ownership rights in the Japanese securities depository system. Therefore, the issuing company can know the ultimate shareholders, while it has to handle the shareholders in the shareholders list as entitled shareholders.

b. Ownership structure of Japanese listed companies

Due to the liquidation of the traditional corporate groups "zaibatsu" after World War II, many stocks were distributed among individual investors. Hence, the ratio of shares held by individuals peaked at 69.1% in 1949. Since the regulation of foreign exchange and capital transfer was liberalized in the 1960s, the publicly listed companies in Japan sought to protect against mergers and acquisitions by foreign capital mainly by constructing a stable ownership structure. Namely, many companies strengthened cross-shareholdings among industrial companies and shareholdings by financial institutions, especially by main banks. The ratio of shareholdings by financial institutions was at a high in 1986, at 61.8%. A bank-centered system formerly characterized the Japanese financial system, in which there was less pressure for management to make technological innovations and instead the aim was to construct a larger corporate group to facilitate bank finance. Nonetheless, the ratio of banks and other financial institutions among others commercial banks has gradually decreased to 31.2% in 2012. Cross-shareholdings are also being unwound. After the burst of the stock bubble in Japanese capital markets, the stock price declined sharply in the late 1990s. That was caused mainly by the banking crisis of 1997-1998 and then, in 2001, banks were forced to release their shareholdings due to new regulations, under which the values of shareholdings must be evaluated at their market prices. Furthermore, banks had to deduct 60% of their unrealized losses from their earned surplus.

On the other hand, in the 2000s, cross-shareholdings among nonfinancial companies started to rise again as defensive measures against hostile takeover bids.

As of March, 2016, the ratio of stocks held by foreign investors is 30.1%,[210] 27.1% by domestic financial institutions, 22.1% by industrial companies, 17.2%

by individuals and others, and only 3.5% by commercial and regional banks.[211] It should be noted that the ratio of stocks held by foreign and domestic financial institutions has been increasing to 60. 7%. This means that shareholdings of listed companies have become highly concentrated and exercising shareholders' rights by financial institutions has become more important from a corporate governance viewpoint. In Japan, it has been pointed out that shareholding by financial institutions contributes to stability of ownership. One reason is the investment strategy known as passive or index management, which large financial institutions usually adopt. Once the portfolio is structured, a fund manager has less incentive to monitor individual companies in the portfolio. The interests of retail investors or ultimate investors are not necessarily aligned with the interests of financial institutions. The Japanese Stewardship Code was introduced in 2014 in response to these circumstances. The Stewardship Code and Corporate Governance Code of 2015 may change the mindset of Japanese financial institutions and the management of issuing companies.

## 3. Disclosure on corporate governance

a. Corporate Governance Statement in Securities Report

Disclosure on corporate governance can address the agency problems between management of listed companies and investors. First, market price pressure could bring about hostile takeovers in the case of equity securities. Secondly, disclosure pertaining to, for example, the structure of the board of directors including independent directors, the compensation structure of managers, cross-shareholdings or self-dealing in corporate assets by managers and other situations related to its corporate governance could reduce agency costs by allowing for more control over managers. Thus, mandatory disclosure on corporate governance could enhance the quality of

---

210 One reason why the Japanese Companies Act was reformed in 2014 with respect to corporate governance was pressure from foreign institutional investors.

211 The Tokyo Stock Exchange, Nagoya Stock Exchange, Fukuoka Stock Exchange and Sapporo Stock Exchange, Summary of Investigation of Ownership Structure in Listed Companies as of March 2016, Figure 3 (20 June 2017). (*2016 nendo kabushiki bunpu jokyo chosa no chosa kekka ni tsuite*) 〈http://www.jpx.co.jp/markets/statistics-equities/examination/01.html〉

Chapter 1   Introduction to the Japanese Financial Instruments and Exchange Act

corporate governance and reduce investors' monitoring costs.

The Financial Instruments and Exchange Act requires a company that has to submit a securities report to disclose information regarding the corporate governance situation in the report. This information must include essential information on the corporate governance arrangements of the company.

b. Corporate governance report based on comply-or-explain rule

The Tokyo Stock Exchange (TSE) has introduced a corporate governance reporting requirement. The TSE requires every listed company to submit a corporate governance report according to a unified form under listing regulations, which are soft law. The following information is to be stated: (1) the basic policy on corporate governance, and other basic information on capital structure; (2) business corporate organization profile and other corporate governance systems regarding decision-making, the execution of business, and oversight in management; (3) implementation of measures for shareholders and other stakeholders; and (4) matters related to the internal control system, etc. The information is disclosed via EDINET and on the website of the exchange.[212]

The TSE introduced the Corporate Governance Code in 2015, which was proposed by the Council of Experts,[213] in order to enhance the value of listed companies through good governance. In a corporate governance report, a listed company must state whether it complies with the principles of the Corporate Governance Code. If a listed company does not adopt a principle or sub-principle in the governance code, it must make a statement to that effect in the report, and, with respect to certain principles and sub-principles, it must state its response to them regardless of its adoption or non-adoption.

The Code was established based on the OECD Principles of Corporate

---

212 JPX, Enhancing Corporate Governance. 〈http://www.jpx.co.jp/english/equities/list-ing/cg/01.html〉

213 The Council of Experts Concerning the Corporate Governance Code, "Japan's Corporate Governance Code [Final Proposal] — Seeking Sustainable Corporate Growth and Increased Corporate Value over the Mid- to Long-Term," March 5th, 2015. 〈http://www.fsa.go.jp/en/refer/councils/corporategovernance/20150306-1/01.pdf.〉

*111*

Governance; therefore, a principles-based approach and a comply-or-explain rule were adopted.[214] The Code includes five general principles, 30 principles and 38 supplementary principles. The Code defines "corporate governance" as a structure for transparent, fair, timely and decisive decision-making by companies, with due attention to the needs and perspectives of shareholders and also customers, employees, and local communities. The enhancement of Japanese corporate governance has been focused on for several years, because of the lower ROE of Japanese listed companies in comparison with other major capital markets, as well as corporate scandals and fraudulent capital raising by third-party allotment with unfair prices. As one of the weaknesses of corporate governance in Japanese listed companies, the lack of independence of the board of directors has been pointed out. Subsequently, listed companies are required to explain the reason they do not have outside directors and will not appoint outside directors under the amendments to the Japanese Companies Act of 2014. The Corporate Governance Code requires a listed company to appoint at least two independent directors (Principle 4. 8).

The Corporate Governance Code is expected to work with the Stewardship Code as the two wheels of a cart, so that the sustainable growth of listed companies is promoted by both sides, institutional investors and listed companies.[215]

## 4. Internal control reports

Issuers of listed shares are required to file an internal control report concurrently with the filing of an annual securities report. Internal controls

---

214 The comply-or-explain rule was originally adopted from the former Combined Code (now Corporate Governance Code and Stewardship Code by Financial Reporting Committee) in the UK. Under the comply-or-explain rule, if a company finds specific principles inappropriate to comply with in view of their individual circumstances, they need not be complied with, provided that the company explains fully the reasons why it does not comply with the principles. Then, the participants in the capital market analyze and evaluate the explanation.

215 "Principles for Responsible Institutional Investors (Japanese Version of the Stewardship Code)" was already established by the Council of Experts Concerning the Japanese Version of the Stewardship Code under the Financial Services Agency in February 2014.

Chapter 1 Introduction to the Japanese Financial Instruments and Exchange Act

mean controls that pertain to the preparation of financial reporting for external purposes that are fairly presented in conformity with generally accepted accounting principles. The internal control report was introduced by the amendments to the FIEA of 2006. An internal control report must include the basic framework of internal control over financial reporting, scope of evaluation, evaluation date and evaluation procedures, the results of evaluation of internal control and the additional statements and special notes. Unlike internal controls under the Companies Act, internal controls under the FIEA are limited to matters concerning financial reporting.

In 2006, the FIEA also introduced internal control audits by a certified public accountant or auditing firm for a company, which is required to submit a securities report. An internal control report has to be examined and reviewed by a certified public accountant or auditing firm. As the auditing of financial statements evolved from a process of detailed testing of transactions and account balances towards a process of sampling and testing, greater consideration of a company's internal controls became necessary in planning an audit. In other words, effective internal control contributes to an enhanced basis of external audit review and is closely related to good corporate governance.

Furthermore, the FIEA of 2006 introduced the requirement for a confirmation letter, which must state that the contents of annual securities reports, quarterly securities reports and semiannual securities reports are appropriate in light of the FIEA. The chief financial officer and the representative of the issuer have to certify the appropriateness of the documents in a confirmation letter. A confirmation letter is supposed to enhance the appropriateness and credibility of the securities reports.

## 5. Takeover bid regulation

Regulation of takeover bid and large-volume shareholdings reports was originally introduced as part of the securities regulation disclosure systems. Takeover bidding was regulated for the first time in Japan in 1971 modeled on the Williams Act in the United States, which aims to enhance the transparency of the transfer of large-volume shareholdings and of the control of a company outside an exchange.

A takeover bid is a means of purchasing a substantial portion of the

*113*

outstanding shares of a listed company outside a stock exchange, by making an offer to purchase all shares up to a specified number, within a specified period at a fixed price, normally at a premium above the market price.

Takeover bids are regulated by the FIEA, as they may affect the price and furthermore changes of control of the target company. First, the regulation of takeover bids aims to protect investors by ensuring transparency and fairness in securities transactions that are conducted outside a stock exchange. Therefore, the FIEA requires a takeover bidder to submit a takeover bid statement (*kokai kaitsuke todokede-sho*), to issue a public notice of commencement of a takeover bid (*kokai kaitsuke kaishi kokoku*) and to provide shareholders tendering their shares with a takeover bid explanation (*kokai kaitsuke setsumei-sho*). A takeover bid explanation must include the purpose and terms and conditions of the takeover bid. The target company has to submit a report on its opinion on the takeover bid (*iken hyomei hokoku-sho*). Secondly, the takeover bid regulation aims to give shareholders an equal opportunity to sell their shares, usually at a premium above the market price. While this aim can be justified by the principle of equal treatment of shareholders, it overlaps with that of company law.

The position of the Japanese takeover bid regulation is complicated and unique, because it is a mixture of the United States model and the European model. At first, the former Securities and Exchange Act (SEA) introduced takeover bid regulation in 1971, on the model of tender offer regulations in the United States. Its purpose was to disclose information necessary to enable the shareholders of the target company's securities to make rational investment decisions and to treat them equally. Since then, the takeover bid regulation under the FIEA has become closer to the European model. In 1990, the FIEA introduced mandatory takeover bids, in cases where a takeover bidder will hold more than one-third of the outstanding voting shares of a target company within 61 days and from fewer than 10 shareholders.[216]

---

216 Hideki Kanda, Comparative Corporate Governance Report: Japan, in Klaus J. Hopt et. al. eds., Comparative Corporate Governance: The State of Art and Emerging Research, Oxford University Press, 1998, pp. 934-5.

Chapter 1　Introduction to the Japanese Financial Instruments and Exchange Act

In 2006, the FIEA was revised to obligate a takeover bidder to solicit and acquire all shares if the bidder will hold more than two-thirds of the outstanding voting shares of the target company after the takeover bid.

The aim of the mandatory takeover bid rule is to prohibit private purchase of controlling shareholdings, in order to make corporate control transactions transparent, which could have significant impact on the stock market and allow the sharing of control premiums.[217] Under the 2006 amendments, disclosure requirements were strengthened. The purpose of the purchase, including the management policy after the acquisition, the basis for deciding the bid price and the arrangement to avoid conflicts of interest in certain cases such as management buyouts (MBO) are required to be disclosed. The target company is required to express its opinion on the takeover bid, whether it has a defense policy against the takeover and, if any, the content thereof.

In 2006, the FIEA was revised to obligate a takeover bidder to solicit and acquire all tendered shares, if the bidder will hold more than two-thirds of the outstanding voting shares of the target company after the takeover bid. These amendments were supposed to ensure minority shareholders an opportunity to exit from a company and share in the control premiums.[218] These amendments concerning mandatory takeover bid regulation seem similar to the European takeover bid regulation, but the Japanese mandatory takeover bid regulation is different from the European rule in three ways. First, a mandatory offer is required after becoming a controlling shareholder in Europe (*ex post* regulation), while in Japan it is required when a takeover bidder will hold more than one-third or two-thirds of the outstanding voting shares, as the case may be (*ex ante* regulation). Second, the Japanese takeover bid regulation applies only to the act of purchasing a target company, not to acquisition due to issuance of shares. Third, the Japanese takeover bid rule does not apply to the purchase of shares of a target company on a stock exchange.[219]

---

**217** Tomotaka Fujita, The takeover bid regulation in Japan: Peculiar Developments in the Mandatory Offer Rule, UT Soft Law Review, No.3, pp. 24, 31–33 (2011).
**218** Id., pp. 33–34.

Therefore, it is difficult to explain clearly the concept of takeover bid regulation in Japan. It is explained by the viewpoint of either the transparency of markets for corporate control or the fair distribution of control premiums.

## 6. Large-volume shareholdings reporting system

A large-volume shareholdings reporting system was introduced in 1990. This system was also based on the Williams Act in the United States.

The large-volume shareholdings reporting system is designed for the disclosure of information when a large-volume shareholding in a listed company of more than five percent of the shares is acquired. When the percentage of such a shareholding increases or decreases by 1% or more, the shareholder must file an alteration shareholdings report indicating the change that occurred in the percentage of such holdings. This regulation is originally aimed at enhancing market transparency, because changes in large-volume shareholdings might have significant effects on the formation of the stock price in the market. Knowing the identity of large-volume shareholders provides investors with important information, for example, about imminent takeovers.

Holders of particular shares or corporate bonds with share options that are listed on a financial instruments exchange whose shareholding exceeds five percent must in principle submit a report to the Prime Minister that contains the matters concerning the holding ratio, the funds for the acquisition, purposes of holding and any other matters specified by cabinet office ordinance, within five business days from the date on which such person has become a large-volume shareholder (Article 27-23(1) of the FIEA).

A large-volume shareholder must in principle submit a report to the Prime Minister, within five business days from the change, pursuant to the provisions of a cabinet office ordinance if the holding ratio of shares has increased or decreased by one percent or more (Article 27-25(1) of the FIEA).

The large-volume shareholdings reporting system aims at disclosure of material information concerning changes in large-volume shareholdings,

---

**219** Id., pp. 28-29.

*116*

Chapter 1    Introduction to the Japanese Financial Instruments and Exchange Act

which can affect the prices and further the control of the company. This information is useful not only for enhancing the transparency of securities as financial products but also for enhancing the transparency of the ownership structure, which relates to corporate governance.

# 7. Proxy solicitation rule

The FIEA bans soliciting proxies in violation of rules and regulations adopted by the Cabinet Office.[220] Shareholders have the right to designate a proxy in connection with the exercise of voting rights in shareholder meetings under the Japanese Companies Act. A person who is going to solicit proxies in connection with voting rights of a listed company has to abide by the proxy solicitation regulation. The main purpose of the regulation is to provide material information concerning proposals for the agenda of a shareholder meeting in order to help shareholders make rational decisions as to whether they will delegate their voting rights to the solicitor. The Cabinet Office Ordinance regulates the proxy form, in which shareholders are able to select "withhold," "approval," or "disapproval." Not only a listed company but also shareholders can solicit proxies and communicate with other shareholders according to the regulation. In cases where the solicitation is made by a listed company, a shareholder may require the company to deliver its proxy materials.[221] Proxy solicitation with proxy materials that contain any false statement or omit any statement on important matters is prohibited.

This regulation is most closely related to the corporate control and corporate governance.

---

**220** Article 36-2(1) of the Financial Instruments and Exchange Act Implementing Order and the Cabinet Office Ordinance on Proxy Solicitation of Listed Companies Shares.
**221** Article 36-5(1) of the Financial Instruments and Exchange Act Implementing Order.

*117*

# Chapter 2

## Scope of application and financial administration

*Hiroyuki Kansaku* (Part A)

*Naohiko Matsuo* (Parts B & C)

# A. Definition of "securities" and "derivatives transactions" under the FIEA

## 1. Definition of "securities"

a. Extension of the scope of securities

The scope of the Japanese Financial Instruments and Exchange Act (FIEA) is basically defined by the concepts of "securities" (A. 1.) and "derivatives transactions" (A. 2.).

The issuers of securities are subject to disclosure requirements. More specifically, public offering or secondary distribution of "securities" is subject to mandatory disclosure regulation under the FIEA. Mandatory disclosure regulation is different for "type I securities" and "type II securities."[1] Mandatory disclosure regulation has been made flexible according to the class of a security depending on its liquidity.[2]

While all financial instruments businesses are required to register under the comprehensive industry regulations, businesses are classified into the four categories of type I and type II financial instruments business, investment advisory and agency business, and investment management business, with separate rules applying to each category. Financial instruments business is also defined by the concept of "securities". For example, the following transactions and other conduct are considered financial instruments business: (1) sale and purchase of securities; (2) intermediary, brokerage or agency services in connection with the sale and purchase of securities; (3) intermediary, brokerage or agency services in connection with the entrustment of the sale and purchase of securities; (4) providing investment advice regarding the values of securities or acting as an agent or broker for the conclusion of investment advisory contracts or discretionary investment in securities; or (5) making investment decisions regarding securities based on the analysis of values of securities on behalf of clients (Article 2(8) of the

---

1    See infra b.
2    Hideki Kanda, *Kinyū shohin torihiki ho no kozo* [Structure of the Financial Instruments and Exchange Act], *Shoji Homu*, No. 1799, pp. 45–46 (2007).

*120*

Chapter 2 Scope of application and financial administration

Financial Instruments and Exchange Act). Financial instruments business operators (investment firms) that are registered with the Prime Minister according to Article 29 of the FIEA, are subject to business conduct regulation and supervisory regulation.

Furthermore, market abuse regulation applies to conduct or transactions related to securities (FIEA Chapter 6 of the FIEA).

The FIEA of 2006 made the structure of the regulatory framework more flexible and the substance of regulations more sophisticated. The scope of the definition of securities under the FIEA has been substantially widened compared with that under the former law, and specifically there is a comprehensive provision applicable to interests in non-strictly-regulated collective investment vehicles, or funds.

b. Type I securities and type II securities

The definition of "security" under the FIEA is divided into two groups based on the degree of liquidity: Type I securities and type II securities. Type I securities consist of the securities prescribed in Article 2, paragraph (1) of the FIEA, the rights as those for which certificates shall be issued but not issued, and designated electronically recorded monetary claims. On the other hand type II securities are so-called deemed securities (*minashi yûka shoken*) (Article 2(2)(i)-(vii) of the FIEA). While the type I securities are characteristic of higher liquidity in the securities market, the type II securities are less liquid. Fundamentally, they conform to different types of rules with respect to disclosure requirements and financial instruments business regulations, with many exceptions.

Securities are a key concept that defines the scope of the various rules and regulations under the FIEA. For example, the FIEA imposes strict disclosure obligations in relation to type I securities due to their high liquidity, strengthening the disclosure obligation in financial reports and verification statements from auditors. In contrast, type II securities are not, in principle, subject to mandatory disclosure regulation, except with regard to such securities whose issuer conducts investment management business investing mainly in other securities. Type II securities that are illiquid, in principle, are exempt from these disclosure regulations due to their having less liquidity. Therefore, significant information about type II securities,

*121*

which, in principle, are not subject to the duty to disclose, cannot be found for investors or prospective investors through the Electronic Disclosure for Investors' NETwork (EDINET), which is managed by the Financial Services Agency of Japan to make important information about issuers and securities available to the public. However, if a type II securities scheme invests mainly in type I securities, then the disclosure requirements for type I securities can be easily avoided. Therefore, when the scheme invests mainly in securities and more than 500 investors participate in it, the units of type II securities should be subject to the disclosure requirements in a similar way as type I securities through EDINET (Article 3(iii) of the FIEA; Article 1-7-2 of the Financial Instruments and Exchange Act Implementing Order). In such cases, the concept of offering for type II securities is different from that of type I securities. In terms of type I securities, "private offering for a small number of investors," which is exempt from the application of disclosure requirements, means any attempt to solicit for asquisition to less than 50 investors. On the other hand, for type II securities, private placement means that less than 500 investors participate in the scheme and hold the units in the end.

A firm engaging in financial instruments business involving type I securities is, in principle, subject to registration requirements such as capital or personnel requirements before it can commence "type I financial instruments business *(dai isshu kinyû shohin torihiki gyo)*." A firm engaging in financial instruments business involving type II securities is usually, in principle, subject to registration requirements before it can commence "type II financial instruments business *(dai nishu kinyû shohin torihiki gyo)*," those requirements are less strict than the regulation of type I financial instruments business. The type I financial instruments business includes, in relation to type I securities, (i) handling in offering and private placement, (ii) sale and purchase, (iii) intermediary, brokerage and agency for sale and purchase, (iv) secondary distribution, and (v) brokerage for clearing (Article 28(1)(i) of the FIEA).[3] Registration is required with the Financial Services Agency of Japan, in order to commence the business (Article 29 of

---

3  There is a similar provision also for type II financial instruments business (Article 28 (2)(ii) of the FIEA).

Chapter 2 Scope of application and financial administration

the FIEA). A financial instruments business firm has to comply with registration requirements such as capital and personnel requirements (Article 29-4(1)(iv) and Article 15-7(1) of the Financial Instruments and Exchange Act Implementation Order).[4] The business code of conduct regulation is the same for all financial instruments firms, including both type I and type II financial instruments business operators.[5] The regulations also generally apply to foreign firms that engage in securities business.

c. Definition of "securities" in the FIEA and in Japanese civil law

In Japan, there is no general definition of securities in civil and commercial law. Generally, the term "security" in civil and commercial law refers to certificates and other physical instruments that give their legal holders the rights to cash flow or other property, as indicated on the security, and are necessary to exercise or assign the rights.[6] They are designed to facilitate and ensure the assignment of such rights and have the characteristic of combining rights and certificates that helps protect the bona fide purchaser. On the other hand, the definition of securities in the FIEA is aimed at the ultimate purposes of the FIEA namely the sound development of the national economy and protection of investors (Article 1 of the FIEA).[7] Therefore,

---

4    The minimum capital requirement is 10 million yen for a type II financial instruments business operator (Article 29-4 (1) (iv) of the FIEA; Article 15-7 (1) (v) of the Financial Instruments and Exchange Act Implementing Order), and from 50 million yen to 3 billion yen for a type I financial instruments business operator (Article 29-4 (1) (iv) of the FIEA, Article 15-7 (1) (i) - (iv) of the Financial Instruments and Exchange Act Implementing Order).

5    For example, the financial instruments business operator including its management and employees owes an obligation of good faith and fair practice to clients (Article 36 of the FIEA). It should collect information about each client and conclude the financial instruments transaction contract in respect of his or her knowledge, experience, assets and the purpose of the client's investment. The firm should not provide inaccurate information or conclusive recommendations about securities they handle (Article 38 (1) (2) of the FIEA) and is subject to the restriction on advertisements (Article 37 of the FIEA).

6    For extensive discussion concerning the concept of securities in civil law, see Takeo Suzuki (supplemented by Hitoshi Maeda), *Tegata ho & Kogitte ho* [Law of Bills, Notes and Checks], *Yuhikaku*, 1992, pp. 1-34.

7    See Chapter 1 A. 1.

*123*

securities in the FIEA are so-called investment securities. For example, bills and notes, checks or bills of lading, those which are securities in civil law, are excluded from the definition of securities in the FIEA. On the other hand, those which are securities in the FIEA, are not always securities in civil law.

d. Type I securities

Type I securities consist of three types of securities, namely (1) securities prescribed in Article 2, paragraph (1) of the FIEA, (2) rights for which certificates shall be, but have not yet been, issued, and (3) designated electronically-recorded monetary claims.

( i ) Securities prescribed in Article 2, paragraph (1) of the FIEA

Article 2, paragraph (1) of the FIEA designates the following securities or certificates as type I securities whose interests or rights are indicated on securities or certificates that are physically issued (Article 2(1)(i)-(xxi) of the FIEA). These securities are deemed not only adequate as investment but also as securities with high liquidity in the capital market.

( a ) Japanese government bonds (JGB) (Article 2(1)(i))

( b ) Municipal bonds (Article 2(1)(ii))

( c ) Debentures issued by a juridical person under a special act (Article 2(1)(iii))

( d ) Specified corporate bonds prescribed in the Act on the Securitization of Assets (Article 2(1)(iv))

( e ) Corporate bonds (Article 2(1)(v))

( f ) Shares issued by a juridical person established under a special act (Article 2(1)(vi))

( g ) Preferred shares prescribed in the Act on Preferred Equity Investment by Cooperative Structured Financial Institutions (Article 2(1)(vii))

( h ) Preferred shares and rights to subscribe for preferred shares prescribed in the Act on the Securitization of Assets (Article 2(1)(viii))

( i ) Shares and share options (Article 2(1)(ix))

( j ) Beneficial interests in investment trusts, shares, share options and

Chapter 2   Scope of application and financial administration

corporate bonds of investment corporations prescribed in the Investment Trust and Investment Corporation Act or other special acts (Article 2(1)(x)-(xiii))

(k)   Beneficial interests in beneficiary certificate-issuing trusts prescribed in the Trust Act (Article 2(1)(xiv))

( l )   Promissory notes issued by a juridical person in order to raise funds necessary to operate its business and which are specified by cabinet office ordinance (Article 2(1)(xv))

(m)   Mortgage securities prescribed in the Mortgage Securities Act (Article 2(1)(xvi))

( n )   Securities or certificates issued by a foreign state or foreign person having the nature of the abovementioned securities and certificates (Article 2(1)(xvii))

( o )   Securities or certificates specified by cabinet office ordinance that have been issued by a foreign person and indicate beneficiary interests in a trust in which loan claims held by persons engaging in banking business or persons otherwise conducting money lending on a regular basis, are entrusted (Article 2(1)(xviii))

( p )   Securities or certificates that indicate rights pertaining to option transactions conducted in a financial instruments market, in accordance with such requirements and by using such methods as prescribed by the operator of the market, rights pertaining to option transactions which are conducted in a foreign financial instruments market or rights pertaining to option transactions conducted in over-the-counter markets (Article 2(1)(xix))

( q )   Securities or certificates that have been issued by a person with whom abovementioned securities or certificates are deposited and in a state other than the state in which the deposited securities or certificates were issued and which indicate the rights pertaining to the deposited securities or certificates (Article 2(1)(xx))

( r )   Certificates designated by cabinet order as those for which it is found, when taking into consideration the liquidity thereof and other factors, necessary in order to protect the public interest or investors (Article 2(1)(xxi))

*125*

Type I securities prescribed in Article 2, paragraph (1) of the FIEA are securities or certificates that are physically issued and classified in the following nine groups.

The first is debt securities. Japanese government bonds (JGB), municipal bonds and debentures issued by a juridical person under a special act are classified as public bonds ((a) – (c)), while specified corporate bonds prescribed in the Act on the Securitization of Assets and corporate bonds are classified as private bonds ((d) and (e)). Both types of securities are called debt securities.

The second is equity and quasi-equity securities. Shares and share options of a stock company are typical examples. Shares issued by a juridical person established under a special act, preferred shares prescribed in the Act on Preferred Equity Investment by Cooperative Structured Financial Institutions, preferred shares and securities indicating a right to subscribe for preferred shares prescribed in the Act on the Securitization of Assets are also called equity or quasi-equity securities ((f)-(i)).

The third is beneficial interests, which indicate beneficiary rights based on trust laws. Beneficial interests in investment trusts prescribed in the Investment Trust and Investment Corporation Act or other special acts, and beneficial interests in certificate-issuing trusts prescribed in the Trust Act ((j) and (k)).

The fourth is commercial papers (CP). CPs are unsecured promissory notes for a specified amount to be paid at a specified date issued by financial institutions and corporations with strong credit ratings. CPs are designated by cabinet office ordinance as promissory notes issued by a juridical person in order to raise funds necessary to operate its business ((l)).

The fifth is mortgage securities. Under the Mortgage Securities Act, mortgage securities include both claims and mortgage ((m)).

The sixth is foreign securities. Securities or certificates issued by a foreign state or foreign person having the nature of the abovementioned securities and certificates and securities or certificates that have been issued by a foreign person, indicate a beneficial interests in a trust to which loan claims held by persons engaging in banking business or persons otherwise conducting money lending on a regular basis are entrusted are classified as type I securities ((n) and (o)).

Chapter 2    Scope of application and financial administration

The seventh is covered warrants. Covered warrants are securities or certificates that indicate rights pertaining to option transactions conducted in a financial instruments market, in accordance with such requirements and using such methods as prescribed by the operator of the market, rights pertaining to option transactions that are conducted in a foreign financial instruments market or rights pertaining to option transactions conducted in over-the-counter markets ((p)).

The eighth is depositary receipts. Depositary receipts are securities or certificates that have been issued by a person with whom the abovementioned securities or certificates are deposited and in a state other than the state in which the deposited securities or certificates were issued and that indicate the rights pertaining to the deposited securities or certificates ((q)).

The ninth is certificates designated by cabinet order. The requirements for designation are liquidity and the necessity to protect public interest or investors ((r)). Negotiable certificates of deposit (CD) issued by foreign juridical persons and bonds issued by private educational institutions are designated as type I securities by cabinet order based on this comprehensive provision (Article 2 (1) (xxi) of the FIEA; Article 1 (i) and (ii) of the Financial Instruments and Exchange Act Implementing Order), in consideration of the reality that these bonds have been sold to a lot of general investors.[8]

( ii )    Rights for which certificates shall be issued but not issued
The following rights or interests are deemed type I securities, even though certificates indicating these have not been physically issued (Article 2(2) of the FIEA). For example, rights or interests that must be indicated on bond certificates or share certificates held under an electronic book-entry transfer system according to the Act on Book-Entry Transfer of Corporate Bonds and Shares are deemed equivalent to those securities listed in Article 2, paragraph (1) even though bonds or shares have not been indicated on certificates.

---

8    Naohiko Matsuo & Keisuke Matsumoto, *Jitsumu ronten kinyû shohin torihiki ho* [Practical Issues], *Kinyû Zaisei Jijo Kenkyû Kai*, 2008, p. 24.

( a ) Japanese government bonds (JGB)

( b ) Municipal bonds

( c ) Debentures issued by a juridical person under a special act

( d ) Specified corporate bonds prescribed in the Act on the Securitization of Assets

( e ) Corporate bonds

( f ) Shares issued by a juridical person established under a special act

( g ) Preferred shares prescribed in the Act on Preferred Equity Investment by Cooperative Structured Financial Institutions

( h ) Preferred shares and rights to subscribe for preferred shares in the Act on the Securitization of Assets

( i ) Shares and share options

( j ) Beneficial interests in investment trusts, shares, share options and corporate bonds of investment corporations prescribed in the Investment Trust and Investment Corporation Act or other special acts

( k ) Beneficial interests in beneficiary certificate-issuing trusts prescribed in the Trust Act

( l ) Promissory notes issued by a juridical person in order to raise funds necessary to operate its business and which are specified by cabinet office ordinance

( m ) Securities or certificates issued by a foreign state or foreign person having the nature of the abovementioned securities and certificates

( n ) Securities or certificates specified by cabinet office ordinance that have been issued by a foreign person and indicate beneficiary interests in a trust in which loan claims held by persons engaging in banking business or persons otherwise conducting money lending on a regular basis are entrusted

Rights and interests for which mortgage securities or foreign mortgage securities must be issued are deemed the type I securities, only when they are designated by cabinet office ordinance. Covered warrants, deposit receipts or certificates designated by cabinet order also become the type I securities, when they are designated by cabinet office ordinance (Article 2 (2) of the FIEA). Nevertheless, there is no such cabinet office ordinance at the moment.

*128*

Chapter 2   Scope of application and financial administration

(ⅲ)   Designated electronically-recorded monetary claims

Electronically-recorded monetary claims are monetary claims for which electronic recording under the Electronically-Recorded Monetary Claims Act is required for accrual or assignment. Electronically-recorded monetary claims are deemed type I securities, when they are designated by cabinet order (Article 2(2) of the FIEA). The requirements for designation are liquidity and the necessity to protect investors. Nevertheless, there is no such cabinet order at the moment.

e.   Type II securities

(ⅰ)   Outline

Article 2, paragraph (2) of the FIEA defines so-called "deemed securities" (*minashi yûka shoken*) (Article 2(2)(ⅰ)-(ⅶ) of the FIEA). These type II securities have less liquidity in the capital market than type I securities, but are adequate for investment objectives. The scope of the definition of the type II securities under the FIEA of 2006 has been substantially widened compared with that of the former law.

Under the FIEA, type II securities are subject not only to limited disclosure regulation,[9] but also to supervisory regulation,[10] business code of conduct regulation,[11] and a ban on market abuses.[12] Under the FIEA, interests in

---

**9**   See Chapter 3 footnote 4.

**10**   The FIEA has introduced regulations on self-offering of the interests or units of non-strictly-regulated CISs and self-investment-management of the assets of the CIS contributed by investors. According to the regulation, a person engaging in self-offering or self-investment-management has to be registered with Financial Services Agency of Japan, irrespective of the categorical attributes of its counterparty (for example a qualified institutional investor, professional investor or non-professional investor). The regulation for the type II financial instruments business, as stated above, will generally apply to self-offering. The regulation for investment management business will generally apply to self-investment-management.

**11**   A person involved in interests or units of a non-strictly-regulated CIS must deliver a written document prior to entry into a financial instruments transaction contract, where matters such as those relating to risks and accounting of the CIS are to be stated. Moreover, the financial instruments business operator has to deliver a written document at the conclusion of the contract. These documents are provided directly to an investor by an investment firm with whom he or she concludes a financial instruments transaction contract.

*129*

non-strictly-regulated CISs are included in the definition of type II securities pursuant to Article 2, paragraph 2, item 5 comprehensively and subject to the limited disclosure regulation, supervisory regulation, business code of conduct regulation, and a ban on market abuses. The significant information about type II securities, which, in principle, are not subject to the duty to disclose, cannot be found for investors or prospective investors through EDINET;[13] but it is provided directly to the investor by the investment firm with whom it concludes a financial instruments transaction contract.[14]

(ii) Beneficial interests of a trust not indicated on a beneficiary certificate

Beneficial interests based on trust contracts are generally deemed type II securities, which are not beneficial certificates[15] based on a trust contract, according to the amendments to the FIEA of 2006 (Article 2(2)(i) of the FIEA). The backdrop of this extension is the increase in the use of trust as financial instruments such as vehicles for asset securitization. In other words, trust is an adequate legal form to provide an investment scheme as well as a juridical person.

Rights that are claimable against a foreign person and which have the nature of the beneficial interests of a trust are also deemed securities (Article 2(2)(ii) of the FIEA).

(iii) Membership rights in a general partnership company, etc.

Membership rights in a general partnership company (*gomei kaisha*) or limited partnership company (*goshi kaisha*) that are specified by Cabinet Order are deemed type II securities, and membership rights in a limited liability company (*godo kaisha*) are always deemed type II securities

---

12  See Chapter 8.

13  〈http://disclosure.edinet-fsa.go.jp/〉

14  The FIEA has categorized an investor according to its attributes; professional investor and non-professional investor. To professional investors, most of the provisions about conduct of business obligations under the FIEA do not apply (Article 45 of the FIEA).

15  Beneficial interests can be indicated on certificates based on a trust contract (Article 185(1) of the Trust Act). Beneficial certificates are type I securities (Article 2(1) (xiv) of the FIEA).

Chapter 2   Scope of application and financial administration

(Article 2 (2) (iii) of the FIEA). According to the prevailing argument, membership rights in a general partnership company, limited partnership company or limited liability company cannot be indicated on certificates as securities in the civil law sense. Nevertheless, these companies are an adequate legal form for investment schemes, as well as stock companies or trusts.

Membership rights in a foreign juridical person having the nature of rights of these companies are also deemed type II securities (Article 2(2) (iv) of the FIEA).

(iv)   Interests in non-strictly-regulated collective investment schemes
ⅰ)   Backdrop

In Japan, there are two categories of collective investment schemes (CISs): strictly regulated CISs and loosely or non-regulated CISs.[16] Regulated CISs are subject to strict laws and regulations. Most important are the Investment Trust and Investment Corporation Act, the Act on the Securitization of Assets, the Real Estate Syndication Act and the Act concerning Regulation of Commodity Investment. These acts each regulate a particular type of collective investment scheme comprehensively. More specifically, they regulate such matters as the setting up of the scheme, the structure and organization of a special purpose vehicle (SPV) in the scheme, filing and overseeing of the fund, the business code of conduct of related parties (for example, arrangers or management of the SPV), disclosure and the qualifications of fund managers. The interests or units of strictly regulated CISs for investment trust and asset-backed securitization have already been deemed "security" by the amendments to the former Securities and Exchange Act of 1990; therefore, they are subject to the provisions of the law, for example, disclosure requirements and prohibition of unfair dealing.

On the other hand, outside strictly-regulated CISs there are various types of non-strictly-regulated CISs that are formed, such as civil law partnerships, anonymous partnerships based on the Commercial Code, trusts, or corporations (both for-profit and not-for-profit). The interests or units of

---

**16**  See Chapter 1 F.

some types of such CISs were at most partly regulated as "securities" by the amendments to the Securities and Exchange Act of 2004, to the extent the scheme was found to invest in securities.

The interests or units of such non-strictly-regulated CISs are sometimes distributed not only to professional investors but also to general investors, and might result in huge financial losses for them. The scheme itself might sometimes be fraudulent and deceitful, because the business plan invested in by the fund is entirely fictitious or very faulty from the beginning.[17]

Exactly what constitutes a non-strictly-regulated CIS is unclear. There is no legal definition of non-strictly-regulated CISs, including hedge funds and private equity funds. According to research by the Financial Services Agency of Japan, non-strictly-regulated CISs in Japan consist mainly of hedge funds, business funds that invest directly in a particular business, private equity funds, venture capital funds, restructuring funds, real estate funds, fund of funds[18] and others. Regarding business funds, a general partner in a civil law partnership or a business person, with whom anonymous partners conclude partnership contracts, engages in particular business by using assets contributed by investors. Examples of the activites of the business fund type are investing in the business of filmmaking (contents fund), leasing for telecommunication facilities or running a chain of Chinese noodle restaurants (business fund).

In Japan, as of the end of March 2015, the number of non-strictly-regulated CISs that were sold to investors from April 2015 to March 2016 was 2,758 and the sales amount was 1.4 trillion yen.[19] The total assets under the management of the funds was about 13.8 trillion yen. About 70% of the non-

---

17 World Ocean Firm, which solicited investments in the shrimp farming business, and Heisei-den-den, which solicited investments in the leasing business in the form of an anonymous partnership contract based on the Japanese Commercial Code are notorious recent cases where many non-professional investors suffered financial losses.

18 The fund governing body has its own investment portfolio, but investments could be allocated across the funds invested in by the same or an external investment manager. The portfolios require being rebalanced when investors enter or exit individual funds. To avoid reallocation and rebalancing, a master-feeder structure is generally used. The portfolio is held and traded at the level of the master fund, and the returns of the master fund will be reflected in the net asset value of the feeder funds.

Chapter 2    Scope of application and financial administration

strictly-regulated CISs had less than one billion yen's worth of investment assets, while the total investment assets of about 8% thereof account for more than 10 billion yen. Real estate funds are prominent among non-strictly-regulated funds, the number of which is 1,024 and the total assets under the management of which is 9.6 trillion yen. The number of hedge funds is 111 and the assets under management of those funds are 2.3 trillion yen.[20]

Non-strictly-regulated CISs in Japan can take a number of legal forms and structures. A civil law partnership (*minpo kumiai*), an anonymous partnership (*tokumei kumiai*) based on the Japanese Commercial Code, for-profit or non-profit corporation such as limited liability company (*godo-kaisha*) or a general incorporated association (*ippan shadan hojin*) or trust (*shintaku*) is usually chosen as the legal form for a non-strictly-regulated CIS. These legal forms and structures are less regulated and are subject to few mandatory rules, giving them a wide realm of freedom of contract and of articles of corporation.

A non-strictly-regulated CIS whose assets are managed by investment managers (an investment-type CIS) normally takes the legal form of a corporation or trust. The fund is required to protect its assets from the bankruptcy of related parties such as the fund manager and the other funds invested in by the same manager. This state of protection from the bankruptcy of related parties is called "bankruptcy remoteness". Therefore, the assets of the fund are expected to be separated from the investment managers and are held by a special purpose vehicle (SPV) for the scheme. This is why corporations and trusts are normally used as SPVs in CISs. Therefore, the abovementioned beneficial interests in a trust, for which no physical certificates are issued, as well as membership rights in a general partnership company (*gomei kaisha*) or limited partnership company (*goshi kaisha*) specified by cabinet order, or a limited liability company (*godo kaisha*), are generally deemed type II securities according to the amendments of 2006.

---

**19** Financial Services Agency of Japan, *Fund Monitoring Chosa* [Research for Monitoring Funds], p. 8 (October, 2016).

**20** FSA, supra note 19, pp. 9-12.

*133*

ii ) Outline

A comprehensive provision was introduced pursuant to the amendments of 2006 to apply to the interests in various types of collective investment vehicles, or funds. The amendments of 2006 extended the scope of application to include interests or membership rights in non-strictly-regulated collective investment schemes, making it possible to implement regulations comprehensively.[21] Interests or membership rights in a non-strictly-regulated collective investment scheme that are deemed securities do not depend on their legal form. Interests or membership rights in a non-strictly-regulated collective investment scheme are deemed type II securities, regardless of whether they are based on a partnership contract under the Civil Code, an anonymous partnership agreement under the Commercial Code, an investment limited partnership agreement under the Investment Limited Partnership Act, a limited liability partnership agreement provided under the Limited Liability Partnership Act, membership rights in an incorporated association or other rights (Article 2 (2) (v) of the FIEA). The rights based on insurance contracts or mutual aid contracts are excluded from the deemed securities (Article 2(2) (v) (c) of the FIEA).

iii ) Requirements

The FIEA of 2006 expanded the definition of securities dramatically to cover any interests or membership rights in non-strictly-regulated CISs. The rights or interests in non-strictly-regulated CISs are deemed type II securities, if the holders thereof can receive distributions of profits arising from the business conducted using the money invested or contributed by them. Specifically, the requirements for classification as the interests of non-

---

21　Various related laws were revised in 2006 to establish a regulatory framework where financial instruments not covered by the FIEA but sharing many of the same attributes, such as variable life insurance, were subject to similar rules regarding sales and solicitation. Another example of the move to cross-sectional application was the revision of the traditionally vertically-compartmentalized regulations to standardize the registration of sales and solicitation, investment advisory, asset management and asset administration, etc., businesses under the umbrella of financial instruments business with the aim of applying as consistant a business conduct rule as possible.

*134*

Chapter 2   Scope of application and financial administration

strictly-regulated securities are as follows.

The first requirement is collecting money or similar property through the interests or membership rights in non-strictly-regulated CIS. The contribution by investors may be not only money but also property designated by cabinet order in order to avoid regulatory arbitrage.

The second requirement is the conduct of business by others using the money or similar property contributed by investors. Interests or membership rights in non-strictly-regulated CISs are exempt from the law if all the investors are involved in the business (Article 2(2)(v)(a) of the FIEA). This exemption is limited to cases where operations relating to the business for investment are conducted with the consent of all equity partners, and they all either engage in the business on a full-time basis or contribute professional skills that are indispensable for maintaining that business to the business, although not on a full-time basis (Article 1-3-2 of the Financial Instruments and Exchange Act Implementing Order). According to the Financial Services Agency of Japan, the exemption pursuant to involvement in the business by all investors is very rare.[22]

The third requirement is distributing profits or properties originating from the business to investors. It is, however, worth noting that there is no distribution of profits or properties to investors if an investor receives no distribution of profits or properties beyond the amount of its original investment based on the interests in the scheme or rights from the contracts (Article 2(2)(v)(b) of the FIEA).

These characteristics of non-strictly-regulated CISs are very similar to the Howey test in American case law to define an "investment contract" under the definition of "securities".[23] In the United States, the term of "investment contract" had been broadly construed so as to afford investors a full measure of protection. In the interpretation of investment contracts, the legal form is

---

22  For example, according to one explanation, an anonymous partner in an anonymous partnership would seem not to engage in the business on a full-time basis due to its legal character. The Financial Services Agency of Japan, *koment no gaiyo oyobi koment ni taisuru kinyu-cho no kangaekata* [Outline of Comments and Responses by the Financial Services Agency on the Comments], p. 11. ⟨http://www.fsa.go.jp/en/news/2007/20071119.html⟩

23  SEC v. W. J. Howey Company, 328 U.S.293 (1946).

*135*

not looked to for substance, and emphasis is rather placed on the economic reality. An investment contract thus came to mean a contract or scheme for the placing of capital or laying out of money in a way intended to secure income or profit from its employment.

Just like the Howey test, under the FIEA, the legal form of a non-strictly-regulated CIS is irrelevant to whether a right or interest in non-strictly-regulated CIS should be included in the definition of type II securities. Moreover, the sorts of assets and property that a fund invests in and holds are indifferent to the definition of type II securities.

On the other hand, rights based on insurance contracts or mutual aid contracts are excluded from the definition of type II securities (Article 2(2) (v) (c) of the FIEA), because the businesses pertinent to these contracts are strictly regulated by the Insurance Business Act. The rights pertaining to the investment or contribution made to a non-profit corporation established under Japanese laws and regulations are, in principle, also excluded from the definition. The exception to this exemption is general incorporated associations other than public interest incorporated associations and general incorporated foundations other than public interest incorporated foundations.[24] This is because these legal forms can be used for the investment-type of CIS, as distribution of residual properties is possible after the liquidation of these corporations.[25] Furthermore, the rights based on the contracts wherein officers or employees, or any other person of the issuer of shares, promise to continuously purchase the shares of the issuer jointly with other officers according to a certain plan without depending on an individual investment decision are also exempted from the type II securities.[26] The rights based on employees and officers stock plans are out of the scope of the FIEA. The reasons for the exemption are that the directors or trustees of the plan have little discretion and the plan contributes to the enhancement of the welfare of employees or officers.[27]

---

24  Article 1-3-3 (ii) of the Financial Instruments and Exchange Act Implementing Order.
25  Matsuo & Matsumoto, supra note 8, p. 20.
26  Article 1-3-3 (v) of the Financial Instruments and Exchange Act Implementing Order.
27  Matsuo & Matsumoto, supra note 8, p. 22.

Chapter 2   Scope of application and financial administration

iv)   Foreign interests in non-strictly-regulated collective investment Schemes

Interests based on laws and regulations of a foreign state that are similar to the interests in non-strictly-regulated collective investment schemes are deemed type II securities (Article 2(2)(vi) of the FIEA).

v )   Rights specified by cabinet order

Rights specified by cabinet order as those for which it is found, when taking into consideration that are economically similar to securities provided for in Article 2, paragraph (1) and rights specified in the above-mentioned (ii) to (iv) and other circumstances, necessary and appropriate to protect the public interest or the investors are deemed securities. This comprehensive provision was extended pursuant to the amendments of 2006 in order to close the loophole of functional regulation of the FIEA.

Claims under loans to educational institutions are deemed securities specified by Cabinet Order (Article 2(2)(vii) of the FIEA; Article 1-3-4 of the Financial Instruments and Exchange Act Implementing Order), if (i) the loans are made by two or more persons, (ii) the interest rate and the time of performance for the loans are the same, (iii) the loans are made by persons other than those who attend any school established by the educational institution, and (iv) transfer of the claims pertaining to the loans to persons other than interested persons is not prohibited.

## 2 . Definition of "derivatives transactions"

### a . Outline

Financial derivatives are instruments whose value is based on or derived from financial assets, variables or indexes. Derivatives transactions may be used to reallocate risk between parties. These transactions can enhance the economic and social welfare of both parties involved when the risk exposure is transferred to a party that is presumably better able to manage it or that is willing to bear it at a lower cost than the party who transferred it. Thus far, financial derivatives transactions have mainly been developed — and financial innovation has taken place — in the over-the-counter (OTC) space, as OTC derivatives can be designed under lax regulation and enjoy freedom of contract. Various complicated derivatives instruments are available in the marketplace to provide hedging techniques against the risk of fluctuations in exchange rates or prices.

In addition to securities, the scope of the FIEA is basically defined by the concept of "derivatives transactions". The FIEA applies to derivatives transactions in domestic financial instrument markets and over-the-counter markets and foreign markets. The FIEA classifies financial derivatives transactions into three categories based on the place of the transaction: market derivatives transactions, foreign market derivatives transactions and over-the-counter (OTC) derivatives transactions (Article 2 (20) of the FIEA). Derivatives transactions are not subject to the mandatory disclosure regulation under the FIEA, unlike securities.

"Market derivatives transactions" are futures of financial instruments or financial indicators capable of being settled by paying or receiving the difference, options to sell or purchase financial instruments, market derivatives transactions in other markets or financial index futures, etc., interest rate, currency or goods swaps, and credit derivatives contracts (Article 2(21) of the FIEA). These transactions are conducted in a financial instruments market in accordance with the requirements of and using the methods prescribed by the operator of the financial instruments market.

"Foreign market derivatives transactions" means transactions that are conducted in a foreign financial instruments market and are similar to market derivatives transactions (Article 2(23) of the FIEA).

"OTC derivatives transactions" are forwards of financial instruments or financial indexes capable of being settled by paying or receiving the difference, options to sell or purchase financial instruments, other OTC derivatives transactions, etc., swaps of interest rate or currency, and credit derivatives contracts, etc., which are conducted in neither a financial instruments market nor a foreign financial instruments market (Article 2 (22) of the FIEA). These transactions are not conducted in a financial instruments market but on a face-to-face basis, which makes tailor-made derivatives transactions possible.[28]

---

28  Hiroyuki Kansaku, Recent Development in the Regulation of Financial Derivatives in Japan, University of Tokyo Journal of Law and Politics, Volume 2, pp. 8-29 (Winter 2014).

Chapter 2 Scope of application and financial administration

b. Regulatory and supervisory framework for derivatives transactions in general

In Japan, financial derivatives are regulated by the Financial Instruments and Exchange Act (FIEA), and commodity-based derivatives are regulated by the Commodity Futures Transaction Act. Formerly, the regulatory framework for derivatives in Japan consisted of three acts, namely the Securities and Exchange Act, the Financial Futures Trading Act and the Commodity Futures Exchange Act. The basic principle of this framework was that derivatives should be regulated and supervised according to the underlying assets from which their value was derived. Therefore, securities-based derivatives were regulated by the former Securities and Exchange Act and supervised by the Financial Services Agency of Japan (FSA), and commodity-based derivatives were regulated by the former Commodity Exchange Act and supervised by the Ministry of Economy, Trade and Industry (METI) and the Ministry of Agriculture, Forestry and Fisheries (MAFF). Foreign-exchange-related and interest-rate-related derivatives involving forwards were regulated by the former Financial Futures Trading Act and supervised by the FSA.

In 2006, the former Financial Futures Trading Act of 1988 was repealed, and foreign exchange and interest-rate-related futures began to be regulated by the FIEA, along with securities-based derivatives. The title of the Act was also changed from the Securities and Exchange Act of 1948 to the Financial Instruments and Exchange Act. The definition of financial derivatives by the FIEA encompasses foreign exchange and interest-rate-related swaps, credit derivatives, weather derivatives and earthquake derivatives;[29] these newer financial derivatives, which had been regulated by neither the former Securities and Exchange Act nor the former Commodity Exchange Act, became objectives of regulation. The aim of the FIEA is to compile comprehensive and cross-sectional rules for investor protection and to respond to the development of newer derivatives appropriately.[30] Newer financial derivatives such as credit default swaps (CDS) were added to the

---

29  By the amendments to the Cabinet Office Ordinance on Financial Instruments Business of 2011, real-estate-based derivatives were brought under the scope of the FIEA.

*139*

list of financial derivatives regulated by the FIEA. The definition of financial derivatives in the FIEA will be provided in c.

On the other hand, the former Commodity Exchange Act of 1950 continues to exist. On January 1, 2011, the title of the Act was changed from the Commodity Exchange Act to the Commodity Futures Trading Act, and not only futures traded on exchange but also OTC commodity-based derivatives were brought under the scope of the Act.

Why was the regulation of commodity derivatives not integrated into the FIEA, unlike foreign exchange and interest-rate-related derivatives? Lawmakers have explained that commodity-based derivatives seem to be closely related to the policy in terms of the production and circulation of underlying commodities.[31] However, the regulatory regime for commodity derivatives in the Commodity Futures Trading Act of 2011 was very similar to that of financial derivatives, as the Commodity Futures Trading Act was modeled after the regulatory framework of the FIEA in terms of derivatives.[32] The basic frameworks of regulation on financial derivatives and commodity derivatives in Japan are therefore almost convergent.

---

**30** For example, under the former regulatory regime, a securities firm needed to be licensed to conduct securities-based OTC derivatives transactions, to submit a notification to conduct foreign exchange or interest-rate-related derivatives transactions and to be approved to conduct credit derivatives transactions. Under the current regulatory regime, an investment firm needs to be only registered to conduct each of these three derivatives transactions. On the other hand, a bank could conduct foreign exchange or interest-rate-related derivatives transactions under the Banking Act before the Financial Futures Trading Act of 1988 was enacted without additional approval or permission, since these derivatives transactions were thought to be essentially ancillary to banking business (Shinsaku Iwahara, *Derivative Torihiki ni kansuru kantoku-ho jo no mondai* [Legal Issues Regarding Supervisory Regulation on Derivatives Transactions], *Kinyū Hō Kenkyū*, No. 14 (1998), p. 26). After the enactment of the FIEA, a bank needs to be registered as a registered financial institution to conduct OTC financial derivatives transactions.

**31** Hidenori Mitsui & Yūichi Ikeda (ed.), *Ichimon Itto, Kinyū shohin torihiki ho* [One Answer to one Question: Financial Instruments and Exchange Act], (Shoji Homu, 2008), p. 11 and p. 464.

**32** For a brief overview of the history of regulation of financial derivatives transactions in Japan, see Hiroyuki Kansaku, *Derivative torihiki kisei no genjo to kadai* [The Actual Stand and Legal Issues of Regulation on Financial Derivatives Transactions in Japan], *Jurist* No. 1444 (2012), pp. 56–58.

*140*

Chapter 2   Scope of application and financial administration

If both financial derivatives and commodity derivatives could be traded and cleared on the same exchange, it would be convenient for investors and could improve the efficiency and liquidity of the market. On February 24, 2012, the FSA, METI and MAFF published a common statement regarding a comprehensive exchange where financial instruments, financial derivatives, commodities, and commodity derivatives (excluding rice) could be traded. This statement includes an agenda for establishing a comprehensive exchange and the intention to cooperate for comprehensive and effective supervision.[33] Through the amendments to the FIEA of 2012, the financial instruments exchange is permitted to handle commodity-related derivatives (Articles 2(24)(iii-ii) and 117(2) of the FIEA).[34] Type I financial instruments business operators are also permitted to intermediate any transaction on a comprehensive exchange, and the clearinghouse is allowed to settle and clear any transaction on a comprehensive exchange, regardless of the asset from which the value of the instrument is derived (Articles 28 (1)(i-ii) and 156-6(2) of the FIEA).[35]

---

33   FSA, METI & MAFF, *Sogoteki na torihikijo kento team torimatome* [Final Report of the Working Group for the universal exchange] (February 24, 2012).

34   A universal exchange has been realized through the extension of the definition of financial instruments and correspondingly the extension of the coverage of financial indexes and market financial derivatives transactions by the amendments to the FIEA of 2012. Under the amendments financial instruments and financial indexes can encompass commodities, which are designated by cabinet order as those for which derivatives transactions pertaining thereto would be useful for the national economy. Therefore, a universal exchange is legally a financial instruments exchange, which is supervised by the FSA with the close cooperation of METI and MAFF. However, an exchange where only commodity-related derivatives are traded is not a financial instruments exchange (Article 2(14) of the FIEA).

35   The definition of "financial instruments business" is also extended to encompass on-exchange traded commodity-related derivatives transactions named "commodity-related market derivatives transactions" (Article 2(8)(i) of the FIEA). To conduct commodity-related market derivatives transactions business is under the definition of "type I financial instruments business" (Article 28(1)(i-ii) of the FIEA). A market, where only commodity-related market derivatives are traded, shall not be a "financial instruments market" (Article 2(14) of the FIEA).

*141*

c. Definition of "derivatives transactions"
　(ⅰ)　Overview

The FIEA classifies financial derivatives transactions into three categories, according to the place of the transaction: market derivatives transactions, foreign market derivatives transactions, and over-the-counter (OTC) derivatives transactions (Article 2(20) of the FIEA).

"Market derivatives transactions" are futures of financial instruments or financial indicators capable of being settled by paying or receiving the difference, options to sell or purchase financial instruments, market derivatives transactions in other markets or financial index futures, etc., interest rate, currency or goods swaps, and credit derivatives contracts (Article 2(21) of the FIEA).

"Foreign market derivatives transactions" means transactions that are conducted in a foreign financial instruments market and are similar to market derivatives transactions (Article 2(23) of the FIEA).

"OTC derivatives transactions" are forwards of financial instruments or financial indexes capable of being settled by paying or receiving the difference, options to sell or purchase financial instruments, other OTC derivatives transactions, etc., swaps of interest or currency, and credit derivative contracts, etc. (Article 2(22) of the FIEA).

　(ⅱ)　Financial instruments and financial indicators

The value of financial derivatives transactions is based on or derived from financial instruments and financial indicators.

　ⅰ)　Financial instruments

The FIEA defines financial instruments as follows (Article 2(24) of the FIEA).

(i)　securities (Article 2(24)(i))
(ii)　claims based on a deposit contract or other rights, or securities or certificates indicating these claims or rights, and specified by cabinet order (Article 2(24)(ii))
(iii)　currencies (Article 2(24)(iii))
(iv)　commodities specified by cabinet order (Article 2(24)(iii-ii))

Chapter 2   Scope of application and financial administration

(v)   assets for which there are many of the same kind, with substantial price volatility and which are specified by cabinet order as those for which it is found necessary to protect investors with regard to derivatives transactions (Article 2(24)(iv))

(vi)  standardized instruments that are created by a financial instruments exchange for the purpose of facilitating market derivatives transactions by standardizing interest rates, the maturity period and/or other conditions (Article 2(24)(v))

Claims based on a deposit contract or other rights, or securities or certificates indicating these claims or rights, were designated as financial instruments under the amendments of 2006, which integrated the regulation of financial derivatives transactions pertaining to interest rates and foreign currencies, etc. under the Financial Futures Trading Act into the FIEA. Not only claims based on a deposit contract, but also the means of payment, the securities and the claims are designated by cabinet oder as underlying assets of financial derivatives transactions (Article 1-17 of the Financial Instruments and Exchange Act Implementing Order).

The commodities are designated by the Commissioner of the Financial Services Agency through consultation with the minister having jurisdiction over the relevant commodities market (Article 1-17-2 of the Financial Instruments and Exchange Act Implementing Order).

The rights to emit carbon dioxide are not at present designated as financial instruments in Japan, because the legal character of such rights is unclear.[36]

ⅱ)   Financial indicators

The FIEA defines financial indicators as follows (Article 2(25) of the FIEA).

(i)   prices of financial instruments or interest rates of financial instruments (Article 2(25)(i))

(ii)  figures pertaining to the results of meteorological observations published by the Meteorological Agency or others (Article 2(25)(ii))

---

**36**  Naohiko Matsuo, *Kinyū shohin torihiki ho* [Financial Instruments and Exchange Act], 5th ed., p. 77 (Shoji Homu, 2018).

*143*

(iii)　indicators the fluctuation of which is impossible or extremely difficult for a person to influence and which may have a material impact on business activities of business operators or statistical figures pertaining to social or economic conditions (Article 2(25)(iii))

(iv)　figures calculated based on those listed in the preceding three items (Article 2(25)(iv))

The figures pertaining to the results of observations on terrestrial phenomena, ground motion, geomagnetism, terrestrial electricity or hydrology published by a Meteorological Agency can be financial indicators of (iii) above. Earthquake derivatives or tsunami derivatives are included in this category.[37] Another example of the indicators of (iii) above is credit derivatives transactions. Other figures pertaining to national accounts statistics prepared by the Cabinet in compliance with the standards specified by the United Nations, foreign statistical figures equivalent to the abovementioned figures and figures that comprehensively indicate the level of the price of real property or prices of two or more real properties announced or provided periodically by an administrative organ, etc. are also financial indicators (Article 1-18 of the Financial Instruments and Exchange Act Implementing Order).

（ⅲ）　Market derivatives transactions

Market derivatives transactions are conducted in a financial instruments market, in accordance with the requirements of and by using methods prescribed by the operator of the financial instruments market. Therefore, market derivatives transactions are standardized. It is assumed that market derivatives transactions are not conducted outside of a "financial instruments exchange market (*torihikijo kinyû shohin sijo*).[38]

Market derivatives transactions are classified into the following categories i)-vi), making it possible to regulate each category of market derivatives transactions in more detail, thereby ensuring appropriate investor protection and enhancing the efficiency and effectiveness of supervision. On the other

---

**37**　Matsuo & Matsumoto, supra note 8, p. 31.

**38**　Matsuo, supra note 36, p. 72.

Chapter 2 Scope of application and financial administration

hand, if the FIEA were to define market derivatives transactions abstractly, there might remain considerable concerns that financial derivatives transactions will constitute illegal gambling under Articles 185 and 186 of the Japanese Criminal Code.[39]

"Market Derivatives Transactions" are defined under the FIEA to include the following (Article 2(21) of the FIEA).

i ) Futures of financial instruments

Futures of financial instruments are transactions in which the parties promise to deliver or receive financial instruments or consideration for them at a fixed time in the future, and when the resale or repurchase of the underlying financial instruments is made, the transaction may be settled by paying or receiving the difference (Article 2(21)(i)). The requirement is the possibility of settlement for difference, regardless of whether a settlement is really made on a spot basis or for the difference.

ii ) Futures of financial indicators

Futures of financial instruments are transactions in which the parties promise to pay or receive an amount of money calculated based on the difference between the value of a financial indicator to which the parties agree in advance and the actual value of the financial indicator at a fixed time in the future (Article 2(21)(ii)). Examples are Nikkei 225 Futures based on the Nikkei Stock Average, the JPX Nikkei Index 400, whose constituents are selected from all the listed companies on the Tokyo Stock Exchange (TSE) based on criteria such as ROE and corporate governance processes, and

---

**39** There is also the legal issue of whether financial derivatives transactions constitute illegal gambling under Articles 185 and 186 of the Japanese Criminal Code. This legal issue is not yet clearly resolved and remains opaque. The Financial Instruments Exchange Act provides that to pay or receive the difference outside the exchange in quotation of financial instruments on the exchange constitutes a crime (Article 202(1) of the FIEA). Nevertheless, it moves outside the category of what may be punished as long as a party is allowed to conduct the relevant transactions as a financial instruments business operator or as a registered financial institution in the course of business (Article 202(2) of the FIEA). This provision is generally understood as a special provision with respect to gambling in the Criminal Code.

*145*

Three-month Euroyen Futures on the Tokyo Financial Exchange.

iii) Options

Options are transactions in which one party grants to another party the option to, unilaterally and at will, sell or purchase financial instruments at a predetermined price or conduct a market derivatives transaction, financial indicator future transaction, and the other party pays money as consideration therefor (Article 2(21)(iii)). Examples are TOPIX Options based on TOPIX, that is a major Japanese stock index, or Nikkei 225 Options based on the Nikkei Stock Average, that is a major Japanese stock index on the Osaka Exchange, and Options on Three-Month Futures on the Tokyo Financial Exchange.

iv) Swaps

Swaps are transactions in which the parties mutually promise that for the amount the parties have agreed to as the principal, one of the parties will pay an amount of money calculated based on the rate of change during the agreed period of the interest rate, etc. of the financial instrument or a financial indicator agreed to, and the other party will pay the amount of money calculated based on the rate of change during the agreed period of the interest rate, etc. of the financial instruments or financial indicator (Article 2 (21)(iv) of the FIEA).

v) Commodity swaps

Commodity swaps were added to the list of market derivatives transactions under the amendments of 2012 (Article 2(21)(iv-ii) of the FIEA).

vi) Credit derivatives

Credit derivatives are transactions in which one of the parties pays money and the other party, as consideration therefor, promises to pay money in cases where a certain event agreed to by the parties in advance and (i) an event pertaining to the credit status of a juridical person or a similar event occurs or (ii) an event of which it is impossible or extremely difficult for either party to influence the occurrence and which may have a serious influence on the business activities of the parties or other business firms

Chapter 2   Scope of application and financial administration

occurs (Article 2(21)(v) of the FIEA). Unlike with an insurance contract, it is not necessary for claims based on credit derivatives to cause damage.

(iv)   Foreign market derivatives transactions
"Foreign market derivatives transactions" means transactions that are conducted in a foreign financial instruments market and are similar to market derivatives transactions (Article 2(23) of the FIEA).

(v)   Over-the-counter (OTC) derivatives transactions
The FIEA defines over-the-counter derivatives transactions as the following transactions, if conducted in neither a financial instruments market nor a foreign financial instruments market (Article 2(22) of the FIEA).
OTC financial derivatives transactions are classified into the following categories i)-vi), making it possible to regulate each category of OTC derivatives transactions in more detail, thereby ensuring appropriate investor protection and enhancing the efficiency and effectiveness of supervision. On the other hand, if the FIEA were to define the OTC financial derivatives abstractly, there might remain considerable concerns that financial derivatives transactions will constitute illegal gambling under Articles 185 and 186 of the Japanese Criminal Code.[40]

i )   Forwards of financial instruments
Forwards of financial instruments are transactions in which the parties promise to deliver or receive financial instruments or consideration for them at a fixed time in the future, and when the resale or repurchase of the underlying financial instruments is made, settlement thereof may be made by paying or receiving the difference. Financial instruments include securities, currencies and other assets for which there are many of the same kind, which have substantial price volatility and which are specified by cabinet order as those for which it is found necessary to ensure the protection of investors (Article 2(22)(i) of the FIEA).
This definition does not include standardized instruments that the financial instruments exchange has structured (Article 2 (22) (i) of the FIEA).

---

40   See supra note 39.

Examples in this category are Forex (foreign exchange) Margin Contracts, and Non-Deliverable Forwards (NDFs).[41] Exchange contracts are not over-the-counter forwards when they cannot be settled for difference.

ii ) Forwards of financial indicators

Forwards of financial indicators are transactions in which the parties promise to pay or receive an amount of money calculated based on the difference between the agreed amount and the actual amount of a predetermined financial indicator[42] or any other similar transactions (Article 2(22)(ii) of the FIEA). Unlike with the definition of forwards of financial indicators in market derivatives transactions, this category in OTC forwards of indicators includes any other similar transactions thereto. Examples in this category are Forward Rate Agreements (FRA)[43] and Contracts for Difference (CFD).

iii ) Financial instruments options

Financial instruments options are transactions in which one party grants to another party the option to, unilaterally and at will, sell or purchase financial instruments or conduct other OTC derivatives transaction at a predetermined price, and the other party pays consideration therefor (Article 2(22)(iii) of the FIEA). Foreign Exchange Options are included in this category.

---

**41**  A non-deliverable forward (NDF) is a foreign exchange derivatives contract that is settled by calculating the difference between the agreed rate and the spot rate at the time of settlement.

**42**  Financial indicators are as follows: (i) prices of financial instruments or interest rates of financial instruments; (ii) figures pertaining to the results of meteorological observations published by the Meteorological Agency or others; (iii) indicators the fluctuation of which is impossible or extremely difficult for a person to influence and which may have a serious influence on business activities of business firms or statistical figures pertaining to social or economic conditions, indicators or figures; or (iv) figures calculated based on (i)-(iii) (Article 2(25) of the FIEA).

**43**  A Forward Rate Agreement (FRA) is a forward contract between parties that determines the rate of interest, or the foreign exchange rate, to be paid or received on an obligation beginning at a future start date.

*148*

Chapter 2   Scope of application and financial administration

iv)   Financial indicators options

Financial indicators options are transactions in which one party grants to another party the option to, unilaterally and at will, effect a transaction wherein the parties pay or receive an amount of money agreed to in advance. This amount is calculated based on the difference between a value that the parties have agreed in advance to use as the agreed value of the financial indicator when such option is exercised and the actual value of the financial indicator at the time of such exercise. The other party pays consideration for such option (Article 2(22)(iv) of the FIEA).

v )   Swaps

Swaps are transactions in which the parties mutually promise that for the amount the parties have agreed to as the principal, the parties will pay an amount of money calculated based on the rate of change during the agreed period of the interest rate, etc. of the financial instrument or a financial indicator agreed to (Article 2 (22) (v) of the FIEA). Examples in this category are Interest Rate Swaps (IRS) and Foreign Exchange Swaps.

vi)   Credit derivatives

Credit derivatives are transactions in which one of the parties pays money and the other party, as consideration therefor, promises to pay money in cases where a certain event agreed to by the parties in advance and (i) an event pertaining to the credit status of a juridical person or a similar event occurs or (ii) an event of which it is impossible or extremely difficult for either party to influence the occurrence and which may have a serious influence on the business activities of the parties or other business firms occurs (Article 2(22)(vi) of the FIEA). The Credit Default Swaps (CDSs) are included in subcategory (i) and Weather Derivatives, Earthquake Derivatives, and other disaster-related derivatives are included in subcategory (ii).

Credit derivatives are similar to insurance contracts. Insurance contracts, guarantee contracts, and loss compensation contracts are generally excluded from the definition of OTC derivatives transactions (Article 2(22) of the FIEA: Article 1-15 of the Financial Instruments Exchange Act Implementing Order), because these contracts do not aim to speculate but to

*149*

compensate for or cover actual damage or loss.[44]

d. Registration requirements

Conducting market derivatives transactions concerning type I securities or providing intermediary, brokerage or agency services in connection with commodity-related market derivatives transactions or conducting OTC financial derivatives transactions is type I financial instruments business (Article 28(1) of the FIEA). On the other hand, the act of, on an exchange or foreign exchange, conducting derivatives transactions regarding type II securities or conducting market derivatives transactions, excluding securities-related derivatives transactions is considered type II financial instruments business (Article 28(2) of the FIEA).[45] Financial instruments business operators must be registered with the Prime Minister (Article 29 of the FIEA). An applicant should clearly identify the categories of financial instruments business that the firm intends to conduct in the application (Article 29-2 (1) (v) of the FIEA). The law sets out the following requirements: capital amount, capital adequacy, personnel qualification, legal form, organization, etc.

In addition, any firm that has registered as a type I financial instruments business operator may sell and purchase currencies and other assets specified by Cabinet Order as being related to financial derivatives transactions, excluding securities-related derivatives transactions, or it may provide intermediary, brokerage or agency services in connection therewith as ancillary business to the type I financial instruments business (Article 35 (1) (xiii) of the FIEA).

Registration to conduct OTC derivatives transactions business is not

---

44  Miho Matsushita, Atsushi Sakai & Daisuke Tachi, *Kinyū shohin toriki ho no taisho shohin torihiki* (Investment Instruments and Transactions to Which the Financial Instruments and Exchange Act Applies), in Naohiko Matsuo (ed.), *Kinyū shohin toriki ho kankei seifurei no kaisetsu* (Explanation of the Financial Instruments and Exchange Act and Related Cabinet Office Ordinances), *Bessatsu Shoji Homu*, No. 318 (2008), p. 148.

45  A type II financial instruments business operator shall be registered by the Prime Minister, but the registration requirements such as capital requirements are laxer than the requirements for the type I financial instruments business (Article 29-4 of the FIEA).

*150*

Chapter 2 Scope of application and financial administration

necessary in the following three cases that do not technically fall within the original scope of the type I financial instruments business. The first is when a counterparty is a type I financial instruments business operator, registered financial institution, qualified institutional investor, or stock company with more than 1 billion yen capital (Article 2(8) of the FIEA; Article 1-8-6(1) (ii) of the Financial Instruments Exchange Act Implementing Order; Article 15 of the Cabinet Office Ordinance Regarding the Definitions of Article 2 of the FIEA). This exemption is granted because there is no need for investor protection in this case and so the speed and efficiency of transactions with clients can be enhanced. These clients are called derivatives transactions professionals. Nevertheless, *de lege ferenda*, maintaining the category of derivatives transactions professionals, outside of the financial instruments business should be examined.[46] The second case is when the counterparty is a business firm that conducts sale and purchases of goods or provides intermediary services in connection with the sale and purchases of goods in the course of business and the aim of the foreign exchange derivatives contracts is to hedge the volatility risk of foreign exchange rates (Article 2 (8) of the FIEA; Article 1-8-6 (1) (iv) of the Financial Instruments Exchange Act Implementing Order; Article 16(1) (iii) of the Cabinet Office Ordinance Regarding the Definitions of Article 2 of the FIEA). The third is when a company that submits financial reports conducts foreign exchange derivatives transactions with its subsidiary aiming to hedge the volatility risk of foreign exchange rates or to provide intermediary, brokerage or agency services in connection with the hedge transaction for its subsidiaries (Article 2(8) of the FIEA; Article 1-8-6(1) (ii) of the Financial Instruments Exchange Act Implementing Order; Article 16(1) (iv) of the Cabinet Office Ordinance Regarding the Definitions of Article 2 of the FIEA).

On the other hand, there is a principle of separation between banking and securities businesses in the Japanese financial regime (Article 33(1) of the

---

**46** Professor Hideki Kanda suggests that the category of derivatives transactions professionals is surplus to requirement and should be abolished because the FIEA already has similar categories, namely qualified financial institution and professional investor. Hideki Kanda, *Derivative torihiki no genjo to kadai – wholesale torihiki* [The Status and Legal Issues on Financial Derivatives Transactions in Japan – Wholesale Transactions], *Jurist* No. 1951 (2012), pp. 58-59.

FIEA). Nevertheless, a bank may, without registration as a type I financial instruments business operator, conduct financial derivatives transactions, excluding securities-related derivatives transactions (Article 33(3)(ii) of the FIEA, insofar as it is a registered financial institution (*toroku kinyû kikan*) (Article 33-2(iii) and Article 33-4(i) of the FIEA).

e. Regulation on OTC financial derivatives transactions
(ⅰ) Overview

In the aftermath of the financial crisis of 2008-9, the FIEA has been amended several times to prevent and control the deterioration of the financial system by regulating OTC derivatives transactions. These amendments have reflected the worldwide trend of coordination for the reform of OTC derivatives regulation and supervision.[47] The first measure is to strengthen the development of the infrastructure of the central counterparty (CCP). The 2010 amendments to the FIEA mandates the use of a clearinghouse as a CCP for certain OTC derivatives transactions, and establishes a system for data storage and reporting of trading information. The 2012 amendments to the FIEA mandate the use of electronic execution facilities for certain OTC financial derivatives transactions. The 2013 amendments to the Deposit Insurance Act introduced a temporary stay on the close-out netting clause to prevent the extension of systemic risk.

(ⅱ) Transparency and reporting requirements

The 2010 amendments to the FIEA require clearinghouse, certain financial instruments business operator and registered financial institutions to maintain data regarding certain types of OTC derivatives transactions and to report this data to the Prime Minister (Articles 156-63 and 156-64 of the FIEA).[48] The information has to be provided in accordance with uniform data standards to the registered derivatives transactions data repositories

---

47  Leaders' Statement: The Pittsburgh Summit (September 24-25, 2009), ⟨http://www. g20.org/images/stories/docs/eng/pittsburgh.pdf⟩; Financial Stability Board, Implementing OTC Derivatives Market Reform (25 October 2010) ⟨http://www.financial stabilityboard.org/publications/r_101025.pdf⟩; Technical Committee of the IOSCO, Report on Trading of OTC Derivatives (February 2011) ⟨http://www.iosco.org/ library/pubdocs/pdf/IOSCOPD345.pdf⟩

Chapter 2   Scope of application and financial administration

(DTDRs: *torihiki joho chikuseki kikan*), which serve as secure, centralized recordkeeping facilities that are accessible by regulators and relevant authorities (Articles 156–65 of the FIEA). DTDRs have to verify and maintain data and the Prime Minister publicly disseminates it in a timely fashion.

The structure of DTDRs is designed to promote transparency and efficiency in the market for certain OTC derivatives and to create an infrastructure to assist regulators in performing their market oversight functions. The opacity of OTC derivatives transactions was highlighted as one of the causes of the financial crisis of 2008–9, since it exacerbated systemic risk.

The Cabinet Office Ordinance for the OTC Derivatives Transactions Regulation provides that information regarding the following OTC derivatives transactions[49] must be stored in DTDRs: forwards of financial instruments, forwards of financial indicators, options, swaps, CDS, etc.[50]

In Japan, it has been mandatory since April 2013 for the financial institutions to store information with respect to the abovementioned OTC derivatives transactions and to report it to the FSA. The DTCC Data Repository Japan (DDRJ)[51] is the only trade repository in Japan that has been designated by the FSA. Transactions not cleared by the JSCC (Japan Securities Clearing Corporation) are required to be reported to authorities either via the DDRJ or directly by financial institutions. As of December 2016, 71 financial institutions have used its service.[52]

(iii)   Centralized clearing

The 2010 amendments to the FIEA required certain financial instruments firms and registered financial institutions to have certain types of OTC

---

48   Regarding the 2010 amendments to the FIEA on OTC derivatives, see Akira WANI, *Derivative kisei no minaoshi* ⟨Review of Derivatives Regulation⟩, *Kinyu Homu Jijo*, No. 1903, pp. 55–57 (2010).

49   See supra A. 2. c. (v).

50   Article 3 and Article 6(1) of the Cabinet Office Ordinance for the OTC Derivatives Transactions Regulation.

51   Data Repository Japan (DDRJ) was established in April 2012 as a subsidiary of Deriv/SERV26 within the Depository Trust and Clearing Corporation (DTCC) Group.

52   ⟨http://www.jscc.co.jp/en/participant/irs.html⟩

*153*

derivatives transactions centrally cleared. When OTC derivatives transactions in Japan that are standardized and liquid are defaulted on, the Japanese capital market may be significantly affected, so these transactions should be centrally cleared through either a foreign CCP or a domestic CCP (Article 156-62 of the FIEA). The aim of a CCP is to have an entity that stands between parties with respect to certain OTC derivatives transactions. While the CCP bears no net market risk, which remains with the original party to each trade, it takes on counterparty risk, which is centralized in the CCP. The parties no longer need to worry about the credit counterparty risk.[53]

Legally, the original contract is automatically replaced by two contracts, each of which arises between one of the original parties and the CCP.[54] The original parties do not have counterparty risk with regard to one another. This risk is borne exclusively by the CCP, which is expected to control the risk efficiently due to adequate evaluation and margin control. Furthermore, contracts traded through the CCP can be netted, which means that a multilateral netting benefit is provided by the CCP. On the other hand, there are some disadvantages of centralized clearing, the most famous of which is that the all the risks are concentrated in the CCP, which then will be too big or too systemic to be allowed to fail.[55]

The Cabinet Office Ordinance for the OTC Derivatives Transactions Regulation requires that the following OTC derivatives transactions must be

---

53   Jon Gregory, *Counterparty Credit Risk* (John Wiley & Sons Ltd., 2010), p. 369.

54   It is controversial how an original contract can be automatically replaced by two contracts under Japanese civil law. In practice, two methods are used: one is novation (*kokai*); and another is acceptance of the obligation (*saimu-hikiuke*) by the CCP. The legal commission for the civil law (the law of obligations) reform discussed a third alternative as a special type of novation (sanmen-kokai), but did not adopt it finally. *Minpo (Saiken Kankei) no Kaisei ni kansuru chūkan-shian* [Interim Proposal for the Civil Law (Law of Obligations) Reform], Art. 24-6. ⟨http://www.moj.go.jp/content/000108853.pdf⟩

55   Regarding the disadvantages of the centralized clearing system, see Mark J. Roe, The Derivatives Market's Payment Priorities as Financial Crisis Accelerator, 63 *Stan. L. Rev.* 539, pp. 586-587 (2011); Wani pointed out from another perspective that especially in Japan, where there was little chaos even during this financial crisis, the introduction to compulsory centralized clearing would not be necessary. Wani, *supra* note 48, p. 58.

Chapter 2　Scope of application and financial administration

cleared in a CCP. The first is the plain-vanilla interest rate swap on the yen, for which three months or six months LIBOR and three months or six months TIBOR is indicated as the floating rate benchmark. The second is iTraxx Japan, which is the indicator financial product for CDS and single-named CDS.[56]

Nevertheless, a substantial portion of OTC derivatives are not standardized or centrally cleared. Therefore, compulsory use of the CCP will not be enough to reduce systemic risk. Bank for International Settlement (BIS) strengthened the capital requirements for OTC derivatives in Basel III.[57] BIS and the International Organization of Securities Commissions (IOSCO) published a paper in which they proposed that appropriate margining practices should be put in place with respect to all derivatives transactions that are not cleared by CCPs. According to the paper, all financial firms and systemically important non-financial entities that engage in non-centrally cleared derivatives must exchange initial and variation margins as appropriate to the counterparty risks posed by such transactions.[58] Japan introduced the margin requirement regulation for non-centrally cleared derivatives in phases since September 1, 2016.

Japan government bond transactions were formerly cleared and settled by the Japan Government Bond Clearing Corporation (JGBCC). On the other hand, stocks, bonds, beneficial interests in investment trusts, and, since October 9, 2012, interest rate swap (IRS) transactions are cleared by the JSCC and the on-exchange traded foreign exchange and interest-rate-related financial derivatives are cleared by the Tokyo Financial Exchange. The segmentation of CCPs presents a disadvantage in that the efficiency of central clearance could be impaired. The combination of three CCPs in Japan

---

56　Article 2 (1) & (2) of the Cabinet Office Ordinance for the OTC Derivatives Transactions Regulation. No. 60 of the Notification of the Financial Services Agency of July 11, 2012.

57　Basel Committee on Banking Supervision, Basel III: A global regulatory framework for more resilient banks and banking systems, pp. 31-37 (December 2010 (rev. June 2011)). 〈http://www.bis.org/publ/bcbs189.pdf〉

58　Basel Committee on Banking Supervision/ Board of the International Organization of Securities Commissions, Margin requirements for non-centrally cleared derivatives (September 2013). 〈http://www.bis.org/publ/bcbs261.pdf〉

*155*

has not yet been realized, but the JGBCC was merged into the JSCC on October 1, 2013. This merger might make it easy to introduce cross-margins between IRS and JGB futures transactions. The JSCC introduced in 2014 a client clearing system for IRSs and a default fund system in order to overcome inefficiencies and vulnerability.[59]

(iv) Trading infrastructure – Electronic derivatives transactions execution facilities

The 2012 amendments to the FIEA required a financial instruments business operator to conduct OTC financial derivatives transactions in the course of business, using electronic derivatives transactions execution facilities (EDTEF) for qualified OTC financial derivatives transactions (Article 40-7 of the FIEA).

EDTEF is intended to play an important role in enhancing the transparency and oversight of the market for these OTC financial derivatives transactions. EDTEF should help further the statutory objective of greater transparency by serving as a conduit for information regarding trading interests in selected OTC financial derivatives transactions.

There are two points of view on EDTEF regulation.[60] From the first point of view, as this concept is adequately expressed later in this sentence, the administration of EDTEF is handled in Japan not as an exchange or PTS but as a type I financial instruments business, unlike the regulation in the US on swap execution facilities (SEF) and in the EU on multilateral trading facilities (MTF). That is, the trading of financial derivatives, excluding securities-based derivatives, in Japan is of only two types: on-exchange traded derivatives and OTC derivatives. In other words, there is no category of PTS in terms of OTC financial derivatives excluding securities-based derivatives in Japan. From the second point of view, with respect to

---

**59** With regard to statistics, see II. B. Takahiro Kaneko, *Kinri swap torihiki no client clearing wo kaisi he* [Introduction of Client Clearing System with Regard to Interests Rate Swap], *Kinyū Zaisei Jijo*, No. 3038 (2013), pp. 18-23.

**60** For more details, see Hiroyuki Kansaku, *Derivative torihiki no genjo to kadai – kinsho-ho ni okeru infura seibi* [The Status and Legal Issues on Financial Transactions in Japan – Establishment of the Infrastructure for Certain Types of OTC Derivatives Transactions], *Jurist*, No. 1951 (2012), pp. 44-55.

*156*

Chapter 2  Scope of application and financial administration

securities-based derivatives, there are three types of trading: on-exchange, OTC, and PTS.

The first point may be related to the second. EDTEF in Japan must not be of the multiple-dealer type. In the US and the EU, the obligatory use of an electronic trading platform is intended to create a more competitive environment for the trading of certain types of OTC derivatives transactions by providing a venue for multiple parties to execute trades in OTC derivatives. SEF in the US and MTF in the EU must be of the multiple-dealer type and therefore be similar to an exchange.

The regulator would have access to information on the trading of certain types of OTC derivatives transactions in EDTEF and information regarding trading by the participants. Thus, EDTEF could be expected to play an important role in helping to oversee the market for certain types of OTC derivatives transactions on an ongoing basis, allowing regulators to quickly assess information regarding the potential for systemic risk across trading venues.

The scope of OTC derivatives transactions traded through EDTEF is a little narrower than that of the derivatives transactions that have to be centrally cleared.[61] Namely, the FSA designated the plain-vanilla interest rate swap on the yen as qualified OTC financial derivatives transactions that must be executed by JSCC and the trading information of those must be disclosed.[62]

(ⅴ)  Temporary stay of close-out netting clause

Due to the close-out netting clause upon the default of one of the two counterparties, all future claims and contractual relations between the two become due, calculated, netted, and then set off. The close-out amount can be smaller. In the case of insolvency, counterparty credit risk is substantially reduced to the resulting net position. This means that close-out netting, by

---

61  FSA, *Tento derivative shijo kisei ni kakaru kentokai ni okeru giron no torimatome* [Concluding the Discussion in the Working Group Regarding Regulation on the OTC Derivatives Market] (December 26, 2011), pp. 3-4.

62  Article 125-7 (1) of the Cabinet Office Ordinance Regarding Financial Instruments Business, No. 67 of the Notification of the Financial Services Agency of July 13, 2015.

*157*

reducing counterparty exposures, can contribute to a reduction in systemic risk. In Japan, the validity of the close-out netting clause is protected by Article 58 of the Bankruptcy Act and the Act Regarding Close-Out Netting in Qualified Financial Transactions by Financial Institutions of 1998.

On the other hand, the close-out netting rights of counterparties could exacerbate a failing bank's position to such an extent that orderly resolution by the authorities would become difficult. This might generate systemic risk. Therefore, it is claimed that a temporary stay on rights to close-out netting will be introduced in order to facilitate the orderly resolution of failing banks in a manner that does not destabilize the counterparties under netting agreements.[63] Authorities should have the legal authority to temporarily stay the operations of contractual early termination clauses in order to complete a transfer of certain financial market contracts to another sound financial institution.

The 2013 amendments to the Deposit Insurance Act (DIA) introduced the temporary stay of early termination clause to conduct close-out netting at an early stage, by which the Prime Minister must make a decision not to give effect to the clause during the period when it is considered to be necessary to take measures to avoid turbulence in the financial system (Article 137-3(1) of the DIA).[64] During the temporary stay, the provisions of Article 58 of the Bankruptcy Act and the Act Regarding Close-Out Netting in Qualified Financial Transactions by Financial Institutions do not apply (Article 137-3 (5) & (6) of the DIA). It is expected that during the temporary stay of early termination clause, authorities will transfer relevant contracts, as part of a resolution measure, to another sound financial institution. This regulation might represent a strong intervention of the state in the area of private law and private autonomy. Therefore, the appropriate implementation and enforcement of this temporary stay should be carefully observed.[65]

---

63  Basel Committee on Banking Supervision, Report and Recommendations of the Cross-border Bank Resolution Group, Recommendation 8 and 9 (2010 March).

64  Atsushi Sawaii & Masamichi Kamijima, *Kinyû shohin torihiki ho no ichibu wo kaisei suru horitu no gaiyo* [Outline of the Act Amending Part of the Financial Instruments and Exchange Act], *Shoji Homu*, No.2006 (2013), p. 2.

*158*

# B. Financial administration bodies and procedures

## 1. Locus of authority for financial administration

### a. The Prime Minister

The Financial Instruments and Exchange Act (FIEA) vests administrative authority in the "Prime Minister." The Prime Minister acts (1) as the head of the Cabinet (Article 66(1) and Article 72 of the Constitution; Article 2(1) and Article 5 of the Cabinet Act) and (2) as joint administrator of administrative affairs in his capacity as the head (minister in charge) of the Cabinet Office (Article 6 of the Act for Establishment of the Cabinet Office). "Prime Minister" as used in the FIEA refers to the Prime Minister in his capacity as head of the Cabinet Office.

Administrative authority under the FIEA is vested not in the Commissioner of the Financial Services Agency but in the Prime Minister in order to clarify administrative accountability to the Diet, and by extension the people, by granting that authority to the Prime Minister in his capacity as the minister in charge of the Cabinet Office.

It should be noted in this regard that affairs under the jurisdiction of the Financial Services Agency (Article 4 of the Act for Establishment of the Financial Services Agency) are included among the affairs under the jurisdiction of the Cabinet Office (Article 4 (3) (lx) of the Act for Establishment of the Cabinet Office).

### b. The Minister of State for Financial Services

The Cabinet Office includes the post of the so-called Minister of State for Financial Services, who assists the Prime Minister as one of the "Ministers of State for Special Missions" (Articles 9 (1) and 11 of the Act for Establishment of the Cabinet Office). The Minister of State for Financial

---

65 Kazuhiko Yamamoto, *Kinyû kikan no chitsujo aru shori no wakugumi* [Legal Framework for Orderly Resolution of Financial Institutions], *Kinyû Homu Jijo*, No. 1975 (2013), p. 35.

Services is appointed from among the Ministers of State (ibid., Article 9(2)) and is a member of the Cabinet (Article 66 of the Constitution; Article 2(1) of the Cabinet Act).

The Minister of State for Financial Services is responsible for administering the following (Article 11 of the Act for Establishment of the Cabinet Office):

( 1 )　affairs relating to formulation, planning, and overall coordination of "matters relating to overall creation of an environment facilitating financial services," which matters are necessary to ensuring coherence of policy measures among the various administrative branches (ibid., Article 4(1)(xv)); and

( 2 )　affairs under the jurisdiction of the Financial Services Agency (ibid., Article 4(3)(lx)).

The Minister of State for Financial Services, although not vested with authority under the FIEA, may be understood to possess authority to supervise the affairs under the jurisdiction of the Financial Services Agency.

　　c . The Commissioner of the Financial Services Agency

Because it is not practical for the Prime Minister, being also the head of the Cabinet, to exercise his administrative authority under the FIEA individually, that authority is, except for its core elements, such as granting and revocation of licenses (as specified by Cabinet Order), delegated to the Commissioner of the Financial Services Agency (Article 194-7(1) of the FIEA). The Commissioner of the Financial Services Agency is the head of the Financial Services Agency (Article 2(2) of the Act for Establishment of the Financial Services Agency).

The Prime Minister has the power to appoint the Commissioner of the Financial Services Agency (Article 55(1) of the National Public Service Act), although in practice the Minister of State for Financial Services appears to exercise influence over the choice of who will fill the position.

*160*

Chapter 2   Scope of application and financial administration

# 2. The Financial Services Agency (FSA)

a. Overview

The Financial Services Agency (FSA) is an external organ of the Cabinet Office (Article 49(3) of the Act for Establishment of the Cabinet Office; Article 2(1) of the Act for Establishment of the Financial Services Agency). The FSA has the functions of (1) ensuring the stable functioning of Japan's financial system; (2) protecting depositors, insurance policyholders, investors in securities, and other such parties; and (3) facilitating financial services (ibid., Article 3).

In fulfillment of those functions, the FSA has jurisdiction over financial regulatory laws and conducts financial administration in accordance with them. Financial regulatory laws include, for example, (1) legislation governing financial institutions that take deposits, such as the Banking Act, the Shinkin Bank Act, the Act on Financial Businesses by Cooperatives, the Act on Engagement in Trust Business by a Financial Institution, and the Deposit Insurance Act, etc.; (2) legislation governing markets and investments, such as the Financial Instruments and Exchange Act, the Act on Investment Trusts and Investment Corporations, the Act on Securitization of Assets, and the Act on Book-Entry Transfer of Company Bonds, Shares, Etc., etc.; (3) legislation governing insurance companies, such as the Insurance Business Act, etc.; and (4) miscellaneous legislation, such as the Trust Business Act, the Money Lending Business Act, the Payment Services Act, and the Act on Special Treatment of Corporate Reorganization Proceedings and Other Insolvency Proceedings of Financial Institutions, Etc., and so on.

b. How the FSA operates

(i) Characteristics of the FSA's organization

The FSA, Japan's sole financial regulatory agency, has several characteristics. First, it has jurisdiction over all banks, securities firms, insurance companies, and nonbanks. It also has jurisdiction over accounting and auditing standards and over certified public accountants and audit corporations. On the other hand, since in Japan finance and commodities are considered separate categories, the FSA does not have jurisdiction over

*161*

commodity exchanges and commodity derivatives business operators, which under the Commodity Derivatives Act fall within the purview of the Ministry of Agriculture, Forestry and Fisheries and the Ministry of Economy, Trade and Industry.

Second, the FSA performs the function of financial system planning and design — a case of the so-called separation of fiscal and financial policy, which is rare anywhere in the world (another example being the Monetary Authority of Singapore, or MAS). In all the G7 countries except Japan, the finance ministry performs the function of financial system planning and design.

Third — and this relates to the financial system planning and design functions of the FSA — is the existence of a Minister of State for Financial Services. This too is a global rarity (another example again being Singapore). In the other G7 countries, the finance minister is the responsible minister. In Japan, such a minister is needed in the Cabinet in that any draft legislation regulating finance must be adopted by the Cabinet and then submitted to the Diet for deliberation. On the other hand, given that, internationally, IOSCO principles call for securities regulators to be "operationally independent," this arrangement could create problems with the political independence of the FSA.

Fourth, the FSA is organized by function. Its internal departments are (1) the Planning and Coordination Bureau, which serves as the agency's secretariat and performs system planning and design functions; (2) the Supervisory Bureau, which performs supervisory functions; and (3) the Inspection Bureau, which performs inspection functions. Each bureau has jurisdiction over all banks, securities firms, insurance companies, and nonbanks, although the Supervisory Bureau has separate divisions for each type of business (Banks Division I, Banks Division II, Securities Business Division, Insurance Business Division, Cooperative Financial Institutions Office, Nonbank Financial Companies Office, etc.). This function-based organization is designed to maintain a healthy tension between different functions, although lately higher priority has tended to be given to coordinating them.

Fifth, one of the FSA's functional arms is the Securities and Exchange Surveillance Commission (SESC), which performs market surveillance

*162*

Chapter 2   Scope of application and financial administration

functions. This arrangement too is rare internationally. The SESC was established in July 1992 to enhance and strengthen the monitoring of compliance with market rules from a neutral, objective standpoint in the wake of the securities scandals, particularly securities firms' compensation for of certain clients' for losses, which came to light in the summer of 1991. The SESC has its own dedicated secretariat.

Sixth, the FSA's function-based organization is characterized by a division between supervisory functions and inspection and surveillance functions. Inspection and surveillance functions are generally considered a means of performing supervisory functions; but in Japan the two have been kept organizationally separate in order to ensure that actual conditions can be ascertained objectively by the inspection and surveillance arm without distortion by the supervisory arm. Recently, however, higher priority has tended to be given to coordinating supervisory and inspection and surveillance functions.

(ⅱ)   Characteristics of the FSA's regional organization

Seventh, the task of supervising, inspecting, and monitoring local financial institutions and such is the job of the local offices of the Ministry of Finance, namely the Local Finance Bureaus and Local Finance Branch Bureau (Article 13(1) and Article 14(2) of the Act for Establishment of the Ministry of Finance). The FSA does not have its own local offices. This is explained from the standpoint of administrative reform as a means of making effective use of the existing Local Finance Bureaus and Branch Bureau; on the other hand, it has resulted in the maintenance and expansion of the local offices of the Ministry of Finance.

Eighth, among the Local Finance Bureaus, the Kanto Local Finance Bureau performs a particularly significant role, being delegated, among others, authority relating to (1) disclosure by domestic companies capitalized at 5 billion yen or more and by all foreign companies (Article 39 (1) (2) of the Financial Instruments and Exchange Act Implementing Order); (2) disclosure of tender offers (ibid., Article 40(1)); and (3) large-volume shareholding reports by nonresidents (ibid., Article 41(1)).

*163*

(ⅲ) Characteristics of the FSA's structure and personnel

Ninth, the FSA, with the SESC, is an administrative agency dedicated to performing administrative functions (supervision, surveillance, and inspection) designed to ensure proper enforcement of the law. Japanese administrative agencies generally concentrate on system planning and design; proper legal enforcement has traditionally not been a high priority. For that reason, rules are not always observed, resulting in numerous problems. The FSA, like the Fair Trade Commission, which administers the Antimonopoly Act, and the National Tax Agency, which enforces taxlaws, is an administrative agency dedicated to due enforcement of the law. Some 75 percent of FSA and SESC personnel are in law enforcement (supervision, inspection, and surveillance), with 55 percent being affiliated with the inspection and surveillance arm.

Tenth, the personnel and organization of the FSA and the SESC have expanded considerably. When the Financial Supervisory Agency was first established on June 22, 1998, it and the SESC had a complement of 403 staff. As of the end of fiscal year 2016, the FSA and the SESC have a complement of 1,571 staff (410 of them affiliated with the SESC). In addition, there are 1,626 staff working in the field of financial administration at Local Finance Bureaus and Branch Bureaus (352 of them in the inspection officer department).

## 3. The Securities and Exchange Surveillance Commission (SESC)

a. Organization

The Securities and Exchange Surveillance Commission (SESC) is a "Council or the like" (Article 54 of the Act for Establishment of the Cabinet Office) set up inside the FSA (Article 6(1) of the Act for Establishment of the Financial Services Agency). It handles matters for which it is assigned authority pursuant to the provisions of the FIEA, the Act on Investment Trusts and Investment Corporations, the Act against Unjustifiable Premiums and Misleading Representations, the Deposit Insurance Act, the Act on Securitization of Assets, the Act on Book-Entry Transfer of Company Bonds, Shares, Etc., and the Act on Prevention of Transfer of Criminal Proceeds (ibid., Article 8).

Chapter 2   Scope of application and financial administration

The SESC is a consultative body consisting of a chairman and two commissioners, who are appointed by the Prime Minister with the consent of both Houses of the Diet for a tenure of three years (ibid., Articles 10-13). The chairman and commissioners have guaranteed status: during their term of office, they are not allowed to in principle be dismissed against their will (ibid., Article 14). Being a consultative body, the SESC is not subject to the control or supervision of the Prime Minister or the Commissioner of the FSA. The independence of the chairman and commissioners in exercising their authority is explicitly confirmed in Article 9.

The SESC has its own secretariat (ibid., Article 19). Originally organized into two divisions, it was expanded to five in July 2006 and the present six divisions in July 2011. These are the Coordination Division, the Market Surveillance Division, the Inspection Division, the Administrative Monetary Penalty Division, the Disclosure Statements Inspection Division, and the Investigation Division.

b. Authority
The authority delegated to the SESC under the law includes:

- the authority to order submission of reports and materials by financial instruments business operators and to conduct inspections (Article 194-7 (2) & (3) of the FIEA; Article 38 and Article 38-2 (2) of the Financial Instruments and Exchange Act Implementing Order);
- the authority to investigate violations and impose administrative monetary penalties (Article 194-7 (2) (viii) of the FIEA);
- the authority to order submission of reports and materials by issuers of disclosure statements, related parties, and witnesses; tender offerors, related parties, and witnesses; and submitters of large-volume shareholdings reports, related parties, and witnesses; and to conduct inspections (Article 194-7 (3) of the FIEA; Article 38-2 (1) of the Financial Instruments and Exchange Act Implementing Order);
- the authority to order submission of reports and materials by issuer companies on large-volume shareholdings reports and by relevant witnesses (ibid.);
- the authority to publicize names, etc. (Article 194-7 (3) of the FIEA;

Article 38-2 (3) of the Financial Instruments and Exchange Act Implementing Order); and

· the authority to petition a court for an emergency prohibition or suspension order, and the authority to conduct investigations for that purpose (Article 194-7(4) of the FIEA).

In addition, SESC officials possess seven independent powers to investigate criminal cases (Articles 210-211 of the FIEA; Article 45 of the Financial Instruments and Exchange Act Implementing Order).

c. Securities inspections and administrative monetary penalty investigations

In performing securities inspections (inspections of operators), the SESC focuses on intensively examining problem cases: for example, (1) operators of real estate investment corporations (J-REITs); (2) validation of management systems, etc. related to restrictions on short-selling (released October 2008); (3) foreign exchange margin trading operators (findings released April 2009); (4) sellers of funds (findings released October 2010); (5) investment advisory and agency service providers (findings released February 2011); and (6) discretionary investment service providers (released April 2012).

Between FY2007 and FY2013, the SESC followed a policy of making more extensive use of the system of administrative monetary penalties in such cases as unfair trading and false statements, thus capitalizing on the system's advantages (speed and efficiency). In FY2012 and 2013, for example, administrative monetary penalty investigations were conducted in cases of insider trading related to new offerings of shares. Since FY2014, on the other hand, the SESC has followed a policy of dealing strictly with serious or blatant violations by exercising its authority to investigate criminal cases.

d. Authority to petition a court for an emergency prohibition or suspension order

The authority to petition a court for an emergency prohibition or suspension order (Article 192 of the FIEA), modeled on the Anglo-American legal institution of the injunction, has been enshrined in law since

Chapter 2   Scope of application and financial administration

the enactment of the Securities and Exchange Act in 1948, but until recently it had never been used.

Enforcement under the FIEA is conducted primarily ex post facto. However, when the FIEA was amended in 2008, this authority to petition the courts (Article 192(1) of the FIEA), along with the authority to conduct investigations for that purpose (Article 187 of the FIEA), was vested in the SESC (Article 194-7(4) of the FIEA) in order to as far as possible forestall violations. When the Act was again amended in 2010, penalties for violations of Article 192 (Article 198 (viii) of the FIEA) were made subject to concurrent liability provisions (Article 207(1) (iii) of the FIEA), and the above authority to petition the courts and conduct investigations was delegated to the Director General of the Local Finance Bureau or Branch Bureau (Article 194-7 (7) of the FIEA; Article 44-5 of the Financial Instruments and Exchange Act Implementing Order).

e. Authority to investigate criminal cases

SESC officials (including an official of a Local Finance Bureau or Branch Bureau designated by the bureau's Director General) may, in order to investigate a criminal case, request that a suspect or witness in the case appear, question that person, or inspect or retain his or her articles (Article 210 and Article 224 of the FIEA). SESC officials may also execute an official inspection, search, or seizure with a permit issued by a judge (Article 211 of the FIEA).

Criminal cases cover certain crimes in violation of the FIEA (Article 45 of the Financial Instruments and Exchange Act Implementing Order), primarily such crimes as submitting a false securities report (so-called window dressing), insider trading, disseminating unfounded rumors, fraud, and manipulating the market.

SESC officials are required to report the results of their investigation of a criminal case to the Commission (Article 223 of the FIEA); if convinced as a result of the investigation that a crime has occurred, the Commission must then file an accusation (Article 226 of the FIEA). Public prosecutors are seconded to the SESC, and SESC officials and prosecutors from the public prosecutors office exchange information and consult through such forums as so-called consultative meetings for criminal prosecutions.

*167*

f . Recommendations and proposals

Unlike the Fair Trade Commission, which under Article 27, paragraph 1, of the Antimonopoly Act is a "commission" established within the Cabinet Office (Article 49(3) of the Act for Establishment of the Cabinet Office), the SESC cannot itself decide and express the will of the state. It cannot therefore issue an administrative action itself; upon conducting a securities transactions inspection or the like, however, it can, based on the results, recommend administrative action or other measure to the Prime Minister or the Commissioner of the FSA if it consider it necessary (Article 20 of the Act for Establishment of the Financial Services Agency).

The SESC can also, if it consider it necessary based on the results of a securities transactions inspection or the like, propose necessary measures to the Prime Minister, the Commissioner of the FSA, or others (ibid., Article 21).

The SESC's recommendations and proposals are not legally binding, nor does the law require the Prime Minister and the Commissioner of the FSA to respect them. In practice, however, the FSA generally respects the SESC's recommendations and proposals when implementing administrative actions and other measures. The SESC secretariat liaises with the relevant departments of the FSA to ensure their smooth execution.

The SESC makes its administrative action recommendations public; hence, the recommendation itself acts as a de facto sanction.

# 4 . Implementation of financial administration

a . Principles governing operation of financial administration

( i ) Basic principles governing operation of financial administration

When the Financial Services Agency was launched on July 1, 2000, it declared its basic approach to implementing financial administration to be "Ensuring transparency and fairness in financial administration based on clear rules (market discipline and the principle of self-responsibility)." That principle seems to fit well in substance even today, when the problem of bad loans held by financial institutions has been cleared up and the global financial crisis dealt with. In conducting supervision, due consideration must be given to respecting voluntary efforts by financial instruments business operators (Article 65-6 of the FIEA).

Chapter 2 Scope of application and financial administration

The FSA has, since releasing "Strategic Directions and Priorities 2015-2016" in September 2015, defined the objectives of financial administration in macro terms, describing its mission as to contribute to national welfare by ensuring sustainable corporate and economic growth and steadily creating wealth. "Strategic Directions and Priorities 2016-2017" (October 2016) defines the guiding principle of financial administration as striking a balance between (1) financial stability and effective financial intermediation; (2) user protection and user benefits; and (3) market integrity and market vigor.

( ii ) Better regulation — improving the quality of financial regulation

In July 2007 the FSA unveiled the policy "Better Regulation — Improving the quality of financial regulation." This policy identifies three objectives of financial administration: (1) ensuring the stability of the financial system; (2) protecting users; and (3) establishing and maintaining a fair, transparent market. It then sets out four pillars of better regulation underpinning the FSA's approach to overseeing financial markets. Specifically, the four pillars are (1) the optimal combination of rules-based and principles-based supervisory approaches; (2) effective responses to high-priority issues by effective use of administrative resources; (3) encouraging voluntary efforts by financial institutions, and placing greater emphasis on incentives for them; and (4) improving the transparency and predictability of regulatory actions. In April 2008, the FSA then released "The Principles in the Financial Services Industry" and "Administrative Action in the Financial Sector."

The Better Regulation policy was inaugurated when the financial system was relatively stable, but even today, having responded to the global financial crisis triggered by the so-called Lehman shock (September 15, 2008), the FSA is still committed to further entrenching and advancing the policy.

( iii ) Market surveillance

The market watchdog charged with establishing a fair market, the Securities and Exchange Surveillance Commission, has for a number of years (2007-2016) conducted market surveillance with the goals of ensuring market integrity and protecting investors. It has recently (in January 2017) also been assigned an additional, broader mission in macro terms:

*169*

contributing to the sound development of capital markets and the sustainable growth of the national economy.

Hitherto priority has been given to these areas, among others: (1) preventing gaps in market surveillance by keeping an overall eye on primary and secondary markets and reinforcing oversight of cross-border transactions (comprehensive, flexible market surveillance); and (2) by actively disseminating information and beefing up cooperation with self-regulating bodies and other organizations, strengthening market discipline through voluntary action by individual market players.

Most recently (as of January 2017) emphasis has been placed on breadth, expeditiousness, and depth of market surveillance.

 b. The practice of financial administration
  ( i ) Practical guidelines of financial administration

Implementation of financial administration by the FSA takes the form of supervision, inspection, and surveillance conducted individually under financial regulatory laws, in accordance with guidelines, supervisory guidelines, and inspection manuals setting out detailed procedures.

The following guidelines have been prepared and released under the FIEA:

- Planning and Coordination Bureau, FSA, "Points to be Considered Regarding Disclosure of Corporate Affairs" (corporate disclosure guidelines) and "Comprehensive Guideline for Supervision of Designated Dispute Resolution Organizations"
- Securities Business Division, Supervisory Bureau, FSA, "Comprehensive Guidelines for Supervision of Financial Instruments Business Operators, etc."
- SESC, "Basic Guidelines on Securities Inspections," "Inspection Manual for Financial Instruments Business Operators, etc." "Basic Guidelines on Investigation of Market Misconduct," and "Basic Guidelines on Disclosure Statements Inspection"

In addition, every administrative year (July through to the following June) the FSA prepares and releases an annual "Strategic Direction and Priorities

Chapter 2 Scope of application and financial administration

of Financial Administration."

In addition, every fiscal year until FY2015 (every administrative year between 2006 and 2008), the Securities and Exchange Surveillance Commission prepared and released a "Securities Inspection Policy and Program," while more recently it has released "Monitoring Priorities for Securities Businesses (July 2016 – June 2017)." A recent policy on monitoring financial instruments business operators, etc. has given priority to (1) seamless on- and off-site monitoring of all operators; (2) risk-based selection of targets for on-site monitoring; and (3) reviewing the suitability and effectiveness of governance systems of financial institutions, etc.

There have also been two reports assessing the progress and results of financial administration over the course of the year by applying the PDCA cycle: the "Financial Monitoring Report" (July 2015) and "Progress and Assessment of the Strategic Directions and Priorities" (September 2016).

Further, the Planning and Coordination Bureau of the FSA releases "Points to be considered regarding the preparation and submission of securities reports" (since the accounting year ended March 2011) and "Implementation of review of securities reports" (since the accounting year ended March 2012) for each accounting year ending in March.

(ⅱ) Validation of systems

The supervisory guidelines and inspection manuals call for institution and due implementation of various "systems." These systems can be schematized hierarchically as in Figure 2-1, although there are differences between the supervisory guidelines and inspection manuals in how they are defined.

This is based on the idea of three lines of defense: (1) as the first line of defense, the front office of the organization conducts risk management directly, having identified operational risks of all types; (2) as the second line of defense, the risk management and compliance arms support the first line of defense and evaluate the effectiveness of its management procedures; (3) as the third line of defense, the internal auditing arm evaluates whether the first and second lines of defense are functioning effectively.

*171*

## Figure 2-1. Structure of a financial institution's systems

Governance system
  Internal management system
    Legal compliance system
      ⇒ Customer management system (customer protection management system, customer information management system)
      ⇒ Outsourcing management system etc.
    Risk management system
      ⇒ Financial risk management system
      ⇒ Operational risk management system
      ⇒ System risk management system
      ⇒ Crisis management system (Business continuity management [BCM] etc.)
    Internal audit system
  Business management system

(ⅲ) The PDCA cycle

When reviewing different systems, the authorities responsible for financial oversight and surveillance assess whether the so-called PDCA cycle functions effectively. To be specific, they determine whether appropriate steps have been taken by management to (1) draw up a policy (Plan); (2) establish organizational structures and institute regulations (Do); (3) conduct evaluations (Check); and (4) make improvements (Action). The PDCA cycle concept is also useful in evaluating the effectiveness of internal controls over financial reporting required of listed companies (Article 24-4-4 of the FIEA).

During validation of different systems by the financial oversight and surveillance authorities, a check is conducted of whether the so-called PDCA cycle functions effectively. To be specific, it is validated whether appropriate steps have been taken by management to (1) draw up a policy (Plan); (2) establish organizational structures and institute regulations (Do); (3) conduct evaluations (Check); and (4) make improvements (Action). The PDCA cycle concept is also useful in evaluating the effectiveness of internal controls over financial reporting required of listed companies (Article 24-4-4 of the FIEA).

Chapter 2 Scope of application and financial administration

c. Legal status of disclosure/supervisory guidelines and inspection manuals

In terms of legal basis, financial regulations take the form of legally binding "laws and regulations," that is, Acts, Cabinet Orders, Cabinet Office Ordinances, and Public Notices established pursuant to Acts (see Article 2 (i) of the Administrative Procedure Act). These are all promulgated in the Official Gazette.

On the other hand, in "The Principles in the Financial Services Industry" released by the FSA on April 18, 2008, financial regulations are defined as "rules such as laws, regulations, the FSA's Inspection Manuals and Supervisory Guidelines." However, disclosure guidelines, supervisory guidelines, and inspection manuals per se fall into the category of "instructions or circular notices," that constitute orders or directions issued by higher-ranking administrative organs to affiliated lower-ranking administrative organs or officials within the government hierarchy for the purpose of directing them to exercise their official authority (Article 58(7) of the Act for Establishment of the Cabinet Office); they are not legally binding on issuing companies and financial service providers. In the supervisory guidelines and inspection manuals themselves, they are described as "manuals" for the use of officials within government.

The disclosure guidelines, supervisory guidelines, and inspection manuals are of practical use to the private sector in that they set out the interpretation of laws and regulations to ensure consistent enforcement by government, describe internal procedures, and identify areas on which the authorities focus. Their transparency is ensured because they are finalized after public comment. They have the further advantage of being more easily comprehensible than laws and regulations. On the other hand, they need to be formulated and applied in a manner entirely consistent with their character as non-legally binding "instructions or circular notices"; in particular, an administrative guidance approach must not be taken to their formulation and application.

On the other hand, administrative guidance toward the private sector is not restricted to the field of financial administration. For example, the government's efforts to sever ties between business and "antisocial forces" (criminal organizations and such) are implemented on the basis of the

*173*

Guideline for How Companies Prevent Damage from Anti-Social Forces (June 19, 2007) agreed upon at a secretarial level meeting of cabinet ministers responsible for anticrime measures; in the field of financial administration, they are promoted by the supervisory authorities (III-2-11 of the Comprehensive Guidelines for Supervision of Financial Instruments Business Operators, etc.).

d. The relationship between supervision and inspections

Given that inspections are a means of supervision, there is no need for separate supervision guidelines and inspection manuals; integrating the two instead would have the advantage of simplifying and streamlining financial administration. In fact, the second revised version of the Three-Year Plan for the Promotion of Regulatory Reform adopted by the Cabinet on March 31, 2009, stated that "supervision guidelines and inspection manuals will be flexibly revised in the direction of greater simplicity and clarity." No subsequent progress was seen until in March 2017 it was finally proposed that both be combined.

In the field of financial supervision and inspection, meanwhile, efforts have been made to seamlessly integrate on-site monitoring and off-site monitoring (conducting interviews and demanding documentation). A "Financial Monitoring Policy" has been prepared and released since the 2014 administrative year, and whereas there were previously separate supervision guidelines for each business category, these have now been combined into one. In the 2015 administrative year, a policy governing all aspects of financial administration, including financial system planning and market surveillance, was drawn up and released under the title "Strategic Directions and Priorities"; cross-sectoral supervision is included in this policy.

Since the 2016 administrative year the Securities and Exchange Surveillance Commission has prepared and released "Monitoring Priorities for Securities Businesses," which emphasizes seamlessness between supervision and inspection of securities businesses.

e. Locus of authority for administrative interpretation

Authority for administrative interpretation of financial regulatory

*174*

Chapter 2　Scope of application and financial administration

legislation within the FSA is understood to lie with the FSA's planning arm (the Planning and Coordination Bureau), which handles planning and drafting of financial regulatory legislation. The planning arm presents its administrative interpretation while consulting as necessary with the Cabinet Legislation Bureau, which is empowered to express views on legal questions within the executive branch of government (Article 3 (iii) of the Act for Establishment of the Cabinet Legislation Bureau).

Conversely, in practical matters, administrative interpretation is conducted not by the planning arm but by the enforcement arm. Requests for no-action letters and written inquiries on the general interpretation of laws and regulations are generally answered by the enforcement arm. On the other hand, there is, in individual cases, a strict partition (a kind of Chinese wall) between the planning and enforcement arms with respect to administrative actions and indications made during inspections (itself an appropriate arrangement), and the SESC in particular is institutionally independent; given that fact, it may be concluded that the enforcement arm engages in administrative interpretation of financial regulatory laws exclusively with respect to practical matters.

Thus, in the practical conduct of administration, the body that plans and drafts financial regulatory legislation is organizationally separate from that which conducts practical interpretation. The challenge thus arises of ensuring consistent interpretation and application of laws and regulations in accordance with the intent with which they were planned and drafted. The grounds for interpretation should also be clearly given. It seems that recently cases have increased in which the enforcement arm consults interpretations of laws and regulations with the planning arm.

　f．Practical implementation of administrative actions
　　( i )　Overview
The FSA has authority to implement administrative actions under financial regulatory laws. In the broad sense, the term "administrative action" may include an order to submit a report or other materials in the sense of an "adverse actions" under the Administrative Procedure Act (Article 2 (iv)) or an "action for the revocation of the original administrative actions" under the Administrative Case Litigation Act (Article 3 (2)); but in

*175*

the narrow sense it refers to an order to improve business operation, a business suspension order, a rescission of registration, or the like.

Unlike a "sanction" by means of criminal punishment, which aims for retribution and deterrence by condemning a past act, with the focus on its antisocial or immoral nature, an administrative action seeks to correct a problematic situation, and prevent the occurrence of future problems, for the purpose of achieving an administrative goal, and thus to effectively enforce regulations. Administrative actions are therefore not intended to act as sanctions, but they undeniably function in effect as such by being made public.

Administrative actions may thus be considered to have the functions of correcting problem situations, preventing problems from occurring, and acting as sanctions.

(ⅱ) Administrative discretion

Because administrative dispositions apply financial regulatory laws to individual cases, they inevitably entail administrative discretion.

Administrative discretion is classified into discretion with respect to conditions (administrative discretion to determine whether necessary conditions are met) and discretion with respect to effects (administrative discretion to determine whether and to what degree to take action). In particular, the provisions granting the power to issue an order to improve business operation in Articles 51-1 and 51-2 of the FIEA, inserted when the Securities and Exchange Act was revised in 2006, allow not only discretion with respect to conditions, but also discretion with respect to effects as regards the indeterminate concept of "necessary and appropriate for the public interest or protection of investors"; although the legislative intent is not to grant broad discretion.

The FSA's exercise of its administrative discretionary powers is sometimes criticized as "discretionary administration." Granted that financial administrators are to a certain extent allowed to make discretionary decisions in specialized technical matters and policy matters, a mechanism needs to be established to ensure that that discretion is appropriately and reasonably exercised. Accordingly it is important, as in the case of administrative interpretation, to ensure (1) clarity of discretionary

Chapter 2　Scope of application and financial administration

criteria; (2) transparency of discretionary decisions; and (3) except in urgent cases, a fair opportunity to summarily challenge discretionary decisions before the administrative disposition takes force.

In these regards, (1) action standards are set out in the FSA's supervisory and disclosure guidelines, etc. in accordance with the requirement to endeavor to establish standards for adverse actions, and make them available to the public, enshrined in the Administrative Procedure Act (Article 12); and (2) the FIEA requires that a hearing be conducted prior to implementation of an administrative action (Articles 9(1), 10(1), 27-8(4), 27-29(1), 57(1)(2), 66-23, etc. of the FIEA). However, the latter procedure appears in practice to be implemented on the assumption that the administrative action will be enforced, and does not really function as a fair opportunity to summarily challenge the decision. Problems thus remain.

On the other hand, as regards administrative monetary penalty payment orders, the provisions of the law are worded in such a way that the Commissioner of the FSA has discretion with respect to neither conditions nor effects. When the system of administrative monetary penalties was first instituted, the SESC administered it pro forma and uniformly, with no real discretion (non-discretionary administration, as it were). However, that approach was undesirable in that it could potentially undermine the functions of preventing illegal conduct (by encouraging respect for the law) and of imposing sanctions. For that reason what might be called discretionary administration is in effect practiced today.

g. Practical implementation of inspections and investigations

Inspections and investigations have the character of administrative investigations — the means whereby administrative organs gather the information required to achieve their administrative goals. The process of determining and ascertaining objective facts and conditions by gathering information through implementation of inspections and investigations is indispensable to achieving the goals of financial regulatory legislation.

Therefore, the authority of the FSA and SESC to conduct inspections and investigations is enshrined in the FIEA (Articles 26, 27-22, 27-30, 56-2, 66-22, 66-45, 75, 151, 156-34, 156-58, 177, 187, etc. of the FIEA). Moreover, to ensure that inspections and investigations are effective, provision is also

*177*

made for indirect coercion through imposition of penalties for refusing, hindering, or avoiding an inspection (Articles 198-6(xi) (xvii-v) ~ (xvii-vii), 205(vi), 205-3(i) & (ii), 207(1)(iv) & (vi) of the FIEA).

Inspections and investigations are legally classified as "voluntary investigations" in the sense that they do not involve direct physical coercion. However, because a party subject to an inspection or investigation is required to undergo it on pain of a penalty, during implementation care must be exercised to avoid what is "in effect tantamount to direct physical coercion" (Supreme Court Judgment of Nov. 22, 1972, *Criminal Cases of the Supreme Court*, Vol. 26, No. 9, p. 554 [Kawasaki Democratic Society of Commerce and Industry case]).

A reasonable balance must be attained between the need to ensure the effectiveness of the inspection or investigation and the need to protect the rights of the party subject to it. From that standpoint the "Basic Policy for Financial Inspection" of the Director General of the FSA's Inspection Bureau and "Basic Guidelines on Securities Inspections" of the SESC go too far in demanding that before consulting with a lawyer on inspection-related matters, the party undergoing inspection obtain prior approval from, e.g., the chief inspector (in the case of financial inspections) or report in advance (in the case of securities inspections). This requirement should be revoked.

h. Publication of names, etc.

Under revisions made to the FIEA in 2013, a new system has been adopted whereby the names and so forth of committers of "violations of the law or regulations" (the FIEA or regulations based on it) are made public (Article 192-2 of the FIEA, Cabinet Office Ordinance on Publication of Names).

This is intended to apply to parties that while involved in insider trading, are not subject to administrative monetary penalties themselves — officers or employees of intermediary service providers, for example, or asset managers at institutional investors. The idea is to forestall further violations by publicizing individual names and so on.

However, there are no specific provisions on the scope of the violations and violators subject to publication. Publication is an effective sanctioning tool for the administrative authorities, and it basically does not constitute an

Chapter 2 Scope of application and financial administration

administrative disposition against which an action for revocation may be filed; appropriate procedures should therefore be followed (see Article 2 of the Ordinance on Publication of Names).

One notable feature is that authority to make public the names, etc. of those involved in cases where administrative monetary penalties have been imposed is vested in the Commissioner of the FSA rather than the SESC (Article 194-7(3) of the FIEA; Enforcement Order, Article 38-2(4) of the Financial Instruments and Exchange Act Implementing Order).

i . Information and documentation, disclosure requests, and submission orders

Information on supervisory activities, inspections, and investigations is basically considered to fall into the category of "Non-Disclosure Information" as defined in Article 5 of the Act on Access to Information Held by Administrative Organs. Specifically, it constitutes information concerning juridical persons or other entities prescribed in item (ii) of that Article, or information concerning administrative affairs, etc. prescribed in item (vi) (see the official FSA directive "Standards for Determinations under the Provisions of Article 9 of the Act on Access to Information Held by Administrative Organs").

Under the Code of Civil Procedure, the holder of a document is required to submit it unless it constitutes an excluded document (Article 220). Types of excluded documents include documents containing official secrets (ibid., (iv) (b)) and documents containing technical or professional secrets (ibid., (iv) (c)). Documents containing official secrets must, besides containing secrets relating to official duties, be of such a nature that their disclosure would specifically hinder the conduct of public duties (Supreme Court Decision of Oct. 14, 2005, *Civil Cases of the Supreme Court*, Vol. 59, No. 8, p. 2265; Supreme Court Decision of Apr. 19, 2013, *Hanrei Jiho*, No. 2194, p. 13).

In Antimonopoly Act cases, a report submitted by an enterprise in accordance with a report order from the Fair Trade Commission is subject to a document submission order, with the exception of preliminary information in cases in which final action has not yet been taken (Tokyo High Court Decision of Feb. 16, 2007, *Kinyu Shoji Hanrei*, No. 1303, p. 58; Osaka District Court Decision of Jun. 15, 2012, *Hanrei Jiho*, No. 2173, p. 58).

*179*

In another court decision, inspection reports relating to administrative monetary penalty-related investigations by the SESC were deemed subject to document submission orders, with the exception of quotations from statements by persons under investigation, descriptions of the initial reason for the inspection or course of the investigation, and reasons for not investigating (Tokyo District Court Decision of May 6, 2010, *Kinyu Shoji Hanrei*, No. 1344, p. 30). Another court decision ruled that a document submission court order also applied to a document containing the results of an internal investigation conducted by a securities company for the purpose of preparing a remedial action report submitted by the securities company in accordance with a business improvement order issued by the Director General of the Local Finance Bureau, as well as to any survey forms submitted by sales personnel at the time of that investigation (Tokyo High Court Decision of August 8, 2014, *Hanrei Jiho*, No. 2252, p. 46).

# C. International scope of application of the FIEA

## 1. International scope of application of Japanese law

### a. Overview

What with the growth in cross-border financial transactions and the accelerating expansion of Japanese and foreign financial institutions into each other's markets, financial instruments transactions and markets have become much more internationalized; hence, the international scope of application of the Financial Instruments and Exchange Act (FIEA) increasingly needs to be considered. This relates to the question of the so-called extraterritorial jurisdiction of domestic law.

The international scope of application of Japanese law can basically be examined in the separate categories of (1) civil law, (2) criminal law, and (3) administrative law.

The international scope of application of civil law is decided in accordance with the rules for determining governing law based on the Act on General Rules for Application of Laws (Act No. 78 of 2006), a complete revision of the previous law (Act No. 10 of 1898). As for the international scope of

Chapter 2　Scope of application and financial administration

application of criminal law, the provisions of the Penal Code apply except as otherwise provided for (Article 8); basically they apply to "anyone who commits a crime within the territory of Japan" (Article 1). Thus, the principle of territoriality is asserted.

By contrast, no law exists governing the international scope of application of administrative law in general. There has been a long-running discussion on the extraterritorial jurisdiction of the Antimonopoly Act, which is instructive in considering the international scope of application of the FIEA. Although the FIEA has civil and criminal aspects as well, the following analysis will focus on the administrative-law provisions that form its core.

b. State jurisdiction

In international law, the power to establish and enforce domestic laws is termed "state jurisdiction." State jurisdiction is classified into (1) *legislative* (or *prescriptive*) *jurisdiction* — the power to pass laws and regulations; (2) *judicial jurisdiction* — the power to adjudicate specific matters; and (3) *enforcement jurisdiction* — the power to enforce laws and regulations.

The international scope of application of the FIEA must accordingly be considered in two separate categories: the international scope of application of the law and regulations (legislative jurisdiction), and that of powers of enforcement (enforcement jurisdiction).

c. The territoriality principle and the effect principle

Several approaches can be cited to understanding the international scope of application of the FIEA and related regulations: (1) the *territoriality principle*, under which the FIEA and related regulations are applied if any of the regulated activity takes place on Japanese territory; (2) the *effect principle*, under which the FIEA and related regulations are applied if any legal interest that they seek to protect may have been violated; and (3) the *modified effect principle*, which is based on the territoriality principle, with the scope of application being modified by factoring in the effect principle if the goals of the FIEA and related regulations cannot otherwise be adequately attained. Specific questions, however, need to be analyzed in accordance with the individual facts.

The territoriality principle is subdivided into the *subjective territoriality*

*181*

*principle*, under which the country in which the actor is located can exercise jurisdiction, and the *objective territoriality principle*, under which the country in which the effects of the act occur can exercise jurisdiction. But because the distinction between act and effect is not always clear, (1) above, the territoriality principle, should be understood to subsume both. To cite Section 9200 (b) of the so-called Dodd-Frank Act enacted by the United States on July 21, 2010, in response to the financial crisis, the effect principle recognizes that Japan has jurisdiction when an act committed outside Japan has a "foreseeable substantial effect" within its borders.

If the "effect" of the effect principle is identified with the "effect" of the objective territoriality principle, the effect principle may be regarded as a subtype of the territoriality principle; the distinction between the two is relative.

## 2. International scope of application of the FIEA and related regulations

### a. Four types

We begin by examining the international scope of application of the FIEA and related regulations in terms of legislative jurisdiction. Before considering specifics, it will be useful to classify transactions into four types depending on the country where the actor is located: (1) internal-internal; (2) internal-external; (3) external-internal; and (4) external-external. It should be kept in mind, however, that what follows is only a rough typology, as there may be cases where the dividing line between the different types is not necessarily clear.

### b. Internal-internal transactions

Internal-internal transactions — transactions conducted domestically in Japan by domestic actors — are subject to the FIEA and related regulations under the (subjective) territoriality principle.

Even if the party with which a domestic actor deals is a "non-resident" (Article 6(1)(vi) of the Foreign Exchange Act), the transaction may still be classified in this category as long as the non-resident in question is, for example, located in Japan.

When determining whether an act constitutes a public offering of

Chapter 2   Scope of application and financial administration

securities, for example, non-residents solicited domestically in Japan are counted in the number of individuals solicited. Whether solicitation is conducted inside Japan or outside Japan is, practically speaking, determined not by whether the individual solicited is a resident or a non-resident, but by whether the securities acquired by the non-resident circulate domestically in Japan.

c. Internal-external transactions

Internal-external transactions — transactions initiated domestically in Japan by a domestic actor, which have a cross-border effect outside Japan — are subject to the FIEA and related regulations under the (subjective) territoriality principle, because the domestic actor may be considered to act domestically in Japan.

To give several specific examples, first, the FIEA is thought generally to protect investors who are "residents" of Japan (Article 6(1)(v) of the Foreign Exchange Act) but not necessarily non-resident foreign investors. However, if, for example, a financial instruments business operator markets and sells a product to a non-resident from within Japan, or conducts investment management within Japan, the non-resident in question is protected. On that assumption, non-residents are included among those targeted by private placements to professional investors (Article 2(3)(ii) (b) (β)), and foreign juridical persons are included among professional investors and professional fund investors (Article 2(31)(iv), 61(1)(i) of the FIEA; Article 17-12(1)(xiii) of the Financial Instruments and Exchange Act Implementing Order; Article 23(x) of the Cabinet Office Ordinance Regarding the Definitions of Article 2 of the FIEA).

Second, it becomes grounds for filing an extraordinary report if an issue or distribution of securities with a total issue value or distribution value of at least one hundred million yen is initiated outside Japan by a company filing an annual securities report (Article 24-5(4) of the FIEA; Article 19(1)(2) (i) of the Cabinet Office Ordinance on Corporate Disclosure).

Third, a foreign investment trust, even if none of its investors are resident in Japan, must be registered as an investment management business if it is directly set up and directed from Japan (see Article 2(8)(xiv) of the FIEA; Article 1-11 of the Financial Instruments and Exchange Act Implementing

Order; Article 16(1)(ix-ii) of the Cabinet Office Ordinance Regarding the Definitions of Article 2 of the FIEA).

Fourth, an officer of a domestic company listed in Japan is guilty of insider trading if, after coming to know about an undisclosed material fact pertaining to business or other matters of that listed company, he or she places an order from Japan to sell or purchase American Depositary Receipts (ADRs) of that company listed on the New York Stock Exchange (NYSE) in the United States (Articles 166(1) and 163(1) of the FIEA; Article 27-4(iv) of the Financial Instruments and Exchange Act Implementing Order).

### d. External-internal transactions

External-internal transactions — transactions initiated outside Japan by an external actor, which have a cross-border effect inside Japan — are also subject to the FIEA and related regulations under the (objective) territoriality principle.

To give several specific examples, first, if, on the Japanese secondary market, a foreign investor invests in share certificates issued by a domestic company listed in Japan, that investor is subject to large-volume shareholdings report regulations, takeover bid regulations, the requirement to file reports of sale and purchase, insider trading restrictions, and so on.

Second, if, outside Japan, a non-resident investor sells or purchases share certificates issued by a domestic company listed in Japan, or even sells or purchases depositary receipts (DRs) for those share certificates issued outside Japan, that investor is subject to takeover bid regulations, large-volume shareholdings report regulations, the requirement to file reports of sale and purchase, insider trading restrictions, and such (Articles 27-2(1), 27-23(1), 163(1) and 166(1) of the FIEA; Articles 6(1)(v), 14-4-2 (iii) and 27-4 (iv) of the Financial Instruments and Exchange Act Implementing Order). This is a case of factoring in the effect principle.

Third, a foreign securities broker is, unless registered, in principle forbidden from conducting any acts constituting securities-related business with a counterparty in Japan (Article 58-2 of the FIEA; Article 17-3 of the Financial Instruments and Exchange Act Implementing Order). In this regard, the posting of notices advertising securities-related business acts on a website or the like by a foreign securities broker is as a rule, for the

Chapter 2 Scope of application and financial administration

purposes of regulatory supervision, classified as "solicitation" (X-1-2 of the Comprehensive Guidelines for Supervision of Financial Instruments Business Operators, Etc.). That classification factors in the effect principle.

Fourth, a system is in place for granting partial permission to conduct underwriting to foreign securities brokers, one condition of which is that, from the standpoint of the territoriality principle, the subject acts be conducted "within Japan" (Article 59(1) of the FIEA; Article 17-4 of the Financial Instruments and Exchange Act Implementing Order).

Fifth, self-management of so-called foreign collective investment schemes (foreign funds) is subject to regulation (Article 2(8)(xv)(c) and (2)(vi) of the FIEA). Further, a person engaged in the investment advisory business or investment management business in a foreign state may, unless registered, engage in that business only with certain specified persons (Article 61 of the FIEA; Article 17-11 of the Financial Instruments and Exchange Act Implementing Order). For example, even if a person engaged in the investment management business in a foreign state engages in the act of managing an investment outside Japan, that person is subject to the FIEA and related regulations if the investor is resident in Japan, regardless of whether or not the investment was solicited in Japan; for the effect of that act is felt by the resident in question.

e. External-external transactions

External-external transactions — transactions conducted between foreign actors outside Japan, whose effect also occurs outside Japan — are, under the territoriality principle, as a rule not subject to the FIEA and related regulations.

To give several specific examples, first, if, outside Japan, a non-resident investor sells or purchases share certificates issued by a foreign company listed in Japan, that investor is understood as a rule not to be subject to large-volume shareholdings report regulations, takeover bid regulations, the requirement to file reports of sale and purchase, insider trading restrictions, and so on.

Second, the FIEA and related regulations do not as a rule apply when (1) outside Japan, a foreign securities broker relays an order from a non-resident client, placing an order for an on-exchange transaction with a

*185*

Japanese financial instruments business operator (entrusted brokerage); (2) outside Japan, a person engaged in the investment management business in a foreign state concludes a discretionary investment contract with a non-resident foreign investor and manages that investor's investments; or (3) outside Japan, a fund manager located outside Japan solicits only non-residents to acquire shares in the fund in question, or manages assets invested in by non-residents only.

Third, a non-Japan-related rating — that is, a credit rating assigned by an overseas location of a credit rating agency that is a foreign corporation — is considered exempt from FIEA regulations if it satisfies each of the following conditions: (1) the credit rating is not of a financial instrument intended for solicitation by a domestic financial instruments business operator; (2) the stakeholders in the rating are not domiciled in Japan; and (3) if the instrument is a securitized product, the main underlying assets are not located in Japan.

Fourth, although a foreign branch of a financial instruments business operator is legally the same entity as a domestic actor, its activities outside Japan should basically be treated as external-external transactions, like activities conducted outside Japan by a foreign affiliate. For example, the FIEA and related regulations do not as a rule apply in cases where, outside Japan, a foreign branch of a financial instruments business operator underwrites securities issued by a foreign corporation. Further, whereas restrictions on banks' scope of business under the Banking Act apply also to foreign branches of banks, registered financial institution regulations under the FIEA do not apply to foreign transactions undertaken by foreign branches of banks with non-residents.

Application of the FIEA and related regulations to external-external transactions should be recognized only in exceptional cases justifiable in light of the effect principle, such as putative attempts to evade the law. For that reason the interpretation of the Financial Services Agency (FSA) — "a domestic operator managing a foreign investment trust through a foreign branch that is legally part of the same entity is itself subject to the FIEA as an investment manager" (response to public comments, Dec. 21, 2010) — should be understood in a limited sense.

*186*

# 3. International enforcement of the FIEA and related regulations

a. Enforcement jurisdiction

Even if the FIEA and related regulations can be applied internationally, however, it is another question whether the FSA and the Securities and Exchange Surveillance Commission (SESC) can enforce them against violators, for the question of enforcement jurisdiction arises. Unlike legislative jurisdiction, the exercise of enforcement jurisdiction in the territory of a foreign state is not considered permitted except with the consent of the state in question.

For example, the FSA has the authority to order submission of reports and materials by major shareholders of financial instruments business operators and to conduct inspections (Article 56-2(2) of the FIEA), but it cannot in practice exercise that authority over major foreign shareholders outside Japan. Conversely, foreign officials have been observed for example visiting financial instruments business operators on Japanese soil, but this is purely voluntary: the authority vested in such officials under foreign laws and regulations to order submission of reports and materials and conduct inspections cannot be exercised in Japan.

b. International exchange of information and Article 189 of the FIEA

On the other hand, given the increasing globalization of financial instruments transactions and markets, the exchange of information with foreign authorities is essential if the authorities regulating financial instruments transactions in a particular country or region are to properly oversee them and regulate the market, thus ensuring their soundness.

The Japanese Financial Services Agency and Securities and Exchange Surveillance Commission exchange information on financial instruments transactions and markets with foreign authorities in the following ways: (1) the Japanese authorities request information from foreign authorities, who then provide that information; (2) the Japanese authorities spontaneously provide information to foreign authorities; (3) foreign authorities request information from the Japanese authorities, who then provide that information; and (4) foreign authorities spontaneously provide information to the Japanese authorities.

The FIEA makes no specific provision for (1), (2), or (4). With regard to (2), the Japanese authorities, while taking care to protect Japan's public interests and the rights and interests of the Japanese people, voluntarily provide information to foreign authorities insofar as is necessary and appropriate and within the bounds of Japanese laws and regulations pertaining to, e.g., the confidentiality obligations of national government employees. For example, the British authorities fined a British hedge fund after being tipped off by the SESC (SESC press release, Aug. 2, 2006).

In the case of (3), the Japanese authorities are voluntarily able to provide foreign authorities with information publicly available in Japan; but if acceding to the request necessitates gathering information anew from the parties concerned, legal grounds are required. Those grounds are provided by Article 189 of the FIEA. If a foreign financial instruments regulatory authority requests cooperation in regard to an administrative investigation being conducted in order to enforce the foreign state's laws and regulations corresponding to the FIEA, the FSA Commissioner or the SESC may, under certain conditions, order persons who conduct sales or purchases of securities or similar transactions, or other persons concerned or witnesses, to submit reports and materials (Article 189(1) of the FIEA; Article 38(9) (ii) of the Financial Instruments and Exchange Act Implementing Order).

c. Securities MOUs

The Japanese Financial Services Agency has, in line with the intent of Article 189 of the FIEA, agreed on a framework for exchange of information with the world's main security regulators by signing several memorandums of understanding — the so-called securities MOUs.

Securities MOUs may be either (1) multilateral or (2) bilateral between two agencies. With respect to the former, the FSA signed the Multilateral MOU of the International Organization of Securities Commissions (IOSCO) on February 5, 2008. With respect to the latter, it has concluded MOUs with seven market regulators (including America's SEC) in six countries and regions.

These securities MOUs, however, have the status of non-legally binding statements of intent, and are implemented only insofar as permitted by

Chapter 2　Scope of application and financial administration

existing domestic laws and regulations such as Article 189 of the FIEA.

d. Memorandum of cooperation on market supervision

The FSA has also signed a Memorandum of Cooperation (MOC) on supervision of the derivatives market with the U.S. Commodity Futures Trading Commission (Mar. 10, 2014), which supplements the securities MOUs.

This memorandum allows for voluntary on-site visits to cross-border covered entities physically located in the other country.

# Chapter 3

## Disclosure requirements
—— Disclosure of corporate affairs and other related matters

*Masao Yanaga*

# A. Disclosure on primary markets — notification for public offerings, secondary distributions, specified procedures related to securities issuance for reorganization, and specified procedures relating to securities delivery for reorganization

Except for exempted securities (1. below), in principle notification through the submission of a securities registration statement is required when conducting a public offering of securities (Article 2 of the Financial Instruments and Exchange Act) or secondary distribution of securities (Article 4(1) of the Financial Instruments and Exchange Act). However, in cases where information regarding the issuer has already been disclosed and in cases where it is considered inappropriate to request notification of the balance of costs and benefits (e.g., where the total issue value or total distribution value is less than ¥100 million), the obligation for notification is waived (2. below). However, even in cases where the obligation for notification is waived, submission of a written notice of securities is still sometimes requested (C. below).

In cases where specified procedures relating to securities issuance for reorganization or specified procedures relating to securities delivery for reorganization are conducted, in principle a securities registration statement must be submitted (Article 4(1) of the Financial Instruments and Exchange Act).

For this purpose, the term "specified procedures relating to securities issuance for reorganization" means maintaining prior disclosure documents based on the Companies Act (procedures relating to securities issuance for reorganization) by a company absorbed in an absorption-type merger, demerger (limited to cases where shares or equity in the surviving company or established company is given as a dividend in kind), wholly-owned subsidiary company in a share exchange, or wholly-owned subsidiary company in a share transfer (company subject to reorganization; Article 2-2 (4) (i) of the Financial Instruments and Exchange Act; Article 2-2 of the

Chapter 3   Disclosure requirements

Implementing Order for the Financial Instruments and Exchange Act Article) in cases where new securities are issued because of company merger, demerger, share exchange or share transfer (collectively, referred to as "reorganization") (including similar cases as specified by a cabinet office ordinance)[1] and there are a large number of holders (company shareholders subject to reorganization, etc.; Article 2-2 (4) (i) of the Financial Instruments and Exchange Act) of the following issued by the company subject to reorganization: (i) shares; (ii) share option certificates; (iii) bonds with share options; (iv) securities trust beneficiary certificates with (i) - (iii) as the entrusted securities; or (v) depository receipts indicating rights pertaining to (i)-(iii) (Article 2-2(4) (i) of the Financial Instruments and Exchange Act; Article 2-3 of the Financial Instruments and Exchange Act Implementing Order) or which meet certain other requirements (Article 2-2(4) of the Financial Instruments and Exchange Act).

When the securities newly issued under the reorganization are shares, bonds (including bonds with share options), share option certificates or other type I securities, they are subject to specified procedures relating to securities issuance for reorganization (i) in cases where there are 50 or more shareholders subject to reorganization (except where they are all qualified institutional investors) (Article 2-2(4) (i) of the Financial Instruments and Exchange Act; Article 2-4 of the Financial Instruments and Exchange Act Implementing Order) and (ii) in cases other than i) those where only qualified institutional investors are shareholders subject to reorganization, and in cases which do not constitute cases where a Cabinet Order provides there is little concern that the securities issued under the procedures relating to securities issuance for reorganization will be transferred to parties other than qualified institutional investors (Article 2-2(4) (i) (a) of the Financial Instruments and Exchange Act; Article 1-4 of the Financial Instruments and Exchange Act Implementing Order; Article 11 of the Cabinet Office Ordinance regarding the Definitions Specified under Article 2 of the Financial Instruments and Exchange Act [hereinafter referred to as

---

1   As of now, none have been specified.

"Cabinet Office Ordinance Regarding Definitions"]) those which do not constitute cases where a Cabinet Order prescribes that there is little concern that the securities issued under the procedures relating to securities issuance for reorganization will be owned by a large number of shareholders (Article 2-2 (4) (ii) (b) Financial Instruments and Exchange Act; Article 2-4-2 (1-7) (ii) of the Financial Instruments and Exchange Act Implementing Order; Article 13 of the Cabinet Office Ordinance Regarding Definitions). On the other hand, when securities issued by the reorganization are type II securities, they are subject to specified procedures relating to securities issuance for reorganization when a cabinet order provides that the shareholders subject to reorganization will be a considerably large number of persons, and a considerably large number of persons is deemed to be 500 persons or more (Article 2-2 (4) (iii) of the Financial Instruments and Exchange Act; Article 2-4 of the Financial Instruments and Exchange Act Implementing Order).

The term "specified procedures relating to securities delivery for reorganization" means maintaining prior disclosure documents (delivery procedures) by a company absorbed in an absorption-type merger, demerger (limited to cases where shares or equity in the surviving company or established company are given as dividends in kind), wholly-owned subsidiary company in a share exchange, or wholly-owned subsidiary company in a share transfer in cases where already-issued securities are offered because of merger, demerger, share exchange or share transfer (excluding cases corresponding to cases similar to procedures relating to securities issuance for reorganization) and there are a large number of shareholders subject to reorganization, or which meet certain other requirements (Article 2-2 (5) of the Financial Instruments and Exchange Act)

Where the already-issued securities delivered because of reorganization are shares, bonds (including bonds with share options), share option certificates or other type I securities, they are subject to specified procedures relating to securities issuance for reorganization (i) when there are 50 or more company shareholders subject to reorganization (except when they are all

Chapter 3  Disclosure requirements

qualified institutional investors) (Article 2-2 (5) (i) of the Financial Instruments and Exchange Act; Article 2-4 of the Financial Instruments and Exchange Act Implementing Order) and (ii) in cases other than i) those where only qualified institutional investors are shareholders subject to reorganization, and in cases which do not constitute cases where a cabinet order provides that there is little concern that the securities offered under the procedures relating to securities delivery for reorganization will be transferred to parties other than qualified institutional investors (Article 2-2 (5) (ii) (a) of the Financial Instruments and Exchange Act; Article 1-7-4 of the Financial Instruments and Exchange Act Implementing Order; Article 13-4 of the Cabinet Office Ordinance Regarding Definitions), and ii) those which do not constitute cases where a Cabinet Order provides that there is little concern that the securities delivered under the procedures relating to securities issuance for reorganization will be owned by a large number of shareholders (Article 2-2 (5) (ii) (b) of the Financial Instruments and Exchange Act; Article 2-6-2(1-8-4) (iii) of the Financial Instruments and Exchange Act Implementing Order; Article 13-7 of the Cabinet Office Ordinance Regarding Definitions).

Where securities offered because of reorganization are type II securities (limited to interests in securities investment business, etc. that are subject to the disclosure requirements), they are subject to specified procedures relating to securities delivery for reorganization when a Cabinet Order provides the shareholders subject to reorganisation are a considerably large number of persons, and a considerably large number of persons is deemed to be 500 persons or more (Article 2-2(5) (iii) of the Financial Instruments and Exchange Act; Article 2-7 of the Financial Instruments and Exchange Act Implementing Order).

Considering that the Financial Instruments and Exchange Act is a statute designed to protect investors inside Japan, in principle the disclosure regulations in Primary Markets prescribed by the Financial Instruments and Exchange Act are considered to apply to public offerings and secondary distributions inside Japan, namely, in cases where acts of solicitation take place inside Japan.[2] This interpretation is also consistent with the request,

*195*

for continuous disclosure companies, to submit an extraordinary report when conducting a public offering or secondary distribution in areas outside Japan.[3] The issue of whether acts of solicitation are conducted inside Japan is determined based on whether the investors subject to solicitation are located within Japan, and for investors subject to solicitation outside Japan it is based on whether the acts of solicitation were conducted inside Japan.

# 1. Exempted securities

Among those securities defined in Article 2 of the Financial Instruments and Exchange Act, the following securities provided in Article 3 of the Act are exempted from the application of disclosure regulations, including the securities registration statement system.

(1) National government bonds (Article 2(1)(i) and Article 3(i) of the Financial Instruments and Exchange Act);

(2) Municipal bonds (Article 2(1)(ii) and Article 3(i) of the Financial Instruments and Exchange Act);

(3) Debentures issued by a juridical person under a special act (excluding specified bonds prescribed in the Act on the Securitization of Assets, investment corporation debentures prescribed in the Investment Trust Act, and social medical corporation bonds prescribed in the Medical Care Act) (Article 2 (1) (iii) and Article 3 (ii) of the Financial Instruments and Exchange Act; Article 2-8 of the Financial Instruments and Exchange Act Implementing Order);

---

2    Regarding the number of holders who should be included in a "considerably large number of persons" for public offerings and secondary distributions of type II securities for the purpose of Article 2, paragraph 3, item 3 and paragraph 4, item 3 of the Financial Instruments and Exchange Act, the Financial Services Agency interprets that these are persons who came to hold securities as a result of acts of solicitation considered to have been conducted inside Japan. "Results of Public Comments on 'Draft Cabinet Orders and Draft Cabinet Office Ordinances regarding the Financial Instruments and Exchange Act System,'" "Outline of Comments and FSA's Position on Comments" (July 31, 2007), p. 29, No. 53.

3    When the issuer is a continuous disclosure company, the submission of extraordinary reports is sometimes required for issuances that do not fall under issuances or public offerings of securities outside Japan, (for details, see D. below).

Chapter 3 Disclosure requirements

(4) Investment securities issued by a juridical person established under a special statute (excluding preferred equity investment certificates prescribed in the Act on Preferred Equity Investment, preferred equity investment certificates and securities indicating preemptive rights for new preferred equity investment prescribed in the Act on Securitization of Assets, and investment securities or foreign investment securities prescribed in the Investment Trust Act (Article 2(1) (vi) and Article 3 (ii) of the Financial Instruments and Exchange Act);

(5) Beneficiary certificates of loan trusts (Article 2(1) (xii) and Article 3 (ii) of the Financial Instruments and Exchange Act);

(6) Type II securities (trust beneficial interests, equity in group investment schemes, etc.) (Article 2(2) of the Financial Instruments and Exchange Act); excluding interests in securities investment business, etc.[4] (Article 3(iii) of the Financial Instruments and Exchange Act; Article 2-9 and 2-10 of the Financial Instruments and Exchange Act Implementing Order).

---

**4** (i) Equity of group investment schemes concerning businesses where it is over 50% of the total amount of money, and other assets invested or contributed by investors is invested in securities as well as rights based on foreign laws and regulations that have a similar characteristics (Article 3(iii) (a) of the Financial Instruments and Exchange Act; Article 2-9(1) and Article 2-10(i) (v) of the Financial Instruments and Exchange Act Implementing Order) (excluding the equity in the product fund in cases where all investments and contributions by the product fund are invested in a single juridical person but the relevant juridical person does not invest over 50% of the amount of the relevant investment and other assets in securities, and the relevant juridical person is prohibited from receiving investments from two or more persons, as well as equity in the group investment scheme in cases where the group investment scheme that received the monetary investment uses contributed funds to acquire race horses, and uses only the race horses as contribution in kind to other persons; and the persons receiving the relevant contribution in kind are prohibited from receiving investments from two or more persons, and the persons receiving the relevant contribution in kind do not use the relevant race horses to acquire securities) (Article 2-9(1) (i) (ii) of the Financial Instruments and Exchange Act Implementing Order; Article 1-3 of the Cabinet Office Ordinance on Specified Securities Disclosure).

(ii) Among trust beneficial interests, beneficial interests to trusts where over 50% of the total amount of assets belonging to the trust assets are invested in securities and managed, as well as rights to foreign persons with similar characteristics to such beneficial interests (however, excluding trust contracts regarding welfare pensions

(7) Bonds for which the government guarantees the redemption of principal or the payment of interest (Article 3 (iv) of the Financial Instruments and Exchange Act); and

(8) As securities specified by a cabinet order, among securities or certificates that have been issued by a foreign state or foreign person and have the characteristics of securities or certificates listed in Article 2, paragraph 1, items 1 to 9 or items 12 to 16 of the Financial Instruments and Exchange Act (Article 2 (1) (xvii) of the Financial Instruments and Exchange Act), those debentures issued by an organ established by a treaty signed by Japan and for which consent of the Government of Japan is required for public offering or secondary distribution inside Japan by the treaty (Article 3 (v) of the Financial

---

based on the Employee's Pension Insurance Act and other pensions, and trust contracts regarding separate management of subscriber protection trust contracts concluded based on the Act on Book-Entry Transfer of Company Bonds, Shares, etc.) (Article 3 (iii) (b) of the Financial Instruments and Exchange Act; Article 2-10(1) (i) & (ii) of the Financial Instruments and Exchange Act Implementing Order).

(iii) Among membership rights of general partnership companies, limited partnership companies and limited liability companies, those conducting business by investing over 50% of the total amount of contributions in securities as well as rights based on foreign laws and regulations that have similar characteristics (Article 3 (iii) (b) of the Financial Instruments and Exchange Act; Article 2-10(i) (iii) (iv) of the Financial Instruments and Exchange Act Implementing Order).

(iv) School loan claims (claims on loans to school corporations) that meet all the following requirements: (1) the interest rate and repayment period of the relevant loans is uniform and the loans are from multiple persons [excluding loans where the relevant loans are interest free], and (2) some or all of the relevant loans are made by parties other than persons enrolled at schools established by the educational foundation receiving the loans concerned or by other interested persons as prescribed by a cabinet office ordinance (parents of persons enrolled, alumni, etc.), or the transfer of the claims on the relevant loans to parties other than interested persons is not prohibited, and (3) some or all of the relevant loans are from persons other than persons who can conduct the loans concerned as a business under banking or other laws, or the transfer of the claims to the relevant loans to persons other than banks (including claim collection companies prescribed by the Act on Special Measures Concerning Claim Management and Collection Business) is not prohibited (Article 3 (iii) (c) of the Financial Instruments and Exchange Act; Article 1-3-4 and Article 2-10(2) of the Financial Instruments and Exchange Act Implementing Order; Article 8 of the Cabinet Office Ordinance Regarding Definitions).

Chapter 3 Disclosure requirements

Instruments and Exchange Act; Article 2-11 of the Financial Instruments and Exchange Act Implementing Order).

## 2. Exemption from obligation to notify

Even in cases where public offerings and secondary distribution of type I securities do not fall under exempted securities, they are exempt from the obligation for notification under the following cases (1) through (5) (proviso to Article 4(1) of the Financial Instruments and Exchange Act). Type II securities are exempt from the obligation for notification under cases (2), (3), and (5).

(1) In cases where the other parties to a public offering or secondary distribution of securities have already obtained or can easily obtain information pertaining to the securities concerned and issuer of the securities concerned as specified by a cabinet order (Article 4(1)(i) of the Financial Instruments and Exchange Act).

This is referred to as the "stock options exception." These are cases where a company that is the issuer of share option certificates or of securities with the characteristics of share option certificates issued by a foreign company (share option certificates, etc.) (Article 2-12 of the Financial Instruments and Exchange Act Implementing Order) which have transfer restrictions conducts solicitation for acquisition or solicitation for sales of the share option certificates only to directors, accounting advisors, company auditors or executive officers or employees of the company or its wholly-owned subsidiaries or wholly-owned subsidiaries of subsidiaries (Article (1)(i) of the Financial Instruments and Exchange Act; Article 2-12 of the Financial Instruments and Exchange Act Implementing Order; Article 2(1)(ii) of the Cabinet Office Ordinance on Disclosure of Corporate Affairs, etc.).[5]

---

5  Even in cases where the obligation for notification is waived, when the total issue price or total distribution price is ¥100 million or more, an extraordinary report must be submitted (Article 24-5(iv) of the Financial Instruments and Exchange Act; Article 19(2)(ii-2) of the Cabinet Office Ordinance on Disclosure of Corporate Affairs, etc.).

*199*

For items subject to transfer restrictions, in cases of share option certificates issued by a domestic company, the matters stated in Article 236, paragraph 1, item 6 of the Companies Act, that are the purport of "the approval of the relevant joint-stock company is required for acquisition of the relevant share option certificates via transfer" must be included as a description of the share option certificates, and in cases of securities with the characteristics of share option certificates issued by a foreign company, they must have a restriction prohibiting transfer of the securities (Article 2-12 of the Financial Instruments and Exchange Act Implementing Order; Article 2(1) of the Cabinet Office Ordinance on Disclosure of Corporate Affairs, etc.), and transfer restrictions in the contract concluded between the company and the counterparty alone do not meet the requirements for exemption of notification.[6]

(2)   Among procedures relating to securities issuance for reorganization and procedures relating to securities delivery for reorganization, (i) cases where disclosure has not been conducted for shares (including share option certificates and other securities specified by a cabinet order[7]) issued by a company absorbed in an absorption-type merger or other company subject to reorganization, and (ii) cases where disclosure has already been conducted for the securities being issued or delivered (Article 4(1)(ii) of the Financial Instruments and Exchange Act).

(3)   Secondary distribution of securities for which disclosure has already been conducted (Article 4 (1) (iii) of the Financial Instruments and Exchange Act).[8]

---

**6**   "Results of Public Comments on 'Draft Cabinet Orders and Draft Cabinet Office Ordinances Regarding the Financial Instruments and Exchange Act System,'" "Outline of Comments and FSA's Position on Comments" (July 31, 2007), p. 122, No. 2.

**7**   Share option certificates, bonds with share options, beneficiary certificates of securities in trust with share certificates, share option certificates, or bonds with share options as the entrusted securities, as well as depository receipts representing rights to shares, share option certificates or bonds with share options.

Chapter 3   Disclosure requirements

1 )   In cases where a notification regarding a public offering, secondary distribution, general solicitation for securities acquired by qualified institutional investors, or general solicitation for securities acquired by professional investors already conducted itself for the securities concerned is still in effect (excluding cases where the issuer of the securities concerned is exempted from the obligation to submit annual securities reports under the proviso to Article 24, paragraph 1 of the Financial Instruments and Exchange Act) (Article 4(7)(i) of the Financial Instruments and Exchange Act).

2 )   In cases where a notification regarding a secondary distribution for the same issue as an issue of the securities concerned that has already been conducted or regarding a public offering or secondary distribution (including general solicitation for securities acquisition by qualified institutional investors as well as general solicitation for securities acquisition by professional investors) (Article 1(xi) of the Cabinet Office Ordinance on Disclosure of Corporate Affairs, etc.; Article 1(xii) of the Cabinet Office Ordinance on Disclosure of Information, etc. on Specified Securities [hereinafter referred to as the "Cabinet Office Ordinance on Specified Securities Disclosure"]) for the same class of securities as the securities concerned (Article 10-2(1) of the Cabinet Office Ordinance Regarding Definitions) is still in effect (excluding cases where the issuer of the securities concerned is exempted from the obligation to submit securities reports under the proviso to Article 24, paragraph 1 of the Financial Instruments and Exchange Act) (Article 4(7)(ii) of the Financial Instruments and Exchange Act; Article 6(i) of the Cabinet Office Ordinance on Disclosure of Corporate Affairs, etc.; Article 7(i) of the Cabinet Office Ordinance on Specified Securities Disclosure).

3 )   In cases where a shelf registration regarding a public offering or secondary distribution for the securities concerned or for the same

---

**8**   A securities written notice must be submitted in certain cases such as the secondary distribution of shares or share option certificates held by the securities issuer or related parties (Article 4(6) of the Financial Instruments and Exchange Act; Article 4 (4) of the Cabinet Office Ordinance on Disclosure of Corporate Affairs, etc.).

*201*

class of securities as the securities concerned that has already been conducted is effective and a shelf-registration supplement regarding the public offering or secondary distribution for any of the securities regarding the shelf registration has already been submitted (excluding cases where the issuer of the securities concerned is exempted from the obligation to submit securities reports under the proviso to Article 24, paragraph 1 of the Financial Instruments and Exchange Act) (Article 4(7)(ii) of the Financial Instruments and Exchange Act; Article 6(ii) of the Cabinet Office Ordinance on Disclosure of Corporate Affairs, etc.).

4) In cases where the securities concerned are listed or over-the-counter registered and a securities report for the business year or specified period immediately before listing or over-the-counter registration is submitted (Article 4 (7) (ii) of the Financial Instruments and Exchange Act; Article 6(iii) of the Cabinet Office Ordinance on Disclosure of Corporate Affairs, etc.; Article 7(ii) of the Cabinet Office Ordinance on Specified Securities Disclosure).

5) In cases where the securities concerned fall under the number of shareholders standard (see D.), where a securities report has been submitted for any business year after the business year in which the securities concerned fell under the standard (excluding cases where the issuer of the securities concerned is exempted from the obligation to submit securities reports under the proviso to Article 24, paragraph 1 of the Financial Instruments and Exchange Act) (Article 4(7)(ii) of the Financial Instruments and Exchange Act; Article 6 (iv) of the Cabinet Office Ordinance on Disclosure of Corporate Affairs, etc.).

Specified securities including type II securities are exempt from notification in cases 1), 2) and 4), but no exemption is provided for cases 3) or 5) (see Article 7 of the Cabinet Office Ordinance on Specified Securities Disclosure).

(4) Among secondary distributions of securities already issued in foreign states or provided by a cabinet order as equivalent (limited to those conducted by financial instruments business operators, etc.), those

Chapter 3   Disclosure requirements

which meet the requirement that information on the sale and purchase prices of the securities concerned can easily be obtained inside Japan (Article 4(1)(iv) of the Financial Instruments and Exchange Act).[9]

Securities to which this exception applies are limited to securities specified in Article 2-12-3 of the Financial Instruments and Exchange Act Implementing Order, and the requirements specified by that article must be met in accordance with the class of securities. Specifically, as requirements are set in accordance with the class of securities, it must be easy to obtain information regarding domestic sales and the purchase prices of the relevant foreign securities using the Internet or other means, the relevant foreign securities must be continuously bought and sold in foreign states, and it must be easy to obtain information regarding the issuer of the securities concerned using the Internet or other means.

(5)   Public offerings or secondary distributions of securities of which the total issue value or total distribution value is less than ¥100 million (Article 4 (1) (v) of the Financial Instruments and Exchange Act; "small-amount exemption").[10,11]

---

9   The submission and disclosure of "information on foreign securities" (see B.4. below) is also mandatory (Article 27-32-2(1) of the Financial Instruments and Exchange Act).

10   In cases where a securities registration statement was not submitted because the total issue price or total distribution price was projected to be less than ¥100 million but the total issue price or total distribution price is subsequently projected to be ¥100 million or more, subsequent public offering or secondary distribution is prohibited as long as a securities registration statement is not submitted (Guidelines on Corporate Affairs Disclosure, B4-15). Conversely, in cases where a total issue price or total distribution price is less than ¥100 million after submitting a securities registration statement, the securities registration statement is withdrawn (Guidelines on Corporate Affairs Disclosure, B-4-13).

11   Even when the small-amount exemption applies, when the total issue price or total distribution price exceeds ¥10 million, a securities written notice (see C. below) must be submitted (Article 4(5) & (6) of the Financial Instruments and Exchange Act; Article 4(5) of the Cabinet Office Ordinance on Disclosure of Corporate Affairs, etc.; Article 5(4) of the Cabinet Office Ordinance on Specified Securities Disclosure).

Registration is not required not only for public offerings and secondary distributions of securities of which the total issue value or total distribution value is less than ¥100 million, but also for specified procedures relating to securities issuance for reorganization and specified procedures relating to securities delivery for reorganization of which the total issue value or total distribution value [12] is less than ¥100 million.

Because an issuer could attempt to gain exemption from the obligation for notification by dividing a public offering or secondary distribution of securities with a total issue value or total distribution value of more than ¥100 million into multiple public offerings or secondary distributions, even where a public offering or secondary distribution of securities has a total issue value or total distribution value of less than ¥100 million, in certain cases, the obligation for notification is not waived and the submission of a securities registration statement is required (Article 4 (1) (v) of the Financial Instruments and Exchange Act; Article 2 (iii) of the Cabinet Office Ordinance on Disclosure of Corporate Affairs, etc.; Article 2 of the Cabinet Office Ordinance on Specified Securities Disclosure).

1 ) Annual sum totals

Notification is required where the sum of the total issue value or total distribution value of a public offering or secondary distribution of securities and the total issue value or total distribution value of public offerings or secondary distributions of the same class of securities within the year before the starting date of the relevant public offering or secondary distribution

---

12　In this case, the total issue price or total distribution price, in principle, is deemed to be the sum of the change in shareholders equity, shareholders equity carried forward and the shareholders equity as prescribed by the Companies Accounting Regulation, and where the amount of shareholders equity is not determined in the relevant procedures relating to securities issuance for reorganization or procedures relating to securities delivery for reorganization, a projected amount calculated using suitable methods is to be used as the total issue price or total distribution price (Guidelines on Corporate Affairs Disclosure, B4-22).

Chapter 3 Disclosure requirements

exceeds ¥100 million (Article 4(1)(v) of the Financial Instruments and Exchange Act; Article 2 (4) (ii) of the Cabinet Office Ordinance on Disclosure of Corporate Affairs, etc.; Article 2 (i) of the Cabinet Office Ordinance on Specified Securities Disclosure; Article 1-2(i) of the Cabinet Office Ordinance on Disclosure of Information etc. of Issuers of Foreign Government Bonds, etc. [hereinafter referred to as the "Cabinet Office Ordinance on Foreign Bonds"]). However, sum totals are not applied to public offerings and secondary distributions for which securities registration statements or shelf-registration supplements have been submitted or for public offerings or secondary distributions conducted before them with a total issue value or total distribution value of less than ¥100 million (Article 2(4)(ii) of the Cabinet Office Ordinance on Disclosure of Corporate Affairs, etc.; Article 2(i) of the Cabinet Office Ordinance on Specified Securities Disclosure; Article 1-2(i) of the Cabinet Office Ordinance on Foreign Bonds; Guidelines on Disclosure of Corporate Affairs, B4-77). Sum totals are also not applied to public offerings and secondary offerings that fall under the stock options exception (Article 2 (4) (ii) of the Cabinet Office Ordinance on Disclosure of Corporate Affairs, etc.).

For this purpose, "public offerings or secondary distributions of securities within the year before the starting date of the relevant public offering or secondary distribution" means public offerings or secondary distributions that were started within the past year (deemed as beginning on the day after the date the written notice of securities was submitted) as well as public offerings or secondary distributions with payment dates or delivery dates within the past year, with the day before the starting date of the relevant public offering or secondary distribution considered the starting date for the calculation (Guidelines on Disclosure of Corporate Affairs, B4-6). The total issue value or total distribution value of public offerings or secondary distributions of securities that have already been completed and must be summed up is calculated from the actual total issue value or total distribution value of the securities issued and sold (Guidelines on Disclosure of Corporate Affairs, B4-8).

Also, "the same class of securities" means the type in the categorisation of securities (shares, bonds, etc.) under each item of Article 2, paragraphs 1 and 2 of the Financial Instruments and Exchange Act that is the same (Article 1 (ii) of the Cabinet Office Ordinance on Disclosure of Corporate Affairs, etc.; Article 1 (x) of the Cabinet Office Ordinance on Specified Securities Disclosure); however, share option certificates are deemed to be the same class of securities as shares (Article 2 (1) (ix) of the Financial Instruments and Exchange Act) and bonds with share options are also deemed to be the same class of securities as shares and share option certificates (Article 2 (4) (ii) of the Cabinet Office Ordinance on Disclosure of Corporate Affairs, etc.). In cases where the sum total of bonds with share options is calculated together with shares for which public offerings have already been conducted, the calculation is made using the total issue value of shares issued or transferred by exercise of the share options attached to bonds with share options (Guidelines on Disclosure of Corporate Affairs, B4-5).

2 ) Public offerings where six-month sum totals apply
In cases of public offerings where six-month sum totals[13] are deemed to apply, notification is required where the sum of the total issue value of securities pertaining to the public offering and the total issue value of the same class of securities that were newly issued within the six months before the date of issuance of the securities exceeds ¥100 million (Article 2 (4) (iii) of the Cabinet Office Ordinance on Disclosure of Corporate Affairs, etc.; Article 2 (ii) of the Cabinet Office Ordinance on Specified Securities Disclosure; Article 1-2 (i-2) of the Cabinet Office Ordinance on Foreign Bonds).

---

13  In cases where there has been a private offering of "the same type" of securities to a small number of investors within the past six months, even when conducting solicitation for acquisition to 49 or fewer investors, where the sum of the number of investors solicited plus the number of investors solicited in the prior private offering to a small number of investors is 50 or more persons, this is not considered a private offering to a small number of investors, and is viewed as a public offering (Article 1-6 of the Financial Instruments and Exchange Act Implementing Order).

Chapter 3    Disclosure requirements

3 )   When secondary distribution monthly sum totals apply

In cases of secondary distributions where monthly sum totals[14] apply, notification is required where the sum of the total distribution value of securities pertaining to the secondary distribution and the total distribution value of the same class of securities that were newly issued within the month before the date of issuance of the securities exceeds ¥100 million (Article 2 (4) (iii-2) of the Cabinet Office Ordinance on Disclosure of Corporate Affairs, etc.; Article 2(ii-2) of the Cabinet Office Ordinance on Specified Securities Disclosure; Article 1-2 (i-3) of the Cabinet Office Ordinance on Foreign Bonds).

4 )   Parallel public offerings and secondary distributions

An obligation for notification arises when the sum of the total issue value or total distribution value of two or more sets of public offerings or secondary distributions of the same class of securities conducted in parallel is at least ¥100 million.

This means that even if either the total issue value of the public offering of securities or the total distribution value of the secondary distribution of securities conducted in parallel is less than ¥100 million, notification is required for each if the total of both is at least ¥100 million (Article 2(4) (iv) of the Cabinet Office Ordinance on Disclosure of Corporate Affairs, etc.; Article 2 (iii) of the Cabinet Office Ordinance on Specified Securities Disclosure; Article 1-2(ii) of the Cabinet Office Ordinance on Foreign Bonds Article). Also, public offerings or secondary distributions of the same class of securities conducted in parallel with public offerings and secondary offerings of securities with a total issue value or total distribution value of at least ¥100 million require notification even if their total issue value or total

---

14   In cases where there has been a private secondary distribution of "the same type" of securities to a small number of investors within the past one month, even when conducting solicitation for secondary distribution to 49 or fewer investors, where the sum of the number of investors solicited plus the number of investors solicited in the prior small number secondary distribution is 50 or more persons, this is not considered a private secondary distribution to a small number of investors (Article 1-8-3 of the Financial Instruments and Exchange Act Implementing Order).

*207*

distribution value is less than ¥100 million (Article 2(4)(v) of the Cabinet Office Ordinance on Disclosure of Corporate Affairs, etc.; Article 2(iv) of the Cabinet Office Ordinance on Specified Securities Disclosure; Article 1-2(iii) of the Cabinet Office Ordinance on Foreign Bonds). Furthermore, even if their total issue value or total distribution value is less than ¥100 million, notification is required for public offerings and secondary distributions of the same class of securities conducted in parallel with public offerings or secondary distributions with an annual sum (1. above) total issue value or total distribution value of ¥100 million or more (Article 2(4)(v) of the Cabinet Office Ordinance on Disclosure of Corporate Affairs, etc.; Article 2 (iv) of the Cabinet Office Ordinance on Specified Securities Disclosure; Article 1-2(iii) of the Cabinet Office Ordinance on Foreign Bonds; Guidelines on Disclosure of Corporate Affairs, B4-12).[15]

For this purpose, public offerings or secondary distributions "conducted in parallel" means that the payment dates or delivery dates are essentially the same (Guidelines on Disclosure of Corporate Affairs, B4-11). "The same class of securities" means that the type in the categorisation of securities under each item of Article 2, paragraphs 1 and 2 of the Financial Instruments and Exchange Act is the same.

5) Cases where the effect of notification has been suspended, etc.

In cases where there are false statements, etc. regarding material matters in a securities registration statement, the Prime Minister may order the suspension of the effect of the notification or extension of the waiting period (Article 10(1) and Article 11(1) of the Financial Instruments and Exchange Act). The Prime Minister may also suspend the effect of the notification or

---

15 In this case, unlike in case (i), the law explicitly states that public offerings and secondary distributions to which the stock option exception applies are not exempt from the application of annual sum totals, but the Financial Services Agency has indicated the opinion that these public offerings and secondary distributions are not included in parallel public offerings and secondary distributions in (4) and public offerings and secondary distributions of ¥100 million or more in (5) ("Outline of Public Comments Regarding the '[Draft] Guidelines Related to Implementing Partial Revision of the Securities and Exchange Act' and FSA's Position" (October 2, 2007), p. 3 No. 11.

*208*

Chapter 3 Disclosure requirements

shelf registration or extend the waiting period of other securities registration statements, shelf-registration statements or shelf-registration supplements submitted by the person who submitted the securities registration statement within one year from the date the statement was submitted (Article 11(1) of the Financial Instruments and Exchange Act). Similarly, in cases where a shelf registration statement or shelf registration supplement contains any false statements on material matters, the Prime Minister may suspend the effect of the shelf registration or extend the waiting period, and also suspend the effect of notification or shelf registration or extend the waiting period of other securities registration statements, shelf-registration statements and shelf-registration supplements submitted within one year (Article 23-10(3) and 23-11(1) of the Financial Instruments and Exchange Act). Notifying persons who are subject to such suspensions of effect or extensions of waiting periods are required to notify new securities public offerings and secondary distributions they conduct during the suspension or extension period even where the total issue value or total distribution value is less than ¥100 million (Article 2(4)(vi) & (vii) of the Cabinet Office Ordinance on Disclosure of Corporate Affairs, etc.; Article 2(v) & (vi) of the Cabinet Office Ordinance on Specified Securities Disclosure; Article 1-2(iv) & (v) of the Cabinet Office Ordinance on Foreign Bonds).

6) Cases of share option certificates

Notification is required when the securities for a public offering or secondary distribution are share option certificates and the sum of the total issue value or total distribution value and the payment amount upon exercise of the share options pertaining to the share option certificates (exercise value) is ¥100 million or more (Article 4(1)(v) of the Financial Instruments and Exchange Act; Article 2(4)(i) of the Cabinet Office Ordinance on Disclosure of Corporate Affairs, etc.). In cases (i) through (v) above as well, where the securities for a public offering or secondary distribution are share option certificates, whether the small-amount exemption applies is determined using the sum of the total issue value or total distribution value and the exercise value of the share options pertaining to the share option certificates (Article 2(4)(ii) of the Cabinet Office Ordinance on Disclosure of Corporate Affairs, etc.).

*209*

7) Cases of public offerings or secondary distributions of share certificates Immediately Before Listing

Companies that intend to list issued shares (including issued preferred-equity investments) on a domestic financial instruments exchange and companies that intend to register issued shares over-the-counter with an authorized financial instruments firms association must give notification when the company is not a continuous disclosure company, even where the sum of the total issue value or total distribution value of the public offering or secondary distribution of issued shares under the regulations of a financial instruments exchange or authorized financial instruments firms association is less than ¥100 million (Article 2(4)(viii) of the Cabinet Office Ordinance on Disclosure of Corporate Affairs, etc.).

## 3. Notifications

a. Persons with notification obligation (issuers)

Issuers of securities subject to public offering or secondary distribution have a notification obligation by submitting a securities registration statement (Article 4(1) of the Financial Instruments and Exchange Act). In cases where foreign companies submit a securities registration statement or amendment, they must specify a person who resides inside Japan as having the authority to represent the relevant foreign company in all acts concerning the notification of the relevant public offering or secondary distribution (Article 7(1) of the Cabinet Office Ordinance on Disclosure of Corporate Affairs, etc.; Guidelines on Disclosure of Corporate Affairs, B7-11). An attorney providing the issuer with advice regarding the notification of securities public offering or secondary distribution often serves as such a representative.

The "issuer" generally means the person who issues or intends to issue the securities (Article 2(5) of the Financial Instruments and Exchange Act).

While the person who corresponds to the issuer is clear regarding such securities as share certificates and bonds, there are cases where it is unclear who the issuer is. Therefore, the Cabinet Office Ordinance Regarding Definitions provides who is considered the issuer for certain Type I

*210*

Chapter 3  Disclosure requirements

Securities (Article 2 (5) parentheses of the Financial Instruments and Exchange Act; Article 14(1) (2) of the Cabinet Office Ordinance Regarding Definitions).[16]

(1)  Among beneficiary securities of specific purpose trusts and securities or certificates issued by a foreign state or a foreign person, for those that have the characteristics of beneficiary securities of special purpose trusts, the original settlor and the trustee of the trust pertaining to the securities are viewed as the issuer (Article 14 (2) (i) of the Cabinet Office Ordinance Regarding Definitions).

(2)  Among beneficiary securities of beneficiary securities issuing trusts (excluding beneficiary certificates of securities in trust) and securities or certificates issued by a foreign state or foreign person, for those that have the characteristics of beneficiary securities of beneficiary securities issuing trusts, the parties specified below are considered the issuer as follows (Article 14 (2) (ii) of the Cabinet Office Ordinance Regarding Definitions):

1 )  In cases based on settlor's instruction, namely, cases where the trust assets are managed and disposed of only at the instruction of the settlor or of a person that has been authorized to give instructions by the settlor (limited to persons other than those listed under each item of Article 2 of the Trust Business Act Implementing Order as persons having a close relationship with the trustee)— The settlor of the trust pertaining to the securities concerned (Article 14 (2) (ii) (a) of the Cabinet Office Ordinance Regarding Definitions).

2 )  In cases of self-benefit trusts not subject to settlor's instruction with money as the trust asset,[17] namely, cases other than those stated in 1) (cases not subject to settlor's instruction) where the beneficiary is the settlor when the act of the trust regarding the

---

16  For type II securities, for each class of securities, the person deemed the issuer and the time when the relevant rights are issued as securities are provided by the Cabinet Office Ordinance Regarding Definitions (Article 2(5) of the Financial Instruments and Exchange Act; Article 14 (3) & (4) of the Cabinet Office Ordinance Regarding Definitions).

*211*

security concerned comes into effect (self-benefit trusts) and money is the trust asset — The trustee of the trust pertaining to the securities concerned (Article 14 (2) (ii) (b) of the Cabinet Office Ordinance Regarding Definitions).

3 ) In cases other than those stated in 1) and 2), namely, in cases of self-benefit trusts not subject to settlor's instruction when the trust assets include assets other than money, and in cases of third-party-benefit-trusts not subject to settlor's instruction when the trust asset is money — The settlor and the trustee of the trust pertaining to the securities concerned (Article 14(2) (ii) (c) of the Cabinet Office Ordinance Regarding Definitions).

(3) Regarding beneficiary certificates of securities in trust,[18] the person who issues or intends to issue the entrusted securities for the securities concerned is deemed to be the issuer (Article 14(2) (iii) of the Cabinet Office Ordinance Regarding Definitions).

(4) Among mortgage securities and securities or certificates issued by a foreign state or foreign person, for those with the characteristics of mortgage securities the person receiving delivery of the securities concerned is deemed to be the issuer (Article 14(2) (iv) of the Cabinet Office Ordinance Regarding Definitions).

(5) For depository receipts, the person who issues or intends to issue securities pertaining to the rights indicated to the securities concerned is deemed to be the issuer (Article 14 (2) (v) of the Cabinet Office Ordinance Regarding Definitions).

---

17　Whether money is the trust asset is determined based on whether the asset transferred from the settlor to the trustee where the trust was established was money ("Regarding the Results of Public Comments on Draft Cabinet Orders and Draft Cabinet Office Ordinances Regarding the Financial Instruments and Exchange Act System," "Outline of Comments and FSA's Position on Comments", (July 31, 2007), p. 31, No. 3).

18　These include, among beneficiary securities of beneficiary securities issuing trusts, those with foreign shares as the trust asset that have rights equivalent to rights pertaining to the foreign shares that are the trust asset concerned as the beneficiary securities of the trust asset concerned (so-called JDR [Japanese Depository Receipts], etc.)..

Chapter 3 Disclosure requirements

b. Due date for notification

In principle, there are no restrictions on the timing of notification.[19]

However, in cases such as the issuance of shares or share options from a rights issue, where a securities public offering or secondary distribution is made to the shareholders recorded in the shareholder register on a certain date or to preferred equity investors as provided in the Act on Preferred Equity Investment and recorded in the preferred equity investor register, notification of the relevant public offering or secondary distribution must be made 25 days before a certain date (reference date) (Article 4(4) of the Financial Instruments and Exchange Act).

Cases where public offering or secondary distribution of securities is made to the shareholders recorded in the shareholder register means cases of conducting a public offering of shares or share options by means of granting the rights to receive allotment of shares or share options to shareholders as of the reference date, as well as cases of conducting a public offering or secondary distribution preferentially granting the qualifications to apply to shareholders as of the reference date. In these cases, a notification must be submitted up to and excluding 25 days before the day before the reference date (Guidelines on Disclosure of Corporate Affairs, B4-18 and B4-19).

In the following cases, however, notification up to and excluding 25 days before the day before the reference date is not required (proviso to Article 4 (4) of the Financial Instruments and Exchange Act; Article 3 of the Cabinet Office Ordinance on Disclosure of Corporate Affairs, etc.).

(1) Securities other than shares (including preferred equity investment certificates, the same hereafter), share option certificates, and bonds

---

**19** However, in cases that correspond to securities public offerings or secondary distributions and which as a result require notification, solicitation before submission of the securities registration statement is prohibited (Article 4(1) of the Financial Instruments and Exchange Act). Contracts for the securities acquisition and purchase cannot be concluded until the notification comes into effect (Article 15(1) of the Financial Instruments and Exchange Act).

*213*

with share options (Article 3 (i) of the Cabinet Office Ordinance on Disclosure of Corporate Affairs, etc.).

(2) Shares issued at the market price or at a certain price close to the market price (Article 3 (ii) of the Cabinet Office Ordinance on Disclosure of Corporate Affairs, etc.).

(3) Bonds with share options granting rights to acquire shares issued and transferred at the market price or at a certain price close to the market price (Article 3 (iii) of the Cabinet Office Ordinance on Disclosure of Corporate Affairs, etc.).

(4) Securities issued by a company other than a company with securities that are listed or over-the-counter registered (excluding securities stated in (1) through (3) and securities listed on an overseas financial instruments exchange) (Article 3 (iv) of the Cabinet Office Ordinance on Disclosure of Corporate Affairs, etc.).

(5) Share option certificates for gratis share option allotment as prescribed in Article 277 of the Companies Act that will be sold and purchased on a financial instruments exchange market (Article 3 (v) of the Cabinet Office Ordinance on Disclosure of Corporate Affairs, etc.).

c. Cases where public offerings and secondary distributions are conducted in parallel

In principle, securities registration statements must be submitted for each public offering or secondary distribution. However, where securities public offerings and secondary distributions that require notification are conducted in parallel, their notification can be made via the same securities registration statement (Guidelines on Disclosure of Corporate Affairs, B5-1). Also, where public offerings of listed shares and secondary distributions that do not require notification but which do require submission of a written notice of securities are conducted in parallel, this can be conducted via the same securities registration statement. In that case, it is deemed that the written notice of securities for the secondary distribution concerned has been submitted (Guidelines on Disclosure of Corporate Affairs, B5-1).

d. Place of submission and public inspection

Notifications regarding public offerings and secondary distributions of

Chapter 3　Disclosure requirements

securities are to be made via submission of a securities registration statement, foreign company registration statement or foreign person registration statement to the Prime Minister (Article 5 (1) (vi) of the Financial Instruments and Exchange Act). The Prime Minister delegates the authority granted under the Financial Instruments and Exchange Act (excluding the authority provided by cabinet order) to the Commissioner of the Financial Services Agency (Article 194-7 (1) of the Financial Instruments and Exchange Act), and the Commissioner of the Financial Services Agency delegates authority concerning the disclosure of corporate affairs including the authority to receive securities registration statements, shelf-registration statements and other offering disclosure documents as well as securities reports and other distribution disclosure documents to the Director General of the relevant Local Finance Bureau and the Local Finance Branch Bureau (Article 194-7 (6) of the Financial Instruments and Exchange Act; Article 39 (2) of the Financial Instruments and Exchange Act Implementing Order). As a result, the place of submission for securities registration statements, foreign company registration statements, and foreign person registration statements is provided as follows (Article 39 (2) of the Financial Instruments and Exchange Act Implementing Order; Article 20 (1) & (2) of the Cabinet Office Ordinance on Disclosure of Corporate Affairs, etc.; Guidelines on Disclosure of Corporate Affairs, B5-42; Article 33 (2) of the Cabinet Office Ordinance on Specified Securities Disclosure; Articles 5 and 6-5 of the Cabinet Office Ordinance on Foreign Bonds).

(1) Among domestic companies, those where the amount of stated capital, total amount of funds and total amount of contributions is at least ¥500 million and which have issued securities that are listed on a financial instruments exchange ─ The Director General of the Kanto Local Finance Bureau.

(2) Among domestic companies, companies other than those under (1) (excluding cases where a company that is the issuer of domestic investment trust beneficiary certificates, domestic investment securities, domestic asset-backed securities, domestic asset trust securitization beneficiary certificates, domestic securities in trust beneficiary certificates, domestic trust bonds, domestic mortgage

*215*

securities, domestic trust beneficial interests, interests in domestic securities investment business, securities in trust beneficiary certificates for specified securities, or regulated depository receipts, issues these securities)— The Director General of the Local Finance Bureau with jurisdiction over the location of the head office or principal office (the Director General of the Fukuoka Local Finance Branch Bureau when the location is within the jurisdiction of the Fukuoka Local Finance Branch Bureau).

(3) Persons other than those in (1) and (2) above (including foreign companies and issuers of foreign bonds)— The Director General of the Kanto Local Finance Bureau

Submitted securities registration statements, foreign company registration statements, foreign person registration statements and the documents attached hereto (this also applies to amendments, foreign company amendments, foreign person amendments, shelf-registration statements, amended shelf-registration statements, shelf-registration supplements and written withdrawals of shelf registrations stated below) will be made available for public inspection. Specifically, documents are to be kept and made available for public inspection for five years after the submission date (one year in cases of incorporation by reference method) at the Kanto Local Finance Bureau and at the Local Finance Bureau (Local Finance Bureau or Fukuoka Local Finance Branch Bureau; Article 21 of the Cabinet Office Ordinance on Disclosure of Corporate Affairs, etc.) (the Kanto Local Finance Bureau for documents submitted by a foreign person) with jurisdiction over the location of the head office or principal office of the company submitting the relevant documents (in the case of a foreign company, of the company's representative) (Article 25(1), Article 5(8) and Article 27 of the Financial Instruments and Exchange Act; Article 21 of the Cabinet Office Ordinance on Disclosure of Corporate Affairs, etc.; Article 31 of the Cabinet Office Ordinance on Specified Securities Disclosure; Article 27 (1) of the Cabinet Office Ordinance on Foreign Bonds).

When an issuer who has listed securities on a financial instruments exchange or over-the-counter traded securities with an authorized financial

Chapter 3   Disclosure requirements

instruments firms association has given notification of a public offering or secondary distribution, the issuer must submit copies of the securities registration statement or foreign company registration statement and attached documents (this also applies to amendments, foreign company amendments, shelf-registration statements, amended shelf-registration statements, shelf-registration supplements, and written withdrawals of shelf registrations stated below) to the financial instruments exchange or authorized financial instruments firms association without delay (Article 6, Article 5(8), and Article 27 of the Financial Instruments and Exchange Act; Article 3 of the Financial Instruments and Exchange Act Implementing Order). The financial instruments exchange or authorized financial instruments firms association that receives copies of the securities registration statement or foreign company registration statement and attached documents must keep these documents at its office and make them available for public inspection for five years after the submission date of those copies (one year in cases of incorporation by reference method) (Article 25(3) and Article 5(8) of the Financial Instruments and Exchange Act; Article 23 of the Cabinet Office Ordinance on Disclosure of Corporate Affairs, etc.; Article 18 (1) of the Cabinet Office Ordinance on Foreign Bonds).

Also, the issuer of securities that gave notification of public offerings or secondary distributions must keep copies of the securities registration statement or foreign company registration statement and attached documents at its head office, principal office and main branches and make them available for public inspection for five years after the submission date (one year in cases of incorporation by reference method) (Article 25(2), Article 5(6) & (8) and Article 27 of the Financial Instruments and Exchange Act; Article 22 (1) of the Cabinet Office Ordinance on Disclosure of Corporate Affairs, etc.; Article 32 of the Cabinet Office Ordinance on Specified Securities Disclosure).

However, the issuer of securities may apply to the Prime Minister for exclusion from public inspection of parts of securities registration statements, foreign company registration statements, foreign person

*217*

registration statements and attached documents made available for public inspection to maintain the confidentiality of business secrets, and when approved by the Prime Minister not make those parts of the documents available for public inspection (Article 25(4), Article 5(6) & (8) and Article 27 of the Financial Instruments and Exchange Act). Also, where the holder of securities for secondary distribution of securities stated on a securities registration statement or foreign person registration statement regarding foreign bonds is an individual, except where the person submitting the relevant documents has applied to the Director General of the Kanto Local Finance Bureau to make the relevant parts of the holder's address available for public inspection, the Director General of the Kanto Local Finance Bureau and the financial instruments exchange or authorised financial instruments firms association will not make available for public inspection the parts of the relevant holder's address beyond the city, town or village (and ward in those parts of Tokyo with special wards and in designated cities) (Article 17(2) and Article 18(2) of the Cabinet Office Ordinance on Foreign Bonds).

In cases where the Prime Minister orders submission of documents concerning amendments to disclosure documents (or of a foreign company registration statement) listed under each item of Article 25, paragraph 1 of the Financial Instruments and Exchange Act, the Prime Minister may choose not to make all or part of the relevant disclosure documents available for public inspection (Article 25(6), Article 27-30-7(1) & (2) and Article 5 (6) & (8) of the Financial Instruments and Exchange Act). In this case, copies are not made available for public inspection at the head office, principal office and main branches of the issuer or at the financial instruments exchange or authorized financial instruments firms association (Article 25(7) & (8) and Article 5(6) & (8) of the Financial Instruments and Exchange Act).

e. Electronic disclosure procedures (EDINET)

The Electronic Disclosure for Investors' NETwork (EDINET) is an electronic data processing system for disclosure which links via telecommunications lines the computers used by the Cabinet Office with the

Chapter 3 Disclosure requirements

input/output devices used by persons who conduct submission procedures for annual securities reports and other disclosure documents, as well as the input/output devices used by financial instruments exchanges and authorized financial instruments firms associations (Article 27-30-2 of the Financial Instruments and Exchange Act). The term "electronic disclosure procedures" refers to disclosure documents submission procedures that require the use of EDINET (Article 27-30-3(1) of the Financial Instruments and Exchange Act). Procedures regarding securities registration statements, foreign company registration statements, foreign person registration statements, shelf-registration statements, shelf-registration supplements, amendments, foreign company amendments, foreign person amendments, amended shelf-registration statements and procedures to apply for exemption of public inspection for confidential matters therein as well as procedures for written withdrawal of shelf registration are electronic disclosure procedures (Article 27-30-2, Article 5(6) & (8), and Article 27 of the Financial Instruments and Exchange Act).

Electronic disclosure procedures must be conducted by input using input/output devices that meet technical standards prescribed by the Commissioner of the Financial Services Agency (Article 14-10(1) of the Financial Instruments and Exchange Act Implementing Order). Persons submitting disclosure documents via EDINET for the first time must submit a registration notification to the Commissioner of the Financial Services Agency (Director General of the Local Finance Bureau or Director-General of the Fukuoka Finance Branch Bureau) beforehand (Article 14-10(2) of the Financial Instruments and Exchange Act Implementing Order; Article 2 of the Cabinet Office Ordinance on Special Provisions etc. for Procedures by Use of Electronic Data Processing System for Disclosure). In the registration notification, the articles of incorporation and certificate of registered matters are deemed to be attached documents (Article 14-10(1) of the Financial Instruments and Exchange Act Implementing Order; Article 2(4) of the Cabinet Office Ordinance on Special Provisions etc. for Procedures by Use of Electronic Data Processing System for Disclosure). These must be submitted every three years (Article 2(6) of the Cabinet Office Ordinance on Special Provisions etc. for Procedures by use of Electronic Data

*219*

Processing System for Disclosure, but continuous disclosure companies are exempted [Article 2-7]). Seals and signatures are not needed when conducting electronic disclosure procedures (proviso to Article 1 and proviso to Article 4 of the Cabinet Office Ordinance on Special Provisions etc. for Procedures by Use of Electronic Data Processing System for Disclosure).

Documents are deemed to have arrived at the Cabinet Office and procedures completed at the time when files are recorded on computers at the Cabinet Office (Article 27-30-3 (3), Article 5 (6) & (8), and Article 27 of the Financial Instruments and Exchange Act). Cases where electronic disclosure procedures are conducted using EDINET are deemed to have carried out the disclosure under the Financial Instruments and Exchange Act prescribed as conducted in writing (Article 27-30-3(4), Article 5(6) & (8), and Article 27 of the Financial Instruments and Exchange Act). As mentioned below, for example, although it is stated that securities registration statements enter into effect 15 days after the date on which they are received by the Prime Minister (Article 8(1), Article 5(6) & (8), and Article 27 of the Financial Instruments and Exchange Act), in cases where EDINET is used the statements are deemed to be "received" when they are recorded by the computers at the Cabinet Office.

When a person who conducts electronic disclosure procedures cannot conduct electronic disclosure using EDINET because of failures in telecommunications lines or other causes, the person may, with the prior approval of the Prime Minister, conduct electronic disclosure procedures by means of submitting a magnetic disk instead of using EDINET (Article 27-30-4(1), Article 5(8), and Article 27 of the Financial Instruments and Exchange Act). When electronic disclosure procedures are conducted via submission of a magnetic disk, the Prime Minister must immediately record the items recorded on the magnetic disk in a file and they are deemed to have arrived at the Cabinet Office when they are recorded in the file (Article 27-30-4 (3), Article 5 (6) & (8), and Article 27 of the Financial Instruments and Exchange Act). With this, just as when using EDINET, in cases where electronic disclosure procedures are conducted via submission of a magnetic disk, the person is deemed to have carried out the disclosure

Chapter 3  Disclosure requirements

under the Financial Instruments and Exchange Act prescribed as conducted in writing (Article 27-30-4(4), Article 5(6) & (8), and Article 27 of the Financial Instruments and Exchange Act).

When a securities registration statement, etc. is submitted to the Prime Minister via EDINET, the Prime Minister must make available for public inspection, instead of these documents, the matters recorded in the file or documents with these matters stated (Article 27-30-7 and Article 5(8) of the Financial Instruments and Exchange Act). The same applies when disclosure is conducted via submission of a magnetic disk. The Commissioner of the Financial Services Agency, having been delegated authority from the Prime Minister, makes these available for public inspection by displaying the relevant matters on the relevant computer input/output devices at the Local Finance Bureau or Fukuoka Local Finance Branch Bureau (Article 14-12 of the Financial Instruments and Exchange Act Implementing Order). As part of its administrative services, the Financial Services Agency may also make these documents available for public inspection on the EDINET homepage.

In cases where securities registration statements, etc. are submitted via EDINET, instead of submitting and sending copies of those documents, notice of the matters stated in the documents must be given to the financial instruments exchange where the securities are listed or the authorized financial instruments firms association where they are over-the-counter registered (Article 27-30-6(1) and Article 5(8) of the Financial Instruments and Exchange Act). Then, the delivery of the relevant notice to other parties is assumed to have occurred once the matters to be stated on these documents are recorded in an EDINET file and the time normally required for their output after the recording has passed (Article 27-30-6(2) and Article 5(8) of the Financial Instruments and Exchange Act). Consequently in cases where these documents are submitted via EDINET, there is no need to submit or send them to a financial instruments exchange or authorized financial instruments firms association using paper media. A financial instruments exchange or authorized financial instruments firms association that receives notice of the matters stated on a securities registration statement, etc. must make the matters notified or documents with the

*221*

matters stated available for public inspection instead of copies of the documents that must be made available for public inspection when submitted using paper media (Article 27-30-8 and Article 5 (8) of the Financial Instruments and Exchange Act). Namely, the financial instruments exchange or authorized financial instruments firms association must make them available for public inspection by displaying the relevant matters on the screen of the input/output devices of the computers at its office (Article 14-13 of the Financial Instruments and Exchange Act Implementing Order).

In cases where it is found that the Cabinet Office computers have failed or there are other causes prescribed by cabinet order (cases where the Cabinet Office computers cannot be operated because of power supply cutoffs or other reasons) (Article 14-11-2 of the Financial Instruments and Exchange Act Implementing Order), and with permission from the Prime Minister, procedures may be conducted paper-based (Article 27-30-5 (1) (i) and Article 5 (8) of the Financial Instruments and Exchange Act). With permission from the Prime Minister, paper-based procedures may also be conducted in cases where conducting electronic disclosure procedures using of EDINET is considered to be conspicuously difficult (Article 27-30-5(1) (ii) and Article 5(8) of the Financial Instruments and Exchange Act).

Also, in cases where the Prime Minister deems it necessary and appropriate for achieving public benefit or investor protection, the Prime Minister may make available for public inspection on EDINET, together with the relevant disclosure documents, a statement to the effect that an order to submit documents regarding amendment of disclosure documents was issued or other related information that could have a material impact on investors' investment decisions (Article 27-30-7(5) and Article 5(8) of the Financial Instruments and Exchange Act).

f. Items to be stated in securities registration statements
A securities registration statement submitted by an issuer that is a company (including a foreign company) must state (1) matters concerning the public offering or secondary distribution of the securities (securities information),

Chapter 3 Disclosure requirements

(2) the trade name of the issuing company, state of financial affairs, corporate group to which the issuing company belongs, status of accounting of the issuing company and other material matters concerning the description of company business (company information), and (3) other matters specified by cabinet office ordinance as necessary and appropriate for the public interest or investor protection (Article 5(1) of the Financial Instruments and Exchange Act).

While preparing a securities registration statement submitted by an issuer that is a company (including a foreign company)[20], not only stating matters including company information (ordinary method), for companies that meet certain conditions the [actual] incorporation method and the incorporation by reference method are also accepted. The forms and matters to be stated on the securities registration statement are prescribed separately for cases of initial public offerings of shares, small-amount public offerings of shares, specified procedures relating to securities issuance for reorganization, and specified procedures relating to securities delivery for reorganization.

Furthermore, the forms and matters to be stated on securities registration statements are prescribed by the Cabinet Office Ordinance on Disclosure of Information, etc. on Issuers of Foreign Government Bonds, etc. (Cabinet Office Ordinance on Foreign Bonds) for foreign bonds, etc.[21] and by the Cabinet Office Ordinance on Disclosure for Specified Securities[22], respectively.

---

20 Because designated juridical persons such as cooperative-type financial institutions that are issuers of preferred equity investment certificates, mutual companies for the purpose of the Insurance Business Act, medical corporations that issue social medical corporation bonds, school corporations that issue school bonds or school loan claims and other designated juridical persons (designated juridical persons provided in Article 1(1) of the Ordinance on Financial Statements, etc.; Article 1(xx-5) of the Cabinet Office Ordinance on Disclosure of Corporate Information, etc.) are not companies, under Article 27 of the Financial Instruments and Exchange Act only of Article 5 of the Act applies. However, regarding the forms and matters to be stated on the securities registration statement, the Cabinet Office Ordinance on Disclosure of Corporate Information, etc. applies (Article 15(1) main body, parentheses of the Cabinet Office Ordinance on Disclosure of Corporate Information, etc.).

( i ) Ordinary method

The ordinary method is the default method that can be used by all persons submitting a notification.

In addition to securities information, unlike the [actual] incorporation method and the incorporation by reference method mentioned below, company information is actually stated in the ordinary method (Article 8(1) as well as Forms 2 and 7 of the Cabinet Office Ordinance on Disclosure of Corporate Affairs, etc.). In cases of using the ordinary method, domestic companies are to use the Form 2 of the Cabinet Office Ordinance on Disclosure of Corporate Affairs, etc. and foreign companies are to use the Form 7 of the Cabinet Office Ordinance on Disclosure of Corporate Affairs, etc. (Article 8(1) (i) (iv) of the Cabinet Office Ordinance on Disclosure of Corporate Affairs, etc.).

i ) Securities Information

For securities information, there are columns for public offering requirements, secondary distribution requirements, special matters in cases of third-party allotment, and other matters to be stated, and the public

---

21  For bonds issued by foreign governments, foreign local governments, international organs, foreign government organs, etc. and depository receipts displaying rights concerning these bonds ("Foreign Bonds, etc.;" Article 1 (i) of the Cabinet Office Ordinance on Foreign Bonds), because the issuer is not a company, while as provided in Article 27 of the Financial Instruments and Exchange Act, Article 5 of the Act applies, the disclosure documents format and matters to be stated are provided by the Cabinet Office Ordinance on Foreign Bonds.

22  So-called asset-finance-type securities such as asset-backed securities and investment trust securities whereby other specific assets held by the issuing body guaranteeing their value require disclosure that differs from shares, bonds, and other so-called company-finance-type securities whereby the assets and profitability of the issuing body itself is the source of their value. Thus, under the Financial Instruments and Exchange Act, asset-finance-type securities require disclosure as specified securities (Article 5(1) (5) of the Financial Instruments and Exchange Act), and the disclosure documents format and items to be stated are specified by the Cabinet Office Ordinance on Disclosure of Information, etc. of Specified Securities. Also, with the exception of school loan claims, interests in securities investment business, etc. are also treated as specified securities (Article 2-13(vii) of the Financial Instruments and Exchange Act Implementing Order).

## Table 3-1

| | Ordinary Method | | [actual] Incorporation Method | | Incorporation by Reference Method | | IPO (cases not under specified procedures for securities issuance or delivery for reorganisation) | IPO (cases under specified procedures for securities issuance or delivery for reorganisation) | Small amount public offering, etc. | Purchases in which specified procedures for securities issuance or delivery for reorganisation or securities are the consideration | | Foreign Company Notification |
|---|---|---|---|---|---|---|---|---|---|---|---|---|
| | Domestic companies | Foreign companies | Domestic companies | Foreign companies | Domestic companies | Foreign companies | Domestic companies | Domestic companies | Domestic companies | Domestic companies | Foreign companies | Foreign companies |
| | Form 2 | Form 7 | Form 2-2 | Form 7-2 | Form 2-3 | Form 7-3 | Form 2-4 | Form 2-7 | Form 2-5 | Form 2-6 | Form 7-4 | Form 7-5 |

Body contents:

| Row group | Information included |
|---|---|
| Securities Information | Information on Takeover Bid |
| | Information on Reorganization (Takeover Bid) |
| Company information | Referenced information |
| | Information regarding subsequent completion of filing |
| | Incorporated information |
| | Issuer information |
| | Information on affiliates |
| | Company information |
| | Information on guarantor company for reporting company |
| | Information on guarantor company for reporting company |
| | Special information on reporting company |
| | Special information |
| Special information | Special information |
| | Stock offering information |
| | Information on company subject to reorganization |
| | Information on company subject to reorganization |
| Foreign Company Notification | In addition to foreign company notification, referenced documents disclosed (i. e., being made available for public inspection in relevant foreign state based on the laws and regulations of the state [including regulations specified by persons operating foreign financial instruments exchange markets or other persons specified by a cabinet office ordinance]) in a foreign state or equivalent to foreign company statements written in English. |

offering or secondary distribution conditions and other descriptions to be stated are prescribed separately by public offering or secondary distribution and by issued securities. For example, for a public offering of share certificates, as public offering requirements, statements are to be made regarding each item of newly issued shares, shares public offering method and conditions, share underwriting, and applications of funds acquired from the new issue. In cases of third-party allotment, as specially recorded matters, the matters to be stated include the state of the intended recipients of the allotment, restrictions on the transfer of share certificates, etc., matters concerning issuance conditions, matters concerning large-scale third-party allotment, and the state of major shareholders after the third-party allotment (Cabinet Office Ordinance on Disclosure of Corporate Affairs, etc., Form 2, Note 23-7; Cabinet Office Ordinance on Disclosure of Corporate Affairs, etc., Form 7, Note 24-2), as well as the necessity of a large-scale third-party allotment, existence and description of any planned reverse stock splits, and other matters that will serve as a reference (Cabinet Office Ordinance on Disclosure of Corporate Affairs, etc., Form 2, Note 23-10; Cabinet Office Ordinance on Disclosure of Corporate Affairs, etc., Form 7, Note 24-2). In the case of third-party allotment through which the subscriber of newly issued shares becomes a new parent company by holding more than half of the shares as a result of the issuance, the issuer company must disclose the name and other information about the subscriber (Cabinet Office Ordinance on Disclosure of Corporate Affairs, etc., Form 2, Note 23-3h).

For this purpose, "third-party allotment" means a method of allocating to specified persons shares or share option certificates pertaining to a public offering or secondary distribution of the shares, share option certificates or bonds with share options of the securities concerned (methods of share allotment under Article 202, paragraph 1 of the Companies Act and of stock options allotment under Article 241, paragraph 1 and Article 277 of the Companies Act [for foreign companies, equivalent methods]; excluding over-allotments and stock options) (Article 19(2)(i) of the Cabinet Office Ordinance on Disclosure of Corporate Affairs, etc.; Guidelines on Corporate Affairs Disclosure, B24-5-29).

Chapter 3   Disclosure requirements

Regarding the state of the intended allottees of the allotment, the matters that must be stated are an outline of the intended allottees of the allotment, relationship between the reporting company and the intended allottees, reasons for selecting the intended allottees, number of shares to be allocatted, policy on holding shares, etc., state of funds, etc. required for payment, and actual status of the intended allottees of the allotment. Regarding the outline of the intended allottees, in cases where the intended allotee is a juridical person, the name, location of the head office and main investments must be stated, However, in cases where the intended allottee is a company that submits a securities report, instead of newly stating the information, the company is to state the date of submission of its latest continuous disclosure documents (Cabinet Office Ordinance on Disclosure of Corporate Affairs, etc., Form 2, Note 23-3a; Cabinet Office Ordinance on Disclosure of Corporate Affairs, etc., Form 7, Note 24-2). Regarding the relationship between the reporting company and the intended allottees of the allotment, the description must be made specifically in cases where there is investment, personnel, capital, technology, trading or other important relationship between the reporting company and the intended allottee of the allotment. In cases where the intended allottee of the allotment is a fund, any important relationship with its managing partners must be stated (Cabinet Office Ordinance on Disclosure of Corporate Affairs, etc., Form 2, Note 23-3b; Cabinet Office Ordinance on Disclosure of Corporate Affairs, etc., Form 7, Note 24-2). Regarding the state of funds, etc. required for payment, the results of confirmations that the intended allottees of the allotment have the funds or assets required for payment for the third-party allotment pertaining to this notification as well as the methods used for that confirmation must be specifically stated (Cabinet Office Ordinance on Disclosure of Corporate Affairs, etc., Form 2, Note 23-3f; Cabinet Office Ordinance on Disclosure of Corporate Affairs, etc., Form 7, Note 24-2). Also, in cases where the intended allottees of the allotment will use loans for payment, the names of the lenders and an outline of the preconditions where there are important preconditions for the loan must be stated.[23] Regarding the actual status of the intended allottees of the allotment, when there are persons who are authorized to exercise rights as shareholders or have *de facto* authority to give instructions to exercise rights or investment authority

*227*

for the shares, etc. of the intended allottees of the allotment, a statement to that effect and the description of the authority must be specifically stated. Also, individuals, juridical persons, and other organisations that act to gain economic benefit using violence or force or conduct fraud or other criminal acts are defined as "specified organisations, etc."; and results confirming whether the intended allottees of the allotment are specified organisations, etc. and whether the intended allottees of the allotment have some sort of relationship with specified organisations, etc., as well as the confirmation method must be specifically stated (Cabinet Office Ordinance on Disclosure of Corporate Affairs, etc., Form 2, Note 23-3g; Cabinet Office Ordinance on Disclosure of Corporate Affairs, etc., Form 7, Note 24-2).

Regarding matters concerning the terms of issuance, the grounds for calculating the issue price and the understanding regarding the rationality of the issuance conditions must be specifically stated (Cabinet Office Ordinance on Disclosure of Corporate Affairs, etc., Form 2, Note 23-5a; Cabinet Office Ordinance on Disclosure of Corporate Affairs, etc., Form 7, Note 24-2). In cases where the issuance of securities by third-party allotment is considered to constitute an issuance offering favourable terms under the Companies Act, the reasons and judgment process as well as the reasons why the issuance is offered on favourable terms must be specifically stated, and in cases where the issuance is considered not to constitute an issuance offering on favourable terms, the reasons and judgment process must be specifically stated. In cases where there is an opinion expressed by a company auditor regarding the legality of the relevant issuance or a valuation[24] by a third party used as reference for the judgment, its description must be included (Cabinet Office Ordinance on Disclosure of Corporate Affairs, etc., Form 2, Note 23-5b; Cabinet Office Ordinance on Disclosure of Corporate Affairs, etc., Form 7, Note 24-2).

---

23 "Results of Public Comments on 'Draft Cabinet Office Ordinance Regarding Partial Revision of the Cabinet Office Ordinance on Disclosure of Corporate Affairs, etc.'" "Outline of Comments and FSA's Position on Comments" (December 11, 2009), p. 2, Nos. 9 and 10.

Chapter 3 Disclosure requirements

Cases where (i) the voting rights dilution ratio in a third-party allotment is 25% or more (Cabinet Office Ordinance on Disclosure of Corporate Affairs, etc., Form 2, Note 23-6a; Cabinet Office Ordinance on Disclosure of Corporate Affairs, etc., Form 7, Note 24-2) or where (ii) the third-party allotment would generate a controlling shareholder (Cabinet Office Ordinance on Disclosure of Corporate Affairs, etc., Form 2, Note 23-6b; Cabinet Office Ordinance on Disclosure of Corporate Affairs, etc., Form 7, Note 24-2) are considered large-scale third-party allotments, and in corresponding cases a statement to that effect and the reasons must be stated. For this purpose, a "controlling shareholder" means a major shareholder that owns directly or indirectly the majority of the voting rights of all shareholders of the parent company of the reporting company or of the reporting company (limited to cases where the sum of the number of voting rights held under its own calculation and the number of voting rights held by certain parties[25] exceeds 50 percent of the voting rights of all shareholders). In cases corresponding to a large-scale third-party allotment, the reasons for conducting the large-scale third-party allotment and the description of the decision of the board of directors regarding the impact of the large-scale third-party allotment on existing shareholders must be specifically stated (Cabinet Office Ordinance on Disclosure of Corporate Affairs, etc., Form 2, Note 23-8a; Cabinet Office Ordinance on Disclosure of Corporate Affairs, etc., Form 7, Note 24-2), and the process of the decision on conducting the large-scale third-party allotment must also be stated (in cases where hearings of opinions regarding the large-scale third-party allotment from

---

24  For example, in cases where a third-party valuation organ evaluates the theoretical price of stock options, the name of the organ conducting the calculation, the subject evaluated by the valuation organ, and an outline of the evaluation must be stated within the range that can be disclosed in a manner easily understandable by investors (Results of Public Comments on 'Draft Cabinet Office Ordinance regarding Partial Revision of the Cabinet Office Ordinance on Disclosure of Corporate Affairs, etc.'" "Outline of Comments and FSA's Position on Comments" (December 11, 2009), p. 3, No. 16).

25  (i) That person's close relatives (within the second degree of kinship) and (ii) juridical persons and other bodies (juridical persons, etc.) where that person or that person's close relatives, under their own calculation, own the majority of the voting rights of all the relevant shareholders and of subsidiaries of the juridical person, etc.

*229*

persons independent of managers, confirmation of the intention of shareholders through a resolution of a shareholders' general meeting[26] or other measures are devised to ensure the appropriateness of the decision of the board of directors (for companies that have one or more outside directors, the opinions of the outside director(s), which is (are) different from that of the board of directors, should also be included) regarding the large-scale third-party allotment, including a statement to that effect and the contents) (Cabinet Office Ordinance on Disclosure of Corporate Affairs, etc., Form 2, Note 23-8b; Cabinet Office Ordinance on Disclosure of Corporate Affairs, etc., Form 7, Note 24-2).

Regarding the existence and description of any plan for reverse stock splits etc., in cases where a reverse stock split that would cause shareholders to lose their voting rights in the shares of the reporting company or other act with a similar effect are planned, the purposes of the act, the scheduled time, method and procedure, the status of shareholders after the act, the consideration granted to shareholders and other description of the act must be specifically stated (Cabinet Office Ordinance on Disclosure of Corporate Affairs, etc., Form 2, Note 23-9; Cabinet Office Ordinance on Disclosure of Corporate Affairs, etc., Form 7, Note 24-2).

Regarding other matters to be stated, in cases where there are photographs or drawings of plants or products, or other matters to appear in particular in a prospectus, a statement to that effect and the locations where they appear in the prospectus are to be indicated (Cabinet Office Ordinance on Disclosure of Corporate Affairs, etc., Form 2, Note 24; Cabinet Office Ordinance on Disclosure of Corporate Affairs, etc., Form 7, Note 25). Moreover, the statement must use easy-to-understand expressions and notations so investors can easily understand. Also, statements that advertise the reporting company (such as, "our company is unique in the XX industry

---

26　After 2014 amendments, the Companies Act requires a resolution of a general meeting in some cases of large-scale third-party allotment in a public company (Article 206-2). In the case where there are objections from shareholders holding more than 10 % of the voting rights, the allotment to the subscriber must be, in principle, approved by an ordinary resolution of the shareholders meeting.

Chapter 3   Disclosure requirements

and the world's leading manufacturer of XX"), statements where the explanations are subjective expressions in the captions attached to photographs (such as, "our company's product XX is the best-known worldwide because of its versatility and other characteristics") and statements of figures whose basis is deemed not to be clear (for example, the operating profit on our company's leading product XX for the month of XX rose XX% year-on-year) or other statements that might cause any misunderstanding as materials for investment judgment are prohibited (Guidelines on Disclosure of Corporate Affairs, B5-10).

In cases where there are matters that are information regarding a public offering or secondary distribution of securities that should be stated in particular, following the secondary distribution requirements a "special notes regarding the public offering or secondary distribution" section can be established and state the relevant matters (Guidelines on Disclosure of Corporate Affairs, B5-3). In practice, matters concerning the listing of securities for a public offering, matters concerning offerings in foreign states in cases of global offerings, matters concerning secondary distributions through over-allotment, matters concerning lockups, and other matters are stated.

In principle, all matters that should be stated on a securities registration statement are to be stated when the securities registration statement is submitted, however in cases where it is necessary to conduct a public offering or secondary distribution before determining the issue price or distribution price and other cases prescribed by the relevant cabinet office ordinance (Article 9 of the Cabinet Office Ordinance on Disclosure of Corporate Affairs, etc.), a securities registration statement can be submitted without stating the matters prescribed by the relevant cabinet office ordinance (proviso to Article 5 (1) of the Financial Instruments and Exchange Act). For example, these cases include those where it is necessary to conduct the public offering before determining the issue price for items where the entrusted certificates are shares or the shares are represented by depository receipts (shares, etc.) among share certificates, securities and beneficiary certificates of securities-in-trust issued at the market price or at

*231*

a fixed price near the market price; and cases where it is necessary to conduct the secondary distribution before determining the distribution price for shares or share option certificates for which the secondary distribution is conducted at the market price or at a fixed price near the market price. In cases where submitting a securities registration statement without stating the issue price or distribution price, etc., the time when it is expected to be determined must be stated (Cabinet Office Ordinance on Disclosure of Corporate Affairs, etc., Form 2, Notes 9c and 10d; Cabinet Office Ordinance on Disclosure of Corporate Affairs, etc., Form 7, Notes 11c and 12d). Also, in cases where items not stated on a securities registration are determined, an amendment must be submitted (Article 7 of the Financial Instruments and Exchange Act; Article 11(iii) of the Cabinet Office Ordinance on Disclosure of Corporate Affairs, etc.).

ii ) Company Information

Regarding company information, domestic companies must state the general condition of the company, state of business, state of facilities, state of the reporting company, status of accounting, and outline of the shareholder service of the reporting company, as well as referenced information on the reporting company. In addition to these, foreign companies must provide an outline of the legal system in their home country and foreign exchange rate movements.

(1) Overview of Company

The changes in the main management indicators, history, description business, status of associated companies and status of employees must be stated.

(2) State of business

Outline of performance, etc.; production, order receipt and sales; business policy, business environment and issues to be addressed, etc.; business and other risk; important contracts, etc. for management; research and development activities; and analyses of financial conditions and management performance must be stated. In cases where a stock company has specified its fundamental policy regarding the approach to persons who control the

Chapter 3 Disclosure requirements

financial and business policy decisions of the stock company, as matters specified in each item of Article 127 of the Implementing Order for the Companies Act, the description of the basic policy and the specific measures (takeover defense measures) must be stated as issues to be addressed (Cabinet Office Ordinance on Disclosure of Corporate Affairs, etc., Form 2, Note 32; Cabinet Office Ordinance on Disclosure of Corporate Affairs, etc., Form 7, Note 37).

(3) State of facilities

An outline of capital investment, etc.; the state of the main facilities; and plans for facilities new construction or removal of facilities, etc. must be stated.

(4) State of reporting companies

Domestic companies must include the status of shares, etc.,[27] the status of share acquisition, etc., dividend policy, share price movement, the status of directors, and the status of corporate governance, etc.; however, foreign companies are not required to state the status of share acquisition, etc.

Here, as a statement of the status of corporate governance, etc. (Cabinet Office Ordinance on Disclosure of Corporate Affairs, etc., Form 2, Note 57; Cabinet Office Ordinance on Disclosure of Corporate Affairs, etc., Form 7, Note 50), regarding the corporate governance system, an outline of the corporate governance system (including the system for securing the proper management in subsidiaries), the reasons for choosing the system, existence of any corporate auditors, audit and supervisory committee members or audit committee members with substantial knowledge of finance and

---

27  In cases where stock options have been issued as part of the measures to prevent control of the relevant company's financial and business policy decisions by persons who are inappropriate in light of the fundamental policy, the contents of the rights plans must be stated (Cabinet Office Ordinance on Disclosure of Corporate Affairs, etc., Form 2, Note 42; Cabinet Office Ordinance on Disclosure of Corporate Affairs, etc., Form 7, Note 43f). However, regarding the "takeover defense measures" themselves, since they are explained as one of the issues to be addressed, the terms of the stock options have to be stated only where the stock options have already been issued.

accounting, coordination of outside directors and outside auditors with the internal control division, state of appointing outside directors and outside auditors and reasons why they are not appointed must be stated; regarding director compensation, the amount of compensation, etc. by type of compensation (monetary compensation, stock options, bonuses, retirement bonuses, etc.) by director (this can be limited to persons receiving at least ¥100 million in compensation, etc.), the amount of compensation etc. by type of compensation by position, and the description of policies and method for determining the amount of compensation and the calculation method must be stated. Also, regarding the status of shareholding, (i) the issue name, number of shares, holding purpose and amounts posted on the balance sheet of shares held for purposes other than pure investment in cases where these amounts posted on the balance sheet account for over 1% of the capital for this period or the prior period or in cases where these are among the top 30 shares posted on the balance sheet by amount, (ii) in cases where the reporting company is a holding company, matters similar to those in (i) for shares of principal consolidated subsidiaries (consolidated subsidiaries with the largest investment share amounts posted among the reporting company and its consolidated subsidiaries) that meet certain requirements, and (iii) the total amounts posted on the balance sheet for this period and the prior period of shares held for pure investment purposes by listed and unlisted shares must be stated.

(5) Status of accounting

In addition to consolidated financial statements and individual financial statements (in the case of foreign companies, financial documents),[28] the

---

**28** Financial statements, quarterly financial statements, interim financial statements, consolidated financial statements, consolidated quarterly financial statements and consolidated interim financial statements included in securities registration statements, etc. and annual securities reports, etc. must be prepared using terminology, forms, and preparation methods generally accepted as fair as specified by cabinet office ordinance (Article 193 of the Financial Instruments and Exchange Act). Ordinance on Terminology, Forms and Preparation Methods of Financial Statements, etc. (Ordinance on Financial Statements, etc.), Ordinance on Terminology, Forms and Preparation Methods of Quarterly Financial Statements, etc. (Ordinance on Quarterly Financial Statements, etc.), Ordinance on Terminology, Forms and Preparation

Chapter 3   Disclosure requirements

Methods of Semiannual Financial Statements etc. (Ordinance on Semiannual Financial Statements, etc.), Ordinance on Terminology, Forms and Preparation Methods of Consolidated Financial Statements (Ordinance on Consolidated Financial Statements), Ordinance on Terminology, Forms and Preparation Methods of Quarterly Consolidated Financial Statements (Ordinance on Quarterly Consolidated Financial Statements), and Ordinance on Terminology, Forms and Preparation Methods of Semiannual Consolidated Financial Statements (Ordinance on Semiannual Consolidated Financial Statements) have been prescribed as delegated by this Article. Matters not stated in these ordinances are in accordance with corporate accounting standards generally accepted as fair and appropriate (Article 1(1) of the Ordinance on Financial Statements, etc., and so on).

The "Corporate Accounting Standards" published by the Business Accounting Deliberation Council have been considered corporate accounting standards generally accepted as fair and appropriate (Article 1(2) of the Ordinance on Terminology, Forms and Preparation Methods of Financial Statements, etc., and so on); and among the corporate accounting standards prepared and published by the Accounting Standards Board of Japan, those specified as business accounting standards in notices by the Commissioner of the Financial Services Agency ("Designation of Corporate Accounting Standards by the Commissioner of the Financial Services Agency Pursuant to the Ordinance on Terminology, Forms and Preparation Methods of Consolidated Financial Statements" [FSA Notice No. 69 of FY 2009] and "Stipulations of Corporate Accounting Standards by the Commissioner of the Financial Services Agency Pursuant to the Ordinance on Terminology, Forms and Preparation Methods of Financial Statements, etc." [FSA Notice No. 70 of FY 2009]) are also considered corporate accounting standards generally accepted as fair and appropriate (Article 1 (2) of the Ordinance on Financial Statements, etc. and so on).

Also, among companies submitting annual securities reports, companies meeting the two requirements of stating special efforts to ensure the appropriateness of financial statements in annual securities reports, etc. and of assigning directors or employees with adequate knowledge of designated international financial reporting standards and preparing systems to appropriately prepare financial statements based on designated international financial reporting standards or the Modified International Standards are classified as specified companies (Articles 1-2-2 and 1-3 of the Ordinance on Consolidated Financial Statements), and the terminology, forms and preparation methods of their consolidated financial statements can follow the designated international financial reporting standards or the Modified International Standards (Articles 93 and 94 of the Ordinance on Consolidated Financial Statements; Articles 93 and 94 of the Ordinance on Quarterly Consolidated Financial Statements; Articles 87 and 88 of the Ordinance on Semiannual Consolidated Financial Statements).

Furthermore, companies that have registered their consolidated financial statements

*235*

prepared in accordance with U.S. GAAP with the U.S. Securities and Exchange Commission may, with the approval of the Commissioner of the Financial Services Agency, prepare their consolidated financial statements in accordance with U.S. GAAP also for the purpose of complying with the Japanese securities regulation (Articles 95 of the Ordinance on Consolidated Financial Statements) (for details, see D.4. below).

On the other hand, concerning the financial documents for foreign companies (Article 1-3 of the Ordinance on Financial Statements, etc.), where considered by the Commissioner of the Financial Services Agency not to harm the public interest or investor protection, the submission of documents on financial accounting disclosed in the home country or in an area other than the home country and other than Japan as financial documents is permitted (Article 131(1) & (2) of the Ordinance on Financial Statements, etc.). Note that the Ordinance on Financial Statements, etc. does not apply to foreign states, foreign local governments and other issuers of foreign bonds.

Financial statements, quarterly financial statements, interim financial statements, consolidated financial statements, consolidated quarterly financial statements and consolidated interim financial statements included in securities registration statements, etc. and securities reports, etc. must receive audit certification from a certified public accountant or auditing firm that has no special relationship with the issuer (Article 193-2 of the Financial Instruments and Exchange Act; Article 1(i)-(vi) & (xvi) of the Cabinet Office Ordinance on Audit Certification of Financial Statements, etc.) However, among these documents, items included in securities registration statements, securities reports, quarterly securities reports, semiannual reports, etc. that were already submitted do not require audit certification (Article 1 (i)-(vi) & (xvi) of the Cabinet Office Ordinance on Audit Certification of Financial Statements, etc.). Also, regarding financial statements, only financial statements pertaining to the most recent business year or the business year immediately before that business year (for specified securities, the most recentry specified period and the period immediately before that special period) require audit certification (Article 1(i) of the Cabinet Office Ordinance on Audit Certification of Financial Statements etc.), and financial statements presented as special information do not require audit certification. The results of the audit of financial statements and consolidated financial statements are to be presented in an audit report,those of the audit of interim financial statements and interim consolidated financial statements are to be presented in an interim audit report, and those of the audit of quarterly financial statements and quarterly consolidated financial statements are to be presented in a quarterly review report (Article 3 (1) of the Cabinet Office Ordinance on Audit Certification of Financial Statements). On the other hand, among securities or certificates issued by a foreign state or foreign person, there is no need to receive audit certification in cases where issuers of items with the characteristics of shares or share option certificates and other securities specified by Article 35, paragraph 2 of the Implementing Order

*236*

Chapter 3   Disclosure requirements

description of main assets and liabilities (in the case of foreign companies, the description of main assets and liabilities and income and expenditures) and other items must be stated.

For domestic companies, in principle, these include consolidated financial statements (consolidated balance sheet, consolidated profit and loss statement, consolidated statement of comprehensive income [or consolidated statement of profit and loss and comprehensive income], statement of changes in shareholders' equity, and consolidated cash flow statement) [29] for the two most recent consolidated fiscal years, as well as the individual financial statements (balance sheet, profit and loss statement, and statement of changes in shareholders' equity) for the two most recent business years (Cabinet Office Ordinance on Disclosure of Corporate Affairs, etc., Form 2, Notes 59 through 75). In cases where consolidated cash flow statements are not prepared, individual cash flow statements are required (Cabinet Office Ordinance on Disclosure of Corporate Affairs, etc. Form 2, Note 67, Note 71).

For foreign companies, in cases where documents on financial accounting of

---

for the Financial Instruments and Exchange Act receive a certificate from a foreign auditing firm, etc. (Article 193-2, item 1 of the Financial Instruments and Exchange Act) deemed equivalent to audit certification as specified by Article 1-2 of the Cabinet Office Ordinance on Audit Certification of Financial Statements, etc. in cases where financial documents of foreign companies, etc. (namely, among the securities and certificates issued by foreign states or foreign persons, financial documents submitted under the Financial Instruments and Exchange Act by the issuers of items that have the characteristics of share certificates or share option certificates [Article 34-35(1) of the Certified Public Accountants Act]), receive any certification deemed equivalent to audit certification as specified by cabinet office ordinance from persons specified by cabinet office ordinance recognized to receive appropriate supervision from foreign administrative institutions that supervise persons conducting business deemed to be equivalent to the audit certification business under Article 2, paragraph 1 of the Certified Public Accountants Act or other equivalent organs (there are presently no such cases specified by any Cabinet Office Ordinance), and in cases where approval received from the Prime Minister under Article 1-3 of the Cabinet Office Ordinance on Audit Certification of Financial Statements, etc. would not harm public interest or investor protection even without audit certification (Article 193-2(1)(i)-(iii) of the Financial Instruments and Exchange Act). Audit certification is not required for foreign bonds, etc. of foreign states, foreign local governments, etc.

*237*

the reporting company disclosed in areas other than Japan are considered under Article 131, paragraphs 1 and 2 of the Ordinance on Financial Statements, etc. not to harm public interest or investor protection, where only consolidated financial statements are disclosed in the relevant area, the consolidated financial statements, where only individual financial statements are disclosed in the relevant area, the individual financial statements; and where both consolidated financial statements and individual financial statements are disclosed in the relevant area, the consolidated financial statements and the individual financial statements must be presented. In these cases, the types of financial documents (balance sheet, profit and loss statement, etc.) are those that must be disclosed in the relevant area. However, reporting companies that are only required to present individual financial statements must prepare consolidated financial statements in accordance with Article 131, paragraph 3 of the Ordinance on Terminology, Forms and Preparation Methods of Financial Statements, etc.[30] and present these together with the relevant individual financial statements (Cabinet Office Ordinance on Disclosure of Corporate Affairs, etc., Form 7, Note 53a). On the other hand, in cases where documents on financial accounting disclosed by a foreign company in its home country or another area outside Japan are not recognised by the Commissioner of the Financial Services Agency in accordance with Article 131, paragraph 1 or 2 of the Ordinance on Financial Statements, etc., the terminology, forms and preparation methods of the financial documents submitted by the relevant foreign company are as directed by the Commissioner of the Financial Services Agency (Article 131

---

29　In cases where the consolidated financial statements are prepared according to the designated international financial reporting standards, the Modified International Standards or U.S. GAAP, the equivalent statements to the consolidated financial statements provided in the Ordinance on Terminology, Forms and Preparation Methods of Consolidated Financial Statements for Japanese GAAP preparers.

30　Where foreign companies for which the Commissioner of the Financial Services Agency has approved the submission of documents on financial accounting disclosed in areas outside Japan as financial documents submit documents on financial accounting other than documents on financial accounting disclosed in the relevant area as financial statements, the terminology, form and preparation methods of the documents on financial accounting are to be as directed by the Commissioner of the Financial Services Agency.

Chapter 3   Disclosure requirements

(4) of the Ordinance on Financial Statements, etc.). In principle, the financial documents for the most recent two business years (for the most recent one business year in cases where information equivalent to comparative information provided in Article 8-3 of the Ordinance on Consolidated Financial Statements, etc. and Article 6 of the Ordinance on Financial Statements, etc. are included [for the most recent two business years in cases where financial documents for the business year prior to the most recent business year are not stated in the notification or annual securities report submitted under Article 5, paragraph 1 or Article 24, paragraphs 1 through 3 of the Financial Instruments and Exchange Act]; for supplementary statements, for the most recent one business year) are to be submitted. However, in cases where the reporting company is not a continuous disclosure company, at the discretion of the company, financial documents for the most recent three business years (for supplementary statements, for the most recent one business year) that have received audit certification from a certified public accountant or auditing firm or certification equivalent to audit certification from a foreign auditing firm may be presented (Cabinet Office Ordinance on Disclosure of Corporate Affairs, etc., Form 7, Note 53b).

Companies submitting quarterly securities reports, in securities registration statements submitted on or after 45 days[31] (Article 4-2-10 (3) of the Financial Instruments and Exchange Act Implementing Order)[32] after three months, six months, and nine months from the beginning of the consolidated business year after the most recent consolidated business year (for foreign companies, the most recent business year), must include quarterly

---

31   However, in cases where the reporting company is a bank, company or other specified operating company (Article 17-5(2) and From 2, Note 61 a of the Cabinet Office Ordinance on Disclosure of Corporate Affairs, etc.), the consolidated interim financial statements for the second half (the individual interim financial statements in cases where consolidated interim financial statements are not prepared) shall also be included in securities registration statements submitted on or after six months and 60 days after the most recent consolidated business year.

32   However, even in cases of submissions before that date, when the most recent consolidated quarterly financial statements, individual quarterly financial statements or quarterly financial documents can be presented, they must be presented.

consolidated financial statements and quarterly individual financial statements (for foreign companies, quarterly financial documents) for the first quarter, second quarter, and third quarter respectively (Cabinet Office Ordinance on Disclosure of Corporate Affairs, etc., Form 2, Notes 61 through 71; Cabinet Office Ordinance on Disclosure of Corporate Affairs, etc., Form 7, Note 53b).

Companies submitting semiannual securities reports, for domestic companies with a business year lasting one year, in securities registration statements submitted on or after the date nine months after the beginning of the consolidated business year after the most recent consolidated business year must include consolidated interim financial statements and individual interim financial statements (Cabinet Office Ordinance on Disclosure of Corporate Affairs, etc., Form 2, Notes 61 through 71). Similarly, companies submitting semiannual securities reports, in cases where foreign companies whose business year is one year long submitted statements on or after the date eight months after the beginning of the next business year (excluding cases where quarterly financial documents were presented when planning to list or register as an over-the-counter traded security), must include the interim financial documents for the next relevant business year (excluding information equivalent to comparative information under Article 4-2 of the Ordinance on Interim Consolidated Financial Statements, etc. or Article 3-2 of the Ordinance on Interim Financial Statements, etc.) (Cabinet Office Ordinance on Disclosure of Corporate Affairs, etc., Form 7, Note 53b). When a foreign company whose business year is one year long (excluding companies submitting quarterly securities reports) that intends to list shares issued on a Japanese financial instruments exchange or to register shares issued as over-the-counter securities with an authorized financial instruments firms association submits a securities registration statement to conduct a public offering or secondary distribution of shares issued under the rules of the relevant financial instruments exchange or the relevant authorized financial instruments firms association, instead of interim financial documents, similar to the case of companies submitting quarterly securities reports, the foreign company may include quarterly financial statements for the first quarter, second quarter, and third quarter

Chapter 3　Disclosure requirements

respectively in securities registration statements submitted on or after 45 days[33] after three months, six months, and nine months from the beginning of the business year after the most recent consolidated business year (Cabinet Office Ordinance on Disclosure of Corporate Affairs, etc., Form 7, Note 53c).

　(6)　Outline of the shareholder services of the reporting company
The business year, timing of the ordinary general shareholders meeting, reference date, types of share certificates, reference date for dividends of surplus, number of shares per unit, registration of transfer of shares and shareholder registry administrator, purchase of shares less than one unit, method of public notice, shareholder privileges, etc. must be stated.

For foreign companies, as an "outline of the shareholder services of reporting companies in Japan," the location in Japan where registration of transfer of shares is conducted, the shareholder registry administrator, shareholder privileges, share transfer restrictions and other matters regarding shareholder services deemed necessary to show investors must be stated. Also, in cases of conducting a public offering or secondary distribution of shares, regarding the procedures, etc. to exercise shareholders' rights in Japan, procedures regarding the exercise of shareholders' voting rights, procedures regarding invoicing of dividends of surplus (including share dividends, etc.), procedures regarding transfer of shares, and in cases where there are rights preferential to other shareholders for the purchase or underwriting of unissued stock or treasury shares of the reporting company, procedures for the exercise of rights, tax treatment of dividends, etc., and other necessary procedures regarding the exercise of shareholders' rights must be stated (Cabinet Office Ordinance on Disclosure of Corporate Affairs, etc., Form 7, Note 57).

　(7)　Outline of laws and regulations in home country
In the case of a foreign company, as an outline of the company system, etc., in

---

**33**　However, even in cases of submissions before that date, where the most recent consolidated quarterly financial statements or individual quarterly financial statements can be presented, they must be presented.

addition to stating the company system in the country, state, etc. to which the reporting company belongs (especially matters concerning the general shareholders meeting, board of directors and other company organs and their authority, matters regarding shares, and matters regarding company accounting, etc.) and the systems prescribed in the articles of incorporation, etc. of the reporting company (in particular, matters concerning voting rights, rights to vote in elections of directors, claims of dividends and other shareholders' rights and their limitations [share transfer restrictions, etc.]), the foreign exchange management system, tax treatment and legal opinions in the home country must be stated (Cabinet Office Ordinance on Disclosure of Corporate Affairs, etc., Form 7). As legal opinions, a summary of the legal opinion letter of a legal expert that the public offering or secondary distribution that the statement covers is legal and the matters regarding the law presented in the statement are true and accurate must be stated (Cabinet Office Ordinance on Disclosure of Corporate Affairs, etc., Form 7, Note 29).

(8) Foreign exchange rate movements

In principle, foreign companies must state foreign exchange rate movements; however, this may be omitted in cases where foreign exchange rates between the currency used in the financial documents and Japanese currency have been published in at least two daily newspapers that publish matters regarding current events inside Japan for the past five business years and for the past six months (Cabinet Office Ordinance on Disclosure of Corporate Affairs, etc., Form 7, Note 56c).

(9) Referenced information on the reporting company

Information on the parent company, etc. of the reporting company and other referenced information are to be stated. Regarding information on the parent company, etc. of the reporting company, the company name, etc. of the parent company, etc. prescribed in Article 24-7, paragraph 1 of the Financial Instruments and Exchange Act must be stated or when there is no relevant parent company a statement to that effect must be presented (Cabinet Office Ordinance on Disclosure of Corporate Affairs, etc., Form 2, Note 76; Cabinet Office Ordinance on Disclosure of Corporate Affairs, etc., Form 7,

Chapter 3   Disclosure requirements

Note 58). As other referenced information, in cases where documents (securities registration statements, securities report, etc.) under each item of Article 25, paragraph 1 of the Financial Instruments and Exchange Act have been submitted between the first day of the most recent business year and the statement submission date, the names and submission dates of the documents; in cases where the documents include an extraordinary report, the reasons for its submission and which provisions the submission was based on (Article 19(2) & (3), or Article 19-2 of the Financial Instruments and Exchange Act); and in cases where the documents include an amendment, which document the amendment pertains to must be stated (Cabinet Office Ordinance on Disclosure of Corporate Affairs, etc., Form 2, Note 77; Cabinet Office Ordinance on Disclosure of Corporate Affairs, etc., Form 7, Note 59).

ⅲ) Information on the guarantor company, etc. for the reporting company Information on the guarantor company, information on companies other than the guarantor company, and information on indices and other information is stated.

Information on the guarantor company is stated about the relevant guarantor company, etc. in cases where bonds pertaining to the relevant notification are the subject of guarantee, etc., and includes the bonds that are the subject of guarantee, etc. (where the relevant notification is regarding a secondary distribution, the bonds that are the subject of guarantee [excluding short-term corporate bonds], bond name, issue date, total face value or total book-entry value, redemption amount, amount unredeemed as of the last day of the most recent business year of the reporting company, and name of the financial instruments exchange where listed or authorised financial instruments firms association where registered), matters concerning the guarantor company in cases where it is a continuous disclosure company (securities report submitted by the guarantor company and attached documents, quarterly securities reports or semiannual securities reports, extraordinary reports and amendment report, as well as the place where these documents are available for inspection), and matters concerning the guarantor company in cases where it is not a continuous

*243*

disclosure company (company name, name and title of representative, location of head office, overview of company, state of business, state of facilities, state of guarantor company, status of accounting; and in the case of foreign companies, an outline of the legal system in the home country) [34].

Regarding information on companies other than the guarantor company, reasons why disclosure of information of company information is necessary, matters regarding the company where it is a continuous disclosure company, and matters regarding the company where it is not a continuous disclosure company shall be disclosed. For the securities pertaining to the relevant notification, company information on tracked subsidiary companies [35] and companies other than the guarantor company but deemed to have a material influence on investment decisions (for example, in cases where the securities pertaining to the notification are covered warrants, the issuer of the securities that are subject to the option exercise, in cases where they are depository receipts the person receiving the deposit; and in cases where they are beneficiary certificates of securities in trust, the trustee) [36] is to be stated (Cabinet Office Ordinance on Disclosure of Corporate Affairs, etc, Form 2, Note 81; Cabinet Office Ordinance on Disclosure of Corporate Affairs, etc., Form 7, Note 63). Then in the case of domestic companies, for tracked subsidiary companies, the consolidated cash flow statements for the two

---

34  For domestic companies, the company information from "overview of company" through "status of accounting" is stated (statement of the consolidated cash flow statement and individual cash flow statement can be omitted). For foreign companies, the company information from "outline of legal system in home country" through "status of accounting" is stated (Cabinet Office Ordinance on Disclosure of Corporate Affairs, etc., Form 2, Note 80; Cabinet Office Ordinance on Disclosure of Corporate Affairs, etc., Form 7, Note 62).

35  Where the articles of incorporation of the relevant reporting company state that the surplus dividends of the shares issued by the reporting company are determined based on the surplus dividends or interim dividends of a specific subsidiary provided by Article 454, paragraph 5 of the Companies Act (Article 19(3) of the Financial Instruments and Exchange Act), the subsidiary.

36  When submitting notification of a public offering, etc. of bonds that can be converted into the shares of another company, the company issuing the shares is considered "a company other than the guarantor company considered to have a material influence on investment decisions" (Guidelines on Corporate Affairs Disclosure, B5-23).

Chapter 3 Disclosure requirements

most recent consolidated fiscal years and the individual cash flow statements for the two most recent business years are to be stated, and in cases where consolidated cash flow statements and individual cash flow statements are not prepared, the equivalent state of consolidated cash flow and cash flow conditions are to be stated (Cabinet Office Ordinance on Disclosure of Corporate Affairs, etc., Form 2, Note 81c).

Regarding information on indices, for the securities pertaining to the relevant notification, concerning indices considered to have a material influence on investment decisions, the reasons why disclosure of information on the relevant indices, etc. is necessary and on the movements of the indices (the highest and lowest annual values of the relevant indices, etc. during the five years immediately before the submission date of the securities registration statement and the highest and lowest monthly values during the six months immediately before the submission date of the statement) are to be stated (Cabinet Office Ordinance on Disclosure of Corporate Affairs, etc., Form 2, Note 82b; Cabinet Office Ordinance on Disclosure of Corporate Affairs, etc., Form 7, Note 64b).

iv) Special Information
In addition to the most recent financial statements or financial documents of the reporting company and the most recent financial statements or financial documents of the guarantor company and tracked subsidiary companies, in the case of foreign companies, the forms of the securities are to be stated (the forms and the contents of matters stated on the face of the securities certificates of securities for which a public offering or secondary distribution is conducted [including securities planned to be issued]) (Cabinet Office Ordinance on Disclosure of Corporate Affairs, etc., Form 7, Note 66).

In the case of domestic companies, regarding the most recent financial statements, among the balance sheet, profit and loss statement (excluding manufacturing cost detailed statements and sales cost detailed statements) for the most recent five business years (10 business years for companies whose business year is six months long), statement of changes in shareholders equity and cash flow statements, documents (excluding

*245*

comparative information provided by Article 6 of the Ordinance on Financial Statements, etc.) other than documents included in company information (including comparative information provided by Article 6 of the Ordinance on Financial Statements, etc.) are to be presented in accordance with the statements of company information; but the statement of cash flow statements can be omitted. In the case of foreign companies, similarly, among the financial documents (excluding supplementary statements) for the most recent five business years (10 business years for companies whose business year is six months long), documents (excluding comparative information provided by Article 6 of the Ordinance on Financial Statements, etc.) other than documents stated in company information (including comparative information provided by Article 6 of the Ordinance on Financial Statements, etc.) are to be presented in accordance with the statements of company information; however, in cases where financial documents for the most recent three years are presented in the corporate information, these are not required.

When reporting companies and guarantor companies, etc. are continuous disclosure companies (companies which intend to submit a securities registration statement [including designated juridical persons], companies submitting a securities registration statement or securities report before the date of the relevant submission [including designated juridical persons] excluding cases where the obligation to submit a securities report is waived under the proviso to Article 24, paragraph 1 of the Financial Instruments and Exchange Act [Article 1 (xxviii) of the Cabinet Office Ordinance on Disclosure of Corporate Affairs, etc.]), it is not required to state financial documents regarding the companies (Cabinet Office Ordinance on Disclosure of Corporate Affairs, etc., Form 2, Note 1e; Cabinet Office Ordinance on Disclosure of Corporate Affairs, etc., Form 7, Note 1h).

v ) Attached documents

The "attached documents" must be, in the case of domestic companies, the articles of incorporation (articles of endowment in the case of domestic issuers that are foundations); in cases where there is a board of directors resolution or general shareholders meeting resolution regarding issuance of

Chapter 3   Disclosure requirements

the securities concerned, a copy of the minutes of the relevant board of directors meeting or a copy of the minutes of the relevant general shareholders meeting, or documents attesting the receipt of authorization of the administrative agency or similar documents; in cases where permission, authorization or approval of the administrative agency is required to change the amount of capital of the company (including designated juridical persons) by issuance of the securities concerned, documents sufficient to show the relevant permission, authorization or approval; in cases where the securities concerned are bonds, social medical-care corporation bonds, school bond certificates or school loan claims (bonds, etc.) or commercial paper with attached guarantees, the articles of incorporation of the company, etc. providing the relevant guarantee (in cases where this is a partnership other than a juridical person, a copy of the partnership agreement) as well as a copy of the minutes, etc. of the board of directors meeting or a copy of the minutes of the general shareholders meeting regarding the resolution by the board of directors or the resolution made at the general shareholders meeting that was adopted in order to provide the guarantee; in cases where the securities concerned are covered warrants and there is a contract concluded regarding the options represented in the covered warrants, a copy of the relevant contract; in cases where the securities concerned are beneficiary certificates of securities in trust, copies of the trust contract concluded regarding the issuance of the relevant beneficiary certificates of securities in trust and of other main contracts; and in cases where the securities concerned are depository receipts, copies of the depository contract concluded regarding the issuance of the concerned depository receipts concerned and of the other main contracts (Article 10(1) (i) of the Cabinet Office Ordinance on Disclosure of Corporate Affairs, etc.).

In the case of foreign companies, in addition to the "attached documents" for domestic companies, the securities registration statement "attached documents" are a document attesting that the representative of the foreign company which intends to submit the relevant securities registration statement is a person with legitimate authority concerning notification of the public offering or secondary distribution of the securities stated on the relevant securities registration statement, a document attesting that the

*247*

relevant foreign company has authorized a person who has residence in Japan to represent the relevant foreign company in all acts concerning notification of the public offering or secondary distribution of the securities, a legal opinion letter from a legal expert that the public offering or secondary distribution of the securities is legal and that the matters stated in the relevant securities registration statement regarding law are true and accurate, a document attesting that the relevant permission has been received in cases where permission provided by Article 21, paragraph 1 or paragraph 2 of the Foreign Exchange and Foreign Trade Act is required, and a copy of the wholesale underwriting contract concluded between the relevant foreign company and a financial instruments business operator; and in cases where the securities concerned are bonds, etc., a copy of the contract in which the relevant foreign company entrusts the duties of administration of claims and other duties to perform acts for obligees or acts for the concerned foreign company concerned and a copy of the contract concerning payment of principal and interest (Article 10 (1) (iv) of the Cabinet Office Ordinance on Disclosure of Corporate Affairs, etc.). In cases where the attached documents are stated in languages other than Japanese, a Japanese translation must be attached (Article 10(2) of the Cabinet Office Ordinance on Disclosure of Corporate Affairs, etc.).

(ⅱ) [Actual] incorporation method
The [actual] incorporation method can be used by persons submitting annual securities reports continuously for at least one year (Article 5(3) of the Financial Instruments and Exchange Act; Article 9-3(1) of the Cabinet Office Ordinance on Disclosure of Corporate Affairs, etc.) (continuous disclosure requirements). "Persons submitting annual securities reports continuously for at least one year" means either (i) persons submitting an annual securities report on the corresponding date for the one year before the submission date of a securities registration statement, or (ii) persons who did not submit an annual securities report as of the corresponding date because the obligation to submit an annual securities report for the immediately preceding business year was waived (Article 16-2 of the Cabinet Office Ordinance on Disclosure of Corporate Affairs, etc.) because three months have passed since the beginning of the business year of the day

Chapter 3　Disclosure requirements

on which the person came to bear the obligation for continuous disclosure or because the financial statements for the immediately preceding business year were stated in the securities registration statement because the person had the obligation to submit a securities registration statement regarding public offering or secondary distribution of the securities issued by a company with no obligation for continuous disclosure; so the person should bear the obligation to submit an annual securities report for the immediately preceding business year without delay and subsequently submitted an annual securities report by the securities registration statement submissions date using the [actual] incorporation method, and appropriately fulfilled the continuous disclosure obligation between the corresponding date and the date for submission of the securities registration statement using the [actual] incorporation method (Guidelines on Corporate Affairs Disclosure, B5-26).

Also, in cases where the person who intends to submit a securities registration statement is a wholly-owning parent company established through share transfer, even in cases where the wholly-owning parent company itself has not submitted annual securities reports continuously for one year or more, the use of the [actual] incorporation method is permitted in certain cases considering the conditions of continuous disclosure by the wholly-owning subsidiary companies (special provision for wholly-owning parent company in a share transfer). Namely, use of the [actual] incorporation method is permitted in cases where the person who intends to submit a securities registration statement is a company established through a share transfer conducted within two years and three months before the submission of the annual securities report regarding the most recent business year of the relevant company, and on the day before the date of the share transfer the total number of eligible wholly-owning subsidiary companies in the share transfer (wholly-owning subsidiary companies in a share transfer which meet qualification requirements for use of the above-mentioned incorporation by reference method on the day before the date of the share transfer; Article 9-3(3) of the Cabinet Office Ordinance on Disclosure of Corporate Affairs, etc.) was at least two-thirds the number of all wholly-owning subsidiary companies in a share transfer or on the day

*249*

before the date of the share transfer the total number of shareholders of eligible wholly-owning subsidiary companies in the share transfer was at least two-thirds the total number of shareholders of all share transfer subsidiary companies, when the relevant wholly-owning parent company in a share transfer and all eligible wholly-owning subsidiary companies in a share transfer properly fulfill their continuous disclosure obligations between the submission date of the most recent annual securities report submitted before the share transfer date by the eligible wholly-owning subsidiary companies in a share transfer (in cases where there are multiple eligible wholly-owning subsidiary companies in a share transfer, the date of the earliest submission) and the securities registration statement submission date by the wholly-owning parent company (Article 9-3(3) of the Cabinet Office Ordinance on Disclosure of Corporate Affairs, etc.; Guidelines on Corporate Affairs Disclosure, B5-27).

In cases where securities for which a company that becomes a wholly-owned subsidiary company in a share transfer is the issuer and which were listed on a financial instruments exchange or registered as over-the-counter trading securities by an authorized financial instruments firms association are delisted from the relevant financial instruments exchange or have their registration rescinded before the date of the share transfer by the relevant authorized financial instruments firms association along with the share transfer, the securities are viewed as having been listed on the relevant financial instruments exchange or registered on the relevant authorized financial instruments firms association as of the day before the date of the share transfer and deemed to meet the requirements for use of the [actual] incorporation method (Guidelines on Corporate Affairs Disclosure, B5-28).

i ) Incorporated information

When using the [actual] incorporation method, domestic companies are to prepare the securities registration statement using Form 2-2 and foreign companies using Form 7-2 of the Cabinet Office Ordinance on Disclosure of Corporate Affairs, etc., respectively (Article 3 (1) of the Cabinet Office Ordinance on Disclosure of Corporate Affairs, etc.). Even with the [actual]

Chapter 3　Disclosure requirements

incorporation method, while securities information must all be stated on the securities registration statement, instead of company information, copies of the most recent securities report and its attached documents as well as copies of the quarterly securities reports or semiannual securities reports submitted after the most recent securities report and any amendment reports are incorporated as incorporated information [37] and material facts that emerge after the submission of the relevant annual securities report are stated as subsequent completion information (Article 5(3) of the Financial Instruments and Exchange Act).

For domestic companies, items that must be stated as follow-up information include: (i) when circumstances emerge that are grounds for submission of an amendment report before the notification prescribed by Article 7, paragraph 1, first sentence of the Financial Instruments and Exchange Act takes effect, the contents thereof; (ii) when circumstances emerge that are grounds for submission of an extraordinary report prescribed by Article 19, paragraph 2 each item or Article 19-2 of the Cabinet Office Ordinance on Disclosure of Corporate Affairs, etc., the contents thereof; (iii) other events with a material impact on financial conditions or operating results; (iv) capital increases or decreases and changes to the statement of "business-related risks etc." between the date of submission of the annual securities report deemed incorporated information and the date of submission of the securities registration statement; (v) when a company that presents consolidated financial statements in its securities report and submits quarterly securities reports submits a securities registration statement on or after the day when roughly three months, six months or nine months have passed since the beginning of the subsequent consolidated business year following the most recent consolidated business year, outlines of performance for the respective three months, six months or nine months after the beginning of the relevant subsequent consolidated business year;

---

37　It is not necessary to include the attached documents in the annual securities report. However, in cases where the articles of incorporation are not included, the relevant articles of incorporation must be attached to the relevant securities registration statement (Guidelines on Disclosure of Corporate Affairs, B5-24).

*251*

and (vi) where there was a general shareholders meeting resolution pertaining to treasury shares at the most recent general shareholders meeting before the submission date of the securities registration statement, the state of the relevant acquisition of the treasury shares between the submission date of the securities report deemed incorporated information and the submission date of the securities registration statement (see Guidelines on Corporate Affairs Disclosure, B5-25) (Cabinet Office Ordinance on Disclosure of Corporate Affairs, etc., Form 2-2, Note 2).

Foreign companies must also state (i), (ii), (iii), (iv), etc.; and in cases where a sufficient period has passed sufficient to state performance in the business year following the most recent business year, an outline of that must be stated in comparison with the same period of the previous business year, and in cases where a notification is submitted after the passage of the business year following the most recent business year, when a statement using financial documents forms is possible, the statement should be made using the financial documents forms (Cabinet Office Ordinance on Disclosure of Corporate Affairs, etc., Form 7-2, Note 3).

ii ) Attached Documents

For domestic companies, in addition to the attached documents required where using the ordinary method (where included in the securities registration statement inclusion documents, excluding the articles of incorporation [Articles of Endowment in the case of domestic issuers which are foundations]), where under the special provision for wholly-owning parent company in a share transfer, the names, representatives' names, stated capital and description of business of the relevant reporting company's relevant wholly-owned subsidiary companies in a share transfer and eligible wholly-owned subsidiary companies in a share transfer, purpose of the relevant share transfer, method of the relevant share transfer and description of resolutions of general shareholders meetings of the relevant eligible wholly-owned subsidiary companies in a share transfer regarding the relevant share transfer, and also in cases of special provision because on the day before the date of the relevant share transfer the total number of shareholders of the eligible wholly-owned subsidiary companies in a share

Chapter 3 Disclosure requirements

transfer was at least two-thirds of the total number of shareholders of the relevant wholly-owned subsidiary companies in a share transfer, a document stating the number of shareholders on the day before the date of the share transfer of the relevant wholly-owned subsidiary companies in a share transfer and eligible wholly-owned subsidiary companies in a share transfer of the relevant reporting company must be included as attached documents (Article 10 (1) (ii) of the Cabinet Office Ordinance on Disclosure of Corporate Affairs, etc.).

Foreign companies other than those that have submitted foreign company reports must submit the following items, in addition to the items submitted by domestic companies, as securities registration statement attached documents: a legal opinion letter from a legal expert stating that the public offering or secondary distribution of the securities is legal; a document attesting that the representative of the foreign company stated in the relevant securities registration statement that intends to submit the relevant securities registration statement is a person with legitimate authority concerning notification of the public offering or secondary distribution of the securities; a document attesting that the relevant foreign company has authorized a person who has residence in Japan to represent the relevant foreign company in all acts concerning notification of the concerned securities public offering or secondary distribution of the securities concerned; a document attesting that the relevant permission has been received in cases where permission provided by Article 21, paragraph 1 or 2 of the Foreign Exchange and Foreign Trade Act is required, and a copy of the wholesale underwriting contract concluded between the concerned foreign company concerned and a financial instruments business operator. In cases where the securities concerned are bonds, etc., a copy of the contract in which the relevant foreign company entrusts the duties of administration of claims and other duties to perform acts for obligees or acts for the relevant foreign company and a copy of the contract concerning payment of the principal and interest (Article 10(1) (v) of the Cabinet Office Ordinance on Disclosure of Corporate Affairs, etc.).

Foreign companies that have submitted foreign company reports must

*253*

submit the following items as securities registration statement attached documents: in cases where there is a board of directors resolution or general shareholders meeting resolution regarding issuance of the securities concerned, a copy of the minutes of the relevant board of directors meeting or of the minutes of the relevant general shareholders meeting, or documents attesting the receipt of authorization of the administrative agency or similar documents; in cases where permission, authorization or approval of an administrative agency is required to change the amount of capital of the company (including designated juridical persons) by issuance of the securities concerned, documents sufficient to show the relevant permission, authorization or approval; a legal opinion letter from a legal expert that the public offering or secondary distribution of the securities is legal; a document attesting that the representative of the foreign company stated on the relevant securities registration statement that intends to submit the relevant securities registration statement is a person with legitimate authority concerning notification of the public offering or secondary distribution of the securities; a document attesting that the relevant foreign company has authorized a person who has residence in Japan to represent the relevant foreign company in all acts concerning notification of the public offering or secondary distribution of the securities; a document attesting that the relevant permission has been received in cases where permission provided by the Article 21, paragraph 1 or 2 of the Foreign Exchange and Foreign Trade Act is required; a copy of the wholesale underwriting contract concluded between the relevant foreign company and a financial instruments business operator; and in cases where the securities concerned are bonds, etc., a copy of the contract in which the relevant foreign company entrusts the duties of administration of claims and other duties to perform acts for obligees or acts for the concerned foreign company concerned and a copy of the contract concerning payment of the principal and interest (Article 10 (1) (v-2) of the Cabinet Office Ordinance on Disclosure of Corporate Affairs, etc.).

(ⅲ) Incorporation by reference method

The incorporation by reference method can be used by persons submitting annual securities reports continuously for at least one year (continuous

Chapter 3 Disclosure requirements

disclosure requirement) and which meet certain criteria (publicity criteria) regarding the trading on financial instruments exchange markets for securities previously issued by the persons as widely providing the public with information on their corporate affairs, etc. (Article 5(4) of the Financial Instruments and Exchange Act (4); Article 9-4 of the Cabinet Office Ordinance on Disclosure of Corporate Affairs, etc.).

The requirement for "submitting annual securities reports continuously for at least one year" is the same as under the [actual] incorporation method. The publicity criteria, in cases where the shares issued by the person submitting the securities registration statement are listed on a domestic financial instruments exchange or are over-the-counter registered securities in an authorized financial instruments firms association, is met in any of the following cases: (i) the average trading value and average market capitalization are both ¥10 billion or more (Article 9-4(5)(i)(a), (b) & (c) of the Cabinet Office Ordinance on Disclosure of Corporate Affairs, etc.); (ii) the market capitalization is ¥25 billion or more (Article 9-4(5)(i)(d) of the Cabinet Office Ordinance on Disclosure of Corporate Affairs, etc.); (iii) the total face value of corporate bond certificates or the total value of bonds issued or delivered in the past five years through submission of a securities registration statement or shelf-registration supplement regarding their public offering or secondary distribution is ¥10 billion or more (Article 9-4 (5)(i)(e) of the Cabinet Office Ordinance on Disclosure of Corporate Affairs, etc. Article); or (iv) corporate bond certificates with preferential payment rights guaranteed by law have already been issued (Article 9-4(5)(i)(f) of the Cabinet Office Ordinance on Disclosure of Corporate Affairs, etc. Article). Also, the publicity criteria is met where the person submitting the securities registration statement issues share certificates listed on a specified foreign financial instruments exchange (among foreign financial instruments exchanges, those specified by the Commissioner of the Financial Services Agency considering the securities listed, state of information disclosure regarding the issuer, trading volume, and other circum stances) (Article 2-12-3(iv)(b) of the Financial Instruments and Exchange Act Implementing Order; Article 2(3)(vi) of the Cabinet Office Ordinance on Disclosure of Corporate Affairs, etc.)[38] and the base time market capitalization for the share certificates on a foreign financial instruments market is at least ¥100 billion (Article 9-4 (5) (iii) of the Cabinet Office Ordinance on Disclosure of Corporate Affairs, etc.). Moreover, in relation to securities registration statements pertaining to corporate bond certificates (including items issued by foreign persons with the same characteristics as corporate bond certificates), even where the issued share certificates are not listed on a financial instruments exchange or registered over-the-counter with an authorized financial instruments firms association in Japan, the communications requirement is deemed to be fulfilled when corporate bond certificates issued or delivered by submission of a securities registration statement or shelf-registration supplement regarding their public offering or secondary distribution within the past five years have a total face value or a total value of ¥10 billion or more (Article 9-4(5) (iv) of the Cabinet Office Ordinance on Disclosure of Corporate Affairs, etc.).

Similar to cases under the [actual] incorporation method, in cases where the person who intends to submit a securities registration statement is a wholly-owning parent company established through share transfer, even in cases where the wholly-owning parent company has not submitted annual securities reports continuously for one year or more, the use of the incorporation by reference method is permitted in certain cases considering

---

**38** In Financial Services Agency Notification No. 41 of 2010 "Specification of Foreign Financial Instruments Exchanges Prescribed in the Implementing Order for Article 2-12-3, item 4b of the Financial Instruments and Exchange Act," the following exchanges are specified: Irish Stock Exchange; Oslo Børs, Deutsche Börse; Nasdaq OMX Stockholm; Nasdaq OMX Helsinki; New York Stock Exchange Euronext Amsterdam; New York Stock Exchange Euronext Paris; New York Stock Exchange Euronext Brussels; BME Spanish Exchanges; Borsa Italiana; Luxembourg Stock Exchange; London Stock Exchange (limited to financial instruments exchanges in the relevant foreign states which operate regulated markets as announced by the European Commission in accordance with Article 47 of the Directive 2004/39/EC of the European Parliament and of the Council), New York Stock Exchange Euronext; Nasdaq OMX; SIX Swiss Exchange; Australian Securities Exchange; Korea Exchange; Singapore Exchange; Taiwan Stock Exchange; Toronto Stock Exchange, Bursa Malaysia; Hong Kong Stock Exchange and Mexican Stock Exchange among foreign financial instruments exchanges registered by the U.S. Securities and Exchange Commission in accordance with Article 6 of the U.S. Securities Exchange Act of 1934.

Chapter 3  Disclosure requirements

the state of ongoing disclosure by the wholly-owned subsidiary companies (special provision for wholly-owning parent company in a share transfer). Namely, in cases where the person who intends to submit a securities registration statement is a company established through a share transfer conducted within two years and three months before the submission of the annual securities report regarding the most recent business year of the relevant person; and on the day before the date of the share transfer the number of eligible wholly-owned subsidiary companies in a share transfer (wholly-owned subsidiary companies in a share transfer which meet the qualification requirements for use of the above-mentioned incorporation by reference method on the day before the date of the share transfer; Article 9-3(3) of the Cabinet Office Ordinance on Disclosure of Corporate Affairs, etc.) was at least two-thirds the number of all wholly-owned subsidiary companies in a share transfer or on the day before the date of the share transfer the total of the number of shareholders of eligible wholly-owned subsidiary companies in a share transfer was at least two-thirds the number of shareholders of all wholly-owned subsidiary companies in a share transfer, as long as the relevant wholly-owning parent company in a share transfer and all eligible wholly-owned subsidiary companies in a share transfer properly fulfill their ongoing disclosure obligation between the submission date of the most recent annual securities report submitted before the share transfer date by the eligible wholly-owned subsidiary company in a share transfer (in cases where there are multiple eligible wholly-owning subsidiary companies in a share transfer, the date of the earliest submission) and the securities registration statement submission date by the wholly-owning parent company, the ongoing disclosure requirements are met; and if the publicity criteria is met the incorporation by reference method can be used (Article 9-4(4) of the Cabinet Office Ordinance on Disclosure of Corporate Affairs, etc.; Guidelines on Corporate Affairs Disclosure, B5-27).

In cases where securities for which a company that becomes a wholly-owned subsidiary company in a share transfer is the issuer and which were listed on a financial instruments exchange or registered as over-the-counter traded securities by an authorized financial instruments

*257*

firms association are delisted from the relevant financial instruments exchange or have their registration rescinded before the date of the share transfer by the relevant authorized financial instruments firms association along with the share transfer, the securities are viewed as having been listed on the concerned financial instruments exchange concerned or registered on the relevant authorized financial instruments firms association as of the day before the date of the share transfer and deemed to meet the requirements for use of the incorporation by reference method (Guidelines on Corporate Affairs Disclosure, B5-28).

In addition to the above, in cases where an issuer of commercial paper intends to submit a securities registration statement concerning a public offering or secondary distribution of its commercial paper, the incorporation by reference method can be used in cases where the total issue value or total distribution value of commercial paper issued or delivered by the issuer in Japan by submitting the securities registration statement or shelf-registration supplement regarding a public offering or secondary distribution within five years before the submission date of the securities registration statement is at least ¥10 billion (Article 9-5 of the Cabinet Office Ordinance on Disclosure of Corporate Affairs, etc.).

ⅰ) Referenced information

When using the incorporation by reference method, domestic companies are to prepare the securities registration statement using Form 2-3 and foreign companies using Form 7-3 of the Cabinet Office Ordinance on Disclosure of Corporate Affairs, etc., respectively (Article 9-4(1) of the Cabinet Office Ordinance on Disclosure of Corporate Affairs, etc.). While securities information must all be stated on the securities report, for company information a statement to refer to copies of the most recent securities report and its attached documents and to quarterly securities reports, semiannual securities reports, and extraordinary reports submitted after the securities report and any amendment reports thereto is viewed as having stated company information (Article 5(4) of the Financial Instruments and Exchange Act).

Chapter 3   Disclosure requirements

While it is not necessary to state, in the securities registration statement, material facts that emerged after submission of the securities report provided for reference as follow-up information, documents stating the description of certain material facts must be attached.

Also, in cases where an extraordinary report or foreign company extraordinary report is included in the reference documents, the reasons for its submission and which provisions the submission was based on Article 19, paragraph 2, each item, or paragraph 3, or Article 19-2 of the Cabinet Office Ordinance on Disclosure of Corporate Affairs, etc.; and in cases where an amendment report is included in the reference documents, which document the amendment report pertains to must be stated; and where there are any changes, etc. to the statement of business-related risks, etc. between the date of submission of the securities report to be referenced and the date of submission of the securities registration statement, a statement to that effect and the description must be stated (Cabinet Office Ordinance on Disclosure of Corporate Affairs, etc., Form 2-3, Note 2; Cabinet Office Ordinance on Disclosure of Corporate Affairs, etc., Form 7-3, Note 2).

ⅱ) Attached documents

For domestic companies, in addition to the attached documents required in using the [actual] incorporation method, a document attesting that the person submitting the relevant securities registration statement fulfills the requirements of each item of Article 5, paragraph 4 of the Financial Instruments and Exchange Act, and in cases where after the submission date of the relevant securities report in which the securities registration statement refers to material facts that occurred prior to the submission date that should have been stated in the relevant annual securities report whose contents could not be stated when the relevant documents were submitted can now be stated, or in cases where material facts concerning items that should be stated in the relevant securities report occur (excluding cases where quarterly securities reports, semiannual securities reports, extraordinary reports or amendment reports which include the description of those material facts are included in the reference documents for the relevant securities registration statement), documents stating the

*259*

description of the relevant material facts, as well as an outline of description of business and a document accurately and simply explaining major management indicators, etc. must be included as attached documents (Article 10 (1) (iii) of the Cabinet Office Ordinance on Disclosure of Corporate Affairs, etc.)

Foreign companies must submit the following items, in addition to the items to be submitted by domestic companies, as securities registration statement attached documents: a legal opinion letter from a legal expert that the public offering or secondary distribution of the securities is legal; a document attesting that the representative of the foreign company stated on the relevant securities registration statement which intends to submit the relevant securities registration statement is a person with legitimate authority concerning notification of the public offering or secondary distribution of the securities; a document attesting that the relevant foreign company has authorized a person who has residence in Japan to represent the relevant foreign company in all acts concerning notification of the public offering or secondary distribution of the securities; a document attesting that the relevant permission has been received in cases where permission provided by Article 21, paragraph 1 or 2 of the Foreign Exchange and Foreign Trade Act is required; and a copy of the wholesale underwriting contract concluded between the relevant foreign company and a financial instruments business operator. In cases where the securities concerned are bonds, etc., a copy of the contract whereby the relevant foreign company entrusts the management of the claims and other acts for the obligees and the duty of acts for the relevant foreign company and a copy of the contract concerning payment of the principal and interest (Article 10(1)(vi) of the Cabinet Office Ordinance on Disclosure of Corporate Affairs, etc.).

In cases where, after the submission date of the annual securities report to be referenced, consolidated financial statements are prepared and disclosed as a summary settlement of accounts, or there has been a change of the parent company or of the representative director of the reporting company, or certain other material facts arise, where quarterly securities reports, semiannual securities reports, extraordinary reports, or amendment reports

Chapter 3 Disclosure requirements

that state the material facts are not included in the reference documents of the securities registration statement, a document stating the description of the material facts must be attached (see Article 10 (1) (iii) (e) of the Cabinet Office Ordinance on Disclosure of Corporate Affairs, etc.; Guidelines on Corporate Affairs Disclosure, B7-3, 7-4, 7-6).

(iv) Stock initial public offering

Companies (limited to domestic companies) that intend to list issued shares on a financial instruments exchange in Japan (including specified juridical persons) or to register issued shares as over-the-counter traded securities in an authorized financial instruments firms association and which intend to submit securities registration statements in order to conduct public offerings or secondary distributions of issued shares under the regulations of the relevant financial instruments exchange or authorized financial instruments association must prepare securities registration statements using Form 2-4 (using Form 2-7 when the relevant public offering or secondary distribution falls under specified procedures relating to securities issuance for reorganization or specified procedures relating to securities issuance for delivery) where the relevant public offering or secondary distribution does not correspond to specified procedures relating to securities issuance for reorganization or specified procedures relating to securities delivery for reorganization (Article 8 (2) (i) of the Cabinet Office Ordinance on Disclosure of Corporate Affairs, etc.).

In Form 2-4, in addition to securities information, company information and special information, as stock offering information the state of transfer of shares, etc. of special stakeholders, etc., an overview of third-party allotments etc. and the status of shareholder must be stated, but efforts are made to simplify the company information and special information.

i ) Differences in company information compared with using the ordinary method

First, regarding the movements of major management indicators, etc., the enumerated movements of major management indicators, etc. of the reporting company for the most recent five business years (ten business

*261*

years for companies whose business year is six months long) must be stated, but among the movements of the main management indicators, etc. for the most recent five business years, aside from those for the most recent two business years (four business years for companies whose business year is six months long), each value can be stated and calculated based on the Companies Accounting Regulation. However, in cases where each value is stated based on the Companies Accounting Regulation, a statement to that effect and a statement that these have not received audit certification specified by Article 193-2, paragraph 1 of the Financial Instruments and Exchange Act must be stated in a note in the margin. Also, cash flow from operating activities, cash flow from investing activities, cash flow from financing activities, and the term-end balance of cash and cash equivalents are not required to be stated for business years where a statement of cash flows is not prepared (Cabinet Office Ordinance on Disclosure of Corporate Affairs, etc., Form 2-4, Note 11b).

Second, in cases where consolidated financial statements are prepared using the designated international financial reporting standards, the movement of indices, etc. corresponding to indices, etc. under the Ordinance on Consolidated Financial Statements must be stated regarding the consolidated fiscal years for the consolidated financial statements (in cases of consolidated financial statements regarding consolidated fiscal years using the designated international financial reporting standards, including the relevant consolidated fiscal years) (Cabinet Office Ordinance on Disclosure of Corporate Affairs, etc., Form 2-4, Note 11a).

ⅱ) Special information
The financial statements of tracked subsidiaries for the past two business years should be included (Cabinet Office Ordinance on Disclosure of Corporate Affairs, etc., Form 2-4, Note 22).

ⅲ) Stock offering information
Regarding the state of transfer of shares, etc. of special stakeholders, etc., in cases where between the date two years before the last day of the most recent business year and the date the notification is submitted, special

Chapter 3 Disclosure requirements

stakeholders, etc.[39] have transferred or accepted shares, share options, or bonds with share options issued by the reporting company (movements of shares, etc; Cabinet Office Ordinance on Disclosure of Corporate Affairs, etc., Form 2-4, Note 24a),[40] the dates of the share transfers, the names and addresses of the shareholders before and after the transfers, the relationships between the person submitting the notification and the shareholders before and after the transfers, the number of shares transferred, the prices, the reasons for the transfers, etc. must be stated.

Regarding an overview of third-party allotment, etc., in cases where between the date two years before the last day of the most recent business year and the date the securities registration statement was submitted, the company issued new shares, share options, or bonds with share options using means other than shareholder allotment (third-party allotment, etc.; Cabinet Office Ordinance on Disclosure of Corporate Affairs, etc., Form 2-4, Note 25a (a)), the description of the issue including the issue date and issue price and an overview of the persons acquiring the shares including their names, addresses and relationship with the reporting company must be stated; and in cases where shares acquired by third-party allotment, etc. were transferred, etc. between the date one year before the last day of the most recent business year and the date the securities registration statement was submitted, then similar to the requirements for the status of shares transfer, etc. of special stakeholders, etc., the status of persons acquiring shares, etc. must be stated.

However, in cases where stock options are granted to employees and the number of granted stock options is small, disclosure of detailed information regarding each individual employee is not required, and it is sufficient to

---

39 These refer to the reporting company's "directors", spouses and relatives of "directors" within the second degree of kinship, top ten shareholders, and certain companies that have a personnel or capital relationship with the relevant company. This judgment is made at the time of the transfer of the shares, etc. (Article 1(xxxi) of the Cabinet Office Ordinance on Disclosure of Corporate Affairs, etc.; Guidelines on Corporate Affairs Disclosure, B5-37).

40 Including exercise of share options or of share options pertaining to bonds with share options, wholesale succession of shares, etc. from succession or merger, etc. (Guidelines on Disclosure of Corporate Affairs, B5-39).

*263*

state the total number of persons and units granted. In other words, where the persons acquiring the shares are employees of the company submitting the securities registration statement or a company under its control, etc. (Article 6(3) of the Cabinet Office Ordinance Regarding Definitions) and do not constitute special stakeholders, etc. of the relevant reporting company, and the acquired securities are share option certificates with transfer restrictions specified by Article 236, paragraph 1, item 6 of the Companies Act, and the total number of shares that are the object of the relevant acquired share option certificates is less than 1,000 shares, it is sufficient to place a note in the margin stating the number of persons and shares for the relevant allotment and to state the total number of persons and number of shares delivered (Cabinet Office Ordinance on Disclosure of Corporate Affairs, etc., Form 2-4, Note 25b(a)).

Regarding shareholders, approximately the top 50 shareholders as of the date the securities registration statement is submitted must be stated in the order of the number of shares held.

In cases where the securities concerned are green-sheet issues under the Japan Securities Dealers Association, these statements (special stakeholders, etc. transfer status of shares, etc.; overview of third-party allotment, etc.; shareholder status) are not required, and a statement to the effect that the securities concerned are a green-sheet issue and a statement of their monthly trading volume and monthly high and low share prices between the date two years before the last day of the most recent business year and the date the securities registration statement was submitted are sufficient (Cabinet Office Ordinance on Disclosure of Corporate Affairs, etc., Form 2-4, Note 23).

ii ) Attached documents
The attached documents are the same as those for securities registration statements submitted by domestic companies using the ordinary method (Article 10(1) (i) (iii-2) of the Cabinet Office Ordinance on Disclosure of Corporate Affairs, etc.).

*264*

Chapter 3   Disclosure requirements

（ⅴ）   Small-amount public offerings, etc.

In cases where domestic companies that are not continuous disclosure companies and which have not submitted securities registration statements, annual securities reports, quarterly securities reports or semiannual securities reports without using the small-amount public offerings, etc. special provision in the past public offerings or secondary distributions with a total issue value or total distribution value of less than ¥500 million (small-amount public offerings, etc.), statement of company information on securities registration statements on an individual basis is permitted (Article 5(2) of the Financial Instruments and Exchange Act).

However, even in cases where the total issue value or total distribution value is less than ¥500 million, the small-amount public offering, etc. special provision cannot be applied in the following cases (Article 5 (2) of the Financial Instruments and Exchange Act; Article 9-2 of the Cabinet Office Ordinance on Disclosure of Corporate Affairs, etc.).

(1)   In cases where the securities pertaining to the public offering or secondary distribution are share option certificates, and the sum of the total issue value or total distribution value of the share option certificates plus the exercise value of the share options pertaining to the share option certificates is ¥500 million or more (Article 9-2(i) of the Cabinet Office Ordinance on Disclosure of Corporate Affairs, etc.).

(2)   In cases where the sum of the total issue value or total distribution value of securities pertaining to a public offering or secondary distribution plus the total issue value or total distribution value of public offerings or secondary distributions of the same class of securities[41]

---

41   The "same class of securities" means the category of securities under each item of Article 2, paragraphs 1 and 2 of the Financial Instruments and Exchange Act that is the same (Article 1(ii) of the Cabinet Office Ordinance on Disclosure of Corporate Affairs, etc.). Share option certificates are deemed the same class of securities as share certificates (Article 2(1)(ix) of the Financial Instruments and Exchange Act) and bonds with share options are also deemed the same class of securities as shares (Article 9-2(ii) of the Cabinet Office Ordinance on Disclosure of Corporate Affairs, etc.).

*265*

conducted within one year from the date the relevant public offering or secondary distribution began (excluding public offerings and secondary distributions for which securities registration statements or shelf-registration supplements were submitted and prior public offerings and secondary distributions) is ¥500 million or more (Article 9-2(ii) of the Cabinet Office Ordinance on Disclosure of Corporate Affairs, etc.).

(3) In cases falling under public offering by six-month summation, when the sum of the total issue value of the securities pertaining to the public offering plus the total issue value of the same class of newly issued securities issued within six months from the issue date of the securities concerned is ¥500 million or more (Article 9-2(iii) of the Cabinet Office Ordinance on Disclosure of Corporate Affairs, etc.).

(4) In cases falling under secondary distribution by one-month summation, when the sum of the total distribution value of the securities pertaining to the secondary distribution plus the total issue value of the same class of securities already issued within one month from the issue date of the securities concerned is ¥500 million or more (Article 9-2 (iii-2) of the Cabinet Office Ordinance on Disclosure of Corporate Affairs, etc.).

(5) In cases where two or more public offerings and secondary distributions of the same class of securities each with a total issue value or total distribution value of less than ¥500 million are conducted in parallel[42] and the sum of the total issue prices or total distribution prices of the securities pertaining to these public offerings or secondary distributions is ¥500 million or more (Article 9-2(iv) of the Cabinet Office Ordinance on Disclosure of Corporate Affairs, etc.).

(6) In cases of public offerings or secondary distributions of securities with a total issue value or total distribution value of ¥500 million or more, and in cases of public offerings or secondary distributions of the same class of securities conducted in parallel with (1) (Article 9-2(v) of the Cabinet Office Ordinance on Disclosure of Corporate Affairs, etc.).

---

42 Public offerings and secondary distributions "conducted in parallel" means those for which the payment date and delivery date are generally the same (Guidelines on Disclosure of Corporate Affairs, B4-10).

Chapter 3   Disclosure requirements

In cases falling under small-amount public offerings, etc., securities registration statements can be prepared using Form 2-5 of the Cabinet Office Ordinance on Disclosure of Corporate Affairs, etc. (Article 8(1)(ii) of the Cabinet Office Ordinance on Disclosure of Corporate Affairs, etc.).

In addition to securities information, company information, information on the guarantor company, etc. of the reporting company and special information, information on associated companies is also to be stated[43], but the statement of company information on an individual basis is distinctive.

ⅰ)   Company information on an individual basis

For company information, in contrast to the ordinary method under which consolidated financial statements and other consolidated basis disclosure is required, in cases of small-amount public offerings, etc. individual basis disclosure is required. Also, while the "status of associated companies" must be included in company information under the ordinary method, in cases of small-amount public offerings, etc. this is to be given not as company information but as "associated companies information" stated after the company information. Regarding the "associated company information" for the associated companies for the most recent business year, the company names, addresses, stated capital and contributions, description of main business, percentage of voting rights of the reporting company, and description of the relationship between the reporting company and the associated companies (for example, the description of the relationship of concurrent "directors", etc., financial support, business trading, facilities lease, business alliances, etc.) must be stated and divided by the parent company, subsidiary companies, affiliated companies and other associated companies. For associated companies with little importance, however, it is permitted to only state the number of those companies (Cabinet Office Ordinance on Disclosure of Corporate Affairs, etc., Form 2-5, Note 53a).

---

43   In cases corresponding to specified procedures relating to securities issuance for reorganization or specified procedures relating to securities delivery for reorganization, in addition information regarding the company subject to reorganization and information regarding the reorganization (takeover bid) is required.

*267*

ⅱ) Attached documents

The attached documents are the same as those for securities registration statements submitted by domestic companies using the ordinary method (Article 10(1)(i)(iii-3) of the Cabinet Office Ordinance on Disclosure of Corporate Affairs, etc.).

(ⅵ) Exchange offers for specified procedures relating to securities issuance for reorganization and specified procedures relating to securities delivery for reorganization

Regarding securities registration statements concerning reorganisation (exchange offers) where the consideration for specified procedures relating to securities issuance for reorganization or specified procedures relating to securities delivery for reorganization are securities that are not specified securities, "information regarding reorganization" and "information regarding company subject to reorganization" must be stated in addition to the same securities information and company information required on securities registration statements pertaining to other public offerings or secondary distributions (Cabinet Office Ordinance on Disclosure of Corporate Affairs, etc., Form 2-6, Form 2-5, Form 2-7, and Form 7-4). In principle, issuers that are domestic companies are to prepare securities registration statements using Form 2-6 and issuers that are foreign companies are to use Form 7-4 (Article 8(1)(iii) & (v) of the Cabinet Office Ordinance on Disclosure of Corporate Affairs, etc.).[44] However, securities registration statements are to be prepared using Form 2-5 in cases corresponding to small-amount public offerings and using Form 2-7 in cases of domestic companies conducting specified procedures relating to securities issuance for reorganization or specified procedures relating to securities delivery for reorganization before an initial public offering (Article 8(1)(ii) and (2)(ii) of the Cabinet Office Ordinance on Disclosure of Corporate Affairs, etc.).

On the other hand, unlike other public offerings or secondary distributions, in cases where securities issued or delivered under specified procedures relating to securities issuance for reorganization or specified procedures relating to securities delivery for reorganization are specified securities,

*268*

Chapter 3    Disclosure requirements

"information regarding reorganization" must be stated; but "information regarding company subject to reorganisation" is not required (Cabinet Office Ordinance on Specified Securities Disclosure, Form 4, Note 63; Form 4-2, Note 69; Form 4-3, Note 77; Form 4-4, Note 85).

ⅰ) Securities information

While it is necessary to state the class of securities and number of shares being issued, etc. in cases of specified procedures relating to securities issuance for reorganization and specified procedures relating to securities delivery for reorganization, in practice for the application period, deposit for subscription, payment deadline, subscription handling office, payments handling office, underwriting and other matters, a statement that they do not apply is generally sufficient.

ⅱ) Information concerning reorganization (Takeover bid)

An outline of the reorganization including takeover bid, integrated financial information, and important contracts between the issuer (or its affiliated parties) and the company subject to reorganization (important contracts between issuer [or its affiliated parties] and subject company) must be

---

**44**  On Form 2-2 ([actual] incorporation method for domestic companies), Form 2-3 (incorporation by reference method for domestic companies), Form 7-2 ([actual] incorporation method for foreign companies) and Form 7-3 (incorporation by reference method for foreign companies), "information regarding the tender offer" must be stated, but the "information regarding reorganization" and "information regarding company subject to reorganization" included in Form 2-6 is not required. This can be understood based on the assumption that in cases of exchange offers, securities registration statements using the inclusion method and using the reference method are permitted; but in cases of specified procedures relating to securities issuance for reorganization and of specified procedures relating to securities delivery for reorganization, securities registration statements using the inclusion method or the reference method are not permitted. Similarly, Form 12, Form 12-2 (shelf-registration supplement for domestic companies) and Form 15 (shelf-registration supplement for foreign companies) also do not require "information regarding reorganization" and "information regarding company subject to reorganization" and this can be understood assuming that the shelf-registration system is not used for specified procedures relating to securities issuance for reorganization or specified procedures relating to securities delivery for reorganization.

*269*

stated. Regarding the outline of the reorganization (takeover bid), the purposes, etc. of the reorganization (takeover bid), an outline of the companies who are a party to the reorganization (takeover bid), contracts concerning the reorganization (takeover bid), the description and calculation basis of the allotment pertaining to the reorganization (takeover bid), differences between the securities issued by the company subject to reorganization and the securities issued (delivered) by the reorganization (differences between the securities issued by the subject company and the securities issued [delivered] by the reporting company pertaining to the takeover bid), matters concerning the issuance (delivery) conditions in cases of takeover bids using securities as consideration, rights held by shareholders of securities issued by the company subject to reorganization, and procedures concerning the reorganization (procedures concerning the takeover bid) must be stated.

Also, as integrated financial information, in cases where securities registration statements are submitted concerning specified procedures relating to securities issuance for reorganization or specified procedures relating to securities delivery for reorganization, for the company subject to reorganization (each newly established company where two or more stock companies or partnership companies will be demerged and jointly established; each wholly-owned subsidiary company in a share transfer in cases where two or more stock companies will jointly transfer shares) and for the reporting company, the major management indicators, etc. for the most recent consolidated fiscal year (the most recent business year in cases where consolidated financial statements are not prepared), and the major management indicators, etc. for the reporting company after the relevant reorganization calculated based on these major management indicators, etc. must be stated. Also, there must be a clear statement to the effect that the major management indicators of the reporting company after the reorganization are based on financial information that has not received an audit certification from a certified public accountant or auditing firm (Cabinet Office Ordinance on Disclosure of Corporate Affairs, etc., Form 2-6, Note 8a; Cabinet Office Ordinance on Disclosure of Corporate Affairs, etc., Form 2-5, Note 25; Cabinet Office Ordinance on Disclosure of Corporate

Chapter 3   Disclosure requirements

Affairs, etc., Form 2-7, Note; Cabinet Office Ordinance on Disclosure of Corporate Affairs, etc., Form 7-4, Note). On the other hand, in cases where the reporting company submits a securities registration statement regarding a takeover bid, the major management indicators for the most recent business year must be stated for the reporting company (in cases where the reporting company is not the takeover bidder, for the company that is the bidder) and for the company that is the subject of the relevant takeover bid.

If an organ that determines the business operation of the company subject to reorganization determines, in the most recent consolidated fiscal year [the most recent business year in cases where consolidated financial statements are not prepared], that the company implementing reorganization [including its associated companies; when the company implementing the reorganization is not the reporting company, including the reporting company and its associated companies] and the company subject to reorganisation [including its associated companies] will conduct reorganization, an important contract between the issuer and the company suject to reorganization (excluding reorganization contracts) must be stated.

For the purpose of this requirement, reorganization includes absorption-type merger, consolidation-type merger, transfer of all or part of important business, receipt of all or part of important business, share exchange, share transfer, absorption-type demerger or incorporation-type demerger (Cabinet Office Ordinance on Disclosure of Corporate Affairs, etc., Form 2-6, Note 9a; Cabinet Office Ordinance on Disclosure of Corporate Affairs, etc., Form 2-5, Note 25; Cabinet Office Ordinance on Disclosure of Corporate Affairs, etc., Form 2-7, Note; Cabinet Office Ordinance on Disclosure of Corporate Affairs, etc., Form 7-4, Note). In cases where the company subject to reorganization and the company implementing the reorganization have concluded contracts for lease or delegation of the management of entire businesses or the main parts thereof, contracts sharing all business profit and loss with other persons, technology assistance contracts or other contracts that are important for management, then an outline of the contracts must be stated; and where there have been important changes or cancellations of the contracts between the first day of the most recent consolidated fiscal year and the date of submission of the

*271*

securities registration statement, those descriptions must be stated (Cabinet Office Ordinance on Disclosure of Corporate Affairs, etc., Form 2-6, Note 9b; Cabinet Office Ordinance on Disclosure of Corporate Affairs, etc., Form 2-5, Note 25; Cabinet Office Ordinance on Disclosure of Corporate Affairs, etc., Form 2-7, Note; Cabinet Office Ordinance on Disclosure of Corporate Affairs, etc., Form 7-4, Note). On the other hand, in cases where the reporting company pertaining to a takeover bid submits a securities registration statement, regarding contracts concluded between the reporting company pertaining to the takeover bid and the subject company of the takeover bid of the reporting company (including its associated companies), equivalent items must be stated (however, this may be omitted in cases where there is a statement for section 4 "transactions, etc. between the takeover bidder and the subject company" in the takeover bid notification) (Cabinet Office Ordinance on Disclosure of Corporate Affairs, etc., Form 2-6, Note 9c; Cabinet Office Ordinance on Disclosure of Corporate Affairs, etc., Form 2-5, Note 25; Cabinet Office Ordinance on Disclosure of Corporate Affairs, etc., Form 2-7, Note; Cabinet Office Ordinance on Disclosure of Corporate Affairs, etc., Form 7-4, Note).

Information regarding the company subject to reorganization is to be stated when the company subject to reorganization is a continuous disclosure company, and the most recent annual securities report of the company subject to reorganization already submitted on the securities registration statement submission date and its attached documents as well as quarterly securities reports or semiannual securities reports and extraordinary reports submitted thereafter and their amendment reports must be stated (Cabinet Office Ordinance on Disclosure of Corporate Affairs, etc., Form 2-6, Notes 10a and 10b; Cabinet Office Ordinance on Disclosure of Corporate Affairs, etc., Form 2-5, Note 56; Cabinet Office Ordinance on Disclosure of Corporate Affairs, etc., Form 2-7, Note; Cabinet Office Ordinance on Disclosure of Corporate Affairs, etc., Form 7-4, Note).

ⅲ) Attached documents

In cases where the issued or delivered securities are securities other than specified securities, in addition to the attached documents for securities

Chapter 3 Disclosure requirements

registration statements by the ordinary method, in cases where the reporting company is not the company conducting the reorganization, the articles of incorporation of the company conducting the reorganization must be submitted as attached documents (Article 10(iii-3), (iii-4), (iii-5), and (vii) of the Cabinet Office Ordinance on Disclosure of Corporate Affairs, etc.). In cases where the issued or delivered securities are specified securities, the attached documents are the same as those for securities registration statements pertaining to public offerings or secondary distributions (Article 12 of the Cabinet Office Ordinance on Specified Securities Disclosure).

(vii)　Foreign bonds, etc.

The Cabinet Office Ordinance on the Disclosure of Information, etc. on Issuers of Foreign Government Bonds, etc. (Cabinet Office Ordinance on Foreign Bonds) regulates, among securities and certificates issued by foreign states or foreign persons, national government bonds, municipal bonds, debentures issued by juridical persons under a special statute, and items with the characteristics of investment securities issued by juridical persons established under a special act (excluding those with the characteristics of medical-care corporation bonds) as well as depository receipts representing rights concerning these securities as foreign government bonds, etc. (Article 1(i) of the Cabinet Office Ordinance on Foreign Bonds).

ⅰ )　Securities registration statements

Regarding securities registration statements concerning foreign bonds, etc., in addition to securities information, the condition of public offering debentures, foreign exchange rate movements[45] and an overview of the issuer must be stated as issuer information (Cabinet Office Ordinance on Foreign Bonds, Form 2). As an overview of the issuer, the matters to be

---

45　This may be omitted in cases where foreign exchange rates between the relevant foreign currency and Japanese currency have been published in at least two daily newspapers that have published matters regarding current events inside Japan for the past five years (or business years) and for the past six months (Cabinet Office Ordinance on Foreign Bonds, Form 2, Note 29c).

*273*

disclosed are prescribed respectively for cases where the issuer is a foreign state, a foreign local government body, and an international organ or government-related organ. In other words, in cases where the issuer is a foreign state, an outline, the economy, the foreign trade and international payments balance, currency and financial systems, government finances, public debt and other items must be stated. In cases where the issuer is a regional or local government body, an outline, the economy, government finances public debt and other items and an outline of its country must be stated. In cases where the issuer is an international organ or government-related organ, its establishment, capital structure, organization, operations overview, status of accounting and other overview of the issuer's country must be stated.

For example, in cases where the issuer is an international organ or government-related organ, statements on finance and accounting for the most recent five years (the most recent two years in cases where the issuer is a person that has submitted a notification or an annual securities report before the date of the relevant notification; the most recent one year in cases where that includes information equivalent to comparative information specified in Article 6 of the Cabinet Office Ordinance on Financial Statements) are required. However, in cases where the issuer is a party that has not submitted a notification or an annual securities report before the date of the relevant notification, at the choice of the issuer, the issuer may submit only statements on finance and accounting for the most recent three years that received certification deemed equivalent to an audit certification from a person equivalent to a certified public accountant or auditing firm. In this case, if there are special accounting handling or unusual items displayed, they must be explained in an easy-to-understand manner (Cabinet Office Ordinance on Foreign Bonds, Form 2, Note 44b). In addition, while audit certification is not required, in cases where the statements on finance and accounting have received certification deemed equivalent to audit certification from a person equivalent to a certified public accountant or auditing firm, a statement to that effect is required (Cabinet Office Ordinance on Foreign Bonds, Form 2, Note 44a).

Chapter 3   Disclosure requirements

Among issuers of foreign government bonds, etc., issuers that have continuously submitted annual securities reports for at least one year can use the [actual] incorporation method (Cabinet Office Ordinance on Foreign Bonds, Form 2-2) for the submission of securities registration statements (Article 5(3) and Article 27 of the Financial Instruments and Exchange Act; Article 6-2 of the Cabinet Office Ordinance on Foreign Bonds). Also, among issuers of foreign government bonds, etc., issuers that have continuously submitted annual securities reports for at least one year and which satisfy the publicity criteria can use the incorporation by reference method (Cabinet Office Ordinance on Foreign Bonds, Form 2-3) for the submission of securities registration statements (Article 5(4) and Article 27 of the Financial Instruments and Exchange Act; Article 6-3 of the Cabinet Office Ordinance on Foreign Bonds).

The publicity criteria is met where the total face value of foreign government bonds, etc. issued or delivered by an issuer of foreign government bonds, etc. by submission of a securities registration statement in Japan is at least ¥10 billion (Article 6-3 (4) of the Cabinet Office Ordinance on Foreign Bonds).

ⅱ） Foreign person registration statement

As mentioned below, in parallel with recognition of a foreign company registration statement by a foreign company, issuers of foreign government bonds, etc. that meet certain requirements can submit a foreign person registration statement instead of a securities registration statement. Namely, foreign persons submitting a notification who must submit a securities registration statement can submit a foreign person registration statement instead of the securities registration statement in cases considered by the Commissioner of the Financial Services Agency not to harm the public interest or investor protection (Article 5(6) and Article 27 of the Financial Instruments and Exchange Act; Article 6-4 of the Cabinet Office Ordinance on Foreign Bonds). The foreign person registration statement includes (i) Japanese language documents stating securities information that should be stated on the securities registration statement, and (ii) English language reference documents and documents similar to securities registration

*275*

statements disclosed in foreign states (offered for public inspection based on the laws and regulations of the relevant foreign state [including regulations of parties establishing foreign financial instruments markets or parties establishing markets with the characteristics of over-the-counter securities markets established in foreign states as equivalent to foreign financial instruments markets]) (Article 6-5 of the Cabinet Office Ordinance on Foreign Bonds).

a ) Documents in Japanese stating securities information that should be stated on the securities registration statement

These must be prepared using Form 2-4 specified by the Cabinet Office Ordinance on Foreign Bonds (Article 6-5 of the Cabinet Office Ordinance on Foreign Bonds). These are to be stated in accordance with Form 2 (Cabinet Office Ordinance on Foreign Bonds, Form 2-4, Note 2).

b ) Supplementary documents

i) Among the matters stated in the documents for (ii) above, a Japanese language translation of a summary of matters equivalent to "state of public offering (secondary distribution) debentures" that should be stated under the second section of Form 2 issuer information), and "overview of operations" and "status of accounting" in cases where the issuer is an international organ or government-related organ, etc.," that should be stated under "overview of issuer" in the second section of Form 2 (issuer information) and other items deemed necessary and appropriate for investor protection; ii) documents in English or Japanese with matters that should be stated on the securities registration statement (excluding matters to be stated as "securities information") that are not stated in the documents under (ii) above (matters not stated) (including a Japanese translation of a summary in cases where the relevant matters fall under i) and the "matters not stated" are prepared in English, and (iii) comparison table between the matters stated on the foreign person registration statement and the corresponding matters stated on the securities registration statement form must be attached (Article 5(7) and Article 27 of the Financial Instruments and Exchange Act; Article 6-5 of the Cabinet Office Ordinance on Foreign Bonds). Regarding the comparison table between the issuer information and

276

Chapter 3   Disclosure requirements

the matters stated on the foreign person registration statement corresponding to the matters, this can be prepared in accordance with the preparation guidelines [46] jointly prepared and published by the Tokyo Stock Exchange and the Japan Securities Dealers Association (Notes regarding Disclosure via Foreign Company Registration Statement, etc., B5-2).

iii) Attached documents

For securities registration statements prepared using Form 2 and From 2-2 of the Cabinet Office Ordinance on Foreign Bonds and foreign person registration statements, the attached documents must be: (1) a document attesting that relevant issuer has authorized a person who resides in Japan to represent the relevant issuer in all acts regarding the notification of the relevant public offering or secondary distribution of the securities concerned; (2) a copy of the wholesale underwriting contract concluded between the relevant issuer or owner and a financial instruments business operator; (3) a copy of the contract in which the relevant issuer entrusts the duties of administration of claims and other duties to perform acts for obligees or acts for the relevant issuer; (4) a copy of the contract concerning payment of the principal and interest and the relevant provisions of the relevant laws and regulations of the country of the issuer regarding the payment of the principal and interest; (5) a legal opinion letter from the manager of the legal department or from a legal expert that the public offering or secondary distribution of the securities concerned is legal and the relevant provisions of the relevant laws and regulations citied in the legal opinion letter; and (6) where foreign government bonds, etc. (excluding national government bonds and items with the characteristics of investment securities issued by juridical persons established by a special statute) have an attached guarantee from the issuer's country for the repayment of the principal and interest, a document stating the description of the relevant guarantee (Article 7(1)(i) of the Cabinet Office Ordinance on Foreign Bonds).

---

**46**   The "Preparation Guidelines for Foreign Company Reports, etc." were prepared by the Research Committee on Preparation Guidelines for Foreign Company Reports, etc. jointly established by the Japan Securities Dealers Association and the Tokyo Stock Exchange.

*277*

For securities registration statements prepared using Form 2-3 of the Cabinet Office Ordinance on Foreign Bonds, in addition to these documents, the attached documents are: (7) a document showing that the person submitting the relevant securities registration statement meets the qualification requirements for using the incorporation by reference method; (8) in cases where after the submission date of the relevant annual securities report which is referenced by the relevant securities registration statement material facts that occurred before the submission date that should have been stated in the relevant annual securities report whose description could not be stated when the relevant documents were submitted can now be stated, and in cases where material facts concerning matters to be stated in the relevant annual securities report occur (excluding cases where quarterly semiannual securities reports, extraordinary reports or amendment reports that have the description of these material facts are included in the reference documents for the relevant securities registration statement), documents stating the description of the relevant material facts; and (9) a document accurately and simply summarizing the main items among the matters stated in "status of issuer" in the annual securities report that is referenced in the securities registration statement (Article 7 (1) (ii) of the Cabinet Office Ordinance on Foreign Bonds).

In cases where (2), (3), or (4) are not attached to the securities registration statement, they can be attached to an amendment and submitted (Article 7 (1) main body of the Cabinet Office Ordinance on Foreign Bonds).

In cases where the attached documents are not stated in Japanese, in principle a Japanese language translation must be attached. However, in cases with submission of securities registration statements prepared using the [actual] incorporation method or the incorporation by reference method or submission of foreign person registration statements, where the attached documents are not stated in Japanese or English, attaching a Japanese or English translation is sufficient (Article 7 (2) of the Cabinet Office Ordinance on Foreign Bonds).

Chapter 3   Disclosure requirements

(viii)   Specified securities

ⅰ)   Definition of "Specified Securities"

Specified securities are "securities specified by a cabinet order as those for which information that will have a material influence on investors' investment decisions is information on assets investment or other similar business conducted by the issuer of the securities" (Article 5(1) of the Financial Instruments and Exchange Act). The securities as follows are specified securities: (i) among specified bonds prescribed in the Act on the Securitization of Assets (Article 2(1)(iv) of the Financial Instruments and Exchange Act), preferred equity investment certificates and securities indicating preemptive rights for new preferred equity investment (Article 2 (1) (viii) of the Financial Instruments and Exchange Act), beneficiary securities of specific purpose trusts (Article 2(1)(xiii) of the Financial Instruments and Exchange Act) and specified promissory notes (Article 2 (1)(xv) of the Financial Instruments and Exchange Act) (Article 2-13(i) of the Financial Instruments and Exchange Act Implementing Order); (ii) beneficiary securities of investment trusts or foreign investment trusts prescribed in the Act on Investment Trusts and Investment Corporations (Article 2 (1) (x) of the Financial Instruments and Exchange Act), investment securities, investment corporation debentures, or foreign investment securities (Article 2(1)(xi) of the Financial Instruments and Exchange Act) (Article 2-13(ii) of the Financial Instruments and Exchange Act Implementing Order); (iii) beneficiary securities of beneficiary securities issuing trusts prescribed in the Trust Act (Article 2(1)(xiv) of the Financial Instruments and Exchange Act) (excluding beneficiary certificates of securities in trust) (Article 2-13 (iii) of the Financial Instruments and Exchange Act Implementing Order); (iv) mortgage securities prescribed in the Mortgage Securities Act (Article 2(1)(xvi) of the Financial Instruments and Exchange Act) (Article 2-13 (iv) of the Financial Instruments and Exchange Act Implementing Order); (v) securities or certificates that are issued by a foreign person, which represent the beneficial interest of a trust in which loan claims held by persons engaging in banking business or persons otherwise conducting money loans in the course of trade are entrusted, or which indicate any other similar rights (foreign loan trust beneficiary certificates, etc.) (Article 2(1)(xviii) of

*279*

the Financial Instruments and Exchange Act; Article 3 of the Cabinet Office Ordinance Regarding Definitions) (Article 2-13 (v) of the Financial Instruments and Exchange Act Implementing Order); (vi) beneficiary certificates of securities in trust (limited to those with the securities listed in (i) through (v) as the entrusted securities) (Article 2-13 (vi) of the Financial Instruments and Exchange Act Implementing Order); (vii) interests in securities investment business, etc. (Article 3 (iii) of the Financial Instruments and Exchange Act; but excluding school loan claims [Article 1-3-4 of the Financial Instruments and Exchange Act Implementing Order]) (Article 2-13(vii) of the Financial Instruments and Exchange Act Article Implementing Order); (viii) trust bonds prescribed in Article 2, paragraph 3, item 17 of the Implementing Order for the Companies Act (Article 2-13 (viii) of the Financial Instruments and Exchange Act Implementing Order; Article 8 (i) of the Cabinet Office Ordinance on Specified Securities Disclosure); (ix) among corporate bond certificates and commercial paper (excluding specified promissory notes in (i) above), those satisfying both of the following requirements: 1) there are monetary claims or other assets (transfer assets) directly or indirectly transferred (or acquired) from owners to juridical persons established and administered for the purpose of issuing the securities concerned (Special Purpose Corporations; Article 8(ii) (a) of the Cabinet Office Ordinance on Specified Securities Disclosure); and 2) Special purpose corporations issue the securities concerned, and regarding performance of obligations for the securities concerned (including those issued for refinancing of the securities concerned) allocate monies obtained by conducting management, administration or disposal of the transferred assets (Article 2-13(viii) of the Financial Instruments and Exchange Act Implementing Order; Article 8(ii) of the Cabinet Office Ordinance on Specified Securities Disclosure); (x) among securities and certificates issued by foreign states or foreign persons, those with the characteristics of trust bonds (Article 2-13 (viii) of the Financial Instruments and Exchange Act Implementing Order; Article 8(iii) of the Cabinet Office Ordinance on Specified Securities Disclosure); (xi) among securities and certificates issued by foreign states or foreign persons, those with the characteristics of corporate bond certificates (Article 2(1) (v) of the Financial Instruments and Exchange Act), investment certificates

Chapter 3   Disclosure requirements

issued by juridical persons established by a special statute (Article 2(1)(vi) of the Financial Instruments and Exchange Act), shares or share option certificates (Article 2(1)(ix) of the Financial Instruments and Exchange Act) or commercial paper (Article 2(1)(xv) of the Financial Instruments and Exchange Act; Article 2 of the Cabinet Office Ordinance Regarding Definitions) which satisfy both of the following requirements: 1) there are monetary claims or other assets (transfer assets) directly or indirectly transferred (or acquired) from owners to special purpose corporations; and 2) Special purpose corporations issue the securities concerned, and regarding performance of obligations for the securities concerned (including those issued for refinancing of the securities concerned) allocate monies obtained by conducting management, administration or disposal of the transferred assets, or items with the characteristics of specified bonds prescribed by the Act on Securitization of Assets (Article 2(1)(iv) of the Financial Instruments and Exchange Act), preferred equity investment certificates or securities indicating preemptive rights for new preferred equity investment (Article 2-13(viii) of the Financial Instruments and Exchange Act Implementing Order; Article 8(iv) of the Cabinet Office Ordinance on Specified Securities Disclosure); (xii) among securities and certificates issued by foreign states or foreign persons, items with the characteristics of beneficiary certificates relating to a specific purpose trust prescribed in the Act on Securitization of Assets (Article 2(1)(xiii) of the Financial Instruments and Exchange Act) and beneficiary securities of beneficiary securities issuing trusts prescribed in the Trust Act (Article 2 (1)(xiv) of the Financial Instruments and Exchange Act) (excluding beneficiary certificates of securities in trust) (Article 2-13(viii) of the Financial Instruments and Exchange Act Implementing Order; Article 8(v) of the Cabinet Office Ordinance on Specified Securities Disclosure); (xiii) among beneficiary certificates of securities in trust beneficiary certificates, those with the securities listed in (viii) through (xii) as the entrusted securities (Article 2-13(viii) of the Financial Instruments and Exchange Act Implementing Order; Article 8(vi) of the Cabinet Office Ordinance on Specified Securities Disclosure), and (xiv) among depository receipts (Article 2(1)(xx) of the Financial Instruments and Exchange Act), those rights to be represented on securities listed in (i) through (v) and (viii)

*281*

through (xii) (Article 2-13(viii) of the Financial Instruments and Exchange Act Implementing Order; Article 8(vii) of the Ordinance on the Disclosure of Specified Securities).

ⅱ) Securities registration statement forms
Securities information and information regarding the description of assets are stated on securities registration statements pertaining to specified securities.

Among the issuers of domestic investment securities, foreign investment securities, regulated domestic asset-backed securities, regulated foreign asset-backed securities, and beneficiary certificates of specified securities in trust with these specified securities as the entrusted securities, or specified depository receipts indicating rights pertaining to these specified securities, persons submitting annual securities reports continuously for at least one year can prepare and submit securities registration statements using the [actual] incorporation method (Article 5 (3) & (5) of the Financial Instruments and Exchange Act; Article 11-2 of the Cabinet Office Ordinance on Specified Securities Disclosure on Specified Securities). In cases of submission by the [actual] incorporation method, the securities registration statement is prepared incorporating the most recent annual securities report (or foreign company report) and its attached documents, with copies of quarterly securities reports and semiannual securities reports submitted after the annual securities report and their amendment reports, and any material facts that occurred after the submission of the relevant annual securities report stated as subsequent completion information (Article 5(3) & (5) of the Financial Instruments and Exchange Act).

Also, among issuers of domestic investment securities, foreign investment securities, regulated domestic asset-backed securities, regulated foreign asset-backed securities, and beneficiary certificates of specified securities in trust with these specified securities as the entrusted securities, or specified depository receipts indicating rights pertaining to these specified securities, those issuers submitting annual securities reports continuously for at least one year and which meet the criteria set to confirm that information on the

Chapter 3  Disclosure requirements

conditions of accounting and the description of the asset regarding the management of assets and similar businesses by that issuer are already broadly provided (publicity criteria) can prepare and submit securities registration statements using the incorporation by reference method (Article 5 (3) (v) of the Financial Instruments and Exchange Act; Article 11-3 of the Cabinet Office Ordinance on Specified Securities Disclosure). The publicity criteria is met in cases where the domestic investment securities or foreign investment securities are listed on a domestic financial instruments exchange or registered over-the-counter on an authorized financial instruments firms association and the average trading value and average market capitalization are both at least ¥10 billion (Article 11-3 (4) (i) (a), (b), and (c) of the Cabinet Office Ordinance on Specified Securities Disclosure), or the average market capitalization is at least ¥25 billion (Article 11-3 (4) (i) (d) of the Cabinet Office Ordinance on Specified Securities Disclosure), or in the most recent five years the face value of corporate bond certificates pertaining to public offerings and secondary distributions for which issuance disclosure was made is at least ¥10 billion (Article 11-3 (4) (i) (e) of the Cabinet Office Ordinance on Specified Securities Disclosure). The publicity criteria is also met for regulated domestic asset-backed securities or regulated foreign asset-backed securities in cases where in the five years before submitting the securities registration statement the total issue value or total distribution value of regulated domestic asset-backed securities or regulated foreign as-set-backed securities issued or delivered by the notifier through submission of a securities registration statement or shelf-registration supplement concerning a public offering or secondary distribution in Japan is at least ¥10 billion (Article 11-3 (4) (ii) of the Cabinet Office Ordinance on Specified Securities Disclosure). Where the publicity criteria are met for specified securities as entrusted securities for the beneficiary certificates of specified securities in trust regarding beneficiary certificates of specified securities in trust, and when the publicity criteria are met for specified securities pertaining to the rights represented in the relevant specified depository receipts regarding specified depository receipts.

In cases using the incorporation by reference method, a statement that

*283*

reference should be made to the most recent securities report (or foreign company report) and its attached documents, and to quarterly securities reports, semiannual securities reports, extraordinary reports submitted after the securities report and their amendment reports is viewed as having stated the company information (Article 5 (4) & (5) of the Financial Instruments and Exchange Act). While it is not necessary to state on the securities registration statement material facts that emerged after submission of the securities report provided for reference as follow-up information, documents stating the description of certain material facts must be attached.

Securities registration statements must be prepared, respectively, regarding beneficiary certificates of specified securities in trust (securities in (vi) - (xiii) above) using forms set in accordance with the category of specified securities for entrusted securities pertaining to the beneficiary certificates of specified securities in trust and regarding specified deposit receipts (securities in (xiv) above) using forms set in accordance with the category of specified securities for specified securities pertaining to the rights represented in the specified depository receipts. In cases using the [actual] incorporation method and cases using the incorporation by reference method as well, regarding beneficiary certificates of specified securities in trust (limited to those with domestic investment securities, foreign investment securities, regulated domestic asset-backed securities or regulated foreign asset-backed securities as the entrusted securities), annual securities reports prepared using forms set in accordance with the category of specified securities for entrusted securities pertaining to the beneficiary certificates of specified securities in trust and submitted to the Director General of the Kanto Local Finance Bureau are deemed to be incorporated information or referenced information; and regarding specified depository receipts (limited to those indicating rights concerning domestic investment securities, foreign investment securities, regulated domestic asset-backed securities or regulated foreign asset-backed securities), annual securities reports prepared using forms set in accordance with the category of specified securities for specified securities pertaining to rights represented in the specified depository receipts and submitted to the Director General of

Chapter 3 Disclosure requirements

the Kanto Local Finance Bureau are deemed to be incorporated information or referenced information.

ⅲ) Attached documents

The attached documents for securities registration statements pertaining to specified securities are prescribed by Article 12, paragraph 1 of the Cabinet Office Ordinance on Specified Securities Disclosure for each issuer and form used.

g. Foreign company registration statement

Foreign companies that must submit a securities registration statement can submit a foreign company registration statement instead of the securities registration statement in cases considered by the Commissioner of the Financial Services Agency not to harm the public interest or investor protection (Article 5(6) of the Financial Instruments and Exchange Act; Article 9-6 of the Cabinet Office Ordinance on Disclosure of Corporate Affairs, etc.; Article 11-4 of the Cabinet Office Ordinance on Specified Securities Disclosure; Article 6-4 of the Cabinet Office Ordinance on Foreign Bonds).[47] The foreign company registration statement consists of (ⅰ) Japanese language documents stating securities information that should be stated on the securities registration statement, and (ⅱ) reference documents and documents similar to securities registration statements disclosed in foreign states in English (offered for public inspection based on the laws and regulations of the relevant foreign state [including regulations of parties establishing foreign financial instruments markets or parties establishing markets with the characteristics of over-the-counter securities markets established in foreign states as equivalent to foreign financial instruments markets]).

As for whether a case corresponds to "considered by the Commissioner of

---

**47** Foreign company reports can also be used for securities registration statements using the [actual] incorporation method or the incorporation by reference method as well as for shelf-registration statements and shelf-registration, supplements (Article 9-3, Article 9-4, Article 14-3, Form 7-2, Form 7-3, Form 14, Form 14-4, and Form 15 of the Cabinet Office Ordinance on Disclosure of Corporate Affairs, etc.).

*285*

## Table 3-2

| | Ordinary Method Forms | [actual] Incorporation Method | | Incorporation by Reference Method | | Form for Securities Information Section in Foreign Company Registration Statement |
|---|---|---|---|---|---|---|
| | | Form | Incorporated information | Referenced information | Form | |
| Domestic investment trust beneficiary certificates | Form 4 | | | | | |
| Foreign investment trust beneficiary certificates | Form 4-2 | | | | | Form 4-2-2 |
| Domestic investment securities | Form 4-3 | Form 4-3-2 | Annual securities report prepared using Form 7-3 and submitted to the Director General of the Kanto Local Finance Bureau | | Form 4-3-3 | |
| Foreign investment securities | Form 4-4 | Form 4-4-2 | When the issuer is a person other than the person who submitted the foreign company report, annual securities report prepared using Form 8 and submitted to the Director General of the Kanto Local Finance Bureau / when the issuer is the person who submitted the foreign company report, foreign company report submitted to the Director General of the Kanto Local Finance Bureau | | Form 5 | Form 4-4-3 |
| Domestic asset-backed securities (specified bonds, preferred equity securities, securities indicating preferred equity subscription rights, specified promissory notes, and securities under (ix) above) | Form 5-2 | Form 5-2-2 | Annual securities report prepared using Form 8-2 and submitted to the Director General of the Kanto Local Finance Bureau | | Form 5-2-3 | |
| Foreign asset-backed securities (securities under (xi) above) | Form 5-3 | Form 5-3-2 | When the issuer is a person other than the person who submitted the foreign company report, annual securities report prepared using Form 8-3 and submitted to the Director General of the Kanto Local Finance Bureau / when the issuer is the person who submitted the foreign company report, foreign company report submitted to the Director General of the Kanto Local Finance Bureau | | Form 5-3-3 | Form 5-3-4 |

# Chapter 3　Disclosure requirements

| | | | |
|---|---|---|---|
| Domestic beneficiary certificates backed by assets in trust (beneficiary securities of specific purpose trusts) | Form 5-4 | | |
| Foreign beneficiary certificates backed by assets in trust (securities under (xiii) above) | Form 5-5 | | Form 5-5-2 |
| Domestic trust beneficiary certificates (beneficiary securities of beneficiary securities issuing trusts [excluding securities under (vi) and (xiii) above]) / domestic trust corporate bond certificates (securities under (viii) above) / domestic trust beneficiary interests (trust beneficial interests that correspond to rights in securities investment business, etc.) | Form 6 | | |
| Foreign trust beneficiary certificates (securities and certificates issued by a foreign state or foreign person that have the characteristics of beneficiary securities of beneficiary securities issuing trusts [excluding securities under (vi) and (xiii) above]) / foreign trust corporate bond certificates / foreign trust beneficial interests / foreign loan trust beneficiary certificates | Form 6-2 | | Form 6-2-2 |
| Domestic mortgage securities | Form 6-3 | | |
| Foreign mortgage securities | Form 6-4 | | Form 6-4-2 |
| Interests in securities investment in domestic business, etc. (membership rights in general partnership, limited partnership or limited liability companies or equity in collective investment schemes that correspond to rights in a securities investment in business, etc.) | Form 6-5 | | |
| Interests in securities investment in foreign business, etc. (membership rights in foreign corporations with the characteristics of membership rights in general partnership, limited partnership or limited liability companies / interests based on the laws and regulations of foreign states that are similar to equity in collective investment schemes, those corresponding to rights in a securities investment in business, etc.) | Form 6-6 | | Form 6-6-2 |

the Financial Services Agency not to harm the public interest or investor protection," the Financial Services Agency inspects and considers in advance, for each statement, whether the foreign states' drafting standards and disclosure standards for reference documents and documents similar to securities registration statements disclosed in a foreign state in English do not harm investor protection compared with those in Japan, and whether the relevant documents were properly disclosed in the foreign state. Also, "the laws and regulations of the foreign state" can be those of a third state when the foreign company is located in a state that is not its home country.[48] Moreover, cases "disclosed in a foreign state" include cases where a public offering or secondary distribution will be conducted simultaneously in Japan and in a foreign state and disclosure is scheduled to be made in the foreign state; and cases where simultaneous listings are planned on financial instruments exchanges in a foreign state and in Japan and a listing examination on the relevant foreign financial instruments exchange and disclosure in the relevant foreign state are scheduled (Notes regarding Disclosure by Foreign Company Registration Statement, etc., A3).

In cases where a foreign company registration statement and supplementary documents are submitted, these are viewed as the securities registration statement (not including the documents attached) and the Financial Instruments and Exchange Act apply (Article 5(8) and Article 27 of the Financial Instruments and Exchange Act).

    ⅰ) Documents in Japanese stating securities information that should be stated on the securities registration statement

Documents in Japanese stating securities information that should be stated on a securities registration statement that constitutes a foreign securities registration statement not pertaining to specified securities or foreign bonds, etc.[49] must be prepared using Form 7-5 prescribed by the Cabinet Office

---

**48**  "Results of Public Comments on Draft Cabinet Orders and Draft Cabinet Office Ordinances (To Be Implemented Within One Year) regarding the 2011 Revision of the Financial Instruments and Exchange Act," "Outline of Comments and FSA's Position on Comments" (February 10, 2012), p. 38, No. 93.

*288*

Chapter 3 Disclosure requirements

Ordinance on Disclosure of Corporate Affairs, etc. (Article 9-7 of the Cabinet Office Ordinance on Disclosure of Corporate Affairs, etc.). Statements are to be made following Part I of Form 7 (Parts 1 and 2 of Form 7-4 in cases of specified procedures relating to securities issuance for reorganization and specified procedures relating to securities delivery for reorganization, and cases where purchases are made using securities as consideration) (Cabinet Office Ordinance on Disclosure of Corporate Affairs, etc., Form 7-5, Note 2).

ⅱ) Supplementary documents

For foreign company requisition statements that do not pertain to specified securities or foreign bonds, etc.,[50] 1) among the matters stated in the documents in (ⅱ) above, Japanese translations of summaries of the movements of major management indicators, description of business, business risk and other items deemed necessary and appropriate for investor protection, 2) documents in English or Japanese with matters that should be stated on the securities registration statement (excluding matters to be stated as "securities information" in Form 7 or as "securities information" or "information regarding reorganization" [takeover bid] in Form 7-4) that are not stated in the documents in (ⅱ) above (matters not stated) (including a Japanese translation of a summary in cases where the relevant matters fall under 1) and the "matters not stated" are prepared in English, and 3) a comparison table between the matters stated on the foreign company registration statement and the corresponding matters stated on the securities registration statement form must be attached (Article 5(7) of the Financial Instruments and Exchange Act; Article 9-7 of the Cabinet Office Ordinance on Disclosure of Corporate Affairs, etc.). Regarding the

---

49  For specified securities, the form prescribed by Cabinet Office Ordinance on Specified Securities Disclosure (Article 11-5 of the Cabinet Office Ordinance on Specified Securities Disclosure); and for foreign bonds, etc., Form 2-4 prescribed by the Cabinet Office Ordinance on Foreign Bonds (Article 6-5 of the Cabinet Office Ordinance on Foreign Bonds).

50  For specified securities the stipulations are provided by Article 11-5 of the Cabinet Office Ordinance on Specified Securities Disclosure; and for foreign government bonds, etc., the reguirements are provided under Article 6-5 of the Cabinet Office Ordinance on Foreign Bonds.

preparation of these supplementary documents, these can be prepared in accordance with the preparation guidelines[51]jointly prepared and published by the Tokyo Stock Exchange and the Japan Securities Dealers Association (Notes Regarding Disclosure by Foreign Company Registration Statement, etc., B4-1, C5-22,[52] D6-1, and D6-2).

iii ) Attached documents

The attached documents for foreign company registration statements that do not pertain to specified securities or foreign bonds, etc.[53] are: in cases where there is a board of directors resolution or general shareholders meeting resolution regarding issuance of the securities concerned, a copy of the minutes of the relevant board of directors meeting or a copy of the minutes of the relevant general shareholders meeting, or documents attesting the receipt of authorization of administrative agency or similar documents; in cases where permission, authorization or approval of the administrative agency is required to change the amount of capital of the company by issuance of the securities concerned, documents sufficient to show the concerned permission, authorization or approval concerned; in cases where the securities concerned are beneficiary certificates of securities in trust, copies of the trust contract concluded regarding the issuance of the relevant beneficiary certificates of securities in trust and of other main contracts; a document attesting that the representative of the foreign company stated on the relevant securities registration statement

---

51 See Fn. 46 above.

52 However, in cases where a Japanese translation of a summary of matters corresponding to matters that should be stated under "status of accounting" in Form 2 of the Cabinet Office Ordinance on Foreign Bonds is prepared, a complete translation of the financial documents (excluding notes) and a summary of the notes are to be prepared. Regarding the summary of the notes, important accounting policies, segment information and subsequent occurrence matters, and other particularly material matters in analyses of financial documents are to be simply summarized (Regarding Notes Concerning Disclosure by Foreign Company Registration Statement, etc., C5-1).

53 These are prescribed, respectively, by Article 12 of the Cabinet Office Ordinance on Specified Securities Disclosure for Specified Securities and by Article 7 of the Cabinet Office Ordinance on Foreign Bonds for Foreign Bonds, etc.

*290*

Chapter 3   Disclosure requirements

which intends to submit the concerned securities registration statement concerned is a person with legitimate authority regarding notification of the public offering or secondary distribution of the securities; a document attesting that the relevant foreign company has authorized a person who has residence in Japan to represent the relevant foreign company in all acts regarding notification of the public offering or secondary distribution of the securities; a document attesting that the relevant permission has been received in cases where permission prescribed by Article 21, paragraph 1 or paragraph 2 of the Foreign Exchange and Foreign Trade Act is required; and in cases where the relevant securities are bonds, etc., a copy of the contract in which the relevant foreign company entrusts the duties of administration of claims and other duties to perform acts for obligees or acts for the relevant foreign company and a copy of the contract concerning payment of the principal and interest; as well as a legal opinion letter from a legal expert that the public offering or secondary distribution of the securities is legal. In addition to the above, in cases where specified procedures relating to securities issuance for reorganization or specified procedures relating to securities delivery for reorganization are being conducted and in cases of purchases using securities as consideration where the reporting company is a company other than the company conducting reorganization, the Articles of Incorporation of the company conducting the relevant reorganization are deemed to be attached documents (Article 10 (1) (xiii) of the Cabinet Office Ordinance on Disclosure of Corporate Affairs, etc.).

For foreign company registration statements, Japanese translations of attached documents stated in English are deemed not to be required (Article 10 (2) (ii) of the Cabinet Office Ordinance on Disclosure of Corporate Affairs, etc.).

h. Amendments
　　( i )　Voluntary submission of amendments
　　 i )　Statutory amendment matters
Amendments must be submitted to the Prime Minister by reporting companies in the following cases: cases where there are changes to material

*291*

facts that should be stated on the securities registration statement or its attached documents after the securities registration statement submission date and before the registration comes into effect; cases where material facts that should have been stated on the relevant securities registration statement or its attached documents that occurred before the submission date whose description could not be made at the time can now be stated; cases where material facts emerge regarding matters that should be stated on the relevant securities registration statement or its attached documents; and cases where the description of matters listed under each item of Article 9 of the Financial Instruments and Exchange Act (for example, issue price) that were not stated on the relevant securities registration statement are decided (Article 7 (1) of the Financial Instruments and Exchange Act; Article 11 of the Cabinet Office Ordinance on Disclosure of Corporate Affairs, etc. Article 11; Article 13 of the Cabinet Office Ordinance on Specified Securities Disclosure; Article 8 of the Cabinet Office Ordinance on Foreign Bonds). In cases where a numerical indication[54] is given for the issue price etc., an amendment must be submitted promptly when the minimum issue value is determined (Guidelines on Corporate Affairs Disclosure, B7-5).

Cases of changes to material facts that should be stated on securities registration statements or their attached documents include, for example, cases of changes in the number of shares issued or in the total amount of the face value and cases of changes that have a material influence on investor decisions such as "application of proceeds from a new issuance," "business-related risks, etc.," "analysis of financial position, operating results and cash flow conditions," and "plans for new construction, expansion, repair, retirement or sale of important facilities" (Guidelines on Corporate Affairs Disclosure, B7-1).

---

54 This is displayed using a formula multiplying the closing securities issue price or distribution price on a given day on a given financial instruments exchange market (in cases where the securities concerned are over-the-counter traded securities, the final price of the relevant over-the-counter traded securities on a given day announced by a given authorized financial instruments firms association) by a given ratio (Article 1 (xxx) of the Cabinet Office Ordinance on Disclosure of Corporate Affairs, etc.,).

Chapter 3  Disclosure requirements

Cases where material facts that should have been stated on the relevant securities registration statement or its attached documents which occurred prior to the submission date whose description could not be made at the time can now be stated include the following cases (Guidelines on Corporate Affairs Disclosure, B7-3).

(1) Cases where consolidated financial statements, quarterly consolidated financial statements or semiannual consolidated financial statements for the consolidated fiscal year following the most recent consolidated fiscal year (or the quarterly consolidated accounting period for the next consolidated fiscal year) have been prepared and the relevant consolidated financial statements, etc. (including an outline thereof) have been disclosed[55] or have received audit certification.

(2) Cases where the proposed settlement for the business year following the most recent business year has been approved by the board of directors, cases where the balance sheet and income statement for the relevant business year have been finalized under Article 439 of the Companies Act,[56] and cases where the settlement for the relevant business year has been finalized and received audit certification.

(3) Cases where quarterly financial statements or semiannual financial statements have been prepared for the quarterly accounting period of the business year following the most recent business year (or for the next business year), and the relevant quarterly financial statements or semiannual financial statements (including an outline thereof) have been disclosed or have received audit certification.

(4) Cases where an important lawsuit under dispute has been resolved.

---

55  For example, these include summary announcements of settlements of accounts that include consolidated financial statements based on financial instruments exchange regulations.

56  At companies with accounting auditors, in cases where the accounting audit report of the accounting auditor expresses an unqualified opinion and the company auditor, board of company auditors, audit committee or committee on audits, etc. (including attached opinions by company auditors, audit committee members, or members of the committee on audits, etc.) do not express the opinion that the methods or results of the audit by the accounting auditor are unsuitable, the financial statements are finalized by approval of the board of directors.

(5) Cases where documents equivalent to documents stated in or that should be stated in "information regarding the guarantor company of the reporting company" are newly submitted (for companies that are not continuous disclosure companies, when the relevant documents are newly prepared).

(6) Cases where there has been an acquisition of treasury shares as stated in Article 155 of the Companies Act (however, submission of an amendment is only required when the relevant securities registration statement pertains to public offering or secondary distribution of shares, share option certificates, or bonds with share options).

(7) Cases where an agreement regarding "derivatives trading or other trading" (trading in cases where the securities and the relevant derivatives trading and other trading is viewed as one action and the securities concerned have the same characteristics as corporate bond certificates with MS warrants[57], etc.) provided in Article 19, paragraph 9 of the Cabinet Office Ordinance on Disclosure of Corporate Affairs, etc., an agreement between an acquirer and the reporting company regarding matters concerning the exercise of rights represented in corporate bond certificates with MS warrants provided in Article 19, paragraph 2, item 1 (i) (4) of the Cabinet Office Ordinance on Disclosure Affairs, etc., or an agreement between an acquirer and the reporting company regarding matters concerning tha sale and purchase of shares of the reporting company provided in Article 19, paragraph 2, item 1 (i) (5) of the Cabinet Office Ordinance on Disclosure Affairs, etc. has been concluded (including cases where securities that did not correspond to corporate bond certificates with MS warrants come to be viewed as corporate bond certificates with MS warrants from the conclusion of the relevant agreement), as well as cases where an agreement between an acquirer and special stakeholders, etc. of the reporting company regarding matters concerning leasing of shares of the reporting company provided in Article 19, paragraph 2, item 1 (i) (6) of the

---

57 MS warrants (Moving strike warrant a direct Japanese-to-English translation) are warrants whose exercise price is tracked to the market price of stocks to the extent that is provided in the terms and conditions.

Chapter 3  Disclosure requirements

Cabinet Office Ordinance on Disclosure Affairs, etc. has come to be known.

Similarly, amendments must be submitted where any documents similar to the reference documents for securities registration statements submitted using the incorporation by reference method are newly submitted (Guidelines on Corporate Affairs Disclosure, B7-10).

For cases where material facts arise regarding matters that should be stated on the relevant securities registration statement or its attached documents, examples given include changes of the reporting company's parent company or specified subsidiaries, changes of representative director, occurrence of material disaster at the reporting company or its consolidated subsidiaries, institution of important lawsuits, company mergers, transfer or receipt of important businesses, and emergence of high-value claims that are not recoverable (Guidelines on Corporate Affairs Disclosure, B7-6).

ⅱ) Voluntary amendment matters

Even where there are no matters to be amended as prescribed by Article 7, paragraph 1 of the Financial Instruments and Exchange Act, amendments must be submitted to the Prime Minister when the reporting company recognizes there are items on the securities registration statement that must be revised (Article 7(1) of the Financial Instruments and Exchange Act). However, in cases where it is ascertained that changes have occurred regarding basic matters (description of securities, intended allotment recipients, etc.) pertaining to the securities public offering or secondary distribution after the submission of the securities registration statement, and an amendment has been submitted, except for minor items, a new securities registration statement is deemed to have been submitted (Guidelines on Corporate Affairs Disclosure, B7-14).[58]

In parallel with the statutory amendment matters, as cases where voluntary submission of an amendment report is required under Article 7, paragraph 1, second sentence, the examples given in the Guidelines on Corporate Affairs Disclosure include cases where the following circumstances occur between

*295*

the time notification takes effect and the time the offer to purchase or subscription for shares[59] is finalized (Guidelines on Corporate Affairs Disclosure, B7-7).[60]

(1) Cases where there have been changes that have an important influence on investor decisions such as "application of proceeds from a new issuance," "business-related risks, etc.," "analysis of financial position, operating results and cash flow conditions," and "plans for new construction, expansion, repair, retirement or sale of important facilities."

(2) Cases where consolidated financial statements, quarterly consolidated financial statements or semiannual consolidated financial statements for the consolidated fiscal year following the most recent consolidated fiscal year (or the quarterly consolidated accounting period for the next consolidated fiscal year) have been prepared and the relevant consolidated financial statements, etc. (including an outline thereof) have been disclosed or have received audit certification.

(3) Cases where the draft accounts for the business year following the most recent business year have been approved by the board of directors, cases where the balance sheet and income statement for the relevant business year have been finalized under Article 439 of the Companies Act, and cases where the accounts for the relevant business year have been finalized and received audit certification.

(4) Cases where quarterly financial statements or semiannual financial statements have been prepared for the quarterly accounting period of

---

58  In stating in the "offer to purchase or subscription for shares column" on the securities registration statement, after stating a given application period, a statement to the effect that changes are being made can be stated in the notes within the range of a certain period (generally about one week). When stating in the "payment date" and other columns, a statement to the effect that payment date changes are being made along with changes to the application period can be stated in the notes (Guidelines on Disclosure of Corporate Affairs, B5-8).

59  These Guidelines do not apply to securities registration statements pertaining to specified procedures relating to securities issuance for reorganization or specified procedures relating to securities delivery for reorganization since there is no act equivalent to "application" in cases of reorganization.

Chapter 3   Disclosure requirements

the business year following the most recent business year (or for the next business year), and the relevant quarterly accounting statements or semiannual accounting statements (including an outline thereof) have been disclosed or have received audit certification.

(5)   Cases where an important lawsuit under dispute has been resolved.

(6)   Cases where there have been changes of the reporting company's

---

**60**   The Financial Services Agency — assuming the interpretation that for rights offerings, investment decisions regarding share option certificates are made not with the pro forma allotment of share option certificates but where the allotted share options are exercised and the subscription is paid — took the position that the submission of amendments is necessary even in cases where reasons that may be grounds for submission of amendments occur after the time the share options are allotted (April 2010 Public Comment "Results of Public Comments on Cabinet Office Ordinance [Draft #8] etc. regarding the Cabinet Office Ordinance on Disclosure of Corporate Affairs, etc." "Outline of Comments and FSA's Position on Comments" (April 21, 2010), "Results of Public Comments on Draft Cabinet Orders and Draft Cabinet Office Ordinances [to be Implemented Within One Year] regarding the 2011 Revision of the Financial Instruments and Exchange Act," "Outline of Comments and FSA's Position on Comments" (February 10, 2012), p. 2 No. 4, p. 3 No. 8). Also, in Guidelines on Disclosure of Corporate Affairs, B7-7, the FSA explained its interpretation that the time limit when circumstances occur which make voluntary amendment necessary under Article 7, Paragraph 1 "from after the notification comes into effect until the application is finalised" is until the expiration of the period in which investors can exercise the share options ("Results of Public Comments on Draft Cabinet Orders and Draft Cabinet Office Ordinances [To Be Implemented within One Year] regarding the 2011 Revision of the Financial Instruments and Exchange Act," "Outline of Comments and FSA's Position on Comments" (February 10, 2012), p. 10, No. 28. However, the Guidelines on Disclosure of Corporate Affairs after the 2012 revision provides that the submission of an amendment report is unnecessary as long as the securities registration statement pertaining to the relevant notification states that ongoing disclosure documents which state the planned disclosure time and consolidated financial statements or quarterly consolidated financial statements will be submitted and their planned submission time even in cases where the circumstances in (ii), (iii) or (iv) above arise after a notification regarding a public offering of share options conducted through allotment of share options without contribution prescribed in Article 277 of the Companies Act comes into effect (B7-7). In cases where there are changes to the planned time of submitting ongoing disclosure documents, etc., submission of an amendment report is necessary; but where ongoing disclosure documents are submitted at the planned time after such amendments, it is not necessary to submit amendment reports regarding the submission of the relevant ongoing disclosure documents.

*297*

parent company or specified subsidiaries, changes of major shareholders, changes of representative director, occurrence of material disaster at the reporting company or its consolidated subsidiaries, institution of important lawsuits, company mergers, share exchanges, share transfers, transfer or receipt of important businesses, or emergence of high-value claims that are not recoverable.

(7) Regarding the "status of accounting" in the matters to be stated on securities registration statements, cases falling under each item of Form 2, Note 74 of the Cabinet Office Ordinance on Disclosure of Corporate Affairs, etc. (such as cases where, between the end of the most recent business year and the report submission date, facts that have caused or that are expected to certainly cause significant changes in assets or liabilities or a material influence on profit and loss have occurred, cases where a certain period has passed since the beginning of the business year following the most recent business year, and cases where there are important lawsuits regarding the reporting company's operations, etc.).

(8) Cases where documents equivalent to documents that are stated or should be stated in "information of the guarantor company of the reporting company" are newly submitted (for companies that are not continuous disclosure companies, when the relevant documents are newly prepared).

(9) Cases where an agreement regarding "derivatives trading or other trading" (trading in cases where the securities and the relevant derivatives trading and other trading is viewed as one action and the securities concerned have the same characteristics as corporate bond certificates with MS warrants, etc.) provided in Article 19, paragraph 9 of the Cabinet Office Ordinance on Disclosure of Corporate Affairs, etc., an agreement between an acquirer and the reporting company regarding matters concerning the exercise of rights represented in corporate bond certificates with MS warrants provided in Article 19, paragraph 2, item 1 (i) (4) of the Cabinet Office Ordinance on Disclosure Affairs, etc., or an agreement between an acquirer and the reporting company regarding matters concerning the sale and purchase of share certificates of the reporting company provided in Article 19, paragraph 2, item 1 (i) (5) of the Cabinet Office Ordinance on Disclosure Affairs,

Chapter 3 Disclosure requirements

etc. has been concluded (including cases where securities that did not correspond to corporate bond certificates with MS warrants come to be viewed as corporate bond certificates with MS warrants from the conclusion of the relevant agreement), as well as cases where an agreement between an acquirer and special stakeholders, etc. of the reporting company regarding matters concerning lease of share certificates of the reporting company prescribed in Article 19, paragraph 2, item 1 (i) (6) of the Cabinet Office Ordinance on Disclosure Affairs, etc. has come to be known.

Also, in cases where numerical indication is given for the issue price or distribution price on the securities registration statement that is submitted, when the issue price or distribution price is finalized, the finalized issue price or distribution price, the amount of the public offering (secondary distribution) based on the issue price, etc., the total issue value (total distribution value) and other related matters are to be stated in the reported prospectus, so in cases where the finalized issue price or distribution price etc. cannot be stated on the amendment submitted just before the securities registration statement comes into effect, an amendment must be promptly submitted voluntarily (Guidelines on Corporate Affairs Disclosure, B7-8).

(ii) Foreign company amendments registration statements

The provisions concerning amendments apply *mutatis mutandis* when a foreign company that submitted a foreign company registration statement or foreign person who submitted a foreign person registration statement submits amendments to the foreign company registration statement or foreign person registration statement and their supplementary documents (Article 7-2, Article 9-2, Article 10-2, Article 5(6) and Article 27 of the Financial Instruments and Exchange Act). Namely, submission of foreign company amendments or foreign person amendments is approved in cases where submission of a foreign company amendment or foreign person amendment (documents similar to the relevant amendments disclosed in a foreign state in English) instead of amendments by a foreign company or foreign person is considered by the Commissioner of the Financial Services Agency not to harm the public interest or investor protection in light of their

*299*

terminology, forms, and preparation methods (Article 11-2 of the Cabinet Office Ordinance on Disclosure of Corporate Affairs, etc.; Article 8-2 of the Cabinet Office Ordinance on Foreign Bonds; Article 13-2 of the Cabinet Office Ordinance on Specified Securities Disclosure).

Foreign company amendments and foreign person amendments must have as attachments, in addition to the same supplementary documents attached to foreign company registration statements and foreign person registration statements, a supplementary document in Japanese stating the submission date of the foreign company registration statement or foreign person registration statement being amended, the reason for the amendment, and the part to be amended and the description of the amendment (Article 11-3 of the Cabinet Office Ordinance on Disclosure of Corporate Affairs, etc.; Article 8-3 of the Cabinet Office Ordinance on Foreign Bonds; Article Article 13-3 of the Cabinet Office Ordinance on Specified Securities Disclosure).

However, in preparing the "part to be amended and the description of the amendment" it is sufficient to state the headings, items etc. in Japanese, and the specified part to be amended and the description of the amendment can be stated in either Japanese or English (Notes Regarding Disclosure by Foreign Company Registration Statement etc., B4-3, C5-4, D6-4).

(ⅲ) Foreign companies and representatives
In cases where a foreign company submits an amendment pursuant to Article 7, paragraph 1, etc. of the Financial Instruments and Exchange Act, the foreign company must designate a person who has residence in Japan and who is authorized to represent the relevant foreign company for all acts regarding submission of the amendment (Guidelines on Corporate Affairs Disclosure, B7-11).

(ⅳ) Amendment orders, orders suspending the effect of notifications, administrative dispositions to extend waiting periods
The Prime Minister can order reporting companies to submit amendments, foreign company amendments or foreign person amendments, suspend the

Chapter 3   Disclosure requirements

effect of notifications, or make administrative decisions to extend waiting periods.

(ⅴ)   Authority to which submission is made and public inspection
The periods for which documents are to be made available for public inspection, the authority to which submission is made and other rules regarding public inspection are the same as those for securities registration statements.

ⅰ. Notifications entry into effect
(ⅰ)   Significance of Notifications Entry into Effect
Even for public offerings and secondary distributions that require notifications, if a securities registration statement is submitted, solicitations and solicitations for selling, etc. to investors can be conducted (Article 4(1) of the Financial Instruments and Exchange Act); however, unless the notification comes into effect, the securities must not be acquired or sold via public offering or secondary distribution (Article 15(1) of the Financial Instruments and Exchange Act).

Similar to cases of conducting other public offerings or secondary distributions of securities, issuers conducting reorganization must not have securities acquired or sold by specified procedures relating to securities issuance for reorganization or specified procedures relating to securities delivery for reorganization before the notification comes into effect (Article 15 (1) of the Financial Instruments and Exchange Act). Incidentally, Guidelines on Corporate Affairs Disclosure B15-1 prescribe "Unless the notification comes into effect, the reorganization pertaining to the relevant specified procedures relating to securities issuance for reorganization or specified procedures relating to securities delivery for reorganization cannot be placed into effect under the Companies Act." In other words, assuming the interpretation that the acquisition and sale of securities in a reorganization means having securities acquired by having the reorganization come into effect, the Financial Services Agency takes the position that it is sufficient if the notification is effective by the date the reorganization comes into effect.

*301*

( ii )  Time of entry into effect

The period from the submission of the securities registration statement until the notification comes into effect is called the waiting period.

In principle, notifications regarding the public offering or secondary distribution of securities, notifications of general solicitation for securities acquired by qualified institutional investors, and notifications of general solicitation for securities acquired by professional investors enter into effect 15 days after the date that the Prime Minister receives the securities registration statement (Article 8 (1) of the Financial Instruments and Exchange Act). However, where the Prime Minister believes that the contents of the notification documents are easily understandable to the public or finds that information on the corporate affairs of the issuer which is the reporting company has already been made widely available to the public, the Prime Minister may designate a period shorter than 15 days for the relevant reporting company, or have the notification enter into effect immediately or on the day after the day when the notification is submitted (Article 8(3) of the Financial Instruments and Exchange Act).

Regarding a case recognizing that information on corporate affairs of the issuing company has already been made widely available to the public, where there is a company that meets the requirements for use of the [actual] incorporation method or the incorporation by reference method and the reporting company applies to shorten the waiting period, the shortening of the waiting period is approved, excluding cases where shortening the period would not be appropriate (Guidelines on Corporate Affairs Disclosure, B8-2). In this case, the notification is deemed to enter into effect on the day approximately seven days after the Prime Minister receives the securities registration statement, but the notification can be held for at least four days excluding government holidays. However, when securities registration statements concerning third-party allotments are subject to examination under guidelines on the handling of statements in the Guidelines on Corporate Affairs Disclosure, C (Individual Guidelines) III "Third Party Allotments Concerning Issuances of Share Certificates, etc.", the period under Article 8, paragraph 3 will not be shortened in principle (Guidelines on

Chapter 3 Disclosure requirements

Corporate Affairs Disclosure, B8-2(4)).

Also, in cases where the following three requirements are all met, the notification can be put into effect immediately, excluding cases in which the handling is deemed to be inappropriate (Guidelines on Corporate Affairs Disclosure, B8-3).

First, the company submitting the securities registration statement must meet each of the following requirements: (i) a company which has submitted an annual report on the corresponding day one year before the submission date of the relevant securities registration statement, and which has properly fulfilled its ongoing disclosure obligation from the corresponding day until the submission date of the relevant securities registration; (ii) a company which has issued shares which correspond to listed share certificates or over-the-counter registered shares; and (iii) the listing date etc. must be a date at least three years and six months before the date of submission of the relevant securities registration statement, and with regard to the shares already issued by the relevant reporting company, the amount obtained by dividing the total trading value within the three years prior to the reference date must be ¥10 billion or more, and the average market capitalization over the three years must be at least ¥10 billion.

Second, the notification must pertain to either (i) public offerings of shares corresponding to listed shares or over-the-counter registered shares, or (ii) public offerings of share option certificates (limited to share option certificates listed on Japanese exchanges [excluding cases of listing as specified listed securities] or scheduled to be listed without delay after issuance and share option certificates registered with an authorized financial instruments firms association as over-the-counter traded securities [excluding cases of registration as specified over-the-counter traded securities] or scheduled to be registered without delay after issuance) for allotment of share options without contribution (including equivalent allotments conducted by foreign companies upon their establishment based on applicable laws of foreign states) indicating share options for shares pertaining to shares corresponding to the listed shares or over-the-counter

*303*

registered shares.

Third, (i) regarding the listed shares or over-the-counter registered shares, the ratio of the total number of shares to be issued or transferred by the public offering pertaining to the relevant notification (in cases where concurrently with the relevant public offering there is an issuance of shares of the same type as the shares pertaining to the relevant public offering or of share option certificates or bonds with share options for shares concerning shares of the same type as the shares pertaining to the public offering concerned, including the total number of relevant issued shares or the expected total number of shares issued or transferred issued from exercising all the share options pertaining to the relevant share option certificates or bonds with share options) divided by the total number of relevant shares (excluding those owned by the issuer) before the relevant public offering is 20% or less, and (ii) regarding share option certificates pertaining to share options without contribution, the ratio of the total number of shares planned to be issued or transferred by the exercise of share options when all the share options pertaining to the share option certificates planned to be issued by the public offering concerning said notification are exercised divided by the total number of shares before the public offering (excluding those owned by the issuer) is 20% or less.

In addition to the above, in cases where notification has been given for an additional public offering, in parallel with the relevant public offering, of unclaimed shares resulting from a public offering of shares for which a notification was submitted, and this would not particularly harm public interest or investor protection, where deemed necessary, the relevant notification can be put into effect on the day one day (not including the number of days of administrative institution holidays) after the submission (Guidelines on Corporate Affairs Disclosure, B8-2(6)).

For notifications concerning reorganization as well, similar to notifications regarding other public offerings and secondary distributions of securities, in principle the notifications come into effect on the day 15 days after the day that the securities registration statement is received by the Prime Minister

*304*

Chapter 3   Disclosure requirements

(Article 8(1) of the Financial Instruments and Exchange Act). However, securities registration statements using Form 2-6, Form 2-7 or Form 7-4 of the Cabinet Office Ordinance on Disclosure of Corporate Affairs, etc. can be put into effect on the day after the submission date of the relevant securities registration statement where the relevant reporting company has requested a shortening of the period, except in cases where the handling is deemed inappropriate (Article 8(3) of the Financial Instruments and Exchange Act; Guidelines on Corporate Affairs Disclosure, B8-2(5)).

In cases where there are false statements, etc. regarding material matters on securities registration statements, the Prime Minister can order suspension of the effect of the notification or extension of the waiting period (Article 10 (1) and Article 11(1) of the Financial Instruments and Exchange Act). The Prime Minister can also order suspension of effect or extension of waiting period for notifications and shelf registrations of other securities registration statements, shelf-registration statements and shelf-registration supplements submitted by that reporting company within one year from the date the relevant securities registration statement was submitted (Article 11(1) of the Financial Instruments and Exchange Act).

(iii)   Time of entering into effect in cases where amendments are submitted

In principle, in cases where securities registration statements omitting statement of the issue price, distribution price, etc. have been submitted, the notification comes into effect 15 days (or 7 days) after the date that an amendment stating the omitted items is received by the Prime Minister (Article 8(1) of the Financial Instruments and Exchange Act) and in cases where an amendment is submitted after the notification comes into effect, the entry into effect occurs 15 days (or 7 days) after the date that the amendment is submitted (Article 8(2) of the Financial Instruments and Exchange Act). However, further reductions in the waiting period can be approved even when amendments are submitted as well (Article 8(3) & (4) of the Financial Instruments and Exchange Act).

First, in cases where securities information is amended, in principle this

*305*

comes into effect within one day (excluding the number of days of government holidays) thereafter (Guidelines on Corporate Affairs Disclosure, B8-4a). However, this does not apply in cases where this handling is considered inappropriate, such as cases where securities registration statements pertaining to third-party allotments are the subject of the examination under handling guidelines concerning statement of the Guidelines on Corporate Affairs Disclosure, C "Third Party Allotments Concerning Issuance of Share Certificates, etc.", and the matters regarding the relevant third-party allotment have been significantly changed (proviso to the Guidelines on Corporate Affairs Disclosure, B8-4, (i)).

Second, among securities information amendments, for issuances by the so-called book building method (including cases where the number of shares issued or the total face value of bonds will change simultaneously with the determination of the issue price, etc. depending on the demand of the relevant investors [limited to cases where the description of the relevant changes can be easily understood by investors and their description is noted]) [61] and for public offerings or secondary distributions that accompany initial public offerings in cases where amendments are submitted when the issue price, distribution price or interest rate that were not decided in the initial notification are decided, the notification is deemed to enter into effect on the submission date or the following date, excluding cases where that handling is deemed inappropriate (Guidelines on Corporate Affairs Disclosure, B8-4b).

Third, excluding minor items and those falling under B8-4b of the Guidelines on Corporate Affairs Disclosure, changes regarding the number of shares issued or the total face value of bonds are deemed to come into effect on the day when three days (excluding the number of days of government holidays) have passed, excluding cases where the handling is deemed inappropriate (Guidelines on Corporate Affairs Disclosure, B8-4c). As

---

61  Issuance after presenting tentative conditions regarding issue price, etc. to investors at the time of solicitation for applications for acquisition of the relevant securities and ascertaining the investor demand state for the relevant securities.

Chapter 3  Disclosure requirements

standards to decide whether items are minor items, in the past one standard was whether the increase in the number of shares issued or total face value was 30% or more, or the decrease was 50% or more. Presently, it is considered inappropriate to make this decision based on the percentage change in the stated number of issued shares, etc. alone ("Results of Public Comments on 'Partial Revision [Draft] of Notes Concerning Disclosure of Corporate Affairs (Guidelines on Corporate Affairs Disclosure),'" "Outline of Comments and FSA's Position on Comments" (June 4, 2000), p. 13, Nos. 64 and 65).

Fourth, in cases where there are amendments for matters other than securities information, in principle these are deemed to come into effect on the day when three days have passed (not including administrative institution holidays) (Guidelines on Corporate Affairs Disclosure, B8-4d). However, in cases where amendments are submitted pursuant to Article 7, paragraph 1, second part of the Financial Instruments and Exchange Act for minor items concerning information other than securities information, these are deemed to come into effect on the day when one day has passed (not including government holidays), except where the handling is deemed inappropriate (for example, in cases where there have been major changes to the contents stated in consolidated financial statements etc.).

The Guidelines on Corporate Affairs Disclosure prescribe the same handling in principle for cases where a foreign person (including persons other than companies) is the issuer for matters other than matters separately prescribed, however, in cases where there are unavoidable circumstances as prescribed under the relevant laws and regulations of a foreign state, etc., other handling is conducted as necessary (Guidelines on Corporate Affairs Disclosure, A1-9-1).

ⅰ. Withdrawal of notification
In cases where after the securities registration statement submission date the total issue value or total distribution value of the securities pertaining to the public offering or secondary distribution by the relevant securities registration statement decreases to an amount that does not require

*307*

notification, and in cases where the securities public offering, secondary distribution or issuance pertaining to the relevant securities registration statement is to be canceled, the person who submitted the relevant securities registration statement must without delay submit to the Commissioner of the Financial Bureau Director General of the Local Finance Bureau or the Director General of the Fukuoka Finance Branch Bureau a "notification withdrawal request" stating that the securities registration statement is being withdrawn. In this case, the public inspection of the relevant securities registration statement and its copies are canceled (Guidelines on Corporate Affairs Disclosure, B4-13). When a notification withdrawal request is submitted, the date the relevant notification withdrawal request was submitted is deemed the date the written notice of securities was submitted. Moreover, securities issued or sold are handled as items that do not correspond to securities under Article 24, paragraph 1, item 3 of the Financial Instruments and Exchange Act (Guidelines on Corporate Affairs Disclosure, B4-14).

# 4. Shelf-registration system

The shelf-registration system is a system whereby parties planning to issue securities that meet certain requirements can submit a shelf-registration statement in advance stating the planned issue period, planned total amount of issue, class of securities to be issued, etc., and at the time of the actual issuance issue the shares by just submitting a shelf-registration supplement with only the issuance conditions and other securities information stated, without submitting a new notification. In other words, because Article 4, paragraph 1 of the Financial Instruments and Exchange Act does not apply to securities public offerings or secondary distributions for which shelf registration has been conducted (Article 23-3 (3) of the Financial Instruments and Exchange Act), solicitation for acquisition and solicitation for sale of the securities concerned can be conducted without notification. Additionally, if the shelf registration is effective, the issuer can have others acquire and sell the securities by submission of a shelf-registration supplement (Article 28-8 (1) of the Financial Instruments and Exchange Act). Shelf registrations are conducted for each security, a single shelf registration cannot be made for different securities, and separate shelf

Chapter 3 Disclosure requirements

registrations are required for public offerings and secondary distributions.

a. Shelf registrations for public offerings and secondary distributions

Among persons planning a securities public offering or secondary distribution, issuers whose qualifications for use of shelf registration are recognized can submit a shelf-registration statement to the Prime Minister and register the relevant public offering or secondary distribution in cases where the total issue value and total distribution value (planned amount of issue) of the securities planned for the relevant public offering or secondary distribution is ¥100 million or more (Article 23-3 (3) of the Financial Instruments and Exchange Act).

However, shelf registration cannot be used in the following cases (1) through (3) (proviso to Article 23-3 (1) of the Financial Instruments and Exchange Act).

(1) The solicitation for acquisition or solicitation for selling, etc. corresponds to solicitation conducted for private placement or private secondary distribution to professional investors or other qualified institutional investors who are excluded as professional investors, and is subject to application of Article 23-13, paragraph 1 of the Financial Instruments and Exchange Act (cases where disclosure has not been conducted of the securities concerned and the planned secondary distribution of the securities has a total issue value or total transfer value of ¥100 million or more).

(2) The solicitation for acquisition or solicitation for selling, etc. corresponds to solicitation for acquisition to professional investors or solicitation for selling, etc. to professional investors, and is subject to application of Article 23-13, paragraph 3 of the Financial Instruments and Exchange Act (cases where secondary distribution is planned for securities where disclosure of the securities concerned has not been conducted).

(3) The solicitation for acquisition or solicitation for selling, etc. corresponds to private placement to a small number of investors or private secondary distribution to a small number of investors, and is

*309*

subject to application of Article 23-13, Paragraph 4 of the Financial Instruments and Exchange Act (cases where secondary distribution is planned for securities where disclosure of the securities concerned has not been conducted and the total issue value or total transfer value is ¥100 million or more).

To conduct shelf registration, the planned amount of issue[62] must be ¥100 million or more, but there is no upper limit prescribed for the planned amount of issue that can be stated. Moreover, it is not always necessary to issue the entire amount of the planned amount of issue that is stated, and while the amount can be reduced by submission of an amended shelf-registration statement, subsequent increases in the planned amount of issue are not permitted (Article 23-4 of the Financial Instruments and Exchange Act; Article 14-5 (3) (i) of the Cabinet Office Ordinance on Disclosure of Corporate Affairs, etc.; Article 18-3(3) (i) of the Cabinet Office Ordinance on Specified Securities Disclosure; Article 11-5 (3) (i) of the Cabinet Office Ordinance on Foreign Bonds).

Because the planned amount of issue fundamentally means the total issue value or total distribution value of the securities planned to be issued by the public offering or secondary distribution pertaining to the relevant shelf registration, if the securities are issued, only the total issue value and total distribution value of the amount that can be issued decrease. However, if the shelf-registration statement states a "maximum amount of outstanding balance," a format (the so-called program amount format) is also recognized whereby in cases where the outstanding balance is reduced from redemptions, etc., the amount that can be issued increases by the amount of the redemptions (Article 23-3 (1) of the Financial Instruments and Exchange Act). In cases where shelf registration is conducted by the program amount format, when the maximum amount of the outstanding

---

62 In cases where the securities for a planned public offering or secondary distribution are share option certificates, add the planned amount of issue of the share option certificates to the total amount to be paid when exercising the share options (Article 23-3(1) of the Financial Instruments and Exchange Act).

Chapter 3   Disclosure requirements

balance during the planned issue period is stated, it is necessary to state the planned amount of redemptions during the planned issue period of bonds issued during past public offerings.

The planned issue period for public offerings or secondary distributions (planned issue period) is one year from the planned date the shelf registration comes into effect[63] for commercial paper, and for other cases either one or two years can be chosen by the issuer (Article 23-6(1) of the Financial Instruments and Exchange Act; Article 14-6(3) of the Cabinet Office Ordinance on Disclosure of Corporate Affairs, etc. ; Article 18-4 of the Cabinet Office Ordinance on Specified Securities Disclosure; Article 11-6 of the Cabinet Office Ordinance on Foreign Bonds). Then, the shelf registration loses its effect on the day when the planned issue period has passed (Article 23-6(2) of the Financial Instruments and Exchange Act). When the total planned amount of issue of securities public offerings or secondary distributions is completed before the date the planned issue period has passed, the shelf registration holder must submit a written withdrawal of shelf registration with a statement to that effect to the Prime Minister, and withdraw the shelf registration (Article 23-6 (1) of the Financial Instruments and Exchange Act).

b．Qualifications to choose shelf-registration system and subject securities

Shelf registration is available only for a person submitting annual securities reports continuously for one year or more, information on whose corporate affairs, etc. has already been widely provided to the public, and the trading, etc. of securities issued by the relevant person already issued on a financial instruments exchange market meet criteria specified by Cabinet Office Ordinance (Article 5(4) and Article 23-3(1) of the Financial Instruments and Exchange Act; Article 9-4 of the Cabinet Office Ordinance on Disclosure of Corporate Affairs, etc.; Article 11-3 of the Cabinet Office Ordinance on Specified Securities Disclosure; Article 6-3 of the Cabinet Office Ordinance

---

**63** Even in cases where the shelf registration comes into effect later than the expected date, this has no impact on the end of the planned issue period.

*311*

on Foreign Bonds).

A company that is the issuer of the securities for which a shelf registration was once made may continue to submit securities reports and their attached documents even after the obligation to submit securities reports ceases, if their submission is necessary to satisfy the eligibility for use of the incorporation by reference method (Article 23-3 (4) of the Financial Instruments and Exchange Act).

Securities for which the shelf-registration system can be used are, among the securities subject to the Cabinet Office Ordinance on Disclosure of Corporate Affairs, etc. (bonds, shares, share options, preferred equity investment certificates under the Act on Preferred Equity Investment by Cooperative Financial Institutions [Preferred Equity Investment Act], commercial paper, etc.), securities subject to the Cabinet Office Ordinance on Foreign Bonds (foreign government bonds, etc.) and specified securities, domestic investment securities, foreign investment securities, specified bonds and preferred equity investment certificates, etc. issued by specific purpose companies under the Act on Securitization of Assets and foreign specific purpose companies and other similar securities issued by foreign specific purpose companies.

c. Items to be stated on shelf-registration statements
Shelf-registration statements must state the matters specified by cabinet office ordinance as necessary and appropriate for the public interest or investor protection including the period in which the relevant public offering or secondary distribution is planned, the class of securities for the public offering or distribution, the planned amount of issue or the maximum amount of issue or distribution, and the names of principal financial instruments business operators or registered financial institutions which plan to underwrite the securities[64] (Article 23-3 of the Financial Instruments and Exchange Act).

The Cabinet Office Ordinance on Disclosure of Corporate Affairs, etc. provides the items to be stated and specifies, respectively, Form 11 for

*312*

Chapter 3 Disclosure requirements

domestic companies that issue bond certificates, preferred equity investment certificates, shares, share option certificates, securities or certificates which represent options, depository receipts, and beneficiary certificates of securities in trust, Form 11-2 for domestic companies which issue commercial paper, Form 11-2-2 for domestic companies that issue short-term bonds, etc., Form 14 for foreign companies, and Form 14-4 for foreign companies which issue short-term foreign bonds (Article 14-3 of the Cabinet Office Ordinance on Disclosure of Corporate Affairs, etc.). Meanwhile, the Cabinet Office Ordinance on Specified Securities Disclosure provides the items to be stated and specifies, respectively, Form 15 for domestic investment securities and Form 16 for foreign investment securities (Article 18 (1) of the Cabinet Office Ordinance on Specified Securities Disclosure). The Cabinet Office Ordinance on Foreign Bonds provides the items to be stated for foreign government bonds, etc. and specifies Form 6 (Article 11-3 of the Cabinet Office Ordinance on Foreign Bonds).

In addition to securities information, as referenced information all the forms require a statement to refer to the most recent reference documents for items concerning the corporate affairs and assets of the issuing company, the general conditions of the issuer, etc. In cases where there is no financial instruments business operator planning to underwrite, those statements are unnecessary (Guidelines on Corporate Affairs Disclosure, B23-3-1) and statement of the other securities information can be omitted in whole or in part (e.g., Cabinet Office Ordinance on Disclosure of Corporate Affairs, etc., Form 11, Note 8).

d. Attached documents for shelf-registration statements
The Cabinet Office Ordinance on Disclosure of Corporate Affairs, etc. provides the attached documents for shelf-registration statements

---

**64** Among the financial instruments business operators or registered financial institutions planning to conclude wholesale underwriting agreements, companies planning to serve as lead underwriters (Guidelines on Disclosure of Corporate Affairs, B23-3-1).

*313*

submitted by domestic companies (Article 14-4(1)(i) and (2)(i)) and the attached documents for shelf-registration statements submitted by foreign companies (Article 14-4(1)(ii) and (2)(ii)). For domestic companies, the attached documents are the articles of incorporation (limited to cases where these are not included in reference documents of the shelf-registration statement), a document indicating qualifications for use of the shelf-registration system, a document stating the description of material facts that could be stated or which occurred after the submission date of the securities report referenced in the relevant shelf-registration statement (excluding cases where a quarterly securities report, semiannual securities report, extraordinary report or amendment report stating the description was included as a reference document of the shelf-registration statement), an outline of description of business, and a document accurately and simply explaining the movement of major management indicators. For foreign companies, the attached documents, in addition to those items included in the attached documents for domestic companies, are a document attesting that the representative of the foreign company has legitimate authority regarding the relevant shelf registration, a document attesting that the relevant foreign company has authorized a person who has residence in Japan to represent the relevant foreign company in all acts regarding the shelf registration, as well as a legal opinion letter from a legal expert that the relevant shelf registration is legal. In cases where the attached documents are prepared in a language other than Japanese, a Japanese language translation must be attached (Article 14-4(3) of the Cabinet Office Ordinance on Disclosure of Corporate Affairs, etc.).

Similarly, the attached documents for shelf-registration statements are prescribed, respectively, by Article 11-4 of the Cabinet Office Ordinance on Foreign Bonds for foreign government bonds, etc. and Article 18-2 of the by Cabinet Office Ordinance on Specified Securities Disclosure for specified securities.

  e. Amendment of shelf registrations
Persons who conducted shelf registrations must submit amended shelf-registration statements where any of the events 1) through 7) below

Chapter 3 Disclosure requirements

occur after the date that the shelf registration was made and before the date that the relevant shelf registration loses effect (Article 23-4 of the Financial Instruments and Exchange Act; Article 14-5 (1) of the Cabinet Office Ordinance on Disclosure of Corporate Affairs, etc.; Article 18-3(1) of the Cabinet Office Ordinance on Specified Securities Disclosure; Article 11-5(1) of the Cabinet Office Ordinance on Foreign Bonds).

1) Documents similar to the referenced documents referenced in the shelf-registration statement are newly submitted.

2) Part of an unissued portion of the planned amount of issue is no longer likely to be issued within the planned issue period.

3) When the maximum amount of the outstanding balance has been stated, and circumstances occur dictating that the maximum amount of the outstanding balance must be reduced.

4) When the maximum amount of the outstanding balance has been stated, and the date and amount of bond redemptions planned within the planned issue period have been stated, and there are changes to the redemption date or redemption amount.

5) There are changes to a principal financial instruments business operator planning to underwrite the issue.[65]

6) There are changes to the planned date the shelf registration comes into effect.

7) The shelf-registration holder otherwise recognizes there are items in the shelf-registration documents that require amendment.

Increases in the planned amount of issue, changes to the planned issue period, and changes to the class of securities cannot be amended (Article 23-4 of the Financial Instruments and Exchange Act; Article 14-5(3) of the Cabinet Office Ordinance on Disclosure of Corporate Affairs, etc.; Article

---

65 However, in cases where the principal financial instruments business operator planning to underwrite the issue was not decided when the shelf-registration statement was submitted and that was subsequently decided during the relevant shelf-registration period, it is not necessary to submit an amended shelf-registration statement regarding the decision on the matter (Guidelines on Disclosure of Corporate Affairs, B23-4-2).

*315*

18-3(3) of the Cabinet Office Ordinance on Specified Securities Disclosure; Article 11-5(3) of the Cabinet Office Ordinance on Foreign Bonds).[66]

f . Shelf registrations entry into effect

The provisions regarding the entry into effect of securities registration statements are applied *mutatis mutandis* to the entry into effect of shelf registrations (Article 23-5(1) of the Financial Instruments and Exchange Act). Namely, in principle shelf registrations should enter into effect on the day when 15 days have passed since the day the Prime Minister receives the shelf registration statement (Article 23-5 (1) and Article 8 (1) of the Financial Instruments and Exchange Act). However, since shelf-registration holders have qualifications to use the incorporation by reference method, shelf registrations correspond to cases where information regarding the corporate affairs of the issuer who is the shelf-registration holder is deemed to be already widely provided to the public (Article 8(3) and Article 23-5(1) of the Financial Instruments and Exchange Act), so when the shelf-registration holder so requests the waiting period is shortened and the shelf-registration statement comes into effect in about seven days (Guidelines on Corporate Affairs Disclosure, B8-1, 23-5-1). Also, notifications can be made stating that shelf registrations pertaining to short-term bonds, etc. and commercial paper will immediately be put into effect (Guidelines on Corporate Affairs Disclosure, B8-1 and 23-5-2).

In cases where an amended shelf-registration statement is submitted before the date a shelf registration comes into effect, the Prime Minister views the date this is received as the date the shelf-registration statement is received; and the relevant shelf-registration statement comes into effect 15 days or seven days from the date (Article 8(2) and Article 23-5(1) of the Financial Instruments and Exchange Act). On the other hand, where an amended shelf registration statement is submitted after a shelf registration comes into

---

66 Consequently, in cases where the shelf-registration holder increases the planned amount of issue, changes the planned issue period, or changes the class of securities, the shelf-registration holder must withdraw the shelf registration and submit a new shelf-registration statement.

*316*

Chapter 3　Disclosure requirements

effect, the Prime Minister can suspend the effect of the shelf registration for a period specified by the Prime Minister that does not exceed 15 days where deemed necessary and appropriate for the public interest or investor protection (Article 23-5 (2) of the Financial Instruments and Exchange Act).[67]

In principle, the periods of suspension of the effect of shelf registrations specified by the Commissioner of the Financial Services Agency are as follows (Guidelines on Corporate Affairs Disclosure, B23-5-3):

(1)　In cases where documents similar to shelf-registration statement reference documents are newly submitted, in accordance with the reasons prescribed in 1) through 4) below, until the date when the periods prescribed, respectively, have passed.

　　1 )　Where an annual securities report is newly submitted — about two days including the date of submission (about four days in cases where the relevant amended shelf-registration statement is submitted not using EDINET)

　　2 )　Where a quarterly securities report or semiannual securities report is newly submitted — about one day including the date of submission (about three days where the relevant amended shelf-registration statement is submitted not using EDINET)

　　3 )　Where an extraordinary report is newly submitted — about one day including the date of submission (about two days where the relevant amended shelf-registration statement is submitted not using EDINET)

　　4 )　Where an amendment report is newly submitted — about one day including the date of submission (about two days where the relevant amended shelf-registration statement is submitted not using

---

**67**　However, Article 23-5, paragraph 2 of the Financial Instruments and Exchange Act does not apply to the suspension of the effect of shelf registrations pertaining to short-term bonds, etc. and commercial paper. Namely, the effect of the registration can be made not to be suspension (Guidelines on Disclosure of Corporate Affairs, B23-5-4).

EDINET)

(2) In cases where an amended shelf-registration statement states the tentative conditions for securities planned to be issued — one day including the submission date.

(3) In cases were an amended shelf-registration statement is submitted for reasons other than those listed in (i) or (ii) — about one day including the submission date (about two days where the relevant amended shelf-registration statement is submitted not using EDINET).

In cases where there are false statements, etc. regarding material matters on a shelf-registration statement or shelf-registration supplement, the Prime Minister may suspend the effect of the shelf registration or extend the waiting period, and may also suspend the effect of notification or shelf registration or extend the waiting period of other securities registration statements, shelf-registration statements and shelf-registration supplements submitted within one year (Article 23-10(3) and Article 23-11(1) of the Financial Instruments and Exchange Act).

g. Shelf-registration supplements

In principle, the issuer cannot have another person acquire securities even for which shelf registration has been made for their public offering or secondary distribution, or sell such securities to another person through public offering or secondary distribution, unless the relevant shelf registration has already come into effect and, for each public offering or secondary distribution, a shelf-registration supplement has been submitted to the Prime Minister (Article 23-10(1) of the Financial Instruments and Exchange Act). However, it is not necessary to submit shelf-registration supplements if the total issue value or total distribution value of securities (calculated over one year, etc.; Article 14-9 of the Cabinet Office Ordinance on Disclosure of Corporate Affairs, etc.) is less than ¥100 million (proviso to Article 23-10(1) of the Financial Instruments and Exchange Act). Also, among book-entry bonds, etc. provided by the Act on Book-entry Transfer of Bonds, etc., for short-term bonds the issuer can have another person acquire them or sell them through public offering or secondary distribution

Chapter 3  Disclosure requirements

without submission of a shelf-registration supplement as long as the shelf registration is effective (Article 23-10(2) of the Financial Instruments and Exchange Act; Article 3-2-2 of the Financial Instruments and Exchange Act Implementing Order; Article 14-9-2 of the Cabinet Office Ordinance on Disclosure of Corporate Affairs, etc.; Article 18-7-2 of the Cabinet Office Ordinance on Specified Securities Disclosure).

In cases where a securities public offering or secondary distribution is conducted for the shareholders registered and recorded in the shareholders register on a given date (the rights allotment reference date), in principle the shelf-registration supplement pertaining to the relevant public offering or secondary distribution must be submitted by 10 days before the relevant rights allotment reference date (Article 23-10(3), main body of the Financial Instruments and Exchange Act). However, submission of a shelf-registration supplement 10 days before the relevant rights allotment reference date is not required for: (i) shares (including preferred equity investment certificates, the same hereafter), share option certificates, and securities other than bonds with share options; (ii) shares issued at a fixed price at or near the market price; (iii) bonds with share options granting share options for the acquisition of shares issued and transferred at a fixed price at or near the market price; (iv) securities issued by a company other than the company listing the shares or registering the shares over-the-counter (excluding securities listed on a foreign financial instruments exchange); and (v) share option certificates pertaining to an allotment of share options without contribution provided by Article 277 of the Companies Act to be bought and sold on a financial instruments exchange market (proviso to Article 23-10(3) of the Financial Instruments and Exchange Act; Article 3 and 14-10 of the Cabinet Office Ordinance on Disclosure of Corporate Affairs, etc.).

Shelf-registration supplements must state the total issue value or total distribution value, conditions of issuance or distribution and other matters specified by cabinet office ordinance as necessary and appropriate for the public interest or investor protection (Article 23-10(1) of the Financial Instruments and Exchange Act). The Cabinet Office Ordinance on

*319*

Disclosure of Corporate Affairs, etc. provides, respectively, the necessary matters to be stated and specifies Form 12 for domestic companies that issue bond certificates, preferred equity investment certificates, shares, share option certificates, securities or certificates indicating options, depository receipts, and beneficiary certificates of securities in trust, Form 12-2 for domestic companies which issue commercial paper, and Form 15 for foreign companies (Article 14-10 of the Cabinet Office Ordinance on Disclosure of Corporate Affairs, etc.). Similarly, the Cabinet Office Ordinance on Specified Securities Disclosure provides the items to be stated in Form 21 for domestic investment securities and Form 22 for foreign investment securities, respectively (Article 18-6 of the Cabinet Office Ordinance on Specified Securities Disclosure). The Cabinet Office Ordinance on Foreign Bonds provides the items to be stated for foreign government bonds, etc. using Form 9 (Article 11-10 of the Cabinet Office Ordinance on Foreign Bonds). On all the forms, the detailed description of the public offering or secondary distribution and each of their referenced information is to be stated as securities information.

In cases where there are minor amendment matters deemed to have no impact on the investment decisions of investors, shelf-registration supplements can be amended using an amended shelf-registration statement (Guidelines on Corporate Affairs Disclosure, B23-8-3).

h. Attached documents for shelf-registration supplements
The Cabinet Office Ordinance on Disclosure of Corporate Affairs, etc. provides the attached documents for shelf-registration supplements submitted by domestic companies (Article 14-12(1)(i)) and the attached documents for shelf-registration supplements submitted by foreign companies (Article 14-12(1)(ii)).

For domestic companies, the attached documents are: in cases where there is a board of directors resolution or general shareholders meeting resolution regarding issuance of the securities concerned, a copy of the minutes of the relevant board of directors meeting or a copy of the minutes of the relevant general shareholders meeting, or documents attesting the receipt of

Chapter 3 Disclosure requirements

authorization of administrative agency; in cases where permission, authorization or approval of administrative agency is required to change the amount of capital of the company (including designated juridical persons) by issuance of the relevant securities, documents sufficient to show the relevant permission, authorization or approval; a document stating the description of material facts that could be stated or which occurred after the submission date of the annual securities report referenced in the relevant shelf-registration supplement (excluding cases where a quarterly securities report, semiannual securities report, extraordinary report or amendment report stating the description was included as a reference document of the shelf-registration supplement), and a document accurately and simply explaining an outline of the description business and the movement of major management indicators; in cases where the relevant securities are bonds, social medical-care corporation bonds, school bond certificates, school loan claims, or commercial paper with guarantees, the articles of incorporation of the company, etc. (including designated juridical persons and partnerships) providing the relevant guarantee (in cases where this is a partnership other than a juridical person, a copy of the partnership agreement) as well as a copy of the minutes, etc. of the board of directors meeting or a copy of the minutes of the general shareholders meeting regarding the resolution by the board of directors or the resolution made at the general shareholders meeting that was adopted in order to provide the guarantee, other documents attesting that a procedure was taken to provide the guarantee, and a document stating the description of the guarantee; in cases where the securities concerned are covered warrants and there is a contract concluded regarding the options represented in the covered warrants, a copy of the relevant contract; in cases where the securities concerned are beneficiary certificates of securities in trust, copies of the trust contract concluded regarding the issuance of the relevant beneficiary certificates of securities in trust and of other main contracts; and in cases where the securities concerned are depository receipts, copies of the depository contract concluded regarding the issuance of the relevant depository receipts and of the other main contracts.

For foreign companies the attached documents, in addition to those items

*321*

included in the attached documents for domestic companies, are: a document attesting that the representative of the foreign company has legitimate authority regarding the submission of the relevant shelf-registration supplement, a document attesting that the relevant foreign company has authorized a person who has residence in Japan to represent the relevant foreign company in all acts regarding the submission of the shelf-registration supplement, a legal opinion letter from a legal expert that the submission of the relevant shelf-registration supplement is legal, a document attesting that the relevant permission has been received in cases where permission provided by Article 21, paragraph 1 or paragraph 2 of the Foreign Exchange and Foreign Trade Act is required, a copy of the wholesale underwriting contract concluded between the relevant foreign company and a financial instruments business operator; and in cases where the securities concerned are bonds, etc., a copy of the contract in which the relevant foreign company entrusts the duties of administration of claims and other duties to perform acts for obligees or acts for the relevant foreign company and a copy of the contract concerning payment of the principal and interest.

In cases where the attached documents are prepared in a language other than Japanese, a Japanese language translation must be attached (Article 14-12(2) of the Cabinet Office Ordinance on Disclosure of Corporate Affairs, etc.).

Items that were attached to the shelf-registration statement do not have to be attached to the shelf-registration supplement (Article 14-12(1) of the Cabinet Office Ordinance on Disclosure of Corporate Affairs, etc. introductory clause).

Similarly, the attached documents to shelf-registration supplements are provided by the Cabinet Office Ordinance on Foreign Bonds (Article 11-11) for foreign bonds, etc. and by the Cabinet Office Ordinance on Specified Securities Disclosure (Article 18-9) for specified securities.

*322*

Chapter 3　Disclosure requirements

ⅰ. Amended shelf-registration statements and amendments to shelf-registration supplements

Persons who conducted shelf registrations must submit amended shelf-registration statements when any of the events (1) through (7) below occur after the date that the shelf registration was made and before the relevant shelf registration loses effect (Article 23-4 of the Financial Instruments and Exchange Act; Article 14-5 (1) of the Cabinet Office Ordinance on Disclosure of Corporate Affairs, etc.; Article 18 (3) of the Cabinet Office Ordinance on Specified Securities Disclosure Article; Article 11-5(1) of the Cabinet Office Ordinance on Foreign Bonds).

(1)　Documents of the same type as the reference documents referenced in the shelf-registration statement are newly submitted (excluding cases when the submission deadline for the relevant same type of documents is stated in the relevant shelf-registration statement, and the same type of documents are submitted by that submission deadline; Article 23-4 of the Financial Instruments and Exchange Act).[68]

(2)　Part of an unissued portion of the planned amount of issue is no longer likely to be issued within the planned issue period.

For example, cases where conditions arise making it necessary to reduce the planned amount of issue because of outstanding changes to production plans, facilities investment plans, capital plans, etc. during the shelf-registration period correspond to this reason (Guidelines on Corporate Affairs Disclosure, B23-4-1).

(3)　When the maximum amount of outstanding balance has been stated, and circumstances occur dictating that the maximum amount of outstanding balance must be reduced.

(4)　When the maximum amount of outstanding balance has been stated, and the date and amount of bond redemptions planned within the planned issue period have been stated, and there are changes to the

---

**68**　Even where documents equivalent to documents where "information on the guarantor company etc." is stated or should be stated are newly submitted, it is necessary to submit an amended shelf-registration statement (Guidelines on Disclosure of Corporate Affairs, B23-4-3).

redemption date or redemption amount.

(5) There are changes to a principal financial instruments business operator that plans to underwrite the issue.

However, in cases where the principal financial instruments business operator that planned to underwrite the issue was not decided when the shelf-registration statement was submitted and that was subsequently decided during the relevant shelf-registration period, it is not necessary to submit an amended shelf-registration statement regarding the decision on the matter (Guidelines on Corporate Affairs Disclosure, B23-4-2).

(6) There are changes to the planned date the shelf registration comes into effect.

(7) The shelf-registration holder otherwise recognizes there are items in the shelf-registration documents that require amendment (Article 23-4, sentence 2).

However, increases in the planned amount of issue, changes to the planned issue period, and changes to the class of securities cannot be amended (Article 23-4 of the Financial Instruments and Exchange Act; Article 14-5 (3) of the Cabinet Office Ordinance on Disclosure of Corporate Affairs, etc.; Article 18-3 (3) of the Cabinet Office Ordinance on Specified Securities Disclosure; Article 11-5 (3) of the Cabinet Office Ordinance on Foreign Bonds).

In cases where there are minor amendment matters deemed to have no impact on the investment decisions of investors, shelf-registration supplements can be amended using an amended shelf-registration statement (Guidelines on Corporate Affairs Disclosure, B23-8-3).

j. Authority to which submission is made and public inspection

Shelf-registration statements, shelf-registration supplements, and amended shelf-registration statements must be made available for public inspection until the shelf registration is no longer in effect (Article 25(1) (iii), Article 5 (8) and Article 27 of the Financial Instruments and Exchange Act), and the authority to which submission is made and other rules regarding public

Chapter 3 Disclosure requirements

inspection are the same as those for securities registration statements.

k. Withdrawal of shelf-registration

In cases where the entire planned amount of issue of a securities public offering or secondary distribution is completed before the planned issue period has passed, the shelf-registration holder must submit a written withdrawal of shelf registration to that effect to the Prime Minister and withdraw the shelf registration (Article 23-7 (1) of the Financial Instruments and Exchange Act). Withdrawal of shelf registration can be permitted in other cases as well (Guidelines on Corporate Affairs Disclosure, B23-7-1). Withdrawal of shelf registration is conducted by submitting a written withdrawal of shelf registration to the Prime Minister (Article 23-7 (1) of the Financial Instruments and Exchange Act). The shelf registration loses its effect on the day when the written withdrawal of shelf registration is received by the Prime Minister (Article 23-7 (2) of the Financial Instruments and Exchange Act).

# B. Regulation of transactions on primary market and provision of information to investors

## 1. Regulation before notification

In principle, the issuer of the securities concerned must submit a securities registration statement (Article 4(1), (2) & (3) of the Financial Instruments and Exchange Act) before beginning solicitation for acquisition (Article 2(3) of the Financial Instruments and Exchange Act), specified procedures relating to securities issuance for reorganization (Article 2-2 (4) of the Financial Instruments and Exchange Act), solicitation for selling, etc. (Article 2(4) of the Financial Instruments and Exchange Act), specified procedures relating to securities delivery for reorganization (Article 2-2(5) of the Financial Instruments and Exchange Act), or general solicitation for securities acquired by qualified institutional investors or general solicitation for securities acquired by professional investors, etc. pertaining to a securities public offering or secondary distribution. Also, in certain cases, written notice of securities must be submitted regarding the secondary

*325*

distribution of securities that have already been disclosed; and in those cases the relevant written notice of securities must be submitted by the day before the relevant secondary distribution begins (namely, the day before conducting solicitation for selling, etc. pertaining to the secondary distribution).[69]

There are no provisions of the Financial Instruments and Exchange Act or of Cabinet Orders or Cabinet Office Ordinances based thereon that define the meaning of "solicitation" in "solicitation for acquisition and solicitation for selling etc. of securities" as used here. However, the Financial Services Agency interprets that distributing documents (including notification of allotment of new shares and application for share subscriptions) regarding the public offering or secondary distribution of securities, giving oral explanations at meetings to explain capital increases to shareholders, etc., and advertising the public offering or secondary distribution of securities using newspapers, magazines, billboards, television, radio, the Internet, etc. constitute acts of "public offering or secondary distribution of securities" (Guidelines on Corporate Affairs Disclosure B4-1). However, the Financial Services Agency interprets that, where third-party allotments (Article 19 (2) (i) (l) of the Cabinet Office Ordinance on Disclosure of Corporate Affairs, etc.) are conducted if the parties expected to receive the allotment are limited and the qualification is met to be considered as corresponding to "cases where there is little concern that the securities pertaining to the relevant third-party allotment will be immediately resold" by the relevant parties expected to receive the allotment, investigations concerning the parties expected to receive the allotment to be conducted before the notification for the purposes of selection of such parties or ascertaining the overall conditions of the relevant parties expected to receive the allotment, consultations with the parties expected to receive the allotment regarding the description, etc. of the relevant third-party allotment, and other similar acts do not constitute solicitation for acquisition or solicitation for selling, etc. of securities (Guidelines on Corporate Affairs Disclosure, B2-12). For

---

69  However, solicitation for acquisition and solicitation for selling, etc. can be conducted without notification for securities whose issuance is covered by shelf registration.

Chapter 3  Disclosure requirements

example, cases where conducting capital alliances and cases where a parent company underwrites the shares of a subsidiary constitute "cases where there is little concern that the securities pertaining to the relevant third-party allotment will be immediately resold," while in all other cases the decision on whether they constitute such cases is made on an individual, specific basis.[70]

## 2. Regulation after notification and provision of information to investors

a. Prohibition of transactions before notification comes into effect

Securities issuers, persons conducting secondary distribution of securities (sellers), underwriters (Article 2 (6) of the Financial Instruments and Exchange Act), financial instruments business operators, registered financial institutions and financial instruments intermediary service providers cannot have another person acquire or cannot sell to another person, by way of public offering or secondary distribution, securities whose public offering or secondary distribution is subject to Article 4, paragraph 1, paragraph 2 or paragraph 3 main body of the Financial Instruments and Exchange Act unless the notification under these provisions is effective (Article 15(1) of the Financial Instruments and Exchange Act). Moreover, even after the notification has come into effect, it is prohibited to have another person acquire or to sell to another person securities through public offering or secondary distribution during periods when the effect of the notification is suspended by the Prime Minister (Article 10 (1) of the Financial Instruments and Exchange Act).

b. Obligation to prepare and deliver a prospectus

Issuers of securities that require notification for their public offering or secondary distribution must prepare a prospectus[71] upon the relevant public offering or secondary distribution, and in principle issuers of securities

---

70 "Results of Public Comments on 'Draft Cabinet Office Ordinance Regarding Partial Revision of the Cabinet Office Ordinance on Disclosure of Corporate Affairs, etc.'" "Outline of Comments and FSA's Position on Comments" (December 11, 2009), p. 5, No. 26.

*327*

pertaining to secondary distributions of securities that have already been disclosed (previously-disclosed securities; Article 13 (1) of the Financial Instruments and Exchange Act) must also prepare a prospectus (Article 13 (1) of the Financial Instruments and Exchange Act). Moreover, in principle, unless a prospectus stating the items provided by cabinet office ordinance is delivered beforehand or concurrently,[72] securities issuers, sellers, underwriters, financial instruments business operators, registered financial institutions or financial instruments intermediary service providers cannot have another person acquire or cannot sell to another person securities that require a notification for their public offering or secondary distribution or previously-disclosed securities through the relevant public offering or secondary distribution[73] (Article 15 (2) of the Financial Instruments and Exchange Act).[74,75]

However, delivery of a prospectus to qualified institutional investors is not

---

71  A prospectus is a document stating explanations regarding the business of the issuer of the security concerned and other matters delivered to counterparties or delivered upon request for delivery from counterparties for public offering or secondary distribution of securities (excluding those listed in Article 4, paragraph 1, item 4 of the Financial Instruments and Exchange Act) or general solicitations of securities acquired by qualified institutional investors under Article 4, paragraph 2 of the Financial Instruments and Exchange Act (excluding those which correspond to secondary distribution of securities) (Article 2(10) of the Financial Instruments and Exchange Act).

72  In cases where a prospectus is used for public offering or secondary distribution of securities for which there is an obligation to submit a securities registration statement or for secondary distribution of previously-disclosed securities, a statutory prospectus that contains false statements or lacks items that should be stated cannot be used (Article 13(4) of the Financial Instruments and Exchange Act).

73  Under Article 4, paragraph 1, in relation to Article 13, paragraphs 1 and 2 of the Financial Instruments and Exchange Act that provide the obligation to prepare a prospectus and Article 15, paragraph 2 that provides the obligation to deliver a prospectus, specified procedures relating to securities issuance for reorganization and specified procedures relating to securities delivery for reorganization are not included in the definition of "public offering or secondary distribution of securities." Consequently, there is no obligation to prepare or deliver a prospectus when conducting specified procedures relating to securities issuance for reorganization or specified procedures relating to securities delivery for reorganization.

*328*

Chapter 3 Disclosure requirements

required (proviso to Article 15(2) and (i) of the Financial Instruments and Exchange Act). Similarly, delivery of a prospectus is not required to persons who hold the same issue as the relevant securities and to persons who live together with persons who have received or are certainly expected to receive the prospectus if they have given their consent not to receive that prospectus (proviso to Article 15(2) and (ii) of the Financial Instruments and Exchange Act). However, even in these cases, when delivery of a prospectus is requested, a prospectus must be delivered.

Also, among cases of rights offerings though allotments of share options without consideration as prescribed in Article 277 of the Companies Act, the issuer is exempted from the obligation to prepare and deliver a prospectus when the share option certificates that are the subject of the allotment of share options without consideration are listed on a financial instruments exchange or are scheduled to be listed without delay after issuance; and a statement to the effect that the securities registration statement has been submitted and other items prescribed by cabinet office ordinance (the date of notification concerning the share option certificates, the EDINET web address, and the issuer's contact for inquiries regarding the issuance of the relevant share option certificates; Article 11-5 of the Cabinet Office Ordinance on Disclosure of Corporate Affairs, etc.) are published after the submission without delay in a daily newspaper that covers matters related to current affairs (proviso to Article 13(1) and Article 15(2)(iii) of the

---

74  For general solicitation for securities acquired by professional investors, etc. (Article 4(3) of the Financial Instruments and Exchange Act) as well, because there is an obligation to submit a securities registration statement, there is also an obligation to prepare and deliver a prospectus (Article 13(1) and Article 15(2) of the Financial Instruments and Exchange Act, Article 13(1), first sentence and Article 15(2)).

75  A prospectus must also be delivered where the remainder (underwriting balance) of securities not listed or over-the-counter traded that were not acquired in a public offering or secondary distribution are acquired by or sold to a person not through public offering or secondary distribution within three months from the date the public offering or secondary distribution notification came into effect (excluding periods when suspensions are in effect in cases where an order has been given to suspend the effect of the notification) (Article 15(6) of the Financial Instruments and Exchange Act).

*329*

Financial Instruments and Exchange Act). On the other hand, such exemptions to the obligation to prepare and deliver a prospectus are not granted when rights offerings are conducted by foreign companies using the share option certificates of a foreign state.

Regarding the secondary distribution of previously-disclosed securities, there is no obligation to prepare a prospectus (i) where the total distribution value is less than ¥100 million (Article 13(1) of the Financial Instruments and Exchange Act), and (ii) where the securities that are the subject of the secondary distribution are securities other than equity securities (shares, share option certificates, securities with share options or which can be converted into shares, or securities with the characteristics of these securities issued by a foreign state or a foreign person) (Article 11-4 of the Cabinet Office Ordinance on Disclosure of Corporate Affairs, etc.). Also, it is provided that, except for cases where stabilizing transactions regarding the secondary distribution of the securities concerned are conducted, the preparation of a prospectus is not required (iii) where the secondary distribution of securities does not correspond to a secondary distribution of securities provided in Article 2, paragraph 4 of the Financial Instruments and Exchange Act (Article 11-4(i) of the Cabinet Office Ordinance on Disclosure of Corporate Affairs, etc., Article 14 of Cabinet Office Ordinance on Specified Securities Disclosure)[76] and (iv) where the secondary distribution of securities does not correspond to a secondary distribution of securities under any of the items 1) through 5) below (Article 11-4(ii) and proviso to the Cabinet Office Ordinance on Disclosure of Corporate Affairs, etc.).

1 ) A secondary distribution of securities conducted by the issuer of the securities concerned who is the owner of the securities pertaining to

---

[76] Including general solicitations for securities acquired by qualified institutional investors and general solicitations for securities acquired by professional investors, etc. within the definition of "secondary distribution" in Article 13, paragraph 1 of the Financial Instruments and Exchange Act that do not correspond to secondary distribution under Article 2, paragraph 4 of the Financial Instruments and Exchange Act.

Chapter 3 Disclosure requirements

the secondary distribution of the securities concerned

2 ) A secondary distribution of securities in cases where the owner of the securities pertaining to the secondary distribution of the relevant securities corresponds to any of the following:

a ) A subsidiary or major shareholder (shareholder who owns 10% or more of the voting rights of all shareholders, etc.; Article 163(1) of the Financial Instruments and Exchange Act) of the issuer of the securities concerned;

b ) A "director"[77] or incorporator of the issuer of the securities concerned;

c ) A "director" or incorporator of a subsidiary of the issuer of the securities concerned;

d ) Persons similar to those listed in a) through c) above in cases where the issuer of the securities concerned is a foreign company or a person other than a company.

3 ) A secondary distribution of securities conducted by a financial instruments business operator, etc. that acquired the securities concerned from persons listed in 1) or 2) for the purposes of having other persons acquire the securities concerned

4 ) A secondary distribution of the securities concerned conducted by a financial instruments business operator corresponding to an underwriter (excluding persons who conduct firm commitment underwriting as provided in Article 2 (6) (i) of the Financial Instruments and Exchange Act).

5 ) A secondary distribution of the relevant share option certificates or securities concerned conducted by a financial instruments business operator, etc. that acquired share option certificates based on a contract in a rights offering implementing the commitment provided in Article 2, paragraph 6, item 3 of the Financial Instruments and Exchange Act, or which acquired securities by exercising the share

---

77 In this chapter, "director" (*yakuin*) or "directors" means directors, accounting advisors, company auditors or executive officers or equivalent persons.

*331*

options pertaining to the relevant share option certificates (limited to persons corresponding to underwriters implementing the contract prescribed in the same item).

Also, for beneficiary certificates of investment trusts and foreign investment trusts (Article 2(1)(x) of the Financial Instruments and Exchange Act), investment securities, investment corporation debentures and foreign investment securities (Article 2(1)(xi) of the Financial Instruments and Exchange Act) (Article 15(3) of the Financial Instrument and Exchange Act; Article 3-3 of the Financial Instruments and Exchange Act Implementing Order), while information which has "an extremely material influence" on investment decisions must be stated in a prospectus for mandatory delivery and delivered to all shareholders (Article 15(2), and Article 13(2)(i) of the Financial Instruments and Exchange Act), it is deemed sufficient as regards information that only has a material influence on investment decisions if a prospectus to be delivered upon request containing such information is delivered to those investors that request a copy (Article 15(3) and Article 13(2)(ii) of the Financial Instruments and Exchange Act).

Furthermore, regarding amended portions of a prospectus, in certain cases their delivery is not required. Namely, in public offerings and secondary distributions using the book-building, etc., in cases where a securities registration statement was submitted without stating the issue price, etc. pursuant to the proviso to Article 5, paragraph 1 of the Financial Instruments and Exchange Act,[78] it is not required to state those items in the prospectus either (proviso to Article 13(2) of the Financial Instruments and Exchange Act); however, a prospectus stating the relevant issue price, etc. must be delivered before or simultaneously with having other persons acquire the securities or selling them to other persons (Article 13(2)(iii) of

---

[78] However, at the time when the price etc. is determined, it is necessary to submit an amendment (Article 7 of the Financial Instruments and Exchange Act) to supplement these matters (Article 11(iii) of the Cabinet Office Ordinance on Disclosure of Corporate Affairs, etc.; Article 13(iv) of the Cabinet Office Ordinance on Specified Securities Disclosure).

Chapter 3   Disclosure requirements

the Financial Instruments and Exchange Act). Nevertheless, delivery of the amended portions is deemed not required where a prospectus delivered without stating the issue price, etc. has a statement to the effect that the issue price, etc.[79] will be publicized (instead of delivering the amended portion) along with the publication method,[80] and the relevant issue price, etc. is then publicized by the relevant publication method (Article 15(5) of the Financial Instruments and Exchange Act). Here, the following three alternatives are provided for publication: (i) publication in two or more daily newspapers that cover matters related to overall current affairs in Japan or newspapers (daily newspapers) that cover general matters related to the Japanese industry and the domestic economy; (ii) publication in one or more daily newspapers, and offering for inspection via a telecommunications line those matters recorded in a file that is stored on a computer used by the issuer or by the person who intends to have the securities acquired and sell them through public offering or secondary distribution (e.g., disclosure on the home page of the issuer or the financial instruments business operator handling the public offering or secondary distribution); and (iii) offering for inspection through the home page of the issuer or of the person who intends to have the securities acquired or to sell them through public offering or secondary distribution, and adding the method of directly confirming by telephone or other means that the counterparties by whom the securities are to be acquired and to whom they are to be sold have inspected the matters or have obtained information regarding the matters through other methods (by delivery of written documents or explanations, communication via facsimile, transmission via electronic mail, oral explanations, spoken guidance by telephone, etc.; Guidelines on Corporate Affairs Disclosure, B15-5) (Article 14-2(1) of the Cabinet Office Ordinance on Disclosure of Corporate Affairs, etc.; Article 17(1) of the Cabinet Office Ordinance on Specified

---

79   Regarding matters to be amended along with the determination of the issue price, etc. as well, it is interpreted that these can be disclosed using the stated publicizing method if there is a statement to that effect on the securities registration statement (Guidelines on Disclosure of Corporate Affairs, B13-1).

80   A statement that the issue price etc. will be publicized (not that the amended matters will be delivered) and the method of publication are stated on the securities registration statement (Guidelines on Disclosure of Corporate Affairs, B7-2).

Securities Disclosure; Article 11-2(1) of the Cabinet Office Ordinance on Foreign Bonds).

c. Items to be stated on a prospectus

The items provided in Article 13, paragraph 2 of the Financial Instruments and Exchange Act must be included in prospectuses that must be prepared pursuant to Article 13, paragraph 1 of the Financial Instruments and Exchange Act (reported prospectuses; Article 1(xv-2) of the Cabinet Office Ordinance on Disclosure of Corporate Affairs, etc.; Article 1(xviii) of the Cabinet Office Ordinance on Specified Securities Disclosure).[81] Excluding (1) and (2) below, reported prospectuses must include the items to be included in the securities registration statement (see Article 12 of the Cabinet Office Ordinance on Disclosure of Corporate Affairs, etc.).[82]

(1) Special information (among financial statements in the five most recent business years, financial statements other than financial statements of the two most recent business years which are stated in

---

[81] In contrast, a prospectus used before the day the notification comes into effect is called a provisionally-submitted prospectus (Article 1(xvi) of the Cabinet Office Ordinance on Disclosure of Corporate Affairs, etc.; Article 1(xix) of the Cabinet Office Ordinance on Specified Securities Disclosure). The items to be stated on a provisional prospectus are fundamentally the same as those to be stated on a submitted prospectus,; but as special instructions, while a submitted prospectus must state that the notification is in effect, a provisional prospectus must state the date of notification and that the notification is not in effect and that amendments may be made to the stated contents (Article 13(1)(ii) and Article 14(1)(ii) of the Cabinet Office Ordinance on Disclosure of Corporate Affairs, etc.; Article 15-2(1)(ii) and Article 15-3(1)(ii) of the Cabinet Office Ordinance on Specified Securities Disclosure). A provisional prospectus can be used as a submitted prospectus after notification comes into effect by, among others, inserting a document stating that the notification concerning the public offering or secondary distribution is in effect (Guidelines on Disclosure of Corporate Affairs, B13-3).

[82] However, regarding beneficiary certificates for investment trusts and foreign investment trusts, investment securities, investment corporation debentures and foreign investment securities, as stated above, for information that only has a material influence on investor decisions, it is deemed sufficient if a requested prospectus including such information is delivered to the investors upon request (Article 15(3) and 13(2)(ii) of the Financial Instruments and Exchange Act).

Chapter 3 Disclosure requirements

the status of accounting, for example, Part 4 of securities registration statements of domestic companies using the ordinary method [Form 2] or Part 4 of securities registration statements of foreign companies using the ordinary method [Form 7]).

(2) Business secrets (the relevant part where the securities issuer makes an application to the Prime Minister not to make available for public inspection part of the disclosure documents because of the necessity to preserve business secrets and this application is approved) (proviso to Article 12 of the Cabinet Office Ordinance on Disclosure of Corporate Affairs, etc.; proviso to Article 15 of the Cabinet Office Ordinance on Specified Securities Disclosure).

Meanwhile, in addition to the matters stated on the securities registration statement, certain matters (special instructions) such as a statement to the effect that notification is effective (for secondary distribution of previously-disclosed securities, a statement to the effect that no notification has been made) must also be stated in the prospectus (Article 13(2)(i)(a) b) of the Financial Instruments and Exchange Act; Article 13(1)(i) and 14 (1)(i) of the Cabinet Office Ordinance on Disclosure of Corporate Affairs, etc.; Article 15-2(1)(i) and 15-3(1)(i) of the Cabinet Office Ordinance on Specified Securities Disclosure Article). These matters must be stated on the cover of the prospectus or at an easily viewable location in the prospectus (Article 13(2) and 14(2) of the Cabinet Office Ordinance on Disclosure of Corporate Affairs, etc.; Article 15-2(2) and 15-3(2) of the Cabinet Office Ordinance on Specified Securities Disclosure).

Also, in cases where the securities registration statement is prepared using the incorporation by reference method, among the attached documents to the securities registration statement, a document showing qualifications to use the incorporation by reference method, an outline of the description of business, and a document stating the movement of major management indicators (highlighted information), as well as the contents of documents stating the description of material facts after the date that the reference documents were submitted (in cases of secondary distributions of previously-disclosed securities, equivalent contents) must be stated in the

*335*

prospectus (Article 13(1) (i) (c) and Article 14(1) (i) (c) of the Cabinet Office Ordinance on Disclosure of Corporate Affairs, etc.). These are to be stated immediately after the referenced information (Article 13(2) and Article 14(2) of the Cabinet Office Ordinance on Disclosure of Corporate Affairs, etc.; Article 15-2(2) and Article 15-3(2) of the Cabinet Office Ordinance on Specified Securities Disclosure).

In cases where a foreign company registration statement and supplementary documents have been submitted, the items to be included in the prospectus are deemed to be the items included in the foreign company registration statement and supplementary documents (Article 12(ii) (e) (f) of the Cabinet Office Ordinance on Disclosure of Corporate Affairs, etc.; Article 9 of the Cabinet Office Ordinance on Foreign Bonds; Article 16(ii) & (iv) of the Cabinet Office Ordinance on Specified Securities Disclosure). Consequently, for the prospectus as well, disclosure in English is permitted.

d. Provision of a prospectus, etc. by electromagnetic means

Instead of providing the prospectus using paper media, a prospectus can be delivered by a method whereby a file containing the matters to be stated in the prospectus that has been prepared using media which is capable of securely recording certain matters by means of magnetic disk, CD-ROM or other equivalent method is delivered (Article 23-2(2) (ii) of the Cabinet Office Ordinance on Disclosure of Corporate Affairs, etc.). The matters stated in the prospectus can also be provided on-line by using an electronic data processing system (Article 27-30-9(1) of the Financial Instruments and Exchange Act). The following four methods are recognized as methods using an electronic data processing system (Article 23-2(2) (i) of the Cabinet Office Ordinance on Disclosure of Corporate Affairs, etc.). However, for a prospectus provider to provide the prospectus to the prospectus recipient using electromagnetic means, the prospectus provider must present the type and contents of the electromagnetic means to the prospectus recipient and obtain consent in writing, by electromagnetic means, or by telephone (Article 27-30-9(1) of the Financial Instruments and Exchange Act; Article 23-2(1) of the Cabinet Office Ordinance on Disclosure of Corporate Affairs, etc.).

Chapter 3 Disclosure requirements

(1) A method whereby items included in the prospectus are transmitted via a telecommunications line that links a computer used by the prospectus provider (solicitor; typically a financial instruments business operator) with a computer used by the prospectus recipient (solicitee) and recorded in the prospectus recipient's file stored on a computer used by the prospectus recipient.

(2) A method whereby items included in the prospectus that have been recorded in a file that is stored on a computer used by the prospectus provider, etc. are offered to the prospectus recipient for inspection via a telecommunications line, and recorded in the prospectus recipient's file stored on a computer used by the prospectus recipient.

(3) A method whereby items included in the prospectus that have been recorded in the prospectus recipient's file stored on a computer used by the prospectus provider are offered to the prospectus recipient for inspection via a telecommunications line.

(4) A method whereby matters stated in the prospectus that have been recorded in an inspection file (meaning a file stored on a computer used by the prospectus provider, etc. in which the items included in the prospectus are recorded for the purposes of offering them to two or more prospectus recipients concurrently) are offered to the prospectus recipient, etc. for inspection via a telecommunications line.

In all these cases, it must be possible to prepare a document by outputting the records (Article 23-2 (3) (i) of the Cabinet Office Ordinance on Disclosure of Corporate Affairs, etc.). Also, in cases using the methods in (1), (2), or (4), in principle the prospectus provider must notify the prospectus recipient to the effect that the matters stated in the prospectus will be recorded or have been recorded in the prospectus recipient's file or the inspection file (Article 23-2 (3) (ii) of the Cabinet Office Ordinance on Disclosure of Corporate Affairs, etc.). However, this does not apply in cases where it has been confirmed that the prospectus recipient has inspected the relevant stated matters (proviso to Article 23-2(3) (ii) of the Cabinet Office Ordinance on Disclosure of Corporate Affairs, etc.). Additionally, in cases using the method in (4), the information required to inspect the inspection file must be recorded in the prospectus recipient's recipient's file (Article

*337*

23-2 (3) (iii) of the Cabinet Office Ordinance on Disclosure of Corporate Affairs, etc.). In addition to the above, in cases using the methods in (3) or (4) above, in principle the stated matters recorded in the file cannot be deleted or altered for five years from the time the prospectus is provided (Article 23-2 (3) (iv) (a) of the Cabinet Office Ordinance on Disclosure of Corporate Affairs, etc.). Moreover, in cases using the method in (4), in principle the file must always be kept available for access over those five years (Article 23-2 (3) (v)) or, instead of this, when there is a request from a prospectus recipient to inspect a prospectus, the prospectus must be provided immediately using the method of transmitting the stated matters by electronic mail, the method of delivering the stated matters using a magnetic disc, etc., or the method of outputting the stated matters on a document and delivering the document (Article 23-2 (3) (iv) (b) of the Cabinet Office Ordinance on Disclosure of Corporate Affairs, etc. Article).

Note that "prospectus provider, etc." includes not only prospectus providers but also persons who under a contract with a prospectus provider store files on computers under their own management and make them available for use by prospectus recipients or prospectus providers (Article 23-2 (2) (i) (a) of the Cabinet Office Ordinance on Disclosure of Corporate Affairs, etc.).

In all cases, persons who provide matters stated in a prospectus are deemed as having delivered the relevant prospectus (Article 27-30-9 (1), second sentence of the Financial Instruments and Exchange Act).

e. Shelf-registration system and prospectuses
When a shelf-registration statement is submitted, acts of solicitation can be initiated regarding public offerings or secondary distributions of the securities that are the subject of the shelf registration without notifying each individual public offering or secondary distribution, and while the shelf registration is effective, it is permitted to have other persons acquire or to sell the securities by submitting a shelf-registration supplement (Article 23-8 (1) of the Financial Instruments and Exchange Act). Then, when concluding a contract for acquisition or for sale by public offering or secondary distribution of securities using the shelf-registration system, a

Chapter 3 Disclosure requirements

supplementary shelf-registration prospectus must be delivered to investors in advance or concurrently (Article 23-12 (3) and Article 15 (2) of the Financial Instruments and Exchange Act). A prospectus must also be delivered when the remainder (underwriting balance) of securities not listed or over-the-counter traded that were not acquired in a public offering or secondary distribution are acquired by or sold to a person not through public offering or secondary distribution while the shelf registration is effective and within three months from the day when the relevant shelf-registration supplement was submitted (Article 23-12 (3) and Article 15 (6) of the Financial Instruments and Exchange Act).

A shelf-registration prospectus[83] is a prospectus used for acts of solicitation until the shelf-registration supplement is submitted presuming the shelf-registration statement, and it states the contents to be stated on the shelf-registration statement and on all amended shelf-registration statements submitted after the shelf-registration statement was submitted. A supplementary shelf-registration prospectus is a prospectus used when having securities acquired or selling securities after submission of a shelf-registration supplement, and it states the contents to be stated on the shelf-registration statement and on all amended shelf-registration statements and shelf-registration supplements submitted after the shelf-registration statement was submitted (Article 23-12(2) and Article 13 (2) of the Financial Instruments and Exchange Act; Guidelines on Corporate Affairs Disclosure, B23-12-1). Also, a shelf-registration prospectus, provisional shelf-registration prospectus or supplementary shelf-registration prospectus can state regarding the company information of the relevant shelf-registration holder the contents stated on reference documents of the relevant shelf-registration statement, etc.. In this case, however, all the contents stated on those documents must be stated (Guidelines on Corporate Affairs Disclosure, B23-12-2).

A shelf-registration prospectus, provisional shelf-registration prospectus or

---

**83** A provisional shelf-registration prospectus when it is to be used before the shelf registration comes into effect.

*339*

supplementary shelf-registration prospectus must also include documents indicating qualifications to use the incorporation by reference method and other special instructions (Article 14-13 of the Cabinet Office Ordinance on Disclosure of Corporate Affairs, etc.; Article 18-10 of the Cabinet Office Ordinance on Specified Securities Disclosure).

In cases where an issuer, seller, underwriter or financial instruments business operator has another person acquire or sells securities for which shelf registration was conducted via public offering or secondary distribution, after submitting a shelf-registration statement or amended shelf-registration statement, (i) documents stating the following must be delivered in advance: 1) among the matters that must be stated on the shelf-registration statement or amended shelf-registration statement, matters other than issue price, etc., 2) a statement to the effect that the issue price, etc. will be publicized, and 3) the method of relevant publication, and (ii) when the relevant issue price, etc. is publicized using the relevant method, the relevant documents are deemed the prospectus and the publication of the relevant issue price, etc. is deemed the delivery of the prospectus (Article 23-12(7) of the Financial Instruments and Exchange Act). This constitutes the exemption for shelf registration of the delivery of amended portions of the prospectus that is equivalent to the exemption permitted for securities registration statements. The following three methods are specified as means of publication: (i) publication in two or more daily newspapers that cover matters related to overall current affairs in Japan or daily newspapers that cover general matters related to the Japanese industry and the domestic economy (daily newspapers); (ii) publication in one or more daily newspapers, and offering for inspection via a telecommunications line those matters recorded in a file that is stored on a computer used by the issuer or by the person who intends to have the securities acquired and to sell the securities through public offering or secondary distribution (publication on the home page of the issuer or the financial instruments business operator handling the public offering or secondary distribution); and (iii) offering for inspection through the home page of the issuer or of the person who intends to have the securities acquired or to sell them through public offering or secondary distribution,

*340*

Chapter 3 Disclosure requirements

and directly confirming by telephone or other means that the counterparties by whom the securities are to be acquired or to whom they are to be sold through public offering or secondary distribution have inspected the matters or have obtained information regarding the matters through other methods (by delivery of written documents or explanations, communication via facsimile, transmission via electronic mail, oral explanations, spoken guidance by telephone, etc.; Guidelines on Corporate Affairs Disclosure, B15-5) (Article 14-2 of the Cabinet Office Ordinance on Disclosure of Corporate Affairs, etc.; Article 17 of the Cabinet Office Ordinance on Specified Securities Disclosure; Article 11-2 of the Cabinet Office Ordinance on Foreign Bonds).

f. Solicitation using materials other than a statutory prospectus
If notification is submitted for a public offering or secondary distribution of securities, solicitation for acquisition and solicitation for selling, etc. of the securities concerned can be conducted; and in carrying out solicitation for acquisition or solicitation for selling, etc. of the securities concerned, documents, drawings, sound, and other materials that are not a statutory prospectus can be used as well. These other materials include indications using television, radio, the Internet, newspaper and magazine advertising, and oral explanations, etc., and a summary of the contents of the prospectus, etc. (Guidelines on Corporate Affairs Disclosure, B13-4). However, false and misleading indications are not permitted (Article 13 (5) of the Financial Instruments and Exchange Act). Also, to avoid the misunderstanding that these other materials are the prospectus, they must include a statement to the effect that reference should be made to the prospectus in order to make investment decisions, as well as the method and location for obtaining the prospectus (Guidelines on Corporate Affairs Disclosure, B13-7).

Documents, drawings, sound and other materials aside from the prospectus can be used for a public offering or secondary distribution pertaining to a shelf registration as well, and in that case, false and misleading indications are prohibited (Article 23-12 (2) and Article 13-5 of the Financial Instruments and Exchange Act).

*341*

g. Reorganisations and prospectuses

In cases where securities are issued or delivered in reorganization, an obligation to prepare and deliver a prospectus is not prescribed. This is because specified procedures relating to securities issuance for reorganization and specified procedures relating to securities delivery for reorganization do not constitute "public offering or secondary distribution of securities" for which the obligation to prepare a prospectus is provided under Article 13, paragraphs 1 and 2 of the Financial Instruments and Exchange Act and for which the obligation to deliver a prospectus is provided under Article 15, paragraph 2 of the Financial Instruments and Exchange Act (Article 4 (1) and (4) of the Financial Instruments and Exchange Act). However, the obligation to prepare and deliver a prospectus is provided in cases of takeover bids with securities as consideration (exchange offers).

h. Obligation to notify in solicitation of qualified institutional investors and solicitation of a small number of investors

In solicitation of qualified institutional investors (cases corresponding to Article 2, paragraph 3, items 2a and 2c, paragraph 4, items 2a and 2c, Article 2-2, paragraph 4, item 2a, or Article 2-2, paragraph 5, item 2a of the Financial Instruments and Exchange Act)[84], excluding cases where disclosure regarding the securities concerned has been made and cases where the total issue value or total transfer value is less than ¥100 million

---

[84] Also, in cases where only qualified institutional investors are shareholders, etc. of the company subject to reorganization and which correspond to cases where cabinet order provides there is little concern that the issue or delivered shares will be transferred to persons other than qualified institutional investors in the procedures relating to securities issuance for reorganization or the procedures relating to securities delivery for reorganization (Article 23-13(1) (v) (vi) and Article 2-2(4) (ii) (a) and (5) (ii) (a) of the Financial Instruments and Exchange Act), the same type of obligation for notification is provided as that for cases of other private placement to qualified institutional investors or private secondary distribution to qualified institutional investors. The notification must be in effect in order to cause securities "acquired" by reorganization, but the date of acquisition is the date that the reorganisation comes into effect, and it is understood that documents stating the matters to be notified must be delivered before the day the reorganization comes into effect.

Chapter 3   Disclosure requirements

that are specified by cabinet office ordinance, the solicitor must notify the person being solicited (i) that the relevant solicitation for acquisition corresponds to a private placement so the notification provided by Article 4, paragraph 1 of the Financial Instruments and Exchange Act is not being made for the relevant solicitation for acquisition, and (ii) the description and terms of resale restrictions attached because there is deemed to be little concern regarding transfer to persons other than qualified institutional investors that limit the rights of the holders of the securities concerned (Article 23-13(1) of the Financial Instruments and Exchange Act; Article 14-14 of the Cabinet Office Ordinance on Disclosure of Corporate Affairs, etc.; Article 19 of the Cabinet Office Ordinance on Specified Securities Disclosure; Article 11-13 of the Cabinet Office Ordinance on Foreign Bonds). Namely, the solicitor must deliver a document stating the matters to be notified to the person being solicited in advance of or concurrently with the solicitation (Article 23-13(2) of the Financial Instruments and Exchange Act), but if consent is received from a person that should receive delivery of this document, instead of delivering the document the resale restriction information to be stated on the document can be provided via electronic mail or other electromagnetic means (Article 27-30-9 of the Financial Instruments and Exchange Act; Articles 23-2 and 23-3 of the Cabinet Office Ordinance on Disclosure of Corporate Affairs, etc.; Articles 32-2 and 32-3 of the Cabinet Office Ordinance on Specified Securities Disclosure; Article 18-3 of the Cabinet Office Ordinance on Foreign Bonds).

In solicitations of a small number of investors (for type I securities, cases corresponding to Article 2, paragraph 3, item 2c, paragraph 4, item 2c, or to Article 2-2, paragraph 4, item 2b, paragraph 5, item 2b of the Financial Instruments and Exchange Act[85], and for type II securities, cases that do not correspond to cases under Article 2, paragraph 3, item 4 or Article 2-2, paragraph 4, item 3 of the Financial Instruments and Exchange Act),

---

[85] Cases corresponding to cases of issuance or delivery of the securities in procedures relating to securities issuance for reorganization or procedures relating to securities delivery for reorganization that are specified by cabinet order as having little likelihood of being owned by a large number of persons (Article 23-13(4)(i)(c) & (d) of the Financial Instruments and Exchange Act).

excluding cases where disclosure regarding the securities concerned has been made or cases where the total issue value or total transfer value is less than ¥100 million that are specified by cabinet office ordinance, the solicitor must notify the person being solicited (i) that the relevant solicitation for acquisition corresponds to a private placement so the notification provided by Article 4, paragraph 1 of the Financial Instruments and Exchange Act is not being made for the relevant solicitation for acquisition, and (ii) among the description and terms of resale restrictions attached because there is deemed to be little concern regarding transfer to a large number of persons, those restrictions that limit the rights of the holders of the relevant securities (Article 23-13(4) of the Financial Instruments and Exchange Act; Article 14-15 of the Cabinet Office Ordinance on Disclosure of Corporate Affairs, etc.; Article 20 of the Cabinet Office Ordinance on Specified Securities Disclosure; Article 11-14 of the Cabinet Office Ordinance on Foreign Bonds). Aside from shares and share option certificates (Article 2(1)(ix) of the Financial Instruments and Exchange Act), there is no obligation for notification for securities indicating preemptive rights for new preferred equity investment, commercial paper, specified short-term bonds, short-term bonds provided by the Act on Transfer of Corporate Bonds, Shares, etc., short-term bonds prescribed by the Insurance Business Act, short-term investment corporation debentures, and short-term foreign bonds (Article 3-3 of the Financial Instruments and Exchange Act Implementing Order).

Where there is an obligation to notify, the solicitor must deliver a document stating the matters to be notified to the person being solicited beforehand or concurrently (Article 23-13(5) of the Financial Instruments and Exchange Act); however, if consent is received from a person that should receive delivery of this document, instead of delivering the document, the persons who are prescribed to deliver such document may provide the resale restriction information to be stated on the document via electronic mail or other electromagnetic means (Article 27-30-9 of the Financial Instruments and Exchange Act; Article 23-2 and 23-3 of the Cabinet Office Ordinance on Disclosure of Corporate Affairs, etc.; Article 32-2 and 32-3 of the Cabinet Office Ordinance on Specified Securities Disclosure; Article 18-3 of the

Chapter 3    Disclosure requirements

Cabinet Office Ordinance on Foreign Bonds).

Also, persons conducting solicitation for acquisition to professional investors or solicitation for selling, etc. to professional investors, unless the disclosure has been made regarding the securities pertaining to the relevant solicitation (Article 23-13(3) (i) of the Financial Instruments and Exchange Act), must notify the parties being solicited, as provided by cabinet office ordinance, that notification provided by Article 4, paragraph 1 of the Financial Instruments and Exchange Act is not being made for the relevant solicitation for acquisition to professional investors or relevant solicitation for selling to professional investors and other matters provided by Cabinet Office Ordinance (Article 14-4-2 of the cabinet office ordinance on Disclosure of Corporate Affairs, etc.; Article 19-2 of the Cabinet Office Ordinance on Specified Securities Disclosure; Article 11-13-2 of the Cabinet Office Ordinance on Foreign Bonds).

In addition, when issuing securities, the obligation to notify is prescribed even in cases where the number of company shareholders subject to reorganization is less than 500 persons that do not correspond to specified procedures relating to securities issuance for reorganization pertaining to type II securities (Article 23-13(4) (ii) (b) of the Financial Instruments and Exchange Act), and in cases having other persons acquire securities by procedures relating to securities issuance for reorganization, a document stating the matters that should be notified must be delivered to the counterparty in advance or concurrently (Article 23-13(5) of the Financial Instruments and Exchange Act). On the other hand, even in cases where securities are delivered, this obligation to notify does not apply in cases where the number of company shareholders subject to reorganization is less than 500 persons that do not correspond to specified procedures relating to securities delivery for reorganization pertaining to type II securities.

# 3. Specified financial instruments exchange markets and obligation to provide and disclose specified information on securities

To conduct specified solicitation for acquisition or specified solicitation for

*345*

selling, etc. (collectively referred to as "specified solicitation, etc"; Article 27-31(1) of the Financial Instruments and Exchange Act), it is sufficient for the issuer of the subject security to provide to counterparties or publicize the information prescribed by cabinet office ordinance (specified information on securities) as basic information to be clarified with investors regarding the relevant securities and the relevant issuer by the time the specified solicitation, etc. is conducted.

Here, specified solicitation for acquisition refers to certain solicitation for acquisition to professional investors[86] and other solicitation for securities issuance, etc. to which Article 4, paragraph 1 of the Financial Instruments and Exchange Act does not apply (solicitation for acquisition or procedures relating to securities issuance for reorganization; Article 4(1)(iv) of the Financial Instruments and Exchange Act) that are specified by cabinet order (Article 27-31(1) of the Financial Instruments and Exchange Act). Presently, however, no such items have been provided as "items prescribed by cabinet order." On the other hand, specified solicitation for selling etc. refers to certain solicitation for selling, etc. to professional investors[87] and other solicitation for securities delivery, etc. to which Article 4, paragraph 1, Article 2, and Article 3 of the Financial Instruments and Exchange Act do not apply (solicitation for selling, etc. or procedures relating to securities delivery for reorganization; Article 4(2) of the Financial Instruments and Exchange Act) that are specified by cabinet order (Article 27-31(1) of the Financial Instruments and Exchange Act). Presently, however, no such items have been provided as "items prescribed by cabinet order."

---

86 Solicitation for acquisition that meets the requirements listed in Article 2, paragraph 3, item 2b of the Financial Instruments and Exchange Act (Article 4(3)(i) of the Financial Instruments and Exchange Act).

87 Solicitation, etc. for sales pertaining to type I securities that meets the requirements listed in Article 2, paragraph 4, item 2b of the Financial Instruments and Exchange Act, excluding the sale and purchase of securities on a financial instruments exchange market or over-the-counter traded securities market and the sale and purchase of listed securities via a proprietary trading system (PTS) (in cases of specified listed securities, limited to cases where the parties are only professional investors, etc.) (Article 2(6) of the Financial Instruments and Exchange Act; Article 1-7-3 of the Financial Instruments and Exchange Act Implementing Order).

Chapter 3  Disclosure requirements

Specified information on securities includes (i) a statement that the relevant information is specified information on securities, (ii) matters regarding the securities concerned, (iii) matters regarding already-issued securities other than the securities concerned (in cases of specified securities, matters regarding the description of the assets under management such as funds and managed assets and the management), as well as (iv) matters concerning the business and accounting of the issuer (in cases of specified securities, matters concerning the person engaged in the investment of the assets under management, etc.) (Article 2(2) of the Cabinet Office Ordinance on the Provision and Publication of Information on Securities). However, the specific contents of specified information on securities are left up to the regulations prescribed by the financial instruments exchange establishing the specified financial instruments exchange market. Namely, specified information on securities is deemed to be: (i) for specified listed securities (securities listed only on a specified financial instruments exchange market; Article 2(33) of the Financial Instruments and Exchange Act) or securities to be listed on a specified financial instruments exchange market, information prescribed by the regulations of the financial instruments exchange for the securities concerned that are listed or to be listed; (ii) for specified over-the-counter traded securities or securities to be registered with an authorized financial instruments firms association, information specified by the regulations of the authorized financial instruments firms association to which the securities concerned are registered or to be registered; and (iii) for other securities, information prescribed by the Commissioner of the Financial Services Agency (Article 2(1) of the Cabinet Office Ordinance on the Provision and Publication of Information on Securities).

Here, "specified financial instruments exchange market" refers to financial instruments exchange markets where members etc. are prohibited from purchasing securities under commission from persons other than professional investors (purchase by general investors; Article 117-2(1) of the Financial Instruments and Exchange Act) (Article 2-32 of the Financial Instruments and Exchange Act), "specified over-the-counter traded securities" means over-the-counter traded securities traded only on an

*347*

over-the-counter securities market whereby the Articles of Association of the authorized financial instruments firms association establishing the relevant over-the-counter securities market members are prohibited from purchasing securities under commission from persons other than professional investors (purchase by general investors; Article 67(3) of the Financial Instruments and Exchange Act) (Article 2-12-4 (3) (ii) of the Financial Instruments and Exchange Act Implementing Order).

Presently, as the specified financial instruments exchange markets in Japan are the stock market TOKYO PRO Market and the bond market TOKYO PRO-BOND Market that have both been established by the Japan Stock Exchange. The "Special Provisions on Securities Listing Regulations regarding Specified Listed Securities" and the "Implementing Order for the Special Provisions on Securities Listing Regulations regarding Specified Listed Securities" provide the forms, etc. for specified information on securities (Articles 110, 130 and 209 of the Special Provisions on Securities Listing Regulations regarding Specified Listed Securities; Article 103(4) & (5) and Article 204 (1) (2) of the Implementing Order for the Special Provisions on Securities Listing Regulations regarding Specified Listed Securities). Either Japanese or English can be chosen as the language (Articles 105 and 202 of the Special Provisions on Securities Listing Regulations regarding Specified Listed Securities). The accounting standards are to be Japanese accounting standards, U. S. accounting standards or international accounting standards, or standards considered equivalent to any of these three standards by the responsible J-Adviser and auditing firm and considered appropriate by the exchange (Article 100(6) and Article 209(5) of the Special Provisions on Securities Listing Regulations regarding Specified Listed Securities; Article 103(7) of the Implementing Order for the Special Provisions on Securities Listing Regulations regarding Specified Listed Securities).

Issuers intending to provide or publicize specified information on securities must provide the relevant specified information on securities themselves or through consignment to another person or publicize the information using the Internet or other methods (Article 27-31 (2) of the Financial

Chapter 3 Disclosure requirements

Instruments and Exchange Act). The specific method of provision and publication are also left up to the regulations, etc. of financial instruments exchanges establishing specified financial instruments exchange markets (Article 3 of the Cabinet Office Ordinance on the Provision and Publication of Information on Securities), and on the TOKYO PRO Market and TOKYO PRO-BOND Market, publication is prescribed to be made by continuous posting on the website of either the Tokyo Stock Exchange or the issuer (Article 130 of the Special Provisions on Securities Listing Regulations regarding Specified Listed Securities; Article 117 and Article 104(1) of the Implementing Order for the Special Provisions on Securities Listing Regulations Regarding Specified Listed Securities). Also, in cases where the issuer has publicized specified information on securities, the relevant specified information on securities and amended specified information on securities (Article 27-31 (4) of the Financial Instruments and Exchange Act) must be continuously publicized for one year from the date of the relevant publication (Article 27-31 (5) of the Financial Instruments and Exchange Act). However, in cases corresponding to cases where disclosure is conducted on the securities concerned or other securities of the relevant issuer and where the securities concerned cease to exist because they are canceled or redeemed, it is sufficient if continuous publication is made until that time (Articles 6 and 5 (1) of the Cabinet Office Ordinance on the Provision and Publication of Information on Securities).

When there are matters that need to be amended in specified information on securities between the date the specified information on securities was provided or publicized and the day that one year has passed from that date, the issuer who provided or publicized the specified information on securities must provide or publicize information, pursuant to cabinet office ordinance, in accordance with the amendment (amended specified information on securities) (Article 27-31 (4) of the Financial Instruments and Exchange Act). However, in certain cases the relevant period is shortened (Article 5 (1) of the Cabinet Office Ordinance on the Provision and Publication of Information on Securities).

Also, when issuers publicizing issuer information continuously for one year

*349*

under Article 27-32, paragraph 1 of the Financial Instruments and Exchange Act indicate in the specified information on securities that reference should be made to the most recent issuer information and amended issuer information (Article 27-32(3) of the Financial Instruments and Exchange Act), the information concerning the issuer is then deemed to have been provided or publicized (Article 27-31(3) of the Financial Instruments and Exchange Act; Article 4(1) of the Cabinet Office Ordinance on the Provision and Publication of Information on Securities).

## 4. Transaction regulation in secondary distributions of foreign securities

a. Obligation to provide or publicize foreign securities information — before selling

When conducting secondary distribution of foreign securities exempt from statutory disclosure (Article 4 (1) (iv) of the Financial Instruments and Exchange Act), a financial instruments business operator, etc., in principle, must provide to the counterparty or publicize foreign securities information (information regarding the securities and its issuer) in advance of or concurrently with selling the securities (Article 27-32-2(1) of the Financial Instruments and Exchange Act); however, the provision and publication of foreign securities information is not required in the following cases (proviso to Article 27-32-2 (1) of the Financial Instruments and Exchange Act; Article 13 of the Cabinet Office Ordinance on the Provision and Publication of Information on Securities):

(1) Cases where the issuer of the securities concerned submits an annual securities report on other securities of the issuer and provides or publicizes securities information on the securities.

(2) Cases where the issuer of the securities concerned has already publicized specified information on securities or issuer information, and has provided or publicized securities information on the securities concerned.

(3) Cases where the securities concerned are foreign government bonds, foreign municipal bonds, or foreign public corporate bonds (limited to those with guarantees) and it can be confirmed pursuant to the

Chapter 3　Disclosure requirements

regulations of an authorized financial instruments firms association that work concerning the sale and purchase of the securities concerned is conducted continuously by two or more financial instruments business operators, etc.

(4) Cases where the counterparties for the secondary distribution of the relevant foreign securities are qualified institutional investors (limited to those who acquire the securities concerned on the condition that they will not be transferred to financial instruments business operators, etc. or non-residents) (excluding cases where the relevant qualified institutional investors request the provision and publication of foreign securities information).

b. Obligation to provide or publicize foreign securities information ─ after selling

A financial instruments business operator, etc. that has conducted secondary distribution of foreign securities must provide or publicize foreign securities information regarding the relevant foreign securities when so requested by a person that acquired securities through the secondary distribution of the relevant foreign securities and has deposited the relevant securities in the custody of the relevant financial instruments business operator, etc. or in cases where facts arise that have a material influence on the investment decisions of investors (merger or initiation of reorganization proceedings of the issuer, etc.) (Article 27-32-2 (2) of the Financial Instruments and Exchange Act; Article 15 of the Cabinet Office Ordinance on the Provision and Publication of Information on Securities); however, the provision and publication of foreign securities information is not required in the following cases (proviso to Article 27-32-2 of the Financial Instruments and Exchange Act; Article 16 of the Cabinet Office Ordinance on the Provision and Publication of Information on Securities):

(1) Cases where annual securities reports on the relevant securities have been submitted.

(2) Cases corresponding to (2), (3) or (4) in "a." above.

(3) Cases where there are less than 50 owners of the relevant securities inside Japan.

*351*

c. Foreign securities information

The Cabinet Office Ordinance on the Provision and Publication of Information on Securities provides the contents of foreign securities information for each class of securities. Foreign securities information comprises "issuer information" ("outline of the fiscal policy of the issuing country" in cases of government bonds; "description of business", "outline of accounting", etc. in cases of share certificates and bonds, etc.) and "securities information" (description of securities, etc.) for the most recent business year (fiscal year) (Article 12(1) (2) and Attached Table of the Cabinet Office Ordinance on the Provision and Publication of Information on Securities).

d. Cases where information can be obtained by internet is permitted

In cases where all or part of the contents of foreign securities information is included in information publicized by the issuer of the securities concerned (limited to cases of publication based on laws and regulations, etc. that can easily be obtained inside Japan via the Internet stated in either Japanese or English), a statement to refer to that information and information on the home page address where that information is publicized can be deemed all or part of the foreign securities information (Article 12(3) of the Cabinet Office Ordinance on the Provision and Publication of Information on Securities).

e. Methods of provision and publication of foreign securities information

Foreign Securities Information must be provided or publicized using one of the methods as follows (Article 17 of the Cabinet Office Ordinance on the Provision and Publication of Information on Securities):

(1) Delivery of written documents.

(2) Transmission via facsimile (limited to cases where the recipient of the foreign securities information gives consent to receive relevant information by this method and where relevant information can be received as a document).

(3) Transmission via electronic mail (limited to cases where the recipient of the foreign securities information gives consent to receive relevant information by this method and where relevant information can be

Chapter 3   Disclosure requirements

received as a document).

(4) Provision and publication of information regarding the home page address where the foreign securities information is publicized and other information on the method of inspection of the foreign securities information (limited to cases where the recipient of the foreign securities information gives consent to receive relevant information by this method).

# C. Written notices of securities and written notices of shelf registration

While not a system for the purpose of disclosure of corporate affairs, etc., the submission of a written notice of securities or written notice of shelf registration is required in certain cases from the perspective of enforcement of the notification of public offerings and secondary distributions of securities, namely, for the authorities to check that public offerings and secondary distributions that require notifications are not being conducted without notifications, that appropriate disclosure is being conducted for secondary distributions of securities for which disclosure is conducted, and that prospectuses are being prepared in accordance with the disclosure documents.

## 1. Obligation for submission of written notice of securities

Even in cases exempted from notification of public offerings or secondary distributions of securities, the issuer must submit a written notice of securities for cases corresponding to "specified public offerings etc." (Article 4(6) of the Financial Instruments and Exchange Act).

Here, "specified public offering" refers to (i) those public offerings and secondary distributions of securities with a total issue value or total distribution value of less than ¥100 million that are specified by cabinet office ordinance (excluding those prescribed in Article 4, paragraph 1, items 1 through 4 of the Financial Instruments and Exchange Act) and (ii) general acquisitions of securities acquired by qualified institutional investors that are exempt from notification under Article 4, paragraph 2 of the Financial

*353*

Instruments and Exchange Act or those general solicitations for securities acquired by professional investors that are exempt from notification under the proviso to Article 4, paragraph 3 of the Financial Instruments and Exchange Act that are neither 1) cases corresponding to secondary distributions, nor 2) cases that do not correspond to secondary distributions but for which disclosure has been made (Article 4(1) (v), proviso to (2), proviso to (3) and (5)). Also, "specified public offering, etc." refers to secondary distribution of securities for which a specified public offering and disclosure have been made (excluding those prescribed in Article 4, paragraph 1, items 1 and 2 of the Financial Instruments and Exchange Act) (Article 4(6) of the Financial Instruments and Exchange Act).

Even when a specified public offering, etc. is to be conducted, submission of written notice of securities is not required in the following cases (proviso to Article 4(6) of the Financial Instruments and Exchange Act; Article 4(5) of the Cabinet Office Ordinance on Disclosure of Corporate Affairs, etc.; Article 5(4) of the Cabinet Office Ordinance on Specified Securities Disclosure):

(1) Cases of secondary distribution of securities for which disclosure has been made (referring to secondary distribution of securities provided by Article 4, paragraph 4 of the Financial Instruments and Exchange Act; including general solicitation of qualified institutional investors and general solicitation for securities acquired by professional investors, etc. which do not correspond to secondary distributions) where the total distribution value is less than ¥100 million.

(2) Cases of secondary distribution of securities for which disclosure has been made by persons other than the issuer of the securities concerned or persons that are specified by cabinet office ordinance (Article 4(4) of the Cabinet Office Ordinance on Disclosure of Corporate Affairs, etc.; Article 5(3) of the Cabinet Office Ordinance on Specified Securities Disclosure).

(3) Cases of public offerings or secondary distributions of securities with a total issue value or total distribution value of ¥100 million or less that are specified by cabinet office ordinance with a total issue value or total distribution value of ¥10 million or less.

Chapter 3 Disclosure requirements

Consequently, for example, in cases of specified procedures relating to securities issuance for reorganization and specified procedures relating to securities delivery for reorganization where the total issue value or total distribution value of the securities is over ¥10 million but less than ¥100 million, written notice of securities must be submitted by the day before the day the specified procedures relating to securities issuance for reorganization or the specified procedures relating to securities offer for reorganization are initiated (Article 4(5) & (6) of the Financial Instruments and Exchange Act; Article 4 (4) of the Cabinet Office Ordinance on Disclosure of Corporate Affairs, etc.).

## 2. Submission of written notice of securities

Written notice of securities must be submitted to the Director General of the Local Finance (Branch) Bureau with jurisdiction over the location of the issuer's headquarters by the day before the day the relevant specified public offering, etc. is initiated (Article 4 (6) of the Financial Instruments and Exchange Act; Article 4(1) of the Cabinet Office Ordinance on Disclosure of Corporate Affairs, etc.). In cases of specified securities, written notice must be submitted to the Director General of the Kanto Local Finance Bureau by the day before the day the relevant specified public offering, etc. is initiated (Article 5 (1) of the Cabinet Office Ordinance on Specified Securities Disclosure).

The contents to be stated on a written notice of securities are prescribed by the Cabinet Office Ordinance on Disclosure of Corporate Affairs, etc., Cabinet Office Ordinance on Specified Securities Disclosure, and Cabinet Office Ordinance on Foreign Bonds (Article 4 (1) of the Cabinet Office Ordinance on Disclosure of Corporate Affairs, etc.; Article 5 (1) of the Cabinet Office Ordinance on Specified Securities Disclosure; Article 2(1) of the Cabinet Office Ordinance on Foreign Bonds). In cases of public offerings and secondary distributions of securities that are neither specified securities or foreign government bonds etc., domestic companies need to state information on the securities for new issuance or secondary distribution, the method and conditions of the securities public offering or secondary distribution, an outline of the securities underwriting, and the state of public

*355*

offerings and secondary distributions within the past one year, using Form 1 of the Cabinet Office Ordinance on Disclosure of Corporate Affairs, etc. Foreign companies also need to state similar matters using Form 6 of the Cabinet Office Ordinance on Disclosure of Corporate Affairs, etc.

Also, written notices of securities require that attached documents be attached as provided separately for domestic companies and foreign companies, and in accordance with the type of securities (Article 4(2) of the Cabinet Office Ordinance on Disclosure of Corporate Affairs, etc.; Article 5 (2) of the Cabinet Office Ordinance on Specified Securities Disclosure; Article 2 (2) of the Cabinet Office Ordinance on Foreign Bonds). For example, in cases of public offerings and secondary distributions of securities that are neither specified securities nor foreign government bonds, etc., the documents that must be attached for domestic companies are: the articles of incorporation; in cases where there is a board of directors resolution or general shareholders meeting resolution, etc. regarding issuance of the securities concerned, a copy of the minutes of the relevant board of directors meeting or a copy of the minutes of the relevant general shareholders meeting, etc.; and in cases where a prospectus is used in the public offering or secondary distribution of the securities concerned, the relevant prospectus (Article 4(2) (i) of the Cabinet Office Ordinance on Disclosure of Corporate Affairs, etc.). For foreign companies, in addition to the attached documents that must be attached for domestic companies, the attached documents include a legal opinion letter from a legal expert that the public offering or secondary distribution of the securities is legal; and in cases where permission provided by Article 21, paragraph 1 or paragraph 2 of the Foreign Exchange and Foreign Trade Act is required, a document attesting that the relevant permission has been received (Article 4 (2) (ii) of the Cabinet Office Ordinance on Disclosure of Corporate Affairs, etc.).

Submitted written notices of securities are not subject to public inspection, unlike securities registration statements.

In principle a written notice of securities must be submitted for each public offering or secondary distribution; however, in cases where public offerings

Chapter 3   Disclosure requirements

# Table 3-3

| Foreign Bonds, Etc. | | Cabinet Office Ordinance on Foreign Bonds, Form 1 |
|---|---|---|
| Specified Securities | Domestic investment trust beneficiary certificates | Cabinet Office Ordinance on Specified Securities Disclosure, Form 1 |
| | Foreign investment trust beneficiary certificates | Cabinet Office Ordinance on Specified Securities Disclosure, Form 1-2 |
| | Domestic investment securities | Cabinet Office Ordinance on Specified Securities Disclosure, Form 1-3 |
| | Foreign investment securities | Cabinet Office Ordinance on Specified Securities Disclosure, Form 2 |
| | Domestic asset backed securities | Cabinet Office Ordinance on Specified Securities Disclosure, Form 2-2 |
| | Foreign asset backed securities | Cabinet Office Ordinance on Specified Securities Disclosure, Form 2-3 |
| | Domestic beneficiary certificates backed by assets in trust | Cabinet Office Ordinance on Specified Securities Disclosure, Form 2-4 |
| | Foreign beneficiary certificates backed by assets in trust | Cabinet Office Ordinance on Specified Securities Disclosure, Form 2-5 |
| | Domestic trust beneficiary certificates / Domestic trust corporate bond certificates / Domestic trust beneficial interests | Cabinet Office Ordinance on Specified Securities Disclosure, Form 3 |
| | Foreign trust beneficiary certificates / Foreign trust corporate bond certificates / Foreign trust beneficial interests | Cabinet Office Ordinance on Specified Securities Disclosure, Form 3-2 |
| | Domestic mortgage securities | Cabinet Office Ordinance on Specified Securities Disclosure, Form 3-3 |
| | Foreign mortgage securities | Cabinet Office Ordinance on Specified Securities Disclosure, Form 3-4 |
| | Interests in securities investment in domestic business | Cabinet Office Ordinance on Specified Securities Disclosure, Form 3-5 |
| | Interests in securities investment in foreign business | Cabinet Office Ordinance on Specified Securities Disclosure, Form 3-6 |
| | Beneficiary certificates of specified securities in trust | Form specified for Specified Securities that are entrusted securities pertaining to the relevant beneficiary certificates of Specified Securities in trust |
| | Specified depository receipts | Form specified for the Specified Securities pertaining to the rights indicated on the relevant specified depository receipts |

*357*

or secondary distributions that require submission of written notices of securities are conducted in parallel, the submission can be made using the same written notice of securities (Guidelines on Corporate Affairs Disclosure, B4-20). Also, in cases where a securities registration statement withdrawal request is submitted because after submission of a securities registration statement the total issue value or total distribution value is less than ¥100 million, the date on which the relevant securities registration statement withdrawal request is made is deemed to be the date of submission of the written notice of securities (Guidelines on Corporate Affairs Disclosure, B4-14).

## 3. Written notice of changes

In cases where there are changes to the contents stated on a written notice of securities after the date the written notice of securities is submitted but before the payment date pertaining to the public offering or secondary distribution under the written notice of securities, the person who submitted the written notice of securities must submit a written notice of changes stating the description of the changes to the Director General of the Local Finance Bureau or the Director General of the Fukuoka Local Finance Branch Bureau (in cases of foreign government bonds, etc., the Director General of the Kanto Local Finance Bureau) without delay (Article 5 of the Cabinet Office Ordinance on Disclosure of Corporate Affairs, etc.; Article 6 of the Cabinet Office Ordinance on Specified Securities Disclosure; Article 3 of the Cabinet Office Ordinance on Foreign Bonds).

## 4. Written notice of shelf registration

Even when shelf registration is conducted, in cases where the total issue value or total distribution value of the securities is less than ¥100 million, it is not necessary to submit a shelf-registration supplement (proviso to Article 23-10(1) of the Financial Instruments and Exchange Act; Article 14-9 of the Cabinet Office Ordinance on Disclosure of Corporate Affairs, etc.; Article 18-7 of the Cabinet Office Ordinance on Specified Securities Disclosure; Article 11-9 of the Cabinet Office Ordinance on Foreign Bonds). However, even in such cases, when the total issue value or total distribution value exceeds ¥10 million, a written notice of shelf registration must be submitted

Chapter 3   Disclosure requirements

# Table 3-4

| Foreign Bonds, Etc. | | Cabinet Office Ordinance on Foreign Bonds, Form 10 |
|---|---|---|
| Specifed Securities | Domestic investment securities | Cabinet Office Ordinance on Regulated Securities Disclosure, Form 23 |
| | Foreign investment securities | Cabinet Office Ordinance on Regulated Securities Disclosure, Form 24 |
| | Specified domestic asset backed securities | Cabinet Office Ordinance on Regulated Securities Disclosure, Form 23-2 |
| | Specified foreign asset backed securities | Cabinet Office Ordinance on Regulated Securities Disclosure, Form 24-2 |
| | Beneficiary certificates of specified securities in trust | Form specified for Specified Securities that are entrusted securities pertaining to the relevant beneficiary certificates of Specified Securities in trust |
| | Specified depository receipts | Form specified for the Specified Securities pertaining to the rights represented in the relevant specified depository receipts |

(Article 4 (6) and Article 23-10 (4) of the Financial Instruments and Exchange Act; Article 14-11 (5) of the Cabinet Office Ordinance on Disclosure of Corporate Affairs, etc.; Article 18-10(5) of the Cabinet Office Ordinance on Specified Securities Disclosure; Article 2(4) of the Cabinet Office Ordinance on Foreign Bonds).

In cases of public offerings and secondary distributions of securities that are

*359*

neither specified securities nor foreign government bonds, etc., the written notice of shelf registration must be prepared using Form 13 for domestic companies and using Form 16 for foreign companies, and submitted to the Director-General of the Local Finance Bureau or the Director General of the Fukuoka Local Finance Branch Bureau (Article 14-11(1) of the Cabinet Office Ordinance on Disclosure of Corporate Affairs, etc.).

In cases where there are changes to contents stated on a written notice of shelf registration, the person who submitted the written notice of shelf registration must submit a written notice of changes stating the description of the changes to the Director General of the Local Finance Bureau or the Director General of the Fukuoka Local Finance Branch Bureau (in cases of foreign government bonds etc., the Director General of the Kanto Local Finance Bureau) without delay (Article 14-11(4) and Article 5 of the Cabinet Office Ordinance on Disclosure of Corporate Affairs, etc.; Article 18-10(4) and Article 6 of the Cabinet Office Ordinance on Specified Securities Disclosure; Article 11-10(3) and Article 3 of the Cabinet Office Ordinance on Foreign Bonds).

# D. Disclosure on secondary markets

## 1. Persons obliged to submit annual securities reports

Issuers of securities that fall under any of the following (1) through (4)[85] must submit annual securities reports, quarterly securities reports (or semiannual securities reports) and extraordinary reports (continuous disclosure obligation) (Article 24(1) of the Financial Instruments and Exchange Act; for specified securities, Article 24(5) of the Act):[86]

---

[85] However, where a company that is an issuer of securities described in (3) ceases to exist due to a consolidation-type merger or an absorption-type merger into a company that does not bear the continuous disclosure obligation, the company incorporated through the consolidation-type merger or the company surviving the absorption-type merger bears the continuous disclosure obligation (Guidelines on Disclosure of Corporate Affairs, B24-5).

*360*

Chapter 3   Disclosure requirements

(1)  Securities listed on a financial instruments exchange (Article 24(1)(i) of the Financial Instruments and Exchange Act; excluding specified listed securities [securities listed only on markets for professional investors. Article 2(33) of the Financial Instruments and Exchange Act]).

(2)  Securities specified by cabinet order of which the characteristics of distribution are equivalent to those of the securities stated in (1) (Article 24(1)(ii) of the Financial Instruments and Exchange Act; over-the-counter traded securities[87] are so specified [Article 3 of the Financial Instruments and Exchange Act Implementing Order]).

(3)  Securities for which a securities registration statement or shelf-registration supplement has been submitted regarding their public offering or secondary distribution (excluding those falling under (1) or (2) above, Article 24(1)(iii) of the Financial Instruments and Exchange Act).

(4)  Securities (limited to shares, beneficiary certificates of securities in trust whose entrusted securities are shares, and depository receipts representing rights pertaining to shares [Article 3-6(3) of the Financial Instruments and Exchange Act Implementing Order], but not including foreign shares, etc.) issued by the relevant issuer that have 1,000 or more holders[88,89] on the last day of that business year or on the last day of any of the business years that began within four years before the day on which that business year began. If the issued securities are interests in securities investment business, etc. that constitute specified securities

---

86  However, in cases where the securities are asset-trust securitisation beneficiary certificates or trust beneficiary certificates or trust beneficial interests, their originator and mandator at the time when the act of trust takes effect do not bear the continuous disclosure obligation (Article 22-2 of the Cabinet Office Ordinance on Specified Securities Disclosure).

87  Over-the-counter traded securities mean securities with their class and issue name registered in a registry of over-the-counter traded securities prepared by an authorized financial instruments firms association as securities purchased and sold on an over-the-counter traded securities market based on Article 67-11 of the Financial Instruments and Exchange Act. These exclude over-the-counter traded securities for professionals (i.e., specified over-the-counter traded securities; Article 2-12-4(3)(ii) of the Financial Instruments and Exchange Act Implementing Order).

*361*

(limited to trust beneficial interests, membership rights of a limited liability company, limited partnership company or general partnership company, and equity in collective investment schemes [Article 2(2)(i), (iii) & (v) of the Financial Instruments and Exchange Act]; Article 4-2 (4) of the Financial Instruments and Exchange Act Implementing Order), in cases where the number of holders is 500 or more on the last day of the relevant specified period (excluding cases falling under any of (1) through (3); Article 24(1)(iv) of the Financial Instruments and Exchange Act; Article 3-6(4) and Article 4-2(5) of the Financial Instruments and Exchange Act Implementing Order)(the number of shareholders criteria).[90]

---

**88** In cases of securities for professional investors, (a) professional investors who cannot choose to be general investors, (b) professional investors who neither fall under (a) nor are known by the issuer to have chosen not to be regarded as professional investors by one or more financial instruments business operators, and (c) general investors known by the issuer to be regarded as professional investors by one or more financial instruments business operators are excluded (Article 15-4 of the Cabinet Office Ordinance on Disclosure of Corporate Affairs, etc.).

**89** The Cabinet Office Ordinance on Disclosure of Corporate Affairs, etc., Cabinet Office Ordinance on Specified Securities Disclosure, and Guidelines on Disclosure of Corporate Affairs prescribe the method for calculating the number of holders of securities by category of securities (Article 24(4) of the Financial Instruments and Exchange Act; Article 16-3 of the Cabinet Office Ordinance on Disclosure of Corporate Affairs, etc.; Guidelines on Disclosure of Corporate Affairs B24-6; Article 26-2 of the Cabinet Office Ordinance on Specified Securities Disclosure). For example, the number of holders of share certificates is calculated based on the number of persons recorded in the shareholders registry.

**90** The obligation to prepare annual securities reports also applies where the number of holders of preferred equity investment certificates was 1,000 or more (however, in cases of securities for professional investors, professional investors within the same scope as the case of shares, etc. are excluded; Article 15-4 of the Cabinet Office Ordinance on Disclosure of Corporate Affairs, etc.) or when the number of holders of school loan claims was 500 or more on the last day of any of the past five business years (Article 24(1)(iv) applicable pursuant to Article 27; Article 4-11(4) & (5) of the Financial Instruments and Exchange Act Implementing Order).

Chapter 3　Disclosure requirements

# 2. Extinguishment and exemption of continuous disclosure obligation

a. Extinguishment due to delisting of securities or cessation of being over-the-counter traded securities

The continuous disclosure obligation extinguishes when the securities falling under 1.(1) above are delisted or when the securities falling under 1.(2) cease to be over-the-counter traded securities. However, the issuers may continue to bear the continuous disclosure obligation because the securities fall under 1.(3) or 1.(4) above.

b. Exemption of obligation to submit annual securities reports for specific business years in cases under the number of shareholders criteria

Issuers obliged to submit annual securities reports under the number of shareholders criteria ((4) above) are not obliged to submit annual securities reports for a business year in cases where the amount of capital at the end of the business year is less than ¥500 million (in cases of school loan claims, where the net assets on the balance sheet of the school corporation, etc. at the end of the business year are less than ¥100 million; in cases where the securities concerned are interests in securities investment business, etc. constituting specified securities, where the amount specified by Article 4-2, paragraph 2 of the Financial Instruments and Exchange Act Implementing Order as the amount of assets of the relevant company on the last day of the relevant specified period[91] is less than ¥100 million); and in cases where the number of holders of the securities on the last day of the business year is less than 300 (proviso to Article 24 (1) of the Financial Instruments and Exchange Act; Article 3-6(1), Article 4-2(1) & (3), and Article 4-11(1) & (2) of the Financial Instruments and Exchange Act Implementing Order).

---

**91**　"Specified period" means the period prescribed by cabinet office ordinance as the period in which issuers of specified securities should submit annual securities reports (Article 24 (5) of the Financial Instruments and Exchange Act). Cabinet Office Ordinances specify the business year of issuers and the calculation period of trusts by class of specified securities (Article 23 of the Cabinet Office Ordinance on Specified Securities Disclosure).

*363*

c . Exemption from continuous disclosure obligation of issuers of securities who submitted securities registration statements, etc.

Issuers of securities who have submitted a securities registration statement or shelf-registration supplement (for (3) above) are exempted from the obligation to submit an annual securities report for the relevant business year onwards in cases where: 1) the securities for which the public offering, etc. was conducted were shares (Article 3-5 (1) (i) of the Financial Instruments and Exchange Act Implementing Order), securities with the characteristics of shares issued by a foreign company or their beneficiary certificates of securities in trust or depository receipts (Article 3-5(1) (ii), (iii) & (iv) of the Financial Instruments and Exchange Act Implementing Order), or preferred equity investment certificates (Article 4-10(1) (i) of the Implementing Order for the Financial Instruments and Exchange Act), or securities with the characteristics of preferred equity investment certificates issued by a foreign issuing body or their beneficiary certificates of securities in trust or depository receipts (Article 4-10(1) (ii) (iii) (iv) of the Implementing Order for the Financial Instruments and Exchange Act); and 2) five years have passed since the end of the business year when submission of securities registration statements occurred;[92] and 3) on the last day of the business year and on each last day of all business years that began within four years from the commencement day of the business year, the number of holders[93] of the securities concerned of the issuer is/was less than 300 (Article 3-5(2) and Article 4-10(2) of the Financial Instruments and Exchange Act Implementing Order); and 4) the issuer has been approved by the Prime Minister pursuant to the Cabinet Office Ordinance not to harm public interest or investor protection if it does not submit an annual securities report (proviso to Article 24 (1) of the Financial Instruments and Exchange Act).[94] In order to receive this exemption approval, domestic companies must submit a written application to the Director-General of the Local Finance Bureau or Local Finance Branch

---

92 This means the business year that includes the date on which notification etc. regarding public offering, etc. of the securities concerned was made. When there are multiple business years in which the relevant reports began to be submitted, the most recent of those business years applies.

Chapter 3  Disclosure requirements

Bureau, together with copies of their articles of incorporation and shareholders register at the time of the application (including the register of preferred equity investors under the Preferred Equity Investment Act) attached (Article 15-3(1)(i) of the Cabinet Office Ordinance on Disclosure of Corporate Affairs, etc.). Foreign companies must, in addition to these attachments, also attach documents attesting the number of holders of the securities concerned (excluding non-residents) as of the last day of the business year immediately preceding the business year that includes the date of application, and as of each of the last days of the business years that commenced within four years before the day that the immediately preceding business year commenced, a statement that the foreign company has disclosed information regarding its accounting and other information for each business year based on the laws and regulations of the relevant foreign

---

93  For domestic companies, the number of persons recorded or registered in the shareholders register (Article 15-3(2) of the Cabinet Office Ordinance on Disclosure of Corporate Affairs). For foreign companies, it is the number of holders of the securities concerned (excluding non-residents) in principle (Article 15-3(3) of the Cabinet Office Ordinance on Disclosure of Corporate Affairs, etc.). However, among cases where the securities concerned issued by the relevant issuer are listed on a foreign financial instruments exchange at the time of application, when the securities concerned have been deemed to be listed on a (Japanese) financial instruments exchange (excluding specified listed securities), companies may use the number of persons holding the securities concerned (excluding non-residents; after the securities concerned cease to be deemed to be listed on a [Japanese] financial instruments exchange, limited to those persons holding the securities concerned on the day of the cessation), and when the securities concerned (excluding specified listed securities) have never been deemed to be listed on a (Japanese) financial instruments exchange, companies may use the number of persons (excluding non-residents; limited to those who acquired the securities concerned in public offerings or secondary distributions) recorded in the registry of holders of the securities concerned held by the financial instruments business operator, etc. that has been entrusted with the custody of the securities (proviso to Article 15-3(3) of the Cabinet Office Ordinance on Disclosure of Corporate Affairs, etc.).

94  Submission of an annual securities report is not required even if the number of holders of the securities concerned on the last day of any business year beginning after the commencement day of the relevant business year becomes 300 or more, provided that the securities concerned do not subsequently newly fall under the category of securities listed in each item of Article 24, paragraph 1 of the Financial Instruments and Exchange Act (Guidelines on Disclosure of Corporate Affairs, B24-12).

state and the regulations of the relevant foreign financial instruments market (limited to cases where the disclosure is made in Japanese or English), a document summarising the relevant laws and regulations of the relevant foreign state and regulations of the relevant foreign financial instruments market and stating the methods whereby the relevant information can be acquired inside Japan (limited to cases where the number of holders of the securities is calculated using the number provided in the proviso to Article 15-3, paragraph 3 of the Cabinet Office Ordinance Disclosure on Corporate Affairs, etc.), a document attesting that the representative of the relevant foreign company stated on the relevant written approval application has legitimate authority to submit the approval application, and a document attesting that the relevant foreign company has authorized a person who has residence in Japan to represent itself in all acts concerning the submission of the relevant approval application (Article 15-3 (1) (ii) of the Cabinet Office Ordinance on Disclosure of Corporate Affairs, etc.) [95].

Regarding the exemption from the obligation to submit an annual securities report because of the number of holders of the securities being less than 300 on each of the last days of all the most recent five business years, even in cases where the number of securities holders subsequently becomes 300 or more, the interpretation is that the issuer does not bear the obligation to submit an annual securities report unless the securities fall under 1. (4) above (Guidelines on Disclosure of Corporate Affairs, B24-12). However, in cases where it is found that the number of holders of securities issued by a foreign company that received approval becomes 1,000 or more on the last day of a business year, the Commissioner of the Financial Services Agency can revoke the relevant approval for the future (Article 15-3 (4) of the Cabinet Office Ordinance on Disclosure of Corporate Affairs, etc.).

---

95　Where the attached documents are not written in Japanese (or when the Articles of Incorporation or the copy of the shareholders registry at the time of application are not written in Japanese or English), a Japanese translation (or a Japanese or English translation of the articles of incorporation or the copy of the shareholders registry at the time of application) must be attached (Article 15-3 (5) of the Cabinet Office Ordinance on Disclosure of Corporate Affairs, etc.).

Chapter 3 Disclosure requirements

d . Exemption because the issuer is in liquidation, etc.

Where the issuer of securities falling under 1. (3) or 1. (4) above is in liquidation or has suspended business for a substantial period of time; or in the case of the issuer of securities falling under 1. (3) above, where the number of holders of securities stated or recorded in its shareholders register or register of holders on the last day of the business year immediately preceding the business year that includes the date of application is less than 25 (Article 16 (2) & (3) of the Cabinet Office Ordinance on Disclosure of Corporate Affairs, etc.; Article 25 (3) & (4) of the Cabinet Office Ordinance on Specified Securities Disclosure), it can be exempted from the obligation to submit annual securities reports by receiving approval from the Prime Minister (Article 4 of the Financial Instruments and Exchange Act Article 4 Implementing Order).[96] For this purpose, the number of holders of securities of a foreign company is calculated as the total of the number of holders of the securities concerned recorded in the customer registers of all financial instruments business operators concluding wholesale underwriting contracts with the issuers and holders of the securities concerned upon public offering or secondary distribution in Japan (Guidelines on Disclosure of Corporate Affairs, B24-3).

When applying for exemption approval, a domestic company must submit a written application to the Commissioner of the Financial Services Agency together with copies of its articles of incorporation and shareholders register at the time of the application; and in cases where the company is in liquidation, a copy of the minutes of the general shareholders meeting where the resolution for dissolution was adopted and a certificate of the registered matters or equivalent documents; or in cases where the company has suspended business for a substantial period of time, a document stating the background to the business suspension and the future outlook, etc. (Article 4 (1) of the Financial Instruments and Exchange Act Implementing Order; Article 16 (1) (i) of the Cabinet Office Ordinance on Disclosure of Corporate Affairs, etc.). In addition to these, if the applicant is a foreign company, it

---

96 This exemption also applies to issuers of specified securities (Article 4-2 (1) of the Financial Instruments and Exchange Act).

*367*

must also attach a document attesting that the representative of the foreign company stated in the written application for approval has legitimate authority to submit the written application and a document attesting that the foreign company has authorized a person who has residence in Japan to represent itself in all acts concerning the written application for approval (Article 16 (1) (ii) of the Cabinet Office Ordinance on Disclosure of Corporate Affairs, etc.).

In cases where the exemption of the obligation for submission is approved, in principle the issuer is not required to submit an annual securities report for the business year that includes the date of application for approval (or the immediately prior business year in cases where that date is within three months [or within six months in principle in cases of foreign issuers] after the commencement of the business year) and thereafter (Article 4(2) of the Financial Instruments and Exchange Act Implementing Order). However, in cases where the issuer has received a decision for commencement of reorganization proceedings and made the application within three months from the day of such decision for commencement of reorganization proceedings, it is not required to submit an annual securities report for the business year that includes the day of the decision of commencement of reorganization proceedings and thereafter (Article 4 (4) of the Financial Instruments and Exchange Act Implementing Order). This approval is granted under the condition that within three months after the end of the business year that includes the date of the application and of the subsequent four business years, respectively, a copy of the shareholders register as of the last date of the relevant business year and financial statements and business reports (i.e., those listed in Article 438 of the Companies Act) of the relevant business year reported or approved at the general shareholders meeting will be submitted to the Commissioner of the Financial Services Agency (Article 4 (3) of the Implementing Order for the Financial Instruments and Exchange Act; Article 16(4) & (5) of the Cabinet Office Ordinance on Disclosure of Corporate Affairs, etc.).[97]

And, if an issuer no longer meets the requirements for exemption, the issuer resumes the obligation to submit annual securities reports from the business

Chapter 3  Disclosure requirements

year that includes the date when the requirements were no longer met (or from the immediately prior business year in cases where that date is within three months [within six months in cases of foreign issuers in principle] after the commencement of the business year) (Article 4(2) and Article 4-2 (1) of the Financial Instruments and Exchange Act Implementing Order).

## 3. Annual securities reports

Annual securities reports are reports that an issuer under the obligation to submit annual securities reports prepares and submits to the Prime Minister each business year stating its trade name, state of accounting of the corporate group to which it belongs and of itself and other material matters concerning its business (or, in cases of specified securities, the status of accounting of assets for asset investment and other similar businesses it conducts, and other material matters concerning its assets) and other matters specified by cabinet office ordinance as necessary and appropriate for the benefit of public interest and investor protection (Article 24(1) & (5) of the Financial Instruments and Exchange Act). An issuer who is not a company but under the ongoing disclosure obligation must also prepare and submit annual securities reports (Article 27 of the Financial Instruments and Exchange Act).

a. Due date for submission

Domestic companies and other domestic issuers must submit annual securities reports to the Prime Minister within three months of the date the relevant business year ends (or, when found that it is not possible to submit the report within the relevant period due to inevitable grounds, within the period set in advance under approval from the Prime Minister pursuant to the relevant provisions of the Cabinet Office Ordinance [i.e., Article 15-2 of the Cabinet Office Ordinance on Disclosure of Corporate Affairs, etc.; Article 24 of the Cabinet Office Ordinance on Specified Securities Disclosure; Article 13 of the Cabinet Office Ordinance on Foreign Bonds]) [98]. Foreign companies

---

97  The same applies to specified securities (Article 4-2(1) of the Financial Instruments and Exchange Act Implementing Order; Article 25(5) & (6) of the Cabinet Office Ordinance on Specified Securities Disclosure).

*369*

and other foreign issuers must submit annual securities reports to the Prime Minister within the period specified by cabinet order as necessary and appropriate for the benefit of public interest and investor protection (Article 24(1) and Article 27 of the Financial Instruments and Exchange Act). The Financial Instruments and Exchange Act Implementing Order states that in principle foreign issuers must submit the report within six months after the end of each business year; however, in cases where it is considered not possible to submit the report within six months because of the laws and

---

**98** The Guidelines on Disclosure of Corporate Affairs provide the following policy on setting of a new due date for submission under approval (B24-13(3)).

In establishing a new due date for submission under approval, in cooperation with the financial instruments exchange or authorized financial instruments firms association and the issuer's auditing firm, etc., it is necessary to ensure that the new date is necessary and appropriate for the benefit of public interest and investor protection, considering on a case-by-case basis the time when the reason for requiring approval of new due date for submission arose, the possibility of recovery, the issuer's business scale, and the complexity of the case. The decision must be made comparing the disadvantages arising if company information is not disclosed and the benefits to be brought by disclosure of accurate company information.

When an application is made to request a postponement of the due date for one month or more on the grounds that: due to false statements discovered concerning material matters in past annual securities reports, etc., past financial statements or consolidated financial statements should be amended to confirm the starting balances, etc. of the relevant business year or consolidated accounting year but such amendments are not completed or relevant audit reports are not received by the due date for submission, and the issuer has published it; or the relevant audit report could not be received by the due date for submission because an auditing firm, etc. identified in the course of audit an error that could cause a material and false indication in the relevant issuer's financial statements or consolidated financial statements or suspicious material and false indications by wrongdoing, and the auditing firm needs to conduct additional audit procedures, and the issuer has published it, decisions on the appropriateness of the postponement should be made considering the harmful impact on investors arising from not disclosing company information, considering also the relevant issuer's information disclosure conditions including whether the issuer has confirmed errors or wrongdoings that may cause a material and false indication in its financial statements or consolidated financial statements disclosed based on the rules of the financial instruments exchange or authorized financial instruments firms association, and whether the issuer admitted false statements of material matters in the past annual securities reports and quickly demonstrated to investors its earnest efforts to resolve or correct them.

Chapter 3   Disclosure requirements

regulations or practices in the state of the foreign company or other inevitable grounds, the foreign company is allowed to submit the report within a period approved in advance by the Commissioner of the Financial Services Agency pursuant to the relevant provisions of the Cabinet Office Ordinance[99] (Article 24(1) of the Financial Instruments and Exchange Act; Article 3-4 of the Financial Instruments and Exchange Act Implementing Order; Article 15-2-2 of the Cabinet Office Ordinance on Disclosure of Corporate Affairs, etc.; Article 24-2 of the Cabinet Office Ordinance on Specified Securities Disclosure; Article 13 of the Cabinet Office Ordinance on Foreign Bonds).

Here, cases where it is found that it is not possible to submit the annual securities report by the due date due to inevitable grounds are interpreted as including: (i) cases where the preparation of financial statements or consolidated financial statements could not be completed or audit reports could not be received by the due date for submission because obligations could not be confirmed, etc. due to suspension of operation of a computer that the issuer uses due to suspension of electricity supply or for other reasons; (ii) cases where the preparation of financial statements or consolidated financial statements could not be completed or audit reports could not be received by the due date for submission because obligations could not be confirmed, etc. because of a petition to initiate rehabilitation proceedings filed in accordance with the Civil Rehabilitation Act, etc.; (iii) cases where false statements were discovered concerning material matters stated in annual securities reports, etc. submitted in the past and the amendments to financial statements or consolidated financial statements of past years needed to confirm the starting balances, etc. for the relevant business year or consolidated business year were not completed or audit reports could not be received by the due date for submission, and the issuer has publicized that matter; (iv) cases where an audit report could not be received by the due date for submission from the relevant auditing firm because additional audit procedures are required to be carried out by the auditing firm, etc. because an audit by the auditing firm, etc. identified an error that could cause a

---

**99** *Ibid.*

material and false indication in the financial statements or consolidated financial statements of the relevant issuer or suspicion of material and false indications through wrongful acts, and the issuer has publicized that matter; and (v) cases where the issuer of securities listed in each item of Article 24, paragraph 1 of the Financial Instruments and Exchange Act is a foreign person, and annual securities reports cannot be submitted by the due date for submission due to any reason in connection with the laws and regulations or practices related to accounting in the status of the foreign person (Guidelines on Disclosure of Corporate Affairs, B24-13(1)).

In cases where parties who have not submitted annual securities reports become obliged to make continuous disclosure by new listing or over-the-counter registration of their securities or by submission of a securities registration statement pertaining to public offering or secondary distribution, they must submit an annual securities report without delay for the business year immediately preceding the business year that includes the day on which they became obliged to submit annual securities reports (Article 24(3) of the Financial Instruments and Exchange Act). However, in cases where an issuer becomes obliged to submit annual securities reports by submission of a securities registration statement pertaining to public offering or secondary distribution, the issuer is not required to submit an annual securities report for the immediately preceding business year; and it is sufficient to submit annual securities reports from the business year in which the submission of the securities registration statement is made when: (i) the submission date of the relevant securities registration statement is at least three months after the starting date of the business year that includes that submission date, or (ii) the relevant securities registration statement presents the financial statements of the business year immediately before the business year that includes the submission date (Article 24 (3), parentheses of the Financial Instruments and Exchange Act; Article 16-2 of the Cabinet Office Ordinance on Disclosure of Corporate Affairs, etc.; Guidelines on Disclosure of Corporate Affairs, B24-1; for specified securities, see Article 26 of the Cabinet Office Ordinance on Specified Securities Disclosure).

Chapter 3   Disclosure requirements

b. Place of submission and public inspection

Annual securities reports must be submitted to the authority to which securities registration statements must be submitted. Details are as follows (Article 20 of the Cabinet Office Ordinance on Disclosure of Corporate Affairs, etc.; Article 22 of the Cabinet Office Ordinance on Specified Securities Disclosure; Article 12 of the Cabinet Office Ordinance on Foreign Bonds):

(1)  Among domestic companies, those where the amount of stated capital, total amount of funds, and total amount of contributions is at least ￥500 million and which have issued securities that are listed on a financial instruments exchange — The Director General of the Kanto Local Finance Bureau.

(2)  Among domestic companies, companies other than those under (1) above (excluding cases where a company which is the issuer of domestic investment trust beneficiary certificates, domestic investment securities, domestic asset-backed securities, domestic asset trust securitization beneficiary certificates, domestic securities in trust beneficiary certificates, domestic trust bonds, domestic mortgage securities, domestic trust beneficial interests, domestic interests in domestic securities investment business, securities in trust beneficiary certificates for specified securities, or regulated depository receipts, issues these securities)— The Director General of the Local Finance Bureau with jurisdiction over the location of the head office or principal office (the Director General of the Fukuoka Local Finance Branch Bureau when the location is within the jurisdiction of the Fukuoka Local Finance Branch Bureau).

(3)  Persons other than those in (1) and (2) above (including foreign companies and issuers of foreign bonds)— The Director General of the Kanto Local Finance Bureau

Annual securities reports are made available for public inspection (Article 25 (1) (iv) of the Financial Instruments and Exchange Act) (the same applies to the below-mentioned quarterly securities reports, semiannual securities reports, confirmation letters, internal control reports and

*373*

extraordinary reports, and to foreign company annual securities reports, foreign company quarterly securities reports, foreign company semiannual securities reports, foreign company confirmation letters, foreign company internal control reports, foreign person annual securities reports and foreign person semiannual securities reports and their supplementary documents, and to foreign company extraordinary reports and foreign person extraordinary reports, and to amendment reports to all these documents, and to parent company's status reports and foreign parent company's status reports and their supplementary documents; hereafter in b., together with annual securities reports and their attached documents, these are collectively referred to as "annual securities reports, etc."). Namely, annual securities reports, etc. are to be retained and made available for public inspection for five years from the date of submission (or one year in cases where the incorporation by reference method applies) at the Kanto Local Finance Bureau and at the Local Finance Bureau (including Fukuoka Local Finance Branch Bureau; Article 21, introductory provision of the Cabinet Office Ordinance on Disclosure of Corporate Affairs, etc.) (Kanto Local Finance Bureau for annual securities reports, etc. submitted by a foreign person) with jurisdiction over the location of the head office or principal office of the company submitting the relevant annual securities reports, etc. (or of the company's representative in the case of a foreign company) (Article 25(1), Article 5(8) and Article 27 of the Financial Instruments and Exchange Act; Article 21 of the Cabinet Office Ordinance on Disclosure of Corporate Affairs, etc.; Article 31 of the Cabinet Office Ordinance on Specified Securities Disclosure; Article 27(1) of the Cabinet Office Ordinance on Foreign Bonds).

Where an issuer who has listed securities on financial instruments exchanges or registered over-the-counter traded securities with authorized financial instruments firms associations submits annual securities reports, etc. to the Prime Minister, the issuer must submit copies of the annual securities reports etc., to those financial instruments exchanges or authorized financial instruments firms associations (Article 6, Article 5(8), Article 27, Article 24 (7), Article 24-2(3), Article 24-4-2(5), Article 24-4-3(2), Article 24-4-4(5), Article 24-4-5 (2), Article 24-4-7 (5), Article 24-5 (6), Article 24-6 (3),

Chapter 3   Disclosure requirements

Article 24-7 (4), Article 24-4-8 (1) & (2) and Article 24-5-2 (1) of the Financial Instruments and Exchange Act; Article 3 of the Financial Instruments and Exchange Act Implementing Order). Financial instruments exchanges and authorized financial instruments firms associations that have received a submission of copies of annual securities reports, etc. must retain those documents at their offices and make them available for public inspection for five years from their date of submission (Article 25 (3) and Article 5 (8) of the Financial Instruments and Exchange Act; Article 23 of the Cabinet Office Ordinance on Disclosure of Corporate Affairs, etc.; Article 18 (1) of the Cabinet Office Ordinance on Foreign Bonds).

Also, an issuer of securities who has submitted annual securities reports, etc. to the Prime Minister must retain copies of the annual securities reports, etc. at its head office, principal office and main branches and make them available for public inspection for five years after the date of the submission (Article 25 (2), Article 5 (6) & (8) and Article 27 of the Financial Instruments and Exchange Act; Article 22 (1) of the Cabinet Office Ordinance on Disclosure of Corporate Affairs, etc.; Article 32 of the Cabinet Office Ordinance on Specified Securities Disclosure).

However, an issuer of securities may be exempted from the obligation to make annual securities reports, etc. available for public inspection in relation to a part thereof if it applies to the Prime Minister because of the necessity to maintain the confidentiality of business secrets and obtains approval from the Prime Minister (Article 25 (4), Article 5 (6) & (8), and Article 27 of the Financial Instruments and Exchange Act).

In cases where the Prime Minister orders submission of documents concerning amendments to annual securities reports, etc., the Prime Minister may allow not to make all or part of the relevant disclosure documents available for public inspection (Article 25 (6), Article 27-30-7 (1) & (2), and Article 5 (6) & (8) of the Financial Instruments and Exchange Act). In this case, their copies are not made available for public inspection at the head office, principal office and main branches of the issuer or at the relevant financial instruments exchange or authorized financial instruments firms

*375*

association (Article 25 (7) (8) and Article 5 (6) & (8) of the Financial Instruments and Exchange Act).

The application for non-disclosure of annual securities reports, etc. or business secrets in relation thereto must be made through EDINET as electronic disclosure procedures (Article 27-30-3 (1) of the Financial Instruments and Exchange Act) (Article 27-30-2, Article 5 (6) & (8) and Article 27 of the Financial Instruments and Exchange Act) (for details of electronic disclosure procedures, see A.3.e above).

c. Items to be included in annual securities reports

Annual securities reports submitted by domestic companies must be prepared using Cabinet Office Ordinance on Disclosure of Corporate Affairs, etc. Form 3 (form to be used in principle), Form 3-2 (form to be used in cases where the special provision pertaining to small-amount public offerings etc. under Article 24-2 of the Financial Instruments and Exchange Act applies), or Form 4 (form to be submitted in accordance with Article 24, paragraph 3 of the Financial Instruments and Exchange Act where a company is an issuer of neither listed securities nor over-the-counter traded securities and has not conducted a public offering or secondary distribution) (Article 15 (i) of the Cabinet Office Ordinance on Disclosure of Corporate Affairs, etc.). Annual securities reports submitted by foreign companies must be prepared using Form 8 (form to be used, in principle) or Form 9 (form to be submitted in accordance with Article 24, paragraph 3 of the Financial Instruments and Exchange Act where a company is an issuer of neither listed securities nor over-the-counter traded securities and has not conducted a public offering or secondary distribution) of the Cabinet Office Ordinance on Disclosure of Corporate Affairs, etc. (Article 15 (ii) of the Cabinet Office Ordinance on Disclosure of Corporate Affairs, etc.).

On the other hand, the forms for annual securities reports pertaining to registered securities are prescribed by the Cabinet Office Ordinance on Specified Securities Disclosure in accordance with the class of specified securities (Article 22 (1) of the Cabinet Office Ordinance on Specified Securities Disclosure). Namely, annual securities reports must be prepared

Chapter 3    Disclosure requirements

using Form 7 for domestic investment trust beneficiary certificates, Form 7-2 for foreign investment trust beneficiary certificates, Form 7-3 for domestic investment securities, Form 8 for foreign investment securities, Form 8-2 for domestic asset-backed securities, Form 8-3 for foreign asset-backed securities, Form 8-4 for domestic trust securitization beneficiary certificates, Form 8-5 for foreign trust securitization beneficiary certificates, Form 9 for domestic securities in trust beneficiary certificates, domestic trust bonds and domestic trust beneficial interests, Form 9-2 for foreign securities in trust beneficiary certificates, foreign trust bonds, foreign trust beneficial interests and foreign loan trust beneficiary certificates, Form 9-3 for domestic mortgage securities, Form 9-4 for foreign mortgage securities, Form 9-5 for interests in domestic securities investment business, and Form 9-6 for interests in foreign securities investment business. Annual securities reports must be prepared for beneficiary certificates of specified securities in trust using the form prescribed for the entrusted securities pertaining to the relevant beneficiary certificates of specified securities in trust, and for specified depository receipts using the form prescribed for the specified securities pertaining to the rights represented on the relevant specified depository receipts.

Moreover, annual securities reports pertaining to foreign bonds, etc. must be prepared using Cabinet Office Ordinance on Foreign Bonds Form 3 (form to be used in principle) or Form 4 (form to be submitted in accordance with Article 24, paragraph 3 of the Financial Instruments and Exchange Act where a person is an issuer of neither listed securities nor over-the-counter traded securities and has not conducted a public offering or secondary distribution) (Article 12 of the Cabinet Office Ordinance on Foreign Bonds).

An annual securities report prepared using Cabinet Office Ordinance on Disclosure of Corporate Affairs, etc. Form 3, which is the form used in principle where domestic companies prepare and submit annual securities reports, comprises of "Part 1 Company Information" (see Tables 5 and 6) and "Part 2 Information on the Guarantor Company of the Reporting Company." The contents to be stated in "Part 1 Company Information" and "Part 2 Information on the Guarantor Company of the Reporting Company"

*377*

## Table 3-5

| Securities Registration Statement | Annual Securities Report | | | | |
|---|---|---|---|---|---|
| Domestic Companies | Domestic Companies | | | Foreign Companies | |
| Form 2 | Form 3 | Form 3-2 | Form 4 | Form 8 | Form 9 |
| Securities Information | | | | | |
| Company Information | | | | | |
| | | | | Outline of legal system in home country | |
| Overview of company | | | | | |
| State of business | | | | | |
| State of Facilities | | | | | |
| Status of reporting company | | | Status of reporting company | | |
| Status of accounting (consolidated and individual) | Status of accounting (individual only) | | Status of accounting (consolidated and individual) | Status of accounting (financial documents) | |
| | | | | Foreign exchange rate movements | |
| Outline of shareholder services of reporting company | | | | Outline of shareholder services of reporting company in Japan | |
| Reference information on reporting company | | | | | |
| | | | Stock offering information | | |
| | | Information on associated companies | | | |
| Information on guarantor company of reporting company | | | | | |
| Special information | | | | | |

*378*

Chapter 3 Disclosure requirements

are almost the same as the contents to be stated in "Part 2 Company Information" and "Part 3 Information on the Guarantor Company of the Reporting Company, etc." of a securities registration statement to be prepared using Form 2 of the Cabinet Office Ordinance on Disclosure of Corporate Affairs, etc..

Aside from annual securities reports not containing securities information, the contents of annual securities reports prepared in the other forms are also almost the same as the contents of the corresponding securities registration statement (for example, Form 4 of the Cabinet Office Ordinance on Disclosure of Corporate Affairs, etc. corresponds to Form 2-4, Form 3-2 corresponds to Form 2-5 [in cases not constituting specified procedures relating to securities issuance for reorganization or specified procedures relating to securities delivery for reorganization], and Form 8 corresponds to Form 7).

d. Attached documents

Domestic companies must attach the articles of incorporation (articles of endowment in cases of domestic issuers that are foundations), financial statements and business reports for the relevant business year that have been reported to or approved by the ordinary general shareholders meeting (in cases where annual securities reports are submitted before the ordinary general shareholders meeting, financial statements and business reports that are planned to be reported to or approved by the ordinary general shareholders meeting); in cases where bonds, etc. (corporate bonds, social medical care corporation bonds, school bond certificates or school loan claims; Article 10(1) (i) (d) of the Cabinet Office Ordinance on Disclosure of Corporate Affairs, etc.) or commercial paper are guaranteed, the Articles of Incorporation of the guarantor company, a copy of the minutes of the board of directors meeting regarding the resolution to provide the guarantee and documents stating the details of the guarantee; in cases where the securities concerned are covered warrants and there is a contract concluded regarding the options represented by the covered warrants, a copy of such contract; in cases where the securities concerned are beneficiary certificates of securities in trust, copies of the trust contract concluded regarding the

*379*

issuance of the relevant beneficiary certificates of securities in trust and of other material contracts; and in cases where the securities concerned are depository receipts, copies of the depository contract concluded regarding the issuance of the relevant depository receipts and of the other material contracts (Article 24(6) of the Financial Instruments and Exchange Act; Article 17(1)(i) of the Cabinet Office Ordinance on Disclosure of Corporate Affairs, etc.). Excluding financial statements and business reports pertaining to the relevant business year, in cases where there are any items that have already been submitted as attached to previous annual securities reports within five years before the submission date of the relevant annual securities report, the rule is to attach only the portions that have different contents.

In the case of foreign companies, in addition to the documents that domestic companies must attach and submit, a company must submit: (i) a document attesting that the representative of the foreign company stated in the relevant annual securities report has legitimate authority to submit the annual securities report; (ii) a document attesting that the relevant foreign company has authorized a person who has residence in Japan to represent the foreign company in all acts regarding submission of the annual securities report; (iii) a legal opinion letter from a legal expert stating that the legal matters in the relevant annual securities report are true and accurate; and (iv) in cases where there are bonds, etc. that require notification regarding their public offering or secondary distribution, a copy of the contract whereby the foreign company entrusts the duties of administration of claims and other acts for obligees or acts for the foreign company and a copy of the contract concerning payment of the principal and interest (Article 17(1)(ii) of the Cabinet Office Ordinance on Disclosure of Corporate Affairs, etc.). In cases where the attached documents are not written in Japanese, excluding items equivalent to financial statements and business reports regarding the relevant business year (which have been reported to or approved by the ordinary general shareholders meeting), a Japanese translation must be attached, and even in cases where a Japanese translation has been sent to domestic shareholders, obligees, and other related parties regarding items equivalent to financial statements or business reports pertaining to the relevant business year (which have been reported to or approved by the

Chapter 3 Disclosure requirements

ordinary general shareholders meeting) or their summaries, such Japanese translation must be attached (Article 17(2) of the Cabinet Office Ordinance on Disclosure of Corporate Affairs, etc.).

# 4. Quarterly securities reports

Quarterly securities reports are documents stating the status of accounting and other matters of the corporate group the relevant company belongs to for each period, dividing a business year into three-month periods.

a. Obligatory submitter and voluntary submitter

Companies issuing shares that are listed or over-the-counter registered or preferred equity investment certificates, securities with the characteristics of shares or preferred equity investment certificates issued by foreign persons, beneficiary certificates of securities in trust whose entrusted securities are shares, preferred equity investment certificates or securities with the characteristics of shares or preferred equity investment certificates issued by foreign persons, or depository receipts representing rights pertaining to shares, preferred equity investment certificates or securities with the characteristics of shares or preferred equity investment certificates issued by foreign persons (i.e., listed companies, etc.) must submit to the Prime Minister quarterly securities reports stating the status of accounting and other matters of the corporate group the relevant company belongs to for each period, dividing a business year into three-month periods (Article 24-4-7(1) of the Financial Instruments and Exchange Act Article 24-4-7, paragraph 1; Article 4-2-10(1) of the Financial Instruments and Exchange Act Implementing Order). Also, companies that must submit annual securities reports can submit quarterly securities reports voluntarily, even if they are not listed companies, etc.[100] (Article 24-4-7 (2) of the Financial

---

100 However, because there are no Cabinet Orders under delegation of Article 24-4-7, paragraph 3 of the Financial Instruments and Exchange Act, the quarterly reporting system does not apply to issuers of specified securities; and they cannot submit quarterly securities reports voluntarily ("Results of Public Comments on 'Draft Cabinet Orders and Draft Cabinet Office Ordinances Regarding the Financial Instruments and Exchange Act System,'" "Outline of Comments and FSA's Position on Comments" (July 31, 2007), p. 133, No. 2).

*381*

Instruments and Exchange Act). In cases where companies that are only obliged to submit semiannual securities reports voluntarily submit quarterly securities reports, they must start the submission from the first quarter of that business year (Guidelines on Disclosure of Corporate Affairs, B24-4-7-4). Also, once a company has started submitting quarterly securities reports voluntarily, except for cases where it attempted to list its shares but failed or other equivalent cases, it must continue to submit quarterly securities reports (Guidelines on Disclosure of Corporate Affairs, B24-4-7-5).

Companies that newly listed its securities or newly registered its securities over-the-counter must submit quarterly securities reports from the quarter in which the new listing or registration took place (Guidelines on Disclosure of Corporate Affairs, B24-4-7-3).

b. Due date for submission, place of submission, and public inspection
Both domestic companies and foreign companies must submit quarterly securities reports within 45 days after the end of each quarter (Article 24-4-7(1) of the Financial Instruments and Exchange Act; Article 4-2-10 (3) of the Financial Instruments and Exchange Act Implementing Order). However, there is no need to submit quarterly securities reports for the last period of the business year (the fourth quarter, in cases where the business year is one year long) (Article 24-4-7(1) of the Financial Instruments and Exchange Act; Article 4-2-10(2) of the Financial Instruments and Exchange Act Implementing Order). Also, companies engaged in the banking business, insurance business, and other businesses specified by cabinet office ordinance (Article 17-15(2) of the Cabinet Office Ordinance on Disclosure of Corporate Affairs, etc.) (specified operating companies) are obliged to include interim financial statements on an individual basis in quarterly securities reports for the second quarter, so they are allowed to submit the quarterly securities report for the second quarter within 60 days after the end of the relevant second quarter (Article 24-4-7 (1) of the Financial Instruments and Exchange Act; Article 4-2-10 (4) (i) of the Financial Instruments and Exchange Act Implementing Order).

*382*

Chapter 3 Disclosure requirements

However, when it is deemed impossible to submit the reports within the due period because of unavoidable reasons, submission may be made within the period approved by the Prime Minister in advance as provided by cabinet office ordinance (Article 24-4-7 (1) of the Financial Instruments and Exchange Act; Article 17-15-2 of the Financial Instruments and Exchange Act Implementing Order).

Quarterly securities reports should be submitted to the same authority as the one to which annual securities reports should be submitted (Article 20 of the Cabinet Office Ordinance on Disclosure of Corporate Affairs, etc.). Similar to annual securities reports, quarterly securities reports must also be made available for public inspection, however, the public inspection period is three years from the date of submission (Article 25(1)(vii) of the Financial Instruments and Exchange Act).

c. Items to be included in quarterly securities reports
Quarterly securities reports must be prepared and submitted by domestic companies using Form 4-3 and by foreign companies using Form 9-3 (Article 17-15 of the Cabinet Office Ordinance on Disclosure of Corporate Affairs, etc.).

The matters to be stated on quarterly securities reports are substantially limited compared with those for semiannual securities reports, with distinctive characteristics including: (i) no requirement to state the status of associated companies as the summary of the company; (ii) as for the state of business, the "outline of business performance," "issues to be addressed" and "research and development activities" that are independent items in semiannual securities reports and annual securities reports can be stated together in "analysis of financial position, business performance and state of cash flow"; and (iii) regarding the status of the reporting company, statement of the status of corporate governance, etc., dividend policy, and status of acquisition of treasury stock, etc. are not required.

Also, regarding the status of accounting, quarterly consolidated financial statements [101] (or, in the case of foreign companies, quarterly financial

*383*

documents) should be included. (Individual) quarterly financial statements should be included only in cases where consolidated quarterly financial statements are not prepared (Cabinet Office Ordinance on Disclosure of Corporate Affairs, etc., Form 4-3, Note 25a). Additionally, as quarterly financial statements, only the quarterly consolidated balance sheet, quarterly consolidated profit and loss statement (regarding the relevant quarterly consolidated cumulative period) and quarterly consolidated statement of comprehensive income (regarding the relevant quarterly consolidated cumulative period) should be included in all quarterly securities reports; and the quarterly consolidated cash flow statement (regarding the relevant quarterly consolidated cumulative period) is required to be included only in the second quarter (Cabinet Office Ordinance on Disclosure of Corporate Affairs, etc., Form 4-3, Notes 19 to 23).[102] However, companies may voluntarily include the first-quarter consolidated cash flow statement and the (cumulative) third-quarter consolidated cash flow statement, quarterly (three-month) consolidated profit and loss statements and quarterly (three-month) consolidated statements of comprehensive income.

The terminology, forms and preparation methods of the quarterly consolidated financial statements that a specified company submits may be in accordance with the designated international financial reporting standards or the Modified International Standards (Articles 93 and 94 of the Ordinance on Quarterly Consolidated Financial Statements). In cases where the Commissioner of the Financial Services Agency approves a company that has registered its consolidated financial statements prepared according to

---

**101** Regarding standards for preparation of quarterly financial statements, the Accounting Standards Board of Japan has published "Accounting Standards for Quarterly Financial Reporting" and "Implementation Guidance for Accounting Standards for Quarterly Financial Reporting." In principle, quarterly financial statements must be prepared according to the accounting principles and procedures applicable to preparation of financial statements (Article 4 (1) of the Ordinance on Quarterly Financial Statements). In their preparation, simplified accounting methods and special accounting methods for quarterly financial statements are permitted to be used.

**102** (Consolidated) statements of changes in shareholders' equity are not required to be prepared as quarterly (consolidated) financial statements; notes are required in cases where there are outstanding changes in shareholders' equity.

Chapter 3   Disclosure requirements

the terminology, forms, and preparation methods that are required regarding issuance, etc. of American Depositary Receipts (U. S. -style consolidated financial statements) with the U.S. Securities and Exchange Commission to submit the U.S.-style consolidated financial statements as the consolidated financial statements under the Financial Instruments and Exchange Act, on finding no risk of harming public interests or investor protection, the terminology, forms, and preparation methods of the consolidated financial statements submitted by the company may, except for matters as instructed by the Commissioner of the Financial Services Agency on finding that they are necessary, be the terminology, forms, and preparation methods required regarding issuance, etc. of American Depository Receipts (Article 95 of the Ordinance on Consolidated Financial Statements; Article 95 of the Ordinance on Quarterly Consolidated Financial Statements; Article 89 of the Ordinance on Semiannual Consolidated Financial Statements).

Also, for foreign companies, even in cases where quarterly financial documents of the reporting company disclosed in an area outside Japan are considered not to harm public interest or investor protection under Article 85, paragraph 1 or 2 of the Ordinance on Terminology, Forms and Preparation Methods of Quarterly Financial Statements, etc., consolidated quarterly financial statements should be included in cases where only consolidated quarterly financial statements are disclosed in the relevant area, [individual] quarterly financial statements should be included in cases where only [individual] quarterly financial statements are disclosed in the relevant area, and both consolidated quarterly financial statements and [individual] quarterly financial statements should be included in cases where both consolidated quarterly financial statements and [individual] quarterly financial statements are disclosed in the relevant area. In these cases, the types of quarterly financial documents (quarterly balance sheet for the quarterly accounting period, quarterly profit and loss statement for the quarterly accounting period and cumulative quarterly accounting period, and cash flow statement for the cumulative quarterly accounting period) are according to those to be disclosed in the relevant area. However, in cases where the terminology, forms and preparation methods of financial

*385*

# Table 3-6

| Annual Securities Report | | | Semiannual Securities Report | | | Quarterly Securities Report | |
|---|---|---|---|---|---|---|---|
| Domestic Company | | Foreign Company | Domestic Company | | Foreign Company | Domestic Company | Foreign Company |
| Form 3 | Form 3-2 | Form 8 | Form 5 | Form 3-2 | Form 10 | Form 4-3 | Form 9-3 |
| Company Information | | | | | | | |
| | | Outline of Legal System in Home Country | | | Outline of Legal System in Home Country | | Outline of Legal System in Home Country |
| Company Overview | | | | | | | |
| [Movement of Principal Management Indicators] | | | | | | | |
| [History] | | | | | | | |
| [Description of Business] | | | | | | | |
| [Status of Employees] | | | | | | | |
| [Status of Associated Companies] | | [Status of Associated Companies] | | | [Status of Associated Companies] | | |
| | [Status of Shares, etc.] | | | [Status of Shares, etc.] | | | |
| | [Share Price Movement] | | | [Share Price Movement] | | | |
| | [Status of Directors] | | | [Status of Directors] | | | |
| | [Status of Corporate Governance, etc.] | | | | | | |
| State of Business | | | | | | | |
| [Outline of Business Performance] | | | | | | | |
| [Status of Production, Orders Received and Sales] | | | | | | | |
| [Issues to be Addressed] | | | | | | | |
| [Business-related Risk, etc.] | | | | | [Business-related Risk etc.] | | |
| [Important Contracts etc. for Management] | | | | | | | |
| [Research and Development Activities] | | | | | | | |
| [Analysis of Financial Position, Operating Results and Cash Flow Conditions] | | | | | [Analysis of Financial Position, Operating Results and Cash Flow Conditions] | | |
| State of Facilities | | | | | | | |
| [Outline of Capital Investment, etc.] | | | | | | | |
| [State of Main Facilities] | | | | | | | |
| [Plan for Facilities Construction, Removal, etc. | | | | | | | |
| Status of Reporting Company | | Status of Reporting Company | | | Status of Reporting Company | | |
| [Status of Shares, etc.] | | [Status of Shares, etc.] | | | [Status of Shares, etc.] | | |
| [Status of Acquisition of Treasury Share, etc.] | | | | | | | |

Chapter 3 Disclosure requirements

| [Dividend Policy] | | [Dividend Policy] | | | | | |
|---|---|---|---|---|---|---|---|
| [Share Price Movement] | | [Share Price Movement] | | | [Share Price Movement] | | |
| [Status of Directors] | | [Status of Directors] | | | [Status of Directors] | | |
| [Status of Corporate Governance, etc.] | | [Status of Corporate Governance, etc.] | | | | | |
| Status of Accounting | | | | | | | |
| [Consolidated Financial Statements, etc.] | | [Financial Documents] | [Semiannual Consolidated Financial Statements, etc.] | | [Semiannual Financial Documents] | [Quarterly Consolidated Financial Statements] | [Quarterly Financial Documents] |
| [Financial Statements, etc.] | [Financial Statements] | [Financial Documents] | [Semiannual Financial Statements, etc.] | [Semiannual Financial Statements] | [Semiannual Financial Documents] | [Quarterly Consolidated Financial Statements] | [Quarterly Financial Documents] |
| [Contents of Main Assets and Liabilities] | | [Contents of Main Assets, Liabilities, Income and Expenditures] | | | | | |
| [Others] | | | | | | | |
| | | Foreign Exchange Rate Movements | | | Foreign Exchange Rate Movements | | Foreign Exchange Rate Movements |
| Outline of Reporting Company's Shareholder Services | | Outline of Reporting Company's Shareholder Services in Japan | | | | | |
| Reference Information on Reporting Company | | | | | | | |
| | Associated Company Information | | | Associated Company Information | | | |
| Information on Guarantor Company, etc. for Reporting Company | | | | | | | |

documents are instructed in Article 85, paragraph 3 of the Ordinance on Quarterly Financial Statements, etc., quarterly financial documents prepared in accordance with those instructions must be included (Cabinet Office Ordinance on Disclosure of Corporate Affairs, etc., Form 9-3, Note 19).

While the quarterly securities reports for the second quarter of specified operating companies should include interim consolidated financial statements and interim [individual] financial statements (including statements of changes in net assets), quarterly consolidated profit and loss statements (quarterly [individual] profit and loss statements in cases where quarterly consolidated profit and loss statements are not prepared) can be included in "others" under "status of accounting" (Cabinet Office Ordinance on Disclosure of Corporate Affairs, etc., Form 4-3, Note 30). Also, for the third-quarter consolidated accounting period, specified operating companies can include the profit and loss statement for the relevant quarterly consolidated accounting period in the form of a quarterly consolidated profit and loss statement and quarterly consolidated statement of comprehensive income, or quarterly consolidated statement of profit, loss and comprehensive income. Also, in cases where quarterly consolidated financial statements are not prepared, the profit and loss statement for the relevant quarterly accounting period can be stated in the form of [individual] quarterly profit and loss statements (Cabinet Office Ordinance on Disclosure of Corporate Affairs, etc., Form 4-3, Notes 24d and 29d).

Quarterly financial statements and quarterly consolidated financial statements must undergo audit certification (quarterly review) by a certified public accountant or auditing firm (Article 193-2 (1) of the Financial Instruments and Exchange Act; Articles 1 and 3 of the Cabinet Office Ordinance on Audit Certification of Financial Statements, etc.). Quarterly reviews give a negative assurance that "there is no matter which causes belief of not being properly stated in any material aspects" (Business Accounting Deliberation Council, "Opinion on Establishing Quarterly Review Standards").

# 5. Semiannual securities reports

Semiannual securities reports are documents stating the status of accounting of the corporate group to which the relevant company belongs and of the company itself, other material matters concerning the business (or, in cases of specified securities, material matters concerning the status of accounting of assets pertaining to asset management and other similar businesses conducted by the relevant company and other details of assets), and other necessary and appropriate matters for the benefit of public interest or investor protection for the first six months of the business year (Article 24-5

*388*

Chapter 3 Disclosure requirements

(1) & (3) of the Financial Instruments and Exchange Act).

a. Parties with an obligation to submit semiannual securities reports
Among companies submitting annual securities reports, those which do not submit quarterly securities reports and which have a business year longer than six months must submit semiannual securities reports (Article 24-5(1) of the Financial Instruments and Exchange Act). Issuers who must submit annual securities reports (excluding persons with an obligation to submit quarterly securities reports) must prepare semiannual securities reports and submit them to the Prime Minister even where they are not companies (Article 27 and Article 24-5 of the Financial Instruments and Exchange Act). In cases where the business year prescribed in the articles of incorporation is changed and the period of that first business year after the change is longer than six months, semiannual securities reports must be submitted. However, in cases where the final day of such first business year comes before the due date for submission of the relevant semiannual securities report, the issuer can choose not to submit the semiannual securities report (Guidelines on Disclosure of Corporate Affairs, B24-5-1).

Also, where the securities issued by companies with a business year longer than six months that did not have an obligation to submit an annual securities report came to fall under the categories of securities listed under Item 1, 2 or 3 or Article 24, paragraph 1 of the Financial Instruments and Exchange Act, a semiannual securities report must be submitted for the six months of the business year only in cases where the date the securities came to fall under the categories of such securities is a date within the first six months of the relevant business year (Guidelines on Disclosure of Corporate Affairs, B24-5-3).

b. Due date for submission, place of submission and public inspection
In principle, semiannual securities reports must be submitted within three months after six months have passed from the beginning of the business year (Article 24-5(1) and Article 27(1) of the Financial Instruments and Exchange Act). Where it is deemed impossible to submit the reports within the due period because of unavoidable reasons, submission must be made

389

within the period approved by the Prime Minister in advance as provided by cabinet office ordinance.

Semiannual securities reports should be submitted to the same authority as the one to which annual securities reports should be submitted (Article 20 of the Cabinet Office Ordinance on Disclosure of Corporate Affairs, etc.; Article 28 (1) of the Cabinet Office Ordinance on Specified Securities Disclosure; Article 12 of the Cabinet Office Ordinance on Foreign Bonds). Similar to annual securities reports, semiannual securities reports and their amendment reports must also be made available for public inspection; however, the public inspection period is three years from the date of submission (Article 25(1)(viii) of the Financial Instruments and Exchange Act).

 c. Items to be included in semiannual securities reports
Semiannual securities reports must be prepared and submitted by domestic companies using Form 5 (ordinary form) or Form 5-2 (form for use in cases of the small-amount public offering pursuant to Article 24, paragraph 2 of the Financial Instruments and Exchange Act) and by foreign companies using Form 10 (Article 18(1) of the Cabinet Office Ordinance on Disclosure of Corporate Affairs, etc.).

However, the forms for semiannual securities reports pertaining to registered securities are prescribed by the Cabinet Office Ordinance on Specified Securities Disclosure in accordance with the category of specified securities (Article 28 (1) of the Cabinet Office Ordinance on Specified Securities Disclosure). Namely, semiannual securities reports must be prepared using Form 10 for domestic investment trust beneficiary certificates, Form 10-2 for foreign investment trust beneficiary certificates, Form 10-3 for domestic investment securities, Form 11 for foreign investment securities, Form 11-2 for domestic asset-backed securities, Form 11-3 for foreign asset-backed securities, Form 11-4 for domestic trust securitization beneficiary certificates, Form 11-5 for foreign trust securitization beneficiary certificates, Form 12 for domestic trust beneficiary certificates, domestic trust bonds and domestic trust beneficial interests,

*390*

Chapter 3   Disclosure requirements

Form 12-2 for foreign securities in trust beneficiary certificates, foreign trust bonds, foreign trust beneficial interests and foreign loan trust beneficiary certificates, Form 12-3 for domestic mortgage securities, Form 12-4 for foreign mortgage securities, Form 12-5 for interests in domestic securities investment business, and Form 12-6 for interests in foreign securities investment business.

Also, semiannual securities reports must be prepared for beneficiary certificates of specified securities in trust using the form provided for the entrusted securities pertaining to the relevant beneficiary certificates of specified securities in trust, and for regulated depository receipts using the form prescribed for the specified securities pertaining to the rights represented on the relevant regulated depository receipts.

Moreover, semiannual securities reports pertaining to foreign bonds etc. must be prepared using Form 5 of the Cabinet Office Ordinance on Foreign Bonds (Article 15 of the Cabinet Office Ordinance on Foreign Bonds).

From the perspective of simplifying the statement compared with annual securities reports reflecting that semiannual securities reports are interim reports, comparing Form 3 of the Cabinet Office Ordinance on Disclosure of Corporate Affairs, etc. with Form 5 and comparing Form 3-2 of the Cabinet Office Ordinance on Disclosure of Corporate Affairs, etc. with Form 5-2, semiannual securities reports do not require a statement of the status of corporate governance or outlines of capital investment, etc.

Also, comparing Form 3 of the Cabinet Office Ordinance on Disclosure of Corporate Affairs, etc. with Form 5, semiannual securities reports do not require a statement of dividend policy or status of acquisition of treasury shares, etc.

Furthermore, in Form 5-2 of the Cabinet Office Ordinance on Disclosure of Corporate Affairs, etc., parallel to Form 3-2 for securities reports (form to be used in cases where the special provision pertaining to small-amount public offerings, etc. applies under Article 24-2 of the Financial Instruments and

*391*

Exchange Act), "status of the reporting company" is not required to be included as an independent item, and the status of shares, etc., changes in share price, and status of "directors" are stated together in "overview of company". From the perspective of simplifying the statements compared with annual securities reports, statements analyzing business risk, financial position, operating results and state of cash flow are not required as "state of business."

Moreover, in semiannual securities reports, there are many items that must be stated only when there are material changes.

d. Attached documents

No attached documents are required for the semiannual securities reports of domestic companies. For the semiannual securities reports of foreign companies, however, (i) a document attesting that the representative of the foreign company stated in the relevant semiannual securities report has legitimate authority to submit the semiannual securities report, and (ii) a document attesting that the relevant foreign company has authorized a person who has residence in Japan to represent the relevant foreign company in all acts regarding the submission of the relevant semiannual securities report must be attached.

In cases where these documents are not written in Japanese, a Japanese translation must be attached (Article 18(2) of the Cabinet Office Ordinance on Disclosure of Corporate Affairs, etc.).

# 6. Extraordinary reports

A company that must submit annual securities reports must submit extraordinary reports without delay stating the contents required by cabinet office ordinance in cases where it conducts public offerings or secondary distributions of its securities in a foreign state and in cases specified by cabinet office ordinance as necessary and appropriate for the benefit of public interest or investor protection (Article 24-5 (4) of the Financial Instruments and Exchange Act; Article 19 of the Cabinet Office Ordinance on Disclosure of Corporate Affairs, etc.; Article 29 of the Cabinet Office

Chapter 3   Disclosure requirements

Ordinance on Specified Securities Disclosure). Persons that must submit annual securities reports must submit extraordinary reports, even if they are not companies (Article 27 of the Financial Instruments and Exchange Act; Article 16 of the Cabinet Office Ordinance on Foreign Bonds).

a. Cases where extraordinary reports must be submitted

Issuers of securities that are neither specified securities nor foreign bonds etc. must submit extraordinary reports when, first pertaining to the reporting company, any of the following events take place: public offering or secondary distribution of securities overseas of which the total issue value or total distribution value is not less than ¥100 million (except for cases where the information on such public offering or private placement is included in the securities registration documents or shelf-registration supplement regarding a parallel public offering or private placement of the same kind of securities in Japan); issuance of securities by private placement of which the total issue value is not less than ¥100 million; issuance of stock options that do not require notification of which the total issue value or total distribution value is not less than ¥100 million; changes in the parent company or specified subsidiary companies; changes in major shareholders; notice of squeeze-out by the special controlling shareholder to the reporting company or the decision of the management body of the reporting company whether the squeeze-out is approved; decision by the management body of the reporting company to convene a shareholders meeting for acquisition of class shares subject to wholly call or reverse stock split that leads to odd lots; occurrence of a serious disaster; filing or settlement of a suit for damages against the reporting company; decisions of share exchange; share transfer; absorption-type demerger; incorporation-type demerger; absorption-type merger or consolidation-type merger; decisions of transfer or acquisition of significant businesses; decisions of acquisitions of subsidiaries; changes of representative director; resolutions of general shareholders meetings; revisions or rejections of matters stated in annual securities reports that require resolutions at ordinary general shareholders meetings; changes in certified public accountants for audits; filing of a petition for the commencement of bankruptcy proceedings, etc. pertaining to the reporting company; emergence of concerns that collection of material claims is likely to become impossible or to be delayed, and occurrence of material post-balance-sheet events (Article 19(2)(i) through (xii) of the Cabinet Office Ordinance on Disclosure of Corporate Affairs, etc.).

Next, where any of the following events occurs pertaining to consolidated subsidiaries, extraordinary reports must be submitted: occurrence of a serious disaster; filing or settling of a suit for damages against a consolidated subsidiary; decisions of share exchange, share transfer; absorption-type demerger; incorporation-type demerger; absorption-type merger or consolidation-type merger; decisions of transfer or acquisition of significant businesses; decisions of acquisitions of subsidiaries; filing of a petition for the commencement of bankruptcy proceedings, etc.; emergence of concerns that collection of material claims is likely to become impossible or to be delayed; and occurrence of material post-balance-sheet events (Article 19(2)(xiii)-(xix) of the Cabinet Office Ordinance on Disclosure of Corporate Affairs, etc.).

In addition to the above, extraordinary reports must be submitted in cases where stock offering information is created or changes (Article 19-2 of the Cabinet Office Ordinance on Disclosure of Corporate Affairs, etc.).

In cases where a reporting company has issued shares (tracking stock) for which the articles of incorporation of the reporting company prescribed that the dividends of surplus of the reporting company shall be determined based on dividends of surplus of its consolidated subsidiary or on its interim dividends as provided by Article 454, paragraph 5 of the Companies Act, the reporting company must submit an extraordinary report when any of the above-mentioned events occurs where the term "reporting company" is replaced by "consolidated subsidiary" (Article 19(3) of the Cabinet Office Ordinance on Disclosure of Corporate Affairs, etc.).

Issuers of specified securities must submit extraordinary reports to the Director General of the Kanto Local Finance Bureau without delay if any of the following events occurs: public offerings or secondary distributions of specified securities overseas; changes in principal affiliated juridical persons;

*394*

Chapter 3   Disclosure requirements

material changes in basic policies regarding the management of funds pertaining to investment trust securities issued by the relevant issuer (excluding cases where a securities registration statement stating that the relevant change occurred, an outline of the change, and the date of the relevant change has already been submitted); in cases where the trust accounting period is less than six months, arrival of the relevant trust accounting period; occurrence of a serious disaster; filing or settlement of a suit for damages against the issuer etc.; decisions of material absorption-type mergers or consolidation-type mergers of the relevant issuer (limited to investment corporations); notifications of fund mergers; filing of a petition for the commencement of bankruptcy proceedings, etc. pertaining to the relevant issuer; emergence of concerns that collection of material claims is likely to become impossible or to be delayed; occurrence of material post-balance-sheet events; cancellation of registration of the relevant issuer, etc. or business suspension order or other equivalent acts by administrative agency under laws and regulations (including equivalent acts under foreign laws and regulations); and decisions of dissolution, etc. of the relevant issuer (Article 24-5(iv) of the Financial Instruments and Exchange Act; Article 29 (1)(2) of the Cabinet Office Ordinance on Specified Securities Disclosure).

Issuers of foreign bonds, etc. must submit extraordinary reports stating the equity investment amounts of each investor and their percentages in the total amount of the equity investments and the date of changes in cases where there are changes in principal equity investors (i.e., equity investors holding 10% or more of total equity investments) (when a person ceases to be an equity investor or when a person becomes a principal equity investor) (Article 16 of the Cabinet Office Ordinance on Foreign Bonds).

Issuers of securities that are neither specified securities nor foreign bonds, etc. must prepare and submit extraordinary reports using Form 5-3 of the Cabinet Office Ordinance on Disclosure of Corporate Affairs, etc. when they are domestic companies and using Form 10-2 when they are foreign companies.

*395*

b. Due date for submission, place of submission, and public inspection extraordinary reports must be submitted without delay

Extraordinary reports should be submitted to the same authority as the one to which annual securities reports should be submitted (Article 20 of the Cabinet Office Ordinance on Disclosure of Corporate Affairs, etc.; Article 29 (1) of the Cabinet Office Ordinance on Specified Securities Disclosure; Article 16 of the Cabinet Office Ordinance on Foreign Bonds). Similar to annual securities reports, extraordinary reports and their amendment reports must also be made available for public inspection; however, the public inspection period is one year from the date of submission (Article 25 (1) (x) of the Financial Instruments and Exchange Act).

c. Attached documents

When a domestic company submits an extraordinary report upon a public offering or secondary distribution of securities overseas, it must attach: (i) in cases where permission, authorization, or approval of an administrative agency is required for the issuance, public offering, or secondary distribution of securities, a document sufficient to show that the permission, authorization or approval has been obtained; (ii) a copy of the minutes, etc. of the board of directors meeting or a copy of the minutes of the general shareholders meeting pertaining to the resolution, etc., by the board of directors or the resolution adopted at the general shareholders meeting for the issuance of the securities concerned; and (iii) in cases where a prospectus is used in the relevant public offering or secondary distribution, a copy of the relevant prospectus, and when a domestic company submits an extraordinary report upon issuance of securities via private placement, it must attach: (i)' in cases where permission, authorisation, or approval of an administrative agency is required for the issuance, public offering or acquisition of the securities, a document sufficient to show that the permission, authorization or approval has been obtained; and (ii) a copy of the minutes, etc. of the board of directors meeting or a copy of the minutes of the general shareholders meeting pertaining to the resolution, etc. by the board of directors or the resolution adopted at the general shareholders meeting for the issuance of the securities concerned (Article 19(4) of the Cabinet Office Ordinance on

Chapter 3   Disclosure requirements

Disclosure of Corporate Affairs, etc.).

In cases where the reporting company is a foreign company, in addition to (i) (or (i)') and (ii) above, it must attach (iv) a document attesting that the representative of the foreign company that is stated in the extraordinary report has legitimate authority to submit the extraordinary report; and (v) a document attesting that the foreign company has authorized a person who has residence in Japan to represent the foreign company in all acts concerning the submission of the relevant extraordinary report (Article 19 (5) of the Cabinet Office Ordinance on Disclosure of Corporate Affairs, etc.). Issuers of foreign specified securities must also submit as attached documents: (iv)' a document attesting that the representative of the foreign company that is stated in the extraordinary report has legitimate authority to submit the relevant extraordinary report; and (v)' a document attesting that the reporting company has authorized a person who has residence in Japan to represent the reporting company in all acts concerning the submission of the relevant extraordinary report (Article 29 (4) of the Cabinet Office Ordinance on Specified Securities Disclosure)

In cases where the attached documents are not written in Japanese, a Japanese translation must be attached (Article 19(6) of the Cabinet Office Ordinance on Disclosure of Corporate Affairs, etc.; Article 29(4) of the Cabinet Office Ordinance on Specified Securities Disclosure).

# 7. Internal control reports

Internal control reports are reports prepared by listed companies for each business year evaluating systems specified by cabinet office ordinance for internal controls over financial reporting as necessary to ensure the adequacy of documents on financial accounting and other information concerning the corporate group to which the company belongs and concerning the company itself (Article 24-4-4 of the Financial Instruments and Exchange Act). Here, "systems specified by cabinet office ordinance as necessary to ensure the adequacy of documents on financial accounting and other information" refers to systems to ensure that the relevant company prepares financial reports adequately in accordance with laws and

*397*

regulations, etc. (Article 3 of the Cabinet Office Ordinance on the System for Ensuring the Adequacy of Documents on Financial Accounting and of Other Information [Cabinet Office Ordinance on Internal Controls]).

The reference date is the last day of the business year of the company that must submit the internal control report (Article 5(1) of the Cabinet Office Ordinance on Internal Controls). In cases where the last day of the business year of a consolidated subsidiary differs from the last day of the company's business year, in principle the evaluation of internal controls concerning the financial reports of the consolidated subsidiary may be conducted as of the last day of the business year of the relevant consolidated subsidiary (Article 5(3) of the Cabinet Office Ordinance on Internal Controls). In cases where there are material changes in the internal controls of the relevant subsidiary such as mergers or other major reorganizations, major changes in settlement methods, or major changes in articles handled; however, in principle these must be subject to the internal control evaluation.

a. Obligatory submitter and voluntary submitter

Companies issuing shares that are listed or over-the-counter registered, preferred equity investment certificates, securities with the characteristics of shares or preferred equity investment certificates issued by a foreign person, beneficiary certificates of securities in trust whose entrusted securities are shares, preferred equity investment certificates or securities with the characteristics of shares or preferred equity investment certificates issued by a foreign person, or depository receipts representing rights pertaining to shares, preferred equity investment certificates or securities with the characteristics of shares or preferred equity investment certificates issued by a foreign person (i.e., listed companies, etc.) must submit internal control reports together with annual securities reports (or with the relevant foreign company annual securities reports, in cases where foreign company annual securities reports are submitted instead of annual securities reports etc.,) to the Prime Minister each business year (Article 24-4-4(1) of the Financial Instruments and Exchange Act; Article 4-2-7(1) of the Financial Instruments and Exchange Act Implementing Order).

Chapter 3 Disclosure requirements

Companies that must submit annual securities reports may submit internal control reports voluntarily, even if they are not listed companies, etc. (Article 24-4-4 (2) of the Financial Instruments and Exchange Act). However, issuers of specified securities are not subject to the internal control reporting system because there is no provision under cabinet order under the delegation of Article 24-4-4, paragraph 3 of the Financial Instruments and Exchange Act, and they cannot submit the reports voluntarily.

Also, it is understood that once a company submits an internal control report voluntarily, it must then continue to submit internal control reports.

b. Due date for submission and place of submission
Because internal control reports should be submitted together with securities reports each business year (Article 24-4-4(1) of the Financial Instruments and Exchange Act; Article 4 of the Cabinet Office Ordinance on Internal Controls), the due date for submission is the same as that of the annual securities report. Submission should be made to the same authority as the one to which the annual securities report should be submitted. Internal control reports must be made available for public inspection for five years after the submission date (Article 25(1)(xi) of the Financial Instruments and Exchange Act).

c. Matters to be stated in internal control reports
The matters to be stated in Internal Control Reports are specified by the Cabinet Office Ordinance on Internal Controls, and those matters not specified by the Cabinet Office Ordinance on Internal Controls should follow internal control evaluation standards pertaining to financial reporting that are generally accepted as fair and appropriate (Article 1(1) of the Cabinet Office Ordinance on Internal Controls). And the standards for evaluation and audits of internal controls over financial reporting published by the Business Accounting Deliberation Council are considered the internal control evaluation standards pertaining to financial reporting that are generally accepted as fair and appropriate (Article 4 (4) of the Cabinet Office Ordinance on Internal Controls).

*399*

Internal control reports must be prepared and submitted by domestic companies using Form 1 of the Cabinet Office Ordinance on Internal Controls and by foreign companies using Form 2 (Article 4 (1) of the Cabinet Office Ordinance on Internal Controls). On both of these forms, the reporting company must state matters regarding the basic framework of internal controls pertaining to financial reporting, the scope of evaluation, matters regarding the reference date and the evaluation procedure, matters regarding the evaluation results, supplementary notes and special notes.

Regarding matters concerning the basic framework of internal controls pertaining to financial reporting, the reporting company must state: (i) that the representative (and the CFO, if the company appoints a CFO) has responsibility for the establishment and operation of internal controls over financial reporting; (ii) the names of the standards used for establishing and operating the internal controls pertaining to financial reporting; and (iii) that there is a possibility that false statements in financial reporting cannot be completely prevented or discovered by the internal controls over financial reporting (Cabinet Office Ordinance on Internal Controls, Form 1, Note 6; Form 2, Note 7).

Regarding matters concerning the scope of evaluation, the reference date and the evaluation procedures, the reporting company must state concisely: (i) the reference date on which the evaluation of internal controls over financial reporting took place, that the evaluation of internal controls over financial reporting followed standards for the evaluation of internal controls over financial reporting which are generally accepted as fair and appropriate; and (ii) an outline of the evaluation procedures for the internal controls over financial reporting, the scope for the evaluation of internal controls over financial reporting and the process, methods, etc. whereby the scope of the relevant evaluation was decided. In cases where sufficient evaluation procedures could not be implemented concerning part of the internal controls over financial reporting because of unavoidable circumstances, the scope of that part and the reasons must be stated (Cabinet Office Ordinance on Internal Controls, Form 1, Note 7; Form 2, Note 8).

Chapter 3　Disclosure requirements

Regarding matters concerning the evaluation results, the results of the evaluation of internal controls over financial reporting should be stated. One of the following should be stated as the conclusion (Cabinet Office Ordinance on Internal Controls, Form 1, Note 8; Form 2, Note 9):

1 ) The internal controls over financial reporting are effective.

2 ) The evaluation procedures could not be conducted on part of the internal controls, but the internal controls over financial reporting are effective, specifying the evaluation procedures that could not be implemented and the reasons why.

3 ) As there are material deficiencies that should be disclosed[103], the internal controls over financial reporting are not effective, specifying the details of the material deficiencies that should be disclosed and the reasons why they were not rectified by the last day of the business year.

4 ) The results of evaluation of internal controls over financial reporting cannot be declared because material evaluation procedures could not be implemented, specifying the evaluation procedures that could not be implemented and the reasons why.

Regarding supplementary notes, the reporting company must state: (i) in cases where events with a significant impact on the evaluation of the effectiveness of internal controls over financial reporting occur between the last day of the business year and the internal control report submission date (post-balance-sheet events), details of the relevant events; and (ii) in cases where there are material deficiencies that should be disclosed on the last day of the business year and it is considered that the internal controls over financial reporting are not effective, where measures were implemented to rectify the stated material deficiencies that should be disclosed after the last day of the business year and before the internal control report submission

---

103 "Material deficiencies that should be disclosed" refers to deficiencies in internal controls pertaining to financial reporting that are highly likely to have a material impact on financial reporting (Article 2(x) of the Cabinet Office Ordinance on Internal Controls).

date, the details of the measures (Cabinet Office Ordinance on Internal Controls, Form 1, Note 9; Form 2, Note 10). Also, where there are matters to be specially noted regarding the evaluation of internal controls over financial reporting (special notes), that fact and the details of the special notes should be included (Cabinet Office Ordinance on Internal Controls, Form 1, Note 10; Form 2, Note 11).

d. Attached documents

No document is required to be attached to internal control reports for domestic companies because there are no specifications by cabinet office ordinance based on Article 24-4-4, paragraph 4 of the Financial Instruments and Exchange Act. Foreign companies, however, must submit as attached documents: (i) a document attesting that the representative of the foreign company stated on the internal control report has legitimate authority to submit the internal control report; and (ii) a document attesting that the relevant foreign company has authorized a person who has residence in Japan to represent it in all acts regarding the submission of the relevant internal control report.[104] In cases where any of the attached documents is not prepared in Japanese, a Japanese translation must be attached (Article 4 (2) of the Cabinet Office Ordinance on Internal Controls).

e. Internal control audits

Internal control reports must be audited by a certified public accountant or auditing firm that has no special interests[105] in the reporting company (Article 193-2 (2) of the Financial Instruments and Exchange Act). The audit certification should be provided as part of an internal control audit

---

104 When foreign companies submit internal control reports, foreign company internal control reports or documents pertaining to their amendments, they must authorize a person with residence in Japan to represent the relevant foreign company in all acts concerning the submission of these documents (Article 3-2 of the Cabinet Office Ordinance on Internal Controls).

105 "Special interest" in the context of internal control audits is defined the same as "special interest" in the context of financial statements audits (Article 2 of the Cabinet Office Ordinance on Audit Certification of Financial Statements) because, in general, internal control audits and financial statements audits are conducted by the same auditor (Article 11 of the Cabinet Office Ordinance on Internal Controls).

Chapter 3 Disclosure requirements

report (Article 1(2) of the Cabinet Office Ordinance on Internal Controls). The internal control audit report must be prepared based on the results of audits implemented following standards and practices regarding the auditing of internal controls over financial reporting specified by the Cabinet Office Ordinance on Internal Controls and generally accepted as fair and appropriate (Article 1 (3) of the Cabinet Office Ordinance on Internal Controls). Here, the standards regarding evaluations and audits of internal controls over financial reporting published by the Business Accounting Deliberation Council are considered the auditing standards on internal controls over financial reporting generally accepted as fair and appropriate (Article 1(4) of the Cabinet Office Ordinance on Internal Controls). The Business Accounting Deliberation Council has published "Standards for Evaluation and Audit of Internal Controls over Financial Reporting," and "Implementation Standards for Evaluation and Audit of Internal Controls over Financial Reporting." In principle, internal control audit reports should be issued by the same auditor who audits financial statements on the same occasion, and prepared together with the audit report on financial statements (Article 7 of the Cabinet Office Ordinance on Internal Controls; Implementation Standards for Evaluation and Audit of Internal Controls over Financial Reporting).

Standards for internal control audits require obtaining reasonable assurance on whether there are any material misstatements in internal control reports (Article 6(4) (iii) of the Cabinet Office Ordinance on Internal Controls). The audit results are to be stated in internal control audit reports in accordance with the categories of unqualified opinions, qualified opinions with exceptions, adverse opinions, and disclaimers (Article 6(5) (7) of the Cabinet Office Ordinance on Internal Controls).

f . Special provisions for foreign companies and companies registered with the U.S. SEC

( i ) Special provisions for foreign companies

In cases where the Commissioner of the Financial Services Agency approves a foreign company to submit documents on financial accounting disclosed in its home country as financial documents considering this not to harm public

*403*

interest or investor protection, and the Commissioner of the Financial Services Agency approves the submission of reports evaluating the internal controls over financial reporting disclosed by the relevant foreign company in its home country (including similar documents) as internal control reports considering this not to harm public interest or investor protection, except for matters considered necessary and instructed by the Commissioner of the Financial Services Agency, the terminology, forms and preparation methods of the internal control report prepared by the foreign company may be the terminology, forms and preparation methods in its home country (Article 12 (1) of the Cabinet Office Ordinance on Internal Controls). Similarly, in cases where the Commissioner of the Financial Services Agency approves a foreign company to submit documents on financial accounting disclosed in a country other than its home country and other than Japan as financial documents considering this not to harm public interest or investor protection, and the Commissioner of the Financial Services Agency approves the submission of reports evaluating the internal controls over financial reporting disclosed by the relevant foreign company in a country other than its home country and other than Japan (including similar documents) as internal control reports considering this not to harm public interest or investor protection, except for matters considered necessary and instructed by the Commissioner of the Financial Services Agency, the terminology, forms and preparation methods of the internal control reports concerning financial reporting prepared by the foreign company may be the terminology, forms and preparation methods in the relevant country other than its home country and other than Japan (Article 12(2) of the Cabinet Office Ordinance on Internal Controls)

In these cases, internal control reports must additionally state: (i) the terminology, forms and preparation methods followed in preparing the relevant internal control reports; (ii) the material differences from reports prepared based on the Cabinet Office Ordinance on Internal Controls; and (iii) in cases where a foreign auditing firm, etc. issues certification regarding the relevant internal control reports that can be considered equivalent to audit certification under Article 193-2(2) (i) of the Financial Instruments and Exchange Act, the material differences from an internal control audit

Chapter 3 Disclosure requirements

(Article 13 of the Cabinet Office Ordinance on Internal Controls).

(ⅱ) Special provisions for companies registered with the U.S. SEC
(1) In cases where specified companies (Article 1-2 of the Ordinance on Terminology, Forms and Preparation Methods of Consolidated Financial Statements) that register with the U.S. Securities and Exchange Commission (SEC) their consolidated financial statements prepared based on designated international financial reporting standards submit those consolidated financial statements; or (2) in cases where the Commissioner of the Financial Services Agency approves reporting companies that register with the U.S. SEC their consolidated financial statements prepared based on the terminology, forms, and preparation methods required for the issuance etc. of U.S. depository receipts (U.S.-style consolidated financial statements) to submit the U.S.-style consolidated financial statements as consolidated financial statements prescribed by the Financial Instruments and Exchange Act, considering this not to harm public interest or investor protection, except for matters found as necessary and instructed by the Commissioner of the Financial Services Agency, the terminology, forms and preparation methods of the internal control reports submitted by the company may be the terminology, forms and preparation methods required for internal control reports in the U.S. (Article 18 of the Cabinet Office Ordinance on Internal Controls). However, in this case, the internal control reports must be prepared in Japanese (Article 19 of the Cabinet Office Ordinance on Internal Controls). Moreover, (i) the terminology, forms and preparation methods followed in preparing the relevant internal control reports, and (ii) the material differences from reports prepared based on the Cabinet Office Ordinance on Internal Control must be stated in addition (Article 20 of the Cabinet Office Ordinance on Internal Controls).

Also, in this case, audit certification for internal control reports prepared by specified companies or prepared by companies registered with the U.S. SEC their U.S. style consolidated financial statements submitted as consolidated financial statements can, except for matters found as necessary and instructed by the Commissioner of the Financial Services Agency, be issued in accordance with the standards and practices regarding audits of internal

*405*

controls over financial reporting generally accepted as fair and appropriate in the U.S. (Article 21 (1) of the Cabinet Office Ordinance on Internal Controls). However, the internal control audit report pertaining to audit certification issued on internal control reports must state (1) the audit standards followed in preparing the relevant internal control audit report, and (2) the major differences from reports prepared based on the Cabinet Office Ordinance on Internal Controls (Article 21(2) of the Cabinet Office Ordinance on Internal Controls).

## 8. Confirmation letters

Confirmation letters are documents by the management of listed companies stating that they themselves have confirmed that the contents stated in annual securities reports, etc. are appropriate (Articles 24-4-2, 24-4-8 and 24-5-2 of the Financial Instruments and Exchange Act).

a. Obligatory submitter and voluntary submitter
Companies issuing shares that are listed or registered over-the-counter, preferred equity investment certificates, securities with the characteristics of shares or preferred equity investment certificates issued by foreign persons, beneficiary certificates of securities in trust whose entrusted securities are shares, preferred equity investment certificates or securities with the characteristics of shares or preferred equity investment certificates issued by foreign persons, or depository receipts representing rights pertaining to shares, preferred equity investment certificates or securities with the characteristics of shares or preferred equity investment certificates issued by foreign persons (i. e., listed companies, etc.) must submit confirmation letters to the Prime Minister together with annual securities reports and quarterly securities reports or semiannual securities reports (Article 24-4-2(1), Article 24-4-8(1) and Article 24-5-2(1) of the Financial Instruments and Exchange Act; Article 4-2-5 (1) of the Financial Instruments and Exchange Act Implementing Order). Also, in cases where they submit amendment reports regarding annual securities reports, quarterly securities reports or semiannual securities reports, they must submit confirmation letters for the amendment reports together with the relevant amendment reports (Article 24-4-2 (4), Article 24-4-8 (1), and

*406*

Chapter 3 Disclosure requirements

Article 24-5-2(1) of the Financial Instruments and Exchange Act).

Companies that must submit annual securities reports can submit confirmation letters voluntarily even if they are not listed companies, etc. (Article 24-4-2 (2) of the Financial Instruments and Exchange Act). However, issuers of specified securities are not subject to the confirmation letters system because there are no specifications by cabinet office ordinance based on Article 24-4-2, paragraph 3 of the Financial Instruments and Exchange Act and cannot submit confirmation letters voluntarily.

b. Due date for submission and place of submission
Because confirmation letters should be submitted together with annual securities reports and quarterly securities reports or semiannual securities reports, the due date for submission is the same as that of the annual securities reports, quarterly securities reports, or semiannual securities reports, and submission should be made to the same authority as the one to which the annual securities report should be submitted, and confirmation letters must be made available for public inspection for five years or for three years from the submission date in accordance with the public inspection period of the disclosed documents that are the subject of the confirmation letter (Article 25(1) (v) (ix) of the Financial Instruments and Exchange Act).

c. Items to be included in confirmation letters
Confirmation letters must be prepared and submitted by domestic companies using Form 4-2 and by foreign companies using Form 9-2 (Article 17-10 of the Cabinet Office Ordinance on Disclosure of Corporate Affairs, etc.). They must state that the representative (and the CFO if the company appoints a CFO) has confirmed that the stated contents in annual securities reports, etc. are appropriate under the Financial Instruments and Exchange Act (Cabinet Office Ordinance on Disclosure of Corporate Affairs, etc., Form 4-2, Note 6b; Form 9-2, Note 7b). In cases where the scope of the stated contents that were confirmed was limited, a statement to that effect and the reasons therefor; and in cases where there are other matters that should be specially noted, a statement to that effect and the details must be

*407*

stated, respectively (Cabinet Office Ordinance on Disclosure of Corporate Affairs, etc., Form 4-2, Notes 6c and 7; Form 9-2, Notes 7c and 8).

# 9. Parent company's status report

A parent company, etc. of a company that must submit annual securities reports because it issues listed securities or over-the-counter traded securities (i.e., a reporting subsidiary) must submit a report stating matters concerning shareholders of the parent company, etc. and other matters prescribed by Cabinet Office Ordinance (Article 19-5 of the Cabinet Office Ordinance on Disclosure of Corporate Affairs, etc.) as necessary and appropriate for the benefit of public interest and investor protection (i.e., a parent company's status report) to the Prime Minister for each business year of the parent company, etc. (Article 24-7 (1) of the Financial Instruments and Exchange Act). It may be necessary to submit a parent company's status report in cases where the reporting subsidiary is not a company as well (Article 27 of the Financial Instruments and Exchange Act), but a parent company, etc. of an issuer of specified securities is not required to submit a parent company's state report.

a. Parties obliged to submit a parent company's status report
The issuer obliged to submit a parent company's status report is the "parent company, etc." of the reporting subsidiary; and "parent company, etc." refers to a company which holds the majority of the voting rights of the reporting subsidiary or other party specified by cabinet order as having close relations with the reporting subsidiary (excluding companies submitting annual securities reports). Specifically, this means (i) a company that holds the majority of the voting rights of all shareholders, etc. (the voting rights of all shareholders, all members, all partners and all equity investors; in the case of stock companies, excluding the voting rights of shares with no voting rights exercisable for all matters that are subject to resolution at general shareholders meetings and including the voting rights of shares for which the reporting companies are deemed to have voting rights under Article 879, paragraph 3 of the Companies Act; Article 29-4 (2) of the Financial Instruments and Exchange Act) of the reporting subsidiary in its own name or in the name of another party (including fictitious names), and (ii) a

Chapter 3  Disclosure requirements

company which, together with another juridical person, etc. (corporation or other entity) in which it holds the majority of the voting rights of all shareholders in its own name or in the name of another party, holds the majority of the voting rights of all shareholders, etc. of the reporting subsidiary in their own name or in the name of another party (Article 4-4(1) of the Financial Instruments and Exchange Act Implementing Order).

In cases where a company, together with other juridical persons, etc. in which it holds the majority of the voting rights of all shareholders in its own name or in the name of another party (i.e., controlled juridical persons, etc.), holds the majority of the voting rights of all shareholders in another juridical person etc in their own name or in the names of other parties, the relevant other juridical person, etc. is viewed as a controlled juridical person of the relevant company (Article 4-4 (2) of the Financial Instruments and Exchange Act Implementing Order).

Also, in cases where the parent company, etc. is a person other than a company (limited to cooperative structured financial institutions, etc.), the person is obliged to submit a parent company's status report (Article 24-7 (6) of the Financial Instruments and Exchange Act; Articles 4-7 and 4-8 of the Financial Instruments and Exchange Act Implementing Order).

b. Due date for submission and place of submission
In principle, the parent company's status report should be submitted within three months from the end of the business year of the relevant parent company, etc. (or, in cases where the relevant parent company, etc. is an issuer of specified securities, the period stated by cabinet office ordinance) (Article 24-7(1) of the Financial Instruments and Exchange Act; Article 4-5 of the Financial Instruments and Exchange Act Implementing Order). However, where a parent company, etc. is a foreign company and it is found that the foreign company cannot submit the parent company's status report within three months from the end of the relevant business year because of the laws, regulations or practices in its home country or for other unavoidable reasons, it may submit the report within the period approved by the Commissioner of the Financial Services Agency as provided by cabinet

*409*

office ordinance (proviso to Article 4-5 of the Financial Instruments and Exchange Act Implementing Order; Article 19-6 of the Cabinet Office Ordinance on Disclosure of Corporate Affairs, etc.). Also, when a company that was not a parent company, etc. becomes a parent company, etc., a parent company's status report for the business year immediately preceding the business year that includes the day when the company becomes a parent company, etc. must be submitted without delay (Article 24-7 (2) of the Financial Instruments and Exchange Act).

The parent company's status report should be submitted to the Director General of the Local Finance Bureau or the Director General of the Fukuoka Local Finance Branch Bureau to which the reporting subsidiary submits its annual securities report (Article 20(3) of the Cabinet Office Ordinance on Disclosure of Corporate Affairs, etc.). Submitted parent company's status reports must be made available for public inspection for five years from the date of submission (Article 25 (1) (xii) of the Financial Instruments and Exchange Act).

Also, in cases where the parent company, etc. submits a parent company's status report or its amendment report, the parent company, etc. must send copies of those documents without delay to the reporting subsidiary and to the relevant financial instruments exchange or authorized financial instruments firms association (Article 24-7(4) of the Financial Instruments and Exchange Act). When a parent company, etc. submits a parent company's status report, the reporting subsidiary must retain and provide copies of these documents for public inspection at the reporting subsidiary's head office or principal offices and principle branch offices for five years (Article 25(1) (xii) and (2) of the Financial Instruments and Exchange Act; Article 22(1) (ii) of the Cabinet Office Ordinance on Disclosure of Corporate Affairs, etc.).

c. Items to be included in parent company's status reports

Parent company's status reports must be prepared and submitted by parent companies, etc. that are residents using Form 5-4 of the Cabinet Office Ordinance on Disclosure of Corporate Affairs, etc., and by parent companies

Chapter 3  Disclosure requirements

etc. that are not residents using Form 10-3 of the Cabinet Office Ordinance on Disclosure of Corporate Affairs, etc. (Article 19-5 (2) of the Cabinet Office Ordinance on Disclosure of Corporate Affairs, etc.).

A parent company that is a resident in Japan must, regarding the status of the reporting company, state the status of shares, etc., the status of major shareholders and the status of "directors", and include financial statements, etc. based on the Companies Act (balance sheet, profit and loss statement, statement of changes in net assets, individual explanatory notes, business reports and their attached detailed statements) (or equivalent documents in cases where the parent company, etc. is not a company; Cabinet Office Ordinance on Disclosure of Corporate Affairs, etc., Form 5-4, Note 3). It must attach an audit report pertaining to the audit by a company auditor (or by the audit committee if it has a nominating committee, etc.; or by the audit, etc. committee if it has an audit, etc. committee) and an audit report pertaining to the audit by its accounting auditor when it has an accounting auditor. Financial statements, etc. based on the Companies Act can be attached rather than included (Cabinet Office Ordinance on Disclosure of Corporate Affairs, etc., Form 5-4, Note 4).

On the other hand, a parent company, etc. that is not a resident in Japan is required to include "financial statements, etc." instead of "financial statements, etc. in accordance with the [Japanese] Companies Act." "Financial statements, etc." refers to statements equivalent to the balance sheet, profit and loss statement, statement of changes in net assets, individual explanatory notes, business reports and their attached detailed statements provided by Article 435, paragraph 2 of the [Japanese] Companies Act and Article 59, paragraph 1 of the Ordinance on Accounting of Companies. Also, documents equivalent to an audit report pertaining to an audit by a company auditor (or by the audit committee if it has a nominating committee, etc.; or by the audit, etc. committee if it has an audit, etc. committee) based on the Companies Act or a report equivalent to an audit report pertaining to the audit if the company has an accounting auditor must be attached to the relevant financial statements, etc. (Cabinet Office Ordinance on Disclosure of Corporate Affairs, etc., Form 10-3, Note 2).

*411*

However, if any of such financial statements, etc. is not required to be prepared in accordance with the laws, regulations or practices of the country of the relevant parent company etc., it is sufficient to state it instead of including the relevant documents (Cabinet Office Ordinance on Disclosure of Corporate Affairs, etc., Form 10-3, Note 2). Also, instead of including financial statements, etc., the concerned financial statements, etc. can be attached to the report, but when the relevant financial statements, etc. are not prepared in Japanese, a Japanese translation must be attached (Cabinet Office Ordinance on Disclosure of Corporate Affairs, etc., Form 10-3, Note 3).

d. Attached documents

There is no document that is required to be attached to the parent company's status reports of parent companies, etc. that have residence in Japan. However, parent companies, etc. that are non-residents must submit as attachments (i) a document attesting that the representative of the relevant foreign parent company, etc. stated in the relevant parent company's status report has legitimate authority to submit the parent company's status report, and (ii) a document attesting that the relevant foreign parent company, etc. has authorized a person who has residence in Japan to represent the relevant parent company, etc. in all acts regarding the submission of the relevant parent company's status report[106]. Also, where any attached documents are not prepared in Japanese, a Japanese translation must be attached (Article 19-5 (3) of the Cabinet Office Ordinance on Disclosure of Corporate Affairs, etc.).

## 10. Documents substituting part of annual securities report for specified securities

In cases where approval is received from the Prime Minister as not harming public interest or investor protection, persons who must submit annual

---

**106** Parent companies, etc. that are non-residents must authorize a person with residence in Japan with the authority to represent the relevant foreign parent company, etc. in all acts concerning the submission of the parent company's status report (Article 19-4 (1) of the Cabinet Office Ordinance on Disclosure of Corporate Affairs, etc.).

Chapter 3 Disclosure requirements

securities reports pertaining to specified securities can submit documents that state part of the matters required to be stated in annual securities reports prepared pursuant to laws, regulations or financial instruments exchange rules (i.e., documents substituting part of an annual securities report) together with an annual securities report not stating the matters stated in the documents substituting part of an annual securities report (i.e., the original annual securities report) to the Director General of the Kanto Local Finance Bureau (Article 24 (14) and Article 27 of the Financial Instruments and Exchange Act; Article 27-4-2 (1) of the Cabinet Office Ordinance on Specified Securities Disclosure). In this case, such a person is deemed to have submitted the documents substituting part of an annual securities report as part of the annual securities report that the issuer is required to submit (Article 24 (15) of the Financial Instruments and Exchange Act).

In order for an issuer of specified securities to receive approval from the Prime Minister to submit documents subsuming part of an annual securities report, immediately after the specified period for the relevant original annual securities report elapses, it must submit a written application for approval to the Commissioner of the Financial Services Agency that states: (i) the specified period of the relevant original annual securities report; (ii) the reasons why it needs the approval regarding submission of documents substituting part of an annual securities report; and (iii) the laws or regulations or the financial instruments exchange regulations that constitute the basis for the preparation of the relevant documents substituting part of an annual securities report (Article 27-4-2 (2) of the Cabinet Office Ordinance on Specified Securities Disclosure). In this case, in addition to its articles of incorporation and basic terms and conditions or the bylaws, an applicant for the approval who is an issuer of foreign specified securities must attach: (i) a document attesting that the representative of the relevant issuer has legitimate authority to submit the written application for approval; (ii) a document attesting that the relevant issuer of foreign specified securities has authorized a person who has residence in Japan to represent itself in all acts regarding the submission of the relevant approval application; and (iii) a legal opinion letter from a legal expert stating that the matters

*413*

concerning laws, regulations and practices stated in the relevant written application for approval are true and accurate, and the relevant provisions of the relevant laws and regulations cited in the relevant legal opinion letter. When these documents are not written in Japanese, a Japanese translation must also be attached (Article 27-4-2(4) of the Cabinet Office Ordinance on Specified Securities Disclosure).

The documents substituting part of an annual securities report can also be used for semiannual securities reports, quarterly securities reports and extraordinary reports pertaining to specified securities (Article 24-4-7(12) & (13) [documents substituting part of a quarterly securities report] and Article 24-5 (xiii) through (xvi) [documents substituting part of a semiannual securities report and documents substituting part of an extraordinary report] of the Financial Instruments and Exchange Act).

## 11. Amendment reports, etc.

In cases where there are changes to material matters that should be stated in annual securities reports, quarterly securities reports, semiannual securities reports, extraordinary reports, internal control reports or confirmation letters, or in their attached documents (hereafter in 11., referred to as "annual securities reports, etc.") or there are conditions otherwise deemed by cabinet office ordinance as necessary to amend the relevant annual securities reports, etc. for the benefit of public interest or investor protection, the reporting company must submit an amendment report (or amendment confirmation letter when concerning a confirmation letter) to the Prime Minister. Even in the absence of these grounds, if the reporting company considers that some of the contents of its annual securities reports, etc. must be revised, it must submit an amendment report or an amendment confirmation letter as the case may be (Article 24-2(1), Article 24-4-3(1), Article 24-4-5(1), Article 24-4-7(4), Article 24-5(5) and Article 7(1) of the Financial Instruments and Exchange Act).

Also, in cases where the Prime Minister finds any deficiencies in formalities in annual securities reports etc., or insufficiencies in statements on material matters to be stated therein, or discovers false statements on material

Chapter 3  Disclosure requirements

matters stated therein, omission of a statement of material matters that should be stated therein, or omission of a statement of material facts that should be stated therein in order to prevent any misunderstanding, the Prime Minister may order the submitter of the reports etc. to submit an amendment report (Article 24-2(1), Article 24-4-3(1), Article 24-4-5(1), Article 24-4-7(4), Article 24-5(5), Article 9(1), and Article 10(1) of the Financial Instruments and Exchange Act).

When a submitter of an annual securities report submits an amendment report regarding material matters stated in the annual securities report, it must make a public notice thereof pursuant to cabinet order regardless of whether the amendment report was submitted voluntarily or in response to an order to submit the amendment report (Article 24-2(2) of the Financial Instruments and Exchange Act). The public notice must be made without delay either by using EDINET whereby it places information to be publicized on a website where a large number of unspecified persons may view it (electronic public notice) or by publishing it in a daily newspaper that publishes matters on current affairs nationwide (Article 4-2-4(1) of the Financial Instruments and Exchange Act Implementing Order; Article 17-5 (2) of the Cabinet Office Ordinance on Disclosure of Corporate Affairs, etc.; Article 27-5 (2) of the Cabinet Office Ordinance on Specified Securities Disclosure). In cases of making the public notice by way of electronic public notice, the public notice must continue until the day five years have passed from the submission date of the annual securities report and its attached documents in relation to which the amendment report was submitted (Article 4-2-4 (2) of the Financial Instruments and Exchange Act Implementing Order).

Amendment reports to annual securities reports, quarterly securities reports, semiannual securities reports, extraordinary reports or internal control reports and amendment confirmation letters for confirmation letters must be made available for public inspection for the same periods as the public inspection periods of the annual securities report, quarterly securities report, semiannual securities report, extraordinary report or internal control report, or confirmation letter in relation to which the amendment

*415*

reports/letters were submitted (Article 25(1) of the Financial Instruments and Exchange Act).

## 12. Foreign company reports, foreign person reports, etc.

In certain cases, foreign companies (or foreign persons in relation to specified securities) are permitted to submit foreign company annual securities reports and their supplementary documents, foreign company quarterly securities reports and their supplementary documents, foreign company semiannual securities reports and their supplementary documents, foreign company internal control reports and their supplementary documents, and amendment reports to these reports, and foreign company confirmation letters and their supplementary documents and amendment confirmation letters, and foreign company extraordinary reports, instead of annual securities reports, quarterly securities reports, semiannual securities reports, internal control reports, and amendment reports thereto, and confirmation letters and their amendment confirmation letters and extraordinary reports (Article 24(8), Article 24-2(4), Article 24-5(7)(8) (12), Article 24-4-7(6)(11), Article 24-5(15), Article 24-4-4(6), Article 24-4-5 (3), Article 24-4-2 (6), and Article 24-4-3 (3) of the Financial Instruments and Exchange Act).

Similarly, in certain cases, issuers of foreign bonds, etc. are permitted to submit foreign person annual securities reports and their supplementary documents, foreign person semiannual securities reports and their supplementary documents, and amendment reports to these reports, and foreign person extraordinary reports, instead of annual securities reports, semiannual securities reports, extraordinary reports, and amendment reports to these reports (Article 27, Article 24(8), Article 24-2(4), Article 24-5(7), (8) & (13), Article 24-4-7(6) & (11) of the Financial Instruments and Exchange Act; Articles 14-2, 14-5, 15-2, and 15-4 and of the Cabinet Office Ordinance on Foreign Bonds).

a. Foreign company reports and foreign person reports

Foreign companies and foreign persons may submit foreign company annual securities reports or foreign person annual securities reports instead of

Chapter 3   Disclosure requirements

annual securities reports, etc. in cases considered by the Commissioner of the Financial Services Agency not to harm public interest or investor protection in light of their terminology, forms, and preparation methods (Article 24(8) and Article 27 of the Financial Instruments and Exchange Act; Article 17-2 of the Cabinet Office Ordinance on Disclosure of Corporate Affairs, etc.; Article 14-2 of the Cabinet Office Ordinance on Foreign Bonds, Article 27-2 of the Cabinet Office Ordinance on Specified Securities Disclosure). When determining whether an applied case may be approved by the Commissioner of the Financial Services Agency as not harming public interest or investor protection, the Financial Services Agency examines in advance and considers on a case-by-case basis whether the foreign preparation standards and disclosure standards pursuant to which the reference materials and documents equivalent to securities registration statements in Japan written in English are prepared and disclosed harm the investor protection compared with those in Japan, and whether those documents are properly disclosed in the foreign state. The same procedure applies to foreign company quarterly securities reports, foreign company semiannual securities reports and foreign person semiannual securities reports (Article 24-4-7(6), Article 24-5(7), and Article 27 of the Financial Instruments and Exchange Act; Article 17-6 and 18-2 of the Cabinet Office Ordinance on Disclosure of Corporate Affairs, etc.; Article 15-2 of the Cabinet Office Ordinance on Foreign Bonds; Article 28-2 of the Cabinet Office Ordinance on Specified Securities Disclosure).

Because foreign company annual securities reports and foreign person annual securities reports are documents similar to annual securities reports etc. written in English and disclosed in a foreign state, the matters required to be stated in foreign company annual securities reports and foreign person annual securities reports are, aside from information on securities not being included, the same as the matters required to be stated in the foreign company registration statement. "Disclosed in a foreign state" means that it is made available for public inspection based on the laws and regulations of the relevant foreign state (including the regulations of operators of foreign financial instruments markets or operators of markets with the characteristics of an over-the-counter traded securities market established

*417*

in a foreign state as equivalent to a foreign financial instruments market).

Also, the supplementary documents to foreign company annual securities reports (a Japanese translation of a summary of the matters specified by cabinet office ordinance as necessary and appropriate for the benefit of public interest or investor protection among the matters stated in the relevant foreign company annual securities report, documents stating matters not stated in the relevant foreign company annual securities report but specified by cabinet office ordinance as necessary and appropriate for the benefit of public interest or investor protection, and other documents specified by cabinet office ordinance) are the same as the supplementary documents (and partly the same as the attached documents) to the foreign company registration statement, except for the requirement for preparation of a cover sheet in accordance with Form 8-2 of the Cabinet Office Ordinance on Disclosure of Corporate Affairs, etc. (Article 17-3 of the Cabinet Office Ordinance on Disclosure of Corporate Affairs, etc.). The supplementary documents to foreign company annual securities reports pertaining to specified securities are also the same as the supplementary documents (and partly the same as the attached documents) to the foreign company registration statement, except for the requirement for preparation of a cover sheet in accordance with Form 7-2-3 of the Cabinet Office Ordinance on Specified Securities Disclosure (Article 27-3(3) of the Cabinet Office Ordinance on Specified Securities Disclosure).

Similarly, the supplementary documents to foreign person annual securities reports are the same as the supplementary documents (and partly the same as the attached documents) to the foreign person registration statement, except for the requirement for preparation of a cover sheet in accordance with Form 4-2 of the Cabinet Office Ordinance on Foreign Bonds (Article 14-3 of the Cabinet Office Ordinance on Foreign Bonds).

Matters Not Stated: Among matters required to be stated in forms of disclosure documents in Japanese, those that are not stated in corresponding disclosure documents in English.

Chapter 3   Disclosure requirements

Comparison Table: Table comparing matters required to be stated in forms of disclosure documents in Japanese with corresponding matters stated in corresponding disclosure documents in English.

Document Certifying Authority of Representative: A document attesting that the representative of the relevant foreign company has legitimate authority to submit the disclosure documents in English (or notification of securities public offering or secondary distribution).

Power of Attorney: A document attesting that the relevant foreign company has authorized a person who has residence in Japan to represent the relevant foreign company in all acts regarding the submission of the relevant disclosure documents in English (or notification of securities public offering or secondary distribution).

*Regarding companies and persons submitting annual securities reports pertaining to specified securities, Article 27-3 (3) of the Cabinet Office Ordinance on Specified Securities Disclosure provides the matters to be included in supplementary documents to foreign company annual securities reports, Article 29-3 of the Cabinet Office Ordinance on Specified Securities Disclosure provides the matters to be included in supplementary documents to foreign company semiannual securities reports, and Article 11-5, paragraph 2 of the Cabinet Office Ordinance on Specified Securities Disclosure provides the matters to be included in supplementary documents to foreign company registration statements, respectively.

** Matters for which a Japanese translation of a summary should be prepared must be written in Japanese.

*** Matters constituting results of evaluations of internal controls pertaining to financial reports in cases where foreign companies do not state such matters in foreign company internal control reports (Notes regarding Disclosure of Foreign Company Registration Statements, etc., E7-2).

Foreign company reports and their supplementary documents and foreign

*419*

# Table 3-7

| | Foreign Company Registration Statement* | Foreign Company Annual Securities Report* | Foreign Company Quarterly Securities Report* | Foreign Company Semiannual Securities Report | Foreign Company Confirmation Letter | Foreign Company Internal Control Report | Foreign Parent Company's Status Report |
|---|---|---|---|---|---|---|---|
| Movement of major management indicators | ○ | ○ | ○ | ○ | | | |
| Description of Business | ○ | ○ | ○ (Cases where there were important changes in the relevant quarterly consolidated cumulative period) | ○ (Cases where there were important changes in the relevant interim consolidated period) | | | |
| Business risk, etc. | ○ | ○ | ○ (Cases where during the relevant quarterly consolidated cumulative period matters with a potential material impact on investors' decisions, such as abnormal changes in financial position, operating results or cash flow conditions, took place, or cases where there were material changes to "business risk.etc." stated in the annual securities report [foreign company report] for the previous business year). | ○ (Cases where during the relevant semiannual consolidated period matters with a potential material impact on investors' decisions, such as abnormal changes in financial position, operating results or cash flow conditions took place, or cases where there were material changes to "business risk, etc." stated in the annual securities report [or foreign company report] for the previous business year). | | | |
| Requirement of Japanese translation of a summary of the matters | Matters other than those above recognised by the reporting foreign company as necessary and appropriate for the benefit of public interest and investor protection | | | | Matters regarding the appropriateness of contents stated in annual securities reports / special instructions | Matters regarding the basic framework of internal controls over financial reports /matters regarding the scope of evaluation, base date and evaluation procedures / matters regarding evaluation results / supplementary matters /special instructions | Financial statements, etc. |

| | | | | | |
|---|---|---|---|---|---|
| Among matters not stated, documents in English or Japanese stating matters for which a Japanese translation of its summary should be prepared (with a Japanese translation of its summary attached when the documents are in English) | | | | | ○* |
| Documents with matters not stated (other than those above) in English or Japanese | | | | | ○ |
| Comparison table | | ○ | | | |
| Document certifying authority of representative / Power of attorney | Submitted as attached documents | ○ | ○ | ○ | ○ |
| Others | Cover sheet prepared using Form 8-2 of the Cabinet Office Ordinance on Disclosure of Corporate Affairs | Cover sheet prepared using Form 8-2 of the Cabinet Office Ordinance on Disclosure of Corporate Affairs | Coversheet prepared using Form 8-2 of the Cabinet Office Ordinance on Disclosure of Corporate Affairs. Matters instructed by the Commissioner of the Financial Services Agency as necessary for the benefit of public interest and investor protection written in Japanese | Cover sheet prepared using Form 3 of the Cabinet Office Ordinance on Disclosure of Internal Controls. / Matters instructed by the Commissioner of the Financial Services Agency as necessary for the benefit of public interest and investor protection written in Japanese*** | Cover sheet prepared using Form 10-4 of the Cabinet Office Ordinance on Disclosure of Corporate Affairs |

person annual securities reports and their supplementary documents must be submitted within four months of the end of the business year in principle (Article 24(10) and Article 27 of the Financial Instruments and Exchange Act; Article 4-2-2 of the Financial Instruments and Exchange Act Implementing Order). However, in cases where it is considered not possible to submit the report within four months because of the laws and regulations or practices in the home country or other inevitable grounds, submission may be made within the period approved by the Commissioner of the Financial Services Agency in advance (proviso to Article 4-2-2 of the Financial Instruments and Exchange Act Implementing Order).

When foreign company annual securities reports and their supplementary documents or foreign person annual securities reports and their supplementary documents are submitted under the Financial Instruments and Exchange Act, they are deemed annual securities reports and their submissions are deemed the submission of annual securities reports and these documents are subject to the Financial Instruments and Exchange Act (Article 24(11) and Article 27 of the Financial Instruments and Exchange Act).

b. Foreign company quarterly securities reports, foreign company semiannual securities reports and foreign person semiannual securities reports

Foreign companies and foreign persons may submit foreign company quarterly securities reports, foreign company semiannual securities reports or foreign person semiannual securities reports instead of quarterly securities reports or semiannual securities reports in cases considered by the Commissioner of the Financial Services Agency not to harm public interest or investor protection in light of their terminology, forms, and preparation methods (Article 24-4-7(6), Article 24-5(7) and Article 27 of the Financial Instruments and Exchange Act; Articles, 17-6 and 18-2 of the Cabinet Office Ordinance on Disclosure of Corporate Affairs, etc.; Article 15-2 of the Cabinet Office Ordinance on Foreign Bonds, Article 28-2 of the Cabinet Office Ordinance on Specified Securities Disclosure).

Chapter 3   Disclosure requirements

Foreign company semiannual securities reports and foreign person semiannual reports are documents similar to semiannual securities reports disclosed in a foreign state written in English, and foreign company quarterly securities reports are documents similar to quarterly securities reports disclosed in a foreign state written in English.

Foreign company quarterly securities reports, foreign company semiannual securities reports and foreign person semiannual securities reports are required to include supplementary documents (Article 24-4-7(7), Article 24-5(8), Article 27 of the Financial Instruments and Exchange Act; Article 17-17 of the Cabinet Office Ordinance on Disclosure of Corporate Affairs, etc.; Article 15-3 of the Cabinet Office Ordinance on Foreign Bonds; Article 28-3 of the Cabinet Office Ordinance on Specified Securities Disclosure) (see Table 7).

The due date and place for submission of foreign company quarterly securities reports, foreign company semiannual securities reports and foreign person semiannual securities reports are the same as those for quarterly securities reports and semiannual securities reports.

When a foreign company submits a foreign company quarterly securities report and its supplementary documents under the Financial Instruments and Exchange Act, the relevant foreign company quarterly securities report and its supplementary documents are deemed a quarterly securities report and their submission is deemed the submission of a quarterly securities report, and these documents are subject to the Financial Instruments and Exchange Act (Article 24-4-7 (8) of the Financial Instruments and Exchange Act). Similarly, when a foreign company submits a foreign company semiannual securities report and its supplementary documents, and when an issuer of foreign bonds, etc. submits a foreign person semiannual securities report and its supplementary documents, the relevant foreign company semiannual securities report or foreign person semiannual securities report and their supplementary documents are deemed a semiannual securities report and their submission is deemed the submission of a semiannual securities report and these documents are subject to the

*423*

Financial Instruments and Exchange Act (Article 24-5(9) and Article 27 of the Financial Instruments and Exchange Act).

　　c . Foreign company extraordinary reports, foreign company confirmation letters and foreign company internal controls reports
Foreign companies may submit foreign company extraordinary reports instead of extraordinary reports where considered by the Commissioner of the Financial Services Agency not to harm public interest or investor protection, including the case where the reasons for submitting the extraordinary report are stated in Japanese (Article 24-5 (15) of the Financial Instruments and Exchange Act; Article 19-2-2(1) of the Cabinet Office Ordinance on Disclosure of Corporate Affairs, etc.; Article 29-2 of the Cabinet Office Ordinance on Specified Securities Disclosure). Foreign company extraordinary reports (excluding those pertaining to specified securities) must be prepared using Form 10-2 of the Cabinet Office Ordinance on Disclosure of Corporate Affairs, etc. and submitted to the Director General of the Kanto Local Finance Bureau (Article 19-2-2(2) of the Cabinet Office Ordinance on Disclosure of Corporate Affairs, etc.).

Also, foreign companies may submit documents written in English containing the matters required to be stated in confirmation letters (foreign company confirmation letters) instead of confirmation letters where considered by the Commissioner of the Financial Services Agency not to harm public interest or investor protection in light of their terminology, forms, and preparation methods (Article 24-4-2(6) and Article 24(8) of the Financial Instruments and Exchange Act; Article 17-11 of the Cabinet Office Ordinance on Disclosure of Corporate Affairs, etc.). Similarly, foreign companies may submit documents written in English containing the matters required to be stated in internal control reports (foreign company internal control reports) instead of internal control reports where considered by the Commissioner of the Financial Services Agency not to harm public interest or investor protection in light of their terminology, forms, and preparation methods (Article 24-4-4(6) and Article 24(8) of the Financial Instruments and Exchange Act; Article 14 of the Cabinet Office Ordinance on Internal Controls).

Chapter 3   Disclosure requirements

Foreign company confirmation letters and foreign company internal control reports may only be submitted in cases where foreign company annual securities reports have been submitted (Article 24-4-2 (6) and Article 24-4-4 (3) of the Financial Instruments and Exchange Act). Also, while there are no clear provisions that allow a foreign company to submit foreign company extraordinary reports only where the foreign company has submitted foreign company annual securities reports, it is considered appropriate that foreign company extraordinary reports may only be submitted in cases where foreign company annual securities reports, etc. have already been submitted ("Results of Public Comments on Draft Cabinet Orders and Draft Cabinet Office Ordinance Regarding the 2011 Revision of the Financial Instruments and Exchange Act [to be Implemented within One Year]," "Outline of Comments and FSA's Position on Comments" [February 10, 2012], p. 41, No. 100). Also, while basically the Commissioner of the Financial Services Agency does not consider in advance each time whether an extraordinary report has been submitted, because it is necessary to confirm that the relevant foreign company has submitted a foreign company annual securities report and other matters, companies are requested to consult with the Kanto Local Finance Bureau before submission (*Ibid.*, p. 42, Nos. 103 and 104).

Foreign company extraordinary reports, foreign company confirmation letters and foreign company internal control reports do not have to have been provided for public inspection in the relevant foreign state based on the laws and regulations of the relevant foreign state, but can be newly prepared in English (Article 24-5(15), Article 24-4-2(6), Article 24-4-3(3), Article 24-4-4(6) and Article 24-4-5(3) of the Financial Instruments and Exchange Act).

Foreign company confirmation letters and foreign company internal control reports must have supplementary documents attached (Article 24-4-2(6), Article 24-4-4 (6) and Article 24 (9) of the Financial Instruments and Exchange Act; Article 17-2 of the Cabinet Office Ordinance on Disclosure of Corporate Affairs, etc.; Article 15 of the Cabinet Office Ordinance on Internal Controls) (see Table 7).

*425*

When a reporting foreign company submits a foreign company extraordinary report under the Financial Instruments and Exchange Act, the foreign company extraordinary report is deemed an extraordinary report and its submission is deemed the submission of an extraordinary report, and the report is subject to the Financial Instruments and Exchange Act (Article 24-5(16) of the Financial Instruments and Exchange Act).

d. Foreign company amendment reports, foreign person amendment reports, and foreign company amendment confirmation letters

The provisions regarding amendment reports apply *mutatis mutandis* to cases where foreign companies that have submitted foreign company annual securities reports or foreign persons that have submitted foreign person annual securities reports submit amendment reports to foreign company annual securities reports or foreign person annual securities reports or to their supplementary documents (Article 24-2(4), Article 24(8), Article 7 (2), Article 9(2), Article 10(2), and Article 27 of the Financial Instruments and Exchange Act). Namely, foreign companies or foreign persons may submit foreign company amendment reports or foreign person amendment reports (i.e., documents similar to the relevant amendment reports which are disclosed in a foreign state written in English) instead of amendment reports in cases considered by the Commissioner of the Financial Services Agency not to harm public interest or investor protection in light of their terminology, forms, and preparation methods (Article 17-8 of the Cabinet Office Ordinance on Disclosure of Corporate Affairs, etc.; Article 14-5 of the Cabinet Office Ordinance on Foreign Bonds; Article 27-8 of the Cabinet Office Ordinance on Specified Securities Disclosure).

Excluding the document certifying the authority of the representative and the power of attorney, the same supplementary documents as those to foreign company annual securities reports and foreign person annual securities reports must be attached to foreign company amendment reports and foreign person amendment reports. In addition, documents stating in Japanese the submission date of the foreign company annual securities report or foreign person annual securities report that is subject to the amendments, and the reasons for and part and details of the amendments

*426*

Chapter 3    Disclosure requirements

must be attached as supplementary documents (Article 24-2(4), Article 24 (9) and Article 27 of the Financial Instruments and Exchange Act; Article 17-9 of the Cabinet Office Ordinance on Disclosure of Corporate Affairs, etc.; Article 14-6 of the Cabinet Office Ordnance on Foreign Bonds; Article 27-9 of the Cabinet Office Ordinance on Specified Securities Disclosure).

Submission of foreign company semiannual amendment reports and foreign person semiannual amendment reports is also permitted under the same conditions (Article 24-5(12)(7) and Article 27 of the Financial Instruments and Exchange Act; Article 18-4 of the Cabinet Office Ordinance on Disclosure of Corporate Affairs, etc.; Article 15-4 of the Cabinet Office Ordinance on Foreign Bonds; Article 28-4 of the Cabinet Office Ordinance on Specified Securities Disclosure), and their supplementary documents are also prescribed in parallel with the supplementary documents to foreign company amendment reports and foreign person amendment reports (Article 18-5 of the Cabinet Office Ordinance on Disclosure of Corporate Affairs, etc.; Article 15-5 of the Cabinet Office Ordinance on Foreign Bonds; Article 28-5 of the Cabinet Office Ordinance on Specified Securities Disclosure).

Submission of foreign company quarterly amendment reports, foreign company internal control amendment reports and foreign company amendment confirmation letters is also permitted (Article 27-4-7(11)(6), Article 24-4-5(3), Article 24-4-3(3) and Article 24(8) of the Financial Instruments and Exchange Act), on condition that submission of such reports or letters instead of the relevant amended quarterly securities reports, amended internal control reports or amended confirmation letters, respectively, is considered by the Commissioner of the Financial Services Agency not to harm public interest or investor protection in light of their terminology, forms, and preparation methods (Articles 17-16 and 17-13 of the Cabinet Office Ordinance on Disclosure of Corporate Affairs, etc.; Article 16 of the Cabinet Office Ordinance on Internal Controls).

In addition to the same supplementary documents as those to foreign company quarterly securities reports and foreign company confirmation letters, documents stating in Japanese the submission date of the foreign company quarterly securities report or foreign company confirmation letter that is subject to the amendments and the reasons for and part and details of the amendments must be attached as supplementary documents to foreign company quarterly amendment reports or foreign company amendment confirmation letters (Articles 17-19 and 17-14 of the Cabinet Office Ordinance on Disclosure of Corporate Affairs, etc.). Documents required to be attached to foreign company internal control amendment reports are a cover sheet (prepared in accordance with Form 3 of the Cabinet Office Ordinance on Internal Controls) and documents stating in Japanese the submission date of the internal control report and its supplementary documents that are subject to the amendment and the reasons for and part and details of the amendments (Article 17 of the Cabinet Office Ordinance on Internal Controls).

However, when describing the "part and details of the amendments" in the supplementary documents of foreign company amendment reports, foreign company amendment confirmation letters, foreign company quarterly amendment reports, foreign company semiannual amendment reports, foreign company internal control amendment reports, foreign person amendment reports and foreign person semiannual amendment reports, it is sufficient to state titles, etc. in Japanese; and the specific part and details can be described in either Japanese or English (Notes regarding Disclosure by Foreign Company Registration Statement, etc., B4-3, B4-4, C5-4, D6-4 and E7-3).

    e. Foreign parent company's status reports
A parent company, etc.[107] that is a foreign company must submit the parent company's status reports. A foreign parent company may submit documents stating the matters that should be stated in a parent company's status report

---

**107** Parent companies, etc. that submit foreign parent company's status reports must authorize a person with residence in Japan to represent the relevant foreign parent company, etc. in all acts concerning the submission of the foreign parent company's status report (Article 19-4 (2) of the Cabinet Office Ordinance on Disclosure of Corporate Affairs, etc.).

Chapter 3  Disclosure requirements

written in English (i.e., a foreign parent company's status report) instead of a parent company's status report where considered by the Commissioner of the Financial Services Agency not to harm public interest or investor protection in light of their terminology, forms, and preparation methods (Article 24-7 (5) and Article 24 (8) of the Financial Instruments and Exchange Act; Article 19-7 of the Cabinet Office Ordinance on Disclosure of Corporate Affairs, etc.). Consequently, the foreign parent company's status reports do not have to be the ones provided for public inspection in the relevant foreign state based on the laws and regulations of the relevant foreign state, and can be newly prepared in English.

Foreign parent company's status reports also require supplementary documents (Article 24-7(5) and Article 24-9 of the Financial Instruments and Exchange Act; Article 19-8 of the Cabinet Office Ordinance on Disclosure of Corporate Affairs, etc.).

The due date for submission is the same as that for the parent company's status report of the parent company, etc. that is a foreign company. The reports should be submitted to the Director General of the Local Finance Bureau or the Director General of the Fukuoka Local Finance Bureau where the reporting company submits its annual securities report (Article 19-10 (1) of the Cabinet Office Ordinance on Disclosure of Corporate Affairs, etc.).

In cases where a parent company, etc. that is a foreign company submits a foreign parent company's status report and its supplementary documents, the foreign parent company's status report and the supplementary documents are deemed a parent company's status report, and their submission is deemed the submission of a parent company's status report, and these documents are subject to the Financial Instruments and Exchange Act (Article 24-7(5) and Article 24(1) of the Financial Instruments and Exchange Act).

# 13. Share buyback reports

a. Grounds for submission and parties obliged to submit reports

A company that issues listed share certificates, etc. must submit a share

*429*

buyback report when it has determined to buy back its shares under agreements with its shareholders, etc. by way of a resolution of a shareholders meeting set forth in Article 156, paragraph 1 of the Companies Act, a resolution of a board of directors meeting (including cases where the resolution is made at a board of directors meeting based on authorization pursuant to the articles of incorporation in accordance with Article 165, paragraph 3 of the Companies Act) or a decision by equivalent organ specified by cabinet order (*i.e.*, a Board of Officers Meeting of an investment corporation; Article 4-3(3) of the Financial Instruments and Exchange Act Implementing Order) (Article 24-6 of the Financial Instruments and Exchange Act).

The securities listed in (1) through (8) below are "listed share certificates, etc.":

(1)　Shares listed on a financial instruments exchange (Article 4-6(1) of the Financial Instruments and Exchange Act)

(2)　Shares that are over-the-counter traded securities (Article 4-3(1) of the Financial Instruments and Exchange Act Implementing Order)

(3)　Investment securities listed on a financial instruments exchange (investment securities prescribed in the Act on Investment Trusts and Investment Corporations) (Article 4-3 (2) (i) of the Financial Instruments and Exchange Act Implementing Order)

(4)　Investment securities that are over-the-counter traded securities (Article 4-3 (2) (ii) of the Financial Instruments and Exchange Act Implementing Order)

(5)　Beneficiary certificates of securities in trust whose entrusted securities are shares listed on a financial instruments exchange or traded over-the-counter or investment securities mentioned in (3) or (4) above (Article 4-3 (2) (iii) of the Financial Instruments and Exchange Act Implementing Order)

(6)　Beneficiary certificates of securities in trust (limited to those whose entrusted securities are shares or investment securities; excluding those falling under (5)) that are listed securities (i.e., securities listed on a financial instruments exchange) or over-the-counter traded securities

Chapter 3　Disclosure requirements

(Article 4-3 (2) (iv) of the Financial Instruments and Exchange Act Implementing Order)

(7) Depository receipts (Article 2(1) (xx) of the Financial Instruments and Exchange Act) of shares listed on a financial instruments exchange or traded over-the-counter or securities that represent rights pertaining to investment securities mentioned in (3) or (4) (Article 4-3 (2) (v) of the Financial Instruments and Exchange Act Implementing Order)

(8) Depository receipts (limited to those which represent rights pertaining to shares or investment securities; excluding those falling under (7)) that are listed securities or over-the-counter traded securities (Article 4-3 (2) (vi) of the Financial Instruments and Exchange Act Implementing Order)

Foreign shares are not listed shares, etc.. Also, persons other than companies are not subject to the provisions prescribing the obligation to submit share buyback reports in principle (Article 27 of the Financial Instruments and Exchange Act). But because those mentioned in (3) and (4) above are deemed to be listed shares, etc., investment corporations may have to submit share buyback reports when buying back or otherwise acquiring their own investment equity in certain cases.

　　b. Due date for submission and place of submission

Share buyback reports must be submitted to the Prime Minister on the 15th day of the month following each month (reporting month), from the month which includes the date of the resolution at a shareholders meeting, board of directors meeting or investment corporation Board of Officers meeting to the month which includes the date when the period in which the company may buy back its listed shares, etc. under the resolution expires (Article 24-6(1) of the Financial Instruments and Exchange Act). The submission should be made to the same authority as the one to which annual securities reports should be submitted (Article 20 of the Cabinet Office Ordinance on Disclosure of Corporate Affairs, etc.). The public inspection period is one year (Article 25(1) (xi) of the Financial Instruments and Exchange Act).

*431*

c. Matters to be stated in share buyback reports

Share buyback reports must state matters concerning purchases of listed shares, etc. representing the company's own shares or equity conducted in each month based on the resolution of a general shareholders meeting, etc. (including cases when no purchase was made) and other matters required by cabinet office ordinance as necessary and appropriate for the public interest and investor protection (Article 24-6 (1) of the Financial Instruments and Exchange Act).

Companies, etc. that issue listed shares, etc. must prepare and submit share buyback reports using Form 17 of the Cabinet Office Ordinance on Disclosure of Corporate Affairs, etc. (Article 19-3 of the Cabinet Office Ordinance on Disclosure of Corporate Affairs, etc.). Namely, they must state the status of acquisition, the status of processing and the status of holdings. In the case of stock companies, the status of acquisition should be stated in two separate parts: the status of acquisition under a resolution of a shareholders meeting; and the status of acquisition under a resolution of a board of directors, etc. meeting. Also, the status of processing should be stated in three separate parts: acquired treasury shares for which the company solicited subscribers; acquired treasury shares that were cancelled; and acquired treasury shares that were transferred in the course of a merger, share exchange or demerger.

d. Amendment reports

Companies that have submitted share buyback reports must submit amendment reports (or amendment confirmation letters, in cases of confirmation letters) to the Prime Minister, in cases where there are changes to material matters that should be stated on a share buyback report and in cases where there are conditions otherwise deemed by cabinet office ordinance as necessary to amend the relevant report for the public interest and investor protection. Even in the absence of these grounds, if the reporting company considers that some of the contents of share buyback reports must be amended, it must submit an amendment report or an amendment confirmation letter as the case may be (Article 24-6(2) and Article 7(1) of the Financial Instruments and Exchange Act). In certain

Chapter 3   Disclosure requirements

cases, the Prime Minister may order submission of an amendment report (Article 24-6 (2), Article 9 (1), and Article 10 (1) of the Financial Instruments and Exchange Act).

## 14. Disclosure of distribution in markets for professional investors

Under cabinet office ordinance, issuers of securities for professional investors[108] must provide information prescribed by cabinet office ordinance as information regarding the issuer (i.e., issuer's information) to persons holding their securities issued for professional investors or publish the information once or more each business year. Also, under Article 27-31, paragraph 2 of the Financial Instruments and Exchange Act, issuers who are not described above but have provided specified information on securities themselves or through consignment to others, or published specified information on securities on the Internet or by other methods, must publish or provide the issuer's information to persons holding securities pertaining to which it provided or published specified information on securities (Article 27-32(1) of the Financial Instruments and Exchange Act). However, such provision or publication of information is not required in cases specified by a cabinet office ordinance as not harming public interest or investor protection considering the marketability of securities and other conditions (proviso to

---

**108** Securities for professional investors means: (i) securities in relation to which solicitation for acquisition was that for professional investors only (i.e. solicitation for acquisition falling under Article 2, paragraph 3, item 2(b) of the Financial Instruments and Exchange Act); (ii) securities in relation to which solicitation for acquisition etc. was that for professional investors only (i.e., solicitation for acquisition of type I securities falling under Article 2, paragraph 4, item 2(b) of the Financial Instruments and Exchange Act; excluding the sale and purchase of securities on a financial instruments exchange market, equivalent transactions, and other securities transactions specified by cabinet order); (iii) securities issued by issuers of securities listed in either (i) or (ii) that are specified by cabinet office ordinance as falling under the same class of securities listed in (i) or (ii); and (iv) specified listed securities and other securities specified by cabinet order as having an equivalent marketability. However, this excludes those falling under any item of Article 24, paragraph 1 of the Financial Instruments and Exchange Act and those specified by cabinet order as having a small prospect of being held by a large number of professional investors (Article 4(3) of the Financial Instruments and Exchange Act).

*433*

Article 27-32(1) of the Financial Instruments and Exchange Act). Namely, the provision and publication of issuer's information is not required in cases where: (i) information is disclosed in relation to the securities concerned or other securities issued by the same issuer; (ii) the Commissioner of the Financial Services Agency has approved that the securities concerned are not considered securities for professional investors; or (iii) the Commissioner of the Financial Services Agency has approved of not providing and publishing the issuer's information because the Commissioner recognizes that the issuer is under liquidation or has suspended business (Article 7 (5) of the Cabinet Office Ordinance on the Provision and Publication of Information on Securities).

Also, when securities that were not for professional investors become securities for professional investors, the issuer must provide issuer's information to persons holding the relevant securities or publish the information without delay (Article 27-32(2) of the Financial Instruments and Exchange Act). However, this obligation does not apply to certain cases specified by cabinet office ordinance as follows: information is disclosed in relation to the securities concerned or other securities of the same issuer; specified information on securities regarding the securities concerned is provided or published and matters concerning the business and accounting in the immediately prior business year are disclosed; and solicitation for acquisition of securities of the same class as the securities concerned has been made only to professional investors (Article 8(1) of the Cabinet Office Ordinance on the Provision and Publication of Information on Securities). In cases where any matters in issuer's information must be amended, the issuer must provide or publish such amendments (i.e., amendment of issuer's information) based on cabinet office ordinance (Article 27-32 (3) of the Financial Instruments and Exchange Act). Once issuer's information is published, the issuer's information and any amendment of the issuer's information must be continuously published from the publication date until the date of provision or publication of issuer's information pertaining to the subsequent business year (Article 27-32(4) of the Financial Instruments and Exchange Act). However, in cases where securities come to fall under any item of Article 7, paragraph 5 of the Cabinet Office Ordinance on the

Chapter 3 Disclosure requirements

Provision and Publication of Information on Securities that provide for cases where the provision or publication of issuer's information is not required, and in cases where the securities concerned cease to exist because they are withdrawn or redeemed, the publication period ends at the time of such event (Article 10 of the Cabinet Office Ordinance on the Provision and Publication of Information on Securities).

"Issuer's information" is: for specified listed securities, etc. (specified listed securities [Article 2(33) of the Financial Instruments and Exchange Act] and securities that the issuer attempts to list on a specified financial instruments exchange market), information specified by the rules set by the financial instruments exchange where the issuer lists or attempts to list its securities; for specified over-the-counter traded securities, etc. (specified over-the-counter traded securities and securities which the issuer attempts to register with an authorized financial instruments firms association), information specified by the rules set by the authorized financial instruments firms association where the issuer registers or attempts to register its securities; and for other securities, information designated by the Commissioner of the Financial Services Agency. However, in cases where any information on specified listed securities, etc. or specified over-the-counter traded securities is considered not appropriate to be treated as issuer's information for the benefit of public interest or investor protection, issuers should follow instructions of the Commissioner of the Financial Services Agency (proviso to Article 7(2) of the Cabinet Office Ordinance on the Provision and Publication of Information on Securities). Also, "issuer's information" must include a statement that the relevant information is issuer's information, matters concerning issued securities other than the securities concerned (in cases of specified securities, matters concerning the details and operation of assets under management including funds and managed assets), and matters concerning business and accounting of the issuer (in cases of specified securities, matters concerning the persons operating assets under management, etc.) (Article 7(3) of the Cabinet Office Ordinance on the Provision and Publication of Information on Securities).

*435*

For example, regarding issuers of securities listed on the TOKYO PRO market or the TOKYO PRO BOND market, Articles 128 and 217 of the Tokyo Stock Exchange Special Regulations of Securities Listing Regulations Concerning Specified Listed Securities stipulate that issuers who list stocks must prepare and publish issuer's information within three months from the end of the immediately preceding business year and the end of the immediately preceding interim accounting period, and issuers who list bonds must prepare and publish issuer's information within three months from the immediately preceding business year (or within the period approved by the Tokyo Stock Exchange under its implementing rules in cases where the relevant stock exchange recognizes that the issuer's information cannot be prepared and published within the prescribed period for unavoidable reasons).

Also, Article 116 of the Implementing Rules for the Special Regulations of Securities Listing Regulations Concerning Specified Listed Securities stipulates as follows regarding issuer's information prescribed by Article 128 of the Special Regulations of Securities Listing Regulations Concerning Specified Listed Securities.

First, the contents of issuer's information are defined as the information prescribed by each item of Article 7, paragraph 3 of the Cabinet Office Ordinance on the Provision and Publication of Information on Securities and other information concerning matters listed in appended Form 4. Second, in preparing issuer's information, listed companies must use attached Form 4 or other forms deemed appropriate by the Tokyo Stock Exchange. Third, the financial documents required for issuer's information must be prepared based on Japanese accounting standards, U.S. accounting standards or international accounting standards, or other accounting standards prescribed by implementing rules. Fourth, the means of publication is via posting on the website of the Tokyo Stock Exchange or on the website of the listed company. In cases of choosing the latter method, the issuer must promptly submit the relevant published documents to the Tokyo Stock Exchange; and in cases where the Tokyo Stock Exchange accepts the published documents it promptly posts the published documents on the Tokyo Stock Exchange

Chapter 3   Disclosure requirements

website. Fifth, audit reports, etc. attached to financial documents required to be included in issuer's information must state unqualified opinions, unqualified conclusions or equivalent opinions or conclusions, and meet all the following requirements: (i) they must state the conclusions of audits or reviews implemented based on audit standards, interim audit standards, quarterly review standards or equivalent standards generally accepted as fair and appropriate in Japan; (ii) they must state a certificate corresponding to an audit certificate specified in Article 193-2 of the Financial Instruments and Exchange Act or an equivalent certificate; (iii) they must be prepared by an audit corporation; and (iv) they must be concerning the most recent business year or consolidated fiscal year.

Attached Form 4 has two sections, namely, company information and special information. The company information comprises an outline of the legal system, etc. in the home country, an overview of the company, state of business, state of facilities, state of the issuer, status of accounting, foreign exchange rate movements, and an outline of the issuer's stock business. This is basically the same as the form to be used in principle for foreign companies' annual securities reports, which is provided in Form 8 of the Cabinet Office Ordinance on Disclosure of Corporate Affairs, etc. The differences are that status of treasury stock acquisition and information about transactions with related parties are required to be included in the issuer's company information, and that information equivalent to the reporting company's referenced information is not required. Also, status of accounting is only required to be disclosed on a consolidated basis. Moreover, there is no section corresponding to information on the guarantor company of the reporting company.

Also, Article 208 of the Implementing Rules for Special Regulations of Securities Listing Regulations Concerning Specified Listed Securities prescribes the as follows regarding issuer's information prescribed by Article 217 of the Special Regulations of Securities Listing Regulations Concerning Specified Listed Securities.

First, the contents of issuer's information are defined as the information prescribed by each item of Article 7, paragraph 3 of the Cabinet Office Ordinance on the Provision and Publication of Information on Securities. Second, in preparing issuer's information, issuers of listed bonds must use attached Form 10 or other forms deemed appropriate by the Tokyo Stock Exchange. Third, the financial documents required for specified information on securities must be prepared based on Japanese accounting standards, U.S. accounting standards or international accountings standards, or other accounting standards prescribed by implementing rules.

Attached Form 10 has two sections, namely company information and matters concerning securities other than the securities concerned. The company information comprises an overview of the company and the state of accounting. The overview of the company comprises three items, namely movements of principal management indicators, description of business, and status of associated companies. The status of accounting is required to be disclosed only on a consolidated basis.

## 15. Fair disclosure rules

On May 24, 2017, the Act amending the Financial Instruments and Exchange Act (Law No. 37 of 2017), which introduced the fair disclosure rule (FD Rules), was promulgated and will come into force within one year on the day that will be designate by cabinet order.

Under the FD Rules, in cases where some types of tipper provides, in relation to its business, insider information before the information is made available to the public, to a business-related parties, such information should be publicly disclosed to other investors (Article 27-36 of the Financial Instruments and Exchange Act).

Tippers to whom the FD Rules apply are 1) "listed companies, etc.", 2) "asset management companies acting for some types of listed companies, etc.", and 3) any officers as well as agents, employees or other personnel (with regard to non-officers, limited to agents, employees or other personnel who are responsible for communicating information to business-related parties) of 1) or 2) above. For the purpose of the Rules, "listed companies,

Chapter 3 Disclosure requirements

etc." includes issuers of bonds, shares, securities with options, investment units, preferred equity investment certificates, securities representing preemptive rights for new preferred equity investment, investment corporation debentures and foreign investment units that are listed on any stock exchange in Japan and over-the-counter traded. "Asset management companies acting for some types of listed companies, etc." means asset management companies retained to manage the assets of investment corporations formed under the Investment Trust and Investment Corporation Act of Japan and whose shares are traded on any stock exchange in Japan.

The information subject to the FD Rules includes non-public material information in relation to the operation, business or property of the listed companies, etc. that has not been made public and may have a material effect on investors in making their investment decisions (material information). Material information covers not only information subject to insider trading regulations but also other non-public information of a precise nature concerning an issuer or its financial products and which, if made public, would be likely to have a significant effect on the price of the relevant securities.[109]

Business-related parties (information recipients that trigger issuer's duty to disclose material information to the public) include 1) financial instruments business operators, registered financial institutions, credit rating agencies, investment corporations or other persons to be specified by cabinet office

---

[109] The Report by Task Force, Working Group on Financial Markets of the Financial System Council, on Fair Disclosure Rule (December 7, 2016) proposed that information that may have an effect on an investment decision combined with other information, but which would have no immediate effect on an investment decision, in of itself ("*mosaic jyoho*", meaning information that is a piece of a mosaic), should not be subject to the FD Rules. Accordingly, in the explanatory materials for the bill amending the Financial Instruments and Exchange Act (March, 2017), the Financial Services Agency is of the view that financial information that has not been made available to the public, should fall under material information; whereas dialogue regarding a company's strategies and explanations of products during a factory tour, and the like should be exempted.

*439*

ordinance, or their personnel, and 2) any person so specified by cabinet office ordinance as one who is highly likely to engage in trades of an issuer's securities based on the material information received by such a person specified in connection with the investor relations activities of such issuer (Article 27-36(1)(i) of the Financial Instruments and Exchange Act) [110].

Moreover, the Financial Instruments and Exchange Act excludes from the scope of business-related parties any persons to be specified by cabinet office ordinance as those who are not engaged in services relating to financial instruments business and who are employed by an entity that takes necessary measures for appropriate management of material information to be specified by cabinet office ordinances (Article 27-36(1)(i) parentheses of the Financial Instruments and Exchange Act). [111]

In addition, an issuer does not need to disclose information to the public in cases where an information recipient, under laws and ordinances or contracts, bears confidentiality obligations and obligations under which he/she is prohibited from selling, purchasing or otherwise transacting in the relevant securities before the information is made available to the public (proviso to Article 27-36(1) of the Financial Instruments and Exchange Act). However, if an information recipient divulges such information received from other business-related parties or engages in sales, purchase, or other transactions of the relevant securities before the information is made available to the public in violation of his/her obligations under the relevant laws, regulations or contracts, and the relevant issuer becomes aware of that, such information would have to be promptly disclosed by the relevant issuer unless the issuer is unable to disclose the material information due to unavoidable reasons or other circumstances to be

---

110 Judging from the discussions in the Task Force, it is expected that a Cabinet Office Ordinance will specify securities analysts as falling under category 1) above and the shareholders of the listed companies, etc. as falling under category 2) above. On the other hand, news media and the issuer's customers/suppliers would be excluded from the scope of business-related parties.

111 Judging from the discussions in the Task Force Report, the exemption will be provided for cases where a Chinese wall is established within securities firms.

*440*

Chapter 3 Disclosure requirements

prescribed by cabinet office ordinance (Article 27-36(3) of the Financial Instruments and Exchange Act).

Any issuer that is a listed company, etc., is required to make disclosure 1) simultaneously in the case of any intentional selective disclosure of material information to a business-related party (Article 27-36(1), main body of the Financial Instruments and Exchange Act); and 2) promptly upon becoming aware that the selectively disclosed information was material information in the case of any unintentional selective disclosure (i.e., communication of material information to a business related party without being aware that it was material information), or in any other cases to be specified by cabinet office ordinance where it is deemed to be difficult to make a public disclosure simultaneously with the selective disclosure (Article 27-36 (2) of the Financial Instruments and Exchange Act).

The public disclosure should be made via the Internet or any other manner to be specified by the cabinet office ordinance (Article 27-36 (3) of the Financial Instruments and Exchange Act). In addition to disclosures made via EDINET in accordance with the Financial Instruments and Exchange Act and timely disclosures in accordance with the listing rules of Japan's stock exchanges made through TDnet (Timely Disclosure network that is operated by the Tokyo Stock Exchange), issuers may make public disclosure on their websites.

Where the Prime Minister finds it necessary and appropriate for public interest or investor protection, he/she may order the person who disclosed or is considered as one who has to disclose any material information, or a witness to submit reports or materials that will be helpful, or have the officials inspect the books and documents or other articles held by these persons (Article 27-37(1) of the Financial Instruments and Exchange Act). He/she, where he/she finds it necessary for the order to report or submit materials as well as the inspection above, may inquire with public offices, or public or private organizations and request these parties to submit reports on necessary matters (Article 27-37(2) of the Financial Instruments and Exchange Act).

*441*

Where the Prime Minister finds that material information to be publicly disclosed has not been disclosed to the public, he/she may instruct the person who has to disclose the material information to the public or to take other appropriate measures (Article 27-38(1) of the Financial Instruments and Exchange Act). Where the person who had been instructed has not taken the measures instructed without any legitimate grounds, the Prime Minister may order the person to take the measures instructed (Article 27-38(2) of the Financial Instruments and Exchange Act).

# E. Civil liability

## 1. Civil liability in offering disclosure

a. False statements, etc. in securities registration statements and shelf-registration statements

( i ) Liability of the person submitting documents

i ) Liability on primary markets

When a securities registration statement (including its attached documents and amendments) or a shelf-registration statement (including amended shelf-registration statements, shelf-registration supplements, attached documents and referenced documents) contains false statements regarding material matters or omits statements of material matters that should be stated or statements of material facts that must be stated to avoid causing misunderstandings (false statements, etc.), the person who submitted the document (i.e., the issuer of the securities) shall be liable for damage suffered due to the false statements, etc. by a person who acquired the securities concerned in response to the relevant public offering or secondary distribution (Article 18 (1) and Article 23-12 (5) of the Financial Instruments and Exchange Act).

Here, a matter's importance is considered by the amount of influence it has on the investment decisions of investors.

The liability of the person who submitted the document is absolute liability;

*442*

Chapter 3   Disclosure requirements

and where the person who acquired the securities did not know about the false statements, etc., regardless of whether he/she inspected the securities registration statement or the shelf-registration statement to acquire the securities and regardless of whether he/she acquired the securities relying on the false statements, etc., the person who submitted the document bears the liability for damage. However, in cases where the person who acquired the securities knew about the false statements, etc. when he/she subscribed to acquire them, the person who submitted the document does not bear the liability for damages (proviso to Article 18 (1); Article 23-12 (5) of the Financial Instruments and Exchange Act). The burden of proof that the person who acquired the securities knew about the false statements, etc. lies with the person who submitted the document.

The amount of compensatory damages is statutory, namely: (i) the amount obtained by subtracting the market price of the securities at the time of the claim for damages (or the estimated disposal value of the securities at that time if there is no market price) from the amount paid by the person who acquired the securities for the acquisition of the securities concerned; or (ii) in cases where the person who acquired the securities disposed of the securities before claiming for damages, the amount obtained by deducting the disposal value from the amount paid for the acquisition of the securities concerned (Article 19(1) and Article 23-12(5) of the Financial Instruments and Exchange Act). However, in cases where the person who submitted the document proves that part or all of the damage suffered by the person who acquired the securities was caused by reasons other than the decline in the price of the securities concerned due to the false statements etc. in the securities registration statement or shelf-registration statements, the person who submitted the document may be relieved from the liability for that part or all of the damages (Article 19-2 and Article 23-12(5) of the Financial Instruments and Exchange Act).

This right to claim damages extinguishes if it is not exercised for three years from the time when the person who acquired the securities comes to know or should have been able to know about the false statements, etc. if exercising reasonable care (Article 20, first sentence and Article 23-12(5) of

*443*

the Financial Instruments and Exchange Act). Also, this right to claim damages extinguishes when it has not been exercised for seven years after the notification concerning the public offering or secondary distribution of the securities comes into effect (or, for shelf-registration statements, after the shelf-registration takes effect and the pertinent shelf registration supplement is submitted) (Article 20 and Article 23-12(5) of the Financial Instruments and Exchange Act). The former is interpreted to be an extinctive prescription, and the latter is interpreted to be a period of exclusion.[112]

ii) Liability on secondary markets

When a securities registration statement (including its attached documents and amendments) or a shelf-registration statement (including amended shelf-registration statements, shelf-registration supplements, attached documents and referenced documents) contains false statements regarding material matters or omits statements of material matters that should be stated or statements of material facts that must be stated to avoid causing any misunderstandings (false statements, etc.), the person who submitted the document shall be liable for damage suffered due to the false statements, etc. by a person who acquired or disposed of the securities concerned during the public inspection period of the disclosure document not through public offering or secondary distribution (Article 21-2 (1) of the Financial Instruments and Exchange Act). However, where the person who submitted

---

112 The differences between the extinctive prescription and the period of exclusion are as follows. First, the extinguishment of rights due to completion of the extinctive prescription takes effect retroactively to the initial date (Article 144 of the Civil Code), but the passage of the period of exclusion has no such retroactive force. Second, the extinctive prescription may be interrupted (Article 147 of the Civil Code). In cases where certain prescribed grounds for the interruption arise, the running period of prescription loses force and a new period of prescription begins from the time when the grounds for interruption end; but there is no interruption of the progress of the period of exclusion. Third, while the extinctive prescription takes effect only when persons receiving benefits of the prescription express the intention to receive the benefits (invocation) from the prescription (Article 145 of the Civil Code), there is no need for invocation in order for a right to extinguish due to the expiration of the period of exclusion because rights automatically extinguish with the passage of time.

*444*

Chapter 3  Disclosure requirements

the document proves that it had no intention or negligence concerning the false statements, etc. in the relevant documents, the person submitting the document does not bear liability for damages (Article 21-2 (2) of the Financial Instruments and Exchange Act).

As long as the person who acquired or disposed of the securities did not know about the false statements, etc., regardless of whether he/she inspected the securities registration statement or the shelf-registration statement to acquire or dispose of the securities and regardless of whether he/she acquired or disposed of the securities relying on the false statements etc., the person who submitted the document bears the liability for damages. However, in cases where the person who acquired or disposed of the securities knew about the false statements, etc. when he/she acquired or disposed of them, the person who submitted the document does not bear the liability for damages (proviso to Article 21-2(1) of the Financial Instruments and Exchange Act). The burden of proof that the person who acquired or disposed of the securities knew about the false statements, etc. lies with the person who submitted the document.

There are presumptive rules for valuing the amount of damage. Namely, if the existence of false statements, etc. is disclosed to the public, the amount obtained by subtracting the average market price of the securities concerned over the one month after the relevant disclosure date from the average market price (or the estimated disposal value where there is no market price) of the securities concerned over the one month before the relevant disclosure date is presumed to be the amount of damage suffered by the person who acquired the securities concerned relying on the relevant false statements, etc. within one year before the disclosure date of the facts of false statements, etc. and continues to hold the securities on the disclosure date (for details, see 2.a below).

However, the amount of damage cannot exceed (i) the amount obtained by subtracting the market price of the securities at the time of the claim for damages (or the estimated disposal value of the securities at that time if there is no market price) from the amount paid by the person for the

*445*

acquisition of the securities, or (ii) in cases where the person who acquired the securities disposed of the securities before claiming the damages, the amount obtained by subtracting the disposal value from the amount paid for the acquisition of the securities concerned (proviso to Article 21-2 (1); Article 19(1) of the Financial Instruments and Exchange Act).

Also, where the person who submitted the document proves that part or all of the damage suffered by the person who claims the damage was caused by reasons other than the decline in the price of the securities concerned due to the false statements, etc. in the relevant document, the person who submitted the document does not bear liability for that part or all of the damages (Article 21-2(4) of the Financial Instruments and Exchange Act). Also, when it is found that part or all of the damage suffered by the person who claims the damage was caused by reasons other than the decline in the price of the securities concerned due to the false statements, etc. in the relevant document and it is extremely difficult to prove the amount of the damage caused by such reasons because of the characteristics of such damage, courts can determine a suitable amount of damage for which the person who submitted the document is not liable based on the entire import of oral arguments and the results of examining evidence (Article 21-2(5) of the Financial Instruments and Exchange Act).

The Supreme Court Judgment of December 21, 2012 (*Hanrei Jiho* No. 2177, p. 51) ruled that when a reporting company announced that it had instituted rehabilitation proceedings on the same date when it disclosed to the public the facts of the false statements, under Article 21-2 (4) & (5) of the Financial Instruments and Exchange Act, there is leeway to reduce the amount of damage suffered by investors who acquired shares of the reporting company on exchange markets before the disclosure of the facts of the false statements, etc. under circumstances where: (i) the reporting company instituted the rehabilitation proceedings because of a worsening of cash flow due to the tightened lending stance of financial institutions, and the worsening of cash flow was not caused by the false statements, etc. or the disclosure of those facts; (ii) the reporting company had begun negotiations on a business and capital alliance with a leading U.S. investment bank from

Chapter 3    Disclosure requirements

about two months before instituting the rehabilitation proceedings and they expected to launch a takeover bid for shares of the company in the near future; therefore, at the time of the false statements, etc., it cannot be that the reporting company was already in a state of bankruptcy or was highly likely to go bankrupt soon; and (iii) the price of the shares of the reporting company almost consistently declined from before the submission of the extraordinary report or annual securities report until the date of the disclosure of the facts of the false statements, etc., and the price decline was caused partly by the management conditions of the reporting company or other factors unrelated to the false statements, etc.

(ⅱ)    Liability of the issuer's "directors"
　ⅰ)    Liability on primary markets

Where a securities registration statement (including its attached documents and amendments) or a shelf-registration statement (including amended shelf-registration statements, shelf-registration supplements, attached documents and referenced documents) contains false statements regarding material matters or omits statements of material matters that should be stated or statements of material facts that must be stated to avoid causing any misunderstandings (false statements, etc.), the "director" (directors, accounting advisors, company auditors or executive officers or equivalent persons) of the company that submitted the relevant disclosure documents at the time of the submission or the incorporators of the company (limited to cases where the relevant disclosure document was submitted before the establishment of the company) shall be liable for damage suffered due to false statements, etc. by a person who acquired the securities concerned in response to the relevant public offering or secondary distribution (Article 21 (1) (i) and Article 23-12 (5) of the Financial Instruments and Exchange Act). However, the "directors" or incorporators may be relieved from the liability for damages if they prove that they did not know and could not know that there were false statements, etc. in the securities registration statement or shelf-registration statement even though exercising reasonable care (Article 21 (2) (i) and Article 23-12 (5) of the Financial Instruments and Exchange Act).

*447*

Also, the "directors" or incorporators may be relieved from the liability for damages if they prove that the person who acquired the securities knew about the false statements, etc. at the time of the acquisition (proviso to Article 21(1); Article 23-12(5) of the Financial Instruments and Exchange Act).

ⅱ) Liability on secondary markets

Where a securities registration statement (including its attached documents and amendments) or a shelf-registration statement (including amended shelf-registration statements, shelf-registration supplements, attached documents and referenced documents) contains false statements, etc., the "directors" (directors, accounting advisors, company auditors, or executive officers or equivalent persons) of the company that submitted such disclosure document at the time of the submission or the incorporators of the relevant company (limited to cases where the relevant disclosure document was submitted before the establishment of the company) shall be liable for damage suffered due to the false statements, etc. by a person who acquired or disposed of the securities issued by the person who submitted the disclosure document not through public offering or secondary distribution without knowing the false statements or the omission of necessary statements (Article 22(1) and Article 23-12(5) of the Financial Instruments and Exchange Act). However, the "directors" or incorporators shall not be liable for the damage in cases where they prove that they did not know and could not know that there were false statements, etc. in the securities registration statement or shelf-registration statement even though exercising reasonable care (Article 21(2)(ⅰ), Article 22(2) and Article 23-12 (5) of the Financial Instruments and Exchange Act).

ⅲ) Burden of proof and timing of extinguishment of liability

Because there are no particular provisions, persons who acquired securities (or disposed of securities in secondary markets) must prove that damage was caused by false statements, etc. and the amount of damage. Also, because there are no particular provisions regarding the timing when the right to claim damages extinguishes, it is widely accepted that Article 724 of the Civil Code which provides for the timing of the extinguishment of the

Chapter 3   Disclosure requirements

right to claim damages in the case of torts in general applies. Namely, the right to claim damages based on Article 21, paragraph 2, item 1; Article 22, paragraph 1, and Article 23-12, paragraph 5 of the Financial Instruments and Exchange Act extinguishes by operation of prescription three years after the time when a person who acquired or disposed of the securities learns of the damage, or due to a period of exclusion 20 years after the time of the tort.

(iii)   Liability of sellers on secondary markets

Where a securities registration statement (including its attached documents and amendments) or a shelf-registration statement (including amended shelf-registration statements, shelf-registration supplements, attached documents and referenced documents) contains false statements regarding material matters or omits statements of material matters that should be stated or statements of material facts that must be stated to avoid causing any misunderstandings (false statements, etc.), sellers of the securities shall be liable for damage suffered due to the false statements, etc. by a person who acquired the securities concerned in response to the relevant secondary distribution (Article 21 (1) (ii) and Article 23-12 (5) of the Financial Instruments and Exchange Act). However, sellers of the securities concerned may be relieved from the liability for damages in cases where they prove that they did not know and could not know that there were false statements etc., in the securities registration statement or shelf-registration statement even though exercising reasonable care (Article 21 (2) (i) and Article 23-12(5) of the Financial Instruments and Exchange Act).

Also, sellers of the securities concerned shall not be liable for damages in cases where they prove the persons who acquired the securities knew about the false statements, etc. at the time of the acquisition (proviso to Article 21 (1); Article 23-12(5) of the Financial Instruments and Exchange Act).

Because there are no particular provisions, persons who acquired securities must prove that damage was caused by false statements, etc. and the amount of damage. Also, because there are no particular provisions regarding the timing when the right to claim damages extinguishes, it is widely accepted that Article 724 of the Civil Code which provides for the

*449*

timing of the extinguishment of the right to claim damages in the case of torts in general applies. Namely, the right to claim damages based on Article 21, paragraph 2, item 2 and Article 23-12, paragraph 5 of the Financial Instruments and Exchange Act extinguishes by operation of prescription three years after the time when a person who acquired or disposed of the securities learns of the damage, or due to a period of exclusion 20 years after the time of the tort.

(iv) Liability of certified public accountants and auditing firms

i ) Liability on primary markets

When financial statements (including balance sheet, profit and loss statement and other documents concerning statements on finance and accounting) pertaining to a securities registration statement or a shelf-registration statement contain false statements or omit statements of material matters that should be stated or statements of material facts that must be stated to avoid causing any misunderstandings (false statements, etc.) and a certified public accountant or auditing firm certified in an audit certification (Article 193-2(1) of the Financial Instruments and Exchange Act) that there are no false statements or the omission of necessary statements in such financial statements, the certified public accountant or auditing firm shall be liable for damage suffered due to the false statements, etc. by persons who acquired the securities concerned in response to the relevant public offering or secondary distribution (Article 21 (1) (iii) and Article 23-12(5) of the Financial Instruments and Exchange Act). However, the certified public accountant or auditing firm may be relieved from the liability for damages if they prove that they did not provide such inappropriate certification intentionally or negligently (Article 21(2) (ii) and Article 23-12(5) of the Financial Instruments and Exchange Act).

Also, the certified public accountant or auditing firm may be relieved from the liability for damages if they prove that the person who acquired the securities knew about the false statements, etc. at the time of the acquisition (proviso to Article 21(1) and Article 23-12(5) of the Financial Instruments and Exchange Act).

Chapter 3 Disclosure requirements

ii ) Liability on secondary markets

Where financial statements pertaining to a securities registration statement or a shelf-registration statement contain false statements or omit statements of material matters that should be stated or statements of material facts that must be stated to avoid causing any misunderstandings (false statements, etc.) and a certified public accountant or auditing firm certifies in an audit certification that there are no false statements or the omission of necessary statements in such financial statements, the certified public accountant or auditing firm shall be liable for damage suffered due to the false statements, etc. by persons who acquired or disposed of the securities concerned issued by the person who submitted the disclosure documents not through public offering or secondary distribution without knowing about the false statements or the omission of necessary statements (Article 22 (1) and Article 23-12(5) of the Financial Instruments and Exchange Act). However, the relevant certified public accountant or auditing firm may be relieved from the liability for damages if they prove that they did not provide such certification intentionally or negligently (Article 21 (2) (iii), Article 22 (2), and Article 23-12(5) of the Financial Instruments and Exchange Act).

iii ) Burden of proof and timing of extinguishment of liability

Because there are no particular provisions, persons who acquired securities (or disposed of securities in secondary markets) must prove that damage was caused by false statements, etc. and the amount of damage. Also, because there are no particular provisions regarding the timing when the right to claim damages extinguishes, it is widely accepted that Article 724 of the Civil Code which provides for the timing of the extinguishment of the right to claim damages in the case of torts in general applies. Namely, the right to claim damages based on Article 21 (2) (iii), Article 22 (1) and Article 23-12(5) of the Financial Instruments and Exchange Act extinguishes by operation of prescription three years after the time when a person who acquired or disposed of the securities learns of the damage, or due to a period of exclusion 20 years after the time of the tort.

*451*

(v) Liability of financial instruments business operators who are wholesale underwriters

When a securities registration statement (including its attached documents and amendments) or a shelf-registration statement (including amended shelf-registration statements, shelf-registration supplements, attached documents and referenced documents) contains false statements regarding material matters or omits statements of material matters that should be stated or statements of material facts that must be stated to avoid causing any misunderstandings (false statements, etc.), financial instruments business operators and registered financial institutions which have concluded a wholesale underwriting contract[113] with the person who issued or distributed the securities through the relevant public offering of secondary distribution shall be liable for damage suffered due to false statements, etc. by persons who acquired the securities in response to the public offering or secondary distribution (Article 21 (1) (iv) and Article 23-12 (5) of the Financial Instruments and Exchange Act). However, the financial instruments business operators and registered financial institutions may be relieved from the liability for damages in cases where they prove

---

113 A "wholesale underwriting contract" is a contract concluded for the public offering or secondary distribution of securities, falling under any of the following categories: (i) a contract in which it is agreed that a party will acquire all or part of the securities from their issuer or holder (excluding cases where the holder is a financial instruments business operator or a registered financial institution; the same shall apply hereinafter) for the purpose of having other persons acquire them (firm commitment underwriting); (ii) a contract in which it is agreed that, with regard to all or part of the securities, a party will acquire all of the remaining securities that are not acquired by any other person (stand-by underwriting); or (iii) a contract concluded for share option certificates (including bonds with share options, securities or instruments issued by foreign persons with the characteristics of share option certificates or bonds with share options; Article 14-2-2(1) of the Cabinet Office Ordinance on Disclosure of Corporate Affairs) in which it is agreed that, when persons who acquired the share option certificates do not exercise all or part of the share options (including rights to foreign persons with the characteristics of share options; Article 14-2-2(2) of the Cabinet Office Ordinance on Disclosure of Corporate Affairs) represented by the share option certificates, a party will acquire the share option certificates representing the share options that are not exercised from the issuer or holder and exercise or have a third party exercise such share options (Article 21(4) of the Financial Instruments and Exchange Act).

Chapter 3    Disclosure requirements

that they did not know that there were false statements or the omission of necessary statements and that they could not know that there were false statements or the omission of necessary statements even though exercising reasonable care anywhere other than the portion of documents on financial accounting as specified in Article 193-2, paragraph 1 of the Financial Instruments and Exchange Act[114] (Article 21(2)(iii) and Article 23-12(5) of the Financial Instruments and Exchange Act).

Tokyo District Court Judgment of December 20, 2016 (*Shiryoban Shoji Homu* No. 396, p. 171) held that Mizuho Securities, who was the lead manager at the time of FOI's listing, is liable for damage suffered by investors due to the misrepresentation in the securities registration statement of FOI despite the fact that the auditor's unqualified opinion being issued. According to Article 21, paragraph 2, item 3 of the Financial Instruments and Exchange Act, the lead manager is not required to examine the very figures in the financial and accounting part. The Court ruled, however, that the screening for underwriting covers the proper disclosure of financial information and the lead manager cannot simply rely on the result of financial audit of the financial and accounting part but is responsible for checking whether there is any circumstance to cast doubt upon the reliability of the result of the financial audit. Based on this, the Court decided that the lead manager had a duty to conduct additional investigation in order to confirm the actual state of sales, since external letters that had suggested

---

114 This means that, to be relieved from the liability for damages arising in relation to parts pertaining to documents concerning statements on finance and accounting it is sufficient for them to prove they did not know there were false statements or omission of necessary statements, and not necessary to prove they could not know even though exercising reasonable care. However, in practice, since financial instruments business operators and registered financial institutions that conclude wholesale underwriting contracts use prospectuses in selling securities and those prospectuses contain financial statements that have received audit certification, in order for them to be relieved from the liability of users of misrepresented prospectuses based on Article 17 of the Financial Instruments and Exchange Act (see below), they must exercise reasonable care as to whether there are false statements, etc. in the financial statements which received audit certification (proviso to Article 17 of the Financial Instruments and Exchange Act).

*453*

FOI's window dressing had occurred twice at the lead manager.

The financial instruments business operators and registered financial institutions may be relieved from the liability for damages in cases where they prove that persons who acquired the securities knew about the false statements, etc. at the time of the acquisition (proviso to Article 21 (1); Article 23-12 (5) of the Financial Instruments and Exchange Act).

    b. False statements in prospectuses, etc.
      ( i ) Liability of issuers preparing prospectuses
In cases where a prospectus contains false statements regarding material matters or omits statements of material matters that should be stated or statements of material facts that must be stated to avoid causing misunderstandings (false statements, etc.), the issuer who prepared the prospectus shall be liable for damage suffered due to false statements, etc. by a person who received the prospectus and acquired securities through the relevant public offering or secondary distribution (Article 18(1) & (2) and Article 23-12(5) of the Financial Instruments and Exchange Act). While this liability is absolute liability, the issuer may be relieved from the liability for the damages if the issuer proves that the person who acquired the securities concerned knew about the false statements, etc. at the time when they subscribed for acquisition of the securities (Article 18(2), proviso to (1), and Article 23-12(5) of the Financial Instruments and Exchange Act).

The amount of compensatory damages is statutory, namely: (i) the amount obtained by subtracting the market price of the securities at the time of the claim for damages (or the estimated disposal value of the securities at that time if there is no market price) from the amount paid by the person who acquired the securities for the acquisition of the securities concerned; or (ii) in cases where the person who acquired the securities disposed of the securities before claiming for damages, the amount obtained by deducting the disposal value from the amount paid for the acquisition of the securities concerned (Article 19(1) and Article 23-12(5) of the Financial Instruments and Exchange Act). However, in cases where the issuer who prepared the prospectus proves that part or all of the damage suffered by the person who

*454*

Chapter 3 Disclosure requirements

acquired the securities was caused by reasons other than the decline in the price of the securities concerned due to the false statements, etc. in the securities registration statement or shelf-registration statement, the issuer may be relieved from the liability for that part or all of the damages (Article 19-2 and Article 23-12(5) of the Financial Instruments and Exchange Act).

This right to claim damages extinguishes if it is not exercised for three years from the time the person who acquired the securities comes to know or should have been able to know about the false statements, etc. if exercising reasonable care (Article 20 and Article 23-12 (5) of the Financial Instruments and Exchange Act). Also, this right to claim damages extinguishes when it has not been exercised for seven years after the notification concerning the public offering or secondary distribution of the securities comes into effect (or, for shelf-registration statements, after the shelf registration takes effect and the pertinent shelf-registration supplement is submitted) (Article 20 and Article 23-12(5) of the Financial Instruments and Exchange Act).

(ⅱ) Liability of the issuer's "directors" and sellers

In cases where a prospectus contains false statements regarding material matters or omits statements of material matters that should be stated or statements of material facts that must be stated to avoid causing any misunderstandings (false statements, etc.), "directors" of the issuer at the time of the preparation of the prospectus and the seller of the securities shall be liable for damage suffered due to false statements, etc., by persons who received the prospectus and acquired securities through the relevant public offering or secondary distribution (Article 21(1) & (3) and Article 23-12(5) of the Financial Instruments and Exchange Act). However, the issuer's "directors" and the secondary distributors may be relieved from the liability for damages if they prove that they did not know and could not know that there were false statements, etc. even though exercising reasonable care (Article 21(3), (2) (i), and Article 23-12(5) of the Financial Instruments and Exchange Act).

Also, the "directors" and the secondary distributors may be relieved from the liability for damages if they prove that the person who acquired the securities knew about the false statements, etc. at the time of the acquisition (proviso to Article 21 (3); and Article 23-12 (5) of the Financial Instruments and Exchange Act).

Because there are no particular provisions, persons who acquired securities must prove that damage was caused by false statements, etc. and the amount of damage. Also, because there are no particular provisions regarding the timing when the right to claim damages extinguishes, the interpretation is that Article 724 of the Civil Code which provides for the timing of the extinguishment of the right to claim damages in the case of torts in general applies. Namely, this right to claim damages extinguishes by operation of prescription three years after the time when a person who acquired or disposed of the securities learns of the damage, or due to a period of exclusion 20 years after the time of the tort.

(iii) Liability of users of prospectus and materials

If a prospectus for a public offering or secondary distribution of securities that requires notification or in which false statements, etc. have already been disclosed regarding material matters or which omits statements of material matters that should be stated or statements of material facts that must be stated to avoid causing any misunderstandings or any materials [115] concerning such public offering or secondary distribution of securities contain false indications regarding material matters or indications that cause misunderstandings or omit necessary indications to avoid any misunderstandings, a person who has others acquire the securities concerned by using such prospectus or materials shall be liable for damage suffered by a person who acquired the securities without knowing about the false statements/information or the omission of necessary statements/information (Article 17

---

[115] Documents, drawings, recorded voice and other materials other than a prospectus used for public offering or secondary distribution of securities requiring notification or securities already disclosed (in cases where prepared using electromagnetic recordings, including written contents of the information recorded in those electromagnetic recordings) (Article 13 (5) of the Financial Instruments and Exchange Act).

Chapter 3 Disclosure requirements

and Article 23-12(5) of the Financial Instruments and Exchange Act).

Here, the ruling in the Tokyo High Court Judgment of August 9, 2006 (*Minshu* Vol. 62 No. 2, p. 418) limited "a person who has others acquire securities" — who is the person subject to the liability under Article 17 of the Financial Instruments and Exchange Act — to the issuer, persons conducting the public offering or secondary distribution of the securities, underwriters, securities companies, etc., and persons deemed equivalent to any of the above (issuers, etc.). However, the Supreme Court judgment of February 15, 2008 (*Minshu* Vol. 62 No. 2, p. 377), which is the judgment of the final appellate court in this case, ruled that Article 17 of the Financial Instruments and Exchange Act has "no expression that restricts the person subject to the liability to issuers, etc.," and that "considering that the [Financial Instruments and Exchange] Act provides that no one may use a prospectus for the public offering or secondary distribution of securities containing any statement different from the statutorily required statement or make any statement different from the statutorily required statement (Article 13(5)) and that the liability for damages of issuers who prepared a prospectus with false statements regarding material matters or without statements of material facts is prescribed in Article 18, paragraph 2 separately from the liability under Article 17, the person who should be liable for damages under Article 17 can be any person who is deemed to have others acquire securities using a prospectus, etc. with false statements, and cannot be limited to issuers, etc."

However, persons who have others acquire securities using a prospectus or materials containing false statements, etc. may be relieved from the liability for damages if they prove that they did not know and could not know that there were false statements or the omission of necessary statements or that there were indications that were false or causing any misunderstanding even though exercising reasonable care (proviso to Article 17 and Article 23-12 (5) of the Financial Instruments and Exchange Act).

In claiming for damages, persons who acquired securities must prove the existence of false statements, etc., the amount of damage, and that the

*457*

damage was caused by the false statements, etc.

c . False statements, etc. in continuous disclosure documents, and the securities registration statement and shelf-registration system using the [actual] incorporation method or the incorporation by reference method

In the case of securities registration statements prepared using the [actual] incorporation method, the annual securities reports, etc. (continuous disclosure documents) are considered to be part of the securities registration statement and the prospectus in which they are included (Article 5 (3) of the Financial Instruments and Exchange Act). Consequently, if there are false statements, etc. in the included continuous disclosure documents, this means that the securities registration statement and the prospectus contain false statements, etc., and the civil liability mentioned in the above section on the offering disclosure arises.

In the case of securities registration statements prepared using the incorporation by reference method, it is prescribed that the materials referenced in a securities registration statement or a prospectus are deemed to be incorporated therein by reference (Article 23-2 of the Financial Instruments and Exchange Act). Consequently, if there are false statements, etc. in the referenced materials, this means that the securities registration statement and the prospectus contain false statements, etc., and the civil liability mentioned in the above section on the offering disclosure arises.

In cases where the shelf registration system is used, civil liability applicable to the offering disclosure arises when there are false statements, etc. in the shelf-registration statement, amended shelf-registration statement or shelf-registration supplement or their attached documents or in reference materials pertaining to these documents (Article 23-12(5) of the Financial Instruments and Exchange Act).

d . Japanese translations included in supplementary documents to foreign company registration statements

When a foreign company submits a foreign company registration statement

Chapter 3  Disclosure requirements

under Article 5, paragraph 6 of the Financial Instruments and Exchange Act and supplementary documents under Article 5, paragraph 7 of the Financial Instruments and Exchange Act, these are viewed as a securities registration statement under Article 5, paragraph 1 of the Financial Instruments and Exchange Act and the Financial Instruments and Exchange Act applies (Article 5 (8) of the Financial Instruments and Exchange Act). The presence or absence of false statements, etc. is to be considered based on the actual conditions of each case. Also, even in cases where there are no errors in the original English document, in cases where there are false statements, etc. regarding material matters in the Japanese summary submitted as supplementary documents, in some cases it is deemed that the foreign company registration statement contains false statements, etc. regarding material matters ("Results of Public Comments on Draft Cabinet Orders and Draft Cabinet Office Ordinances Regarding the 2011 Revision of the Financial Instruments and Exchange Act [to be Implemented within One Year]," "Outline of Comments and FSA's Position on Comments" [February 10, 2012], p. 43, No. 110).

# 2. Civil liability in continuous disclosure

### a. Liability of the person submitting documents

When an annual securities report or its attached documents (or a foreign company annual securities report or foreign person annual securities report or their supplementary documents or attached documents) or amendment reports to these documents contain false statements regarding material matters or omit statements of material matters that should be stated or statements of material facts that must be stated to avoid causing misunderstandings, the person who submitted the annual securities report shall be liable for damage suffered by persons who acquired or disposed of its securities not through public offering or secondary distribution during the public inspection period of the relevant reports due to the false statements or the omission of statements of material matters or of material facts that must be stated to avoid any misunderstandings, except when the person who submitted the documents proves that it was neither intentional or negligent concerning the false statements, etc. in the relevant documents (Article 21-2 (1) and (2), Article 25(1)(iv), Article 24(11), Article 24-2(4), and Article

*459*

27 of the Financial Instruments and Exchange Act).

Also, in cases where there are false statements, etc. in internal control reports, foreign company internal control reports, quarterly securities reports, foreign company quarterly securities reports, semiannual securities reports, foreign company semiannual securities reports, foreign person semiannual securities reports, extraordinary reports, foreign company extraordinary reports, share buyback reports and parent company's status reports[116] or the amendment reports to these documents, the person who submitted such documents shall bear the same liability (Article 21-2(1), main body and (2), Article 25(1)(vi)(vii)(viii)(x)(xi) & (xii), Article 24-4-7(4), Article 24-5(5), Article 24-6(2), Article 24(11), Article 24-4-2 (6), Article 24-4-3(3), Article 24-4-4(6), Article 24-4-5(3), Article 24-4-7 (8), Article 24-4-8(2), Article 24-5(9) & (16), Article 24-5-2(2), Article 27 of the Financial Instruments and Exchange Act).

Where receiving a claim for damages, persons who submitted the document cannot be relieved from the liability even if they prove that the persons who acquired or disposed of the securities did not inspect the annual securities report, etc., but may be relieved from the liability for damages when they prove that the persons who acquired or disposed of the securities knew about the false statements, etc. at the time of the acquisition or the disposal (proviso to Article 21-2(1) of the Financial Instruments and Exchange Act).

The Supreme Court Judgment of March 13, 2012 (*Minshu* Vol. 66 No. 5, p. 1957), ruled that " 'damages' provided for in Article 21-2, paragraph 1 of the Financial Instruments and Exchange Act means, like damage that should be compensated for under the provisions for torts in general, all damage that is substantially caused by false statements, etc."

---

**116** Because the person who submits the parent company's status report is a parent company, etc., it is the parent company, etc., and not the issuer of the securities, which shall be liable for damage for false statements, etc. in the parent company's status report.

*460*

Chapter 3   Disclosure requirements

However, there are presumptive rules for valuing the amount of damage (Article 21-2(3) of the Financial Instruments and Exchange Act). Namely, if the existence of false statements, etc. is disclosed to the public, the amount obtained by subtracting the average market price of the securities concerned over the one month after the relevant disclosure date from the average market price (or the estimated disposal value when there is no market price) of the securities concerned over the one month before the relevant disclosure date is presumed to be the amount of damages suffered by persons who acquired the securities concerned relying on the relevant false statements, etc. within one year before the disclosure date of the facts of false statements, etc. and continue to hold the securities concerned on the disclosure date.

Here, the "disclosure" of the existence of false statements, etc. means that the person who submitted the relevant documents or persons with statutory authority over the business or assets of the person who submitted the documents have taken measures to place the material matters that should be stated regarding the false statements in the relevant documents or the material facts that must be stated to avoid causing any misunderstanding regarding the same, under conditions which allow a large number of persons to learn of the material matters through the public inspection provided in Article 25, paragraph 1 of the Financial Instruments and Exchange Act or through other means (Article 21-2(4) of the Financial Instruments and Exchange Act).

The Supreme Court Judgment of March 13, 2012 above ruled that just disclosing the fact that there are false statements, etc. in the relevant annual securities report, etc. without disclosing details does not constitute "disclosure" as provided in the Act; however, "taking the above-mentioned measures regarding basic facts sufficient to clarify the misevaluation in the exchange market of the securities issued by the person who submitted the annual securities reports, etc. with false statements, etc. is sufficient to constitute the same."

The "person with statutory authority over the business or assets of the person who submitted the documents" is considered to refer to the Prime Minister, the Financial Services Agency and the Securities and Exchange Surveillance Commission; and in cases of listed companies or over-the-counter registered companies, financial instruments exchanges and authorized financial instruments firms associations. Trustees in bankruptcy or corporate reorganization and various authorities legally authorized for supervision, inspection and the hearing of reports under various industry laws are also considered to be such person. The Supreme Court Judgment of March 13, 2012, above illustrated the interpretation that public prosecutors are also considered to be such persons because "public prosecutors have various investigative powers under the Code of Criminal Procedure regarding the crime of making false statements, etc. in annual securities reports, etc.; and based on those powers they can obtain information amending false statements, etc. in annual securities reports, etc. and correct information that should be stated in annual securities reports, etc., and that information is typically recognised as highly reliable."

Moreover, in addition to making the information available for public inspection, "measures to place ... under conditions which allow a large number of persons to learn of the material matters" include press releases, press conferences and posting on home pages by the person who submitted the relevant documents or supervisory authorities.

Even in cases where this presumptive provision applies, in cases where a person who submitted a document containing false statements, etc. proves that part or all of the damage suffered by a person who acquired the securities was caused by reasons other than the decline in the price of the securities concerned due to the false statements, etc., the person who submitted the document may be relieved from the liability for that part or all of the damage (Article 21-2(5) of the Financial Instruments and Exchange Act). Also, in cases where it is found that part or all of the damage suffered by the person who acquired the securities was caused by reasons other than the decline in the price of the securities concerned due to the false statements, etc. and it is extremely difficult to prove the amount of damage caused by such reason because of the characteristics of such damage, courts

*462*

Chapter 3   Disclosure requirements

can reduce the amount from the amount of compensatory damages based on the entire import of oral arguments and the results of examining evidence (Article 21-2(6) of the Financial Instruments and Exchange Act).

When persons who acquired securities prove that they suffered damage beyond the statutorily presumed amount, they can claim compensatory damages; however, this is limited to (i) the amount obtained by subtracting the market price of the securities at the time of the claim for damages (or the estimated disposal value of the securities at that time if there is no market price) from the amount paid for the acquisition of the securities concerned, or (ii) in cases where the persons who acquired the securities disposed of the securities before claiming for damages, the amount obtained by deducting the disposal value from the amount paid for the acquisition of the securities concerned (Article 21-2(1) and Article 19(1) of the Financial Instruments and Exchange Act).

The right to claim damages concerning false statements, etc. in annual securities reports, etc. based on Article 21-2 of the Financial Instruments and Exchange Act extinguishes if it is not exercised for two years from the time when the person who acquired the securities comes to know or should have been able to know about the false statements, etc. if exercising reasonable care (Article 21-3 and Article 20 of the Financial Instruments and Exchange Act). Also, this right to claim damages extinguishes when it has not been exercised for five years after the submission of the annual securities report, etc. (Article 21-3 and Article 20 of the Financial Instruments and Exchange Act).

The Supreme Court Judgment of March 13, 2012, above ruled that Article 21-2, paragraph 3 (paragraph 2 at that time) of the Financial Instruments and Exchange Act "is a provision presuming the amount of damages arising from false statements, etc. on the premise of paragraph 1 of the same Article and therefore" the "damages" in paragraph 3 of the same Article "should be interpreted to include all damage substantially caused by false statements, etc., and there are no grounds to limit these to the difference between the amount paid for the acquisition and the estimated market price if there were

*463*

no false statements, etc. of the securities concerned," and that the "decline in the price of the securities concerned due to the false statements, etc." in paragraph 6 (paragraph 5 at that time) of the same Article "should be interpreted to include all price declines substantially caused by false statements, etc. in the annual securities report, etc., rather than limited to the difference between the amount paid for the acquisition."

b. Liability of "directors" of person submitting documents, certified public accountants and auditing firms

In cases where an annual securities report (including its amendment reports but excluding its attached documents; Article 24-3 of the Financial Instruments and Exchange Act) or a foreign company annual securities report or foreign person annual securities report (including its supplementary documents and amendment reports) contains false statements regarding material matters or omits statements of material matters that should be stated or statements of material facts that must be stated to avoid causing any misunderstandings, the "directors" of the issuer of the securities when the annual securities report was submitted shall be liable for damage suffered due to the false statements, etc. by persons who acquired or disposed of the securities concerned of the issuer without knowing about the false statements, etc. (Article 24-4, Article 22(1), Article 24 (1), Article 24-2 (4), and Article 27 of the Financial Instruments and Exchange Act). Also, when financial statements incorporated in an annual securities report contain false statements or omit statements of material matters that should be stated or statements of material facts that must be stated to avoid causing any misunderstanding and a certified public accountant or auditing firm certifies in an audit certification that there are no false statements or the omission of necessary statements in such financial statements, the certified public accountant or auditing firm shall be liable for damage suffered due to false statements, etc. by persons who acquired or disposed of the securities concerned of the issuer without knowing about the false statements, etc. (Article 24-4, Article 22(1), Article 24(1), Article 24-2 (4), and Article 27 of the Financial Instruments and Exchange Act).[117]

The "directors" of the issuer of the securities may be relieved from the

Chapter 3 Disclosure requirements

liability for damages in cases where they prove that they did not know and could not know that there were false statements, etc. even though exercising reasonable care (Article 24-4, Article 22(2), and Article 21(2)(i) of the Financial Instruments and Exchange Act). Similarly, the certified public accountant or auditing firm may be relieved from the liability for damages if it proves that it did not intentionally or negligently certify that the financial statements contained no false statements, etc. even though they actually contained false statements, etc. (Article 24-4, Article 22(2), and Article 21 (2)(ii) of the Financial Instruments and Exchange Act).

Also, in cases where there are false statements etc. in internal control reports, foreign company internal control reports, quarterly securities reports, foreign company quarterly securities reports, semiannual securities reports, foreign company semiannual securities reports, foreign person semiannual securities reports, extraordinary reports, foreign company extraordinary reports, share buyback reports or the amendment reports to these documents, the issuer's "directors" shall bear the same liability for damages (Article 24-2(4), Article 24-4-6, Article 24-4-7(4), Article 24-5 (5), Article 24-6(2), Article 24(11), Article 24-4-2(6), Article 24-4-3(3), Article 24-4-4(6), Article 24-4-5(3), Article 24-4-7(8), Article 24-4-8(2), Article 24-5(9) & (16), Article 24-5-2(2), and Article 27 of the Financial Instruments and Exchange Act). Similarly, a certified public accountant or auditing firm that certifies in an audit certification that there are no false

---

117 One court ruling (Tokyo District Court Judgment of May 21, 2009, above) found that in cases where the auditor is an auditing firm, assuming that the auditing firm bears liability for damages under the Financial Instruments and Exchange Act, the member of the auditing firm who signed the audit report without fulfilling their duty of care as a certified public accountant shall be liable in tort for compensatory damages that arose from the false statements to persons who acquired the securities without knowing about the false statements in the annual securities report (Article 709 of the Civil Code). On the other hand, members of the auditing firm who did not sign the audit report should be directly liable to investors in stock markets for the statement in the audit report only when they are considered to be involved in the formulation of the audit opinion stated in the audit report equivalent to those members who signed the report, and members who were not viewed as such shall bear unlimited liability in relation to the liability of the auditing firm (Article 34-10-6(1) of the Certified Public Accountant Act).

465

statements or omission of necessary statements in financial statements incorporated in quarterly securities reports or semiannual securities reports even though there are false statements or the omission of statements of material matters that should be stated or material facts that must be stated to avoid causing any misunderstandings shall bear the same liability (Article 24-4-7(4) and Article 24-5(5) of the Financial Instruments and Exchange Act).

Whether "directors" "exercised reasonable care" shall be determined on an individual basis considering the position of the relevant "director" in the relevant company, the function and the factual knowledge of the "director" at that time (Tokyo District Court Judgment of May 21, 2009 [*Hanrei Jiho* No. 2047, p. 36; the appeal by the defendants was dismissed by the Tokyo High Court Judgment of November 30, 2011 ⟨*Hanrei Jiho* No. 2152, p. 116⟩]; Tokyo District Court Judgment of June 22, 2012 [*Kinyu Shoji Hanrei* No. 1397, p. 30]). Also, there is a court ruling that since whether an outline of the transactions should be stated in the section on the application of funds in an extraordinary report was closely related to the execution of such transactions which was an agenda item of the board of directors meeting and also material information that would influence reasonable judgment on investment and lending by stakeholders of the person submitting documents, a "director" attending the board of directors meeting was in a position to supervise the proper statement of the application of funds in the relevant extraordinary report through deliberations at the board of directors meeting (Tokyo District Court Judgment of June 22, 2012, above). There is also a court ruling that in order to avoid making false statements in an annual securities report, the representative director of the reporting company should have specifically instructed the chief financial officer and the director responsible for the company's finance operation to examine the appropriateness of the accounting for a certain transaction, or otherwise should have taken specific examination measures such as confirming with the accounting auditor (Tokyo District Court Judgment of May 21, 2009, above). On the other hand, focusing on the fact that the liability for the accounting audit of large companies under the former Act on Exceptions to the Commercial Code (and companies with accounting auditors under the

Chapter 3   Disclosure requirements

present Companies Act) being primarily borne by the accounting auditor, many court rulings uphold the defense of reliance by company auditors of the issuers (Tokyo District Court Judgment of May 21, 2009, above; Tokyo District Court Judgment of October 15, 2013 [unpublished]). Also, there is a lower court ruling that as long as the allocation of duties set by the audit committee is reasonable in light of the duty of care of a prudent manager, each company auditor shall not be charged for negligence of care concerning establishing such allocation of duties itself; and unless there are specific and special circumstances that cause doubts regarding the appropriateness of execution of the duty of other company auditors, etc., and if a company auditor fulfills his or her prescribed duties with the care of a prudent manager assuming that the other company auditors fulfill their duties appropriately, the company auditor is deemed to have "exercised due care" (Tokyo District Court Judgment of October 15, 2013 [unpublished]).

## 3. Civil liability for information provision on markets for professional investors

a. Civil liability for false information, etc. on primary markets

( i ) Issuer's liability

When specified information on securities, referenced information pertaining to specified information on securities, amended specified information on securities or referenced information pertaining to the relevant amended specified information on securities (i.e., specified information on securities, etc.; Article 27-33 of the Financial Instruments and Exchange Act) contains false information regarding material matters or omits material matters that should be provided or publicized or omits information regarding material facts that must be stated to avoid any misunderstanding, the issuer who provided or publicized the relevant specified information on securities, etc. shall be liable for damage suffered by persons who acquired the securities concerned in response to the specified solicitation, etc. (Article 27-31(1) of the Financial Instruments and Exchange Act) pertaining to the relevant specified information on securities, etc. (Article 27-33 and Article 18(1) of the Financial Instruments and Exchange Act). However, where the relevant specified information on securities, etc. has not been publicized, the issuer shall be liable only to persons who were provided with the relevant specified

*467*

information on securities, etc. Also, the issuer shall not be liable to persons who acquired the securities concerned knowing that the information was false or that the information was omitted on material matters that should be provided or publicized or information regarding material facts that must be provided or publicized to avoid any misunderstanding (false information, etc.). The amount of liability for damages and the extinctive prescription and period of exclusion of the right to claim damages are provided by laws in line with the liability for damages in the case of false statements, etc. in securities registration statements, (Articles 27-33, 19, and 20 of the Financial Instruments and Exchange Act).

(ⅱ) Liability of "directors", etc., securities holders, and financial instruments business operators, etc. who are wholesale underwrites

Where specified information on securities, etc. contains false information regarding material matters or omits material matters that should be provided or publicized or information on material facts that must be provided or publicized to avoid causing misunderstandings, 1) the "directors" and incorporators of the issuer and equivalent persons, 2) holders of securities pertaining to specified solicitation for selling, etc. (Article 27-31(1) of the Financial Instruments and Exchange Act), and 3) financial instruments business operators or registered financial institutions that concluded a wholesale underwriting contract with issuers of securities pertaining to specified solicitation for acquisition (Article 27-31(1) of the Financial Instruments and Exchange Act) or persons listed in 2) shall be liable for damage caused by false information or the omission of information to persons who acquired the securities concerned in response to specified solicitation, etc. (Articles 27-33 and 21 of the Financial Instruments and Exchange Act). However, in cases where the relevant specified information on securities, etc. is not publicized, they shall be liable only to persons who were provided with the relevant specified information on securities, etc. They shall not be liable to persons who acquired the relevent securities knowing the existence of false information, etc.

However, the persons in 1)-3) above may be relieved from the liability for damages in cases where they prove that they did not know and could not

Chapter 3 Disclosure requirements

know that there was false information, etc. even though exercising reasonable care.

b. Civil liability for false information etc. on secondary markets

( i ) Issuer's liability

Where specified information on securities etc. or issuer information, etc, (i.e., issuer information or amended issuer information) (i.e., specified information; Article 27-34 of the Financial Instruments and Exchange Act) that has been publicized (publicized information) contains false information regarding material matters or omits material matters that should be provided or publicized or information regarding material facts that must be provided or publicized to avoid causing any misunderstandings, the issuer who publicized the relevant publicized information shall be liable for damage suffered due to the false information, etc. by persons that acquired or disposed of the securities of the relevant issuer not through public offering or secondary distribution or specified solicitation, etc. (Article 27-31(1) of the Financial Instruments and Exchange Act) during the publication period of the relevant publicized information (Article 27-34 and Article 21-2(1) of the Financial Instruments and Exchange Act). However, in cases where the relevant specified information on securities, etc. is not publicized, they shall be liable only to persons who were provided with the relevant specified information on securities, etc. They shall not be liable to persons who acquired the securities concerned knowing about the false information, etc.

The presumptive provisions regarding the amount of damages in the case of false statements, etc. in annual securities reports, etc. on secondary markets provided in Article 21-2, paragraph 3 of the Financial Instruments and Exchange Act applies *mutatis mutandis* (Article 27-34 of the Financial Instruments and Exchange Act); however, the amounts of damage shall not exceed the amounts calculated under Article 19, paragraph 1 of the Financial Instruments and Exchange Act. The right to claim damages extinguishes if it is not exercised for two years after the false information, etc. came to be known or could have been known by exercising reasonable care (Article 27-34, Article 21-3 and Article 20 of the Financial Instruments and Exchange Act), or if it is not exercised for five years from the publication date of the publicized information (Article 27-34, Article 21-3, and Article 20 of the Financial Instruments and Exchange Act).

(ii) Liability of "directors" and incorporators

Where specified information contains false information regarding material matters or omits material matters that should be provided or publicized or information regarding material facts that must be provided or publicized to avoid causing misunderstandings, the "directors" of the issuer that provided or publicized the relevant specified information at the time of the provision or the publication and the incorporators of the relevant issuer and other equivalent persons shall be liable for damage suffered due to the false information, etc. by persons that acquired or disposed of the securities of the issuer which provided or publicized the relevant specified information without knowing about the false information, etc. (Article 27-34 and Article 22(1) of the Financial Instruments and Exchange Act). However, in cases where the relevant specified information on securities, etc., is not publicized, they shall be liable only to persons who were provided with the relevent specified information on securities, etc. Also, in cases where the relevant specified information is specified information on securities, etc. (Article 27-33 of the Financial Instruments and Exchange Act), they shall be liable only to persons who acquired the securities not through public offering, secondary distribution or specified solicitation, etc.

The "directors" of the issuer that provided or publicized the relevant specified information at the time of the provision or the publication and the incorporators of the relevant issuer and other equivalent persons shall not be liable for damages in cases where they prove that they did not know and could not know that there was false information, etc. even though exercising reasonable care (Article 27-34 and Article 22 (2) of the Financial Instruments and Exchange Act).

# 4. Civil liability pertaining to the provision of information in secondary distributions of foreign securities

In secondary distributions of foreign securities, financial instruments business operators, etc. that offered securities for sale without providing or

Chapter 3   Disclosure requirements

publicizing foreign securities information shall be liable for damages arising from the relevant illegal act to persons who purchased these securities (Article 27-34-2(1) of the Financial Instruments and Exchange Act).

Also, in the secondary distribution of foreign securities, financial instruments business operators, etc. that offered securities for sale using foreign securities information which contains false information regarding material matters or omits material matters that should be provided or publicized or information regarding material facts that must be provided or publicized to avoid causing any misunderstandings shall be liable for damage suffered by persons who purchased the securities concerned without knowing about the false information or the omission of information (Article 27-34-2(2) of the Financial Instruments and Exchange Act). Furthermore, when there is false information in foreign securities information publicized in accordance with Article 27-33-2, paragraph 3 of the Financial Instruments and Exchange Act (publicized information), financial instruments business operators, etc. who publicized the relevant publicized information shall be liable for damages arising from the false information or the omission of information to persons who purchased or disposed of these securities pertaining to the relevant publicized information from the relevant financial instruments business operator during the publication period of the relevant publicized information under those provisions not through public offering or secondary distribution or specified solicitation, etc. without knowing about the false information or the omission of information (Article 27-34-2(3) of the Financial Instruments and Exchange Act). However, in both cases, the relevant financial instruments business operators, etc. may be relieved from the liability if they prove that they did not know and could not know that there were false statements, etc. or the omission of information even though exercising reasonable care (proviso to Article 27-34-2(2) of the Financial Instruments and Exchange Act).

# F. Administrative measures, etc.

## 1. Offering disclosures

a. Amendment orders for securities registration statements

In cases where the Prime Minister recognizes that there are deficiencies in formalities or that statements of material matters which should be stated are insufficient in a securities registration statement (including attached documents and amendments), foreign company registration statement (including supplementary documents, attached documents and amendments), foreign person registration statement (including supplementary documents, attached documents and amendments), shelf-registration statement (including attached documents and referenced documents), or amended shelf-registration statement (including referenced documents) (Article 9(1), Article 5(8), Article 27, and Article 23-9(1) of the Financial Instruments and Exchange Act),[118] the Prime Minister may order the person who submitted the document to submit an amendment or amended shelf-registration statement. It should be noted that an amendment order cannot be issued on the grounds that there are deficiencies in formalities or that statements of material matters which should be stated are insufficient in a securities registration statement or amendments (foreign company registration statement or foreign person registration statement or amendments to these documents) after a notification comes into effect. However, in cases where after a notification comes into effect the Prime Minister recognizes that regarding an amendment voluntarily submitted by the person who submitted the documents there are deficiencies in formalities or that statements of material matters which should be stated are insufficient (Article 7 of the Financial Instruments and Exchange Act), an amendment order can be issued even after a notification comes into effect (Article 9(5) of the Financial Instruments and Exchange Act). On the other hand, in cases where the Prime Minister recognizes that in a shelf-registration statement or amended shelf-registration statement there are deficiencies in formalities or that statements of material matters are

*472*

Chapter 3 Disclosure requirements

insufficient, the Prime Minister may order submission of an amended shelf-registration statement during the period until the shelf registration loses effect (Article 23-9(1) of the Financial Instruments and Exchange Act).

---

**118** When the Prime Minister finds it necessary and appropriate for the public interest or protection of investors, the Prime Minister may order persons who submitted or who it is deemed should submit disclosure documents listed in each item of Article 25 paragraph 1 of the Financial Instruments and Exchange Act (these include annual securities reports, etc. and other ongoing disclosure documents in addition to securities registration statements, foreign company registration statements, foreign person registration statements, shelf-registration statement and the amendments, etc. to these documents and shelf-registration supplements, etc.), and underwriters of securities and other persons concerned or witnesses (for example, financial institutions which have business relationship with the person submitting the documents) to submit reports or materials that will be helpful, or have the officials inspect the books and documents or other articles held by these persons (Article 26 (1) of the Financial Instruments and Exchange Act). Also, where the Prime Minister finds it necessary in connection with these orders for submission of reports or materials or with these inspections, the Prime Minister may inquire with public offices or public or private organisations and request submission of reports on the necessary matters (Article 26 (2) and Article 27-35 (2) of the Financial Instruments and Exchange Act). In addition, where the Prime Minister finds it necessary and appropriate for the public interest or protection of investors, the Prime Minister may order a certified public accountant or auditing firm that conducted an audit certification of financial statements stated in a securities registration statement or of an internal control report to submit reports or materials that will be helpful (Article 193-2(6) of the Financial Instruments and Exchange Act).

These powers are delegated by the Prime Minister to the Commissioner of the Financial Services Agency and then from the Commissioner of the Financial Services Agency as follows: For securities registration statements and shelf-registration statements (also for foreign company registration statements and foreign person registration statements), inspections before these disclosure documents come into effect are implemented by the Director General of a Local Finance Bureau or Fukuoka Local Finance Branch Bureau, and inspections, etc. after they come into effect and inspections, etc. of other documents are implemented by the Securities and Exchange Surveillance Commission (Article 194-7 (3) (5) of the Financial Instruments and Exchange Act, Article 38-2(1) (i) & (ii) and Article 39(2) (xvi) of the Financial Instruments and Exchange Act Implementing Order).

Presently, issuers that provided and publicized or should provide and publicize specified information, underwriters of the subject securities and other persons concerned and witnesses are similarly subject to the submission of reports and site inspections (Article 27-35 of the Financial Instruments and Exchange Act).

*473*

In cases where it is discovered that there are false statements regarding material matters or that statements are omitted on material matters to be stated or statements of material facts required to avoid any misunderstandings in a securities registration statement (including attached documents and amendments), foreign company registration statement (including supplementary documents, attached documents and amendments), foreign person registration statement (including supplementary documents, attached documents and amendments), shelf-registration statement (including attached documents and referenced documents), amended shelf-registration statement (including referenced documents), or shelf-registration supplement (including attached documents and referenced documents), the Prime Minister may order the person who submitted the document to submit an amendment or amended shelf-registration statement at any time (even after the notification comes into effect) (Article 10 (1), Article 5 (8), Article 27 and Article 23-10 (1) of the Financial Instruments and Exchange Act) [119]

In cases where an amendment order is issued for a securities registration statement, etc., the Prime Minister must hold a hearing irrespective of the categories of procedures for hearing statements of opinion under Article 13, paragraph 1 of the Administrative Procedures Act (Article 9(1), Article 10 (1), Article 23-9(1), Article 23-10(1), Article 5(8), and Article 27 of the Financial Instruments and Exchange Act). Here, the hearing is a procedure to seek the presence of the subject person, confirm the facts of the violation that is the subject of the administrative disciplinary action, and give the subject person an opportunity to offer a defense or explanations. The provisions regarding the hearing procedures are specified in the Administrative Procedures Act (Articles 15 through 28 of the Administrative Procedures Act) [120]

In cases where the Prime Minister issues an order to submit a securities registration statement (including attached documents and amendments),

---

**119** There are also penal provisions prescribed for non-compliance with an order (Article 200(ii) & (iv) of the Financial Instruments and Exchange Act).

Chapter 3 Disclosure requirements

foreign company registration statement (including supplementary documents, attached documents and amendments), foreign person registration statement (including supplementary documents, attached documents and amendments), shelf-registration statement (including attached documents and referenced documents), or amended shelf-registration statement (including referenced documents), the Prime Minister may make all or part of the relevant disclosure documents not available for public inspection (Article 25(6), Article 27-30-7(1) & (2), Article 5(6) & (8), and Article 27 of the Financial Instruments and Exchange Act). In this case, copies are also not made available for public inspection at the head office, principal offices and main branches of the issuer or at the financial instruments exchange or authorized financial instruments firms association (Article 25(7) & (8), Article 5(6) & (8), and Article 27 of the Financial Instruments and Exchange Act). Also, in cases where the Prime Minister recognizes as necessary and appropriate for the public interest or investor protection, the fact that an order to submit documents pertaining to the revision of disclosure documents has been issued and other related information that could have a material influence on investors' investment decisions can be made available for public inspection on EDINET together with the relevant disclosure documents (Article 27-30-7(5), Article 5(8), and Article 27 of the Financial Instruments and Exchange Act).

---

**120** The Financial Services Agency takes the following type of policy regarding hearings (Guidelines on Disclosure of Corporate Affairs, A1-8-3). (i) The hearings are open to the public in accordance with Article 186-2 of the Financial Instruments and Exchange Act; but in cases where the person subject to the hearing requests that the hearing be closed to the public because of reasonable grounds, this is permitted. Note that even in cases where the person subject to the hearing does not request that the hearing be closed to the public, examinations regarding making the details of the hearing open to the public must be conducted from the perspective of public interest. (ii) Presentation of the reason for action in accordance with Article 14 of the Administrative Procedures Act is presented in the written notification of hearing provided by Article 15, paragraph 1 of the Administrative Procedures Act. (iii) In accordance with Article 15, paragraph 1 of the Administrative Procedures Act, a reasonable period must be set from the issuance of the written notification of hearing to the hearing date, but the reasonable period is decided in accordance with each case.

*475*

b. Notification effect suspension orders

In cases where there are false statements, etc. concerning material matters in a securities registration statement (including attached documents and amendments), foreign company registration statement (including supplementary documents, attached documents and amendments), or foreign person registration statement (including supplementary documents, attached documents and amendments), where considered necessary the Prime Minister may order suspension of the effect of the notification (Article 10 (1), Article 5 (8) and Article 27 of the Financial Instruments and Exchange Act). Also, in cases where an amendment has been submitted based on an amendment order and the Prime Minister recognizes this as appropriate, the Prime Minister may cancel the suspension order (Article 10 (4), Article 5 (8), and Article 27 of the Financial Instruments and Exchange Act).

There are similar provisions for cases where an amended shelf-registration statement submission order is issued after the date a shelf-registration comes into effect (Article 23-10 (3) & (4) of the Financial Instruments and Exchange Act).

In cases where an order to suspend the effect of a securities registration statement, etc. is issued, the Prime Minister must hold a hearing irrespective of the categories of procedures for hearing statements of opinion in accordance with Article 13, paragraph 1 of the Administrative Procedures Act. (Article 10 (1), Article 23-10 (1), Article 5 (8), and Article 27 of the Financial Instruments and Exchange Act).

c. Suspension of effect and extensions of waiting periods regarding other offering disclosure documents

In cases where there are false statements etc. concerning material matters in a securities registration statement (including attached documents and amendments), foreign company registration statement (including supplementary documents, attached documents and amendments), or foreign person registration statement (including supplementary documents, attached documents and amendments), where considered necessary and

*476*

Chapter 3 Disclosure requirements

appropriate for the public interest or investor protection, the Prime Minister may suspend the effect not only of the relevant securities registration statement, etc. but also of notifications pertaining to securities registration statements, foreign company registration statements, foreign person registration statements, shelf-registration statements, or shelf-registration supplements submitted by the person who submitted the documents within one year from the date the documents were submitted or of the shelf-registration pertaining to the relevent shelf-registration statement or shelf-registration supplement for a period considered suitable for the public interest or investor protection, or extend the waiting period until the document comes into effect (Article 11(1), Article 5(8), and Article 27 of the Financial Instruments and Exchange Act).

In cases where such measures are taken, the Prime Minister must hold a hearing irrespective of the categories of procedures for hearing in accordance with Article 13, paragraph 1 of the Administrative Procedures Act (Article 11(1), Article 5(8) and Article 27 of the Financial Instruments and Exchange Act).

In cases where such measures were taken, the Prime Minister may, however, cancel the disciplinary action when the Prime Minister recognizes that the amendments submitted pursuant to Article 7, paragraph 1 or Article 10, paragraph 1 of the Financial Instruments and Exchange Act are appropriate and that sale or having others acquire securities issued by the person who submitted the statements through public offering or secondary distribution would not harm the public interest or investor protection (Article 11(2), Article 5(8), and Article 27 of the Financial Instruments and Exchange Act).

Also, in cases where there are false statements, etc. concerning material matters in a shelf-registration statement (including attached documents and amended shelf-registration statements) or shelf-registration supplement (including attached documents) or in referenced documents pertaining to these documents, the Prime Minister may suspend the effect not only of the relevant shelf-registration statement documents, etc. but also of securities

*477*

registration statements, foreign company registration statements, foreign person registration statements, shelf-registration statements, or shelf-registration supplements submitted by the person who submitted the relevant shelf-registration statement, etc. within one year from the date the statement was submitted for a period considered suitable for the public interest or investor protection, or extend the waiting period until the document comes into effect (Article 23-11(1) of the Financial Instruments and Exchange Act).

In cases where such measures are taken, the Prime Minister must hold a hearing irrespective of the categories of procedures for hearing in accordance with Article 13, paragraph 1 of the Administrative Procedures Act (Article 23-11(1) of the Financial Instruments and Exchange Act).

In cases where such measures were taken, the Prime Minister may cancel the disciplinary action if the Prime Minister recognizes that the amended shelf-registration statement (including referenced documents to the relevant amended shelf-registration statement) submitted pursuant to Article 23-4 or Article 23-10, paragraph 1 (including cases applied *mutatis mutandis* under Article 23-10, paragraph 5 of the Financial Instruments and Exchange Act) are appropriate and the sale or having another person acquire securities issued by the person who submitted the statements through public offering or secondary distribution would not harm the public interest or investor protection (Article 2-11(2) of the Financial Instruments and Exchange Act).

## 2. Continuous disclosure

In cases where the Prime Minister recognizes there are deficiencies in formalities or that statements of material matters which should be stated are insufficient in an annual securities report (including attached documents), a confirmation letter pertaining to the contents stated in an annual securities report, etc., internal control report (including attached documents), quarterly securities report, semiannual securities report, extraordinary report, foreign company report (including supplementary documents and attached documents), foreign person report (including supplementary

Chapter 3   Disclosure requirements

documents and attached documents), foreign company confirmation letter
(including supplementary documents), foreign company internal control
report (including supplementary documents and attached documents),
foreign company quarterly securities reports (including supplementary
documents), foreign company semiannual securities report (including
supplementary documents), foreign person semiannual securities report
(including supplementary documents), foreign company extraordinary
report, foreign person ad-hoc report, share buyback report, parent
company's status report or foreign parent company's status report
(including supplementary documents), the Prime Minister may order the
company submitting these ongoing disclosure documents to submit an
amendment report or amended confirmation letter (Article 24-2(1), Article
24-4-3(1), Article 24-4-5(1), Article 24-4-7(4), Article 24-5(5), Article
24-6(2), Article 24-7(3), Article 9(1), Article 5(8), and Article 27 of the
Financial Instruments and Exchange Act).

Also in cases where the Prime Minister discovers there are false statements
regarding material matters or a statement is omitted on material matters
that should be stated or on material facts necessary to avoid causing any
misunderstanding in an annual securities report (including attached
documents), a confirmation letter pertaining to the contents stated in an
annual securities report, etc., internal control report (including attached
documents), quarterly securities report, semiannual securities report,
extraordinary report, foreign company report (including supplementary
documents and attached documents), foreign person report (including
supplementary documents and attached documents), foreign company
confirmation letter (including supplementary documents), foreign company
internal control report (including supplementary documents and attached
documents), foreign company quarterly securities reports (including
supplementary documents), foreign company semiannual securities report
(including supplementary documents), foreign person semiannual securities
report (including supplementary documents), foreign company extraordinary report, foreign person extraordinary report, share buyback report,
parent company's status report or foreign parent company's status report
(including supplementary documents), the Prime Minister may order the

company that submitted these documents to submit an amendment report or amended confirmation letter (Article 24-2(1), Article 24-4-3(1), Article 24-4-5(1), Article 24-4-7(4), Article 24-5(5), Article 24-6(2), Article 24-7 (3), Article 10(1), Article 5(8), and Article 27 of the Financial Instruments and Exchange Act).

Also, in cases where there are false statements concerning material matters in an annual securities report, foreign company report (including supplementary documents) or foreign person report (including supplementary documents) or in amendment reports pertaining to these reports and where considered necessary and appropriate for the public interest or investor protection, the Prime Minister may suspend the effect of securities registration statements, foreign company registration statements, foreign person registration statements, shelf-registration statements, or shelf-registration supplements submitted within one year from the date the amendment report regarding the relevant false statements was submitted (when by amendment order, the date of the relevant order) or suspension of the effect of the shelf-registration pertaining to the relevant shelf-registration statement or shelf-registration supplement, or extend the waiting period for a suitable period until the document comes into effect (Article 24-3 and Article 11(1) of the Financial Instruments and Exchange Act).

In cases where such measures are taken, the Prime Minister must hold a hearing irrespective of the categories of procedures for hearing in accordance with the Administrative Procedures Act (Article 13(1), Article 24-2(1), Article 24-3, Article 24-4-3(1), Article 24-4-5(1), Article 24-4-7 (4), Article 24-5(5), Article 24-6(2), Article 24-7(3), Article 9(1), Article 10(1), Article 11(1), Article 5(8) and Article 27 of the Financial Instruments and Exchange Act).

In cases where the effect of offering disclosure documents has been suspended and the waiting period extended, the Prime Minister may, however, cancel the disciplinary action if the Prime Minister recognizes that the amendment reports submitted pursuant to Article 24-2, paragraph 1 of the Financial Instruments and Exchange Act are appropriate and that the

Chapter 3   Disclosure requirements

sale or having other persons acquire securities of the relevant company through public offering or secondary distribution would not harm the public interest or investor protection (Article 24-3, Article 11(2), Article 5(8) and Article 27 of the Financial Instruments and Exchange Act).

# 3. Appeals against administrative dispositions

Requests for administrative review can be filed in accordance with Article 5 of the Administrative Appeal Act in response to report submission orders, amendment and amendment report submission orders and other disciplinary actions. Also, lawsuits to revoke report submission orders, amendment and amendment report submission orders and other disciplinary actions can be instituted in accordance with Article 8 of the Administrative Case Litigation Act.

To date, there are no examples known where an order has been revoked through requests for administrative review or an action to revoke a disciplinary action has been approved. However, in April 2013 Japan Wind Development Company, Ltd. had filed a lawsuit in accordance with Article 8 of the Administrative Case Litigation Act to revoke an amendment report submission order and asked for an administrative stay of execution in accordance with Article 25 of the same Act (The JWDC withdrew the latter application, and the Tokyo District Court dismissed the former claim (Judgment of February 26, 2016 [unpublished])).

# 4. Urgent provisional suspension court orders and cease-and-desist orders

When urgently necessary and also necessary and appropriate for public benefit and investor protection, a court may order a person who has conducted or plans to conduct any act in violation of the Financial Instruments and Exchange Act or orders in accordance with the Financial Instruments and Exchange Act to prohibit or suspend that act, subject to the filing of a petition by the Prime Minister or by the Prime Minister and the Minister of Finance (Article 192 of the Financial Instruments and Exchange Act). For example, cases where a person plans to conduct a public offering or secondary distribution in violation of the Financial Instruments and

*481*

Exchange Act or an order based on the Financial Instruments and Exchange Act are subject to urgent provisional suspension orders and cease-and-desist orders by courts.

The Prime Minister's authority to file a petition is consigned to the Commissioner of the Financial Services Agency (Article 194-7 (1) of the Financial Instruments and Exchange Act), and then consigned from the Commissioner of the Financial Services Agency to the Securities and Exchange Surveillance Commission (Article 194-7 (4) (ii) of the Financial Instruments and Exchange Act). In recent years, the Securities and Exchange Surveillance Commission has actively filed petitions and made use of court urgent provisional suspension orders and cease-and-desist orders (for example, Tokyo District Court Judgment of November 26, 2010 [*Hanrei Jiho* No. 2104, p. 130]; Kofu District Court Judgment of December 15, 2010 [unpublished]; Sapporo District Court Judgment of May 13, 2011 [unpublished]; Tokyo District Court Judgment of July 5, 2011 [unpublished]; Tokyo District Court Judgment of July 15, 2011 [unpublished]; and Tokyo District Court Judgment of February 3, 2012 [unpublished]).

# G. Criminal penalties and administrative fines

In accordance with the general principles of criminal law, only crimes committed intentionally are subject to criminal penalties (intention is not a requirement for administrative monetary penalties).

## 1. Submission of securities registration statements, etc. with false statements

a. Offering disclosure documents and annual securities reports, etc.
Persons who have submitted false statements regarding material matters in any of the following documents (1) through (6) will be punished by imprisonment with work for not more than ten years or by a fine of not more than ¥10 million or both (Article 197 (1) (i), Article 5 (8), Article 24 (11), Article 24-2 (4), and Article 27 of the Financial Instruments and Exchange

Chapter 3 Disclosure requirements

Act). Here, "persons who have submitted" is limited to natural persons, and is interpreted to include not only the representative director and person responsible for preparing documents within the accounting division, but also persons who approved the documents at the board of directors (Tokyo District Court Judgment of December 24, 1976 [*Kinyu Shoji Hanrei* No. 524, p. 32]; Kobe District Court Judgment of December 26, 1978 [*Kinyu Shoji Hanrei* No. 568, p. 43]; Tokyo District Court Judgment of February 25, 1982 [*Keiji Saiban Geppo* Vol. 14 No. 1 No. 2, p. 194]; Niigata District Court Judgment of May 17, 1984 [*Hanrei Jiho* No. 1123, p. 3]; Tokyo District Court Judgment of March 12, 1987, [*Shiryoban Shojihomu* No. 37, p. 49]; Supreme Court Decision of April 25, 2011 [unpublished], etc.). Certified public accountants who were involved in the false statements as joint accomplices or as aiders or abettors to the crime are also subject to punishment (Supreme Court Decision of May 31, 2010 [*Hanrei Jiho* No. 2174, p. 127]; Tokyo High Court Judgment of January 11, 2013 [unpublished]). Also, in cases where the representative of a juridical person or an agent, employee or other worker of a juridical person or individual has made a submission regarding the business or property of the juridical person or individual, the relevant juridical person is also punished by a fine of not more than ¥700 million (Article 207(1)(i), Article 5(8), Article 24(11), Article 24-2(4), and Article 27 of the Financial Instruments and Exchange Act).

(1)  Securities registration statement (including referenced documents and attached documents), foreign company registration statement, or foreign person registration statement

(2)  Amendment (including amendments and referenced documents under Article 7, paragraph 1; Article 9, paragraph 1 and Article 10, paragraph 1 of the Financial Instruments and Exchange Act)

(3)  Shelf-registration statement (including referenced documents and attached documents)

(4)  Amended shelf-registration statement (including amended shelf-registration statements and referenced documents under Article 23-4, Article 23-9, paragraph 1; Article 23-10, paragraph 1 or paragraph 5 of the Financial Instruments and Exchange Act)

(5)  Shelf-registration supplement (including referenced documents and

*483*

attached documents)

(6) Annual securities report, foreign company report, or foreign person report (each excluding attached documents) and its amendment reports (amendment reports under Article 24-2, paragraph 1 of the Financial Instruments and Exchange Act)

b. Provision of specified information on securities, etc. with false statements

Persons who have provided or publicized false statements regarding material matters in specified information on securities (including referenced information), amended specified information on securities (including referenced information), issuer information or amended issuer information will be punished by imprisonment with work for not more than 10 years or by a fine of not more than ¥10 million or both (Article 197(1)(iv-2) of the Financial Instruments and Exchange Act). Also, in cases where the representative of a juridical person or an agent, employee or other worker of a juridical person or individual has made a provision or publication regarding the business or property of the juridical person or individual, the relevant juridical person is also punished by a fine of not more than ¥700 million (Article 207(1)(i) of the Financial Instruments and Exchange Act).

c. Annual securities report attached documents, semiannual securities reports, quarterly securities reports, extraordinary reports, etc.

Persons who have submitted false statements regarding material matters in any of the following documents (1) through (8) will be punished by imprisonment with work for not more than five years or by a fine of not more than ¥5 million or both (Article 197-2(vi), Article (18), Article 24(11), Article 24-2(4), Article 24-4-2(6), Article 24-4-3(3), Article 24-4-4(6), Article 24-4-5(3), Article 24-4-7(8), Article 24-4-8(2), Article 24-5(9) (16), Article 24-5-2(2), Article 2-7(5) & (6), and Article 27 of the Financial Instruments and Exchange Act). Also, in cases where the representative of a juridical person or an agent, employee or other worker of a juridical person or individual has made a submission regarding the business or property of the juridical person or individual, the relevant juridical person is also punished by a fine of not more than ¥500 million (Article 207(1)(ii), Article

Chapter 3　Disclosure requirements

5(8), Article 24(11), Article 24-2(4), Article 24-4-2(6), Article 24-4-3(3), Article 24-4-4(6), Article 24-4-5(3), Article 24-4-7(8), Article 24-4-8(2), Article 24-5(9) & (16), Article 24-5-2(2), Article 24-7(5)(vi), and Article 27 of the Financial Instruments and Exchange Act).

(1) The attached documents to an annual securities report, foreign company report, or foreign person report (attached documents pursuant to Article 24, paragraph 6 of the Financial Instruments and Exchange Act)

(2) Amendment reports to the attached documents to an annual securities report, foreign company report, or foreign person report (amendment reports pursuant to Article 24-2 (1) of the Financial Instruments and Exchange Act)

(3) Internal control report or foreign company internal control reports (including attached documents and their amendment reports)

(4) Quarterly securities reports or foreign company quarterly securities reports (including their amendment reports)

(5) Semiannual securities reports, foreign company semiannual securities reports, or foreign person semiannual securities reports (including their amendment reports)

(6) extraordinary reports, foreign company extraordinary reports, or foreign person extraordinary reports (including their amendment reports)

(7) Share buyback reports (including their amendment reports)

(8) Parent company's status reports or foreign parent company's status reports (including their amendment reports)

# 2. Public offerings, secondary distributions, etc. without notification

Persons who conducted public offerings or secondary distributions of securities that require notification under Article 4, paragraph 1 of the Financial Instruments and Exchange Act, or general solicitations for securities acquired by qualified institutional investors which require notification under Article 4, paragraph 2 of the Financial Instruments and

Exchange Act, or general solicitation for securities acquired by professional investors which require notification under Article 4, paragraph 3 of the Financial Instruments and Exchange Act even though the pertinent notifications have not been accepted, or persons who dealt with these, will be punished by imprisonment with work for not more than five years or by a fine of not more than ¥5 million, or both (Article 197-2(i) of the Financial Instruments and Exchange Act). Also, in cases where the representative of a juridical person or an agent, employee or other worker of a juridical person or individual has conducted any of these acts regarding the business or property of the juridical person or individual, the relevant juridical person is also punished by a fine of not more than ¥500 million (Article 207(1)(ii) of the Financial Instruments and Exchange Act).

Similarly, persons who sold or had other persons acquire securities through public offering or secondary distribution even though the required securities notification for that public offering or secondary distribution is not in effect in violation of Article 15, paragraph 1 of the Financial Instruments and Exchange Act, and persons who sold or had other persons acquire securities through public offering or secondary distribution even though the shelf-registration is not effective or the shelf-registration supplement has not been submitted in violation of Article 23-8, paragraph 1 of the Financial Instruments and Exchange Act will be punished by imprisonment with work for not more than five years or by a fine of not more than ¥5 million, or both (Article 197-2(iii) of the Financial Instruments and Exchange Act). Also, in cases where the representative of a juridical person or an agent, employee or other worker of a juridical person or individual has conducted any of these acts regarding the business or property of the juridical person or individual, the relevant juridical person is also punished by a fine of not more than ¥500 million (Article 207(1)(ii) of the Financial Instruments and Exchange Act).

In parallel with these, regarding specified solicitations, etc. (Article 27-31(1) of the Financial Instruments and Exchange Act), persons who conducted specified solicitations, etc. or persons who dealt with these even though the specified information on securities pertaining to the relevant specified solicitation, etc. has not been provided or publicized will be punished by

Chapter 3  Disclosure requirements

imprisonment with work for not more than five years or by a fine of not more than ¥5 million, or both (Article 197-2 (x-20) of the Financial Instruments and Exchange Act). Also, in cases where the representative of a juridical person or an agent, employee or other worker of a juridical person or individual has conducted any of these acts regarding the business or property of the juridical person or individual, the relevant juridical person is also punished by a fine of not more than ¥500 million (Article 207(1)(ii) of the Financial Instruments and Exchange Act).

## 3. Non-submission of annual securities reports, etc.

a. Non-submission of annual securities reports and internal control reports

Persons who do not submit annual securities reports (including attached documents) or their amendment reports (amendment reports pursuant to amendment orders, in cases where there were false statements, etc. in material matters based on Article 10, paragraph 1 applied *mutatis mutandis* under Article 24-2, paragraph 1 of the Financial Instruments and Exchange Act) or internal control reports (including attached documents) or their amendment reports (amendment reports pursuant to amendment orders, in cases where there were false statements, etc. in material matters based on Article 10, paragraph 1 applied *mutatis mutandis* under Article 24-4-5, paragraph 1 of the Financial Instruments and Exchange Act) will be punished by imprisonment with work for not more than five years or by a fine of not more than ¥5 million, or both (Article 197-2(v) of the Financial Instruments and Exchange Act). Also, in cases where the representative of a juridical person or an agent, employee or other worker of a juridical person or individual does not submit any of these documents regarding the business or property of the juridical person or individual, the relevant juridical person is also punished by a fine of not more than ¥500 million (Article 207(1)(ii) of the Financial Instruments and Exchange Act).

b. Non-provision and non-publication of issuer information

Persons who do not provide and do not publicize issuer information (Article 27-32(1) & (2) of the Financial Instruments and Exchange Act) or who do not continuously disclose issuer information (Article 27-32 (4) of the

*487*

Financial Instruments and Exchange) will be punished by imprisonment with work for not more than five years or by a fine of not more than ¥5 million, or both (Article 197-2 (x-30) of the Financial Instruments and Exchange Act). Also, in cases where the representative of a juridical person or an agent, employee or other worker of a juridical person or individual does not provide or publicize information regarding the business or property of the juridical person or individual, the relevant juridical person is also punished by a fine of not more than ¥500 million (Article 207(1)(ii) of the Financial Instruments and Exchange Act).

c. Non-submission of amendments and amended shelf-registration statements

Persons who do not submit amendments (amendments in accordance with Article 7, paragraph 1, first sentence and Article 9, paragraph 1 or Article 10, paragraph 1 of the Financial Instruments and Exchange Act) or amended statements (amended shelf-registration statements in accordance with Article 23-4, Article 23-9, paragraph 1, or Article 23-10, paragraph 1 or paragraph 5 where paragraph 1 applied *mutatis mutandis* of the Financial Instruments and Exchange Act) will be punished by imprisonment with work for not more than one year or by a fine of not more than ¥1 million, or both (Article 20(ii) & (iv) of the Financial Instruments and Exchange Act). Also, in cases where the representative of a juridical person or an agent, employee or other worker of a juridical person or individual does not submit any of these documents regarding the business or property of the juridical person or individual, the relevant juridical person is also punished by a fine of not more than ¥100 million (Article 207(1)(v) of the Financial Instruments and Exchange Act).

d. Non-provision and non-publication of amended specified information on securities

Persons who do not provide and do not publicize amended specified information on securities regarding material matters (Article 27-31(4) of the Financial Instruments and Exchange Act) or who do not continuously publicize amended specified information on securities (Article 27-31(5) of the Financial Instruments and Exchange Act) will be punished by

Chapter 3 Disclosure requirements

imprisonment with work for not more than one year or by a fine of not more than ¥1 million, or both (Article 200(xii-20) of the Financial Instruments and Exchange Act). Also, in cases where the representative of a juridical person or an agent, employee or other worker of a juridical person or individual does not provide or publicize information regarding the business or property of the juridical person or individual, the relevant juridical person is also punished by a fine of not more than ¥100 million (Article 207(1)(v) of the Financial Instruments and Exchange Act).

e. Non-submission of amendment reports by amendment order when there were deficiencies in formalities or other ongoing disclosure documents, etc.

Persons who do not submit any of the following disclosure documents (1) through (6) will be punished by imprisonment with work for not more than one year or by a fine of not more than ¥1 million, or both (Article 200(v) of the Financial Instruments and Exchange Act). Also, in cases where the representative of a juridical person or an agent, employee or other worker of a juridical person or individual does not submit any of these documents regarding the business or property of the juridical person or individual, the relevant juridical person is also punished by a fine of not more than ¥100 million (Article 207(1)(v) of the Financial Instruments and Exchange Act).

(1) Amendment reports to annual securities reports (including attached documents) (amendment reports pursuant to amendment orders, in cases where there were inadequacies in form, etc. based on Article 9, paragraph 1 applied *mutatis mutandis* under Article 24-2, paragraph 1 of the Financial Instruments and Exchange Act)

(2) Amendment reports to internal control reports (included attached documents) (amendment reports pursuant to amendment orders, in cases where there were inadequacies in form, etc. based on Article 9, paragraph 1 applied *mutatis mutandis* under Article 24-4-5, paragraph 1 of the Financial Instruments and Exchange Act)

(3) Quarterly securities reports and amendment reports to quarterly securities reports (amendment reports pursuant to amendment orders, in cases where there were inadequacies in form etc. based on Article 9,

paragraph 1 or Article 10, paragraph 1 applied *mutatis mutandis* under Article 24-4-7, paragraph 4 of the Financial Instruments and Exchange Act)

(4) Semiannual securities reports, extraordinary reports or amendment reports to these reports (amendment reports pursuant to amendment orders based on Article 9, paragraph 1 or Article 10, paragraph 1 of the Financial Instruments and Exchange Act applied *mutatis mutandis* under Article 24-5, paragraph 5 of the Financial Instruments and Exchange Act)

(5) Share buyback reports or amendment reports to share buyback reports (amendment reports pursuant to amendment orders based on Article 9, paragraph 1 or Article 10, paragraph 1 applied *mutatis mutandis* under Article 24-6, paragraph 2 of the Financial Instruments and Exchange Act)

(6) Parent company's status reports or amendment reports to parent company's status reports (amendment reports pursuant to amendment orders based on Article 9, paragraph 1 or Article 10, paragraph 1 applied *mutatis mutandis* under Article 24-7, paragraph 3 of the Financial Instruments and Exchange Act).

f. Non-submission of confirmation letters pertaining to the contents of statements of annual securities reports and amended confirmation letters pursuant to amendment orders

Persons who do not submit confirmation letters pertaining to the contents of statements of annual securities reports or amended confirmation letters (amended confirmation letters pursuant to amendment orders based on Article 9, paragraph 1 or Article 10, paragraph 1 applied *mutatis mutandis* under Article 24-4-3, paragraph 1 or Article 24-5-2, paragraph 2 of the Financial Instruments and Exchange Act) will be punished by an administrative fine of not more than ¥300,000 (Article 208 (ii) of the Financial Instruments and Exchange Act).

Chapter 3 Disclosure requirements

g. Non-submission of confirmation letters pertaining to the contents of statements of quarterly securities reports and semiannual securities reports and amended confirmation letters pursuant to amendment orders

Persons who do not submit confirmation letters pertaining to the contents of statements of quarterly securities reports or semiannual securities reports or amended confirmation letters (amended confirmation letters pursuant to Article 9, paragraph 1 or Article 10, paragraph 1 applied *mutatis mutandis* under Article 24-4-8, paragraph 2 and Article 24-5-2, paragraph 2 of the Financial Instruments and Exchange Act) will be punished by an administrative fine of not more than ¥100,000 (Article 209 (iv) of the Financial Instruments and Exchange Act).

# 4. Submission of false copies of securities registration statements, etc.

In submitting or sending copies of securities registration statements etc. to a financial instruments exchange or authorized financial instruments firms association, persons who submit or send a copy of a document containing falsehoods regarding material matters and which have contents that differ from the original document will be punished by imprisonment with work for not more than five years or by a fine of not more than ¥5 million, or both (Article 197-2(ii) of the Financial Instruments and Exchange Act). Also, in cases where the representative of a juridical person or an agent, employee or other worker of a juridical person or individual submits such a document regarding the business or property of the juridical person or individual, the relevant juridical person is also punished by a fine of not more than ¥500 million (Article 207(1)(ii) of the Financial Instruments and Exchange Act).

Similarly, in making copies of a securities registration statement available for public inspection at the head office and main branches of the issuer of the securities concerned, a person who makes documents available for public inspection which contain false statements regarding material matters and have contents that differ from the original documents as copies of the securities registration statement will be punished by imprisonment with work for not more than five years or by a fine of not more than ¥5 million, or

*491*

both (Article 197-2(vii) of the Financial Instruments and Exchange Act). Also, in cases where the representative of a juridical person or an agent, employee or other worker of a juridical person or individual makes copies of such documents available for public inspection regarding the business or property of the juridical person or individual, the relevant juridical person is also punished by a fine of not more than ¥500 million (Article 207(1)(ii) of the Financial Instruments and Exchange Act).

Moreover, persons who do not submit copies of securities registration statements, etc. pertaining to issuers of listed securities or issuers of over-the-counter traded securities to a financial instruments exchange or authorized financial instruments association will be punished by imprisonment with work for not more than one year or by a fine of not more than ¥1 million, or both (Article 200(i) of the Financial Instruments and Exchange Act). Also, in cases where the representative of a juridical person or an agent, employee or other worker of a juridical person or individual does not submit such documents regarding the business or property of the juridical person or individual, the relevant juridical person is also punished by a fine of not more than ¥100 million (Article 207(1)(v) of the Financial Instruments and Exchange Act).

Similarly, persons who do not make copies of a submitted securities registration statement, etc. available for public inspection at the relevant company's head office and main branches will be punished by imprisonment with work for not more than one year or by a fine of not more than ¥1 million, or both (Article 200(vi) of the Financial Instruments and Exchange Act). Also, in cases where the representative of a juridical person or an agent, employee or other worker of a juridical person does not make copies of such documents available for public inspection regarding the business or property of the juridical person or individual, the relevant juridical person is also punished by a fine of not more than ¥100 million (Article 207(1)(v) of the Financial Instruments and Exchange Act).

## 5. Non-delivery of prospectuses

In cases where issuers or sellers, underwriters, financial instruments

Chapter 3 Disclosure requirements

business operators, registered financial institutions or financial instruments intermediary service providers sell or have another person acquire through public offering or secondary distribution securities that require notification regarding their public offering or secondary distribution without delivering a prospectus in advance or concurrently in violation of Article 15, paragraph 2 through 4 of the Financial Instruments and Exchange Act, they will be punished by imprisonment with work for not more than one year or by a fine of not more than ¥1 million, or both (Article 200 (iii) of the Financial Instruments and Exchange Act). Also, in cases where the representative of a juridical person or an agent, employee or other worker of a juridical person or individual sells or has another person acquire through public offering or secondary distribution such securities without delivering a prospectus in advance or concurrently regarding the business or property of the juridical person or individual, the relevant juridical person is also punished by a fine of not more than ¥100 million (Article 207(1)(v) of the Financial Instruments and Exchange Act). These also apply in cases where persons sell or have another person acquire through public offering or secondary distribution securities for which shelf registration has been conducted without delivering the shelf-registration prospectus and supplementary shelf-registration prospectus in advance or concurrently (violation of Article 15, paragraphs 2 and 6 applied *mutatis mutandis* under Article 23-12, paragraph 3 of the Financial Instruments and Exchange Act).

Also, in cases where persons sell or have another person acquire the remainder of a public offering or secondary distribution not through public offering or secondary distribution within three months from the date the notification pertaining to the relevant public offering or secondary distribution comes into effect (Article 15(6) of the Financial Instruments and Exchange Act) in violation of the obligation to use a prospectus, they will be punished by imprisonment with work for not more than six months or by a fine of not more than ¥500,000, or both (Article 205(i) of the Financial Instruments and Exchange Act). Also, in cases where the representative of a juridical person or an agent, employee or other worker of a juridical person or individual sells or has another person acquire not through public offering or secondary distribution such securities without delivering a prospectus in

*493*

advance or concurrently regarding the business or property of the juridical person or individual, the relevant juridical person is also punished by a fine of not more than ¥500,000 (Article 207(1)(vi) of the Financial Instruments and Exchange Act).

Similarly, persons who used a prospectus for public offering or secondary distribution of securities that require notification regarding public offering or secondary distribution or which have already been disclosed that has false statements or omits statements of matters that should be stated (violation of Article 13, paragraph 4 of the Financial Instruments and Exchange Act), persons who used a shelf-registration prospectus, shelf-registration provisional prospectus, or supplementary shelf-registration prospectus which has false statements or omits statements of matters that should be stated (violation of Article 13, paragraph 4 applied *mutatis mutandis* under Article 23-12, paragraph 2 of the Financial Instruments and Exchange Act), and persons who used documents other than the prospectus, drawings, sound and other materials with false indications or indications that cause misunderstanding (violation of Article 13, paragraph 5 of the Financial Instruments and Exchange Act) will be punished by imprisonment with work for not more than six months or by a fine of not more than ¥500,000, or both (Article 205(i) of the Financial Instruments and Exchange Act). Also, in cases where the representative of a juridical person or an agent, employee or other worker of a juridical person or individual uses a prospectus with false statements, etc. or has made false indications or indications that cause any misunderstanding with regard to the business or property of the juridical person or individual, the relevant juridical person is also punished by a fine of not more than ¥500,000 (Article 207 (1) (vi) of the Financial Instruments and Exchange Act). These penal provisions are similarly applied to shelf-registration prospectuses, provisional shelf-registration prospectuses, and supplementary shelf-registration prospectuses.

Persons who did not state that the relevant specified public offering, etc. is not subject to Article 4, paragraphs 1 and 2 of the Financial Instruments and Exchange Act in a prospectus used for a specified public offering or to sell or have another person acquire securities pertaining to the relevant specified

Chapter 3　Disclosure requirements

public offering (violation of Article 4, paragraph 5 of the Financial Instruments and Exchange Act) will be punished by an administrative fine of not more than ¥300,000. (Article 208(i) of the Financial Instruments and Exchange Act). This also applies to persons who did not make such a statement in prospectuses used for public offerings and secondary distributions that do not require submission of a shelf-registration statement (Article 4, paragraph 5 applied *mutatis mutandis* by Article 23-8, paragraph 4 of the Financial Instruments and Exchange Act).

# 6. Others

a. Non-submission of securities registration statements for rights issues, non-submission of foreign securities information, etc.

In the following cases, persons will be punished by imprisonment with work for not more than six months or by a fine of not more than ¥500,000, or both (Article 205(i), (vi-2), (vi-3), and (vi-4) of the Financial Instruments and Exchange Act)

(1) Cases where a securities public offering or secondary distribution is conducted for shareholders recorded in the shareholders register on a given date, where persons do not submit a securities registration statement by 25 days before that date (violation of Article 4, paragraph 4 of the Financial Instruments and Exchange Act)

(2) Cases where persons do not submit a written notice of securities or written notice of shelf registration pertaining to a specified public offering, etc. by the day before the day the relevant specified public offering, public offering, or secondary distribution begins (violation of Article 4, paragraph 6 and Article 23-10, paragraph 4 of the Financial Instruments and Exchange Act)

(3) Cases where persons indicate that the Prime Minister certifies that statements of the securities registration statement are true and accurate or that it does not omit any statements on material matters or guarantees or approves the value of the securities concerned because a notification or shelf registration has come into effect or an order to suspend its effect has been canceled (violation of Article 23, paragraph 2 or Article 23-12, paragraph 5 of the Financial Instruments and

*495*

Exchange Act)

(4) Cases where a securities public offering or secondary distribution is conducted for shareholders recorded in the shareholders register on a given date, where persons do not submit a shelf-registration supplement by 10 days before that date (violation of Article 23-10, paragraph 3 of the Financial Instruments and Exchange Act)

(5) Cases where persons failed to make a public notice without delay where they submitted an amendment report regarding material matters among those stated in an annual securities report (violation of Article 4, paragraph 6 and Article 24-2, paragraph 2 of the Financial Instruments and Exchange Act)

(6) Cases where persons provided or publicized foreign securities information with falsehoods concerning material matters (violation of Article 27-32-2, paragraphs 1 and 2 of the Financial Instruments and Exchange Act)

(7) Cases where persons sold securities pertaining to a secondary distribution of foreign securities even though they did not provide or publicize foreign securities information pertaining to the relevant secondary distribution of foreign securities (violation of Article 27-32-2, paragraph 1 of the Financial Instruments and Exchange Act)

(8) Cases where persons did not provide or publicize foreign securities information (violation of Article 27-32-2, paragraph 2 of the Financial Instruments and Exchange Act)

b. Violations of obligation for notification

In the following cases, persons will be punished by an administrative fine of not more than ¥100,000 (Article 209(i) & (ii) of the Financial Instruments and Exchange Act).

(1) Cases where persons do not indicate that no notification has been made etc., in solicitations, etc. of qualified institutional investors that do not require notification (violation of Article 23-13(1) of the Financial Instruments and Exchange Act)

(2) Cases where persons do not indicate that no notification has been made etc., in solicitations, etc. of professional investors that do not

Chapter 3  Disclosure requirements

require notification (violation of Article 23-13 (3) of the Financial Instruments and Exchange Act)

(3) Cases where persons do not indicate that no notification has been made etc., in solicitations, etc. of a small number of investors that do not require notification (violation of Article 23-13 (4) of the Financial Instruments and Exchange Act)

(4) Cases of selling or having another person acquire securities through solicitation of qualified institutional investors that does not require notification, where persons do not deliver in advance or concurrently any documents stating that notification has not been made, etc. (violation of Article 23-13 (2) of the Financial Instruments and Exchange Act)

(5) Cases of selling or having another person acquire securities through solicitation of a small number of investors that does not require notification, where persons do not deliver in advance or concurrently any documents stating that notification has not been made, etc. (violation of Article 23-13 (5) of the Financial Instruments and Exchange Act)


c. Failure to comply with Prime Minister's order to disclose material information, etc. (violation of the FD Rules)

Any person who 1) fails to submit a report or materials, or submits a false report or materials under Article 27-37(1) of the Financial Instruments and Exchange Act, 2) refuses, impedes, or avoids the inspections under Article 27-37 (1) of the Financial Instruments and Exchange Act, or 3) fails to comply with the order to disclose material information (violation of Article 27-38, paragraph 2 of the Financial Instruments and Exchange Act), will be punished by imprisonment with work for not more than six months or a fine of not more than ¥500,000, or both (Article 205(v), (vi), and (vi-5) of the Financial Instruments and Exchange Act).

# H. Administrative monetary penalties

## 1. False statements, etc. in offering disclosures

a. Issuers in cases with false statements, etc. in offering disclosure documents

Where issuers who submitted offering disclosure documents with false statements concerning material matters or without statements of material matters that should be stated [121] sell or have another person acquire securities by public offering or secondary distribution based on the relevant offering disclosure documents (limited to secondary distributions of securities held by the relevant issuer), the Prime Minister must order the relevant issuer to pay administrative monetary penalties to the national treasury (Article 172-2(1) of the Financial Instruments and Exchange Act). Here, offering disclosure documents corresponds to securities registration statements (including referenced documents and attached documents), foreign company registration statements (including supplementary documents and attached documents), foreign person registration statements (including supplementary documents and attached documents), amendments (including referenced documents), foreign company amendments (including supplementary documents), foreign person amendments (including supplementary documents), shelf-registration statements (including referenced documents and attached documents), amended shelf-registration statements (including referenced documents), and shelf-registration supplements (including referenced documents and attached documents) (Article 172-2(3) of the Financial Instruments and Exchange Act).

---

121 Administrative monetary penalties are not imposed in cases where statements of material facts necessary to avoid causing any misunderstanding are omitted. This is on the grounds that there is a range in determining the requirement of "not causing any misunderstanding."

Chapter 3 Disclosure requirements

The administrative monetary penalties will be an amount equivalent to: (i) in cases where the issuer has others acquire securities by public offering, 2. 25% of the total issue value where the securities concerned are securities other than shares, etc. (shares, preferred equity investment certificates and other securities specified as equivalent by a cabinet order; Article 33-5(1) of the Financial Instruments and Exchange Act Implementing Order) (where the securities concerned are share option certificates or other securities specified as equivalent by a cabinet office ordinance, including the amount to be paid upon exercising the share options pertaining to the relevant share option certificates and other amounts specified as equivalent by cabinet office ordinance; the same in 2., 3., and 4. below) and 4.5% of the total issue value where the securities concerned are shares, etc. (Article 172-2(1)(i) of the Financial Instruments and Exchange Act); (ii) in cases where the issuer sells securities it holds by secondary distribution, 2.25% of the total amount of the offer value when the securities concerned are securities other than shares, etc., and 4.5% of the total amount of the offer value where the securities concerned are shares, etc. (Article 172-2(1)(ii) of the Financial Instruments and Exchange Act).

b. "Directors", etc. of issuers in cases with false statements, etc. in offering disclosure documents

Where "directors" (directors, agents, employees or other personnel; the same in 2 below) of the issuer that submitted the relevant offering disclosure documents which have false statements regarding material matters or omit statements of material matters that should be stated and who were involved in the submission of the relevant offering disclosure documents while knowing that there were false statements or that statements that should be stated were omitted in the relevant offering disclosure documents sold securities held by the relevant "directors", etc. via secondary distribution based on the relevant offering disclosure documents, the Prime Minister must order the relevant "directors", etc. to pay administrative monetary penalties to the national treasury (Article 172-2 (2) of the Financial Instruments and Exchange Act). The amount of the administrative monetary penalties will be equivalent to 2.25% of the total amount of the offer value where the securities concerned sold are securities other than

*499*

shares, etc. and 4.5% of the total amount of the offer value price where the securities concerned are shares, etc.

c. Issuers who use prospectuses with false statements, etc. regarding important matters

In cases where issuers who used a prospectus with false statements regarding material matters (limited to matters listed in each item of Article 5, paragraph 1 of the Financial Instruments and Exchange Act) or without statements of material matters that should be stated sell securities held by the relevant issuers through secondary distribution pertaining to the relevant prospectus, the Prime Minister must order the relevant issuer to pay administrative monetary penalties to the national treasury (Article 172-2(4) of the Financial Instruments and Exchange Act). The amount of the administrative monetary penalties will be equivalent to 2.25% of the total amount of the offer value where the securities concerned are securities other than shares, etc., and 4.5% of the total amount of the offer value where the securities concerned are shares, etc.

d. "Directors", etc. of issuers using prospectuses with false statements regarding important matters

In cases where "directors", etc. of issuers who used a prospectus with false statements regarding material matters or without statements of material matters that should be stated who were involved in the preparation of the relevant prospectus while knowing that there were false statements or that statements that should be stated were omitted sell securities held by the relevant "directors", etc. by secondary distribution pertaining to the relevant prospectus, the Prime Minister must order the relevant "directors", etc. to pay administrative monetary penalties to the national treasury (Article 172-2(5) of the Financial Instruments and Exchange Act).

## 2. False statements, etc. in continuous disclosure

a. Issuers in cases of false statements, etc. in annual securities reports

Where issuers of securities submit annual securities reports, etc. with false statements concerning material matters or without statements of material matters that should be stated, the Prime Minister must order the relevant

Chapter 3 Disclosure requirements

issuer to pay administrative monetary penalties to the national treasury (Article 172-4(1) of the Financial Instruments and Exchange Act). Here, annual securities reports, etc. refer to annual securities reports and their attached documents, foreign company reports and their supplementary documents and attached documents, and foreign person reports and their supplementary documents and attached documents and amendment reports.

The amount of administrative monetary penalties will be (i) ¥6 million or (ii) in cases where 6/100,000 of the total amount of the market price of index securities for calculation issued by the issuer exceeds ¥6 million, that amount. Here, index securities for calculation refer to share certificates, preferred equity investment certificates provided by the Act on Preferred Equity Investment, and other equivalent securities prescribed by Article 33-5-2 of the Financial Instruments and Exchange Act Implementing Order. Also, the total amount of the market price is calculated in accordance with the Cabinet Office Ordinance on Administrative Monetary Penalties under Chapter 6-2 of the Financial Instruments and Exchange Act (Cabinet Office Ordinance on Administrative Monetary Penalties) Article 1ter, but in cases where no market price or no index securities for calculation have been issued, in accordance with Article 33-5-3 of the Financial Instruments and Exchange Act Implementing Order, it is the amount calculated by subtracting the total amount of liabilities from the total amount of assets posted on the balance sheet specified in Article 1-4 of the Cabinet Office Ordinance on Administrative Monetary Penalties

b. Issuers in cases of false statements, etc. in quarterly securities reports, semiannual securities reports, extraordinary reports, etc.

In cases where issuers submit quarterly securities reports, foreign company quarterly securities reports (including supplementary documents), semiannual securities reports, foreign company semiannual securities reports (including supplementary documents), extraordinary reports, foreign company extraordinary reports or foreign person extraordinary reports or amendment reports to these reports with false statements concerning material matters or without statements of material matters that should be stated, the Prime Minister must order the relevant issuer to pay

*501*

administrative monetary penalties to the national treasury (Article 172-4(1) of the Financial Instruments and Exchange Act).

The amount of administrative monetary penalties is equivalent to one-half of the amount in cases of false statements in annual securities reports, etc. There are provisions established to adjust the amounts of the administrative monetary penalties for submitting continuous disclosure documents (annual securities reports [including attached documents], foreign company reports [including supplementary documents and attached documents], foreign person reports [including supplementary documents and attached documents] and amendment reports to these reports, as well as quarterly securities reports, foreign company quarterly securities reports [including supplementary documents], semiannual securities reports, foreign company semiannual securities reports [including supplementary documents], foreign person semiannual securities reports [including supplementary documents], extraordinary reports, foreign company extraordinary reports, and foreign person extraordinary reports and the amendment reports to these reports) with two or more false statements in the same business year (Article 185-7 (6) & (7) of the Financial Instruments and Exchange Act). Also, when there is a final and binding court decision concerning a fine for the same case of submission of continuous disclosure documents with false statements, etc. for which administrative monetary penalties should be imposed, the amount of administrative monetary penalties to be paid is the amount after subtracting the amount of the fine from the amount of the administrative monetary penalties (Article 185-7 (4) and Article 185-8 (6) of the Financial Instruments and Exchange Act).[122]

## 3. Non-delivery of prospectuses in solicitation before notification, transactions before notification comes into effect, and secondary distribution of previously-disclosed securities

Regarding public offerings and secondary distributions of securities that

---

122 There are no provisions for adjustments of criminal penalties and administrative monetary penalties concerning false statements, etc. in offering disclosure documents.

Chapter 3  Disclosure requirements

require notification (Article 4(1) of the Financial Instruments and Exchange Act), general solicitations for securities acquired by qualified institutional investors that require notification (Article 4(2) of the Financial Instruments and Exchange Act), and general solicitations for securities acquired by professional investors that require notification (Article 4(3) of the Financial Instruments and Exchange Act), the Prime Minister must order persons who conduct the relevant public offering, secondary distribution, general solicitation for securities acquired by qualified institutional investors or general solicitation for securities acquired by professional investors (for persons who conduct secondary distributions, general solicitations for securities acquired by qualified institutional investors, and general solicitation for securities acquired by professional investors secondary distributions, limited to persons who conducted these acts pertaining to securities they hold themselves) even though their notification has not been accepted to pay administrative monetary penalties to the national treasury (Article 172(1) of the Financial Instruments and Exchange Act).

The administrative monetary penalties will be an amount equivalent to: (i) in cases where the issuer has others acquire securities by public offering, 2. 25% of the total issue value where the securities concerned are securities other than shares, etc. and 4.5% of the total issue value where the securities concerned are shares, (Article 172(1)(i) of the Financial Instruments and Exchange Act); and (ii) in cases where the issuer sells securities by secondary distribution, general solicitation for securities acquired by qualified institutional investors, or general solicitation for securities acquired by professional investors, 2.25% of the total amount of the offer value where the securities concerned are securities other than shares, etc., and 4.5% of the total amount of the offer value where the securities concerned are shares, etc. (Article 172(1)(ii) of the Financial Instruments and Exchange Act).

Also, the Prime Minister must order issuers who had others acquire by public offering securities prescribed in Article 4, paragraph 1 of the Financial Instruments and Exchange Act and persons who sold by secondary distribution securities prescribed in Article 4, paragraph 4 (limited to persons who sold securities that they hold themselves) of the Financial

Instruments and Exchange Act before notification comes into effect in violation of Article 15, paragraph 1 of the Financial Instruments and Exchange Act to pay administrative monetary penalties to the national treasury (Article 172(2) of the Financial Instruments and Exchange Act). The amount of the administrative monetary penalties is the same as the amount of administrative monetary penalties in cases of solicitation before notification (Article 172(1) of the Financial Instruments and Exchange Act). There are provisions established to adjust the amount of administrative monetary penalties where there are violations of both Article 172, paragraphs 1 and 2 of the Financial Instruments and Exchange Act in the same public offering or secondary distribution (Article 185-7(2) & (3) of the Financial Instruments and Exchange Act).

Moreover, the Prime Minister must order issuers who had others acquire securities by public offering and persons who sold securities by secondary distribution (limited to persons who sold securities they hold themselves) before a shelf registration comes into effect or before submission of a shelf-registration supplement to pay administrative monetary penalties to the national treasury (Article 172(2) & (4) of the Financial Instruments and Exchange Act). The amount of the administrative monetary penalties is the same as the amount in cases of solicitation before notification (Article 172(1) of the Financial Instruments and Exchange Act).

In addition to the above, the Prime Minister must order persons who sold securities they hold themselves via secondary distribution without delivering a prospectus in violation of Article 15, paragraph 2 of the Financial Instruments and Exchange Act to pay administrative monetary penalties to the national treasury (Article 172 (3) of the Financial Instruments and Exchange Act). The amount of administrative monetary penalties is the same as that amount in cases of secondary distribution before notification (Article 172(1) of the Financial Instruments and Exchange Act).

## 4. Non-submission of continuous disclosure documents

The Prime Minister must order issuers who do not submit annual securities reports, foreign company reports or foreign person reports to pay

Chapter 3 Disclosure requirements

administrative monetary penalties of an amount equivalent to the audit certification fee for the business year immediately before the business year of the annual securities report, etc. that should have been submitted under these regulations (money paid or that should be paid as consideration for audit certification prescribed in Article 193-2 (1) of the Financial Instruments and Exchange Act and amounts prescribed by a cabinet office ordinance as the value of other assets) (¥4 million in cases where there is no immediately prior business year that should receive audit certification or equivalent cases prescribed by a cabinet office ordinance) to the national treasury (Article 173(1) of the Financial Instruments and Exchange Act).

Similarly, the Prime Minister must order issuers who do not submit quarterly securities reports or foreign company quarterly securities reports, and issuers that do not submit semiannual securities reports or foreign company semiannual securities reports or foreign person semiannual securities reports to pay administrative monetary penalties of an amount equivalent to one half of the audit certification fee for the business year immediately before the business year of the period of the quarterly or semiannual securities report that should have been submitted under these regulations (money paid or that should be paid as consideration for audit certification prescribed in Article 193-2, paragraph 1 of the Financial Instruments and Exchange Act and amounts prescribed by a cabinet office ordinance as the value of other assets) (¥2 million in cases where there is no immediately prior business year that should receive audit certification or equivalent cases prescribed by a cabinet office ordinance) to the national treasury (Article 172-3(2) of the Financial Instruments and Exchange Act).

There are provisions established to adjust the amount of administrative monetary penalties when there are two or more non-submissions of annual securities reports, etc., quarterly securities reports, or semiannual securities reports, etc. in the same business year (Article 18-7(4) of the Financial Instruments and Exchange Act).

Issuers who do not submit extraordinary reports that should state matters specified by the Cabinet Office Ordinance on Administrative Monetary

Penalties as having a material influence on investors' investment decisions are subject to administrative monetary penalties similar to those for false statements, etc. in extraordinary reports (Article 172-4(3) of the Financial Instruments and Exchange Act). However, the Cabinet Office Ordinance on Administrative Monetary Penalties prescribes that all matters that should be stated have a material influence on investors' investment decisions (Article 1-5 of the Cabinet Office Ordinance on Administrative Monetary Penalties), and cases where an extraordinary report, etc. is not submitted without delay are all subject to administrative monetary penalties.

# 5. Administrative monetary penalties payment orders concerning markets for professionals

a. Specified solicitation, etc. without providing or publicizing specified information on securities

The Prime Minister must order persons who conducted specified solicitation etc. even though the issuer of the securities has not provided or publicized specified information on securities pertaining to the securities concerned to the counterparties (for persons who conducted specified offers to sell etc., limited to persons who conducted specified offers to sell concerning securities they hold themselves) to pay administrative monetary penalties to the national treasury (Article 172-9 of the Financial Instruments and Exchange Act).

The amount of the administrative monetary penalties will be equivalent to 2. 25% of the total issue value or total securities sales price where the securities concerned are securities other than shares, etc. and 4.5% of the total issue value or total securities sales price where the securities concerned are shares, etc. (Article 172-9 (i) & (ii) of the Financial Instruments and Exchange Act).

b. False statements, etc. in specified information on securities, etc.

Where issuers who submitted or publicized false specified information on securities, etc. regarding material matters or did not submit or publicize information regarding material matters that should be provided or publicized (for persons who conducted specified offers to sell, etc., limited to

Chapter 3 Disclosure requirements

persons who conducted specified offers to sell, etc. regarding securities they hold themselves) sold or had another person acquire securities by specified solicitation, etc. pertaining to the specified information on securities, etc. with the relevant false statements, etc., the Prime Minister must order these persons to pay administrative monetary penalties to the national treasury (Article 172-10(1) of the Financial Instruments and Exchange Act).

The amount of the administrative monetary penalties will be: (i) in cases where specified information on securities, etc. with false statements, etc. has been publicized, an amount equivalent to 2.25% of the total issue value or total securities sales price where the securities concerned are securities other than shares, etc. and 4.5% of the total issue value or total securities sales price where the securities concerned shares, etc.; and (ii) in cases where specified information on securities, etc. with false statements, etc. has not been publicized, the amount calculated by multiplying the amount in (i) by the number calculated by dividing the number of persons who received the specified information on securities, etc. with false statements, etc. by the number of counterparties to the relevant specified solicitation (Article 172-10(1)(i) & (ii) of the Financial Instruments and Exchange Act).

Also, where "directors", etc. (directors, agents, employees or other workers) who were involved in the false statements, etc. and were involved in the provision or publication of the relevant specified information on securities, etc. while knowing the relevant false statements, etc. sold securities held by the relevant "directors" by specified offers to sell, etc. pertaining to the relevant specified information on securities, etc., the Prime Minister must order these "directors" to pay administrative monetary penalties to the national treasury (Article 172-10 (2) of the Financial Instruments and Exchange Act).

The amount of administrative monetary penalties will be an amount equivalent to 2.25% of the total offer value where the securities concerned sold are securities other than shares, etc. and 4.5% of the total offer value where the securities concerned are shares, etc.

*507*

c . False statements, etc. in issuer information, etc.

The Prime Minister must order issuers who provided or publicized false issuer information, etc. regarding material matters or did not provide or publicize information regarding material matters that should be provided or publicized to pay administrative monetary penalties to the national treasury (Article 172-11(1) of the Financial Instruments and Exchange Act).

The amount of administrative monetary penalties will be (i) in cases where issuer information, etc. with false statements, etc. has been publicized, ¥6 million; or (ii) in cases where an amount equivalent to 6/100,000 of the total market price of index securities for calculation issued by the issuer exceeds ¥6 million, that amount. In cases where there is no market price or no index securities for calculation have been issued, it is the amount calculated as specified by cabinet order.

In cases where the issuer information, etc. with false statements, etc. has not been publicized, the amount of administrative monetary penalties will be the amount calculated by multiplying the amount above by the number calculated by dividing the number of persons who received the issuer information, etc. with false statements, etc. by the number of counterparties who should receive the issuer information, etc. (Article 172-11(1)(i) & (ii) of the Financial Instruments and Exchange Act).

# 6 . Acts of assistance in submission of false disclosure documents, etc.

In cases where an issuer submitted, provided or publicized offering disclosure documents (Article 172-2(3) of the Financial Instruments and Exchange Act), misrepresented annual securities reports, etc., quarterly or semiannual or extraordinary securities reports, etc., specified information on securities, etc. or issuer information that has false statements regarding material matters or omitted statements regarding material matters that should be stated (Article 172-12(1)(i) of the Financial Instruments and Exchange Act), where there is a person who committed a specified act of involvement, the Prime Minister must order the relevant person who committed the specified act of involvement to pay as administrative

*508*

Chapter 3 Disclosure requirements

monetary penalties an amount equivalent to the money paid or that should be paid as fees, rewards and other consideration regarding the relevant specified act of involvement and the value of other assets as specified by a cabinet office ordinance to the national treasury (Article 172-12(1) of the Financial Instruments and Exchange Act).

Here "specified act of involvement" is an act that assists the issuer in submitting, providing or publicizing false disclosure documents, etc. and refers to either (i) the provision of advice regarding the preparation of the relevant false disclosure documents to persons who take a series of actions to conceal or disguise all or part of the facts that are the basis for the accounting treatment necessary to prepare the relevant false disclosure documents and then prepare the relevant false disclosure documents based on those actions to conceal or disguise; or (ii) taking a series of actions to conceal or disguise while knowing all or part of the series of actions to conceal or disguise prescribed in (i) (excluding acts for audit certification prescribed in Article 193-2(1) of the Financial Instruments and Exchange Act), or the act of encouraging the submission, provision or publication of false disclosure documents, etc. by the person submitting the disclosure documents (Article 172-12(2) of the Financial Instruments and Exchange Act).

In this case, the amount of administrative monetary penalties will be an amount equivalent to the amounts paid or that should be paid as fees, rewards and other consideration regarding the relevant specified act of involvement and the value of other assets as specified by a cabinet office ordinance (Article 172-12(1) of the Financial Instruments and Exchange Act).

*509*

# Chapter 4

The takeover bid system and
the system of disclosure of the
status of large-volume holdings

*Masakazu Shirai*

# A. The takeover bid system

## 1. Overview of the takeover bid system

### a. What is a takeover bid?

The term "takeover bid" means offering to effect purchase, etc. of shares, etc. or soliciting offers to sell them, etc. from many unspecified persons through a public notice, and then effecting their purchase, etc. outside of a financial instruments exchange market (Article 27-2 (6) of the Financial Instruments and Exchange Act). Such purchase, etc. of shares, etc. is effected primarily with the intent of acquiring or strengthening control of a company. When a takeover bid is made, the provisions of the Financial Instruments and Exchange Act ensure that all shareholders are treated equally by giving them the opportunity to sell the shares in their possession on equal terms, and enables shareholders to decide whether to sell their shares based on adequate information.

Under the Japanese takeover bid system, when shares, etc. issued by an issuer required to submit an annual report (or other such issuer) are purchased outside a financial instruments exchange market by a person other than the issuer from more than ten persons within 61 days, and after that purchase the ownership ratio of shares, etc. of the person who effects the purchase will exceed five percent, the purchase, etc. of those shares, etc. must be effected by means of a takeover bid (Article 27-2 (1) (i) of the Financial Instruments and Exchange Act; Article 6-2 (3) of the Financial Instruments and Exchange Act Implementing Order). Further, even if shares, etc. issued by an issuer required to submit an annual report (or other such issuer) are purchased outside of a financial instruments exchange market by a person other than the issuer from ten or fewer persons within 61 days, the purchase, etc. of those shares, etc. must be effected by means of a takeover bid if after that purchase the ownership ratio of shares, etc. of the person who effects the purchase will exceed one-third (Article 27-2(1) (ii) of the Financial Instruments and Exchange Act; Article 6-2 (3) of the Financial Instruments and Exchange Act Implementing Order). The former

*512*

Chapter 4   The takeover bid system and the system of disclosure of the status of large-volume holdings

rule governing when implementation of a takeover bid is compulsory is generally referred to as the "five-percent rule"; the latter as the "one-third rule".

When conducting a takeover bid in accordance with the above rules, the takeover bidder need purchase only the number of shares, etc. required, with one exception: if the takeover bidder's ownership ratio of shares, etc. will be two-thirds or more after the purchase, a requirement to purchase all the tendered shares, etc. (the buy-all requirement) is imposed on it (Article 27-13 (4) parenthesis of the Financial Instruments and Exchange Act; Article 14-2-2 of the Financial Instruments and Exchange Act Implementing Order). The Financial Instruments and Exchange Act also defines cases where a solicit-all requirement is imposed on takeover bidders on the same principle as the buy-all requirement. If the takeover bidder's ownership ratio of shares, etc. will be two-thirds or more after the purchase, it must in principle implement a takeover bid for all the shares, etc. issued by the issuer of the shares, etc. in question (Article 27-2(5) of the Financial Instruments and Exchange Act; Article 8 (5) (iii) of the Financial Instruments and Exchange Act Implementing Order).

b. Characteristics of the Japanese takeover bid system

The following three general observations may be made on the characteristics of the takeover bid system adopted in Japan as compared to that of other countries.

First, the Japanese takeover bid system regulates cases of purchase, etc. of shares, etc. outside a financial instruments exchange market; implementation of a takeover bid is not in principle compulsory if the purchase, etc. of shares, etc. is effected, for example, through a transaction on a financial instruments exchange market or by issuing shares for subscription. Thus, in determining when it is compulsory to implement a takeover bid, a distinction is made based on whether the transaction occurs outside a financial instruments exchange market: only certain purchases, etc. of shares, etc. effected outside a financial instruments exchange market are subject to regulation, whereas transactions effected on financial instruments exchange markets are not.

Second, in Japan the conditions for making implementation of a takeover bid compulsory and the conditions for imposing the buy-all requirement or the solicit-all requirement differ; the latter may be characterized as stricter than the former. Specifically, under the one-third rule, implementation of a takeover bid is compulsory if the ownership ratio of the person purchasing the shares, etc. will be one-third or more after the purchase. But even in that case, unless the takeover bidder's ownership ratio will be two-thirds or more after the purchase, the solicit-all requirement or the buy-all requirement is not imposed, and the takeover bidder need purchase only the number of shares, etc. required.

Third, under the takeover bid system adopted in Japan, when implementation of a takeover bid is compulsory under the five-percent rule or the one-third rule, the purchase, etc. whereby the ownership ratio of the person conducting it will increase to more than five percent or one-third must itself be effected by means of a takeover bid. Thus, in Japan the requirement is not that, upon achieving an ownership ratio of more than five percent or one-third, one must then implement a takeover bid for all the remaining shares; the purchase, etc. of shares, etc. as a result of which the ownership ratio increases to more than five percent or one-third must itself be effected by means of a takeover bid. This regulatory approach may be characterized as a so-called ex ante regulation in that it requires that the purchase, etc. of shares, etc. be effected by means of a takeover bid at the stage before the ownership ratio of the person conducting the purchase increases to more than five percent or one-third, unlike a regulatory approach requiring that a takeover bid be made after the ownership ratio increases to that level.

c . Rationale behind the takeover bid system

These, then, are the characteristics of the Japanese takeover bid system. What may be considered the rationale behind it? Concisely explaining the rationale behind the Japanese takeover bid system is no simple task, for it involves a complex welter of regulations, and the regulatory goals of each cannot always be understood in a way that is consistent with the rest. Nonetheless, its rationale can generally be summarized as follows.

The first point that may be cited as part of the rationale behind the Japanese takeover bid system is the need to treat shareholders equally and the need to provide adequate information to them (primarily in order to

Chapter 4   The takeover bid system and the system of disclosure of the status of large-volume holdings

protect shareholders who have received a purchase offer). Where equal negotiations cannot be expected due to disparities in information between the parties, shareholders may feel pressured to sell the shares in their possession, resulting in unfairness; in such situations, therefore, the need arises to protect shareholders by compelling the party that has the information advantage to release the information and give shareholders equal opportunities to sell.[1] Thus, by making a takeover bid compulsory in such situations, it is necessary to ensure, based on the provisions of the Financial Instruments and Exchange Act, that all shareholders are treated equally through the provision of opportunities to sell their shares on equal terms[2] and that they are provided with enough information to decide whether to sell their shares. These needs can be adduced as grounds justifying compulsory implementation of a takeover bid primarily under the five-percent rule.

The need to treat shareholders equally and the need to provide adequate information to them can thus be cited as part of the rationale behind the Japanese takeover bid system. How is that to be reconciled with the fact that under the Japanese takeover bid system, only certain purchases, etc. of shares, etc. effected outside a financial instruments exchange market are subject to regulation, while transactions effected on a financial instruments exchange market are not? In this regard it may be argued that shareholders (investors) are in general treated fairly and equally in financial instruments exchange markets in that transactions on them are (a) public in that anyone may participate in them, (b) transparent in that volumes and prices are publicly disclosed, and (c) fair in that they are by auction.[3] Thus in the case of transactions effected on a financial instruments exchange market, it can be

---

1   Kuronuma Etsuro and Ota Yo, eds., *Ronten taikei: Kinyū shōhin torihiki hō 1* (Point by point: The Financial Instruments and Exchange Act 1) (Dai-Ichi Hoki, 2014), pp. 286-287 (written by Noda Masaki).

2   Nonetheless, in Japan, where as briefly described in Section A.1 (b) the buy-all requirement and solicit-all requirement are imposed in only limited situations, the takeover bid system cannot be said to guarantee shareholders the opportunity to sell all the shares in their possession. Even in cases where implementing a takeover bid is compulsory, unless the buy-all requirement or solicit-all requirement applies, shareholders are given only the opportunity to sell their shares on equal terms; it cannot be argued that they are actually guaranteed the opportunity to sell them.

reasonable to think that shareholders (investors) will be treated fairly and equally through the market even if implementing a takeover bid is not compulsory when purchasing shares, etc.[4]; the Financial Instruments and Exchange Act therefore exempts transactions effected on a financial instruments exchange market from the requirement to implement a takeover bid. By contrast, transactions effected outside a financial instruments exchange market (typically over-the-counter transactions) are not always highly public, transparent, and fair, and it cannot really be claimed that shareholders (investors) are treated fairly and equally with regard to them; hence, the need to make implementation of a takeover bid compulsory in certain cases.

Second, besides the need to treat shareholders equally and the need to provide adequate information to them, another point that may be cited as part of the rationale behind the Japanese takeover bid system is the need for equal distribution of control premiums (in order to protect not shareholders who have received a purchase offer but those who have not). This need for equal distribution of control premiums can be adduced as grounds justifying compulsory implementation of a takeover bid particularly under the one-third rule.

A control premium is the difference between price (per share) of control stock and its market price. A block of shares large enough to enable one to acquire control of a company is generally referred to as "control stock". When ownership of control stock is transferred, the transfer price is often set

---

3    Yamashita Tomonobu and Kanda Hideki, *Kinyū shōhin torihiki hō gaisetsu* (Overview of the Financial Instruments and Exchange Act) (Yuhikaku, 2010), p. 243 (written by Kato Takahito); Kondo Mitsuo et al., *Kinyū shōhin torihiki hō nyūmon* (Introduction to the Financial Instruments and Exchange Act), 4th ed. (Shojihomu, 2015), p. 368, etc.

4    Likewise, with regard to provision of information to shareholders, if a large volume of shares is acquired through a transaction conducted on a financial instruments exchange market, information on that large share acquisition will be reflected in the share price of the target company; thus, shareholders (investors) can trade on the assumption that the share price reflects information on large share acquisitions. Therefore, in the case of transactions effected on a financial instruments exchange market, it can be reasonable to think that less need exists to provide information to shareholders than in the case of transactions effected outside of a financial instruments exchange market.

*516*

Chapter 4  The takeover bid system and the system of disclosure of the status of large-volume holdings

higher than the market price of the shares in question (hence the control premium is usually a positive value). If transfer of ownership of the control stock is effected by means of an over-the-counter transaction outside a financial instruments exchange market, the control premium is enjoyed solely by the transferor of the control stock (the controlling shareholder); but if implementing a takeover bid is compulsory when transferring ownership of control stock, all shareholders can enjoy a share of the control premium.

By adopting the one-third rule as one condition under which implementation of a takeover bid is compulsory, the Japanese takeover bid system requires that the control premium be equally distributed among all shareholders instead of letting the transferor of the control stock (the controlling shareholder) monopolize it. As for situations in which the one-third rule applies, only certain purchases, etc. of shares, etc. effected outside a financial instruments exchange market are subject to regulation under it; in principle, transactions effected on a financial instruments exchange market are not. This is presumably on the grounds that if enough shares are bought up through transactions effected on a financial instruments exchange market to constitute control stock, that can be expected to drive up the target company's share price by being reflected in it, allowing shareholders to enjoy a share (albeit imperfect) of the control premium through the rise in share price. Of course, distribution of the control premium through a rise in share price certainly does not guarantee its perfectly equal distribution to shareholders to the same extent as distribution through compulsory implementation of a takeover bid does. However, given that implementation of a takeover bid entails various costs, making it compulsory in a broad range of cases could in certain regards hinder transactions in control stock per se;[5] thus, the adoption of the above approach by the Japanese takeover bid system is, though there is room for dissent, an understandable policy decision.

d. Evolution of the takeover bid system

The Japanese takeover bid system was introduced in 1971 by a revision of

---

5　See Yamashita and Kanda (supra, n. 3), p. 249 (Kato Takahito).

the Securities and Exchange Act, taking as its model the Williams Act enacted by the United States in 1968. In the United States before the Williams Act was enacted, it often happened that, in a takeover strategy termed the Saturday Night Special, a short tender deadline was set over the weekend and shares were bought up on a first come, first served basis; it was accordingly feared that shareholders could be induced to sell without being able to reach an informed decision on the reasonableness of the purchase terms. In Japan in around 1970, meanwhile, overseas investors were expected to start buying up listed companies in Japan as the liberalization of capital progressed, and it was considered necessary to establish corresponding regulations; hence, the adoption of the takeover bid system under the above revision of the law.

However, for some time after the takeover bid system was brought in through the 1971 amendment to the Securities and Exchange Act, there were only a handful of cases of takeover bids actually being made in Japan.[6] The Japanese takeover bid system was cumbersome at the time, and it was criticized in particular by foreign companies as actually making corporate acquisitions more difficult.[7] Given those circumstances, the takeover bid system was completely overhauled by the 1990 revision of the Securities and Exchange Act with a view to bringing it into line with the takeover bid systems of other countries, and the one-third rule on compulsory implementation of takeover bids was introduced mainly on the model of the European takeover bid system.

Following the 1990 revision of the Securities and Exchange Act, the takeover bid system came into wide use in Japan as well. But as use of the system spread, problems gradually arose that exposed its defects; to remedy those problems, an attempt was made to improve the system under the 2006 revision of the Financial Instruments and Exchange Act, chiefly with the goals of ensuring fair competition for company control and enhancing

---

6   Kawamoto Ichiro et al., *Shin Kinyū shōhin torihiki hō tokuhon* (New readings in the Financial Instruments and Exchange Act) (Yuhikaku, 2014), p. 109.

7   Kondo Mitsuo, "Kōkai kaitsuke seido" (The takeover bid system) in Kawamoto Ichiro and Tatsuta Misao, eds., *Kinyū shōhin torihiki hō no ronri to jitsumu* (Theory and practice of the Financial Instruments and Exchange Act) (Economic Legal Research Institute, 2007), p. 40.

Chapter 4　The takeover bid system and the system of disclosure of the status of large-volume holdings

provision of information to shareholders. For example, the 2006 revision of the Financial Instruments and Exchange Act mandated takeover bids in the case of transactions combining on- and off-market transactions and in the case of competition between different bidders, and it brought in the buy-all requirement. The 2006 revision of the Financial Instruments and Exchange Act was implemented with the goal of remedying problems that had actually occurred in cases of acquisitions in Japan, and the improvements so made in the takeover bid system make a certain amount of sense. On the other hand, however, it is also a fact that the 2006 revision of the Financial Instruments and Exchange Act has considerably complicated the Japanese takeover bid system.

## 2. Scope of application of takeover bid regulations

a. Securities subject to takeover bid regulations

The securities subject to takeover bid regulations in Japan are (i) "shares, etc." issued by an issuer required to submit an annual report (see Article 24 (1) of the Financial Instruments and Exchange Act), and (ii) "shares, etc." issued by an issuer of specified listed securities or of specified over-the-counter traded securities[8] (Article 27-2 (1) main clause of the Financial Instruments and Exchange Act; Article 6 (2) of the Financial Instruments and Exchange Act Implementing Order). Note also that even after securities have been delisted, "shares, etc." issued by the issuer thereof are still subject to takeover bid regulations as long as that issuer is required to submit an annual report.

What specifically constitute "shares, etc." are prescribed in Article 6, paragraph 1 of the Financial Instruments and Exchange Act Implementing Order. There "shares, etc." are defined as (a) shares, share options, and corporate bonds with share options (Article 6 (1) (i) of the Financial Instruments and Exchange Act Implementing Order); (b) securities or certificates issued by a foreign person that have the nature of the securities set forth in (a) (ibid. (ii)); (c) investment securities, etc. and investment

---

**8**　Category (ii) means essentially "shares, etc." listed solely on a specified financial instruments exchange market (the so-called pro market) and "shares, etc." registered solely on a specified over-the-counter traded securities market.

*519*

equity subscription rights, etc. (ibid. (iii)); (d) beneficiary certificates of securities in trust of which the entrusted securities constitute securities in any of categories (a)-(c) (termed "beneficiary certificates of shares, etc. in trust") (ibid. (iv)); and (e) depositary receipts or certificates that represent rights pertaining to securities in any of categories (a) - (c) (termed "depository receipts for shares, etc.") (ibid. (v)).[9]

However, given that takeover bids are implemented primarily for the purpose of acquiring or strengthening control of a company, securities pertaining to shares with no voting rights on all the matters that may be resolved at a shareholders meeting (shares with no voting rights) are excluded from the "shares, etc." subject to takeover bid regulations (Article 6(1) of the Financial Instruments and Exchange Act Implementing Order; Article 2 of the Cabinet Office Ordinance on Disclosure Required for Takeover Bid for Shares, etc. by Person Other than Issuer). Specifically, (1) shares with no voting rights for which issuance of shares with voting rights in exchange for acquisition of the shares is not provided in the articles of incorporation; (2) share options or corporate bonds with share options with the rights to acquire only the shares set forth in (1); (3) securities or certificates issued by a foreign person that have the nature of the securities set forth in (1) or (2); (4) beneficiary certificates of shares, etc. in trust of which the entrusted securities constitute securities in any of categories (1)-(3); and (5) depository receipts for shares, etc. which represent rights pertaining to securities in any of categories (1)-(3) are excluded from the "shares, etc." subject to takeover bid regulations.

b. Basic concepts defining scope of application of takeover bid regulations

( i ) "Purchase, etc."

A "purchase, etc." subject to takeover bid regulations means a purchase or other acquisition for compensation (i. e., in exchange for something of economic value) of shares, etc., and includes acts specified by cabinet order

---

9 Note also that even shares for which no share certificate is issued, such as book-entry transfer shares, constitute "shares, etc." This is because they are "deemed securities" (Article 2(2) of the Financial Instruments and Exchange Act).

Chapter 4   The takeover bid system and the system of disclosure of the status of large-volume holdings

as being similar to this (Article 27-2(1) of the Financial Instruments and Exchange Act). Specifically the acts "similar to" a purchase or other acquisition for compensation of shares, etc. comprise specifically (a) pre-contract for the sale or purchase of shares, etc. exercisable by one party (limited to cases wherein the party holds the rights to complete the sale or purchase and acquires the position as a buyer through the exercise of the rights); (b) acquisition of options pertaining to the sale and purchase of shares, etc. (limited to options wherein the person who exercises the options acquires the position as a buyer in such sale and purchase through the exercise of the options); and (c) acquisition of corporate bonds (limited to the acquisition of the right, as a right pertaining to the corporate bonds, to have the corporate bonds redeemed through shares, etc. of which the issuer is other than that of the corporate bonds, but only when the person acquiring such corporate bonds acquires the right to have the issuer of such corporate bonds redeem them by such shares, etc.) (Article 6(3) of the Financial Instruments and Exchange Act Implementing Order; Article 2-2 of the Cabinet Office Ordinance on Disclosure Required for Takeover Bid for Shares, etc. by Person Other than Issuer).

Note also that whereas the acquisition of shares, etc. newly issued by an issuer of shares, etc. does not constitute "purchase, etc.", the acquisition of shares, etc. in connection with disposal of treasury shares by an issuer of shares, etc. does in principle constitute "purchase, etc.," since it is a transaction relating to already-issued securities.[10]

(ⅱ)  "Ownership ratio of shares, etc."

The percentage of shares owned, an important criterion for determining the scope of application of takeover bid regulations, is described in the Financial Instruments and Exchange Act as the "ownership ratio of shares, etc." The number of voting rights serves as the criterion for calculating the ownership ratio of shares, etc., and the ownership ratio of shares, etc. of specially related parties is added to the post-purchase ownership ratio of the person effecting the purchase of the shares, etc. (the bidder) (Article 27-2

---

10   Matsuo Naohiko, *Kinyū shōhin torihiki hō* (The Financial Instruments and Exchange Act), 4th ed. (Shojihomu, 2016), p. 227.

*521*

(1) (i) of the Financial Instruments and Exchange Act).

Specially related parties are defined according to either formal or substantial criteria. A specially related party by formal criteria is any person with a shareholding relationship, familial relationship, or other special relationship specified by cabinet order to the bidder (Article 27-2(7) (i) of the Financial Instruments and Exchange Act; Article 9 of the Financial Instruments and Exchange Act Implementing Order); an example is a stock company in which the bidder owns shares representing at least twenty percent of the voting rights of all shareholders, etc. (Article 29-4(2) of the Financial Instruments and Exchange Act). A specially related party by substantial criteria is any party with which the bidder has agreed on so-called joint action. Specifically, (a) a person with which the bidder has agreed to jointly acquire or transfer the shares, etc.; (b) a person with which the bidder has agreed to jointly exercise voting rights or other rights as shareholders in the issuer of the shares, etc.; or (c) a person with which the bidder has agreed to transfer the shares, etc. to or acquire them from the other after the purchase, etc. of the shares, etc. constitutes a specially related party by substantial criteria (Article 27-2 (7) (ii) of the Financial Instruments and Exchange Act).

The ownership ratio of shares, etc. is calculated as a fraction, with the denominator comprising the sum of the number of voting rights of all shareholders, etc. of the issuer of the shares, etc. plus the number of voting rights pertaining to securities with potential voting rights owned by the bidder and any specially related party thereto (excluding those included in the number of voting rights of all shareholders, etc. of the issuer), and the numerator comprising the number of voting rights pertaining to shares, etc. owned by the bidder or any specially related party thereto (Article 27-2(8) of the Financial Instruments and Exchange Act; Article 6, Article 7 of the Cabinet Office Ordinance on Disclosure Required for Takeover Bid for Shares, etc. by Person Other than Issuer). Securities with potential voting rights include (a) corporate bonds with share options; (b) share options; (c) shares pertaining to shares with put options; (d) shares pertaining to shares subject to call; (e) securities or certificates issued by a foreign person which have the nature of any of the securities set forth in (a) – (d); and (f) investment equity subscription rights, etc. (Article 9-2 of the Financial

Chapter 4 The takeover bid system and the system of disclosure of the status of large-volume holdings

Instruments and Exchange Act Implementing Order).

c. Types of transactions subject to takeover bid regulations
（ⅰ） General observations

Transactions subject to takeover bid regulations in Japan can be broadly divided into three types (Article 27-2(1) of the Financial Instruments and Exchange Act): first, the purchase, etc. of shares, etc. effected outside of a financial instruments exchange market (ibid. (i)-(iii)); second, the purchase, etc. of shares, etc. effected by combining transactions on and off a financial instruments exchange market over a specified period (ibid. (iv)); and third, the purchase, etc. of shares, etc. that are already the object of a takeover bid, which purchase, etc. is effected by an investor owning more than a specified volume of those shares, etc. (ibid. (v)).

Below we will review the types of transactions subject to takeover bid regulations as defined in each item of Article 27-2, paragraph 1 of the Financial Instruments and Exchange Act.

（ⅱ） Purchases, etc. meeting the five-percent rule (Article 27-2(1)(i) of the Financial Instruments and Exchange Act)

The first type of transaction subject to takeover bid regulations is transactions meeting the criterion known as the five-percent rule. Specifically, when shares, etc. issued by an issuer required to submit an annual report (or other such issuer) are purchased outside of a financial instruments exchange market by a person other than the issuer from more than ten persons within 61 days,[11] and after that purchase the ownership ratio of shares, etc. of the person who effects the purchase will exceed five percent, the purchase, etc. of those shares, etc. must be effected by means of a takeover bid (Article 27-2 (1) (i) of the Financial Instruments and Exchange Act; Article 6-2(3) of the Financial Instruments and Exchange Act Implementing Order). The main rationale that can be cited for requiring

---

11 To be more precise, where the total of the number of persons who are counterparties to the purchase, etc. of the shares, etc., and the number of counterparties of purchases, etc. of shares, etc. issued by the issuer of the shares, etc. made outside the financial instruments exchange market during the 60 days prior to the day on which that purchase, etc. is to be made is more than ten persons.

*523*

implementation of a takeover bid based on the five-percent rule is the need to treat shareholders equally and the need to provide adequate information to them (see Section A.1. (c) of this chapter for details).

However, even if a purchase, etc. of shares, etc. meets the five-percent rule, implementing a takeover bid is not compulsory in the cases specified by cabinet order as being equivalent to the purchase and sale, etc. of securities on a financial instruments exchange market (Article 27-2(1)(i) parenthesis of the Financial Instruments and Exchange Act). Specifically, transactions on an over-the-counter securities market,[12] and transactions through a proprietary trading system (PTS) designated by the Commissioner of the Financial Services Agency as fulfilling certain conditions, are specified by cabinet order as being equivalent to the purchase and sale, etc. of securities on a financial instruments exchange market (Article 6-2(2) of the Financial Instruments and Exchange Act Implementing Order).

The reason adduced for making implementation of a takeover bid compulsory under the five-percent rule only in cases where shares, etc. are purchased from more than ten persons outside a financial instruments exchange market is that if the number of investors (shareholders) receiving purchase bids for shares, etc. is small, there is relatively little need to protect investors.[13] The fewer the investors, the more able they are to act in unison. As a result investors who receive bids can acquire bargaining power equal or almost equal to that of the bidder; and the parties can negotiate over information disclosure demands and purchase price.

(ⅲ) Purchases, etc. meeting the one-third rule (Article 27-2(1)(ii) of the Financial Instruments and Exchange Act)

The next type of transaction subject to takeover bid regulations comprises transactions meeting the criterion known as the one-third rule. Specifically, even if shares, etc. issued by an issuer required to submit an annual report (or other such issuer) are purchased outside of a financial instruments

---

12 However, because the JASDAQ was reorganized as an exchange securities market in December 2004, there are no over-the-counter securities markets as of the writing of this chapter.

13 Yamashita and Kanda (supra, n. 3), p. 254 (Kato Takahito).

Chapter 4   The takeover bid system and the system of disclosure of the status of large-volume holdings

exchange market by a person other than the issuer from ten or fewer persons within 61 days (such a purchase, etc. of shares, etc. from an extremely small number of persons effected outside of the market is termed a "specified purchase, etc.": Article 6-2(1)(iv) and (3) of the Financial Instruments and Exchange Act Implementing Order), the purchase, etc. of those shares, etc. must be effected by means of a takeover bid if after that purchase the ownership ratio of shares, etc. of the person who effects the purchase will exceed one-third (Article 27-2(1)(ii) of the Financial Instruments and Exchange Act; Article 6-2(3) of the Financial Instruments and Exchange Act Implementing Order). The main rationale that can be cited for requiring implementation of a takeover bid based on the one-third rule is the need for equal distribution of control premiums (see Section A.1. (c) of this chapter for details). In this case implementation of a takeover bid is required primarily with a view to protecting the interests of investors (shareholders) who have not received a purchase bid for shares, etc.

Even if a specified purchase, etc. meets the above one-third rule, implementing a takeover bid is, as with the five-percent rule, not compulsory in the cases specified by cabinet order as being equivalent to the purchase and sale, etc. of securities on a financial instruments exchange market (Article 27-2(1)(ii) of the Financial Instruments and Exchange Act). In this case, however, while transactions on an over-the-counter securities market are "equivalent to the purchase and sale, etc. of securities on a financial instruments exchange market" as with the five-percent rule, transactions over a proprietary trading system (PTS) are not (Article 6-2(4) of the Financial Instruments and Exchange Act Implementing Order), unlike in the case of the five-percent rule. Thus, it must be noted, the one-third rule applies to transactions over a proprietary trading system (PTS).

(iv)   Purchase, etc. by means of specified purchase and sale, etc. (Article 27-2(1)(iii) of the Financial Instruments and Exchange Act)

When shares, etc. issued by an issuer required to submit an annual report (or other such issuer) are purchased by a person other than the issuer by means of specified purchase and sale, etc., and as a result the ownership ratio of shares, etc. of the person who effects the purchase will, after that purchase, exceed one-third, the purchase, etc. of those shares, etc. must be

*525*

effected by means of a takeover bid (Article 27-2(1) (iii) of the Financial Instruments and Exchange Act).

"Specified purchase and sale, etc." here is defined as a purchase and sale, etc. of securities on a financial instruments exchange market that is specified by the Prime Minister as being a purchase and sale, etc. of securities based on a method other than an auction method (Article 27-2 (1) (iii) of the Financial Instruments and Exchange Act). Specifically, off-floor transactions conducted on financial instruments exchanges nationwide, such as ToSTNeT transactions on the Tokyo Stock Exchange, are classified as "specified purchase and sale, etc." These off-floor transactions formally constitute transactions on a financial instruments exchange market, but because neither time priority nor price priority applies, they are considered to be in effect over-the-counter transactions not conducted by auction; hence, if the ownership ratio of shares, etc. will exceed one-third as a result, implementation of a takeover bid is required. To prevent overregulation of off-floor trading, off-floor transactions are not subject to takeover bid regulations as long as the ownership ratio of shares, etc. after the purchase remains within one-third.

(ⅴ) Rapid purchases, etc. combining on- and off-market transactions
(Article 27-2(1) (iv) of the Financial Instruments and Exchange Act)

Under the one-third rule, implementation of a takeover bid is compulsory if the ownership ratio of shares, etc. will exceed one-third as a result of the purchase, etc. of shares, etc. outside a financial instruments exchange market. It thus used to be easy to circumvent the regulations based on the one-third rule by, for example, purchasing 32 percent of the shares outside of the market, then purchasing 2 percent on the market or acquiring 2 percent through a private placement of new shares. Therefore, to prevent such evasive transactions that circumvent the one-third rule, the 2006 revision of the Financial Instruments and Exchange Act introduced a new regulation governing rapid purchases, etc. combining on- and off-market transactions.

This regulation governing rapid purchases, etc. combining transactions on and off a financial instruments exchange market is specifically as follows. If (a) more than ten percent of the total number of shares, etc. issued by the issuer of the shares, etc. subject to acquisition are acquired within three

Chapter 4　The takeover bid system and the system of disclosure of the status of large-volume holdings

months through the purchase, etc. of shares, etc. or through the "acquisition of a new issue" (meaning the acquisition of shares, etc. newly issued by their issuer); and (b) in the transaction in (a), more than five percent of the total number of shares, etc. issued by the issuer of the shares, etc. subject to acquisition are acquired through a purchase, etc. of shares, etc. that is effected through a "specified purchase and sale, etc." (i.e., off-floor trading) or that is effected outside a financial instruments exchange market (excluding one effected through a takeover bid); and (c) as a result of the transaction in (a), the ownership ratio of shares, etc. will exceed one-third, then the purchase, etc. of the shares, etc. included in the transaction in (a) must be effected by means of a takeover bid (Article 27-2(1)(iv) of the Financial Instruments and Exchange Act; Article 7(2)-(4) of the Financial Instruments and Exchange Act Implementing Order). Thus, to prevent circumvention of the one-third rule, acquisition of more than ten percent of shares, etc. within three months is regarded as a single series of acts, and if all of the conditions (a) through (c) are met, implementation of a takeover bid is compulsory for the purchase, etc. of the shares, etc. included in the transaction in (a).

Because the above regulation makes implementation of a takeover bid compulsory for the purchase, etc. of the shares, etc. included in the transaction in (a), the regulation governing rapid purchases, etc. combining transactions on and off financial instruments exchange markets serves not only to prevent circumvention of the one-third rule but also to limit the speed of corporate buyouts. For example, if a person already owning 25 percent of the shares purchases a further seven percent off the market, that person cannot acquire new shares in excess of three percent through a private placement until three months have elapsed from that purchase of seven percent off the market.[14] That is because, if the person did acquire new shares in excess of three percent through a private placement within three months, the regulation governing rapid purchases, etc. combining

---

14　Note also that this prohibition on acquisition of more than three percent of the shares, etc. within three months applies not only in the case of private placements of new shares as explained in the text; it also applies in the case of acquisition of shares, etc. on the market or by takeover bid.

*527*

transactions on and off financial instruments exchange markets would apply, as a result of which the original purchase of the seven percent outside the market would have had to be effected by means of a takeover bid. For that reason, the regulation governing rapid purchases, etc. combining transactions on and off financial instruments exchange markets is sometimes referred to as the "speed regulation".

(vi) Competing purchases, etc. during the takeover bid period (Article 27-2(1)(v) of the Financial Instruments and Exchange Act)

In principle, a takeover bidder, etc. (including a specially related party, etc.) must not purchase, etc. shares, etc. subject to the takeover bid, other than through the takeover bid, during the takeover bid period (Article 27-5 main clause of the Financial Instruments and Exchange Act). This is the so-called prohibition of separate purchase. The prohibition of separate purchase has been established because the acquisition by a single bidder of the same shares, etc. on different terms, whether on or off the market, would result in unfairness to shareholders offering their shares, etc.

On the other hand, until the 2006 revision of the Financial Instruments and Exchange Act, a person other than the takeover bidder was able, during the takeover bid period, to acquire shares, etc. subject to a takeover bid by a means other than a takeover bid, even if that person was a major shareholder of the company issuing those shares, etc. However, it seems unfair that during a struggle for control of a company, the takeover bidder is required to acquire shares, etc. through a takeover bid, yet other major shareholders can freely buy up large numbers of shares, etc. from the market without being required to implement a takeover bid.[15] Therefore a regulation governing competing purchases, etc. during the takeover bid period was adopted in the 2006 revision of the Financial Instruments and Exchange Act with the objectives of ensuring equality between buyers during corporate buyouts and enabling investors (shareholders) to decide, in light of adequate information, which party is better suited to controlling the company.[16]

Specifically, when, during the period of a takeover bid by a certain person, a shareholder whose ownership ratio of the shares, etc. subject to the

---

**15** Kondo et al. (supra, n. 3), p. 373.

Chapter 4 The takeover bid system and the system of disclosure of the status of large-volume holdings

takeover bid exceeds one-third effects a purchase, etc. in excess of five percent of those shares, etc., whether on or off a financial instruments exchange market, that purchase, etc. must be effected by means of a takeover bid (Article 27-2 (1) (v) of the Financial Instruments and Exchange Act; Article 7 (5) & (6) of the Financial Instruments and Exchange Act Implementing Order). The reason for restricting the scope of the regulation to large shareholders whose ownership ratio already exceeds one-third is to avoid overregulation that could adversely affect the secondary market. The applicable takeover bid period is understood to be from the first to the last day of the takeover bid period recorded on the takeover bid statement, and not to include any extension of that period.[17]

(vii)  Other (Article 27-2 (1) (vi) of the Financial Instruments and Exchange Act)

Additionally, in the case of purchases, etc. of shares, etc. through a proprietary trading system (PTS) designated by the Commissioner of the Financial Services Agency, which are exempt from the five-percent rule, implementation of a takeover bid is required if after that purchase, etc. the ownership ratio of shares, etc. will exceed one-third (Article 27-2(1)(vi) of the Financial Instruments and Exchange Act; Article 7 (7) (i) of the Financial Instruments and Exchange Act Implementing Order).

---

16  However, ensuring the provision of adequate information to shareholders must be understood as merely a secondary objective of the regulation governing competing purchases, etc. during the takeover bid period (see Kuronuma Etsuro, "Kigyō baishū rūru toshite no kōkai kaitsuke kisei" [Takeover bid regulations as corporate buyout rules], *Jurist*, No. 1346 [2007], p. 28), for if the preceding purchase, etc. of shares, etc. takes place on a financial instruments exchange market, major shareholders are not required to implement a takeover bid. Thus requiring major shareholders to implement a takeover bid through the regulation governing competing purchases, etc. during the takeover bid period dovetails primarily with the imposition of certain trade restrictions on the takeover bidder in a preceding takeover bid (Yamashita and Kanda [supra, n. 3], p. 260 [Kato Takahito]).

17  Matsuo (supra, n. 10), p. 242.

*529*

d. Exclusions from application of takeover bid regulations

( i ) General observations

Even in cases where a transaction constitutes a purchase, etc. of shares, etc. as defined in each item of Article 27-1, paragraph 1 of the Financial Instruments and Exchange Act, if, for the purpose of protecting investors, there is little need to effect it by means of a takeover bid, it is not subject to takeover bid regulations as an excluded purchase, etc. (proviso to Article 27-1(1) of the Financial Instruments and Exchange Act). The main types of purchases, etc. defined as excluded purchases, etc. are specifically described below.

( ii ) Purchase, etc. through the exercise of rights

Purchase, etc. of shares, etc. through the exercise of rights is, as an excluded purchase, etc., not subject to takeover bid regulations. The reason for this is that shares, etc. acquirable through exercise of rights are, at the time of acquisition of those rights, factored into calculation of the ownership ratio of shares, etc. as potential voting rights. Specifically, typical transactions defined as excluded purchases, etc. are (a) the purchase, etc. of shares, etc. made through the exercise of share options; (b) the purchase, etc. of shares, etc. made through the exercise of the right to receive an allotment of shares by the person who holds such rights; (c) the purchase, etc. of shares, etc. that are delivered in exchange for the redemption of shares; and (d) the purchase, etc. of shares, etc. which are delivered in exchange for the redemption of shares subject to call or share options subject to call (proviso to Article 27-1(1) of the Financial Instruments and Exchange Act; Article 6-2 (1) (i), (xi), (xii) of the Financial Instruments and Exchange Act Implementing Order).

( iii ) Purchase, etc. from specially related parties

The purchase, etc. of shares, etc. from a person who has, for a continuous period of one year prior to the date on which the purchase, etc. of the shares, etc. is to be conducted, held the relationship of a specially related party (by formal criteria) [18] with the person to conduct the purchase, etc. is, as an excluded purchase, etc., not subject to takeover bid regulations (proviso to Article 27-1(1) of the Financial Instruments and Exchange Act; Article 3(1)

Chapter 4   The takeover bid system and the system of disclosure of the status of large-volume holdings

of the Cabinet Office Ordinance on Disclosure Required for Takeover Bid for Shares, etc. by Person Other than Issuer). Similarly, a specified purchase, etc.[19] from a sister juridical person, etc. is, as an excluded purchase, etc., not subject to takeover bid regulations (proviso to Article 27-1 (1) of the Financial Instruments and Exchange Act; Article 6-2(1) (v) of the Financial Instruments and Exchange Act Implementing Order; Article 2-3 of the Cabinet Office Ordinance on Disclosure Required for Takeover Bid for Shares, etc. by Person Other than Issuer). A sister juridical person, etc. means another juridical person over which the parent juridical person, etc. of the juridical person, etc. that is the offeror holds a special controlling interest (meaning the position of holding voting rights exceeding 50 percent of the total number of the voting rights held by all the shareholders, etc., which position has been held for a continuous period of one year prior to the date on which the specified purchase, etc. is to be conducted). The reason is that in these cases control of the company is unlikely to be effectively transferred as a result of the purchase, etc.[20]

(iv)   Purchase, etc. with the consent of all of less than 25 shareholders

A specified purchase, etc. is, as an excluded purchase, etc., not subject to takeover bid regulations if the number of holders of shares, etc. is small (less than 25), and all the holders of the shares, etc. covered by the specified purchase, etc. have given written consent to make the specified purchase, etc. pertaining to the shares, etc. by means other than a takeover bid (proviso to Article 27-1(1) of the Financial Instruments and Exchange Act; Article 6-2 (vii) of the Financial Instruments and Exchange Act Implementing Order; Article 2-5 of the Cabinet Office Ordinance on

---

**18**   A specially related party by formal criteria is any person with a shareholding relationship, familial relationship, or other special relationship specified by cabinet order to the bidder (Article 27-1(7) (i) of the Financial Instruments and Exchange Act; Article 9 of the Financial Instruments and Exchange Act Implementing Order); an example is a stock company in which the bidder owns shares representing at least twenty percent of the voting rights of all shareholders, etc.

**19**   A "specified purchase, etc." means a purchase, etc. of shares, etc. from an extremely small number of persons effected outside of the market (Article 6-2(1) (iv), (3) of the Financial Instruments and Exchange Act Implementing Order).

**20**   Matsuo (supra, n. 10), p. 244.

Disclosure Required for Takeover Bid for Shares, etc. by Person Other than Issuer). The reasons are that if the number of holders of shares, etc. is small, it is relatively unlikely that asymmetry of information will exist between the party seeking consent and those giving it; and if all the holders are in agreement, there is little need to guarantee equal selling opportunities through a takeover bid.[21]

The term "shares, etc." as the criterion for determining that the less-than-25 requirement is met means, in the case of a company issuing class shares, shares, etc. of the class covered by the specified purchase, etc.; it does not mean all shares, etc. including those of classes not covered by the specified purchase, etc. (Supreme Court Decision of Oct. 22, 2010, *Civil Cases of the Supreme Court*, Vol. 64, No. 7, p. 1843). Therefore, if the holders of shares, etc. of the class covered by the specified purchase, etc. amount to less than 25, and the consent of all holders of shares, etc. of that class has been obtained, the consent of the holders of shares, etc. of other classes is in principle unnecessary, unless the ownership ratio of shares, etc. after the specified purchase, etc. will be more than two-thirds; in that case, not only must all the holders of the shares, etc. of the class covered by the specified purchase, etc. give written consent to make the specified purchase, etc. in question by means other than a takeover bid, it is further required that consent be given by a class meeting concerning classes of shares, etc. not covered by the specified purchase, etc. in question ("shares, etc. not covered"), or that written consent be given by all the holders of the shares, etc. not covered (Article 2-5 (2) of the Cabinet Office Ordinance on Disclosure Required for Takeover Bid for Shares, etc. by Person Other than Issuer).

## 3. Regulations governing takeover bids

a. Information disclosure regulations governing takeover bids

To enable investors (shareholders) to make a reasonable decision on whether to accept a takeover bid, the Financial Instruments and Exchange Act establishes detailed information disclosure regulations governing takeover bids. Below, an overview is first provided of the information

---

21  Matsuo (supra, n. 10), pp. 245-246.

*532*

Chapter 4   The takeover bid system and the system of disclosure of the status of large-volume holdings

disclosure regulations governing takeover bids, and the content of the main disclosure documents required by the Financial Instruments and Exchange Act is described; then the special information disclosure provisions pertaining to cases of exchange bids and MBOs, etc. are explained.

( i )   Overview of information disclosure regulations

A takeover bidder must issue a public notice of the commencement of a takeover bid before implementing that bid (Article 27-3(1) of the Financial Instruments and Exchange Act), and, on the same day (or, if that day is not a business day, on the following business day), submit a takeover bid statement to the Prime Minister (ibid. (2)). If there is a formal deficiency in the content of the public notice of the commencement of a takeover bid or the takeover bid statement, or any particular thereof conflicts with the facts of the matter, an amended public notice must be issued or an amended statement submitted; in the case of failure to do that voluntarily, the Prime Minister may order it to be done (Article 27-7(2) and Article 27-8(3) of the Financial Instruments and Exchange Act).

Additionally, when effecting a purchase, etc. of shares, etc. through a takeover bid, the takeover bidder must, in advance or at the same time, deliver a takeover bid explanation to any investor (shareholder) seeking to sell, etc. those shares, etc. (Article 27-9(2) of the Financial Instruments and Exchange Act; Article 24(4) of the Cabinet Office Ordinance on Disclosure Required for Takeover Bid for Shares, etc. by Person Other than Issuer).

On the other hand, the issuer of the shares, etc. covered by the takeover bid (the target company of the takeover bid) must, within ten business days of the date on which the public notice of the commencement of the takeover bid is issued, submit the target company's position statement to the Prime Minister stating its opinion on the takeover bid (Article 27-10(1) of the Financial Instruments and Exchange Act; Article 13-2(1) of the Financial Instruments and Exchange Act Implementing Order). The takeover bidder must, if questions from the target company are included in the target company's position statement, submit the takeover bidder's answer to the Prime Minister within five business days of the date on which it receives a copy of the target company's position statement (Article 27-10 (11) of the Financial Instruments and Exchange Act; Article 13-2(2) of the Financial

*533*

Instruments and Exchange Act Implementing Order).

Finally, when the takeover bid period has ended, the takeover bidder must, on the day following the last day of the takeover bid period, issue a public notice or public announcement of the results of the takeover bid, and submit a takeover bid report to the Prime Minister (Article 27-13(1) & (2) of the Financial Instruments and Exchange Act). In addition, when the takeover bid period has ended, the takeover bidder must, without delay, send to the tendering shareholders a written notice of purchase, etc. containing the prescribed items, including the number of shares, etc. of which purchase, etc. is to be made (Article 27-2(5) of the Financial Instruments and Exchange Act; Article 8 (5) (i) of the Financial Instruments and Exchange Act Implementing Order).

(ii) Public notice of the commencement of a takeover bid

Takeover bid procedures begin with the issuance of a public notice of the commencement of a takeover bid by the takeover bidder (Article 27-3(1) of the Financial Instruments and Exchange Act). The public notice of the commencement of a takeover bid is an important means of notifying investors (shareholders) of the implementation of a takeover bid and its specifics. It contains such basic information on the takeover bid as the name and address of the takeover bidder, the purpose of the takeover bid, the price of purchase, etc., the number of shares, etc. to be purchased, and the period of purchase, etc. (Article 10 of the Cabinet Office Ordinance on Disclosure Required for Takeover Bid for Shares, etc. by Person Other than Issuer).

The public notice of the commencement of a takeover bid may be given either by electronic public notice or by publication in a daily newspaper that publishes matters on current affairs (Article 9-3 (1) of the Financial Instruments and Exchange Act Implementing Order). If the notice is given by electronic public notice, the fact that the public notice has been given, the Internet address for the electronic public notice, etc., must, without delay after the public notice is given, be published in a daily newspaper that publishes matters on current affairs (Article 9-3 (3) of the Financial Instruments and Exchange Act Implementing Order; Article 9-2 of the Cabinet Office Ordinance on Disclosure Required for Takeover Bid for Shares, etc. by Person Other than Issuer). The electronic public notice must

Chapter 4   The takeover bid system and the system of disclosure of the status of large-volume holdings

continue being given until the last day of the takeover bid period (Article 9-3 (4) of the Financial Instruments and Exchange Act Implementing Order).

(iii)   The takeover bid statement

The takeover bid statement consists of a document stating the particulars prescribed in Article 27-3, paragraph 2 of the Financial Instruments and Exchange Act, along with the accompanying documents. The takeover bidder must submit the takeover bid statement to the Prime Minister on the day on which it issues the public notice of the commencement of the takeover bid (or, if that day is not a business day, on the following business day) (Article 27-3(2) of the Financial Instruments and Exchange Act). The submitted takeover bid statement is made available for public inspection for five years from the close of the takeover bid (Article 27-14 (1) of the Financial Instruments and Exchange Act). Unless the takeover bid statement has been submitted, the takeover bidder, a specially related party thereto, or any other such party is not allowed to solicit offers to sell, etc. shares, etc. or perform certain other acts on or after the day following the day on which the public notice of the commencement of the takeover bid is issued (Article 27-3(3) of the Financial Instruments and Exchange Act; Article 10 of the Financial Instruments and Exchange Act Implementing Order; Article 15 of the Cabinet Office Ordinance on Disclosure Required for Takeover Bid for Shares, etc. by Person Other than Issuer).

The takeover bid statement states (a) the purchase, etc. price, the number of shares, etc. sought for purchase, the purchase, etc. period, the terms of delivery in connection with the purchase, etc., and other terms of settlement and purchase, etc. set by the takeover bidder; (b) the details of any contract to purchase, etc. the shares, etc. that are subject to the takeover bid, other than through the takeover bid, on or after the day on which the takeover bidder issues the public notice of the commencement of the takeover bid; and (c) the purpose of the takeover bid, the particulars of the takeover bidder, etc. (Article 27-3 (2) (i) - (iii) of the Financial Instruments and Exchange Act). The more detailed particulars to be recorded on the takeover bid statement are specified by cabinet office ordinance as being in accordance with Form 2[22] (Article 12 of the Cabinet Office Ordinance on Disclosure Required for Takeover Bid for Shares, etc. by Person Other than Issuer).

*535*

Immediately after the submission of the takeover bid statement, the takeover bidder must send a copy of it to the issuer of the shares, etc. covered by the takeover bid (the target company of the takeover bid), to any person that has already submitted a takeover bid statement for the shares, etc. in question, and to the financial instruments exchange, etc. on which the shares, etc. are listed (Article 27-3 (4) of the Financial Instruments and Exchange Act). This provision takes account of several factors: when a takeover bid is made, the target company must state its opinion about the takeover bid (by submitting the target company's position statement), any competing takeover bidder may need to reconsider its conditions of purchase, etc., and the financial instruments exchange, etc. will need to examine the takeover bid from the viewpoint of maintaining market order.[23]

Finally, if the takeover bidder is a non-resident, it must, when submitting a takeover bid statement, appoint a representative with an address or office in Japan (Article 27-3 (2) of the Financial Instruments and Exchange Act; Article 11 of the Cabinet Office Ordinance on Disclosure Required for Takeover Bid for Shares, etc. by Person Other than Issuer) to facilitate examination of the takeover bid statement.

(iv)　The takeover bid explanation

The takeover bid explanation must record all the particulars stated on the takeover bid statement excluding those that shall not be made available for public inspection (Article 24 (1) of the Cabinet Office Ordinance on Disclosure Required for Takeover Bid for Shares, etc. by Person Other than Issuer). When effecting a purchase, etc. of shares, etc. through a takeover bid, the takeover bidder must, in advance or at the same time, deliver a takeover bid explanation to the investors (shareholders) seeking to sell, etc.

---

22　According to Form 2, the takeover bid statement broadly consists of these items: summary of the takeover bid, situation of the takeover bidder, holdings of and transactions in shares, etc. by the takeover bidder and specially related parties thereto, transactions, etc. between the takeover bidder and the target company, and situation of the target company. When preparing the statement, one should take careful note of the "Instructions for Completion" on Form 2.

23　Kondo et al. (supra, n. 3), p. 375.

*536*

Chapter 4 The takeover bid system and the system of disclosure of the status of large-volume holdings

those shares, etc. (Article 27-9 (2) of the Financial Instruments and Exchange Act; Article 24(4) of the Cabinet Office Ordinance on Disclosure Required for Takeover Bid for Shares, etc. by Person Other than Issuer). Thus, the takeover bid explanation has the function of directly disclosing to investors (shareholders) the information that they require to decide whether to accept the takeover bid.

(ⅴ) The target company's position statement

What the present management of the issuer of the shares, etc. subject to a takeover bid (the target company of the takeover bid) thinks about the takeover bid, or about the future running of the target company, is information of the greatest importance for investors (shareholders) deciding whether to accept the takeover bid.[24] With that in mind, the Financial Instruments and Exchange Act prescribes that the target company of the takeover bid must submit a statement of its position on the takeover bid (the target company's position statement) to the Prime Minister within ten business days of the date on which the public notice of the commencement of the takeover bid is issued (Article 27-10(1) of the Financial Instruments and Exchange Act; Article 13-2(1) of the Financial Instruments and Exchange Act Implementing Order). The submitted target company's position statement is made available for public inspection (Article 27-14(1) of the Financial Instruments and Exchange Act).

Immediately after the submission of the target company's position statement, the target company of the takeover bid must send a copy of it to the takeover bidder involved in the takeover bid, to any person other than the takeover bidder that has already submitted a takeover bid statement for the shares, etc. covered by the takeover bid in question, and to the financial instruments exchange, etc. on which the shares, etc. are listed (Article 27-10 (9) and Article 27-3(4) of the Financial Instruments and Exchange Act).

The target company's position statement states (a) the target company's opinion on the takeover bid and the grounds for it; (b) in cases where efforts are made to prevent the decision on financial and business policies of the target company from being controlled by any inappropriate person in light of

---

24  Kondo et al. (supra, n. 3), p. 383.

*537*

the basic policy concerning the requirements for the person controlling the decision on the financial and business policies of the target company (adoption of a so-called defense against takeovers), the details of those efforts; (c) questions for the takeover bidder; and (d) any request for extension of the takeover bid period and the reason, etc. (Article 27-10(1) & (2) of the Financial Instruments and Exchange Act; Article 25(1) & (2), Form 4 of the Cabinet Office Ordinance on Disclosure Required for Takeover Bid for Shares, etc. by Person Other than Issuer). Of these, (c) means that the target company is given the opportunity to question the takeover bidder and is thus practically speaking of great importance. However, only one opportunity for the target company to ask questions is prescribed under law; the ability to engage in discussion through multiple questions and answers is not guaranteed as a matter of course. As for (d), this dovetails with the provision that if the takeover bid period set by the takeover bidder is shorter than 30 business days, the target company may request an extension of that period on the target company's position statement (Article 27-10(2) (ii), (3) of the Financial Instruments and Exchange Act; Article 9-3 (6) of the Financial Instruments and Exchange Act Implementing Order).

(vi) The takeover bidder's answer

The takeover bidder must, if questions from the target company are included in the target company's position statement, submit the takeover bidder's answer to the Prime Minister within five business days of the date on which it receives a copy of the target company's position statement (Article 27-10 (11) of the Financial Instruments and Exchange Act; Article 13-2 (2) of the Financial Instruments and Exchange Act Implementing Order). The takeover bidder's answer must record the responses of the takeover bidder to the target company's questions, although the answer may be deferred as long as the reason is given (Article 25(3), (4), Form 8 of the Cabinet Office Ordinance on Disclosure Required for Takeover Bid for Shares, etc. by Person Other than Issuer).

(vii) End of the takeover bid period and the takeover bid report

When the takeover bid period has ended, the takeover bidder must, without delay, send to the shareholders who have accepted the takeover bid

*538*

Chapter 4   The takeover bid system and the system of disclosure of the status of large-volume holdings

a written notice of purchase, etc. recording the number of shares, etc. for which the purchase, etc. is to be made and any other matters specified by the relevant cabinet office ordinance (Article 5 (1) of the Cabinet Office Ordinance on Disclosure Required for Takeover Bid for Shares, etc. by Person Other than Issuer), and complete the transfer or other settlement procedures for purchase, etc. (Article 27-2(5) of the Financial Instruments and Exchange Act; Article 8(5) (i) & (ii) of the Financial Instruments and Exchange Act Implementing Order).

The takeover bidder must then issue a public notice or public announcement of the number of tendered shares, etc. and other particulars on the day following the last day of the takeover bid period (Article 27-13(1) of the Financial Instruments and Exchange Act), and submit a takeover bid report to the Prime Minister, stating the results of the takeover bid and other particulars specified by cabinet office ordinance, on the day on which it issues the public notice or public announcement (ibid. (2); Article 31, Form 6 of the Cabinet Office Ordinance on Disclosure Required for Takeover Bid for Shares, etc. by Person Other than Issuer). The rationale behind the Financial Instruments and Exchange Act's establishment of such disclosure regulations is that the outcome of a takeover bid is material information affecting the stock market immediately after.[25]

(viii)   Information disclosure regulations pertaining to cases of exchange bids

Takeover bids do not always involve consideration in cash. The takeover bidder may make a takeover bid involving consideration in securities instead. A takeover bid involving consideration in securities is specifically called an exchange bid.

Where an exchange bid takes place, the exchange bid may also constitute a public offering or secondary distribution of securities, since the securities are generally issued to many unspecified persons. Therefore, not only regulations governing exchange bids but also those governing public offering

---

[25]   Kawamura Masayuki, ed., *Kinyū shōhin torihiki hō* (The Financial Instruments and Exchange Act), 5th ed. (Chuokeizai-sha, 2014), p. 262 (written by Furuyama Masaaki).

or secondary distribution of securities usually apply; thus, even if the takeover bidder submits a takeover bid statement and so on, it cannot solicit investors (shareholders) to accept the exchange bid unless it also submits a securities registration statement, etc. (Article 27-4(1) & (2) of the Financial Instruments and Exchange Act; Article 15 of the Cabinet Office Ordinance on Disclosure Required for Takeover Bid for Shares, etc. by Person Other than Issuer). If, however, a registration statement, etc. has been submitted, some of the particulars that the takeover bid statement is required to include, and certain accompanying documents, may be omitted as specified by cabinet office ordinance (Article 27-4(3) of the Financial Instruments and Exchange Act; Article 17 of the Cabinet Office Ordinance on Disclosure Required for Takeover Bid for Shares, etc. by Person Other than Issuer).

(ix) FIEA information disclosure regulations pertaining to cases of MBOs

In a management buyout (MBO), the directors of the target company, who are by right supposed to represent shareholders' interests by increasing enterprise value, themselves acquire the company's shares from its shareholders; hence, a structural conflict of interest arises between shareholders and directors. In addition, because the directors possess relatively accurate, full information on the target company, asymmetry of information exists between the buyers of the shares, the directors, and the sellers, the shareholders.[26] Such a structural conflict of interest and asymmetry of information are thought to occur likewise when the controlling shareholder freezes out minority shareholders,[27] since in such cases the target company's directors, being in the position of being appointed by the controlling shareholder, may harm the interests of minority shareholders by favoring those of the controlling shareholder.

It is argued, then, that in cases of MBOs and of the freezing out minority shareholders by the controlling shareholder, there is typically a possibility that directors will, far from seeking to maximize shareholders' interests,

---

26 Ministry of Economy, Trade and Industry (METI), *Kigyō kachi no kōjō oyobi kōsei na tetsuzuki kakuho no tame no keieisha ni yoru kigyō baishū (MBO) ni kansuru shishin* (Guidelines on Management Buyouts [MBOs] for Increasing Enterprise Value and Ensuring Fair Process), pp. 3-4 (released Sept. 4, 2007).

27 METI (supra, n. 26), pp. 20-21.

*540*

Chapter 4　The takeover bid system and the system of disclosure of the status of large-volume holdings

conduct transactions at times and on terms favorable to themselves, to the detriment of shareholders, owing to the existence of a structural conflict of interest and asymmetry of information between shareholders and directors.

Due to that concern, the Financial Instruments and Exchange Act seeks to make regulations on information disclosure stronger in cases of takeover bids conducted through MBOs and takeover bids by parent companies for their subsidiaries' shares[28] than in other cases of takeover bids.

Specifically, in cases of takeover bids conducted through MBOs and takeover bids by parent companies for their subsidiaries' shares, the takeover bidder is required, when submitting the takeover bid statement, to attach a copy of any written appraisal, written opinion, or document similar thereto that has been prepared by a third party and has been referred to for calculating the purchase price (Article 27-3(2) of the Financial Instruments and Exchange Act; Article 13(1)(viii) of the Cabinet Office Ordinance on Disclosure Required for Takeover Bid for Shares, etc. by Person Other than Issuer); to record the specific details of any measures taken to guarantee the fairness of the purchase price (Article 27-3(2) of the Financial Instruments and Exchange Act; Article 12; Form 2, Instructions for Completing, (6)f of the Cabinet Office Ordinance on Disclosure Required for Takeover Bid for Shares, etc. by Person Other than Issuer); and to disclose the decision-making process whereby it was decided to implement the takeover bid and to record the specific details of any measures taken to avoid conflict of interest (Article 27-3(2) of the Financial Instruments and Exchange Act; Article 12; Form 2, Instructions for Completion, (27) of the Cabinet Office Ordinance on Disclosure Required for Takeover Bid for Shares, etc. by Person Other than Issuer). Similarly, in the target company's position statement, the target company is required to record the specific details of

---

28　To be more precise, if the takeover bidder is (a) an officer of the target company, (b) a person who conducts the takeover bid based on the request of an officer of the target company and has a common interest with the officer of the target company, or (c) a company or other juridical person that holds the target company as its subsidiary, the disclosure of the information specified in the text is required (Article 13(1)(viii) of the Cabinet Office Ordinance on Disclosure Required for Takeover Bid for Shares, etc. by Person Other than Issuer). It appears that (a) and (b) have in mind takeover bids through MBOs, while (c) has in mind takeover bids by parent companies for their subsidiaries' shares.

*541*

any measures taken on its part to avoid conflict of interest (Article 27-10(1) of the Financial Instruments and Exchange Act; Article 25(2); Form 4, Instructions for Completion, (3) d of the Cabinet Office Ordinance on Disclosure Required for Takeover Bid for Shares, etc. by Person Other than Issuer).

(x) Financial instruments exchange regulations on disclosure in cases of MBOs, etc.

Given that mergers and other such organizational changes, takeover bids, and statements of position regarding takeover bids may directly affect the share price and control of listed companies, the Tokyo Stock Exchange (TSE) has from before required companies listed on it to engage in timely, appropriate disclosure in the interests of protecting investors. Particularly with regard to cases of takeover bids through MBOs and takeover bids by controlling shareholders, where a structural conflict of interest and asymmetry of information exists between shareholders and directors, the TSE requires that companies listed on it make timely disclosure in a necessary and sufficient manner (Rule 441 and Rule 441-2 (2) of the Securities Listing Regulations).

With the release of the "Guidelines on Management Buyouts (MBOs) for Increasing Enterprise Value and Ensuring Fair Process" by the Ministry of Economy, Trade and Industry on September 4, 2007, some progress was seen on the practical front in protecting the interests of shareholders of target companies in cases of MBOs and in cases where minority shareholders were frozen out by the controlling shareholder. In the wake of these practical advances the TSE, in a document of July 8, 2013, entitled "Enhancing Timely Disclosure Relating to MBOs and so on" (*Tosho Jokai*, No. 752), revised the information normally to be disclosed in cases of takeover bids conducted through MBOs or by controlling shareholders and targeting companies listed on the TSE,[29] expanding and clarifying the range of that information.[30] Below, we provide the details of the TSE's 2013 revisions to matters subject to timely disclosure, and review the general

---

29  The revisions applied from October 1, 2013, and all transactions decided or disclosed on or after that date were subject to them.

Chapter 4    The takeover bid system and the system of disclosure of the status of large-volume holdings

outlines of current disclosure regulations as enshrined in financial instruments exchange rules.

The first major pillar in the revision of matters subject to timely disclosure was an increase in the range of information to be recorded relating to calculation of the price of the purchase, etc. In cases of takeover bids by MBO and takeover bids by the controlling shareholder, the TSE has from before required, during any statement of position, timely disclosure materials record, among other items relating to the calculation on the written appraisal obtained from the appraising agency, the specific methods of calculation used, the grounds for using those methods, and the figure (or range) obtained by each method. Likewise, in terms of key conditions on which the calculation is predicated, there has been from before a requirement that, if for example, the discounted cash flow (DCF) method is used, and the financial forecasts on which calculation of the price of the purchase, etc. is predicated foresee a significant increase or decrease in profits, a summary of those financial forecasts be provided along with the factors justifying the increase or decrease. However, when for example using the DCF method, previously there was no requirement to disclose, among key conditions on which the calculation was predicated, the exact content of the financial forecasts on which the calculation was predicated or the discount rate used; and in practice they were not usually disclosed.[31] The 2013 revision of matters subject to timely disclosure endeavored to expand and clarify what was to be disclosed. In particular, when using the DCF method, one is now required to disclose the exact figures for the financial forecasts[32] (of sales,

---

**30**    On the revisions to matters subject to timely disclosure at the TSE, see Sagawa Yuki, "MBO tō ni kansuru tekiji kaiji naiyō no minaoshi tō no gaiyō" (Summary of revisions, etc. to timely disclosure content relating to MBOs, etc.), *Shoji Homu* No. 2006 (2013), p. 76, and Fujiwara Soichiro and Anzai Nobuhiro, "Tōshō 'MBO tō ni kansuru tekiji kaiji naiyō no jūjitsu tō nitsuite' no kaisetsu" (Commentary on the TSE's 'Enhancing Timely Disclosure Relating to MBOs and so on'), *Business Homu* Vol. 13, No. 11 (2013), p. 53.

**31**    Fujiwara and Anzai (supra, n. 30), p. 54.

**32**    But the exact figures for the financial forecasts need not be disclosed if the company is to remain listed. The reason cited for this is that if a company is to remain listed, minority shareholders can retain their shares without accepting the takeover bid (Sagawa [supra, n. 30], p. 79).

operating income, EBITDA, and free cash flow for each business year) on which the calculation is predicated and the exact figure for (or range of) the discount rate used, as well as the method of calculating terminal value and the exact figures for (or range of) the parameters used for that calculation.

Second, the information to be recorded on the process leading up to the decision was clarified. Even before the 2013 revision of matters subject to timely disclosure, it was required in cases of takeover bids by MBO and takeover bids by the controlling shareholder that, during any statement of position, timely disclosure materials record the details of one's assessment regarding the increase in enterprise value resulting from the buyout, and specifically include an explanation on the respect for shareholders' interests through a fair process. The 2013 revision of matters subject to timely disclosure makes clear that, in the case of a takeover bid by MBO or by the controlling shareholder, it is necessary, when stating a position recommending acceptance of that bid, to record the reasons for one's assessment regarding purchase price (for example, having verified the reasonableness of the results of the calculation by the appraising agency, to explain the reasons for that assessment in terms of whether the purchase price is reasonable relative to those results). This is explained as being intended to make clear that when stating a position recommending acceptance of a takeover bid, one must not only provide an explanation of procedures but also record one's assessment regarding the purchase price itself.[33]

Finally, the information to be recorded about steps taken to guarantee fairness and prevent conflicts of interest was clarified.[34] Given the increasing tendency in recent years, in Japan as well, to set up a special committee in cases of takeover bids by MBO and takeover bids by the controlling shareholder, it is now required, when a special committee is established, to provide a general outline of it (such as the names and occupations of the members of whom it is composed); if the committee is consulted on the statement of position, to record the details of what it was asked and the specifics of and reasons for its recommendations in response; and if it is

---

**33** Sagawa (supra, n. 30), pp. 79–80.
**34** Sagawa (supra, n. 30), p. 80.

Chapter 4   The takeover bid system and the system of disclosure of the status of large-volume holdings

entrusted with the task of negotiating with the takeover bidder, to record that fact.

b. Transaction regulations governing takeover bids

In the case of takeover bids, besides the disclosure regulations just surveyed, regulations governing the exact form of the transaction have also been established with a view to ensuring substantial equality between takeover bidders and investors (shareholders) and among investors themselves.[35] Here we review the specifics of the regulations governing the exact form of the transaction in cases of takeover bids.

(ⅰ) The takeover bid period and extension thereof

The takeover bidder must set a takeover bid period of not less than 20 business days but within 60 business days from the day on which public notice of the commencement of the takeover bid was given (Article 27-2(2) of the Financial Instruments and Exchange Act; Article 8(1) of the Financial Instruments and Exchange Act Implementing Order). The takeover bid period means the period from the day on which the takeover bidder issues the public notice of the commencement of the takeover bid to the last day of the purchase, etc., and including the extended period, if any (Article 27-5 parenthesis of the Financial Instruments and Exchange Act).

Thus, the Financial Instruments and Exchange Act prescribes a minimum and a maximum takeover bid period. The reason for mandating a minimum period of not less than 20 business days is the necessity, in order to protect investors (shareholders), of giving them time to ponder carefully whether to accept the takeover bid. The reasons for mandating a maximum period of not more than 60 business days are these: it would be undesirable to leave investors who had accepted the takeover bid in an unstable position for too long; in addition, uncertainty about the success or failure of the takeover bid for prolonged periods could be disruptive to smooth circulation and fair price formation of the shares, etc. subject to the takeover bid.[36]

---

**35** Kawamura, ed. (supra, n. 25), p. 262 (Furuyama Masaaki).
**36** Kondo et al. (supra, n. 3), p. 377; Kawamura, ed. (supra, n. 25), p. 264 (Furuyama Masaaki).

*545*

As regards extensions of the takeover bid period, broadly speaking two cases are defined. First, if a rival takeover bid is initiated in competition with the original takeover bid, the original takeover bidder is permitted to extend its own takeover bid period until the last day of the takeover bid period pertaining to the competing takeover bid (Article 27-6 (1) (iv) of the Financial Instruments and Exchange Act; Article 13 (2) (ii) (b) of the Financial Instruments and Exchange Act Implementing Order). The reason for this is that not allowing any extension of the takeover bid period pertaining to the original takeover bid when a competing takeover bid was initiated would leave the original takeover bidder unable to compete adequately against the competing bid. Thus, an extension of the takeover bid period is permitted in order to enable rival takeover bids to compete on equal terms.

Second, if certain conditions are met, the target company of the takeover bid is permitted to demand an extension of the takeover bid period. To be specific, the target company of the takeover bid may, if the takeover bid period set by the takeover bidder is less than 30 business days, request an extension thereof in the target company's position statement (Article 27-10 (2) (ii) of the Financial Instruments and Exchange Act; Article 9-3(6) of the Financial Instruments and Exchange Act Implementing Order); if the target company's position statement including that request for an extension is made available for public inspection, the takeover bidder is required to extend the takeover bid period to 30 business days (Article 27-10(3) of the Financial Instruments and Exchange Act; Article 9-3(6) of the Financial Instruments and Exchange Act Implementing Order). The reason for this is that if the takeover bid period is set for a shorter length than 30 business days, it is necessary to allow sufficient time for management of the target company in particular to present a counterproposal to investors (shareholders), and for investors to ponder carefully on that basis and reach an appropriate decision.[37] Any takeover bid period extended at the request of the target company is a uniform 30 business days; the target company cannot specifically choose the length of the extension.

---

37　Matsuo (supra, n. 10), p. 249.

Chapter 4    The takeover bid system and the system of disclosure of the status of large-volume holdings

(ⅱ)    Uniformity of purchase price

If a purchase, etc. is effected through a takeover bid, the purchase, etc. price must be on the same conditions for all tendering shareholders (Article 27-2(3) of the Financial Instruments and Exchange Act; Article 8(3) of the Financial Instruments and Exchange Act Implementing Order). This is because all tendering shareholders need to be treated equally in a takeover bid. When anything other than money is delivered as the consideration of the purchase, etc., the ratio of exchange and any difference that arises in such exchange must be on the same conditions for all tendering shareholders (Article 8(2) of the Financial Instruments and Exchange Act Implementing Order).

(ⅲ)    Prohibition of separate purchase

Another systematic measure designed, like uniformity of purchase price, to ensure equality between shareholders of the target company of the takeover bid is the prohibition of separate purchase: takeover bidders (including specially related parties, etc.) must not, in principle, purchase, etc. shares, etc. subject to the takeover bid, other than through the takeover bid, during the takeover bid period (Article 27-5 main clause of the Financial Instruments and Exchange Act). The prohibition of separate purchase has been adopted in consideration of the unfairness that would result to shareholders tendering their shares, etc. if the same bidder were to acquire the same shares, etc. on different terms, whether on or off the market.

As an alternative method of regulating separate purchase, it would in theory be conceivable, while permitting separate purchase, to deem the takeover bid price to have been raised if separate purchase were made for more than the takeover bid price, and to require the takeover bidder to purchase the tendered shares, etc. from all tendering shareholders at the higher price. For the sake of ease of enforcement, however, the Financial Instruments and Exchange Act has decided to uniformly prohibit separate purchase. Moreover, takeover bidders that make separate purchases may be subject to criminal penalties (Article 200(ⅲ); Article 207(1)(ⅴ) of the Financial Instruments and Exchange Act); from a civil law perspective, too, they may be held liable to provide compensatory damages to shareholders who have accepted the takeover bid (Article 27-17 (1) of the Financial

*547*

Instruments and Exchange Act). The amount of compensatory damages in such instances is the price that the takeover bidder, etc. paid for the separate purchase less the takeover bid price, multiplied by the number of shares, etc. tendered by the shareholder claiming compensation (ibid. (2)).

A separate purchase is thus, in principle, forbidden, but certain cases are given where, exceptionally, it is permitted, including (a) if a contract for effecting separate purchase is concluded prior to the public notice of the commencement of the takeover bid, and the existence and details of that contract are stated in the takeover bid statement; and (b) if a specially related party by formal criteria notifies the Prime Minister that the person does not fall under the category of a specially related party by substantial criteria (proviso to Article 27-5 of the Financial Instruments and Exchange Act; Article 12 of the Financial Instruments and Exchange Act Implementing Order; Article 18 of the Cabinet Office Ordinance on Disclosure Required for Takeover Bid for Shares, etc. by Person Other than Issuer). The reason for (b) is that cases are conceivable where a specially related party by formal criteria could buy up shares, etc. of the target company not as an ally of the takeover bidder but rather as an ally of the target company of the takeover bid, with the goal of countering that bid.[38]

(iv)  Changes to the terms of purchase

If after commencement of a takeover bid the takeover bidder could change the terms of purchase at will in a way disadvantageous to investors (shareholders), not only might that cause unforeseen losses to investors who accepted the takeover bid, it could also seriously affect trading on the secondary market for the shares, etc. subject to the takeover bid; thus, the share price of the target company of the takeover bid could be liable to wild fluctuations or manipulation. Therefore, the Financial Instruments and Exchange Act, while in principle allowing changes to the terms of purchase after commencement of the takeover bid (Article 27-6(2) of the Financial Instruments and Exchange Act), states that certain changes to the terms of purchase disadvantageous to investors are not allowed to be made (ibid. (1)).

---

**38**  Kondo et al. (supra, n. 3), p. 385.

Chapter 4 The takeover bid system and the system of disclosure of the status of large-volume holdings

Specifically, the takeover bidder is not allowed to (a) lower the purchase, etc. price; (b) reduce the number of shares, etc. sought for purchase; (c) shorten the purchase, etc. period; or (d) make any other changes specified by cabinet order to the terms of purchase, etc. (Article 27-6 (1) of the Financial Instruments and Exchange Act; Article 13 (2) of the Financial Instruments and Exchange Act Implementing Order). An exception is, however, allowed with regard to (a) the lowering of the purchase, etc. price: if the target company of the takeover bid conducts a share split, or conducts an allotment of new shares or share options without contribution, thus reducing the target company's price per share, the bidder may lower the purchase price to a certain degree as long as it states beforehand, in the public notice of the commencement of the takeover bid and the takeover bid statement, that it may do so in those circumstances (Article 27-6 (1) (i) parenthesis of the Financial Instruments and Exchange Act; Article 13 (1) of the Financial Instruments and Exchange Act Implementing Order). This is because, given that the target company's share price per share is reduced in such cases, it would make no sense to maintain the original purchase price to the detriment of the bidder. The minimum level to which the price may be lowered in such cases is set on the basis of the increase in number of shares (Article 19 (1) of the Cabinet Office Ordinance on Disclosure Required for Takeover Bid for Shares, etc. by Person Other than Issuer), so even after the price is lowered, investors (shareholders) are effectively guaranteed the same terms as the original purchase price.[39] For example, if the takeover bidder commences a takeover bid with a purchase price of 100, and the target company of the takeover bid then conducts a two-for-one share split, the takeover bidder may lower the purchase price to a minimum level of 50 ($=100 \times 1/2$).

The prohibition against (d) any other changes specified by cabinet order to the terms of purchase, etc. applies, for example, to increasing the number of shares, etc. sought for purchase where the condition is imposed that, if the total number of tendered shares, etc. does not reach the number of shares, etc. sought for purchase designated in advance in the public notice of the commencement of the takeover bid and in the takeover bid statement, the

---

**39** Yamashita and Kanda (supra, n. 3), p. 270 (Kato Takahito).

*549*

takeover bidder will not purchase, etc. any of the tendered shares, etc. (Article 13 (2) of the Financial Instruments and Exchange Act Implementing Order). This is because increasing the number of shares, etc. sought for purchase under such conditions would for investors (shareholders) be a disadvantageous change to the terms of purchase in that it would make the takeover bid less likely to succeed. An exception is, however, allowed even in such cases: if, after public notice of the commencement of a takeover bid is given, a third party other than the takeover bidder or the target company commences a takeover bid competing with the original takeover bid, or a third party conducting a competing takeover bid increases the number of shares, etc. sought for purchase, the takeover bidder of the original takeover bid may increase the number of shares, etc. sought for purchase (proviso to Article 13(2) (i) of the Financial Instruments and Exchange Act Implementing Order).

Finally, when changing the terms of purchase of the takeover bid pursuant to the above rules, the takeover bidder must issue public notice of the details of the change during the takeover bid period (Article 27-6 (2) of the Financial Instruments and Exchange Act; Article 19(2) of the Cabinet Office Ordinance on Disclosure Required for Takeover Bid for Shares, etc. by Person Other than Issuer), and must immediately submit an amended statement to the Prime Minister (Article 27-8 (2) of the Financial Instruments and Exchange Act).

(ⅴ) Takeover bid withdrawal, etc.

In principle, a takeover bidder is not allowed to withdraw bids or cancel contracts in connection with a takeover bid (takeover bid withdrawal, etc.) after having issued public notice of the commencement of the takeover bid (Article 27-11(1) main clause of the Financial Instruments and Exchange Act). This is because enabling a takeover bidder to effect a takeover bid withdrawal, etc. at will would place investors (shareholders) in an uncertain position and could allow the casual commencement and withdrawal of takeover bidders to be used as a means of market manipulation.[40]

As exceptions to this principle, however, the Financial Instruments and

---

**40** Kondo et al. (supra, n. 3), p. 382.

*550*

Chapter 4   The takeover bid system and the system of disclosure of the status of large-volume holdings

Exchange Act does allow a takeover bid withdrawal, etc. by the takeover bidder in, broadly speaking, two cases. First, if any circumstance specified by cabinet order occurs that would significantly compromise the takeover bidder's ability to achieve the purpose of the takeover bid, the takeover bidder may effect a takeover bid withdrawal, etc. as long as it states beforehand, in the public notice of the commencement of the takeover bid and the takeover bid statement, that it may do so in those circumstances (proviso to Article 27-11(1) of the Financial Instruments and Exchange Act; Article 14(1) of the Financial Instruments and Exchange Act Implementing Order). For example, if the takeover bidder's ability to achieve the purpose of the takeover bid is significantly compromised as the result of measures taken by the target company to defend itself against the takeover, or if the takeover bidder is unable to obtain from an administrative agency the permission, etc. necessary under other laws and regulations for the acquisition of the target company's shares, etc., the takeover bidder may effect a takeover bid withdrawal, etc. as long as it states beforehand, in the public notice of the commencement of the takeover bid and the takeover bid statement, that it may do so in those circumstances (Article 14(1) of the Financial Instruments and Exchange Act Implementing Order; Article 26 of the Cabinet Office Ordinance on Disclosure Required for Takeover Bid for Shares, etc. by Person Other than Issuer). Second, if an order to commence bankruptcy proceedings is issued against the takeover bidder or any other material change in circumstances specified by cabinet order occurs, a takeover bid withdrawal, etc. may be effected (even if the possibility of doing so is not stated in the public notice of the commencement of the takeover bid and the takeover bid statement) based on the fact that the bid would be difficult to implement (proviso to Article 27-11 (1) of the Financial Instruments and Exchange Act; Article 14 and Article 2 of the Financial Instruments and Exchange Act Implementing Order).

Finally, when seeking to effect a takeover bid withdrawal, etc. pursuant to the above rules, the takeover bidder must, in principle, issue a public notice indicating that it will effect a takeover bid withdrawal, etc., the reason for this, etc., by the last day of the takeover bid period (Article 27-11(2) of the Financial Instruments and Exchange Act; Article 27 of the Cabinet Office Ordinance on Disclosure Required for Takeover Bid for Shares, etc. by

Person Other than Issuer), and must submit a written takeover bid withdrawal notice to the Prime Minister on the day on which it issues that public notice (Article 27-11(3) of the Financial Instruments and Exchange Act).

(vi) Cancellation of a contract by a tendering shareholder, etc.

A person that accepts a bid to purchase, etc. the shares, etc. involved in a takeover bid or that offers to sell them, etc. may cancel a contract involving a takeover bid at any time during the takeover bid period (Article 27-12(1) of the Financial Instruments and Exchange Act). This is designed to allow shareholders who have accepted a takeover bid to change their investment decision afterwards (and particularly to accept a different takeover bid initiated by a competing takeover bidder). If a tendering shareholder cancels a contract, the takeover bidder is not allowed to claim payment for damages or penalties (ibid. (3)).

(vii) The buy-all requirement and solicit-all requirement

When effecting a takeover bid, a takeover bidder can in principle purchase only the number of shares, etc. required. Thus, so-called partial takeover bids are permitted. Specifically, a takeover bidder is able to acquire only the number of shares, etc. required, without having to acquire them all, as long as it has included in the public notice of the commencement of the takeover bid and the takeover bid statement the condition that if the total number of tendered shares, etc. exceeds the number of shares, etc. sought for purchase, it will not purchase, etc. all or any of the shares, etc. tendered in excess of the number of shares, etc. sought for purchase (Article 27-13 (4) (ii) of the Financial Instruments and Exchange Act). Further, if a partial takeover bid is effected and the total number of tendered shares, etc. exceeds the number of shares, etc. sought for purchase, the Financial Instruments and Exchange Act requires that the tendered shares, etc. be acquired using a pro rata method[41] (Article 27-13(5) of the Financial Instruments and Exchange Act; Article 32 of the Cabinet Office Ordinance on Disclosure Required for Takeover Bid for Shares, etc. by Person Other than Issuer) in order to ensure that tendering shareholders are treated equally regardless of when they accept the bid.

Chapter 4   The takeover bid system and the system of disclosure of the status of large-volume holdings

There is, however, an important exception to the above principle: if the takeover bidder's ownership ratio of shares, etc. will be two-thirds or more after the purchase, a requirement to purchase all the tendered shares, etc. (the buy-all requirement) is imposed on it (Article 27-13(4) parenthesis of the Financial Instruments and Exchange Act; Article 14-2-2 of the Financial Instruments and Exchange Act Implementing Order). The rationale for thus restricting the implementation of partial takeover bids and imposing a buy-all requirement on the takeover bidder is to protect the interests of investors (shareholders) who, after the close of the takeover bid, are forced to hold on to shares, etc. that were not subject to purchase, etc. If the takeover bidder's ownership ratio of shares, etc. is two-thirds or more after the purchase, the target company's shares, etc. may be difficult to dispose of because if they have been delisted, and under the Companies Act shareholders other than the takeover bidder will basically lose their veto on extraordinary resolutions of shareholders meetings; in this case alone, then, it was thought appropriate to impose a buy-all requirement on takeover bidders in addition to restricting partial takeover bids.[42]

The Financial Instruments and Exchange Act also defines cases where a solicit-all requirement is imposed on takeover bidders on the same principle as the buy-all requirement. Specifically, if the takeover bidder's ownership ratio of shares, etc. will be two-thirds or more after the purchase, it must in principle offer to effect a purchase, etc. of, or solicit offers to sell, etc., all the shares, etc. issued by the issuer of the shares, etc. in question (Article 27-2 (5) of the Financial Instruments and Exchange Act; Article 8(5)(iii) of the Financial Instruments and Exchange Act Implementing Order).

---

41   The pro rata method entails multiplying the number of shares, etc. that the tendering shareholder actually tenders by the ratio of the shares, etc. for which purchase, etc. is to be made to the total number of voting rights pertaining to all the shares, etc. tendered (Article 32(1) of the Cabinet Office Ordinance on Disclosure Required for Takeover Bid for Shares, etc. by Person Other than Issuer). If the number obtained by this calculation includes a fraction of less than one share, it is rounded off to a whole number.

42   Kondo et al. (supra, n. 3), p. 379.

*553*

# 4. Ensuring effective implementation of takeover bid regulations

a. Civil liability

Provisions governing civil liability in the case of violations of takeover bid regulations cover, broadly speaking, (a) compensatory liability on the grounds of an act of solicitation before submission of a takeover bid statement, etc.; (b) compensatory liability on the grounds of a violation of the prohibition of separate purchase; (c) compensatory liability on the grounds of unfair settlement; (d) compensatory liability of a person using a takeover bid explanation that contains a false statement, etc.; and (e) compensatory liability on the grounds of a public notice of the commencement of a takeover bid, etc. that contains a false statement, etc.. Below we briefly review each of these provisions on compensatory liability.

(ⅰ) Compensatory liability on the grounds of an act of solicitation before submission of a takeover bid statement, etc.

If, on or after the day following the day on which the public notice of the commencement of the takeover bid is issued, but before submission of the takeover bid statement, the takeover bidder (including a specially related party, etc.) offers to effect a purchase, etc. of shares, etc. or solicits offers to sell them, etc. or conducts any other act specified by cabinet office ordinance (Article 15 of the Cabinet Office Ordinance on Disclosure Required for Takeover Bid for Shares, etc. by Person Other than Issuer), that takeover bidder is liable to compensate any person that sells, etc. its shares, etc. in response to the takeover bid for damages arising from the violation (Article 27-16, Article 16 of the Financial Instruments and Exchange Act). This also applies if an order to submit an amended statement has been issued, and the takeover bidder offers to effect purchase, etc. of shares, etc. or solicits offers to sell them, etc. or conducts any other act specified by cabinet office ordinance (Article 15 of the Cabinet Office Ordinance on Disclosure Required for Takeover Bid for Shares, etc. by Person Other than Issuer), before submitting the amended statement.

Chapter 4　The takeover bid system and the system of disclosure of the status of large-volume holdings

(ⅱ)　Compensatory liability on the grounds of a violation of the prohibition of separate purchase

A takeover bidder (including a specially related party, etc.) that effects separate purchase is liable to compensate any person that sells, etc. its shares, etc. in response to the takeover bid for damages sustained (Article 27-17(1) of the Financial Instruments and Exchange Act). The amount of compensatory damages in such instances is the price that the takeover bidder, etc. paid for the separate purchase less the takeover bid price, multiplied by the number of shares, etc. tendered by the shareholder claiming compensation (ibid. (2)).

(ⅲ)　Compensatory liability on the grounds of unfair settlement

If a takeover bidder (1) purchases, etc. shares, etc. at a price that is more favorable than the takeover bid price from only some of the persons selling, etc. their shares, etc. in response to the takeover bid, or (2) purchases, etc. shares, etc. through a method that is different from the pro rata method stated in the takeover bid statement, that takeover bidder is liable to compensate any person that sells, etc. its shares, etc. in response to the takeover bid for damages sustained (Article 27-18 (1) of the Financial Instruments and Exchange Act).

The amount of compensatory damages is, in the case of (1), the favorable price less the takeover bid price, multiplied by the number of shares, etc. tendered by the shareholder claiming compensation (Article 27-18(2) (i) of the Financial Instruments and Exchange Act); and in the case of (2), the number of shares, etc. that should have been purchased, etc. from the shareholder claiming compensation had the pro rata method stated in the takeover bid statement been followed, less the number of shares, etc. actually purchased, etc. from that shareholder, multiplied by the difference between the takeover bid price and the market price of the shares, etc. in question (ibid. (ii)).

(ⅳ)　Compensatory liability of a person using a takeover bid explanation that contains a false statement, etc.

A person that has caused a person to sell, etc. shares, etc. through the use of a takeover bid explanation or other representation that contains a false

*555*

statement about a material particular, omits a representation as to a material particular that is required to be represented, or omits a representation of a material particular that is necessary to prevent deception is liable to compensate any person that sells, etc. its shares, etc. in response to the takeover bid without knowing that the statement is false, etc. for damages sustained (Article 27-19, Article 17 of the Financial Instruments and Exchange Act), unless the person that would be liable to compensate proves it did not know, and in the exercise of reasonable care could not have known, that the statement was false, etc.

(ⅴ) Compensatory liability on the grounds of a public notice of the commencement of a takeover bid, etc. that contains a false statement, etc.

If (1) a public notice of the commencement of a takeover bid, (2) a takeover bid statement, (3) a takeover bid explanation, or (4) the takeover bidder's answer contains a false statement about a material particular, omits a statement as to a material particular that is required to be represented, or omits a statement of a material particular that is necessary to prevent deception, the issuer of (1), the submitter of (2), the preparer of (3), or the submitter of (4) is liable to compensate any person that sells, etc. its shares, etc. in response to the takeover bid without knowing that the statement is false, etc. for damages sustained (Article 27-20(1) and Article 18(1) of the Financial Instruments and Exchange Act).

b. Criminal liability

Besides the above provisions on civil liability, for many violations of takeover bid regulations there are also provisions for criminal penalties. Typical provisions for criminal penalties are these: (a) a person that makes a false statement, etc. about a material particular on a public notice of the commencement of a takeover bid or other such document is subject to punishment by imprisonment with required labor for not more than ten years, a fine of not more than ten million yen, or both (Article 197(1)(ii) of the Financial Instruments and Exchange Act); (b) a person that fails to issue a public notice of the commencement of a takeover bid or to submit a takeover bid statement is subject to punishment by imprisonment with

Chapter 4   The takeover bid system and the system of disclosure of the status of large-volume holdings

required labor for not more than five years, a fine of not more than five million yen, or both (Article 197-2(iv) & (v) of the Financial Instruments and Exchange Act); and (c) a person that fails to deliver a takeover bid explanation or violates the prohibition of separate purchase is subject to punishment by imprisonment with required labor for not more than one year, a fine of not more than one million yen, or both (Article 200(iii) & (ix) of the Financial Instruments and Exchange Act). These provisions on criminal penalties entail dual liability (Article 207 (1) of the Financial Instruments and Exchange Act).

    c . Administrative monetary penalties

    Finally, let us review the provisions on issuance of an administrative monetary penalty in the case of a violation of takeover bid regulations. Broadly speaking, two types of such administrative monetary penalties can be cited.

    First, a person effecting a purchase, etc. of shares, etc. without issuing a public notice of the commencement of a takeover bid is subject to an administrative monetary penalty (Article 172-5 of the Financial Instruments and Exchange Act). The penalty in this case is equivalent to the total amount of the purchase, etc. multiplied by 25 percent.

    Second, (a) a person making a public notice of the commencement of a takeover bid, etc. that contains a false representation about a material particular or that omits a representation as to a material particular that is required to be represented, (b) a person submitting a takeover bid statement, etc. that contains a false statement about a material particular or that omits a statement as to a material particular that is required to be stated, or (c) a person failing to submit a takeover bid statement, etc. is subject to an administrative monetary penalty (Article 172-6(1) & (2) of the Financial Instruments and Exchange Act). The penalty in this case is equivalent to the amount arrived at when the closing price of the shares, etc. subject to the takeover bid as of the day immediately preceding the day of the public notice of the commencement of the takeover bid is multiplied by the number of shares, etc. that the person purchases, etc. through that takeover bid, further multiplied by 25 percent.

*557*

## 5. Takeover bids by issuers

### a. Overview of the system

As in the case examined so far of the purchase, etc. of shares, etc. outside a financial instruments exchange market by a person other than the issuer, implementing a takeover bid may also be compulsory when an issuer effects purchase, etc. of its own shares outside a financial instruments exchange market.

To be specific, a purchase, etc. of listed shares, etc. outside a financial instruments exchange market by the issuer of those listed shares, etc. must in principle be effected by means of a takeover bid if (a) the purchase, etc. is effected by resolution of a shareholders meeting under Article 156, paragraph 1 of the Companies Act (or of a board of directors meeting under Article 165, paragraph 3 of the Companies Act); or (b) the issuer is a foreign company, and the purchase, etc. is one of which the particulars are to be made available to a large number of persons through publication in a newspaper or magazine, in writing, through broadcasting, in film, or by any other means (Article 27-22-2(1) of the Financial Instruments and Exchange Act; Article 14-3-2 (3) of the Financial Instruments and Exchange Act Implementing Order). In other words, when an issuer effects a purchase, etc. of its own shares outside a financial instruments exchange market, implementing a takeover bid is in principle compulsory except in the case of the purchase of shares, etc. from specific shareholders (Article 160 of the Companies Act).

This provision was established because even in the case of an issuer's purchase, etc. of its own shares, it is still necessary to treat investors (shareholders) equally and ensure appropriate disclosure of information. Besides, a takeover bid by the issuer does not fundamentally differ from a takeover bid by a person other than the issuer insofar as investors are still forced to make an investment decision on whether to sell the shares, etc. in their possession within a limited time.[43] The Financial Instruments and Exchange Act accordingly applies, mutatis mutandis, most of the provisions

---

43  Yamashita and Kanda (supra, n. 3), p. 278 (Kato Takahito); Kawamura (supra, n. 25), p. 269 (Furuyama Masaaki).

Chapter 4 The takeover bid system and the system of disclosure of the status of large-volume holdings

governing takeover bids by persons other than the issuer to takeover bids by issuers as well (Article 27-22-2 (2) ff. of the Financial Instruments and Exchange Act).

b. Characteristics of regulations applying to takeover bids by issuers

( i ) Listed shares, etc. subject to a takeover bid

"Listed shares, etc." subject to a takeover bid by the issuer constitute (a) shares that are listed on a financial instruments exchange, and (b) shares specified by cabinet order as having equivalent distribution statuses to shares listed on a financial instruments exchange, such as over-the-counter traded securities (Article 24-6 (1) of the Financial Instruments and Exchange Act; Article 4-3 (1) & (2) of the Financial Instruments and Exchange Act Implementing Order). The objective of making implementing a takeover bid compulsory in the event of purchase, etc. by the issuer of its own shares is to guarantee all investors (shareholders) equal opportunity to sell their listed shares, etc.; therefore, unlike in the case of takeover bids effected by a person other than the issuer, share options and corporate bonds with share options are not included in the "listed shares, etc." subject to the takeover bid.[44]

( ii ) Requirement to disclose material facts and extension of the takeover
       bid period

When an issuer implements a takeover bid in order to effect the purchase, etc. of its own shares, it must, as the takeover bidder, issue a public notice of the commencement of the takeover bid and submit a takeover bid statement to the Prime Minister (Article 27-22-2(2) of the Financial Instruments and Exchange Act). In a takeover bid by the issuer, it is further required that all material facts known to the issuer (namely the material facts about business specified in Article 166(1) of the Financial Instruments and Exchange Act) be disclosed at the time of submission of the takeover bid statement (Article 27-22-3 (1) of the Financial Instruments and Exchange Act). This is because, in the case of a takeover bid by the issuer, there is a particular risk that the issuer of the shares, etc. subject to purchase, etc., possessing as it

---

**44** Yamashita and Kanda (supra, n. 3), p. 278 (Kato Takahito).

*559*

does extensive information relating to them, could effect their purchase, etc. while intentionally concealing information likely to affect its own share price.

For similar reasons, if, during the takeover bid period, a new material fact arises or the existence of an undisclosed material fact comes to light, the issuer, as the takeover bidder, must immediately disclose that material fact, and must also notify persons that have accepted the bid to purchase, etc. listed shares, etc. through the takeover bid, persons that have offered to sell, etc. their listed shares, etc. in connection with the takeover bid, and persons seeking to sell, etc. such listed shares, etc., of the content of what it has disclosed, regardless of whether they have already accepted the takeover bid (Article 27-22-3(2) of the Financial Instruments and Exchange Act).

Disclosure of any material fact pursuant to the above provision must be conducted by means of two or more of the following media organizations: (a) news publishers engaged in the sale of daily newspapers that publish matters on current affairs in the course of trade; (b) news agencies engaged in comprehensively supplying information on current affairs to the news publishers in (a) in the course of trade; and (c) NHK and key broadcasters (Article 11 of the Cabinet Office Ordinance on Disclosure Required for Takeover Bid for Listed Shares, etc. by Issuer). Further, in order to guarantee investors (shareholders) the opportunity for careful considera- tion, if the issuer, as the takeover bidder, discloses a new material fact, or a material fact found not yet to have been made public, when there are ten or fewer days remaining in the takeover bid period, the issuer must extend the purchase, etc. period from the day following the last day of the takeover bid period to the date on which ten business days have elapsed from the day on which that disclosure was made, and must immediately issue public notice of that extension or publicly announce it (Article 27-22-3(4) and Article 27-8 (8) of the Financial Instruments and Exchange Act; Article 25 of the Cabinet Office Ordinance on Disclosure Required for Takeover Bid for Listed Shares, etc. by Issuer).

An issuer that fails to make a disclosure or issue a notice (collectively referred to as "disclosure") of a material fact under the above provisions, or makes a false disclosure, is liable to compensate any person that sells, etc. its listed shares, etc. in response to the takeover bid for damages arising from its failure to make disclosure or from its false disclosure (Article 27-22-4(1)

Chapter 4 The takeover bid system and the system of disclosure of the status of large-volume holdings

main clause of the Financial Instruments and Exchange Act), except if (a) the person that makes the sale, etc. knows that the material fact has occurred within the issuer or knows that the content of the disclosure is false, or (b) the issuer proves that it did not know that the material fact had occurred within it or that the content of the disclosure was false, and that in the exercise of reasonable care it could not have known this at the time of the takeover bid; in which cases the issuer is exempt from liability for damages (ibid., proviso).

An officer (Article 21(1)(i) of the Financial Instruments and Exchange Act) of an issuer at the time of a takeover bid in which the issuer fails to make a disclosure of a material fact under the above provisions, or makes a false disclosure, is jointly and severally liable with the issuer for compensatory damages (Article 27-22-4(2) main clause of the Financial Instruments and Exchange Act), except if the officer proves that he/she did not know that the material fact had occurred within the issuer or that the content of the disclosure was false, and that in the exercise of reasonable care he/she could not have known this at the time of the takeover bid; in which case the officer is exempt from liability for damages (ibid. proviso).

As for criminal penalties, a person that fails to make a disclosure of a material fact under the above provisions, or that makes a false disclosure, is subject to punishment by imprisonment with required labor for not more than ten years, a fine of not more than ten million yen, or both (Article 197 (1)(iv) of the Financial Instruments and Exchange Act). These provisions on criminal penalties entail dual liability (Article 207(1) of the Financial Instruments and Exchange Act).

(iii)   Other salient characteristics

Because a takeover bid by an issuer is not a transaction relating to transfer of company control, the provisions on specially related parties (Article 27-2(7) of the Financial Instruments and Exchange Act) and on ownership ratio of shares, etc. (ibid. (8)) do not apply (see Article 27-22-2 (2) of the Financial Instruments and Exchange Act).

Because in this type of takeover bid the takeover bidder is the issuer, the provisions on submission of the target company's position statement (Article 27-10(1) of the Financial Instruments and Exchange Act) and the rest of the

*561*

back-and-forth between takeover bidder and target company do not apply (see Article 27-22-2(2) of the Financial Instruments and Exchange Act).

Finally, setting a minimum number of shares, etc. sought for purchase (Article 27-13(4) (i) of the Financial Instruments and Exchange Act) is not permitted (see Article 27-22-2 (2) of the Financial Instruments and Exchange Act), and a takeover bid may be withdrawn only in cases where purchase, etc. by a takeover bid would violate another law or regulation (Article 27-22-2 (2) and proviso to Article 27-11 (1) of the Financial Instruments and Exchange Act).

# B. The system of disclosure of the status of large-volume holdings

## 1. Overview of the system of disclosure of the status of large-volume holdings

### a. What is the system of disclosure of the status of large-volume holdings?

Under the system of disclosure of the status of large-volume holdings, if a person's "ownership ratio of shares, etc." (roughly speaking, the number of shares, etc. held by that person divided by the total number of issued shares) issued by a corporation that is the issuer of share-related securities listed on a financial instruments exchange or issued over the counter exceeds five percent, that person is required to submit a statement of large-volume holdings stating the purpose of the holdings, the breakdown of the shares, etc. held, the funds used to acquire them, and other matters (Article 27-23 (1) of the Financial Instruments and Exchange Act). If, after the holder of shares, etc. submits a statement of large-volume holdings, its ownership ratio of shares, etc. increases or decreases by one percent or more, the holder is further required to submit a statement of changes; this ensures that any changes in ownership of the shares, etc. after submission of a statement of large-volume holdings are disclosed (Article 27-25 (1) of the Financial Instruments and Exchange Act). Statements of large-volume holdings and statements of changes are made available for public inspection for five years from the day on which they are accepted (Article 27-28(1) of the Financial

Chapter 4   The takeover bid system and the system of disclosure of the status of large-volume holdings

Instruments and Exchange Act).

In addition to the above ordinary reporting system, there is also a special reporting system applying primarily to institutional investors (Article 27-26 (1) of the Financial Instruments and Exchange Act). To ensure that disclosure does not place an excessive administrative burden on institutional investors that trade shares, etc. continually in the course of their daily business, this system has special provisions on the frequency of and deadlines for disclosure of the status of large-volume holdings in shares, etc. in place of those of the ordinary reporting system, as long as certain conditions are met.

b.  Objectives of the system of disclosure of the status of large-volume holdings

The system of disclosure of the status of large-volume holdings in shares, etc. imposes the requirement to disclose information relating to shares, etc. on the investor who holds them, rather than on the issuer. Broadly speaking, two grounds are cited for this imposition of the duty to disclose information on the investor.[45]

First, there is the need to provide information on large-volume holdings in shares, etc. to ordinary investors. If the number of shares, etc. held by a particular investor exceeds a certain percentage, that investor may influence the control of the issuer of the shares, etc. through the exercise of its voting rights; it may also influence demand for those shares, etc. on the market, and by extension their price. In other words, the acquisition, possession, or disposal of large numbers of shares, etc. may cause their price on the market to fluctuate wildly. For that reason, it was required that information on the acquisition, possession, and disposal of large numbers of shares, etc. be disclosed to ordinary investors with a view to preventing the occurrence of unexpected losses to them.

Second, there is the need to provide information on large-volume holdings

---

**45**   Yamashita Tomonobu and Kanda Hideki, *Kinyū shōhin torihiki hō gaisetsu* (Overview of the Financial Instruments and Exchange Act) (Yuhikaku, 2010), p. 229 (written by Kato Takahito); Kawamura Masayuki, ed., *Kinyū shōhin torihiki hō* (The Financial Instruments and Exchange Act), 5th ed. (Chuokeizai-sha, 2014), pp. 277-278 (written by Furuyama Masaaki), etc.

*563*

in shares, etc. to the managers of the corporation that issued them. In recent years hostile takeovers and institutional investors that make aggressive use of shareholders' rights have become more common in Japan; given that fact, there is a growing need to ensure managers of corporations that are issuers of shares, etc. have the opportunity and time to negotiate directly with investors holding large numbers of shares or offer alternatives to proposals by them. Moves have been seen toward turning the system of disclosure of the status of large-volume holdings in shares, etc. into a means to that end. [46]

c. Evolution of the system of disclosure of the status of large-volume holdings

The Japanese system of disclosure of the status of large-volume holdings in shares, etc., modeled on that of the United States and other countries, was adopted through the 1990 revision of the Securities and Exchange Act with the goals of increasing the fairness and transparency of the market and advancing investor protection.

Subsequently cases of large numbers of listed shares, etc. being acquired over a short period increased, and problems were pointed out with the speed and flexibility of the system of disclosure of the status of large-volume holdings in shares, etc.; hostile buyouts too became more common. With that background the need for swifter, more accurate disclosure by means of statements of large-volume holdings increased. [47] The 2006 revision of the Financial Instruments and Exchange Act primarily overhauled the special reporting system, increasing the frequency of reporting and shortening deadlines.

The 2014 revision of the Financial Instruments and Exchange Act made wide-ranging changes in order to remedy general problems with the system

---

46 However, consideration of the need to protect the interests of companies issuing shares, etc. when designing the system of disclosure of the status of large-volume holdings, as opposed to the need to protect their shareholders (investors), has been criticized by some (Kuronuma Etsuro, "Kōkai kaitsuke seido, tairyō hoyū hōkoku seido no kaisei" [Reforms to the takeover bid system and the system of disclosure of the status of large-volume holdings], *Hōritsu no hiroba*, Nov. 2006, pp. 26-27).

47 Matsuo Naohiko, *Kinyū shōhin torihiki hō* (The Financial Instruments and Exchange Act), 4th ed. (Shojihomu, 2016), p. 285.

Chapter 4   The takeover bid system and the system of disclosure of the status of large-volume holdings

of disclosure of the status of large-volume holdings in shares, etc.; it excluded treasury shares from the scope of the system, for example, and abolished the provision requiring that if, by the day before submission of a statement of changes, a new cause for submission arose, a new statement of changes had to be submitted at the same time.

## 2. The ordinary reporting system

a. The requirement to submit a statement of large-volume holdings

(ⅰ) Securities subject to the system

The Financial Instruments and Exchange Act, having defined shares, corporate bonds with share options, and other securities specified by cabinet order (Article 14-4 of the Financial Instruments and Exchange Act Implementing Order) as "share-related securities," requires that any person that holds more than a certain percentage of such "shares, etc." issued by a corporation that is the issuer of share-related securities listed on a financial instruments exchange or issued over the counter submit a statement of large-volume holdings (Article 27-23(1) of the Financial Instruments and Exchange Act).

The "shares, etc." subject to the system of disclosure of the status of large-volume holdings include "subject securities" consisting of (a) shares (excluding shares with no voting rights); (b) share options and corporate bonds with share options (excluding those with the right to acquire only shares with no voting rights as the share option); (c) securities or certificates issued by a foreign person that have the nature of the securities set forth in (a) or (b); (d) investment securities, etc.; and (e) investment equity subscription rights, etc. (Article 27-23 (2) of the Financial Instruments and Exchange Act; Article 14-5-2 of the Financial Instruments and Exchange Act Implementing Order). In addition, they also include securities indicating options pertaining to "subject securities" (limited to options of which the exerciser acquires the position of buyer through their exercise) (Article 27-23(1) of the Financial Instruments and Exchange Act; Article 14-4-2 of the Financial Instruments and Exchange Act Implementing Order). Thus, any investor that holds more than a certain percentage of such securities (shares, etc.) issued by a corporation that is the issuer of share-related securities listed on a financial instruments

*565*

exchange or issued over the counter is required to submit a statement of large-volume holdings.

The above explanation of the scope of application of the system of disclosure of the status of large-volume holdings in shares, etc. needs to be supplemented by noting two further points. First, under the system of disclosure of the status of large-volume holdings in shares, etc., the disclosure requirement is imposed on an investor only if that investor holds shares, etc. issued by a corporation that is the issuer of share-related securities listed on a financial instruments exchange or issued over the counter — in other words, a corporation that is the issuer of securities that can easily be traded and presumably interest many investors.[48] Second, the "shares, etc." subject to the system of disclosure of the status of large-volume holdings need not necessarily be listed or issued over the counter, but they do have to be securities pertaining to shares with voting rights (or enabling the acquisition of shares with voting rights through the exercise of rights, etc.). The reason adduced for this is that the system of disclosure of the status of large-volume holdings in shares, etc. has the object of ensuring that the impact of large-volume holdings in shares, etc. on control of an issuer is disclosed.[49]

(ii) Ownership ratio of shares, etc.

The requirement to submit a statement of large-volume holdings is imposed on persons whose "ownership ratio of shares, etc." of a certain type exceeds five percent (Article 27-23(1) of the Financial Instruments and Exchange Act). This five-percent benchmark has been set for policy reasons in view of the impact of such holdings on control of companies and on the market supply-and-demand environment.[50] It also appears to take into account that most other countries with advanced capital markets impose

---

48 Note also that this first point pertains to the condition governing the issuer, which is a separate question from the condition governing the range of "shares, etc." subject to the system of disclosure of the status of large-volume holdings in shares, etc. (the second point).

49 Kawamoto Ichiro et al., *Shin Kinyū shōhin torihiki hō tokuhon* (New readings in the Financial Instruments and Exchange Act) (Yuhikaku, 2014), p. 141.

50 Yamashita and Kanda (supra, n. 45), p. 231 (Kato Takahito).

Chapter 4   The takeover bid system and the system of disclosure of the status of large-volume holdings

reporting requirements based on actual ownership levels of roughly five percent.[51]

The "ownership ratio of shares, etc." is the ratio of shares, etc. held that serves as the criterion for determining whether the holder thereof is required to submit a statement of large-volume holdings. The "ownership ratio of shares, etc." is basically calculated as a fraction in which the numerator comprises the number of shares, etc. held by the holder, plus the number of shares, etc. held by joint holders, and the denominator comprises the total number of shares issued by the issuer of those shares, etc.[52] To elaborate in more detail, rights such as share options through the exercise of which shares with voting rights may be acquired in the future (potential shares) are included in calculating the numerator: they are, after being converted to shares, added to the number of shares, etc. held. Similarly, any shares, etc. which the holder is obligated to transfer due to their conveyance through a margin transaction, etc. are, in calculating the numerator, deducted from the number of shares, etc. held.[53] Then, in calculating the denominator, the number of potential shares held by the holder or any joint holders is added to the total number of shares issued by the issuer of the shares, etc.

Note also that this "ownership ratio of shares, etc.," unlike the ownership ratio of shares, etc. used for takeover bids (Article 27-2(8) of the Financial Instruments and Exchange Act), is based on the number of shares, etc., not the number of voting rights. Being thus based on the number of shares, etc. irrespective of the number of voting rights per share, the "ownership ratio of

---

51   Kawamoto et al. (supra, n. 49), p. 142.
52   Note that the 2014 revision of the Financial Instruments and Exchange Act excludes treasury shares from the range of shares, etc. subject to the system of disclosure of the status of large-volume holdings in shares, etc. (Article 27-23(4), parenthesis of the Financial Instruments and Exchange Act).
53   However, shares, etc. that the holder is obligated to transfer to a joint holder are not deducted from the number of shares, etc. held. In such cases shares, etc. for which a right to request delivery or any other right specified by cabinet order (Article 14-6-2 of the Financial Instruments and Exchange Act Implementing Order) exists between the holder and a joint holder are deducted from the number of shares, etc. held by the joint holder that are added to those of the holder (Article 27-23(4) of the Financial Instruments and Exchange Act).

*567*

shares, etc." does not necessarily reflect the weight of the holder's voting rights. Two reasons are cited for making the number of shares, etc. the benchmark: (a) given the system's objective of disclosing information relating to supply of and demand for shares, etc., it is preferable to make the number of shares, etc. the benchmark; and (b) in the case of an ordinary report, it would be difficult for holders promptly and accurately to ascertain their own proportion of voting rights.[54]

(iii) Large-volume holders

The requirement to submit a statement of large-volume holdings is imposed on "holders" whose ownership ratio of shares, etc. of a certain type exceeds five percent (Article 27-23(1) of the Financial Instruments and Exchange Act); such holders are specifically called "large-volume holders." The concept of a "holder" is defined not formally, by the title to the shares, etc., but substantially. Thus, given the purpose of the system of disclosure of the status of large-volume holdings in shares, etc., the criterion for determining whether a person constitutes a "holder" is whether in actual fact that person has the ultimate decision-making power over investment decisions and the exercise of shareholders' rights.[55]

Specifically, the term "holder" includes (a) in addition to persons that own shares, etc. in their own name, persons who own shares, etc. in the name of another (whether an actual person or under a fictitious name), as well as any person that holds the right to request the delivery of shares, etc. under a purchase and sale contract or any other contract, or any other person specified by cabinet order (Article 14-6 of the Financial Instruments and Exchange Act Implementing Order) as being equivalent (Article 27-23(3) of the Financial Instruments and Exchange Act). The purport of this is to define the actual possessor of the shares, etc. as their "holder," regardless of title.

In addition to any person falling into category (a) above, a person may in

---

**54** Kawamura, ed. (supra, n. 45), p. 281 (Furuyama Masaaki), etc.
**55** Yamashita and Kanda (supra, n. 45), p. 232 (Kato Takahito). See also Kondo Mitsuo et al., *Kinyū shōhin torihiki hō nyūmon* (Introduction to the Financial Instruments and Exchange Act), 4th ed. (Shojihomu, 2015), p. 392.

Chapter 4　The takeover bid system and the system of disclosure of the status of large-volume holdings

certain cases be considered a "holder" even if the shares, etc. in question are owned by another, on the grounds that that person has a certain degree of authority over that other party. Specifically, the term "holder" also includes (b) a person that has the authority to exercise voting rights or any other rights as a shareholder in the issuer of the shares, etc., or to give instructions concerning the exercise of the voting rights or any other rights, based on a money trust contract or any other contract or the provisions of law, and that has the aim of controlling the business activities of the issuer; and (c) a person that has the necessary authority to invest in shares, etc., based on a discretionary investment contract or any other contract or the provisions of law (Article 27-23 (3) of the Financial Instruments and Exchange Act). Given the purpose of the system of disclosure of the status of large-volume holdings in shares, etc., category (b) exists because of the need to bring to light persons that could influence control of the issuer of the shares, etc. by exercising voting rights, etc. or giving instructions, while Category (c) exists because of the need to bring to light persons that could influence the supply of and demand for the shares, etc. on the market by exercising their authority over investment decisions.

(iv)　Joint holders

As already noted, shares, etc. held by joint holders are added to the number of shares, etc. held that comprises the numerator when calculating the ownership ratio of shares, etc. The reason is this: when multiple investors act in concert to attain a common end, the shares, etc. in their possession are generally governed by a single decision-making process; therefore, if their ownership ratio of shares, etc. exceeds five percent when the total number of shares, etc. in their possession is combined, it is possible that they could, as when a single investor's ownership ratio of shares, etc. exceeds five percent, exert control over the issuer of the shares, etc. or exert influence on their market price.[56]

"Joint holders" are of two types: actual joint holders as determined by the existence of a separate agreement, and deemed joint holders as determined

---

56　See Yamashita and Kanda (supra, n. 45), p. 232 (Kato Takahito), and Kawamura, ed. (supra, n. 45), p. 282 (Furuyama Masaaki).

*569*

by the existence of a specific relationship. "Actual joint holder" means the other holder in a case in which a holder of shares, etc. has agreed with another holder of shares, etc. issued by the issuer of those shares, etc. to jointly acquire or transfer those shares, etc., or to jointly exercise voting rights and other rights as shareholders in the issuer (Article 27-23(5) of the Financial Instruments and Exchange Act). In other words, investors that have agreed to take concerted action must, when deciding whether they are required to submit a statement of large-volume holdings, calculate their ownership ratio of shares, etc. by combining the number of shares, etc. in the possession of each. Note that shareholders (investors) are basically not considered to be actual joint holders if they merely discuss how, at a shareholders meeting, they will exercise their voting rights, or if they simply agree on general action as shareholders, as opposed to the exercise of their voting rights or other shareholders' rights under laws and regulations (for example, if they jointly ask a company in which they have invested to establish a forum for dialog).[57]

Next, "deemed joint holder" means the other holder if a first holder of shares, etc. and another holder of shares, etc. that are issued by the issuer of those shares, etc. are related to each other through a shareholding relationship, familial relationship, or other special relationship specified by cabinet order (Article 14-7 of the Financial Instruments and Exchange Act Implementing Order); the deemed joint holder is then considered a joint holder with the first holder (Article 27-23(6) main clause of the Financial Instruments and Exchange Act). This provision is designed to ensure the effectiveness of the system of disclosure of the status of large-volume holdings in shares, etc. by deeming parties in a specific relationship to be joint holders with each other even if no agreement to take concerted action can be identified, since it is difficult to prove the existence of such an

---

**57** Financial Services Agency, *Nihon-ban suchuwādoshippu kōdo no sakutei o fumaeta hōteki ronten ni kakaru kangaekata no seiri* (Summary of reasoning on legal issues based on formulation of the Japanese Stewardship Code) (released Feb. 26, 2014), pp. 10-11. See also Kawamoto et al. (supra, n. 49), p. 144. Conversely, if shareholders, as a result of having discussed how they will exercise their voting rights at a shareholders meeting, agree to exercise those rights in concert, they become as of that point in time actual joint holders.

*570*

Chapter 4   The takeover bid system and the system of disclosure of the status of large-volume holdings

agreement, and it seems highly probable that parties in a specific relationship such as a shareholding relationship or a familial relationship will make such an agreement. Nevertheless, even if two parties formally meet the definition of deemed joint holders, they are not deemed joint holders if the number of shares, etc. held by either the first holder or the other holder is small (in case of shares, etc. issued by a domestic corporation, an individual ownership ratio of shares, etc. of 0.1% or less) (proviso to Article 27-23(6) of the Financial Instruments and Exchange Act; Article 6(i) of the Cabinet Office Ordinance on Disclosure of the Status of Large-Volume Holdings in Share Certificates, etc.).

(ⅴ)  Exclusions

Even if an investor's ownership ratio of shares, etc. exceeds five percent, that investor is not required to submit a statement of large-volume holdings in the following cases, since the increase in the ratio is not the result of positive action by the investor (proviso to Article 27-23(1) of the Financial Instruments and Exchange Act; Article 3 of the Cabinet Office Ordinance on Disclosure of the Status of Large-Volume Holdings in Share Certificates, etc.). The first is any case where there is no increase in the total number of shares, etc. held. One conceivable example would be where the total number of issued shares decreased due to the issuer's acquisition and cancellation of its own shares, so that the investor's ownership ratio of shares exceeded five percent. The second is any case where the total number of shares, etc. held increases only as a result of the adjustment of the issue price of the shares underlying the share options or corporate bonds with share options held by the investor (including cases where the total number of shares, etc. held increases only as a result of the adjustment of the issue price of investment equity underlying investment equity subscription rights).

b.  Disclosure by means of a statement of large-volume holdings

(ⅰ)  Submission of a statement of large-volume holdings

A holder of shares, etc. whose ownership ratio of shares, etc. with respect to the relevant shares, etc. exceeds five percent (a large-volume holder) must submit a statement of large-volume holdings to the Prime Minister within five days (excluding Saturdays, Sundays, national holidays, and the

*571*

period from December 29th to January 3rd of the following year) of the date on which it becomes a large-volume holder (Article 27-23 (1) of the Financial Instruments and Exchange Act; Article 14-5 of the Financial Instruments and Exchange Act Implementing Order). The submitted statement of large-volume holdings is made available for public inspection for five years from the day on which it is accepted (Article 27-28(1) of the Financial Instruments and Exchange Act).

The statement of large-volume holdings must be submitted using the electronic data processing system for disclosure (EDINET) (Article 27-30-2 and Article 27-30-3(1) of the Financial Instruments and Exchange Act).

(ii) Contents of the statement of large-volume holdings

The statement of large-volume holdings must be prepared using Form 1 prescribed by the Cabinet Office Ordinance on Disclosure of the Status of Large-Volume Holdings in Share Certificates, etc. (Article 27-23(1) of the Financial Instruments and Exchange Act; Article 2 of the Cabinet Office Ordinance on Disclosure of the Status of Large-Volume Holdings in Share Certificates, etc.). For ordinary reporting purposes, the statement of large-volume holdings records, in addition to the name of the issuer and the name, address, and so on[58] of the submitter (a large-volume holder), (a) the purpose for which the shares, etc. are held; (b) material proposals; (c) the breakdown of shares, etc. held by the submitter and the quantity of each; (d) status of acquisition or disposal of shares, etc. issued by the issuer of the relevant shares, etc. over the past sixty days; (e) collateral agreements and other important contracts relating to the relevant shares, etc.; (f) the funds used for acquisition of the shares, etc. held; (g) particulars relating to any joint holders; and (h) a summary table on the submitter and any joint holders (Form 1 of the Cabinet Office Ordinance on Disclosure of the Status

---

58 However, under the 2015 revision of the Cabinet Office Ordinance, if the submitter of the statement of large-volume holdings is an individual, the street number of the address and date of birth are, in the interests of protecting personal privacy, excluded from the items made available for public inspection (Form 1 of the Cabinet Office Ordinance on Disclosure of the Status of Large-Volume Holdings in Share Certificates, etc.).

Chapter 4   The takeover bid system and the system of disclosure of the status of large-volume holdings

of Large-Volume Holdings in Shares, Etc.). Of these Items (a) through (h), those requiring particular care during completion are explained below.

First, under (a) the purpose for which the shares, etc. are held, the purpose and its details must be recorded as specifically as possible: for example, portfolio investment (investment for the purpose of making a profit from increases in share price or distributions of surplus), or relationship investment (investment as a vehicle for a business or capital partnership with the issuer). If there is more than one purpose, each must be recorded.

Next, under (b) material proposals, any material proposal that institutional investors and so on intend to make must be recorded. A material proposal is an act specified by cabinet order as something that materially changes or materially influences the business activities of the issuer of the shares, etc.; this is defined as the act of suggesting at the shareholders meeting (including the investors' meeting) or to the officers such matters related to the issuer or a subsidiary thereof as, for example, (i) the disposal or acceptance of transfer of important assets, (ii) borrowing in a significant amount, or (iii) selection or removal of a representative director (Article 27-26(1) of the Financial Instruments and Exchange Act; Article 14-8-2(1) of the Financial Instruments and Exchange Act Implementing Order; Article 16 of the Cabinet Office Ordinance on Disclosure of the Status of Large-Volume Holdings in Share Certificates, etc.). Even if the holder of the relevant shares, etc. is an institutional investor, it is not allowed to use the special reporting system described next in Section 3 if its purpose in holding the shares, etc. is to make a material proposal (Article 27-26(1) of the Financial Instruments and Exchange Act).

Under (e) collateral agreements and other important contracts, the details must be recorded of any loan contract, collateral agreement, repurchase agreement, selling contract, or any other important contract or agreement relating to the shares, etc. held, including the type of contract, the counterparty, and the number of shares, etc. covered by the contract. This is because information on such important contracts is valuable in determining, to some extent objectively, the nature of the transactions in shares, etc. in which the submitter (a large-volume holder) engages and its future behavior, as well as in identifying parties that may exercise influence behind the submitter.[59] Note also that an agreement to accept a takeover bid

*573*

concluded by the submitter with the takeover bidder is considered to constitute an important contract that must be recorded under (e).

Finally, under (f) the funds used for acquisition of the shares, etc. held, one must provide a breakdown of those funds (the amount of one's own funds used, the amount borrowed, etc.), a breakdown of the amount borrowed, and the name and so on of the lender. Investment decisions and decisions on the exercise of voting rights are in reality, it appears, frequently conducted on the instructions of the supplier of the funds used for acquisition of the shares, etc.;[60] the objective of this requirement is, given that fact, to identify the true interested party that bought the shares, etc. by ensuring that the statement of large-volume holdings indicates who is the party that actually put up the funds used for their acquisition.[61] At the same time, this information also serves to clarify whether the purchaser of the shares, etc. still has the wherewithal to continue purchasing them in future.[62] However, if the funds used for acquisition of the shares, etc. have been borrowed from a bank, cooperative financial institution, or any other financial institution specified by cabinet order (Article 1-9 of the Financial Instruments and Exchange Act Implementing Order), and if the large-volume holder did not clearly indicate to the financial institution, before borrowing those funds, that it was doing so in order to acquire those shares, etc., the name of the financial institution is not made available for public inspection[63] (Article 27-28(3) of the Financial Instruments and Exchange Act; Article 22 of the Cabinet Office Ordinance on Disclosure of the Status of Large-Volume Holdings in Share Certificates, etc.). This is in consideration of the impact on financial institutions' normal

---

**59**  Matsuo (supra, n. 47), p. 300.

**60**  Yamashita and Kanda (supra, n. 45), p. 234 (Kato Takahito).

**61**  Kondo et al. (supra, n. 55), p. 397; Kawamura, ed. (supra, n. 45), p. 284 (Furuyama Masaaki).

**62**  Kondo et al. (supra, n. 55), p. 397; Yamashita and Kanda (supra, n. 45), p. 234 (Kato Takahito).

**63**  In addition, the holder of the shares, etc. must, after submitting a statement of large-volume holdings, without delay send copies of it to the issuer of the shares, etc. and to the financial instruments exchange (or in the case of over-the-counter registration, to the authorized financial instruments business association); however, if the conditions given in the text are met, the holder is to delete the name of the financial institution when sending those copies.

Chapter 4 The takeover bid system and the system of disclosure of the status of large-volume holdings

lending operations.[64]

c. Disclosure by means of a statement of changes
( i ) Submission of a statement of changes

If, after the day on which a person that is required to submit a statement of large-volume holdings has become a large-volume holder, that person's ownership ratio of shares, etc. has increased or decreased by one percent or more, or if there has been any other change that is specified by cabinet order (Article 14-7-2 of the Financial Instruments and Exchange Act Implementing Order; Article 9-2 of the Cabinet Office Ordinance on Disclosure of the Status of Large-Volume Holdings in Share Certificates, etc.) as a change in a material particular that is required to be stated in the statement of large-volume holdings, such person must submit[65] a statement of changes to the Prime Minister within five days (excluding Saturdays, Sundays, national holidays, and the period from December 29th to January 3rd of the following year) after the day of the change (Article 27-25(1) of the Financial Instruments and Exchange Act). The submitted statement of changes is made available for public inspection for five years from the day on which it is accepted (Article 27-28 (1) of the Financial Instruments and Exchange Act). These provisions are designed to ensure that any changes in holdings of shares, etc. after submission of the statement of large-volume holdings are disclosed.

Notwithstanding the above, the requirement to submit a statement of changes does not arise if (a) the total number of shares, etc. held does not increase or decrease; (b) a statement of changes has already been submitted stating that the person's ownership ratio of shares, etc. is five percent or less; or (c) the total number of shares, etc. held increases or decreases only as a result of the adjustment of the issue price of the shares underlying the share options or corporate bonds with share options (including cases where the total number of shares, etc. held increases or decreases solely as a result of

---

64 Yamashita and Kanda (supra, n. 45), p. 234, n. 216 (Kato Takahito); Kawamura, ed. (supra, n. 45), p. 285 (Furuyama Masaaki).

65 The statement of changes must be submitted using the electronic data processing system for disclosure (EDINET) (Article 27-30-2 and Article 27-30-3 (1) of the Financial Instruments and Exchange Act).

the adjustment of the issue price of investment equity underlying investment equity subscription rights) (Article 27-25(1) of the Financial Instruments and Exchange Act; Article 9 of the Cabinet Office Ordinance on Disclosure of the Status of Large-Volume Holdings in Share Certificates, etc.).

It used to be required that if, by the day before submission of a statement of large-volume holdings or a statement of changes, a new cause for submitting a statement of changes arose, the statement of changes pertaining to that new cause for submission had to be submitted at the same time as the statement of large-volume holdings or statement of changes pertaining to the original cause for submission. However, this requirement for simultaneous submission of the new statement of changes was abolished by the 2014 revision of the Financial Instruments and Exchange Act, in response to criticism that, practically speaking, it might in some cases be difficult to meet that requirement for such reasons as the existence of an overseas subsidiary. At present, therefore, even if a new cause for submitting a statement of changes arises by the day before submission of a statement of large-volume holdings or a statement of changes, the statement of changes pertaining to that new cause for submission need only be submitted within five days (excluding Saturdays, Sundays, national holidays, and the period from December 29th to January 3rd of the following year) of the day of its occurrence.

(ⅱ) Contents of the statement of changes

The statement of changes must be prepared using Form 1 prescribed by the Cabinet Office Ordinance on Disclosure of the Status of Large-Volume Holdings in Shares, Etc. (Article 27-25(1) of the Financial Instruments and Exchange Act; Article 8 of the Cabinet Office Ordinance on Disclosure of the Status of Large-Volume Holdings in Share Certificates, etc.). When the statement of changes is submitted, all the particulars stated in the statement of large-volume holdings must be recorded in accordance with the situation as of the day on which the obligation to submit the statement of changes arose (Form 1 of the Cabinet Office Ordinance on Disclosure of the Status of Large-Volume Holdings in Share Certificates, etc.); it is insufficient to record only the change giving rise to the obligation to submit the statement of changes itself. In addition, the change giving rise to the obligation to submit

Chapter 4   The takeover bid system and the system of disclosure of the status of large-volume holdings

the statement of changes must be recorded under the particular of Cause for Submission of a Statement of Changes in Form 1.

In a case that falls under the criteria specified by cabinet order (Article 14-8 (1) of the Financial Instruments and Exchange Act Implementing Order) as a case in which a large number of shares, etc. have been transferred within a short period, a person that submits a statement of changes due to a decrease in the ownership ratio of shares, etc. must also state in the statement of changes the particulars of the party to which the shares, etc. have been transferred and of the consideration received (Article 27-25(2) of the Financial Instruments and Exchange Act). Specifically, in a case that falls under the criteria specified by cabinet order as a case in which a large number of shares, etc. have been transferred within a short period, these matters must be included in Form 2 in lieu of "The status of the acquisition or disposition over the past 60 days regarding shares, etc. issued by the issuer of the shares, etc." in Form 1 (Article 27-25(2) of the Financial Instruments and Exchange Act; Article 10 of the Cabinet Office Ordinance on Disclosure of the Status of Large-Volume Holdings in Share Certificates, etc.).

In cases where a large number of shares, etc. have been transferred within a short period, disclosure of the transferee and the consideration received is required because of the many instances seen in the past where a party, having bought up shares, etc., got the issuer, its officers, or an affiliated company to buy them from it at a high price; it is intended to curtail such demands to buy shares at a premium.[66] Another reason is adduced for requiring special information disclosure in cases where a large number of shares, etc. have been transferred within a short period: such transfers may greatly alter the supply of and demand for the relevant shares, etc. on the market, because the party that has bought up the shares, etc. often conducts such transfers to lock in profits.[67] Note, however, that under the 2014 revision of the Financial Instruments and Exchange Act, in the case of a person specified by cabinet order (Article 14-8 (2) of the Financial Instruments and Exchange Act Implementing Order) as a person to which

---

66   Kondo et al. (supra, n. 55), p. 399; Kawamoto et al. (supra, n. 49), p. 150.
67   Yamashita and Kanda (supra, n. 45), p. 235 (Kato Takahito).

*577*

an insignificant number of shares, etc. have been transferred, only the particulars of the consideration received need be stated (Article 27-25(2) parenthesis of the Financial Instruments and Exchange Act). The reason is that there is little utility in requiring disclosure of parties to which an insignificant number of shares, etc. have been transferred.

A case that falls under the criteria specified by cabinet order as a case in which a large number of shares, etc. have been transferred within a short period means a case in which the ownership ratio of shares, etc. after the change which should be stated in the statement of changes (a) falls to less than half of the highest ownership ratio of shares, etc. that has been stated or should have been stated in the statement of large-volume holdings related to the statement of changes or in another statement of changes related to the statement of large-volume holdings in the sixty days prior to the day of the transfer of the shares, etc., and (b) has decreased by an amount of more than five percent in comparison with the highest ownership ratio of shares, etc. (Article 14-8(1) main clause of the Financial Instruments and Exchange Act Implementing Order). However, a decrease in the ownership ratio of shares, etc. can occur for reasons other than their transfer, such as a private placement of new shares by the issuer; therefore, even if both criteria, (a) and (b), are met, cases where the decrease in the ownership ratio of shares, etc. due to their transfer is not large do not fall under the criteria specified by cabinet order for cases in which a large number of shares, etc. have been transferred within a short period (proviso to Article 14-8(1) of the Financial Instruments and Exchange Act Implementing Order).

d. Amended reports

If a person that has submitted a statement of large-volume holdings or a statement of changes finds that its content conflicts with the facts of the matter, that such a document insufficiently states or omits a statement concerning a material particular that is required to be stated, or that such a document insufficiently states or omits a statement as to a material fact that is necessary to prevent deception, that person must submit an amended report to the Prime Minister (Article 27-25(3) of the Financial Instruments and Exchange Act). This provision imposes on the submitter the obligation to submit an amended report if it determines that there is a cause for

Chapter 4    The takeover bid system and the system of disclosure of the status of large-volume holdings

amendment.

In the case where the submitter fails to submit an amended report voluntarily upon determining that there is a cause for amendment, there is a further provision empowering the Prime Minister, at any time, to order the submitter of a statement of large-volume holdings or a statement of changes to submit an amended report if (a) the Prime Minister finds a formal deficiency in that statement, or finds that it insufficiently states a material fact that is required to be stated, or (b) if he discovers that that statement contains a false statement about a material particular, omits a statement as to a material particular that is required to be stated, or omits a statement of material fact that is necessary to prevent deception (Article 27-29(1) of the Financial Instruments and Exchange Act).

Submitted amended reports are made available for public inspection (Article 27-28(1) of the Financial Instruments and Exchange Act). Note also that under the 2014 revision of the Financial Instruments and Exchange Act, the last day of the period of public inspection of an amended report was made the same as the last day of the period of public inspection of the statement amended.

e. Sending of copies of the statement of large-volume holdings, etc.

If a holder of shares, etc. has submitted to the Prime Minister a statement of large-volume holdings, statement of changes, or amended report in connection with it (a statement of large-volume holdings, etc.), that holder must send a copy without delay to the issuer of the relevant shares, etc., and to the financial instruments exchange (or in the case of over-the-counter registration, to the authorized financial instruments firms association) (Article 27-27 of the Financial Instruments and Exchange Act). The reason for requiring that a copy of the statement of large-volume holdings, etc. also be sent to the issuer is to enable the issuer to furnish information on large-volume holdings to shareholders and others through an extraordinary report or the like.[68] Note, however, that under the 2014 revision of the Financial Instruments and Exchange Act, if procedures for submitting a statement of large-volume holdings, etc. to the Prime Minister are

---

**68**    Kondo et al. (supra, n. 55), p. 397.

*579*

completed using the electronic data processing system for disclosure (EDINET), it is no longer necessary to send a copy of that statement to the issuer (Article 27-30-6(3) of the Financial Instruments and Exchange Act), since the issuer can easily access it via EDINET.

Financial instruments exchanges (and in the case of over-the-counter registration, authorized financial instruments business associations) must keep at their offices the copies of statements of large-volume holdings, etc. that have been sent to them, and must make them available for public inspection for five years from the day on which they receive them (Article 27-28(2) of the Financial Instruments and Exchange Act; Article 21 of the Cabinet Office Ordinance on Disclosure of the Status of Large-Volume Holdings in Share Certificates, etc.).

## 3. The special reporting system

### a. Overview of the special reporting system

Financial institutions and institutional investors trade shares, etc. continually in the course of their daily business; disclosure would therefore very likely impose an excessive administrative burden on them were they required to submit statements of large-volume holdings and statements of changes in accordance with the ordinary reporting system described in Section 2. Thus, imposing disclosure requirements under the ordinary reporting system would be liable to discourage the activities of institutional investors and the like that trade shares, etc. on a routine basis, and consequently impair the efficiency and liquidity of the stock market (to the detriment also of ordinary investors). Hence, special provisions on the frequency of and deadlines for disclosure of large-volume holdings, in place of those of the ordinary reporting system, are recognized for institutional investors and such that meet certain conditions (Article 27-26(1) of the Financial Instruments and Exchange Act).

### b. Conditions for using the special reporting system

( i ) Conditions

To use the special reporting system, the holder of the shares, etc. (the investor) must be either (a) a financial services provider, a bank, or other person specified by cabinet office ordinance,[69] or (b) the State, a local

*580*

Chapter 4   The takeover bid system and the system of disclosure of the status of large-volume holdings

government, or other person specified by cabinet office ordinance[70] (Article 27-26(1) of the Financial Instruments and Exchange Act). Thus, use of the special reporting system is restricted first in terms of the party holding the shares, etc.

Of the above, (a) a financial services provider, a bank, or other person specified by cabinet office ordinance may use the special reporting system only if all the following three conditions are met. First, it must not hold the shares, etc. for the purpose of performing an act specified by cabinet order (Article 14-8-2 (1) of the Financial Instruments and Exchange Act Implementing Order; Article 16 of the Cabinet Office Ordinance on Disclosure of the Status of Large-Volume Holdings in Shares, etc.) as something that materially changes or materially influences the business activities of the issuer of the shares, etc. (a material proposal) (Article 27-26 (1) of the Financial Instruments and Exchange Act). The reason that may be cited for this is that the need for information disclosure is greater when the holder of the shares, etc. seeks to exercise a certain degree of influence over the management of the issuer than when it does not; therefore it was considered appropriate to require in such cases that information be disclosed in accordance with the ordinary reporting system rather than the special reporting system. Material proposals are explained in detail in the next section, Section (ii).

---

69   Including specifically (a) persons engaging in type I financial instruments business in the form of securities services, (b) persons who engage in certain forms of investment management, (c) banks, (d) trust companies that have obtained a license, (e) insurance companies, (f) the Norinchukin Bank, (g) the Shoko Chukin Bank Limited, (h) persons engaging in type I financial instruments business in the form of securities services, certain forms of investment management, banking business, trust business, or insurance business in foreign states in accordance with the laws thereof, (i) the Banks' Shareholdings Purchase Corporation and the Deposit Insurance Corporation of Japan, as well as persons who are joint holders with any person set forth in (a) through (i) (a financial services provider, etc.) (Article 11 of the Cabinet Office Ordinance on Disclosure of the Status of Large-Volume Holdings in Share Certificates, etc.).

70   Including specifically the national or local government, as well as any person who is a joint holder with the national or local government (Article 14 of the Cabinet Office Ordinance on Disclosure of the Status of Large-Volume Holdings in Share Certificates, etc.).

Second, the ownership ratio of shares, etc. of a financial services provider, a bank, or other person specified by cabinet office ordinance must not exceed ten percent (Article 27-26(1) of the Financial Instruments and Exchange Act; Article 12 of the Cabinet Office Ordinance on Disclosure of the Status of Large-Volume Holdings in Share Certificates, etc.). That is because if the ownership ratio of shares, etc. rises above a certain level, the influence on supply and demand for them on the market and on company management cannot be ignored, whatever the purpose for which they are held.[71]

Third, in cases where a financial services provider, etc. (Article 11(iv) of the Cabinet Office Ordinance on Disclosure of the Status of Large-Volume Holdings in Share Certificates, etc.) has a joint holder who is not a financial services provider, etc., the ownership ratio of shares, etc. of that joint holder as calculated by deeming that joint holder to have no joint holder who is a financial services provider, etc., must not exceed one percent (Article 27-26 (1) of the Financial Instruments and Exchange Act; Article 13(i) of the Cabinet Office Ordinance on Disclosure of the Status of Large-Volume Holdings in Share Certificates, etc.). This third condition requires that the ownership ratio of shares, etc. of a joint holder that is not a financial services provider, etc. be one percent or less, in order to prevent it from taking advantage of the special reporting system by using a financial services provider, etc. as a joint holder, thus circumventing the law.[72]

By contrast, (b) the State, a local government, or another person specified by cabinet office ordinance need not fulfill the preceding three conditions imposed on persons in category (a), but may automatically use the special reporting system by virtue of belonging to category (b).

(ⅱ) Material proposals

A material proposal means an act specified by cabinet order as something that materially changes or materially influences the business activities of the issuer of the shares, etc. Specifically, it means any act in which certain matters related to the issuer of the shares, etc. or a subsidiary thereof[73] are suggested at the shareholders meeting (including the investors' meeting) or

---

71  Yamashita and Kanda (supra, n. 45), p. 235 (Kato Takahito).
72  Kawamura, ed. (supra, n. 45), p. 291 (Furuyama Masaaki).

Chapter 4   The takeover bid system and the system of disclosure of the status of large-volume holdings

to the officers (Article 14-8-2(1) of the Financial Instruments and Exchange Act Implementing Order; Article 16 of the Cabinet Office Ordinance on Disclosure of the Status of Large-Volume Holdings in Share Certificates, etc.). If the purpose for which the shares, etc. are held is to make a material proposal, information disclosure must be conducted under the ordinary reporting system even if the holder of the shares, etc. is (a) a financial services provider, a bank, or other person specified by cabinet office ordinance; the special reporting system is not allowed to be used (Article 27-26(1) of the Financial Instruments and Exchange Act).

In 2014, the Japanese Stewardship Code was drawn up and released. Under the Code, institutional investors are now called on to engage in constructive dialog with their portfolio companies with a view to promoting the latter's sustained growth. There is some concern that implementation of such dialog could render investors ineligible to use the special reporting system; but if, for instance, a shareholder passively states its own views in response to a request to do so by the issuer of the shares, etc., or if it states its views in a forum for dialog with shareholders (such as a briefing on financial results) arranged by the issuer of its own accord, such statements of opinion are made for the purpose of complying with the issuer's wishes, and it is therefore unlikely that they would meet the criteria for cases where

---

**73**  The matters related to the issuer of the shares, etc. or a subsidiary thereof enumerated in the relevant provisions are (a) the disposal or acceptance of transfer of important assets; (b) borrowing in a significant amount; (c) selection or removal of a representative director; (d) important changes in the constitution of officers; (e) appointment or dismissal of a manager or any other important employee; (f) establishment, changes in, or abolition of a branch office or any other important organization; (g) share exchange, share transfer, or split or merger of the company; (h) the transfer, acquisition, suspension, or abolition of the business in whole or in part; (i) important changes in the policy concerning dividend distribution; (j) important changes relating to capital policy, including the policy concerning increases in or reduction of the amount of stated capital; (k) delisting of issued securities or rescission of their over-the-counter registration; (l) listing of issued securities or their registration over-the-counter; (m) dissolution; and (n) a petition for the commencement of bankruptcy proceedings, rehabilitation proceedings, or reorganization proceedings (Article 14-8-2 of the Financial Instruments and Exchange Act Implementing Order; Article 16 of the Cabinet Office Ordinance on Disclosure of the Status of Large-Volume Holdings in Share Certificates, etc.).

*583*

the purpose for which the shares, etc. are held is to make a material proposal.[74]

c . Disclosure under the special reporting system
( i ) Disclosure procedures and information disclosed

An investor meeting the conditions for using the special reporting system may use that system upon providing notification of its reference dates (Article 27-26(1) parenthesis of the Financial Instruments and Exchange Act). Specifically, a holder of shares, etc. must select one of the combinations of two or more days in each month[75] designated pursuant to the cabinet order (Article 14-8-2(2) of the Financial Instruments and Exchange Act Implementing Order) and notify the Prime Minister of them as its reference dates (Article 27-26(3) of the Financial Instruments and Exchange Act). Notification of reference dates must be provided by preparing a written notification using Form 4 prescribed by the Cabinet Office Ordinance on Disclosure of the Status of Large-Volume Holdings in Share Certificates, etc. (Article 18(1)).

Under the special reporting system, an investor meeting the conditions for using that system needs to submit a statement of large-volume holdings to the Prime Minister only within five days (excluding Saturdays, Sundays, national holidays, and the period from December 29th to January 3rd of the following year) of any notified reference date as of which its ownership ratio of shares, etc. comes to exceed five percent for the first time (Article 27-26 (1) of the Financial Instruments and Exchange Act).

Further, under the special reporting system, whether the requirement to submit a statement of changes applies is determined as of the notified reference dates. If it does apply — if, for example, as of any reference date

---

74 Financial Services Agency (supra, n. 57), p. 5. See also Kawamoto et al. (supra, n. 49), p. 154.

75 The combinations of two or more days in each month designated pursuant to the cabinet order are: the combination of the second and fourth Monday of each month (in cases where there is a fifth Monday, the second, fourth and fifth Monday); or the combination of the fifteenth and last day of each month (in cases where such days fall on a Saturday, the previous day thereto, and in cases where such days fall on a Sunday, the day two days before) (Article 14-8-2 (2) of the Financial Instruments and Exchange Act Implementing Order).

*584*

Chapter 4 The takeover bid system and the system of disclosure of the status of large-volume holdings

the investor's ownership ratio of shares, etc. has increased or decreased by one percent or more compared to the level recorded on the statement of large-volume holdings — the investor needs to submit a statement of changes to the Prime Minister only within five days (excluding Saturdays, Sundays, national holidays, and the period from December 29th to January 3rd of the following year) of that reference date (Article 27-26(2) (i) & (ii) of the Financial Instruments and Exchange Act). However, if a holder of shares, etc. that previously used the special reporting system ceases to meet the conditions for doing so — if, for example, the purpose for which it holds the shares, etc. changes to that of making a material proposal, or if its ownership ratio of shares, etc. comes to exceed ten percent — it must submit a statement of changes to the Prime Minister under the ordinary reporting system, not the special reporting system (Article 27-26(2) parenthesis of the Financial Instruments and Exchange Act).

Statements of large-volume holdings and statements of changes under the special reporting system are in principle to be prepared using Form 3 prescribed by the Cabinet Office Ordinance on Disclosure of the Status of Large-Volume Holdings in Shares, Etc. (ibid., Article 15). The information to be recorded is slightly reduced compared to that required for ordinary reporting: for example, one is not required to record the status of acquisition or disposal of shares, etc. issued by the issuer of the relevant shares, etc. over the past sixty days; collateral agreements and other important contracts relating to the relevant shares, etc.; or the funds used for acquisition of the shares, etc. held (Form 3 of the Cabinet Office Ordinance on Disclosure of the Status of Large-Volume Holdings in Share Certificates, etc.). In addition, what must be recorded is the state of ownership of the shares, etc. as of the reference date (Article 27-26(1) of the Financial Instruments and Exchange Act). Public inspection and so forth of statements of large-volume holdings, statements of changes, and amended reports are subject to the same provisions under the special reporting system as under the ordinary reporting system (Article 27-27 through 27-30 of the Financial Instruments and Exchange Act).

(ⅱ) Material proposals by investors using the special reporting system
If a person meeting the conditions for using the special reporting system,

*585*

which person is a financial services provider, a bank, or other person specified by cabinet office ordinance, makes a material proposal within the period until five days (excluding Saturdays, Sundays, national holidays, and the period from December 29th to January 3rd of the following year) have elapsed from the first reference date falling on or after the date on which its ownership ratio of shares comes to exceed five percent, that person must submit a statement of large-volume holdings to the Prime Minister by five days (excluding Saturdays, Sundays, national holidays, and the period from December 29th to January 3rd of the following year) prior to the date on which it actually makes that material proposal (Article 27-26(4) of the Financial Instruments and Exchange Act; Article 14-8-2(3) of the Financial Instruments and Exchange Act Implementing Order).

Similarly, if the ownership ratio of shares, etc. of a person meeting the conditions for using the special reporting system, which person is a financial services provider, a bank, or other person specified by cabinet office ordinance, increases by one percent or more after the submission of a statement of large-volume holdings or a statement of changes under the special reporting system, and that person makes a material proposal within the period until five days (excluding Saturdays, Sundays, national holidays, and the period from December 29th to January 3rd of the following year) have elapsed from the first reference date falling on or after the date of the increase, that person must submit a statement of changes to the Prime Minister by five days (excluding Saturdays, Sundays, national holidays, and the period from December 29th to January 3rd of the following year) prior to the date on which it actually makes that material proposal (Article 27-26(5) of the Financial Instruments and Exchange Act; Article 14-8-2(3) of the Financial Instruments and Exchange Act Implementing Order).

These provisions are intended to prevent users of the special reporting system from making a material proposal without disclosing their latest ownership level of shares, etc., as recorded in a statement of large-volume holding or statement of changes, by making that material proposal before the deadline for submitting a statement of large-volume holdings or statement of changes under the special reporting system.[76] In other words, they are designed to prevent use of the special reporting system as a means of making a material proposal while concealing one's ownership level of shares,

Chapter 4　The takeover bid system and the system of disclosure of the status of large-volume holdings

etc. as of the time of that proposal. Statements of large-volume holdings and statements of changes to be submitted under these provisions are prepared using Form 1 prescribed by the Cabinet Office Ordinance on Disclosure of the Status of Large-Volume Holdings in Share Certificates, etc. (ibid., Article 2(1) and Article 8(1)).

## 4. Regulatory powers, administrative monetary penalties, and criminal penalties

### a. General observations

To guarantee the effectiveness of the system of disclosure of the status of large-volume holdings in shares, etc., the Financial Instruments and Exchange Act contains provisions pertaining to the regulatory powers of administrative organs, administrative monetary penalties, and criminal penalties, as surveyed below. These provisions apply uniformly to both ordinary reporting and special reporting.

### b. Regulatory powers of administrative organs

The regulatory powers of administrative organs over the system of disclosure of the status of large-volume holdings in shares, etc. are, broadly speaking, twofold: the power to order submission of an amended report, and the power to collect and inspect reports.

First we examine the power to order submission of an amended report. The Prime Minister may, at any time, order the submitter of a statement of large-volume holdings or a statement of changes to submit an amended report if (a) he finds a formal deficiency in that statement, or finds it to insufficiently state a material fact that is required to be stated, or (b) if he discovers that that statement contains a false statement about a material particular, omits a statement as to a material particular that is required to be stated, or omits a statement of material fact that is necessary to prevent deception (Article 27-29(1) of the Financial Instruments and Exchange Act).

In connection with the above power, if the Prime Minister orders the

---

76　Kawamoto et al. (supra, n. 49), p. 155; Kawamura, ed. (supra, n. 45), pp. 291-293 (Furuyama Masaaki).

*587*

submission of an amended report, the Prime Minister may decide not to make all or part of the statement of large-volume holdings or statement of changes to which the submission order pertains available for public inspection (Article 27-28(4) of the Financial Instruments and Exchange Act). This provision is designed to prevent investors from making erroneous investment decisions because a statement of large-volume holdings or statement of changes containing errors or the like remains available for public inspection.[77]

Next we examine the power to collect and inspect reports. Whenever the Prime Minister finds it to be necessary and appropriate in the public interest or for the protection of investors, the Prime Minister may order (a) a person that has submitted a statement of large-volume holdings or a person that is found to be required to submit the same, or (b) a joint holder with (a), or any other relevant party or witness, to submit reports or materials that should serve as a reference, and may have the relevant officials inspect the books, documents or any other articles of persons falling under (a) or (b) above (Article 27-30(1) of the Financial Instruments and Exchange Act). Further, whenever the Prime Minister finds it to be necessary and appropriate in the public interest or for the protection of investors, the Prime Minister may order the issuer of shares, etc. to which a statement of large-volume holdings pertains, or a witness, to submit reports or materials that should serve as a reference (Article 27-30 (2) of the Financial Instruments and Exchange Act).

In connection with such powers, the 2013 revision of the Financial Instruments and Exchange Act further empowers the Prime Minister, whenever he finds it to be necessary in relation to an order to submit the above reports or materials, or their inspection, to inquire with public offices or public and private organizations, and require that these parties report the necessary particulars (Article 27-30(3) of the Financial Instruments and Exchange Act).

c . Administrative monetary penalties

The 2008 revision of the Financial Instruments and Exchange Act

---

77　Yamashita and Kanda (supra, n. 45), p. 242 (Kato Takahito).

Chapter 4   The takeover bid system and the system of disclosure of the status of large-volume holdings

instituted administrative monetary penalties for violations of the system of disclosure of the status of large-volume holdings in shares, etc. First, if a person required to submit a statement of large-volume holdings or a statement of changes fails to do so, an administrative monetary penalty is levied that is equivalent to one hundred thousandth of the market capitalization of the issuer of the relevant shares, etc. on the day after that on which the person is required to submit the statement (Article 172-7 of the Financial Instruments and Exchange Act; Article 1-7 of the Cabinet Office Ordinance on Administrative Monetary Penalty under the Provisions of Chapter IV-2 of the Financial Instruments and Exchange Act). Further, if a person submits a statement of large-volume holdings, statement of changes, or amended report that contains a false statement about a material particular or that omits a statement as to a material particular that is required to be stated, an administrative monetary penalty is levied that is equivalent to one hundred thousandth of the market capitalization of the issuer of the relevant shares, etc. on the day after that on which the person is required to submit the statement (Article 172-8 of the Financial Instruments and Exchange Act; Article 1-7 of the Cabinet Office Ordinance on Administrative Monetary Penalty under the Provisions of Chapter IV-2 of the Financial Instruments and Exchange Act).

d. Criminal penalties

If a person required to submit a statement of large-volume holdings or a statement of changes fails to do so, or if that person submits a statement of large-volume holdings, statement of changes, or amended report that contains a false statement about a material particular, the prescribed penalty is punishment by imprisonment with required labor for not more than five years, a fine of not more than five million yen, or both (Article 197-2(v) & (vi) of the Financial Instruments and Exchange Act). There is also a dual liability provision imposing a fine of not more than 500 million yen on the corporation (Article 207(1)(ii) of the Financial Instruments and Exchange Act).

*589*

# Chapter 5

Business regulations on financial instruments business operators, etc.

*Naohiko Matsuo*

# A. The concept of "financial instruments business"

## 1. "Financial instruments business" and "financial instruments business operators"

### a. Overview

The FIEA, in fulfillment of its objectives of protecting investors and ensuring the soundness of capital markets, defines certain acts conducted in the course of business as "financial instruments business" (Article 2(8) of the FIEA). A financial instruments business can be conducted only by persons registered by the Prime Minister (Article 29 of the FIEA) (with authority delegated to the Director General of the Local Finance Bureau or Branch Bureau).

Any person so registered is deemed a "financial instruments business operator" (Article 2(9) of the FIEA).

### b. Background

Under the FIEA legislative framework established in 2006, the FIEA integrates several existing types of businesses into the "financial instruments business" category with a view to establishing a comprehensive, cross-sectoral legal framework for regulating business activities. These are: (1) "securities business" under the revised Securities and Exchange Act and the now-repealed Act on Foreign Securities Brokers; (2) "investment trust entrustment" and "investment corporation asset management" under the revised Investment Trust Act; (3) "investment advisory services" and "discretionary investment management services" under the now-repealed Act on Regulation, etc. of Investment Advisory Business Pertaining to Securities (Investment Advisory Business Act); (4) "financial futures trading" under the now-repealed Financial Futures Exchange Act; (5) "sale of trust beneficial interests" under the revised Trust Business Act; (6) "mortgage security services" under the now-repealed Act on Regulation, etc. of Mortgage Security Business (Mortgage Security Business Act); and (7) "commodity investment sales" under the revised Act on Control for

Chapter 5   Business regulations on financial instruments business operators, etc.

Business Pertaining to Commodity Investment (Commodity Fund Act). Several other new activities are also subsumed under the concept of "financial instruments business": specifically, so-called direct placement and private placement (Article 2(8)(vii) of the FIEA); provision of agency or intermediary service for conclusion of an investment advisory contract or a discretionary investment contract; and so-called asset custody of money and securities (ibid., Article 2(8)(xiii)) (ibid., Article 2(8)(xvi) & (xvii)).

On the other hand, the regulatory framework governing "real-estate specified joint enterprises" under the Real Estate Specified Joint Enterprise Act has, given that the act imposes many restrictions specific to real estate, been maintained without being absorbed into the FIEA. Banking, insurance, and trust services have likewise not been integrated into the FIEA, because all of the following are still important points of debate: (1) the Banking Act, the Insurance Business Act, and the Trust Business Act impose more stringent business regulations such as licensing; (2) non-investment products — e.g., payment and settlement deposits, insurance with no cash value (so-called term insurance), and charitable trusts — which are also subject to regulation; and (3) the possibility of a conflict of interest and banks' abuse of their dominant position, the grounds for the so-called separation of the banking and securities sectors.

c.  "Securities companies"

Stock companies registered as securities brokers were termed "securities companies" in the Securities and Exchange Act, but that term is not used in the FIEA. Financial instruments business operators that conduct securities-related business (limited to those engaged in a type I financial instruments business) are the equivalent of securities companies.

# 2.  "Registered financial institutions"

Activities conducted by banks, cooperative structured financial institutions, insurance companies (including foreign insurance companies etc.), mutual loan companies, securities finance companies, the Shoko Chukin Bank, and designated call-loan dealers falling into the category of investment management business (Article 2(8) (xii), (xiv) & (xv) of the FIEA), or falling into the category of securities-related business (Article 28(8) of the

FIEA), are excluded from the definition of "financial instruments business" (Article 2(8) of the FIEA; Article 1-9 of the Financial Instruments and Exchange Implementing Order [hereinafter, the "Implementing Order"]).

The conduct of any such excluded act in the course of trade by any such "financial institution" does not constitute a "financial instruments business." On the other hand, financial institutions are in principle prohibited from engaging in securities-related business or investment management business (Article 33(1) of the FIEA; Article 1-9 of the Implementing Order), with the exception of certain securities-related businesses in which they are permitted to engage (Article 33(2) of the FIEA) upon being registered by the Prime Minister (Article 33-2 of the FIEA) (with authority delegated to the Director General of the Local Finance Bureau or Branch Bureau). Financial institutions that have been so registered are termed "registered financial institutions" (Article 2(11) of the FIEA). The business registered to financial institutions is registered to conduct is termed "registered financial institution business" (Article 33-5(1)(iii) of the FIEA).

The operations of financial institutions are regulated by other industry legislation such as the Banking Act. The FIEA does not regulate the overall operations of registered financial institutions; rather, it specifically regulates registered financial institution business and related operations (see Articles 44-2(2) and 52-2(1)(iii) of the FIEA).

## 3. "Financial instruments business operators, etc."

Financial instruments business operators and registered financial institutions are collectively termed "financial instruments business operators, etc." (Article 34 of the FIEA).

Financial instruments business operators, etc. perform the function of linking seekers of funding such as investors and companies with capital markets. They thus play an important role in protecting investors, ensuring the soundness of capital markets, and promoting healthy development of capital markets and the national economy. The advisory committee of the Financial Services Agency (FSA) on the market intermediary functions of securities companies, in its summary report of June 30, 2006, sets forth the principle that ensuring securities companies' proper performance of their market intermediary and other functions is necessary for establishing a

*594*

Chapter 5　Business regulations on financial instruments business operators, etc.

dependable securities market (IV-3-2 of the Comprehensive Guidelines for Supervision of Financial Instruments Business Operators, Etc.).

## 4. "Financial instruments intermediary service" and "financial instruments intermediary service provider"

a. "Financial instruments intermediary service"

Under the FIEA, any "financial instruments business" falling into the category of an "act of financial instruments intermediation" and conducted on entrustment from and on behalf of an "entrusting financial instruments business operator, etc." — a financial instruments business operator engaged in type I financial instruments business (excluding type I crowdfunding business) or the investment management business (excluding investment management business for qualified investors) or registered financial institution — is classified as a "financial instruments intermediary service" (Articles 2(11), 29-4-2(7), 29-5(5), 66-2(1)(iv) and 66-11 of the FIEA).

b. "Acts of financial instruments intermediation"

"Acts of financial instruments intermediation" constitute (1) intermediary services for the sale and purchase of securities (excluding proprietary trading system [PTS] acts); (2) intermediary services for entrustment of the sale and purchase of securities and market transactions of derivatives in financial instruments exchange markets, and of sales and purchase of securities and foreign market derivatives transactions in foreign financial instruments markets; (3) dealing in public offering, secondary distribution, and private placement of securities, and solicitation for selling, etc. only for professional investors; and (4) intermediary service for conclusion of an investment advisory contract or a discretionary investment contract (Articles 2(11) and 66-11 of the FIEA).

"Financial instruments intermediary service" is the business of conducting acts of financial instruments intermediation (Article 1(4)(xiii) of the Cabinet Office Ordinance on Financial Instruments Services, Etc.).

c. "Financial instruments intermediary service provider"

A person duly registered by the Prime Minister (with authority delegated to the Director General of the Local Finance Bureau or Branch Bureau) is

*595*

termed a "financial instruments intermediary service provider" (Article 2 (12) of the FIEA). Registration requirements are simpler than for registration as a financial instruments business operator (Articles 66 and 66-4 of the FIEA).

A financial institution can engage in financial instruments intermediary services as a registered financial institution rather than a financial instruments intermediary service provider (Articles 33 (2) (iii) (c), 33 (2) (iv) (b) and 33-2 (ii) of the FIEA). An "entrusting financial instruments business operator" is a financial instruments business operator engaged in type I financial instruments business, by which a registered financial institution is entrusted with financial instruments intermediary services (Article 44 (vi) of the Cabinet Office Ordinance on Financial Instruments Services, Etc.).

On the other hand, a financial instruments business operator engaged in type I financial instruments business cannot become a financial instruments intermediary service provider (Articles 66, 66-4 (vi) and 66-19 (2) of the FIEA).

d. Objectives and features of the financial instruments intermediary services system

The financial instruments intermediary services system was established at the time of the 2006 revision of the Securities and Exchange Act, being an expanded version of the "securities intermediation" system established when the Securities and Exchange Act was revised in 2003. It is designed to expand the sales channel functions of financial instruments business operators, etc. with a view to promoting broad market participation by a wide range of investors; the hope is that thereby client access to financial instruments business operators, etc. will be simplified and services diversified through competition. The system is also inspired by the idea of promoting the functional separation of the business of producing financial instruments from that of providing financial services.

The features of the financial instruments intermediary services system are as follows: First, it takes the form of an "entrusting financial instruments business operator, etc." system, in which services are provided on entrustment from a particular financial instruments business operator, etc.

Chapter 5　Business regulations on financial instruments business operators, etc.

Second, acts of financial instruments intermediation are basically limited to "intermediary services"; "brokerage" and "agency services" are not permitted. They constitute acts not of "contracting commercial agents" but of "intermediary commercial agents" (see Article 27 of the Commercial Code). The party concluding the contract for financial instruments transaction with the client through the intermediation of a provider of financial instruments intermediary services is the entrusting financial instruments business operator, etc., not the provider of financial instruments intermediary services.

Third, in the case of market transactions of derivatives and foreign market derivatives transactions, intermediation of the transaction itself is not permitted, only intermediation of "entrustment."

Fourth, intermediation of over-the-counter transactions in derivatives is not permitted.

# 5. Requirements for classification as "business" (*gyo*)

a. Abolition of the for-profit requirement

Traditional "securities business," "investment trust entrustment," and so on were deemed "businesses," and being for profit was a requirement for classification as such (Article 2(8) of the Securities and Exchange Act; Article 6 of the Act on Investment Trusts and Investment Corporations [prior to revision]). On the other hand, traditional "financial futures business" was classified as "business," and being for profit was not a requirement for classification as such (Article 2(12) of the Financial Futures Trading Act [prior to repeal]).

The term used in the items of Article 2, paragraph 8 of the FIEA, by contrast, is "acts." "Financial instruments business" is defined as conducting any of these acts "in the course of business" (Article 2(8) of the FIEA). Because such acts are not deemed "businesses," being for profit is not a requirement for classification as such.

b. Meaning of "in the course of business"

(i) Overview

The phrase "in the course of business" is understood to mean that the act is *directed at the public* conducted repeatedly and continuously. In addition to

*597*

being *repeated and continuous*, it must also be *directed at the public*.

( ii ) Purpose of the requirement to be *directed at the public*

The requirement to be *directed at the public* was evidently established primarily to avoid the application of business regulations to securities purchases and sales and derivatives transactions often conducted by ordinary individuals and companies on their own account for investment or asset management purposes, on the grounds that such frequent trades for investment purposes are performed simply to improve one's portfolio.

The provision of the FIEA (proviso to Article 33, paragraph 1) that financial institutions may conduct sales or purchase of securities or transactions of securities-related derivatives for the purpose of investment pursuant to the other Acts (e.g., Article 10(2) (ii) of the Banking Act) is a confirmatory provision predicated on that interpretation. On the other hand, dealing operations and trading operations conducted by financial instruments business operators, etc., which are operators, are understood to meet the "in the course of business" requirement because of the need to regulate them.

( iii ) Function of the requirement to be *directed at the public*

Practically speaking, the requirement to be directed at the public serves merely as a means of excluding acts that could not reasonably be deemed, by the ordinary standards of society, to be conducted in the course of business. For example, an act to which only a parent company and its wholly owned subsidiary are parties may be understood not to be conducted "in the course of business" in that it is not in principle directed at the public.

On the other hand, it is denied by some that being directed at the public is a requirement for classification as an act conducted in the course of business. Taking into account that view, even if the requirement to be directed at the public is accepted, careful consideration is required before an act may be deemed not to be conducted in the course of business on the grounds that it is not directed at the public. It would be particularly inappropriate to understand "directed at the public" broadly to mean directed at an unspecified audience or at a multitude of people; the phrase must be interpreted in the strict sense. A transaction is not excluded from the

*598*

Chapter 5   Business regulations on financial instruments business operators, etc.

definition of an act conducted in the course of business just because the clients are all qualified institutional investors or professional investors.

(iv)   Interpretation of the requirements *directed at the public* and *repeated and continuous*

Acts *directed at the public* and conducted *repeatedly and continuously* include not only acts that are in fact directed at the public and conducted repeatedly and continuously, but also acts that may be assumed to be. Whether a specific act is directed at the public and conducted repeatedly and continuously must be determined individually in each case in accordance with the actual nature of the act.

With the establishment of a civil rule applying to unregistered operators (Article 171-2 of the FIEA), determining in practice whether an act can be defined as conducted "in the course of business" requires greater care than ever.

# 6. Acts constituting "financial instruments business"

a. Sale and purchase of securities, market transactions of derivatives, and foreign market derivatives transactions

Sale and purchase of securities, market transactions of derivatives, and foreign market derivatives transactions are deemed acts constituting "financial instruments business" (Article 2(8)(i) of the FIEA).

Because futures and forward transactions with underlying assets in the form of securities notionally constitute "sale and purchase of securities," transactions falling into the category of derivatives transactions are excluded from "sale and purchase of securities." Similarly, "commodity-related market transactions of derivatives" are excluded from market transactions of derivatives (2012 revision of the FIEA). Commodity-related market transactions of derivatives conducted on one's own account are thus excluded from the scope of "financial instruments business."

Sale and purchase of securities, market transactions of derivatives, and foreign market derivatives transactions all constitute consensual contracts that take effect upon agreement (Article 555 of the Civil Code; Article 2(21) & (23) of the FIEA). This is understood to mean transactions on one's own account and exclude transactions on another's account. In the case of sales

*599*

and purchase of securities, it does not matter whether the transaction is a transaction at exchange or an over-the-counter transaction. Nor does it matter whether any of these types of transactions is undertaken as a long-term investment or short-term speculation.

b. Intermediary, brokerage, and agency services for the sale and purchase of securities, market transactions of derivatives, and foreign market derivatives transactions

( i ) Overview

Intermediary, brokerage, and agency services for the sale and purchase of securities, market transactions of derivatives, and foreign market derivatives transactions are deemed acts constituting "financial instruments business" (Article 2(8)(ii) of the FIEA).

( ii ) "Intermediary service"

"Intermediary service," meaning acting as a so-called go-between, refers to the real act of endeavoring to effectuate a juridical act by intermediating between other parties (see Article 543 of the Commercial Code). It differs from "agency service" in that it does not involve acting as agent for another; it differs from "brokerage" in that the juridical act is not performed in one's own name. The intermediary is not a party to the transaction.

Any performance of the real act of endeavoring to effectuate a juridical act constitutes "intermediary service." The effectuation of the juridical act in question is not a requirement. Nor is active solicitation a requirement: for example, the act of setting up a bulletin board on the Internet and mechanically effecting transactions may constitute intermediary service. Information vendors that provide share price and financial information are also understood to offer intermediary services if indicative prices provided by several financial instruments business operators, etc. are listed (price competition) and order-matching methods on transaction terms are provided, including distribution of dedicated terminals and posting of links for order placement and negotiation (IV-4-2-1 (i) of the Comprehensive Guidelines for Supervision of Financial Instruments Business Operators, Etc.).

Intermediary service for the sale and purchase of securities (excluding

Chapter 5　Business regulations on financial instruments business operators, etc.

PTS acts) constitutes an act of financial instruments intermediation (Articles 2(11)(i) and 66-11 of the FIEA).

(ⅲ) "Brokerage"

"Brokerage" means the act of undertaking to perform a juridical act on another's account in one's own name (see Article 502(xi) of the Commercial Code). "In one's own name" means that the brokering party assumes the relevant rights and obligations (ibid., Article 552 (1)). "On another's account" means that the economic profits and losses accrue to another party.

If a financial instruments business operator, under entrustment by a customer, undertakes the sale or purchase of securities in a financial instruments exchange market established by a financial instruments exchange that is one of its members, etc. (meaning members or trading participants [Article 81 (1) (ⅲ) of the FIEA]), that act constitutes "brokerage."

(ⅳ) "Agency service"

"Agency service" means that the principal is directly subject to the legal effect of an agent's manifestation of intention made by an agent within his/her authority, or of a manifestation of intention to an agent by a third party (Article 99 of the Civil Code; Article 504 of the Commercial Code). The agent makes a manifestation of intention in another's name and on another's account.

c. Intermediary, brokerage or agency service for entrustment of sale and purchase of securities, market transactions of derivatives, and foreign market derivatives transactions

Intermediary, brokerage or agency service for entrustment of the sale and purchase of securities or market transactions of derivatives conducted in a financial instruments exchange market, and intermediary, brokerage or agency service for entrustment of the sale and purchase of securities or foreign market derivatives transactions conducted in a foreign financial instruments market, are deemed acts constituting "financial instruments business" (Article 2(8)(iii) of the FIEA).

A "financial instruments exchange market" means a financial instruments

*601*

market established by a financial instruments exchange (ibid., Article 2 (17)). A "financial instruments market" means a market in which the sale and purchase of securities or market transactions of derivatives are conducted (ibid., Article 2(14)). A "foreign financial instruments market" means a market in a foreign state similar to a financial instruments exchange market (ibid., Article 2 (8) (iii)). "Entrustment" means requesting the performance of a juridical act or real act by another person.

The sale and purchase of securities and market transactions of derivatives in a financial instruments exchange market may, in principle, be conducted only by a member, etc. (member or trading participant) of the financial instruments exchange which has established the financial instruments exchange market (Article 111(1) of the FIEA). Therefore, when a financial instruments business operator, etc. that is not a member, etc. of the financial instruments exchange is entrusted by a customer with the sale or purchase of securities or a market transaction of derivatives in the financial instruments exchange market in question, it acts as the customer's intermediary, broker, or agent in entrusting the transaction to a member, etc. In this case, the entrusting party is the customer.

    d. Over-the-counter transactions in derivatives and intermediary, brokerage, and agency service therefor

    ( i ) Overview

Over-the-counter transactions in derivatives and intermediary, brokerage, and agency service therefor ("over-the-counter transactions of derivatives, etc.") are deemed acts constituting "financial instruments business" (Article 2(8)(iv) of the FIEA).

    ( ii ) Electronic trading platforms

The Leaders' Statement of the G20 Pittsburgh summit (September 24-25, 2009) agreed that "all standardized OTC derivatives contracts should be traded on exchanges or electronic trading platforms."

An electronic trading platform is a system for electronically placing orders for and executing over-the-counter transactions in derivatives. Providing an electronic trading platform constitutes "over-the-counter transaction of derivatives, etc.," being termed "business in electronic over-the-counter

Chapter 5   Business regulations on financial instruments business operators, etc.

transactions of derivatives, etc." (see Article 60-14(1) of the FIEA).

e . Brokerage for clearing of securities, etc.
( i )   Overview
Brokerage for clearing of securities, etc. is deemed an act constituting "financial instruments business" (Article 2(8)(v) of the FIEA). When a financial instruments transaction such as the sale or purchase of securities or a derivatives transaction is conducted, settlement is made once the transaction is agreed on between the parties. Settlement consists of the transfer of rights (securities settlement, etc.) and transfer of funds (cash settlement). Settlement of the sale or purchase of securities consists of transfer of the securities (securities settlement) and cash settlement. Derivatives transactions can be settled by delivery (transfer of the financial instrument [Article 2(24) of the FIEA] constituting the underlying asset, or of the right to that financial instrument), but typically the difference in value is settled through payment of cash only; such settlement of the difference takes the form of cash settlement alone.

The parties to a transaction are exposed to settlement risk (counterparty risk, the risk of sustaining a loss due to the other party's failure to settle). Settlement risk needs to be reduced in order to ensure the stable, smooth implementation of financial instruments transactions.

For that reason, a system of financial instruments clearing organizations and foreign financial instruments clearing organizations is enshrined in the FIEA (Chapter V-3). Under this system, financial instruments transactions proceed as follows: (1) effectuation of the transaction agreement, (2) clearing, and (3) settlement. Clearing organizations perform (2) clearing functions as so-called central counter parties (CCPs). The term "clearing functions" refers to the process whereby the clearing organization completes settlement as a party to it, assuming the obligations of the seller and the buyer.

Currently, the period for settling share transactions is T+3 (settlement takes place on the fourth business day after the trade date); that for settling government bond transactions is T+2. The goal is to shorten this to T+2 for share transactions during 2019 and to T+1 for government bond transactions in the first half of 2018.

*603*

( ii ) "Financial instruments obligation assumption service"

The FIEA refers to the performance of these clearing functions as "financial instruments obligation assumption service" (Article 2(28) of the FIEA). A financial instruments clearing organization is a person licensed or approved to provide financial instruments obligation assumption service (Articles 2 (29), 156-2 and 156-19 (1) of the FIEA); a foreign financial instruments clearing organization is a person licensed to provide a financial instruments obligation assumption service (Articles 2(29) and 156-20-2 of the FIEA).

"Financial instruments obligation assumption service" means provision of service, which involves assuming, novating, or by any other method bearing obligations arising from a "subject transaction," such as the sale or purchase of securities or a derivatives transaction, conducted by a financial instruments business operator, registered financial institution, or securities finance company ("business operator covered by financial instruments obligation assumption service"), in the course of trade, to business operators covered by financial instruments obligation assumption service (Article 2 (28) of the FIEA; Article 1-19 of the Implementing Order).

When, under the 2010 revision of the FIEA, foreign clearing organizations were permitted to enter the clearing business in the Japanese market, the concept of "financial instruments obligation assumption service" was given substance through the addition of novating and other methods to the traditional methods of assuming obligations under the Civil Code. This revision also established exclusions from "financial instruments obligation assumption service": those transactions cleared by foreign clearing organizations that are designated by the Commissioner of the FSA are excluded (Article 1-18-2 of the Implementing Order; Article 2 of the Public Notice of the FSA No. 105 of 2011).

( iii ) "Brokerage for clearing of securities, etc."

The other party to the financial instruments obligation assumption service provided by a clearing organization is referred to as the "clearing participant" (Article 156-7 (2) (iii) of the FIEA). In the case of a subject transaction conducted by a trading participant or member of a financial instruments exchange that is a clearing participant (financial instruments

604

Chapter 5   Business regulations on financial instruments business operators, etc.

business operator or registered financial institution), a financial instruments clearing organization or foreign financial instruments clearing organization bears the obligations; but in the case of a transaction conducted by a "non-clearing participant" unable to settle with a clearing organization, the obligations arising from the transaction need to be treated as obligations of a clearing participant.

The FIEA therefore adopts the legal framework of "brokerage." In formal terms, a clearing participant conducts the transaction of the non-clearing participant on the non-clearing participant's account, becoming the legal performer of the transaction under entrustment by the non-clearing participant. The clearing participant thus "brokers" the transaction with the clearing organization. When the legal framework of "brokerage" is adopted, it likewise constitutes "brokerage" for a clearing participant entrusted with the sale or purchase of securities or a derivatives transaction by a general customer other than a non-clearing participant to have a clearing organization bear the obligations.

Thus, it constitutes "brokerage for clearing of securities, etc." when a clearing participant brokers a transaction of a customer (whether a non-clearing participant or a general customer) who is the entrusting person in order to effect the transaction in its own name and have the clearing organization bear the obligations. It is required that (1) the subject transaction is effected by the customer on behalf of the financial instruments business operator or registered financial institution; or (2) the customer identifies the other party in the subject transaction and certain other matters in advance at the time of the entrustment (Article 2(27) of the FIEA).

These two requirements are designed to ensure that the specifics of the subject transaction are essentially decided by the customer who is the entrusting person rather than by the clearing participant. The first requirement adopts a legal framework whereby the clearing participant (the financial instruments business operator or registered financial institution in question) is nominally the performer (principal) of the subject transaction, and the subject transaction is effected by the customer (agent) on behalf of the clearing participant that is the principal. This arrangement is basically intended for use in exchange transactions. Under the second requirement, unlike the first, the customer, at the time of entrustment, identifies in

*605*

advance the other party to the subject transaction, whether it is a purchase or a sale, the issue, the volume or amount, the price, and the date of delivery (in the case of sale or purchase of securities) (Article 2(27)(ii) of the FIEA; Article 22 of the Cabinet Office Ordinance on Definitions). This arrangement is used, for example, for the book-entry transfer system for corporate bonds operated by the Japan Securities Depository Center; it is characterized as the securities equivalent, as it were, of payment order contracts.

f. Underwriting of securities
( i ) "Underwriting of securities"
Underwriting of securities is deemed an act constituting "financial instruments business" (Article 2(8)(vi) of the FIEA).

"Underwriting of securities" means, at the time of public offering, secondary distribution, or private placement of securities, or solicitation for selling, etc. only for professional investors, either (1) acquiring all or part of the securities for the purpose of having other persons acquire them; (2) concluding a contract in which, with regard to all or part of the securities, the underwriter promises to acquire all of the remaining securities that are not acquired by any other person; or (3) if the securities are share option certificates, concluding a contract stipulating that, if the person who has acquired them does not exercise the relevant share options in whole or in part, the underwriter will acquire the share option certificates for the unexercised share options, and the underwriter or a third party will exercise the share options in question (ibid. and Article 2(6) of the FIEA).

Category (1) constitutes what in Japan is called purchase underwriting (i. e., a firm commitment); category (2) constitutes so-called standby underwriting. In the case of (1), the act must be for distribution purposes. If the acquirer of the securities resells them, and the acquisition is only temporary, until the securities are resold to another party, the act might be considered for distribution purposes (see Article 44-4 of the FIEA). If the acquirer intends to transfer them to another party several years later as an so-called "exit," the act does not basically constitute "underwriting."

Category (3) relates to a type of capital increase through allotment, without contribution, of share option or investment equity option certificates (a so-called rights offering), the so-called commitment-type (a scheme in

606

Chapter 5 Business regulations on financial instruments business operators, etc.

which the issuer acquires unexercised share options or investment equity options in accordance with a call option, and then sells them to a financial instruments business operator, which operator then sells the shares acquired by exercising the options on the market or elsewhere). This scheme, while falling into neither Category (1) nor Category (2) above, resembles the latter in terms of the manner in which the act is conducted and the risks involved; therefore, when the FIEA was revised in 2011, this category was added to include the act of the committing party (the acquisition and exercise of the unexercised share options or investment equity options) under "underwriting of securities" (Article 2(6)(iii) of the FIEA; Article 14-2 of the Cabinet Office Ordinance on Definitions). The provision is not restricted to cases of commitment-type rights offerings.

A person who, at the time of public offering, secondary distribution, or private placement of securities, or solicitation for selling, etc. only for professional investors, conducts any of the acts in (1)-(3) above is termed an "underwriter" (Article 2(6) of the FIEA).

A public offering or secondary distribution by an issuer in Japan begun outside Japan basically does not constitute a public offering or secondary distribution of securities (see Article 19 (2) (i) of the Cabinet Office Ordinance on Disclosure of Corporate Affairs, Etc.). The acts of overseas underwriting companies do not constitute "underwriting of securities," and they are not "underwriters."

(ⅱ) "Wholesale underwriting of securities"
Underwriting of securities is classified into "wholesale underwriting of securities" and acts other than wholesale underwriting of securities (Article 28(1)(iii)(a)-(c) of the FIEA).

Wholesale underwriting of securities means engaging in any of the forms of underwriting of securities in (1)-(3) above with an issuer or with a holder other than a financial instruments business operator or registered financial institution (ibid., Article 28(7)).

Wholesale underwriting contracts for securities are classified into those for which management of risks is highly necessary and other (ibid., Article 28 (1) (iii) (a) & (b)), and different minimum capital levels as financial instruments business operators are set for each (three billion yen and 500

*607*

million yen) (Article 29-4(1)(iv) of the FIEA; Article 15-7(1)(i-ii) of the Implementing Order).

Wholesale underwriting for which management of risks is highly necessary means types of underwriting for which discussions are held with the issuer or holder (secondary distributor) of the securities for fixing the terms of the wholesale underwriting contract when the contract is concluded, except if the total amount underwritten is ten billion yen or less, or if it is more than ten billion yen, but the amount underwritten by the underwriter itself is ten billion yen or less (Article 28(1)(iii)(a) of the FIEA; Article 15 of the Implementing Order; Article 4 of the Cabinet Office Ordinance on Financial Instruments Services, Etc.). Wholesale underwriting contracts are contracts concluded at the time of public offering or secondary distribution of securities, or solicitation for acquisition only for professional investors or solicitation for selling, etc. only for professional investors; they do not include contracts concluded at the time of private placement or secondary distribution other than solicitation for acquisition only for professional investors and solicitation for selling, etc. only for professional investors.

Any party that holds discussions with the issuer or holder of the securities for fixing the terms of the wholesale underwriting contract when the contract is concluded is referred to as a "managing underwriter" (Article 147(iii) of the Cabinet Office Ordinance on Financial Instruments Services, Etc.). The party that underwrites an amount not less than that underwritten by the other managing underwriters, or that receives a fee, remuneration, or other type of consideration not less than that received by the other managing underwriters, is referred to as the "lead managing underwriter" (ibid.; see also Article 153(1)(iv) of the Ordinance). On the other hand, the Rules Concerning Underwriting, Etc. of Securities issued by the Japan Securities Dealers Association defines as the "lead managing regular member underwriter" the "regular member underwriter" (a regular member who is an underwriter: see Article 2(8) of the Rules) appointed by the issuer or the secondary distributor to negotiate on the underwriting agreement with the issuer or the secondary distributor of the securities related to the underwriting agreement at the time of concluding the underwriting agreement of the securities (ibid., Article 2(9)); this is a

Chapter 5   Business regulations on financial instruments business operators, etc.

broader concept than that of "lead managing underwriter." If there is only a single underwriter, it constitutes the "lead managing underwriter" or "lead managing regular member underwriter."

Financial instruments business operators or registered financial institutions concluding wholesale underwriting contracts with either the issuer of securities for which a public offering is made or the holder of securities of which secondary distribution is made have civil liability (Article 21 (1) (iv) of the FIEA) only with respect to "wholesale underwriting contracts" concluded for a public offering or secondary distribution of securities (ibid., Article 21 (4); Article 14-2-2 of the Cabinet Office Ordinance on Disclosure of Corporate Affairs, Etc.).

(iii)   Underwriting other than wholesale underwriting of securities

Underwriting other than wholesale underwriting of securities (Article 28 (1) (iii) (c) of the FIEA) constitutes so-called sub-underwriting. Specifically, it constitutes the act of either purchase underwriting or standby underwriting for an underwriter conducting wholesale underwriting of securities.

If foreign securities are brought into Japan, the acquisition of those foreign securities by a securities company in Japan is basically not considered to constitute "underwriting of securities" unless they are acquired from an issuer, secondary distributor, or the like that conducts public offering, secondary distribution, etc. of securities.

g.  Public offering and private placement of certain securities

Public offering and private placement of certain securities are deemed acts constituting "financial instruments business" (Article 2 (8) (vii) of the FIEA). This makes acts conducted by the securities issuer itself (Article 2 (3) of the FIEA) financial instruments business.

The types of securities subject to the "public offering or private placement" constituting "financial instruments business" are, given the need to protect investors and out of consideration for the benefit of issuers seeking to raise funds, limited to (1) beneficiary certificates of trusts for investment based on settlor's instructions; (2) beneficiary certificates of foreign investment trusts; (3) mortgage securities; (4) foreign mortgage securities;

*609*

(5) rights to be indicated on the securities in (1) and (2), which rights are regarded as securities (the rights to be indicated on (3) and (4) are not specified by cabinet office ordinance); (6) equity in a collective investment scheme, or equity in a foreign collective investment scheme; and (7) equity in a trust-type commodity fund (Article 2(8)(vii)(a)-(g) of the FIEA; Article 1-9-2 of the Implementing Order).

Categories (1) and (2) make so-called direct selling of investment trusts a financial instruments business, because the issuer of the beneficiary certificates of a trust for investment based on settlor's instructions is the settlor (settlor company of an investment trust) (Article 2(7) & (11) of the Act on Investment Trusts and Investment Corporations). Category (6) is included because in the case of fund equity, structuring of the product is often integrated with sale and solicitation.

On the other hand, direct placement and private placement using trust schemes such as trust beneficial interests are considered financial instruments business only in the case of beneficial interests from trust-type commodity funds, as in category (7). Further, direct placement and private placement of share certificates, share option certificates, corporate bond certificates, and so forth are not deemed financial instruments business lest companies' ability to raise funds be impeded, and direct placement and private placement of investment securities issued by investment corporations and foreign investment securities issued by foreign investment corporations are not deemed financial instruments business, although securities may be added by cabinet order if necessary to protect investors (Article 2(8)(vii)(g) of the FIEA).

Public offering and private placement consist in "solicitation for acquisition" (Article 2(3) of the FIEA). "Solicitation" refers to the real act of encouraging another to engage in a certain act, but the concept is not necessarily clearly defined. Under disclosure regulations, such acts of providing information as distributing documentation, giving explanations during briefing sessions, and advertising are also categorized as "solicitation" (B4-1 of the Guideline for the Disclosure of Corporate Affairs); but for the purpose of business regulations, the concept needs to be interpreted more strictly.

*610*

Chapter 5   Business regulations on financial instruments business operators, etc.

h. Secondary distribution of securities and solicitation for selling, etc. only for professional investors

Secondary distribution of securities and solicitation for selling, etc. only for professional investors are deemed acts constituting "financial instruments business" (Article 2(8)(viii) of the FIEA).

"Secondary distribution of securities" means, among solicitations of applications to sell or purchase already-issued securities (excluding solicitations falling under acts similar to solicitation for acquisition and certain other acts) ("solicitation for selling, etc."), those meeting certain requirements (Article 2(4) of the FIEA). Solicitation for selling, etc. conducted with regard to certain securities transactions is excluded (ibid; Article 1-7-3 of the Implementing Order).

"Solicitation for selling, etc. only for professional investors" means solicitation for selling, etc. of paragraph 1 securities made only to professional investors and meeting certain requirements (excluding transactions excluded from secondary distribution of securities) (Article 2(6) of the FIEA; Article 1-7-3 of the Implementing Order). Those requirements are (1) when the other party to the solicitation for selling, etc. is not the State, the Bank of Japan, or a qualified institutional investor, that the solicitation for selling, etc. is made by a financial instruments business operator, etc. based on entrustment by a customer or for itself; and (2) that the solicited securities are not likely to be transferred from the person who acquired them to any person other than a "professional investor, etc." (Article 2(4) (ii)(b) of the FIEA; Article 1-8-2 of the Implementing Order).

Under the 2008 revision of the FIEA, when "solicitation for selling, etc. only for professional investors" (so-called private secondary distribution to professional investors) was excluded from the definition of "secondary distribution of securities" (Article 2(4)(ii)(b) of the FIEA), solicitation for selling, etc. only for professional investors and dealing therein were added to the definition of financial instruments business alongside secondary distribution of securities and dealing therein (Article 2(8)(viii)-(ix) of the FIEA).

The act of distributing securities for which a financial instruments business operator has conducted purchase underwriting (the securities being already issued at the time of purchase), while formally meeting the

*611*

definition of "secondary distribution," is considered to be a "public offering" rather than "secondary distribution" on the grounds that it forms part of the process of distributing newly issued securities.

ⅰ. Dealing in public offering or secondary distribution of securities, and dealing in private placement of securities or solicitation for selling, etc. only for professional investors

Dealing in public offering or secondary distribution of securities, and dealing in private placement of securities or solicitation for selling, etc. only for professional investors, are deemed acts constituting "financial instruments business" (Article 2(8)(ix) of the FIEA).

"Dealing" is interpreted to mean acting on behalf of another person, such as an issuer of securities, in conducting a public offering, secondary distribution, or private placement of securities, or solicitation for selling, etc. only for professional investors (proxy solicitation). Simple provision of information unaccompanied by "solicitation" does not as a rule constitute "dealing."

For example, over-the-counter sales of investment trusts by financial instruments business operators and registered financial institutions constitute dealing in public offerings of beneficiary certificates in investment trusts. The seller is not a party to the "investment trust contract" (Article 3 (1) of the Act on Investment Trusts and Investment Corporations); the relationship between the seller and the settlor company of the investment trust is determined by the public offering and sale entrustment contract, while that between the seller and the investor (beneficiary) is determined by a contract based on general business rules on investment trusts (Supreme Court Decision of Dec. 14, 2006, *Civil Cases of the Supreme Court*, Vol. 60, No. 10, p. 3,914).

Similarly, over-the-counter sales of jointly managed money trusts (excluding those with guaranteed principal) by financial instruments business operators, etc. constitute dealing in public offering or private placement rather than "trust agreement agency business" (see Article 2(8) of the Trust Business Act). In such cases, the financial instruments business operator, etc. is subject to the conduct regulations of the FIEA, while the trustee is subject to the conduct regulations of the Trust Business Act

Chapter 5   Business regulations on financial instruments business operators, etc.

(including, in the case of "specific trust agreements," the FIEA as applied *mutatis mutandis*) (see ibid, Article 24-2, and Article 2-2 of the Act on Engagement in Trust Business by a Financial Institution). The FIEA does not, by contrast, apply to over-the-counter sales of trusts with guaranteed principal, which constitute trust agreement agency business (see Article 14 (4) (i) (a) of the Cabinet Office Ordinance on Definitions (revised in April 2014)).

Further, when a security trust is used in a syndicated loan by financial institutions, the participating financial institutions have a beneficial interest in the trust as beneficiaries of the trust (a third-party beneficiary trust); thus, the act of the arranger formally constitutes dealing in private placement of trust beneficial interests. It is not, however, considered to fall into the category of type II financial instruments business if the trust beneficial interests are inseparably united with the loan.

The acts in this provision constitute acts of financial instruments intermediation (Articles 2(11) (iii) and 66-11 of the FIEA).

ｊ. Proprietary trading systems (PTSs)

（ⅰ） Overview

The sale and purchase of securities, or an intermediary, brokerage, or agency service therefor, which is conducted through an electronic data processing system, by using certain specified price formation methods or other similar methods, and in which a large number of persons participate simultaneously as one or more parties to the transaction, are deemed acts constituting "financial instruments business" (Article 2(8) (x) of the FIEA).

These are "proprietary trading system (PTS)" acts. After the abolition of the requirement to trade listed securities through stock exchanges took effect on December 1, 1998, it was expected that PTSs such as those that had spread in the United States and elsewhere would be established in Japan as well. (A PTS is an electronic trading system unlike a traditional exchange, through which a private organization provides trading services using electronic technology.) These PTSs, it was anticipated, would promote competition between markets and help enhance convenience for investors. In the 1998 revision of the Securities and Exchange Act (Financial System Reform Act), PTSs were classified as "securities businesses" ("financial instruments business" in the FIEA) so as to create a legal framework to ensure the fairness of the transactions conducted on them. PTSs have in the United States recently come to be called "alternative trading systems" (ATSs); in the EU they are referred to as "multilateral trading facilities" (MTFs).

Derivatives transactions are not allowed on PTSs. Further, the FSA has established a supervisory guideline requiring that in order to be authorized for PTS management business, operators should not handle margin trading (IV-4-2-1(ii) of the Comprehensive Guidelines for Supervision of Financial Instruments Business Operators, Etc.). Margin trading on PTSs is expected to be allowed under certain conditions.

(ii) PTS price formation methods

Certain price formation methods are designated for PTSs (Article 2(8)(x) (a)-(e) of the FIEA; Article 1-10 of the Implementing Order; Article 17 of the Cabinet Office Ordinance on Definitions). This is because of the necessity to distinguish PTSs as enterprises conducted in the course of trade from financial instruments exchanges, because if a PTS were to possess the same high level of price formation functions as do financial instruments exchanges, it would need to obtain a license as a financial instruments exchange.

Specifically, these methods are: (1) a method of auction (limited to cases where the trading volume of securities does not exceed certain specified criteria); (2) with regard to securities listed in a financial instruments exchange, a method using the trading price of the securities in the financial instruments exchange market operated by the financial instruments exchange (market price trading); (3) with regard to over-the-counter traded securities, a method using the trading price of the securities published by the authorized financial instruments firms association to which the securities are registered (market price trading); (4) a method using the price decided by negotiation between customers (price negotiated between customers); (5) a method that uses the figures presented by a customer, in cases where the figure presented by the customer corresponds to that presented by the other customer who becomes a counterparty to the transaction (matching customer orders); and (6) a method by which a financial instruments business operator offers more than one asked and

*614*

Chapter 5   Business regulations on financial instruments business operators, etc.

bidding quotations of its own or of any other financial instruments business operators, etc. for a single issue, and uses an indicative price based on the asked and bidding quotations (offering asked and bidding quotations).

Excluded from (6) are cases where more than one financial instruments business operator, etc. constantly offers asked and bidding quotations, and has obligations to conduct a purchase and sale on the basis of the asked and bidding quotations (so-called market making) (Article 2(8)(x)(e) of the FIEA; Article 17(ii) of the Cabinet Office Ordinance on Definitions). That requires a license as a financial instruments exchange, except if conducted in an over-the-counter securities market.

(iii)   Relationship with the financial instruments exchange system

No person, other than an authorized financial instruments firms association authorized to establish an over-the-counter securities market, may establish a financial instruments market unless the person has obtained a license as a financial instruments exchange (Article 80(1) of the FIEA). Although a PTS, being a market in which the sale and purchase of securities are conducted, constitutes a financial instruments market (Article 2(14) of the FIEA), it requires no license (Article 80(2) of the FIEA).

The definition of "financial instruments market" (Article 2(14) of the FIEA) does not embrace markets in which over-the-counter transactions in derivatives are conducted, and over-the-counter transactions in derivatives are not included in PTS business; therefore, a financial instruments business operator does not require a license either as a financial instruments exchange or for PTS management business (Article 30(1) of the FIEA) in order to conduct over-the-counter transactions in derivatives, or intermediary, brokerage, or agency services therefor, with a large number of persons as one or more parties to the transaction.

(iv)   What constitutes a PTS

A system that brokers the sale and purchase of securities in a financial instruments exchange market, or brokers the sale and purchase of securities to another financial instruments business operator, is basically not considered to be a PTS or a financial instruments exchange market. For example, a system that simultaneously brokers sell and buy orders of the

*615*

same volume by two customers outside trading sessions of a financial instruments exchange does not as a rule constitute either, although it may be considered to do so if orders are integrated, offset, or otherwise combined within the system (IV-4-2-1 (i) of the Comprehensive Guidelines for Supervision of Financial Instruments Business Operators, Etc.) (revised in March 2012).

Thus, a dark pool (a matching system in which a securities company matches orders of institutional investors in house without offering quotations) basically does not constitute a PTS if it brokers transactions outside trading sessions of a financial instruments exchange in cross-trading format.

k. Investment advice

( i ) Overview

Concluding an investment advisory contract and providing advice under that contract is deemed an act constituting "financial instruments business" (Article 2 (8) (xi) of the FIEA). Solicitation to conclude an investment advisory contract by a person seeking to be one of the parties to the contract also basically constitutes investment advice.

( ii ) Definition of "investment advisory contract"

An "investment advisory contract" is a contract in which one of the parties promises to provide the other party with advice orally, in writing (excluding newspapers, magazines, books, or others which are issued to be sold to many unspecified persons and many unspecified persons can buy as needed), or otherwise, on (1) "values, etc. of securities" (the value of securities, amount receivable for securities-related options, or movement of securities indicators), or (2) investment decisions based on analysis of "values, etc. of financial instruments" (the value of financial instruments, amount receivable for options, or movement of financial indicators); and the other party promises to pay remuneration therefor (ibid.; Article 18 of the Cabinet Office Ordinance on Definitions).

In (1) above, "securities-related options" means rights pertaining to securities-related option transactions (Article 28(8) (iii) (c) of the FIEA) conducted in a financial instruments market in accordance with the

*616*

Chapter 5   Business regulations on financial instruments business operators, etc.

requirements and by using the methods prescribed by the operator of the financial instruments market; rights pertaining to transactions similar to such option transactions (ibid.) conducted in a foreign financial instruments market; or the amount receivable for over-the-counter option transactions (ibid., (iv) (c) & (d)) conducted in neither a financial instruments market nor a foreign financial instruments market. "Securities indicators" means the price or interest rates of securities, percentages of the distribution of profit pertaining to securities or the equivalent thereof, and the discount rate of securities issued on a discount basis (Article 2 (8) (xi) (a) of the FIEA; Article 18 of the Cabinet Office Ordinance on Definitions).

Of the "values, etc. of financial instruments" in (2) above, those pertaining to commodities (as designated by cabinet order) are restricted to those of instruments listed on a financial instruments exchange (2012 revision of the FIEA).

(iii)   "Values, etc. of securities"

With regard to securities and derivatives transactions related to securities, even providing advice simply on "values, etc. of securities" constitutes investment advice. Providing advice on "investment decisions" is not a requirement.

The term "values, etc. of securities" is generally interpreted to mean the profits to be gained in future from investing in securities, namely, economic value such as capital gains, interest, and dividends. Economic trends, corporate results, and present and past securities prices do not immediately fall into that category, but they are considered to do so if they are deemed to implicitly indicate future economic value.

A so-called financial planner (FP) advising a customer on the asset allocation of his or her investment portfolio will, as long as the advice is only general and does not touch on specific securities issues, usually fall outside the category of advice on "values, etc. of securities." On the other hand, an analyst report on individual shares, for example, constitutes advice on "values, etc. of securities."

*617*

(iv) "Investment decisions based on analysis of values, etc. of financial instruments"

With regard to derivatives transactions unrelated to securities, merely advising on the value of the financial instruments that are the underlying assets, or the movement of financial indicators that serve as benchmarks, does not on its own constitute investment advice, but it does constitute investment advice, if accompanied by advice on investment decisions. For example, in the case of weather derivatives, merely advising about trends in average summer temperatures (the equivalent of financial indicators) in Japan this year does not on its own constitute investment advising.

On the other hand, so-called analysts are considered to engage in at least the "analysis of values, etc. of financial instruments" (see Article 72(i) of the Cabinet Office Ordinance on Financial Instruments Services, Etc.).

(v) "Investment decisions"

"Investment decisions" means decisions on classes, issues, volume, or prices of securities to be invested in as well as whether the securities shall be purchased or sold, by what method, and at what timing, and decisions on the contents and timing of derivatives transactions to be conducted (Article 2 (8)(xi) of the FIEA).

Decisions on the exercise of voting rights, in themselves, are understood not to be included in "investment decisions." Therefore, advice by so-called proxy advisory firms on the exercise of voting rights is basically understood not per se to constitute investment advice.

(vi) The exclusion of what "many unspecified persons can buy as needed"

This exclusion is out of respect for freedom of speech and the press as guaranteed by the Constitution. It is considered to suffice if the material in question is available for "many unspecified persons" to buy at any time in store, say, or on the Internet; it does not matter whether it is purchased regularly or on a one-time basis, and it is not necessary for "many unspecified persons" actually to have bought it.

On the other hand, documents generally distributed to only specific members, or presentations to gatherings of many unspecified persons,

*618*

Chapter 5   Business regulations on financial instruments business operators, etc.

cannot really be described as available to many unspecified persons as needed. In one administrative action case, a developer of software used to select issues of shares to invest in was ruled to be an unregistered investment advisor and agent (administrative action by the Tokai Local Finance Bureau, Dec. 4, 2012; see VII-3-1(2)(ii)A(b) of the Comprehensive Guidelines for Supervision of Financial Instruments Business Operators, Etc.).

(vii)   Remuneration

Since an investment advisory contract is an agreement on payment of remuneration, anything unremunerated does not constitute investment advising. Whether something constitutes "remuneration" is determined substantively; it does not matter what it is called, whether a "fee" or something else. So-called securities companies sometimes provide advice to customers in the course of performing intermediary, brokerage, and agency services for the sale and purchase of securities, but because that advice may usually be regarded as unremunerated, it is not considered to constitute investment advising (see Article 35(1)(viii) of the FIEA).

Even if the advice is remunerated, it does not constitute investment advice unless the remuneration is received from the recipient of the advice. For example, giving advice in return for remuneration from the organizer of a lecture does not constitute investment advice, except if the remuneration may be deemed to be effectively received from the recipient of the advice even though it is formally received from a third party; in that case it does constitute investment advice.

(viii)   Advice

"Advice" has traditionally been interpreted to mean explicitly or implicitly communicating, in whole or in part, "values, etc. of securities" or "investment decisions based on analysis of values, etc. of financial instruments." However, "advice" is generally defined as recommending carrying out a certain act or making helpful suggestions about matters necessary to the performance of a certain act; it thus requires an active element, and caution should be exercised in deeming an act advice by implication.

*619*

For example, it is thought that simply analyzing and appraising the value of individual securities in an analyst report and assigning a rating basically does not constitute "advice"; on the other hand, appending a recommendation such as "Buy," "Sell," or "Neutral" may basically constitute "advice." However, the borderline between the two is undeniably not always clear.

Cases are seen in forex system trading where the provision of buy and sell signals (strategies) to customers by financial instruments business operators engaged in over-the-counter foreign exchange margin trading is treated as advice.

1. Management of investment corporation assets and discretionary investment management

(ⅰ) Overview

Conclusion of an entrustment contract for asset investments (Article 188 (1)(iv) of the Act on Investment Trusts and Investment Corporations) with a registered investment corporation, or of a discretionary investment contract, and investment (including instructions of investment) of money or other properties in securities or rights pertaining to derivatives transactions conducted under investment decisions based on analysis of values, etc. of financial instruments under such a contract, is deemed an act constituting "financial instruments business" (Article 2(8)(xii) of the FIEA).

It is clearly stated that the term "investment" as used in the FIEA includes "instructions on investment." Investment instructions are basically assumed to mean instructions on investment of a trust property.

(ⅱ) Management of investment corporation assets

A financial instruments business operator that conducts business affairs related to asset investment under entrustment from a registered investment corporation is termed an "asset management company" (Article 2(21) of the Act on Investment Trusts and Investment Corporations). In cases where an asset management company invests assets of a registered investment corporation as an investment in securities or in assets other than rights pertaining to derivatives transactions in the course of business, that investment is deemed to fall under management of investment corporation

*620*

Chapter 5   Business regulations on financial instruments business operators, etc.

assets (ibid., Article 223-3(3)). The requisite conduct regulations of the FIEA are thereby applied to such investments.

(iii)   Discretionary investment management

A "discretionary investment contract" is a contract wherein one of the parties is fully or partly entrusted by the other party with discretion in making investment decisions based on analysis of values, etc. of financial instruments and is also entrusted with the authority necessary for making investment on behalf of the other party based on such investment decisions (Article 2(8)(xii)(b) of the FIEA).

Discretionary investment management takes one of two forms, agency or brokerage. In the case of agency, the transaction is conducted in the customer's name and on the customer's account; in the case of brokerage, it is conducted in the operator's name and on the customer's account.

(iv)   Distinction between discretionary investment management and investment advice

Discretionary investment management and investment advice differ in whether the operator itself makes investment decisions or only provides advice on investment decisions. Just because the party making the investment decision does so in accordance with the investment advice received, that in itself does not immediately lead to the conclusion that the provider of the investment advice is effectively the maker of the investment decision. Similarly, being fully or partly entrusted with discretion in making investment decisions does not constitute discretionary investment management unless investment authority is delegated.

The borderline between the two is not always clear, however. For example, there is debate over whether, in a so-called real-estate securitization scheme, the services provided by a so-called asset manager (AM) to a special-purpose company (SPC) investing in beneficial interests in a real estate trust constitute discretionary investment management or investment advice. In this regard, whether the AM is entrusted, fully or partly, by the SPC with discretion in making investment decisions and delegated investment authority must be determined substantively depending on the case in accordance with the actual facts, rather than simply

*621*

in light of the wording of the contract, the design of the scheme, and other formal aspects.

(ⅴ) Distinction between discretionary investment management and discretionary trading acts

The FIEA abolishes the so-called prohibition on discretionary trading enshrined in the old Securities and Exchange Act and related regulations (Article 42(1) (v) & (vi) of the Securities and Exchange Act). On the other hand, the acts previously exempted from this prohibition formally meet the requirement for partial delegation of discretion in making investment decisions. Of these, first, acts performed on behalf of group foreign operators ("affiliated foreign financial instruments business operators") — so-called offshore booking — are explicitly excluded from acts constituting financial instruments business (Article 2(8) of the FIEA; Article 1-8-6(1) (iv) of the Implementing Order; Article 16(1) (vii) (a) & (b) and (3) of the Cabinet Office Ordinance on Definitions).

Second, certain discretionary trading acts remain outside the scope of discretionary investment management; these are classified as able to be conducted as type I financial instruments business or type II financial instruments business, not as investment management business (see Article 40 (ii) of the FIEA; Article 123 (1) (xiii) (a) – (e) of the Cabinet Office Ordinance on Financial Instruments Services, Etc.).

To engage in any of the above discretionary trading acts, financial instruments business operators, etc. are required to establish a sufficient internal control system (ibid., Article 123(1) (xiii)).

(ⅵ) Soliciting to conclude discretionary investment contracts

A financial instruments business operator conducting business under discretionary investment contracts may solicit to conclude discretionary investment contracts. Even if, upon conclusion of such a contract, the operator intends to invest in specific issues of target securities on the basis of that contract, such solicitation does not constitute dealing in public offering or private placement of those securities (see Article 96(2) of the Cabinet Office Ordinance on Financial Instruments Services, Etc.).

*622*

Chapter 5   Business regulations on financial instruments business operators, etc.

(vii)   Incidental business

Certain acts that financial instruments business operators conducting business under discretionary investment contracts perform with respect to foreign-registered funds managed by group foreign investment specialists — various forms of consulting (surveys of domestic demand in Japan, advice on structuring of instruments, negotiations with sales companies), provision of information (preparation and sending of analyst reports on Japanese stocks), and accepting entrustment of various tasks and performing them on another's behalf (translating sales materials, liaising between that party and customers) — constitute incidental business (Article 35 (1) (viii), (ix) & (xii) of the FIEA).

m.   Agency or intermediary service for conclusion of an investment advisory contract or a discretionary investment contract

Agency or intermediary service for conclusion of an investment advisory contract or a discretionary investment contract is deemed an act constituting "financial instruments business" (Article 2 (8) (xiii) of the FIEA). This means the act of providing agency or intermediary service for conclusion of a contract on behalf of another party (a party concluding an investment advisory contract or a discretionary investment contract).

The intermediary service defined in this provision constitutes an act of financial instruments intermediation (Articles 2 (11) (iv) and 66-11 of the FIEA).

Simple distribution and provision of fliers, pamphlets, contract application forms, etc.; receipt and collection of contract applications, attached documents, etc. (excluding cases where the business operator checks the contents of the documents); and general explanations provided at seminars for financial instruments with regard to the structures, schemes, and the utilization methods of financial instruments are not considered to constitute agency or intermediary services for conclusion of an investment advisory contract or a discretionary investment contract (VII-3-1 (2) (ii) B of the Comprehensive Guidelines for Supervision of Financial Instruments Business Operators, Etc.).

*623*

n. Investment trust management

Investment of money or other properties (including giving instructions on their investment) contributed from a person who holds rights indicated on beneficiary certificates of investment trusts or other rights specified by cabinet order, as an investment in securities or rights pertaining to derivatives transactions conducted under investment decisions based on analysis of values, etc. of financial instruments, is deemed an act constituting "financial instruments business" (Article 2(8)(xiv) of the FIEA). To avoid redundancy, acts constituting management of investment corporation assets or discretionary investment management (ibid., Article (8) (xii)) are excluded.

The Cabinet Order in question specifies rights indicated on beneficiary certificates of investment trusts and beneficiary certificates of foreign investment trusts (Article 1-11 of the Implementing Order).

Therefore, first, investment management business relating to investment trusts constitutes financial instruments business. The financial instruments business operator that is the settlor of a trust for investment based on settlor's instruction is termed the "settlor company of an investment trust" (Article 2 (11) of the Act on Investment Trusts and Investment Corporations).

Second, rights indicated on beneficiary certificates of foreign investment trusts were added when the 2010 revision of the FIEA came into force (April 1, 2011). The intent is not to classify investment management business relating to foreign investment trusts as financial instruments business as a general principle, but rather only if the foreign investment trust is established and instructed directly from Japan (Article 16(1)(ix-ii) of the Cabinet Office Ordinance on Definitions). Note also that a trust that does not meet the definition of a foreign investment trust (a trust "similar to an Investment Trust": Article 2(24) of the Act on Investment Trusts and Investment Corporations) constitutes a financial instruments business (self-management of funds) (Article 2(8)(xv)(a)-(b) of the FIEA).

Third, in cases where the settlor company of an investment trust gives instructions in the course of business for investment to be made in assets other than securities or the rights pertaining to derivatives transactions, as an investment of the trust property of an investment trust managed under

*624*

Chapter 5   Business regulations on financial instruments business operators, etc.

instructions from the settlor, that investment is considered to constitute investment trust management (Article 223-3(2) of the Act on Investment Trusts and Investment Corporations). The requisite conduct regulations of the FIEA are thereby applied to such investments.

Note also that instructions on exercise of voting rights pertaining to securities held as investment trust property of a trust managed under instructions from the settlor are considered to be included in the term "investment" or "management" (*unyo*) (see ibid., Article 10(1)).

o. Self-management of funds

Investment of money or other properties (including giving instructions on their investment) invested or contributed from a person who holds certain rights, as an investment mainly in securities or rights pertaining to derivatives transactions conducted under investment decisions based on analysis of values, etc. of financial instruments, is deemed an act constituting "financial instruments business" (Article 2(8)(xv) of the FIEA). To avoid redundancy, acts constituting management of investment corporation assets or discretionary investment management (ibid., Article 2(8)(xii)) and acts constituting investment trust management (ibid., Article 2(8)(xiv)) are excluded.

Those rights are (1) beneficiary certificates of beneficiary certificates issuing trusts, or foreign securities or certificates of a similar nature; (2) trust beneficial interests or foreign trust beneficial interests; and (3) collective investment scheme equity or foreign group investment scheme equity (ibid., Article 2(8)(xv)(a)-(c)). The acquirer or holder of those rights is the investor.

Such acts constitute so-called self-management of funds. Conducting self-management in the course of business constitutes "financial instruments business" if the investment is mainly in securities or rights pertaining to derivatives transactions; organizing a fund and investing mainly in other assets such as real estate does not constitute "financial instruments business," even if conducted in the course of business (see Article 35(1)(xv) and (2)(i), (ii), (v-ii) & (vi) of the FIEA). "Mainly" means basically more than 50 percent of the investment property.

In the case of, for example, a so-called investment fund, "investment" or

*625*

"management" likely includes identifying possible investment targets, negotiating with possible investment targets about investing, deciding which investment targets to invest in, executing investments, and disposing of securities acquired through those investments. Soliciting investments or contributions of money or other properties with the intention of oneself investing the assets so invested or contributed can also basically be considered engaging in "investment" or "management."

On the other hand, the business conducted by the trustee of a trust of which the trust property is managed and disposed of in accordance with the instructions solely of the settlor or of the person entrusted with authority to give instructions by the settlor (custodian-type trust business: Article 2(3) of the Trust Business Act) does not constitute "investment" or "management." With regard to investment funds, dispatching an officer or employee of one's own organization, or dispatching a third party, to an investment target, attending a board of directors meeting or other important meeting of an investment target, exercising the right to make proposals as a shareholder, and soliciting powers of attorney constitute incidental business.

p. Acceptance of deposits of money or securities

Acceptance of deposits of money or securities or certificates listed in the items of Article 2, paragraph 1 of the FIEA from customers in relation to acts listed in Article 2, paragraph 8, items (i) to (x) inclusive of the FIEA performed by oneself, is deemed an act constituting "financial instruments business" (Article 2(8)(xvi) of the FIEA).

Such acts, corresponding to safe custody in the old Securities and Exchange Act, were previously classified as incidental business of securities companies (Article 34(1)(i) of the Securities and Exchange Act), but in the FIEA they are included in their core business as financial instruments business. Accepting security deposits from customers in relation to derivatives transactions, for example, falls into this category. In the 2012 revision of the FIEA, accepting deposits of commodities, or of securities or certificates issued in relation to deposited commodities, from customers in relation to acts listed in Article 2, paragraph 8, items (ii), (iii), and (v) of the FIEA conducted with respect to commodity-related market transactions of derivatives was added to the list of acts constituting "financial instruments

Chapter 5   Business regulations on financial instruments business operators, etc.

business."

The provision specifies "acts⋯performed by oneself"; thus, an act does not fall into this category unless the doer itself conducts any of the acts listed in Article 2, paragraph 8, items (i) to (x) of the FIEA. Therefore the simple act of accepting deposits of money or securities in itself does not fall into this category. For example, in the case of beneficiary certificates of an investment trust directly placed by the investment trust settlor company, (1) a cancellation fee, if the customer cancels, or (2) sale proceeds, if purchase is made from the customer, may be temporarily withheld from the customer; but since such acts are basically unrelated to the acts listed in Article 2, paragraph 8, items (i) to (x) of the FIEA, they do not fall into the category of acts specified in Article 2, paragraph 8, item (xvi).

Book-entry bonds and so on are considered to be included among the items subject to "deposit." This holds true also of "safe custody" of securities (Article 35(1)(iii) of the FIEA).

q . Transfer of bonds, etc.

Transfer of bonds, etc. conducted in response to opening of an account for transfer of "bonds, etc." defined in Article 2, paragraph 1 of the Act on Book-Entry Transfer of Corporate Bonds and Shares, Etc. is deemed an act constituting "financial instruments business" (Article 2 (8) (xvii) of the FIEA).

Under the Act on Transfer of Corporate Bonds, etc., securities companies and so on used to be allowed to open an account for the transfer of bonds, etc. for another party at the request of that party (Article 44(1) of the old Act on Transfer of Corporate Bonds, Etc.). Under this provision of the FIEA, however, the service conducted by an account management institution is, like safe custody service, classified as an act constituting financial instruments business, since it resembles safe custody service in that both involve managing the location and transfer of another's rights (or the securities displaying them), as well as in their actual economic nature, although they differ in whether the asset is possessed in tangible form.

So-called global custody services (the provision by overseas custody banks or the like of custody services to Japanese institutional investors and so forth outside Japan, such as securities settlement and custody services,

*627*

and receipt of principal, interest, and dividends on their behalf) are generally not conducted in relation to overseas custody banks' own acts listed in Article 2, paragraph 8, items (i) to (x) of the FIEA, nor are they conducted on the basis of the Act on Transfer of Corporate Bonds, etc.

r. Acts specified by cabinet order

Acts specified by cabinet order as being similar to acts listed in Article 2, paragraph 8, items (i) - (xvii) of the FIEA are deemed acts constituting "financial instruments business" (Article 2(8)(xviii) of the FIEA).

The Cabinet Order in question specifies the purchase without the purpose of resale of beneficiary certificates of a trust for investment based on settlor's instruction or beneficiary certificates of a foreign investment trust by a person who has conducted direct placement or private placement of those beneficiary certificates (Article 1-12 of the Implementing Order).

This means that such purchases are not classified under the sale and purchase of securities (Article 2(8)(i) of the FIEA). On the other hand, cancellation of an investment trust contract or a foreign investment trust contract, being the rescission of an existing agreement (a contract to obtain beneficiary certificates of an investment trust), does not constitute financial instruments business (see Article 98(1)(i) of the Cabinet Office Ordinance on Financial Instruments Services, Etc.).

# 7. Acts excluded from "financial instruments business"

a. Overview

In order to establish a comprehensive, cross-sectoral framework for protecting investors covering a broad range of financial instruments and transactions, and simplify regulations by overhauling previously compartmentalized industry legislation, the FIEA defines relevant trades as "financial instruments business" (Article 2 (8) of the FIEA) and comprehensively enumerates acts subject to the law's regulations. On the other hand, by such a definition financial instruments business could formally embrace acts that would not necessarily hinder protection of investors even if unregulated.

Therefore the Cabinet Order and Cabinet Office Ordinance based on the introductory section of Article 2, paragraph 8 of the FIEA explicitly exclude

Chapter 5 Business regulations on financial instruments business operators, etc.

from "financial instruments business" any activity deemed, in light of its nature and other factors, not to hinder protection of investors (Article 1-8-6 of the Implementing Order; Articles 15 and 16 of the Cabinet Office Ordinance on Definitions).

Thus, under the FIEA, explicit exclusions are enshrined in the legislative framework in order to exempt certain acts formally meeting the definition of "financial instruments business" from the regulations, thereby increasing their clarity and predictability.

b. How exclusions are administered

In practical terms, certain acts formally meeting the definition of "financial instruments business" may be found not to substantially hinder protection of investors. In such cases, the act may be deemed not to constitute "financial instruments business" if a substantive interpretation can reasonably be made within the wording of the legislation.

On the other hand, substantive interpretations must not be made where they may go beyond the wording of the legislation. In such cases, it is important that the FSA flexibly establish exclusions from "financial instruments business" while heeding the views of the business community. It must be kept in mind that exclusions are enshrined in the cabinet order and the cabinet office ordinance based on it to enable such flexibility.

c. Application of the FIEA to acts excluded from "financial instruments business"

Whether the provisions of the FIEA apply to acts excluded from the definition of "financial instruments business" should be determined in light of the purport of each provision.

Basically, such acts are neither directly subject to business regulations and conduct regulations (the requirement to deliver documentation before and when concluding a contract, the requirement to prepare and deliver investment reports, etc.), nor are they directly subject to the requirement to prepare and preserve books and documents. For example, non-securities-related over-the-counter transactions of derivatives, etc. conducted with so-called professional customers excluded from financial instruments business (Article 1-8-6(1)(ii) of the Implementing Order) do not require

*629*

registration of sales representatives.

In the case of some acts excluded from the definition of "financial instruments business," the agent of the act is restricted under the provisions of legislation, and such acts are excluded only if performed by the designated agent; thus, financial instruments business operators cannot engage uniformly in all excluded acts. If, however, a business activity fulfills the conditions of the specific provision, it may basically be conducted as an "incidental business" (Article 35(1) of the FIEA) of a financial instruments business operator (a person who conducts type I financial instruments business or investment management business). The act in question can then be conducted without providing notification of subsidiary business (ibid., Article 35(3)) or obtaining approval for subsidiary business (Article 35(4)).

Nonetheless, the general supervisory provisions of Article 51 of the FIEA are thought to apply also to such business activities, which may therefore be subject to an order to improve business operation under that provision.

Further, even if a bank or the like engages in an act excluded from the definition of "financial instruments business," it does not require registration as a registered financial institution (Article 33-2 of the FIEA) except if financial institutions are not among the excluded agents of the act.

d. Specific acts excluded from "financial instruments business"

Acts specifically excluded from the definition of "financial instruments business" are listed in Table 5-1.

These acts may be classified as follows: first, acts excluded from the overall range of acts constituting "financial instruments business" (Article 2 (8) of the FIEA) — Table 5-1(1); second, acts excluded from the sale and purchase of securities (ibid., Article 2(8)(i)) and intermediary, brokerage, or agency service for the sale and purchase of securities, etc. (ibid., Article 2 (8)(ii)) — (4); third, acts excluded from intermediary, brokerage, or agency service, etc. for foreign market derivatives transactions (ibid., Article 2(8) (ii) & (iii)) — (5); fourth, acts excluded from intermediary, brokerage, or agency service, etc. for the sale and purchase of securities, etc. (ibid., Article 2(8)(ii), (iii) & (iv)) — (6); fifth, acts excluded from over-the-counter transactions in derivatives, etc. (ibid., Article 2(8)(iv)) — (2), (7), and (8); sixth, acts excluded from underwriting of securities (ibid., Article 2(8)(vi))

Chapter 5   Business regulations on financial instruments business operators, etc.

## Table 5-1.   Acts excluded from "financial instruments business"

（1）  Acts carried out by the State, local governments, the Bank of Japan, foreign governments, foreign local governments, and foreign central banks (Article 1-8-6(1) (i) of Implementing Order).

（2）  Non-securities-related over-the-counter transactions of derivatives, etc., or intermediary, brokerage, or agency service therefor (excluding business in electronic over-the-counter transactions of derivatives, etc.), conducted with professional customers such as financial instruments business operators, etc., qualified institutional investors, and stock companies with stated capital of one billion yen or more (Article 1-8-6 (1) (ii) of the Implementing Order; Article 15 of the Cabinet Office Ordinance on Definitions).

（3）  Investment management in a double-decker commodity fund scheme, in which all the assets are invested in a single juridical person (Article 1-8-6 (1) (iii) of the Implementing Order).

（4）  The sale of trust beneficial interests conducted through the agency or intermediation of a financial instruments business operator, etc. without any solicitation (limited to cases where it is clearly specified in the contract for the entrustment of business activities, etc. that the entirety of the solicitation is entrusted) (Article 1-8-6(1) (iv) of the Implementing Order; Article 16 (1) (i) of the Cabinet Office Ordinance on Definitions).

（5）  Non-securities-related foreign market derivatives transactions, etc. conducted with a financial instruments business operator or the like, or with a professional customer without any solicitation, conducted from a foreign state by a person who conducts non-securities-related foreign market derivatives transactions, etc. in the course of business in a foreign state (ibid., Article 16(1) (i-ii)).

（6）  Intermediary, brokerage or agency service for entrustment of transactions, conducted by a registered investment manager under entrustment by a foreign investment manager ("affiliated foreign investment operator") (ibid., Article 16(1) (ii) (2)).

（7）  Over-the-counter currency derivatives transactions (forward transactions or option transactions) performed by a person who conducts the purchase and sale of goods or other activities as part of its business, and in association with any of those transactions, conducted with a service provider as the counterparty, for the purpose of hedging the service provider's foreign exchange risk (ibid., Article 16(1) (iii)).

*631*

( 8 ) Over-the-counter currency derivatives transactions (forward transactions or option transactions), or intermediary, brokerage, or agency service therefor, performed by a listed company, etc. required to submit an internal control report, conducted with a subsidiary company or on its behalf for the purpose of hedging the subsidiary company's foreign exchange risk (ibid., Article 16(1)(iv)).

( 9 ) Underwriting of rights that are based on an anonymous partnership agreement, conducted by a financial instruments business operator (limited to a juridical person engaged in type II financial instruments business whose amount of stated capital or such is fifty million yen or more) for a wholly owned subsidiary company (stock company) in the leasing business (special underwriting) (ibid., Article 16(1)(v)).

(10) Underwriting of anonymous partnership investment equity in a so-called privately placed real-estate fund (equivalent to a so-called baby fund), conducted by a financial instruments business operator (limited to a juridical person engaged in type II financial instruments business) for the purpose of causing another anonymous partnership proprietor (equivalent to the so-called mother fund) to acquire the equity (ibid., Article 16(1)(vi)).

(11) Underwriting by an investment-based trust company or a foreign trust company of trust beneficial interests of which it is itself the trustee at the time of public offering or private placement of those beneficial interests (ibid., Article 16(1)(vii)).

(12) Acquiring share certificates so that they can be purchased by a type of holding company (in either partnership or trust format) termed a Japanese employee stock ownership plan (ESOP) (ibid., Article 16(1)(vii-ii)).

(13) Acts conducted under a discretionary investment contract on behalf of a group foreign operator ("affiliated foreign financial instruments business operator") (so-called offshore booking) (ibid., Article 16(1)(viii)(3)).

(14) Acts under a discretionary investment contract whereby a commodity trading advisor, etc. invests in a "currency derivative transaction" in association with a commodity investment for the purpose of hedging foreign exchange risk (ibid., Article 16(1)(ix)(4)).

(15) Conducting investment management business relating to a foreign investment trust in a foreign state under foreign laws and regulations (ibid., Article 16(1)(ix-ii)).

(16) Self-management in cases of collective investment schemes where all investment authority is entrusted to a registered investment manager under a discretionary investment contract, and the necessary notification, etc. has

Chapter 5　Business regulations on financial instruments business operators, etc.

been filed (ibid., Article 16(1)(x)).

(17)　Self-management in cases of collective investment schemes where, in a so-called double-decker real estate fund (baby fund), the manager of the mother fund (an anonymous partnership proprietor who is a registered investment manager, a notifier of specially permitted business activities, or a person engaged in special investment management business as prescribed in Article 48, paragraph 1 of the Supplementary Provisions of the 2006 Act for Partial Revision of the Securities and Exchange Act, etc.) has filed the necessary notification, etc. (Article 16 (1) (xi) of the Cabinet Office Ordinance on Definitions).

(18)　Self-management in a racehorse fund scheme (ibid., Article 16(1)(xii); Article 7(iv)(d) of the Cabinet Office Ordinance on Financial Instruments Services, Etc.).

(19)　Self-management in cases of foreign collective investment schemes where the equity investors (direct equity investors and indirect equity investors) are limited to a total of less than ten qualified institutional investors and notifiers of specially permitted business activities, and the amount invested by them does not exceed one-third of the total amount invested in the foreign collective investment scheme (Article 16(1) (xiii) of the Cabinet Office Ordinance on Definitions).

(20)　The acceptance of money deposits from a customer by a financial instruments business operator (limited to a juridical person engaged in type II financial instruments business whose amount of stated capital or such is fifty million yen or more) in connection with dealing in public offering or private placement in relation to trust beneficial interests or collective investment scheme equity, which money is separately managed (special securities, etc. management) (ibid., Article 16(1)(xiv)).

(21)　The acceptance of money deposits from a customer by a financial instruments business operator ((20) above) in connection with crowdfunding business, etc. with electronic means for customers' applications, which money is in custody in trust separately from the operator's own assets (special securities, etc. custody) (ibid., Article 16(1)(xiv-ii)).

(22)　Transfer of bonds, etc. by a foreign account management institution (ibid., Article 16(1)(xv)).

(23)　Transfer of investment trust beneficial interests in cases where the financial instruments business operator that directly markets those investment trust beneficial interests manages them separately (ibid., Article 16(1)(xvi)).

— (9) - (12); seventh, acts excluded from discretionary investment management (ibid., Article 2(8)(xii)) — (13)-(14); eighth, acts excluded from foreign investment trust management (ibid., Article 2(8)(xiv)) — (15); ninth, acts excluded from self-management of funds (ibid., Article 2(8)(xv)) — (3) and (16) - (19); tenth, acts excluded from acceptance of deposits of money or securities (ibid., Article 2(8)(xvi)) — (20)-(21); and eleventh, acts excluded from transfer of bonds, etc. (ibid., Article 2(8)(xvii)) — (22)-(23).

# 8. Categories of financial instruments business

### a. Overview

The FIEA classifies "financial instruments business" (Article 2(8) of the FIEA) into the categories "type I financial instruments business," "type II financial instruments business," "investment advisory and agency business," and "investment management business" (Article 28(1)-(4) of the FIEA).

The extent to which it is necessary to ensure a financial instruments business operator has a firm financial basis, and thus protect investors, differs depending on the nature of the services it provides. Business regulations have therefore been made structurally flexible by classifying financial instruments business according to the range of their business operations and establishing start-up regulations and conduct regulations for each category (Articles 29-4, 30(1) and 31-2 of the FIEA).

Registration requirements for financial instruments business operators are strictest for "type I financial instruments business" and become progressively less strict for "investment management business," "type II financial instruments business," and "investment advisory and agency business," in that order.

### b. Description of each category

( i ) "Type I financial instruments business"

Generally speaking, the term "type I financial instruments business" means, among financial instruments business, conducting any of the following in the course of business (Article 28(1) of the FIEA): (1) with respect to type I securities, sale and purchase, market transactions of derivatives, foreign market derivatives transactions, etc.; secondary

Chapter 5   Business regulations on financial instruments business operators, etc.

distribution of securities or solicitation for selling, etc. only for professional investors; or dealing in public offering, secondary distribution, or private placement of securities, or solicitation for selling, etc. only for professional investors (Article 2 (8) (i) – (iii), (v), (viii) & (ix) of the FIEA); (2) intermediary, brokerage, or agency service for commodity–related market transactions of derivatives; intermediary, brokerage, or agency service for entrustment; or brokerage for clearing of securities, etc. (ibid., Article 2(8) (ii), (iii) & (v)) (the 2012 revision of the FIEA); (3) over–the–counter transactions in derivatives, etc. (ibid., Article 2 (8) (iv) & (v)); (4) underwriting of securities (ibid., Article 2(8)(vi)); (5) proprietary trading system (PTS) acts (ibid., Article 2(8)(x)); or (6) acceptance of deposits of money or securities, or transfer of bonds, etc. (ibid., Article 2(8)(xvi) & (xvii)).

The sixth of these is termed "securities, etc. custody business" (Article 28 (5) of the FIEA).

These acts can be conducted only by a financial instruments business operator that is registered as an operator of a type I financial instruments business. This is because (1) transactions in type I securities with their high liquidity involve many parties; (2) over–the–counter transactions in derivatives are particularly highly specialized and risky; (3) underwriting of securities is highly specialized and entails underwriting risks; (4) proprietary trading systems (PTSs) are intended for many people to participate in, making smooth, stable operations management especially essential; and (5) in the case of securities etc. custody business, the proper right holders are at serious risk of losing their rights unless financial soundness is ensured.

(ⅱ)   Type II financial instruments business

Generally speaking, the term "type II financial instruments business" means, among financial instruments business, conducting any of the following in the course of business (Article 28(2) of the FIEA): (1) direct placement or private placement of securities (Article 2 (8) (vii) of the FIEA); (2) with respect to paragraph 2 securities, sale and purchase, market transactions of derivatives, foreign market derivatives transactions, etc.; secondary distribution of securities or solicitation for selling, etc. only for

*635*

professional investors; or dealing in public offering, secondary distribution, or private placement of securities, or solicitation for selling, etc. only for professional investors (Article 2(8)(i)-(iii), (v), (viii) & (ix) of the FIEA); (3) market transactions of derivatives (excluding commodity-related market transactions of derivatives), foreign market derivatives transactions, etc. unrelated to securities (ibid., Article 2(8)(i)-(iii) & (v)); or (4) the purchase without the purpose of resale of beneficiary certificates of investment trusts or beneficiary certificates of foreign investment trusts that have been directly placed or privately placed (ibid., Article 2(8)(xviii)).

(iii) Investment advisory and agency business

The term "investment advisory and agency business" means, among financial instruments business, conducting any of the following in the course of business (Article 28(3) of the FIEA): (1) investment advising (Article 2 (8)(xi) of the FIEA); or (2) agency or intermediary service for conclusion of an investment advisory contract or a discretionary investment contract (ibid., Article 2(8)(xiii)).

The first of these is termed "investment advisory business" (Article 28 (6) of the FIEA).

(iv) Investment management business

The term "investment management business" means, among financial instruments business, conducting any of the following in the course of business (Article 28(4) of the FIEA): (1) management of investment corporation assets (Article 2(8)(xii)(a) of the FIEA); (2) discretionary investment management (ibid., Article 2(8)(xii)(b)); (3) investment trust management (ibid., Article 2(8)(xiv)); or (4) self-management of funds (ibid., Article 2(8)(xv)).

The conduct of acts constituting investment management business by a financial institution is excluded from the definition of acts constituting "financial instruments business" (Article 2(8) of the FIEA), but it is made clear that such business is covered by the definition of "investment management business" (in the wording "among financial instruments business": Article 28(4) of the FIEA). Financial institutions are then prohibited from engaging in "investment management business" (Article 33

Chapter 5　Business regulations on financial instruments business operators, etc.

(1) of the FIEA).

Investors (including registered investment corporations) with respect to investment management business are termed "right holders" (Article 42(1) of the FIEA), and the property invested in is termed "investment property" (Article 35 (1) (xv) of the FIEA). The assets in which the investment property is invested are the invested assets (see ibid., Article 35(1) (xv) & (2) (vi)).

c . Securities-related business

(ⅰ) Intent

In the FIEA, the term "financial instruments business" is substituted for the "securities business" of the old Securities and Exchange Act, and its range is expanded to include businesses unrelated to securities. On the other hand, the so-called separation of the banking and securities sectors enshrined in Article 65 of the old Securities and Exchange Act is basically maintained (Article 33(1) of the FIEA). Accordingly, in order to define the range of acts that relate to "securities" and clearly delineate the range of business activities that financial institutions are in principle prohibited from conducting, the FIEA sets out the definition "securities-related business" as the equivalent of the old "securities business" (Article 28(8) of the FIEA).

Further, the conduct in the course of business of any of the acts constituting securities-related business (ibid., each item) by a financial institution is excluded from the definition of "financial instruments business" (Article 2(8) of the FIEA), but acts conducted by financial institutions are included in the definition of "securities-related business" (Article 28(8) of the FIEA); the conduct of securities-related business by financial institutions is then prohibited (Article 33(1) of the FIEA).

(ⅱ) Scope

The term "securities-related business" means conducting any of the following in the course of business: (1) sale and purchase of securities, or intermediary, brokerage, or agency service therefor; (2) intermediary, brokerage, or agency service for the entrustment of the sale and purchase of securities on financial instruments exchange markets or foreign financial instruments markets; (3) market transactions of derivatives relating to

*637*

securities; (4) over-the-counter transactions in derivatives relating to securities; (5) foreign market derivatives transactions relating to securities; (6) intermediary, brokerage, or agency service of "transactions of securities-related derivatives" ((3)-(5) above), or intermediary, brokerage, or agency service of the entrustment of the transactions in (3) and (5); (7) certain types of brokerage for clearing of securities, etc.; or (8) underwriting of securities; secondary distribution of securities or solicitation for selling, etc. only for professional investors; or dealing in public offering, secondary distribution, or private placement of securities, or solicitation for selling, etc. only for professional investors (Article 28(8) (i)-(viii) of the FIEA; Article 15-2 and Article 15-3 of the Implementing Order).

The sixth, seventh, and eighth of these are termed "underwriting of securities, etc." (Article 130(1) (ix) of the Cabinet Office Ordinance on Financial Instruments Services, Etc.).

(iii) Distinctions between type I financial instruments business

Within the financial instruments business category, both persons conducting securities business as defined in the old Securities and Exchange Act and persons accepting entrustment of over-the-counter financial futures transactions in the course of business as defined in the old Financial Futures Exchange Act are classified as financial instruments business operators engaged in "type I financial instruments business" (Article 28(1) of the FIEA). On the other hand, considering how these two have been treated in the past and the actual nature of what they do, it may not necessarily be appropriate to treat both identically.

For that reason, the FIEA distinguishes between financial instruments business operators engaged in type I financial instruments business depending on whether they engage in securities-related business. Specifically, (1) money and securities deposited by customers in connection with securities-related business remain subject to a strict separate-custody requirement, and a new external-audit requirement has been adopted (Article 43-2 of the FIEA); (2) financial instruments business operators (operators of a type I financial instruments business) engaged in securities-related business are subject to a requirement to join an investor protection fund (Articles 79-27(1) and 79-20(1) of the FIEA; Article 18-7-2(1) of the

Chapter 5    Business regulations on financial instruments business operators, etc.

Implementing Order); (3) the name "securities company" may be used by financial instruments business operators engaged in securities-related business (which are assumed to be operators of a type I financial instruments business) (Article 25 of the Supplementary Provisions of the 2006 Act for Partial Revision of the Securities and Exchange Act, Etc.); and (4) the category of business related to registration of financial instruments business is different (Articles 29-2(1) (v), 28(1) (i), (i-ii) & (ii) and 31(4) of the FIEA).

# B. Start-up regulations for financial instruments businesses

## 1. The registration system

### a. "Permission systems" in administrative law theory

In administrative law theory, the term "permission system" refers to a legal framework whereby a general prohibition on the conduct of certain types of activities by citizens is, upon application by a citizen, lifted in individual, specific cases if after examination certain requirements are found to be met. Licenses and registrations under the FIEA both constitute the lifting of general prohibitions in individual, specific cases under such a permission system.

Under the FIEA, financial instruments business is not allowed to be conducted by any person who is not registered (Article 29 of the FIEA); this constitutes a general prohibition. A person who has obtained registration (lifting the prohibition in an individual, specific case) — a financial instruments business operator — may engage in financial instruments business (Articles 29-3, 35 (1) and 35-2 (1) of the FIEA). The FIEA prescribes no system for renewing registration.

### b. Licensing systems and registration systems

Generally, insofar as start-up regulations under financial regulatory laws are concerned, the rules for licensing are stricter than those for registration, while permission and authorization lie midway between the two.

As regards start-up regulations for "securities businesses" under the

*639*

Securities and Exchange Act, a licensing system was introduced when the law was revised in 1965. Four types of licenses were established: for dealing, brokerage, underwriting, and selling. The start-up regulations of a general, preventive nature imposed under this licensing system were relaxed in the 1998 revision of the Securities and Exchange Act (Financial System Reform Act) as the transition was made to ex post facto checks under a registration system. Asset management (investment trust management, discretionary investment business) remained subject to authorization.

With licensing systems, administrative discretion with respect to conditions is often allowed because the requirements for commencing business are abstract; administrative discretion with respect to effects is also allowed in that often there is no requirement to grant a license even if licensing criteria are met (see, however, Article 80(2) of the FIEA). With a registration system, by contrast, there is little discretion with respect to conditions because the requirements are specifically set out, and discretion with respect to effects is basically not allowed in that granting of registration is required unless it must be denied because certain conditions for refusal of registration are met (Articles 29-3 and Article 29-4 of the FIEA).

c. Design of start-up regulations

The FIEA imposes start-up regulations on operators in the form of a registration system. That is because, unless start-up regulations were imposed, unqualified operators could not be debarred from entering the business at the "gateway," and operators that engaged in unsuitable conduct after entering the business could not be forced to "exit" by canceling their license or registration; moreover, it is not always easy for the supervisory authorities to gather information on operators.

Such start-up regulations do not constitute the only approach to regulatory oversight of operators. The Act on Specified Commercial Transactions, for example, prescribes no start-up regulations; instead it imposes conduct regulations on operators and defines the supervisory powers of the administrative authorities over operators: to order submission of reports and materials, to conduct inspections, to give instructions, and to issue business suspension orders. The FIEA, by contrast, continues to employ the start-up regulation-based approach for the reasons cited above.

Chapter 5   Business regulations on financial instruments business operators, etc.

ｄ. Administrative action against unregistered operators

With the start-up regulation-based approach, it is registered operators that are subject to administrative oversight. The administrative authorities therefore used to deal with unregistered operators engaging in so-called fraudulent solicitation of unlisted shares or the like by issuing a warning or notifying the investigative authorities (II-1-1 (6) and (7) of the Comprehensive Guidelines for Supervision of Financial Instruments Business Operators, Etc.), and criminal penalties were basically the only recourse.

Recently, however, steps have been taken to beef up administrative action against unregistered operators while maintaining the start-up regulation-based approach. First, the Securities and Exchange Surveillance Commission now petitions courts for emergency prohibition or suspension orders against unregistered operators (Article 192 of the FIEA). Second, in addition to the ban on the use of confusing trade names or names by unregistered operators (Article 31-3 of the FIEA), a series of measures was adopted in the 2011 revision of the FIEA. Specifically, (1) sales, etc. of unlisted securities (corporate bond certificates, share certificates, share option certificates, etc.) by unregistered operators have in principle been invalidated (Article 171-2 of the FIEA; Article 33-4-4 and Article 33-4-5 of the Implementing Order; establishment of a so-called civil rule); (2) advertising and soliciting by unregistered operators have been prohibited (Article 31-3-2 of the FIEA); and (3) penalties on unregistered operators and so on have been increased (from imprisonment with work for not more than three years or a fine of not more than three million yen, with a fine on juridical persons of not more than three million yen under dual liability, to imprisonment with work for not more than five years or a fine of not more than five million yen, with a fine on juridical persons of not more than 500 million yen under dual liability; Articles 197-2(x-iv)-(x-vi), 207(1)(ii) of the FIEA).

The civil rule in (1) above is explained as in principle invalidating a purchase contract or the like, on the presumption that the sale of unlisted securities by an unregistered operator is an act of profiteering, a type of violation of public policy (Article 90 of the Civil Code), even if the investor does not specifically prove it to be so.

*641*

e. Optional registration system for credit rating businesses

（ⅰ） Overview

The registration system for financial instruments business is compulsory: engaging in financial instruments business requires obtaining registration. By contrast, the system of regulatory oversight of credit rating agencies established under the 2009 revision of the FIEA (Chapter III-3) employs an optional registration system allowing juridical persons engaged in "credit rating business" to obtain registration from the Commissioner of the FSA (Article 2(34), (35) and 66-27 of the FIEA). A person who has obtained such registration is a "credit rating agency" (Article 2(36) of the FIEA). Credit rating business does not constitute a financial instruments business.

This system has been adopted to ensure that regulations apply specifically to rating agencies whose credit ratings are widely used in financial and capital markets and that are thus in a position to exert a significant influence on investors' investment decisions; the idea is thereby to restrict their scope of application to what is necessary and reasonable, in order to avoid having a chilling effect on overall discussion about credit risk.

Because the system *allows* one to register, there is no penalty for engaging in credit rating business without being registered. Persons who obtain registration by wrongful means are subject to imprisonment with work for not more than three years or a fine of not more than three million yen, with a fine on juridical persons of not more than 300 million yen under dual liability (Articles 198(ii) and 207(1)(iii) of the FIEA).

（ⅱ） Conduct regulations for financial instruments business operators, etc.

Under this optional registration system, it must be ensured that investment decisions are not distorted due to investors confusing credit ratings determined by registered credit rating agencies with credit ratings determined by unregistered credit rating companies. To that end financial instruments business operators, etc. and their officers and employees are prohibited from the act of providing a customer with a credit rating determined by a person engaged in a credit rating business other than a credit rating agency, without informing the customer of the fact that the person who has determined the credit rating has not obtained registration, the significance of the registration, and any other matters, thereby soliciting

Chapter 5   Business regulations on financial instruments business operators, etc.

him/her to conclude a contract for financial instruments transaction (Article 38 (iii) of the FIEA; Articles 116-2 and 116-3 of the Cabinet Office Ordinance on Financial Instruments Services, Etc.).

This prohibition is expected to be effective in encouraging juridical persons engaged in a credit rating business, especially credit rating companies in a position to exert a significant influence on investors' investment decisions, to voluntarily obtain registration. Indeed, the major credit rating companies (including the Japanese affiliates of foreign rating company groups) have all obtained registration.

(iii)   Special provision for foreign rating company groups

In the case of foreign rating company groups (Moody's, Standards & Poor's, and Fitch Ratings), only the groups' Japanese affiliates are registered as credit rating agencies; other juridical persons in each group are not registered. These other juridical persons are thus unregistered operators, making it necessary for financial instruments business operators, etc. to explain to customers the matters prescribed by law; but to streamline procedures for financial instruments business operators, etc., a special provision has been established allowing group designation with respect to the matters to be explained (Article 116-3 (2) of the Cabinet Office Ordinance on Financial Instruments Services, Etc.).

This special provision had to be established in order to prevent disruptions in administrative procedures, since the FIEA prescribes a system that assumes, on the principle of reciprocity, registration also of foreign juridical person within foreign rating company groups. Another conceivable legislative approach would be to adopt a system of providing notification such as that for foreign audit firms, etc. (Articles 1-3 (7) and 34-35 (1) of the Certified Public Accountants Act).

## 2. Comprehensiveness of start-up regulations

a. Overview

In order to overhaul previously compartmentalized industry legislation and establish a comprehensive, cross-sectoral legislative framework, the FIEA expands the range of businesses subject to regulation by subsuming them under financial instruments business (Article 2 (8) of the FIEA). In line with the trend toward relaxing entry regulations, it then integrates start-up regulations into a single registration system for financial instruments business (Article 29 of the FIEA) except proprietary trading system (PTS) business, for which a system of authorization has been maintained (Article 30(1) of the FIEA).

A financial instruments business operator may in principle conduct a business constituting a financial instruments business with a single registration. Authorization for PTS management business can also be obtained after obtaining registration (Article 30(1) of the FIEA).

b. Exclusion of "undesirable operators"

The shift to a registration system is expected to lead to the provision of a greater range of financial instruments and services to users by encouraging new market entry by "desirable operators," as it were. On the other hand, it also undeniably makes it easier for "undesirable operators," as it were, to enter the market, increasing the regulatory burden of conducting oversight and surveillance through ex post facto checks.

In consideration of such concerns, the FIEA takes several steps to ensure that "undesirable operators" are properly supervised and monitored. First, minimum capital levels are maintained for businesses previously subject to authorization (Article 29-4(1)(iv) of the FIEA; Article 15-7(1)(i)-(iii) of the Implementing Order) with the exception of over-the-counter transactions of derivatives, etc.

Second, new criteria have been established for examining whether, among conditions for refusal of registration, that one personnel structure applies (Article 29-4 (1) (i) (e) of the FIEA; Article 13 of the Cabinet Office Ordinance on Financial Instruments Services, Etc.). The condition on personnel structure was included among the conditions for refusal of registration in order to prevent entry of unqualified operators into the financial instruments business from creating obstacles to protection of investors, thus undermining public trust in the financial instruments business. Whether an operator who is "a person who does not have a personnel structure sufficient to conduct business in an appropriate manner" is not alone is necessarily sufficient in terms of preventing the entry of unqualified operators and ensuring that criteria are clear and predictable.

Chapter 5   Business regulations on financial instruments business operators, etc.

Based on the Securities and Exchange Surveillance Commission's inspection results and proposal of February 8, 2011, a condition on personnel structure was established also for the investment advisory and agency business under the 2011 revision of the FIEA (Article 29-4(1)(i)(e)).

Third, under the 2014 revision of the FIEA, a condition on operational organization was added to the conditions for refusal of registration (Article 29-4(1)(i)(f) of the FIEA).

## 3. Structurally flexible start-up regulations

A graded set of conditions for refusal of registration depending on the type of business in which the financial instruments business operator will engage has been established (Article 29-4(1) of the FIEA); thus a person who has obtained registration as a financial instruments business operator cannot necessarily engage in all forms of financial instruments business. It therefore has to be determined whether the person who intends to obtain registration as a financial instruments business meets the conditions for refusal of registration in the "category of business" recorded on the written application for registration (Article 29-2(1)(v) of the FIEA).

To add a new "category of business," a financial instruments business operator must complete the procedures for registration of change (Article 31(4) of the FIEA; Article 22 and Appended Form 1 of the Cabinet Office Ordinance on Financial Instruments Services, Etc.). It is then determined whether the operator meets the conditions for refusal of registration in the newly added "category of business" (Articles 31(5) and 29-4 of the FIEA).

The term "categories of business" means (1) business relating to type I securities; (2) business relating to commodity-related market transactions of derivatives; (3) business relating to over-the-counter transactions of derivatives, etc.; (4) wholesale underwriting that involves holding discussions to fix the terms of wholesale underwriting contracts; (5) other forms of wholesale underwriting; (6) underwriting other than wholesale underwriting; (7) proprietary trading system (PTS) management business; (8) securities etc. custody business; (9) type II financial instruments business; (10) investment advisory and agency business; and (11) investment management (Article 29-2(1)(v) of the FIEA).

*645*

# 4. Special provisions on start-up regulations

a. Overview

A number of special provisions relating to the duty to register as a financial instruments business have been established. Specifically, these are (1) the special provision on registration requirements for type I crowdfunding business (Article 29-4-2 of the FIEA); (2) the special provision on registration requirements for type II crowdfunding business (Article 29-4-3 of the FIEA); (3) the special provision on registration requirements for investment management businesses serving qualified investors (Article 29-5 of the FIEA); (4) exclusion from application for acts constituting securities-related business of foreign securities brokers (Article 58-2 of the FIEA); (5) the permission system for foreign securities brokers to engage in part of the underwriting business (Article 59(1) of the FIEA); (6) the permission system for foreign securities brokers to engage in transaction-at-exchange operations (Article 60(1) of the FIEA); (7) the permission system for business in electronic over-the-counter transactions of derivatives, etc. (Article 60-14 of the FIEA); (8) exclusion from application for persons engaged in investment advisory business or investment management business in a foreign state (Article 61 of the FIEA); (9) the notification system for specially permitted businesses for qualified institutional investors, etc. (Article 63(1) & (2) of the FIEA); (10) exclusion from application for sale and purchase, etc. of trust beneficial interests by trust companies and foreign trust companies, etc. (Article 65-5 (1) of the FIEA); (11) exclusion from application for the sale of trust beneficial interests by the Japan Housing Finance Agency (ibid., Article 65-5 (3)); (12) the registration system for financial instruments intermediary services (Article 66 of the FIEA); and (13) exemption of the Japan Finance Corporation from the duty to register (Article 63(1) of the Japan Finance Corporation Act).

b. Special provisions for acts constituting securities-related business of foreign securities brokers

(i) Foreign securities brokers

The term "foreign securities broker" means a person other than financial

646

Chapter 5   Business regulations on financial instruments business operators, etc.

instruments business operators and financial institutions able to become registered financial institutions, which is governed by the laws and regulations of a foreign state, and which engages in securities-related business in a foreign state (Article 58 of the FIEA; Article 1-9 of the Implementing Order).

A person that does not engage in securities-related business in a foreign state is not a foreign securities broker. For example, a person who conducts only derivatives transactions unrelated to securities in a foreign state is not a foreign securities broker.

( ii )　The in-principle prohibition on foreign securities brokers conducting acts constituting securities-related business

Foreign securities brokers are in principle forbidden from conducting acts constituting securities-related business (Article 28 (8) (i) - (xviii) of the FIEA) with a person in Japan as the counterparty (Article 58-2 of the FIEA).

This prohibition is carried over from the old Act on Foreign Securities Brokers enacted in 1971. Foreign securities brokers are prohibited from conducting such acts not only in Japan but also directly from outside Japan, regardless of whether they do so in the course of business. This is because even one-time acts not clearly intended to be conducted repeatedly and continuously in Japan need to be deemed a form of business, as it were, and restricted in order to protect investors in Japan, since the principals of those acts are business operators.

However, foreign securities brokers may conduct such acts with a financial instruments business operator engaged in securities-related business as the counterparty, or in any other cases specified by cabinet order (ibid., proviso). That applies even if a foreign securities broker conducts those acts in the course of business, in which case registration as a financial instruments business is not required. Conduct regulations on financial instruments business operators, etc. are not applied in cases where foreign securities brokers conduct acts and business operations covered by this special provision.

This special provision pertains to securities-related business conducted by foreign securities brokers; it is not applied in cases where foreign operators

*647*

other than foreign securities brokers conduct such acts, or foreign securities brokers conduct financial instruments business other than securities-related business.

(iii) Special provision for cases where the other party is a financial institution, etc.

The Cabinet Order in question specifies, first, cases where a foreign securities broker carries out certain acts from a foreign state with the government or the Bank of Japan, certain financial institutions, and financial instruments business operators engaged in investment management business, etc. (Article 17-3(i) of the Implementing Order; Article 208-36 - 212 of the Cabinet Office Ordinance on Financial Instruments Services, Etc.).

(iv) Special provisions for cases where no solicitation takes place

Second, the Cabinet Order specifies cases where a foreign securities broker carries out the following acts from a foreign state without solicitation: (1) intermediary, brokerage, or agency service, etc. for the sale and purchase of securities or securities-related foreign market derivatives transactions, based on an order from a customer in Japan; and (2) through agency or intermediary service performed by a financial instruments business operator engaged in securities-related business (operator of a type I financial instruments business), sale and purchase of securities, securities-related foreign market derivatives transactions, or securities-related over-the-counter transactions in derivatives carried out with a customer in Japan (in the case of over-the-counter derivatives transactions, limited to a financial instruments business operator, etc., a qualified institutional investor, a stock company with stated capital of not less than one billion yen, etc.) (Article 17-3 (ii) of the Implementing Order; Article 213 of the Cabinet Office Ordinance on Financial Instruments Services, Etc.).

Instances in which a financial instruments business operator brokers the transaction are not specified in (2) above because in the case of brokerage the principal of the act conducted with the customer in Japan is not the foreign securities broker but the financial instruments business operator. Cases of agency and intermediary services performed for registered financial institutions are not covered by the special provision in (2).

648

Chapter 5   Business regulations on financial instruments business operators, etc.

The old Foreign Securities Brokers Act and related regulations required that, in addition to not conducting "solicitation," foreign brokers also not conduct "acts similar to solicitation" in order to be eligible for the special provisions (Article 3(2) of the old Act on Foreign Securities Brokers; Article 2(ii) of the Implementing Order on the old Act on Foreign Securities Brokers). "Acts similar to solicitation" were defined specifically as (1) conducting advertising on investment in securities through such media as newspapers, magazines, television, and radio (excluding advertising directed primarily at persons outside Japan); (2) holding briefing sessions on investment in securities; (3) providing information on investment in securities orally, in writing, by telephone, or by other means of communication; and (4) conducting acts similar to (1)-(3) (Article 7 of the Cabinet Office Ordinance on the old Act on Foreign Securities Brokers). No such requirement, however, is imposed under the FIEA and related regulations; thus, these special provisions may apply even to a foreign broker conducting "acts similar to solicitation," although they do not of course apply if the broker conducts what is effectively "solicitation" under the guise of "acts similar to solicitation."

In contrast, registration as a financial instruments business is not required for the conduct of non-securities-related over-the-counter transactions in derivatives, etc. by a foreign securities broker only if the customer is a financial instruments business operator, etc., a qualified institutional investor, a stock company with stated capital of not less than one billion yen, or the like (Article 2(8) of the FIEA; Article 1-8-6(1)(ii) of the Implementing Order; Article 15 of the Cabinet Office Ordinance on Definitions).

(ⅴ)   Special provision on discussions for fixing the terms of wholesale underwriting contracts

Third, the Cabinet Order specifies cases where a foreign securities broker, among its business of underwriting securities, holds a discussion solely to fix the terms of the "wholesale underwriting contract" with the issuer or holder of the securities (excluding a financial instruments business operator, etc.) in Japan (Article 17-3(iii) of the Implementing Order).

This special provision enables a foreign securities broker to act as a so-called managing underwriter and hold discussions to fix the terms of a wholesale underwriting contract in Japan. Wholesale underwriting of securities can be divided into three stages: (1) discussions for fixing the terms of the wholesale underwriting contract; (2) conclusion of the wholesale underwriting contract; and (3) execution of the wholesale underwriting contract. This special provision permits only the first of these acts in Japan; the foreign securities broker in question is not allowed to engage in the second, concluding the wholesale underwriting contract, in Japan. Further, cases of secondary distribution of the securities or solicitation for selling, etc. only for professional investors, or dealing in public offering, private placement, or secondary distribution of the securities or in solicitation for selling, etc. only for professional investors, are excluded if conducted in Japan. Therefore, this special provision is not recognized if the underwritten securities are sold in Japan; it is recognized only if they are sold outside Japan.

c. Permission system for foreign securities brokers to engage in part of the underwriting business

A foreign securities broker may, without obtaining registration as a financial instruments business and with the permission of the Commissioner of the FSA, participate in a "wholesale underwriting contract" (limited to a contract concluded for public offering or secondary distribution of securities: Article 21 (4) of the FIEA) — what is referred to as "underwriting business" — in Japan, amongst its business of underwriting of securities, in cases where it does not hold a discussion to fix the terms of the wholesale underwriting contract with the issuer or holder of the securities, and in Japan, does not conduct secondary distribution of the securities, solicitation for selling, etc. only for professional investors, or dealing in public offering, private placement, or secondary distribution of the securities or in solicitation for selling, etc. only for professional investors (Article 59(1) of the FIEA; Article 17-4 of the Implementing Order).

Such permission is in principle required for each individual act. Participation in a wholesale underwriting contract, the permitted act, means the conclusion of a wholesale underwriting contract. The foreign securities broker granted permission may conclude a wholesale underwriting contract in Japan as long as it does not act as managing underwriter and engages in

Chapter 5   Business regulations on financial instruments business operators, etc.

no selling of the underwritten securities in Japan. In other words, the foreign securities broker in question may participate in the underwriting syndicate as an ordinary underwriter if the wholesale underwriting contract is concluded in Japan with the condition that the securities are sold outside Japan.

This permission system was established at the time of the enactment of the Act on Foreign Securities Brokers in 1971 with the goal of promoting the development of Japan's capital markets, being a less cumbersome arrangement than the licensing system for establishing branches of foreign securities companies. Today, however, it must be admitted that it has little real purpose.

In practice, this permission system has now fallen into disuse; instead a securities company in Japan "intermediates" underwriting by an "overseas affiliated company" (see Article 37 of the Japan Securities Dealers Association, Rules Concerning Underwriting, Etc. of Securities), and the overseas affiliated company neither holds discussions to fix the terms of, nor concludes, a wholesale underwriting contract in Japan.

d. Permission system for foreign securities brokers to engage in transaction-at-exchange operations

A Foreign Securities Broker may, without obtaining registration as a financial instruments business and with the permission of the Commissioner of the FSA, engage in the sale and purchase of securities and market transactions of derivatives ("transaction at exchange") on a financial instruments exchange in the course of business ("transaction-at-exchange operations") (Article 60(1) of the FIEA).

The permission system for transaction-at-exchange operations makes possible so-called remote membership of financial instruments exchanges. It was established by the 2003 revision of the Securities and Exchange Act with the goals of (1) increasing liquidity on Japanese exchange markets by allowing direct participation by foreign securities brokers; and (2) boosting the international competitiveness of Japanese exchanges by enabling cooperation between Japanese and overseas exchanges by such means as cross-membership (whereby exchanges mutually recognize securities companies from the partner country or region as qualified members, thus

651

enabling participation by overseas securities brokers).

Foreign securities brokers are not allowed to conduct intermediary, brokerage, or agency service for transactions by investors who are residents of Japan. On the other hand, if, outside Japan, a foreign securities broker conducts intermediary, brokerage, or agency service for entrustment of a transaction by a non-resident on a Japanese exchange, that act is basically outside the scope of FIEA regulations.

Two special requirements are prescribed for permission to engage in transaction-at-exchange operations: (1) mutual assurance of investigative cooperation (Article 189 (2) (i) of the FIEA) by the foreign financial instruments regulatory authority of a state where the head office or "transaction-at-exchange office" (the business office or office where transaction-at-exchange operations are conducted: Article 60-2(1) (iii) of the FIEA) of the applicant for permission is located; and (2) the conclusion of an agreement on provision of information between the "establisher of a foreign financial instruments exchange market" (Article 60-2(1) (vi) of the FIEA) of which the transaction-at-exchange office of the applicant for permission is a member and the financial instruments exchange in which the applicant for permission will become a trading participant, or the implementation of similar measures (Article 60-3 (1) (ii) & (iii) of the FIEA).

With respect to the measures in (2), the financial instruments exchange in question may, under the laws and regulations of the state concerned, need to obtain the required action from the foreign financial instruments regulatory authority (such as the issue of a no-action letter or a license). In February 2009, the Tokyo Stock Exchange brought in a "Remote Trading Participant System," which awards trading qualifications to foreign securities brokers that have obtained permission to engage in transaction-at-exchange operations ("authorized transaction-at-exchange operators": Article 60-4 (1) of the FIEA); and in November 2010, it was certified by the Securities and Futures Commission (SFC) of Hong Kong. In May 2015, the business operator in Hong Kong became the first authorized transaction-at-exchange operator.

Chapter 5　Business regulations on financial instruments business operators, etc.

e. The permission system for foreign operators engaged in business in electronic over-the-counter transactions of derivatives, etc.

To enable financial instruments business operators, etc., and the like in Japan to make use of electronic trading platforms available abroad, the 2012 revision of the FIEA established a permission system for foreign operators engaged in "business in electronic over-the-counter transactions of derivatives, etc." (specified over-the-counter transactions in derivatives using an electronic data processing system, or intermediary, brokerage, or agency service therefor) (Article 60-14(1) of the FIEA; Article 17-10-2 of the Implementing Order).

Under this system, "authorized implementers of electronic over-the-counter transactions of derivatives, etc." (ibid., Article 60-14(2) of the FIEA) are not required to register as type I financial instruments business, and their electronic trading platforms are specified among those whose use is required for "specified over-the-counter transactions in derivatives" (Article 40-7 of the FIEA).

When engaging in business in electronic over-the-counter transactions of derivatives, etc., foreign securities brokers are not eligible for the system of special exemptions for foreign securities brokers (Article 58-2 of the FIEA; Article 17-3 of the Implementing Order).

f. Special provisions for persons engaged in investment advisory business or investment management business in a foreign state

(i) Special provision for persons engaged in investment advisory business in a foreign state

A person engaged in investment advisory business in a foreign state may, without obtaining registration as a financial instruments business, perform investment advisory business exclusively for financial instruments business operators engaged in investment management business or registered financial institutions engaged in investment management business (Article 61(1) of the FIEA; Article 17-11(1) of the Implementing Order).

This is because the other parties in such cases possess sufficient specialized knowledge and experience, so there is little need for investor protection through regulation.

*653*

( ii ) Special provision for persons engaged in discretionary investment business in a foreign state

A person engaged in investment management business (discretionary investment business) in a foreign state may, without being registered, perform discretionary investment business exclusively for financial instruments business operators engaged in discretionary investment business, financial instruments business operators engaged in investment management business other than discretionary investment business, or registered financial institutions engaged in investment management business (Article 61(2) of the FIEA; Article 17-11(2) of the Implementing Order).

This special provision is available even if the person in question has obtained registration only for the investment advisory and agency business in Japan, and such persons are not subject to conduct regulations on investment management business, as the law clearly states (Article 61(2) & (4) of the FIEA).

( iii ) Special provision for persons engaged in the business of self-management of group investment scheme equity in a foreign state

A person engaged in the business of self-management of collective investment scheme equity in a foreign state (Article 2(8)(xv) of the FIEA) may, without being registered, perform self-management business exclusively for financial instruments business operators engaged in investment management business or registered financial institutions engaged in investment management business (Article 61(3) of the FIEA; Article 17-11(1) of the Implementing Order).

This special provision is available even if the person in question has obtained registration only for the investment advisory and agency business in Japan, and such persons are not subject to conduct regulations on investment management business, as the law clearly states (Article 61(3) & (4) of the FIEA).

On the other hand, this special provision is not allowed if the other party is a notifier of specially permitted business activities with respect to a so-called fund for professional investors (a person engaged in the business of self-management), since whether it meets the condition on personnel

Chapter 5   Business regulations on financial instruments business operators, etc.

structure (Article 29-4(1) (i) (e) of the FIEA) for investment management business is unconfirmed, and it is not necessarily guaranteed to have sufficient specialized knowledge and experience.

(iv)  Duty of foreign operators to provide notification of establishment of facilities for collecting information

To promote the public interest and protect investors by promptly assessing the state of foreign operators active in Japan, a foreign securities broker (including "those whose business is closely related to securities-related business") or a person who conducts investment advisory business or investment management business in a foreign state is, when it establishes a representative office or any other facility in Japan for the purposes of collection or provision of information, required to provide notification in advance (Article 62 of the FIEA; Article 233 (1) of the Cabinet Office Ordinance on Financial Instruments Services, Etc.).

The collection and provision of information in Japan, and facilities for that purpose such as a representative office, do not basically constitute financial instruments business; therefore, this duty to provide notification in advance is not a special provision on registration as a financial instruments business.

g.  The notification system for specially permitted businesses for qualified institutional investors, etc.

( i )  Intent

The sale or solicitation (including direct placement or private placement) of collective investment scheme (fund) equity (Article 2(2) (v) (vi) of the FIEA) is a type II financial instruments business (Article 28(2) (i) (ii) of the FIEA), and self-management of those assets mainly for investment in securities or derivatives transactions constitutes investment management business (ibid., Article 2 (4) (iii) and (8) (xv)); hence, registration as a financial instruments business is required.

By contrast, when the Securities and Exchange Act was revised in 2006, the FIEA, in order to ensure the soundness of capital markets while promoting financial innovations through funds engaged in healthy activities, did not impose a registration system on persons engaged in the business of direct private placement or self-management of so-called funds for

*655*

professional investors ("specially permitted businesses for qualified institutional investors, etc."); instead, in a bid to make business regulations more structurally flexible, it required them to register as "notifiers of specially permitted business activities" so that it would be possible to accurately assess their situation (Article 63(1) & (2) of the FIEA).

On the other hand, in view of the increase in fraudulent solicitation and victimization of general (amateur) investors, regulations were beefed up under the 2015 revision of the FIEA. While the notification system has been maintained, start-up regulations, conduct regulations, and supervisory measures have been imposed similar to those for registered operators (financial instruments business operators); thus, such businesses are in effect regulated and supervised on a par with registered operators.

( ii ) Condition for classification as a specially permitted business

The condition for classification as a specially permitted business for qualified institutional investors, etc. is the conduct of either (1) the business of direct private placement for "qualified institutional investors, etc." (one or more qualified institutional investors, or no more than 49 persons other than qualified institutional investors — termed "investors served by specially permitted businesses"), or (2) the business of self-management of money, etc. invested or contributed exclusively by qualified institutional investors, etc. (Article 63 (1) of the FIEA; Article 17-12 (1), (2) & (3) of the Implementing Order).

Originally only the number of persons was limited — to no more than 49 general investors — but with the 2015 revision of the FIEA, the 49 or fewer investors have been restricted to certain investors able to make investment decisions and persons closely connected with the specially permitted business. Specifically, they are restricted to, at the time of solicitation and transfer: (1) the State, the Bank of Japan, local governments, special corporations, and independent administrative agencies; (2) financial instruments business operators, etc., listed companies, corporations capitalized at 50 million yen or more, corporations with net assets of 50 million yen or more, and subsidiaries and affiliates of such corporations; (3) fund managers, etc. and parties closely connected with them; (4) specific purpose companies (TMK); (5) corporate pension funds and surviving

Chapter 5   Business regulations on financial instruments business operators, etc.

employees' pension funds with at least 10 billion yen in financial investment assets; (6) foreign corporations; (7) individuals possessing at least 100 million yen in assets who have had a brokerage account for at least a year; (8) corporations with at least 100 million yen in assets; and (9) asset custody companies, etc. (Article 17-12(1) of the Implementing Order; Article 233-2 of the Cabinet Office Ordinance on Financial Instruments Services, Etc.).

The definition of venture funds (investing in excess of 80 percent of assets in unlisted shares, etc.) has exceptionally been expanded to include certain persons possessing investment knowledge and experience (Article 17-12(2) of the Implementing Order; Articles 233-3 and 233-4 of the Cabinet Office Ordinance on Financial Instruments Services, Etc.), and measures have been established to protect them (Article 63(9)(10) of the FIEA; Article 17-13-2 of the Implementing Order; Article 239-2 of the Cabinet Office Ordinance on Financial Instruments Services, Etc.).

(ⅲ)   Special provisions governing the restriction on number of persons

To prevent the restriction to no more than 49 investors being circumvented through adoption of a fund-of-funds (FOF) format, first, if the equity investors (the mother fund) in the fund (the baby fund) include a *tokutei mokuteki kaisha* (TMK, or special purpose company), an anonymous partnership proprietor, a special purpose company (SPC), or another collective investment scheme (e.g., a Civil Code partnership) in which even a single person who is not a qualified institutional investor (i.e., who is a general investor) has invested, the operation of the baby fund does not constitute a specially permitted business for qualified institutional investors, etc., and use of the notification system is not permitted (Article 63(1)(i)(a)- (c)(ii) of the FIEA; Article 235(i) of the Cabinet Office Ordinance on Financial Instruments Services, Etc.). Trusts are not mentioned.

Second, if the mother fund consists solely of limited partnerships (LPSs) or limited liability partnerships (LLPs) (or similar partnerships based on foreign laws and regulations) in which general investors have invested, and the total number of general investors in the mother fund and the baby fund combined is no more than 49, the requirement on the number of investors is fulfilled with respect to the operator of the baby fund (Article 235(ii)(a) of the Cabinet Office Ordinance on Financial Instruments Services, Etc.).

*657*

Furthermore, if the operator of the mother fund (the LPS or LLP) is a financial instruments business operator, etc. engaged in the investment management business, there is no need to total up the number of general investors in the mother fund (ibid., Article 235 (ii) (a) (β)). This measure can be described as giving preferential policy treatment to LPSs and LLPs, for which a registration system and so on have been established under special governing legislation.

Third, if the operator of the mother fund and of the baby fund are the same (except if an anonymous partnership), and the total number of general investors in the mother fund and the baby fund combined is no more than 49, the requirement on the number of investors is fulfilled with respect to the operator of the baby fund (Article 235 (ii) (b) of the Cabinet Office Ordinance on Financial Instruments Services, Etc.).

(iv) Exclusions from the use of specially permitted business services

With the 2015 revision of the FIEA, certain exclusions from use of specially permitted business services have been established to protect investors (Article 63(1)(i) & (ii) of the FIEA; Article 234-2 of the Office Ordinance on Financial Instruments Services, Etc.).

First, in order to exclude limited partnerships (LPSs) that are not genuine investors, use is not allowed if the qualified institutional investors are all LPSs (ibid., Article 234-2(1)(i) and (2)(i)), although LPSs with total assets of at least 500 million yen (excluding borrowings) may make use of such services.

Second, in view of the purpose of the system of specially permitted businesses — basically to serve qualified institutional investors — use is not allowed if at least half the total amount invested is contributed by persons under the control of fund managers, etc. or by certain persons possessing investment knowledge and experience (ibid., Article 234-2(1)(ii) and (2) (ii)).

(v) Start-up regulations governing specially permitted business

Persons to whom certain conditions for refusal of registration or other grounds for disqualification apply, excluding financial instruments business operators, etc., are prohibited from conducting specially permitted business

Chapter 5　Business regulations on financial instruments business operators, etc.

(Article 63(7) of the FIEA) (2015 revision of the FIEA). Penalties for violations have also been beefed up (Article 197-2(x-viii) & (x-ix) of the FIEA).

(vi)　Notification requirements for specially permitted business activities

Notifiers of specially permitted business activities are required to provide notification of the names of the business holdings (funds) invested in and, for each fund, the names and number of qualified institutional investors (Articles 63(2)(ix) & (3) and 63-3(1) of the FIEA; Articles 238, 238-2 and 244(2) & (3) of the Cabinet Office Ordinance on Financial Instruments Services, Etc.).

(vii)　Conduct regulations governing notifiers of specially permitted business activities

Notifiers of specially permitted business activities that are operators handling funds for professional investors were originally subject only to limited conduct regulations designed to ensure the fairness of transactions: the prohibition on providing false information (Article 38(i) of the FIEA), and the prohibition of compensations for loss, etc. (Article 39 of the FIEA). Under the 2015 revision of the FIEA, however, they are, if they engage in specially permitted business activities, regarded as financial instruments business operators, and conduct regulations governing them have been strengthened considerably (Article 63(11) of the FIEA); in addition, disclosure requirements have been instituted for notifiable items (ibid., Article 63(6)).

Disclosure requirements have also been imposed on financial instruments business operators, etc. engaging in specially permitted business activities (Article 63-3(2) of the FIEA), and inappropriate conduct of specially permitted business is prohibited (Article 40(2) of the FIEA; Article 123(1) (xxx) of the Cabinet Office Ordinance on Financial Instruments Services, Etc.).

In addition, a notifier of specially permitted business activities is required, under the Act on Prevention of Transfer of Criminal Proceeds, to conduct verification at the time of a transaction and to report suspicious transactions (Articles 2(2)(xxiii), 4, 6, 7 and 8(1)).

*659*

(viii)  Oversight of notifiers of specially permitted business activities

Oversight of notifiers of specially permitted business activities by the administrative authorities was originally limited to orders to submit reports and materials and to inspections (of management of their own investments only); the 2015 revision of the FIEA, however, provides for orders to submit reports and materials and for on-site inspections (Article 63-6 of the FIEA), and for orders to improve business operation, suspend business, and discontinue business (Article 63-5(1), (2) & (3) of the FIEA).

For the purpose of administrative oversight, a notifier of specially permitted business activities is required to submit a "monitoring survey report" to enable assessment of its situation (Article 63-6 of the FIEA). A List of Notifying Business Operators and a List of Notifying Business Operators with Recognized Problems, etc. are posted on the FSA website (IX-2-2 of the Comprehensive Guidelines for Supervision of Financial Instruments Business Operators, Etc.).

(ix)  Handling of structural regulations

The FIEA adopts a regulatory approach to collective investment schemes (funds) that involves imposing business regulations on fund managers rather than "structural regulations" of funds, themselves.

This is in consideration of several factors: (1) business regulations are regarded as more practically effective in protecting investors; (2) a system of registration or notification of the structure or mechanism itself would risk imposing a massive administrative burden on both the administrative authorities and the business community; (3) in other major countries, regulations on funds other than traditional funds such as investment trusts chiefly take the form of business regulations; (4) the FIEA is basically not structural regulatory legislation but rather legislation applying administrative regulations — disclosure regulations, business regulations, unfair trade regulations — within the framework of structural regulatory legislation such as the Civil Code, the Commercial Code, the Companies Act, and the Trust Act; and (5) whereas the FSA has jurisdiction over such structural regulatory legislation as the Act on Investment Trusts and Investment Corporations and the Act on Securitization of Assets, it does not necessarily have jurisdiction over structural regulatory legislation in general.

*660*

Chapter 5   Business regulations on financial instruments business operators, etc.

# 5. Registration of financial instruments business

a. Submission of a registration application and registration

A person who intends to obtain registration as a financial instruments business must submit a written application for registration to the Director General of the Local Finance Bureau or Branch Bureau (Article 29-2(1) of the FIEA; Article 5 and Appended Form 1 of the Cabinet Office Ordinance on Financial Instruments Services, Etc.).

To enable the authorities to examine whether conditions for refusal of registration apply, this written application for registration must record (1) the category of business as well as (2) if the person intends to engage in "crowdfunding business," that fact; (3) if the person intends to engage in "securities-related business," certain matters; (4) if the person intends to engage in "electronic trading platform operations," that fact; (5) if the person intends to engage in "commodity-related business," certain matters; (6) if the person intends to engage in "commodity investment-related business," certain matters; (7) if the person intends to engage in "the business of the sale and purchase of beneficial interests in real estate trusts etc.," that fact; (8) if the person intends to engage in "real-estate-related specified investment management business," that fact; (9) if the person intends to engage in "special underwriting acts," that fact; and (10) if the person intends to engage in "specified securities etc. custody acts," that fact (Article 29-2(1)(v), (vi) & (ix) of the FIEA; Article 7 of the Cabinet Office Ordinance on Financial Instruments Services, Etc.). Items (6), (7), and (8) are designed to enable examination of whether the condition on personnel structure is met (Article 13(iii)-(v) of the Cabinet Office Ordinance on Financial Instruments Services, Etc.).

In addition, so-called business rules must be attached to the written application for registration (Article 29-2(2)(ii) of the FIEA; Article 8 of the Cabinet Office Ordinance on Financial Instruments Services, Etc.).

When an application for registration has been filed, the Director General of the Local Finance Bureau or Branch Bureau must, except when he/she refuses registration, register certain matters in a registry of financial instruments business operators and make that registry available for public inspection (Article 29-3 of the FIEA; Article 12 of the Cabinet Office

*661*

Ordinance on Financial Instruments Services, Etc.). The standard time to process a registration is two months (Article 329(1)(i) of the Cabinet Office Ordinance on Financial Instruments Services, Etc.), but it takes longer in practice (see ibid., Article 329(2)).

b. Overview of conditions for refusal of registration

The Director General of the Local Finance Bureau or Branch Bureau must refuse registration when (1) an applicant meets any of the conditions for refusal of registration, or (2) a written application for registration or the attached documents or records contain untrue statements or records, or lack statements or records about important matters (Article 29-4(1) of the FIEA).

In addition, if a registered operator (financial instruments business operator) meets the conditions for refusal of registration, its registration may be rescinded or it may be subject to a business suspension order (Article 52(1)(i)-(iv) of the FIEA).

The FIEA establishes a graded set of conditions for refusal of registration depending on the type of financial instruments business (Article 29-4 of the FIEA). Specifically, (1) general conditions for refusal of registration are prescribed in Article 29-4, paragraph 1, items (i)-(iii) of the FIEA, and additional conditions for refusal of registration are prescribed (2) in ibid., item (iv) for persons (excluding individuals) intending to engage in type I financial instruments business, type II financial instruments business, or investment management business; (3) in ibid., item (v) for persons intending to engage in type I financial instruments business or investment management business; and (4) in ibid., item (vi) for persons intending to engage in type I financial instruments business.

For example, a person intending to engage exclusively in investment advisory and agency business is subject only to the conditions for refusal of registration in (1); a person intending to engage in type I financial instruments business, on the other hand, is subject to all four types of conditions for refusal of registration. Thus start-up regulations are made structurally flexible by clearly defining different levels of application. An overview is provided in Table 5-2.

Stricter conditions are generally imposed on type I financial instruments

Chapter 5　Business regulations on financial instruments business operators, etc.

## Table 5-2.　Necessary conditions for registration as a financial instruments business

| | | Type I financial instruments business | Investment management business | Type II financial instruments business | Investment advisory and agency business |
|---|---|---|---|---|---|
| Condition on personnel structure? Condition on operational organization? | | Yes | | | |
| Required to be a corporation? | | Yes (stock company) | | No | |
| Required to have an office or business office in Japan? Required to adopt Association regulations in house? | | Yes | | Yes (corporations) | No |
| Asset conditions | Condition on minimum stated capital or capital contributions? | Yes (50 million-3 billion yen) | Yes (50 million yen) | Yes (corporations) (10 million yen) | No |
| | Condition on net assets? | Yes (50 million-3 billion yen) | Yes (50 million yen) | Yes (corporations) (10 million yen) | No |
| | Condition on capital-to-risk ratio? | Yes | No | | |
| Conditions on major shareholders? Conditions on subsidiary business? | | Yes | | No | |
| Condition on trade name? | | Yes | No | | |

business and investment management business due to the high necessity of ensuring the soundness of their business operations, because (1) type I financial instruments businesses are the linchpin linking investors and capital markets and regularly accept deposits of assets from customers; and (2) investment management businesses are directly involved in building wealth for the nation's people by managing assets on behalf of customers.

c . Conditions on major shareholders

( i ) Overview

A person intending to engage in type I financial instruments business or investment management business is subject to certain conditions for refusal of registration relating to major shareholders (Article 29-4(1) & (5) (v) (d)- (f) of the FIEA). These conditions for refusal of registration were established under the 2003 revision of the Securities and Exchange Act in order to verify in advance the competence of major shareholders with substantial influence over management. Conditions on major shareholders are not, however, imposed on foreign juridical persons. Most major shareholders of foreign juridical persons are assumed to be located outside Japan, making it difficult to ensure the effectiveness of regulations on major shareholders; it was therefore evidently decided to leave the task of verifying their competence and regulating them to foreign financial instruments regulatory authorities.

The term "major shareholder" means a person who holds voting rights (excluding certain voting rights; referred to as "subject voting rights") equivalent to not less than 20 percent (or 15 percent when certain facts apply) of the voting rights held by all the shareholders, etc. of the company (ibid., Article 29-4(2); Articles 15 and 16 of the Cabinet Office Ordinance on Financial Instruments Services, etc.). This threshold of 20 percent or 15 percent of voting rights was decided in light of the so-called criteria of influence used in corporate accounting (Article 8(6) of the Ordinance on Financial Statements, Etc.).

Whether a person holds subject voting rights is determined substantively. A person holds subject voting rights, even if they are in another's name or held under a fictitious name, as long as the person can be considered effectively to hold them. In addition, certain subject voting rights are deemed to be held by a person even if the person cannot be considered to hold them in reality (Article 29-4(4) of the FIEA). Thus there are both "deemed holders" according to substantive criteria (ibid., Article 29-4(4) (i)) and "deemed holders" according to formal criteria (ibid., Article 29-4(4) (ii); Article 15-10 of the Implementing Order).

Chapter 5   Business regulations on financial instruments business operators, etc.

(ⅱ)   Oversight with respect to major shareholders

A person who has become a major shareholder of a financial instruments business operator (excluding a foreign juridical person) engaged in type Ⅰ financial instruments business or investment management business must submit a "notification of holding subject voting rights" to the Director General of the Local Finance Bureau or Branch Bureau (Article 32(1) & (2) of the FIEA; Articles 36, 37 and 38 of the Cabinet Office Ordinance on Financial Instruments Services, Etc.). When a major shareholder ceases to be a major shareholder, he/she is required to provide notification to that effect (Article 32-3 of the FIEA).

The administrative authorities have authority (1) to order major shareholders to submit reports and materials and to conduct inspections (Article 56-2 (2) of the FIEA), and (2) to order unqualified major shareholders to take measures such as selling their shares (Article 32-2(1) of the FIEA).

These regulations are looser than those on major shareholders of banks and insurance companies, which are subject to authorization (Articles 2(10) and 52-9 (1) of the Banking Act; Articles 2 (14) and 271-10 (1) of the Insurance Business Act).

However, deteriorating finances at a major shareholder can restrict the cash flow of an affiliated financial instruments business operator, and a legal violation by or conflict of interest at a major shareholder can adversely affect its business. Therefore, measures to strengthen regulations on major shareholders were adopted in the 2010 revision of the FIEA, including a system for ordering major shareholders holding a majority of the voting rights of a financial instruments business operator ("specified major shareholders") to implement improvement measures (Articles 32(3) & (4) and 32-2(2) & (3) of the FIEA).

Regulations on major shareholders of financial instruments business operators, except those relating to specified major shareholders, apply mutatis mutandis to shareholders of or equity investors in a holding company that holds a financial instruments business operator as a subsidiary company (Article 32-4 of the FIEA).

*665*

d. Condition on capital-to-risk ratio

( i ) Overview

In terms of property regulations, if a person intends to engage in type I financial instruments business, in addition to conditions on stated capital or capital contributions (Article 29-4(1)(iv) of the FIEA) and on net assets (ibid., Article 29-4(1)(v)(b)), a further condition for refusal of registration is a capital-to-risk ratio of less than 120 percent (ibid., Article 29-4(1)(vi) (a)).

Financial instruments business operators engaged in type I financial instruments business must keep the capital-to-risk ratio at no less than 120 percent (Article 46-6(2) of the FIEA).

( ii ) Capital-to-risk ratio

The capital-to-risk ratio is the ratio of (1) the numerator, equity capital minus fixed assets, etc. to be deducted to (2) the denominator, risk equivalent, which equals market risk equivalent plus counterparty risk equivalent plus basic risk equivalent (Article 46-6(1) of the FIEA; Articles 176, 177 and 178 of the Cabinet Office Ordinance on Financial Instruments Services, Etc.; Public Notice of the FSA No. 59 of 2007, "Notice of the Establishment of Criteria for the Calculation of Financial Instruments Business Operators' Market Risk Equivalent, Counterparty Risk Equivalent and Basic Risk Equivalent").

( iii ) Oversight with respect to capital-to-risk ratio

A financial instruments business operator engaged in type I financial instruments business must notify the administrative authorities (1) of its capital-to-risk ratio as of the end of each month by the 20th of the following month; (2) immediately and on every business day if its capital-to-risk ratio falls below 140 percent; and (3) without delay when the ratio returns to 140 percent or above (Article 46-6(1) of the FIEA; Article 179 of the Cabinet Office Ordinance on Financial Instruments Services, Etc.). The financial instruments business operator must also make its capital-to-risk ratio available for public inspection at the end of each March, June, September, and December (Article 46-6(3) of the FIEA; Article 180 of the Cabinet Office Ordinance on Financial Instruments Services, Etc.).

Chapter 5   Business regulations on financial instruments business operators, etc.

The administrative authorities may (1) if the capital-to-risk ratio of a financial instruments business operator engaged in type I financial instruments business is less than 120 percent, order it to make improvements; (2) if the ratio is less than 100 percent, issue it a business suspension order; and (3) if on the day when three months have passed since the business suspension order was issued the ratio continues to be less than 100 percent and is not likely to recover, rescind its registration (Article 53 of the FIEA). These supervisory measures using the criterion of capital-to-risk ratio are parallel to prompt corrective action for banks (Article 26(2) of the Banking Act).

e . Condition on trade name

Another condition for refusal of registration in the case of type I financial instruments business is intending to use the same trade name another financial instruments business operator engaged in type I financial instruments business has already used or a trade name that may be misidentified as another financial instruments business operator (Article 29-4(1)(vi)(b) of the FIEA).

Further, a person who is not a financial instruments business operator is forbidden from using a trade name or name as a financial instruments business operator or any trade name or name confusingly similar thereto (Article 31-3 of the FIEA). This is to prevent unregistered operators from harming investors' interests by engaging in fraudulent business using the trade name or name of a financial instruments business operator.

The Securities and Exchange Act required that the word *shoken* ("securities") be used in the trade names of securities companies, but the FIEA has no provision requiring the use of a specific term in the trade names of financial instruments business operators. However, the name "securities company" may be used only by financial instruments business operators engaged in securities-related business (which are assumed to be operators registered as type I financial instruments businesses) (Article 25 of the Supplementary Provisions of the 2006 Act for Partial Revision of the Securities and Exchange Act, Etc.).

*667*

f. Conditions for refusal of registration of registered financial institution business

Registered financial institution business is subject to oversight under other industry legislation; given that and other factors, the fact that an officer or employee is disqualified is not deemed a condition for refusal of registration, but a condition on personnel structure is prescribed (Article 33-5(1)(iii) of the FIEA; Article 49 of the Cabinet Office Ordinance on Financial Instruments Services, Etc.). A condition on operational organization was added under the 2014 revision of the FIEA (Article 33-5(1)(v) of the FIEA).

g. Special provisions on conditions for refusal of registration of investment management business for qualified investors

When the FIEA was revised in 2011, special provisions relaxing conditions for refusal of registration as an "investment management business for qualified investors" were established (Article 29-5 of the FIEA) as a deregulatory measure intended to promote investment management business start-ups. These special provisions are not available to financial instruments business operators registered as ordinary investment management businesses.

Investment management business for qualified investors means a business in which the investors of all the invested assets are exclusively "qualified investors" and the total value of all the invested assets does not exceed twenty billion yen (ibid., Article 29-5 (1) (ii); Article 15-10-5 of the Implementing Order). Qualified investors include, besides professional investors, individuals who possess financial assets of no less than 300 million yen and have at least a year of trading experience, and officers of financial instruments business operators (Article 29-5 (3) of the FIEA; Article 15-10-7 of the Implementing Order; Articles 16-5-2 and 16-6 of the Cabinet Office Ordinance on Financial Instruments Services, Etc.) (enlarged in March 2016).

An investment management business for qualified investors, first, is not required to be a company with a board of directors (Article 29-4(1)(5)(a) of the FIEA); it need only be a company with audit & supervisory board members (Article 29-5(1) of the FIEA).

668

Chapter 5   Business regulations on financial instruments business operators, etc.

Second, when a financial instruments business operator registered as an investment management business for qualified investors is, under a discretionary investment contract, completely entrusted with authority to invest certain paragraph 1 securities, such as beneficiary certificates of investment trusts or foreign investment trusts, and that operator deals in private placement for qualified investors, such dealings are deemed not type I financial instruments business but type II financial instruments business (ibid., Article 29-5(2); Article 15-10-6 of the Implementing Order).

Third, for investment management business for qualified investors, the minimum amount of stated capital and amount of net assets are set at (not the usual fifty million yen but) ten million yen (Article 29-4(1)(iv)(a)(v) (b) of the FIEA; Articles 15-7(1)(v) and 15-9(1) of the Implementing Order).

These special provisions were evidently established to increase the international competitiveness of the Japanese market, given moves by Japanese players to start up investment management businesses in Singapore and elsewhere. However, if their use is to be promoted, heed will need to paid to concerns about the clarity and predictability of administrative oversight and surveillance.

h. Special provisions on conditions for refusal of registration of investment crowdfunding

Special provisions on conditions for refusal of registration as a "crowdfunding business" were established in the 2014 revision of the FIEA in order to promote certain "investment crowdfunding" — raising small amounts of funds over the Internet (with a total issue size of less than 100 million yen and an investment of no more than 500,000 yen per person).

Specifically, dealing in public offering or private placement of unlisted share certificates or share option certificates, or accepting deposits from customers in connection with such business, is defined as "type I crowdfunding business." Among the conditions for refusal of registration as a type I financial instruments business, those on subsidiary business (Article 29-4(1)(v)(c) of the FIEA) and capital-to-risk ratio (ibid., Article 29-4(1) (vi)(a)) are not applied (Article 29-4-2(1), (2) & (10) of the FIEA), while those on the minimum amount of stated capital and net assets have been

*669*

relaxed to ten million yen (Articles 15-7 (1) (vi) and 15-9 (1) of the Implementing Order). Financial instruments business operators that engage exclusively in type I crowdfunding business are "type I crowdfunding operators" (Article 29-4-2(9) of the FIEA).

Dealing in public offering or private placement of securities exempt from disclosure (Article 3(iii) of the FIEA) or unlisted fund equity is defined as "type II crowdfunding business" (Article 29-4-3(1) & (4) of the FIEA). The condition on minimum amount of stated capital has been relaxed to ten million yen (Article 15-7 (1) (viii) of the Implementing Order). Financial instruments business operators that engage exclusively in type II crowdfunding business are "type II crowdfunding operators" (Article 29-4-3(2) of the FIEA).

# 6. Start-up-related regulations on financial instruments business operators, etc.

a. Changes in registered matters

( i ) Notification of changes

When there are any changes in the matters recorded on the written application for registration (excluding category of business), a financial instruments business operator must provide notification to that effect within two weeks (Article 31 (1) of the FIEA; Article 20 of the Cabinet Office Ordinance on Financial Instruments Services, Etc.).

When there are any changes in contents and methods of business stated in the business rules, a financial instruments business operator must provide notification to that effect without delay (Article 31(3) of the FIEA; Article 21 of the Cabinet Office Ordinance on Financial Instruments Services, Etc.). Article 37 of the Administrative Procedure Act (that procedural obligations are fulfilled upon arrival of notification) applies to notification procedures, although it appears that in practice consultations on the draft notification are held beforehand with the supervisory authorities and it is examined in advance.

A similar system for providing notification of changes has been established for registered financial institutions (Article 33-6 (1) & (3) of the FIEA; Articles 51 and 52 of the Cabinet Office Ordinance on Financial Instruments Services, Etc.).

*670*

Chapter 5　Business regulations on financial instruments business operators, etc.

(ⅱ)　Registration of change

When a financial instruments business operator intends to change the category of business or engagement in crowdfunding business regarding securities exempt from disclosure or unlisted fund equity, he/she must obtain registration of change (Articles 31(4) and 29-2(1)(v) & (vi) of the FIEA; Article 22 of the Cabinet Office Ordinance on Financial Instruments Services, Etc.), because it must be determined whether any of the conditions for refusal of registration prescribed for the category of financial instruments business, etc. in question applies.

The standard time to process a registration of change is one month (Article 329(1)(ii) of the Cabinet Office Ordinance on Financial Instruments Services, Etc.), but it takes longer in practice (see ibid., Article 329(2)).

No system for registering changes has been established for registered financial institutions.

b.　Authorization of PTS business

When a financial instruments business operator intends to engage in acts involving a proprietary trading system (PTS) (Article 2(8)(x) of the FIEA) in the course of business ("proprietary trading system operations"), he/she must obtain authorization (Articles 30 to 30-4 of the FIEA; Articles 17, 18 and 19 of the Cabinet Office Ordinance on Financial Instruments Services, Etc.). Engaging in PTS management business requires registering as a financial instruments business operator before obtaining authorization.

Whereas changes in the contents and methods of business of financial instruments business operators are notifiable items (Article 31(3) of the FIEA), changes in important matters relating to PTS management business are subject to authorization (ibid., Article 31(6); Article 19 of the Cabinet Office Ordinance on Financial Instruments Services, Etc.).

Registered financial institutions are not permitted to engage in PTS business.

c.　Regulations on deposits for operation

Among financial instruments business operators, individuals engaged in type II financial instruments business and juridical persons and individuals engaged only in investment advisory and agency business are subject to

*671*

regulations on deposits for operation (Article 31-2 of the FIEA). Regulations on deposits for operation do not constitute conditions for refusal of registration. No regulations on deposits for operation are prescribed for financial instruments business operators engaged in a type I financial instruments business or investment management business or for juridical persons engaged in a type II financial instruments business, since they are subject to regulations on the minimum amount of stated capital.

To protect investors, the deposit-for-operation system grants customers who have concluded contracts with applicable financial instruments business operators the right to preferential payment (the right to receive payment in preference over other creditors) with regard to claims incurred under such contracts (ibid., Article 31-2(6)).

The amount of the deposit for operation is ten million yen for individuals engaged in a type II financial instruments business and five million yen for persons engaged only in investment advisory and agency business (ibid., Article 31-2(2); Article 15-12 of the Implementing Order).

An applicable financial instruments business operator must not start financial instruments business until he/she deposits a deposit for operation, for which certain securities may be substituted (or instead of depositing a deposit, concludes a contract with a bank, etc.), and files a notification to that effect (Article 31-2(3), (5) & (9) of the FIEA).

No regulations on deposits for operation are prescribed for registered financial institutions.

# 7. Membership in financial instruments and exchange system organizations (market infrastructure organizations)

a. Market infrastructure organizations: Overview

Under the FIEA and related regulations, various systems have been established that serve as infrastructure for financial instruments transactions and financial instruments markets; some of these relate to the organizations responsible for the operation of such systems (financial instruments and exchange system organizations or market infrastructure organizations, as it were).

Because financial instruments business operators, etc. play a key role as

*672*

Chapter 5   Business regulations on financial instruments business operators, etc.

market intermediaries linking investors and capital markets, they are required to join market infrastructure organizations when doing business; they may also in some cases join such organizations voluntarily. Many financial instruments business operators engaged in type I financial instruments business and securities-related business (so-called securities companies) in particular are members of market infrastructure organizations.

b.  Types of market infrastructure organizations

Market infrastructure organizations, which are examined in detail in Chapter 7, are categorized as follows. The first type comprises "designated dispute resolution organizations": financial ADR bodies that financial instruments business operators, etc. and securities finance companies are in principle required to join under the FIEA (Article 156-38(1)).

The second type comprises "financial instruments firms associations" ("authorized financial instruments firms associations" and "certified financial instruments firms associations"): self-regulatory organizations that financial instruments business operators, etc. may join as "member firms" or "members" under the FIEA (Article 67(1); Article 78(2)).

The third type comprises "certified investor protection organizations": financial ADR bodies that financial instruments business operators, etc. and financial instruments intermediary service providers may join as "members" under the FIEA (Article 79-10(1)).

The fourth type comprises "investor protection funds": funds for protection of investors that securities companies are required to join under the FIEA (Article 79-21).

The fifth type comprises "financial instruments exchanges" and "foreign financial instruments exchanges": establishers of markets of which financial instruments business operators, etc. and registered financial institutions may become "members, etc." (members or trading participants) under the FIEA (Article 2(16) & (26)).

The sixth type comprises "financial instruments clearing organizations" and "foreign financial instruments clearing organizations": clearing organizations in which financial instruments business operators, etc. and securities finance companies may participate as "clearing participants"

*673*

under the FIEA (ibid., Article 2(29)).

The seventh type comprises "book-entry transfer institutions": settlement institutions of which financial instruments business operators engaged in type I financial instruments business and banks etc. may become "account management institutions" under the Act on Book-Entry Transfer of Corporate Bonds and Shares, Etc. (Article 2(2)).

The eighth type comprises "securities finance companies": persons who, under the FIEA, engage in the business of lending money or securities as necessary for settlement of margin transactions, etc. to a member, etc. of a financial instruments exchange by utilizing settlement systems of, for example, a financial instruments exchange market established by the financial instruments exchange (Article 2(30) of the FIEA).

The ninth type comprises "trade repositories" and "designated foreign trade repositories": institutions where, under the FIEA, the Financial Services Agency collects transaction information on over-the-counter transactions of derivatives (Article 156-64(3) of the FIEA).

The tenth type comprises "calculators of specified securities indicators," to which financial instruments business operators, etc. are assumed to be providers, under contract, of the information based on which specified financial indicators are calculated (Articles 38(vii), 156-85(1), 156-87(2)(iii) & (iv) of the FIEA).

# C. Regulations on scope of business of financial instruments business operators, etc.

## 1. Regulations on scope of business of financial instruments business operators engaged in type I financial instruments business or investment management business

Under the FIEA, the business of financial instruments business operators engaged in type I financial instruments business or investment management business is classified into core business, incidental business, notifiable business, and approved business (Article 35 of the FIEA). Regulations on scope of business are not, however, applied to type I crowdfunding operators (Article 29-4-2(3) & (4) of the FIEA).

*674*

Chapter 5   Business regulations on financial instruments business operators, etc.

Under the licensing system established by the 1965 revision of the Securities and Exchange Act, securities companies were required to specialize in the business and obtain approval for subsidiary business; that was in order to prevent conflicts of interest between securities companies and customers and improve the quality of the securities business through specialization. The 1998 revision of the Securities and Exchange Act (the Financial System Reform Act) abolished the requirement to specialize, with the aim of empowering securities companies to conduct operations independently by being innovative, and established the same operational regime as exists today. The present operational regime for investment management business came into being when the FIEA legislative framework was established in 2006.

This operational regime has several characteristics. First, an applicable financial instruments business operator may, in addition to its core business of "financial instruments business," also engage as a matter of course in "other business incidental to Financial Instruments Business," or incidental business (Article 35(1) of the FIEA). The acts listed in that paragraph are examples; incidental business encompasses also "other business incidental to Financial Instruments Business" besides that listed. Operations occurring as a matter of course in the process of performing listed acts are included in "other incidental business." Whether an act constitutes "other incidental business" is determined substantively depending on the case in accordance with the actual facts, taking into consideration, among other factors, the degree to which the act is concomitant to core business or the incidental business acts listed, the degree to which it approximates them in content (its proximity), and the similarity and extent of the risks it entails. Even if a business act constituting incidental business is conducted in isolation from the core business, that does not negate its character as incidental business.

Second, an applicable financial instruments business operator may, upon providing notification, engage in the business acts listed in Article 35, paragraph 2 of the FIEA, or notifiable business (ibid., Article 35(2) & (3); Articles 68 and 69 of the Cabinet Office Ordinance on Financial Instruments Services, Etc.). Notifiable business is restricted to the acts listed, although it also includes business incidental to them (Article 68(xxiv) of the Cabinet Office Ordinance on Financial Instruments Services, Etc.). Notifiable items

*675*

include the method of managing risk of losses from the business in question, or risk management method (ibid., Article 69(i)(b)).

Third, an applicable financial instruments business operator may engage in a business other than incidental business or notifiable business upon obtaining approval, or approved business (Article 35(4) of the FIEA; Article 70 of the Cabinet Office Ordinance on Financial Instruments Services, Etc.). Upon receipt of an application for approval, the authorities may choose not to grant approval only where the business in question is found to go against the public interest or hinder the protection of investors due to the difficulty in management of the risks of loss (Article 35(5) of the FIEA).

The conduct by a financial instruments business operator of the business of managing the trust property of a trust for investment based on settlor's instruction, or the assets of a registered investment corporation, as an investment in real estate, etc. (the business of conducting "specified investment management acts") is classified not as notifiable business (Article 35(2)(vi) of the FIEA) but as approved business (Article 223-3(1) of the Act on Investment Trusts and Investment Corporations). The requisite conduct regulations of the FIEA are applied to such business (ibid., Article 223-3(2) & (3)).

Legally, the administrative authorities have no discretion with regard to notifiable business and only limited discretion with regard to approved business; in the actual practice of administrative oversight, however, it appears that notifiable businesses are examined in advance, while discretion is exercised in the case of approved businesses.

## 2. Regulations on scope of business of financial instruments business operators engaged only in type II financial instruments business or investment advisory and agency business

Under the FIEA, no regulations on scope of business are imposed on financial instruments business operators engaged only in type II financial instruments business or investment advisory and agency business (Article 35-2 of the FIEA). Therefore, such financial instruments business operators may, in addition to financial instruments business (limited to type II financial instruments business or investment advisory and agency business), also

Chapter 5   Business regulations on financial instruments business operators, etc.

engage in any other business as a subsidiary business (ibid., Article 35-2 (1)). However, such financial instruments business operators are not allowed to engage in business found to be against public interest (Articles 29-4(1)(i)(d), 52(1)(i)).

An interpretative provision is included for confirmatory purposes stating that where a financial instruments business operator engages in any other business as a subsidiary business, the above provision is not to be construed to preclude the application of Acts concerning that business (Article 35-2(2) of the FIEA).

# 3. Scope of business of registered financial institutions

## a. Overview

Regulations on the scope of business of financial institutions are enshrined in the legislation governing each type of business (for example, Articles 10-12 of the Banking Act and Articles 97-100 of the Insurance Business Act).

Within the framework of that industry legislation, Articles 33 through 33-8 of the FIEA prescribe regulations on the scope of business of registered financial institutions. The core of those provisions comprises regulations on the so-called separation of the banking and securities sectors. When under the 2006 revision of the Securities and Exchange Act "securities business" was expanded to "financial instruments business," the scope of business of registered financial institutions was also expanded.

First, while acts by financial institutions constituting "investment management business" or "securities-related business" are excluded from the range of acts constituting "financial instruments business" (Article 2(8) of the FIEA), financial institutions are in principle forbidden from engaging in securities-related business or investment management business (Article 33(1) of the FIEA). Financial institutions are thus explicitly prohibited from conducting investment management business, because it entails the conduct of securities transactions.

Second, a financial institution may, without obtaining registration as a registered financial institution, conduct sales or purchase of securities or "transactions of securities-related derivatives" (Article 28(8)(vi) of the FIEA) for the purpose of investment pursuant to the provisions of other

677

Acts or on the account of a person who entrusts based on a trust contract (Article 33(1) of the FIEA). This provision is interpreted as confirmatory. It makes clear that, since the sale and purchase of securities and other such transactions by ordinary companies and individuals are understood not to meet the definition of "financial instruments business" (in that they are not conducted "in the course of business"), the sale and purchase of securities and other such transactions for the purpose of investment shall be similarly treated. The phrase "other Acts" refers to, for example, Article 10, paragraph 2, item (ii) of the Banking Act. Transactions conducted on "specified trading accounts" (Article 13-6-3 (1) of the Ordinance for Implementation of the Banking Act) are not generally classified as being for the purpose of investment (VIII-1-1(1) of the Comprehensive Guidelines for Supervision of Financial Instruments Business Operators, Etc.).

Third, a financial institution may, upon obtaining registration as a registered financial institution, conduct in the course of business (1) brokerage with written orders or (2) certain acts with regard to certain securities or transactions of securities-related derivatives (Articles 33(2) and 33-2(i) & (ii) of the FIEA).

Fourth, a financial institution may, upon obtaining registration as a registered financial institution, (1) conduct, in the course of trade, "derivatives transactions, etc." other than "transactions of securities-related derivatives, etc." (excluding those conducted for the purpose of investment pursuant to other Acts or on the account of a person who entrusts based on a trust contract); (2) conduct, in the course of business, brokerage for clearing of securities, etc. other than that falling into the category of securities-related business; (3) conduct, in the course of business, direct placement or private placement; (4) conduct investment advisory and agency business; and (5) conduct securities, etc. custody business (Articles 33(3), 33-2(iii) & (iv) of the FIEA). The ban on the conduct of investment advisory and agency business by financial institutions was lifted when investment advisory business was added to the scope of business of banks and insurance companies under the 2008 revisions of the FIEA and related regulations (Article 11 (i) of the Banking Act; Article 99 (2) (iii) of the Insurance Business Act).

Fifth, a financial institution conducting trust business may conduct certain

*678*

Chapter 5   Business regulations on financial instruments business operators, etc.

investment management business (namely discretionary investment business) as registered financial institution business, and may, without obtaining registration, conduct certain investment management business (namely management of investment trusts managed without instructions from the settlor or self-management) as a trustee (Articles 33-8(1) and 2 (8) of the FIEA). This maintains the policy established under the 2003 revision of the Securities and Exchange Act of lifting the ban on the conduct of discretionary investment business (wrap accounts, etc.) by trust banks. Note also that the Development Bank of Japan can conduct investment management business in the form of self-management (Article 3(1)(xvi) of the Development Bank of Japan Act; Article 33-8 (1) of the FIEA as reinterpreted in light of ibid., Article 4(1)).

Sixth, a life insurance solicitor or non-life insurance agent does not require registration as a financial instruments business when conducting "specified financial instruments business" on behalf of a registered financial institution (Article 33-8(2) of the FIEA; Article 15-21 of the Implementing Order). Specified financial instruments business comprises the sale of investment trusts and foreign investment trusts and transactions in weather derivatives. This provision was established for the convenience of customers and out of consideration for the operations of life insurance solicitors and non-life insurance agents. In this case, the provisions of the FIEA apply to the person who conducts specified financial instruments business, who is deemed to be an employee of the registered financial institution he/she represents.

Seventh, a confirmatory provision is included stating that a person the majority of whose voting rights held by all the shareholders, etc. are held by a financial institution may be granted registration or authorization with respect to financial instruments business (Article 33-7 of the FIEA; Article 1-9 of the Implementing Order).

b. Intent of regulations on the separation of the banking and securities sectors

Article 33 of the FIEA assumes the regulations on the separation of the banking and securities sectors imposed under Article 65 of the old Securities and Exchange Act. Financial institutions were in principle forbidden from themselves conducting acts such as the sale and purchase of securities or intermediary, brokerage, or agency service therefor in the course of business (Article 65(1) of the Securities and Exchange Act), out of concerns about the detrimental effects of conflicts of interest — such as financial institutions attempting to recover loans by having borrowers issue securities — and fears about their gaining excessive influence over industry by effectively controlling companies' methods of procuring funds. Only in certain cases where the risk of such detrimental outcomes was considered low were financial institutions permitted to engage in such acts upon obtaining registration (ibid., Article 65(2) and Article 65-2).

In academic circles, it was argued that the in-principle prohibition on the conduct of securities business by financial institutions enshrined in Article 65 of the Securities and Exchange Act was imposed in an effort to protect savers by detaching the inherently risky business of underwriting securities from financial institutions, in line with the thinking behind the U.S. Banking Act (the Glass–Steagall Act) separating commercial banking from the securities business; but (it was asserted) that its actual effect was primarily to furnish securities brokers with systemic infrastructure for achieving healthy growth in their field of business by requiring financial institutions to withdraw from the securities business, and the underwriting business in particular, while protecting savers was ultimately merely a secondary goal. Others countered that the prohibition aimed to eliminate financial institutions' excessive control of the economy resulting from their simultaneous engagement in banking and securities business and prevent harm to the interests of savers.

The Fundamental Research Committee of the Securities and Exchange Council, in its report "The Design of the Basic System Relating to Securities Transactions" (May 24, 1991), asserted, "Due attention should be paid to the fact that the basic principles underlying Article 65 of the Securities and Exchange Act (preventing conflict of interest, preventing market dominance and influence over corporations, ensuring the soundness of banks, and so forth) still retain great significance today." More recently, the First Subcommittee of the Sectional Committee on Financial System of the Financial System Council, in its report "Toward a Financial System Centered on Market Functions" (December 24, 2003), noted, "The chief role in financial intermediation in the financial system is still played by banks, and

Chapter 5   Business regulations on financial instruments business operators, etc.

the possibility of the conflict of interest and banks abusing their dominant position that were the grounds for Article 65 remains an important issue today···It does not appear to be the time to implement revisions affecting the fundamental scope of business." (The December 18, 2007 report of the First Subcommittee of the Sectional Committee on Financial System of the Financial System Council made a similar argument.)

The FIEA, maintaining these principles in the belief that the regulations on the separation of the banking and securities sectors enshrined in Article 65 of the Securities and Exchange Act have not lost their significance, contains provisions of similar import (Articles 33 and 33-2 of the FIEA). Moreover, the Banking Act, for example, establishes regulations on banks' scope of business (Article 10(2), Article 11(i) & (ii)) predicated on the regulations on the separation of the banking and securities sectors in the FIEA. On the other hand, regulations on the separation of the banking and securities sectors have undergone considerable change since the Securities and Exchange Act was enacted in 1948.

c. Changes in regulations on the separation of the banking and securities sectors
( i ) Expansion of securities business conducted by financial institutions themselves

The types of securities business that financial institutions were exceptionally permitted to conduct when the Securities and Exchange Act was enacted in 1948 were (1) brokerage with written orders (Article 65(1) of the Securities and Exchange Act); (2) the sale and purchase of securities on an account of a person who entrusts based on a trust contract (ibid.); (3) the sale and purchase of securities for the purpose of investment (ibid.); and (4) securities business in general relating to public bonds (ibid., Article 65 (2)). When the Banking Act was completely revised in 1981, it was explicitly stated in it and other industry legislation that financial institutions could engage in the types of securities business permitted to them under the Securities and Exchange Act. At the same time, in the 1981 revision of the Securities and Exchange Act, a system of authorization was adopted for securities business relating to public bonds conducted by financial institutions (Article 65-2).

*681*

The range of securities business that financial institutions are exceptionally permitted to conduct themselves has subsequently gradually expanded. (1) Trading in securities index futures, etc., trading in securities options, and securities futures trading in foreign markets, relating to public bonds were added under the 1988 revision of the Securities and Exchange Act (Article 65(1) & (2)(ii)). (2) Dealing in securities business and private placement relating to commercial paper and certain securitization-related products (such as CARDs) was added in the 1992 revision of the Securities and Exchange Act (Financial Systems Reform Act) (Article 65 (2) (ii) – (iv)); it was also made clear that Article 65 of the Act did not preclude the granting of a license to conduct securities business to a subsidiary company of a financial institution (Article 65-3). (3) Dealing, etc. in public offering of beneficiary certificates of a securities investment trust or investment securities of a securities investment corporation, and certain over-the-counter transactions in securities derivatives, were added under the 1998 revision of the Securities and Exchange Act (Financial System Reform Act) (Article 65(2)(iv) & (vii)). In addition, (4) the ban on securities intermediation by financial institutions was lifted by the 2004 revision to the Securities and Exchange Act (Article 65(2)(iii)(c) & (iv)(b)).

Therefore the types of securities business (securities-related business) that financial institutions are currently prohibited from themselves conducting are restricted to, among others: (1) sale and purchase, brokerage (excluding brokerage with written orders) of sale and purchase, agency services, underwriting, and secondary distribution of share certificates, share option certificates, corporate bond certificates, covered warrants, and depositary receipts (DRs); (2) dealing in private placement of covered warrants relating to share certificates; (3) certain over-the-counter transactions in derivatives relating to securities conducted with a large number of persons (50 or more); and (4) proprietary trading system (PTS) management business (see Article 33 (2) of the FIEA; Article 15-18 to Article 15-20 of the Implementing Order; Article 42 of the Cabinet Office Ordinance on Financial Instruments Services, Etc.).

*682*

Chapter 5   Business regulations on financial instruments business operators, etc.

(ⅱ)  Expansion of securities business conducted by financial institution groups

As the range of securities business conducted by financial institutions themselves has expanded, so too has the range of that conducted by financial institution groups.

First, the 1992 Financial Systems Reform Act, to promote healthy development of capital markets by fostering effective and proper competition, allowed banks and securities companies to enter each other's markets through the establishment of separate subsidiaries in different business categories. Under the revisions to the Securities and Exchange Act enacted by that law, (1) the Minister of Finance was empowered to grant a securities business license to a stock company of which a financial institution held the majority of the shares (Article 65-3); and (2) a securities company was, with the authorization of the Minister of Finance, allowed to acquire and hold the majority of the shares in a financial institution (Article 43-2). However, with regard to (1), when a new license was granted to the subsidiary company of a financial institution, for the time being the condition was attached that it not engage in brokerage, underwriting, or secondary distribution of share certificates, etc. (Article 19(1) of the Supplementary Provisions of the 1992 Financial Systems Reform Act); when a financial institution made an existing securities company a subsidiary, this condition could be attached to the securities company's license (ibid., Article 19(2)).

Second, after the ban on holding companies was lifted under the 1997 revision of the Antimonopoly Act, cross-entry took place through establishment of holding companies. A system of bank holding companies was instituted by the 1997 revision of the Banking Act, allowing bank holding companies to turn securities companies into subsidiaries. Further, the 1997 revision of the Insurance Business Act enabled insurance companies to turn securities companies into subsidiaries, and instituted a system of insurance holding companies allowing insurance holding companies to turn securities companies into subsidiaries. The Securities and Exchange Act, by contrast, instituted no system of securities holding companies, and operators were free to establish holding companies with securities companies as subsidiaries.

Third, Article 5 of the 1998 Financial System Reform Act abolished Article 19 of the Supplementary Provisions of the 1992 Financial Systems Reform

Act; with this all restrictions on the scope of business of securities subsidiaries of financial institutions were eliminated.

d. Current state of regulations on separation of the banking and securities sectors

Given these developments, regulations separating the banking and securities sectors by restricting the scope of business have in reality lost much of their significance. Practical interest has now shifted to the question of relaxing the restriction on concurrent holding of positions by officers and employees, and restrictions on acts in which parent juridical persons, etc. and subsidiary juridical persons, etc. are involved; these were imposed by the 1992 revision of the Securities and Exchange Act (Financial Systems Reform Act) as preventive measures against the adverse effects of parent-subsidiary relations, to create a so-called firewall between banking and securities.

Thus, with regard to the provisions of Article 33 of the FIEA, one possible idea would have been to replace the existing regulatory approach — in principle prohibiting banks and so on from engaging in securities business except where expressly allowed — with an alternative approach more in accordance with reality: in principle allowing them to engage in securities business except where expressly prohibited. However, the question of which is the principle and which the exception is an important yardstick of legislative thinking. Given the series of debates on financial system reform since the late 1980s, the existing regulatory approach has symbolic significance for the Japanese financial system; it was therefore felt that changing it without sufficient discussion by a broad range of stakeholders would be inappropriate. Hence it was decided to maintain this approach in the 2006 revision to the Securities and Exchange Act.

The question ultimately boils down to one of policy. In order to promote the healthy development of Japanese capital markets, to what degree, from the viewpoint of the users of capital markets (investors, corporations, etc.), should a market structure be permitted in which market intermediaries belonging to financial institution groups can exercise de facto dominance? How important should healthy competition between market intermediaries belonging to financial institution groups and independent market intermediaries be considered? The current FIEA attaches greater

*684*

Chapter 5   Business regulations on financial instruments business operators, etc.

importance to the latter, healthy competition.

# 4 . Notification of concurrent holding of positions by officers and employees

### a . Intent

Previously the concurrent holding of positions by officers and employees of securities companies was restricted or prohibited in line with (1) the requirement to specialize in the securities business imposed by the 1965 revision of the Securities and Exchange Act, and the need to prevent evasions of its prohibition on the conduct of subsidiary business by securities companies; and (2) the preventive measures against the adverse effects of dealings exploiting the relationship between parent and subsidiary established by the 1992 revision of the Securities and Exchange Act (Financial Systems Reform Act).

Then the 1998 revision of the Securities and Exchange Act (Financial System Reform Act) abolished all restrictions and prohibitions on concurrent holding of positions, except the prohibition rooted in the separation of the banking and securities sectors, and a system of ex post facto notification was adopted instead. Finally, the 2008 revision of the FIEA abolished also the prohibition rooted in the separation of the banking and securities sectors, leaving only the requirement to provide ex post facto notification of concurrent holding of positions by officers.

### b . Overview

First, a director or executive officer of a financial instruments business operator engaged in a type I financial instruments business or an investment management business must, in cases where he/she has assumed or resigned from the position of director, accounting advisor, audit & supervisory board member, or executive officer of another company, provide notification to that effect without delay (Article 31-4(1) of the FIEA; Article 31 of the Cabinet Office Ordinance on Financial Instruments Services, Etc.).

Second, a director or executive officer of a financial instruments business operator engaged in a securities-related business other than a type I financial instruments business must, in cases where he/she has assumed or resigned from the position of director, accounting advisor, audit &

*685*

supervisory board member, or executive officer of a parent bank, etc. or subsidiary bank, etc. of that operator, provide notification to that effect without delay (Article 31-4(2) of the FIEA; Article 31 of the Cabinet Office Ordinance on Financial Instruments Services, Etc.).

    c . Definitions of "parent bank, etc.," "parent juridical person, etc.," "subsidiary bank, etc.," "subsidiary juridical person, etc.," and related terms
        ( i ) Definitions of "parent bank, etc." and "subsidiary bank, etc."
"Parent bank, etc." means a "parent juridical person, etc." that is a "financial institution" (Article 31-4 (3) of the FIEA; Article 1-9 of the Implementing Order). "Subsidiary bank, etc." means a "subsidiary juridical person, etc." that is a "financial institution" (Article 31-4(4) of the FIEA; Article 1-9 of the Implementing Order).

        ( ii ) Definitions of "parent juridical person, etc." and "subsidiary juridical person, etc."
    The definitions of "parent juridical person, etc." and "subsidiary juridical person, etc." have greater significance with regard to preventive measures against adverse effects (firewall regulations) (Article 44-3 of the FIEA).
    The term "parent juridical person, etc." in principle encompasses (1) the parent company, etc. of the person; (2) a subsidiary company, etc. of the parent company, etc. thereof (excluding the person himself/herself, etc.); (3) an affiliated company, etc. of the parent company, etc. thereof; and (4) a "company, etc." (meaning a company, partnership, or any other business entity equivalent thereto, including those equivalent thereto in a foreign state) (including a subsidiary company, etc. or affiliated company, etc. of the company, etc.) of which more than 50 percent of the voting rights are held by a "specified individual shareholder" of the person (meaning an individual who holds voting rights exceeding 50 percent of the voting rights held by all the shareholders, etc. thereof), or a company, etc. of which not less than 20 percent but not more than 50 percent of the voting rights are held by a specified individual shareholder of the person (Article 31-4(3) of the FIEA; Article 15-16(1) of the Implementing Order).
    The term "subsidiary juridical person, etc." in principle encompasses (1) a

Chapter 5 Business regulations on financial instruments business operators, etc.

subsidiary company, etc. of the person, and (2) an affiliated company, etc. thereof (Article 31-4(4) of the FIEA; Article 15-16(2) of the Implementing Order).

Excluded from the scope of the terms "parent juridical person, etc." and "subsidiary juridical person, etc." are (1) so-called dependent operators (persons engaged exclusively in operations for the purpose of execution of operations by the person himself/herself, or by the person himself/herself and the parent juridical person, etc. or a subsidiary juridical person, etc. thereof); and (2) foreign juridical persons and other organizations having no business offices, offices, or equivalent facilities in Japan (Article 32 of the Cabinet Office Ordinance on Financial Instruments Services, Etc.).

(ⅲ) Definitions of "parent company, etc.," "subsidiary company, etc.," and "affiliated company, etc."

The terms "parent company, etc.," "subsidiary company, etc.," and "affiliated company, etc." are defined by the same "criteria of control" and "criteria of influence" as contained in the Ordinance on Financial Statements, Etc. (Article 8(3) through (7)). This is in order to achieve consistency with the definitions of "parent juridical person, etc.," "subsidiary juridical person, etc.," and "affiliated juridical person, etc." in the Banking Act and related regulations (Article 13-2 of the Banking Act; Article 4-2(2) & (3) of the Order for Enforcement of the Banking Act; Article 14-7 of the Ordinance for Enforcement of the Banking Act).

Specifically, the term "parent company, etc." means a specified company, etc. which has control over the organ (meaning the shareholders meeting and any other organs equivalent thereto; referred to as the "decision making body") which is responsible for deciding the policies for finance, operations, and business of another company, etc. (Article 15-16 (3) of the Implementing Order; Article 33 of the Cabinet Office Ordinance on Financial Instruments Services, Etc.).

The term "subsidiary company, etc." means another company, etc. whose decision-making body is controlled by a parent company, etc. (Article 15-16 (3) of the Implementing Order). Where the parent company, etc. and subsidiary company, etc. or the subsidiary company, etc. has control over the decision making body of another company, etc., such other company, etc. is deemed to be the subsidiary company, etc. of the parent company, etc. (ibid.).

The term "affiliated company, etc." means a specified company, etc. (excluding a subsidiary company, etc.) over which another company, etc. (including a subsidiary company, etc. of such company, etc.) may have a material influence on the decisions about the policies for finance, operations, or business, through investment, assumption of office as a director or other position equivalent thereto by a person who is or has been an officer or employee of the other company, etc., provision of financing, guarantee of obligations, or collateral, provision of technology, or operational or business transactions, etc. (Article 15-16(4) of the Implementing Order; Article 34 of the Cabinet Office Ordinance on Financial Instruments Services, Etc.).

## 5. Consolidated regulatory oversight

### a. Overview

In the case of banks and insurance companies, start-up regulations are imposed on bank holding companies and insurance holding companies of which they are subsidiaries in the form of a system of authorization (Articles 2(13) and 52-17(1) & (3) of the Banking Act; Articles 2(16) and 271-18(1) & (3) of the Insurance Business Act). Thus, in addition to regulatory oversight at the individual company level, a system of consolidated (group-wide) regulatory oversight is also in place.

By contrast, the system of regulatory oversight of financial instruments business operators enshrined in the FIEA previously focused on the individual company level; holding companies of which financial instruments business operators, etc. were subsidiaries and were subject only to reporting and inspection requirements (Article 56-2 (1) of the FIEA). The FSA implemented consolidated oversight on a supervisory basis, drawing up a Guideline for Financial Conglomerates (June 24, 2005) for that purpose.

In the case of banking groups, the 2016 revision of the Banking Act has clarified the function of "management and control" of subsidiary companies by bank holding companies or banks (Articles 16-3 and 52-21(1) & (4) of the Banking Act; Articles 17-5-3 and 34-14-2 of the Ordinance for Implementation of the Banking Act).

However, as securities companies grew more colossal and complex

Chapter 5   Business regulations on financial instruments business operators, etc.

(taking the form of corporate groups), the need came to be felt, in the aftermath of the so-called Lehman shock (September 15, 2008), for a system of regulatory oversight enabling the supervisory authorities to assess the business and risk profile of securities groups on a consolidated basis, in order to ensure the stability and soundness of the financial system.

To that end, the 2010 revision of the FIEA established a system of consolidated regulatory oversight of "downstream consolidation" and "upstream consolidation."

b. Regulatory oversight of "downstream consolidation"

Under the system of regulatory oversight of "downstream consolidation," a financial instruments business operator (excluding a foreign juridical person) engaged in type I financial instruments business with total assets in excess of one trillion yen is (1) required to provide notification (Article 57-2 (1) of the FIEA; Article 17-2-2 of the Implementing Order; Article 208-2 of the Cabinet Office Ordinance on Financial Instruments Services, Etc.); then (2) required to submit materials (each quarter) on its parent company group (Article 57-2 (2) through (9) of the FIEA); and (3) required to submit (each business year) a consolidated business report on the special financial instruments business operator and its subsidiary juridical persons, etc., prepare consolidated explanatory documents and make them available for public inspection (each business year), and provide notification of its 〈consolidated capital-to-risk ratio〉 and make it available for public inspection (each quarter). In addition, it is subject to supervisory actions according to consolidated capital adequacy requirements (Article 57-3 to Article 57-11 of the FIEA).

Foreign juridical persons are excluded from regulatory oversight of "downstream consolidation" on the principle that their regulatory oversight should be left to the authorities in their home country rather than duplicated by the Japanese administrative authorities.

A financial instruments business operator that has provided the notification in (1) above is termed a "special financial instruments business operator" (Article 57-2 (2) of the FIEA). Taking the special financial instruments business operator as the reference point, the third pillar of regulatory oversight above relates to "downstream consolidation" in the

*689*

strict sense of the term, whereas the second contains an element of oversight of "upstream consolidation." The second pillar is needed in order for the administrative authorities to assess the overall state of operations and finances of the parent company group to which the special financial instruments business operator belongs, as well as determine whether it needs to be subjected to regulatory oversight of "upstream consolidation." The term "parent company" means a company which has another company as its subsidiary company (meaning a subsidiary company prescribed in Article 29-4, paragraph 3 of the FIEA) (Article 57-2(8) of the FIEA); the term "subsidiary juridical person, etc." means a subsidiary company, etc. or an affiliated company, etc. (ibid., Article 57-2 (9); Articles 17-2-4 and 15-16-2(1) of the Implementing Order).

The specific materials that must be submitted under (2) above include the state of the operations and assets of the parent company group (comprising the parent company of the special financial instruments business operator and the parent company's subsidiary juridical persons, etc.); the nature and method of management and control of the special financial instruments business operator by the parent company; and the nature and methods of funding assistance to the special financial instruments business operator by the parent company and its subsidiary juridical persons, etc. (Article 57-2 (2) of the FIEA; Articles 208-4 to 208-6 of the Cabinet Office Ordinance on Financial Instruments Services, Etc.).

c. Regulatory oversight of "upstream consolidation"

Under the system of regulatory oversight of "upstream consolidation," the Commissioner of the FSA may designate a parent company as being subject to consolidated regulatory oversight if it is found necessary to assess the business and risk profile of the group as a whole, including the parent company (Article 57-12 (1) of the FIEA) — if, for example, the special financial instruments business operator's parent company, or a subsidiary juridical person, etc. of that parent company, conducts financial business integrally with the special financial instruments business operator. Regulatory oversight of "upstream consolidation" is compatible with the strengthening of regulatory oversight of "systemically important financial institutions" agreed on in the Leaders' Statement adopted at the G20

Chapter 5   Business regulations on financial instruments business operators, etc.

Pittsburgh summit (September 24-25, 2009) in the wake of the global financial crisis.

The parent company so designated is termed a "designated parent company," and the special financial instruments business operator with respect to which the designation is made is termed a "subject special financial instruments business operator" (ibid., Article 57-12 (3)). The "parent company" may be a foreign company (Article 57-27 of the FIEA; Article 17-2-12 of the Implementing Order). Currently there are two designated parent companies; Nomura Holdings, Inc., and Daiwa Securities Group Inc. (Public Notice of the FSA No. 46 of 2011). These two companies are designated as domestic systemically important banks (D-SIBs) (December 2015).

Bank holding company groups and insurance holding company groups, as well as foreign-owned securities groups overseen by foreign administrative agencies, are exempt from oversight of "upstream consolidation" (Article 57-12(2) of the FIEA). The parent company of a foreign-owned securities group may be ordered to implement improvement measures as a "specified major shareholder" (Article 32-2(2) & (3) of the FIEA), and supervisory monitoring of a "foreign holding company, etc. group" as a whole is conducted through the type I financial instruments business operator which is the Japanese base of the group (IV-7 of the Comprehensive Guidelines for Supervision of Financial Instruments Business Operators, Etc.).

The requirement for designation as a parent company is either (1) that the parent company conducts management and control of the special financial instruments business operator as a business, or (2) that the parent company or its subsidiary juridical person, etc. provides funding assistance to the special financial instruments business operator for the purpose of its business operations, which, if suspended, has the risk of causing substantial detriment to the operation of the business of the special financial instruments business operator.

A designated parent company (1) is required to provide notification of certain matters and submit a consolidated business report (each business year), prepare consolidated explanatory documents and make them available for public inspection (each business year), and provide notification of its consolidated capital-to-risk ratio and make it available for public

*691*

inspection (each quarter); (2) is subject to orders to improve business operation, take measures, suspend business, and dismiss directors and officers, as well as regarding supervisory actions according to consolidated capital adequacy requirements; and (3) is subject to regulatory oversight of major shareholders (Articles 57-13 to 57-26 of the FIEA).

# 6. The sales representative system

### a. Overview

To ensure that the sale and solicitation of securities and derivatives transactions are appropriately conducted and to protect investors, the FIEA institutes a registration system for sales representatives under which the only officers and employees who may engage in sale and solicitation on behalf of financial instruments business operators, etc. are those who are registered.

### b. "Sales representative"

The term "sales representative" means an officer or employee of a financial instruments business operator, etc. who conducts certain acts on its behalf, irrespective of his/her title such as solicitor, sales person, agent, or others (Article 64 (1) (i), (ii) & (iii) of the FIEA; Article 17-14 of the Implementing Order).

Currently the acts covered comprise, in the main, (1) in the area of type I financial instruments business, sale and solicitation with respect to type I securities, type I securities-related market transactions of derivatives and foreign market derivatives transactions, and over-the-counter transactions in derivatives; and (2) in the area of type II financial instruments business, sale and solicitation with respect to market transactions of derivatives and foreign market derivatives transactions that are related to "deemed securities" or are not securities-related. On the other hand, they do not include sale and solicitation with respect to type II securities in the area of Type II financial instruments business, or sale and solicitation with respect to investment management business, investment advisory and agency business, and securities etc. custody business. Acts covered can, however, be added by cabinet order.

Characteristically, covered acts include not only certain acts constituting

*692*

Chapter 5　Business regulations on financial instruments business operators, etc.

"financial instruments business" but also "solicitation for application" for transactions in type I securities and derivatives, or intermediary, brokerage, or agency service therefor, as well as "solicitation for the entrustment" of market transactions of derivatives or foreign market derivatives transactions. Transactions conducted for one's own account are also included.

c. Authority of sales representatives

A sales representatives has the authority to conduct any extra-judicial acts concerning subject acts on behalf of the financial instruments business operator, etc. to which he/she belongs (so-called general authority of representation) (Article 64-3(1) of the FIEA). This provision was added under the 1965 revision of the Securities and Exchange Act for the purpose of defining more clearly the scope of authority of sales representatives, in order to protect investors (Supreme Court Decision of Dec. 3, 1963, *Civil Cases of the Supreme Court*, Vol. 17, No. 12, p. 1596).

Courts have ruled in the past that the authority of sales representatives (1) includes authority with respect to incidental business such as transfer of title or deposits for the purpose of safe custody (Nagoya High Court Decision of Dec. 27, 1976, *Hanrei Jiho*, No. 856, p. 85; Osaka High Court Decision of Mar. 25, 1993, *Hanrei Times*, No. 829, p. 171); (2) must be within the scope of business actually conducted by the securities company to which the representative belongs (Tokyo District Court Decision of Feb. 16, 1995, *Hanrei Jiho*, No. 1550, p. 65); and (3) does not include acts involving accepting money from a customer for deposit in a fictitious transaction account (Supreme Court Decision of Mar. 25, 2003; *Hanrei Jiho*, No. 1822, p. 63).

A sales representative does not have general authority of representation in cases where the other party has acted in bad faith (Article 64-3(2) of the FIEA). "Bad faith" includes not only cases where the other party knows that the sales representative's authority of representation is defective or restricted, but also cases where the sales representative does not conduct the transaction on behalf of the securities company in question and cases where he/she has acted as the customer's agent out of a special personal relationship of trust (Tokyo District Court Decision of Feb. 26, 1982, *Hanrei*

*Times*, No. 474, p. 132; Takamatsu High Court Decision of Apr. 12, 1983, *Hanrei Times*, No. 498, p. 106). "Bad faith" includes gross negligence (ibid.; Osaka High Court Decision of Mar. 30, 1989, *Hanrei Times*, No. 701, p. 265).

The acts of a sales representative may be held subject not only to the contractual liability of the financial instruments business operator, etc. to which he/she belongs, but also to liability for tort in the form of employer liability (Article 715 of the Civil Code). Many past court decisions have, in cases where an act is considered to fall within the apparent range of business of the employer (under the apparent-range theory), denied bad faith or gross negligence by the other party to the act and found the employer liable (e.g., Tokyo High Court Decision of Nov. 20, 1995, *Hanrei Times*, No. 918, p. 171; Osaka District Court Decision of Sept. 30, 1996, *Hanrei Times*, No. 937, p. 195; Tokyo High Court Decision of Aug. 11, 2003, *Shoken Torihiki Higai Hanrei Serekuto*, Vol. 22, p. 139 — in the retrial after the Supreme Court, in its above Decision of Mar. 25, 2003, referred the case back to the court of second instance), but some have recognized it and denied the liability of the employer (Tokyo District Court Decision of Aug. 5, 1993, *Hanrei Times*, No. 839, p. 225; Tokyo District Court Decision of Jun. 26, 1997, *Hanrei Jiho*, No. 1641, p. 94; Tokyo District Court Decision of Mar. 26, 1998, *Hanrei Times*, No. 1042, p. 191).

### d. Registration of sales representatives

A financial instruments business operator, etc. must have its sales representatives registered in the registry of sales representatives ("registry") (Article 64(1) of the FIEA).

This registry is kept at the Local Finance Bureau or Fukuoka Local Finance Branch Bureau, except if it is of sales representatives of financial instruments business operators, etc. that have an "association" (meaning an authorized financial instruments firms association or recognized financial instruments firms association) conduct registration procedures, in which case it is kept at the association in question (ibid.; Article 248 of the Cabinet Office Ordinance on Financial Instruments Services, Etc.).

A financial instruments business operator, etc. must not have a person other than those registered conduct duties of sales representatives (Article 64 (2) of the FIEA). A sales representative can belong to only a single

Chapter 5   Business regulations on financial instruments business operators, etc.

operator (see Article 64-2(1)(iii) of the FIEA); it is thus made clear where liability with respect to sales representatives lies. Sales representatives are classified into sales representatives belonging to financial instruments business operators, etc. (who have authority of representation) and sales representatives belonging to financial instruments intermediary service providers (who perform only intermediary services) (see ibid.).

e. Delegation of sales representative registration procedures

The Commissioner of the FSA has an association conduct procedures for registration of sales representatives of a financial instruments business operator, etc. belonging to that association ("registration procedures") (Article 64-7(1) of the FIEA; Article 254 of the Cabinet Office Ordinance on Financial Instruments Services, Etc.). The registration procedures delegated to the association are as follows: accepting written applications for registration; conducting registration and providing notification to that effect; refusing registration, providing notification to that effect, and conducting relevant hearings; accepting notification of changes etc. in registered matters; rescinding registration of a sales representative or ordering suspension of his/her business, providing notification to that effect, and conducting relevant hearings; and deleting registration (ibid., each item). When the Commissioner of the FSA has decided to have an association conduct registration procedures, he/she does not conduct the registration procedures (Article 64-7(3) of the FIEA).

Sales representative registration procedures are currently delegated to the Japan Securities Dealers Association (JSDA) and the Financial Futures Association of Japan (FFAJ), which both constitute associations. For practical purposes, registration procedures under the FIEA are conducted in accordance with the rules of these associations: specifically, the "Rules Concerning Qualification and Registration, Etc. of Sales Representatives of Association Members" of the Japan Securities Dealers Association (below referred to as the "JSDA sales representative rules") and the "Rules on Registration, Etc. of Sales Representatives" of the Financial Futures Association of Japan (below referred to as the "FFAJ sales representative rules").

*695*

f . Qualifications of sales representatives

Alongside the conditions for refusal of registration of a sales representative contained in the FIEA (Article 64-2, paragraph 1), the rules of the two associations (the Japan Securities Dealers Association and the Financial Futures Association of Japan) set out a system of qualifications for sales representatives. An officer or employee of an association member is not allowed to be registered as a sales representative unless he/she possesses sales representative qualifications (Article 4 of the JSDA sales representative rules; Article 4 of the FFAJ sales representative rules).

The qualification system for sales representatives is administered by the associations in their capacity as self-regulatory organizations; it is not based on the authority delegated to them to conduct registration procedures under the FIEA. To qualify as a sales representative, one is required, for example, to pass the sales representative qualification exam administered by each association. Each association has several categories of sales representative qualifications.

Each association requires registered sales representatives to take a "training course for renewal of the sales representative qualification" every five years; if a person fails to complete this training course within the prescribed period, the effectiveness of his/her sales representative qualification is suspended (Article 18 of the JSDA sales representative rules; Article 18 of the FFAJ sales representative rules).

g . Supervisory actions for sales representatives

In cases where a registered sales representative has violated laws and regulations concerning financial instruments business (or registered financial institution business in the case of registered financial institutions) involving the conduct of acts requiring registration as a sales representative (Article 64(1)(i), (ii) & (iii) of the FIEA), or a business incidental thereto, or is found to have conducted other extremely inappropriate acts concerning duties of sales representatives, the relevant association may rescind his/her registration or order suspension of his/her business specifying a period not exceeding two years (Article 64-5(1) of the FIEA).

In addition to the above actions based on the FIEA (e.g., Article 11 of the JSDA sales representative rules), each association prescribes the following

Chapter 5   Business regulations on financial instruments business operators, etc.

action under its own rules: (1) revocation or suspension of sales representative qualifications (ibid., Article 6); (2) public announcement of disciplinary action against sales representatives recommended by the Securities and Exchange Surveillance Commission (ibid., Article 12); and (3) requiring association members to make disciplined persons take the designated training courses (ibid., Article 13).

h. System of officers administered by self-regulatory organizations

Through self-regulations, financial instruments firms associations administer a system of officers with a view to strengthening the internal control system of member financial instruments business operators, etc. The Japan Securities Dealers Association and the Financial Futures Association of Japan have established a system of qualification exams for such officers.

For example, the Japan Securities Dealers Association has a system of exams for internal administration supervisors, internal administration assistant supervisors, sales managers, and internal administrators.

*697*

# Chapter 6

Conduct regulations on
financial instruments business
operators, etc.

*Naohiko Matsuo*

# 1. Structure of conduct regulations on financial instruments business operators, etc.

### a. Basic thinking behind conduct regulations

To ensure the effectiveness of rules for protecting users, the FIEA legislative framework established in 2006 takes a functional approach whereby financial instruments and transactions of the same economic nature are subject to the same rules; thus, conduct regulations on financial instruments business operators, etc. are applied on a cross-sectoral basis, regardless of preexisting business categories.

In accordance with the same functional, cross-sectoral approach, the FIEA is defined as having a general character with respect to sale and solicitation of financial instruments and transactions. Financial regulatory laws such as the Banking Act, the Insurance Business Act, and the Trust Business Act are equipped with the requisite provisions on, for example, the application mutatis mutandis of the FIEA conduct regulations to forms of business not constituting financial instruments business or registered financial institution business — banking business conducted by banks, insurance business conducted by insurance companies, and trust business conducted by trust companies (Article 13-4 of the Banking Act; Article 300-2 of the Insurance Business Act; Article 24-2 of the Trust Business Act). This ensures equivalence with the conduct regulations in the FIEA.

On the other hand, just as business regulations are made structurally flexible through the classification of "financial instruments business" into "type I financial instruments business," "type II financial instruments business," "investment advisory and agency business," and "investment management business," conduct regulations are made structurally flexible by following the same classification.

### b. Structure of provisions on conduct regulations

To protect investors and ensure the soundness of capital markets, conduct regulations on financial instruments business operators, etc. prohibit or restrict the performance of certain acts by those operators in the course of their business, or require them to perform certain acts or establish certain systems.

*700*

Chapter 6   Conduct regulations on financial instruments business operators, etc.

The provisions on conduct regulations on financial instruments business operators, etc. enshrined in the FIEA are structured as follows. First, there are conduct regulations applying in common to all financial instruments business operators, etc. (Article 35-3 to Article 40-5 of the FIEA). These conduct regulations prohibit not only financial instruments business operators, etc. but also their officers and employees from conducting certain acts (Articles 36(1) and 38 of the FIEA). They also include a prohibition of compensation for loss, etc. applying not only to financial instruments business operators, etc. but also to their customers (Article 39(2) of the FIEA).

On the other hand, these conduct regulations include certain regulations that, by their nature, apply only to certain types of financial instruments business operators, etc.

Specifically, these are (1) the obligation of "specified financial instruments business operators, etc." (securities companies and registered financial institutions) to establish a conflict-of-interest management system (Article 36(2) to (5) of the FIEA; Article 15-27 of the Financial Instruments and Exchange Act Implementing Order [hereinafter, the "Implementing Order"]); (2) the prohibition on bond management, etc. by financial instruments business operators engaged in securities-related business (Article 36-4 of the FIEA); (3) the obligation of financial instruments business operators, etc. engaged in securities etc. custody business to deliver documentation upon receipt of a security deposit (Article 37-5 of the FIEA); (4) the obligation of financial instruments business operators in type I financial instruments business or type II financial instruments business and registered financial institutions engaged to clarify conditions of transactions in advance (Article 37-2 of the FIEA), the obligation to establish the best execution policy (Article 40-2 of the FIEA), the prohibition on their conducting sale and purchase, etc. where separate custody of assets is not ensured (Article 40-3 of the FIEA), the prohibition on their engaging in public offering, etc. where money is diverted (Article 40-3-2 of the FIEA), restrictions on their selling, purchasing, or otherwise dealing in securities for professional investors (Article 40-4 of the FIEA), and the obligation to provide notification with regard to securities for professional investors (Article 40-5 of the FIEA), the prohibition on bucketing (Article 40-6 of the FIEA), and the obligation to use an electronic data processing system, etc.

*701*

for over-the-counter transactions of derivatives (Article 40-7 of the FIEA); (5) the provision on cancellation by means of document (cooling off) applying to financial instruments business operators, etc. engaged in investment advisory and agency business (Article 37-6 of the FIEA; Article 16-3(1) of the Implementing Order); and (6) the prohibition on the conduct of certain acts by financial instruments business operators, etc. engaged in investment advisory and agency business or investment management business (Article 38-2 of the FIEA).

Second, there are conduct regulations applying to financial instruments business operators, etc. engaged in investment advisory business (Article 41 to Article 41-5 of the FIEA).

Third, there are conduct regulations applying to financial instruments business operators, etc. engaged in investment management business (Article 42 to Article 42-8 of the FIEA).

Fourth, there are conduct regulations applying to financial instruments business operators, etc. engaged in securities, etc. custody business (Article 43 to Article 43-4 of the FIEA).

Fifth, there is the obligation to provide information applying to financial instruments business operators, etc. engaged in crowdfunding business (the business of handling investment crowdfunding) (Article 43-5 of the FIEA).

Sixth, there are preventive measures against adverse effects and related provisions (such as so-called firewall regulations) (Article 44 to Article 44-4 of the FIEA).

Seventh, there are certain conduct regulations from which professional investors are exempt (Article 45 of the FIEA).

c. Fiduciary duty and its core elements
( i ) Fiduciary duty as legal obligation

The conduct regulations on financial instruments business operators, etc. contained in the FIEA are founded on the concept of "fiduciary duty." The term "fiduciary" in this context means, broadly, anyone who performs a task on behalf of another. "Fiduciary duty" has four core elements: "duty of care," "duty of loyalty," "duty not to delegate," and "duty of segregation".

The five core elements of fiduciary duty in the FIEA are: (1) the basic duty to act in good faith that is fairly imposed on all financial instruments

Chapter 6   Conduct regulations on financial instruments business operators, etc.

business operators, etc. (Article 36 (1) of the FIEA); (2) with respect to investment advisory business and investment management business, the duty of care of a prudent manager and the duty of loyalty (Articles 41 and 42 of the FIEA); (3) with respect to securities, etc. custody business, the duty of care of a prudent manager (Article 43 of the FIEA); (4) with respect to investment management business, the duty not to delegate (Article 42-3 of the FIEA); and (5) with respect to investment management business relating to self-management of collective investment schemes (funds) and securities, etc. custody business, the duty of segregation (Articles 42-4, 43, 43-1, 43-2 and 43-3 of the FIEA).

( ii )   Fiduciary duty as a principle

The subject of fiduciary duty in the broad sense (customer-oriented business conduct) is treated in the Financial Services Agency's Strategic Directions and Priorities for 2015-2016 and for 2016-2017.

Fiduciary duty in the broad sense is defined as the general term for the wide range of roles and responsibilities that a person performing certain functions must fulfill in order to live up to the trust placed in him or her by another. Unlike fiduciary duty in the narrow sense, it is not a legal obligation (although it may overlap with the duty to act in good faith and fairly); it may be considered rather a principle of financial services, which aims to ensure best practices in providing financial products and services that are in the best interest of the customer. "Principle" here means any of the key norms and standards of conduct that underlie individual legal and other regulations and that should be respected by financial institutions in conducting business and by the authorities in regulating it (FSA, Apr. 18, 2008).

Fiduciary duty in the broad sense requests that all financial operators anywhere in the investment chain, whether they sell financial products, provide advice, develop products, provide asset custody, or manage assets, always conduct business in the best interest of the costomer (i.e., in the best interest of the person who ultimately supplies the funds and is the beneficiary).

The Principles of Fiduciary Duty compiled by the FSA are these: (1) establish and release a policy on fiduciary duties; (2) pursue the best interest of the customer; (3) appropriately manage conflicts of interest; (4) clearly

*703*

state fees, etc.; (5) provide material information in a manner that is easily understandable; (6) provide services suitable to the client; and (7) establish an appropriate framework for motivating personnel to comply (FSA, March 30, 2017).

d. Conflict-of-interest regulations

The FIEA establishes regulations on conflict of interest founded on the principle of fiduciary duty (particularly the duty of loyalty).

First, specified financial instruments business operators, etc. (securities companies and registered financial institutions) are required to establish a conflict-of-interest management system (Article 36(2) to (5) of the FIEA). This requirement was imposed by the 2008 revision of the FIEA as an effective means of preventing the adverse effects of conflict of interest, when firewall regulations separating banking and securities sectors were relaxed and the scope of business of banking groups and insurance company groups expanded. A mechanism for avoiding conflicts of interest is also a required element of the operational control systems to be established by credit rating agencies (Article 66-33 of the FIEA; Article 306(1)(vii) of the Cabinet Office Ordinance on Financial Instruments Services, Etc.).

Second, concrete provisions have been established prohibiting conflicts of interest by financial instruments business operators, etc. Specifically, these are (1) the prohibition on selling, purchasing, or otherwise dealing in securities on one's own account in preference to orders on consignment (Article 38(viii) of the FIEA; Article 117(1)(x) of the Cabinet Office Ordinance on Financial Instruments Services, Etc.); (2) the prohibition of conflicts of interest with respect to investment advisory business (Article 41-2(i), (ii), (iii), (iv) & (vi) of the FIEA; Article 126(i) of the Cabinet Office Ordinance on Financial Instruments Services, Etc.); (3) the prohibition of conflicts of interest with respect to investment management business (Article 42-2(i), (ii), (iii), (iv), (v) & (vii) of the FIEA; Article 130(1)(i), (ii), (iii) & (vi) of the Cabinet Office Ordinance on Financial Instruments Services, Etc.); and (4) the prohibition of conflicts of interest with respect to preventive measures against adverse effects (Articles 44(i) (ii), 44-2(1)(ii), 44-3(1)(iii) and (2)(iii), etc.). These provisions, in line with their objective of prohibiting conflicts of interest, define conditions of purpose

*704*

Chapter 6   Conduct regulations on financial instruments business operators, etc.

(the act must be conducted "for the purpose of gaining profit" for oneself or a third party) and of legally sufficient cause (it must involve "utilizing" information or such). Whether these conditions are met should be determined substantively in light of the objective facts.

Third, provisions designed to restrict conflicts of interest by financial instruments business operators, etc. include (1) the prohibition on bond management, etc. by financial instruments business operators engaged in securities-related business (Article 36-4 of the FIEA); (2) the obligation of financial instruments business operators, etc. to clarify conditions of transactions in advance (Article 37-2 of the FIEA); (3) restrictions on the act of furnishing as security or loaning a customer's securities or instruments (Article 43-4 of the FIEA); and (4) restrictions on granting of credit by underwriters (Article 44-4 of the FIEA).

Fourth, when the best execution requirement was imposed on securities companies by the 2004 revision of the Securities and Exchange Act, two prohibitions intended to restrict conflicts of interest were deleted: the prohibition on dual trading (in which, in a securities sale or purchase transaction or an over-the-counter derivatives transaction in securities, the same securities company is both the principal and simultaneously the broker or agent of the counterparty) in Article 39 of the old Securities and Exchange Act, and the prohibition on bucketing (in which a member, etc. of an exchange securities market entrusted with a securities sale or purchase transaction on that market effects the transaction by becoming the counterparty to it off that market) in Article 129 of the old Securities and Exchange Act. Derivatives transactions are exempt from the best execution requirement (Article 40-2 (1) of the FIEA; Article 16-6 (1) (ii) of the Implementing Order). On the other hand, the 2012 revision of the FIEA newly imposed a prohibition on bucketing with respect to "commodity-related market transactions of derivatives, etc." (Article 40-6 of the FIEA).

   e . Individual conduct regulations and system establishment requirements
      ( i )   Individual conduct regulations
Conduct regulations on financial instruments business operators, etc. can be classified into individual conduct regulations and system establishment

*705*

requirements.

Individual conduct regulations prohibit or restrict the performance of specific acts by financial instruments business operators, etc., or require them to perform specific acts. Individual conduct regulations make up the lion's share of conduct regulations.

( ii ) System establishment requirements

System establishment requirements either require financial instruments business operators, etc. to establish certain systems or prohibit them from doing so.

An example of the former (positive system establishment requirements) is the obligation of specified financial instruments business operators, etc. to establish a conflict of interest management system (Article 36(2) to (5) of the FIEA). Similarly, credit rating agencies have an obligation to establish an operational control system (Article 66-33 of the FIEA). The 2014 revision of the FIEA imposes a new obligation on financial instruments business operators, etc. to establish an operational control system (Article 35-3 of the FIEA, Article 70-2 of the Cabinet Office Ordinance on Financial Instruments Services, Etc.).

The latter (negative system establishment requirements) are exemplified by the prohibition on certain states of business operation (Article 40(ii) of the FIEA; Article 123 of the Cabinet Office Ordinance on Financial Instruments Services, etc.). Note that the principle of suitability (Article 40 (i) of the FIEA) constitutes an individual conduct regulation.

Even if an individual act by an officer or employee of a financial instruments business operator, etc. is problematic as judged by the intent of the system establishment requirements, that does not in itself constitute a violation of system establishment requirements (a violation of laws and regulations, etc.); on the other hand, if the occurrence of a single problematic act leads to the conclusion that an appropriate system is not in place, system establishment requirements are considered to have been violated.

(iii) Obligation to provide notification of "incident, etc."

When the officer or employee of a financial instruments business operator, etc. has committed an act that violates "laws and regulations, etc." (Article

Chapter 6   Conduct regulations on financial instruments business operators, etc.

13 (iv) (a) (γ) of the Cabinet Office Ordinance on Financial Instruments Services, etc.), notification must be provided of the "incident, etc." and its details (Article 50(1) (viii) of the FIEA; Articles 199(vii) & (viii) and 200 (vi) & (vii) of the Cabinet Office Ordinance on Financial Instruments Services, Etc.).

In the term "laws and regulations, etc.," "laws and regulations" means the laws and regulations of Japan; foreign laws and regulations are excluded (see Article 117 (1) (xv) (a) (α) Cabinet Office Ordinance on Financial Instruments Services, etc.). The term "laws and regulations" is not limited to financial regulatory laws and regulations, but refers to all laws and regulations. "Articles of incorporation and other rules" means the rules of financial instruments firms associations and financial instruments exchanges, which are self-regulatory organizations.

In terms of administrative oversight, financial instruments business operators, etc. are required to provide notification of incident, etc. in financial instruments business, etc. (III-2-2 and VIII-1 of the Comprehensive Guidelines for Supervision of Financial Instruments Business Operators, Etc.). "Incident, etc. in financial instruments business, etc." comprises (1) acts that constitute violations of laws and regulations, etc., (2) cases of criminal accusation, and (3) other similar acts.

(iv)   Obligation of association members to submit reports on incidents

Members of the Japan Securities Dealers Association (JSDA) are required to submit a "report on incidents" and a "report on incident resolution" concerning any "incident" by an "employee, etc." (meaning any person who is currently, or who has been, an employee of the member) (JSDA, Articles 9 and 10 of the Rules Concerning Employees of Association Members).

The JSDA deems any employee, etc. who has committed an act that greatly impairs public confidence in the financial instruments business a "perpetrator of an inappropriate act" and keeps a list of perpetrators of such acts; association members are prohibited from hiring a class-1 perpetrator of an inappropriate act in perpetuity and from hiring a class-2 perpetrator of an inappropriate act for five years (ibid., Articles 4(2) & (3), 12(1) and 13-3).

f . The professional investor system

Conduct regulations on operators under financial regulatory laws such as the old Securities and Exchange Act were applied across the board, regardless of the characteristics of investors. Under the 2006 revision of the Securities and Exchange Act, however, the FIEA, primarily following the example of the European Union (EU), classifies investors into "professional investors" (so-called pros) and general investors, or "customers other than professional investors" (so-called amateurs), and applies conduct regulations to financial instruments business operators, etc. in accordance with that classification, in order to ensure the structural flexibility of those regulations.

Specifically, first, when financial instruments business operators, etc. conduct transactions with general investors, the FIEA conduct regulations are fully applied in the interests of investor protection.

Second, persons who, in light of their knowledge, experience, and state of property, are considered capable of appropriately managing the risks associated with financial transactions are defined as "professional investors" (Article 2(31) of the FIEA). When financial instruments business operators, etc. conduct transactions with professional investors, they are exempt from conduct regulations designed to rectify the information gap, such as for example the obligation to deliver a pre-contract document prior to conclusion of the contract; but they are not exempt from conduct regulations also intended to ensure the fairness of capital markets, such as the prohibition of compensation for loss (Article 45 of the FIEA). However, the FIEA's exemption of transactions with professional investors from conduct regulations merely prescribes how such transactions are to be handled for the purpose of administrative regulation; it does not prohibit financial instruments business operators, etc. from voluntarily treating professional investors in the same manner as general investors.

Third, in certain cases a customer may, for each kind of contract, elect to change its status from general investor to professional investor or from professional investor to general investor (Article 34 to Article 34-5 of the FIEA; Article 53 of the Cabinet Office Ordinance on Financial Instruments Services, Etc.). Thus, there are four categories of investors (Table 6-1). The shift in status between professional investor and general investor is relative

Chapter 6　Conduct regulations on financial instruments business operators, etc.

## Table 6-1.　The four categories of investors under the professional investor system

I . Professional investors (cannot change status to general investor)
　⇒　Qualified institutional investors, the State, and the Bank of Japan
II . Professional investors (can elect to change status to general investor)
　⇒　Juridical persons as defined in Cabinet Office Ordinance on Definitions, Article 23
III. General investors (can elect to change status to professional investor)
　⇒　Juridical persons other than those in categories I and II, and individuals meeting the conditions in Cabinet Office Ordinance on Financial Instruments Services, Etc., Articles 61 and 62 (net assets of at least 300 million yen and invested financial assets of at least 300 million yen, etc.)
IV. General investors (cannot change status to professional investor)
　⇒　Individuals (excluding individuals in category III)

depending on the individual financial instruments business operator, etc.

Fourth, in the interests of protecting investors, the principle is adopted that full protection by the conduct regulations enshrined in law as enjoyed by general investors is the rule, while the treatment of professional investors is the exception. In accordance with that principle, straightforward procedures have been established for changing status from professional investor to general investor: professional investors must be notified that they can request to change their status, and such a request must be accepted when it is made, there is no fixed term of validity for the change, and procedures exist for application for reinstatement (Articles 34 and 34-2 of the FIEA). Under the 2009 revision of the FIEA, the change is valid indefinitely (it was previously valid for one year), and application may be made for reinstatement as a professional investor at any time.

Conversely, rigorous procedures have been established for changing status from general investor to professional investor: notification must be provided but there is no obligation to accept the request, written consent must be obtained, there is a fixed term of validity for the change, and procedures exist for requesting renewal (Articles 34-3 and 34-4 of the FIEA). Under the 2009 revision of the FIEA, application may be made for reinstatement as a general investor at any time, even before the expiration date. If a financial instruments business operator, etc. violates the latter procedures, the change in status to professional investor is invalid. In the aftermath of the AIJ Investment Advisors incident, which came to light in February 2012, welfare pension funds are, for the time being, in principle unable to request a change in status to professional investor (Article 3-2 of the Supplementary Provisions of the 2013 Act for Partial Revision of the FIEA, Etc.).

g. Characteristics of recently established conduct regulations

Recent revisions to the FIEA have tended to establish conduct regulations on financial instruments business operators, etc. with the goal of ensuring the effectiveness of other systems and regulations.

Specifically, first there are the conduct regulations relating to the system of "securities for professional investors" (Article 4 (3) of the FIEA) established under the 2008 revision of the FIEA. Since securities for professional investors are in principle to be traded only among professional investors, etc., these prescribe (1) the limitation on sale and purchase, etc. of securities for professional investors to general investors (Article 40-4 of the FIEA); and (2) the obligation to notify the counterparty in relation to securities for professional investors (Article 40-5 of the FIEA).

Second, there is the conduct regulation compelling the use of the system of designated dispute resolution organizations (financial ADR system) established under the 2009 revision of the FIEA, namely the obligation of financial instruments business operators, etc. to conclude a contract with a designated dispute resolution organization (Article 37-7 of the FIEA).

Third, there is the conduct regulation relating to the system of credit rating agencies established under the 2009 revision of the FIEA. Given that a credit rating business can but need not be registered, this prohibits a financial instruments business operator, etc. from providing a customer with a credit rating determined by a person engaged in a credit rating business other than a credit rating agency without informing the customer that the person who has determined the credit rating has not obtained registration and other matters, thereby soliciting him/her to conclude a contract (Article 38(iii) of the FIEA).

Fourth, under the 2012 revision of the FIEA, in order to enforce the

Chapter 6   Conduct regulations on financial instruments business operators, etc.

obligation to use an electronic trading platform for standardized over-the-counter transactions in derivatives, a financial instruments business operator, etc. that conducts over-the-counter transactions in derivatives in the course of business is, when engaging in "specified over-the-counter transactions in derivatives" (plain-vanilla yen interest rate swaps), required to use an electronic transaction system and publicize transaction information (Article 40-7 of the FIEA; Articles 125-7 and 125-8 of the Cabinet Office Ordinance on Financial Instruments Services, etc.; 2015 FSA Notice No. 67).

## 2. Fiduciary duty and its core elements

### a. The duty to act in good faith and fairly

The bedrock of "fiduciary duty" in the FIEA is the duty to act in good faith and fairly, understood to be a general provision embracing the conduct regulations on financial instruments business operators, etc. In the FIEA, the provision prescribing the duty to act in good faith and fairly (Article 36(1) of the FIEA) immediately precedes the specific conduct regulations (Articles 36(2) to (5) and 36-2 of the FIEA); thus, the arrangement of the articles makes clear that the specific conduct regulations concretize the duty to act in good faith and fairly. The duty to act in good faith and fairly is prescribed also for financial instruments intermediary service providers and credit rating agencies (Articles 66-7 and 66-32 of the FIEA).

The duty to act in good faith and fairly, established by the 1992 revision of the Securities and Exchange Act, enshrines as a legal obligation, for the purpose of administrative regulation, the principle of honesty and fairness that is the first of the seven "International Conduct of Business Principles" applying to securities brokers approved by the International Organization of Securities Commissions (IOSCO) at a general meeting in November 1990 (which principles are referred to below as the "IOSCO Conduct of Business Principles"). The IOSCO Conduct of Business Principles are (1) honesty and fairness, (2) diligence, (3) capabilities, (4) information about customers, (5) information for customers, (6) conflicts of interest, and (7) compliance.

The duty to act in good faith and fairly is, for the purpose of administrative regulation, a legal obligation, and any breach thereof is a violation of laws and regulations. On the other hand, for practical purposes it serves as a principle to be followed in interpreting specific conduct regulations or as a means of

*711*

supplementing them.

Exemplifying the latter, a court ruling has found that, in cases of frequent switching between investment trusts and "churning" of shares, if an account manager at a securities company, in order to make a profit for him/herself or the company by earning commission fees and so forth, engages in solicitation of transactions that make little or no sense for the customer and are largely or wholly unnecessary, such solicitation is also illegal under tort law in that it constitutes a serious breach of the duty to act in good faith and fairly (Yokohama District Court Decision of Mar. 25, 2009, *Shoken Torihiki Higai Hanrei Serekuto*, Vol. 35, p. 1). On the other hand, a breach of the duty to act in good faith and fairly has never been cited as direct grounds in an administrative action case, although one case did cite "dealings violating the intent of the duty to act in good faith and fairly towards customers" (FSA administrative action of Jun. 11, 2007).

The first of the IOSCO Conduct of Business Principles states that "a firm should act honestly and fairly in the best interests of its customers and the integrity of the market"; hence the duty to act in good faith and fairly enshrined in the FIEA should similarly be interpreted in terms of ensuring the integrity of the market. In the IOSCO Conduct of Business Principles it is further explained that the first principle includes any obligation to avoid deception and deceptive acts of representations; this too aids in understanding the duty to act in good faith and fairly enshrined in the FIEA.

The provisions of the law do not restrict the duty to act in good faith and fairly or the types of "business" subject to it; therefore, it should be understood to apply even to a business other than financial instruments business conducted by a financial instruments business operator, etc. if that business could seriously affect the operator's ability to execute financial instruments business in good faith and fairly.

b. The duty of care of a prudent manager and the duty of loyalty

(ⅰ) The duties of care and loyalty as conduct regulations

Whereas the duty to act in good faith and fairly applies to all financial instruments business operators, etc., the duty of due care of a prudent manager and the duty of loyalty are prescribed only for certain types of such operators (Articles 41, 42 and 43 of the FIEA). The FIEA does not impose

Chapter 6   Conduct regulations on financial instruments business operators, etc.

the duty of care of a prudent manager and the duty of loyalty in the case of business relating to sale and solicitation, dealing, brokerage, underwriting, and secondary distribution (selling).

This is because (1) these types of businesses are not necessarily conducted on entrustment by the customer (in the case of sale and solicitation); (2) even if they are conducted on entrustment by the customer — if the duty of care of a prudent manager under civil law (Article 644 of the Civil Code; Article 552 (2) of the Commercial Code) applies — the relationship is not necessarily one in which the business is conducted with reasonable discretionary judgment (in the case of brokerage), or is a relationship between equal parties (in the case of underwriting and secondary distribution), or is a relationship in which the business is not necessarily conducted solely for the customer's profit (in the case of brokerage, underwriting, and secondary distribution); and (3) in the case of brokerage, the duty to act in good faith and fairly was thought to suffice (general mandatory provisions imposing the duty of care of a prudent manager and the duty of loyalty were considered unnecessary), since the 2004 revision to the Securities and Exchange Act imposed the obligation to establish and publicize a best execution policy and the obligation to execute orders in accordance with that policy, etc. (Article 40-2 of the FIEA) in accordance with the intent of the duty of due care of a prudent manager.

The duty of care of a prudent manager and the duty of loyalty explicitly imposed on financial instruments business operators, etc. can be interpreted as duties deriving from the duty to act in good faith and fairly. Conversely, the duty to act in good faith and fairly can be understood as embracing the intent of the duty of care of a prudent manager and the duty of loyalty while differing from both per se. Citing Article 213 of the old Commodity Exchange Act (Article 213 of the current Commodity Futures Trading Act) prescribing a duty to act in good faith and fairly toward customers, a Supreme Court Decision of July 16, 2009 (*Civil Cases of the Supreme Court*, Vol. 63, No. 6, p. 1280) ruled that "futures commission merchants have a duty to the entrusting person to execute business in good faith and fairly, in accordance with the main purpose for which the entrustment was made and with the care of a prudent manager (Article 644 of the Civil Code)." This ruling defines the duty to act in good faith and fairly as part of the duty of care of a prudent manager under civil law.

The duty of care of a prudent manager and the duty of loyalty too are legal obligations for the purpose of administrative regulation, and there have been cases of administrative action against violations of them, primarily in the investment management business.

The party to which the duty of care of a prudent manager and the duty of loyalty are owed is basically the customer or right holder (investor) (Articles 41, 42 and 43 of the FIEA); but in the case of management of assets of an investment corporation (Article 2(8) (xii) (a) of the FIEA) the party to which they are owed is the registered investment corporation that is the other party to the asset management entrustment agreement, not the investor (Article 42(1) (i) of the FIEA).

( ii )　The duties of care and loyalty as structural regulations

A registered investment corporation must entrust business pertaining to the custody of assets to an "asset custody company" (Article 208(1) of the Act on Investment Trusts and Investment Corporations). An asset custody company is a juridical person who conducts business pertaining to the custody of assets under entrustment from a registered investment corporation (ibid., Article 2(20)), and must be a trust company, etc. or a financial instruments business operator, etc. engaged in securities etc. custody business (ibid., Article 208(2)). An asset custody company owes a duty of care of a prudent manager and a duty of loyalty to the investment corporation (ibid., Article 209).

c ．The duty not to delegate
( i )　The duty not to delegate as a conduct regulation

When conducting investment management business, a financial instruments business operator, etc. has a fiduciary duty not to delegate. As an exception to the duty not to delegate, a financial instruments business operator, etc. may, only where the requisite matters are set forth in the contract, entrust all or part of its investment authority to a third party (limited to another financial business operator, etc. engaged in an investment management business or a foreign juridical person engaged in an investment management business in a foreign state) (Article 42-3 (1) of the FIEA;

*714*

Chapter 6   Conduct regulations on financial instruments business operators, etc.

Article 16-12 of the Implementing Order; Article 131 of the Cabinet Office Ordinance on Financial Instruments Services, Etc.). Notwithstanding the above, the operator is prohibited from entrusting the whole of its investment authority pertaining to all the investment property (Article 42-3(2) of the FIEA).

The investment authority so regulated is investment management authority with regard to rights pertaining to securities or derivatives transactions, which also includes the authority to give instructions on exercise of voting rights. On the other hand, investment management authority with regard to assets other than these rights is outside the scope of the regulation.

A financial instruments business operator, etc. is prohibited from re-entrusting to another party all of the investment authority entrusted to it with regard to investment management business, or from re-entrusting to another party the whole or part of the authority re-entrusted to it; on the other hand, it may re-entrust to another party part of the investment authority entrusted to it (see Article 42-2(vii) of the FIEA; Articles 130(1) (x) and 131(i) of the Cabinet Office Ordinance on Financial Instruments Services, Etc.).

(ii)   The duty not to delegate as a structural regulation

With regard to investment trusts, the range of persons to which authority to give investment instructions may be entrusted and the allowance of partial re-entrustment are treated consistently with the above (Articles 2 (1)(2), 4(2)(xviii) and 49(2)(xix) of the Act on Investment Trusts and Investment Corporations; Articles 2(i) and 4(i) of the Order for Enforcement of the Act on Investment Trusts and Investment Corporations; Articles 7(v) & (vi) and 78(iv) & (v) of the Ordinance for Enforcement of the Act on Investment Trusts and Investment Corporations).

The asset management company of a registered investment corporation may re-entrust to another party part of the asset investment authority entrusted to it by that investment corporation, but it is prohibited from re-entrusting the whole of it (Article 202 of the Act on Investment Trusts and Investment Corporations).

*715*

d. Duty of segregation

( i ) Investment management business

When conducting investment management business, a financial instruments business operator, etc. has a fiduciary duty of segregation.

In the case of investment management business pertaining to an investment trust, the trust property must be separately managed (Article 28 (3) of the Trust Business Act). In the case of investment management business pertaining to a registered investment corporation, business pertaining to the custody of assets must be entrusted to an asset custody company (Article 208 of the Act on Investment Trusts and Investment Corporations), which company has a duty to retain those assets separately from its own (ibid., Article 209-2). In the case of discretionary investment business, a financial instruments business operator, etc. is prohibited from receiving deposits of money or securities (Article 42-5 of the FIEA; Articles 16-9 and 16-10 of the Implementing Order).

Therefore, with respect to self-management by financial instruments business operators, etc. (Article 2 (8) (xv) of the FIEA), the FIEA prescribes a duty of segregation (Article 42-4 of the FIEA).

Managing a so-called business-type fund does not constitute investment management business, and no duty of segregation is prescribed. On the other hand, a financial instruments business operator, etc. is prohibited from selling or soliciting equity in a domestic or foreign collective investment scheme, including in a business-type fund, unless it is ensured that the money invested is separately managed (Articles 40-3 and 40-3-2 of the FIEA; Article 16-7 of the Implementing Order; Article 125 of the Cabinet Office Ordinance on Financial Instruments Services, Etc.); thus, separate custody of assets is ensured indirectly via the seller.

( ii ) Securities, etc. custody business

When conducting securities, etc. custody business, a financial instruments business operator, etc. has a fiduciary duty of segregation.

First, securities deposited with an operator in connection with a transaction of securities-related derivatives, a margin transaction, etc., or a "subject securities-related transaction" (a transaction pertaining to securities-related business or incidental business, excluding over-the-coun-

Chapter 6   Conduct regulations on financial instruments business operators, etc.

ter transactions in derivatives with a certain type of party) are subject to the duty of segregation (Article 43-2(1) of the FIEA; Article 16-15 of the Implementing Order; Articles 136 to 137-2 of the Cabinet Office Ordinance on Financial Instruments Services, Etc.). With the appearance of contracts for difference (CFDs) in securities concluded with individual customers, the 2009 revision of the FIEA imposed a duty of segregation for over-the-counter transactions in securities derivatives and foreign market derivatives transactions as well. Book-entry bonds, etc. for which a financial instruments business operator, etc. opens an account and keeps records on behalf of the customer as the account management institution are also understood to be subject to the duty of segregation as being "securities deposited from a customer."

Second, money deposited in connection with such transactions, and securities furnished as security for them, are required to be separately managed by means of a trust for separate custody of customers (Article 43-2(2) of the FIEA; Articles 138 to 141-3 of the Cabinet Office Ordinance on Financial Instruments Services, Etc.). A financial instruments business operator, etc. must, every day, calculate the amount returnable to each customer and the total amount returnable required (the total of the amounts returnable to each customer) (Articles 141-3, 141(1)(vi) of the Cabinet Office Ordinance).

Third, given the existence of an investor protection fund system that, while predicated on the assumption of this strict duty of segregation, is designed to supplement it, financial instruments business operators are required to undergo an external audit of such procedures separately for custody assets, or a segregated custody audit (Article 43-2(3) of the FIEA; Article 142 of the Cabinet Office Ordinance on Financial Instruments Services, Etc.) (enacted when the FIEA legislative framework was established in 2006). Registered financial institutions are, not being subject to the investor protection fund system (Article 79-20(1) of the FIEA), also not subject to the requirement to undergo a segregated custody audit.

Fourth, the 2012 revision of the FIEA establishes a duty of segregation like that in Article 43-2, paragraph 1 of the law for "transactions relating to subject commodity derivatives transactions" (Article 43-2-2 of the FIEA; Articles 142-2 to 142-5 of the Cabinet Office Ordinance on Financial

*717*

Instruments Services, Etc.). Segregated custody by means of a "trust for segregated custody of commodity customers" is required (Articles 142-4(1) and 142-5(1) of the Cabinet Office Ordinance).

Fifth, money or securities deposited by a customer in connection with derivatives transactions, etc. (excluding transactions of securities-related derivatives, etc., commodity-related market transactions of derivatives, and "brokerage etc. of commodity-related market transactions of derivatives") are subject to a duty of segregated custody (Article 43-3 of the FIEA; Articles 143, 144 and 145 of the Cabinet Office Ordinance on Financial Instruments Services, Etc.). For "currency-related derivatives transactions, etc." (foreign exchange margin trading), a single method of segregated custody of money deposited as a security deposit is prescribed, namely the use of a money trust ("trust for segregated customer custody") (Articles 143(1)(i)(3) and 143-2(1) of the Cabinet Office Ordinance).

(iii)　The duty to retain assets separately as a structural regulation

An asset custody company is subject to the duty to retain the assets of an investment corporation separately from its own (Article 209-2 of the Act on Investment Trusts and Investment Corporations).

## 3. Obligation to establish a conflict-of-interest management system

### a. Intent

Article 36, paragraph 2 of the FIEA is generally understood to impose on specified financial instruments business operators, etc. the obligation to establish a conflict-of-interest management system (e.g., IV-1-3 of the Comprehensive Guidelines for Supervision of Financial Instruments Business Operators, Etc.). However, the provisions of the law and related regulations do not use the term "conflict of interest" but prescribe only that measures be taken "so that the interests of the customers... would not be unjustly impaired." Thus, it is possible to interpret more broadly as an obligation to establish a system for protecting customers' interests.

This obligation is prescribed immediately after the duty to act in good faith and fairly (Article 36(1) of the FIEA), which is taken to indicate that it is a basic obligation deriving from the duty to act in good faith and fairly and

*718*

Chapter 6   Conduct regulations on financial instruments business operators, etc.

relating to the "fiduciary duty" of financial instruments business operators, etc. The already-cited Supreme Court Decision of July 16, 2009, in light of the duty of care of a prudent manager in civil law, which embraces also the duty to act in good faith and fairly, affirms the duty of a futures commission merchant to explain to an entrusting person that there is a high likelihood of a conflict of interest arising between them.

This obligation is grounded in the notion that conflicts of interest are something to be managed rather than forbidden, which notion is consistent with standard international thinking on the handling of conflicts of interest in financial regulatory laws.

This obligation is by its nature a principles-based regulation that, in order to protect customers' interests, calls on specified financial instruments business operators, etc. to exercise their ingenuity in voluntarily establishing a conflict-of-interest management system (a type of internal management system) consistent with the nature, characteristics, and scale of their own and their group companies' business operations. It is to be hoped that in the course of oversight and surveillance, the administrative authorities will take care not to undermine the intent of such principles-based regulation in the process of conducting meticulous ex post facto checks on the state of conflict-of-interest management with respect to specific activities.

b. Overview of relevant regulations

The regulations embodying the obligation to establish a conflict-of-interest management system are complexly structured. First, the specified financial instruments business operators, etc. required to fulfill the obligation are, because it constitutes a new system establishment requirement, restricted to securities companies or registered financial institutions (Article 36(2) & (3) of the FIEA; Article 15-27 of the Implementing Order). That is because these organizations commonly experience situations where conflicts of interest arise in the area of financial business, and given the nature of their business the need for them to establish appropriate systems is generally high. Financial instruments business operators engaged solely in investment management business are exempt. Banks that are registered financial institutions are in addition subject to the obligation to establish a conflict-of-interest management system as banks (Article 13-3-2 of the Banking Act).

*719*

Second, customers with respect to whom conflict-of-interest management may be required are restricted in range to those on whose behalf "financial instruments related business" is conducted by an applicable specified financial instruments business operator, etc. or a "subsidiary financial institutions, etc." thereof (Article 36(2) & (5) of the FIEA; Article 15-28(2) & (3) of the Implementing Order). Customers of "parent financial institutions, etc." (Article 36(4) of the FIEA; Article 15-28(1) & (2) of the Implementing Order) are excluded. Parent financial institutions, etc. and subsidiary financial institutions, etc. include foreign group companies with no base in Japan. Financial instruments related business is restricted in scope to financial instruments business or incidental business thereto, or registered financial institution business (Article 36(2) of the FIEA; Article 70-2 of the Cabinet Office Ordinance on Financial Instruments Services, Etc.). Where securities companies engage in investment advisory business or investment management business, these too constitute financial instruments related business.

Third, transactions with applicable customers with respect to which conflict-of-interest management may be required ("subject transactions") comprise any transactions conducted by an applicable specified financial instruments business operator, etc. or the parent financial institution, etc. or subsidiary financial institution, etc. thereof. Their scope is thus broadly defined at the group level (Article 36(2) of the FIEA; Article 70-3(3) of the Cabinet Office Ordinance on Financial Instruments Services, Etc.).

Fourth, the phrase "so that the interests of the customers...would not be unjustly impaired" is undefined, and it is left to the specified financial instruments business operators, etc. to identify the range of "conflicts of interest" to be managed. Since it is impracticable to manage all the diverse types of conflict of interest that could arise, a risk-based approach can be adopted that involves identifying those types of conflict of interest that may be considered "unjust" from the viewpoint of protecting customers and managing them intensively.

Fifth, the contents of the obligation are defined in the FIEA as establishing a system for properly managing information on financial instruments related business, establishing a system for properly supervising the status of that business's implementation, and "any other measures necessary." In the

*720*

Chapter 6    Conduct regulations on financial instruments business operators, etc.

Cabinet Office Ordinance they are summarized as: (1) establishing a system for identifying subject transactions by appropriate means; (2) establishing a system for properly ensuring that customers are protected by such means as separating departments with a Chinese wall, modifying or suspending transactions, and disclosure to customers; (3) formulating a policy for implementing the first two (a conflict-of-interest management policy) and publicizing a summary thereof; and (4) keeping records (for five years) on identification of subject transactions and on measures taken to ensure proper protection of customers (Article 70-3 (1) & (2) of the Cabinet Office Ordinance on Financial Instruments Services, Etc.).

The summary of the conflict-of-interest management policy to be publicized must specify the types of transactions involving the risk of conflict of interest, methods of conflict-of-interest management, the conflict of interest management system, and scope of companies subject to conflict of interest management (IV-1-3(4)(ii) of the Comprehensive Guidelines for Supervision of Financial Instruments Business Operators, Etc.).

## 4. Structure of regulations on sale and solicitation

### a. Contracts for financial instruments transaction

(ⅰ)  Overview

A "contract for financial instruments transaction" means a contract to conduct "acts of financial instruments transaction" (meaning acts listed in the items of Article 2, paragraph 8 of the FIEA) with a customer as the other party or on behalf of a customer (Article 34 of the FIEA). Here the phrase "with a customer as the other party" designates cases where the financial instruments business operator, etc. is the counterparty to the contract with the customer, while "on behalf of a customer" designates cases where the financial instruments business operator, etc. conducts intermediary services, agency services, or brokerage on the customer's behalf.

(ⅱ)  Status of entrustment agreements between operators

When a financial instruments business operator, etc. is entrusted with business by another financial instruments business operator, etc., the entrustment agreement per se is understood not to constitute a contract for

*721*

financial instruments transaction (see Article 2(11) of the FIEA). On the other hand, the contract relating to the act of financial instruments transaction conducted by the financial instruments business operator, etc. on the basis of that entrustment agreement does constitute a contract for financial instruments transaction.

(ⅲ) Changes in content of contracts for financial instruments transaction

Making partial changes in the content of a contract for financial instruments transaction is treated as the conclusion of a new contract for financial instruments transaction (see Article 37-3(1) of the FIEA; Article 110 (1) (ⅵ) of the Cabinet Office Ordinance on Financial Instruments Services, Etc.), although minor changes need not be so treated.

(ⅳ) Change in the counterparty to a contract for financial instruments transaction

A change in the counterparty to a contract for financial instruments transaction is not per se an act of financial instruments transaction.

Whether the change in party is due to general succession (inheritance, merger, or company split) or specific succession (business transfer, etc.), formally it does not constitute the conclusion of a new contract for financial instruments transaction with the successor.

(ⅴ) Cancellation of a contract for financial instruments transaction

The cancellation of an existing contract for financial instruments transaction is understood not to constitute the conclusion of a contract for financial instruments transaction (see Article 37-6(1) of the FIEA).

(ⅵ) Relation between acts of financial instruments intermediation and the contract for financial instruments transaction

When a financial instruments intermediary service provider conducts an act of financial instruments intermediation under entrustment by an entrusting financial instruments business operator, etc., the party that concludes the contract for the financial instruments transaction is the entrusting financial instruments business operator, etc.

When, among acts of financial instruments intermediation, a registered

Chapter 6 Conduct regulations on financial instruments business operators, etc.

financial institution conducts the act of "intermediary service" under entrustment by an entrusting financial instruments business operator (Article 2(11) (i) & (ii) of the FIEA), the party that concludes the contract for the financial instruments transaction is the entrusting financial instruments business operator. On the other hand, when, among acts of financial instruments intermediation, a registered financial institution conducts the act of "dealing" under entrustment by an entrusting financial instruments business operator (ibid, Article 2 (11) (iii)), the party that concludes the contract for the financial instruments transaction is the registered financial institution.

b. Protection of investors and the principle of individual investor responsibility

A financial instruments transaction between an investor and a financial instruments business operator, etc. is based on a contract between the parties, and the principle of individual investor responsibility applies in accordance with the *principle of private autonomy*, which may be described as a cornerstone of capitalism, and the *principle of freedom of contract*, one of its manifestations.

Under the FIEA, on the other hand, the principle of individual investor responsibility is modified in the interests of protecting investors, and both in financial administration and in court decisions pertaining to financial instruments transactions there appears to be a growing trend toward keeping a protective eye on investors. It is to be hoped that a proper balance can be struck between the requirements of the principle of individual investor responsibility and the need to protect investors, thus ensuring the sustainability of legal regulation and enforcement.

In this regard the Supreme Court Decision of March 7, 2013 (*Hanrei Jiho*, No. 2185, p. 64) is noteworthy. This cited the client's "individual responsibility" when reversing a ruling by the Fukuoka High Court (decision of Apr. 27, 2011, *Hanrei Jiho*, No. 2136, p. 58) which found that a bank had violated its duty of accountability to a corporate client in a plain-vanilla interest rate swap transaction. The Supreme Court denied that there had been any such violation.

*723*

c . The process of concluding a contract for financial instruments transaction

The process whereby a financial instruments business operator, etc. sells or solicits a financial instrument or service to a customer (investor) can be conceived as the process of concluding and continuing a contract for financial instruments transaction with that customer. To protect investors, the FIEA imposes conduct regulations on acts such as sale and solicitation by financial instruments business operators, etc., because a structural disparity exists between customers and operators concerning access to information, analytical ability, and bargaining power, and operators are incentivized to make a profit through the conclusion of contracts for financial instruments transaction with customers.

These conduct regulations can be broadly classified into (1) regulations on provision of information prior to solicitation to conclude a contract for financial instruments transaction; (2) prohibitions of solicitation per se; (3) prohibition of inappropriate solicitation, etc.; (4) the obligation to provide information (duty of accountability) at the sales stage following solicitation; (5) the obligation to provide information upon conclusion of the contract; (6) the obligation to provide information following conclusion of the contract; and (7) the regulation on cancellation of contract following conclusion.

d . Regulations on provision of information prior to solicitation

( i ) Overview

The following regulations on provision of information prior to solicitation to conclude a contract for financial instruments transaction apply to financial instruments business operators, etc.: (1) the obligation to post a sign (Article 36-2(1) of the FIEA); (2) the prohibition of name lending (Article 36-3 of the FIEA); and (3) regulation of advertising, etc. (Article 37 of the FIEA). The advertising regulation does not apply to professional investors (Article 45(i) of the FIEA).

Type I crowdfunding operators and type II crowdfunding operators are exempt from the obligation to post a sign and instead required to post an electronic notice (Articles 29-4-2(5) & (8) and 29-4-3(2) & (3) of the FIEA).

Chapter 6   Conduct regulations on financial instruments business operators, etc.

(ⅱ)   Regulation of advertising, etc.

Regulation of advertising, etc. applies to advertising and "acts similar to advertising" (the provision of similar information to a large number of persons), which are considered "provision of information" (Article 72 of the Cabinet Office Ordinance on Financial Instruments Services, Etc.). Acts similar to advertising include the provision of marketing materials and so on.

Regulation of advertising, etc. does not require financial instruments business operators, etc. to provide information in the form of advertising and the like; rather, it requires that, when engaging in advertising or similar acts, they indicate the prescribed matters, including risk information (the fact that there is a risk of loss of principal and of the loss exceeding the principal, along with the indicator that is the direct cause thereof and its grounds) and the fees and so on that the customer will be charged (Article 37(1) of the FIEA; Article 16 of the Implementing Order). It also prohibits so-called misleading advertising, etc. (Article 37 (2) of the FIEA). A financial instruments business operator, etc. is subject to regulation of advertising, etc. as long as the act in question is effectively conducted by it, even if not formally in its name.

(ⅲ)   Prohibition of indications by unregistered operators

Under the 2011 revision of the FIEA, persons other than financial instruments business operators, etc., financial instruments intermediary service providers, and other persons permitted to conduct financial instruments business under the provisions of the law and regulations are prohibited from posting the prescribed sign or a sign similar thereto, or otherwise indicating that they conduct financial instruments business (Article 31-3-2(ⅰ) of the FIEA).

This prohibition applies only to claims to conduct financial instruments business; it does not apply to indications about the content of financial instruments business. Thus, for example, newspapers, magazines, books, and Internet-based information vendors are understood not to be prohibited from the act per se of providing information on financial instruments and transactions (see Article 35(1)(ⅷ) of the FIEA).

*725*

e . Main prohibitions of solicitation per se
( i )　Overview

The following prohibitions on solicitation per se to conclude a contract for financial instruments transaction apply to financial instruments business operators, etc. and their officers and employees: (1) the prohibition of uninvited solicitation, etc. (Article 38(iv) & (viii) of the FIEA; Article 117 (1) (viii) of the Cabinet Office Ordinance on Financial Instruments Services, Etc.); (2) the prohibition of solicitation without confirming intention to receive solicitation (Article 38 (v) & (viii) of the FIEA; Article 117 (1) (viii-ii) of the Cabinet Office Ordinance on Financial Instruments Services, Etc.); (3) the prohibition of repeated solicitation, etc. (Article 38(vi) & (viii) of the FIEA; Article 117(1) (iv) of the Cabinet Office Ordinance on Financial Instruments Services, Etc.); and (4) the principle of suitability (Article 40(i) of the FIEA). None of these applies to professional investors (Article 45(i), etc. of the FIEA).

( ii )　Prohibited transactions

Transactions subject to the first three prohibitions enumerated in Section (i) above are restricted to those specified by cabinet order. In the specification of those transactions, the factors primarily considered are whether the instrument in question is highly leveraged and its other characteristics, and the actual occurrence of persistent solicitation and of harm to the interests of users; heed is also paid to the impact on the freedom of business of financial instruments business operators, etc. and to the fact that such prohibitions may have a detrimental effect on new entrants to the market. For these reasons, the first prohibition applies only to over-the-counter financial futures transactions and over-the-counter transactions in derivatives with individual customers (Article 16-4(1) of the Implementing Order); the second and third apply only to financial futures transaction (financial futures transactions on a domestic or foreign exchange and over-the-counter financial futures transactions), commodity-related market transactions of derivatives and over-the-counter transactions in derivatives with individual customers (ibid., Article 16-4(2)).

By contrast, there is no restriction on the types of transactions subject to the principle of suitability.

Chapter 6   Conduct regulations on financial instruments business operators, etc.

(ⅲ)   The principle of suitability

The principle of suitability in the FIEA, which prohibits situations such as the conduct of "solicitation...found to be inappropriate," is understood to mean the principle of suitability in the narrow sense of the term (the rule against engaging in sale and solicitation of certain instruments to certain types of users no matter how full the explanation).

The Supreme Court, in its first case to deal with the principle of suitability in the field of administrative regulation and recognize a civil rule prohibiting its violation (as being illegal under tort law) (Supreme Court decision of Jul. 14, 2005, *Civil Cases of the Supreme Court*, Vol. 59, No. 6, p. 1323), has ruled that "where an account manager of a securities company, against the customer's intentions and circumstances, actively solicits a transaction clearly entailing excessive risk, or otherwise engages in solicitation of a securities transaction seriously deviating from the principle of suitability, and causes the customer to undertake the transaction, that act is understood to be also illegal under tort law." This ruling makes clear that the essence of the principle of suitability is the principle of suitability in the narrow sense of the term.

(ⅳ)   Interrelationship between the various prohibitions

The principle of suitability is an individuated rule prohibiting solicitation: it takes into consideration the attributes of the customer. The first three prohibitions in Section (ⅰ), by contrast, are rules applied across the board, regardless of the attributes of the customer, forbidding solicitation of transactions where the principle of suitability is alone considered insufficient to protect investors.

The second and third requirements lie somewhere between the principle of suitability and the first prohibition. The first prohibition is restricted in its application to acts of solicitation by visit or telephone, whereas there is no restriction on the acts of solicitation to which the second and third prohibitions apply. Further, the second prohibition serves as the basis on which the third is predicated.

(ⅴ)   Prohibition of solicitation by unregistered operators

Under the 2011 revision of the FIEA, persons other than financial

*727*

instruments business operators, etc., financial instruments intermediary service providers, and other persons permitted to conduct financial instruments business under the provisions of the law and regulations are prohibited from soliciting conclusion of a contract for financial instruments transaction for the purpose of engaging in financial instruments business (Article 31-3-2 (ii) of the FIEA). The acts enumerated in each item of Article 2, paragraph 8 of the FIEA are exempted from the prohibition, but only because the conduct of those acts without obtaining the requisite registration is prohibited as a matter of course.

f . Prohibition of inappropriate solicitation, etc.

( i ) Overview

Prohibitions relating to solicitation to conclude a contract for financial instruments transaction applying to financial instruments business operators, etc. and their officers and employees include (1) the prohibition on providing false information (Article 38(i) of the FIEA; this applies also with regard to conclusion of a contract); (2) the prohibition on providing conclusive evaluations, etc. (ibid., Article 38(ii)); (3) the prohibition of false indications and of misleading indications on important matters (Article 38 (viii) of the FIEA; Article 117(1) (ii) of the Cabinet Office Ordinance on Financial Instruments Services, Etc.); (4) the prohibition on promising to provide or providing special profits (ibid., Article 117 (1) (iii)); (5) the prohibition on using fraudulent means and committing assault or intimidation (ibid., Article 117 (1) (iv)); (6) the prohibition on soliciting individual customers, etc. at inconvenient hours (ibid., Article 117(1) (vii)); (7) restrictions on sale and solicitation of excessively speculative transactions; (8) the prohibition on provision of corporate information (ibid., Article 117(1) (xiv)); (9) the prohibition on provision to an acquirer of share options, by a securities company underwriting a commitment-type rights offering, of false information and conclusive evaluations with regard to solicitation to exercise those share options (ibid., Article 117(1) (xxxiii)); (10) the prohibition on soliciting conclusion of a contract when entrusted by a financial instruments business operator, etc. engaged in investment management business with intermediating conclusion of a discretionary investment contract, without stating that and specifying the name of the

Chapter 6   Conduct regulations on financial instruments business operators, etc.

operator (ibid., Article 117(1)(xxxiv)); and (11) in the case of commodity-related market transactions of derivatives, the prohibition on solicitation of cross order, the prohibition on accepting entrustment of transactions similar to cross order, the prohibition on trading against the customer, and the duty to explain in person (ibid., Article 117(1)(xxxv)-(xxxviii)).

These prohibitions apply also in the case of professional investors. Only the first entails penalties (Articles 198(ii-ii), 198-6(ii) and 207(1)(iii) & (iv) of the FIEA).

The tenth prohibition, prompted by the AIJ Investment Advisors incident, was instituted to prevent similar conflicts of interest. In addition, under the 2013 revision of the FIEA, penalties for violations of the prohibition on using fraudulent means or committing assault or intimidation with regard to the conclusion, etc. of a discretionary investment contract (Article 38-2(i) of the FIEA) were increased (Articles 197-3, Article 198-3 and Article 207(1)(ii) & (iii) of the FIEA).

( ii )  Prohibition of false indications and of misleading indications on important matters

Whereas the first of the prohibitions in Section (i) above, that on providing false information, forbids the direct provision of such information to individual customers, the prohibition of false indications in (3) forbids either directly or indirectly making such indications to a large number of persons. It appears, however, that in recent administrative action cases relating to providing false information, false statements in writing are, when particularly blatant, also regarded as provision of false information.

The term "false" means not according with truth or fact, being normally used in cases where there is a subjective awareness of the untruth of the statement.

In the prohibition of misleading indications on important matters in (3), the term "important matters" means matters that may significantly affect the customer's investment decisions. Whether something constitutes an "important matter" or "a representation that would cause a misunderstanding" is determined in light of whether, by the ordinary standards of society, it is important for or may cause misunderstanding among investors in general.

For example, using the term "principal secure" to describe an instrument

*729*

when the principal is not guaranteed in yen could be considered a misleading indication on an important matter.

(ⅲ) The prohibition on promising to provide or providing special profits

As for the fourth prohibition in Section (i) above, that on promising to provide or providing special profits, originally the act of soliciting while promising to provide special profits was forbidden, but under the FIEA and related regulations the acts of promising to provide and providing special profits are themselves prohibited. The primary intent of the prohibition is to guarantee fair treatment between customers (with a view to ensuring the soundness of capital markets) and ensure appropriate investment decisions by customers (with a view to protecting investors), rather than to ensure the soundness of financial instruments business operators, etc. and to guarantee fair competition among them.

Given that intent, whether an act constitutes "providing special profits" is in each case determined substantively in accordance with the facts — the nature of the case, the purpose of the act, and so forth — considering the ordinary standards of society. For example, discounting fees for customers meeting specific conditions, or offering extra interest, giving premiums, or providing cash rebates to them, is not prohibited across the board; such acts basically do not constitute "providing special profits" as long as they may be considered within reasonable bounds by the ordinary standards of society — as long as the specified conditions are not illicit, other customers doing business on the same transaction terms are treated likewise, the benefit provided is not excessive, and so forth.

There have been cases where repeatedly entertaining officers of a pension fund has been deemed providing special profits, indicating that the ordinary standards of society have become stricter in the aftermath of the AIJ Investment Advisors incident.

(ⅳ) Prohibition on soliciting at inconvenient hours

The sixth prohibition in Section (i) above, that on soliciting individual customers, etc. at inconvenient hours, unlike prohibitions on solicitation per se, simply imposes certain restrictions on concrete methods of solicitation based on the ordinary standards of society, including solicitation of

Chapter 6   Conduct regulations on financial instruments business operators, etc.

customers who have requested it.

The prohibition on soliciting at inconvenient hours applies only to solicitation by phone or visit. Acts of solicitation by electronic mail, for example, are not covered, although acts of solicitation by facsimile should be considered included in solicitation by phone.

Whether a time may be considered inconvenient for a customer must in each case be determined substantively in accordance with the facts considering the ordinary standards of society. Instructive in this regard are, for example, the Money Lending Business Act and related regulations, under which "hours found to be clearly inappropriate in terms of general social norms" are defined as "the period between the hours of 9 p.m. to 8 a.m." (Article 21(1)(i) of the Money Lending Business Act; Article 19(1) of the Ordinance for Implementation of the Money Lending Business Act).

（ⅴ） Restrictions on solicitation and sale of excessively speculative transactions

As for the seventh category in Section (i) above, restrictions on excessively speculative transactions, there are several of these. First, in the interests of customer protection, risk management of business operators and prevention of excessive speculation on financial instruments business operators, etc. have, since August 2010, been subject to a leverage restriction on foreign exchange margin transactions ("currency-related derivatives transactions") with individual customers (Article 38(viii) of the FIEA; Article 117(1)(xxvii) to (xxviii)(3) to (12) of the Cabinet Office Ordinance on Financial Instruments Services, Etc.). Since August 1, 2011, the maximum allowable leverage has been twenty-five times (with a clearing margin of at least 4% of the notional value). Currency-related derivatives transactions with individual customers have, since August 2009, been subject to a loss-cutting rule (Article 40(ii) of the FIEA; Article 123(1)(xxi-ii) and Item (xxi-iii) of the Cabinet Office Ordinance on Financial Instruments Services, Etc.).

Second, financial instruments business operators, etc. are subject to a leverage restriction on "securities-related over-the-counter transactions in derivatives" with individual customers (Article 38(viii) of the FIEA; Article 117(1)(xxix) to (xxx)(13) to (22) of the Cabinet Office Ordinance on

*731*

Financial Instruments Services, Etc.). Since January 2011 the maximum allowable leverage has been five times for transactions in which the underlying asset comprises individual stocks, ten times for transactions in which a share price index serves as the benchmark, fifty times for transactions in which the underlying asset comprises bonds, and five times for other securities.

Third, in the interests of risk management by operators, financial instruments business operators, etc. have, since February 2017, been subject to a leverage restriction on foreign exchange margin transactions ("over-the-counter transactions of derivatives in specified currencies") with corporate customers (Article 38(viii) of the FIEA; Article 117(1)(xxxix) to (xl)(23) to (32) of the Cabinet Office Ordinance on Financial Instruments Services, Etc.) (announced June 2016). The necessary margin rate ("assumed foreign exchange risk ratio") is calculated each week by the operator (Article 3(iii) of the Public Notice of the FSA No. 25 of 2016).

Fourth, in "specified over-the-counter option transactions" (so-called binary options, etc.) with individual customers, financial instruments business operators, etc. are required to notify the customer in advance of the exercise price and set an appropriate transaction period and maturity date (Article 40(ii) of the FIEA; Article 123(1)(xxi-iv)(6) of the Cabinet Office Ordinance on Financial Instruments Services, Etc.).

Fifth, "Accepting an Entrustment, etc." for the sale and purchase of securities on the condition of provision of credit is in principle prohibited (Article 44-2(1)(i) & (2)(i) of the FIEA; Articles 148 and 149-2 of the Cabinet Office Ordinance on Financial Instruments Services, Etc.).

Sixth, in order to prevent market manipulation, etc. and ensure the soundness of capital markets, financial instruments business operators, etc. are, when engaging in the sale and purchase of securities, market transactions of derivatives, or over-the-counter transactions in derivatives based on a discretionary investment contract, whether on their own account or on entrustment, prohibited from doing so in a manner found to disturb the order of a financial instruments exchange market or an over-the-counter securities market through what may be considered, in light of the main purpose of the entrustment under the contract or the contract amount, to be excessive volumes of sales or purchases (Article 161 of the FIEA; Article 9

Chapter 6 Conduct regulations on financial instruments business operators, etc.

of the Cabinet Office Ordinance on Restrictions on Securities Transactions, Etc.).

Seventh, for similar purposes, the act of engaging simultaneously in excessive solicitation of many unspecified persons for a continuous period is prohibited (Article 38(iii) of the FIEA; Article 117(1)(xvii) & (xviii) of the Cabinet Office Ordinance on Financial Instruments Services, Etc.).

Eighth, in conduct of investment trust management, forms of management that violate restrictions on risk with respect to derivatives transactions, or violate appropriate management of credit risk, are prohibited (Article 42-2 (vii) of the FIEA; Article 130(1)(viii) & (viii-ii) of the Cabinet Office Ordinance on Financial Instruments Services, Etc.).

Ninth, as a measure for managing the risks of "uncleared over-the-counter transactions in derivatives," from September 2016 the requirement is imposed (1) to accept an amount equivalent to the fluctuation in market value as "variation margin" (Article 40(ii) of the FIEA; Article 123(1) (xxi-v) & (10) of the Cabinet Office Ordinance on Financial Instruments Services, Etc.); and (2) to accept the "estimated amount of potential losses, etc." as "initial margin" (ibid., Article 123(1)(xxi-vi) & (11)).

Tenth, in addition to acts prohibited under business regulations, courts have found "churning," in which an operator solicits a customer to engage in transactions of excessive frequency and volume considering the customer's attributes, to be illegal under private law; the conditions cited for being so deemed are excessiveness of the transaction, control of the account (dominant position of the operator), and malice (fraudulent intentions or disregard for the customer's interests) (e.g., Tokyo District Court Decision of Mar. 31, 1987, *Kinyu Shoji Hanrei*, No. 813, p. 28; Osaka High Court Decision of Sept. 29, 2000, *Hanrei Times*, No. 1055, p. 181).

Eleventh, in terms of restrictions on speculative acts under regulations on unfair trade, the law includes a provision under which restrictions may be placed on the conduct, by financial instruments business operators, etc. or authorized transaction-at-exchange operators, of transactions on their own account or of excessive volumes of transactions (Article 161(1) & (2) of the FIEA). In reality, only the conduct of excessive volumes of transactions based on a contract relating to discretionary trading acts (Article 16(1)(viii) (a) & (b) of the Cabinet Office Ordinance on Definitions; Article 123(1)

*733*

(xiii)(b) to (e) of the Cabinet Office Ordinance on Financial Instruments Services, Etc.) by financial instruments business operators, etc. is prohibited (Article 9 of the Cabinet Office Ordinance on Restrictions on Securities Transactions, etc.). The 2012 revision of the FIEA incorporated a new provision under which restrictions may be placed on similar trading by commodity trading participants (Article 151 of the FIEA) with respect to commodity-related market transactions of derivatives (Article 161(3) of the FIEA).

    g. Duty to provide information at the sales stage following solicitation (accountability)
      (ⅰ) Overview
The duty to provide information to the customer at the sales stage following solicitation to conclude a contract for financial instruments transaction (namely the stage directly leading to conclusion of the contract) is imposed in the form of a duty of accountability. Specifically, this includes (1) the obligation to deliver a pre-contract document prior to conclusion of the contract (Article 37-3 (1) of the FIEA); (2) a substantial duty of accountability (Article 38(viii) of the FIEA; Article 117(1) (i) of the Cabinet Office Ordinance on Financial Instruments Services, Etc.); (3) the obligation to establish a control environment for providing explanations on switching investment trusts and so on (Article 40(ii) of the FIEA; Article 123(1) (ix) of the Cabinet Office Ordinance on Financial Instruments Services, Etc.); (4) the obligation to establish a control environment for providing explanations to individual customers of material events occurring during the period of application for corporate bonds and so on (ibid., Article 123(1) (xi)); and (5) the obligation to establish a control environment for ensuring substantial accountability to welfare pension funds (ibid., Article 123(1) (xxviii)).

      (ⅱ) Accountability
Accountability is basically understood to designate the duty to provide important information considered necessary to allow investors to make investment decisions regarding financial instruments and transactions, but it is sometimes taken also to include ensuring that the investor comprehends the information provided (accurately understands the nature of the financial

Chapter 6   Conduct regulations on financial instruments business operators, etc.

instrument or transaction as a result of the provision of that information) or is satisfied with it. The duty of accountability is intended to rectify the structural gap between operators and investors in their informedness about financial instruments and transactions (the disparity between them in access to information and analytical ability) as the precondition for ensuring the effectiveness of the principle of individual investor responsibility.

The Supreme Court, in its decision of April 22, 2011, on a case regarding solicitation to invest in a credit cooperative (*Civil Cases of the Supreme Court*, Vol. 65, No. 3, p. 1405), has ruled that good-faith accountability prior to conclusion of a civil contract means providing the counterparty with "information that may affect the decision whether to conclude the contract."

(ⅲ)   Obligation to deliver a pre-contract document prior to conclusion of contract

Accountability is defined in the FIEA as the obligation to deliver a pre-contract document prior to conclusion of the contract (Item (1) in Section (i) above). This is based on such considerations as these: consistency is thereby ensured with the obligation to deliver a prospectus, a face-to-face disclosure requirement under disclosure regulations; in non-face-to-face transactions using electronic media, explanation is primarily by means of documentation delivered electronically; and under the old financial regulatory laws, accountability likewise took the form of an obligation to deliver a pre-contract document prior to conclusion of the contract. This obligation to deliver a document constitutes as it were an accountability requirement under administrative legislation; it is therefore not waived even if the customer indicates that he or she does not require delivery of such documentation.

The matters to be contained in the pre-contract document are prescribed in detail (Article 37-3(1)(i) to (vii) of the FIEA; Articles 81 to 96 of the Cabinet Office Ordinance on Financial Instruments Services, Etc.). The main matters to be recorded include an outline of the contract, the fees, etc. to be borne by the customer, and information on risk. Three different formats are prescribed depending on the importance of the content (Article 79 of the Cabinet Office Ordinance).

Since the objective is to provide customers with the information they

*735*

require to make investment decisions, it is desirable that financial instruments business operators, etc., while fulfilling legal requirements, take creative steps of their own accord when drawing up the pre-contract document (such as using boxes, underlining, bold typeface, and conspicuous colors) so as to attract customers' attention and ensure that they accurately understand the information.

Delivering the document by electronic means is permitted as long as the customer consents. Two forms of electronic delivery are allowed: (1) by the Internet or similar means (sending e-mail, file download by the customer, access to a dedicated customer file, access to an inspection file); and (2) by information media (floppy disk, CD-ROM, USB memory stick, etc.) (Articles 37-3(2) and 34-2(4) of the FIEA; Articles 15-22 and Article 15-23 of the Implementing Order; Articles 56 and 57 of the Cabinet Office Ordinance on Financial Instruments Services, Etc.).

(iv) Exemptions from the obligation to deliver a pre-contract document

Exemptions from the obligation to deliver a pre-contract document prior to conclusion of the contract are prescribed if (1) a "record of listed securities, etc." has been delivered within the past year; (2) a pre-contract document pertaining to a contract for financial instruments transaction on the same terms has been delivered within the past year; (3) a prospectus has been delivered; or (4) a "contract change document" has been delivered (Article 37-3(1) of the FIEA; Article 80 of the Cabinet Office Ordinance on Financial Instruments Services, Etc.).

(v) Substantial duty of accountability

Given the intent of the duty of accountability, it is not enough for financial instruments business operators, etc. merely to deliver pro forma to the customer documentation containing the statutory matters prescribed; the customer must be actually provided with the information required to decide whether to conclude a contract for financial instruments transaction. For that reason, a substantial duty of accountability is imposed with respect to delivery of the pre-contract document, record of listed securities, etc., and other such documentation (Item (2) in Section (i) above). The "principle of suitability in the broad sense" (the rule that operators must engage in sale

*736*

Chapter 6   Conduct regulations on financial instruments business operators, etc.

and solicitation in a manner suited to the knowledge, experience, assets, and objectives of the user) is thus incorporated into the duty of accountability.

(vi)  Obligation to establish a control environment for providing explanations

Items (3) – (5) in Section (i) above, by prohibiting certain states of business operation, effectively require financial instruments business operators, etc. to establish a specific control environment for providing explanations.

h.  Obligation to provide information upon conclusion of contract

An obligation is imposed on financial instruments business operators, etc. to provide information to the customer upon conclusion of a contract for financial instruments transaction in the form of an obligation to deliver a document at that time (Article 37-4 (1) of the FIEA). This document delivered upon conclusion of the contract is for the purpose of confirming the details of the contract for financial instruments transaction concluded by the customer. The matters to be contained therein are prescribed in detail (Articles 99 to 107 of the Cabinet Office Ordinance on Financial Instruments Services, Etc.).

In addition, financial instruments business operators, etc. are required to deliver documentation pertaining to receipt of security deposits (Article 37-5 of the FIEA). The types of security deposits for which such documentation must be delivered comprise money, securities, or other property deposited by the customer with respect to certain transactions (Article 113 of the Cabinet Office Ordinance on Financial Instruments Services, Etc.), namely over-the-counter financial futures transaction, financial futures transactions on exchanges, and over-the-counter transactions in derivatives with individual customers (Article 16-4(2) of the Implementation Order).

i.  Obligation to provide information following conclusion of contract

(i)  Overview

An obligation is imposed on financial instruments business operators, etc. to provide information following conclusion of a contract for financial

*737*

instruments transaction in the form of (1) the obligation to deliver a report on outstanding transaction balance (Article 37-4(1) of the FIEA; Articles 98 (1)(iii) and 108 of the Cabinet Office Ordinance on Financial Instruments Services, Etc.); and (2) the obligation to prepare and deliver an investment report on investment management operations (Article 42-7(1) of the FIEA; Article 134 of the Cabinet Office Ordinance on Financial Instruments Services, etc.).

In the case of investment trusts, the obligation to deliver an investment report under the Act on Investment Trusts and Investment Corporations (Article 14(1) & (7)) applies. The 2013 revision to the Act makes this a two-tiered obligation, under which the investment report for delivery purposes must be delivered, while the full edition must be delivered if requested (ibid., Article 14(2), (3) & (4); Article 25-3 of the Ordinance for Enforcement of the Act on Investment Trusts and Investment Corporations).

( ii ) Obligation to provide after-sales service

No so-called obligation to provide after-sales service is imposed in a general form. The obligation to provide after-sales service means being required, after a transaction takes effect, to provide market price information on the financial instrument or transaction, information relating to decisions about the appropriate time to sell, and so forth. Like the "best-advice" requirement, the obligation to provide after-sales service can generally be thought to apply in cases where the user may, owing to the existence of an ongoing transaction or for other reasons, be considered to have a relationship of trust and dependency (equivalent to a kind of fiduciary relationship) with the operator as a provider of professional services. In the case of financial instruments business, however, no such fiduciary relationship can be recognized to exist, except with regard to investment advisory business, investment management business, and the like; therefore no consensus has emerged broadly recognizing the obligation to provide after-sales service in general terms.

Noteworthy in this regard is a concurring opinion to the aforementioned Supreme Court Decision of July 14, 2005, dealing with the principle of suitability, which states that in certain cases securities companies have the

Chapter 6   Conduct regulations on financial instruments business operators, etc.

obligation, under civil law, to provide guidance and advice based on the principle of good faith. Whereas several subsequent court decisions denied the obligation to provide guidance and advice after a transaction unless special circumstances exist and any violation of the obligation after the transaction of the listed company bonds (MYCAL bonds) (Tokyo High Court Decision of Apr. 16, 2009, *Hanrei Jiho*, No. 2078, p. 25, and Nagoya High Court Decision of May 28, 2009, *Hanrei Jiho*, No. 2073, p. 42), one decision recognized that "churning" occurred in the case of solicitation of margin trading of shares and the obligation to provide guidance and advice was violated (Osaka High Court Decision of Aug. 27, 2008, *Hanrei Jiho*, No. 2051, p. 61).

In terms of administrative oversight, when dealing in over-the-counter derivatives transactions and such financial instruments business operators, etc. are, if requested to do so by the customer, expected to provide customers with market price information on their position or notify them of the amount of settlement money on cancellation at a particular time on a periodic or as-needed basis (IV-3-2-2 (6) (vi) of the Comprehensive Guidelines for Supervision of Financial Instruments Business Operators, Etc.). They are not required to provide market price information at the time when the contract is concluded.

j . The regulation on cancellation of contract following conclusion

The regulation on cancellation of contract following conclusion takes the form of a system of cooling off (cancellation by means of document), which allows a customer who has concluded a contract for financial instruments transaction with a financial instruments business operator, etc. to cancel that contract (Article 37-6 of the FIEA).

Cooling off, in consideration of its unsuitability to certain types of financial instruments and transactions, such as those entailing risk of price fluctuations, applies specifically to "investment advisory contracts" (Article 16-3 (1) of the Implementing Order). A customer who has concluded an investment advisory contract may cancel it by means of a document until ten days have elapsed from the day when the customer received the document for delivery upon conclusion of the contract (Article 37-6(1) of the FIEA; Article 16-3(2) of the Implementing Order).

# 5. Meaning of the term "solicitation"

### a. Distinction between "solicitation" and "provision of information"
#### (i) Overview

In the application of conduct regulations to financial instruments business operators, etc., the key question is often whether an act constitutes "solicitation." Although "solicitation" is not defined in the FIEA, the provision of information on financial instruments and transactions is understood not to be prohibited per se.

Solicitation is generally distinguished from advertising, etc. (provision of information) in that the former targets specific users, while the latter targets large numbers of users. Advertising, etc. is in turn classified into that which aims simply to provide information and that which aims to induce engagement in a financial transaction. The latter is further classified into that concerning instruments in general and that concerning specific instruments; this resembles solicitation in character.

Solicitation can accordingly be defined as any act targeting specific users with the aim of inducing them to engage in a financial transaction. Whether an act aims to induce engagement in a financial transaction is determined substantively in light of the objective circumstances, with ordinary investors as the yardstick.

#### (ii) The concept of "acts similar to solicitation"

Instructive in this regard is the concept of "acts similar to solicitation" enshrined in the old Act on Foreign Securities Brokers (Article 3(2) of the old Act on Foreign Securities Brokers; Article 2(ii) of the Implementing Order on the old Act on Foreign Securities Brokers). "Acts similar to solicitation" were defined specifically as (1) conducting advertising on investment in securities through such media as newspapers, magazines, television, and radio; (2) holding briefing sessions on investment in securities; (3) providing information on investment in securities orally, in writing, by telephone, or by other means of communication; and (4) conducting acts similar to (1) – (3) (Article 7 of the old Cabinet Office Ordinance on the Act on Foreign Securities Brokers). These acts, although included in the concept of "solicitation" under disclosure regulations (B4-1 of

Chapter 6 Conduct regulations on financial instruments business operators, etc.

the Guideline for the Disclosure of Corporate Affairs), may be considered excluded from the concept of "solicitation" under business regulations (see VII-3-1(2)(ii)B and VIII-2-5(2)(i)A of the Comprehensive Guidelines for Supervision of Financial Instruments Business Operators, Etc.).

It should, however, be noted that these acts too may constitute "solicitation" in substance. For example, the posting of advertisements regarding "foreign securities companies' cross-border transactions using the Internet" is deemed in principle to constitute solicitation (X-1-2 of the Comprehensive Guidelines for Supervision of Financial Instruments Business Operators, Etc.).

(iii) Guidance by the U.S. FINRA

Also instructive is the Regulatory Notice released by the Financial Industry Regulatory Authority (FINRA), a U.S. self-regulatory organization, in January 2011 announcing Rule 2090 (Know Your Customer) and Rule 2111 (Suitability) (with follow-up guidance in May 2011 and May 2012). This notice, while noting that the determination of the existence of a "recommendation" — corresponding to "solicitation" in Japan — subject to the suitability rule is based on the facts and circumstances of the particular case, sets out several guiding principles for making that determination.

Specifically, (1) a communication's content, context, and presentation are important aspects; (2) the determination of whether a "recommendation" has been made is an objective rather than subjective inquiry (obligations cannot be avoided through a disclaimer); (3) an important factor is whether — given its content, context and manner of presentation — a particular communication from a firm or associated person to a customer reasonably would be viewed as a suggestion that the customer take action or refrain from taking action regarding a security or investment strategy; (4) the more individually tailored the communication is to a particular customer or customers about a specific security or investment strategy, the more likely the communication will be viewed as a recommendation; (5) a series of actions that may not constitute recommendations when viewed individually may amount to a recommendation when considered in the aggregate; and (6) it makes no difference whether the communication was initiated by a person or a computer software program.

*741*

(iv) "Solicitation" under the principle of suitability

The principle of suitability (in the narrow sense), being a conduct regulation governing "solicitation" (Article 40(i) of the FIEA), does not apply in cases where no "solicitation" occurs. For example, (1) explaining an instrument at the customer's own request, within the bounds of that request, does not necessarily constitute "solicitation." Similarly, (2) the simple act of passively providing sales materials to a customer in response to an individual request by that customer basically does not constitute "solicitation." Likewise, (3) the act of merely explaining the nature of an instrument at a briefing session attended by large numbers of customers, while entrusting "solicitation" to another operator, basically does not constitute "solicitation." However, it basically does constitute "solicitation," for example, for a financial instruments business operator engaged in investment management business to provide investment advice to individual investors during a "consultation session" following a briefing given at an investment seminar (which basically does not constitute "solicitation").

Whether an act constitutes "solicitation" should be carefully determined substantively in each case on the basis of the actual circumstances. Further, it is inappropriate for financial instruments business operators, etc. to assent to a transaction upon obtaining confirmation in writing from the customer that solicitation is unnecessary.

b. Distinction between "solicitation " and "introduction"

(i) Overview

Persons other than financial instruments business operators, etc., financial instruments intermediary service providers, and other persons permitted to conduct financial instruments business under the provisions of the law and regulations are not allowed to engage in "solicitation" of contracts for financial instruments transaction (Article 31-3-2(ii) of the FIEA). On the other hand, the act by a third party of introducing a customer to a financial instruments business operator, etc. does not constitute financial instruments business as long as it does not constitute in substance, for example, "intermediating" conclusion of a contract for financial instruments transaction or dealing in a public offering. One may thus do so even without being registered.

*742*

Chapter 6   Conduct regulations on financial instruments business operators, etc.

(ⅱ)   Meaning of the term "introduction"

The act by a third party of merely providing individual customer information to a financial instruments business operator, etc., without being directly involved in the contract for financial instruments transaction, basically constitutes only an "introduction" (see VIII-2-5(1)(i)(B) of the Comprehensive Guidelines for Supervision of Financial Instruments Business Operators, Etc.).

Further, even if involved in the contract for financial instruments transaction, the acts by a third party of (1) distribution and provision of fliers, pamphlets, contract application forms, etc. (without explaining how to fill out the documents), (2) receipt and collection of contract applications, attached documents, etc. (without checking the contents of the documents), and (3) providing general explanations at seminars for financial instruments with regard to the structures, schemes, and the utilization methods of financial instruments are basically "activities not constituting brokerage" and as such constitute only "introductions" (see VII-3-1 (2) (ii) B and VII-2-5(1) (ii) of the Comprehensive Guidelines for Supervision of Financial Instruments Business Operators, Etc.).

Court rulings have found that they constitute "introductions" by banks (denying that they constitute "solicitation") (Tokyo District Court Decision of Jan. 28, 2011, *Kinyu Homu Jijo*, No. 1925, p. 117; Tokyo District Court Decision of Nov. 18, 2013, *Kinyu Shoji Hanrei*, No. 1438, p. 44).

(ⅲ)   The limits of "introductions" by financial instruments business operators, etc.

To avoid being considered to engage in "intermediary services" or "brokerage" when making "introductions," financial instruments business operators, etc. must refrain from explaining individual financial instruments. Special care is required if introduction fees are accepted (see VII-2-1-1, note of the Comprehensive Guidelines for Supervision of Financial Instruments Business Operators, Etc.).

In one case a financial instruments business operator engaged solely in investment advisory and agency business was found to have conducted the act of solicitation when it explained the product details of a foreign fund and accepted introduction fees for it from the sales agent (administrative action

*743*

by the Kinki Local Finance Bureau of the Ministry of Finance, Dec. 21, 2012).

# 6. Principle of suitability and accountability

## a. A two-tiered approach

Under the principle of suitability, financial instruments business operators, etc. must take a two-tiered approach to the actual task of selling and soliciting financial instruments and transactions. Specifically, (1) they must determine whether, considering the attributes of the customer, it is acceptable to engage in the sale and solicitation of a particular instrument or transaction to that customer (Article 40(i) of the FIEA; the "principle of suitability in the narrow sense"); (2) even if they conclude that it is acceptable to do so, they must provide an explanation in a manner and to the extent necessary for the customer to understand, in light of his or her attributes (Article 38(viii) of the FIEA; Article 117(1)(i) of the Cabinet Office Ordinance on Financial Instruments Services, Etc.; the "principle of suitability in the broad sense").

Under tort law, too, in accordance with the aforementioned Supreme Court Decision of July 14, 2005, an act is illegal whether or not it violates the duty of accountability as long as it can be deemed to deviate seriously from the principle of suitability. Since that Supreme Court decision, some courts have cited a serious deviation from the principle of suitability as grounds for deeming an act illegal under tort law without ruling on whether it violated the duty of accountability (Tokyo High Court Decision of May 30, 2007, *Kinyu Shoji Hanrei*, No. 1287, p. 37; Nagoya District Court Decision of Sept. 8, 2010, *Kinyu Shoji Hanrei*, No. 1356, p. 40); others have continued to find both a serious deviation from the principle of suitability and a violation of the duty of accountability (Osaka District Court Decision of Apr. 26, 2006, *Hanrei Jiho*, No. 1947, p. 122; Osaka High Court Decision of Jun. 3, 2008, *Kinyu Shoji Hanrei*, No. 1300, p. 45; Osaka District Court Decision of Aug. 26, 2010, *Hanrei Jiho*, No. 2106, p. 69).

## b. Acquisition of information on customer attributes

In order to engage in actual sale and solicitation in an appropriate manner while paying due attention to suitability, as a financial instruments business operator, etc. it is necessary to "know your customer," i.e., understand his or

Chapter 6   Conduct regulations on financial instruments business operators, etc.

her attributes (knowledge, experience, asset profile, and objectives in concluding the contract). The FIEA does not, however, impose on financial instruments business operators, etc. the obligation to investigate or endeavor to investigate their customers' attributes.

In this regard, members of the Japan Securities Dealers Association (JSDA), under the "Rules Concerning Solicitation for Investments and Management of Customers, etc. by Association Members" (below referred to as the "Investment Solicitation Rules"), maintain a customer card for those customers who conduct sale and purchase or other transactions of securities, etc. (excluding professional investors), which card records the customer's name or appellation, address or domicile and mailing address, date of birth (if the customer is a natural person), occupation, purpose of investment, asset condition, experience of investments, type of transaction, motive behind becoming a customer, and other matters deemed necessary by the association member (Article 5).

If the customer is a juridical person, its investment knowledge can, besides being surmised from the juridical person's investment experience, be gauged by postulating what officers or employees can reasonably be assumed to possess authority to participate in the decision-making process leading to conclusion of contracts within that juridical person, taking into account its size and line of business.

As for when financial instruments business operators, etc. should go about acquiring such information on customer attributes, if, considering the convenience of the customer, it is not possible to do so adequately before initiating solicitation, it is acceptable to do so by the sales stage.

c. Determination of suitability

The aforementioned Supreme Court Decision of July 14, 2005, stated, "When determining a customer's suitability in order to ascertain whether a tort has occurred because the solicitation of sale of options by the representative of a securities company seriously deviated from the principle of suitability, it is not enough to consider only the general, abstract risks of the sale of options as a type of transaction; rather, it is necessary to consider in aggregate the customer's investment experience, knowledge of securities transactions, investment intentions, state of assets, and other such factors in

*745*

light of the actual characteristics of the instrument — What is the product underlying the options? Are the options listed? — and in relation to them."

Financial instruments business operators, etc. must, in determining a customer's suitability, take overall account of the customer's knowledge, experience, state of assets, and objectives in relation to the characteristics of the actual instrument or transaction (degree of risk, etc.). The principle of suitability demands a varied, flexible response tailored to the individual customer's attributes. When selling to a customer with extensive investment experience, it is not necessary to give exactly the same explanation by the same means as when selling to a customer with little investment experience.

On the other hand, elderly people often lack investment knowledge and experience despite possessing considerable savings and other assets; caution on the part of financial instruments business operators, etc. is therefore desirable during solicitation of risky financial instruments and transactions to the elderly. Many of the court decisions finding serious deviations from the principle of suitability in the wake of the aforementioned Supreme Court decision of July 14, 2005, relate to elderly customers. The JSDA has drawn up a guideline on solicitation and sale to elderly customers (October 2013).

There was a case of administrative action for violating the principle of suitability when soliciting transactions in Nikkei 225 options (Kanto Local Finance Bureau, Mar. 12, 2004).

d. Determination of civil accountability

While the aforementioned Supreme Court Decision of March 7, 2013, does not define a general framework for determining civil accountability, a similar approach should be taken as in the analytical framework of the aforementioned Supreme Court Decision of July 14, 2005, dealing with the principle of suitability.

The aforementioned Tokyo High Court Decision of January 26, 2015, takes that approach, ruling, "Any representative of a financial instruments business operator, or of a financial institution conducting sales on its behalf, soliciting a client who is a general investor for an investment transaction has, as the precondition for the client to make an investment decision at his or her own responsibility, a civil duty of good faith to explain, to the extent that will be specifically understood by the client, the structure and characteristics of

Chapter 6   Conduct regulations on financial instruments business operators, etc.

the product in question and the nature and extent of the risks involved in view of the client's attributes, that is, such factors as his or her investment experience, knowledge of financial instrument transactions, investment intentions, and the state of his or her assets. A violation of that duty constitutes tort."

The Supreme Court Decision of March 15, 2016 (*Hanrei Jiho*, No. 2302, p. 43) denies that a securities company violated the duty of accountability when a client (a financial corporation) engaged in a series of transactions including a trust agreement for managing financial assets consisting of structured bonds sold by the securities company.

    e. "Reasonable-basis suitability" and "solicitation commencement standards"

Based on the FSA's "Approaches to Regulation of Unsolicited Offers of Derivatives Transactions" (Sept. 13, 2010), the JSDA has, to ensure full observance of the principle of suitability during solicitation, revised the Investment Solicitation Rules by newly incorporating "reasonable-basis suitability" and "solicitation commencement standards" into them.

Reasonable-basis suitability requires that when conducting the sale of securities, etc. (including securities, securities-related derivatives transactions, etc., and specified OTC derivatives transactions, etc.) that are new for an association member, the association member fully understands the characteristics and risks of such securities, etc., and prohibits selling them if it is unable to identify suitable customers (Article 3-3 of the Investment Solicitation Rules). The solicitation commencement standards prohibit solicitation of the sale of complex structured bonds/investment trusts similar to OTC derivatives transactions and of leveraged investment trusts to individual customers (excluding professional investors) if they do not meet the standards (ibid., Article 5-2).

Because the principle of suitability (in the narrow sense) applies separately to each customer, one may regard the solicitation commencement standards as setting the criteria used in applying the principle of suitability and reasonable-basis suitability as the assumption on which the principle of suitability is predicated.

The JSDA's Investment Solicitation Rules require association members to

*747*

establish "transaction commencement standards" for margin transactions, sale and purchases or other transactions in stock subscription rights, securities-related derivatives transactions, etc., specified OTC derivatives transactions, etc., over-the-counter handled securities, and so forth (ibid., Article 6). They do not, however, require association members to establish transaction commencement standards for transactions subject to the solicitation commencement standards.

f. "Alert documents" and "confirmation documents"

Likewise based on the above FSA policy, the JSDA requires association members (1) when selling securities-related derivatives transactions, etc., specified OTC derivatives transactions, etc., or complex structured bonds and investment trusts to customers excluding professional investors, to deliver an alert document to the customer in advance including, among other matters, a warning about the associated risks and explain the matters included in the alert document (Article 6-2 of the Investment Solicitation Rules); and (2) when selling OTC derivatives transactions, etc. or complex structured bonds and investment trusts, to obtain a "confirmation document" from the customer (ibid., Article 8(2) & (3)).

However, in the pre-contract document, financial instruments business operators, etc. are required (1) to state plainly at the beginning, in characters and numerals of point size 12 or above, that the content of the document should be read carefully and particularly important matters (that there is a risk of loss of principal and of the loss exceeding the principal, etc.); and (2) clearly and accurately to record, in characters and numerals of point size 12 or above, a fee summary, risk information, and so on in boxes (Article 37-3(1) of the FIEA; Article 79(2) & (3) of the Cabinet Office Ordinance on Financial Instruments Services, Etc.). The need for an alert document overlapping with the pre-contract document is questionable; the matter should be properly handled by being creative in drawing up the statutory pre-contract document.

g. Strengthening the control environment for sale and solicitation of derivatives

In terms of administrative oversight, financial instruments business

*748*

Chapter 6   Conduct regulations on financial instruments business operators, etc.

operators, etc. are, when selling and soliciting over-the-counter derivatives transactions, and structured bonds and investment trusts with a similar risk profile, required (1) to explain to the customer the maximum anticipated loss, along with the tentatively calculated amount of the settlement money on cancellation in the worst-case scenario; (2) to confirm the amount of losses and amount of settlement money on cancellation acceptable to the customer; (3) if the transaction is for the purpose of hedging, to confirm with the customer its effectiveness as a hedging instrument; and (4) to confirm the customer's intention to enter into a contract (IV-3-3-2 (6) of the Comprehensive Guidelines for Supervision of Financial Instruments Business Operators, Etc.).

This framework may be seen positively as, in one regard, standardizing application of the civil rule (the civil accountability requirement based on the principle of good faith) cited in court decisions, based on, among others, the Tokyo District Court decision of March 31, 2009 (*Hanrei Jiho*, No. 2060, p. 102) finding that a securities company had violated its duty to be accountable to a corporate customer in an interest-rate swap transaction; but its retroactive application should be avoided.

# 7 . The Act on Sales, etc. of Financial Instruments

a . Overview of the Financial Instruments Sales Act

The Act on Sales, etc. of Financial Instruments (Financial Instruments Sales Act), in order to protect customers, imposes liability for damages (strict liability and direct liability) on financial instrument providers, etc. that violate their duty of accountability to the customer or provide conclusive evaluations, etc., and establishes a provision on the presumed amount of loss that shifts the burden of proof (Article 1). The law was enacted in 2000.

The Financial Instruments Sales Act has two main characteristics. First, it has the character of civil legislation that, by establishing special provisions under the tort provisions in Article 709 and Article 715 of the Civil Code, is designed to contribute to civil relief of customers who have sustained losses because a financial instrument provider, etc. has violated the duty of accountability or provided conclusive evaluations, etc. The Act does not designate a competent minister, and enforcement against violations of the

*749*

Act's regulatory framework is conducted solely through claims for damages. In this regard it differs in character from financial regulatory laws such as the FIEA, for which there is a competent minister and which are enforced against violations primarily through administrative action.

Second, the Financial Instruments Sales Act covers a wide range of financial instruments and transactions, including deposits and savings in general and all forms of insurance, for it is conceived as a Japanese version of the Financial Services Act designed to establish a set of functional, cross-sectoral rules governing financial instruments and transactions overall.

b. Scope of application of the Financial Instruments Sales Act

The acts subject to the Financial Instruments Sales Act are defined as "sale (s), etc. of financial instruments," meaning "sale (s) of financial instruments" or agency or intermediary service therefor (Article 2(1) & (2)). The Financial Instruments Sales Act does not define the term "financial instruments."

"Sale (s) of financial instruments" include, in addition to the act of causing one to acquire securities and derivatives transactions, concluding a deposit or savings contract, concluding an insurance or mutual aid contract, concluding a real estate specified joint enterprise contract (with contributions made and redeemed in money), transactions involving payment or receipt of the difference (excluding commodities futures transactions, etc.), and financial and other derivatives transactions (Article 2 (1) of the Financial Instruments Sales Act; Article 2-5 of the Order for Implementation of the Financial Instruments Sales Act).

Operators subject to the Financial Instruments Sales Act are defined as "financial instrument providers, etc." (persons carrying out sales, etc. of financial instruments in the course of business) (Article 2(3)). The term "customer" means the counterparty to sales of financial instruments (ibid., Article 2(4)).

c. Accountability

Financial instrument providers, etc. have a civil duty to explain important matters to the customer (Article 3(1) of the Financial Instruments Sales Act). That explanation must be provided in a manner and to the extent

Chapter 6   Conduct regulations on financial instruments business operators, etc.

necessary for the customer to understand, in light of his/her knowledge and experience or the status of his/her property or the purpose of concluding the contract (ibid., Article 3(2)). A substantial duty of accountability is thus imposed.

The important matters that must be explained are (1) that there is a "Risk of Incurring a Loss of Principal" or that there is a "Risk of Incurring a Loss Exceeding the Initial Principal" due to market risk or credit risk; (2) the indicator or person that is the direct cause thereof; (3) "the important portions of the Structure of Transactions Pertaining to the Sales of Financial Instruments" that generate the risk in (1); and (4) the fact that the period during which the rights can be exercised or the contract cancelled is limited (ibid., Article 3(1), (3), (4) & (5)). Of these, the matters relating to losses exceeding the principal and the third were added under the 2006 revision of the Financial Instruments Sales Act in order to expand the range of accountability.

With regard to (1) and (2), a court has ruled that the duty to explain the market risks of an anonymous partnership agreement relating to lease of aircraft did not extend to aircraft marketability trends per se, and that the duty to explain credit risks did not include explaining the extent of the risk of actually losing principal considering the business and state of property of the person in question (Tokyo District Court Decision of Feb. 23, 2004, *Hanrei Times*, No. 1156, p. 256). Nonetheless, if a customer is concerned about the extent of the potential loss, providing an explanation thereof may be necessary in order to ensure that the customer understands the important portions of the structure of the transaction.

Another court decision denied that the risk of loss of principal from early withdrawal of a structured deposit was subject to the duty of accountability in Article 3, paragraph 1, item (i) of the Financial Instruments Sales Act (Tokyo District Court Decision of Sept. 14, 2011; *Hanrei Times*, No. 1397, p. 168).

With respect to (4), it was found in another court case that the time required for a securities company, when structured bonds marketed by it were sold before maturity, to confirm with the customer that the customer possessed no insider information did not constitute a limit on the period (Tokyo District Court Decision of Oct. 31, 2011; *Hanrei Times*, No. 1374, p.

187).

The duty of accountability does not apply (1) when the customer is a "specified customer" having expert knowledge and experience (a financial instrument provider, etc. or professional investor), or (2) when the customer has manifested his/her intention not to require an explanation of important matters (Article 3(7) of the Financial Instruments Sales Act; Article 10 of the Order for Implementation of the Financial Instruments Sales Act). With regard to (1), in order, for practical purposes, to enable uniform handling of the duty of accountability under administrative regulations and the duty of accountability under civil law, the Financial Instruments Sales Act also exempts transactions with professional investors from the scope of accountability.

It is permissible for an operator to deliver one and the same document to the customer as a means of fulfilling the duty of accountability under the Financial Instruments Sales Act and the obligation under the FIEA to deliver a pre-contract document prior to conclusion of the contract. This basically applies also to documentation prescribed under exemptions to the obligation under the FIEA to deliver a pre-contract document prior to conclusion of the contract (such as the record of listed securities, etc.).

Although the Financial Instruments Sales Act was enacted to contribute to civil relief of customers, a review of court decisions since it took effect in April 2001 in which operators have been found liable for damages due to violations of their duty of accountability to the customer during sale of financial instruments reveals that hardly any were based on the Financial Instruments Sales Act (among published cases only the Tokyo District Court decision of Apr. 9, 2003, relating to MYCAL bonds, *Hanrei Jiho*, No. 1846, p. 76); virtually all cited violations of the duty of accountability based on the principle of good faith under the Civil Code. This is presumably because, in reaching the conclusion that an operator is liable for tort, judges find it sufficient to rely on the duty of accountability based on the principle of good faith under the Civil Code as established by legal precedent, and consider it unnecessary to invoke the Financial Instruments Sales Act as well. Conversely, the Osaka High Court decision of December 10, 2015 (*Kinyu Shoji Hanrei*, No. 1483, p. 26) recognized a securities company's liability for damages pursuant to Article 5 of the Financial Instruments Sales Act on the

Chapter 6 Conduct regulations on financial instruments business operators, etc.

grounds that, when selling exchangeable bonds, it failed to deliver a pre-contract document to the client prior to conclusion of the contract and to explain the risk of loss of principal if redeemed by the shares and important features of the transaction's structure that could result in loss of principal.

### d. Provision of conclusive evaluations, etc.

A financial instrument provider, etc. is prohibited from providing a customer with conclusive evaluations, etc. (the act of providing a customer with conclusive evaluations on uncertain matters or with information that misleads him/her into believing the certainty of such matters) (Article 4 of the Financial Instruments Sales Act). This provision was added under the 2006 revision of the Financial Instruments Sales Act.

Note also that one court ruling found solicitation illegal because a conclusive evaluation was provided by a securities company employee (Sapporo District Court Decision of Jan. 30, 2015, *Hanrei Jiho*, No. 2276, p. 138) (although this was not deemed to be a violation of Article 4 of the Financial Instruments Sales Act).

### e. Liability for damages of financial instrument providers, etc.

When a financial instruments business operator, etc. violates the duty of accountability or provides conclusive evaluations, etc., he/she bears strict liability and direct liability for damages to the customer (Article 5 of the Financial Instruments Sales Act). Strict liability means liability without fault. Direct liability means that the liability is not that of the employer as defined in the Civil Code, Article 715, paragraph 1.

The law includes a provision on the presumed amount of loss with respect to the liability for damages: the "Amount of Loss of Principal" is presumed to be the amount of loss incurred (Article 6 of the Financial Instruments Sales Act). This presumes the existence of a causal relationship. Although one court decision has denied that presumption (Tokyo District Court Decision of Nov. 30, 2010, *Hanrei Jiho*, No. 2104, p. 62), the wording "shall be presumed to be the amount of loss incurred by the Customer due to" (ibid., Article 6(1)) makes clear that a causal relationship is presumed.

This presumption requires the operator (not the customer) to prove the nonexistence of a causal relationship between the violation and the loss,

*753*

namely that no loss occurred or that the amount of the loss is less than the amount of loss of principal. Thus, the burden of proof is shifted. One court decision denied an operator's claim that no causal relationship existed (aforementioned Tokyo District Court Decision of Apr. 9, 2003).

Comparative negligence (Article 722(2) of the Civil Code) applies to the above liability for damages (Article 7 of the Financial Instruments Sales Act; aforementioned Tokyo District Court Decision of Apr. 9, 2003). Liability of joint tortfeasors (Article 719 of the Civil Code), the principle of monetary compensation (Articles 722(1) and 417 of the Civil Code), and operation of prescription (Article 724) also apply.

Because the Financial Instruments Sales Act has the character of civil legislation, it does not fall within the scope of "laws and regulations, etc." under the FIEA (Article 13(iv)(a)($\gamma$) of the Cabinet Office Ordinance on Financial Instruments Services, Etc.), although a violation of the Financial Instruments Sales Act by a financial instruments business operator, etc. may be subject to an order to improve business operation (Articles 51 and 51-2 of the FIEA).

f. Ensuring the appropriateness of solicitation

Financial instruments providers, etc. are, in making a solicitation for sales, etc. of financial instruments that are conducted in the course of business, required to endeavor to ensure the appropriateness thereof (Article 8 of the Financial Instruments Sales Act). As specific measures to that end, they are required to establish and publicize a solicitation policy (ibid., Article 9(1) & (3); Article 12 of the Order for Implementation of the Financial Instruments Sales Act). Among the matters to be inclued in the solicitation policy are the principle of suitability and the method and time of the solicitation (Article 9 (2) of the Financial Instruments Sales Act).

The specific content of the solicitation policy is left up to the financial instrument provider, etc.: it is a principles-based measure. For that reason it risks becoming a mere formality of inadequate effectiveness.

Chapter 6　Conduct regulations on financial instruments business operators, etc.

# 8. Prohibition of compensation for loss, etc.

　　a. Overview of the prohibition of compensation for loss in securities transactions

　　　　(ⅰ) "Sale and purchase or other transactions of securities, etc."

Article 39 of the FIEA prohibits compensation for loss, etc. with respect to sale and purchase or other transactions of securities, etc. The term "sale and purchase or other transactions of securities, etc." means sale and purchase or other transactions of securities or derivatives transactions (ibid., Article 39 (1)(i)). It is understood not to include transactions that constitute incidental business or notifiable or approved business of financial instruments business operators. So-called repurchase transactions (sale and purchase of bonds, etc. on condition of repurchase) are, because they effectively constitute lending transactions carried out by a financial instruments business operator, etc. for the purpose of procuring funds, exempted from the prohibition of compensation for loss, etc. (Article 16-5 of the Implementing Order).

　　　　(ⅱ) Prohibition of compensation of loss, etc. by operators

The provision by financial instruments business operators, etc. of compensation for loss, etc. is prohibited (Article 39 (1) of the FIEA). Specifically, it is prohibited (1) in advance, to make an offer or promise to provide a property benefit in order to guarantee against losses or guarantee a profit (ibid., Article 39 (1) (i)); (2) ex post facto, to make an offer or promise to provide a property benefit in order to compensate for a loss or make an addition to the profit (ibid., Article 39(1) (ii)); and (3) ex post facto, to provide a property benefit in order to compensate for a loss or make an addition to the profit (prohibition on implementing compensation for loss, etc.) (ibid., Article 39(1) (iii)). The first and second prohibitions apply not only to making a promise but even to the very act of making an offer.

The term "loss" covers not only losses realized from sale or purchase but also losses in valuation.

The term "property benefit" means the provision of anything of economic value: giving cash or goods, for example, as well as selling goods at a lower price or purchasing them at a higher price than usual, and allotting commodities likely to go up in price. It does not, however, include the

*755*

provision of such for fair value.

(iii)　Prohibition of compensation for loss, etc. at a customer's request

The provision of compensation for loss, etc. at the request of a customer of a financial instruments business operator, etc. is prohibited (Article 39(2) of the FIEA). Specifically, it is prohibited, at the request of a customer, (1) in advance, to make a promise to provide a property benefit in order to guarantee against losses or guarantee a profit (ibid., Article 39(2)(i)); (2) ex post facto, to make a promise to provide a property benefit in order to compensate for a loss or make an addition to the profit (ibid., Article 39(2) (ii)); and (3) ex post facto, to receive a property benefit in order to compensate for a loss or make an addition to the profit (ibid., Article 39(2) (iii)). The first and second prohibit the making of the promise, not merely the making of the request.

(iv)　Purpose of compensation for loss, etc.

The prohibitions in both (ii) and (iii) above forbid the specified acts if they are performed for a certain purpose (to guarantee against losses, guarantee a profit, compensate for a loss, or make an addition to the profit). An act is not prohibited if no such purpose can be identified. If, conversely, such a purpose can be identified, the act is understood to be prohibited even if that purpose coexists with others.

This is a subjective condition (it is interpreted to refer to "intention"), but whether it is met is determined in light of the objective act and circumstances. For example, an act is basically denied to be for the purpose of compensation for loss, etc. if (1) it entails providing a service deemed reasonable by the ordinary standards of society to a customer in order to deal with a complaint (but see III-2-5-1(2)(iii)(G) of the Comprehensive Guidelines for Supervision of Financial Instruments Business Operators, Etc.); (2) it has the legitimate purpose of assisting in business revitalization (see the FSA response of Jan. 25, 2013); or (3) it entails managing or disposing of the property in a business-type fund as ordinarily required.

(v)　Prohibition of compensation for loss, etc. via a third party

These prohibitions apply also in the case of intervention by a third party

*756*

Chapter 6   Conduct regulations on financial instruments business operators, etc.

other than the financial instruments business operator, etc. or the customer (Article 39(1) & (2) of the FIEA).

(vi)   Exceptions due to "problematic conduct"

A financial instruments business operator, etc. may offer, promise, or provide compensation for loss, etc. if it is due to "problematic conduct," but only if certain procedures are followed, such as obtaining confirmation of the problematic conduct (Article 39(3) & (5) of the FIEA).

Similarly, a customer of a financial instruments business operator, etc. may accept a promise of compensation for loss, etc. or receive a property benefit if it is due to "problematic conduct" (Article 39(4) of the FIEA). There is no requirement to follow certain procedures such as obtaining confirmation of the problematic conduct.

(vii)   Exceptions due to "problematic conduct"

Violations of the prohibition of compensation for loss, etc. are subject to penal provisions (Articles 198-3, 200(xiv) and 207(1)(iii)(v) of the FIEA). Also, the property benefit received by the customer in question or a third party who knows the circumstances is subject to mandatory confiscation or collection of equivalent value (Articles 200-2, 209-2 to 209-7 of the FIEA).

b.  History

Under the 1965 revision of the Securities and Exchange Act, securities companies and their officers and employees were prohibited from the act of soliciting customers to engage in the sale or purchase of securities or other securities transactions while guaranteeing them against losses or promising to provide special profits (Article 50(ii) & (iii); Article 1(ii) of the then Ministerial Ordinance on Rules on the Soundness of Securities Companies). These prohibited acts, although subject to administrative actions, were not subject to penal provisions. Further, there were no provisions prohibiting compensation for loss, etc. ex post facto (the act of compensating the customer for a loss after it has been incurred).

In June 1991, the so-called securities scandal came to light when it transpired that Japan's Big Four securities companies and many other securities firms had provided massive guarantees against and compensation

*757*

for losses. Therefore, as the emergency measure to prevent a recurrence, the 1991 revision of the Securities and Exchange Act prohibited, on pain of punishment, guaranteeing against and compensating for losses.

c. Legislative intent

The prohibition of compensation for loss, etc. is intended to maintain the fair price formation functions of the market by ensuring that investors make investment decisions in accordance with the principle of individual responsibility. It is also intended to prevent loss of trust in the neutrality and fairness of the market among ordinary investors as a result of compensating only certain investors for their losses, and to guarantee the degree of liquidity necessary to smooth price formation on the market without hindering market participation by a broad cross section of investors (see Supreme Court Decision of Apr. 18, 2003, *Civil Cases of the Supreme Court*, Vol. 57, No. 4, p. 366).

In line with that intent, financial instruments business operators, etc., which as market intermediaries have the responsibility to maintain fair price formation in capital markets, are prohibited from providing compensation for losses, etc.; and their customers, while not obligated to be fair and neutral as market intermediaries, are prohibited from actively distorting the price formation functions of the market and undermining the fairness and neutrality of financial instruments business operators, etc. by requesting that they engage in illegal acts such as compensating losses.

d. Court decisions

The Supreme Court has issued several decisions dealing with compensation for loss, etc.

First, in a decision of April 24, 1997 (*Hanrei Jiho*, No. 1618, p. 48) relating to losses on a securities transaction conducted under a promise to guarantee profits made in January 1991, before the 1991 revision of the Securities and Exchange Act took effect in January 1992, the Supreme Court ascribed those losses to tort on the part of the securities company and, on the grounds that the illegality of the securities company employees' conduct was far greater than that of the investor's, recognized the employer liability of the securities company without analogously applying Article 708 of the Civil Code

758

Chapter 6   Conduct regulations on financial instruments business operators, etc.

(performance for illegal causes).

Second, the Supreme Court Decision of September 4, 1997 (*Civil Cases of the Supreme Court*, Vol. 51, No. 8, p. 3619) found a securities company contract guaranteeing against losses concluded before the 1991 Revision of the Securities and Exchange Act (in August 1990) to violate public policy and be null and void.

Third, in a decision of July 7, 2000 (*Civil Cases of the Supreme Court*, Vol. 54, No. 6, p. 1767 — a shareholders' class action suit relating to compensation for losses by Nomura Securities), the Supreme Court ruled that compensation for losses provided ex post facto in March 1990, prior to the 1991 revision of the Securities and Exchange Act, while not violating the provisions of the pre-revision law, to wit Article 50, paragraph 1, items (iii) and (iv) (the prohibition on guarantees against losses) and Article 58, item (i) (Article 157(i) of the current Act), did constitute luring customers with unjust profits and as such violated Article 19 of the Antimonopoly Act (prohibition of unfair trade practices). The original decision by the Tokyo High Court (decision of Sept. 26, 1995, *Hanrei Jiho*, No. 1549, p. 11) ruled that the instruction to refrain from providing compensation for losses ex post facto contained in the circular notice of December 26, 1989, from the Director General of the Securities Bureau of the Ministry of Finance was simply administrative guidance with no basis in law.

Fourth, the aforementioned Supreme Court Decision of April 18, 2003, ruled that it would be difficult to conclude that in June 1985, when the contract guaranteeing against losses was concluded, the perception already existed in society that acts such as guaranteeing against losses were highly antisocial acts impermissible within the securities trading system; therefore, the contract could not be considered to violate public policy and be null and void. The decision also ruled that Article 42-2, paragraph 1, item (iii) of the Securities and Exchange Act (Article 39(1)(iii) of the current Act) did not violate Article 29 of the Constitution in not permitting the exercise of the right to claim compensation from a securities company based on a valid contract guaranteeing against losses.

*759*

e. Exclusion from application in cases of problematic conduct

（ⅰ） Overview

The prohibition of compensation for loss, etc. by financial instruments business operators, etc. does not apply where the offer, promise, or provision is made or conducted in order to compensate in whole or in part a loss incurred from "problematic conduct" (Article 39(3) of the FIEA). Similarly, the prohibition of compensation for loss, etc. at the request of a customer of a financial instruments business operator, etc. does not apply where the promise is made in order to compensate in whole or in part a loss incurred from "problematic conduct" or where the provision of the property benefit is conducted in order to compensate for all or part of a loss incurred from "problematic conduct" (ibid., Article 39(4)).

This is because financial instruments business operators, etc. should naturally pay for losses due to "problematic conduct," and it would be unreasonable to prohibit them from doing so on the grounds that it constituted compensation for loss.

（ⅱ） "Problematic conduct"

"Problematic conduct" means an illegal or unjust act conducted by a financial instruments business operator, etc. or an officer or employee thereof that is specified as a potential cause of a dispute between the financial instruments business operator, etc. and his/her customer (Article 39(3) of the FIEA). Specifically, it means an act whereby a "representative, etc." (a representative person, agent, employee, or other worker) of a financial instruments business operator, etc. causes a customer a loss by committing any specific acts with regard to the business of the financial instruments business operator, etc. concerning sale and purchase or other transactions of securities, etc. (Article 118 (i) of the Cabinet Office Ordinance on Financial Instruments Services, Etc.).

With regard to the meaning of "acts in violation of laws and regulations" (ibid., Article 118(i)(e)), one of the categories of problematic conduct, the aforementioned Supreme Court Decision of April 18, 2003, ruled that failure to perform a contract guaranteeing against losses, which was prohibited under the Securities and Exchange Act, did not constitute "problematic conduct." Court decisions have found that the term "does not encompass all

*760*

Chapter 6   Conduct regulations on financial instruments business operators, etc.

other violations of laws and regulations; rather, in addition to fraud, embezzlement in the pursuit of social activities, other violations of the Penal Code, it refers generally to violations of laws and regulations of which it would be unjust, under the principle of individual responsibility, to make the customer bear the cost, that is, violations of laws and regulations where, in cases not meeting any of the descriptions in items (i) through (iv), a disjuncture has arisen between the nature of the customer's intentions and the nature of the transaction" (Tokyo District Court Decision of Oct. 15, 1993, *Kinyu Shoji Hanrei*, No. 951, p. 31; Tokyo District Court Decision of Jan. 27, 1994, *Hanrei Jiho*, No. 1517, p. 70; Tokyo District Court Decision of Apr. 28, 2004, *Hanrei Jiho*, No. 1529, p. 90).

(iii)   Confirmation of the problematic conduct

Ex-post-facto compensation for loss due to problematic conduct is excluded from application of the prohibition of compensation for loss, etc. by financial instruments business operators, etc. only in cases where the financial instruments business operator, etc. has obtained confirmation from the Director General of the Local Finance Bureau or Branch Bureau in advance to the effect that the loss to be compensated was incurred due to problematic conduct or other specified cases (Article 39(3) of the FIEA). This is because it is necessary to prevent problematic conduct from being used as a means of evading the prohibition of compensation of loss.

Confirmation of the problematic conduct is, under the law and regulations, to be conducted by the Director General of the Local Finance Bureau or Branch Bureau (Article 39(5) of the FIEA; Article 120 of the Cabinet Office Ordinance on Financial Instruments Services, Etc.), but practically speaking it is carried out through the Japan Securities Dealers Association (JSDA) in accordance with its "Rules Concerning Application for Confirmation, Examination, Confirmation, Etc. of Incidents."

On the other hand, in cases where the prohibition of compensation for loss, etc. at a customer's request is excluded from application due to problematic conduct, no procedures such as obtaining confirmation of the problematic conduct are prescribed (Article 39(4) of the FIEA).

*761*

(iv) Cases where confirmation of the problematic conduct is unnecessary

In order to streamline compensation for customers' losses in cases of problematic conduct, confirmation of the problematic conduct is deemed unnecessary in certain cases, namely where objective procedures are implemented that make it possible to presume that the compensation for loss is due to problematic conduct, even if the Director General of the Local Finance Bureau or Branch Bureau does not confirm it (Article 39(3) of the FIEA).

Specifically, these cases are: (1) court-related proceedings (Article 119 (1)(i), (ii) & (iii) of the Cabinet Office Ordinance on Financial Instruments Services, Etc.); (2) alternative dispute resolution (ADR) proceedings (ibid., Article 119(1)(iv), (v), (vi) & (vii)); (3) a settlement mediated by an attorney or a judicial scrivener worth no more than a certain amount (ten million yen or 1.4 million yen) or a similar arrangement (ibid., Article 119(1) (viii) & (ix)); (4) where the amount of the loss incurred by the customer during one day's trading is no more than one hundred thousand yen (ibid., Article 119(1)(x)); and (5) what is clearly problematic conduct (ibid., Article 119(1)(xi)).

A financial instruments business operator, etc. is required to report ex-post facto in cases of ibid., item (ix)-Item (xi) (ibid., Article 119(3)).

f. Prohibition of compensation in investment advisory/agency and management business
(i) Prohibition on promising to guarantee against losses

A financial instruments business operator, etc. is prohibited, with regard to his/her investment advisory and agency business or investment management business, from the act of making a promise to a customer, when soliciting him/her, to guarantee beforehand against losses (Article 38-2(ii) of the FIEA). Offering to guarantee against losses beforehand is not prohibited. A promise to guarantee profit is not prohibited either, but if the promise to guarantee a profit includes a promise to guarantee against losses, it violates this article. Customers are not subject to regulation.

This article says nothing about intervention by a third party. Nonetheless, even if, formally, a third party other than a financial instruments business operator, etc. makes a promise to guarantee against losses to the customer

Chapter 6  Conduct regulations on financial instruments business operators, etc.

or a third party other than the customer, that act violates this article if it may be considered effectively a promise to the customer by the financial instruments business operator, etc. to guarantee against losses.

On the other hand, a sponsor letter provided to a lender by an asset manager would not be regarded as a promise to guarantee against losses in many cases.

This article does not explicitly prescribe exceptions in cases of problematic conduct. Promising to guarantee against losses in the case of problematic conduct in the future does not constitute a violation of this article, except if the promise effectively includes a commitment to guarantee against losses in cases other than problematic conduct.

A representative person, agent, employee or other worker of a financial instruments business operator, etc. who violates this prohibition, or a financial instruments business operator that does so, is subject to penal provisions (Articles 198-3 and 207(1)(iii) of the FIEA).

(ii)  Prohibition on implementing compensation for loss, etc.

A financial instruments business operator, etc. is prohibited, with regard to his/her investment advisory business or investment management business, from implementing compensation for loss, etc. ex post facto (Articles 41-2 (v) and 42-2 (vi) of the FIEA). This prohibition applies not only to compensation for loss but also to making an addition to the profit; it does not apply, however, to making an offer or promise of compensation for loss, etc. ex post facto. Investment agency business (Article 28(3)(ii) of the FIEA) and customers are not subject to regulation.

Cases of problematic conduct are excluded from application of the prohibition, but there is no provision on confirmation of the problematic conduct; the question needs to be appropriately determined by the individual financial instruments business operator, etc.

Under the 2013 revision of the FIEA, the purchase of deteriorated investment assets of a money reserve fund (MRF) by the settlor company of an investment trust was excluded from application of the prohibition on implementing compensation for loss (ibid.; Article 129-2 of the Cabinet Office Ordinance on Financial Instruments Services, Etc.). In other cases the purchase of a fund's deteriorated investment assets by the fund manager

*763*

may constitute compensation for loss, etc. Direct compensation for loss, etc. to investors of MRF is not allowed.

(iii) Relationship with the prohibition of compensation for loss in securities transactions

The prohibition of compensation for loss, etc. with respect to sale and purchase or other transactions of securities, etc. (Article 39 of the FIEA) is taken over by the FIEA from the provisions of the old Securities and Exchange Act. The prohibition of compensation for loss, etc. with respect to investment advisory and agency business and investment management business is taken over by the FIEA from the provisions of the old Investment Advisory Business Act. The relationship between the two is not necessarily clear.

This comes down to a question of the application of Article 38-2, item (ii), Article 41-2, item (v), and Article 42-2, item (vi) of the FIEA to investment advisory and agency business and investment management business. It is reasonable to conclude that Article 39 does not apply.

# 9. Regulations to prevent insider trading

## a. Overview

### (i) Prohibited acts

Conduct regulations on financial instruments business operators, etc. include regulations to prevent insider trading.

Specifically, first, financial instruments business operators, etc. are prohibited from the following acts: (1) "accepting an entrustment, etc." (see Articles 44-2(1)(i) and 44(i) of the FIEA) of "sale and purchase or other transactions of securities, etc." (see Article 41-2(iv) of the FIEA) of a customer while knowing that that transaction violates or may violate insider trading regulations (Article 38(viii) of the FIEA; Article 117(1)(xiii) of the Cabinet Office Ordinance on Financial Instruments Services, Etc.); (2) soliciting a customer with respect to the sale, purchase, or other transactions of securities, derivatives transactions relating to securities, or intermediary, brokerage, or agency service therefor, while providing him/her with corporate information on the issuer (ibid., Article 117 (1) (xiv)); (3) soliciting a customer with respect to the sale, purchase, or other transactions

Chapter 6   Conduct regulations on financial instruments business operators, etc.

of securities, derivatives transactions relating to securities (sale, purchase, etc.), or intermediary, brokerage, or agency service therefor, for the purpose of acquiring a profit or avoiding a loss for the customer by having him/her conduct the sale, purchase, etc. before corporate information is made public (ibid., Article 117 (1) (xiv-ii)); (4) when conducting an investigation of potential investor demand (a so-called pre-hearing) prior to the public announcement of the decision to make a public offering of securities, providing corporate information relating to that public offering without taking certain measures (ibid., Article 117(1) (xv)); and (5) on the basis of corporate information, engaging on one's own account in the sale, purchase, or other transactions of securities, etc. to which that corporate information relates (ibid., Article 117(1) (xvi)).

The first, second, and fifth of these were introduced at the time of the 1988 revision of the Securities and Exchange Act, the second at the time of the 2013 revision of the FIEA. The fourth was introduced in November 2006.

In the case of the fifth, the agent of the act can only be a securities company or an officer or employee thereof. The FSA, in applying this provision, appears to interpret "on the basis of" to mean "knowing," but that remains questionable in terms of wording.

( ii )   Prohibited states of operation

Next, the state of operation of the business of a financial instruments business operator, etc. is deemed inappropriate where (1) with regard to management of corporate information or management of securities transactions, etc. of customers, the operator is found to have failed to take necessary and appropriate measures to prevent unfair transactions relating to corporate information; or (2) if engaging in the act of buying up as conducted by securities companies to broker block trading (which act meets the "minor influence" criteria [Article 167(2) of the FIEA; Article 62(ii) of the Cabinet Office Ordinance on Restrictions on Securities Transactions, Etc.] for exclusion from "facts concerning takeover bid, etc."), the operator is found to have failed to take certain measures ── promising that the buy-up is for resale purposes, and if immediate resale may not be possible, making a public announcement after the buy-up (Article 40(ii) of the FIEA; Article 123 (1) (v) & (xxvii) of the Cabinet Office Ordinance on Financial

*765*

Instruments Services, Etc.).

The first of these was introduced in October 1988, the second at the time of the 2011 revision of the FIEA (the part that took effect in April 2012).

b . Intent

The regulations to prevent insider trading all relate to "corporate information." Introduced largely in tandem with the adoption of insider trading regulations under the 1988 revision of the Securities and Exchange Act, they are designed to strengthen securities companies' systems for preventing insider trading so that information on issuer companies acquired in the course of their operations is not passed on to sales divisions and branches and used for insider trading, since securities companies are particularly in a position to gain access to information on issuer companies through their corporate operations.

c . "Corporate information"

"Corporate information" means (1) unpublicized material information on the operations, business, or property of a listed company, etc., which information is considered to affect customers' investment decisions; and (2) unpublicized information (except that meeting the "minor influence" criteria) relating to a decision to execute or terminate a takeover bid or an equivalent buy-up of share certificates, etc. (Article 1 (4) (xiv) of the Cabinet Office Ordinance on Financial Instruments Services, etc.). In order to facilitate block trading by securities companies, information meeting the "minor influence" criteria for exclusion from "facts concerning takeover bid, etc." (Article 167(2) of the FIEA) is excluded from (2).

Two points that corporate information ((1) above) has in common with "material facts pertaining to business or other matters" (Article 166(2) of the FIEA) under insider trading regulations on corporate insiders, etc. are (1) materiality, and (2) influence on investment decisions. Both also have in common the fact that they include information from sources other than listed companies, etc., while excluding information on market supply and demand. However, insofar as regulations on corporate information are intended to prevent insider trading, and the latter are listed individually and the so-called basket clause of the latter sets "a significant influence on investment

Chapter 6   Conduct regulations on financial instruments business operators, etc.

decisions" as a condition, the former covers a wider range of facts than the latter.

Practically speaking, whether something constitutes corporate information appears to be determined in light of such factors as the source of the information and its specificity and potential influence on share prices. However, what corporate information denotes is unclear; thus, an overly broad interpretation would undermine predictability and have a chilling effect on the practical conduct of business. For that reason the condition "information considered to affect customers' investment decisions" (not "may affect") needs to be interpreted rationally in line with the intent of preventing insider trading, so that the wording is not overstepped and virtually all unpublicized information relating to listed companies is not in effect included.

Because corporate information is defined as "unpublicized material information," once publicized a fact no longer constitutes corporate information. The FSA appears to interpret "publicize" here identically to "publicize" in insider trading regulations (Article 166 (4) of the FIEA; Article 30 of the Implementing Order), but it need not necessarily be so interpreted with regard to corporate information not meeting the definition of a material fact under insider trading regulations. According to the FSA's interpretation, something previously reported in the media may constitute corporate information. At least if a fact becomes public knowledge by a means whereby the accuracy of information is typically ensured, it should be considered "publicized."

d. Management of corporate information
   ( i )   Control environment of corporate information
   The Japan Securities Dealers Association (JSDA) has prepared a set of self-regulatory guidelines on management of corporate information, "Rules Concerning Establishment of Confidential Corporate Information" (April 20, 2010).

These rules contain provisions on (1) designating a section to manage corporate information; (2) establishment of internal rules; (3) procedures at the time of acquiring the corporate information (such as immediately reporting it to the Management Section); (4) management of corporate

*767*

information (including establishing a Chinese wall); and (5) enhancement of the management system (such as regular in-house inspections). Meanwhile a new section has been added to the Comprehensive Guidelines for Supervision of Financial Instruments Business Operators, Etc., section III-2-4(3), "Points of Attention Regarding the Prevention of Insider Trading and Other Unfair Acts Using Corporate-Related Information" (June 4, 2010).

The JSDA has released a set of model in-house rules, "Rules on Management of Corporate Information." Further, in a position paper of April 16, 2013, on the Rules Concerning Establishment of Confidential Corporate Information, it has set out several points on the implementation of those rules in the aftermath of the cases of insider trading involving public offerings.

This position paper defines the concepts of (1) "information that is not currently corporate information but is considered highly likely to become so in the future" (highly probable information); (2) "information that does not in itself constitute corporate information but may become so in combination with other information" (implicit information, etc.); and (3) related information ((1) and (2)). It then suggests managing all three as a single package in the form of "corporate information, etc."

Because what corporate information denotes is unclear, it is desirable that for practical purposes "corporate information, etc." (corporate information and information that may constitute corporate information) be managed as a single package.

( ii ) System for managing analyst-related information

The JSDA, in Article 8 of the Rules Concerning Handling of Analyst Reports, requires that association members appropriately manage "material information" including corporate information. It has also released a document entitled Stance on Rules Concerning Handling of Analyst Reports (Feb. 17, 2015).

The JSDA's Guidelines concerning Association Member Analysts' Interviews, etc. with Issuers and Communication of Information (Sept. 20, 2016) were released in the aftermath of violations of regulations on analyst-related corporate information. These prohibit "preview interviews" (interviews with issuers to obtain information relating to undisclosed

Chapter 6   Conduct regulations on financial instruments business operators, etc.

accounting period earnings) and selective provision of "hot news" (provision of that information to specific investors).

e . Chinese walls

Major financial institutions and the like (securities companies, trust banks, etc.) erect an information barrier called a Chinese wall in order to prevent insider trading by properly managing insider information (unpublicized material information). The Chinese wall is installed between divisions possessing corporate information such as the business division (the private arm) and divisions that trade in regulated securities of listed companies and so forth such as the investment, long-term investment, and proprietary trading divisions (the public arm).

In the case of foreign financial institutions, a compliance section termed the "control room" manages a database listing corporate information called a "watch list." Supervisors who, for management purposes, need to have access to corporate information are assigned "above the wall" status. Officers and employees of divisions that regularly handle corporate information, such as investment banking, are assigned "behind the wall" status. "Over the wall" procedures are in place for providing corporate information to people outside the Chinese wall as necessary for business purposes with the approval of the control room.

Where the Chinese wall is properly installed and administered, even if, within the same corporation, the business division, for example, possesses insider information, giving instructions to buy or sell regulated securities is basically not thought to constitute a case of trading with knowledge of insider information as long as the person giving the instructions is not aware of the insider information; insider trading is thus not considered to have taken place. It has been argued that in such cases the department responsible for managing insider information should halt the trade, and if it does not, the trade may constitute a trade conducted due to inaction on the part of one with knowledge; and except if that conduct is for the purpose of evading the law, such a conclusion is unnecessary.

Nonetheless, in 2012 there were cases of public offerings of new shares of listed companies that called into question the effectiveness of using a Chinese wall for systematically managing information at financial instruments

*769*

business operators. The "need to know" principle, whereby information is not disclosed to anyone in-house to whom it does not need to be for business purposes, should be emphasized, and "over the wall" procedures should be strictly enforced.

## 10. Preventive measures against adverse effects (firewall regulations)

a. Intent

Under the 1992 revision of the Securities and Exchange Act (Financial Systems Reform Act), banks and securities companies were permitted to enter each other's markets by establishing separate subsidiaries in different business categories. At the same time preventive measures against adverse effects (firewall regulations) were introduced to prevent such undesirable consequences as a distortion of market functions through transactions exploiting the parent–subsidiary relationship. Regulations on activities not considered particularly deleterious were then gradually relaxed in light of actual circumstances.

Going beyond preventing the adverse effects of interactions between banking and securities, firewall regulations are intended to prevent the adverse effects of interactions between parent juridical persons, etc. and subsidiary juridical persons, etc. in general (Article 44-3 of the FIEA). Firewall regulations have several objectives. Specifically, these include (1) ensuring independence and soundness of management; (2) preventing conflicts of interest; (3) ensuring fair competition between market intermediaries (taking into consideration the influence of parent and subsidiary juridical persons, etc. on issuers and investors); and (4) protecting customers.

Preventive measures against adverse effects apply to financial instruments business operators, etc. They do not directly apply to parent juridical persons, etc. and subsidiary juridical persons, etc.

b. Regulatory firewall measures
  ( i ) Measures primarily ensuring independence and soundness of management

Regulatory firewall measures designed primarily to ensure independence

Chapter 6   Conduct regulations on financial instruments business operators, etc.

and soundness of management have been established in the form of arm's-length rules (mandating transactions on regular terms) applying to securities transactions, over-the-counter transactions in derivatives, and ordinary transactions between a financial instruments business operator, etc. and a parent or subsidiary juridical person, etc. (Article 44-3(1)(i) & (iv) and (2)(i) of the FIEA; Article 153(1)(i) of the Cabinet Office Ordinance on Financial Instruments Services, Etc.).

For securities transactions and over-the-counter transactions in derivatives, terms and conditions that are different from ordinary terms and conditions and detrimental to the fairness of transactions constitute the criterion. For ordinary transactions, terms and conditions that are significantly different from ordinary terms and conditions constitute the criterion.

The Banking Act also imposes an arm's-length rule on transactions between banks and specified related persons (Article 13-2; Article 14-11(ii) & (iii) of the Ordinance for Implementation of the Banking Act). Ordinary transaction terms and conditions constitute the criterion (ibid., Article 14-10).

(ii)   Measures primarily preventing conflict of interest

There are several regulatory firewall measures designed primarily to prevent conflict of interest. First, it is prohibited to give investment advice to conduct, or make an investment in conducting, an unnecessary transaction for the purpose of securing the interest of a parent or subsidiary juridical person, etc. (Article 44-3(1)(iii) & (2)(iii) of the FIEA).

Second is so-called disclosure of conflict of interest: when acting as the underwriter of securities issued by a person having an obligation to a parent or subsidiary juridical person, etc. in the form of borrowings, it is prohibited, if aware that the proceeds will be used to pay off that obligation, to sell those securities without providing an explanation to that effect to the customer (Article 44-3(1)(iv) of the FIEA; Article 153(1)(iii) of the Cabinet Office Ordinance on Financial Instruments Services, Etc.). Where there is considerable likelihood that the money raised will be used to repay the parent or subsidiary juridical person, etc., the operator is regarded as being aware of that even if ignorant of it (FSA administrative action of Mar. 20,

*771*

2003).

Third is the restriction on becoming the "lead managing underwriter" (Article 147 (iii) of the Cabinet Office Ordinance) in the underwriting of securities issued by a parent or subsidiary juridical person, etc. (Article 153 (1) (iv) of the Cabinet Office Ordinance). There are two exceptions: (1) if trading at a certain volume continuously takes place on the market (ibid., Article 153 (1) (iv) ($\alpha$) ($\beta$) ($\gamma$)); and (2) if an independent managing underwriter is involved in deciding the issue price (ibid., Article 153(1) (iv) ($\delta$); Note (11)d on completing Form 2 of the Cabinet Office Ordinance on Disclosure of Corporate Affairs) (added under the 2008 revision of the FIEA).

Fourth, when a parent or subsidiary juridical person, etc. acts as lead managing underwriter, it is prohibited to give investment advice or make an investment for the purpose of manipulating the price in a way not reflecting actual market conditions in order to influence the conditions of the transaction (ibid., Articles 153(1)(xii) and 154(vi)).

Fifth, when a parent or subsidiary juridical person, etc. conducts "underwriting of securities, etc." (Article 130(1)(ix) of the Cabinet Office Ordinance), it is prohibited, where the amount is not expected to reach that planned by the parent or subsidiary juridical person, etc., to give investment advice to acquire or purchase, or make an investment in acquiring or purchasing, the securities in question at the request of that parent or subsidiary juridical person, etc. (Articles 153 (1) (xiii) and 154 (vii) of the Cabinet Office Ordinance).

Sixth, it is prohibited to engage in crowdfunding, etc. with electronic means for customers' applications for securities issued by a parent or subsidiary juridical person, etc. (ibid., Articles 153 (1) (xiv) and 154 (iii) (added under the 2014 revision of the FIEA)).

(iii) Measures primarily ensuring fair competition between market intermediaries

There are several regulatory firewall measures designed primarily to ensure fair competition between market intermediaries. First, a financial instruments business operator is prohibited from concluding a contract for a financial instruments transaction knowing that a parent or subsidiary

Chapter 6　Conduct regulations on financial instruments business operators, etc.

juridical person, etc. has granted credit to, or conducts ordinary transactions with, the customer on a tie-in basis (Article 44-3(1) (ii) & (iv) of the FIEA; Article 153(1) (ii) of the Cabinet Office Ordinance on Financial Instruments Services, etc.). A registered financial institution is prohibited from conducting financial instruments intermediary service while granting credit to, or conducting ordinary transactions with, the customer on a tie-in basis (Article 44-3(2) (ii) & (iv) of the FIEA; Article 154(i) of the Cabinet Office Ordinance on Financial Instruments Services, Etc.); it is likewise prohibited from concluding a contract for financial instruments transaction knowing that a parent or subsidiary juridical person, etc. conducts ordinary transactions with the customer on a tie-in basis (ibid., Article 154(ii)). The phrase "on the condition that" means that if the former is not the case, then neither is the latter.

The Banking Act too prohibits tie-in arrangements with customers of banks or specified related persons (Articles 13-2(ii) and 13-3(iii); Articles 14-11(i) & (iii) and 14-11-2 of the Ordinance for Implementation of the Banking Act).

Second is the prohibition on so-called seller-backed financing: it is prohibited, within six months of becoming an underwriter of securities, to sell those securities to a customer knowing that a parent or subsidiary juridical person, etc. has granted credit to that customer for the purchase price (Article 153(1) (v) of the Cabinet Office Ordinance). This has the same intent as the restriction on granting of credit by underwriters (Article 44-4 of the FIEA).

Third, it is in principle prohibited, within six months of becoming an underwriter of securities, to sell those securities to a parent or subsidiary juridical person, etc. (Article 153(1) (vi) of the Cabinet Office Ordinance on Financial Instruments Services, Etc.).

Fourth, a securities company is prohibited from concluding or soliciting a contract for financial instruments transaction while unjustly taking advantage of the dominant position of a parent or subsidiary bank, etc. (ibid., Article 153(1) (x)). This prohibition is intended also to protect customers.

(iv)　Measures primarily protecting customers
The following regulatory firewall measures are primarily designed to

*773*

protect customers; they are also intended to ensure fair competition among market intermediaries. Restrictions with respect to undisclosed information apply only to securities companies and to officers and employees of registered financial institutions who conduct financial instruments intermediary services.

First, a securities company, or an officer or employee of a registered financial institution who is engaged in financial instruments intermediary services, is in principle prohibited from receiving from or providing to a parent or subsidiary juridical person, etc. undisclosed information relating to an issuer, etc. (Articles 153 (1) (vii) and 154 (iv) of the Cabinet Office Ordinance on Financial Instruments Services, Etc.).

Second, a securities company, or an officer or employee of a registered financial institution who is engaged in financial instruments intermediary services, is prohibited from soliciting the conclusion of a contract for financial instruments transaction using undisclosed information relating to a customer obtained from a parent or subsidiary juridical person, etc. (but only if the information is provided by that parent or subsidiary juridical person, etc. without obtaining written consent from the customer) (Articles 153(1) (viii) and 154(v) of the Cabinet Office Ordinance).

Third, a securities company is prohibited from using undisclosed information relating to an issuer, etc. obtained (for the purpose of system maintenance and management or internal management) from a parent or subsidiary juridical person, etc. for other than for its intended purpose (Article 153(1) (ix) of the Cabinet Office Ordinance).

Fourth, when visiting a customer with a parent or subsidiary bank, etc., a financial instruments business operator is prohibited from failing to disclose that it is a separate juridical person from its parent or subsidiary, etc. and thus misleading the customer into believing that both are the same juridical person (ibid., Article 153(1) (xi)).

（ⅴ） Prohibition of evasion of the law

Evading any of the above prohibitions (evasion of the law) is prohibited irrespective of the nominal reason (ibid., Article 153(1) (xv) and Article 154 (ix)).

Chapter 6   Conduct regulations on financial instruments business operators, etc.

c. Regulations on sharing of undisclosed information by securities companies

( i )   Overview

The regulations on sharing of undisclosed information applying to securities companies (financial instruments business operators engaged in securities-related business that conduct type I financial instruments business) restrict their receipt from or provision to a parent juridical person, etc. or subsidiary juridical person, etc. of "undisclosed information relating to an issuer, etc." (Article 44-3(1) (iv) of the FIEA; Article 153(1) (vii) of the Cabinet Office Ordinance on Financial Instruments Services, Etc.).

( ii )   "Undisclosed information relating to an issuer, etc."

The term "issuer, etc." means a securities issuer or customer to whom undisclosed information relates (Article 147 (ii) of the Cabinet Office Ordinance on Financial Instruments Services, Etc.). The term "customer," although not defined, includes not only persons who are actually party to a contract but also persons about to become so and persons for whom a financial instruments business operator executes administrative procedures.

"Undisclosed information" means (1) unpublicized material information on the operations, business, or property of the issuing company, which information is considered to affect customers' investment decisions; and (2) ordering trends on sale and purchase or other transactions of securities, etc. made by a customer or other special information learned by an officer or employee of the company itself or a parent or subsidiary juridical person, etc. in the course of duties (Article 1(4) (xii) of the Cabinet Office Ordinance).

It is not clear what "undisclosed information relating to an issuer, etc." denotes. The FSA has made clear its view that unpublicized financial and management information and transaction information on a customer should generally be treated as undisclosed information. However, an overly broad interpretation would undermine predictability and have a chilling effect on the practical conduct of business. For that reason, the condition "material information...which information is considered to affect customers' investment decisions" (not "may affect") in the first category of undisclosed information, and the condition "special information" in the second, both need to be interpreted rationally in light of the intent of the regulations on sharing

775

of undisclosed information, namely to protect issuers, etc. and ensure fair competition among market intermediaries.

From this standpoint, first, the information must be of such a degree of importance or specificity that its receipt from or provision to a parent or subsidiary juridical persons, etc. without the customer's consent would typically be considered to pose the risk of harming the customer's interests.

Second, the fact itself that a particular person is the customer of a financial instruments business operator, or of a parent or subsidiary juridical person, etc. thereof, should not be regarded as constituting undisclosed information; nor should the presence or absence of written consent from a particular customer on sharing of undisclosed information, or the fact that a corporate customer has opted out.

Third, where a securities company acquires unpublicized material information relating to an issuing company indirectly from a customer, it may in some cases be difficult to obtain the written consent of the issuer as it is not the company's own customer. Such "hearsay (indirectly obtained information)" (information regarded as such by the customer) can in many cases be treated as undisclosed information relating to the customer (rather than to the issuer). The issuer's consent is, however, considered necessary if the customer, as the issuer's messenger or agent, provides the securities company in turn with information provided to it (the customer) by the issuer, or if the issuer itself constitutes the securities company's "customer in the specific case." Even if the issuer's consent is not necessary, the establishment of an appropriate system for managing conflicts of interest is required in order to ensure that the information so provided is not illicitly used for the purpose of marketing, etc. to the issuer.

Fourth, information on investors can be classified into information relating to opinions and information relating to orders; information relating to opinions may basically be considered not to fall into the second category of undisclosed information.

Further, the first category of undisclosed information relates to "unpublicized information." Because the regulations on sharing of undisclosed information are not regulations to prevent insider trading, "publicize" need not be limited to taking the measures for publication listed under insider trading regulations (Article 166(4) of the FIEA; Article 30 of

*776*

Chapter 6   Conduct regulations on financial instruments business operators, etc.

the Implementing Order).

(iii)   "Receipt" and "provision" of undisclosed information

The acts subject to the regulations on sharing of undisclosed information are "receipt" from and "provision" to a parent or subsidiary juridical person, etc. of undisclosed information.

This may become a problem when an officer or employee of a securities company serves concurrently as an officer or employee of a parent or subsidiary juridical person, etc.; but when such an officer or employee of a securities company acquires undisclosed information, the parent or subsidiary juridical person, etc. at which he/she concurrently holds a position is not considered to have received that information simply by virtue of his/her holding that position.

The FSA, adopting a purely formal interpretation of the concepts "receipt" and "provision," classifies accepting undisclosed information as a messenger or agent of another party (i.e. the parent or subsidiary juridical person, etc.) as the "receipt" of that information by the messenger or agent (i.e. the securities company) in question.

(iv)   Sharing of information with the consent of the issuer, etc.

Because the regulations on sharing of undisclosed information are intended primarily to protect customers, receiving or providing undisclosed information is permitted with "written consent" from the issuer, etc. (Article 153 (1) (vii) (a) of the Cabinet Office Ordinance on Financial Instruments Services, Etc.). A so-called opt-in system is employed, under which the issuer, etc. must actively consent to sharing of undisclosed information. Blanket consent in advance is considered adequate. Consent may also be obtained electronically (Article 155 of the Cabinet Office Ordinance).

With a view to relaxing firewall regulations, the 2008 revision of the FIEA brought in an opt-out system for cases where the issuer, etc. is a juridical person, under which the issuer, etc. is informed in advance that undisclosed information will be shared, and may request that its provision be halted if it does not wish it to be shared (Article 153 (2) of the Cabinet Office Ordinance).

In such cases the securities company or parent or subsidiary juridical person, etc. must "appropriately provide opportunities [to corporate customers] to request that provision of undisclosed information be halted" (ibid.). Practically speaking, it is required to notify and re-notify corporate customers of, and regularly provide them with information on, the opportunity to opt out (IV-3-1-4(1) of the Comprehensive Guidelines for Supervision of Financial Instruments Business Operators, Etc.). For that reason some financial groups continue to seek consent from corporate customers even after the revision.

If the customer is a foreign juridical person, the requirement that consent be in writing is relaxed: consent may be by electronic mail, and it is even acceptable if the customer may reasonably be considered to have consented (Article 153(1)(vii)(a) of the Cabinet Office Ordinance).

(v) Sharing of information without the consent of the issuer, etc.

Receiving or providing undisclosed information is permissible even without the consent of the issuer, etc. in certain cases where doing so is highly necessary and would typically be considered to pose little risk of harming the interests of the issuer, etc.

Specifically, these cases are: (1) when entrusting financial instruments intermediary services to a parent or subsidiary juridical person, etc.; (2) when entrusting financial instruments intermediary services to a parent or subsidiary bank, etc.; (3) when a parent or subsidiary bank, etc. conducts financial institution agency services under entrustment by a principal financial institution; (4) when providing a parent or subsidiary bank, etc. with the amount of credit for a customer for a calculation needed to place restrictions on major extensions of credit, etc.; (5) when necessary for preparing a confirmation letter or internal control report; (6) when necessary for system maintenance and management; (7) when based on "laws and regulations, etc." (including foreign laws and regulations, etc.: Article 117(1)(xv)(a)(α) of the Cabinet Office Ordinance on Financial Instruments Services, Etc.); and (8) when necessary for the conduct of operations relating to internal management and administration (in which case the information may be provided only to a "specified related person" such as a holding company or a parent or subsidiary bank, etc.) (Article 153

Chapter 6   Conduct regulations on financial instruments business operators, etc.

(1) (vii) (b) to (i), (3) & (4) of the Cabinet Office Ordinance on Financial Instruments Services, Etc.).

Cases (6) and (8) apply only if measures are appropriately taken to prevent leakage of undisclosed information from the division in question, although the receipt of undisclosed information by an officer, etc. for the purpose of business administration and internal management operations does not itself constitute leakage (IV-3-1-4(3) (iv) of the Comprehensive Guidelines for Supervision of Financial Instruments Business Operators, etc.).

(vi)   Internal management and control operations

"Operations relating to internal management and control" comprise (1) legal compliance management; (2) management of the risk of losses; (3) internal audits and internal inspections; (4) financial administration; (5) accounting; (6) tax administration; (7) operations relating to the administration of business of a subsidiary juridical person, etc.; and (8) settlement of the sale and purchase of securities, derivatives transactions, and other transactions, and related operations (Article 153(3) of the Cabinet Office Ordinance on Financial Instruments Services, Etc.).

The seventh of these applies only to the receipt of undisclosed information from a subsidiary juridical person, etc. of the financial instruments business operator or the provision of undisclosed information to the financial instruments business operator's parent juridical person, etc. (ibid., Article 153(1) (vii) (i)).

(vii)   Management of sharing of undisclosed information

The Comprehensive Guidelines for Supervision of Financial Instruments Business Operators, etc., includes a section entitled "Points of Attention Regarding Exchange of Non-Disclosure Information with Parent/Subsidiary Corporations." This requires that centralized systems for management of undisclosed information be developed and that "non-shared information" (undisclosed information relating to corporate customers that have opted out or customers who have not opted in) be managed separately from other undisclosed information (IV-3-1-4(2) (iii) of the Comprehensive Guidelines for Supervision of Financial Instruments Business Operators, Etc.). Such

779

separate management is important to ensure the effectiveness of regulations on sharing of undisclosed information; as one means to that end officers and employees are to be restricted from accessing non-shared information (ibid., IV-3-1-4(2)(vi)A), which in itself is reasonable.

The Comprehensive Guidelines for Supervision of Financial Instruments Business Operators, etc. require that securities companies be unable to access non-shared information managed by a parent or subsidiary juridical person, etc., as opposed to that which they manage themselves. Given, however, that concurrent holding of positions by officers and employees is permitted (Article 31-4 of the FIEA), legally speaking it is not prohibited in itself for an employee concurrently holding positions, for example, at a bank and a securities company to have access as a bank employee to non-shared information held by the bank while also having access as a securities employee to non-shared information held by the securities company; therefore, the stipulation of the Comprehensive Guidelines in question should be regarded as merely intended to prevent evasion of the law.

(viii)   Prohibition of solicitation using undisclosed information

Securities companies are prohibited from solicitation using undisclosed information relating to customers obtained from a parent or subsidiary juridical person, etc. (Article 153 (1) (viii) & (2) of the Cabinet Office Ordinance on Financial Instruments Services, Etc.). Such acts by the parent or subsidiary juridical person, etc. (a bank, for example) are not prohibited.

The Comprehensive Guidelines for Supervision of Financial Instruments Business Operators, etc. require the imposition of restrictions on solicitation using non-shared information: customers whose non-shared information is managed by a parent or subsidiary juridical person, etc. of a securities company are not to be solicited by an officer or employee of that securities company using that non-shared information (IV-3-1-4 (2) (vi) B of the Comprehensive Guidelines). However, this stipulation should be considered a confirmatory one prohibiting, for example, an employee concurrently holding positions at a bank and a securities company from, as a securities employee, soliciting securities business using undisclosed information held by the bank. Rather than prohibiting such an employee from the act itself of, as a bank employee, soliciting banking business using undisclosed information held by

Chapter 6   Conduct regulations on financial instruments business operators, etc.

the securities company, it should be regarded as merely intended to prevent one form of evasion of regulations on sharing of undisclosed information: an employee who concurrently holds positions at a bank and a securities company taking advantage of that to use, as a bank employee, undisclosed information held by the securities company of which he/she has gained knowledge as a securities employee (Article 153 (1) (vii) of the Cabinet Office Ordinance on Financial Instruments Services, Etc.).

(ix) Prohibition of investment advice or management based on undisclosed information

A financial instruments business operator, etc. is, with regard to investment advisory business or investment management business, prohibited from providing advice or conducting management based on undisclosed information for the purpose of securing the interest of a customer or right holder (Article 44 (iii) of the FIEA; Article 147 (ii) of the Cabinet Office Ordinance on Financial Instruments Services, Etc.). This is a preventive measure against the adverse effects of interactions within the same juridical person.

d. Regulations on sharing of non-public loan information, etc. by registered financial institutions

( i ) Overview

An officer or employee engaged in financial instruments intermediary services at a registered financial institution is, first, as a preventive measure against the adverse effects of interactions within the same juridical person, in principle prohibited from sharing "non-public loan information, etc. of a customer who is an issuer of securities" with an officer or employee engaged in loan services or financial institution agency services (Article 44-2(2) (iii) of the FIEA; Article 150 (v) of the Cabinet Office Ordinance on Financial Instruments Services, Etc.).

Next, as a preventive measure against the adverse effects of interactions between parent and subsidiary juridical persons, etc., he/she is in principle prohibited from (1) providing a parent or subsidiary juridical person, etc. with "undisclosed information relating to an issuer, etc." (limited to ordering trends on sale and purchase or other transactions of securities, etc. made by

*781*

a customer or other special information [learned in the course of duties]);
and (2) receiving "non-public loan information, etc. of a customer who is an
issuer of securities" from a parent or subsidiary juridical person, etc.
(Article 44-3 (2) (iv) of the FIEA; Article 154 (iv) of the Cabinet Office
Ordinance on Financial Instruments Services, Etc.).

This prohibition was brought in as a preventive measure against the
adverse effects of interactions between financial instruments intermediary
services and loan services when the ban on registered financial institutions
engaging in securities intermediation business was lifted under the 2004
revision of the Securities and Exchange Act. No opt-out system has been
established for corporate customers (see Article 123 (2) of the Cabinet Office
Ordinance on Financial Instruments Services, Etc.).

(ⅱ) "Non-public loan information, etc."

"Non-public loan information, etc." comprises (1) unpublicized
information relating to the business conducted by a customer or other
special information learned by an officer or employee engaged in loan
services or financial institution agency services in the course of duties, which
information is considered to affect customers' investment decisions with
respect to securities solicited by employees or officers engaged in financial
instruments business or financial instruments intermediary services
(corporate bond certificates, share certificates, share option certificates,
investment trust beneficiary certificates, investment securities, covered
warrants, depositary receipts, etc.); and (2) ordering trends on sale and
purchase or other transactions of securities, etc. made by a customer or
other special information learned by an officer or employee engaged in
financial instruments business or financial instruments intermediary
services in the course of duties, which information is considered to
significantly affect loan services or financial institution agency services
relating to the issuer of those securities (Article 1 (4) (xiii) of the Cabinet
Office Ordinance on Financial Instruments Services, Etc.).

Examples of information in Category (1) include unpublicized information
on a customer issuing securities that constitutes a material fact pertaining to
business or other matters under insider trading regulations (Article 166 (2)
of the FIEA), and unpublicized information on long-term cash flow.

Chapter 6   Conduct regulations on financial instruments business operators, etc.

(ⅲ)   Meaning of "learned in the course of duties"

The "undisclosed information" that an officer or employee engaged in financial instruments intermediary services at a registered financial institution is prohibited from providing (Prohibition (1) in Section (i) above) is described as "learned in the course of duties" (Article 1 (4) (xii) of the Cabinet Office Ordinance on Financial Instruments Services, etc.). This is understood to mean information learned with respect to, among types of registered financial institution business, financial instruments intermediary services in particular, since the regulations in question are regulations on registered financial institution business (Article 44-3 (2) (iv) of the FIEA).

e. Restrictions on the exchange of information between registered financial institutions and entrustor financial instruments business operators, and on its use

Registered financial institutions and entrustor financial instruments business operators are in principle prohibited from exchanging "other undisclosed special information on the customers properties" without the prior written consent of the customer, and are prohibited from solicitation using that information (Article 40 (ii) of the FIEA; Article 123 (1) (xviii) & (xxiv) of the Cabinet Office Ordinance on Financial Instruments Services, Etc.).

If the registered financial institution and entrustor financial instruments business operator are parent and subsidiary juridical persons, etc., there is an opt-out relating to corporate clients (ibid, Article 123 (2) (ii)), but this is not available for officers and employees of registered financial institutions who are engaged in financial instruments intermediary service (proviso to that Paragraph).

# Chapter 7

Regulation of exchanges and clearing and settlement organizations

*Sadakazu Osaki*

# A. Financial instruments exchanges

## 1. Role of financial instruments exchanges

a. Various types of exchanges

In general, exchanges are institutions designed to facilitate the smooth conduct of trading and the formation of fair prices by bringing together purchasers and sellers of securities or other financial products. Exchanges are broadly divided into securities exchanges (or stock exchanges), which establish markets for the trading of stocks, bonds and other securities, and futures exchanges for derivatives transactions based on securities, currencies, interest rates, commodities and other underlying assets.

Traditionally, Japanese law sets forth three classifications of exchange. First, securities exchanges (or stock exchanges) handle the trading of securities and their related derivatives. Second, financial futures exchanges handle the trading of currencies, interest rate-related instruments and other financial derivatives. Third, commodity exchanges handle the trading of grains, precious metals and other commodity derivatives.

However, the Financial Instruments and Exchange Act (hereafter, the "FIEA") enacted in 2006 established a new concept of "financial instruments exchanges" that includes securities exchanges and financial futures exchanges. Commodity exchanges, which are established under the Commodity Derivatives Act, are distinguished from these financial instruments exchanges. Commodity exchanges are not only defined in an act other than the FIEA, but also regulated and supervised by government ministries other than the Financial Services Agency (hereafter, the "FSA").

The direct origins of Japan's current exchanges are the exchanges created in the Meiji period (1868-1912), following the establishment of the Tokyo Stock Exchange and the Osaka Securities Exchange in 1878. These were modelled after the modern exchanges at the time in Europe and the United States.

*786*

Chapter 7　Regulation of exchanges and clearing and settlement organizations

Currently, there are six financial instruments exchanges in Japan — the four stock exchanges in Tokyo, Nagoya, Sapporo and Fukuoka — and the Tokyo Financial Exchange and Osaka Exchange (which specializes in derivatives trading). Both the Tokyo and Osaka exchanges are owned by a holding company called Japan Exchange Group (JPX), which was established on January 1, 2013, by the merger of the two exchanges.

b. Establishment of financial instruments markets

Under the FIEA, organized markets for the sale and purchase of securities and derivatives transactions of financial instruments, (i.e., stocks, bonds, J-REITs and other securities, and financial indices with clear trading rules and frameworks for the supervision of trading), are called financial instruments markets. In principle, financial instruments markets can only be established by persons who have obtained a license from the Prime Minister (Article 80 of the Financial Instruments and Exchange Act (FIEA)).

In financial instruments markets, investor protection is accomplished by maintaining the fair and orderly trading of securities and derivatives. These markets also ensure efficient price discovery and a high degree of liquidity by concentrating a large volume of trading. The fair prices formed on financial instruments markets (market values) are used as standards for asset assessment and as criteria for securities issuance prices, so they also lead to efficient resource allocation. In this way, the establishment of financial instruments markets is highly important from the perspective of the public interest. This is the reason there is a licensing system for the establishment of markets by financial instruments exchanges.

The sale and purchase of securities and derivatives transactions are also conducted through means other than financial instruments markets, in what is known as off-exchange or over-the-counter (OTC) trading. While off-exchange trading is sometimes conducted through direct negotiations between investors, securities companies are often involved in these trades as intermediaries.

There are two types of off-exchange or OTC trading. One is off-exchange or

*787*

OTC trading of listed securities, and the other is off-exchange or OTC trading of unlisted securities. For the former type of trading, there are rules established by the Japan Securities Dealers Association (JSDA), which is a self-regulatory organization under the FIEA and an authorized financial instruments association.[1] For the latter type of off-exchange or OTC trading, there are no specific trading rules, though the FIEA is generally applicable to such transactions.

The FIEA provides that "over-the-counter securities markets" are to be established by authorized financial instruments firms associations (Article 67 of the FIEA, discussed in Section 3 below). This is a special type of OTC trading market place for unlisted stocks meeting certain criteria established by authorized financial instruments firms associations. Until 2004, the JSDA operated the JASDAQ market under this provision. However, the market was reorganized into a financial instruments market operated by a securities exchange; and as a result of this reorganization, no over-the-counter securities market exists today.[2]

With the FIEA amendment in 2008, it became possible for financial instruments exchanges to establish, in addition to existing financial instruments markets, new specified financial instruments exchange markets that only handle consignment orders from specified investors; i. e., professional investors meeting certain criteria prescribed in the FIEA (Article 117-2 of the FIEA). Based on this provision, the TOKYO AIM Exchange, a new financial instruments exchange operated by a joint venture of the Tokyo Stock Exchange and the London Stock Exchange, was launched in June 2009. The exchange was dissolved in 2012, and the market for professional investors was reorganized into the TOKYO PRO Market operated by the Tokyo Stock Exchange.

In contrast to the situation with regular listed securities, the issuers of

---

1    The JSDA Rule on Off-Exchange Trading of Listed Stocks is applicable.
2    The JASDAQ market was reorganized into JASDAQ Stock Exchange, which was later merged with the Osaka Securities Exchange.

Chapter 7　Regulation of exchanges and clearing and settlement organizations

securities traded on markets for professionals (specified listed securities) are not required to file securities reports or other continuous disclosure documents provided by law (Article 24 (1) (i) and (ii) of the FIEA). Alternatively, certain types of information disclosure take place based on the rules of the exchange (Article 117-2 (2) of the FIEA). Specifically, in addition to timely disclosure of material facts, there are requirements to disclose financial results in Japanese or English at least twice per year, and to use a format that is similar to securities reports prescribed by the exchange rules, among others.

c . Prohibition of business unrelated to exchange markets

As financial instruments exchanges engage in the business of establishing exchange markets, which has a significant impact on public interest, they are subject to strict limitations on the scope of the business they are allowed to conduct. This is the so-called exclusive business obligation. In other words, financial instruments exchanges are not allowed to engage in any forms of business other than the establishment of financial instruments exchange markets and business associated with the establishment of the markets (Article 87-2(1) of the FIEA). The same restrictions are placed on their subsidiaries (Article 87-3 of the FIEA). However, financial instruments exchanges can establish companies that conduct business related to the establishment of financial instruments exchange markets into subsidiaries with authorization from the Prime Minister (Article 87-3(1) of the FIEA). These same restrictions apply to financial instruments exchange holding companies, which are discussed below (Article 106-24 of the FIEA).

It is believed that such restrictions were imposed to prevent exchanges from taking on any excessive business risk and distorting fairness and neutrality in market administration by engaging in business unrelated to the establishment of financial instruments exchange markets. As described below, however, the operation of exchanges by for-profit companies has been increasing worldwide in recent years, and there are concerns that restrictions limiting the scope of business too severely could hinder the exchanges' development of business strategy and render profit growth difficult.

*789*

Thus, in 2008 the FIEA was revised so that financial instruments exchanges could establish emissions rights trading and other markets with approval from the Prime Minister (Article 87-2(1) of the FIEA). The FIEA was revised again in 2009 to permit the establishment of commodity exchanges by financial instruments exchanges and the placing of financial instruments exchanges and commodity exchanges under the same parent holding company (Article 87-2(1) and Article 87-3 of the FIEA). Additionally, in 2012 the law was revised to add provisions regarding mergers of financial instruments exchanges and commodity exchanges and to permit the establishment of commodities derivatives markets under the supervision of the FSA (the Prime Minister). This opened the path to creating so-called comprehensive exchanges that handle a wide range of derivatives transactions in addition to cash trading.

## 2. Trading on financial instruments exchange markets

### a. Trading flow

The following explains the financial instruments exchange market framework using the example of the sale and purchase of shares, which are the typical subjects of trading on financial instruments exchanges. The flow is basically similar for the sale and purchase of securities other than shares and for derivatives transactions.

Investors who wish to buy or sell shares place purchase or sales orders on financial instruments exchange markets through securities companies (financial instruments business operators). Investors place orders via securities companies because the parties who are granted qualifications as trading participants in financial instruments exchange market trading are limited to financial instruments business operators, authorized transaction-at-exchange operators and registered financial institutions (Article 2 (19), Article 112 (1), and Article 113 (1) of the FIEA). Here, securities companies fulfill the role of wholesalers (Article 551 of the Commercial Code) who conclude trades on financial instruments markets in their own names on behalf of investors.

Chapter 7   Regulation of exchanges and clearing and settlement organizations

The acceptance of entrustment of sale and purchase orders by securities companies must comply with the brokerage contract rules prescribed by the financial instruments exchange (Article 133 of the FIEA). Sale and purchase orders include limit orders that stipulate price and volume, as well as market orders that do not stipulate price. The orders are placed orally at securities company branches or by telephone call, and recently, many investors have been directly entering orders via the Internet. Orders are also placed by financial instruments intermediary service providers on behalf of securities companies.

The matching of sale and purchase orders on exchange markets is executed via an auction process. In such auctions, a single agreement price is determined at the start of trading (the opening) and the end of trading (the closing) using the *itayose* or call auction method giving priority to price. Between opening and closing, prices are set by matching orders under the *zaraba* or continuous session method giving priority to price and time. When orders are placed at the same time, they are processed giving priority to market orders over limit orders.

A sales order and purchase contract is executed when sales order and purchase prices and volumes match up. In market orders, sales orders are matched with the highest purchase order price at the time, and buy orders are matched with the lowest sales order price at the time.

After an order has been executed, the seller delivers the shares to the buyer and the buyer pays money to the seller (transfer and settlement). This transfer and settlement must take place three days after the day upon which the agreement is concluded (T+3). Exchange markets aim for the smooth circulation of large volumes of securities, so centralized trading is conducted anonymously. Thus, the settlements for all trading are conducted through netting (clearing) with a clearing organization (the Japan Securities Clearing Corporation serves as a unified clearing organization, but some exchanges also act as clearing organizations) as the counterparty.

In the past, transfer and settlement generally involved the physical

*791*

movement of share certificates, but printed share certificates of listed companies were abolished and dematerialized in Japan on January 5, 2009. Since then, all transfer and settlement is conducted by account transfer at an institution for book-entry transfer (specifically, the Japan Securities Depository Center, Inc.).

In order to ensure the safety of transactions, sale and purchase orders cannot be rescinded after an agreement has been concluded. This point was viewed as problematic following the "fat finger" or erroneous order incident involving J-Com shares in December 2005, and rules were formed whereby orders may in exceptional cases be canceled after conclusion of an agreement when large-scale erroneous orders occur (Article 13(1), among other provisions, of the Tokyo Stock Exchange Business Regulations).

  b. Various price formation methods
Sometimes, trading on exchange markets is not conducted by auction. Market making is an alternative mechanism through which securities companies called "market makers" continuously present ask and bid double-sided quotes, (i.e., indicative prices for sale and purchase) and promise to trade up to a certain volume of shares at the relevant prices, which facilitates smooth transactions of securities. Under the auction system, sale and purchase prices are determined based on prices presented by investors (an order-driven system). In contrast, with market making, sale and purchase prices are determined based on the prices presented by market making securities companies (a quote-driven system).

Under the market-making system, while minimal liquidity is always ensured, because the differential between the indicative sale and purchase prices (the spread) is the securities companies' revenue source, investors sometimes lose opportunities for potential price improvement. However, if there are multiple market makers presenting quotes for the same security, the spread may narrow due to competition among market makers, which works to improve prices for investors.

Market making used to be the main price formation method on the U.S.

*792*

Chapter 7   Regulation of exchanges and clearing and settlement organizations

NASDAQ market (which was an OTC market but is now an exchange market), and market making was also formerly used for a wide range of securities listed on the London Stock Exchange.

Recently, under competitive pressure imposed by newly established electronic trading systems such as PTSs, which will be discussed below, traditional exchanges have started operating trading systems for after-hours trading in addition to their regular trading platforms. For example, the Tokyo Stock Exchange provides three systems — ToSTNeT-1 for large-lot trading (cross-trading) at prices agreed upon beforehand and for basket trading for the sale and purchase of a portfolio comprising 15 issues, ToSTNeT-2 for trading at the closing price and ToSTNeT-3 for purchases of treasury stock by listed companies.

The treatment of these after-hours trading systems in the regulations for takeover bids (hereinafter, "TOB") was revised, following the acquisition of a large quantity of Nippon Broadcasting System shares without the making of an official bid by Livedoor using ToSTNeT-1 in February 2005. Currently, if investors use these systems to acquire shares that would lead to an ownership ratio of more than one-third of outstanding shares, a TOB must be implemented (Article 27-2(1)(iii) of the FIEA).

# 3. Listing on the exchange markets

### a. Listing examination and listing supervision

Financial instruments exchanges only engage in the sale and purchase of securities that have met certain standards; i.e., listed securities, as well as listed derivatives transactions approved by the exchange. Exchanges provide the standards that must be met by the issuers of the listed securities in their rules. Such standards are for judging whether the securities are suitable investment instruments to be traded widely by general investors, and include factors such as the financial conditions and management structure of the issuers. Based on these standards, exchanges carry out listing examinations to confirm that each security or derivative trading subject asset meets such standards. After the securities are listed, exchanges monitor whether there are any violations of the continued listing standards.

*793*

These standards are normally more lenient than the primary listing standards. If any situation arises that is in conflict with the continued listing standards, the securities will be delisted in accordance with the formal procedures.

When the shares of a listed company are delisted, the existing shareholders lose the opportunity to sell their holdings smoothly, and their economic interests are significantly harmed. In the past, almost all delistings in Japanese exchanges were the result of business failures or buyouts; but in recent years an increasing number of companies with ongoing business have been considered for delisting, and the advantages and disadvantages of judgments by exchanges regarding delisting or continued listing have been highlighted as topics for discussions. Famous cases include Seibu Railway Co. (delisting decided November 2004), Kanebo Ltd. (delisting decided May 2005), Livedoor Co., Ltd. (delisting decided March 2006), and Nikko Cordial Corp. (continued listing decided March 2007). In these cases, the regulatory issue focused on was whether the companies had fallen under the then Article 601(11) of the Tokyo Stock Exchange Securities Listing Rules, which prescribes that securities shall be delisted "when an issuer company has made a false disclosure in a securities report or other document and this Exchange recognizes that has had a material influence." In the case of Paint House, which was delisted in July 2006, the company filed for a temporary court injunction against the exchange delisting and instituted an action to declare the delisting invalid, though the claim was denied in a Tokyo District Court decision.[3]

The Tokyo Stock Exchange revised its rules in August 2013 so that, when a listed company has made a false disclosure in a securities report or other document or the Exchange otherwise recognizes a strong need for the listed company to improve its internal controls or other systems, in principle, the securities issued by the company are designated as "securities on alert" (Article 501 of the Securities Listing Rules). After being so designated, the securities will be delisted if the issuer company does not improve its internal

---

3   Tokyo District Court Decision of July 7, 2006, *Hanrei Times* No. 1232, p. 341.

Chapter 7 Regulation of exchanges and clearing and settlement organizations

control systems during a one-year improvement period and the company is not projected to make future improvements. In cases in which it is clear that it would be difficult to maintain an orderly market if the securities were not immediately delisted, however, the securities can be delisted without being placed on the list of the securities on alert (Article 601 (11) of the Securities Listing Rules).

When a listed company does not properly carry out the timely disclosure required by an exchange, the exchange may demand the submission of an improvement report on timely disclosure (Article 502 of the Securities Listing Rules). Moreover, when a listed company does not fulfill those obligations under the code of conduct on corporate governance and when other issues prescribed in the listing rules apply (Articles 432-452 of the Securities Listing Rules), the exchange may implement public censure or impose financial penalties (Article 509 of the Securities Listing Rules).

b. Market sections
Major securities exchanges have established market sections whereby shares that meet stricter criteria on liquidity, etc. are listed on the first section, and other shares are listed on the second section. Aside from the first and second section markets, there are markets such as the Tokyo Stock Exchange MOTHERS and the JASDAQ market, the Nagoya Stock Exchange Centrex market and other new markets for high-growth emerging companies that set looser listing standards than the traditional standards.[4]

c. Regulations on listing
In the past, listing and delisting from exchange markets required the approval of the competent minister (Articles 110 and 112 of the Securities and Exchange Act prior to the 1998 revisions). In order to attain a greater degree of freedom in the management of the exchanges, this framework was

---

4   In the past, securities exchanges were prohibited from opening two or more markets (Article 87 of the Securities and Exchange Act prior to the revision of 1998), but this provision was deleted in the revision of 1998.

*795*

revised through the amendments to the Securities and Exchange Act (the so-called "Japanese Big Bang") under the Financial System Reform Act of 1998, which prescribes that the exchanges are only required to notify the competent minister on listing and delisting of securities. Further, in the 2006 revision, a notification system was also adopted for listing and delisting of derivatives transactions (Articles 121 and 126 of the FIEA).

Permission for listing by the government is still sought in cases in which it is deemed inappropriate for an exchange to conduct a listing examination. For example, approval from the Prime Minister is required when acting to list securities issued by an exchange itself or by a holding company that owns the exchange as a subsidiary (Articles 122 and 124 of the FIEA).

The listing fees collected from the issuers of listed securities during examinations and the dues for maintaining listings collected each year are important revenue sources for exchanges. For this very reason, the possibility that exchanges may arbitrarily apply listing standards and delisting standards in order to maximize their own profits cannot be excluded from consideration. Therefore, there is a legal provision (Article 127 of the FIEA) stating that in cases in which an exchange acts to list or delist financial instruments in violation of its own rules, the Prime Minister can order the delisting or relisting of such financial instruments. There is also a provision (Article 125 of the FIEA) allowing the Prime Minister to order an exchange to list shares and other securities issued by listed companies that are not listed on the exchange when it is necessary and proper for the public interest or protection of investors.[5]

---

5    This provision was enacted after so-called rights securities (potential shares), which are new shares expected to be issued in the future became the subject of speculative off-exchange sales and purchases in the 1950s, and resulted in transactions that could not be settled and other conditions. Hideki Kanda, Nomura Shoken and Kazuo Kawamura (eds.), *Chukai shoken torihiki ho* [Commentary on the Securities and Exchange Act], (Yuhikaku, 1997) p. 989.

Chapter 7   Regulation of exchanges and clearing and settlement organizations

## 4. Organization of financial instruments exchanges

a. Membership organization and limited company organization

There are two forms for the organization of financial instrument exchanges: those operated by a financial instruments membership corporation, which is a non-profit membership organization, and those operated by a kabushiki kaisha or for-profit limited company (Article 83-2 of the FIEA).

Under the 1792 Buttonwood Agreement, which is the origin of the New York Stock Exchange (NYSE), the world's largest stock exchange, trading with parties other than the 24 stock brokers who were members of the agreement was prohibited (obligation for market centralization) and a fixed commission system was adopted. As this episode illustrates, stock exchanges tend to maintain the characteristics of broker-dealers' cartels or clubs. For a long time, most exchanges have maintained a membership organization with such cartel or club characteristics globally.

However, in Japan, the limited company organization of exchanges was common from their beginnings in the Meiji Era (1868-1912). On Japanese stock exchange markets prior to the Second World War, shares of the exchanges themselves were actively traded for speculative purposes; however, the exchanges did not act to restrict such trading, which was linked to boosting their own profits. In order to change the market structure, when enacting the Securities and Exchange Act after the Second World War, a provision was included providing that stock exchanges must be operated by non-profit membership associations (Article 80 of the Securities and Exchange Act prior to the revision of 2000). The Financial Futures Trading Act enacted in 1988 also adopted the same manner of regulating the organizational form of financial futures exchanges.

It became clear in the early 1980s in the process of negotiations toward opening membership in the Tokyo Stock Exchange to foreign broker-dealers that membership organizations have the flaw of tending to develop a closed mind aiming to protect their members' vested interests due to their club-like nature. Moreover, international competition among market operators has

*797*

intensified with the emergence of the proprietary trading systems discussed in Section B and the globalization of stock trading since the second half of the 1980s. As a result, exchanges in most countries with developed securities markets have been moving to switch from a non-profit membership organization to a for-profit company organization to achieve faster decision making and diversify their fundraising means.

Amid these developments, through the 2000 revisions to the Securities and Exchange Act, Japan also enabled the establishment of limited company organization exchanges as well as the conversion of membership organization exchanges to limited company organization exchanges. At present, Tokyo and Nagoya stock exchanges and the Tokyo Financial Exchange, and Osaka Exchange are limited company-type financial instruments exchanges that have a limited company organizational format, while the two Sapporo and Fukuoka stock exchanges are membership-type financial instruments exchanges that have maintained a non-profit, membership format.

   b. Membership-type financial instruments exchanges
Financial instruments membership corporations, which become member-ship-type financial instruments exchanges, are non-profit corporations established by financial instruments business operators and other businesses (financial instruments business operators and registered financial institutions) of which only financial instruments business operators and other businesses can be members (Articles 88, 88-2, 91, 97 of the FIEA).

Members contribute capital as provided by the articles of incorporation and only bear liability up to the amount of their contribution, in principle (Article 92 of the FIEA). Member's equity can only be transferred when the member withdraws (Article 93 of the FIEA). Members have the qualifications to participate in trading on the financial instruments markets established by the exchange, but parties other than members can also acquire trading qualifications as prescribed by the exchange's articles of incorporation (Articles 111 and 112 of the FIEA). Membership rights and trading participation qualifications were treated collectively in membership system

Chapter 7   Regulation of exchanges and clearing and settlement organizations

exchanges in the past, but those rights have now been separated.

The officers of financial instruments membership corporations are the chairperson of the board of directors, the directors and the auditors, but the business of the corporation is entirely determined through resolutions of general meetings of the members, except for those matters entrusted to the officers by the articles of incorporation (Articles 98 and 88-17 of the FIEA). In principle, the voting rights of each member are equal (Article 88-19(1) of the FIEA). In practice, the daily business is entrusted to the directors and other officers; but this structure, which emphasizes the role of the general meeting of the members, may be said to reflect the club-like nature of the membership exchanges.

Financial instruments membership corporations can switch their organizational structure to a corporate organization based on approval of at least three-quarters of all members and with approval from the Prime Minister. The law has detailed provisions regarding the relevant procedures (Article 101 of the FIEA).

Also, membership-type financial instruments exchanges may conclude contracts to merge with other membership-type financial instruments exchanges or limited company-type financial instruments exchanges and consummate mergers with approval from the general meeting and with authorization from the Prime Minister (Article 136 of the FIEA). In the latter case, the exchange which continues or is established by the merger must be a limited company-type financial instruments exchange (Article 136(2) of the FIEA). The provisions regarding mergers were set forth in the 1998 amendment to the Act. Following this amendment, the Hiroshima Stock Exchange and the Niigata Stock Exchange were merged into the Tokyo Stock Exchange in 2000, and the Kyoto Stock Exchange was merged into the Osaka Securities Exchange in 2001.

c. Limited company-type financial instruments exchanges
The organization and structure of limited companies that operate financial instruments exchanges is regulated under the Companies Act, like those of

*799*

normal limited companies, except for certain provisions regarding disqualification of directors and self-regulatory committees mentioned below. They must have ¥1.0 billion or more in capital (Article 83-2 of the FIEA; Article 19 of the Financial Instruments and Exchange Act Implementing Order (hereafter, the "Implementing Order")).

The establishment and operation of exchange markets is a business with a potentially strong influence on the public interest, and certain restrictions are placed on the shareholding of limited company-type financial instruments exchanges to prevent excessive influence by a single party. For example, in principle, holding more than 20% of the voting rights of financial instruments exchange shares is prohibited (Article 103-2 of the FIEA). This threshold becomes 15% when a material influence on decisions concerning the exchange's finances or business policies is presumed. However, these prohibitions do not apply to authorized financial instruments firms associations, financial instruments exchanges or financial instruments exchange holding companies.

Here, a financial instruments exchange holding company is a company that has a limited company-type financial instruments exchange as a subsidiary, and its establishment requires authorization from the Prime Minister (Article 106-10 of the FIEA). The only example of such a holding company is the Japan Exchange Group formed by a merger between the Tokyo Stock Exchange Group, which was the holding company of the Tokyo Stock Exchange, and the Osaka Securities Exchange in January 2013.

However, local governments and other parties specified by government order (specified in Article 19-3-3 of the Order as local governments, foreign financial instruments exchange market operators that meet certain conditions and foreign financial instrument exchange market operator holding companies) can hold 20% or more but not more than 50% of the shares of limited company-type financial instruments exchanges with authorization from the Prime Minister (Article 106-3 of the FIEA).

These provisions restricting share ownership changed greatly over a short

*800*

Chapter 7  Regulation of exchanges and clearing and settlement organizations

period of time. When it first became possible to establish limited company-type financial instrument exchanges through the 2000 amendment of the FIEA, the regulations were strict, prohibiting individual holdings exceeding 5%. However, the 2003 amendments to the Act changed these provisions to prohibit individual holdings exceeding 50% and require authorization for principal shareholders with holdings of more than 20%. The present framework was adopted in 2006 following the refusal by the FSA of a 2005 authorization application by the Murakami Fund to own more than 20% of the Osaka Securities Exchange.

The framework of placing certain restrictions on the ownership of exchange shares to protect the public interest is also seen in countries other than Japan. However, under conditions in which share ownership by specific individuals is restricted and hostile takeovers and other transfers of management control cannot occur, there are concerns regarding the harmful effects such as deterioration of management discipline and inefficient management of exchanges. Moreover, international capital alliances, acquisitions and mergers between exchanges are becoming popular with the intensified competition among global markets. The existing legal system in Japan limits the strategic options of Japanese exchanges, and one cannot deny the possibility that such regime could possibly lead to the hindrance of their international competitiveness.

# 5. Self-regulation of financial instruments exchanges

### a. Importance of self-regulation

As financial instruments exchanges engage in the business of establishing and operating financial instruments markets, which is important to the public interest, they have power to provide, in addition to articles of incorporation, rules such as business regulations that set trading rules and other matters, securities listing rules regarding securities listing and delisting standards and brokerage contract rules for the handling of orders from investors by market participants, among otherthings. To ensure the effectiveness of such articles of incorporation and regulations, exchanges have their members and trading participants observe laws, administrative dispositions and the exchanges' articles of incorporation and regulations, as

*801*

well as the good faith principle, and in the event the member or participant commits an act that is contrary to or in violation of such rules and regulations, the exchange must impose sanctions such as financial penalties, suspension of trading, expulsion or cancellation of trading participation qualifications (Article 87 of the FIEA).

Self-regulatory organizations are organs that are private organizations but regulate themselves for certain public interest purposes by stipulating rules for self-governance. The law holds self-regulation as one of the important tasks of exchanges (Article 84(1) of the FIEA).

Because the contents of the articles of incorporation and various rules and regulations of exchanges are important to the public interest, it is not appropriate for exchanges to be able to revise and abolish them solely at their own discretion. For this reason, when an application for an exchange license is filed, the Prime Minister must examine whether the provisions of the articles of incorporation and various rules and regulations conform with the law, and are sufficient for achieving fair and smooth trading of securities and transactions of listed derivatives, as well as for protection of investors (Article 82 (1) (i) of the FIEA). Also, amendments to the articles of incorporation and various rules and regulations require the approval of the Prime Minister (Article 149(1) of the FIEA). Furthermore, when necessary, the Prime Minister may order changes to the articles of incorporation and various rules and regulations of exchanges, has the right to dismiss directors, and is given other strong supervisory powers (Articles 150 through 153 of the FIEA).

   b . Self-regulation under the Financial Instruments and Exchange Act
In general, the self-regulatory function of exchanges includes monitoring of transactions, which prevents unfair trading, member supervision to prevent improprieties by trading participants and ensure the soundness of their finances, listing examinations, which confirm that listed securities and derivatives are suitable for trading on exchange markets and listing supervision to uphold continued listing standards and proper information disclosure by the issuers.

Chapter 7    Regulation of exchanges and clearing and settlement organizations

For this reason, the Act (Article 84 (2) of the FIEA) describes the self-regulatory functions carried out by financial instruments exchanges as pertaining to the following three business areas: (1) business related to the listing and delisting of financial instruments, financial indices and options (excluding items provided by cabinet office ordinance); (2) items related to investigating the status of legal compliance by trading participants; and (3) other items specified by cabinet office ordinance as necessary for ensuring fair trading on financial instruments exchange markets. The particular business activities specified include screening of trading other than the real time surveillance under each item of Article 7 of the FIEA, member credentials examinations, disciplinary measures for members and participants, and listed company disclosure information inspections and dispositions.

As stated above, the recent global trend has been toward turning exchanges into for-profit companies. One cannot deny the risk of a limited company exchange overemphasizing business profit, which may lead to the distortion of self-regulatory functions with high degrees of public interest. For example, to secure fee income, an exchange might overlook unfair trading by large-lot trading participants or allow continued listing by a company that has violated the continued listing requirements.

For this reason, to ensure the fairness of self-regulatory functions, the FIEA allows self-regulation-related business to be consigned to an independent self-regulatory organization or the establishment of self-regulation committees that determine matters concerning the self-regulation-related business.

Note that while the nature of the self-regulation business provided by law more or less corresponds to what has been cited as the self-regulation functions of exchanges in general, some caution is required concerning business related to listing and delisting.

Decisions regarding listing and delisting of securities and derivatives are among the most important self-regulatory functions. However, at the same

*803*

time, setting listing standards and establishing market sections or new markets have become extremely important for exchange growth strategy in the current competitive environment. This can be easily understood by looking at the competition among exchanges in establishing markets for emerging companies in Japan after the NASDAQ Japan project was announced in June 1999.

The Cabinet Office Ordinance on Financial Instruments Exchanges situates the drafting, change and abolition of business rules and other regulations concerning self-regulation-related business and the preparation of summaries of draft resolutions for general meetings regarding changes to articles of incorporation concerning self-regulation-related business as aspects of the self-regulatory function of the exchanges, but excludes matters regarding the listing and delisting standards (Article 7(v) and (vi) of the Cabinet Office Ordinance on Financial Instruments Exchanges). Specifically, decisions related to listing standards are to be conducted by the exchange's market operation division, which will normally be more business oriented. As explained below, however, the consent of self-regulatory organizations or self-regulation committees is to be sought for the change or abolition of listing and delisting standards.

c. Entrustment to self-regulatory corporations
Self-regulatory corporations are membership corporations established by financial instruments exchanges or financial instruments exchange holding companies who become their members, approved by the Prime Minister, and they engage in self-regulation-related business (Articles 102-2, 102-3, 102-12 and 102-14 of the FIEA). Financial instruments exchanges can receive permission from the Prime Minister to entrust their self-regulation-related business in whole or in part to a self-regulatory corporation (Article 85 of the FIEA).

Exchanges that have entrusted self-regulation-related business to a self-regulatory corporation must gain consent from such self-regulatory corporation before important matters related to self-regulation business are changed or abolished (Article 102-32 of the FIEA).

*804*

Chapter 7  Regulation of exchanges and clearing and settlement organizations

Self-regulatory corporations are administered by the chairman of the board of directors, the directors and the auditors appointed at a general meeting of the members, but a majority of the directors must be outside directors (directors who are not officers or former officers of the financial instruments exchange entrusting the self-regulation business or its subsidiaries) (Article 102-23(3) of the FIEA). The aim of having this structure is to ensure the independence and neutrality of the self-regulatory corporations.

For the same reason, there are strict procedures for the dismissal of directors by the general meeting of the members, which require a majority of members in attendance and approval from at least four-fifths of the members in attendance (Article 102-25(3) of the FIEA). However, actual self-regulatory corporations tend to receive work from exchanges under a single exchange group, and there are doubts as to whether such provisions effectively function to secure the independence of self-regulatory corporations.

On the other hand, the ways in which the fees paid by exchanges are set for the entrustment of self-regulation business and ensuring there is no improper reduction of the fees are also important for ensuring the independence of self-regulatory corporations. Nevertheless, the Act has no clear provisions regarding this point.

The financial instruments firms associations described below are also self-regulatory organizations with the goal of ensuring fair trading and protection of investors, but the Act does not allow exchanges to entrust self-regulation business to these associations. In the 2008 revision, however, there is a provision allowing entrustment of business concerning specified financial instruments exchange markets to parties other than self-regulatory corporations (Article 85(4) of the FIEA). The objective of the amendment was to introduce a system similar to the nominated advisor (Nomad) system on the U.K.'S AIM (Alternative Investment Market) in the new TOKYO AIM Exchange market for professional investors.

*805*

d. Self-regulation committees

Limited-company-type financial instruments exchanges may establish self-regulation committees pursuant to their articles of incorporation (Article 105-4 of the FIEA).

Self-regulation committees make decisions in place of the board of directors for items concerning the self-regulation business of exchanges (Article 105-4 (2) and (3) of the FIEA). Among such items provided by the exchange's articles of incorporation, by business regulations and by other regulations, items related to the self-regulation business require the approval of self-regulation committees before they can be amended or abolished (Article 105-11 of the FIEA). The specific range is the same as that which requires the consent of self-regulatory corporations as stated above (Article 50 of the Cabinet Office Ordinance on Financial Instruments Exchanges). Also, when there are concerns that an officer or director of an exchange may engage in acts that violate a decision of the self-regulation committee, the members of the self-regulation committee may demand cessation of the acts (Article 105-10(1) of the FIEA).

It is believed that this provision was included in the Act because, unlike the three committees under the Companies Act (the nomination committee, the compensation committee and the auditing committee), whose respective authorities are clearly provided by law, self-regulation committees cannot be given this authority solely through the provisions of the articles of incorporation of the exchange corporation.

Self-regulation committees are comprised of three or more self-regulation committee members appointed from among the directors by resolution of the board of directors of the exchange, and a majority must be outside directors (Article 105-5(1) and (2) of the FIEA). The exchange board of directors can dismiss self-regulation committee members, but the resolution requirements include the approval of the majority of members of the self-regulation committee attending the board of directors meeting, unlike other ordinary resolutions (Article 105-7(1) and (2) of the FIEA).

*806*

Chapter 7  Regulation of exchanges and clearing and settlement organizations

# 6. Foreign financial instruments exchanges

In the past, the matching of sale and purchase orders on exchange markets was conducted exclusively on the floor of the exchange, and the movements and gestures of people on the floor were considered important clues for understanding market trends. With the advance of computers and information technology, however, it has become possible to match orders directly by computer systems, without bringing order slips to the exchange floor.

The NASDAQ market, which was launched in 1971, is considered to be the first exchange in the world without a trading floor. Since the 1980s, the computerization and automation of trading and the closing of trading floors have proceeded for markets that use the auction system as well. The Tokyo Stock Exchange, which is Japan's leading financial instruments exchange, also introduced of automated trading systems in stages starting in 1982, and it closed its trading floor at the end of April 1999.

Once trading is computerized and automated, it becomes technically possible, by having foreign stock exchanges place terminals inside Japanese territory, to directly participate in trading on foreign markets from Japan; therefore, under the 2003 revision of the Securities and Exchange Act, foreign financial instruments exchanges may, with authorization from the Prime Minister, have domestic financial instruments business operators and registered financial institutions (hereafter, "financial instruments business operators, etc.") conduct the sale and purchase of securities and derivatives transactions on foreign financial instruments markets (Article 155 of the FIEA).

Conversely, by having domestic financial instruments exchanges install trading terminals abroad, it is also technically possible for foreign broker-dealers to participate in trading on Japanese exchange markets.

Thus, the Act allows foreign securities brokers (business operators with permission to trade on exchanges), with the permission of the Prime

*807*

Minister, to participate in trading on domestic exchange markets without being registered as domestic financial instruments business operators (Article 60 of the FIEA).

# B. Proprietary trading systems (PTS)

## 1. Role of proprietary trading systems (PTS)

Proprietary trading systems (hereafter "PTS" in singular form and "PTSs" in plural form) are computerized electronic trading systems operated by securities companies for the matching of sale and purchase orders for stocks and bonds. The matching of customer orders by securities companies may be considered a business conducted as part of the brokerage function, which is one of their main business activities. However, when computer systems are used for the efficient processing of a large volume of orders, this function becomes extremely similar to the matching of orders performed by exchanges. PTSs operated by broker-dealers are different from exchange markets in that they allow investors to directly participate in trading and they lack self-regulatory functions.

The first PTS to become operational was Instinet, which started trading in NYSE listed shares in 1969. The aim of its launch was to provide order matching for institutional investors outside the exchange, as at that time the exchange imposed fixed commissions on transactions on its market. (Commissions were liberalized in the U.S. in 1975 and in Japan in 1999.) Under current laws and regulations, "PTSs" are referred to as "ATSs" (alternative trading systems) in the United States and "MTFs" (multilateral trading facilities) in the EU. They play important roles as alternatives to exchange markets.

## 2. Removal of the ban on PTSs

Until the 1998 amendment of the Securities and Exchange Act, PTSs, which may fulfill the same functions as exchanges, were considered to fall under "facilities similar to markets" prohibited under the Act, and thus, securities

Chapter 7   Regulation of exchanges and clearing and settlement organizations

companies were not allowed to operate PTSs (Article 167-2 of the Securities and Exchange Act prior to the 2000 revision). However, the 1998 revision of the Act allowed securities companies to operate PTSs as business permitted by the law (Article 2(8)(x) and Article 30(1) of the FIEA). This made it clear that the provision prohibiting the establishment of facilities similar to markets did not apply to PTSs, which received permission to conduct business in addition to regular registration as securities companies. (The current Article 80 (2) of the FIEA has the same purport.) The first approvals for PTS businesses were issued to two companies in June 2000.

Initially, the role of PTSs was considered to be that of trading systems that did not possess sophisticated price-formation mechanisms like those of markets established by exchanges. For this reason, the sale and purchase price determination methods that could be adopted by PTSs were limited (Article 2(8)(ii) of the FIEA prior to the 2004 revision). Specifically, these were limited to the three methods: (1) determining prices using prices formed on an exchange market; (2) determining prices using prices published by a securities dealers association for securities registered on an OTC market; and (3) using prices based on negotiations between customers. The law permitted another method, to "determine prices based on other methods specified by ordinance of the Prime Minister's Office or the Ministry of Finance"; however, in practice, no ordinances were promptly issued based on this provision.

Consequently, the first two PTSs that received authorization had to take illogical measures to assume the appearance that their price formation was taking place "using prices based on negotiations between customers," including the intentional use of a system that did not allow automatic matching of orders even if it received sell and buy orders for the same price and volume. It was one of the reasons why the investors' use of PTSs did not increase to the extent that the organizers had expected, and in a short period of time both PTSs had to cease operations. Later, in December 2000, the ordinance and working guidelines from the Prime Minister's Office newly permitted the matching of customer limit orders and other price determination methods, although there was no change in the framework to

*809*

restrict the price formation functions of PTSs compared to those of exchange markets.

## 3. Legislation of best execution obligation

Regulations to restrict PTS price determination methods were introduced based on the idea that since systems for publication of indicative prices and reporting of real-time trading information had not been developed for the Japanese market, expansion of PTS trading and other types of off-exchange trading could cause market fragmentation, which would hinder efficient price formation.

At that time, there was an assumption that the exchange markets were the core of price formation. Therefore, despite the lifting of the prohibition of off-exchange trading of listed stocks, securities companies were not allowed to execute orders for listed stocks outside exchange markets without explicit directions from their customers (Article 37 of the Securities and Exchange Act prior to the 2004 revision). Similarly, for off-exchange trading ordered by customers, securities dealer associations imposed regulations on the prices used for such trading executed during normal trading hours, such that the price fluctuation of such trading must fall within a certain range of the trading prices on the exchange markets.

However, concerns regarding market fragmentation are groundless as long as the scale of off-exchange trading is small. If the regulations maintained the assumption that the exchange markets were at the core of the price formation function, healthy competition between PTSs or other off-exchange trading facilities and exchange markets would be prevented, and improvement of the efficiency of the market overall could be hindered.

Accordingly, the 2004 revisions to the Securities and Exchange Act removed the prohibition on "bucketing," which prevented securities companies from freely acting as dealers (Article 39 of the Securities and Exchange Act prior to the 2004 revision), the provision requiring explicit customer orders for off-exchange trading, and price restriction regulations, as well as revising other provisions that formed the basis of the exchange-centric regulatory

*810*

Chapter 7 Regulation of exchanges and clearing and settlement organizations

framework. In addition, the revision allowed PTSs to employ the auction method, which is commonly used on exchange markets for price determination (Article 2(8)(x)(a) of the FIEA).

In the U.S. and other markets in which PTSs and other off-exchange trading facilities are widely available for investors, it is understood that securities companies, which are entrusted with purchase and sale orders from customers, have a best execution obligation to ensure that the orders are executed under the most preferable conditions for the customer (in terms of price, execution speed, execution certainty, etc.). Regarding this point, in addition to the revisions to provisions that kept trading centered on exchanges, the law also provides that securities companies have a best execution duty, which obligates them to set, announce and execute a policy for the best execution of customer orders (Article 40-2 of the FIEA).

Yet, even after the 2004 revision, there are distinctions between the regulation of PTSs and exchanges. For instance, PTSs that use the auction method are prohibited from handling trades of an individual issue exceeding 10% of the entire market average sales volume of the issue over six months, or, from the total sale and purchase volume for all issues handled exceeding 1% of the entire market total (Article 1-10 of the Order). In such cases, a PTS must reorganize itself into a financial instruments exchange and obtain the license required therefor.[6]

---

6   The Financial Services Agency's "Comprehensive Guidelines for Supervision of Financial Instruments Business Operators, etc." also requires obtaining a license to establish a financial instruments market for those PTS that conduct price setting using methods aside from auction in cases where their transaction volume share exceeds 20% of the total volume of an individual issue or 10% of the total volume of all issues handled.

*811*

# C. Financial instruments firms associations

## 1. Importance of self-regulation in securities markets

While financial instruments exchanges are private organizations, they also fulfill roles as self-regulatory organizations that may prescribe self-governing regulations in accordance with the public interest. In addition, the FIEA assigns roles as self-regulatory organizations to financial instruments firms associations established for the purposes of the fair and smooth sale and purchase of securities and derivatives transactions as well as promoting the sound development of financial instruments trading and the protection of investors (Article 67 of the FIEA).

Such institutionalization of self-regulatory organizations based on public laws and ordinances is seldom seen outside securities market regulation. To be sure, self-regulation incorporated in the public law also exists in the United States and other foreign countries, and not only in Japan. The reasons self-regulation is emphasized in securities market regulation in such a manner include the following.

First, for effective regulation of securities markets, which are complex and highly technical, the regulator will be required to have a high level of expertise, including thorough knowledge of trading mechanisms. Since a regulator, as a government body, must be incorporated into the general civil service system, it is not easy to deploy experts flexibly. In contrast, self-regulatory organizations can set up their own systems for personnel, salary, etc. enabling more flexible recruitment of appropriate human resources in a timely manner.

Second, although direct regulation by the government has the strength of ensuring appropriate legal procedures and exercising democratic control through parliamentary bodies, such characteristics also lead to a lack of regulatory flexibility. Self-regulatory organizations are expected to be able

*812*

Chapter 7  Regulation of exchanges and clearing and settlement organizations

to change, interpret and apply rules more flexibly than the government.

Third, it is expected that investors' confidence in market fairness would be increased by having securities brokers taking responsibility for self-regulation, as they play leading roles in the markets. In principle, the cost of self-regulation is born by the regulated entities themselves. Since trust in markets is believed to increase as a result of self-regulation and may lead to expansion of the business of securities brokers, the cost may be considered a form of financial burden passed on to the beneficiaries.

## 2. Authorized associations and recognized associations

The FIEA designates two types of financial instruments firms associations as self-regulatory organizations. There are authorized financial instruments firms associations (hereinafter "Authorized associations"), which are special corporate bodies under the FIEA, and there are also recognized financial instruments firms associations (hereinafter "Recognized associations"), which are regular incorporated bodies.

### a. Authorized associations

Authorized associations are established by financial instruments business operators with authorization from the Prime Minister (Article 67-2 of the FIEA). At present, the Japan Securities Dealers Association (hereafter the "JSDA"), established in July 1973 through the merger of 10 local securities dealers associations, is the only Authorized association.

Authorized associations have the power to establish regulations, to impose fines on financial instruments business operators who are members, to suspend or limit the rights of members and to expel members (Article 67-8 (1) (x) and Article 68-2 of the FIEA). The JSDA enacts binding regulations including Self-regulation Regulations, Uniform Practices Regulations (the two used to be called "Fair Practice Rules" before being separated) and Dispute Resolution Regulations, responds to questions based on board resolutions and a business rules inquiry system and otherwise works toward appropriate practices.

*813*

A major characteristic of Authorized associations is that they are allowed to establish organized over-the-counter securities markets, and the law sets out many provisions regarding the market operation (Article 67-11 forward of the FIEA). The OTC stock market operated by the JSDA was first established in 1963, and it was reorganized into the JASDAQ market with an electronic trading system in 1983. However, the market was reorganized into an exchange market in 2004. Therefore, there is presently no organized over-the-counter securities market in Japan.

Over-the-counter trading of bonds is regulated by JSDA regulations (which include announcement of reference prices for over-the-counter sale and purchases of bonds, and regulations concerning sale and purchase prices). The JSDA also plays a major role in the over-the-counter trading of unlisted stocks, namely green sheet issues (securities prescribed by Article 67-18 (iv) of the FIEA) (Rules Concerning Green Sheet Issues and Phoenix Issues). Moreover, the JSDA has established rules for the suspension of sale and purchases and for reporting regarding off-exchange trading of listed securities including PTS trading (Rules Concerning Sale and Purchas, etc. of Listed Share Certificates, etc. Conducted Outside of a Financial Instruments Exchange Market).

Authorized associations receive complaints from investors and mediate disputes concerning trading of securities and derivatives transactions conducted by association member firms (Articles 77 and 77-2 of the FIEA). The Financial Instruments Mediation Assistance Center (FINMAC) presently handles mediation work under entrustment from the JSDA.

Article 25, paragraph 2 of the JSDA's self-regulation rules, "Rules Concerning Mediation of Resolution of Disputes Between Members and Customers," states that when customers accept a mediation plan, the association member that is the other party in the dispute must accept the mediation plan, unless it deposits the funds it would pay under the mediation plan and initiates a lawsuit.

*814*

Chapter 7 Regulation of exchanges and clearing and settlement organizations

b. Recognized associations

Recognized associations are self-regulatory organizations authorized by the Prime Minister after financial instruments business operators establish them as regular corporate bodies (Article 78(1) and Article 78-2(1) of the FIEA). Currently, there are four recognized associations in Japan: The Investment Trust Association, Japan; the Japan Investment Advisers Association; the Financial Futures Association of Japan; and the Type II Financial Instruments Firms Association. The role of Recognized Associations is (i) to provide guidance and recommendations to members and financial instruments intermediary service providers acting under consignment from members, for the purpose of having them observe legal compliance, (ii) to establish the necessary regulations for correct trading solicitation, (iii) to investigate compliance with laws and other regulations, and (iv) to mediate and resolve complaints (Article 78 (2) of the FIEA). They have many characteristics in common with Authorized Associations; for instance, they are also given the power to impose fines on members that violate laws, association articles of incorporation or other regulations (Article 79-2 of the FIEA). However, unlike Authorized Associations, Recognized Associations cannot establish organized over-the-counter securities markets.

While the distinction between Authorized Associations and Recognized Associations was primarily established in accordance with the actual conditions of the self-regulatory organizations based on the Act prior to the 2006 revision, it is difficult to find a positive reason for such distinction based only on consideration of the roles and functions expected of the associations.

c. Membership of financial instruments firms associations

Financial instruments firms associations as the self-regulatory organizations of financial instruments business operators, are expected to play an important role in investor protection and ensuring fair trading; however, joining these associations is entirely voluntary under the current law.

While membership in self-regulatory organizations is not mandatory, it has a stipulation regarding the supervision of type I financial instruments business operators, investment managers and registered financial institutions that do

*815*

not belong to associations or exchanges that are self-regulatory organizations: the Prime Minister must conduct appropriate supervision of such institutions taking into account the articles of incorporation and other regulations of associations or exchanges (Article 56-4 of the FIEA). The purpose of this provision is to prevent any large differences between the supervision of business operators who join self-regulatory organizations and the supervision of those who do not.

However, in the current environment, in which multiple self-regulatory organizations exist, it is not so simple to determine which self-regulatory organization's articles of incorporation and other regulations should be used in the supervision of individual business operators that do not belong to any self-regulatory organization. In particular, coordination may be particularly difficult when business operators that are not members conduct business across fields regulated by multiple associations. For this reason, it is important for self-regulatory organizations to cooperate, work to set the same rules for the same products and services, and ensure that there are no areas that are not covered by regulations.

## 3. Certified investor protection organizations

In addition to self-regulatory organizations, the FIEA has also established a system of certified investor protection organizations (hereinafter "Certified Organizations") for mediation to resolve complaints from users and to resolve disputes (Article 79-7 of the FIEA).

Certified Organizations were established in order to provide alternative dispute resolution (hereinafter "ADR") functions such as the mediation undertaken by financial instruments firms associations. Industry associations, consumer groups, NPO corporations conducting activities relating to finance and other bodies that do not become authorized associations, as well as public interest organizations, are expected to receive this certification.

The members of Certified Organizations are not limited to financial instruments business operators and financial instruments intermediary service providers, but the FIEA identifies financial instruments business

*816*

Chapter 7   Regulation of exchanges and clearing and settlement organizations

operators and others that have agreed to be subject to the mediation business of Certified Organizations, and the list of such business operators must be available to the public (Article 79-11 of the FIEA).

The Cabinet Office Ordinance on Financial Instruments Firms Associations states that parties other than financial instruments business operators and financial instruments intermediary service providers can be subject business operators of Certified Organizations if they conduct business under the application of sales and solicitation rules equivalent to those specified by law (Article 31 of the Cabinet Office Ordinance on Financial Instruments Firms Associations). Among those bodies that have received certification as Certified Organizations are the Financial Instruments Mediation Association Center (FINMAC), the Life Insurance Association of Japan and the General Insurance Association of Japan (SONPO).

# D. Clearing and settlement organizations

## 1. Financial instruments clearing organizations

### a. Role of clearing organizations

When the sale and purchase of securities is executed on a financial instruments exchange market, the seller transfers the security to the buyer and funds or money are paid by the buyer to the seller. On exchange markets where sales and purchases take place continuously in large volumes, it would not be efficient to transfer securities and funds for each individual transaction. Therefore, after the closing of each day's trading, the trading participants (securities companies) confirm the net credits and debts between them and confirm the necessary quantities and amounts for transfer and settlement.

The transfer and settlement for the residuals after the netting are carried out through the central counterparty, as there remains some risk that the settlement will not be implemented, due to a decline in the payment capacity of a trading participant. Financial instruments clearing organizations that act

*817*

as central counterparties for trading participants assume obligations to deliver securities from sellers and obligations to make payments from buyers. In other words, the clearing organizations become the counterparties for all trading participants and ensure proper execution of all individual transactions.

Through this mechanism, trading participants can participate in market trading without concerns about the credit risk of the other participants. Clearing organizations perform similar functions for market derivatives transactions as well, by becoming the counterparties who pay or receive margins and other money required for the settlement of transactions.

On the other hand, the clearing organizations bear the risk of non-fulfillment of settlement from all trading participants, so they are required to have a certain financial foundation (described in detail below). Also, to limit the risk created by clearing organizations to within a certain range, parties that do not have sufficient credit to directly settle with clearing organizations, even financial instruments business operators with the right to participate in trading, must be non-clearing trading participants who cannot directly participate in clearing. Considering the existence of trading participants that cannot participate in settlements, the law defines the work of conducting clearance with clearing organizations under entrustment from non-clearing trading participants as brokerage for clearance of securities (Article 2(27) of the FIEA). The FIEA prescribes such act as being among the work of type I financial instruments business (Article 28(1)(i) of the FIEA).

In the past, direct netting was conducted among trading participants on the Japanese stock market. In May 1999, the Tokyo Stock Exchange introduced a clearing system with the exchange itself acting as the clearing organization. This is called an "in-house clearing" system.

Alternatively, an "external clearing house" system is another possible system in which an organization other than the exchange carries out the clearing work. However, there was no legislation regarding independent clearing organizations in Japan until the 2002 revisions to the Securities and

*818*

Chapter 7 Regulation of exchanges and clearing and settlement organizations

Exchange Act.

b. Regulations concerning clearing organizations
The law refers to the service provided by clearing organizations as "financial instruments obligation assumption service" (Article 2(28) of the FIEA) that requires a license from the Prime Minister (Article 156-2 of the FIEA). Financial instruments exchanges may also conduct financial instruments obligation assumption services and ancillary businesses with approval from the Prime Minister (Article 156-19 of the FIEA).

The Japan Securities Clearing Corporation (JSCC), which is part of the Japan Exchange Group, currently provides clearing functions for stocks traded on exchanges and PTSs, and for derivatives transactions on the Osaka Exchange as an external clearing house. Tokyo Financial Exchange Inc. undertakes obligations for derivatives transactions on its own market as an in-house clearing organization. JSCC also conducts clearance work for over-the-counter trading of government bonds. JASDEC DVP Clearing Corporation, which is a subsidiary of Japan Securities Depository Center, Inc., a depository trust company (discussed below), provides delivery versus payment (DVP) settlement services for OTC transactions. DVP settlement is a framework for securing settlement safety by mutually linking securities transfer and the payment of settlement funds.

Since clearing organizations have become the sole bodies for handling the credits and debts that arise among many trading participants, market risk is concentrated in the clearing organizations. For that reason, if clearing organizations were to fall into bankruptcy, chaos in the market would inevitably break out.

To address this problem, the law provides that clearing organizations must be stock companies with sufficient provisions in their articles of incorporation and business rules and an adequate personnel structure to properly and safely execute financial instruments obligation assumption services and an adequate financial basis for the sound implementation of financial instruments obligation assumptions services (Article 156-4 of the

*819*

FIEA). Their own capital must be at least ¥1.0 billion (Article 156-5-2 of the FIEA, Article 19-4-2 of the Implementing Order), and in principle main shareholders holding 20% or more of the voting rights of clearing organizations must receive approval from the Prime Minister in advance (Article 156-5-5 of the FIEA). The law also mandates that clearing organizations work exclusively for clearing and that in principle they cannot engage in work other than financial instruments obligation assumption services and ancillary work (Article 156-6 of the FIEA).

Clearing organizations bear the risk of default of the counterparties from whom they have assumed obligations (clearing participants). Thus, they typically require deposits from the clearing participants for clearing funds to guarantee the execution of obligations, in order to eliminate moral hazard.[7] If a clearing participant causes damage to a clearing organization by not fulfilling its obligations, the clearing organization may seek repayment from the deposits made by the clearing participant ahead of other creditors (Article 156-11 of the FIEA).

The method of calculating the amounts of deposits with clearing funds and other reserve fund systems is determined by the clearing organization to cover the expected losses. Even then, it is possible for losses to be incurred that cannot be covered by deposits in exceptional circumstances. For this reason, the FIEA (Article 156-10 of the FIEA) requires clearing organizations to provide in their business rules that, when a clearing organization suffers a loss, the clearing participant must bear the entirety of such loss, and to establish a mutual guarantee system (subscription format) whereby, in emergencies, all clearing participants may cover losses.

---

7    In the case of Japan Securities Clearing Corporation (JSCC), which is the unified clearing organization for stock markets in Japan, losses that cannot be compensated by clearing participants' deposits for non-performance of obligations are compensated using accumulated reserves for breach of contract losses, etc. at the financial instruments exchange and JSCC's earned surplus. Of course, in extremely exceptional cases, conditions could arise where there are losses that could not be compensated by these.

Chapter 7  Regulation of exchanges and clearing and settlement organizations

In addition, there are provisions (Article 156-20-2 of the FIEA) regarding corporate bodies established under the laws of foreign countries engaged in work similar to financial instruments obligation assumption services overseas (foreign financial instrument clearing organizations) conducting financial instruments obligation assumption services in Japan with a license from the Prime Minister.

c . Centralization of clearing for over-the-counter derivatives transactions

Clearing organizations are important parts of market infrastructure that reduce the settlement risk accompanying securities and derivatives transactions. However, in Japan, there were no regulations mandating their use in the past. The global financial crisis of 2007-2008 revealed that while financial institutions traded vast quantities of over-the-counter derivatives among themselves, their risk assessments regarding individual transactions were not conducted appropriately, with such weakness leading to the intensification of the crisis. Hence, an international consensus was reached to ensure market stability by concentrating the settlement of standardized over-the-counter derivatives transactions in a clearing organization.

In the 2010 revision of the Act, it became mandatory for financial instruments business operators and other participants to centralize clearing work for certain over-the-counter derivatives transactions (Article 156-62 of the FIEA). Also, to integrate trading information on over-the-counter derivatives transactions and enhance market transparency, clearing organizations were obligated to prepare and store records and report to the Financial Services Agency information concerning certain transactions subject to clearing (Article 156-63 of the FIEA).

Furthermore, in the 2012 revision of the Act, it became obligatory to use electronic transaction systems when conducting trading for certain over-the-counter derivatives transactions (Article 40-7 of the FIEA). This may evoke the systems under the prior principle of centralizing trading, but the systems also account for the same derivatives transactions being processed through multiple electronic trading systems. Therefore, it should not be

*821*

considered to mandate the centralization of trading.

# E. Institutions for book-entry transfer of securities

## 1. From paper-based trading to book-entry system

When the sale and purchase of securities are executed on financial instruments exchange markets, transfer and settlement take place following netting through the above-mentioned clearing procedures.

In the past, transfer and settlement typically took the form of the seller turning over share certificates to the buyer and the buyer sending funds to a clearing bank account. However, turning over share certificates to the buyer requires the storage and transport of such share certificates, with the risks of share certificate theft, loss and damage. Although the certificates are produced using sophisticated printing technologies, the risk of forgery or alteration cannot be completely eliminated.

To resolve these problems, book-entry transfer based on the depositary system was introduced, whereby genuine certificates are deposited at a specific institution (called a depositary institution for book-entry transfer) and rights are transferred through records on the books kept by the institution. The switchover to the depositary system means that the physical movement of securities is no longer necessary.

The introduction of the book-entry system has greatly contributed to improving the efficiency and reducing the risk of securities transaction settlement. However, in the current era of commercialization of computer technologies, especially databases with huge storage capacity, it has become possible to take this one step further by eliminating securities certificates themselves. In fact, France enacted a law in 1981 (implemented in 1984) which abolished share certificates for listed companies.

*822*

Chapter 7　Regulation of exchanges and clearing and settlement organizations

## 2. Development of the transfer system in Japan

In Japan, a depositary system enabling book-entry transfer of stocks and other securities was implemented in 1991 by the Japan Securities Depository Center, based on the Act concerning the Storage and Transfer of Stock Certificates enacted in 1984 (initially limited to 50 issues listed on the Tokyo Stock Exchange). Thereafter, book-entry transfer settlements were expanded to include all listed and over-the-counter stocks, as well as convertible bonds.

As for corporate bonds, settlement via the book-entry system of registered corporate bonds was formerly conducted based on the Corporate Bond Registration Act enacted in 1942. Moreover, Japanese government bonds have been traded through a book-entry system operated via the Bank of Japan network since 1980. Nevertheless, the book-entry system under the Corporate Bond Registration Act was inefficient, as the law was passed during wartime primarily to reduce the labor required for the printing of securities certificates, rather than for improving the settlement system.

To address this issue, the preparation of laws for a complete shift to paperless transfer of various securities has been promoted since 2000, when the report of the Financial System Council Working Group on Securities Settlement System Reform was published. First, the Act on Transfer of Short-term Corporate Bonds was enacted in 2001 facilitating the issuance of electronic CP (Commercial Paper) and settlement via a book-entry system. This act was revised in 2002 and became the Act on Transfer of Corporate Bonds (the Corporate Bonds Transfer Act), expanding the range of the book-entry transfer settlement system to cover corporate bonds, government bonds and investment trust beneficiary certificates.

Additionally, the so-called Settlement Rationalization Act of 2004 significantly revised the Corporate Bonds Transfer Act to include shares as a subject of transfer settlement, as well as stipulating that all companies listed on exchanges be companies without share certificates from the date the revised law came into effect. This revision came into effect on January 5,

*823*

2009, making Japan the first among the world's developed countries to have its major securities traded in a completely paperless manner on exchanges.

## 3. Regulations concerning institutions for book-entry transfer

Under the current Act on Book-Entry Transfer of Corporate Bonds and Shares (hereafter "Corporate Bonds and Shares Transfer Act"), the rights that should be displayed on shares and other securities are transferred via recording them in transfer account books kept by institutions for book-entry transfer (Article 8, paragraph 1 of the Corporate Bonds and Shares Transfer Act). Specifically, the transferee acquires the rights to the shares or other securities when, based on a transfer application from the transferor, the reduced number of shares or other securities is recorded in the transferor's account book and the increased number of shares or other securities is recorded in the transferee's account book (Articles 70 and 132 of the Corporate Bonds and Shares Transfer Act).

The institutions for book-entry transfer must be stock companies specified by the competent minister with capital of at least ¥500 million (Article 3 paragraph 1 and Article 5, paragraph 1 of the Corporate Bonds and Shares Transfer Act). Specifically, the Japan Securities Depository Center, which had functioned as a depositary institution for book-entry transfer for share certificates, was designated as an institution for book-entry transfer.

If each individual investor holding shares were to directly open accounts at institutions for book-entry transfer, the number of accounts would be massive, and the burden on systems at institutions for book-entry transfer would be excessive. Therefore, the law introduced a two-level framework. The parties that can open direct accounts in institutions for book-entry transfer (members) are limited to financial instruments business operators (securities companies), banks, etc., whereas general investors may open accounts with the members of the institutions for book-entry transfer. The financial instruments business operators and other parties that can open transfer accounts for others are referred to as "account management institutions" (Article 44, paragraph 1 of the Corporate Bonds and Shares

Chapter 7   Regulation of exchanges and clearing and settlement organizations

Transfer Act), and the customer accounts opened by customers at account management institutions are separated from the accounts of the account management institutions themselves where they record their own shares and other securities.

Under the book-entry transfer system without physical share certificates, because the rights concerning shares and other securities are determined by records in transfer accounts, incorrect recording of the details could cause major problems. For this reason, the Corporate Bonds and Shares Transfer Act includes provisions for good faith acquisition by members (because transfer recording is conducted based on application from the transferor), as well as mandatory erasure of excess recordings by institutions for book-entry transfer and account management institutions when there are errors in recording by institutions for book-entry transfer or account management institutions (Articles 77 and 79 of the Corporate Bonds and Shares Transfer Act). Moreover, a member protection trust system is in place to provide for cases in which institutions for book-entry transfer or account management institutions fall into bankruptcy without being able to execute mandatory erasure, so that members suffering losses may be compensated (Articles 51 of the Corporate Bonds and Shares Transfer Act).

*825*

# Chapter **8**

## Market abuse regulation

*Sadakazu Osaki* (Part A)

*Yoko Manzawa* (Parts B, C & D)

# A. Regulation of insider trading

## 1. Historical background of the regulation

In Japan, regulations expressly prohibiting insider trading were introduced by the revisions to the Securities and Exchange Act in 1988 (the Securities and Exchange Act was further revised and renamed to the Financial Instruments and Exchange Act in 2006, and the latter shall be referred to as the "FIEA"). Before this revision, there existed regulation aimed at preventing insider trading, which demanded restitution of profits arising from the sale and purchas of a listed company's shares conducted in the short-term where an officer or the major shareholder owns 10% or more of the company's shares (Article 164 of the current FIEA). Some academics held the opinion that the general provision for preventing unfair trading, (i.e., Article 157 of the current FIEA) could also be applied to insider trading. However, there had been no actual prosecution of insider trading cases in Japan until then.[1]

The Tateho Chemical Industries incident that was discovered in 1987 drastically changed the situation. Tateho Chemical Industries, which was listed on the First Section of the Osaka Securities Exchange at the time, had posted a loss of ¥28.5 billion in JGB futures trading, an amount exceeding four times its annual sales, in its September 1987 interim results. When this news was disclosed, the "Tateho shock" brought chaos to the financial markets and the company's share price dropped sharply. Another shocking revelation was that the company's main bank had sold off almost all the Tateho shares it owned one day before the company announced its losses, which was harshly criticized by the public.[2]

While this incident itself was closed without any prosecution under the general provision for preventing unfair trading, it triggered a discussion by

---

[1] That does not mean there was almost no insider trading on Japanese markets. On the contrary, the view that profits from insider trading were overlooked as a kind of perk seems to be the correct understanding (Kawamoto and Otake, p. 433).

Chapter 8  Market abuse regulation

the (then) Securities and Exchange Council as well as the revision of the
Securities and Exchange Act the following year, explicitly stipulating the
prohibition against insider trading.

It should be recalled that there is no such provision explicitly prohibiting
insider trading in particular under U.S. law. Generally speaking, Japanese
securities regulation is strongly influenced by the U.S. law. Therefore, it is
not surprising that there was no explicit provision prohibiting insider trading
in Japanese law until the 1988 amendment to the Securities and Exchange
Act.

## 2. Contents of insider trading regulations

### a. Structure of the regulations

The FIEA has two provisions that directly regulate insider trading. One is
the provision prohibiting corporate insiders who have special relations with a
listed company from trading securities issued by the company, when they
have come to know undisclosed material facts pertaining to business or other
matters of a listed company (Article 166 of the FIEA). The purpose of this
article can be described as the prohibition of a typical insider trading.

The other provision prescribes prohibited actions of persons involved in a
takeover bid.[3] In the case of a launch of takeover bidder of a listed company,

---

2   At that time, the main bank that sold the shares explained it had received a phone call
from Tateho saying, "Our company president would like to discuss something, so we
are asking our eight relationship banks to meet." The main bank further explained
that they ascertained that some seriously abnormal situation had occurred, and sold all
their share holdings the following morning. The main bank said they first learned
about the specific circumstances that Tateho had suffered a huge loss on bond futures
trading after it sold the shares, at the time when Tateho explained the circumstances
to all its relationship banks. Based on this explanation, while noting that the behavior
of the main bank "has a substantial problem with moral responsibility," the Ministry of
Finance reached the decision that it would be difficult to prosecute the case based on
the general provision for prohibiting wrongful transactions. If the main bank's
assertions are all true, there are fine points of law regarding this case as to whether it
could be considered a violation of insider trading regulations even under current law.
This is because, as stated below in the main text, "material facts" that are subject to
regulation are defined in detail, and it is difficult to judge the information that "The
president says he wants to meet the banking syndicate to discuss something" as
falling under "material facts."

*829*

or purchases of shares including volume equivalent to a launch of a takeover bid, persons involved in a takeover bid, who have special relations with a takeover bidder are prohibited from trading securities issued by the listed company subjected to the takeover bid (Article 167 of the FIEA).

In this case, the persons subject to the trading prohibition are not insiders of the company issuing the securities, which is the target of the takeover bid. Therefore, such trading is considered to belong to a different category from that of typical insider trading. Nevertheless, this type of trading can be considered unfair trading similar to typical insider trading, to the extent that such trading is executed by persons possessing information not disclosed publicly to general investors. Thus, the FIEA also places regulations on this type of trading similar to those imposed on typical insider trading.

Both provisions have the same structure: (i) corporate insiders or persons concerned with takeover bids (hereafter, collectively referred to as "Insiders"), (ii) knowledge of material facts pertaining to the business or other matters of a listed company or facts regarding the implementation or suspension of a takeover bid; and, (iii) prohibition of trading the securities of the listed company or of the company subject to the takeover bid before such information is publicized.[4] Accordingly, the three most important questions to be addressed for better understanding of the insider trading regulations are, (i) Who are "Insiders"? (ii) What is a material fact? and (iii) What is publication? These are described below.

---

3    This includes purchases to buy up shares so that the total number of shares held becomes 5% or more of the voting rights of all shareholders without going through takeover bid procedures (Article 31 of the Financial Instruments and Exchange Act Implementing Order). Also, even purchases that are subject to regulation are exempt from regulation in cases where the shares bought up in one year account for less than 2.5% of the voting rights of all shareholders because this is deemed to have only a minor influence on investors' investment decisions (Article 62 of the Cabinet Office Ordinance on Restrictions on Securities Transactions, etc.).

4    The Financial Instruments and Exchange Act prohibits persons who come to know undisclosed material facts from buying and selling shares, etc. subject to regulation in general. So even transactions from which based on common sense one cannot gain profit, such as knowing that a listed company will file for application of the Civil Rehabilitation Act and buying shares of the relevant company, constitute violations of insider trading regulations.

Chapter 8　Market abuse regulation

b. Persons subject to the regulations

Insiders who are subject to insider trading regulations are divided into three categories: (i) typical insiders such as the officers and employees of listed companies or takeover bidders;[5] (ii) quasi-insiders who are subject to regulation because they are under contract with listed companies or takeover bidders, or they possess statutory authority over the said listed companies or takeover bidders; and (iii) information recipients who are recipients of the information from insiders or quasi-insiders.

( i ) Insiders

Typical insiders include (a) officers, agents, employees or other workers of a listed company or takeover bidders who come to know an undisclosed material fact pertaining to the business or other matters of the listed company or a fact regarding the implementation or suspension of a takeover bid (collectively referred to as "Material Fact(s)") and (b) shareholders who have the right to view the account books of the issuing company or takeover bidder (as prescribed in Article 433(1) of the Companies Act) who come to know Material Facts in the course of exercising the right[6] (Articles 166(1)(i), 166(1)(ii), 167(1)(i), and 167(1)(ii) of the FIEA).[7] There have

---

**5** Listed companies themselves do not fall under corporate insiders subject to regulation. However, acquisition of treasury shares by a listed company is conducted by having a director who comes to know the material fact of a resolution to acquire treasury shares purchase them as a representative of the company, so there is a possibility of violations of insider trading regulations. To address this, an exclusion provision is set (Article 166(6), item (iv)-2 of the FIEA) that grants exclusion from insider trading regulations provided that the resolution to acquire treasury shares has been disclosed. However, if there are material facts aside from the resolution to acquire treasury shares, the possibility that acquisition of treasury shares violates insider trading regulations remains. The Komatsu case presented below in the main text (column) is an example where acquisition of treasury shares was recognized as insider trading.

**6** In principle, these are persons who own 3% or more of the voting rights of all shareholders. Also, in cases where a shareholder that can exercise the right to view the account books is a corporation, officers, agents, employees and other workers of the relevant corporation aside from persons who came to know the inside information by exercise of the rights are subject to regulation in cases where they come to know the inside information in the course of their work duties (Article 166(1)(v) and Article 167(1)(v) of the FIEA).

*831*

been many cases where trading by parties including the typical insider category became an issue, starting with the Macross Corporation (Tokyo District Court Judgment of September 25, 1992, Tokyo District Court Case 1438, p. 151), which was the first trial case following the introduction of insider trading regulations.

In the Macross case, a managing director of a listed company came to know that a large amount of fictitious sales had been posted from a report presented at an extraordinary meeting of the board of directors of his company, and subsequently sold off the shares of this company held under his name and his family members names before that was disclosed.

( ii ) Quasi-insiders

Quasi-insiders include (a) persons with statutory authority over the issuing company or takeover bidder who came to know Material Facts in the course of exercising the authority, and (b) persons who have concluded a contract or are negotiating a contract with the issuing company or takeover bidder who came to know Material Facts in the conclusion or negotiation or exercise of the contract (Articles 166(1)(iii), 166(1)(iv), 167(1)(iii), and 167(1)(iv) of the FIEA).[8]

A typical case of insider trading by a person having statutory authority is the case of a section chief at the Ministry of Economy, Trade and Industry who was in charge of screening and certifying firms eligible for funding under the Act on Special Measures for Industrial Revitalization. The person

---

7　For both categories, whether persons are subject to regulation depends on the type of conditions whereby they come to know the inside information. This is because if insiders and quasi-insiders were defined only by their attributes, such as officer of a listed company or person in a contractual relationship with the company, the regulations would wind up applying to cases where persons come to know material facts by chance or otherwise in no relation to their own duties, and that is considered inappropriate.

8　Like the case of a shareholder who has the right to view the company's account books, in cases where a person who has concluded, or is in negotiations to conclude, a contract with the company is a corporation, the officers, agents, employees and other workers of the relevant corporation aside from persons who came to know the inside information in the course of concluding or negotiating or fulfilling the contract are also subject to regulation in cases where they come to know the inside information in the course of their duties (Article 166(1)(v) and Article 167(1)(v) of the FIEA)

Chapter 8  Market abuse regulation

came to know of a takeover bid based on the application of the Act and subsequently bought shares of the target company.[9]

On the other hand, the INTEC case is an example involving a person who has concluded a contract with a listed company (Supreme Court Judgment December 3, 2003, Case 1845, p. 147). In this case, a person related to the conclusion of a contract was accused of insider trading, and whether the transaction in question constituted trading where the person "has come to know a material fact in the course of conclusion of, negotiation for, or performance of the contract" was disputed.

In this case, Company A and Company B reached a basic agreement regarding the acquisition of exclusive sales rights of a non-contact IC Card. While both parties negotiated the specific method for acquiring the sales rights following the agreement, a representative director and executive director of Company A named Y learned that a decision was made to acquire the sales rights through the merger of Company A and Company B, and subsequently purchased shares of Company B. Y argued that the basic agreement had no relation to the subsequent merger between the companies and it was not possible to say that he came to know that the merger was decided "in the course of performance of" the basic agreement. However, the Supreme Court decided that "a contract" referred to in the law is not limited to a contract concluded based on Material Facts," and ruled against Y.

(ⅲ)  Information Recipients

Persons who receive Material Facts from insiders or quasi-insiders are also subject to insider trading regulations (Articles 166(3) and 167(3) of the FIEA). Such person is called an information recipient. In principle, information recipients are limited to persons who directly received Material Facts from insiders or quasi-insiders (primary information recipients), whereas the persons who received information on Material Facts from other information recipients (secondary information recipients) are not subject to

---

9  Tokyo District Court Decision October 28, 2005, not included in case books. In January 2012, criminal charges were filed by the Securities and Exchange Surveillance Commission against a Ministry of Economy, Trade and Industry deputy director general who purchased shares after coming to know about undisclosed material facts regarding the exercise of authority in the course of his duties.

*833*

insider trading regulation. Similarly, as illustrated by the case of someone who happened to overhear the contents discussed by insiders or quasi-insiders, persons who came to know Material Facts under circumstances that are not considered the case where the person directly "received information" are not subject to the regulations.

However, the case of information recipients who received Material Facts *ex officio* in the course of their duty is treated differently. An officer, etc. of a juridical person who comes to know such Material Facts in relation to the duty of a person who also belongs to the juridical person and has received information on the Material Facts in the course of his/her duty is subject to the insider trading regulation, although strictly speaking, the person did not directly receive information from insiders or quasi-insiders (Articles 166(3) and 167(3) of the FIEA).[10]

The rationale for the above provisions is the concern that the scope of the regulation may become too broad by including persons who did not directly receive information from insiders or quasi-insiders. By including such persons, all persons who ultimately came to know Material Facts would be subject to the regulation, even if they had received information with a low level of reliability through an indirect method. Obtaining and analyzing a wide array of information, including market hearsay, is generally considered a legitimate activity for investors. Therefore, penalizing a person who happened to obtain information that originated from corporate insiders would only result in discouraging market participants.

Finally, an act whereby insiders or quasi-insiders transmit Material Facts to information recipients is regulated under Article 167-2 of the FIEA discussed below, and it may also constitute complicity if it is accompanied by facts such as collusion related to insider trading or the instructions regarding share trading by the insider or quasi-insider.

---

10 One specific example, which was not a criminal case, was the Kappa Create case (order for payment of administrative monetary penalty dated March 19, 2008). In this case, through a reporting information terminal installed at the broadcasting station and other means, an employee of a broadcasting station learned inside information conveyed from an employee of a listed company to a reporter of the broadcasting station in the course of his duties, and conducted trading.

*834*

Chapter 8  Market abuse regulation

c. Information subject to the regulations

The Material Facts subject to the insider trading regulations are stipulated in detail in the FIEA and the relevant Cabinet Office Ordinances. Basically, these are divided into the four groups: (i) decisions (Article 166 (2) (i) of the FIEA); (ii) occurrence of facts (Article 166 (2) (ii) of the FIEA); (iii) changes in business performance (Article 166 (2) (iii) of the FIEA); and (iv) subsidiary company information (Article 166 (2) (v) – (viii) of the FIEA). In addition, the regulations have a so-called basket clause for "material facts concerning operations, business or property of the listed company that may have a significant influence on investors' investment decisions." (Articles 166 (2) (iv) and 166 (2) (viii) of the FIEA).

( i ) Decisions

A decision by an organ responsible for making decisions on the execution of the operations of the listed company to carry out any of the following matters, or a decision by the organ not to carry out a decision that has already been publicized, constitutes a Material Fact.

(i)   Solicitation of subscriptions for shares or share options
(ii)  Reduction of the amount of stated capital or capital reserves
(iii) Acquisition of its own shares by the listed company
(iv)  Allotment of shares without contribution
(v)   Share split
(vi)  Dividend of surplus
(vii) Share exchange
(viii) Share transfer
(ix)  Merger
(x)   Company split
(xi)  Transfer or acquisition of transfer of business in whole or in part
(xii) Dissolution (excluding dissolution as a result of merger)
(xiii) Commercialization of new products or new technology
(xiv)  Business alliance or other matters specified by cabinet order as those equivalent to the matters listed above[11]

Regarding these decisions, minor criteria have been set by cabinet order to

*835*

exclude items from the Material Facts that have a minor influence on investor's investment decisions (Article 49 of the Cabinet Office Ordinance on Restrictions on Securities Transactions). For example, an issue of shares for subscription for which the total amount to be paid is expected to be less than ¥100 million is deemed to be minor; therefore, such issue does not constitute a Material Fact.

Regarding these decisions, the main issues in question would be what is meant by "the organ of a Listed Company, etc. which is responsible for making decisions on the execution of operations of the Listed Company, etc.," and "a decision" made by the organ. The case of Nippon Orimono Kako Co., Ltd. (Supreme Court Judgment of June 10, 1999, Criminal Cases of the Supreme Court, Vol. 53, No. 5, p. 415) is considered a leading case on these points.

In this case, the defendant Y, who was the auditor and legal advisor of Company B, came to know that a listed Company A, which had fallen into financial difficulties, was planning a third-party share issuance by allocating new shares to Company B; subsequently, it purchased Company A shares using the name of an acquaintance before public disclosure of the capital increase. Defendant Y alleged that Company A had not made a decision as an organ to issue shares as of the purchase date. The Supreme Court ruled that "an organ which is responsible for making decisions on the execution of the operations" is not limited to the organ legally authorized to make decisions pursuant to the Commercial Code, and that the "decision" to issue shares means that such organ made a decision to issue shares itself or to take preparatory action to do so as a matter of company business; whereas the expectation that the issue will be carried out reliably is not required. In this case, the Court ruled that the "decision" by the "organ which is responsible for making decisions on the execution of operations" was made when the president dispatched from the de facto parent company to Company A for business restructuring made a statement to the managing director of the

---

11  The matters specified by cabinet order include a business alliance or cancellation of a business alliance, transfer or acquisition of shares etc. involving change in a subsidiary company, transfer or acquisition of fixed assets, suspension or abolition of a business in whole or in part, and application for delisting of shares (Article 28 of the Financial Instruments and Exchange Act Implementing Order).

Chapter 8　Market abuse regulation

parent company that a third-party share issuance would take place. [12]

（ⅱ）　Occurrence of facts

The occurrence of facts that have a major influence on investors' investment decisions is also considered a Material Fact. Specifically, the occurrence of the following facts is prescribed.

(i)　Damage arising from disaster or in the course of performing operations
(ii)　Any change of major shareholders of the relevant listed company
(iii)　Facts that may be grounds for delisting or recession of registration of specified securities [13] (including options pertaining thereto)
(iv)　Matters specified by cabinet order as those equivalent to the matters listed above [14]

Minor criteria have also been set for the above facts to exclude those items with minor influence on investor's investment decisions (Article 50 of the Cabinet Office Ordinance on Restrictions on Securities Transactions). For example, damages arising from disaster or in the course of performing operations with a total value of less than 3% of the net assets at the end of the most recent fiscal year are deemed minor.

---

12　In the Murakami Fund case (Supreme Court Decision of June 6, 2011; *Hanrei Times* No. 1353, p. 92) in which violation of Article 167 was questioned, the Court ruled that a decision to conduct a takeover bid, etc. or conduct work, etc. toward a takeover bid etc. as company work with the intention of realizing a takeover bid, etc. is sufficient as having decided to conduct a takeover bid, etc., and specific recognition that the takeover bid, etc. is feasible is not required.

13　Specified securities refer to the corporate bond certificates, preferred equity securities, share certificates and share option certificates of listed companies, etc. (Article 163(1) of the FIEA).

14　The matters specified by cabinet order include institution of and judgment in a suit concerning claims on property rights, petition for injunction against a business, and rescission of license or other administrative punishment (Article 28-2 of the Financial Instruments and Exchange Act Implementing Order).

*837*

(iii)　Changes in business performance

Regarding the business performance of listed companies, the occurrence of a difference that is likely to influence investors' investment decisions, i.e. between the actual figures of the preceding business year or latest publicized forecasts and the new forecasts newly prepared by the company or results in the settlement of accounts for the business year, also constitutes a Material Fact.

In this case, a difference of 10% or higher in net sales or of 30% or higher in current profits or net income is deemed to have an influence on investment decisions (Article 55 of the Cabinet Office Ordinance on Restrictions on Securities Transactions).[15]

Today, the brief financial results statement form required by stock exchanges for timely disclosure of settlement information has columns for projections of business performance such as net sales, net income and other figures, and virtually all listed companies disclose some sort of performance projection. Hence, insider trading regulation violation problems sometimes emerge regarding corrections to the publicized projection or differences between the figures in the projection and the actual settlement.

In the Macross case cited above, a report that a large amount of fictitious sales had been posted was considered to be the preparation of new forecasts by the company with a material difference compared with the sales projections that had already been publicized, and the report corresponded to the Material Fact.

(iv)　Subsidiary information

While the above Material Facts pertain to the listed company itself, the following decisions and occurrence of facts are also prescribed regarding the subsidiary company of the listed company. In addition, if the subsidiary itself is a listed company, changes in the business performance of the subsidiary also constitute a material fact for the parent company.

---

15　As for ordinary profit, however, in cases where the difference is less than 5% of the amount of net assets or the amount of capital, whichever is bigger, and as for net profit, in cases where the difference is similarly less than 2.5%, the influence on investment decisions is deemed to be minor.

Chapter 8   Market abuse regulation

· Decisions

(i)    Share exchange

(ii)   Share transfer

(iii)  Merger

(iv)   Company split

(v)    Transfer or receipt of business in whole or in part

(vi)   Dissolution (excluding dissolution as a result of merger)

(vii)  Commercialization of new products or new technology

(viii) Business alliance or other matters specified by cabinet order as equivalent to the matters listed above

· Occurrence of facts

(i)    Damage arising from disaster or in the course of performing operations

(ii)   Matters specified by cabinet order as equivalent to the matters listed above

(ⅴ)  Basket clauses

As described above, the insider trading regulations of the FIEA prescribe highly detailed and technical requirements on the definition of information deemed to be Material Facts. However, this does not mean that they necessarily provide comprehensive coverage of all information having a material influence on investors' investment decisions. Therefore, the FIEA has basket clauses providing that "in addition to the facts specified in the preceding three items, material facts concerning operation, business or property of the listed company that may have a significant influence on investors' investment decisions" are regarded as Material Facts (Articles 166 (2) (iv) and 166 (2) (viii) of the FIEA for subsidiaries of listed companies).

The Nippon Shoji Kaisha Ltd. case (Supreme Court Judgment of February 16, 1999, Criminal Cases of the Supreme Court, Vol. 53, No. 2, p. 1) is an example where this provision was applied. In this case, defendant Y came to know from an employee of listed Company A that a medicine which was virtually the company's first attempt at new drug development caused severe side effects including patient deaths, and subsequently short sold

*839*

Company A's shares.

In this case, if the incidence of side effects was viewed as the occurrence of damage arising in the course of Company A performing its operations, the damage amount was considered not to exceed the minor criteria (less than 3% of the net assets at the end of the most recent fiscal year). Therefore, whether it could be considered a Material Fact by applying the basket clause became an issue.

The Supreme Court ruled that the side effects in this case were likely to cause further deterioration of Company A's credibility as a pharmaceutical manufacturer and had a significant influence on its future business development and asset conditions; therefore, they could be deemed facts with separate and important aspects aside from those connoted by and assessed for the occurrence of damages; thus, the basket clause could be applied.

### d. Publication

The term "publicized" is interpreted to mean measures were taken specified by cabinet order as those for making information subject to the regulations available to a large number of persons or for making extraordinary reports, takeover bid notifications and other statutory disclosure documents available for public inspection (Articles 166 (4) and 167 (4) of the FIEA).

What is meant here by the measures to make these documents available to a large number of persons is either (i) Material Facts were provided by an authorized person at the listed company, etc. to at least two media sources and 12 hours have passed since then, or (ii) Material Facts were notified to the stock exchange where the company is listed and the stock exchange made the material facts available for public inspection (Article 30 of the Financial Instruments and Exchange Act Implementing Order, hereafter the "Implementing Order"). Of the two methods, (ii) is a new method approved in the 2003 revisions to the Order, whereas (i) used to be the prevailing method of "publication" in the past.

Method (i) is also mentioned as the "12-hour rule." It was set based on the reasoning that it would take about half a day for facts to become widely known to investors after such facts were reported by newspapers and other

*840*

Chapter 8 Market abuse regulation

media sources based on information received from companies.

This regulation is reasonable assuming an information flow such as the case where a Material Fact, which was notified to a newspaper company in the evening after normal trading hours on the stock exchange have ended, is printed in the morning edition on the following day. However, the rule has aspects that are not compatible with the Internet era when the listed company can publish real-time information on its own website.

Under the 12-hour rule, if a listed company published a material fact on its website at the same time it notified media sources, investors who directly accessed the information on the website will be regarded as receiving undisclosed information (since 12 hours have not yet passed) from corporate insiders, and thus be subject to the insider trading regulations. On the other hand, if a media source that received the notification immediately published the information on its own website or information terminal, then investors who came to know the information by accessing these sources will have received undisclosed information (since 12 hours have not yet passed) as in the former case; however, they will not be subject to the insider regulations because they are secondary information recipients who did not receive information directly from corporate insiders.

Thus, since the end of the 1990s through to the early 2000s when the Internet started to be used widely, listed companies have adopted practical measures related to the 12-hour rule such as placing warnings on their websites that "the information on this website may be regarded as insider information," or, waiting 12 hours after notifying media sources before publishing information on their own websites. Increasingly, these measures came to be criticized as not rational, leading to the revision of the Order.

Today, virtually all listed companies use the newly-approved method (ii) above to disclose material facts via the stock exchange timely disclosure information system TDnet.

In a related matter, media sources often make "scoop" reports. The sources of "scoop" articles about listed companies are usually corporate insiders, but a "scoop" is not information disclosed using regular procedures for public announcements by representatives or public relations managers. Therefore, it is not at all unusual that information which was widely reported on the front page of a newspaper actually is undisclosed Material Facts

*841*

under the insider trading regulations. Thus, in practice when there are "scoop" reports likely to cause a major influence on share prices, stock exchanges respond by confirming the facts with the listed company and urging swift publication.

e. Liability from violating regulations

A person who engages in insider trading in violation of the regulations of the FIEA is subject to criminal penalty; such person shall be punished by imprisonment with work for not more than five years or a fine of not more than five million yen, or both (Article 197-2(xiii) of the FIEA). The profits gained from illegal trading shall be confiscated or collected from the offender.[16]

In addition to regular penalties, there are also provisions stipulating administrative monetary penalties for violations of insider trading regulations (Article 175 (1) (ii) of the FIEA). The amount of the administrative monetary penalty is determined regardless of the amounts of profits actually gained by the offender using the following calculation method. The difference between the price of sales and purchases conducted on the offender's own account within six months before the date of publication of the information subject to the regulations and the lowest and highest prices within two weeks after publication of the relevant information is calculated as the base amount, which is then multiplied by the actual trading volume.

Whether civil liability may be asserted against a person who violated insider trading regulations is a difficult issue. If it may be considered that the insider trading regulations impose obligations on a person possessing important undisclosed information to choose either to "disclose or abstain" from trading, one could argue that other persons who engaged in market trading during the period when the insider trading took place suffered damages because they were forced to trade at improper prices from the violation of the duty to disclose by the offender.

---

16  Since violations of insider trading regulations only come into existence with sales and purchases prior to disclosure of material facts, there are cases where there is no profit to be confiscated or additionally collected.

*842*

Chapter 8  Market abuse regulation

Unlike the provisions prescribed for violation of disclosure regulations, the FIEA has no specific provisions regarding civil liability for violations of insider trading regulations. If persons who believe they have suffered damage from insider trading try to claim tort liability against an offender, it is considered extremely difficult to prove a causal relationship between the trading acts of the offender and their own losses, at least in the case of stock market trading.

f. Prohibition of tipping

In the 2013 amendments to the FIEA, a new provision prohibiting the tipping of information deemed to be Material Facts by insiders and quasi-insiders was introduced (Article 167-2 of the FIEA). This amendment reflected the criticism against the ineffectiveness of existing regulations brought to light by a series of cases of insider trading involving institutional investors in 2012.

In these cases, employees of the investment banks acting as lead managers in public offering deals for listed companies tipped off their institutional clients about unpublished deal information. Institutional investors tipped off by this information sold their shares in order to avoid losses or profited through short-selling.

Although administrative monetary penalties were imposed on the institutional investors engaged in insider trading in violation of the FIEA, no particular sanctions were imposed on the investment banks, as there was no concept of "aiding and abetting" in the administrative monetary penalty cases.

Under the new provision, insiders and quasi-insiders shall not give away unpublished Material Facts in order to enable others to profit or to avoid losses through buying or selling securities, nor recommend buying or selling particular securities based on unpublished Material Facts. A person who violates this provision is subject to criminal penalty or administrative monetary penalty.

*843*

## 3. Regulations aimed at preventing insider trading

a. System for demanding restitution of profits arising from sales and purchases conducted in a short-term sales and purchases

(ⅰ) Outline of the system

Under the system for demanding restitution of profits arising from sales and purchases, when an officer or major shareholder who owns at least 10% of the voting rights of a listed company makes short-term profits from sales of stock or other securities of the company within six months after purchasing them, the listed company may request the officer or major shareholder to provide the company with profits earned by such sales (Article 164 of the FIEA). Listed companies may also demand such restitution from partnerships (specified partnerships, etc.) that are de facto major shareholders (Article 165-2 of the FIEA).

The article includes wording stating that the purpose of the regulation is to prevent the officers or major shareholders of a listed company from "wrongful use of secret information they have obtained" in the course of their duty or by virtue of their position. Thus, the purpose of this regulation is considered to be the prevention of insider trading.[17]

This system was established using the U.S. law as a model. In the U.S., officers and major shareholders bear the duty of loyalty and other fiduciary duties to their companies, so using their duty or position to gain personal profit is a violation of their fiduciary duties. Thus, it is interpreted that such profits must be restituted to the company in the U.S.

For a listed company to use this system to demand restitution of profits from short-term sales and purchases, the company needs to be aware of the stock trading activities of its officers and major shareholders. Accordingly, the FIEA provides that officers and major shareholders of listed companies must submit reports to the Prime Minister on sales, purchases, and other transactions of specified securities (as prescribed above) and other instruments on their own account (Article 163(1) of the FIEA).[18]

---

17  However, as stated below, this wording only clarified the purpose of the system, and the use of the acquired secret is not a requirement for claiming restoration.

*844*

Chapter 8  Market abuse regulation

(ⅱ)  Constitutionality of the regulations

Regarding this system for demanding restitution of profits from short-term sales and purchases, there was a case where it was disputed whether the system violated the right to property guaranteed by Article 29 of the Constitution of Japan for the purpose of preventing insider trading in as much as it forces parties to give up profits although there was no actual exploitation of secrets by the parties (Giken Kogyo Co., Ltd. incident, Grand Bench Supreme Court Judgment of February 13, 2002, Civil Cases of the Supreme Court, Vol. 56, No. 2, p. 331).

The Supreme Court ruled that the regulatory purpose of this system, namely, preventing improper sales and purchases using insider information by the officers and major shareholders of listed companies, is legitimate and consistent with public welfare. It also ruled that the regulation contents allowed demands for restitution of profits from trading with the external appearance of exploitation of secret information in order to remove the inducement for such trading, so the system neither lacks necessity nor rationality as a means to achieving the purpose. Thus, the Supreme Court dismissed the appeal that the system is unconstitutional.

(ⅲ)  Conflicts regarding controlling interests and the restitution demand
system

Nonetheless, observations of the conditions where the system for demanding restitution of profits from short-term sales and purchases has been used in practice reveal aspects that raise questions concerning the rationality of the system, even if it is not unconstitutional. This is because in many cases, the demands for restitution of profits based on this system are made against major shareholders who are in conflict with the company's management team, and not against the officers of a listed company.

An underlying factor that could explain the above is that the demand for restitution of profits is not obligatory. Hence, listed companies can freely decide whether to demand restitution. There is an alternative provision that

---

**18** The same holds true when a partner of a specified partnership, etc. has conducted sales or purchases, etc. pertaining to the asset of the relevant specified partnership (Article 165-2(1) of the FIEA).

*845*

a shareholder of a listed company may make the request in subrogation of the company if the company fails to make the demand within 60 days from the day when the shareholder requested that the company make the demand for restitution (Article 164 (2) of the FIEA). In reality, shareholder derivative actions based on this provision are extremely rare, which is considered to be another factor influencing how the system is actually used.

Specifically, there are cases where once a buyer seeking a hostile takeover of a listed company acquires 10% or more of the voting rights of the target company and becomes a major shareholder, the management team of the listed company starts monitoring the buyer's trading activities in order to demand restitution of any accrued profits from short-term purchases and sales. Here, the goal of the management team is to degrade the buyer's reputation and cause economic damage by demanding restitution.

The Giken Kogyo case ruled on by the Supreme Court seems to have had such background. As a more recent example, in July 2008, the first demand for restitution based on Article 165-2 of the FIEA that had been prescribed by the revision in 2006 was requested. The case involves a U.S. affiliated investment fund Y that acquired approximately 26% of the shares of listed Company X.

In such cases, even if a buyer is a major shareholder in form, the buyer is likely to face difficulty in obtaining information from the opposing management team regarding Material Facts with major influence on share prices. Hence, it would be difficult to argue that the restitution demand system is functioning rationally, even in light of the purpose of the system to prevent insider trading. Now that regulations expressly prohibiting insider trading have been enacted, there is room for debate as to whether keeping such systems aimed at prior prevention is necessary.

b . Prohibition of short-selling by officers of listed companies

The officers and major shareholders, etc. of listed companies, etc. (hereinafter "Officers and Major Shareholders of Listed Companies") who are subject to demands for restitution of profits from short-term sales and purchases are also prohibited from short-selling shares of the listed company (Articles 165 and 165-2(15) of the FIEA). Regarding short-selling, while there are price and other regulations as general market regulations (Article

Chapter 8　Market abuse regulation

162(1) (i) of the FIEA; Articles 26-2 to 26-5 of the Implementing Order), in the case of Officers and Major Shareholders of Listed Companies, the act of short-selling itself is prohibited.

In principle, Officers and Major Shareholders of Listed Companies should strive to increase corporate value and share prices. As such, the act to gain profit from the decline in share prices through short sales may be viewed as violation of the duty of fidelity. Also, when Officers and Major Shareholders of Listed Companies intentionally conduct short-selling, it is highly likely that they possess some form of undisclosed Material Fact with major negative influence on the share price. Similar to Article 164 of the FIEA, this provision does not require parties subject to the regulation to have knowledge of an undisclosed Material Fact, but it can be viewed as a system for prevention of insider trading beforehand.

Officers and Major Shareholders of Listed Companies who conduct short sales in violation of this provision are subject to criminal penalties of imprisonment with work for not more than six months or a fine of not more than five hundred thousand yen, or both (Article 205(xx) of the FIEA).

# 4. Regulations for the prevention of acts of market manipulation

The FIEA does not merely provide direct prohibition of market manipulation and other unfair trading, but it also aims to prevent unfair trading beforehand by setting certain restrictions on trading methods that are likely to lead to acts of market manipulation, even though they cannot be called wrongful transactions themselves. Specifically, the FIEA includes regulations on (i) short-selling and stop orders, (ii) proprietary trading, etc. by financial instruments trading business operators, and (iii) the purchase of treasury shares by listed companies.

### a. Regulations on short sales and stop orders

Short-selling refers to a trading method whereby a party sells shares it does not currently own by borrowing them from another party. It is a trading method with legitimate economic function that allows the market price of the shares to reflect investment decisions of investors who do not hold shares as well, and enhances market liquidity. However, it is possible to

*847*

use short-selling for "bear raids," an investment strategy to artificially drive down stock prices, through intensive short-selling over a brief period of time. There is also the risk of causing chaos in the security settlement system, if the short-seller cannot acquire the required number of shares for settlement.

Stop order refers to a trade method to buy or sell a security when its market price surpasses a particular point, comprising buy stop order and sell stop order. A buy stop order is executed when the market price surpasses an entry price predetermined by the investor. A sell stop order is executed when the market price falls below the exit price predetermined by the investor. Buy stop orders are used in a rising market so as to keep up with the trend. Sell stop orders, also called "stop loss orders," are used to limit losses within a certain range when the market is falling. However, there is criticism that wide use of these types of orders accelerates market moves in a given direction.

While short sales and stop orders are expected to fulfill legitimate economic purposes, they are by nature prone to be used for market manipulation activities. Accordingly, the FIEA sets a provision (Article 162 (1) of the FIEA) that prohibits short sales and stop orders "in violation of a cabinet order."

Regarding short-selling, regulations have been prescribed that oblige securities companies that receive short sales orders to expressly specify and confirm that these are short sales orders (Article 26-3 of the Implementing Order), as well as those intended for price restriction (Article 26-4 of the Implementing Order).[19] Subsequent to the confusion including sudden drops in share prices that were experienced in Japanese markets due to the 2007-2008 global monetary crisis, the FSA introduced emergency restrictions for short-selling from October 30, 2008, including the prohibition of short-selling without devising measures for the specific hand over of securities (the "naked short-selling") (Article 26-2-2 of the Implementing Order), and, the obligation to report and publicize short-selling of more than a certain percentage (0.25% in principle) of issued shares (Article 26-5 of

---

**19** This is called the "uptick rule" because it prevents short sales of stocks at or below the most recent contract price.

Chapter 8   Market abuse regulation

the Implementing Order).

Contrarily, no cabinet order corresponding to the regulations for stop-orders prescribed in the FIEA has been prescribed to date. For that reason some securities companies have interpreted the language preventing stop orders "in violation of a Cabinet Order" as meaning stop orders are "acceptable" since no relevant cabinet orders exist, and they are handling stop orders from their customers.

b. Regulations on proprietary trading by businesses operators

Proprietary trading by securities companies, that is, trading on their own accounts, has a positive meaning such as increasing market liquidity and assisting the formation of fair prices.

In the Japanese stock markets, the traditional philosophy has been that the principal role of securities companies is taking orders from customers and executing them in stock markets. However, the role of securities companies as "market makers" who continuously transmit market signals has been emphasized in the U.S. stock markets. Even in Japan, the market making function of securities companies plays an important role in other markets including the bond market.

Securities companies are market professionals with an advantageous position as traders in trading markets, as they can obtain trading information more easily than general investors. Therefore, they have the capacity to induce the market to move in their desired direction by engaging in excessive proprietary trading. Accordingly, the FIEA allows regulations by cabinet order, "to restrict the sale and purchase of the securities by financial instruments operators, etc. on its own account" as well as to restrict "excessive volumes of sales and purchases to be conducted," if "such sale and purchase is found to disturb the order" of the markets (Article 161 of the FIEA).

Based on this regulation, the Cabinet Office Ordinance on Restrictions on Securities Transactions provides that when financial business trading operators, etc. conduct trading using their discretionary accounts, they are prohibited from trading in volumes deemed excessive in light of the purport or the amount of the consignment of the relevant trading contract and deemed to impair market order (Article 9 of the Cabinet Office Ordinance

*849*

on Restrictions on Securities Transactions). On the other hand, there have been no corresponding cabinet orders enacted regarding limits on proprietary trading by business operators[20].

c. Regulations on purchases of treasury stock by listed companies

In principle, Japan's Companies Act (Commercial Code) prohibited purchases of treasury stock by joint stock corporations. However, the regulations restricting purchases of treasury stock have been gradually eased since the 1994 revision of the Commercial Code, in order to respond to social needs, such as the introduction of equity-linked compensation systems including stock option and the allowance of more flexible corporate finance strategies. Furthermore, in the 2001 revision of the Commercial Code, purchases of treasury shares were fully liberalized in principle, contrary to the former regulations (Article 155 of the Companies Act).

However, concerns that listed companies might manipulate stock prices to their advantage when they acquire treasury stock in the market could not be ignored. So in the 2001 revision of the FIEA, a provision was added to allow matters to be prescribed which are found to be necessary and appropriate to secure the fairness in transactions by cabinet order regarding the purchase of treasury stock by listed companies (Article 162-2 of the FIEA).

Based on this provision, the Cabinet Office Ordinance on Restrictions on Securities Transactions prohibits listed companies from placing purchase orders for treasury stock via multiple securities companies on the same day, and from placing purchase orders less than 30 minutes before the end of floor trading; it also sets detailed regulations on order prices and volumes (Articles 16 to 23 of the Cabinet Office Ordinance on Restrictions on Securities Transactions). Among these regulations, those regarding purchasing time limits and maximum purchasing volumes are now being relaxed, in conjunction with the emergency measures introduced after the financial crisis to beef up regulation of short-selling, as explained earlier.

---

20  While not under this provision, the Cabinet Office Ordinance on Financial Instruments Business etc. prohibits acts that could lead to market manipulation such as involvement in large-volume recommended sales and artificial market formation by financial instruments business operators and others (Article 177(1)(xvii) to (xx) of the Cabinet Office Ordinance on Financial Instruments Business, etc.).

*850*

Chapter 8 Market abuse regulation

# B. Market manipulation (Article 159)

## 1. Background and purpose of enactment of Article 159 of the FIEA

Article 159 was drafted with reference to Section 9 of the U.S. Securities Exchange Act of 1934. Section 9 of that Act, which has the title "Prohibition against Manipulation of Security Prices," regulates market manipulation.

The primary significance of regulating market manipulation is because investors trade believing that the prices of securities and other financial instruments on markets are formed by supply and demand under conditions that are not artificially controlled. So to protect credibility, these regulations seek to exclude rigged trading and guarantee the maintenance of markets where prices are formed freely by the natural relation of supply and demand. Specifically, Article 159 of the FIEA bans the following acts as acts of market manipulation that prevent price formation by the natural relation between supply and demand: false purchases and sales, collusion purchases and sales (Article 159(1)), transactions to mislead the market (Article 159(2)(i)), market manipulation through representation (Article 159(2)(ii)(iii)), and market manipulation to stabilize prices (Article 159(3)). These are addressed in order below.

## 2. Interpretation of Article 159 of the FIEA

a. False purchases and sales and collusion purchases and sales

Article 159, paragraph 1 of the FIEA prohibits purchases and sales of securities and market derivatives transactions and over-the-counter derivatives transactions with the aim of misleading others into believing that the trading is thriving or otherwise misleading others about the state of these transactions,[21] that is: (1) false purchases and sales (Article 159(1)(i)-(iii)); (2) collusion purchases and sales (Article 159(1)(iv)-(viii)); and (3) entrustment or being entrusted with (1) or (2) (Article 159(1)(ix)).

*851*

( i ) False purchases and sales

False purchases and sales refer to transactions where the same party purchases and sells the same securities, etc. at the same price at around the same time, creating a transaction record that cannot be distinguished by other market investors from a real transaction between an independent buyer and seller. Specifically, Article 159 prohibits conducting false purchases and sales of securities and false market derivatives transactions or over-the-counter derivatives transactions without the intent to transfer the rights (Article 159(1)(i)), conducting false market derivatives transactions or over-the-counter derivatives transactions without the intent to pay or receive money (Article 159(1)(ii)), and conducting false market derivatives transactions or over-the-counter derivatives transactions without the intent to grant or acquire the options (Article 159(1)(iii)).

( ii ) Collusion purchases and sales

Collusion purchases and sales refer to transactions whereby multiple parties collude beforehand and purchase, sell, etc. the same securities, etc. at the same price at around the same time, substantially creating the same result as false purchases and sales. Specifically, Article 159 of the FIEA prohibits selling financial instruments after colluding in advance with another party that promises to purchase the financial instruments at the same price and around the same time as the sale (Article 159(1)(iv)), purchasing financial instruments after colluding in advance with another party that promises to sell the financial instruments at the same price and around the same time as the purchase (Article 159(1)(v)), making an offer in connection with a

---

21  Because in practice it is almost impossible to believe that false purchases and sales and collusion purchases and sales would be conducted for any other purposes, the interpretation is that once the external form of false purchases and sales or collusion purchases and sales has been proven, the party denying market manipulation must prove that their acts were not for these purposes. Misao Tatsuta, "Shoken torihiki no hoteki kisei [Legal Regulation of Securities Transactions]" in *Gendai no keizai kozo to ho* [Contemporary Economic Structure and Law] (Chikuma Shobo, 1975), p. 519. Also, so long as the act had these purposes, the act is still illegal as market manipulation even if the party had other purposes. Katsuro Kanzaki, Masashi Shitani and Yasuhiro Kawaguchi, *Kinyu shohin torihiki ho* [Financial Instruments and Exchange Act] (Seirin Shoin, 2012) p. 1298.

Chapter 8 Market abuse regulation

market or over-the-counter derivatives transaction after colluding in advance with another party that promises to become the other party to the transaction at around the same time as the offer and at the same agreed figure as in the offered transaction (Article 159(1)(vi)), making an offer in connection with a market or over-the-counter derivatives transaction after colluding in advance with another party that promises to become the other party to the transaction at around the same time as the offer and for the same amount of consideration as in the offered transaction (Article 159(1) (vii)), and making an offer in connection with a market or over-the-counter derivatives transaction after colluding in advance with another party that promises to become the other party to the transaction at around the same time as the offer and with the same conditions as in the offered transaction (Article 159(1)(viii)).

In this way, collusion transactions require multiple parties that have colluded to purchase and sell the same securities, etc. in the same time period at the same price. As for the same time period, however, it is sufficient if the relevant orders remain in effect within the same time period; and for the same price it is sufficient if both orders are within a range that could be matched and settled.[22]

The collusion can also be partial or implicit.[23] Colluding and then conducting or ordering a purchase or sale is itself illegal, and the probability or certainty that the transaction will be concluded between the parties that colluded is not required.[24] It is also not always necessary that the party the transaction

---

[22] Ichiro Kawamoto and Kaname Seki, *Chikujo kaisetsu shoken torihiki ho 3-tei ban* [Article by Article Commentary on the Securities and Exchange Act, (3rd Edition)] (Shoji Homu, 2008), p. 1272; Katsuro Kanzaki, Masashi Shitani and Yasuhiro Kawaguchi, *Kinyu shohin torihiki ho* [Financial Instruments and Exchange Act] (Seirin Shoin, 2012), p. 1298.

[23] Hideki Kanda, Etsuro Kuronuma and Naohiko Matsuo, *Kinyu shohin torihiki ho konmentaru 4* [Financial Instruments and Exchange Act Commentary 4] (Shoji Homu, 2011), p. 25 (Tomotaka Fujita).

[24] Masayuki Kawamura (ed.), *Kinyu shohin torihiki ho dai-5 han* [Financial Instruments and Exchange Act 5th Edition] (Chuo Keizaisha, 2014), p. 551 (Tokuya Shinatani).

*853*

is actually concluded with be the party with which the collusion was made.[25]

(iii) Entrusting or being entrusted with false purchases and sales or collusion purchases and sales

Entrusting or being entrusted with the above-prescribed false purchases and sales or collusion purchases and sales is also prohibited. Because entrusting or being entrusted is prohibited separately from the false purchases and sales and collusion purchases and sales, regardless of whether the entrustment is executed, the entrusting or being entrusted with such purchases and sales itself violates the prohibition on market manipulation. However, for being entrusted with such a purchase or sale to be illegal, the party to which the purchase or sale is entrusted must know that the transaction is a false purchase or sale or collusion purchase or sale (for entrusting to be illegal, the party to which the purchase or sale is entrusted need not know about the falsity).[26]

b. Market manipulation through actual purchases and sales

Article 159, paragraph 2, item (1) of the FIEA prohibits, for the purpose of inducing purchases and sales of securities or market or over-the-counter derivatives transactions (purpose of inducement): (1) conducting a series of purchases and sales of securities, etc. that are likely to mislead a person into believing that purchases and sales of securities, etc. are thriving, or offering to conduct such transactions, or entrusting a person with conducting such transactions or becoming entrusted with conducting such transactions; or (2) conducting a series of purchases and sales of securities to cause fluctuations in market prices (of securities listed on a financial instruments exchange market or over-the-counter traded securities on an

---

25  Shoken Torihiki Ho Kenkyu Kai, "Chapter 5 Securities Exchanges (25)," *Investment* Vol. 19 No. 1 (1966), pp. 117-118; Hideki Kanda, Etsuro Kuronuma and Naohiko Matsuo, *Kinyu shohin torihiki ho konmentaru 4* [Financial Instruments and Exchange Act Commentary 4] (Shoji Homu, 2011), p. 25 (Tomotaka Fujita).

26  Katsuro Kanzaki, Masashi Shitani and Yasuhiro Kawaguchi, *Kinyu shohin torihiki ho* [Financial Instruments and Exchange Act] (Seirin Shoin, 2012), p. 1297; Takeo Suzuki=Ichiro Kawamoto, *Shoken Torihiki Ho Shinban* [Financial Instruments and Exchange Act New Edition] (Yuhikaku, 1984) p. 529.

Chapter 8　Market abuse regulation

over-the-counter securities market), or offering to conduct such transactions, or entrusting a person with conducting such transactions or becoming entrusted with conducting such transactions (transactions to cause price changes). Even with normal purchases and sales, large-volume transactions move market prices, and trading while recognizing that fact is not itself illegal. To be interpreted as illegal, the above-mentioned purpose of inducement and either (1) or (2) are required. However, in practice because the factor (1) "likely to mislead a person into believing that purchases and sales of securities, etc. are thriving" alone is almost never deemed to be an issue, and in judicial precedents, the problem arises when (2) "cause fluctuations in market prices" (transactions to cause price changes) occurs, considering (2) alone is sufficient.[27]

　( i )　Purpose of inducement and transactions to cause price changes
One well-known precedent which interpreted this point is the case of Kyodo Shiryo Co. Ltd. In this case when the company's board of directors decided to increase its capital by ¥1.2 billion including a public offering at the market price to secure ¥3.0 billion in capital, the company planned to push up the price of its shares which had been trading at between ¥170 and ¥180 to around ¥280 in around just two months, to price the public market offering at around ¥200 per share, and gain a premium of around ¥1.8 billion. During those two months, the company continuously purchased around 6.15 million shares pushing up prices and holding up prices (and also conducted false purchases and sales of a total of around 100,000 shares of the same stock) and the issue was whether this violated then Article 125, paragraph 2 item (i) of the Securities and Exchange Act (the present Article 159(2)(i) of the Financial Instruments and Exchange Act).[28]

---

**27** Katsuro Kanzaki, Masashi Shitani and Yasuhiro Kawaguchi, *Kinyu shohin torihiki ho* [Financial Instruments and Exchange Act] (Seirin Shoin, 2012), p. 1303.

**28** In this case, the relevant company, with the purpose of stabilizing the market price of the company's shares raised by the above-stated purchases, thereafter bought up sell orders at or below the buying limit for approximately one month, acquiring about 870, 000 of the company's shares, and that is also considered stabilization manipulation. (Article 159(3) of the FIEA).

*855*

The judgment by the court of second instance (the high court) [29] interpreted the purpose of inducement as "the intent to induce third parties to purchase and sell the relevant securities" and held that the intent to mislead investors and induce purchase and sales transactions by artificially changing market prices is not a necessary factor. On the other hand, this judgment restricted the interpretation of transactions to cause price changes to "transactions that could change market prices made with the intent to control market prices on securities markets," and "not simply transactions where the transaction itself has the potential to change market prices." In contrast, the Supreme Court decision in this same case [30] interpreted the purpose of inducement as "the purpose of inducing sales and purchases of securities on a securities market while misleading investors that the market prices are formed by the natural relation between supply and demand, regardless of changing the market price through artificial manipulation" and interpreted transactions to cause price changes as "purchases, sales and other transactions with the potential to change market prices." [31] While the Supreme Court judgment differed from the judgment by the high court by including artificial manipulation to change market prices and thus misleading investors in the interpretation of purpose of inducement, it took the broad interpretation of transactions to cause price changes as "sales, purchases and other transactions with the potential to change market prices" and did not include the requirement of intent to control market prices cited by the high court. In other words, in contrast to the high court's restrictive

---

29 Tokyo High Court Judgment of July 26, 1988 (High Courts Reports (criminal cases) Vol. 41 No. 2, p. 269).

30 Supreme Court Decision of July 20, 1994 (Supreme Court Reports (criminal cases) Vol. 48 No. 5, p. 201).

31 The potential to change market prices is sufficient. Actually changing the market prices is not always required. Shoken Torihiki Ho Kenkyu Kai, "Chapter 5 Securities Exchanges (26)," *Investment* Vol. 19 No. 2 (1966), pp. 41-42; Hideki Kanda, Etsuro Kuronuma and Naohiko Matsuo, *Kinyu shohin torihiki ho konmentaru 4* [Financial Instruments and Exchange Act Commentary 4] (Shoji Homu, 2011), p. 29 (Tomotaka Fujita). The "series of purchases and sales" in "series of purchases and sales of securities to cause fluctuations in market prices" (transactions to cause price changes) requires two or more sales or purchases of the same securities, etc. Katsuro Kanzaki, Masashi Shitani and Yasuhiro Kawaguchi, *Kinyu shohin torihiki ho* [Financial Instruments and Exchange Act] (Seirin Shoin, 2012), p. 1302.

*856*

Chapter 8　Market abuse regulation

interpretation of transactions to cause price changes, the Supreme Court ruling took a restrictive interpretation of the purpose of inducement.[32]

The Supreme Court's above-stated interpretations of the purpose of inducement and transactions to cause price changes are supported by legal theory as well.

（ⅱ）　Response to layering and spoofing

"Layering and spoofing" are one of the methods of market manipulation. These are orders placed on the market with no intention of concluding the transactions that are canceled before being settled, and have been a problem in many market manipulation cases. Prior to the 2006 revision, Article 159, paragraph 2, item (i) of the FIEA prescribed "sales, purchases and other transactions of securities or entrusting or being entrusted with such transactions" as a prohibited act, and "layering and spoofing" by customers that correspond to "entrusting" here were prohibited. However, it was not clear if "layering and spoofing" by financial services providers on their own account, that is offering for purchases or sales not leading to the conclusion of a purchase and sale or other contract, were included in this provision. So the 2006 revision added "offering" for the purchase, sale or other transaction of securities to the prohibited actions and clarified that this is prohibited.

c．Market manipulation through representation

Article 159, paragraph 2, item (ii) of the FIEA prohibits spreading a rumor that the market prices of securities will fluctuate due to one's own or another party's market manipulation for the purpose of inducing purchases and sales of securities or market derivatives transactions or over-the-counter derivatives transactions (purpose of inducement). Article 159, paragraph 2, item (iii) prohibits intentionally making a misrepresentation about a

---

**32**　This has posed doubts regarding the extent of differences of proof required in specific cases by these two positions. Katsuro Kanzaki, "Genjitsu torihiki niyoru soba soju [Market Manipulation through Actual Transactions]," *Hoso Jiho* Vol. 44 No. 3, p. 575 (1992); Hideki Kanda, Etsuro Kuronuma and Naohiko Matsuo, *Kinyu shohin torihiki ho konmentaru 4* [Financial Instruments and Exchange Act Commentary 4] (Shoji Homu, 2011), p. 28 (Tomotaka Fujita).

important matters or a representation that is likely to mislead in conducting purchases and sales of securities, etc. for the purpose of inducing purchases and sales of securities or market derivatives transactions or over-the-counter derivatives transactions (purpose of inducement). Under the former (Article 159 (2) (ii)), the rumor that market prices will change based on one's own or another party's market manipulation must be conveyed to a large number of unspecified persons or to a large number of persons, but that spread of information does not have to accompany the purchase and sale of the securities.[33] In fact, manipulation of the market does not have to take place, and even if market prices actually change as a result of manipulation, that does not render this market manipulation through representation legal.[34] On the other hand, representation that is false about important matters or that is likely to mislead might be made to a small number of specified persons, but only when that representation accompanies the listed financial instruments, etc.[35]; the relevant representation does not have to be made directly to the counterparty of the securities purchase and sale, etc. Also, "important matters" are interpreted as matters important enough to make other persons consider, through purchases, sales, and other transactions of the securities and their representation, that the increase or decrease in market prices may be taking place.[36]

Here again, the purpose of inducing trading that is also required for market manipulation through actual purchases and sales (see (2) above) is required. However, concerning the purpose of inducement, some caution is required for the same interpretation of market manipulation through representation, etc. as in the Kyodo Shiryo case Supreme Court decision. For example, in the Kyodo Shiryo case Supreme Court decision, the purpose of inducement was

---

33  Katsuro Kanzaki, Masashi Shitani and Yasuhiro Kawaguchi, *Kinyu shohin torihiki ho* [Financial Instruments and Exchange Act] (Seirin Shoin, 2012), pp. 1291-1292.
34  Id., p. 1293.
35  Id., p. 1292. The reason presented was that even in cases where the indication is to a small number of specified persons, those sales and purchases can easily induce other persons, and have a large danger of market manipulation.
36  Id., p. 1293 Masao Kishida (ed.), *Chushaku kinyu shohin torihiki ho dai-3 kan* [Financial Instruments and Exchange Act annotated: volume 3] (Kinyu Zaisei Jijo Kenkyukai, 2010), p. 36 (Yoshifumi Imagawa).

*858*

Chapter 8   Market abuse regulation

interpreted as "the purpose of inducing the sales and purchases of securities on a securities market while misleading investors that the market prices are formed by the natural relation between supply and demand, regardless of changing the market price through artificial manipulation." However, here the persons who come into contact with the rumored information are not "misled that the market prices are formed by the natural relation between supply and demand, regardless of changing the market price through artificial manipulation" under Article 159, paragraph 2, item (ii); and the purpose of inducement is not to induce trading by the parties receiving the false indication under Article 159, paragraph 2, item (iii) of the FIEA.[37]

d. Manipulation to stabilize prices

Article 159, paragraph 3 of the FIEA prohibits a series of purchases and sales of securities, offering to conduct such transactions, and entrusting and becoming entrusted with conducting such transactions, for the purpose of pegging, fixing or stabilizing market prices. This is known as manipulation to stabilize prices. While this is not an effort to actively raise or lower market prices, it is still an act that prevents the natural formation of prices by the relation of supply and demand, which is the main purpose of regulations on market manipulation. Moreover, this is regulated because the prices of securities that have been the target of manipulation to stabilize prices often drop greatly after the manipulation to stabilize prices ends, and so the manipulation may cause investors who purchase the shares during the manipulation to suffer unexpected losses.[38] On the other hand, manipulation to stabilize prices is considered necessary under certain conditions. Specifically, sometimes when a large volume of securities is supplied to the market through a public offering or secondary distribution of securities, etc., the supply-demand balance is temporarily destroyed from excessive supply,

---

37   Hideki Kanda, Etsuro Kuronuma and Naohiko Matsuo, *Kinyu shohin torihiki ho konmentaru 4* [Financial Instruments and Exchange Act Commentary 4] (Shoji Homu, 2011), p. 31 (Tomotaka Fujita).

38   Cases where this provision was applied to permit stabilization manipulation include, for example, Osaka District Court Judgment of June 28, 1977 (*Shoji Homu* No. 780 p. 30) "Nippon Netsugaku Kogyo case," and Tokyo District Court Judgment of Dec. 24, 1976 (*Kinyu Shoji Hanrei* No. 524, p. 32) "Tokyo Tokei Seizo case."

*859*

the price drops, and it becomes difficult for the enterprise to raise funds.[39] In such cases, manipulation to stabilize prices is permitted under the conditions that the (i) purposes, (ii) body, (iii) location and period, and (iv) price range are restricted and (v) disclosure of the manipulation to stabilize prices is made to investors. The main purpose of restricting the body and period of the stabilizing transactions is not to restrict the persons who can conduct stabilizing transactions or the period, but rather, within the period when price stabilization manipulation can be conducted, to prohibit financial services providers from purchases and sales of the public offering and secondary distribution securities through means other than stabilizing transactions, and to prohibit financial services providers from being entrusted with the purchase of the relevant securities through means other than stabilizing transactions by persons who can entrust stabilizing transactions, etc. (Article 38(7) of the FIEA, and Article 117(xix) of the Cabinet Office Ordinance on Financial Instruments Business, etc.).[40]

(ⅰ) Purposes

First, the purposes permitted for manipulation to stabilize prices are to facilitate public offerings and secondary distributions of securities.[41] For other purposes, acts "to effect a series of purchases and sales of securities, etc. or to offer to conduct such transactions, or to entrust, etc. or become entrusted, etc. with conducting such transactions for the purposes of pegging, fixing, or stabilizing market prices" are all deemed to be illegal.[42]

---

39  As for why stabilization manipulation is permitted to avert difficulties in raising funds, this is interpreted to be for the protection of the interests of the existing shareholders of the issuing company. Hideki Kanda, Etsuro Kuronuma and Naohiko Matsuo, *Kinyu shohin torihiki ho konmentaru 4* [Financial Instruments and Exchange Act Commentary 4] (Shoji Homu, 2011), p. 32 (Tomotaka Fujita).
40  Katsuro Kanzaki, Masashi Shitani and Yasuhiro Kawaguchi, *Kinyu shohin torihiki ho* [Financial Instruments and Exchange Act] (Seirin Shoin, 2012), p. 1336.
41  Article 20 (1) of the Order for Enforcement of the Financial Instruments and Exchange Act.
42  The stabilizing transactions under Article 159, paragraph 3 of the FIEA do not require the purpose of inducement required by paragraph 2 of the same article (this is also clearly stated and confirmed in the Kyodo Shiryo case Supreme Court decision).

*860*

Chapter 8   Market abuse regulation

(ⅱ)   Body

Next, the regulations of the bodies that are allowed to conduct manipulation to stabilize prices are divided into those for bodies that can conduct stabilizing transactions on their own account and those that can entrust stabilizing transactions to others. Apparently, this is to permit only parties that are within the necessary range as reasonable for achieving the above purposes. First, the parties that can conduct stabilizing transactions on their own account must be financial services providers that are members, etc. of financial instruments exchanges, because stabilization manipulation is implemented through the sale and purchases of securities, etc. on financial instruments exchange markets and over-the-counter securities markets (Article 22 (1) of the Financial Instruments and Exchange Act Implementing Order). Among these, in cases where securities registration statements are submitted regarding a public offering or secondary distribution, the financial services provider recorded on the securities registration statement as the financial services provider who will conclude an underwriting contract is permitted to do so. In other cases, only the financial services provider which, pursuant to the regulations of the financial instruments exchange or authorized financial instruments business association where the issuer has listed or registered the securities, has been registered in advance with the financial instruments exchange or authorized financial instruments business association as the financial services provider who will conclude an underwriting contract is permitted to do so (Article 20 (2) of the Financial Instruments and Exchange Act Implementing Order). Next, the parties that can entrust, etc. stabilizing transactions are directors of the issuer, owners of securities related to the relevant secondary distribution, etc., directors of companies that have close relations with the issuer and their companies, and parties which, pursuant to the regulations of the financial instruments exchange, have been registered in advance with the relevant financial instruments exchange as parties to which the issuer entrusts, etc. the stabilizing transactions (Article 20 (3) of the Financial Instruments and Exchange Act Implementing Order).

(ⅲ)   Location and period

As for the location, stabilizing transactions may be effected only through sale

*861*

and purchase of securities or market transactions of derivatives conducted on the financial instruments exchange market that has been stated or recorded in the prospectus, etc. (Article 22(1) of the Financial Instruments and Exchange Act Implementing Order). The period, in cases of public offerings or secondary distributions of securities, fundamentally must be from 20 days prior to the date on which the period for the application for acquisition of securities related to the public offering or secondary distribution ends until the day on which such period ends (Article 22(2)).

(iv) Price

Price is central to the regulations on stabilizing transactions, and this is regulated in the following three parts. To begin with, the first stabilizing transaction effected on the commencement day of stabilizing transactions cannot exceed the lesser of the closing price of the relevant securities on the principal financial instruments exchange market or over-the-counter securities market on the day before the first day of the period in which stabilizing transactions can be conducted, or the closing price of the relevant securities on the principal financial instruments exchange market or over-the-counter securities market on the day before the commencement day of stabilizing transactions (Article 24(1)(i)(a) and (2) of the Financial Instruments and Exchange Act Implementing Order). As for the public offering or secondary distribution price of the securities concerned in the stabilizing transactions and the market price immediately prior to conducting stabilizing transactions, any purchases and sales, etc. exceeding the relevant issue price or secondary distribution price can be made regardless of the price restrictions of the stabilizing transactions, and sales and purchases, etc. that exceed the immediately previous price and will lift the market price of the securities are even allowed.[43]

Second, stabilizing transactions effected after the first stabilizing transaction on the commencement day cannot exceed the price of the initial stabilizing transaction conducted by the financial services provider (Article 24(1)(i)

---

43  Katsuro Kanzaki, Masashi Shitani and Yasuhiro Kawaguchi, *Kinyu shohin torihiki ho* [Financial Instruments and Exchange Act] (Seirin Shoin, 2012), pp. 1338-1339.

Chapter 8　Market abuse regulation

(b) and (2) of the Financial Instruments and Exchange Act Implementing Order). Third, stabilizing transactions effected after the commencement day of stabilizing transactions cannot exceed the lesser of the price at the commencement of the stabilizing transaction or the closing price of the relevant securities on the principal financial instruments exchange market or over-the-counter securities market on the day before the stabilizing transaction is scheduled (Article 24 (1) (ii) and (2) of the Financial Instruments and Exchange Act Implementing Order). Furthermore, regarding these provisions as well, stated differently, as long as these prices are not exceeded, any sales and purchases exceeding the immediately previous price of the relevant securities can be conducted as stabilizing transactions.[44]

（ⅴ） Disclosure to investors regarding manipulation to stabilize prices

Disclosure to investors regarding manipulation to stabilize prices is conducted via i) prospectus, ii) stabilizing transaction notification, iii) stabilizing transaction report, and iv) individual representation by financial services providers.

ⅰ） Prospectus

First, as for stabilizing transactions or their offering, or entrustment or being entrusted, the following must be stated in the prospectus regarding the public offering or secondary distribution of securities that is being facilitated by the relevant stabilizing transactions (Article 21 of the Financial Instruments and Exchange Act Implementing Order): a statement that stabilizing transactions may be conducted (Article 21 (i)); in cases where the relevant securities are listed securities (or over-the-counter listed securities), all names and trade names of the financial instruments exchange markets (or over-the-counter securities markets) on which stabilizing transactions occur and of the financial instruments exchanges (or authorized financial instruments business associations) that establish such financial instruments exchange markets (or such over-the-counter securities markets) and the name or trade name of the financial instruments exchange

---

44　Id., pp. 1339-1340.

*863*

market (or over-the-counter securities market) whereon the principal stabilizing transactions are expected to occur and of the financial instruments exchange (or authorized financial instruments business association) that establishes such financial instruments exchange market (or such over-the-counter securities market) (Article 21 (ii) (iii)). When these statements are lacking, no person can legally conduct or entrust or be entrusted with stabilizing transactions. This still applies in cases where the delivery of a prospectus for making persons acquire or sell the securities thorough public offering or secondary distribution is not required. That is, even in cases where it is not required to submit a report to the Prime Minister regarding a public offering or secondary distribution of securities, to legally conduct, entrust or be entrusted with stabilizing transactions to facilitate the public offering or secondary distribution requires preparation of a prospectus and statement of the above-mentioned items. [45]

ⅱ) Stabilizing transaction notification

The financial services provider that conducted stabilizing transactions on the commencement day of stabilizing transactions must, immediately after conducting the first stabilizing transaction, submit a stabilizing transaction notification stating the relevant financial services provider's trade name, the issue of the securities subject to the relevant stabilizing transaction, the concluded transaction price, etc. to the Commissioner of the Financial Services Agency and to each financial instruments exchange that lists the securities (and each authorized financial instruments business association where the securities are registered) (Article 23 of the Financial Instruments and Exchange Act Implementing Order).

In cases where multiple financial services providers conduct stabilizing transactions on the commencement day of stabilizing transactions, all of these financial services providers are required to submit a stabilizing transaction notification, regardless of whether before or after those transactions. [46] In contrast, financial services providers that conduct stabilizing transactions after the date on which another financial services

---

**45** Id., p. 1349.

Chapter 8　Market abuse regulation

provider already conducted a stabilizing transaction are not required to submit a stabilizing transaction notification.

Stabilizing transaction notifications must be made available for public inspection for one month from the date they are received by the Commissioner of the Financial Services Agency (Article 26 (1) (i) of the Financial Instruments and Exchange Act Implementing Order), and they must also be made available for public inspection for one month from the date of submission at the financial instruments exchanges and authorized financial instruments business associations to which they are submitted. The relevant documents are made available for public inspection after the first stabilizing transaction is conducted, and they may be considered an effort to inform the market about the names of the securities for which stabilizing transactions were conducted as well as about the high likelihood that another stabilizing transaction will be conducted for those securities (financial services providers that have conducted stabilizing transactions even once are deemed to be highly likely to conduct stabilizing transactions thereafter).[47]

  ⅲ）　Stabilizing transaction report

Financial services providers that have conducted stabilizing transactions must, with regard to the sale and purchases of securities subject to stabilizing transactions made during the period between the day the first stabilizing transaction is conducted and the last day of the stabilizing transaction period, submit stabilizing transaction reports stating the details of the relevant purchases and sales to the Commissioner of the Financial Services Agency and to the financial instruments exchange or authorized financial instruments business association that operates the financial instruments exchange market or over-the-counter securities market where

---

46　Id., p. 1344. Persons who entrusted stabilizing transactions to a financial services provider on the commencement day of stabilizing transactions are not persons who directly conducted stabilizing transactions, so they are not required to submit a stabilizing transaction notification (this is submitted by the entrusted financial services provider).

47　Id., p. 1345.

*865*

the relevant stabilizing transactions took place by the day after the day the relevant purchases and sales were conducted (Article 25 of the Financial Instruments and Exchange Act Implementing Order). The relevant documents must be submitted for all sales and purchases during the relevant stabilizing transaction period, even if a financial services provider conducts a stabilizing transaction of given securities only once, regardless of whether the subsequent transactions are stabilizing transactions. The purpose of requiring financial services providers that conduct stabilizing transactions to report all sales and purchases of the subject securities during the stabilizing transaction period in this way is apparently from the understanding that a financial services provider that conducted stabilizing transactions even once has a large potential for artificially manipulating the market price of the relevant securities thereafter. [48]

Stabilizing transaction reports must be made available for public inspection for one month from the day after the last day of the stabilizing transaction period (Article 26 (1) (ii) of the Financial Instruments and Exchange Act Implementing Order), and they must also be made available for public inspection for one month at the financial instruments exchanges and authorized financial instruments business associations to which they are submitted.

iv) Individual representations by financial services providers
Financial services providers that have conducted or been entrusted, etc. with stabilizing transactions must represent that stabilizing transactions have taken place, when selling or being entrusted with the purchase of shares, etc. issued by the issuer of the securities that are the subject of the relevant stabilizing transactions or when being entrusted with securities-related derivatives transactions concerning the sale and purchase of the relevant securities from the time the first stabilizing transaction is conducted until the last day of the period in which stabilizing transactions can be conducted (Article 38 (vii) of the Financial Instruments and Exchange Act, and Article 117 (xxiii) of the Cabinet Office Ordinance on Financial Instruments

---

[48]  Id., pp. 1346-1347.

Chapter 8　Market abuse regulation

Business, etc.). This is to ensure that persons acting to purchase the relevant securities from or entrust the purchase of such securities to financial services providers know that stabilizing transactions have been conducted, to ensure that their purchasing decisions are rational.[49]

## 3. Liability for violation of Article 159 of the FIEA

### a. Criminal liability

Persons who violate Article 159 are subject to punishment by imprisonment with required labor for not more than 10 years or a fine of not more than ¥10 million, or both (Article 197 (1) (v) of the FIEA). Corporations are also subject to dual criminal liability of a fine of not more than ¥700 million (Article 207 (1) (i)).[50] Persons that, by committing the crime referred to in Article 197, paragraph 1, item (v) and for the purpose of gaining economic benefit, cause the market price of securities, etc. to fluctuate and conduct sales, purchases, etc. of those securities, etc. at the market price they have caused to fluctuate are subject to punishment by imprisonment with required labor for not more than ten years or a fine of not more than ¥30 million (Article 197 (2) of the FIEA). Also, the assets gained through the crime set forth in FIEA Article 197, paragraph 1, item (v) of the FIEA are subject to confiscation or collection in principle (Article 198-2).[51]

### b. Civil liability and administrative monetary penalties

In addition, violations of Article 159 are subject to administrative monetary penalties (Articles 174, 174-2 and 174-3 of the FIEA) and civil liability (Article 160). The number of cases where orders to pay administrative monetary penalties are issued has been on a rising trend year by year.[52] Like the cases with criminal penalties, these are almost all cases of market manipulation through the actual purchase and sale of shares.[53] As for civil liability, persons who violate the regulations prohibiting market manipulation (Article 159) are liable to compensate for damages suffered from purchases and sales of securities, etc. in connection with a financial instrument whose price the person formed through that violation, which damages are incurred by any person that conducts or entrusts another person with conducting

---

**49** Id., p. 1347.

*867*

50  In fact, many cases where criminal penalties are imposed for violations of this article are cases of market manipulation where shares were actually bought and sold (or simultaneously with false purchases and sales, collusion purchases and sales, or stabilizing transactions): for example, Tokyo District Court Judgment of May 19, 1993 (*Hanrei Times* No. 817, p. 221) [Fujita Kanko share price manipulation case / case of market manipulation through actual purchases and sales]; Tokyo District Court Judgment of December 7, 1981 (*Hanrei Jiho* No. 1048, p. 164) [Japan Drop Forge share manipulation case / case where market manipulation through actual purchases and sales, false sales and purchases, and collusion sales and purchases were recognized]; Supreme Court Decision of July 20, 1994 (Supreme Court Reports (criminal cases) Vol. 48 No. 5, p. 201) [Kyodo Shiryo market manipulation case / case where market manipulation through actual purchases and sales and stabilization manipulation were recognized]; Tokyo District Court Judgment of October 3, 1994 (*Hanrei Times* No. 875, p. 285) [Nihon Unisys share price manipulation case / case where market manipulation through actual purchases and sales and false purchases and sales were recognized]; Osaka District Court Judgment of June 24, 1999 (*Shiryoban Shoji Homu* No. 187, p. 204) [Showa Chemical Industry market manipulation case / case where market manipulation through actual purchases and sales and false purchases and sales were recognized]; Tokyo District Court Judgment of Nov. 11, 2003 (*Hanrei Jiho* No. 1850, p. 151) [Shimura Kako share price manipulation case / case where market manipulation through actual purchases and sales, false purchases and sales, and collusion purchases and sales were recognized]; Tokyo High Court Judgment of Sept. 7, 2005 (*Hanrei Times* No. 1208, p. 314) [Cats illegal share manipulation case / case where market manipulation through actual purchases and sales, false purchases and sales, and collusion purchases and sales were recognized]; Tokyo District Court Judgment of April 28, 2010 (*Hanrei Times* No. 1365, p. 251); and Tokyo District Court Judgment of July 4, 2014 [ID 28223049] [case where market manipulation through actual purchases and sales and false purchase and sales were recognized]. One case where criminal penalties were imposed which recognized false purchases and sales and collusion purchases and sales concerning share options transactions is the Supreme Court Judgment of July 12, 2007 (Supreme Court Reports (criminal cases) Vol. 61 No. 5, p. 456) [Osaka Securities Exchange false and collusion transactions case].

51  Cases primarily concerning Article 198-2 of the FIEA include the Tokyo High Court Judgment of Sept. 7, 2005 (*Hanrei Times* No. 1208, p. 314) "Cats illegal share manipulation case" and Fukuoka High Court ruling of Jan. 25, 2013 (*Koken Sokuho* 2013, p. 237).

52  The numbers of market manipulation cases where orders to pay administrative surcharges were issued were five cases in 2010, four in 2011, 10 in 2012, 10 in 2013, 10 in 2014, 9 in 2015, 11 in 2016 and 2 in 2017. Financial Services Agency "Table of Administrative Surcharge Orders, Etc." http://www.fsa.go.jp/policy/kachoukin/05. html (last accessed Sep. 15, 2017).

Chapter 8 Market abuse regulation

such a purchase and sale of securities, etc. at the so-formed price (Article 160(1)). This right to claim compensatory damages extinguishes if it is not exercised within one year from when the claimant learns that a violation has taken place or within three years from when the violation place (Article 160 (2)). This provision is designed to protect investors who suffer damage from transactions relying on illegally manipulated market prices; and while it may be said to demonstrate a harsh stance toward market manipulation, it is not easy for investors to obtain relief as long as the interpretation is that the investor bears the burden of proof.[54]

# C. Prohibition on the spreading of rumors, and use of fraudulent means (Article 158 of the FIEA)

## 1. Background and purpose of enactment of Article 158 of the FIEA

Article 158 of the Financial Instruments and Exchange Act (FIEA) prohibits "spreading of rumors, use of fraudulent means, or assault or intimidation." Its origin is traced to Article 32, paragraph 4 of Japan's former Commodity Exchange Act initially enacted in 1914.[55] Article 158 prohibits the spreading of false rumors, use of fraudulent means, or assault or intimidation for the purpose of causing a fluctuation in market price. The intent of this provision was to regulate market manipulation in general, a matter that had not been previously addressed under Japanese law.[56] On the

---

53 Id.

54 Mitsuo Kondo, Kazushi Yoshihara and Etsuro Kuronuma, *Kinyushohin torihiki ho nyumon dai-4 han* [Financial Instruments and Exchange Act Introduction 4th Edition] (Shoji Homu, 2015), p. 333; Katsuro Kanzaki, Masashi Shitani and Yasuhiro Kawaguchi, *Kinyu shohin torihiki ho* [Financial Instruments and Exchange Act] (Seirin Shoin, 2012), pp. 1314-1315. For example, the Mitsubishi Estate case (Tokyo District Court Judgment of April 27, 1981, *Hanrei Jiho* No. 1020, p. 129) was a civil suit regarding market manipulation, but it was dismissed.

55 Etsuro Kuronuma, [Commentary] *Shoji Homu* No. 1557, p. 25; Yasuhiko Kubota in Masao Kishida (ed.), *Chushaku kinyu shohin torihiki ho dai-3 kan* [Financial Instruments and Exchange Act annotated: volume 3] (Kinyu Zaisei Jijo Kenkyu Kai, 2010), p. 10.

*869*

other hand, the Securities and Exchange Act enacted in 1948 contained general prohibitions against market manipulation under Article 159,[57] which was effectively patterned after U.S. law. Notably, Article 159, paragraph 2 prohibited market manipulation by means of misrepresentation. Consequently, the scope of its provisions overlapped extensively with the scope of Article 158 of the FIEA. However, the application of Article 159, paragraph 2 of the FIEA was predicated on "the purpose of inducing transaction," while Article 158 of the FIEA is predicated on "the purpose of carrying out a Public Offering, Secondary Distribution, purchase and sale or other transactions of Securities, or a Derivatives Transaction," or "the purpose of causing a fluctuation in the market price." Moreover, there are some differences between the requirements applicable to the acts prohibited by Article 159 and those applicable to the "spreading of rumors" and "use of fraudulent means" as prescribed by Article 158. Due to this difference, an act that does not come under the requirements of Article 159 may be considered a violation of the FIEA under Article 158.

## 2. Interpretation of Article 158 of the FIEA

Article 158 of the FIEA provides as follows: "It is prohibited for any person to spread rumors, to use fraudulent means, or to commit assault or use intimidation for the purpose of carrying out a Public Offering, Secondary Distribution, purchase and sale or other transaction of Securities, or a Derivatives Transaction, etc. or for the purpose of causing a fluctuation in the market price of a Security, etc. ..." To consider what these provisions specifically prohibit, the following sections shall separately examine "for the purpose of carrying out a Public Offering, Secondary Distribution, purchase and sale or other transaction of Securities, or a Derivatives Transaction, etc.," or "for the purpose of causing a fluctuation in the market price of a Security, etc.," "spread rumors," and "use fraudulent means."

---

**56** At the time, regulation of market manipulation was left to self-regulation by exchanges. Etsuro Kuronuma, [Commentary] *Shoji Homu* No. 1557, pp. 24–25.

**57** At the time of enactment, the relevant provisions were prescribed by Article 125 of the Securities and Exchange Act.

*870*

Chapter 8   Market abuse regulation

a. "... [F]or the purpose of carrying out a public offering, secondary distribution, purchase and sale or other transaction of securities, or a derivatives transaction, etc.," or "for the purpose of causing a fluctuation in the market price of a security, etc. ..."

Article 158 of the FIEA applies when either one of the following two requirements is met: (i) "for the purpose of carrying out a Public Offering, Secondary Distribution, purchase and sale or other transaction of Securities, or a Derivatives Transaction, etc.," or (ii) "for the purpose of causing a fluctuation in the market price of a Security, etc." Requirement (i) is interpreted to mean for conducting securities transactions that are advantageous to self or a third party, or causing a third party to conduct a securities transaction (purchase, sales and exchange of Securities, takeover bid and exercise of stock option, etc., or any other transactional actions causing the party to acquire or lose, change rights of Securities) that is disadvantageous to a third party. It does not necessitate the offender to have undertaken a transaction.[58] (ii) is interpreted to mean the intent to cause the market price to rise or to fall. In this context, "market" is not limited to stock exchanges and OTC "markets" for securities transactions, and the sufficient condition for "market" is interpreted to be any situation where demand and supply for the securities in question is objectively reflected.[59] Requirement (ii) necessitates a decision to be made on the intent to cause a fluctuation in the market price of a security, etc. based on circumstantial evidence.[60] The intent to even stabilize the market price is also interpreted to come under "for the purpose of causing a fluctuation in the market price of a Security, etc.," as this is also considered to be a form of artificial manipulation.[61]

---

58  Mitsuo Kondo in Kanda, Matsuo and Kuronuma (eds.), *Kinyu shohin torihiki ho konmentaru* ⟨4⟩ [Financial Instruments and Exchange Act: commentary ⟨4⟩] (Shoji Homu, 2011), p. 16; Yasuhiko Kubota in Kishida (ed.), p. 12. Takeo Suzuki and Ichiro Kawamoto, *Shoken torihiki ho (Shinpan)* [Securities and Exchange Act (revised)] (Yuhikaku, 1984), p. 553.

59  Tetsuo Seki, *Hanrei Times* No. 971 (1998), p. 95, 97.

60  Shoken Hosei Kenkyukai (ed.), *Chikujo kaisetsu shoken torihiki ho* [Securities and Exchange Act annotated] (Shoji Homu, 1995), p. 1267.

61  Mitsuo Kondo in Kanda, Matsuo and Kuronuma (eds.), p. 17; Yasuhiko Kubota in Kishida (ed.), p. 13. Court rulings affirming this interpretation include Tokyo District Court Judgment of February 18, 2010 (*Hanrei Times* No. 1330, p. 275).

*871*

b. Spreading of rumors

"Spreading of rumors" is interpreted to constitute the act of causing to propagate (with the possibility of propagation, of which possibility the violator is aware) rumors that are without any rationale to the general public or to a large number of persons.[62] There is no requirement for the rumor to be false. However, it is necessary for the violator to know that the rumor is without any rationale.[63]

"Spreading of rumors" has been affirmed in a number of court rulings. The TSD Case and the TOH-TEN-KOH Case are reviewed below.

(ⅰ) TSD Case[64]

[Facts of the Case]

The defendant in this case was the representative director (hereinafter, Defendant Y) of Company A, a computer software company. Pressured to procure funds for the redemption of convertible bonds, Defendant Y released the following information to journalists of the Z Broadcasting Company and others at the Tokyo Stock Exchange press club. Company A had acquired the patent rights to an AIDS vaccine developed by Professor C of Medical School B. A joint venture company had already been established in Thailand for the purpose of manufacturing the AIDS vaccine, and clinical trials had been launched. A decision had also been made in Russia to launch clinical trials and participate in joint research. In reality, however, clinical trials had not started in Thailand, and a joint venture company for manufacturing the AIDS vaccine had not been established. Moreover, a formal agreement had not yet been signed for clinical trials or joint research in Russia.

---

62  Kuniji Shibahara, *Keizai keiho kenkyu (ge)* [Studies in business criminal law (vol. 2)], p. 654; Masao Yanaga, *Jurist* No. 1414 (2011), p. 242; Kuronuma, p. 24, 26; Kubota in Kishida (ed.), pp. 11-12.

63  Shoken Hosei Kenkyukai (ed.), p. 701; Mitsuo Kondo in Kanda, Matsuo and Kuronuma, 17. Note that, as discussed in subsequent sections, the conveyance of false statements was recognized in almost all court rulings that affirmed the spreading of rumors.

64  Tokyo District Court Judgment of March 22, 1996 (*Hanrei Jiho* No. 1566, 143; *Hanrei Times* No. 912, p. 264). Commentaries on this judgment include: Akira Morita, *Jurist* special edition: commentary on important judgment of 1996 (No. 1113, 1996), p. 105; Tetsuo Seki, p. 95; Takeaki Kasahara, *Jurist* No. 1152 (1999), p. 174; Kuronuma, p. 24.

*872*

Chapter 8　Market abuse regulation

Defendant Y was aware that the announced information was false, and had made the announcement with the intent to push up the price of the shares of Company A and to thereby promote the conversion of convertible bonds issued by Company A to shares. Defendant Y was prosecuted for the spreading of rumors in violation of Article 158 of the Securities and Exchange Act for the purpose of causing a fluctuation in the market price of shares.

[Judgment]

"The details of the announcement in this case were, without exception, falsehoods without any rationale. As Defendant Y was cognizant of this matter, it is clear that Defendant Y engaged in the spreading of rumors.... The defense attorney claimed that the announcement was no more than an exaggeration and did not constitute the spreading of rumors in that the announcement merely represented future possibilities as if they had already taken place. However, the announcement in this case was not presented as a projection of future events predicated on certain conditions, and clearly constituted a falsehood in that it represented future possibilities as realized facts. A clear difference in reliability exists between future possibilities and realized facts, and it is obvious that this has a material impact on investors. Therefore, it must be concluded that the act of publicizing future possibilities as realized facts constitutes the spreading of rumors."

(ⅱ)　TOH-TEN-KOH Case[65]

[Facts of the Case]

The defendant in this case (hereinafter, Defendant Y) had purchased a large number of shares of Company A in margin transactions, and had submitted the shares of Company A to the securities company as substitute securities in lieu of cash collateral. A decline in the price of the said shares resulted in a deposit shortage, at which time the securities company issued strong demands for the submission of additional collateral. At this time, Defendant Y conspired with Z and others and caused Z to submit a false Report of

---

**65**　Tokyo District Court Judgment of November 8, 2002 (*Hanrei Jiho* No. 1828, p. 142). For commentary on this judgment, see Hideyuki Matsui, *Jurist* No. 1279 (2004), p. 147.

*873*

Possession of Large Volume of Shares averring that Z had come to possess the equivalent of approximately 20 percent of the shares of Company A. Defendant Y then conspired to push up the price of the shares by announcing a takeover bid for the shares of Company A. Thereupon, Defendant Y transmitted a facsimile (hereinafter, Document) in the name of Z to the coordinating manager of the Tokyo Stock Exchange press club announcing the takeover bid. In a press conference held four days later at the Tokyo Stock Exchange press club, Defendant Y announced the postponement of the takeover bid.[66] Defendant Y was prosecuted for the spreading of rumors in violation of Article 158 of the Securities and Exchange Act and other crimes for the purpose of causing a fluctuation in the market price of shares.

[Judgment]

"While having absolutely no intention to undertake a takeover bid, Defendant Y publicized the intent to launch a takeover bid in a press announcement with the intent to push up the price of the shares of Company A. In the first instance, the purpose of this action was to increase the collateral value of the shares of Company A that had been submitted as substitute securities in lieu of cash collateral, and to thereby create conditions for engaging in further securities transactions by raising the limit on margin transactions. Furthermore, Defendant Y intended to realize profits at an appropriate timing by selling his shares of Company A at a high price. In other words, Defendant Y and others conspired with common intent to cause a fluctuation in the market price of the shares of Company A, and cooperated in publicizing a fictitious plan for launching a takeover bid for the shares of Company A. It can be determined that by transmitting the Document containing related falsehoods to the Tokyo Stock Exchange press club, Defendant Y and others created a condition in which the falsehoods could be propagated to the general public. Therefore, it is clear that the acts of Defendant Y and others constitute the spreading of rumors as prescribed by Article 158 of the Securities and Exchange Act."

---

**66** This was the first case in which a violation of regulations on the disclosure of large-volume holdings of shares was recognized. Although important issues were argued in this case, these are not discussed in the present paper.

*874*

Chapter 8　Market abuse regulation

（ⅲ）　Other court cases

As shown above, in the TSD Case, the act of publicizing false statements concerning the start of clinical trials and other claims, and in the TOH-TEN-KOH Case, the act of publicizing false statements concerning plans to launch a takeover bid were determined to constitute the "spreading of rumors" upon causing the false statements to be conveyed to the general public. In numerous other court cases, the conveyance of false statements has been determined to constitute the "spreading of rumors," and violators have been found liable.

Instances involving charges of spreading rumors that preceded the TSD Case include the Nihon Rare Metals Industry Case.[67] In this instance, whereas Company A was experiencing poor business performance, the representative director of Company A acted to procure operating funds by spreading exaggerated reports claiming that the future prospects of the company were extremely favorable in order to push up the price of the shares of Company A that were traded on the "special stock market." Specifically, the representative director provided fictitious explanations to more than ten members of the securities industry and securities journalists claiming that Company A had entered into a capital alliance with a major trading company for launching a new business. The Tokyo District Court determined that the presentation of fictitious explanations constituted the spreading of rumors for the purpose of causing a fluctuation in market price and handed down a guilty verdict.

Another case is the Ohmori Company Case,[68] an instance involving the effective owner of Company A, who conveyed false news releases and other materials with the intent to maintain the upward trend in the price of the shares of its parent company, a publicly listed company. The news releases claimed that the company was set to start fixed-rate services for IP mobile

---

**67**　Tokyo District Court Judgment of April 5, 1965 (not recorded in law reports). See Rokuro Tsuruta, "Shoken torihiki wo meguru keiji hanrei no doko" [Trends in criminal judgment on securities transactions], *Jurist* No. 920 (1988), p. 15.

**68**　Tokyo District Court Judgment of September 17, 2008 (*Hanrei Times* No. 1286, p. 331).

*875*

telephone services, for which there was no possibility at the time. It was determined that the "conveyance of news releases, etc. containing false information" constituted the "spreading of rumors."

A third case is the Media Lynks Case,[69] an instance involving representative director Y of Company A, who made false announcements in writing and through the company website with the intent to cause a fluctuation in market price aimed at pushing up the price of the shares of Company A. Firstly, it was announced that payments for the purchase of an issue of convertible bonds with equity purchase warrants had been received in full, whereas payments had not been received for the full amount of the issue. Secondly, it was announced that a portion of the convertible bonds had been converted, and that a capital increase had been implemented. It was determined that these acts constituted the spreading of rumors and the use of fraudulent means. The Judgment stated that the spreading of rumors was recognized in that "...Defendant Company A pretended that payments for the purchase of an issue of convertible bonds had proceeded favorably and had been completed, that the procurement of funds had been implemented smoothly, that a portion of the convertible bonds had been converted, and that Company A had thereupon increased and reinforced its capital. False announcements to this effect were made with the intent to cause a fluctuation in the price of the shares of Company A."

In the Livedoor Case[70] and the Dream Technologies Case,[71] the release of false statements was determined to constitute the spreading of rumors. The Livedoor Case can be outlined as follows. Defendant Y was the representative director and chief executive officer of Company A, whose shares were traded on the Mothers Section of the Tokyo Stock Exchange,

---

**69** Osaka District Court Judgment of May 2, 2005, accessible on the website of the Osaka District Court.

**70** Tokyo High Court Judgment of July 25, 2008 (*Hanrei Times* No. 1302, p. 297). For commentary on this judgment, see Masao Yanaga, p. 242; Kanako Takayama, *Hanrei Jiho* No. 2048, p. 169. Note that the Supreme Court dismissed the appeal (Supreme Court Decision of April 25, 2011, not recorded in law reports).

**71** *Katsudo Jokyo* [Status of activities], August 2003 edition, p. 18.

*876*

Chapter 8   Market abuse regulation

and concurrently a director of Company B, whose shares were also traded on the Mothers Section of the Tokyo Stock Exchange, and which was a subsidiary of Company A. Defendant Y conspired with the directors and employees of Company A to perpetrate the acts described below with the intent to promote the sale or purchase of the shares of Company B and to maintain or increase the price of the shares of Company B. Company C was a wholly owned subsidiary of Company A, and was engaged in the corporate mergers and acquisitions business and other operations, and had previously acquired Company D as a subsidiary. In undertaking an exchange of shares between Company D and Company B to render Company D a wholly owned subsidiary of Company B, Defendant Y exaggerated the corporate value of Company D, and released statements containing falsehoods purporting that "the rate at which shares will be exchanged (1: 1) was based on computations carried out by a third party, and determined based on consultation between the two companies." Upon carrying out a 1:100 split of the shares of Company B, an announcement was made revising the abovementioned rate of the exchange of shares to 100:1. Furthermore, the third quarter business results of Company B were falsified by registering revenues from fake transactions. It was determined that the publication of false information constituted the spreading of rumors as well as the use of fraudulent means.

The Dream Technologies Case can be outlined as follows. Using the Internet, Defendant Y signed up members to his investment advisory service. Thereupon, Defendant Y transmitted emails containing false information to members recommending them to undertake transactions in the shares of Company A with the intent to cause a fluctuation in the price of the shares of Company A and to use such fluctuations to profit from transactions in the shares of Company A. Specifically, Defendant Y transmitted emails containing false information to several dozen members stating, "A very negative development affecting the very existence of Company A has come to my attention. You are advised to sell all your shares in Company A at the opening of tomorrow's trading session." Defendant Y later sent a second email informing the members that the negative news turned out to be false, and instructed members to buy back their shares. It was determined that

*877*

this constituted the spreading of rumors as well as the use of fraudulent means. In this instance, the statement of the existence of a "very negative development affecting the very existence of Company A," whereas no such negative development existed, was deemed to be a falsehood. Unlike other court cases, Defendant Y was in a position to provide his opinion, and not necessarily the facts. However, the falsehood was affirmed in this case on the grounds that the opinion provided by Defendant Y was based on falsehoods.

In almost all past cases,[72] affirmation of the "spreading of rumors" has been based on the conveyance and propagation of false statements to the general public or a large number of persons.

   c. Use of fraudulent means

Next, the "use of fraudulent means" will be examined. This term has been

---

[72] On the other hand, the crime of "spreading of rumors" was affirmed in a certain case notwithstanding that no determination was made on the presentation of false statements. This was the case involving the magazine, *Gyanburu Taitei* (Tokyo Summary Court Judgment of January 30, 1997; *Katsudo Jokyo*, October 1997 edition, p. 6). The case involved Defendant Y, a writer of articles recommending stock transactions and concurrently the representative officer of a registered investment advisory company. After purchasing the shares of Company A and others, Defendant Y schemed to push up the price of the shares so as to sell his holdings at a high price. With regard to articles placed in the securities column of the sealed pages of *Gyanburu Taitei*, a magazine for which Defendant Y served as general editor, the court determined that the articles had been used to spread rumors concerning Company A and others for the purpose of engaging in securities transactions and causing a fluctuation in market price. Specifically, the court found that prior to publishing the articles recommending the purchase of shares, Defendant Y had already purchased the shares he planned to recommend with the intent to profit from the sale of the shares at a high price by using the articles to push up the price of the shares. Because the facts and arguments of the case have not been reported in detail, it remains unclear what grounds were cited in the determination of the "spreading of rumors." (Defendant Y stated his opinion on the purchase of a specific issue. In the Dream Technologies Case, the public release of an unsubstantiated opinion was equated with the propagation of a false statement. It is unclear whether the same reasoning was used in judgment against Defendant Y.) If the "spreading of rumors" was affirmed in the absence of any false statement, it is possible to interpret that this ruling affirmed the "spreading of rumors" based on the conveyance of statements that could not be rationally substantiated.

Chapter 8   Market abuse regulation

interpreted by some to connote "false calculations," as in use of the personal calculations of a corporate director in undertaking securities transactions that should be based on the calculations of the company.[73] However, it is generally understood that the "standard interpretation is that this term denotes trickery or unfair deception or means intended to cause an error in judgment in others."[74]

Though not large in number, there are several court rulings that present interpretations of the "use of fraudulent means." First, there is the Cresvale Securities Case[75] in which the court made two separate determinations of the use of fraudulent means. The first instance of the use of fraudulent means can be outlined as follows: Defendant Y1 was a director of and Defendant Y2 was a vice president of Securities Company A. In selling Princeton Bonds to customers, the two presented materials containing falsehoods claiming that the "instrument had been approved by the authorities," whereas no such approval had been given to Princeton Bonds by either the Ministry of Finance or the Bank of Japan. The second instance of the use of fraudulent means can be outlined as follows: Defendant Y3 was the representative director and chairman of Securities Company A. Defendant Y3 was aware that the mark-to-market value of outstanding assets as reported in the monthly investment management reports of Princeton Bonds received from Princeton Economics in the United States was falsified and exaggerated, or that it was highly likely that the bonds were not being redeemed prior to maturity as indicated in the investment agreement. Notwithstanding this knowledge, in selling Princeton Bonds to customers, Defendant Y3 provided such false explanations as, "Ensuring the safety of customer assets is the primary concern in the management of Princeton Bonds." That is to say, in the Cresvale Securities Case, the presentation of materials containing false information (claiming that the

---

73   Hideki Kanda, Nomura Shoken and Kazuo Kawamura (eds.), *Chukai shoken torihiki ho* [Securities and Exchange Act annotated] (Yuhikaku, 1997), pp. 1141–1142.

74   Kubota in Kishida (ed.), p. 12.

75   *Katsudo Jokyo*, September 2000 edition, "I: Kanshi iinkai no katsudo jokyo, dai 2 sho dai 2 no 2 (5) & (6)" [I: Status of activities of the Surveillance Commission, Ch. 2 Sect. 2-2 (5) & (6)]

*879*

financial instrument in question had been approved by the authorities), and the provision of false explanations claiming that Princeton Bonds were safe were determined to constitute the use of fraudulent means. Also, in other cases also, the conveyance of false information has been recognized as constituting the use of fraudulent means.

A case in point is the MTCI Case,[76] which can be outlined as follows. Defendant Y was the representative director and chairman of Company A. Upon a public offering of new shares in Company A, Defendant Y schemed to convey false information to cause a large number of general investors to subscribe to the public offering. Thereupon, at speeches given in seminars and other opportunities, Defendant Y publicized falsehoods by stating to large numbers of general investors that Company A was debt free, and that Company A was committed to thorough disclosure. It was determined that fraudulent means had been used to promote the public offering of shares. A second instance is found in the case of the use of fraudulent means in the acquisition of ICF Securities,[77] which can be outlined as follows. Defendants Y1, Y2, Y3 and Y4 conspired to conduct an exchange of shares between Company A, a company effectively owned by one of the defendants, and Company B in an exchange that would render Company A a wholly owned subsidiary of Company B. Thereupon, the defendants conspired to overstate the corporate value of Company A, and used fraudulent means to publicize that the rate of the exchange of shares based on the agreement concluded between Company A and Company B on the exchange of shares, and the number of new shares to be issued subsequent to the exchange were justified. For this purpose, fake transactions and profits purportedly generated by these fake transactions were registered in the accounts of Company A to convey the impression that the business performance of Company A would dramatically improve in the future. Furthermore, while Company A was actually in a state of negative net worth, the defendants overstated the corporate value of Company A by using the guise of the issuance of new capital and other means. Following the decision of the board

---

76  *Katsudo Jokyo*, August 2003 edition, pp. 19-20.
77  *Katsudo Jokyo*, August 2008 edition, pp. 84-85.

Chapter 8  Market abuse regulation

of directors of Company B, an agreement was concluded for rendering Company A a wholly owned subsidiary of Company B. It was determined that the release of information containing falsehoods constituted the use of fraudulent means for the purpose of the transaction of securities. Moreover, the use of fraudulent means has also been recognized in cases involving simultaneous determination of the spreading of rumors and use of fraudulent means (the above-mentioned Dream Technologies Case, Media Lynks Case, and Livedoor Case).

It has been pointed out that there has been a trend in recent years to make a determination of "use of fraudulent means" as defined under Article 158 of the FIEA in cases involving fictitious capital increase.[78] Such cases can be typically outlined as follows. As the first step, the first party asks a publicly listed company to make a third-party share allocation to the first party. The listed company announces the successful completion of the capital increase but, concurrently, is led to return the payments it has previously received. Meanwhile, the first party sells the shares obtained through the capital increase to realize a profit.

A case in point is the Paint House Case,[79] which can be outlined as follows. Whereas Company A was experiencing poor business performances, Defendant Y, an operator of an investment advisory service and other businesses, was requested to provide support for the rehabilitation of Company A. Thereupon, Defendant Y caused Company A to make a third-party share allocation to Company B, an investment fund controlled by Defendant Y. The funds paid into Company A for the purchase of the newly

---

78  For details, see Tsukasa Okamoto, "Fukosei fainansu ni kakaru gikei no kokuhatsu" [Prosecution of use of fraudulent means in unlawful finance] (*Kinyu Homu Jijo* No. 1900), p. 64; Kazuhiro Takei and Teruhisa Ishii, "Nihonban 10b-5 to shiteno kinshoho 158 jo (jo) (chu) (ge)" [Article 158 of the Financial Instruments and Exchange Act as the Japanese version of 10b-5 (vol. 1), (vol. 2), (vol. 3)] (2010), *Shoji Homu* No. 1904, p. 22; No. 1906, p. 104.

79  Tokyo District Court Judgment of February 18, 2010 (*Hanren Times* No. 1330, p. 275). Another case is the Union Holding Case (Osaka District Court Judgment of August 18, 2010), accessible on the website of the Osaka District Court. For details, see Okamoto, p. 71; Takei and Ishii, *Shoji Homu* No. 1904, pp. 22-23.

*881*

issued shares were immediately transferred outside the company. Notwithstanding this fact, false information was announced to the effect that Company A had procured substantial amounts through the capital increase, which would now be used in the acquisition of assets, payment of expenses and other purposes. Concurrently, the shares acquired by Company B were sold to realize a profit. The adjudicating court ruled as follows on the question of the use of fraudulent means. "Whereas Company B acquired 278, 000 newly issued shares through the exercise of share acquisition rights, arrangements had already been made prior to the completion of payments on May 26, 2005 to immediately remove without compensation most of the funds that were to be paid for the acquisition of new shares. The removal of funds was carried out on the next day, May 27, as scheduled. This fact was concealed and the transfer of these funds was outwardly disguised as representing payment for the acquisition of assets. The capital increase was disclosed in an announcement made on May 26, and this was followed by an announcement made on May 31 disclosing that the capital increase was being used to reinforce the capital structure of Company A. These announcements publicized information resulting in the erroneous judgment that the capital increase involving the issuance of 278,000 shares ensured access to substantial funds to be used by Company A for the acquisition of assets, payment of expenses and other purposes. The abovementioned disclosures constitute the use of 'fraudulent means' through the publication of false information."

## 3. Legal liability of violation of article 158 of the FIEA

### a. Criminal liability

A person found in violation of Article 158 of the FIEA is subject to punishment by imprisonment with required labor for not more than ten years or a fine of not more than ten million yen, or both (Article 197-1-5 and 197-2). A corporation found in violation is subject to dual criminal liability of a fine of not more than 700 million yen (Article 207-1-1). As in the case of violations of Article 157, these represent the highest level of criminal penalty prescribed by the FIEA. Property obtained through the commission of criminal acts is subject to confiscation or collection (Article 198-2).

Chapter 8   Market abuse regulation

b. Civil liability and administrative monetary penalties

As in the case of Article 157 or Article 158 of the FIEA does not provide for the filing of claims for compensatory damages due to violation of its provisions.[80] However, under other provisions contained in the FIEA (Article 21-2, Article 24-2, etc.), it is possible to pursue the civil liability of an offending publicly listed company and its directors, etc. if an act determined to constitute the "spreading of rumors" or "use of fraudulent means" comes under the inclusion of a "false statement about a material matter" in a statutory disclosure document or the omission of a "statement of material fact, or a statement of fact that is necessary to prevent it from being misleading" in a statutory disclosure document. In fact, in the Livedoor Case, the factitious nature of statutory disclosure documents, including the Annual Securities Report, was a point of contention.[81] A problem remains when the "spreading of rumors" or "use of fraudulent means" does not meet the above requirements. It is notable that the cases described above include instances of the "spreading of rumors" and "use of fraudulent means" by persons other than the issuer of shares, as well as the "spreading of rumors" and "use of fraudulent means" that take forms other than the inclusion of false statements in statutory disclosure documents by the issuer of shares. In such instances, as in the case of violations of Article 157, claims for compensatory damages have to be filed under Article 709 and other provisions of the Civil Code.

Administrative monetary penalties may be applied when the spreading of rumors or the use of fraudulent means has impacted the price of securities, etc. (Article 173). On the other hand, administrative monetary penalties do not apply on instances of assault or intimidation.[82]

---

80   It appears that civil liability for violation of Article 158 has not been discussed because no civil case has ever been filed for violation of Article 158. (Articles 157 and 158 differ on this point.)

81   Tokyo District Court Judgment of June 13, 2008 (*Hanrei Times* No. 1294, p. 119); Tokyo High Court Judgment of December 16, 2009 (*Kinyu Shoji Hanrei* No. 1332, p. 7); Tokyo District Court Judgment of May 21, 2009 (*Hanrei Times* No. 1306, p. 124); Tokyo District Court Judgment of June 18, 2009 (*Hanrei Times* No. 1310, p. 198), etc.

*883*

# D. General provision prohibiting "wrongful acts" (Article 157 of the FIEA)

## 1. Background and purpose of enactment of Article 157 of the FIEA

Article 157 of the Financial Instruments and Exchange Act (FIEA) constitutes a general provision prohibiting "wrongful acts." Article 157 in effect carries forward the intent of Article 58 of the Securities and Exchange Act prior to the revision of 2006 as it stood from the time of its original enactment.[83] Article 58 is said to have been modeled after Section 10(b)[84] of the U.S. Securities Exchange Act of 1934, which constitutes the U.S. general provision rule, and SEC Rule 10b-5[85] (hereinafter 10b-5) that comes under this section.[86] Section 10(b) comprises provisions for "regulation of the use of manipulative and deceptive devices." Based on this, the SEC formulated 10b-5 and prohibited the following three matters as related to the purchase or sale of securities: to employ any device, scheme, or artifice to defraud; to make any untrue statement of a material fact or to omit to state a material fact; and to engage in any act, practice, or course of business which operates or would operate as a fraud or deceit upon any person. Pursuant to the

---

82 This is based on the reasoning that the effects of assault and intimidation are limited to their immediate victims, while the effects of the spreading of rumors and use of fraudulent means can extend more widely to the broader market. However, this reasoning has been disputed by some. See Tomonobu Yamashita and Hideki Kanda, *Kinyu shohin torihiki ho gaisetsu* [Outline of the Financial Instruments and Exchange Act] (Yuhikaku, 2010). p. 339.

83 Article 58 of the Securities and Exchange Act became Article 157 in the revision of 1992, and was carried forward as Article 157 of the Financial Instruments and Exchange Act in the revision of 2006. Unless otherwise specified, this chapter uses the text of the article at the time of judicial ruling cited. "Article 58" points to Article 58 of the Securities and Exchange Act prior to the revision of 1992, and "Article 157" points to either Article 157 of the Securities and Exchange Act after the revision of 1992 or Article 157 of the Financial Instruments and Exchange Act. The discussions in this chapter apply equally to the provisions of both articles.

84 15 U.S.C. § 78j(b) (2014).

85 17 C.F.R. 240.10b-5 (2014).

Chapter 8   Market abuse regulation

development of legal precedent, violation of Section 10(b) and 10b-5 has come to be understood to require an act of deception,[87] and the three abovementioned acts can be said to be examples of forms of deception.

The FIEA contains separate and concrete provisions pertaining to unfair transactions (such as Article 158 prohibiting the spreading of rumors, use of fraudulent means, etc.; Article 159 regulating market manipulation, etc.; and Articles 166, 167 and 167-2 regulating insider trading). While the relation between the provisions of Article 157 and those of the other articles may appear to pose some problems, it should be noted that while the other articles regulate the "wrongful acts" prohibited under Article 157, they only address specific aspects and do not encompass all "wrongful acts." On the other hand, the significance of Article 157 can be said to lie in the fact that it is designed to comprehensively regulate "wrongful acts" that cannot be covered by separate and concrete provisions alone.[88] However, as discussed below, the significance of this point has not been fully utilized in practice.[89]

## 2. Interpretation of Article 157 of the FIEA

Article 157 of the FIEA prohibits any person to engage in the following three acts in the course of the purchase and sale or other transaction of securities or a derivatives transaction: using wrongful means, schemes, or techniques (Article 157 (i)); acquiring money or other property through false representation or omission of representation about a material particular (Article 157 (ii)); using false quotations in order to induce transactions (Article 157(iii)). Details of each of the prohibitions are outlined below.

---

**86** Mitsuo Kondo, "Fukosei na shoken torihiki kisei ni kansuru ichikosatsu — shoken Torikiho 157 jo to Kisoku 10b-5 no hikaku" [A study of regulation of unfair securities transactions — a comparison of Article 157 of the Securities and Exchange Act and Rule 10b-5] in *Kawamoto Ichiro sensei koki shukuga: gendai kigyo to yukashoken no hori* [Celebration of 70th birthday of Professor Ichiro Komoto — judicial principles of the modern corporation and securities] (Yuhikaku, 1994), p.172. Some have argued that Section 17(a) of the Securities Act of 1933 also served as a model. See Tetsuo Seki, *Hanrei Times* No.971 (1998), p.95, 97. Actually, as stated below, Article 157 item (iii) is almost a verbatim rendering of Section 17(a)(2) of the Securities Act of 1933.

**87** Santa Fe Industries, Inc. v. Green, 430 U.S. 462 (1977).

a. Article 157, item (i)

Article 157, item (i) prohibits the use of "wrongful means, schemes, or techniques." The term "wrongful" as used in this context is said to be derived from "to defraud" as used in the wording of 10b-5, "to employ any device, scheme, or artifice to defraud."[90] In fact, in much of the academic literature, "wrongful" as used in Item (i) is understood to convey the same significance as 10b-5, so that "wrongful means" is interpreted to denote an "act of deception causing others to fall into error in the purchase or sale of securities."[91]

An early case affirming this interpretation is the Nasu Sulfur Mining Company Case, which involved fake transactions undertaken with no intent to execute the transfer of rights. The fake transactions were executed to

---

**88** Regarding the possible overlap of the scope of application of Article 157 with that of Article 158 (prohibition of spreading of rumors, use of fraudulent means, or assault or intimidation) and Article 159 (prohibition of market manipulation), an argument has been made that the scope of each of these articles was primarily intended to cover the following mutually exclusive areas: Article 157 applies to the informal secondary markets; Article 158 applies to the primary market; and Article 159 applies to transactions executed in formal exchanges or on equivalent over-the-counter markets (Hideki Kanda, Nomura Shoken and Kazuo Kawamura (eds.), *Chukai shoken toriki ho* [Securities and Exchange Act annotated] pp. 1136-1137 (Yuhikaku, 1997)). This has been criticized on the grounds that the provisions of the three articles should be interpreted from the perspective of preventing loopholes in the application of the law, and not from the perspective of avoiding overlap in their scope of application. Yasuhiko Kubota in Masao Kishida (ed.), *Chushaku kinyu shohin torihiki ho dai-3 kan* [Financial Instruments and Exchange Act annotated: volume 3] (Kinyu Zaisei Jijo Kenkyu Kai, 2010), p. 4. See also Katsuro Kanzaki, Masashi Shitani, and Yasuhiro Kawaguchi, *Kinyu shohin torihiki ho* [The Financial Instruments and Exchange Act], (Seirin Shoin, 2012), p. 1193; Mitsuo Kondo in Hideki Kanda, Naohiko Matsuo, and Etsuro Kuronuma (eds.), *Kinyu shohin torihiki ho konmentaru ⟨4⟩* [Financial Instruments and Exchange Act: commentary ⟨4⟩] (Shoji Homu, 2011), p. 6.

**89** However, some scholars have found Article 157 meaningful because this general clause may have some potential to regulate "wrongful means" which is not listed in the FIEA comprehensively. Mitsuo Kondo in Hideki Kanda, Naohiko Matsuo, and Etsuro Kuronuma (eds.) p. 12.

**90** Yasuhiko Kubota in Kishida (ed.), p. 4.

**91** Id.; Kanzaki et al., p. 1195. Note that some room remains for considering whether this is consistent with interpretations given in lower court rulings as discussed below.

*886*

Chapter 8　Market abuse regulation

give the appearance that the shares of a company that actually were of almost no value were marketable. The point of contention in this case was whether the fake transactions violated Article 58 item (i) of the Securities and Exchange Act. The Tokyo High Court[92] ruled as follows on this matter. "It is appropriate to interpret 'wrongful means' to denote... an act of deception causing others to fall into error in the purchase and sale or other transaction of securities for the purpose of realizing a profit for oneself or a third party." While some understand that this represents the majority opinion in academic circles,[93] others argue that "for the purpose of realizing a profit for oneself or a third party" does not constitute a condition, and that the two are not the same.[94] On the other hand, the Supreme Court[95] has determined that "wrongful means" as used in Article 58, item (i) denotes "as limited to and pertaining to securities transactions, any means recognized as wrongful under social norms." This interpretation is recognized to be the closest to the intent of Article 58, item (i), and is also widely accepted in academic circles.[96]

Notwithstanding the broad definition given to Article 58, item (i) by the Supreme Court, this definition has almost never been utilized in subsequent cases. This may be because the wording was equivocal compared to the weight of the statutory penalty.[97] While the argument was made in some civil suits that these provisions had been violated, the number of such cases was minimal. Moreover, even when claimed, the courts did not necessarily

---

92　Tokyo High Court Judgment of July 10, 1963 (Tokyo High Court Criminal Case Newsletter Vol. 14 No. 7, p. 116).

93　Yasuhiko Kubota in Kishida (ed.), p. 5.

94　Kanzaki et al., pp. 1196–1197, fn. 7.

95　Judgment of the Third Petty Bench of the Supreme Court of May 25, 1965 (Supreme Court criminal report No. 155, p. 831).

96　Yasuhiko Kubota in Kishida (ed.), p. 5; Mitsuo Kondo in Hideki Kanda, Naohiko Matsuo, and Etsuro Kuronuma (eds.) p. 8.

97　Violation of this article is punishable by imprisonment with required labor for not more than ten years, a fine of not more than ten million yen, or both, as prescribed by Article 197, paragraph 1, item (v). A corporation found in violation is subject to dual criminal liability of a fine of not more than 700 million yen as prescribed by Article 207, paragraph 1, item (i).

*887*

respond to this argument in all instances.[98] Consequently, interpretations (or some form of suggestion as to the meaning) of Article 58, item (i) can be found in only a very small number of judgment.

In the following two cases, this provision was cited as grounds for, or as a relevant article for, finding the defendant liable. The first case involved a claim for compensatory damages brought against a securities company by a person who had been solicited by the employee of the securities company to engage in transactions in warrants, etc.[99] The employer's liability was recognized based on findings of excessive transaction volumes and violation of obligation of explanation, and the Court referred to Article 157 as an article relevant to the prohibition of excessive volumes of transaction. The second case involved a claim for compensatory damages brought against a securities company by a person who had suffered losses after being solicited by the employee of the securities company to engage in margin transactions, etc.[100] In its judgment, the Court clearly stated that solicitation to engage in excessive transaction volumes was in violation of Article 157, item (i).[101]

On the other hand, there are judgments in which the courts did not find the acts of defendants to be in violation of the provisions of Article 58, item (i) or Article 157, item (i). Examples of this include a case involving ex-post compensation for losses incurred in securities transactions,[102] and a case involving a stock split undertaken to counter a hostile takeover bid.[103] This is the extent of available cases involving some form of interpretation of these

---

**98** The courts did not respond to claims made regarding violation of Article 58 or Article 157 in the following cases: Tokyo High Court Judgment of October 20, 1988 (*Kinyu Shoji Hanrei* No. 813, p. 24) (case involving liability for non-performance of obligation pertaining to solicitation of investment by securities company employee); Osaka High Court Judgment of February 18, 1994 (*Hanrei Jiho* No. 1524, p. 51) (case involving liability for unlawful act of securities company employee who recommended purchase of so-called speculative shares through a different securities company); Tokyo District Court Judgment of February 23, 1998 (*Kinyu Shoji Hanrei* No. 1050, p. 49) (case involving liability for compensatory damages for solicitation of investment trust by securities company employee).

**99** Osaka District Court Judgment of August 29, 1997 (*Hanrei Jiho* No. 1646, p. 113).

**100** Fukuoka District Court Judgment of March 29, 1999 (*Hanrei Times* No. 1026, p. 227).

Chapter 8 Market abuse regulation

provisions, regardless of whether violation of the provisions of Article 58, item (i) or Article 157, item (i) was affirmed or negated.[104]

To be illegal based on this clause, the wrongdoer is interpreted to need not conduct a transaction of securities (with the injured party) by itself while it must know that the transaction in question is wrongful.[105] Moreover, the wrongdoer is interpreted to need not hold securities by itself because this article prohibits "any person" to exercise "wrongful means". Also, Securities relating to "wrongful means" are not necessarily listed.[106]

Furthermore, it is interesting to note the standard response of the legislature when a wrongful act comes to light that had not been originally postulated when the law was enacted. That is, it can be said that, instead of utilizing the

---

101 The Tokyo District Court Judgment of March 31, 1987 (*Kinyu Shoji Hanrei* No. 813, p. 28) (first instance judgment corresponding to the Tokyo High Court Judgment of October 20, 1988) also explicitly states that excessive transaction volumes are in violation of Article 58 item (i). However, as stated above, the Tokyo High Court appellate judgment of October 20, 1988 did not contain any reference to violation of Article 58. The Osaka High Court Judgment of December 26, 2003 (not recorded in law reports) is the appellate judgment corresponding to the first instance judgment rendered by the Wakayama District Court Shingu Branch of June 30, 2003 (not recorded in law reports) that found solicitation by a securities company employee to be in violation of Article 157. While the appellate judgment did recognize the illegality of the solicitation and affirmed liability for the commission of unlawful acts, here again the appellate ruling did not contain any reference to violation of Article 157. Kanda, Kansaku, Osaki, and Matsuo (eds.), *Kinshoho jitsumu keisubukku I hanrei hen* [Casebook of Financial Instruments and Exchange Act in practice, law report I] (Shoji Homu, 2008), p. 291.

102 Tokyo District Court Judgment of May 14, 1998 (*Hanrei Times* No. 976, p. 277); Tokyo High Court Judgment of January 27, 1999 (*Kinyu Shoji Hanrei* No. 1064, p. 21); Supreme Court Judgment of July 7, 2000 (*Kinyu Shoji Hanrei* No. 1096, p. 9; No. 1105, p. 14).

103 Tokyo District Court Judgment of July 29, 2005 (*Hanrei Jiho* No. 1909, p. 87).

104 For judgments pertaining to Article 157, see Kishida, Morita, and Kondo (eds.), *Chikujo shoken torihiki ho — hanrei to gakusetu* [Securities and Exchange Act annotated — judgments and academic theories] (Shoji Homu, 1999), pp. 448-453.

105 Kondo in Kanda et al. (eds.) pp. 8-9; Kubota in Kishida (ed.) p. 3; Kanzaki et al., pp. 1194-1195. However, "wrongful means" in question is interpreted to need to have some relation to purchases, sales, and other transactions of securities. *See supra n. 103.*

106 Kondo in Kanda et al. (eds.) p. 9; Kubota in Kishida (ed.) p. 3; Kanzaki et al., p. 1194.

*889*

general provision found under Article 58 of the Securities and Exchange Act, the legislature has chosen to respond by creating additional rules. A case in point is the Tateho Chemical Industries Company Case, which occurred in 1987 prior to the enactment of explicit provisions regulating insider trading.[107] In this case, the price of the shares of the company plummeted after the company announced in September 1987 that it had incurred large losses in transactions in bond futures. However, a number of insiders, consisting of persons affiliated to the company and its counterparties, who had learned of the loss immediately before the announcement, had sold their shares before the price fell. This incident triggered extensive discussion on how to regulate insider trading. Ultimately, the decision was made to revise the Securities and Exchange Act in three places by adding the following provisions. "Submission of reports on purchase or sale of securities, etc." (Article 188); "Acts prohibited for persons affiliated with a company" (Article 190-2); and "Acts prohibited for persons affiliated with the takeover bid or, etc." (Article 190-3).[108] This is indeed a very interesting fact[109] because while Article 58 did not contain explicit provisions for the regulation of insider trading, it was interpreted that insider trading came under the provisions of Article 58, item (i) that regulates the use of "wrongful means, schemes, or techniques"[110] and the status of this interpretation was such that it was reported that "interpretations contrary to this are hardly ever seen in academic circles."[111]

The same legislative response was seen in various instances of securities scandals, including the ex-post compensation of investor losses and the

---

**107** Such provisions as Article 189, "Request for restitution of wrongful profits earned by an officer or a major shareholder," and Article 190, "Prohibition of short-selling of a company by its officer or major shareholder" did exist at the time. However, from the perspectives of scope of application and effectiveness, these provisions were not sufficient for regulating insider trading.

**108** Provisions with the same intent as these three provisions are prescribed by the current law as follows: "Submission of reports on purchase and sales of specified securities, etc. by the officer of a listed company, etc." (Article 163 of the FIEA), "Acts prohibited for a company insider" (Article 166 of the FIEA), and "Acts prohibited for persons affiliated with the tender offeror, etc." (Article 167 of the FIEA).

*890*

Chapter 8　Market abuse regulation

execution of large-volume sale by recommendation. In both of these instances, the provisions of Articles 157 and Article 58 were not used. Instead, new provisions worded to separately prohibit specific acts were added to the law.[112]

b. Article 157, items (ii) and (iii)

Whereas Article 157, item (i) is an abstract and general provision, Article 157, items (ii) and (iii) exist as derivative provisions designed to facilitate and ensure the realization of the general prohibition of deception contained in item (i).[113]

---

**109** Article 58 of the Securities and Exchange Act was never applied to an insider trading case. Misao Tatsuta, "Naibusha torihiki no koka ni kansuru ripporon teki kosatsu" [Study of the impact of insider trading from the perspective of legislative theory] in *Osumi Kenichiro sensei koki kinen: kigyo ho no kenkyu* [Celebration of 70th birthday of Professor Kenichiro Osumi — study of corporate law] (Yuhikaku, 1977), p. 700. In no instance has administrative disposition, let alone criminal liability, been determined on the basis of Article 58. In academic discussions, it has been argued that Article 709 of the Civil Code can be applied in claiming compensation for damage against a person violating Article 58 through willful negligence. However, it appears that violation of Article 58 has been used as grounds for a civil suit in only one case (Japan Line Case: Tokyo District Court Judgment of October 29, 1991 (*Kinyu Homu Jijo* No. 1321 p. 23)). Akio Takeuchi, "Naibusha torihiki" [Insider trading] in *Kaishaho no riron I* [Theory of Companies Act I] (Yuhikaku, 1984), p. 315; Takeo Suzuki and Ichiro Kawamoto, *Shoken torihiki ho (shinpan)* [Securities and Exchange Act (revised)] (Yuhikaku, 1984), pp. 554–555.

**110** This interpretation is based on the following reasoning. "If it is clear that the counterparty will not undertake a transaction under the same conditions if yet to be announced material information with an impact on a securities investment decision were to be disclosed to the counterparty, undertaking a transaction without disclosing the material information is equivalent to deceiving the counterparty." Katsuro Kanzaki, *Shoken torihiki ho (shinpan)* [Securities and Exchange Act (revised)] (Seirin Shoin, 1987), p. 611.

**111** Suzuki and Kawamoto, p. 554.

**112** Kondo (1994), p. 172. Article 50 prohibiting securities companies and their officers and employees from engaging in specific acts was also added in the revision to address certain problems that were occurring relatively frequently at the time. Seiji Tanaka and Wataru Horiguchi, *Saizentei konmentaru: Shoken torihiki ho* [Commentary on second comprehensive revision: Securities and Exchange Act] (Keiso Shobo, 1996), p. 943.

*891*

Specifically, Item (ii) prohibits the acquisition of money or other property through false representation or omission of representation about important matters.[114] "Important matters" include all matters that may influence reasonable investors judgment. In this context, "important" is generally understood to be determined based on the standard of reasonable investors.[115] Examples of instances in which item (ii) applies are as follows. Whereas the price of the shares of Company A is slumping, a person holding these shares pushes up the price of the shares by using a fake document to claim that Company A is thriving, and thereupon sells his shares. In a similar situation, item (ii) applies when Company A uses a fake document in undertaking the issuance of new shares.[116]

Consequently, these provisions overlap with various other provisions concerning false representation, such as liability for inclusion of false statements, etc. in statutory disclosures (Articles 18, 21, 21-2, 22), and market manipulation by means of representation (Article 159). However, item (ii) differs in that, under its provisions, a violation does not occur if no property has been acquired by means of false representation.[117]

Moving next to item (iii), its provisions prohibit the use of false quotations for the purpose of inducing the purchase and sale or other transaction of securities or a derivatives transaction. As in the case of item (iii), the prohibition of market manipulation by means of actual transaction or by

---

113 Shoken Hosei Kenkyukai (ed.), *Chikujo kaisetsu shoken torihiki ho* [Securities and Exchange Act annotated] (Shoji Homu, 1995), p. 699.

114 Moreover, forecasting without reasonable grounds would be "false representation". Kanzaki et al., p. 1200.

115 Kanzaki et al., pp. 1198-1199.

116 Tomonobu Yamashita and Hideki Kanda (eds.), *Kinyu shohin torihiki ho gaisetu Dai-5han* [Outline of the Financial Instruments and Exchange Act, 5th ed.] (Yuhikaku, 2010), p. 362.

117 The wording of this item is almost identical to the wording of section 17(a)(2) of the U.S. Securities Exchange Act (15 U.S.C. § 77q(a)(2) (2014)), which provides that it is illegal "to obtain money or property by means of any untrue statement of a material fact or any omission to state a material fact necessary in order to make the statements made... not misleading."

*892*

Chapter 8　Market abuse regulation

means of representation (Article 159) becomes applicable only when there is intent to induce transactions. However, an act may be found in violation of item (iii) even if it does not come under the prohibition of market manipulation.

## 3. Legal liability for violation of Article 157 of the FIEA

### a. Criminal liability

A person found in violation of the provisions of Article 157 is subject to punishment by imprisonment with required labor for not more than ten years, a fine of not more than ten million yen, or both (Article 197, paragraph 1, item (v)). A corporation found in violation is subject to dual criminal liability of a fine of not more than 700 million yen (Article 207, paragraph 1, item (i)). These represent the highest level of criminal penal provisions prescribed by the FIEA. Furthermore, property obtained through the commission of criminal acts is subject to confiscation or collection (Article 198-2).

### b. Civil liability and administrative monetary penalty

Article 157 does not provide for a private party to file for compensatory damages incurred as a result of violation of Article 157.[118] As a result, claims for compensatory damages have to be filed under Article 709 and other provisions of the Civil Code.

Furthermore, administrative monetary penalty do not apply to violations of Article 157.

---

**118** At one time, the same held true in the United States. However, shortly after 10b-5 was enacted, a U.S. District Court Judgment handed down in 1946 determined that a private party does have the right to sue under 10b-5. (This is referred to as the "implied private cause of action.") Kardon v. National Gypsum Co. (69 F. Supp. 512 (E.D. Pen. 1946)). No such interpretation has been made in Japan.

*893*

# Chapter **9**

## Enforcement under the FIEA

*Yoko Manzawa*

# A. Legal basis of enforcement

## 1. Overview

The Financial Instruments and Exchange Act (FIEA) is primarily enforced by the Financial Services Agency (FSA) and the Securities and Exchange Surveillance Commission (SESC) by means of criminal penalty, administrative disposition, administrative monetary penalty, prohibition order or order of suspension issued by courts, and civil liability.[1] Additionally, under the supervision of the government, more detailed and flexible enforcement is carried out by self-regulatory organizations (Financial Instruments Exchanges, Authorized Financial Instruments Firms Associations, Certified Financial Instruments Firms Associations). It should be noted that this enforcement system was not operative at all times during the history of enforcement in Japan, and that an enforcement framework unique to Japan was maintained for many years.

The Securities and Exchange Act (renamed the Financial Instruments and Exchange Act in the revision of 2006) was enacted shortly after the end of the Second World War (in 1948) under the direction of the General Headquarters of the Supreme Commander for the Allied Powers (GHQ) and was modeled after the securities exchange legislation of the United States. Enforcement was initially delegated to the Securities and Exchange Commission, an independent body patterned after the Securities and Exchange Commission (SEC) of the United States. However, Japan's Securities and Exchange Commission was abolished in the revision of 1952, and all its powers and administrative functions were transferred to the Ministry of Finance, which thereafter remained responsible for enforcement. Enforcement by the Ministry of Finance was undertaken through numerous directives issued under the name of the Director of the Securities Bureau

---

1 The official announcement of violators was also adopted in the revision of 2013 (Article 192-2 of the FIEA).

Chapter 9   Enforcement under the FIEA

and was complemented with orally conveyed administrative guidance. In total, enforcement was based on a system of protective administration featuring ex-ante preventative measures. The advantage of this approach was that it facilitated very flexible application of the law. On the other hand, it lacked transparency and was prone to the excesses of discretionary administration. This system of centralized securities administration under the Ministry of Finance was harshly criticized as a consequence of the series of securities scandals that occurred in 1991 involving such practices as compensation of investor losses, the hiding of bad loans, and large-volume sales by recommendation. The consensus that emerged was that the Ministry of Finance had not properly supervised the securities companies under its jurisdiction. To improve market supervision and to maintain investor confidence in the markets, the Securities and Exchange Surveillance Commission (SESC) was established in 1992, and responsibility for supervising the securities markets was transferred from the Ministry of Finance to the SESC.

A further step was taken in 1997 when the Financial Supervisory Agency was established in line with the policy of separating the administration of the financial industry from the Ministry of Finance. At this point, the SESC was placed under the Financial Supervisory Agency, but certain functions of financial administration pertaining to the planning and design of the financial system still remained with the Ministry of Finance. However, the Financial Supervisory Agency was reorganized into the Financial Services Agency (FSA) in 2000 with these functions also transferred to the FSA. Finally, the SESC was brought under the FSA. The current system was created as a consequence of this process that ultimately placed the greater part of Japan's securities business administration under the jurisdiction of the FSA and the SESC.

The basic approach to regulation also underwent a change as the enforcement framework shifted from ex-ante preventative administration to ex-post supervisory administration. Pursuant to this change, the FSA worked to increase transparency by compiling and publishing the "Comprehensive Guidelines for Supervision of Financial Instruments

*897*

Business Operators, etc.", a document that sets forth the basic thinking on individual regulations and identifies key points in the supervisory process, as well as the "Inspection Manual for Financial Instruments Business Operators", which explains the basic approach to the inspection of financial instruments business operators.[2]

The previous system of enforcement stipulated enforcement through criminal penalty. This dependence on criminal penalty resulted in the exercise of caution in the application of the system, which undermined effective enforcement. To rectify this situation, measures were taken to reduce the dependence on criminal penalty and diversify the means of enforcement. Specifically, an administrative monetary penalty system was adopted and expanded, legal provisions were made for civil liability, and a financial ADR system was created. Japan had previously adopted a system of prohibition orders and orders of suspension issued by courts that was patterned after the U.S. system of court injunctions. But the system remained unused for many years. As an additional measure, a movement toward active use of prohibition orders and orders of suspension has been seen in recent years.

## 2. Enforcement agencies

### a. Financial Services Agency

By law, authority over the administration of the Financial Instruments and Exchange Act (FIEA) is assigned to the Prime Minister. However, with the exception of certain functions prescribed in Cabinet Orders,[3] a broad range

---

2　Other guidelines have also been formulated that extend beyond regulation for financial instruments business operators to regulation for disclosure and unfair transactions, an example of which is the Points to be Considered Regarding Disclosure of Corporate Affairs (Guideline for the Disclosure of Corporate Affairs). Other procedures have also been established, such as the Prior Confirmation Procedures on the Application of Laws and Regulations (no-action letter system) that allow businesses and others to request prior confirmation on whether their planned actions would be subject to the application of laws and regulations, as well as "written inquiry procedures for general legal interpretation," which complement the no-action letter system by allowing businesses and others to inquire about abstract legal interpretations applicable to hypothetical cases.

*898*

Chapter 9   Enforcement under the FIEA

of authority is delegated to the Commissioner of the FSA (Article 194-7(1) of the FIEA). The FSA, with the Commissioner as its head and functioning as an external bureau of the Cabinet Office, is in this way positioned to function as the enforcement agency of the FIEA. Of the authorities delegated to the FSA, the law provides that those related to ensuring fairness in transactions and acts shall be delegated to the SESC (Article 194-7(2) & (4)). Moreover, authorities related to the collection of reports and inspection may be delegated to the SESC (Article 194-7(3)). Furthermore, of the authorities delegated by the Prime Minister to the FSA Commissioner, the FSA Commissioner may delegate certain authorities to the Director General of the Local Finance Bureau or to the Director General of the Local Finance Branch Bureau (Article 194-7 (6)). Similarly, among the authorities delegated to the SESC, the SESC may delegate certain authorities to the Director General of the Local Finance Bureau or to the Director General of the Local Finance Branch Bureau (Article 194-7(7)).

　　b．Securities and Exchange Surveillance Commission
　　　（i）　Organization
As described above, under the previous system, the administration of securities businesses was centralized under the Ministry of Finance. Consequently, the supervision of securities companies and other operators and the monitoring of the fair management of markets were placed under the jurisdiction of a single government organization. Under this arrangement, the latter monitoring function and powers in many instances were not sufficiently exercised. To rectify this problem, the SESC was established as an agency mandated to monitor legal and regulatory compliance in the markets.

Based on Article 8 of the National Government Organization Act (NGOA),

---

**3**　Article 37-3 of the Financial Instruments and Exchange Act Implementing Order provides the powers related to authorization and rescission of authorization, and licensing and rescission of licensing, including the authorization of the establishment of Authorized Financial Instruments Business Associations and rescission of authorization of the same, and the authorization of the establishment of investor protection funds and rescission of authorization of the same.

*899*

the SESC exists as an agency within the FSA (Article 6(1) of the Financial Services Agency Establishment Act (FSAE)) and functions under a collegiate system with one chairman and two commissioners (Article 10 of the FSAE). The reason that the organization of the SESC was not separated from government ministries[4] is said to reflect the thinking that it would be inappropriate to completely separate market supervision for ensuring fairness from financial administration conducted by the FSA.[5] On the other hand, the independence of the SESC chairman and commissioners in the conduct of their duties is guaranteed by law (Article 9 of the FSAE). Specifically, the status of the chairman and commissioners is protected, so that these officers cannot be dismissed against their will at any time during their tenure (Article 14 of the FSAE), with the exception of such instances as when an officer is deemed unable to perform his or her duties due to a mental or physical disorder, or when an officer is found to have violated one of its obligations in the course of his or her duties or other misconduct unbecoming of the chairman or commissioner. The chairman and commissioners are appointed by the Prime Minister with the consent of both Houses of the Diet (Article 12(1) of the FSAE), and serve a term of three years (with the possibility of re-appointment) (Article 13 of the FSAE).

To facilitate the conduct of its operations, the SESC has an Executive Bureau (Article 19(1) of the FSAE), which oversees the Coordination Division, Market Surveillance Division, Financial Instruments Inspection Division, Administrative Monetary Penalty Division, Disclosure Statements Inspection Division, and Investigation Division. As of fiscal 2017, the Executive Bureau had a personnel quota of 406 staff members. An additional quota of 342 staff members is assigned to perform local SESC operations conducted by the Securities and Exchange Surveillance Department established within local finance bureaus and other agencies. Thus, in total, the SESC Executive Bureau currently has a personnel quota of 748.

---

4   The Japan Fair Trade Commission in charge of the enforcement of the Anti-Monopoly Act, for example, is an independent organization based on Article 3 of the NGOA (a so-called Article 3 commission).

5   Tomonobu Yamashita and Hideki Kanda, *Kinyu shohin torihiki ho gaisetu* [Outline of the Financial Instruments and Exchange Act, 2nd ed.] (Yuhikaku, 2017), p. 477.

*900*

Chapter 9　Enforcement under the FIEA

（ⅱ）　Activities

The activities of the SESC can be summarized as follows.

ⅰ）　Market surveillance

Market surveillance functions as the SESC's "entry point of information." In addition to receiving information from general investors, the SESC cooperates with self-regulatory organizations to collect and analyze various types of information pertaining to the markets. Another function of market surveillance is to uncover transactions and other activities suspected of constituting unfair transactions. Specifically, problems occurring in the markets are identified, and comprehensive and flexible modes of market supervision are developed in order to effectively cope with such problems. In cases of suspected unfair transactions, such as insider trading, the transactions in question are investigated.

ⅱ）　Financial instruments inspection

Financial instruments inspection involves the inspection of financial instruments business operators and others for the purpose of maintaining a safe environment for investment by investors. The SESC has a very wide mandate for inspection that covers a total of about 7,000 businesses as of fiscal 2016. A total of 61 inspections were initiated during fiscal 2016. These comprise financial instruments business operators, etc. (including major shareholders), financial instruments exchanges, authorized and certified financial instruments business associations, credit rating institutions, designated dispute resolution organizations, investment trust management companies, investment companies (including the asset custody companies, etc., and the executive officers of investment companies), and specially permitted business notifying persons.

Depending on the outcome of its inspections, the SESC has two courses of action. First, it may recommend the administrative disposition of offenders to the Commissioner of the FSA (Article 20(1) of the FSAE). Secondly, it may petition the courts for issuance of prohibition orders, etc. (Article 192 of the FSAE). For instance, during fiscal 2016, notifications were issued to 67 businesses pointing out problems related to legal and regulatory compliance,

*901*

internal governance systems, and other issues. During fiscal 2016, the SESC also issued recommendations for administrative disposition in 35 cases involving serious legal and regulatory violations (Articles 51, 51-2, 52, 52-2 of the FIEA). These included a case in which a type II financial instruments business operator lent its name to an unregistered business operator, and a case in which an investment advisory and agency service provider handled a public offering and private placement of an overseas fund without registration. Furthermore, in a number of cases, the SESC found (based on the proper exercise of the powers of inquiry granted under Article 187 of the FIEA) unregistered business operators and persons filing notification for specially permitted services for qualified institutional investors to be in violation of the FIEA, and petitioned the courts for the issuance of prohibition orders, etc. in a total of one case where the probability of continued violation was deemed to be high.

iii） Investigation of transactions and international transactions

The investigation of transactions applies to certain types of unfair transactions that are subject to administrative monetary penalty. These are insider trading, market manipulation, the spreading of rumors, and the use of fraudulent means. Under Article 177 and Article 194-7, paragraph 2, item (viii) of the FIEA, the SESC may question persons concerned with a case, or have these persons submit materials. Based on these investigations, the SESC may recommend to the Commissioner of the FSA to issue orders for the payment of administrative monetary penalties (Article 20 (1) of the FSAE). In fiscal 2016, it recommended the issuance of orders for the payment of administrative monetary penalties for unfair transactions in a total of 47 cases. To strengthen its response to the globalization of markets, the SESC has in recent years investigated cases of unfair transactions involving cross-border transactions (investigation of international transactions), and has recommended the issuance of orders for the payment of administrative monetary penalties. In fiscal 2016, recommendations were issued in four such cases.

iv） Disclosure inspection

The purpose of disclosure inspection is to ensure the accurate, fair and

*902*

Chapter 9 Enforcement under the FIEA

timely disclosure of information pertaining to the business and financial conditions of securities issuers and others so as to enable investors to make appropriate investment decisions in the markets. To realize this objective, whenever the Commissioner of the FSA (the SESC on the Director General of the Local Finance Bureau) finds it to be necessary and appropriate, they may order any person who has filed a notification of a securities registration statement, any person who has submitted an annual securities report, any person who has submitted a shelf-registration statement, a takeover bidder, or any person who has submitted a statement of large-volume holdings to submit reports or materials, and may have the relevant books and documents or any other articles inspected. If as a result of disclosure inspection, for example, it is found that disclosure documents contain a false statement with regard to a material particular, the SESC may recommend to the Commissioner of the FSA to issue an administrative monetary penalty payment order. Furthermore, as deemed necessary, the SESC may also recommend the issuance of an order for the submission of an amendment.[6] If amendment of a disclosure document is deemed necessary, the SESC may prompt voluntary amendment even if no false statement with regard to a material particular is found. For example, disclosure inspection of 15 companies was completed during fiscal 2016. Recommendations for the issuance of administrative monetary penalty payment orders were issued in five cases, and voluntary amendment was prompted in two cases.

v ) Investigation and prosecution of criminal cases

The authority to investigate criminal cases has been granted for the purpose of protecting investors by investigating the truth about malicious acts that are detrimental to fairness in the markets and by strictly punishing violators. SESC officers have been granted certain investigative powers in criminal cases. These comprise the right to conduct voluntary inquiry, including questioning, inspection and retention (Article 210 of the FIEA), and the right to conduct compulsory investigation, including official inspection,

---

6　The Commissioner of the FSA (the Director General of the Local Finance Bureau) may issue an order for submitting an amendment, if necessary (Articles 10 and 27-8 etc., of the FIEA).

*903*

search and seizure under court warrant (Article 211 et seq. of the FIEA). Persons subject to investigation are persons acting to the detriment of fair transaction as prescribed in Cabinet Orders (Article 45 of the Financial Instruments and Exchange Act Implementing Order). This includes persons who have submitted annual securities reports containing misstatements, and persons who have engaged in insider trading, the spreading of rumors, the use of fraudulent means, and market manipulation. Additionally, certain acts prescribed under the Act on Prevention of Transfer of Criminal Proceeds that relate to the regulation of international money laundering also come under the scope of the investigative powers of the SESC. SESC officers are mandated to report the findings of their investigations of criminal cases to the SESC (Article 223 of the FIEA, Article 30 of the Act on Prevention of Transfer of Criminal Proceeds). When the SESC becomes convinced of a criminal violation based on such investigation, it files an accusation with public prosecutors. The SESC may also retain or seize articles, in which case it takes these articles over with a retention list or seizure list (Article 226 of the FIEA, Article 30 of the Act on Prevention of Transfer of Criminal Proceeds). For example, in fiscal 2016, a total of seven accusations were filed for such violations as the submission of false annual securities reports and market manipulation.

## 3. Criminal penalty

### a. Penal servitude and fines

As mentioned above, the means of enforcement under the FIEA has become more diverse. Nevertheless, criminal penalty remains an effective means of enforcement. Specifically, serious violations of the FIEA are subject to criminal penalty (Articles 197 and 207-2 of the FIEA). In general, the heaviest criminal penalty provided under the FIEA consists of a sentence of imprisonment with required labor for not more than ten years, a fine of not more than ten million yen, or both (Article 197). This criminal penalty is applicable to the submission of annual securities reports containing false statements, and such instances of unfair transaction as the spreading of rumors, the use of fraudulent means, and market manipulation. The second heaviest criminal penalty provided under the FIEA consists of a sentence of imprisonment with required labor for not more than five years, a fine of not

Chapter 9  Enforcement under the FIEA

more than five million yen, or both (Articles 197-2 and 197-3). This penalty is applicable to public offering and secondary distribution of securities without notification, failure to submit annual securities reports, submission of quarterly reports or internal control reports containing false statements, insider trading (Article 197-2), and the use of fraudulent means, or the commission of assault or intimidation (Article 197-3) in the conclusion or interpretation of investment advisory contracts in the investment management business. The third heaviest criminal penalty provided under the FIEA consists of a sentence of imprisonment with required labor for not more than three years, a fine of not more than three million yen, or both (Articles 198 and 198-3). This penalty is applicable to the act of conducting operations requiring registration, license, or permission without obtaining the same (Article 198), including persons receiving registration or licensing by fraudulent means, and persons operating without obtaining registration, permission, etc., and to highly malicious acts, such as providing investors with compensation for losses (Article 198-3). Next, criminal penalty of a sentence of imprisonment with required labor for not more than two years, a fine of not more than three million yen, or both (Articles 198-4 and 198-5) is applicable to persons who have established a company that has a stock-company type financial instruments exchange as its subsidiary company without authorization of the Prime Minister (Article 198-4), and persons violating the obligation of financial instruments business operators to separately manage customer assets (Article 198-5). Criminal penalty of a sentence of imprisonment with required labor for not more than one year, a fine of not more than three million yen, or both (Articles 198-6 and 199) is applicable to persons who have entered misstatements into written applications (Article 198-6) and financial instruments firms associations that have made false reports (Article 199). Criminal penalty of a sentence of imprisonment with required labor for not more than one year, a fine of not more than one million yen, or both (Articles 200, 201, and 202) is applicable to persons failing to submit quarterly reports, persons violating the obligation to deliver prospectus (Article 200), financial instruments business operators conducting PTS operations without authorization of the Prime Minister (Article 201), and persons conducting acts for the purpose of paying or receiving differences by using quotations on a financial

905

instruments exchange market instead of through a financial instruments exchange market (Article 202). Criminal penalty of a sentence of imprisonment with required labor for not more than six months, a fine of not more than 500,000 yen, or both (Article 205) is applicable to persons refusing or obstructing inspection, and persons violating the obligation to deliver documents to customers. A fine of not more than 300,000 yen (Article 205-2-3) is applicable to persons violating the obligation of financial instruments business operators and others to submit notifications of various types of changes. Finally, a fine of not more than 200,000 yen (Article 205-3) is applicable to persons violating regulations related to investigation and trial procedures pertaining to administrative monetary penalties (Articles 177 and 185, etc.).

Furthermore, dual criminal liability is provided for corporations for each act of violation as described below (Article 207). Among the abovementioned provisions for criminal penalty, a fine of not more than 700 million yen applies to violations of Article 197 of the FIEA. A fine of not more than 500 million yen applies to violations of Article 197-2 (with the exception of certain violations) or Article 197-3. A fine of not more than 300 million yen applies to violations of Article 198 (with the exception of certain violations) or Article 198-3 through Article 198-5. A fine of not more than 200 million yen applies to violations of Article 198-6 (with the exception of certain violations) or Article 199. A fine of not more than 100 million yen applies to violations of Article 200 and Article 201 (in both instances, with the exception of certain violations). Consequently, for example, when a director of a corporation is found to have made a false statement in the annual securities report (Article 197(1)(i)), the corporation may be deemed to have committed an "unlawful act" pertaining to its "business or property," and may be fined an amount not more than 700 million yen (Article 207(1)(i)).

b. Confiscation or collection

Among the above-mentioned acts, the law provides for the confiscation or collection of property gained through criminal acts. For example, confiscation or collection applies to the following acts: unfair transaction (Article 157), spreading of rumors (Article 158), market manipulation

(Article 159), insider trading (Articles 166 and 167) (Article 198-2), and a customer receiving compensation for losses from a financial instruments business operator and any third party that is aware of this fact (Article 39 (2) and Article 200-2). In principle, property gained through criminal acts is subject to confiscation. The law provides that when the property cannot be confiscated, a value equivalent to the property that otherwise should have been confiscated shall be collected (Articles 198-2 and 200-2). Because such criminal acts are generally committed for the purpose of gaining profit, it was believed that deprivation of the economic benefits gained through criminal acts would have a deterrent effect.

The system of administrative monetary penalties discussed below is also intended to deprive violators of wrongfully gained benefits through the application of monetary penalties. In the above-mentioned instances, when an administrative monetary penalty is charged in addition to confiscation or collection, the amount of the administrative monetary penalty is adjusted by subtracting the total amount confiscated or collected (Articles 185-7 (17) and 185-8 (7)). However, criminal penalties and administrative monetary penalties are applied as mutually exclusive measures in the enforcement of the law. Consequently, the problem of adjustment seldom arises in practice.

## 4. Administrative disposition

Various categories of persons come under the jurisdiction of the FIEA. Specifically, these include financial instruments business operators (Chapter III of the FIEA), financial instruments intermediary service providers (Chapter III-2), credit rating organizations (Chapter III-3), financial instruments firms associations (Chapter IV), investor protection funds (Chapter IV-2), financial instruments exchanges (Chapter V), and designated dispute resolution organizations (Chapter V-5). For example, the following provisions apply to financial instruments business operators. A financial instruments business operator must be registered with the Prime Minister (the Commissioner of the FSA) (certain businesses require authorization) (Articles 29 and 30), must file notification of any changes in registration (Article 31), must comply with regulations pertaining to the performance of specific operations (Article 35, etc.), and must produce reports and submit to inspection when deemed necessary by the Prime Minister (the Commissioner of the FSA) (Article 56-2). An administrative disposition applies when a financial instruments business operator is found to have violated laws or regulations. When deemed necessary and appropriate for the public interest or protection of investors, the Prime Minister (the Commissioner of the FSA) may issue a business improvement order regarding the management of operations or the status of property[7] (Article 51). Depending on the cause for action, such supervisory dispositions as the rescission of registration or authorization or issuance of order for suspension of operations may be imposed (Article 52). Registered financial institutions are basically subject to the same provisions (also see Articles 33-2 and 33-6, etc.). Violations of laws or regulations are subject to business improvement orders and other supervisory dispositions (Articles 51-2 and 52-2).

In order to ensure fairness and transparency in decisions on whether to impose administrative dispositions, the FSA has adopted certain standards based on the following criteria. The first criterion relates to the seriousness or maliciousness of the act (extent of violation of public interest and damage suffered by users; the duration and repetition of the act; intentionality, organizational involvement, concealment, and involvement of anti-social forces). The second criterion relates to the appropriateness of the management control system and operations management system that are in place and which define the environment in which the acts in question have been committed (sufficient awareness and involvement of the board of directors in statutory compliance; sufficient development of internal control, compliance and risk management departments and systems; the achievement of appropriate levels of functionality; sufficient provision of internal education and training). The FSA also takes into consideration any mitigating circumstances (such as whether a financial institution has voluntarily taken necessary measures for the protection of users prior to administrative responses, and whether the financial institution is voluntarily taking appropriate action based on principles shared with the administrative

---

7   Issuance of business improvement orders is conditioned on these requirements, and therefore does not require the commission of acts in violation of laws or regulations.

Chapter 9 Enforcement under the FIEA

authorities).[8]

For the purpose of the explicit presentation of the details of its rules and interpretations, the FSA has published the Comprehensive Guidelines for Supervision of Financial Instruments Business Operators, etc., and Inspection Manual for Financial Instruments Business Operators. Furthermore, the FSA has adopted a no-action letter system and "written inquiry procedures for general legal interpretation" that complement the no-action letter system and allow for case-by-case inquiry. Information on past instances of administrative disposition is published in "*Gyosei shobun jirei-shu*" (Cases of Administrative Disposition). The published information includes the cause and details of administrative disposition.[9]

## 5. Administrative monetary penalty system

### a. Developments leading to introduction

The administrative monetary penalty system was adopted in the 2004 revision. As discussed above, various criminal penalties and administrative dispositions for enforcement did exist prior to the 2004 revision. However, criminal penalties had limited functionality due to the severity of their impact and consequent difficulty in application. The imposition of administrative dispositions was also problematic because such actions could create inconvenience for customers that were unrelated to violations. In light of these drawbacks, the system that was newly introduced in 2004 featured the imposition of monetary penalties on violators. In the beginning, the administrative monetary penalty system applied to making false statements in offering disclosure documents, spreading of rumors, use of fraudulent means, market manipulation and insider trading. At a later date, making false statements in continuous disclosure documents was added to the scope of application. It also became possible to apply administrative monetary penalties to certified public accountants and auditing firms who have falsely certified corporate disclosure documents due to either intent or failure to pay

---

**8**  Financial Services Agency, "Administrative Action in the Financial Sector." http://www.fsa.go.jp/en/refer/guide/action.html

**9**  http://www.fsa.go.jp/status/s_jirei/kouhyou.html (last accessed Sep. 15, 2017).

reasonable attention. Furthermore, in the revision of 2008, the scope of application was significantly extended to include the failure to submit offering disclosure documents and continuous disclosure documents, and failure to submit documents or making false statements in documents pertaining to takeover bids. At the same time, the system was reinforced by raising the level of administrative monetary penalties by revising the calculation method for such violations as making false statements in offering and continuous disclosure documents and insider trading.

 b. Acts subject to administrative monetary penalty system and trial procedures
Acts subject to administrative monetary penalty payment orders fall under two major categories. The first category comprises unfair transactions, such as spreading of rumors, insider trading (including the conveyance of information and recommendation of purchases and sales), and market manipulation (Articles 173, 174, 174-2, 174-3, 175 and 175-2 of the FIEA).[10] The second category comprises failure to submit and the making of false statements in various disclosure documents, etc. Specifically, these comprise securities registration statements and annual securities reports (Articles 172, 172-2, 172-3 and 172-4), public notices for commencing takeover bid and takeover bid notifications (Articles 172-5 and 172-6), a large-volume of shareholding report (Articles 172-7 and 172-8), designated securities information and information on issuers for professional investors (Articles 172-9, 172-10 and 172-11), and the participation of outside persons in the inclusion of false statements in disclosure documents (Article 172-12[11]).

When evidence of any such acts has been recognized, the FSA Commissioner must make a decision on the commencement of trial procedures[12] (Article

---

10 Among unfair transactions, violation of Article 157 (Prohibition of Wrongful Acts) of the FIEA is not subject to administrative monetary penalty. This is believed to be because details of violating acts cannot be said to be unambiguous. *Kinnyu-Shingi-kai Kinnyu-Bunka-Kai Dai-ichi Bukai, Housei working Group Houkoku – Kacho-Kin Seido No Arikata ni tuite –* [Council of the FSA, 1st section, Legal Working Group report –Administrative Monetary Penalty System–] (Dec. 18, 2007) P. 5. http://www.fsa.go.jp/singi/singi_kinyu/tosin/20071218-1/02.pdf (last accessed Sep. 15, 2017).

*910*

Chapter 9   Enforcement under the FIEA

178(1)). Trial procedures commence with the delivery of a Written Decision on Commencement of Trial Procedures to the person to whom the administrative monetary penalty payment order is to be issued (hereinafter referred to as the "respondent") (Article 179(3)). This document contains the date and place of the trial, the facts pertaining to the administrative monetary penalty, the amount of the administrative monetary penalty to be paid, and the basis for its computation (Article 179(2)). As a rule, trial procedures are conducted by a panel of three trial examiners and are open to the public (Articles 180(1) and 182). When served with a Written Decision on Commencement of Trial Procedures, the respondent is required to produce a written response (Article 183(1)). The respondent is also given the opportunity to make a statement of opinion (Article 184) and to submit evidentiary documents, etc. (Article 185-3). The trial examiners may question witnesses and the respondent (Articles 185 and 185-2). The trial examiners may also conduct hearings of expert witnesses (Article 185-4) and conduct on-site inspections (Article 185-5). After completing these procedures, the trial examiners produce a draft decision (Article 185-6). Based on this draft decision, the Prime Minister (the Commissioner of the FSA) is required to make a decision on the issuance of an administrative monetary penalty payment order (Article 185-7). Once the facts pertaining to the imposition of an administrative monetary penalty have been established, the Prime Minister (the Commissioner of the FSA) is understood to have no discretion in deciding whether to order the payment of administrative monetary penalties as well as the amount of such penalties. [13] When a respondent is to pay an administrative monetary penalty

---

11   The revision of 2012 made it possible to impose administrative monetary penalties on persons participating in the concealment, disguising, etc. of the inclusion of false statements in statutory disclosure documents (Article 172-12 of the FIEA). The amount of monetary penalty is to be equivalent to the value of fees, compensation and other consideration and property received for participation in such acts (Article 172-12(1)).

12   The Securities and Exchange Surveillance Commission (SESC) investigates acts suspected of being subject to the imposition of administrative monetary penalty. When it considers that the issuance of an administrative monetary penalty payment order is warranted, the SESC makes a recommendation to the Prime Minister and the Commissioner of the Financial Services Agency (Article 20 of the FSAE).

*911*

pursuant to a decision made to issue a payment order, the due date for payment is set at two months from the date of issuance of the transcript of the decision (Article 185-7 (21)). The decision takes effect when the transcript is served on the respondent (Article 185-7(22) of the FIEA). If payment is not made by the due date, a demand for payment is issued (Article 185-14 (1)). Furthermore, if payment is not made by the date designated in the demand for payment, the payment order has the same effect as an enforceable title of obligation (Article 185-15). If the respondent objects to the decision, the respondent may file an appeal for rescission of the administrative monetary penalty payment order. Such an appeal must be filed with the courts within 30 days (Article 185-18).

When a decision has been made to commence trial procedures, interested persons may request to inspect or to copy the case record as well as the written decision pertaining to the administrative monetary penalty payment order (Article 185-13). Consequently, in a case in which an administrative monetary penalty payment order has been issued, it would be possible for any person pursuing civil liability to inspect or copy the case record and use the same in a civil suit.[14]

　c . Legal nature of administrative monetary penalty
Under the administrative monetary penalty system, the government forcibly collects money from persons committing unlawful acts. In this respect, this system appears to be similar to fines collected as criminal penalties. If so, this would give rise to the problem of the prohibition of double jeopardy (Article 39 of the Constitution of Japan), which states, "No person shall be placed in double jeopardy." However, for the following reasons, it is interpreted that

---

**13** Three types of decisions can be made. In addition to deciding to issue an administrative monetary penalty payment order, a decision can be made determining that there has been no violation, and a decision can be made not to issue an administrative monetary penalty payment order (FIEA Article 185-7(1), (18)). For details of the procedures pertaining to the administrative monetary penalty system, see the Financial Services Agency's *Kachokin seido ni tsuite* (Regarding the Administrative Monetary Penalty System). http://www.fsa.go.jp/policy/kachoukin/ 02.html (last accessed Sep. 15, 2017).

**14** Yamashita and Kanda, p. 493.

*912*

Chapter 9  Enforcement under the FIEA

administrative monetary penalties are essentially different from criminal penalties and therefore do not infringe on the prohibition of double jeopardy.[15] First, administrative monetary penalties under FIEA share the same legal nature as surcharge payments under the Antimonopoly Act and penalty taxes under tax laws (they are found to be constitutional by the Supreme Court). Extrapolating from discussions pertaining to surcharge payments and penalty taxes, the purpose of the administrative monetary penalty system is to deter unlawful acts, and does not contain the intent of moral reproach. For this reason, administrative monetary penalties do not take into account the intent or negligence of a violator, or the form or nature of an unlawful act. Second, an administrative monetary penalty is imposed upon a violator whenever a violation as prescribed by law is established. That is to say, the administrative agency that issues payment orders has no discretion over whether to issue a payment order, or the amount of the administrative monetary payment. Third, the amount of the administrative monetary penalty is essentially determined as a means to confiscate the benefits gained through criminal acts. In these ways, administrative monetary penalties are interpreted to differ from fines as criminal penalties, which focus on the anti-social and immoral nature of an act and are calibrated to correspond to the form and nature of an unlawful act, and thus not to violate the prohibition of double jeopardy.[16]

However, subsequent revisions of the law have come to cast doubt on whether the abovementioned objectives, intent and thinking on the administrative monetary penalty system as originally explained are sustainable. For example, the 2008 revision of the FIEA added provisions for imposing heavier monetary penalties on repeat violators (the applicable administrative monetary penalty is increased by 50 percent when a person has committed a second violation within five years of receiving an earlier

---

15 Meanwhile, the provisions for the adjustment of criminal penalties and administrative monetary penalties for the same violation of continuous disclosure obligations were added in the 2005 revision. See *infra* n 17.

16 Hideki Kanda, Naohiko Mastuo and Etsuro Kuronuma, *Kinyu shohin torihiki ho konmentaru 4* [Financial Instruments and Exchange Act: commentary 4] (Shoji Homu 2011), p. 209 (Masayoshi Ishida).

*913*

administrative monetary penalty payment order: Article 185-7(15) of the FIEA). On the other hand, the 2008 revision provides for reducing the monetary penalty amount when a person voluntarily comes forward to admit to a violation (the applicable administrative monetary penalty is diminished by 50 percent when a violator reports its own violation to the SESC prior to the commencement of investigations by the authorities; this provision only applies to certain acts of violation, such as making false statements in offering and ongoing disclosure documents: Article 185-7(14) of the FIEA). While in its original form, the nature of the law was to deter acts of violation through confiscation of benefits gained, these revisions are understood to have added an element of sanctions to the law.[17]

The 2007 revision of the Certified Public Accountants Act introduced an administrative monetary penalty to be imposed on certified public accountants and auditing firms providing false audit certifications. The amount of penalty is basically computed to be equivalent to the amount of remuneration that has been received for providing a false audit certification. However, in the case of deliberate falsification, the penalty is increased to 1.5 times the amount of remuneration received (Article 31-2 (1) (i) of the Certified Public Accountants Act). In the case of failure to pay reasonable attention, the penalty amount is equivalent to the amount of remuneration (Article 31-2(1) (ii)). It has been pointed out that this system also contains an element of sanctions not included in the FIEA in its original form.[18]

Further additions were made in the 2013 revision of the FIEA. Specifically, the administrative monetary penalty applicable to an asset management business operator conducting unfair transactions on the account of others was increased to three times the amount of its asset management remuneration (monthly remuneration amount).[19] This revision resulted from a review of the law undertaken against the backdrop of incidents of so-called "zoushi (capital increase) insider trading" and criticism that administrative monetary penalties imposed on asset management business

---

17 Yamashita and Kanda, p. 486; Kanda, Matsuo and Kuronuma, p. 208.
18 Kanda, Matsuo and Kuronuma, p. 205.

*914*

Chapter 9   Enforcement under the FIEA

operators conducting unfair transactions on the account of others were too low to act as a proper deterrent.[20] Thus, while the basic standard of determining the amount of administrative monetary penalties to be equivalent to the value of economic benefits gained has been maintained, it may be said that the law as it stands has become less constrained by this standard.[21]

As a result of the series of revisions that have been made in the FIEA, it can

---

19  Originally, administrative monetary penalties were applicable only to violators conducting unfair transactions on their own account. However, the FIEA revision of 2008 expanded the scope of application by deeming unfair transactions conducted on the account of members of the same household and subsidiary companies to constitute own account violations (Article 173(5), Article 174(5), Article 174-2(6), Article 174-3 (5) to (7), Article 175(10) and (11) of the FIEA). The scope of application was further expanded in the 2012 revision so that unfair transactions conducted on the account of others also became generally subject to administrative monetary penalties (Article 173(1)(iv), Article 174(1)(iv), Article 174-2(1)(ii)(d), Article 174-3(1)(ii) (d), Article 175(1)(iii), and Article 175(2)(iii)).

20  As this revision was made in response to incidents of so-called "zoushi (capital increase) insider trading," the review of the law was directly focused on insider trading. However, similar revisions were made to cover other violations, such as acts of spreading rumors and market manipulation. The same capital increase insider-trading incidents also instigated revisions for regulating the conveyance of information and acts of issuing recommendations on transactions, which were made subject to administrative monetary penalty payment orders (Article 175-2). Penalty amounts are prescribed as follows: When the violator is a securities company or other intermediary service providers, a penalty equivalent to three months of intermediary fees is charged in cases involving violations related to intermediary operations. In cases involving the sale and distribution of shares pertaining to a capital increase, the penalty charged is equivalent to three months of intermediary fees plus an amount equivalent to 50 percent of underwriting commissions received (Article 175-2(1)(i) & (ii), and (2)(i) & (ii)).

21  Under the 2005 revision of the Securities and Exchange Act, administrative monetary penalties became applicable to the act of making false statements in continuous disclosure documents. At this time, a provision was added for the adjustment of criminal penalties and administrative monetary penalties applicable to the same violation of the continuous disclosure obligation (Article 185-7(16), Article 185-8(6)). Given the doubtfulness of whether administrative monetary penalties can be said to confiscate economic benefits gained through unlawful acts, the intent of this provision has been interpreted to be avoidance of the problem of double jeopardy. Yamashita and Kanda, p. 492, fn. 32; Kanda, Matsuo and Kuronuma, p. 210.

*915*

be said that the original position that the administrative monetary penalty system is essentially different from criminal penalties that are intended to impose sanctions on acts of an anti-social or immoral nature is being gradually eroded. However, in more recent years, compelling arguments are being made to the effect that even if administrative monetary penalties were to take on an increasing sanctionary function and were to be jointly imposed with criminal penalties, this would not infringe upon the prohibition of double jeopardy as prescribed by Article 39 of the Constitution.[22] According to these arguments, joint imposition of administrative monetary penalty and criminal penalty is a problem that should be addressed and regulated from the perspective of whether the resulting sanctions are excessive as determined on the basis of the principle of commensurate punishment or the principle of proportionality.

# 6. Prohibition orders and orders for suspension issued by courts

When a violation of laws and regulations has been committed or is likely to be committed, ex-post imposition of criminal penalty, administrative disposition, or pursuit of civil liability may not be sufficiently effective in preserving the public interest or protecting investors. In such instances, it is useful to be able to suspend acts that have already been committed or to order ex-ante prohibition of acts that may be committed in the future. For this purpose, the FIEA has adopted provisions for court issuance of prohibition orders and orders of suspension, which have been patterned after the injunction order system of the United States. Specifically, when a court finds that there is an urgent necessity and that it is necessary and appropriate for the public interest and protection of investors, it may issue an order to a person who has conducted or will conduct an act in violation of the FIEA or orders issued under the FIEA for prohibition or suspension of such an act. However, until recently, these provisions were never utilized. To address this problem, the following change was made in the 2008 revision of the FIEA. Prior to revision, the authority to petition the courts for issuance

---

22　Kanda, Matsuo and Kuronuma, p. 210; Hitoshi Saeki, *Seisai ron* [Theory of sanctions] (Yuhikaku, 2009), p. 94 onward.

Chapter 9   Enforcement under the FIEA

of prohibition orders and orders for suspension and to conduct investigations constituting the premise for such petitions was given to the Prime Minister and Minister of Finance or delegated to the Commissioner of the FSA by the Prime Minister (Articles 187 and 192(1)). In the revision of 2008, this authority was assigned to the SESC (Article 194-7(4)).[23] Given that the SESC is engaged in day-to-day surveillance of the markets, the purpose of assigning the authority to petition the courts to the SESC is to facilitate speedy and flexible responses to acts of violation.[24] Acting on these developments, on November 17, 2010, the SESC petitioned the Tokyo District Court for an emergency injunction in the case of violation of Article 29 of the FIEA involving the purchase and sale of securities, intermediation in the purchase and sale of securities, or public offering or private placement as a business operation by a non-registered entity, where it was deemed highly probable that the said acts of violation would be repeated in the future.[25] This was followed by a second court petition filed on November 26, 2010 with the Kofu District Court for an emergency injunction in the case of violation of Article 4, paragraph 1 et seq. of the FIEA involving public offering of securities without filing securities registration statements, where it was deemed highly probable that the act of violation would be repeated in the future.[26] In the ensuing years, a number of petitions for emergency injunctions have been filed every year in cases involving violation by non-registered persons and violation for public offering without Securities Registration Statements. In all instances, petitions have been accepted and

---

**23**  Furthermore, the FIEA revision of 2010 empowered the SESC to delegate the authority to petition the courts for issuance of prohibition orders and orders for suspension to the Director General of Local Finance Bureaus and others (Article 194-7(7) of the FIEA Article 44-5 of the Financial Instruments and Exchange Act Implementing Order).

**24**  Kanda, Matsuo and Kuronuma, p. 475 (Tomotaka Fujita).

**25**  Securities and Exchange Surveillance Commission, *Kabushiki kaisha daikei oyobi sono yakuin ni taisuru kinyu shohin torihikiho dai 192 jo dai 1 ko ni motozuku saibansho eno moshitate ni tsuite* [Regarding petition filed with court against Daikei Co., Ltd. and its senior management based on Article 192(1) of the Financial Instruments and Exchange Act], November 18, 2010. (http://www.fsa.go.jp/sesc/news/c_2010/2010/20101118-1.htm (last accessed Sep. 15, 2017)) In response to this, the Tokyo District Court issued an order exactly as requested in the SESC petition. Tokyo District Court decision of November 26, 2010, (*Kinyu Shoji Hanrei* No. 1357, p. 28).

*917*

acted on by the courts.[27]

## 7. Civil liability

The filing of civil suits pertaining to specific transactions by investors who have incurred damage constitutes one of the principal means by which the purposes of the FIEA are achieved. The FIEA explicitly provides for civil action in a number of instances, including making false statements in disclosure documents and market manipulation (Articles 16, 17, 18, 21, 21-2, 22, 24-4, 24-4-7(4), 24-5(5) and 160 of the FIEA).

While provisions for civil action have not been made for other acts of violation (such as violation of the suitability rule by securities company employees), investors who have incurred damage are able to file civil suits under Articles 709 and 715 of the Civil Code.

# B. Enforcement through self-regulation

Self-regulatory organizations are private organizations that voluntarily establish and enforce rules for the realization of certain public interests. Self-regulatory organizations in Japan's securities markets include Financial Instruments Exchanges and the Japan Securities Dealers Association, which are engaged in self-regulatory activities under the supervision of the Prime Minister.

---

26 Securities and Exchange Surveillance Commission, *Kabushiki kaisha seibutsu kagaku kenkyujo ni taisuru kinyu shohin torihikiho ihan koi ni kakaru saibansho no kinkyu sashitome meirei (doho dai 192 jo dai 1 ko) no hatsurei ni tsuite* [Regarding the issuance of a court order for an emergency injunction against Biochemical Laboratory Co.,Ltd. for violation of the Financial Instruments and Exchange Act (FIEA Article 192 Paragraph 1)], December 16, 2010. (http://www.fsa.go.jp/sesc/news/c_2010/2010/20101216-1.htm (last accessed Sep. 15, 2017))

27 A total of 18 petitions have been filed as of July 31, 2017. Securities and Exchange Surveillance Commission, *Saibansho eno moshitate* [Court petitions filed] (http://www.fsa.go.jp/sesc/actions/moushitate.htm (last accessed Sep. 15, 2017))

*918*

Chapter 9  Enforcement under the FIEA

# 1. Japan Securities Dealers Association

The Japan Securities Dealers Association (JSDA) is authorized by the Prime Minister to operate as an authorized financial instruments firms association (Article 67-2(2) of the FIEA). JSDA membership is comprised of financial instruments business operators and registered financial institutions. Its purpose is to ensure fair and smooth trading in securities, promote the sound development of Japan's financial instruments business, and protect investors. The JSDA has established numerous rules for the achievement of these objectives. For example, these include self-regulatory rules, uniform practice rules, and dispute resolution rules. Members who violate these rules or the JSDA Articles of Association, or violate laws and regulations or the dispositions of government ministries and agencies may be subjected to disciplinary action (reprimand, imposition of a fine, suspension or limitation of membership rights, or expulsion) or may be admonished (Articles 28 and 29 of the Articles of Association of the JSDA).[28]

# 2. Financial instruments exchanges

The Japan Exchange Group (JPX) is a joint-stock company that operates financial instruments markets under a license granted by the Prime Minister (Articles 2(16) and 80(1) of the FIEA), and is Japan's principal financial instruments exchange. With the authorization of the Prime Minister (Article 85), JPX has entrusted its self-regulation related services to the Japan Exchange Regulation, which is its self-regulation organization. As prescribed by the FIEA, self-regulation related services comprise the following: business related to listing and delisting of financial instruments; investigation of the status of compliance of JPX members with laws and regulations, and fair and equitable principles of transactions; and other businesses specified by a cabinet office ordinance as may be necessary for ensuring fairness in transactions (Article 84 (2)). The organizational structure of the Japan

---

28  For record of disciplinary actions taken, see Japan Securities Dealers Association, *Kyokai-in gaimu-in shobun* [Disciplinary actions against members and registered sales representatives] (http://www.jsda.or.jp/shiru/syobun/index.html (last accessed Sep. 15, 2017)).

*919*

Exchange Regulation encompasses the following departments and functions. The Listing Examination Department examines qualifications and determines eligibility for listing. The Listed Company Compliance Department is responsible for maintaining and enhancing the quality of listed financial instruments. The Market Surveillance and Compliance Department is charged with preventing unfair transactions. Finally, the Trading Participants Examination and Inspection Department is responsible for investigating the compliance status of trading participants and the disciplining of trading participants. The Japan Exchange Regulation may take a number of disciplinary actions against trading participants found in violation of laws and regulations, or rules. These consist of revocation of trading qualification, suspension or restriction of transactions, imposition of fines, and censure (Rule 34 of the Trading Participant Regulations).[29] Disciplinary actions that may be taken against listed companies consist of the following: designation of the listed securities of a company as a "Security on Alert" (Rule 501 of the Securities Listing Regulations [Tokyo Stock Exchange]); order to submit Improvement Report or Improvement Status Report (Rules 502 through 505); public announcement measure (Rule 508); order to pay Listing Agreement violation penalty (Rule 509); and delisting (Rules 602 through 604-5).[30]

---

**29** For record of disciplinary actions taken, see Japan Exchange Regulation, "Disciplinary Actions" (http://www.jpx.co.jp/english/rules-participants/participants/actions/index.html (last accessed Sep. 15, 2017)). Because trading participants on the Tokyo Stock Exchange are simultaneously members of the Japan Securities Dealers Association, these entities may be subjected to disciplinary actions imposed by either both or only one of the two self-regulation organizations.

**30** For record of disciplinary actions taken, see Japan Exchange Regulation, "Disciplinary Action on Listed Companies" (http://www.jpx.co.jp/english/regulation/ensuring/activity/measure/ (last accessed Sep. 15, 2017)).

# Chapter **10**

## Proxy solicitation

*Masao Yanaga*

# A. The role of proxy solicitation regulation

Pursuant to Article 194 of the Financial Instruments and Exchange Act (the "FIEA"), solicitation for exercise of voting rights by proxy pertaining to shares of a company that issues shares listed on a financial instruments exchange shall be conducted in accordance with the relevant cabinet order. Accordingly, Articles 36-2 et seq. of the Financial Instruments and Exchange Act Implementing Order (the "FIEA Implementing Order"), establishes rules to conduct solicitation to have the person or a third party exercise by proxy the voting rights of shares of companies that issue shares listed on financial instruments exchanges.

The reason why these regulations have been adopted is to enable shareholders to exercise voting rights by proxy based on sufficient information.[1] Namely, the purport of regulating proxy solicitation is to prevent shareholders from authorizing the exercise of voting rights by proxy without knowing the contents of proposals, or to prevent the abuse of proxy solicitation for the benefit of solicitors by misleading other shareholders, as well as to prevent solicitors from exercising undue influence on share prices by obtaining proxies from other shareholders with little information or knowledge so as to be able to exercise voting rights at will.[2]

---

1  Katsuro Kanzaki, Yasuhiro Kawaguchi and Masashi Shitani, *Kinyu Shohin torihiki ho* [Financial Instruments and Exchange Act], p. 430 (Seirin-Shoin: 2012).

2  Seiji Tanaka and Wataru Horiguchi, *Sai-zentei konmentar Shoken torihiki ho* [Commentary on the Securities and Exchange Act: Third Fully Revised Edition], p. 1139 (Keiso Shobo: 1996); Hideki Kanda (ed.), *Chukai Shoken torihiki ho* [Securities and Exchange Act annotated], p. 1343 (Yuhikaku: 1997); Ichiro Kawamoto and Kaname Seki (eds.), *Santei-ban Chikujo-kaisetsu Shoken torihiki ho* [Article by Article Commentary on the Securities and Exchange Act (3rd Edition)], p. 1468 (Shoji Homu, 2008).

# B. Meaning of solicitation

As for the meaning of "solicitation," while case law has not been compiled, "On the Regulations Revising Part of the Regulation Concerning Solicitation of the Exercise of Voting Rights by Proxy of Listed Shares," promulgated by the Securities and Exchange Commission of Japan (at the time) stated that simply proffering a proxy card along with a convocation of a general shareholders meeting constitutes "solicitation." A famous scholar[3] argues that "solicitation" includes the act of proffering a proxy card and seeking a shareholder's signature, the act of asking a shareholder to prepare and/or deliver a proxy for the exercise of voting rights by proxy, as well as the act of asking shareholders not to respond to proxy solicitations from others.[4] On the other hand, the prevailing doctrine holds that acts whereby shareholders do not seek delivery of a proxy for themselves while working with other shareholders to exercise voting rights in line with those shareholders do not constitute "solicitation" subject to solicitation regulation as defined under the FIEA.[5]

---

[3] Misao Tatsuta, "Proxy in Joint-Stock Company", *Investment*, vol. 21, No. 1, p. 18 (1968).

[4] However, some argue that it is difficult to include the act of asking shareholders not to respond to proxy solicitation being conducted by others, the act of asking shareholders to retract proxies granted to others, or the act of recommending voting in writing as in the exercise of solicitation for voting rights by proxy. On the other hand, in principle, acts applying pressure on management outside of general shareholders meetings and acts confirming the movements of other shareholders in preparation for proxy solicitation do not constitute "solicitation," although "the act of notifying shareholders of information sessions when for the purpose of proxy solicitation" and "acts announcing plans for proxy solicitation with a disclaimer that they are not for the purpose of proxy solicitation (e.g., "this announcement is not for the purpose of proxy solicitation,") are considered solicitation (Takahito Kato, Issues in Regulating Proxy Solicitation, http://www.ose.or.jp/f/ose/rules/doc_ktgj/ktgj_20091204.pdf (2009)).

# C. Exemption

The rules specified in Article 36-2 through Article 36-5 of the FIEA Implementing Order shall not apply in the following cases (Article 36-6(1) of the FIEA Implementing Order).

(1) A solicitation to exercise voting rights of listed shares by proxy made by persons other than the company issuing the respective shares or the officers thereof and in which the Solicited Persons are less than 10 persons. The rationale for this provision is because the cost-benefit balance is lost when proxy solicitation regulation is applied to a case with a very small number of solicited persons.

(2) A solicitation to exercise voting rights of listed shares by proxy made through an advertisement in a daily newspaper that publishes items on current affairs that indicates only the name of the issuer company, the reason for the advertisement, the subject matter of the shareholders meeting, and the place where the Proxy Card, etc. shall be provided. This is based on a decision that such advertising merely serves as an intermediary for solicitation, and itself has little need to be covered by proxy solicitation regulation.

(3) Cases where the person who holds shares in another person's name makes a solicitation to exercise voting rights of listed shares by proxy to the other person with regard to the voting rights of shares. This type of solicitation for the exercise of voting rights by proxy is to complete the formal requirements for the exercise of voting rights by parties who are not the shareholders on the shareholders register but who have become shareholders, and such cases should not fundamentally be subject to proxy solicitation regulation. This provision assumes the case where a

---

5   Haruka Matsuyama, *Tekitai-teki kabunushi teian to proxy fight* [Hostile Shareholder Proposals and Proxy Fights (2nd Edition)] (Shoji Homu: 2014), p. 84; Kenjiro Egashira, *Kabushiki kaisha ho* [Stock Corporation Law (7th Edition)] (Yuhikaku: 2017), p.344, footnote 8. Some argue that the Financial Instruments and Exchange Act does apply (Mitsuhiro Kamiya and Akira Kumaki, "Issues and Handling in Proxy Solicitation in Hostile Takeovers", *Shoji Homu*, No. 1827, p. 19 (2008)).

Chapter 10   Proxy solicitation

shareholder who has not completed registration of shares as of the record date solicits the person who transferred the shares and is still recorded as the shareholder on the shareholders' registry.

# D. Regulation of proxy solicitation and foreign companies

There are many provisions in the FIEA that presuppose that shares issued by foreign companies are included in "shares" for the purpose of the Act, for example, "a report which [...] specifies matters pertaining to persons who hold shares of the Parent Company, etc. [...] within three months after the end of each business year (in cases where the Parent Company, etc. is a foreign company)" (Article 24-7(1) of the FIEA), and, "acquisition of its own shares by the listed company, etc. [...] or under laws and regulations in a foreign state [...] (limited to cases where the listed company, etc. is a foreign company)" (Article 166(2)(i)(d) of the FIEA). Moreover, it is evident that "an issuer company of securities listed on a financial instruments exchange or any other person specified by a cabinet order" in Article 193-2, paragraphs 1 and 2 of the FIEA includes listed foreign companies for the purpose of Article 35, paragraph 1 and Article 35-2 of the FIEA Implementing Order. Thus, the wording of the FIEA does not provide a sufficient basis to interpret that proxy solicitation regulation does not apply to listed foreign companies, considering that the focus of proxy solicitation regulation is on "shares listed on financial instruments exchanges".

On the other hand, some have argued that proxy solicitation regulation regarding a foreign company should be left to the law governing the incorporation of the foreign company, since regulations regarding the exercise of the voting rights of the issuing company are matters concerning company organization and administration; nevertheless, proxy solicitation regulation nevertheless serves to provide and disclose information to investors. However, others have pointed out that it is clear that only domestic joint-stock companies are considered as subject of proxy solicitation regulation[6], based on the wording of Articles 36-2 through 36-6 of the FIEA Implementing Order and those of the Cabinet Office Ordinance on Solicitation to Exercise Voting Rights of Listed Shares by Proxy (the "Proxy Solicitation Cabinet Office Ordinance") both prescribed based on the delegation in Article 194 of the FIEA.

# E. Details of proxy solicitation regulations

## 1. Delivery of proxy cards and reference documents

A person who intends to make solicitations for the exercise of voting rights by proxy shall deliver to the solicited persons, concurrently with or before the solicitation, a proxy card and documents stating matters prescribed by Proxy Solicitation Cabinet Office Ordinance since that would be helpful for granting the authority of representation ("Reference Documents") (Article 36-2(1) of the FIEA Implementing Order). However, a solicitor may, in lieu of delivering the proxy card or Reference Documents, provide the items to be contained in the proxy card or Reference Documents by electromagnetic means[7] with the consent of the solicited persons (Article 36-2(2) of the FIEA Implementing Order).

A solicitor shall not make a Solicitation to Exercise Voting Rights of Listed Shares by Proxy by using a proxy card, Reference Documents or any other documents, or an electromagnetic record that contains false statements or records of important items, or which lacks a statement or record of

---

6  Please see Financial Law Board, Foreign Companies and Proxy Solicitation Regulation, http://www.flb.gr.jp/jdoc/publication38-j.pdf, Sept. 5, 2011.

7  Electromagnetic means are (1) the method of using electronic data processing systems linking the computer used by the sender with the computer used by the receiver through telecommunications circuits, whereby information is transmitted via the telecommunications circuits and the information is recorded in files in the computer used by the user, and (2) the method whereby information is recorded on files using methods that can certainly record certain information using magnetic disks or other equivalent methods and delivered (Article 42(1) of the Proxy Solicitation Cabinet Office Ordinance), and the recipient must be able to output the information recorded in the file and prepare written copies (Article 42(2) of the Proxy Solicitation Cabinet Office Ordinance).

Chapter 10  Proxy solicitation

important items that should be stated, or a material fact that is necessary to avoid causing any misunderstanding (Article 36-4 of the FIEA Implementing Order).

Regarding the items that shall be stated in the Reference Documents for a general shareholders meeting provided to solicited persons, items that are stated in Reference Documents for a general shareholders meeting (Article 301(1) and Article 325 of the Companies Act), documents to be used by the shareholder to exercise the votes ("Voting Forms") (Article 301(1) and Article 325 of the Companies Act), other documents related to the general shareholders meeting or which are provided by electromagnetic means do not have to be stated in the Reference Documents provided to solicited persons; however, in such a case, the fact that there are items stated in the Reference Documents for the general shareholders meeting or Voting Forms, or which are provided by electromagnetic means (Article 1(2) of the Proxy Solicitation Cabinet Office Ordinance) shall be clearly stated. Also, among the items that should be stated in the Reference Documents, where there are matters for which the company issuing the shares has made a public announcement, or items for which measures are taken by the issuing company so that a large number of unspecified persons in Japan may continuously receive them via electromagnetic means, these items do not have to be stated in the Reference Documents; although the date on which the announcement was published in the official gazette, the name of the daily newspaper used and the date of publication, and the items prescribed by ordinance of the Ministry of Justice required for a large number of unspecified persons to receive such information via electromagnetic disclosure or electronic announcement shall be stated (Article 1(3) of the Proxy Solicitation Cabinet Office Ordinance). Additionally, where there are matters among those that shall be stated in the Reference Documents regarding which the issuing company takes measures, in accordance with the company's articles of incorporation, so that shareholders may continuously receive the information via electromagnetic means from the day of issuance of the notice of convocation of the general shareholders meeting until the day when three months have elapsed from the date of the shareholders' meeting, these matters do not have to be stated on the

*927*

Reference Documents. Instead, the parties receiving the information may view and download the contents thereof disclosed by the issuing company via a website over the Internet and this URL shall be stated in the Reference Documents (Article 1(4) of the Proxy Solicitation Cabinet Office Ordinance). These requirements have been provided because there is no need to provide duplicate information as the solicited persons may acquire the necessary information by either means.

In cases where the Solicitation to Exercise Voting Rights of Listed Shares by Proxy is made by or for the company issuing shares, the shareholders of the company may request the company to deliver the Reference Documents by paying the costs fixed by the company (Article 36-5 (1) of the FIEA Implementing Order). On the one hand, this provision envisions the case where the issuing company only solicits certain shareholders for exercise of voting rights by proxy, so that shareholders who did not receive solicitation may obtain the same information as those who were solicited. On the other hand, in cases where shareholders solicit for the exercise of voting rights by proxy in opposition to the issuing company, the information stated on the Reference Documents may be useful for the solicitation to be effective.

## 2. Approval or disapproval columns in proxy cards

The proxy cards provided by solicitors to solicited persons shall allow solicited persons to express their approval or disapproval for each proposal in a general shareholders meeting (Article 43 of the Proxy Solicitation Cabinet Office Ordinance). It is also possible to provide a column for abstentions (proviso to Article 43 of the Proxy Solicitation Cabinet Office Ordinance). However, noting the extreme difficulty of shareholders conducting proxy solicitation after they receive notice of convocation of a general shareholders meeting from the company, there is a court precedent which pointed out that "the interpretation that shareholders shall always prepare proxy cards with columns for approval or disapproval of company proposals where the shareholders solicit the exercise of voting rights by proxy with descriptions against company proposals concurrently with approving the shareholders' proposals would result in a conspicuous violation of the fairness between the company and shareholders regarding solicitation

Chapter 10  Proxy solicitation

of shareholders for the exercise of voting rights by proxy ." (Tokyo District
Court Decision of December 6, 2007, *Shoji Homu* No. 1820, p. 32);[8] the ruling
is a precedent that interprets that such Proxy Card does not impact the
efficacy of granting representation rights.

In cases where the delegated person (the solicitor) exercises a voting right
opposite from that stated in the approval/disapproval column on the proxy
(for example, voting "yes" while the entry on the proxy is "no"), the
doctrines are divided as to whether the exercise of voting rights becomes
invalidated as unauthorized representation[9], and there is no published court
precedent. In the case where the exercise of voting rights becomes invalid as
unauthorized representation, this would lead to the general shareholders
resolution having grounds for revocation, but may leave room for
discretionary dismissal.

Additionally, there are issues regarding proxy cards with questionable
wording even though there are columns where solicited persons may state
approval/disapproval for each proposal. Examples of such cases are: (1)
validity of proxy cards with the wording "when 'yes' or 'no' is not indicated,
this becomes a blank proxy" added; (2) validity of proxy cards with the
wording "this becomes a blank proxy when original proposals are revised or
there are motions regarding the handling of original proposals concerning
administration of the general shareholders meeting" added; and (3) whether

---

8　When the proxy solicitation concerning company proposals or counterproposals takes
　　place before the delivery of written voting forms by the company, shareholders may
　　respond to the proxy solicitation without knowing about the existence of
　　counterproposals, and that could be criticized as violating the purport of proxy
　　solicitation regulations. However, because private law states that proxy authorizations
　　can be withdrawn freely, and shareholders have the opportunity to make new
　　decisions after they learn of the existence of counterproposals, this does not violate the
　　purport of proxy solicitation regulations. (Yo Ota, "*Ininjo kanyu ni kansuru jitsumujo
　　no shomondai*" [Practical Issues concerning Proxy Solicitation], in: Research Group
　　on Securities and Exchange Act, *Shoken kaisha hosei no choryu* [Trends in Securities
　　and Company Legislation], p. 232 (Japan Securities Research Institute: 2007).

9　Hiroshi Imai, *Giketsuken dairi koshi no kanyu* [Solicitation of Exercise of Voting Rights
　　by Proxy], p. 308 (Shoji Homu Kenkyukai: 1971).

*929*

the company is allowed to obtain an *en-bloc* proxy to respond to motions submitted for procedural purposes. Regarding these points, no published precedents have been found denying the acceptability of (3), and the doctrines generally agree that such practice is permissible. However, regarding the validity of the wording in above (1) and (2) that state "when proposals are revised [...] this becomes a blank proxy," some scholars take restrictive view. Nor is the view of the courts necessarily clear. The Tokyo District Court ruled on December 6, 2007 that "since the proxy states, as a matter of delegation, 'when approval or disapproval is not instructed, this becomes a blank proxy,' under the above conditions, there is nothing to prevent the interpretation that the shareholders who submitted the proxy leaving the approval or disapproval column blank granted proxy to exercise voting rights to the plaintiff (the shareholders — added by the author) with the purport to disapprove the company's proposal while approving the shareholders' proposal," and acknowledged the intention of the shareholders who submitted the proxy. In other words, the Court made no judgment regarding whether the blank proxy is justifiable.

## 3. Submission of copies to the Commissioner of the Financial Services Agency

When solicitors deliver the Reference Documents and proxy cards to shareholders, copies of these documents [10] (including electromagnetic records [11] prepared as specified by cabinet office ordinance or documents stating the matters recorded on the electromagnetic records in case electromagnetic records may be prepared in lieu of preparing the documents) shall be submitted to the Commissioner of the Financial Services Agency (hereinafter, the "FSA") [12] in principle (Article 36-3 of the FIEA Implementing Order). However, submission is not required when the

---

10 When some types of documents other than proxy forms and reference materials are delivered, while the legal basis is unclear, in practice it seems these must all be delivered to the supervisory authorities.

11 The electromagnetic record must be on a magnetic disk with a 90 mm flexible disk cartridge structure that conforms with JIS X6223, using a track format prescribed by JIS X6225, with a volume and file structure prescribed by JIS X0605 (Article 45 of the Proxy Solicitation Cabinet Office Ordinance).

*930*

Chapter 10 Proxy solicitation

Reference Documents and Voting Forms concerning the same general shareholders meeting have been delivered to all shareholders of the company that issued the shares (limited to shareholders that may exercise voting rights at the general shareholders meeting) (Article 44 of the Proxy Solicitation Cabinet Office Ordinance).

The submitted Reference Documents and proxy cards are subject to review. However, even when the Reference Documents contain false statements of important matters or statements that would cause a misunderstanding, the Commissioner of the FSA cannot issue an order to suspend the solicitation, or an order to amend the Reference Documents. Consequently, the Commissioner of the FSA may advise solicitors to deliver the revised Reference Documents to solicited persons; if the solicitors do not follow this advice, the Prime Minister or the Minister of Finance may only request that the court issue an order forbidding the exercise of voting rights by proxy in response to the solicitation using those Reference Documents and the granting of power of representation based thereon (Article 192(1) of the FIEA).

# F. Other issues regarding solicitation for exercise of voting rights by proxy

Due to possible concerns regarding confusion in tallying votes for proposals when voting rights are exercised through the exercise of voting rights by proxy for some proposals while Voting Forms were used for others,[13] doctrines are divided as to whether it is possible to conduct solicitations for the exercise of voting rights by proxy for certain proposals only where more than one proposal is expected for voting at a given general shareholders

---

12  The authority to accept the documents lies with the Director General of the Local Finance Bureau with jurisdiction over the solicitor's address (Article 43-11 of the FIEA Implementing Order).

13  Research Group on the Securities and Exchange Act, "*Ininjo kanyu ni kansuru jitsumujo no shomondai*" [Practical Issues concerning Proxy Solicitation], in: *Shoken torihiki ho kenkyu-kai kenkyu kiroku* [Minutes of the Securities and Exchange Act Research Group], No. 10, p. 32. (remark by Prof. Kansaku).

*931*

meeting. However, some interpret that solicitation for proxy cards for some items at a shareholders meeting while not soliciting for other matters is permitted[14]. It is considered natural that power of representation may be granted for each proposal, as a shareholder exercises his/her voting right for each proposal even when there are multiple proposals at a single general shareholders meeting.[15] The Tokyo District Court Judgment of December 6, 2007 above is consistent with this interpretation.

As for the issuing company soliciting proxies only from certain shareholders, initially the "common view" was that solicitation by directors in order to secure votes for the approval of proposals within the scope necessary in cases where he/she believed it was beneficial for the company, as an exercise of the duty of care of a prudent manager, does not fall under the principle of equal treatment of shareholder.[16] Subsequently, however, opinion that solicitation of proxies using company expense should be made to all shareholders became dominant, based on the view which emphasized that solicitation for exercise of voting rights by proxy was a function which ensured opportunities for shareholders to exercise their voting rights.[17] Incidentally, the Act on Special Provisions of the Commercial Code was revised in 1981, which required certain large companies to approve the exercise of voting rights in writing. This caused some to argue that, in cases where exercising voting rights in writing is allowed whereby all shareholders have been granted the opportunity to exercise voting rights in writing through the distribution of Voting Forms, the issuing companies do not violate the principle of equal treatment of shareholders even when they have conducted proxy solicitation only for certain shareholders.[18] The Tokyo

---

14 Imai, note 9 above, p. 134.

15 Ota, note 8 above, p. 32, and Masahiro Hishida, *Shinpan chushaku kaisya ho dai-go kan* [Commentary on Company Law, New Edition ], vol. 5, p. 185 (Yuhikaku: 1986).

16 Tatsuta, note 3 above, p. 25.

17 Seiji Tanaka, *Kaisha ho shoron jokan* [Detailed Analysis of Company Law, Vol. 1], p. 391 (Keiso Shobo: 1967); Shigeru Morimoto, *"Shomen tohyo seido no igi to kino"* [Institutional Significance and Function of Voting in Writing], in: *Ueyanagi Katsuro sensei kanreki kinen Shoji ho no kaishaku to tenbo* [Prof. Katsuro Ueyanagi's 60th Birthday Memorial Research Paper Collection: Interpretation and Outlook of Commercial Law], p. 136 (Yuhikaku: 1984).

*932*

Chapter 10   Proxy solicitation

District Court Judgment on December 6, 2007 took the view that such partial solicitation does not violate the purport of proxy solicitation regulation (*Hanrei Times*, No. 1258, p. 69).

# G. Items that should be stated in reference documents

## 1. Proxy Solicitation Cabinet Office Ordinance and material facts necessary to avoid misunderstanding

Reference Documents that solicitors provide to solicited persons shall be prepared pursuant to the Proxy Solicitation Cabinet Office Ordinance (Article 36-2(1) of the FIEA Implementing Order). The Proxy Solicitation Cabinet Office Ordinance prescribes general matters to be stated (Article 1), items to be stated concerning the proposals submitted by the company (Articles 2 through 38), items to be stated when the issuing company, etc., makes solicitations concerning shareholder proposals (Article 39), and items to be stated when parties other than the issuing company conduct solicitations regarding shareholder proposals (Article 40). Article 41 states that all of the above apply to the provisions for Reference Documents at class shareholders meetings.

However, Article 36-4 of the FIEA Implementing Order prohibits solicitors from conducting solicitation of voting rights by proxy using proxy cards, Reference Documents, or other documents or electromagnetic records that contain false statements or records on important matters, or which lack a statement or record of important items that should be stated, or material facts that are necessary to avoid causing any misunderstanding. Reference Documents should not only accurately state the items specifically prescribed in the Proxy Solicitation Cabinet Office Ordinance, but also state material

---

**18**   Kenichiro Osumi and Hiroshi Imai, *Kaisha ho ron chu-kan* [Theory of Company Law (3rd Edition), vol. 2], p. 67 (Yuhikaku: 1994); Takeo Inaba *et al.*, *Jitsumusodan Kabushiki Kaisha ho 2* [Practical Q&A on Stock Corporation Law, vol. 2], p. 683 (Shoji Homu Kenkyukai: 1992).

*933*

facts necessary to avoid causing any misunderstanding by the solicited persons.

In addition to the items prescribed by the Proxy Solicitation Cabinet Office Ordinance, the Reference Documents may include information that are helpful as a reference for granting the power of representation concerning the exercise of voting rights (Article 1(5) of the Proxy Solicitation Cabinet Office Ordinance).

## 2. General matters to be stated

When the exercise of voting rights by proxy is solicited by the company issuing shares or its officers, its purport, the proposals proposed, as well as the summary and result of the review by auditors, if any, to be reported to the shareholders meeting shall be stated in the Reference Documents. If the proposals are submitted by the company's directors, the Reference Documents shall also state the reasons for the submission (including descriptions in the case of a proposal that requires certain matters to be explained at the general shareholders meeting) (Article 1 (1) (i) of the Proxy Solicitation Cabinet Office Ordinance). On the other hand, when the exercise of voting rights by proxy is solicited by other parties, the proposals and the name or business name and address of the solicitor shall be stated in the Reference Documents (Article 1(1) (ii) of the Proxy Solicitation Cabinet Office Ordinance).

## 3. Individual items to be stated concerning proposals submitted by the company — when solicitation is conducted by or for the issuing company

When proposals are submitted by the directors of the company issuing shares, and solicitations are conducted for the exercise of voting rights by proxy concerning those shares by the company or for the company, certain items shall be stated regarding the descriptions of each proposal. These items to be stated are prescribed in parallel with the items to be stated in the Reference Documents for general shareholders meeting that shall be provided in the case where the exercise of voting rights in writing or via electromagnetic means is permitted under the Companies Act (Articles 73

Chapter 10   Proxy solicitation

through 92 of the Implementing Ordinance for the Companies Act).

a. Election of directors

The candidate's name, date of birth, and brief personal history shall be stated; if the candidate has not agreed to assume office, that shall also be stated (Article 2(1) and Article 2-3(1) of the Proxy Solicitation Cabinet Office Ordinance). The following shall also be stated: the number of shares in the issuing company owned by the candidate; a summary of the agreement for limitation of liability between the candidate and the company if such agreement has been or is going to be concluded; the fact, if any, that the candidate holds material concurrent positions in other entities, a summary of that fact if there is any special relationship between the candidate and the issuing company, and the candidate's position and responsibilities at the issuing company if he/she currently serves as a director of the issuing company (Article 2(1) and Article 2-3(1) of the Proxy Solicitation Cabinet Office Ordinance). Where the issuing company is a subsidiary, etc. of another person (namely, a parent company, etc.), the following shall be stated: the fact, if any, that the candidate is the parent company, etc. (limited to a natural person); if the candidate currently serves as an executive officer of the parent company, etc. (and sister companies), the candidate's position and responsibilities at that company; if the issuing company is aware that the candidate has served as an executive officer of the parent company, etc. (including sister companies) within the past five years, the candidate's position and responsibilities at that company (Article 2(2) and Article 2-3 (2) of the Proxy Solicitation Cabinet Office Ordinance).

In the case of a candidate for outside director, the following shall be stated: the fact that the candidate is an outside director candidate, the reasons why the candidate was nominated as an outside director candidate; where the candidate currently serves as an outside director (limited to outside executives) of the issuing company, any evidence of violating the laws and regulations or articles of incorporation or other evidence of improper execution of business at the company (excluding instances that are not material) during the candidate's term of office since the candidate's most recent appointment, these facts and a summary of the acts taken by the candidate to prevent the occurrence of the facts as well as the acts taken in

*935*

response after the occurrence of such facts shall be stated; in the case where the candidate has been appointed as a director, executive officer or auditor of another stock corporation within the past five years and the issuing company is aware of any evidence of violating the laws and regulations or the articles of incorporation or other evidence of improper execution of business at the company (excluding instances that are not material) during the candidate's term at the company, the evidence (excluding instances that are not material; if the candidate was an outside director or auditor at the joint-stock company, an outline of the acts taken by the candidate to prevent the occurrence of those facts as well as the acts taken in response after the occurrence of such facts are to be included). In the case where the candidate has not been involved with company management in the past (including that of foreign companies) in ways other than serving as an outside director or outside auditor, the reasons why the solicitor determined that the candidate is capable of appropriately executing duties as an outside director without previous experience in management shall be stated. If the issuing company is aware of any of the following facts, the fact shall be stated: (a) the candidate is or has been an executive or officer of the issuing company or a subsidiary of the issuing company; (b) the candidate is or has been within the past five years the parent company, etc. (limited to a natural person); (c) the candidate is an executive or officer of a business operator that has a special relationship with the issuing company or has been an executive or officer of a business operator that has a special relationship with the issuing company (except for a subsidiary of the issuing company) within the past five years; (d) the candidate is scheduled to receive or has received a significant amount of money or other assets within the past two years from the issuing company or the business operator that has a specific relationship with the issuing company (excluding remuneration or fees as director, accounting advisor, auditor, executive officer or other equivalent party of those companies); (e) the candidate is a spouse or relative within the third degree of kinship or equivalent person of the parent company, etc. or an executive or officer of the issuing company or a business operator that has a special relationship with the company (excluding instances that are not material); (f) the candidate was not an outside director or auditor of the issuing company at the time although he/she was an executive officer of another

Chapter 10   Proxy solicitation

stock corporation where the issuing company has succeeded or received rights and responsibilities concerning businesses owned by the other joint-stock companies from a merger, absorption-type demerger, incorporation-type demerger or business transfer within the past two years. Where the candidate currently serves as an outside director or auditor of the issuing company, the number of years since the candidate assumed the position shall be stated. In the case where the candidate has an opinion regarding these statements, the contents of his/her opinion shall be stated (Article 2 (3) and Article 2-3 (3) of the Proxy Solicitation Cabinet Office Ordinance).

In a company with audit and supervisory committee, a member of the audit and supervisory committee may issue opinions regarding the nomination of directors who are members of the committee. The audit and supervisory committee may issue opinions regarding the nomination of directors who are not members of the committee (Article 342-2 (1) & (4) of the Companies Act). Thus, the summary of such opinions shall be stated, if a member of the audit and supervisory committee or the audit and supervisory committee, respectively, chooses to state opinions (Article 2 (1) (iii) and Article 2-3 (1) (viii) of the Proxy Solicitation Cabinet Office Ordinance). The fact, if any, that the proposal has been submitted at the request of the audit and supervisory committee (Article 344-2 (2) of the Companies Act) is also included in the Reference Documents (Article 2-3 (1) (viii) of the Proxy Solicitation Cabinet Office Ordinance).

A large company with auditor (s) subject to the duty to submit an annual securities report to the Prime Minister shall state "the reason which makes appointment of an outside director unreasonable for that company" in the Reference Documents where it has no outside director (including the case where it will no longer have one at the closing of the shareholders' meeting) and does not propose a candidate who will be eligible to be an outside director in electing directors (Article 2-2 (1) of the Proxy Solicitation Cabinet Office Ordinance).

b. Election of auditors

The items to be stated are prescribed in parallel with the items concerning the election of directors. Each candidate's name, date of birth, and brief

*937*

personal history shall be stated; and where the candidate has not yet agreed to assume office, there shall also be a statement to that effect. In addition, the following shall be stated: if there is any special relationship between the candidate and the issuing company, an outline of such facts, if a proposal has been submitted at the request of auditors, an outline of such opinion (Article 343 (2) of the Companies Act); and, if there is an auditor's opinion, a summary of such opinion. In addition, the following shall be stated: the number of shares of the issuing company owned by the candidate; the fact, if any, that a candidate holds material concurrent positions in other entities.; a summary of the agreement for limitation of liability between the candidate and the company if such agreement has been or is going to be concluded; and the fact, if a candidate currently serves as an auditor of the issuing company, the candidate's position and responsibilities at the issuing company (Article 4(1) of the Proxy Solicitation Cabinet Office Ordinance). The items to be stated when the issuing company is the subsidiary, etc.[19] of another person, and the items to be stated when the candidate is an outside auditor candidate are provided in parallel with the facts to be stated in the case of director election proposals (Article 4(2) & (3) of the Proxy Solicitation Cabinet Office Ordinance).

c. Dismissal of directors or auditors

In the case of the dismissal of directors or auditors, the names of the directors or auditors, as well as the reasons for his/her dismissal shall be stated (Articles 6, 6-2 and 8 of the Proxy Solicitation Cabinet Office Ordinance). Regarding the dismissal of auditors, an auditor may state opinions (Article 345(4) (i) of the Companies Act). In the same fashion, in a company with an audit and supervisory committee, a member of the audit and supervisory committee may state opinions regarding the dismissal of directors who are members of the committee. The audit and supervisory committee may state opinions regarding the dismissal of directors who are

---

19 "Subsidiary, etc." is a subsidiary or any juridical person whose management is controlled by a person other than a company as prescribed by the applicable Ordinance of the Ministry of Justice (Article 2(iii-2) of the Companies Act: Article 3-2(1) & (3) of the Implementing Ordinance for the Companies Act).

Chapter 10 Proxy solicitation

not members of the Committee (Article 345-2(1) & (4) of the Companies Act). Thus, a summary of such opinions shall be stated, if a member of the audit and supervisory committee, the audit and supervisory committee or an auditor, respectively, choose to state opinions (Article 6(iii); Article 6-2(iii); and Article 8(iii) of the Proxy Solicitation Cabinet Office Ordinance).

d . Election of accounting advisors and accounting auditors
In the case where an accounting advisor candidate is a certified public accountant or certified public tax accountant, the candidate's name, business address, date of birth and brief personal history shall be stated; where the candidate is an auditing firm or certified public tax accountant corporation, its name, address of main office, and organizational history shall be stated (Article 3(i) of the Proxy Solicitation Cabinet Office Ordinance). Similarly, where an accounting auditor candidate is a certified public accountant, the candidate's name, place of business address, date of birth, and brief personal history shall be stated; and in the case where the candidate is an auditing firm, its name, address of the main office and history shall be stated (Article 5(i) of the Proxy Solicitation Cabinet Office Ordinance). In either case, if a candidate has not yet agreed to assume office, that shall be stated (Article 3 (ii) and Article 5(ii) of the Proxy Solicitation Cabinet Office Ordinance). If there is an opinion from an accounting advisor or accounting auditor, a summary of such opinion (Article 3 (iii) and Article 5 (iv) of the Proxy Solicitation Cabinet Office Ordinance) and a summary of the agreement for limitation of liability between the candidate and the company if such agreement has been or is going to be concluded shall be stated (Article 3(iv) and Article 5(v) of the Proxy Solicitation Cabinet Office Ordinance). If the candidate has been ordered to suspend practice within the past two years, any item that the solicitors deem appropriate to be stated in the Reference Documents among the matters concerning the suspension shall be stated (Article 3 (v) and Article 5 (vii) of the Proxy Solicitation Cabinet Office Ordinance).

There are additional matters to be stated for proposals regarding the election of accounting auditors. Reasons for nomination shall be stated in the Reference Documents (Article 5(iii) of the Proxy Solicitation Cabinet Office

*939*

Ordinance). In the case where a candidate has been ordered to suspend practice and the period for such order has not yet expired, matters concerning the order (Article 5(vi) of the Proxy Solicitation Cabinet Office Ordinance). In the case where the candidate is scheduled to receive or has received within the past two years a significant amount of money or other financial benefits from the issuing company, the issuing company's parent company, etc.,[20] a subsidiary (excluding the issuing company) or an affiliated company of the issuing company's parent company (where the issuing company does not have a parent company, the issuing company itself) (including any company equivalent to a subsidiary company or a related company if the parent company is not a corporation), excluding compensation received from these parties as an accounting auditor (including those who are equivalent thereto under laws and regulations other than the Companies Act) and audit fees, the details of such receipt shall be stated in the Reference Documents (Article 5(viii) of the Proxy Solicitation Cabinet Office Ordinance).

e . Dismissal of accounting advisors, dismissal and non-reappointment of accounting auditors

In such a case, the names or business names of accounting advisors, and the names or business names of accounting auditors and reasons for dismissal or non-reappointment shall be stated in the Reference Documents (Article 9(i) (ii) and Article 7 (i) & (ii) of the Proxy Solicitation Cabinet Office Ordinance). In the case where there is an opinion from an accounting advisor or accounting auditor, a summary of such opinion shall be stated (Article 9 (iii) and Article 7(iii) of the Proxy Solicitation Cabinet Office Ordinance).

f . Approval of financial statements[21]

In the case where there is an opinion from an accounting auditor (Article 398 (1) of the Companies Act), the opinion shall be stated in the Reference

---

20  "Parent company, etc." is the parent company or any person (except for any juridical person) that controls the management of a stock corporation as prescribed by the applicable Ordinance of the Ministry of Justice (Article 2(iii-2) of the Companies Act; Article 4-2(2) & (3) of the Implementing Ordinance for the Companies Act).

Chapter 10   Proxy solicitation

Documents (Article 13 (i) of the Proxy Solicitation Cabinet Office Ordinance). In the case where the issuing company is a company with a board of directors, if there is an opinion from the board of directors, a summary of the opinion shall also be stated (Article 13 (ii) of the Proxy Solicitation Cabinet Office Ordinance).

g. Remuneration of directors, accounting advisors and auditors
Standards for calculating amounts of compensation, and the reasons for any change in such standards shall be stated (Article 10 (1) (i) & (ii); Article 10-2 (1) (i) & (ii); Article 11 (1) (i) & (ii) and Article 12 (1) (i) & (ii) of the Proxy Solicitation Cabinet Office Ordinance). In the case of proposals regarding two or more directors, accounting advisors or auditors, the number of directors, accounting advisors or auditors concerning the proposal shall be stated (Article 10 (1) (iii); Article 10-2 (1) (iii); Article 11 (1) (iii) and Article 12 (1) (iii) of the Proxy Solicitation Cabinet Office Ordinance).

In the case where an accounting advisor has an opinion regarding accounting advisor remuneration, or where an auditor has an opinion regarding auditor remuneration, a summary of the opinion shall be stated (Article 11 (1) (v) and Article 12 (1) (v) of the Proxy Solicitation Cabinet Office Ordinance). In a company with an audit and supervisory committee, in the case where the audit and supervisory committee has an opinion regarding remuneration of directors who are not members of the audit and supervisory committee, or where a member of the audit and supervisory committee has an opinion regarding remuneration of directors who are members of the audit and supervisory committee, a summary of the opinion shall be stated (Article 10 (1) (v) and Article 10-2 (1) (v) of the Proxy Solicitation Cabinet Office Ordinance).

---

21   They include the balance sheet on the date of incorporation, annual accounts (balance sheet, profit and loss statement, statement of changes in shareholders' equity and individual notes) for each business year and the annexes thereto, interim accounts and consolidated accounts. However, consolidated accounts shall be reported only, without approval. The annexes to the balance sheet as of the date of incorporation as well as to annual accounts for each business year are also not subject to approval.

In the case where a proposal concerns the retirement bonus for a director, accounting advisor or auditor, a brief personal history of each retiring director, accounting advisor or auditor shall be stated (Article 10(1)(iv); Article 10-2(1)(iv); Article 11(1)(iv) and Article 12(1)(iv) of the Proxy Solicitation Cabinet Office Ordinance). In the case where a proposal entrusts directors, auditors or other third parties with the determination of retirement bonus based on a predetermined formula, the formula shall be stated in principle (Article 10(2), Article 10-2(2), Article 11(2) and Article 12(2) of the Proxy Solicitation Cabinet Office Ordinance). However, if appropriate measures have been taken to enable each shareholder to know the formula, the descriptions do not have to be stated. In practice, companies keep documents stating the formula at their head offices for viewing by shareholders; maintain electromagnetic records of the formula at their head offices so the descriptions of the information recorded in the electromagnetic records can be displayed on paper or on the screens of output devices for viewing by shareholders. Thus, the formula is usually not stated in the Reference Documents in practice.

Under the Companies Act, after part of the liability of an officer, etc. to the company is exempted through a special resolution of general shareholders meeting or through directors' consent or resolution of board of directors based on the articles of incorporation thereby indemnifying the officer, etc. against liability for amounts exceeding the maximum liability amount set by the liability limitation agreement, provision of retirement bonus or other financial benefits prescribed by a Ministry of Justice Ordinance to the officer, etc. shall be approved by a general shareholders meeting resolution (Article 425(4), Article 426(6), and Article 427(5) of the Companies Act). In the case where the exercise of voting rights by proxy regarding such proposals concerning the payment of retirement bonuses is solicited, the Reference Documents shall state the details of the retirement bonus to be received by the officer, etc. who has been exempted from liability or indemnified against liability (Article 12-2 of the Proxy Solicitation Cabinet Office Ordinance).

Chapter 10 Proxy solicitation

h. Acquisition of class shares subject to wholly call and reverse stock split

For proposals regarding acquisition of class shares subject to wholly call and reverse stock split that leads to odd lots, the reasons for conducting those acts, the particulars of the acts to be decided by a resolution of shareholders' meeting, and, if appropriate, an outline of matters as of the date of decision to be disclosed at the head office in accordance with Article 171-2, paragraph 1 or Article 182-2, paragraph 1 of the Companies Act shall be stated in the Reference Documents (Articles 13-2 and 13-3 of the Proxy Solicitation Cabinet Office Ordinance).

i. Resolutions approving restructuring, etc.

For proposals regarding approval of agreements concerning absorption-type merger agreements, absorption-type demerger agreements, share exchange agreements, consolidation-type merger, incorporation-type demerger plans, share transfer plans and business transfer plans, the reasons for conducting those acts and an outline of the terms of the agreement or plan shall be stated in the Reference Documents (Article 14(i) & (ii), Article 15(i) & (ii); Article 16(i) & (ii), Article 17(i) & (ii), Article 18(i) & (ii), Article 19(i) & (ii), and Article 20 (i) & (ii) of the Proxy Solicitation Cabinet Office Ordinance).

In cases where the company is a company absorbed in an absorption-type merger, a demerging company in an absorption-type demerger or a wholly-owned subsidiary company in a share exchange, the following matters shall be stated: items concerning the appropriateness of the compensation for reorganization on the determination date of convocation of the general shareholders meeting to approve the reorganization, items helpful as reference concerning the compensation for reorganization, items concerning the appropriateness of the provision of share options concerning the act of reorganization, and a summary of the contents of any items concerning annual accounts (Article 14(iii), Article 15(iii), and Article 16(iii) of the Proxy Solicitation Cabinet Office Ordinance). In the cases where the company is the surviving company in an absorption-type merger, succeeding company in an absorption-type demerger, or wholly-owning

*943*

parent company in share exchange, the following matters shall be stated: provision concerning the appropriateness of the compensation for reorganization on the determination date of convocation of the general shareholders meeting to approve the reorganization as well as the allotment of such compensation (where such provision is omitted, the appropriateness of the omission), provision on the appropriateness of the value to be delivered to the share purchase option holders and for its allotment (excluding a provision stipulating that no value will be delivered to all share purchase holders for all of the share purchase options), contents of financial statements, etc. of the company absorbed in an absorption-type merger, a demerging company in an absorption-type demerger or a wholly-owned subsidiary company in a share exchange, or, any material subsequent event regarding the surving company in an absorption-type merger, the succeeding company in an absorption-type demerger, or the wholly-owning parent company in a share exchange (Article 14 (iv), Article 15 (iv), and Article 16 (iv) of the Proxy Solicitation Cabinet Office Ordinance).

Similarly, when the company is a new company incorporated by consolidation-type merger, a company incorporated by incorporation-type demerger, or a wholly-owned subsidiary in a share transfer, items concerning the appropriateness of the compensation as of the determination date of convocation of the general shareholders meeting to approve the reorganization shall be stated, items that should be referred to for the compensation for the reorganization, or a summary of the description of items concerning annual accounts, if any. (Article 17 (iii), Article 18 (iii), and Article 19 (iii) of the Proxy Solicitation Cabinet Office Ordinance). Similarly, in the case of proposals to approve the agreement concerning business transfer, etc., a summary of the matters concerning the appropriateness of the calculation of the compensation to be delivered to the counterparty of such agreement shall be stated (Article 20 (iii) of the Proxy Solicitation Cabinet Office Ordinance).

Additionally, for resolutions to approve an agreement on consolidation-type merger or a share transfer plan, information regarding the persons who will become directors (Article 17 (iv), Article 19 (iv), and Article 2 of the Proxy

944

Chapter 10　Proxy solicitation

Solicitation Cabinet Office Ordinance) shall be stated. In the case where the new company incorporated through consolidation-type merger or the wholly-owning parent company in a share transfer is a company with accounting advisors, information regarding the persons who will become accounting advisors shall be stated (Article 17(v), Article 19(v), and Article 3 of the Proxy Solicitation Cabinet Office Ordinance); whereas if the company is a company with auditors (including stock corporations with articles of incorporation limiting the scope of audits by auditors to accounting), information regarding persons who will become the auditors shall be stated (Article 17(vi), Article 19(vi), and Article 4 of the Proxy Solicitation Cabinet Office Ordinance), and where the company is a company with accounting auditors, information regarding parties that will become the accounting auditors shall be stated (Article 17(vii), Article 19(vii), and Article 5 of the Proxy Solicitation Cabinet Office Ordinance).

# 4. Individual items to be stated regarding proposals submitted by companies — excluding the case where solicitation is conducted by or for the issuing company

In cases other than where solicitation is conducted by or for the issuing company, the items to be stated in Reference Documents are simplified compared to where solicitation is conducted by or for the issuing company. This reflects that it may not be easy to obtain information in the former case. Also, in the case where voting rights may be executed in writing or via electromagnetic means, because the issuing company shall provide the Reference Documents to comply with the Companies Act, the solicited persons may obtain information through these materials.

### a. Election of directors
The candidate's name, date of birth, and brief personal history shall be stated. In the case where the candidate holds material concurrent positions in other entities, that fact shall be stated; where there is any special relationship between the candidate and the issuing company, a summary of that fact shall be stated; and where the candidate is currently a director of the issuing company, the candidate's position and responsibilities at the issuing company shall be stated (Articles 21 and 21-2 of the Proxy

*945*

Solicitation Cabinet Office Ordinance).

b. Election of auditors

The candidate's name, date of birth, and brief personal history shall be stated, and where there is any special relationship between the candidate and the issuing company, a summary of that shall be stated. In the case where the candidate holds material concurrent positions in other entities, that shall be stated; and where the candidate is currently an auditor of the issuing company, the candidate's position and responsibilities at the issuing company shall be stated (Article 23 of the Proxy Solicitation Cabinet Office Ordinance).

c. Dismissal of directors and auditors

The names and brief personal history of the relevant directors or auditors shall be stated (Articles 25, 25-2, and 27 of the Proxy Solicitation Cabinet Office Ordinance).

d. Election of accounting advisors and accounting auditors

In the case where an accounting advisor candidate is a certified public accountant or certified public tax accountant, the candidate's name, place of business address, date of birth and brief personal history shall be stated; and where the candidate is an auditing firm or certified public tax accountant corporation, its name, address of main office, and organizational history shall be stated (Article 22(i) of the Proxy Solicitation Cabinet Office Ordinance). Similarly, where an accounting auditor candidate is a certified public accountant, the candidate's name, business address, date of birth, and brief personal history shall be stated; and where the candidate is an auditing firm, its name, address of main office and organizational history shall be stated (Article 24(i) of the Proxy Solicitation Cabinet Office Ordinance). In the case where the candidate has been ordered to suspend practice within the past two years, information that the solicitor deems appropriate to be stated in Reference Documents among the matters concerning the suspension shall be stated (Article 22(ii), and Article 24(iii) of the Proxy Solicitation Cabinet Office Ordinance).

Chapter 10  Proxy solicitation

For proposals regarding the election of accounting auditors, where a candidate has been ordered to suspend practice and the period for such order has not yet expired, information concerning the order shall be stated (Article 24(ii) of the Proxy Solicitation Cabinet Office Ordinance).

e . Dismissal of accounting advisors and dismissal/non-reappointment of accounting auditors

In the case where the accounting advisor is a certified public accountant or certified public tax accountant, the accounting advisor's name and brief personal history shall be stated, and where the accounting advisor is an auditing firm or a tax accounting corporation, its business name and organizational history shall be stated (Articles 26 and 28 of the Proxy Solicitation Cabinet Office Ordinance).

f . Remuneration of directors, accounting advisors and auditors

For directors (excluding those who are members of the audit and supervisory committee) and auditors, the name and brief personal history shall be stated; where the accounting advisor is a certified public accountant or certified public tax accountant, the name and brief personal history shall be stated; and where the accounting advisor is an auditing firm or tax accounting corporation, its name and history shall be stated (Article 29(i), Article 30(i), and Article 31(i) of the Proxy Solicitation Cabinet Office Ordinance). In the case where the proposal is the provision of two or more directors (those who are members of the audit and supervisory committee and those who are not, respectively), accounting advisors or auditors, the number of the directors, accounting advisors or auditors to be provided shall be stated (Article 29(ii), Article 29-2(i), Article 30(ii), and Article 31(ii) of the Proxy Solicitation Cabinet Office Ordinance). Further, in the case where the proposal is regarding the retirement bonuses of directors (those who are members of the audit and supervisory committee and those who are not, respectively), accounting advisors or auditors, the brief personal histories of each retiring director, accounting advisor or auditor shall be stated (Article 29 (iii), Article 29-2 (ii), Article 30 (iii), and Article 31 (iii) of the Proxy Solicitation Cabinet Office Ordinance).

*947*

g. Resolutions approving reorganization, etc.

For proposals regarding approval of agreements concerning absorption-type merger agreement, absorption-type demerger agreement, share exchange agreements, consolidation-type merger agreements, incorporation-type demerger plans, share transfer plans or business transfer plans, a summary of the agreement or plan shall be stated in the reference documents (Article 32, Article 33, Article 34, Article 35(i), Article 36, Article 37(i), and Article 38 of the Proxy Solicitation Cabinet Office Ordinance). In the case of proposals approving consolidation-type merger agreements and share transfer plans, information concerning the persons who will become directors shall be stated (Article 35(ii), Article 37(ii), and Article 21). In the case where a stock corporation formed by consolidation-type merger or wholly-owning parent company incorporated through a share transfer is a company with accounting advisors, information concerning the persons who will become accounting advisors shall be stated (Article 35(iii), Article 37 (iii), and Article 22); whereas it is a company with auditors (including stock corporations with articles of incorporation limiting the scope of audits by auditors to accounting), information regarding persons who will become auditors shall be stated (Article 35(iv), Article 37(iv), and Article 23); if it is a company with accounting auditors, information regarding parties that will become accounting auditors shall be stated (Article 35(v), Article 37(v), and Article 24).

## 5. Individual items to be stated regarding proposals submitted by shareholders — when solicitation is conducted by or for the issuing company

In cases where proposals are submitted by shareholders of the company issuing shares, and solicitations for the exercise of voting rights are by proxy concerning those shares and made by or for the issuing company, the fact that these proposals were submitted by shareholders shall be stated in the Reference Documents; additionally, if directors (the board of directors in the case of companies with boards of directors) have opinions regarding those proposals, the contents of the opinions shall be stated (Article 39(1)(i) & (ii) of the Proxy Solicitation Cabinet Office Ordinance). However, in cases where proposals with the same purport are submitted by two or more shareholders,

Chapter 10   Proxy solicitation

it is not required to state each proposal as well as any opinion regarding each proposal from directors (board of directors in the case of companies with boards of directors) individually, if the fact that there were proposals with the same purport from two or more shareholders is stated (Article 39(2) of the Proxy Solicitation Cabinet Office Ordinance).

In cases where shareholders notify the issuing company of the reasons for proposals when making demands under Article 305, paragraph 1 of the Companies Act, except for cases where the reasons for the proposals are deemed to be clearly false or merely insult or violate a person's reputation, the reasons for proposals shall be stated; in cases where the proposal is on election of directors, accounting advisors, auditors or accounting auditors, acquisition of class shares subject to wholly call or the reverse stock split that leads to odd lots and where information pertaining to the candidates (referring to Articles 2 through 5), the acquisition of class shares subject to wholly call and the reverse stock split that leads to odd lots are provided, the contents of the provided information shall be stated except where the content is obviously false (Article 39 (1) (iii) through (v) of the Proxy Solicitation Cabinet Office Ordinance). However, if such information comprises a significantly large number of letters, symbols, etc. in the Reference Documents (including cases where the number exceeds the amount the issuing company has prescribed as appropriate for statement in full), it is sufficient to state only the summary of the information. Also, when two or more shareholders submit reasons for proposals with the same purport, it is not necessary to respectively state each of the reasons for proposals in the Reference Documents (Article 39 (3) of the Proxy Solicitation Cabinet Office Ordinance).
These requirements are in parallel with Article 93 of the Implementing Ordinance for Companies Act.

# 6. Individual items to be stated regarding proposals submitted by shareholders — excluding solicitation conducted by or for the issuing company

In the case where proposals are submitted by shareholders of the company issuing shares and solicitation is conducted to exercise voting rights by

*949*

proxy for the shares, if such solicitation is not conducted by or for the issuing company to exercise voting rights by proxy for the shares, the fact that the proposal is a shareholder submission and the reasons for the submission shall be stated in the Reference Documents; in addition, in the case of proposals concerning the election of directors (those who are members of the audit and supervisory committee and those who are not, respectively), accounting advisors, auditors or accounting auditors, information concerning the candidates (referring to Articles 21 through 24) shall be stated in the Reference Documents (Article 40 of the Proxy Solicitation Cabinet Office Ordinance).

# H. Effect of violating proxy solicitation regulations

In cases where a company conducts solicitation in violation of regulations concerning proxy solicitation, shareholders may demand that the directors or executive officers cease the act of solicitation, if such act is likely to cause irrevocable damage to the company (Article 360 of the Companies Act). Also in cases where the company or other parties conduct solicitation in violation of proxy solicitation regulations and receive the power to exercise voting rights by proxy, and where such authorization can be provisionally interpreted as invalid[22], it is considered possible to request a provisional order to prohibit the exercise of voting rights by proxy (Article 23(2) of the Civil Provisional Remedies Act).

On the other hand, in cases where solicitation in violation of regulations concerning proxy solicitation has been conducted and the voting rights by proxy have been exercised, whether the exercise affects the validity of the general shareholders meeting resolutions becomes an issue. The case precedents hold that, since proxy solicitation regulations are provisions

---

22  Michiyo Hamada, *"Ininjo kanyu to shomen tohyo"* [Proxies and Voting in Writing], in: *Kawamoto Ichiro sensei kanreki kinen ronbun-shu Shoken torihiki ho taikei* [Prof. Ichiro Kawamoto's 60th Birthday Memorial Research Paper Collection : Securities and Exchange Act], p. 255 (Shoji Homu Kenkyukai: 1986).

Chapter 10　Proxy solicitation

stipulating the methods that should be observed during solicitation for the exercise of voting rights by proxy, and solicitation for the exercise of voting rights by proxy is an actual act at the stage before general shareholders meeting resolutions, it cannot be deemed a method of a general shareholders meeting resolution[23]; according to this rationale, the court ruling maintained that the Proxy Solicitation Cabinet Office Ordinance does not correspond to "laws and regulations" for the purpose of Article 831 paragraph 1, item 1 of the Companies Act; therefore, the resolution method cannot be regarded as conspicuously unfair (Tokyo District Court Judgment of July 7, 2005, *Hanrei Jiho* No. 1915, p. 150). However, the prevailing doctrine holds that, at least where solicitation for the exercise of voting rights by proxy has been conducted in lieu of allowing the exercise of voting rights in writing, if the solicitation has violated the proxy solicitation regulations, the method of resolution has flaws that lead to revocation of the resolution (Article 831 (1) (i) of the Companies Act).[24] It is also possible to point out the flaws in the resolution method as voting rights were exercised without valid power of representation, from the viewpoint that the proxy is invalid where such proxy has been granted through solicitation in violation of the regulations concerning proxy solicitation. Furthermore, some hold that resolutions may

---

**23**　Tadao Omori, *"Giketsu ken"* [Voting Rights], in: Kotaro Tanaka (ed.), *Kabushiki kaisya ho koza dai san-kan* [Lectures on Stock Corporation Law Vol. 3], p. 934 (Yuhikaku: 1956) and Ichiro Sakai, "Regarding Solicitation of the Exercise of Voting Rights by Proxy at Stock Corporations" (*Kobe Shodai Ronshu* Vol. 7, p. 77) are of the same opinion. On the other hand, there was also the prevailing view based on the grounds as follows that the act by the issuing company in violation of proxy solicitation regulation is equivalent to a cause for revocation of resolutions at a general shareholders meeting: (i) if the issuing company conducts solicitation for exercise of voting rights, such act constitutes part of the procedure for the adoption of resolution in a general shareholders meeting; therefore, it forms part of the "process for approving resolutions"; (ii) unless one denies the efficacy of any acts in violation of proxy solicitation regulations, it becomes impossible to ensure the effectiveness of the regulation; and (iii) the Securities and Exchange Act and the proxy solicitation regulations (at the time) were also *de facto* part of the Companies Act. (Tatsuta, note 3 above, p. 36; Hamada, note 20 above, p. 256; Mitsuko Shibuya, "Commercial Code Regulation and Securities and Exchange Act Regulation", *Shoken Kenkyu* No. 57, p. 246-251 (1979).

**24**　Egashira, note 5 above, p. 346 footnote 11.

*951*

be revoked in cases such as the delivery of proxy cards not conforming with the requirements or unconditional proxy cards or Reference Documents containing false statements because resolutions have been approved conspicuously unfairly.[25]

On the other hand, violations of regulations concerning proxy solicitation shall be punished by a fine of not more than 300,000 yen (Article 205-2-3 (ii) of the Financial Instruments and Exchange Act).

---

**25** Masahiro Hishida, *Kabunushi no giketsu-ken koshi to kaisha shihai* [Shareholder Exercise of Voting Rights and Company Control], p. 108 (Sakai Shoten: 1960); Makoto Yazawa, "Exercise of Voting Rights by Proxy", *Tokyo Kabushiki Konwakai Kaiho* [Tokyo Shares Forum Report] No. 119, p. 36 (1961); Imai, note 9 above, p. 90, Osumi and Imai, note 18 above, p. 67, etc.

# Index

## Number

12-hour rule ·········································· 840

## A

abuse of the dominant power ············73

account for clients ······················· 107

account management institution ······ 18,
107,627,674,717,824

accountability ···························· 734,744

accounting documents ··············· 50,51

accounting standards················51,348

acquisition of a new issue·············· 527

Act Concerning Assets
Liquidation ···························· 17,80

Act Concerning Securitization of
Specified Assets by Special
Purpose Companies (the SPC
Law) ····································80

Act Concerning the Regulation of
Business Relating to Specified
Claims ···································78

Act on Book-Entry Transfer of
Corporate Bonds and Shares ····· 18,
107,127,627,824

Act on Prevention of Transfer of
Criminal Proceeds ················· 659

Act on Sales, etc. of Financial
Instruments ························· 749

activist shareholders ···················· 106

acts of financial instruments
intermediation ····················· 595

acts of financial instruments
transaction··························· 721

acts similar to advertising ············· 725

acts similar to solicitation ············· 740

actual incorporation method ····224,248,
458

actual joint holder ················· 569,570

administrative action············· 175,177

Administrative Appeal Act ········· 481

Administrative Case Litigation
Act ···································· 481

administrative discretion··············· 176

administrative disposition ······896,901,
907

administrative guidance ················ 173

administrative interpretation ········ 174

administrative investigations···· 177,188

administrative monetary penalties ····9,
15,89,91,165,166,177,180,498,557,
589,842,896,898,907,909
  investigations ···························· 166
  payment order···················· 903,910
  system ······································ 909

Administrative Procedures Act······ 480

administrative review ·················· 481

administrative stay of execution ····· 481

ADR — see alternative dispute resolution

advertising ···························· 725,740

advertising regulation ····················62

advice································· 619

affiliated company, etc.············ 687,688

after-sales service ······················ 738

agency service ··············· 597,600,601

aider································ 483

alert document ························· 748

allotments of share options············· 329

already-issued securities··········48,521

alternative dispute
resolution (ADR) ··· 97,710,762,816,
898

alternative trading systems
(ATSs) ······························· 614,808

*953*

amateurs 708

amended report 578,587

amended specified information 349, 467,484

amended statements 488

amendment confirmation letter 414, 426,432

amendment order 414,472,474,479,480
  submission orders 481

American Depositary Receipts 184, 385

analyst report 617,620,768

analyst 440,617

ancillary business 87,150,819

annual securities report 84,105,112, 311,360,363,364,369,376,392,398,408, 412,459,464,487,504
  Form 3 376
  Form 3-2 376
  Form 4 376,379
  Form 8 376
  Form 9 376

anonymous partnerships 131

Antimonopoly Act 164,168,179,181, 683

antisocial forces 173

appeals 481

application for share
  subscriptions 326

approved business 674,676,755

arms-length transaction rule 73

assault 869

asset custody company 714

asset management 640

asset management CISs 17

asset management company 620,715

asset-backed securities 282

asset-backed securitization CISs 17

assumed foreign exchange risk
  ratio 732

asymmetry of information 21,43,532, 540

attached documents 217,246,252,259, 268,272,277,285,313

auction method 526,791,811

auction process 791

audit & supervisory board 105,668, 685

audit certification 105,236,402,404, 405,450

audit report 371,403,411

auditing firm 450,464

authorization 639,640,671,800

authorized financial instruments
  firms association 19,27,30,32,36, 217,219,375,579,615,673,788,813,896, 919

authorized implementers of
  electronic over-the-counter
  transactions of derivatives,
  etc. 653

authorized transaction-at-exchange
  operators 652,733,790

autonomy principle 42,44

### B

bad faith 693

balance sheet 50

ban on transmission of undisclosed
  material information 73

bank 72,73

bank holding company 683,691

bank-centered system 109

Banking Act 67,71,74,593,683

banking crisis 109

bankruptcy remoteness 79,133

Basel III 155

basket clause 766,835,839

best execution 701,713,810
  duty 29,89,811
  policy 701,713

requirement ·················· 705

best practices ·················· 703

best-advice requirement ·············· 738

better regulation ···················· 169

Big Bang ··························87

binary options, etc. ···················· 732

BIS ······························ 155

blank proxy ······················· 929

book-entry system ············18,107,822

book-entry transfer ······18,107,606,792

book-entry transfer institutions······ 18, 674

brief financial results statement ····· 838

brokerage ················ 597,600,601,605

brokerage contract rules ········· 791,801

brokerage for clearing of
securities ·················· 603,604,605

bucketing························· 701,705,810

business···························· 597
in the course of ···················· 597

business conduct regulation ········ 45,61

business conduct standards········· 61,94

business improvement order ···· 180,908

business in electronic
over-the-counter transactions
of derivatives, etc. ········ 638,646,653

business secrets ···················· 218,335

business suspension order ············· 176

business-related parties ·············· 438

buy-all requirement····513,514,519,552, 553

## C

Cabinet Office ···················· 160

Cabinet Office Ordinance on
Disclosure of Corporate
Affairs·························· 376

Cabinet Office Ordinance on
Foreign Bonds················ 205,377

Cabinet Office Ordinance on

Specified Securities
Disclosure························ 201,390

Cabinet Office Ordinance
Regarding on Definitions···· 16,193, 631

cabinet office ordinances ················16

cabinet order ·······················16

calculators of specified securities
indicators ···················· 674

call auction method ····················· 791

capital adequacy requirements ···98,689

capital markets ····························20
efficiency···························22
semi-strong efficiency············· 24,44
strong-form efficiency··················24
weak-form efficiency ··················23

capital markets regulation ··············14

capital requirements ·····················93

capital-to-risk ratio ·············· 666,689

CARDs ···························· 682

carbon dioxide — see rights to emit
carbon dioxide

category of business ·········· 639,645,661

CCP — see central counterparty

CDSs — see credit default swaps

cease-and-desist orders ········· 481,482

central counterparty (CCP) ···· 97,152, 154,603,817,818

central depository institution········· 107

Centrex ···························· 795

certified financial instruments
firms associations············· 673,896

certified investor protection
organizations ··················· 673,816

certified organizations ················· 816

certified public accountants······ 450,464

changes in business performance ···835, 838

charitable trusts···················· 593

chief financial officer ············· 113,466

*955*

Chinese walls ·········· 721, 768, 769
churning ··············· 712, 733
CIS — see collective investment scheme
civil action ··············· 918
Civil Code ··············· 65
civil law partnerships ········· 131
civil liability ···442, 459, 867, 883, 896, 898, 912, 918
class shares ··············· 532
clearing funds ··············· 820
clearing organization ········ 791, 817, 818
clearing participant ········· 604, 820
clearinghouse ········· 100, 141, 152
close-out netting ········· 152, 157
collection ··············· 906
collective investment
    scheme (CIS) ········· 17, 74, 131, 610
    for asset management ·········75
    for asset-backed securitization···· 75, 78
    non-strictly-regulated ······· 61, 69, 131
    strictly regulated ·········· 17, 75
collective-action problems ·········43
collusion purchases and sales ···· 851, 852
combining on- and off-market
    transactions ··············· 526
commercial paper ·······86, 126, 258, 682
Commissioner of the
    Financial Services Agency ·····160, 482, 899
commitment-type — see rights offering
commodities ··············25, 617
commodities market ···············97
Commodity Derivatives Act ········· 162
commodity derivatives business······ 162
Commodity Exchange Act ·············82
commodity exchange ········· 162, 786, 790
Commodity Futures Exchange
    Act ··············· 139

Commodity Futures Trading Act···· 140
commodity swaps ··············· 146
commodity-related derivatives···26, 141
commodity-related market
    transactions of derivatives······· 599
Companies Act ···50, 105, 108, 112, 113, 117
companies registered with the U.S.
    SEC ··············· 405
company information··············· 223, 232
compensation for losses ····· 62, 701, 755, 888
compensatory damages··········· 547, 561
competing purchases··············· 528
competing takeover bidder ··········· 552
comply or explain··············34, 111, 112
comprehensive exchanges ······· 26, 100, 141, 790
Comprehensive Guidelines for
    Supervision of Financial
    Instruments Business
    Operators, etc. ··············· 897, 909
concentration duty of orders on an
    exchange ···············35
conclusive evaluations ··············63, 753
confirmation documents ··············· 748
confirmation letter ······113, 406, 407, 490, 491
confirmation of the problematic
    conduct··············· 761
confiscation··············· 9, 906
conflict of interest ···· 19, 73, 540, 541, 542, 544, 593, 680, 704, 771
    management policy··············· 721
    management system ············· 701, 718
    regulation ···············65
consolidated business report ····· 689, 691
consolidated capital adequacy
    requirements ··············· 689, 692
consolidated capital-to-risk ratio···689, 691
consolidated explanatory

*956*

Index

documents ·················· 689,691
consolidated financial statements ··· 86,
87,234
consolidated oversight ················ 688
continuous disclosure ··· 22,46,49,85,86,
459
documents ························· 458
obligation ······················· 360,363
system ···························84
continuous session method ············· 791
contract for financial instruments
transaction ························· 721
contracting commercial agents ······· 597
contracts for difference (CFD) ······· 148
control premium ···· 115,116,516,517,525
control stock ····················· 516
controlling shareholder ·····229,517,540,
542
cooling off ····················· 739
core business ···················· 674,675
corporate bonds ·················· 37,41
corporate control ········· 9,106,116,117
market ······················ 106
transactions ·················· 115
corporate governance ······ 9,89,104,110,
117,233
Corporate Governance Code ······33,34,
110,111
corporate governance report ···· 106,111
corporate governance statement ····· 110
corporate information ······764,765,766,
769
corporate information
memorandum ················ 38,39
corporate insider ·················55,829
Corporate Reorganization Act ········79
counterparty risk ·················· 603
court injunctions ····················96
covered warrants ···················11,127
Credit Associations Act ···············67

credit default swaps (CDSs) ····· 139,149
credit derivatives ···················· 146,149
credit derivatives transactions ······· 144
credit rating agency ····8,78,97,186,642,
710
credit rating business ················· 642
criminal penalties ····96,482,896,898,904
cross-membership ···················· 651
cross-shareholdings ···················· 109
cross-trading ························ 793
crowdfunding ························ 702,772
business ························· 661,669
investment ························· 669
type I — see type I crowdfunding
business
type II — see type II crowdfunding
business
platform operators ····················· 101
scheme ·························38
currencies ·························25
currency-related derivatives
transactions ···················· 731
custody services ···················· 627
customers ···················· 720,750
customer card ···················· 745
customer-oriented business
conducts ···················· 703

D

dark pool ···················· 616
dealing ···················· 612
deception ···················· 891
decisions ···················· 835
deemed holders ···················· 664
deemed joint holders ············· 569,570
deemed securities ················· 121,129
delisting ················· 794,795,803
delivery versus payment (DVP)
settlement ···················· 819
deposit for operation ···················· 672

957

deposit insurance ·········· 71
Deposit Insurance Act ·········· 152,158
Deposit Insurance Corporation ······· 101
depositary institution for
  book-entry transfer ········· 822,824
depositary receipts ················· 127,184
depository financial institutions ······· 67
deposits for operation ················ 671
derivatives transactions ···· 10,13,22,29,
  63,71,120,137,138,142
derivatives transactions
  professionals ························· 151
designated dispute resolution
  organizations ············· 8,97,673,710
designated electronically-recorded
  monetary claims ··············· 124,129
designated foreign trade
  repositories ························· 674
designated international financial
  reporting standards ····· 262,384,405
designated parent company ············ 691
dialogue with management ············· 106
direct disclosure ·····················48
direct placement ········· 593,610,635,678
direct selling································ 610
Director General of the relevant
  Local Finance Bureau ············· 215
disciplinary action······447,478,480,481,
  919
disclosure ·····························42,105
  documents ····· 47,88,90,194,353,458,
  479,498
  documents for a takeover bid ··········94
  duty ································· 77,87
  inspection ····························· 902
  requirements················96,122,659
  system ····························· 45,91
discounted cash flow (DCF)
  method ····························· 543
discretionary administration ···· 176,897
discretionary investment

contract ···· 186,593,620,621,622,623,
  732
discretionary investment
  management ················60,620,636
discretionary trading acts ······· 622,733
discretionary-account trading ········· 9
distributable amount ······················51
distribution price ··················· 231,299
distributors ························48,455
document delivered upon
  conclusion of the contract ········ 737
document submission order ············ 179
domestic systemically important
  banks (D-SIBs) ····················· 691
downstream consolidation ············· 689
DTCC Data Repository Japan
  (DDRJ) ································· 153
DTDRs — see registered derivatives
  transactions data repositories
dual criminal liability ········ 867,882,906
dual trading ························· 705
duty not to delegate ··········· 702,703,714
duty of accountability ········ 723,734,736
duty of care···················65,702,703,712
duty of good faith ···················62,746
duty of loyalty········· 65,77,702,703,712
duty of segregation············· 702,703,716
duty to act in good faith and
  fairly ······························ 702,711
duty to explain ······················· 63,64
DVP settlement — see delivery versus
  payment settlement

E

early termination clause ·············· 158
earthquake derivatives ······· 139,144,149
EBITDA ····························· 544
EDINET — see Electronic Disclosure
  for Investors' NETwork
EDTEF — see electronic derivatives

Index

transactions execution facilities
effect principle ·················· 181,184
elderly customers ···················· 746
electronic book-entry transfer
system ····························· 127
electronic CP (commercial
paper) ···························· 823
electronic data processing system ··· 336
electronic data processing system
for disclosure ················· 218,572
electronic derivatives transactions
execution facilities
(EDTEF) ····················30,156
Electronic Disclosure for Investors'
NETwork (EDINET) ····· 7,47,111,
122,218,317,415,441,475,580
electronic execution facilities ········ 152
electronic public notice ··········· 415,534
electronic solicitation ················· 101
electronic trading platform ····· 99,602,
653,711
electronic transaction systems ·······711,
821
electronically recorded monetary
claims ························· 124,129
emergency injunction ················· 917
emergency prohibition ··········· 166,641
emissions rights trading ·············· 790
enforcement·············· 9,164,353,896
enforcement jurisdiction ········· 181,187
English-language disclosure···········91
enterprise value ················· 540,544
entrusting financial instruments
business operator ············· 595,722
entry regulation ·············59,87,93,644
ETF — see exchange traded fund
ex-ante preventative
administration ···················· 897
exaggerated promotional campaigns
etc. ······························· 9

excessively speculative
transactions ···················· 731
Exchange Act ······················81
exchange bid······················ 533,539
exchange market···················· 22,25
exchange offers····················· 268,342
Exchange Ordinance ·····················81
exchange traded fund (ETF) ··········78
excluded purchase, etc. ·············· 530
exempted securities ·············· 192,196
external clearing house ··············· 818
extinctive prescription ············· 444,468
extraordinary reporting system·······84
extraordinary reports ······ 196,360,392,
460,505,579,840
extraterritorial jurisdiction ··········· 180

F

fair competition ·················· 73,92,772
fair disclosure rule (FD rule) ·······104,
438,497
fair price formation················· 545,758
false indications ·········· 494,728,729,859
false information ···················· 467,471
false purchases and sales ········ 851,852
false quotations ················54,885,892
false representation············· 557,885,892
false statements ······89,99,305,318,371,
400,442,444,447,454,458,464,474,476,
477,479,482,484,491,494,498,499,500,
501,507,508,555,556,579,587,589,875,
904,918,926,933

FD rules — see fair disclosure rules
fee ····································· 619,803
fictitious capital increase··············· 881
fiduciary···························· 702
fiduciary duty ················· 702,711,719
FIEA — see Financial Instruments and
Exchange Act
FIEA Implementing Order — see

959

Financial Instruments and
Exchange Act Implementing Order

financial benchmarks ·················· 102

financial conglomerates ············· 72,96
  significant ······························98

financial crisis ········· 96,99,152,168,821

Financial Crisis Response Council··· 100

financial derivatives··············· 5,139,786

financial derivatives markets······ 25,29

financial derivatives
  transactions ··············29,35,69,137

Financial Futures Association
  of Japan ·····················20,695,815

financial futures exchanges ············ 786

financial indicators············ 142,143,148

financial institutions······67-69,580,593,
                                              750

financial instrument providers,
  etc. ····································· 750

financial instruments ···············25,142

Financial Instruments and
  Exchange Act (FIEA) ······2,16,17,
                                          67,91
  legal character····························14
  purposes································2,21
  scope ·································10
  structure ································· 5

Financial Instruments and Exchange
  Act Implementing Order ······16,922

financial instruments business ····· 5,11,
  29,57,69,92,120,592,593,594,599,609,
                  611,622,636,643,700
  definition ····························57
  type I — see type I financial
    instruments business
  type II — see type II financial
    instruments business

financial instruments business
  operator····8,11,27,29,32,59,67,452,
  470,592,594,596,607,611,620,630,639,
                                          700,790
  foreign type II ·························· 102

financial instruments clearing
  organization······· 8,604,605,673,817

financial instruments exchange···5,7,8,
  18,25,31,33,35,36,96,97,100,141,216,
  375,536,537,579,602,614,615,673,786,
                  811,819,896,919
  limited company-type ············ 799,806
  membership-type ···············35,798
  remote membership··················· 651

financial instruments exchange
  holding company ·············· 789,800

financial instruments exchange
  market···· 26,27,31,144,512,523,525,
                                          558,601,803

financial instruments firms
  association ············8,19,673,805,812
  recognized ····························· 813

financial instruments inspection ····· 901

financial instruments intermediary
  service································· 595

financial instruments intermediary
  service provider ············· 8,595,596

financial instruments
  intermediation ················ 595,613

financial instruments market···· 25,602,
                                          615,787,919
  operator ································ 617

Financial Instruments Mediation
  Assistance Center
  (FINMAC) ····················· 814,817

financial instruments membership
  corporation ························25,797

financial instruments obligation
  assumption service············ 604,819

financial instruments options ········· 148

Financial Instruments Sales
  Act ·································65,749

financial instruments transaction···· 62,
                  64,597,603,672,721,724

financial intermediaries ··················74

financial literacy ·····················45

Financial Monitoring Policy ········· 174

960

financial penalties ················ 795,802

financial planner (FP) ··············· 617

financial reporting ··············· 88,95

Financial Services Agency
(FSA) ···15,45,122,159,161,168,896,
897,898

Financial Supervisory Agency ····87,897

Financial System Reform Act
(1998) ················ 613,682,685,796

Financial Systems Reform Act
(1992) ················ 682,685,770

fines ·································· 904

FINRA ······························ 741

firewall regulations ··· 73,74,96,686,704,
770

firm commitment ····················· 606

five-percent rule ··· 513,514,523,524,529

foreign affiliate ····················· 186

foreign asset-backed securities······ 282

foreign bonds, etc. ·················· 273,395

foreign branch ······················ 186

foreign collective investment
scheme ························· 185,610

foreign companies ······199,210,232,233,
234,237,240,241,245,246,247,250,252,
253,258,260,268,300,314,320,321,330,
335,356,364,365,367,369,380,385,390,
392,395,397,400,402,403,409,458,518,
558
listed ···························· 925

foreign company amendments
registration statements ··········· 299

foreign company amendment
reports ························· 426

foreign company annual securities
report ··············· 374,398,416,464

foreign company confirmation
letters··························· 424

foreign company extraordinary
reports ························· 424,460

foreign company internal control

reports ······················· 424,460

foreign company quarterly securities
reports ················· 422,460,501

foreign company registration
statements ······· 215,216,285,336,458

foreign company semiannual
securities reports ··················· 422

foreign exchange·························· 155

foreign exchange margin
transactions ··················· 731,732

foreign exchange swaps················· 149

foreign financial instruments clearing
organizations ········· 603,604,673,821

foreign financial instruments
exchanges ··················· 7,673,807

foreign financial instruments
markets ··················· 417,602,807

foreign government bonds ············· 275

foreign holding company, etc.
group······························ 691

foreign investment trusts ·······183,186,
332,624

foreign juridical persons ···· 664,689,778

foreign loan trust beneficiary
certificates ····················· 279

foreign market derivatives
transactions ······13,14,138,142,147,
599

foreign parent company·················· 412

foreign parent company's status
reports ························· 428

foreign person·························· 198

foreign person amendment
reports ························· 426

foreign person annual securities
reports ························· 416

foreign person registration············ 215

foreign person registration
statements ····················· 216,275

foreign person semiannual securities
reports ························· 422

*961*

foreign rating company groups ······ 643

foreign securities ·····42,126,203,350,470

foreign securities brokers ······646,648, 807

foreign securities firms ················60

foreign securities information ····· 350,351,352,471,496

foreign state················· 198,202,280

foreign type II financial instruments business operator ···················· 102

foreign-registered funds ·············· 623

Forex (foreign exchange) margin contracts·································· 148

forward rate agreements (FRA) ···· 148

forwards
financial indicators···················· 148
financial instruments···················· 147

fraud ································52,884
fraudulent acts······················ 52,55
fraudulent information··················63
fraudulent means ·············52,869,879
fraudulent securities trading············90
in the capital markets····················52

free cash flow······························ 544

free-riders ·······························43

Fukuoka Stock Exchange (FSE) ·······35

functional regulatory approach·······68

fund-of-funds (FOF) ·················· 657

funds business for qualified institutional investors··········61,104

futures of financial instruments ····· 145

## G

General Headquarters (GHQ) ·····82,896

General Insurance Association of Japan (SONPO) ···················· 817

general investors ················ 66,94,708

general partnership company ·····13,130

general shareholder notification ····· 108

general shareholders meeting··· 927,928

general solicitations ········· 325,485,503

GHQ — *see* General Headquarters

global custody services················· 627

Green Sheet ····················· 39.89.814

group foreign operators················· 622

Guideline for Financial Conglomerates ······················ 688

## H

hearing·············· 474,476,477,478,480

high frequency traders················ 8,104

holding companies···················· 683

hostile buyouts ·························· 564

hostile takeover··············· 106,110,564

Howey-test ···························· 135

## I

illegal gambling ······················ 145

improvement report on timely disclosure ······················ 795

in-house clearing ···················· 818

incidental business ·····623,626,630,674, 675

incorporated information··············· 250

incorporation (by reference) method ·······85,223,224,254,335,458

independent commission··················83

independent directors ··················· 112

independent self-regulatory organization ························ 803

indirect disclosure ····················48

individual shareholder notification ······················ 108

information barrier···················· 769

information recipient ·····55,439,831,833

initial margin ·························· 733

initial public offering (IPO) ····· 21,101, 261

injection of public capital················71

insiders ·····················55,830,831

insider information ·················24,769

*962*

Index

transmission·····100

insider trading·····3,8,40,52,53,54,90, 99,167,184,764,782,828,901
regulation·····85,104

Inspection Manual for Financial Instruments Business Operators·····898,909

inspections·····174,177,179,497

Instinet·····808

institutional investors·····563,573,580,583

institutional regulatory approach·····69

instructions on investment·····620

Insurance Business Act·····67,683

insurance contracts·····134

intentional selective disclosure·····441

interest rate swaps (IRS)·····149,155
plain vanilla·····97,155,157

interest-rate-related derivatives·····139,155

interlocking directors·····96

intermediary commercial agents·····597

intermediary service·····597,600

internal administration supervisors·····697

internal control·····112,172
audit·····95,113,402
audit report·····402
evaluation standards·····399
report·····95,105,113,397,399,460
system·····105,622

internal management system·····719

international accounting standards·····436,438

International Conduct of Business Principles·····711

International Organization of Securities Commissions (IOSCO)·····155,188,711
Conduct of Business Principles·····711

intimidation·····869

introduction·····742,743

introduction fees·····743

investigation·····177,179,902
into a criminal case·····9

investment·····620

investment advice·····616,618,621

investment advisor·····77

investment advisory and agency business·····59,93,120,634,636,700

investment advisory business·····636,702

investment advisory contract·····593,616, 623,739

investment contract·····135

investment corporation·····76,88

investment decisions·····552,558,618,621

investment firms·····62,63

investment limited partnership·····134

investment management business·····59, 60,70,93,98,120,593,594,595,622,624, 630,634,636,677,700,702,716
qualified investors·····595,668

investment managers·····815

investment securities·····124

Investment Solicitation Rules·····745

investment trust·····75,76,78,624,715

Investment Trust and Investment Corporation Act·····17,76,77,78

investment trust management company·····77

Investment Trusts Association, Japan·····20

investor protection·····69,92

investor protection association·····96

investor protection fund·····8,88,638, 673,717

IOSCO — see International Organization of Securities Commissions

issue price·····231,299,340,575,862

issuer information·····487,508

issuers·····46,210

963

issuing market ·····················37
iTraxx Japan ·····················97,155

## J

J-REITs ··························· 166

Japan Exchange Group (JPX) ·······787, 800,919

Japan Exchange Regulation ··········· 919

Japan Government Bond Clearing Corporation (JGBCC) ·············· 155

Japan Investment Advisers Association ····················20,815

Japan Securities Clearing Corporation (JSCC) ····· 153,156,791

Japan Securities Dealers Association (JSDA) ····· 19,30,34,38,96,695,707, 745,746,748,761,767,788,813,918,919

Japan Securities Depository Center, Inc. (JASDEC) ····107,792, 819,824

Japanese accounting standards·······436, 438

Japanese Big Bang·················72,796

Japanese government bonds (JGB) ····················· 12,37,41,71

JASDAQ market ·············36,788,795

JASDEC DVP Clearing················ 819

JBA TIBOR Administration ·········· 103

joint accomplices····················· 483

joint action ························· 522

joint holders············· 567,569,572,581

joint stock company ·················31

JPX-R ···························34

JSCC — see Japan Securities Clearing Corporation

JSDA — see Japan Securities Dealers Association

## K

Kanto Local Finance Bureau ·········· 163
know your customer ················ 744

## L

large-scale third-party allotments ···················· 229

large-volume (share) holders·······116, 568,571,572,573,575

large-volume (share) holdings ······ 562

large-volume (share) holdings reporting ············· 9,10,15,113,116
  ordinary reporting system ······ 563,565
  special reporting system ········ 580,584

large-volume (share) holdings statement·······562,565,571,572,575, 578,586,589
  revised ······························10

layering·····························857

lead manager ······················ 453

lead managing underwriter ····· 608,772

legislative jurisdiction ············· 181,187

Lehman shock ·················· 169,689

leverage restriction···················· 731

liberalization of capital ················· 518

LIBOR···························· 155
  manipulation scandal·················· 102

license ···············31,84,87,615,639

Life Insurance Association of Japan ························· 817

limited company organization ········ 797

limited liability company ···········13,130

limited partnership company ·····13,130

list of notifying business operators ···················· 660

listed foreign companies ··············· 925

listed securities····················18,793

listed shares····················· 431,559

listing ···························· 795,803
  examination ···················· 793
  fees ························· 796
  requirements····················27,803
  rules ·························· 795

Local Finance Branch Bureau ··· 163,899

Index

Local Finance Bureaus ·············· 163,900
loss compensation ···················· 86,149
loss-cutting rule ························· 731

## M

major shareholders ···················· 98,664
management buyout (MBO) ···· 115,533, 540,542
managing underwriter ·············· 608,649
mandatory disclosure regulation ······· 6, 10,14,88,93,120
manipulation to stabilize prices ······· 859
margin requirement ···················· 155
margin transactions ···················· 84
market abuse ·········· 3,8,11,14,45,52,121
market derivatives transactions ····· 13, 14,26,29,30,138,142,144,145
market fragmentation ·················· 810
market infrastructure
  organizations ························· 672
market makers ······················· 792,849
market making ······················· 615,792
market manipulation ······ 3,8,52,53,550, 851,854,867,892,918
  information-based ···················· 53
  through representation ··········· 851,857
  to stabilize prices ···················· 851
  transaction-based ···················· 53
market surveillance ·················· 169,901
markets for professional investors ·· 433
material facts ·············· 56,766,831,835
material information ·············· 439,442
  non-public ··························· 439
material proposals ······ 581,582,585,586, 572,573
MBO — see management buyout
mediation plan ························· 814
member protection trust ·············· 825
membership organization ·········· 31,797
memorandum of cooperation ·········· 189

memorandums of understanding ····· 188
minimum capital ···················· 607,644
Minister of State for Financial
  Services ····························· 159
Minister of Finance ···················· 481
Ministry of Finance ···················· 896
minor criteria ························· 835,837
minority shareholders ·············· 540,542
misleading advertising, etc. ············· 725
misleading indications ······· 341,728,729
misrepresentation ···················· 52,90
Modified International Standards ···· 384
money laundering ························ 904
money reserve fund (MRF) ·········· 763
moving striking convertible bonds
  (MSCB) ····························· 33
multilateral trading facilities
  (MTFs) ····················· 156,614,808
municipal bonds ····················· 37,41
mutual aid contracts ···················· 134
mutual guarantee system ·············· 820

## N

Nagoya Stock Exchange (NSE) ········· 35
naked short-selling ···················· 848
name lending ························· 62,724
NASDAQ market ···················· 793,807
need to know principle ·············· 770
New York Stock Exchange
  (NYSE) ····························· 797
Nihon Stock Exchange ················· 82
Nikkei 225 Futures ···················· 145
Nikkei 225 Options ················ 146,746
no-action letters ···················· 175,909
nominated advisor ···················· 805
non-clearing trading participants ··· 818
Non-Deliverable Forwards
  (NDFs) ····························· 148
non-professional investors ····· 61,66,96

*965*

non-profit membership
organization ･･････････････････････････ 797

non-public loan information, etc. ････ 782

non-public material information ････ 439

non-registered entity ･･･････････････ 917

non-resident ････････････････････････ 182

non-shared information ･･････････････ 779

notice of securities ･･････ 192,214,308,325

notifiable business ･･････････････ 674,675

notification ･････ 61,202,204,207,208,210,
327,472,485,496,503,504,689,691,707,
796,901
  allotment of new shares ･･････････ 326
  changes ････････････････････････ 670
  of holding subject voting rights ･･････ 665
  obligation ･･････････････････････ 210
  requirements ･･･････････････････ 659
  withdrawal ･･･････････････････ 307

notification effect suspension
orders ･･････････････････････････ 476

notifiers of specially permitted
business activities ･･･････････････ 656

## O

occurrence of facts ･･････････････ 835,837

off-exchange trading ･･･････････････ 810

off-floor trading ･･････････････････ 527

offering ･･････････････････････････ 122

offering disclosure ･･･････････22,46,85,442

offering disclosure documents ･･････498,
499

offshore booking ･･･････････････････ 622

omission
  representation ･･･････････････ 885,892
  statements ･･････････････････････ 52

on-exchange traded derivatives ･････ 156

one-stop shopping ･････････････････ 73

one-third rule ･･････513,514,517,524,525,
526

operational control system ･･････････62,706

options ･･････････････････････････ 146

order
  to disclose material information ･･････ 497
  suspension of operations ･･････････ 908

order-driven system ･･･････････････ 792

orderly resolution ･･････････････････ 158

orderly resolution regime ･･････････ 101

ordinary method ････････････････ 223,224

originator ･･････････････････････････75

Osaka Exchange ････････････････････35

OTC derivatives ･･････････････････ 156

OTC derivatives transactions — see
over-the-counter (OTC) derivatives transactions

OTC financial futures ･･････････････63

OTC securities market ･･･30,32,36,39,49

OTC-handled securities ･･････････ 38,39

other business ･････････････････････70

outside director ･････････････････ 935

over-the-counter (OTC) derivatives
transactions ････ 13,30,63,97,99,138,
147,150,152,602,711
  standardized ･･････････････････ 821

over-the-counter transactions in
derivatives ･･････････････ 594,602,711
  specified ････････････････････ 653
  standardized ･･････････････････ 711
  uncleared ････････････････････ 733

over-the-counter (OTC) markets ････22

over-the-counter foreign exchange
margin trading ･･････････････････ 620

over-the-counter securities
market ･･･････ 27,32,524,525,615,788
  organized ･･････････････････ 814,815

over-the-counter traded
securities ････････････････････ 559

over-the-counter transactions ･･････ 516

ownership ratio of shares, etc. ･･････521,
562,566,567

## P

paragraph 1 securities ･･････････････10,611

paragraph 2 securities ·············· 10, 635

parallel public offerings ············· 207

parent bank, etc. ······················· 686

parent company's status report ······ 408, 410

parent financial institutions, etc. ····· 720

parent juridical person, etc. ··········· 686

PDCA cycle ····························· 171

penal provisions ························· 9

penal servitude ························· 904

performance projection ··············· 838

period of exclusion ··················· 444

permission ······· 222, 248, 639, 796, 804, 809

personnel structure···················· 644

Phoenix ································· 39

planned issue period ·················· 311

power of representation ··············· 934

pre-contract document······734, 735, 748, 752

preventive measures against adverse effects ··············· 686, 770

previously-disclosed securities······· 330

price formation functions ············· 614

primary information recipients ····· 833

primary markets······21, 192, 442, 447, 450

Prime Minister ·············· 159, 481, 898

principle of commensurate punishment ························· 916

principle of equal treatment of shareholders ···················· 932

principle of freedom of contract····· 723

principle of good faith ················ 752

principle of individual investor responsibility··················· 723

principle of private autonomy ········ 723

principle of proportionality ·········· 916

principle of suitability ······706, 727, 742, 744, 745, 754

in the broad sense···················· 744

in the narrow sense ···················· 744

Principles of Fiduciary Duty ········ 703

principles-based approach ············· 112

principles-based regulation ············ 719

private placement ····· 47, 72, 89, 122, 183, 309, 343, 344, 527, 593, 606, 609, 612

handling ································99

to professional investors ············· 611

pro rata method ···················· 552, 555

problematic conduct··············· 757, 760

professional fund investors ············ 183

professional investors·······66, 89, 94, 99, 183, 345, 346, 347, 433, 434, 467, 503, 599, 611, 612, 708

profit and loss statement·················50

program amount format ··············· 310

Program for Publishing Reference Prices (Yields) ····················41

prohibited transactions················· 726

prohibition

compensation for loss ··········· 708, 755

double jeopardy ···················· 912, 916

separate purchase ··········· 528, 547, 555

tipping ······························· 843

loans of money ······················65

receiving deposit of money ············65

prohibition orders ······· 896, 898, 901, 916

promising to provide or providing special profits ·················· 728, 730

proprietary trading···················· 849

system (PTS) ···· 26, 27, 29, 34, 35, 524, 525, 529, 613, 644, 671, 808

management business ····· 645, 671, 682

system operations ···················· 671

prospectus ···· 10, 49, 50, 64, 88, 89, 98, 230, 327, 334, 338, 353, 454, 458, 492, 493, 500, 504, 863

Form 2································ 335

Form 7································ 335

provision (providing)

conclusive evaluations, etc. ····· 728, 753

false information ···················· 728

*967*

information ·························· 725
special profits ······················ 730
**proxy**··································· 922
advisory firms ····················· 618
cards ························· 923,926,928
solicitation ················ 106,117,922
Proxy Solicitation Cabinet
Office Ordinance··············· 926,933
PTS — *see* proprietary trading system
public bonds······························ 681
public censure···························· 795
public goods·······························43
public inspection ···216,221,324,373,383,
390,396,407,410,415,417,425,429,444,
461,475,491,535,537,546,562,572,575,
579,580,588,661,666,689,691,840,865,
866
public notice ···415,496,534,539,545,550,
551,552,554,556,557
public offering ······21,37,48,86,120,192,
199,210,327,342,353,485,539,606,609,
860
publication····························· 840
method ···························· 333
names··························· 178
purchase underwriting······ 606,609,611
purchase, etc. ······················ 520
purchases of treasury stock ··········· 850
purpose for which the shares,
etc. are held ················ 572,573
purpose of inducement ················ 854

## Q

qualified institutional investors···39,61,
66,94,104,328,496,503,599,611,656
qualified investors······················ 668
qualified OTC financial
derivatives transactions ·······30,156
quarterly consolidated financial
statements ··················· 383
quarterly review ······················ 388
quarterly securities reports·······49,93,

239,360,381,383,460,501
Form 4-3································· 383
Form 9-3································· 383
quasi-insiders ······················ 831,832
quote-driven system ···················· 792

## R

rapid purchases, etc. ···················· 526
Real Estate Syndication Act···············76
real-estate investments ···············78
reasonable-basis suitability ··········· 747
recognized associations ··········· 813,815
reference documents ···926,933,945,948,
950
reference method ························85
referenced information ················ 258
registered derivatives transactions
data repositories (DTDRs) ······· 152
registered financial institution····62,63,
72,151,186,452,593,594,595,596,668,
677,783,790,815
registered investment
corporation ···················· 620,714
registered securities ····················32
registration·····························61,639
application ···························· 661
notification··························· 219
of change ···························· 671
refusal ····················· 645,661,662
requirements························· 596
rescission··························· 176,908
statement ···························· 299,540
system ························· 84,87,639
volantary·······························97
regulatory arbitrage ················ 92,97
related parties ················ 530,548,561
remote trading participant
system ···························· 652
remuneration························· 619
reorganization ····················· 268
exchange offers····················· 268
securities delivery ·············· 194,268

*968*

Index

securities issuance·············· 192,268
report submission orders············· 481
representation — *see* power of
representation
representatives ························· 300
request in subrogation ··············· 846
restitution of profits ··················· 844
reverse stock splits ···················· 230
revocation of the resolution ········· 951
rights allotment reference date······ 319
rights issue — *see* rights offering
rights offering ············· 37,98,329,606
commitment-type ·············· 606,607
rights to emit carbon dioxide ········ 143
risk-based approach···················· 720
Rule 10b-5— *see* SEC Rule 10b-5

**S**

sales representatives··············19,692
registration ·························· 694
Sapporo Stock Exchange (SSE) ·······35
Sarbanes-Oxley Act···················· 105
Saturday Night Special ················ 518
scoop reports ·························· 841
SEC Rule 10b-5························· 884
secondary distribution····· 21,48,97,120,
192,199,200,202,210,327,342,350,353,
471,485,539,606,609,611,860
secondary information recipients···833,
841
secondary markets···21,22,360,444,448,
451
securities·······10,11,25,75,76,86,88,92,
120,121,134,667
definition ····························69
sale and purchase ····················· 599
same class ···························· 205
type I — *see* type I securities
type II — *see* type II securities
Securities and Exchange Act ···2,28,70,
82,83,114

Securities and Exchange
Commission ························· 896
Securities and Exchange Surveillance
Commission (SESC) ······86,96,162,
164,482,896,897,899
securities business ···················· 88,92
Securities Business Control Act·······81
Securities Commission ················82
securities companies ···· 593,639,667,775
securities custody business·············66
securities depository system··········· 109
securities exchanges ···················· 786
securities finance companies······· 8,674
securities for professional
investors···························· 710
securities indicators ···················· 617
securities information ············· 222,224
securities inspections ·················· 166
securities intermediary business ······89
Securities Investment Advisory
Act ································77
securities investment business ···46,48,
195,197,361
securities investment trust ···········77
securities markets····················25
securities MOUs ······················· 188
securities on alert ····················· 794
securities registration
statements ······7,10,48,49,50,84,88,
90,192,196,204,208,210,215,216,222,
261,273,282,325,329,335,358,361,364,
372,442,444,458,472,491,495,498,861,
917
securities reports ·····38,49,50,51,85,88,
111,167,202,312,406,478,500,789
securities settlement ··················· 627
Securities Trading Commission·······83
Securities Underwriting Business
Act ································81
securities-based derivatives ····· 139,156

*969*

securities-related business ······ 60,184, 593,594,637,677

securities-related derivatives
exchange market ······················35
transactions ······························72

securities-related options ·············· 616

securities, etc. custody business ··················· 635,702,716

securitization of finance ················68

security deposits ························· 626

security trust······························ 613

selective disclosure ····················· 441

self-execution duty ······················65

self-management ··········61,185,624,625

self-management business ·············· 654

self-offering ······················ 61,72,103

self-regulation ······18,32,33,801,812,918

self-regulation committees ······ 803,806

self-regulation-related business ····803, 804

self-regulatory committee ····· 33,95,800

self-regulatory corporation ·····8,33,95, 804

self-regulatory organization
(SRO) ······ 8,18,45,96,102,696,802, 805,812,896,901,918

self-responsibility principle — see
principle of individual investor responsibility

seller-backed financing ················ 773

semiannual securities reports ·······240, 360,382,383,388,390,414,460,484
Form 5······························· 390,391
Form 5-2···························· 390,391
Form 10 ································· 390

separate purchase ············· 528,547,555

separation of fiscal and financial policy ······························· 162

separation of the banking and securities ···················70,637,677

settlement··················· 603,791,817,822

settlor company of an investment trust ································· 624

share buyback reports············· 429,432

share option certificates ················ 209

share split································· 549

share-related securities ················ 565

shareholder community·············· 38,40

shareholder proposals ················· 933

shareholders list ······················· 108

shareholders meeting·······241,553,558, 570,573,582

shareholder's rights ···················· 107

shares································· 519,521
with no voting rights ················· 520

shelf registration ·······201,209,308,338, 353,458,486,504
amendment····························· 314
prospectus ························ 339,493
provisional prospectus················· 494
statements········· 312,340,442,472,495
amended ···························· 472
Form 11 ····························· 312
Form 11-2 ··························· 313
Form 11-2-2 ························· 313
Form 14 ····························· 313
Form 14-4 ··························· 313
Form 15 ····························· 313
Form 16 ····························· 313
supplements······· 308,318,361,498,504
Form 9··························· 320
Form 12 ····························· 320
Form 12-2 ··························· 320
Form 21 ····························· 320
Form 22 ····························· 320
systems···················· 308,338,458
withdrawal ···························· 325
written notice············· 353,358,495

short sales································· 847

short-selling ······················ 846,847

short-term profits······················ 844

short-term sales and purchases ····· 844

significant financial conglomerates ···98

small-amount

electronic offering handling
businesses ·········· 101
exemption ·········· 203
public offering ·········· 265,268,376,391

solicit-all requirement ········ 513,514,552

solicitation ········ 21,38,48,62,63,185,309,
325,326,434,496,610,611,612,740,742,
780,783,922
a small number of investors ·········· 342
commencement standards ·········· 747
inappropriate·········· 728
policy·········· 754
qualified institutional investors ········ 342

SOX Act (Japanese version) ·········· 105

special financial instruments business
operator·········· 689

special purpose corporations ·········· 280

special purpose vehicle (SPV) ········ 131

special reporting system ····· 563,573,580

specially permitted business ·········· 656
for qualified institutional investors,
etc. ·········· 655,656

specially related parties ·········· 521,547

specified act of involvement·········· 508

specified customer ·········· 752

specified financial indicator
calculation agent ·········· 8,103

specified financial indicators ·········· 103

specified financial instruments
business operators, etc.····· 701,704,
718

specified financial instruments
exchange market···· 96,345,347,435,
788,805

specified information···· 345,467,469,506

specified investment management
acts·········· 676

specified investors ·········· 788

specified listed securities ··· 347,435,789

specified major shareholder····· 665,691

specified operating companies ········ 382

specified over-the-counter traded
securities·········· 347,435,519

specified public offering ·········· 353,494

specified purchase and sale, etc.····· 525,
527

specified purchase, etc. ·········· 525,531

specified securities····· 279,361,388,390,
394,413

specified solicitation····345,467,468,469,
486,506

speculative acts·········· 52
overly ·········· 53

speed regulation·········· 528

spoofing·········· 857

spreading of rumors ····· 52,869,872,883,
885,904,909

SRO — see self-regulatory organization

stabilizing market prices·········· 859

stabilizing transactions·········· 330,860
notification·········· 863,864
report ·········· 863,865

state jurisdiction ·········· 181

statement of changes ···237,411,562,565,
575,578,579,587,589

statutory disclosure documents····· 840,
883

Stewardship Code ·········· 110,583

stock exchange holding companies ····89

Stock Exchange Ordinance ·········· 80

stock options ·········· 263

stock options exception·········· 199

stock splits·········· 33

Stock Trading Commission ·········· 82

Stock Trading Ordinance ·········· 80

stop orders·········· 847

sub-underwriting ·········· 609

subprime mortgage crisis·········· 96

subsidiary bank, etc.·········· 686

subsidiary business ·········· 630,675

*971*

subsidiary company, etc. ·············· 686

subsidiary financial institutions,
etc. ························ 720

subsidiary information ··············· 838

subsidiary juridical person, etc. ·····686,
771

suitability — *see* principle of suitability

suitability rule — *see* principle of
suitability

supplementary shelf-registration
prospectus ··············· 339,493,494

suspension of effect ··············· 305,476

suspension of trading················· 802

suspension order ···· 166,176,395,476,640

swaps ································ 146,149

system establishment
requirements ························· 706

systemic risk ···················· 152,158

systemically important financial
institutions···················· 690

## T

T+1 ································· 603

T+2 ································· 603

T+3 ···························· 603,791

takeover bid····· 9,56,84,106,113,269,512
by the issuer ··················86,559
commencement ················· 550,554
-public notice ················· 9,533,534
competing····························· 546
explanation ········· 9,114,533,536,554
mandatory ················ 90,94,114,115
opinion ························· 9,114
partial····························· 552
period ······528,535,538,545,550,551,
552,560
price································ 555
regulation ···················· 15,94,184
report ······················ 534,539
statement ······9,114,533,535,536,537,
541,548,549,551,552,554,556,559
withdrawal ······················ 550

takeover bidder ····513,528,533,534,535,
538,541,545,551,552,554

takeover bidder's answer ··· 533,538,556

takeover defense measures ········33,233

target company's position
statement··· 533,536,537,538,541,561

TDnet — *see* Timely Disclosure
Network

temporary stay ··························· 158

term insurance·························· 593

territoriality principle ··············· 181

third-party allotment ··· 36,112,224,226,
261,302,326,881

TIBOR ····························· 103,155

timely disclosure·········33,441,542,789

Timely Disclosure Network
(TDnet) ················ 34,51,441,841

TMK (tokutei mokuteki kaisha) ····· 80,
656

TMS (tokutei mokuteki shintaku) ·····80

Tokyo AIM ···························94

TOKYO AIM Exchange ·········· 788,805

Tokyo Financial Exchange ···35,155,819

Tokyo Pro Bond Market ······94,348,436

Tokyo Stock Exchange ·····20,33,35,38,
40,51,106,111,436,526,542,652,786,
788,794,807,823,872,920
First Section ·····················38,795
Mothers ····················40,795,876
Second Section·····················38,795

TOPIX Options ····················· 146

tort law·······················64,712,744

ToSTNeT ····························· 526

ToSTNeT-1·····················90,793

ToSTNeT-2···················· 793

ToSTNeT-3···················· 793

total distribution value ····· 192,203,258,
265,299,307

total issue value··············· 203,207,258

tracking stock ························· 394

*972*

Index

trade name ⋯⋯⋯⋯⋯⋯⋯⋯⋯⋯ 667
trade repositories ⋯⋯⋯⋯⋯⋯⋯ 8,674
trading floor ⋯⋯⋯⋯⋯⋯⋯⋯⋯ 807
trading markets ⋯⋯⋯⋯⋯⋯⋯⋯38
trading participants ⋯⋯⋯⋯⋯ 801,817
transaction at exchange ⋯⋯⋯⋯ 651
transactions to mislead the
    market⋯⋯⋯⋯⋯⋯⋯⋯⋯⋯⋯ 851
transfer ⋯⋯⋯⋯⋯⋯⋯⋯⋯⋯⋯ 791
treasury shares (stocks) ⋯⋯ 99,102,432,
    565,847,850
trial examiners ⋯⋯⋯⋯⋯⋯⋯⋯ 911
trial procedures ⋯⋯⋯⋯⋯⋯⋯⋯ 910
true sale⋯⋯⋯⋯⋯⋯⋯⋯⋯⋯⋯⋯79
Trust Business Act ⋯⋯⋯70,76,592,612,
    626,700
trusts⋯⋯⋯⋯⋯⋯⋯⋯⋯⋯⋯⋯⋯78
two reporting systems ⋯⋯⋯⋯⋯⋯51
type I crowdfunding business ⋯⋯⋯595,
    646,669
type I financial instruments
    business ⋯⋯ 30,59,61,69,93,122,150,
    156,595,622,630,634,648,662,674,685,
    689,692,700,815,818
type I securities ⋯⋯⋯10,17,46,59,76,93,
    120,193,199,210,343,634
type II crowdfunding business ⋯⋯⋯646,
    670
type II crowdfunding operators ⋯⋯670,
    724
type II financial instruments
    business ⋯⋯ 59,61,69,93,99,120,122,
    150,613,622,634,700
Type II Financial Instruments
    Firms Association ⋯⋯⋯⋯⋯⋯20,815
type II securities ⋯10,46,59,93,120,129,
    150,194,197,199,343,692

U

U.S. accounting standards⋯⋯⋯⋯⋯ 436
U.S. Sarbanes-Oxley Act ⋯⋯⋯⋯⋯89

U.S. Securities Exchange Act of
    1934 ⋯⋯⋯⋯⋯⋯⋯⋯⋯⋯ 851,884
underwriter⋯⋯⋯⋯⋯⋯⋯⋯⋯⋯ 607
underwriting ⋯⋯⋯⋯⋯⋯⋯⋯98,606
    business ⋯⋯⋯⋯⋯⋯⋯⋯⋯⋯ 650
    contract ⋯⋯⋯⋯⋯⋯⋯⋯⋯⋯ 861
    standby⋯⋯⋯⋯⋯⋯⋯⋯⋯ 606,609
undisclosed information⋯⋯⋯⋯⋯ 774
unfair trading ⋯⋯⋯⋯⋯⋯⋯⋯96,802
unfair transactions ⋯⋯⋯⋯⋯ 885,901,910
Uniform Practices Regulations ⋯⋯⋯ 813
unpublished material information ⋯ 104
unregistered operators ⋯⋯⋯599,641,725,
    727
unsophisticated investors ⋯⋯⋯⋯⋯45
upstream consolidation ⋯⋯⋯⋯⋯⋯ 689
urgent provisional suspension court
    orders⋯⋯⋯⋯⋯⋯⋯⋯⋯⋯⋯ 481

V

variation margin ⋯⋯⋯⋯⋯⋯⋯ 155,733
venture funds⋯⋯⋯⋯⋯⋯⋯⋯⋯ 657
voluntary investigations ⋯⋯⋯⋯⋯ 178
voting forms ⋯⋯⋯⋯⋯⋯⋯⋯ 927,931
voting rights ⋯⋯⋯⋯⋯⋯⋯ 922,931,950

W

waiting period⋯⋯⋯⋯48,208,300,316,476
    extensions ⋯⋯⋯⋯⋯⋯⋯⋯⋯ 476
weather derivatives ⋯⋯ 139,149,618,679
welfare pension funds⋯⋯⋯⋯⋯⋯ 710
wholesale underwriters⋯⋯⋯⋯ 452,468
wholesale underwriting⋯⋯⋯⋯98,607
    contract ⋯⋯⋯⋯⋯ 452,468,645,650
Williams Act⋯⋯⋯⋯⋯⋯⋯ 113,116,518
written inquiry procedures ⋯⋯⋯⋯ 909
written notice
    changes⋯⋯⋯⋯⋯⋯⋯⋯⋯⋯ 358
    purchase ⋯⋯⋯⋯⋯⋯⋯⋯ 534,539
    securities ⋯⋯ 192,205,308,325,353,355,
    495

*973*

wrongful acts ································ 884
wrongful means ····························· 885

## Z

zaibatsu ······································· 109